1 MONTH OF
FREE
READING

at

www.ForgottenBooks.com

By purchasing this book you are eligible for one month membership to ForgottenBooks.com, giving you unlimited access to our entire collection of over 1,000,000 titles via our web site and mobile apps.

To claim your free month visit:
www.forgottenbooks.com/free1088196

ISBN 978-0-331-46529-7
PIBN 11088196

CATALOGUE

OF

YALE UNIVERSITY

1907-08

NEW HAVEN
THE TUTTLE, MOREHOUSE & TAYLOR COMPANY
1907

CONTENTS

Office Hours	7
General Information	8
Calendar	11
Chronological Table	12

PART I.—OFFICERS OF THE UNIVERSITY

Members and Officers of the Corporation	15
Committees of the Corporation	16
Alumni Advisory Board	17
Administrative Officers of the University and its Departments	19
The University Council	20
Officers of Instruction and Administration :	
Professors	21
Assistant Professors	29
Instructors, including Lecturers, etc.	32
Assistants in Instruction	41
Assistants in Administration	45
Graduate Fellows and Scholars	50

PART II.—GOVERNMENT OF THE UNIVERSITY

The Charter of the Collegiate School	55
The Additional Act of 1723	57
The Charter of Yale College	58
Later Acts of the Legislature	61
The Government of the different Departments	63

PART III.—DEPARTMENTS OF INSTRUCTION

The Department of Philosophy and the Arts :	
The Academical Department (Yale College)	67
The Sheffield Scientific School	200
The Graduate School	295
The School of the Fine Arts	385
The Department of Music	393
The Department of Forestry	403
The Summer School of Forestry	419
The Department of Theology	422
The Department of Medicine	452
The Department of Law	481
Yale-Columbia Courses in preparation for Foreign Service	528

197798

PART IV.—INSTITUTIONS CONNECTED WITH THE UNIVERSITY

Libraries 533
The Peabody Museum of Natural History 538
The Observatory 545
The Botanical Garden 547
The University Church 548
The Infirmary 551
The Dining Hall 551
The Gymnasium 552
The Athletic Field 555
The Yale University Christian Association 557
The Yale Station, United States Post Office 559
The Bureau of Self-Help 560
The Alumni Associations 561

PART V.—LECTURE COURSES AND PRIZES

The Public Lecture Course 569
University Lectures and Concerts 571
University Prizes 575

PART VI.—DEGREES AND HONORS, 1907

Degrees Conferred in Course 581
Honorary Degrees Conferred 594
Honors in the Several Departments 596
Awards of Prizes and Scholarships 606

PART VII.—LISTS OF STUDENTS, DIRECTORY, AND INDEX

Lists of Students:
    The Graduate School 615
    The Academical Department (Yale College) . . . 633
    The Sheffield Scientific School 665
    The School of the Fine Arts 703
    The Department of Music 705
    The Department of Forestry 710
    The Department of Theology 714
    The Department of Medicine 719
    The Department of Law 723
    The Summer School 733
General Summary of Officers and Students 737
Summary of Students, by States 738
              by Cities and Towns 739
              by Degrees Represented . . . 740
Directory of Officers and Students 743
Index 787

OFFICE HOURS

The PRESIDENT OF THE UNIVERSITY—Absent until about March 10. Thereafter Woodbridge Hall, 8.30 A. M. to 1.00 P. M. (Students not having an appointment are advised to call between 10.15 and 11.15 A. M.)

The SECRETARY OF THE UNIVERSITY—Woodbridge Hall, 10.00 A. M. to 1.00 P. M. (Secretary's Office, 9.00 A. M. to 1.00 P. M. and 2.00 to 4.30 P. M. Saturday and in vacation, 9.00 A. M. to 1.00 P. M.)

The TREASURER OF THE UNIVERSITY—Woodbridge Hall, 9.00 A. M. to 5.00 P. M. (Office closes Saturday and in vacation at 1.00 P. M.)

ACADEMICAL DEPARTMENT (Yale College)—The DEAN, Lampson Hall, 10.30 A. M. to 1.00 P. M.

SHEFFIELD SCIENTIFIC SCHOOL—The DIRECTOR and TREASURER, 3 Sheffield Hall, 9.00 A. M. to 1.00 P. M. (Treasurer's Office 8.00 A. M. to 5.00 P. M.)

GRADUATE SCHOOL—The DEAN, 90 High st., daily, except Saturday, 10.30 A. M. to 12.00 M. (Dean's Office also 2.00 to 3.00 P. M., except Saturday.)

SCHOOL OF THE FINE ARTS—The DIRECTOR, 9.00 A. M. to 12.00 M., 2.00 to 4.00 P. M.

DEPARTMENT OF MUSIC—The DEAN, 126 College st., Wednesday, 12.30 to 1.00 P. M.; Tuesday, Wednesday, Thursday, and Friday, 2.00 to 3.00 P. M.

DEPARTMENT OF FORESTRY—The DIRECTOR, 360 Prospect st., daily, 9.00 A. M. to 12.00 M.

DEPARTMENT OF THEOLOGY—ACTING DEAN, 668 West Divinity Hall, daily, except Saturday, 9.30 to 10.30 A. M.

DEPARTMENT OF MEDICINE—The DEAN, Room 25, 150 York st., 9.00 to 11.00 A. M.

DEPARTMENT OF LAW—The DEAN, Hendrie Hall, 9.30 A. M. to 12.30 P. M. The SECRETARY, Room 17, Hendrie Hall, 8.00 to 11.00 A. M.

OBSERVATORY—The DIRECTOR, The Observatory, cor. Prospect and Canner streets, 11.00 A. M. to 1.00 P. M.

COLLEGE BURSAR'S OFFICE—Lampson Hall, 9.00 A. M. to 3.00 P. M.
BUREAU OF SELF-HELP—4 Phelps Hall, 9.30 A. M. to 12.30 P. M.

GENERAL INFORMATION

The CATALOGUE OF YALE UNIVERSITY is published in December. Price, fifty cents. (A copy will be sent free of charge to any graduate desiring it.)

The CATALOGUE OF OFFICERS AND GRADUATES, heretofore generally known as The TRIENNIAL CATALOGUE, was last issued in October, 1904. Price, one dollar.

The DIRECTORY OF LIVING GRADUATES was last issued in November, 1904. Price, one dollar. A SUPPLEMENT, containing Class Lists, etc., revised to date, was published in December, 1906. Price, fifty cents. (Distribution limited at the discretion of the officers of the University.)

The PAMPHLETS of any Department of the University are furnished without charge. These contain detailed information not given in the University Catalogue, especially regarding the individual courses offered.

The UNIVERSITY BULLETIN, published weekly in term time and containing announcements of lectures, prizes, etc., is posted on local bulletin boards, and sent to subscribers for one dollar a year.

———

For Catalogues and general information, address THE SECRETARY OF YALE UNIVERSITY, YALE STATION, NEW HAVEN, CONNECTICUT.

———

To find the position or address of any officer, consult page references in DIRECTORY at the back of this Catalogue.

ABBREVIATIONS

A. Absent on leave.
A.H. Alumni Hall.
A.S. Art School.
B. Berkeley Hall.
B.C. Battell Chapel.
B.G. Botanical Gardens.
B.M.H. Byers Memorial Hall.
C. Connecticut Hall.
C.D. Carpentry Department.
C.S.H. College Street Hall.
D. Durfee Hall.
DW. Dwight Hall.
E.D. East Divinity Hall.
F. Farnam Hall.
FW. Fayerweather Hall.
G. Gymnasium.
H.M.L. Hammond Metallurgical
    Laboratory.
HEN. Hendrie Hall.
HER. Herrick Hall.
K. Kirtland Hall.
K.C.L. Kent Chemical Laboratory.
L. Lawrance Hall.
LAM. Lampson Hall (containing
    Lampson Lyceum).
LIB. University Library.

M.S. Medical School.
MAR. Marsh Hall.
MEM. Memorial Hall.
N.S.H. North Sheffield Hall.
O. Osborn Hall.
P. Pierson Hall.
PEAB. Peabody Museum.
PH. Phelps Hall.
P.O. Post Office (Yale Station).
S.B.L. Sheffield Biological Lab'y.
S.C.L. Sheffield Chemical Lab'y.
S.H. Sheffield Hall.
S.P.L. Sloane Physical Lab'y.
U.C. University Clinic.
U.H. University Hall (Dining
    Hall).
V. Vanderbilt Hall.
V-S. Vanderbilt-Scientific Halls.
W. Welch Hall.
W.D. West Divinity Hall.
W.O. Winchester Observatory.
WH. White Hall.
WIN. Winchester Hall.
WOOD. Woodbridge Hall.
WOOL. Woolsey Hall.

NUMBERING OF ROOMS
COLLEGE DORMITORIES

1- 69. Vanderbilt Hall.	233-272. Durfee Hall.	
70- 93. Connecticut Hall.	331-382. White Hall.	
94-141. Welch Hall.	383-422. Berkeley Hall.	
142-183. Lawrance Hall.	423-470. Fayerweather Hall.	
184-232. Farnam Hall.	521-600. Pierson Hall.	

SHEFFIELD SCIENTIFIC SCHOOL BUILDINGS

1- 21. Sheffield Hall.	175-193. Kirtland Hall.
25- 58. North Sheffield Hall.	1- 14. Byers Hall, dormitory
60- 79. Sheffield Biological Lab'y.	floor.
100-135. Winchester Hall.	100-153. Vanderbilt-Scientific
140-162. Sheffield Chemical Lab'y.	Halls.

DIVINITY SCHOOL

601-654. East Divinity Hall.	655-724. West Divinity Hall.

1907

	SUN.	MON.	TUE.	WED.	THU.	FRI.	SAT.
JULY		1	2	3	4	5	6
	7	8	9	10	11	12	13
	14	15	16	17	18	19	20
	21	22	23	24	25	26	27
	28	29	30	31			
AUG.					1	2	3
	4	5	6	7	8	9	10
	11	12	13	14	15	16	17
	18	19	20	21	22	23	24
	25	26	27	28	29	30	31
SEPT.	1	2	3	4	5	6	7
	8	9	10	11	12	13	14
	15	16	17	18	19	20	21
	22	23	24	25	26	27	28
	29	30					
OCT.			1	2	3	4	5
	6	7	8	9	10	11	12
	13	14	15	16	17	18	19
	20	21	22	23	24	25	26
	27	28	29	30	31		
NOV.						1	2
	3	4	5	6	7	8	9
	10	11	12	13	14	15	16
	17	18	19	20	21	22	23
	24	25	26	27	28	29	30
DEC.	1	2	3	4	5	6	7
	8	9	10	11	12	13	14
	15	16	17	18	19	20	21
	22	23	24	25	26	27	28
	29	30	31				

1908

	SUN.	MON.	TUE.	WED.	THU.	FRI.	SAT.
JAN.				1	2	3	4
	5	6	7	8	9	10	11
	12	13	14	15	16	17	18
	19	20	21	22	23	24	25
	26	27	28	29	30	31	
FEB.							1
	2	3	4	5	6	7	8
	9	10	11	12	13	14	15
	16	17	18	19	20	21	22
	23	24	25	26	27	28	29
MAR.	1	2	3	4	5	6	7
	8	9	10	11	12	13	14
	15	16	17	18	19	20	21
	22	23	24	25	26	27	28
	29	30	31				
APR.				1	2	3	4
	5	6	7	8	9	10	11
	12	13	14	15	16	17	18
	19	20	21	22	23	24	25
	26	27	28	29	30		
MAY						1	2
	3	4	5	6	7	8	9
	10	11	12	13	14	15	16
	17	18	19	20	21	22	23
	24	25	26	27	28	29	30
	31						
JUNE		1	2	3	4	5	6
	7	8	9	10	11	12	13
	14	15	16	17	18	19	20
	21	22	23	24	25	26	27
	28	29	30				

	SUN.	MON.	TUE.	WED.	THU.	FRI.	SAT.
JULY				1	2	3	4
	5	6	7	8	9	10	11
	12	13	14	15	16	17	18
	19	20	21	22	23	24	25
	26	27	28	29	30	31	
AUG.							1
	2	3	4	5	6	7	8
	9	10	11	12	13	14	15
	16	17	18	19	20	21	22
	23	24	25	26	27	28	29
	30	31					
SEPT.			1	2	3	4	5
	6	7	8	9	10	11	12
	13	14	15	16	17	18	19
	20	21	22	23	24	25	26
	27	28	29	30			
OCT.					1	2	3
	4	5	6	7	8	9	10
	11	12	13	14	15	16	17
	18	19	20	21	22	23	24
	25	26	27	28	29	30	31
NOV.	1	2	3	4	5	6	7
	8	9	10	11	12	13	14
	15	16	17	18	19	20	21
	22	23	24	25	26	27	28
	29	30					
DEC.			1	2	3	4	5
	6	7	8	9	10	11	12
	13	14	15	16	17	18	19
	20	21	22	23	24	25	26
	27	28	29	30	31		

UNIVERSITY CALENDAR

1907

26 Sept.	Thursday	First Term begins.
7 Oct.	Monday	Yale Corporation Meeting.
18 Nov.	Monday	Yale Corporation Meeting.
27 Nov.	Wednesday	Thanksgiving Recess begins, 1.20 P. M.
29 Nov.	Friday	Recess ends, 8.00 A. M.
18 Dec.	Wednesday	First Term ends, 6.00 P. M.

1908   **Winter Vacation**

8 Jan.	Wednesday	Second Term begins, 8.00 A. M.
17 Feb.	Monday	Yale Corporation Meeting.
16 March	Monday	Yale Corporation Meeting.
10 April	Friday	Junior Exhibition.
15 April	Wednesday	Spring Recess begins, 1.20 P. M.
23 April	Thursday	Recess ends, 8.00 A. M.
4 May	Monday	DeForest Prize Speaking.
18 May	Monday	Yale Corporation Meeting.
30 May	Saturday	Memorial Day.
1 June	Monday	School of the Fine Arts, Term ends.
3 June	Wednesday	Anniversary of the Divinity School.
21 June	Sunday	Baccalaureate Sermon.
22 June	Monday	College Class-Day Exercises.
22 June	Monday	Scientific School Class-Day Exercises.
22 June	Monday	Anniversary of the Law School.
22 June	Monday	Anniversary of the Medical School.
22 June	Monday	Yale Corporation Meeting.
23 June	Tuesday	Anniversary Meeting of the Alumni.
24 June	Wednesday	Commencement.
24 June	Wednesday	Examination for Admission to Yale College begins, 2.00 P. M.
25 June	Thursday	Examinations for Admission to other Departments begin.

Summer Vacation

19 Sept.	Saturday	Examination for Admission to Yale College begins, 10.30 A. M.
21 Sept.	Monday	Examinations for Admission to other Departments begin.
24 Sept.	Thursday	First Term begins.
16 Dec.	Wednesday	First Term ends.

CHRONOLOGICAL TABLE

Meeting of Ministers in Branford, for founding a College   1700–1701

Charter of the Collegiate School of Connecticut   .   .   .   1701

Organization under the Charter   1701

Beginning of instruction at Saybrook   1702

Removal to New Haven   1716

The Collegiate School named Yale College   .   .   .   1718

Revised Charter   1745

Act of the General Assembly of Connecticut by which State
    Officers became members of the Corporation   .   .   1792

Charter of the Medical School   1810

Beginning of instruction in the Medical School   .   .   1813

Charter confirmed by new Constitution of the State   .   1818

Beginning of instruction in the Divinity School   .   .   1822

Law School affiliated to the College   1824

Graduate Courses in Philosophy and the Arts organized   .   1846

Scientific section of the Department of Philosophy and the
    Arts named the Sheffield Scientific School   .   .   .   1861

School of the Fine Arts established   1866

Act of the General Assembly providing for the election of six
    members of the Corporation by the Alumni .   .   .   1871

Act of the General Assembly authorizing the name Yale
    University   1887

Department of Music established   1894

Forest School established   ˜   1900

Bicentennial Celebration   1901

PART I

OFFICERS OF THE UNIVERSITY

CORPORATION

COMMITTEES OF THE CORPORATION

PRUDENTIAL COMMITTEE

THE PRESIDENT OF THE UNIVERSITY, *Chairman*
REV. CHARLES RAY PALMER, D.D.
REV. EDWIN POND PARKER, D.D.
HENRY FARNAM DIMOCK, M.A.
REV. JAMES WESLEY COOPER, D.D.
HON. ELI WHITNEY, M.A.
ALFRED LAWRENCE RIPLEY, M.A.

———

THE SECRETARY OF THE UNIVERSITY, *Secretary*

———

COMMITTEE ON INVESTMENTS

THE PRESIDENT OF THE UNIVERSITY, *Chairman*
THE TREASURER OF THE UNIVERSITY
HENRY FARNAM DIMOCK, M.A., New York City
HON. ELI WHITNEY, M.A., New Haven
ALFRED LAWRENCE RIPLEY, M.A., Boston, Mass.

—

OTTO TREMONT BANNARD, LL.B., New York City
CLARENCE HILL KELSEY, M.A., New York City

ALUMNI ADVISORY BOARD

CHAIRMAN

HON. FREDERICK NEWTON JUDSON, LL.D., St. Louis, Mo.

MEMBERS

THE PRESIDENT OF THE UNIVERSITY.
THE SECRETARY OF THE UNIVERSITY.
THE TREASURER OF THE UNIVERSITY.
THE CHAIRMAN OF THE BOARD OF DIRECTORS OF THE YALE ALUMNI
UNIVERSITY FUND ASSOCIATION.

Boston, *Yale Alumni Association* of, and *Yale Club* of,
ELMER PARKER HOWE, B.A., 53 State st.

Buffalo, *Yale Alumni Association* of,
EDWARD BUCKINGHAM GUTHRIE, B.A., 159 North Pearl st.

Central and Western Massachusetts, *Yale Alumni Association* of,
THOMAS BOND SHAW, B.A., M.D., 47 Pleasant st., Worcester.

Central New York Federation (Auburn, Syracuse, and Utica),
FRANK ERASTUS WHEELER, B.A., Utica.

Central Pennsylvania, *Yale Alumni Association* of,
EDWARD BAILEY, PH.B., Harrisburg.

Chicago, *Yale Club* of,
EDWARD JOHNSON PHELPS, M.A., 172 La Salle st.

Cincinnati, *Yale Club* of,
CALEB WRIGHT SHIPLEY, B.A., Risor av., Clifton.

Cleveland, *Yale Alumni Association* of,
EDWARD BELDEN GREENE, B.A., 520 Franklin av.

Colorado, *Yale Alumni Association* of,
HENRY TREAT ROGERS, M.A., Boston Bldg., Denver.

Essex County (N. J.), *Yale Alumni Association* of,
JOHN OXENBRIDGE HEALD, B.A., Orange.

Hartford, *Yale Alumni Association* of,
CHARLES HOPKINS CLARK, M.A., Courant Office.

Indiana, *Yale Alumni Association* of,
JOHN ORLANDO PERRIN, B.A., American National Bank, Indianapolis.

Kansas City, *Yale Alumni Association* of,
JAMES PERKINS RICHARDSON, M.A., Prosso Preparatory School.

Kentucky, *Yale Alumni Association* of,
LAFON ALLEN, B.A., Kenyon Bldg., Louisville.

Long Island, *Yale Alumni Association* of,
HON. WILLIAM BATES DAVENPORT, M.A., 189 Montague st., Brooklyn, N. Y.

Maryland, *Yale Alumni Association* of,
WILLIAM MCCULLOH BROWN, PH.B., Oakland, Garrett County.

New York City, *Yale Club* of,
THOMAS THACHER, LL.D., 25 Broad st.

Northeastern New York, *Yale Alumni Association* of,
JOHN KASSON HOWE, B.A., 37 State st., Albany.

Northwest, *Yale Alumni Association* (Minnesota, Iowa, North Dakota, South Dakota, Montana, and part of Washington),·
MARCUS DATY MUNN, PH.B., LL.B., Despatch Bldg., St.Paul, Minn.

Philadelphia, *Yale Alumni Association* of,
·THOMAS DEWITT CUYLER, B.A., 701 Arcade Bldg.

Scranton and Wilkes-Barré.
HON. JOSEPH BENJAMIN DIMMICK, M.A., Scranton.

Southeastern Federation (Tennessee, Alabama, Georgia, South Carolina, and Savannah),
ANTONIO JOHNSTON WARING, B.A., 3 Perry st., W., Savannah, Ga.

Southern California, *Yale Alumni Association* of,
WILLIAM LARNED THACHER, B.A., Nordhoff.

St.Louis, *Yale Alumni Association* of,
HON. FREDERICK NEWTON JUDSON, LL.D., 500 Rialto Bldg.

Washington, D. C., *Yale Alumni Association* of,
GEORGE XAVIER MCLANAHAN, M.L., D.C.L., 2031 Q st.

Wisconsin, *Yale Alumni Association* of,
JAMES GREELEY FLANDERS, B.A., LL.B., 161 Prospect st., Milwaukee.

EXECUTIVE COMMITTEE

Mr. JUDSON, St.Louis, Chairman, and Messrs. HOWE, Boston ; PHELPS, Chicago ; ROGERS, Colorado ; PERRIN, Indiana ; THACHER, New York ; FLANDERS, Wisconsin.

.ADMINISTRATIVE OFFICERS

THE UNIVERSITY
ARTHUR TWINING HADLEY, LL.D., *President*
ANSON PHELPS STOKES, JR., M.A., *Secretary*
LEE McCLUNG, M.A., *Treasurer*

THE DEPARTMENTS
Academical Department
HENRY PARKS WRIGHT, PH.D., LL.D., *Dean*
ALFRED KINDRED MERRITT, B.A., *Registrar*
HOLLON AUGUSTINE FARR, PH.D., *Chairman of the Freshman Faculty*

Sheffield Scientific School
RUSSELL HENRY CHITTENDEN, PH.D., Sc.D., LL.D., *Director and Treasurer*
ARTHUR MARVIN, M.A., *Registrar*
LOUIS VALENTINE PIRSSON, M.A., *Class Officer, Senior Class*
WILBUR LUCIUS CROSS, PH.D., *Class Officer, Junior Class*
PERCEY FRANKLYN SMITH, PH.D., *Class Officer, Freshman Class*

Graduate School
ANDREW WHEELER PHILLIPS, PH.D., *Dean*

School of the Fine Arts
JOHN FERGUSON WEIR, N.A., M.A., *Director*

Department of Music
HORATIO WILLIAM PARKER, MUS.D., *Dean*

Department of Forestry
HENRY SOLON GRAVES, M.A., *Director*

Department of Theology
REV. EDWARD LEWIS CURTIS, PH.D., D.D., *Acting Dean*

Department of Medicine
HERBERT EUGENE SMITH, M.D., *Dean*

Department of Law
HENRY WADE ROGERS, LL.D., *Dean*

University Library
JOHN CHRISTOPHER SCHWAB, PH.D., *Librarian*

UNIVERSITY COUNCIL ·

THE PRESIDENT OF THE UNIVERSITY, *Chairman*
THE SECRETARY OF THE UNIVERSITY, *Secretary*
THE TREASURER OF THE UNIVERSITY
THE UNIVERSITY LIBRARIAN

Academical Department

PROFESSOR H. P. WRIGHT   PROFESSOR MORRIS
PROFESSOR GOOCH   PROFESSOR WARREN

Sheffield Scientific School

PROFESSOR CHITTENDEN   PROFESSOR DU BOIS
PROFESSOR PIRSSON

Graduate School

PROFESSOR PHILLIPS

School of the Fine Arts

PROFESSOR WEIR

Department of Music

PROFESSOR PARKER   PROFESSOR SANFORD

Department of Forestry

PROFESSOR GRAVES

Department of Theology

PROFESSOR CURTIS   PROFESSOR WALKER

Department of Medicine

PROFESSOR SMITH   PROFESSOR BLUMER

Department of Law

PROFESSOR ROGERS   PROFESSOR BALDWIN

Athletic Organizations

MR. CAMP

OFFICERS OF
INSTRUCTION AND ADMINISTRATION

In the lists which follow, the Officers of Instruction and Administration in the University are divided into five groups, as follows:

PROFESSORS, including other officers on permanent University appointments.

ASSISTANT PROFESSORS, and officers of equivalent rank.

INSTRUCTORS, including Tutors, Demonstrators and Lecturers.

ASSISTANTS IN INSTRUCTION.

ASSISTANTS IN ADMINISTRATION.

Names are arranged alphabetically in each of these lists, except in the first, where the order is based on collegiate seniority.

PROFESSORS

ARTHUR TWINING HADLEY, LL.D.
PRESIDENT   (WOOD.)   93 Whitney av.

Rev. GEORGE PARK FISHER, D.D., LL.D.
Titus Street Professor of Ecclesiastical History, Emeritus   A.

GEORGE JARVIS BRUSH, LL.D.
Professor of Mineralogy, Emeritus   14 Trumbull st.

SAMUEL WILLIAM JOHNSON, M.A.
Professor of Agricultural Chemistry, Emeritus   54 Trumbull st.

WILLIAM HENRY BREWER, PH.D., LL.D.
Norton Professor of Agriculture, Emeritus   418 Orange st.

JOHN EMORY CLARK, M.A.
James E. English Professor of Mathematics, Emeritus
Longmeadow, Mass.

ARTHUR MARTIN WHEELER, LL.D.
Durfee Professor of History, Emeritus, and Lecturer on
European History   (H, C.)   86 Trumbull st.

ROBERT BROWN, M.A.
Secretary of the Observatory, Emeritus   Observatory pl.

Rev. LEWIS ORSMOND BRASTOW, D.D.
Professor of Practical Theology, Emeritus
(601 R. D.)   146 Cottage st.

ADDISON VanNAME, M.A.
Librarian, Emeritus (LIB.) 121 High st.

JOHN FERGUSON WEIR, M.A., N.A.
William Leffingwell Professor of Painting and Design,
and Director of the School of the Fine Arts
(9 A. S.) 58 Trumbull st.

CHARLES BRINCKERHOFF RICHARDS, M.A.
Higgin Professor of Mechanical Engineering
(111 WIN.) 227 Edwards st.

ARTHUR WILLIAMS WRIGHT, PH.D.
Professor of Experimental Physics, Emeritus 73 York sq.

THOMAS RAYNESFORD LOUNSBURY, LL.D., L.H.D.
Professor of English, Emeritus 22 Lincoln st.

EUGENE LAMB RICHARDS, M.A.
Professor of Mathematics, Emeritus Woodbridge

DANIEL CADY EATON, M.A.
Professor of the History and Criticism of Art, Emeritus
218 Prospect st.

JOHN HENRY NIEMEYER, M.A., A.N.A.
Street Professor of Drawing (8 A. S.) 251 Lawrence st.

FRANKLIN BOWDITCH DEXTER, LITT.D.
Assistant Librarian (LIB.) 178 Prospect st.

Hon. SIMEON EBEN BALDWIN, LL.D.
Professor of American Constitutional and Private
International Law (69 Church st.) 44 Wall st.

TRACY PECK, LL.D.
Professor of the Latin Language and Literature 124 High st.

WILLIAM HENRY CARMALT, M.D.
Professor of the Principles and Practice of Surgery, Emeritus
87 Elm st.

ADDISON EMERY VERRILL, M.A.
Professor of Zoology, Emeritus 86 Whalley av.

WILLIAM GRAHAM SUMNER, LL.D.
Pelatiah Perit Professor of Political and Social Science
240 Edwards st.

Rev. GEORGE TRUMBULL LADD, D.D., LL.D.
Professor of Moral Philosophy and Metaphysics, Emeritus
204 Prospect st.

CHARLES HENRY SMITH, LL.D.
Larned Professor of American History (177 L.) 284 Orange st.

SIDNEY IRVING SMITH, M.A.
Professor of Comparative Anatomy, Emeritus   147 Whalley av.

WILLIAM GILBERT MIXTER, M.A.
Professor of Chemistry   (160 S. C. L.)   250 Edwards st.

HENRY PARKS WRIGHT, PH.D., LL.D.
Dunham Professor of the Latin Language and Literature,
and Dean of the College Faculty   (LAM.)   128 York st.

HENRY AUGUSTIN BEERS, M.A.
Professor of English Literature   65 York sq.

AUGUSTUS JAY DUBOIS, C.E., PH.D.
Professor of Civil Engineering   (129 WIN.)   334 Edwards st.

BERNADOTTE PERRIN, PH.D., LL.D.
Lampson Professor of Greek Literature and History
                                        (191 F.)   463 Whitney av.

EDWARD SALISBURY DANA, PH.D.
Professor of Physics, and Curator of the Mineralogical
        Collection   (4 PEAB.)   24 Hillhouse av.

THOMAS DAY SEYMOUR, LL.D.
Hillhouse Professor of the Greek Language and Literature
                                        (22 PH.)   34 Hillhouse av.

CHARLES SHELDON HASTINGS, PH.D.
Professor of Physics   (120 WIN.) ʼ248 Bradley st.

THEODORE SALISBURY WOOLSEY, LL.D.
Professor of International Law

THOMAS HUBBARD RUSSELL, M.D.
Professor of Clinical Surgery, and Lecturer on
        Surgical Anatomy   137 Elm st.

FRANK AUSTIN GOOCH, PH.D.
Professor of Chemistry, and Director of the Kent Chemical
        Laboratory   (K. C. L.)   291 Edwards st.

ALBERT STANBURROUGH COOK, PH.D., L.H.D., LL.D.
Professor of the English Language and Literature
                                    (135 Elm st.)   219 Bishop st.

WILLIAM BEEBE, M.A.
Professor of Mathematics, and Instructor in Astronomy
                                                    262 Bradley st.

ANDREW WHEELER PHILLIPS, PH.D.
Professor of Mathematics, and Dean of the Graduate School
                                    (90 High st.)   137 Wall st.

GEORGE BURTON ADAMS, PH.D., LITT.D.
Professor of History   57 Edgehill road

Hon. SAMUEL OSCAR PRENTICE, B.A., LL.B.
Professor of Pleading   Hartford
SAMUEL SIMONS SANFORD, M.A.
Professor of Applied Music   50 W. 52d st., New York City
HENRY WALCOTT FARNAM, M.A., R.P.D.
Professor of Political Economy
EDWARD PARMELEE MORRIS, L.H.D.
Professor of the Latin Language and Literature
                                    (194 F.)   53 Edgehill road
Rev. EDWARD LEWIS CURTIS, PH.D., D.D.
*Holmes Professor of the Hebrew Language and Literature,
    and Acting Dean of the Divinity School*
                                    (668 W. D.)   61 Trumbull st.
HENRY WADE ROGERS, LL.D.
*Professor of Equity and Corporations,
    and Dean of the Law School*   (HEN.)   413 Orange st.
HENRY ROSEMANN LANG, PH.D.
*Benjamin F. Barge Professor of the Romance Languages
    and Literature*   (176 L.)   60 Trumbull st.
RUSSELL HENRY CHITTENDEN, PH.D., LL.D., Sc.D.
*Professor of Physiological Chemistry, and Director
    of the Sheffield Scientific School*   (3 S. H.)   83 Trumbull st.
JOHN HAYS HAMMOND, M.A.
Professor of Mining Engineering   New York City
MAX MAILHOUSE, M.D.
Clinical Professor of Neurology   45 Elm st.
HORACE LEMUEL WELLS, Sc.D.
Professor of Analytical Chemistry and Metallurgy
                                    (151 S. C. L.)   445 Orange st.
THOMAS DWIGHT GOODELL, PH.D.
Professor of the Greek Language and Literature   35 Edgehill road
WILLIAM LEWIS ELKIN, PH.D.
Director of the Observatory   477 Prospect st.
Hon. EDWIN BAKER GAGER, M.A.
*Professor of General Jurisprudence, Mortgages, and the
    Law of Public Service Companies*   Derby
EDWARD WASHBURN HOPKINS, PH.D., LL.D.
Professor of Sanskrit and Comparative Philology   299 Lawrence st.
Rev. HARLAN PAGE BEACH, M.A.
Professor of the Theory and Practice of Missions

HERBERT EUGENE SMITH, M.D.
Professor of Chemistry, and Dean of the Medical School
(25 Medical School)   430 George st.

ARTHUR HUBBELL PALMER, M.A.
Professor of the German Language and Literature
149 East Rock road

GEORGE DUTTON WATROUS, D.C.L.
Professor of Torts   (121 Church st.)   261 Bradley st.

HORATIO MCLEOD REYNOLDS, M.A.
Talcott Professor of the Greek Language and Literature
(3 PH.)   85 Trumbull st.

Rev. FRANK CHAMBERLIN PORTER, PH.D., D.D.
Winkley Professor of Biblical Theology   (611 E. D.)   266 Bradley st.

FREDERICK MORRIS WARREN, PH.D., L.H.D.
Street Professor of Modern Languages   (208 F.)   46 Mansfield st.

EDWARD VILETTE RAYNOLDS, D.C.L.
Professor of Comparative Law   168 Prospect st.

WALTER CAMP, B.A.
Treasurer of the Yale Field   New Haven House

GEORGE MARTIN DUNCAN, LL.D.
Professor of Logic and Metaphysics   299 Edwards st.

Rev. BENJAMIN WISNER BACON, D.D., LL.D., LITT.D.
Buckingham Professor of New Testament Criticism and
Interpretation   (605 E. D.)   244 Edwards st.

LOUIS VALENTINE PIRSSON, M.A.
Professor of Physical Geology   (186 K.)   41 Trumbull st.

EDWARD GAYLORD BOURNE, PH.D.
Professor of History

WILLISTON WALKER, PH.D., D.D.
Titus Street Professor of Ecclesiastical History
(668 W. D.)   281 Edwards st.

WILLIAM GILBERT ANDERSON, M.D., M.A.
Director of the Gymnasium   (G.)   1151 Chapel st.

GUSTAV GRUENER, PH.D.
Professor of German   (78 Pearl st.)   146 L.

OLIVER THOMAS OSBORNE, M.D., M.A.
Professor of Materia Medica and Therapeutics,
also Clinical Professor in Medicine   252 York st.

CHARLES CUTLER TORREY, PH.D., D.D.
Professor of the Semitic Languages   (232 F.)   67 Mansfield st.

HENRY LAWRENCE SWAIN, M.D.
Clinical Professor of Laryngology and Otology   232 York st.

HORATIO WILLIAM PARKER, MUS.D.
*Battell Professor of the Theory of Music, and Dean of
    the Department of Music*   (126 College st.) 420 Temple st.

JOHN WURTS, M.A., M.L.
LaFayette S. Foster Professor of the English Common Law
            (16 HEN.) 654 Savin av., West Haven

WILBUR LUCIUS CROSS, PH.D.
*Professor of English, and Librarian of the Sheffield Scientific
    School*   (22 S. H.) 24 Edgehill road

JOHN CHRISTOPHER SCHWAB, PH.D.
Librarian   (LIB.) 310 Prospect st.

CHARLTON MINER LEWIS, PH.D.
Emily Sanford Professor of English Literature
            (190 F.) 425 St.Ronan st.

ARTHUR NATHANIEL ALLING, M.D.
Clinical Professor of Ophthalmology   199 York st.

HARRY BURR FERRIS, M.D.
Hunt Professor of Anatomy   (M. S.) 395 St.Ronan st.

WILLIAM LYON PHELPS, PH.D.
Lampson Professor of English Literature   (A, C.) 44 High st.

ROBERT NELSON CORWIN, PH.D.
Professor of German

ERNEST WILLIAM BROWN, SC.D.
Professor of Mathematics   389 Temple st.

GEORGE LINCOLN HENDRICKSON, L.H.D.
Professor of the Latin Language and Literature

IRVING FISHER, PH.D.
Professor of Political Economy   460 Prospect st.

JAMES PIERPONT, PH.D.
Professor of Mathematics   42 Mansfield st.

HANNS OERTEL, PH.D.
Professor of Linguistics and Comparative Philology
            (2 PH.) New Haven House

PERCEY FRANKLYN SMITH, PH.D.
James E. English Professor of Mathematics
            (26 S. H.) 330 Willow st.

JAMES WILLIAM TOUMEY, M.A., M.S.
*Professor of Forestry, and Director of the Yale
    Botanical Garden*   (MAR.) Prospect st.

CHARLES FOSTER KENT, PH.D.
  Woolsey Professor of Biblical Literature
                                    (145 L.)   406 Humphrey st.

GIFFORD PINCHOT, SC.D.
  Professor of Forestry   Washington, D. C.

CHARLES MONTAGUE BAKEWELL, PH.D.
  Professor of Philosophy   (G, C.)   305 Lawrence st.

ROSS GRANVILLE HARRISON, M.D., PH.D.
  Bronson Professor of Comparative Anatomy   306 York st.

OTTO GUSTAF RAMSAY, M.D.
  Professor of Obstetrics and Gynecology   251 Church st.

RALPH AUGUSTINE MCDONNELL, M.D.
  Clinical Professor of Dermatology   1142 Chapel st.   •

ALEXANDER WILLIAM EVANS, M.D., PH.D.
  Eaton Professor of Botany   (18 S. H.)   67 Mansfield st.

CHARLES SCHUCHERT, M.A.
  *Professor of Paleontology, Curator of the Geological Collec-
      tion, and Professor of Historical Geology in the Sheffield
      Scientific School*   (9 PEAB.)   59 Wall st.

GUY STEVENS CALLENDER, PH.D.
  Professor of Political Economy   (D. C.)   Forest st.

LAFAYETTE BENEDICT MENDEL, PH.D.
  · *Professor of Physiological Chemistry* (63 S. B. L.)   18 Trumbull st.

Rev. AMBROSE WHITE VERNON, D.D.
  *Professor of Practical Theology, and Acting Pastor
      of the University Church*   (632 E. D.)   339 Humphrey st.

HENRY ANDREWS BUMSTEAD, PH.D.
  *Professor of Physics, and Director of the Sloane
      Physical Laboratory*   (S. P. L.)   45 Edgehill road

GEORGE BLUMER, M.D.
  Professor of the Theory and Practice of Medicine   204 York st.

LEE MCCLUNG, M.A.
  Treasurer of the University   (WOOD.)   284 Orange st.

CHARLES JOSEPH BARTLETT, M.D.
  Professor of Pathology   209 York st.

HENRY SOLON GRAVES, M.A.
  *Pinchot Professor of Forestry, and Director of the
      Forest School*   (MAR.)   68 Trumbull st.

HENRY CROSBY EMERY, PH.D.
  Professor of Political Economy   270 Crown st.

CLIVE DAY, PH.D.
Professor of Economic History (D, c.) 44 Highland st.

HARRY BENJAMIN JEPSON, M.A., MUS.B.
Professor of Applied Music, and
    University Organist (MEM.) 294 Lawrence st.

CHARLES HUBBARD JUDD, PH.D.
Professor of Psychology, and Director of the
    Psychological Laboratory (6 HER.) 318 Willow st.

JOSEPH MARSHALL FLINT, M.D.
Professor of the Principles and Practice of Surgery 77 Elm st.

HERBERT ERNEST GREGORY, PH.D.
Silliman Professor of Geology (6 PEAB.) 399 B.

ALBERT GALLOWAY KELLER, PH.D.
Professor of the Science of Society (I HER.) 55 Huntington st.

REV. ANSON PHELPS STOKES, JR., M.A.
Secretary of the University (WOOD.) 73 Elm st.

JOHN DUER IRVING, PH.D.
Professor of Economic Geology (191 K.) 76 Wall st.

ASSISTANT PROFESSORS

WILLIAM BACON BAILEY, PH.D.
Assistant Professor of Political Economy   26 Edgewood av.

CHARLES SEARS BALDWIN, PH.D.
Assistant Professor of Rhetoric   (15 WH.)   57 Wall st.

SAMUEL EBEN BARNEY, C.E.
Assistant Professor of Civil Engineering (132 WIN.) 346 Whitney av.

JOSEPH BARRELL, PH.D.
Assistant Professor of Geology   (1 PEAB.)   85 Avon st.

PAUL VICTOR CHRISTOPHER BAUR, PH.D.
Assistant Professor of Classical Archæology   246 Church st.

FREDERICK ELIJAH BEACH, PH.D.
Assistant Professor of Physics   44 Lyon st.

GEORGE EMERSON BEERS, M.A., M.L.
Assistant Professor of Elementary Law and Real Property
(15 HEN.)   42 Church st.

BERTRAM BORDEN BOLTWOOD, PH.D.
Assistant Professor of Physics   (S. P. L.)   43 Livingston st.

PHILIP EMBURY BROWNING, PH.D.
Assistant Professor of Chemistry   (K. C. L.)   23 Edgehill road

REV. MARION LEROY BURTON, PH.D.
Assistant Professor of Systematic Theology (607 E. D.) 93 Cottage st.

HERMAN HAUPT CHAPMAN, M.F.
Assistant Professor of Forestry   17 Tryon st.

FREDERICK LINCOLN CHASE, PH.D.
Assistant Astronomer in the Observatory   Observatory

CHARLES UPSON CLARK, PH.D.
Assistant Professor of Latin   (194 F.)   473 Edgewood av.

CHARLES CAMERON CLARKE, JR., B.A.
Assistant Professor of French   254 Bradley st.

WESLEY ROSWELL COE, PH.D.
Assistant Professor of Comparative Anatomy
(75 S. B. L.)   484 Orange st.

ARTHUR LINTON CORBIN, B.A., LL.B.
Assistant Professor of Contracts   285 Willow st.

ALBERT EUGENE CURDY, PH.D.
Assistant Professor of French   361 Elm st.

HOLLON AUGUSTINE FARR, PH.D.
Assistant Professor of German   351 WH.

HARRY WARD FOOTE, PH.D.
Assistant Professor of Physical Chemistry   209 Livingston st.

WILLIAM EBENEZER FORD, JR., PH.D.
　Assistant Professor of Mineralogy　　　(183 K.)　16 Lynwood pl.

CLYDE CHEW GLASCOCK, PH.D.
　Assistant Professor of German　　　　　　　　138 V-S.

HERBERT EDWIN HAWKES, PH.D.
　Assistant Professor of Mathematics　　　　45 Huntington st.

YANDELL HENDERSON, PH.D.
　Assistant Professor of Physiology　　　　400 Prospect st.

WILLIAM ERNEST HOCKING, PH.D.
　Assistant Professor of Philosophy

LOUIS DOREMUS HUNTOON, M.E.
　Assistant Professor of Mining and Metallurgy　　284 Orange st.

JAMES W. D. INGERSOLL, PH.D.
　Assistant Professor of Latin　　　　(D, C.)　139 York st.

ANDREW KEOGH, M.A.
　Reference Librarian, and Lecturer in Bibliography
　　　　　　　　　　　　(LIB.)　49 Huntington st.

Rev. CORNELIUS LADD KITCHEL, M.A.
　Secretary of the Bureau of Self-Help and Appointments
　　　　　　　　　　　　(4 PH.)　253 Lawrence st.

HENRY STANLEY KNIGHT
　Assistant Professor of Applied Music　　(C. S. H.).　258 Bradley st.

DAVID ALBERT KREIDER, PH.D.
　Assistant Professor of Physics　　　　(S. P. L.)　298 Lawrence st.

EDWIN HOYT LOCKWOOD, M.E., PH.D.
　Assistant Professor of Mechanical Engineering
　　　　　　　　　　　　(110 WIN.)　79 Division st.　　　　.

RICHARD SWANN LULL, PH.D.
　Assistant Professor of Vertebrate Paleontology, and Associate
　　　　Curator in Vertebrate Paleontology (9 PEAB.)　327 Willow st.

FREDERICK BLISS LUQUIENS, PH.D.
　Assistant Professor of Spanish　　　　　　595 Orange st.

KENNETH MCKENZIE, PH.D.
　Assistant Professor of Italian　　　　　　67 Mansfield st.

WILLIAM CROSBY MARSHALL, M.E., C.E.
　Assistant Professor of Drawing and Descriptive Geometry
　　　　　　　　　　　　(114 WIN.)　201 Edwards st.

ARTHUR MARVIN, M.A.
　Registrar of the Sheffield Scientific School　　(1 S. H.)　40 Lake pl.

MAX MASON, PH.D.
　Assistant Professor of Mathematics　　　　87 Cottage st.

ALFRED KINDRED MERRITT, B.A.
　Registrar of the College Faculty　　　　(LAM.)　38 V.

GEORGE HENRY NETTLETON, PH.D.
  Assistant Professor of English   339 Prospect st.

JOHN PEASE NORTON, PH.D.
  Assistant Professor of Political Economy   551 Orange st.

EDWARD BLISS REED, PH.D.
  Assistant Professor of English   (B, C.)   215 Bishop st.

LEO FREDERICK RETTGER, PH.D.
  Assistant Professor of Bacteriology and Hygiene
                              (12 S. H.)   370 Edgewood av.

OLIVER HUNTINGTON RICHARDSON, PH.D.
  Assistant Professor of History   284 Orange st.

ROBERT LOUIS SANDERSON, M.A.
  Assistant Professor of French   (228 F.)   277 Willow st.

RUDOLPH SCHEVILL, PH.D.
  *Assistant Professor of the Spanish Language
    and Literature*   431 FW.

CHARLES PHINEAS SHERMAN, D.C.L.
  *Assistant Professor of Roman Law, and
    Librarian of the Law School*   438 Edgewood av.

JOHN CLAYTON TRACY, C.E.
  Assistant Professor of Structural Engineering
                              (131 WIN.)   345 Winthrop av.

ISIDOR TROOSTWYK
  *Assistant Professor of Applied Music, and Instructor in
      Violin-Playing*   (C. S. H.)   179 Bradley st.

FRANK PELL UNDERHILL, PH.D.
  Assistant Professor of Physiological Chemistry
                              (63 S. B. L.)   91 Clark st.

PERCY TALBOT WALDEN, PH.D.
  Assistant Professor of Chemistry   (159 S. C. L.)   367 Prospect st.

HENRY LORD WHEELER, PH.D.
  Assistant Professor of Organic Chemistry (S. C. L.) 45 Trumbull st.

LYNDE PHELPS WHEELER, PH.D.
  Assistant Professor of Physics   (118 WIN.)   124 Linden st.

FREDERICK WELLS WILLIAMS, B.A.
  Assistant Professor of Modern Oriental History

HENRY BURT WRIGHT, PH.D.
  Assistant Professor of Roman History and Latin Literature   A.

GEORGE ZAHM, M.L.
  Assistant Professor of Mercantile Law and Insurance
                                              New York City

INSTRUCTORS

JOHN CHESTER ADAMS, PH.D.
Instructor in English (A, C.) 75 Mansfield st.

HENRY SCHUYLER ANDERSON
Instructor in Gymnastics 350 Humphrey st.

ROSWELL PARKER ANGIER, PH.D.
Instructor in Psychology (7 HER.) 44 Elm st.

ERNST HERMANN ARNOLD, M.D.
Instructor in Orthopædic Surgery 46 York sq.

KAN-ICHI ASAKAWA, PH.D.
Instructor in the History of Japanese Civilization, and
Curator of the Japanese and Chinese Collections
385 Winthrop av.

FRANCIS BACON, M.D., SC D.
Lecturer on Medical Jurisprudence 32 High st.

GEORGE MERRICK BAKER, PH.D.
Instructor in German

Professor JOHN SPENCER BASSETT, PH.D.
Lecturer on American History (90 High st.) Northampton, Mass.

WILLIAM BATESON, M.A., F.R.S.
Silliman Memorial Lecturer Cambridge, England

JOHN KIMBERLY BEACH, B.A., LL.B.
Lecturer on Patents, Admiralty, Copyright, and Trade Mark
450 Temple st.

WILLIAM HILL BEAN, M.D.
Instructor in Materia Medica 252 York st.

FRANK HERBERT BEEDE, B.A.
Lecturer on School Organization and Administration
424 Temple st.

JOHN MILTON BERDAN, PH.D.
Instructor in Rhetoric (11 WH.) 681 Orange st.

ANDREW TEW BIERKAN, D.C.L.
Instructor in Commercial Accounts 42 Church st.

HIRAM BINGHAM, PH.D.
Lecturer on South American Geography and History
(201 F.) 58 Everitt st.

AVARD LONGLEY BISHOP, PH.D.
Instructor in Commercial Geography 120 York st.

LOUIS BENNETT BISHOP, M.D.
Instructor in Pediatrics 356 Orange st.

RICHARD MERVIN BISSELL, B.A.
Lecturer on Insurance   Hartford

THEODORE HARDING BOGGS, B.A.
Instructor in Commercial Geography   (HER.) 115 Park st.

FRANK JOSEPH BORN, M.A., M.D.
Medical Assistant at the Gymnasium   125 High st.

EDWARD AUGUSTUS BOWERS, B.A., LL.B.
Lecturer on Forest Law   209 Crown st.

ISAIAH BOWMAN, B.S.
Instructor in Geography   (I PEAB.) 203 York st.

Rev. Professor BORDEN PARKER BOWNE, D.D., LL.D.
Lecturer on Systematic Theology   Boston, Mass.

RALPH CLEMENT BRYANT, F.E.
Instructor in Forestry   217 St. Ronan st.

HORACE THOMAS BURGESS, M.A.
Instructor in Mathematics   700 W. D.

EDWARD HERBERT CAMERON, PH.D.
Instructor in Psychology   (10 HER.) 67 Howe st.

HENRY SEIDEL CANBY, PH.D.
Instructor in English   105 Mansfield st.

HOWARD WADSWORTH CHURCH, M.A.
Instructor in German   78 Lake pl.

RAYMOND GILMORE CLAPP, B.D., M.A.
*Instructor in Biblical Literature, and Director of
Religious Work in the Divinity School*   613 E. D.

LEON JACOB COLE, PH.D.
Instructor in Zoology   (14 PEAB.) 186 Lawrence st.

WILLIAM JAMES COMSTOCK, PH.B.
Instructor in Organic Chemistry   43 Trumbull st.

FRANK LAWRENCE COOPER, PH.D.
Instructor in Physics   40 Lake pl.

MACGRANE COXE, B.A., LL.B.
Lecturer on Bankruptcy   63 Wall st., New York City

PAUL CURTS, M.A.
Instructor in German   3 Hillhouse av.

HAROUTUNE MUGURDICH DADOURIAN, PH.D.
Instructor in Physics   299 York st.

LEONARD MAYHEW DAGGETT, B.A., LL.B.
Instructor in Wills   (42 Church st.) 60 Wall st.

2

WILLIAM GIBBONS DAGGETT, M.D.
Clinical Lecturer on Medicine   189 Church st.

HENRY BRONSON DEWING, M.A.
Instructor in Greek   219 F.

ALLEN ROSS DIEFENDORF, M.D.
Lecturer on Psychiatry   Middletown

EDWARD LEWIS DURFEE, B.A.
Instructor in History   95 Cottage st.

WILLARD HIGLEY DURHAM, B.A.
Instructor in English   701 W. D.

GEORGE FRANCIS EATON, PH.D.
*Instructor in Comparative Osteology, Curator of the Osteological
      Collection, and Associate Curator in Vertebrate Paleontology*
            (9 PEAB.)   80 Sachem st.

JOHN WARREN EDGERTON, M.A., LL.B.
*Instructor in Mercantile Law, and Secretary of the
      Law Faculty*   (HEN.)   77 Elm st.

FRED ROGERS FAIRCHILD, PH.D.
Instructor in Political Economy   1233 Chapel st.

CHARLES SHERMAN FARNHAM, C.E.
Instructor in Civil Engineering   671 W. D.

Rev. President WILLIAM HERBERT PERRY FAUNCE, D.D., LL.D.
Lyman Beecher Lecturer on Preaching   Providence, R. I.

EMERSON DAVID FITE, PH.D.
Instructor in History   85 Cottage st.

JOHN PIERREPONT CODRINGTON FOSTER, M.D.
Instructor in Anatomy   109 College st.

ROGER FOSTER, M.A., LL.B.
Lecturer on Federal Jurisprudence   79 W. 54th st., New York City

MILTON STAHL GARVER, PH.D.
Instructor in French   3 B. M. H.

LOUIS MICHAEL GOMPERTZ, M.D.
Clinical Instructor in Medicine   1195 Chapel st.

WILLIAM ANTHONY GRANVILLE, PH.D.
Instructor in Mathematics   (46 N. S. H.)   118 Howe st.

ARTHUR HARMOUNT GRAVES, PH.D.
Instructor in Botany   97 Grove st.

ALBERT EDWARD GUBELMANN, PH.D.
Instructor in German   95 Brownell st.

WILLIAM DAMERON GUTHRIE, M.A.
W. L. Storrs Lecturer on Municipal Law   New York City

WILLIAM EDWIN HAESCHE, MUS.B.
  Instructor in Instrumentation   19 Whitney av.

WILLIAM LOGAN HALL
  Lecturer on Tree Planting   Washington, D. C.

EDWARD AVERY HARRIMAN, LL.B.
  Instructor in Comparative Administrative Law   Derby

RALPH CHIPMAN HAWLEY, M.F.
  Instructor in Forestry   634 E. D.

CHARLES WILLARD HAYES, PH.D.
  Lecturer on Appalachian Geology   Washington, D. C.

CARLE WILLIAM HENZE, M.D.
  Clinical Instructor in Medicine   22 Trumbull st.

LAURENCE ILSLEY HEWES, PH.D.
  Instructor in Mathematics   Hamden

JOHN MARSHALL HOLCOMBE, M.A.
  Lecturer on Insurance   Hartford

LUCIUS HUDSON HOLT, PH.D.
  Instructor in English   315 Crown st.

WILLIAM BRIAN HOOKER, M.A.
  Instructor in Rhetoric   (15 WH.)   121 W.

ANDREW DELMAR HOPKINS, PH.D.
  Lecturer on Forest Entomology   Washington, D. C.

REV. EDWARD SACKETT HUME, M.A.
  Instructor in Missions   (606 E. D.)   79 Howe st.

ELLSWORTH HUNTINGTON, M.A.
  Instructor in Geography   708 W. D.

Professor CHARLES CHENEY HYDE, M.A., LL.B.
  Lecturer on International Law   Chicago, Ill.

THOMAS VINCENT HYNES, M.D.
  Clinical Instructor in Obstetrics   27 College st.

GEORGE SAMUEL JAMIESON, PH.D.
  Instructor in Analytical Chemistry   162 S. C. L.

ROSS JEWELL, PH.B.
  Instructor in German   Newtown

CARL OSCAR JOHNS, PH.D.
  Instructor in Chemistry   162 S. C. L.

TREAT BALDWIN JOHNSON, PH.D.
  Instructor in Chemistry   (151 S. C. L.)   120 Dwight st.

WILLIAM SAVAGE JOHNSON, PH.D.
  Instructor in English   361 Elm st.

Rev. HERBERT ATCHINSON JUMP, B.D.
  Alumni Lecturer in the Divinity School   Brunswick, Me.

RICHARD SHELTON KIRBY, C.E.
  Instructor in Sanitary Engineering   297 Crown st.

HOWARD HOYT KNAPP, B.A., LL.B.
  Lecturer on Connecticut Practice

BEVERLY WAUGH KUNKEL, PH.D.
  Instructor in Biology   179 V-S.

GEORGE HENRY LANGZETTEL, B.F.A.
  Instructor in Drawing, and Secretary of the Art School
                                    (A. S.)   725 Whitney av.

IRVILLE CHARLES LeCOMPTE, PH.D.
  Instructor in French   35 Beers st.

DWIGHT MILTON LEWIS, M.D.
  Clinical Instructor in Medicine   438 George st.

EDWARD MORGAN LEWIS, M.A.
  Instructor in Elocution   (610 E. D.) Williamstown, Mass.

WILLIAM ALBERT LILLEY, JR., M.E.
  Instructor in Mechanical Engineering   781 Orange st.

WILLIAM RAYMOND LONGLEY, PH.D.
  Instructor in Mathematics   121 Brownell st.

GEORGE BLAKEMAN LOVELL, M.A.
  Instructor in German   765 Whitney av.

JOHN BODINE LUNGER
  Lecturer on Insurance   Hartford

DAVID RUSSELL LYMAN, M.D.
  Clinical Lecturer on Tuberculosis   Wallingford

EDWARD MICHAEL McCABE, M.D.
  Clinical Instructor on Ophthalmology   22 Elm st.

GEORGE GRANT MacCURDY, PH.D.
  Lecturer on Anthropology, and Curator of the Anthropological
    Collection   (10 PEAB.)   237 Church st.

Rev. ERNEST FRANK McGREGOR, M.A.
  Instructor in Sociology   Clinton

EVERETT JAMES McKNIGHT, M.D.
  Instructor in Surgery   Hartford

Rev. ALBERT ALONZO MADSEN, PH.D.
  Instructor in Palestinian Geography   Durham

MAX SOLOMON MANDELL
  Instructor in Russian   101 Orange st.

CARLTON HOWARD MARYOTT, B.A.
Instructor in Chemistry   U. C.

LAWRENCE MASON, B.A.
Instructor in English   245 York st.

CHAMPION HERBERT MATHEWSON, PH.D.
Instructor in Chemistry and Metallography
(H. M. L.) 666 Chapel st.

CLARENCE WHITTLESEY MENDELL, M.A.
Instructor in Latin   86 c.

STEWART LEA MIMS, B.A.
Instructor in History   701 W. D.

SYDNEY KNOX MITCHELL, PH.D.
Instructor in History   152 Whalley av.

ROBERT CLARK MORRIS, D.C.L.
Lecturer on International Arbitration
767 Fifth av., New York City

CYRUS LaRUE MUNSON, M.A., LL.B.
Lecturer on General Legal Practice   Williamsport, Pa.

GEORGE HEWITT MYERS, M.F.
Lecturer on Forestry Abroad   Washington, D. C.

FREDERICK HAYNES NEWELL, B.S.
Lecturer on Forest Hydrography   Washington, D. C.

WATSON NICHOLSON, PH.D.
Instructor in English   329 Whalley av.

HERBERT BRINKERHOFF NORTH, PH.B.
Instructor in Drawing and Descriptive Geometry   250 Whalley av.

Hon. EPAPHRODITUS PECK, LL.B.
Instructor in Evidence, Practice, Procedure, and
Domestic Relations   Bristol

Hon. JOHN HOYT PERRY, M.A., LL.B.
Lecturer on Parliamentary Law   Southport

CHARLES DICKINSON PHELPS, M.D.
Instructor in Physical Diagnosis   642 Campbell av., West Haven

ISAAC KING PHELPS, PH.D.
Instructor in Chemistry   (K. C. L.) 84 Wall st.

FREDERICK ERASTUS PIERCE, M.A.
Instructor in English and Debating
622 Washington av., West Haven

OVERTON WESTFELDT PRICE, B.A.
Lecturer on Government Forestry   Washington, D. C.

CHARLES RABOLD
Instructor in Singing 141 E. 16th st., New York City

JOSEPH CHAPPELL RAYWORTH, M.A.
*Instructor in Mathematics in the Academical Department, and
Assistant in Mathematics in the Sheffield Scientific School*
120 York st.

JOHN DOUGAN REA, M.A.
Instructor in Latin 351 Crown st.

CHAUNCEY BREWSTER RICE, PH.D.
Instructor in Applied Electricity (56 N. S. H.) 61 Huntington st.

JOHN PIERREPONT RICE, M.A.
Instructor in French 179 V-S.

FREDERICK OSCAR ROBBINS, B.A.
Instructor in French 215 Livingston st.

CHALFANT ROBINSON, PH.D.
Instructor in History 233 Edwards st.

HENRY HOLLISTER ROBINSON, C.E., PH.D.
Instructor in Geology

JOSEPH WICKHAM ROE, M.E.
Instructor in Mechanical Engineering 79 Trumbull st.

EDWARD KING ROOT, M.D.
*Lecturer on Life Insurance Examinations in the
Medical School* Hartford

Professor JOSIAH ROYCE, PH.D., LL.D.
Lecturer on Philosophy Cambridge, Mass.

LEONARD CUTLER SANFORD, M.D.
Instructor in Operative Surgery 347 Temple st.

HERMANN VON SCHRENK, PH.D.
Lecturer on Wood Preservation St. Louis, Mo.

LEO SCHULZ
Instructor in Violoncello-Playing Woodcliff, Bergen Co., N. J.

ROBERT LIVINGSTON SCHUYLER, M.A.
Instructor in History 879 Elm st.

ERNEST WILSON SHELDON, B.A.
Instructor in Mathematics 542 P.

WILLIAM KENT SHEPARD, PH.D.
Instructor in Mechanics 321 Willow st.

DAVID STANLEY SMITH, B.A., MUS.B.
*Instructor in the Theory of Music, and Secretary of the
Department of Music* (126 College st.) 120 Linden st.

CLARENCE GILMAN SPALDING, PH.B.
  Demonstrator of Pharmacy   9 High st.
FREDERICK NOYES SPERRY, M.D.
  Clinical Instructor in Laryngology   42 College st.
WILLIAM SPRENGER, M.D.
  Demonstrator of the Uses of the X-Rays   366 George st.
THOMAS THACHER, LL.D.
  Lecturer on Corporations   62 Cedar st., New York City
ELBERT NEVIUS SÈBRING THOMPSON, PH.D.
  Instructor in Rhetoric   (11 WH.)   732 Elm st.
GEORGE ALBERT THOMPSON, B.F.A.
  Instructor in Painting   (A. S.)   79 Clinton av.
WILMOT HAINES THOMPSON, JR., PH.D.
  Tutor in Greek   157 L.
EDWARD THORSTENBERG, PH.D.
  Instructor in German   35 Lynwood pl.
HARRY DONALD TIEMANN, M.E., M.F.
  Lecturer on Forest Technology   MAR.
CHAUNCEY BREWSTER TINKER, PH.D.
  Instructor in English   245 D.
JAMES MULFORD TOWNSEND, B.A., LL.B.
  Lecturer on Transfer of Monetary Securities
                                 318 West 75th st., New York City
THOMAS ALLEN TULLY, B.A.
  Recorder of the College Faculty   (LAM.)   130 Howe st.
HORACE SCUDDER UHLER, PH.D.
  Instructor in Physics   (S. P. L.) 86 Avon st.
ALBERT WILLIAM VANBUREN, B.A.
  Instructor in the History of Roman Religion   9 Trumbull st.
RALPH GIBBS VANNAME, PH.D.
  Instructor in Chemistry   (K. C. L.) 121 High st.
AXEL EBENEZER VESTLING, PH.D.
  Instructor in German   73 Avon st.
CURTIS HOWE WALKER, PH.D.
  Instructor in History   399 B.
ARTHUR GUSTAVUS WARD, PH.D.
  Instructor in German   152 Whalley av.
FREEMAN WARD, B.A.
  Instructor in Geology and Mineralogy   106 Howe st.

JAMES HENRY WEBB, B.S., LL.B.
Instructor in Criminal Procedure and Criminal Law　42 Church st.

JOHN WESLEY WETZEL, PH.B.
Instructor in Public Speaking　　　　　(HEN.)　16 Dwight st.

JAMES EVERETT WHEELER, B.A., LL.B.
Lecturer on Looking up the Law　　　　　　82 Edgehill road

GEORGE REBER WIELAND, PH.D.
Lecturer on Paleobotany　　　　　(27 PEAB.)　Woodmont

LEWIS WILLIAMS
Instructor in Piano-Playing　　　　　　　284 Orange st.

Professor GEORG WOBBERMIN, PH.D.
Nathaniel William Taylor Lecturer　　　　Breslau, Germany

LORANDE LOSS WOODRUFF, PH.D.
Instructor in Biology　　　　(73 S. B. L.)　835 Orange st.

LESTER WILLIAM ZARTMAN, PH.D.
Instructor in Insurance and Political Economy　　100 Brownell st.

ASSISTANTS IN INSTRUCTION

CLARENCE EDWARD ANDREWS, B.A.
Assistant in English 12 France st., Norwalk

HAROLD SEARS ARNOLD, M.D.
Assistant in Pathology and Bacteriology 36 Dwight st.

CLIFFORD WHITMAN BATES, PH.B.
Assistant in Physics 293 York st.

FREDERICK GEORGE BECK, M.D.
Clinical Assistant in Gynecology 821 Congress av.

GEORGE ELBERT BECK, B.A.
Assistant in Physical Geography 7 Library st.

HORACE DOOLITTLE BELLIS
Assistant in Gymnastics G.

STANLEY ROSSITER BENEDICT, B.A.
Laboratory Assistant in Biology (64 S. B. I.) 77 Grove st.

SAMUEL JOHN BERARD
*Assistant in Descriptive Geometry and Machine Design, and
Assistant Librarian of the Sheffield Scientific School*
813 Orange st.

EARL GORDON BILL, B.A.
Assistant in Mathematics 122 Howe st.

SETH DANIELS BINGHAM, JR., B.A.
Assistant in Organ-Playing 94 Prospect st.

EUGENE MAURICE BLAKE, M.D.
Clinical Assistant in Ophthalmology 199 York st.

FREDERIC THOMAS BLANCHARD, B.L.
Assistant in Rhetoric (15 WH.) 650 E. D.

WALTER MINOR BRADLEY, PH.B.
Assistant in Mineralogy 1346 Chapel st.

CHARLES ALEXANDER COCKAYNE, M.A.
Assistant in Philosophy 105 Park st.

CHARLTON DOWS COOKSEY, PH.B.
Assistant in Physics 284 Orange st.

WILLIS HANFORD CROWE, M.D.
Clinical Assistant in Ophthalmology 106 Whalley av.

JOHN HAMILTON DERBY, JR., PH.B.
Laboratory Assistant in Chemistry 110 Wall st.

WILLIAM COLLIER DOLE
Assistant in the Gymnasium 331 Edgewood av.

WILLIAM ALLEN DRUSHEL, B.S., B.A., LL.B.
Assistant in the Kent Chemical Laboratory　　47 Lake pl.

HENRY PRATT FAIRCHILD, B.A.
Assistant in Commercial Geography　　(3a HER.)　1233 Chapel st.

WILLIAM RUTHVEN FLINT, M.A.
Assistant in the Kent Chemical Laboratory　　121 Dwight st.

FRANK NUGENT FREEMAN, M.A.
Assistant in the Psychological Laboratory, and Proctor　　227 F.

GEORGE EDWARD GAGE, B.A.
Laboratory Assistant in Bacteriology　　(12 S. H.)　642 E. D.

RUSSELL TYNER GARD, PH.B.
Laboratory Assistant in Mining and Metallurgy　　685 W. D.

ASA RUSSELL GIFFORD, M.A.
Assistant in Philosophy　　227 F.

JOSEPH LEO GILMORE, M.D.
Clinical Assistant in Pediatrics　　198 Main st., West Haven

GEORGE FREDERICK GUNDELFINGER, PH.B.
Assistant in Mathematics　　124 Wall st.

WILLIS ELLIS HARTSHORN, M.D.
Clinical Assistant in Surgery　　1138 Chapel st.

FRED HARVEY HEATH, B.S.
Assistant in the Kent Chemical Laboratory　　712 W. D.

ARCHIBALD CECIL HERBERT, M.D.
Clinical Assistant in Medicine　　159 Elm st.

ALBERT WALLACE HULL, B.A.
Assistant in the Sloane Physical Laboratory; and
　　Sloane Fellow　　120 York st.

LON LEWIS HUTCHISON, B.A.
Assistant in Geology　　(PRAB.)　127 Dwight st.

FLORENCE BINGHAM KINNE, M.A.
Laboratory Assistant in Pathology　　96 Sherman av.

ISRAEL SIMON KLEINER, PH.B.
Assistant in Physiological Chemistry　　39 Howe st.

HENRY FREDERICK KLENKE, M.D.
Clinical Assistant in Dermatology　　11 Wooster pl.

CLARENCE MOORE KNOX, PH.B.
Assistant in Drawing　　685 Yale P. O.

JOHN EDWARD LANE, M.D.
Clinical Assistant in Medicine　　203 York st.

WALTER SIDDERS LAY, M.D.
Clinical Assistant in Pediatrics   Centerville

WILLIAM HARDING LONGLEY, B.A.
Laboratory Assistant in Biology   120 York st.

JOHN FRANKLIN LYMAN, B.S.
Laboratory Assistant in Biology   706 W. D.

KENNETH GERARD MACKENZIE, PH.B.
Laboratory Assistant in Chemistry   162 S. C. L.

EDWIN CYRUS MILLER, B.A.
Laboratory Assistant in Botany   7 Library st.

FOSTER STEBBINS NAETHING, PH.B.
Laboratory Assistant in Mining and Metallurgy   124 Prospect st.

HOWARD DOUGLASS NEWTON, B.S.
Assistant in the Kent Chemical Laboratory   117 Wall st.

GEORGE ELWOOD NICHOLS, B.A.
Assistant in Botany, and Proctor   569 P.

LOUIS ADOLPH NOTKINS, M.D.
Assistant in Physical Diagnosis   704 Howard av.

THOMAS AUGUSTINE O'BRIEN, M.D.
Clinical Assistant in Neurology   230 Oak st.

RAYMOND WILLIAM OSBORNE, B.A.
Assistant in the Kent Chemical Laboratory   K. C. L.

WILLIAM ARNOLD PALMER
Assistant in Gymnastics   (G.) 333 York st.

CLARENCE CURTISS PERRY, PH.B.
Assistant in Physics and Steam Engine   121 Maple st.

RICHARD FOSTER RAND, M.D.
Clinical Assistant in Gynecology and Surgery   246 Church st.

EDWIN JAY ROBERTS, B.S.
Assistant in the Kent Chemical Laboratory   712 W. D.

HEATON RIDGEWAY ROBERTSON, B.A., PH.B.
Assistant in Mining and Metallurgy

MAX SCHWARTZ
Assistant in the Gymnasium   465 Dixwell av.

HERBERT LEE SEWARD, PH.B.
Assistant in Shop Visiting and Drawing   116 V-S.

EDWIN KINMOUTH SMITH, PH.B.
Laboratory Assistant in Chemistry   51 Prospect st.

CARL FRANK SPEH, PH.B.
Laboratory Assistant in Chemistry   (S. C. L.) Short Beach

SEYMOUR LEOPOLD SPIER, M.D.
Clinical Assistant in Surgery 359 Crown st.

FRANK BILLINGS STANDISH, M.D.
Clinical Assistant in Medicine 312 Elm st.

HARRY MERRIMAN STEELE, M.D.
Clinical Assistant in Pediatrics 226 Church st.

THOMAS SMITH TAYLOR, B.A.
Assistant in the Sloane Physical Laboratory 687 W. D.

BURTON ISAAC TOLLES, M.D.
Assistant in Anatomy 196 York st.

ROBERT GRAHAM TRACY, M.D.
Clinical Assistant in Surgery 407 Howard av.

HIRAM LEE WARD, B.A.
Assistant in the Kent Chemical Laboratory 205 F.

HARRY LITTLE WELCH, M.D.
Clinical Assistant in Gynecology . 44 College st.

FRANK ELBERT WHEELOCK, B.A.
Assistant in the Sloane Physical Laboratory 120 York st.

RALPH WILLIAM YOUNG, PH.B.
Laboratory Assistant in Mining and Metallurgy 665 W. D.

ASSISTANTS IN ADMINISTRATION

DONALD ALLISON ADAMS, B.A.
 Proctor 569 P.

MRS. EUNICE M. ANDERSON
 Matron of the Infirmary 276 Prospect st.

HENRY A. BARNES
 Superintendent of the University Engineering Department
  (rear HER.) 80 Admiral st.

WILLIAM DELUCE BARNES, JR., B.A.
 Secretary of the Academical Department of the Yale
  University Christian Association, and
  Superintendent of Dwight Hall Dwight Hall

CLARA LOUISA BARNUM, B.A.
 Assistant in the University Secretary's Office 344 Humphrey st.

THOMAS ROSSITER BARNUM, B.A.
 Assistant to the Secretary of the University
  (WOOD.) 344 Humphrey st.

MARSHALL MOORE BARTHOLOMEW, PH.B.
 Secretary of the Scientific Department of the Yale
  University Christian Association B. M. H.

JOHN BAUER, B.A.
 Proctor 565 P.

GEORGE MERWIN BEERS
 Clerk in the Treasurer's Office of the Sheffield Scientific School
  (3 S. H.) 130 Cottage st.

ELIZABETH DESHLER BOGGS
 Assistant in the Library (LIB.) 327 Willow st.

THOMAS ATTWATER BOSTWICK
 Assistant in the Peabody Museum (9 PEAB.) 43 Livingston st.

CHARLES CLARK BROWN, PH.B.
 Private Secretary to the Secretary of the University
  (WOOD.) 22 Lynwood pl.

KATHARINE JEANNETTE BUSH, PH.D.
 Assistant in the Peabody Museum (13 PEAB.) 133 Howe st.

GEORGE HANFORD BUTLER
 Cashier in the Bursar's Office (25 LAM.) 136 Dwight st.

PAUL MORGAN BUTTERFIELD, B.A.
 Proctor 589 P.

MRS. JENNIE CAMPBELL
 Cataloguer in the Library (LIB.) 142 Norton st.

RUBY MCINTYRE CHATFIELD
Assistant in the University Secretary's Office
(WOOD.) 102 Dwight st.

RUTH LOUISE COMES
Cataloguer in the Library (LIB.) 382 Dixwell av.

JAMES ALOYSIUS DELACEY
Assistant in the Library (LIB.) 179 Exchange st.

KARL DIEHL
Assistant in the Library (LIB.) 43 Sylvan av.

A. PAMELIA DINGMAN
Cataloguer in the Library (LIB.) 78 Lake pl.

JOHN IRELAND HOWE DOWNES, B.F.A.
Librarian of the Art School 345 Whitney av.

WILLIAM ALFRED DUDLEY
Cashier in the Gymnasium (G.) Guilford

JOEL NELSON ENO, M.A.
Cataloguer in the Library (LIB.) 130 Howe st.

CHARLES DAVID FAIRMAN
Assistant in the Library (LIB.) 208 Whalley av.

CLIFFORD PIERPONT FOOTE
Clerk in the Bursar's Office (25 LAM.) Stony Creek

JANE ADALINE FORBES
Clerk in the Registrar's Office of the Sheffield Scientific School
Kimberly av., East Haven

HUGH GIBB
Assistant in the Peabody Museum (26 PEAB.) 229 Lloyd st.

MRS. HENRIETTA CLARK GILBERT
Assistant in the Library (LIB.) 26 Kensington st.

EDNA MAY GILLETTE
Private Secretary to the Librarian (LIB.) 252 Winthrop av.

HENRY ROBERT GRUENER
Assistant in the Library . (LIB.) 78 Pearl st.

CHARLES WATSON HAWTHORN HAND
Assistant at the Gymnasium 158 York st.

MRS. JESSIE CRAIG HARGER
Cataloguer in the Library (LIB.) 14 University pl.

ELLEN A. HEDRICK, B.A.
Catalogue Reviser in the Library (LIB.) 65 Grove st.

ARABELLA ENSIGN HORTON
Cataloguer in the Library (LIB.) 202 Crown st.

ADA SUSAN HOTCHKISS
  Private Secretary to the President   ·   (WOOD.) 45 Lake pl.

FRANK EDWIN HOTCHKISS   ·
  Superintendent of the Grounds and Buildings   104 High st.

ANNIE ELIZA HUTCHINS
  Catalogue Reviser in the Library   Library

JAMES READE HUTCHINSON
  *Assistant Clerk in the Treasurer's Office of the
    Sheffield Scientific School*   (3 S. H.) Branford

SARA GARDNER HYDE
  Catalogue Reviser in the Library   (LIB.) 65 Grove st.

EDWARD CRANDALL JOHNSON   ·
  Superintendent of the University Dining Hall   1361 Chapel st.

GEORGE ALEXANDER JOHNSON
  Assistant in the Library   (LIB.) 1916 State st.

ELIZABETH CULLEN KAVANAUGH
  Clerk in the Forest School   14 Compton st.

CONSTANCE KERSCHNER
  Cataloguer in the Library   (LIB.) 261 Winthrop av.

ARNE KILDAL, PH.B., B.L.S.
  Catalogue Reviser in the Library   Library

MRS. CHARLES TODD LINCOLN
  Private Secretary to the Dean of the Academical Department
    126 McKinley av.

MAY B. LYON
  Private Secretary to the Faculty of the Divinity School
    (668 W. D.) 100 Howe st.

BENEDICT EDWARD LYONS, B.A.
  Registrar of the Law School   (HEN.) 155 Elm st.

JAMES STERLING MCCLELLAND
  Private Secretary to the Treasurer
    (WOOD.) 70 Smith st., West Haven

JOHN GILLESPIE MAGEE, B.A.
  *University General Secretary of the Yale University Christian
    Association*   2 Dwight Hall

ARTHUR LAUREN MALTBY
  Assistant Registrar of the Law School   (HEN.) 187 F.

JOHN MAUTTE
  Engineer of the Sheffield Scientific School
    32 Dudley st., Highwood

MARY M. MAYER
  Private Secretary to the Director of the Sheffield Scientific School
                                          (3 S. H.)   475 Elm st.

WILBUR ALLEN MAYNARD
  Assistant in the Bursar's Office   (25 LAM.)   68 Gilbert av.

EZRA PECK MERRIAM
  Superintendent of the Divinity Buildings   108 College st.

MARY GRACE MERRITT
  Resident Nurse at the Infirmary   276 Prospect st.

ANNA MARIE MONRAD, B.S.
  Cataloguer in the Library   146 Norton st.

JOHN E. MOXLEY
  Machinist of the Sheffield Scientific School
                                          411 Blohm st., West Haven

JAMES ALLAN MUNRO
  Superintendent of the Buildings and Maintenance Department
                                          (88 High st.)   88 Lake pl.

JOHN HILL MURRAY
  Head Gardener of the Yale Botanical Garden   227 Mansfield st.

LILLIE BELLE NASON
  Accountant in the University Steam Department   84 Park st.

EDWARD THEODORE NEWELL. B.A.
  Curator of tho Numismatic Collections   (LIB.)   Kenosha, Wisc.

CORNELIA E. NOTZ, B.A.
  Cataloguer in the Library   (LIB.)   221 Orchard st.

HENRY MINOTT OSBORN
  College Bursar   (25 LAM.)   406 Orange st.

HARRY JUDD OSTRANDER
  Clerk in the Treasurer's Office   (WOOD.)   328 Humphrey st.

JESSIE AGNES PARSONS
  Cataloguer in the Library   (LIB.)   917 Howard av.

HARRIET BENTON PHELPS
  Cataloguer in the Library   (LIB.)   67 Dwight st.

CAROLYN QUENTIN
  Private Secretary to the Dean of the Department of Music
                                          (126 College st.)   Whitneyville

WILLIAM EUSTIS ROWLAND
  Cashier in the Treasurer's Office   (WOOD.)   480 Winthrop av.

MAYNARD RAY SANBORN
  Assistant in the Library   (LIB.)   25 Woodland st.

MASON FOOTE SMITH, PH.B.
Assistant in the Observatory W. O.

JAMES PRESTON STRONG
Accountant in the Treasurer's Office (WOOD.) 222 Sherman av.

SARA ELIZABETH THACHER
Accountant in the Department of Buildings and Maintenance
441 Second av., West Haven

MRS. ALEPH KIMBALL THOMPSON
Clerk of the Medical School, and Private Secretary to
the Dean of the Medical School 96 Park st.

I. MAUDE TISDALE
Cataloguer in the Library (LIB.) 268 Orchard st.

CLARA BEATRICE UNDERWOOD
Private Secretary to the Dean of the Graduate School
(90 High st.) 130 Howe st.

ADRIENNE VAN WINKLE
Catalogue Reviser in the Library (LIB.) 98 Howe st.

ALICE AMELIA WOOD, B.S.
Cataloguer in the Library (LIB.) 1305 Chapel st.

CECIL WRIGHT
Proctor 542 P.

GRADUATE FELLOWS AND SCHOLARS

HARRY L. AGARD, B.A., *Graduate Scholar* 711 W. D.

MAY A. ALLEN, B.A., *University Fellow* 256 Edgewood av.

CLARENCE E. ANDREWS, B.A., *Cuyler Fellow in Yale College* 1026 Yale P. O.

ARTHUR H. BASYE, M.A., *Bulkley Fellow in Yale College* 204 F.

JOHN BAUER, B.A., *Eldridge Fellow in Yale College* 565 P.

STANLEY D. BEARD, PH.B., *Sheffield Graduate Scholar* A.

GEORGE E. BECK, B.A., *Foote Fellow in Yale College* .7 Library st.

THEODORE H. BOGGS, M.A., *Eldridge Fellow in Yale College* 115 Park st.

HARRY G. BROWN, B.A., *University Fellow* 82 Whalley av.

HORACE T. BURGESS, M.A., *Foote Fellow in Yale College* 700 Yale P. O.

JOSEPHINE M. BURNHAM, PH.B., *University Fellow* 142 York st.

HENRY H. CARTER, B.A., *Graduate Scholar* 129 Mansfield st.

LOIS CLARK, B.A., *Graduate Scholar* 130 Howe st.

CHARLES A. COCKAYNE, M.A., *University Fellow* 105 Park st.

HENRY B. DEWING, M.A., *University Fellow* 219 F.

WILLIAM A. DRUSHEL, B.A., LL.B., *Silliman Fellow in Yale College* 47 Lake pl.

GRAHAM EDGAR, B.S., *Graduate Scholar* 144 Dwight st.

MARION G. ELKINS, B.S., *Graduate Scholar* 568 Chapel st.

JOSEPH R. ELLIS, B.A., *Graduate Scholar* 679 W. D.

HENRY P. FAIRCHILD, B.A., *University Fellow* 1233 Chapel st.

JAMES F. FERGUSON, M.A., *Larned Fellow in Yale College* 197 F.

EDNA L. FERRY, B.A., *Graduate Scholar* 24 Edgewood av.

ARTHUR S. FIELD, M.A., *Graduate Scholar* 100 Howe st.

EVERETT H. FITCH, M.A., *Graduate Scholar* 148 Whalley av.

WILLIAM R. FLINT, M.A., *Graduate Scholar* 121 Dwight st.

ROY L. FRENCH, PH.B., *Graduate Scholar* 210 F.

ANDREW C. FURBUSH, M.A., B.D., *Graduate Scholar* Georgetown

THOMAS T. GIFFEN, B.A., *Foote Fellow in Yale College* 213 F.

ASA R. GIFFORD, M.A., *Robinson Fellow* 227 F.

HIRAM GILLESPIE, M.A., *Graduate Scholar* 219 F.

CHARLES W. HALL, B.A., *University Fellow* 81 Yale P. O.

EDWIN DEEKS HARVEY, B.A., *Mead Scholar*   625 E. D.
RUTH S. HARVEY, B.A., *University Fellow*   142 York st.
SAMUEL C. HARVEY, PH.B., *Sheffield Graduate Scholar*   114 High st.
JESSIE HAYS, B.A., *University Fellow*   158 York st.
HARRY C. HEATON, B.A., *Scott-Hurtt Fellow in Yale*
    College   Paris, France
JOHN D. HOLM, M.S., *Graduate Scholar*   ·   47 Lake pl.
ALBERT W. HULL, B.A., *Sloane Fellow in Yale College*   120 York st.
LON L. HUTCHISON, B.A., *Graduate Scholar*   127 Dwight st.
SEIMIN INAOKA, B.A., *Graduate Scholar*   350 George st.
JACOB L. JACOBS, PH.B., *Sheffield Graduate Scholar*   128 Lafayette st.
WILLIAM O. KEIRSTEAD, B.A., *Graduate Scholar*   Montowese
SABURO KOSHIBA, B.A., B.D., *Graduate Scholar*   639 E. D.
JAMES A. KUMON, M.A., *Graduate Scholar*   993 Yale P. O.
WALTER E. LAGERQUIST, M.A., *Graduate Scholar*   198 Hamilton st.
JOHN K. LAMOND, M.A., *Graduate Scholar*   103 Park st.
KENNETH S. LATOURETTE, M.A., *Foote Fellow in Yale College*   197 F.
HENRY W. LAWRENCE, JR., M.A., *Macy Fellow in Yale*
    College   125 Dwight st.
LOUIS E. LORD, M.A., *Graduate Scholar*   35 Sherland av.
ERNEST B. LYTLE, M.A., *University Fellow*   120 York st.
WILLIAM P. MCCUNE, M.A., *Douglas Fellow in Yale College*   384 B.
ERNEST F. MCGREGOR, B.D., M.A., *Graduate Scholar* 760 Yale P. O.
JOHN W. MADDEN, PH.B., *Sheffield Graduate Scholar*   88 Wall st.
ALFRED A. MAY, M.A., *University Fellow*   132 Howe st.
EDWIN C. MILLER, B.A., *Graduate Scholar*   728 Yale P. O.
CLIFFORD J. MONAHAN, PH.B., *Sheffield Graduate Scholar*   686 W. D.
VICTOR C. MYERS, M.A., *University Fellow*   707 W. D.
SIDNEY PAIGE, *Graduate Scholar*   217 York st.
HOWARD E. PALMER, B.A., *Larned Fellow in Yale College*   Branford
CLAUDE C. PERKINS, B.A., *Graduate Scholar*   118 Howe st.
PERRY B. PERKINS, M.A., *Loomis Fellow in Yale College* 102 DeWitt st.
CLYDE PHARR, B.A., *Abernethy Fellow in Yale College*   98 York sq.
FREDERICK W. PIERCE, PH.B., *Graduate Scholar*   373 Crown st.
FRANK W. PITMAN, M.A., *University Fellow*   ·   646 George st.
JOSEPH E. POGUE, JR., M.S., *Graduate Scholar*   1305 Chapel st.

GEORGE E. PUTNAM, B.A., *Graduate Scholar* — 176 Meadow st.

KATHARINE M. QUINT, M.A., *Graduate Scholar* — ₹90 Whalley av.

CHESTER A. REEDS, M.S., *University Fellow* — 204 F.

EDWIN J. ROBERTS, B.S., *Graduate Scholar* — 712 W. D.

ANTON R. ROSE, B.S., *Graduate Scholar* — 342 Crown st.

JOSEPH ROSENBAUM, PH.B., *Sheffield Graduate Scholar* — 68 Park st.

TADASU SAIKI, PH.D., *University Fellow* — 462 Elm st.

THOMAS E. SAVAGE, M.S., *Graduate Scholar* — West Haven

HOWARD A. SECKERSON, B.A., *Graduate Scholar* — 178 Ellsworth av.

NOBUJI SEKIDO, *Graduate Scholar* — 385 Winthrop av.

ERNEST W. SHELDON, B.A., *DeForest Prize Man* — 542 P.

GEORGE C. SHERWOOD, B.A., *Graduate Scholar* — 276 Elm st.

GUY A. SIMMONS, M.A., *Graduate Scholar* — 142 Edgewood av.

MARY D. SWARTZ, B.S., *Graduate Scholar* — 25 Whalley av.

LUDWIG E. SWENSON, B.A., *Graduate Scholar* — 272 Winthrop av.

SENJIRO TAKAGI, B.A., *Eldridge Fellow in Yale College* — 228 Crown st.

ARTHUR H. TAYLOR, M.A., *Foote Fellow in Yale College* — 892 Yale P. O.

EDWIN W. TILLOTSON, JR., B.A., *H. B. Loomis Fellow in Yale
College* — 846 Yale P. O.

JOHN K. TOWLES, M.A., *University Fellow* — 706 W. D.

THOMAS A. TULLY, B.A., *Abernethy Fellow in Yale College* — 130 Howe st.

MARY S. WALKER, M.A., *University Fellow* — North Haven

ROOSEVELT P. WALKER, B.A., *Graduate Scholar* — 79 Howe st.

HENRY F. WALRADT, B.A., *Graduate Scholar* — 417 B.

HENRY A. WHITE, M.A., *Graduate Scholar* — 82 Whalley av.

JOHN A. WHITE, B.A., *DeForest Prize Man and Clark Scholar* — 82 C.

RAYMOND H. WHITE, M.A., *Soldiers' Memorial Fellow in
Yale College* — 411 B.

ROBERT D. WILLIAMS, M.A., *University Fellow* — 213 F.

EUPHEMIA R. WORTHINGTON, B.A., *University Fellow* — 37 Howe st.

HARRY C. YORK, M.A., *Larned Fellow in Yale College* — 125 Dwight st.

PART II

GOVERNMENT OF THE UNIVERSITY

GOVERNMENT OF THE UNIVERSITY

The legal designation of the Corporation is "THE PRESI-
DENT AND FELLOWS OF YALE COLLEGE IN NEW HAVEN,"
or "YALE UNIVERSITY"; the powers of this body have
been granted and confirmed in the following order.

CHARTER OF THE COLLEGIATE SCHOOL

THE COLLEGIATE SCHOOL OF CONNECTICUT, subsequently
named YALE COLLEGE, and now called YALE UNIVERSITY,
was founded by the combined action of a few of the
ministers in Connecticut, who obtained in October, 1701,
a Charter from the Colony Legislature, which runs as
follows :—

AN ACT FOR LIBERTY TO ERECT A COLLEGIATE SCHOOL.

WHEREAS several well disposed, and Publick spirited Persons of
their sincere regard to & Zeal for upholding & Propagating of
the Christian Protestant Religion by a succession of Learned & Ortho-
dox men have expressed by Petition their earnest desires that full Liberty and Priveledge be granted unto certain Undertakers for the founding, suitably endowing & ordering a Collegiate School within his Maj^{ties}
Colony of Connecticot wherin Youth may be instructed in the Arts &
Sciences who thorough the blessing of Almighty God may be fitted for
Publick employment both in Church & Civil State. To the intent
therefore that all due incouragement be Given to such Pious Resolu-
tions and that so necessary & Religious an undertakeing may be sett
forward, supported and well managed :—

BE IT ENACTED by the Govern^r & Company of the s^d Colony of
Connecticot in General Court now Assembled, And it is enacted &
ordained by the Authority of the same that there be & hereby is full
Liberty, Right and Priveledge Granted unto the Reverend M^r· James
Noyes of Stonnington, M^r· Israel Chauncey of Stratford, M^r· Thomas
Buckingham of Saybrook, M^r· Abraham Pierson of Kennelworth,
M^r· Samuel Mather of Windsor, M^r· Samuel Andrew of Milford, M^r·
Timothy Woodbridge of Hartford, M^r· James Pierpont of New Haven,
M^r· Noadiah Russel of Middletown, M^r· Joseph Webb of Fairfield,
being Rev^rd Ministers of the Gospel & inhabitants within ye s^d Colony,

proposed to stand as Trustees, Partners or Undertakers for the s^d School, to them and their successors, To ERECT, form, direct, order, establish, improve and att all times in all suitable wayes for the future to encourage the s^d School in such convenient place or Places, & in such form & manner & under such orders & Rules as to them shall seem meet & most conducive to the afores^d end thereof, so as such Rules or Orders be not repugnant to the Laws of the Civil Goverm^t, as also to employ the moneys or any other estate which shall be Granted by this Court or otherwise Contributed to that use according to their discretion for the benefit of the s^d Collegiate School from time to time & att all times henceforward.

And be it further ENACTED by the Authority afores^d that the before named Trustees, Partners or Undertakers together with such others as they shall associate to themselves (not exceeding the number of Eleven or att any time being less than Seven. Provided also that Persons nominated or associated from time to time to fill up s^d number be ministers of the gospel inhabiting within this Colony & above the Age of forty years) or the major Part of them, the s^d M^{r·} James Noyes, [etc.] undertakers, & of such Persons so chosen & associated as aboves^d att any time hereafter, HAVE and shall have henceforward the oversight, full & compleat Right, Liberty, power & Priveledge to furnish, direct, manage, order, improve & encourage from time to time & in all times hereafter the s^d Collegiate School so Erected & formed by them in such ways, orders & manner & by such Persons, Rector or Master and officers appointed by them, as shall according to their best discretion be most conducible to attainé the afores^d mentioned end thereof. . . . . .

It is also further Enacted by the Authority afores^d that the s^d Undertakers & Partners & their successors be & hereby are further empowered to have, accept, acquire, purchase or otherwise lawfully enter upon Any Lands, Tenements & Hereditam^{ts} to the use of the s^d School, not exceeding the value of five hundred Pounds p^r Ann, & any Goods, Chattels, Sum or Sums of money whatsoever as have heretofore already been Granted, bestowed, bequeathed or given, or as from time to time shall be freely given, bequeathed, devised or settled by any Person or Persons whatsoever upon & to & for the use of ye s^d School towards the founding, erecting or endowing the same, & to sue for, Recover & receiv all such Gifts, Legacies, bequests, annuities, Rents, issues & profits arising therefrom & to imploy the same accordingly, & out of ye estate, Revenues, Rents, profits, incoms accrueing & belonging to s^d School to support & pay as the s^d Undertakers shall agree & see cause, the s^d Rector or Master, Tutors, Ushers or other officers their Respective annual Salaries or Allowances. As also for the encouragem^t of the Students to grant degrees or Licences as they or those deputed by them shall see cause to order & appoint.

Under this Charter the Collegiate School was begun in November, 1701, at Saybrook, where it continued until its removal to New Haven, in October, 1716. In September, 1718, the name of YALE COLLEGE was given by the Trustees to the School, in honor of the benefactions of ELIHU YALE, of London, lately Governor of the East India Company's settlement at Madras.

ADDITIONAL ACT OF 1723

In 1723 an "ACT IN EXPLANATION OF AND ADDITION TO THE ACT FOR ERECTING A COLLEGIATE SCHOOL" was passed by the General Assembly, with the following provisions;—

WHEREAS Pursuant to the Powers and Priviledges granted to Certain Trustees for Erecting a Collegiate School in this Colony Entituled an Act for a Collegiate School, the Said Trustees have Erected the said School in the Town of New-Haven which School is now known by the Name of Yale Colledge ; And Whereas it appears to this Assembly that an Explanation and Enlargement of the powers and priviledges granted by Said Act is necessary for the Carrying on the Affairs of the Said Colledge, for want of which it has Laboured under great difficulties very much to the prevention of that Order and good Education which is to be desired there:

Bee it therefore Enacted by the Governour, Council and Representatives in Generall Court assembled and by the Authority of the Same that the Said Act which provides that the Number of the Said Trustees be not under Seven nor above Eleven is not to be Understood or Taken so as to be restrictive of the power of the Said Trustees Never to Choose any person to be a Trustee, when there is of Such persons as have been Chosen and Acted as Trustees Eleven persons Living in the Colony or Elsewhere, but that in Case any person so Chosen be by Providence Incapacitated from attending that Service or shall himself decline the Same thro' the Necessity of his own Affairs or for any other such Reason as he shall Judge requisite, the Trustees in any of their Meetings Lawfully Called may be Understood to have and it is hereby Enacted and declared that they shall be Taken to have full power by the Majority of Such Meeting to proceed to the Choice of Another Trustee in the Room of any such person. And it is hereby further declared and Enacted to be the True Intent and Meaning of the Act afores[d] that the said Trustees shall be Impowered and they are hereby declared to have power to Meet Together for Considering, Advising about and Resolving upon all Matters belonging to the Trust of the Said Colledge committed unto them as afores[d] and to Agree and Conclude, Order and determine Concerning them by the Majority of the Said Meeting, and by the same Majority to Choose and Appoint a Clerk who shall, in a fair book prepared for that End, Register and Carefully preserve the Acts of all such Meetings.

And WHEREAS it has been doubted what Number of the Said Trustees may be Lookt upon as a Sufficient or full Meeting, Inasmuch as there is not in the afores[d] Act any Express mention made of any Meeting of the said Trustees; It is therefore to prevent all Scruple of that kind for the future hereby provided and declared that due Notice being given to the Trustees by Consent of any three of them of a Meeting of the Trustees desired at any Time or place, and Seven or more of the Trustees present at such Time and place shall be Esteemed a full Meeting. And it is hereby declared and Enacted that in all such Meetings, so Called, or Otherwise as the said Trustees in any such Meeting shall agree, all affairs under the Care of the said Trustees shall be determined by the majority of such meeting.

And WHEREAS it has been found Inconvenient that in the Election of Persons to be Trustees, the Trustees Election by the afores[d] Act should be Limited and restrained so as that the Person who shall be Chosen must Necessarily be fourty Years of age; It is hereby declared and Enacted that for the future the said Trustees in any Election of a person into that Trust shall not be Esteemed or held Obliged by said Act to choose such a person as shall be above fourty Years of Age, but may Choose such a person otherwise Qualifyed According to said Act, Provided he is thirty Years of Age. And it is further hereby Allowed, Enacted, Granted and Provided that whosoever shall be Chosen and made a Rector of the said Colledge shall by Virtue thereof become a Trustee of the same and be so Esteemed and Taken during his continuance in the said Rectorship.

CHARTER OF YALE COLLEGE

In 1745 a thoroughly revised Charter was granted by the Assembly; the provisions of permanent interest are as follows:—

An ACT *for the more full and complete Establishment of* YALE COLLEGE *in* NEW HAVEN, *and for enlarging the Powers and Privileges thereof.*

WHEREAS upon the Petition of several well-disposed and public-spirited Persons expressing their desire that full Liberty and Privilege might be granted unto Certain Undertakers for the founding, suitably endowing and ordering a *Collegiate School*, within this Colony, wherein Youth might be instructed in the Arts and Sciences, the Governor and Company of the said Colony in General Court assembled at *New Haven*, on the Ninth Day of October, in the Year of our Lord 1701, Granted unto the Rev'd Messrs. *James Noyes* [etc.], who were proposed to stand as Trustees, Partners, or Undertakers for the Society, and to their Successors, full Liberty, Right and Privilege to erect, form, direct, order, establish, improve, and at all Times in all suitable Ways to encourage the said School in some convenient Place in this Colony, and granted sundry Powers and Privileges for the attaining the End aforesaid ;

And Whereas the said Trustees, Partners or Undertakers in pursuance of the aforesaid Grant, Liberty and License, founded a *Collegiate School* at *New Haven*, known by the Name of YALE COLLEGE, which has received the favorable Benefactions of many Liberal and piously disposed Persons, and under the Blessing of Almighty God has trained up many worthy Persons for the Service of God in the State as well as in the Church ;

And Whereas the General Court of this Colony assembled at *New Haven*, the Tenth day of October, in the Year of our Lord 1723, did explain and enlarge the aforesaid Powers and Privileges granted to the aforesaid Partners, Trustees or Undertakers and their Successors, for the Purpose aforesaid ; as by the respective Acts, reference thereto being had, more fully and at large may appear ;

And Whereas the Rev'd Messrs. *Thomas Clap, Samuel Whitman, Jared Eliot, Ebenezer Williams, Jonathan Marsh, Samuel Cooke, Samuel Whittelsey, Joseph Noyes, Anthony Stoddard, Benjamin Lord,* and *Daniel Wadsworth,* the present Trustees, Partners and Undertakers of the said School, and Successors of those beforementioned, have petitioned, that the said School, with all the Rights, Powers, Privileges and Interests thereof, may be confirmed, and that such other additional Powers and Privileges may be granted as shall be necessary for the Ordering and Managing the said School, in the most advantageous and beneficial Manner for the promoting all good Literature in the present and succeeding Generations : Therefore,

THE GOVERNOR and COMPANY of his Majesty's said English Colony of *Connecticut* in General Court assembled, this Ninth Day of *May*, in the Year of our Lord 1745, enact, ordain, and declare, and by these Presents it is enacted, ordained, and declared—

That the said *Thomas Clap* [etc.], shall be an *Incorporate Society* or *Body Corporate and Politic,* and shall hereafter be called and known by the name of THE PRESIDENT AND FELLOWS OF YALE COLLEGE IN NEW HAVEN, and that by the same Name they and their Successors shall and may have perpetual Succession, and shall and may be Persons in the Law capable to plead and be impleaded, defend and be defended, and answer and be answered unto; and also to have, take, possess, acquire, purchase, or otherwise receive Lands, Tenements, Hereditaments, Goods, Chattels, or other Estates, and the same Lands, Tenements, Hereditaments, Goods, Chattels, or other Estates to grant, demise, lease, use, manage or improye for the Good and benefit of the said *College*, according to the Tenor of the Donation, and their discretion.

That all Gifts, Grants, Bequests, and Donations of Lands, Tenements, or Hereditaments, of Goods and Chattels heretofore made to or for the Use, Benefit and Advantage of the *Collegiate School* aforesaid, whether the ame be expressed to be made to the President or Rector, and to the rest of the Incorporate Society of *Yale College*, or to the Trustees or Undertakers of the *Collegiate School* in *New Haven*, or to the Trustees by any other Name, Style or Title whatsoever, whereby it may be clearly known and understood that the true Intent and Design of such Gifts, Grants, Bequests and Donations, was to or for the Use, Benefit and Advantage of the Collegiate School aforesaid, and to be under the Care and Disposal of the Governors thereof, shall be confirmed, and the same hereby are confirmed, and shall be and remain to, and be vested in the President and Fellows of the *College* aforesaid, and their Successors, as to the true and lawful Successors of the original Grantees.

That the said PRESIDENT AND FELLOWS and their Successors shall and may hereafter have a common Seal, to serve and use for all Causes, Matters and Affairs of them and their Successors, and the same Seal to alter, break, and make new as they shall think fit.

That the said THOMAS CLAP shall be, and he is hereby established the present PRESIDENT, and the said *Samuel Whitman* [etc.] shall be, and they are hereby established the present FELLOWS of the said College, and that they and their Successors shall continue in their respective Places during Life, or until they or either of them shall resign, or be removed, or displaced, as in this Act is hereafter expressed.

That there shall be a General Meeting of the *President* and *Fellows* of said *College*, in the College Library on the second Wednesday of September annually, or at any other Time and Place which they shall see Cause to appoint, to consult, advise and act in and about the Affairs and Business of the said College ; and that on any special Emergency, the President and two of the Fellows, or any four of the Fellows, may appoint a Meeting of the said College, provided they give Notice thereof to the Rest by Letters sent and Left with them, or at the Places of their respective Abode, five Days before such Meeting ; and that the President and six Fellows, or in Case of the Death, Absence, or Incapacity of the President, seven Fellows, convened as aforesaid (in which Case the eldest Fellow shall preside), shall be deemed a Meeting of the President and Fellows of said College, and that in all the said Meetings, the Major Vote of the Members present shall be deemed the Act of the

Whole, and where an Equivote happens, the President shall have a casting vote.

That the President and Fellows of the said College and their Successors, in any of their Meetings assembled as aforesaid, shall and may from Time to Time, as Occasion shall require, elect and appoint a President or Fellow in the Room and Place of any President or Fellow who shall die, resign, or be removed from his office, Place or Trust (whom the said Governor and Company hereby declare, for any Misdemeanor, Unfaithfulness, Default or Incapacity, shall be removable by the President and Fellows of the said College; Six of them, at least, concurring in such Act): and shall have Power to appoint a Scribe or Register, a Treasurer, Tutors, Professors, Steward, and all such other Officers and Servants, usually appointed in Colleges or Universities, as they shall find necessary and think fit to appoint for the promoting good Literature, and the well ordering and managing the Affairs of said College; and them or any of them, at their Discretion, to remove; and to prescribe and administer such Forms of Oaths (not being contrary to the Laws of England or of this Colony) as they shall think proper, to be administered to all the Officers and Instructors of the said College, or to such and so many of them as they shall think proper, for the faithful Execution of their respective Places, Offices and Trusts.

That the President and Fellows shall have the Government, Care and Management of the said College and all the Matters and Affairs thereunto belonging, and shall have Power from Time to Time, as Occasion shall require, to make, ordain and establish all such wholesome and reasonable Laws, Rules and Ordinances, not repugnant to the Laws of England, nor the Laws of this Colony, as they shall think fit and proper for the Instruction and Education of the Students, and Ordering, Governing, Ruling and Managing the said College, and all Matters, Affairs, and Things thereunto belonging, and the same to Repeal and alter as they shall think fit; which shall be laid before this Assembly as often as required, and may also be repealed or disallowed by this Assembly when they shall think proper.

That the President of said College, with the Consent of the Fellows, shall have Power to give and confer all such Honors, Degrees or Licenses as are usually given in Colleges or Universities, upon such as they shall think worthy thereof.

LATER ACTS OF THE LEGISLATURE

In 1792 a grant of money from the State of Connecticut was received, upon the condition that certain State officials should become members of the Board of Fellows, as below expressed:

In case this grant shall be accepted, in manner as hereinafter provided, the Governor, Lieutenant Governor, and six senior assistants in the Council* of this State, for the time being, shall ever hereafter, by virtue of their said offices, be trustees or fellows of said College; and shall together with the present President and Fellows of said College, and their successors, constitute one corporation, by the name and style mentioned in the charter of said College; and shall have and enjoy the same powers, privileges, and authority, in as full and ample a manner, as though they had been expressly named and included in said charter; And that in case of vacancy, by the death, or resignation, or in any other way, of any of the present Fellows of said College, and their successors, every such vacancy shall forever hereafter be supplied by them, and their successors, by election, in the same manner as though this act had never passed.

In the State Constitution, adopted in 1818, the privileges conferred by the Charter were reaffirmed, as follows:—

ARTICLE VIII, SECT. I.

The charter of Yale College, as modified by agreement with the Corporation thereof, in pursuance of an Act of the General Assembly, passed in May, 1792, is hereby confirmed.

In 1872, at the request of the Corporation, an Act was passed by the General Assembly, providing (as follows) for the substitution of graduates in the place of the six senators among the Fellows:—

SECTION I.—All graduates of the first degree, of five or more years' standing, in any of the departments of Yale College, and all persons who have been admitted to any degree higher than the first in Yale College, whether honorary or in course, may, on the day next preceding the public commencement day of said College, in the year of our Lord 1872, cast their votes, under such regulations as the President and Fellows may prescribe, for six persons to be chosen from among such graduates; and the six persons who shall be found to be elected by a plurality of the votes cast, shall be the Fellows of Yale College in the stead of the six senior senators of the State, and shall have all the rights, duties, and privileges as Fellows which are now by law conferred upon said senators. In case of an equality of votes between two or more candidates, the person who shall hold the said office of Fellow shall be designated by lot from among the persons receiving such equality of votes.

* Changed in 1819 to the six senior senators.

SECTION 2.—The Fellows thus elected shall enroll themselves by lot in six classes, one holding the office for six years, another for five years, another for four years, another for three years, another for two years, and another for one year, eligible for re-election; and every year as a vacancy occurs, all graduates of the first degree, of five or more years' standing, in any of the departments of Yale College, and all persons who have been admitted to any degree higher than the first in Yale College, whether honorary or in course, may, upon the day next preceding commencement day, in the manner heretofore prescribed, elect by a plurality of votes a person to fill the vacancy, and hold the office of Fellow for a period of six years, eligible for re-election; and so whenever a vacancy shall occur from death, resignation, or any other cause, such graduates may elect a person at the next commencement to fill the office of Fellow for the remainder of the term in which a vacancy has occurred. The official year of such Fellows shall end with the day next preceding each commencement day.

In March, 1887, an Act passed the General Assembly of the State, authorizing the use of the title " YALE UNIVERSITY " by the President and Fellows of Yale College, and providing that gifts to, contracts with, conveyances to or by, and other acts affecting said Corporation by either of the names specified shall be valid. •

GOVERNMENT OF THE DIFFERENT DEPARTMENTS

The courses of study offered in the University are comprehended in four Departments, under the control of the Corporation, each Department being also under the administration of a distinct Faculty of instruction. The Departments are as follows:—

THE DEPARTMENT OF PHILOSOPHY AND THE ARTS;

THE DEPARTMENT OF THEOLOGY;

THE DEPARTMENT OF MEDICINE;

THE DEPARTMENT OF LAW.

Under the first-named Department are included two separately organized sections in which instruction for undergraduates is provided, viz:—

THE ACADEMICAL DEPARTMENT, and

THE SHEFFIELD SCIENTIFIC SCHOOL;

also, THE SCHOOL OF THE FINE ARTS, the DEPARTMENT OF MUSIC, and the FOREST SCHOOL, each with a special organization, and THE GRADUATE SCHOOL, under the combined Faculty of the Department.

It is to be understood that the courses of study above described are open to men only, except when both sexes are specifically included.

The LIBRARY, the PEABODY MUSEUM OF NATURAL HISTORY, the OBSERVATORY, and the BOTANICAL GARDEN are severally organized independently of the special Departments, and are designed to contribute, in their appropriate spheres, to the instruction and advancement of the whole institution. These Institutions and others connected with the University, and open to all of its students, are described in Part IV of this Catalogue.

PART III

DEPARTMENTS OF INSTRUCTION

ACADEMICAL DEPARTMENT
(YALE COLLEGE)
FACULTY

ARTHUR TWINING HADLEY, LL.D., *President*

HENRY PARKS WRIGHT, PH.D., LL.D., *Dunham Professor of the Latin Language and Literature, and Dean of the College Faculty*

ARTHUR MARTIN WHEELER, LL.D., *Durfee Professor of History, Emeritus, and Lecturer on European History*

ARTHUR WILLIAMS WRIGHT, PH.D., *Professor of Experimental Physics, Emeritus*

EUGENE LAMB RICHARDS, M.A., *Professor of Mathematics, Emeritus*

TRACY PECK, LL.D., *Professor of the Latin Language and Literature*

REV. CORNELIUS LADD KITCHEL, M.A., *Secretary of the Bureau of Self-Help and Appointments*

WILLIAM GRAHAM SUMNER, LL.D., *Pelatiah Perit Professor of Political and Social Science*

CHARLES HENRY SMITH, LL.D., *Larned Professor of American History*

HENRY AUGUSTIN BEERS, M.A., *Professor of English Literature*

BERNADOTTE PERRIN, PH.D., LL.D., *Lampson Professor of Greek Literature and History*

EDWARD SALISBURY DANA, PH.D., *Professor of Physics, and Curator of the Mineralogical Collection*

THOMAS DAY SEYMOUR, LL.D., *Hillhouse Professor of the Greek Language and Literature*

FRANK AUSTIN GOOCH, PH.D., *Professor of Chemistry, and Director of the Kent Chemical Laboratory*

WILLIAM BEEBE, M.A., *Professor of Mathematics, and Instructor in Astronomy*

ANDREW WHEELER PHILLIPS, PH.D., *Professor of Mathematics, and Dean of the Graduate School*

GEORGE BURTON ADAMS, PH.D., LITT.D., *Professor of History*

EDWARD PARMELEE MORRIS, L.H.D., *Professor of the Latin Language and Literature*

HENRY ROSEMANN LANG, PH.D., *Benjamin F. Barge Professor of the Romance Languages and Literature*

— 67 —

ROBERT LOUIS SANDERSON, M.A., *Assistant Professor of French*

THOMAS DWIGHT GOODELL, PH.D., *Professor of the Greek Language and Literature*

ARTHUR HUBBELL PALMER, M.A., *Professor of the German Language and Literature*

FREDERICK WELLS WILLIAMS, B.A., *Assistant Professor of Modern Oriental History*

HORATIO MCLEOD REYNOLDS, M.A., *Talcott Professor of the Greek Language and Literature*

FREDERICK MORRIS WARREN, PH.D., L.H.D., *Street Professor of Modern Languages*

GEORGE MARTIN DUNCAN, LL.D., *Professor of Logic and Metaphysics*

EDWARD GAYLORD BOURNE, PH.D., *Professor of History*

GUSTAV GRUENER, PH.D., *Professor of German*

ALBERT EUGENE CURDY, PH.D., *Assistant Professor of French*

CHARLTON MINER LEWIS, PH.D., *Emily Sanford Professor of English Literature*

WILLIAM LYON PHELPS, PH.D., *Lampson Professor of English Literature*

ERNEST WILLIAM BROWN, SC.D., *Professor of Mathematics*

GEORGE LINCOLN HENDRICKSON, L H.D., *Professor of the Latin Language and Literature*

IRVING FISHER, PH.D., *Professor of Political Economy*

JAMES PIERPONT, PH.D., *Professor of Mathematics*

HANNS OERTEL, PH.D., *Professor of Linguistics and Comparative Philology*

CHARLES SEARS BALDWIN, PH.D., *Assistant Professor of Rhetoric*

PHILIP EMBURY BROWNING, PH.D., *Assistant Professor of Chemistry*

OLIVER HUNTINGTON RICHARDSON, PH.D., *Assistant Professor of History*

CHARLES FOSTER KENT, PH.D., *Woolsey Professor of Biblical Literature*

CHARLES MONTAGUE BAKEWELL, PH.D., *Professor of Philosophy*

ROSS GRANVILLE HARRISON, PH.D., M.D., *Bronson Professor of Comparative Anatomy*

KENNETH MCKENZIE, PH.D., *Assistant Professor of Italian*

HENRY ANDREWS BUMSTEAD, PH.D., *Professor of Physics, and Director of the Sloane Physical Laboratory*

JAMES W. D. INGERSOLL, PH.D., *Assistant Professor of Latin*

JOSEPH BARRELL, PH.D., *Assistant Professor of Geology*

DAVID ALBERT KREIDER, PH.D., *Assistant Professor of Physics*

HENRY CROSBY EMERY, PH.D., *Professor of Political Economy*

CLIVE DAY, PH.D., *Professor of Economic History*

BERTRAM BORDEN BOLTWOOD, PH.D., *Assistant Professor of Physics*

ALFRED KINDRED MERRITT, B.A., *Registrar of the College Faculty*

RICHARD SWANN LULL, PH.D., *Assistant Professor of Vertebrate Paleontology, and Associate Curator of the Collection in Vertebrate Paleontology*

CHALFANT ROBINSON, PH.D., *Instructor in History*

EDWARD BLISS REED, PH.D., *Assistant Professor of English*

WILLIAM BACON BAILEY, PH.D., *Assistant Professor of Political Economy*	.

ISAAC KING PHELPS, PH.D., *Instructor in Chemistry*

PAUL VICTOR CHRISTOPHER BAUR, PH.D., *Assistant Professor of Classical Archæology*

CHARLES HUBBARD JUDD, PH.D., *Professor of Psychology, and Director of the Psychological Laboratory*

JOHN WESLEY WETZEL, PH.B., *Instructor in Public Speaking*

HORACE SCUDDER UHLER, PH.D., *Instructor in Physics*

HENRY HOLLISTER ROBINSON, C.E., PH.D., *Instructor in Geology*

ALBERT GALLOWAY KELLER, PH.D., *Professor of the Science of Society*

HOLLON AUGUSTINE FARR, PH.D., *Assistant Professor of German*

RUDOLPH SCHEVILL, PH.D., *Assistant Professor of the Spanish Language and Literature*

HERBERT ERNEST GREGORY, PH.D., *Silliman Professor of Geology*

JOHN CHESTER ADAMS, PH.D., *Instructor in English*

HERBERT EDWIN HAWKES, PH.D., *Assistant Professor of Mathematics*

EDWARD LEWIS DURFEE, B.A., *Instructor in History*

JOHN MILTON BERDAN, PH.D., *Instructor in Rhetoric*

CHARLES UPSON CLARK, PH.D., *Assistant Professor of Latin*

ALBERT EDWARD GUBELMANN, PH.D., *Instructor in German*

EMERSON DAVID FITE, PH.D., *Instructor in History*

IRVILLE CHARLES LeCOMPTE, PH.D., *Instructor in French*

ELLSWORTH HUNTINGTON, M.A., *Instructor in Geography*

HENRY BURT WRIGHT, PH.D., *Assistant Professor of Roman History and Latin Literature*

FRED ROGERS FAIRCHILD, PH.D., *Instructor in Political Economy*

WILMOT HAINES THOMPSON, JR., PH.D., *Instructor in Greek*

SYDNEY KNOX MITCHELL, PH.D., *Instructor in History*

JOHN PEASE NORTON, PH.D., *Assistant Professor of Political Economy*

RALPH GIBBS VANNAME, PH.D., *Instructor in Chemistry*

CHAUNCEY BREWSTER TINKER, PH.D., *Instructor in English*

CURTIS HOWE WALKER, PH.D., *Instructor in History*

ROSWELL PARKER ANGIER, PH.D., *Instructor in Psychology*

GEORGE MERRICK BAKER, PH.D., *Instructor in German*

WILLIAM SAVAGE JOHNSON, PH.D., *Instructor in English*

ELBERT NEVIUS SEBRING THOMPSON, PH.D., *Instructor in Rhetoric*

WILLIAM ERNEST HOCKING, PH.D., *Assistant Professor of Philosophy*

LUCIUS HUDSON HOLT, PH.D., *Instructor in English*

WILLIAM BRIAN HOOKER, M.A., *Instructor in Rhetoric*

AVARD LONGLEY BISHOP, PH.D., *Instructor in Commercial Geography*

AXEL EBENEZER VESTLING, PH.D., *Instructor in German*

EDWARD HERBERT CAMERON, PH.D., *Instructor in Psychology*

JOHN DOUGAN REA, M.A., *Instructor in Latin*

ROBERT LIVINGSTON SCHUYLER, M.A., *Instructor in History*

LESTER WILLIAM ZARTMAN, PH.D., *Instructor in Insurance and Economics*

CLARENCE WHITTLESEY MENDELL, M.A., *Instructor in Latin*

LAWRENCE MASON, B.A., *Instructor in English*

ISAIAH BOWMAN, B.S., *Instructor in Geography*

THOMAS ALLEN TULLY, B.A., *Recorder of the College Faculty*

ADDITIONAL INSTRUCTORS

WILLIAM GILBERT ANDERSON, M.A., M.D., *Director of the Gymnasium*

CLARENCE EDWARD ANDREWS, B.A., *Assistant in English*

KAN-ICHI ASAKAWA, PH.D., *Instructor in the History of Japanese Civilization*

Rev. BENJAMIN WISNER BACON, D.D., LL.D., LITT.D., *Buckingham Professor of New Testament Criticism and Interpretation*

Hon. SIMEON EBEN BALDWIN, LL.D., *Professor of American Constitutional Law and Private International Law*

CHARLES JOSEPH BARTLETT, M.D., *Professor of Pathology*

GEORGE ELBERT BECK, B.A., *Assistant in Physical Geography*

HIRAM BINGHAM, PH.D., *Lecturer on South American Geography and History*

SETH DANIELS BINGHAM, JR., B.A., *Assistant in Organ-Playing*

RICHARD MERVIN BISSELL, B.A., *Lecturer on Insurance*

FREDERIC THOMAS BLANCHARD, B.L., *Assistant in Rhetoric*

THEODORE HARDING BOGGS, M.A., *Instructor in Commercial Geography*

HORACE THOMAS BURGESS, M.A., *Instructor in Mathematics*

GUY STEVENS CALLENDER, PH.D. *Professor of Political Economy*

RUSSELL HENRY CHITTENDEN, PH.D., LL.D., SC.D., *Professor of Physiological Chemistry, and Director of the Sheffield Scientific School*

HOWARD WADSWORTH CHURCH, M.A., *Instructor in German* ·

RAYMOND GILMORE CLAPP, B.D., M.A., *Instructor in Biblical Literature, and Director of Religious Work in the Divinity School*

CHARLES ALEXANDER COCKAYNE, M.A., *Assistant in Philosophy*

WESLEY ROSWELL COE, PH.D, *Assistant Professor of Comparative Anatomy*

ALBERT STANBURROUGH COOK, PH.D., L.H.D., LL.D., *Professor of the English Language and Literature*

ARTHUR LINTON CORBIN, B.A., LL.B., *Assistant Professor of Contracts*

Rev. EDWARD LEWIS CURTIS, PH.D., D.D., *Holmes Professor of the Hebrew Language and Literature, and Acting Dean of the Divinity School*

HENRY BRONSON DEWING, M.A., *Instructor in Greek*

WILLIAM ALLEN DRUSHEL, B.S., B.A., LL.B., *Assistant in the Kent Chemical Laboratory*

JOHN WARREN EDGERTON, M.A., LL.B., *Instructor in Mercantile Law, and Secretary of the Law Faculty*

ALEXANDER WILLIAM EVANS, M.D., PH.D., *Eaton Professor of Botany*

HENRY PRATT FAIRCHILD, B.A., *Assistant in Commercial Geography*

HARRY BURR FERRIS, M.D., *Hunt Professor of Anatomy*

WILLIAM RUTHVEN FLINT, M.A., *Assistant in the Kent Chemical Laboratory*

FRANK NUGENT FREEMAN, M.A., *Assistant in Psychology*

ASA RUSSELL GIFFORD, M.A., *Assistant in Philosophy*

WILLIAM EDWIN HAESCHE, MUS.B., *Instructor in Instrumentation*

FRED HARVEY HEATH, B.S., *Assistant in the Kent Chemical Laboratory*

YANDELL HENDERSON, PH.D., *Assistant Professor of Physiology*

JOHN MARSHALL HOLCOMBE, M.A., *Lecturer on Insurance*

EDWARD WASHBURN HOPKINS, PH.D., LL.D., *Professor of Sanskrit and Comparative Philology*

ALBERT WALLACE HULL, B.A., *Assistant in the Sloane Physical Laboratory*

LON LEWIS HUTCHISON, B.A., *Assistant in Geology*

Professor CHARLES CHENEY HYDE, LL.B., M.A., *Lecturer on International Law*

HARRY BENJAMIN JEPSON, B.A., MUS.B., *Professor of Applied Music, and University Organist*

ROSS JEWELL, PH B , *Instructor in German*

HENRY STANLEY KNIGHT, *Assistant Professor of Applied Music*

BEVERLY WAUGH KUNKEL, PH.D., *Instructor in Biology*

JOHN BODINE LUNGER, *Lecturer on Insurance*

MAX SOLOMON MANDELL, *Instructor in Russian*

WILLIAM CROSBY MARSHALL, M.E., C.E., *Assistant Professor of Drawing and Descriptive Geometry*

HOWARD DOUGLAS NEWTON, B.S., *Assistant in the Kent Chemical Laboratory*

JOHN HENRY NIEMEYER, M.A., A.N.A., *Street Professor of Drawing*

RAYMOND WILLIAM OSBORNE, B.A., *Assistant in the Kent Chemical Laboratory*

HORATIO WILLIAM PARKER, MUS.D., *Battell Professor of the Theory of Music, and Dean of the Department of Music*

Hon. EPAPHRODITUS PECK, LL.B., *Instructor in Evidence, Practice, Procedure, and Domestic Relations*

FREDERICK ERASTUS PIERCE, M.A., *Instructor in English and Debating*

CHARLES RABOLD, *Instructor in Singing*

JOSEPH CHAPPELL RAYWORTH, M.A., *Instructor in Mathematics*

CHARLES BRINCKERHOFF RICHARDS, M.A., *Higgin Professor of Mechanical Engineering*

EDWIN JAY ROBERTS, B.S., *Assistant in the Kent Chemical Laboratory*

Professor JOSIAH ROYCE, PH.D., LL.D., *Lecturer on Philosophy*

SAMUEL SIMONS SANFORD, M.A., *Professor of Applied Music*

CHARLES SCHUCHERT, M.A., *Professor of Paleontology, Curator of the Geological Collection, and Professor of Historical Geology in the Sheffield Scientific School.*

LEO SCHULZ, *Instructor in Violoncello-Playing*

ERNEST WILSON SHELDON, B.A., *Instructor in Mathematics*

DAVID STANLEY SMITH, B.A., MUS.B., *Instructor in the Theory of Music*

THOMAS SMITH TAYLOR, B.A., *Assistant in the Sloane Physical Laboratory*

EDWARD THORSTENBERG, PH.D., *Instructor in German and Swedish*

CHARLES CUTLER TORREY, PH.D., D.D., *Professor of the Semitic Languages*

ISIDOR TROOSTWYK, *Assistant Professor of Applied Music, and Instructor in Violin-Playing*

FRANK PELL UNDERHILL, PH.D., *Assistant Professor of Physiological Chemistry*

Rev. AMBROSE WHITE VERNON, D.D., *Professor of Practical Theology, and Acting Pastor of the University Church*

HIRAM LEE WARD, B.A., *Assistant in the Kent Chemical Laboratory*

GEORGE DUTTON WATROUS, D.C.L., *Professor of Torts*

JOHN FERGUSON WEIR, N.A., M.A., *William Leffingwell Professor of Painting and Design, and Director of the School of the Fine Arts*

FRANK ELBERT WHEELOCK, B.A., *Assistant in the Sloane Physical Laboratory*

LEWIS WILLIAMS, *Instructor in Piano-Playing*

LORANDE LOSS WOODRUFF, PH.D., *Instructor in Biology*

THEODORE SALISBURY WOOLSEY, LL.D., *Professor of International Law*

JOHN WURTS, M.A., M.L., *Lafayette S. Foster Professor of the English Common Law*

OTHER OFFICERS

DONALD ALLISON ADAMS, B.A., *Proctor*

JOHN BAUER, B.A., *Proctor*

GEORGE HANFORD BUTLER, *Cashier in the Bursar's Office*

PAUL MORGAN BUTTERFIELD, B.A., *Proctor*

CLIFFORD PIERPONT FOOTE, *Clerk in the Bursar's Office*

FRANK EDWIN HOTCHKISS, *Superintendent of Grounds and Buildings*

MRS. CHARLES TODD LINCOLN, *Private Secretary to the Dean*

WILBUR ALLEN MAYNARD, *Assistant in the Bursar's Office*

GEORGE ELWOOD NICHOLS, B.A., *Proctor*

HENRY MINOTT OSBORN, *College Bursar*

CECIL WRIGHT, *Proctor*

STANDING COMMITTEES

On Admission—Professor GRUENER, Chairman ; Professors PERRIN, GOODELL, WARREN, and INGERSOLL, Mr. MERRITT, Professor HAWKES, and Dr. TINKER.

On Freshman Class Administration—Professor FARR, Chairman ; Professors CURDY and HAWKES, Mr. DURFEE, Dr. W. H. THOMPSON, JR., and Dr. VANNAME.

On Sophomore Class Administration—Professors MORRIS, GOODELL, REYNOLDS, INGERSOLL, KREIDER, DAY, and EMERY, Dr. C. ROBINSON, Professor REED, Dr. I. K. PHELPS, Professor SCHEVILL, Dr. J. C. ADAMS, Dr. BERDAN, Dr. FITE, Dr. WALKER, and Mr. HOOKER.

On the Course of Study—Professors DANA, MORRIS, and FISHER.

On Schedules, the Announcement of Courses, and the College Catalogue—Professor INGERSOLL, Mr. MERRITT, and Dr. J. C. ADAMS.

On Changes in the Choice of Courses—Professor BEEBE, Mr. MERRITT, and Professor FARR.

On Enrollment—Professors GOOCH, G. B. ADAMS, and DUNCAN.

On Semi-Annual Examinations—Professors INGERSOLL, DAY, and BAUR.

On Honors—Professors GOOCH, PALMER, and BOURNE.

On Undergraduate Scholarships—Professors GOODELL, DUNCAN, and EMERY.

On the B.A. Degree—Professors C. H. SMITH, DUNCAN, and LEWIS.

On the M.A. Degree—Professors C. H. SMITH and PHILLIPS.

On Public Entertainments—Professors REYNOLDS, EMERY, FARR, CLARK, and H. B. WRIGHT.

On the College Choir—Professors SEYMOUR, PERRIN, and PARKER.

On the Andrews Memorial Library—Professor SEYMOUR, Chairman ; Mr. KITCHEL, and Professor GRUENER.

On Ways and Means—Professors H. P. WRIGHT, DANA, WARREN, and FISHER.

HISTORY OF THE COLLEGE

From the date of the original Charter, in 1701, a course of instruction leading to the degree of Bachelor of Arts has been continuously offered at the College. At first only three years of undergraduate study were required, but before 1710 a four years' course was provided, which has since been maintained.

Until 1813, when a Medical School was organized, no other course of study for a degree was marked out at Yale College. After the incorporation of the Medical Institution (as it was originally styled) the older Department began to be called the Academical Institution (or Department), and it continued to be so named until at length, with the growth of other Schools about it and the expansion of the whole into Yale University, it recovered its original title of Yale College, which is now applied distinctively to the Academical Department of the University.

TERMS OF ADMISSION
SUBJECTS OF THE EXAMINATION FOR ADMISSION TO THE FRESHMAN CLASS

Candidates are admitted to the Freshman class on passing a satisfactory examination in the subjects listed in detail below, under the following six heads : (i) Latin, (ii) Greek or Substitutes for Greek, (iii) French or German, (iv) English, (v) Mathematics, (vi) Ancient History.

In 1908, and thereafter until further notice, candidates may meet the requirements also by passing with satisfactory grades the equivalent subjects in the examination set by the College Entrance Examination Board and presenting their Board certificates for credit. (A candidate may take his preliminary examination with the Board and his final in the Yale examination, or *vice versa*. A combination of the Yale examination and the Board examination *in June of the same year*, however, is not allowed, and a candidate who offers such a combination will be judged solely by his work in the Yale examination. In no case will Board papers be re-read by the Yale examiners.) A detailed list of the equivalent subjects in the Board examination is given below, immediately after the detailed statement of the subjects of the Yale examination. Board certificates may be sent for exchange to the Registrar of Yale College, New Haven, Connecticut. Credits, both preliminary and final, will be granted in accordance with the regulations which govern the Yale examination; for example, at least five subjects must be satisfactorily passed in order to secure a preliminary certificate. Requests for blank forms of application for admission to the Board examination may be sent to the Secretary of the College Entrance Examination Board, Sub-station 84, New York City.

SUBJECTS OF THE YALE EXAMINATION
I. LATIN

1. Latin Grammar and Composition. In three parts (which, however, may not be taken separately): (*a*) Questions on forms; (*b*) Questions on syntax; (*c*) A connected passage of English prose to be translated into Latin.

The examination in 1908 will be based upon the second, third, and fourth orations of Cicero against Catiline.

2. The translation, at sight, of passages from Cæsar and Nepos.

3. Cicero: the orations against Catiline and for Archias, and, in addition, either the *Milo*, or the *Manilian Law*, or the *Cato Maior*, or both the *Marcellus* and the *14th Philippic*.

4 Vergil: the first six books of the *Æneid* (including prosody), and, in addition, either the *Bucolics* or the eighth and ninth books of the *Æneid*.

NOTES ON ALL THE CLASSICAL PAPERS

In the examinations in Latin and Greek much weight is given to the papers in Grammar and Composition (papers 1 and 5). Deficiencies in these subjects render it difficult or impossible to take up and carry on successfully the work in Latin or Greek of Freshman year. The questions on forms and syntax call for a good knowledge of all regular inflections and all common irregular forms, and of the ordinary syntax of Cicero and of Xenophon, respectively. The passages for translation into Latin and Greek call further for acquaintance with the ordinary vocabulary of Cicero and of Xenophon, respectively; but the chief object of this part of the examination is to supplement the examination in formal grammar by testing the candidate's *working knowledge* of inflections, syntax, and the most common forms of sentence-connection. Teachers are urged to combine exercises in composition, both oral and written, with all the prose reading of the school course. Frequent short exercises in retroversion should have a prominent place among the means of obtaining the needed facility.

On the other classical papers grammatical questions are asked only to test the candidate's understanding of a passage, or on poetic forms and constructions (including prosody) in Vergil and Homer. But good translation, even of prepared passages, requires a practical knowledge of grammatical principles.

The translations of Latin and Greek at sight (paper 2 and parts of papers 6 and 7) are read with especial care, as testing the candidate's ability to get at the author's meaning without help. It is intended to give on the papers the meanings of such words (if there be any) as the candidate cannot fairly be expected to know. Exercises in reading at sight should begin early in the school course, and from the outset particular attention should be given to developing the ability to take in the full meaning of each word—and so, gradually, of the whole passage—just as it stands, *i. e.*, in the original order and with full appreciation of the force of each word as it comes, both as to its dictionary meaning and as to its relation to, and force in, its context. The habit of reading in this way should, in fact, be encouraged and cultivated in all the translating that the student has to do. But no translation should be a mere loose paraphrase. The full meaning of the passage to be translated, gathered in the way described above, should be expressed in clear and natural English.

A written examination cannot test the ear and tongue, but proper instruction in any language will necessarily include the training of these organs. The school work in Latin and Greek, therefore, should include much reading aloud, writing from dictation, and translating from the teacher's reading. Learning fine passages by heart is also very useful and should be more practiced.

In order to allow the schools freedom in arranging their courses of work, alternative equivalents are provided in the authors set. Thus, the paper on Cicero contains questions on all the orations named in the list above, and in the Vergil paper passages are set from the eighth and ninth books of the *Æneid* as a substitute for the *Bucolics*. Papers will be prepared also on other parts of Vergil, on other orations of Cicero, on other portions of the works of Xenophon than the first four books of the *Anabasis*, and on other books of Homer than the first three of the *Iliad* and the first four of the *Odyssey*, provided information be given to the Registrar of the College, before May 1 of the calendar year in which the examination is to be taken, that such a paper is desired.

II. GREEK OR SUBSTITUTES FOR GREEK:
GREEK

5. Greek Grammar and Composition. In two parts (which, however, may not be taken separately): (*a*) Questions on forms and syntax; (*b*) A passage of simple English prose to be translated into Attic Greek.

The examination in 1908 will be based upon the first three books of Xenophon's *Anabasis*.

6. Xenophon : four books of the *Anabasis*. This paper includes also a passage from some work of Xenophon to test the candidate's ability to read easy Greek at sight.

7. Homer : three books of the *Iliad* (including prosody). This paper includes also a passage from the poems of Homer to be translated at sight. Four books of the *Odyssey* may be substituted for three books of the *Iliad*.

Notes on all the classical papers are given above.

SUBSTITUTES FOR GREEK

In place of Greek (papers 5–7) the following substitutes are accepted .

A candidate who wishes to omit only Homer must offer two of the three parts of Mathematics A1, described below. It is to be noted that under (3) there is an option between Advanced Algebra and Analytical Geometry. A candidate who wishes to omit the entire Greek requirement (papers 5–7, above, *but not Greek History, which is required of all candidates*) must offer both French (*a*) and German (*a*) and, in addition, one of the three following alternatives :

1. Two of the three parts of Mathematics A1 and either French (*b*) or German (*b*).
2. French (*b*) and German (*b*).
3. German (*b*) and German (*c*).

The requirements in these substitutes are as follows :

MATHEMATICS A1

N. B. A candidate who expects to continue Mathematics in College and who offers two of the three parts of Mathematics A1 in partial satisfaction of the entrance requirement should offer parts (1) and (2).

(1) Solid Geometry : the usual text demonstrations, omitting the theorems on spherical angles and triangles.

(2) Plane Trigonometry : fundamental definitions and properties of the trigonometric functions, with the usual formulæ ; application of the same to simple problems of reduction ; solution of trigonometric

equations ; solution of right and oblique triangles by use of natural or logarithmic tables.

(3) Advanced Algebra *or* Analytical Geometry :

Advanced Algebra : properties of quadratic equations, permutations and combinations, principles of logarithms, partial fractions ; graphical representation of functions of one variable and approximation to incommensurable roots ; simple theorems regarding the relation between the roots of an equation and its coefficients and factors.

Analytical Geometry : plotting of equations in rectangular and polar coördinates ; intersection of loci and interpretation of the same ; equation of straight line in its various forms and problems involving parallelism and perpendicularity of lines ; equation of circle, and conic sections in rectangular and polar coördinates ; transformation of coördinates and reduction of general equation of second degree to normal forms.

FRENCH

French (*a*). See under III. French or German, below.

French (*b*). In addition to the elementary requirements, candidates who offer French for advanced standing, or as a partial substitute for Greek at entrance, are expected to possess a thorough knowledge of French grammar and idioms and the ability to translate connected passages from English into French, and to have read the following texts : Hugo's *Les Misérables*, pp. 1-124 of Super's edition (Heath & Co.) ; Zola's *La Débâcle*, pp. 1-155 of Wells's edition (Heath & Co.) ; Dumas *fils*'s *La Question d'Argent ;* Daudet's *Contes*, pp. 1-133 of Cameron's edition (Holt & Co.). Equivalents : Balzac's *Eugénie Grandet*, pp. 1-115 of Bergeron's edition (Holt & Co.) is accepted for Hugo ; Sandeau's *Mlle. de la Seiglière* is accepted for Dumas *fils*.

Practice in reading French aloud and in writing from dictation is recommended.

[Credit is not given for French (*b*) before French (*a*) is passed.]

GERMAN

German (*a*). See under III. French or German, below.

German (*b*). The examination is designed to test the proficiency of those who have read, in addition to the amount specified under German (*a*), not less than 350 pages of classical and contemporary prose and verse. It consists of two parts (which, however, may not be taken separately) :

(i) The translation at sight of ordinary German.

The suggestions of the Report of the Committee of Twelve as to reading-matter for the Intermediate Course in German should be followed in general. The following selection is recommended : (1) one of Riehl's or Keller's tales ; (2) Freytag's *Die Journalisten* or Lessing's

Minna von Barnhelm ; (3) Heine's Poems and Prose (such extracts, for example, as are contained in *Die Harzreise, Buch Le Grand*, and *Englische Fragmente* in ordinary school editions of Heine's Prose); (4) Goethe's *Hermann und Dorothea.*

(ii) The translation into German of a connected passage of simple English prose, to test the candidate's familiarity with grammar. Proficiency in grammar may be tested also by direct questions.

In the translation into German, candidates are expected to show a thorough knowledge of accidence, the elements of word-formation, the principal uses of prepositions and conjunctions, and the essentials of syntax, especially the use of the modal auxiliaries and of the subjunctive and infinitive moods.

[Credit is not given for German (*b*) before German (*a*) is passed.]

German (*c*). The examination is designed to test the proficiency of those who have read, in addition to the amounts specified under German (*a*) and German (*b*), about 500 pages of difficult prose and of good literature in prose and verse. (The reading should be done with a view to acquiring facility in reading German for advanced work in other subjects, and to gaining an intelligent general appreciation of the purely literary works read.) The examination consists of two parts (which, however, may not be taken separately):

(i) The translation at sight of difficult German prose (not technical) and verse, whether recent or classical.

The suggestions of the Report of the Committee of Twelve as to reading-matter for the Advanced Course should be followed in general, though greater stress should be laid upon acquiring facility in translating and understanding German prose, such as would be necessary for advanced work in other branches.

(ii) The translation into German of a connected passage of ordinary English prose, or the writing in German of a short theme upon some assigned topic.

[Credit is not given for German (*c*) before German (*a*) and (*b*) are passed.]

III. FRENCH OR GERMAN:

8. French (*a*) *or* German (*a*). The candidate is at liberty to decide for himself in which of the two languages he shall be examined.

FRENCH

French (*a*), *Elementary*. Candidates are required to translate simple prose selections from French authors (Kuhns's *French Reading* and Mérimée's *Colomba* are suggested), and to show familiarity with the elements of French grammar; that is, with the forms of the articles, adjectives, nouns, and pronouns, with the conjugation of the regular and the most frequent irregular verbs, and with ordinary syntactical constructions. Simple English sentences are set to be rendered into French, and the candidate's knowledge of the principles of pronunciation is tested.

GERMAN

German (a), *Elementary*. The examination is designed to test the proficiency of those who have studied German in the equivalent of a systematic course of five periods a week for one year. It consists of two parts (which, however, may not be taken separately):

(i) The translation at sight of a passage of easy prose containing no rare words.

The passages set for translation are suited to candidates who have read (including sight-reading done in class) not less than two hundred duodecimo pages of simple German, chiefly narrative prose. It is important that all translation be done into clear and idiomatic English.

(ii) The translation into German of simple English sentences, to test the candidate's familiarity with elementary grammar.

Elementary grammar is understood to include the conjugation of the weak and the more usual strong verbs; the declension of articles, adjectives, pronouns, and such nouns as are readily classified; the uses of the more common prepositions; the simpler uses of modal auxiliaries; the elements of syntax and word-order. Proficiency may be tested also by direct questions.

Practice in pronunciation by reading aloud as much as possible from the texts used in the class is recommended; also the writing of German from dictation.

IV. ENGLISH

No candidate is accepted in either English (a) or English (b) whose work is notably defective in point of spelling, capitalization, punctuation, idiom, or division into paragraphs. An entrance condition imposed in English (a) is removed only upon evidence of marked improvement in the ability to write English correctly.

9. English (a). The candidate should read the books prescribed below with a view to understanding and enjoying them. The examination is designed especially to test the candidate's power of clear and accurate expression, but calls also for a reasonable degree of familiarity with the substance of the books read. The form of the examination is usually the writing of a paragraph or two on each of several topics, to be chosen by the candidate from a considerable number set before him in the examination paper.

The books set for this part of the examination are as follows:

For the preliminary examination in 1907, for the class entering in 1908 : Shakespeare's *Macbeth* and *Merchant of Venice ;* the Sir Roger

•

de Coverley Papers in *The Spectator ;* Irving's *Life of Goldsmith ;* Coleridge's *Ancient Mariner ;* Scott's *Ivanhoe* and *Lady of the Lake ;* Tennyson's *Gareth and Lynette, Lancelot and Elaine,* and *Passing of Arthur ;* Lowell's *Vision of Sir Launfal ;* George Eliot's *Silas Marner.*

For the preliminary examination in 1908, for the class entering in 1909 : Shakespeare's *Merchant of Venice* and *Julius Cæsar ;* Bunyan's *Pilgrim's Progress, Part I ;* the Sir Roger de Coverley Papers in *The Spectator ;* Scott's *Ivanhoe* and *Lady of the Lake ;* Irving's *Sketch Book ;* Macaulay's *Lays of Ancient Rome ;* Tennyson's *Gareth and Lynette, Lancelot and Elaine,* and *Passing of Arthur ;* George Eliot's *Silas Marner.*

For the preliminary examination in 1909, for the class entering in 1910 : Shakespeare's *Merchant of Venice* and *Julius Cæsar ;* the Sir Roger de Coverley Papers in *The Spectator ;* Franklin's *Autobiography ;* Scott's *Ivanhoe* and *Lady of the Lake ;* either Irving's *Sketch Book* or Hawthorne's *House of the Seven Gables ;* Macaulay's *Lays of Ancient Rome ;* Tennyson's *Gareth and Lynette, Lancelot and Elaine,* and *Passing of Arthur ;* either George Eliot's *Silas Marner* or Dickens's *Tale of Two Cities.*

For the preliminary examination in 1910, for the class entering in 1911 : Shakespeare's *Merchant of Venice* and *Julius Cæsar ;* the Sir Roger de Coverley Papers in *The Spectator ;* either Franklin's *Autobiography* or Goldsmith's *Vicar of Wakefield ;* Scott's *Ivanhoe* and *Lady of the Lake ;* Hawthorne's *House of the Seven Gables ;* Macaulay's *Lays of Ancient Rome ;* Tennyson's *Gareth and Lynette, Lancelot and Elaine,* and *Passing of Arthur ;* either George Eliot's *Silas Marner* or Dickens's *Tale of Two Cities.*

10. English (*b*). The candidate should read the books prescribed for this part of the examination with the view of acquiring such knowledge of their contents as will enable him to answer specific questions with accuracy and some detail. The examination tests also the candidate's ability to express his knowledge with clearness and accuracy. It is not designed, however, to require minute drill in difficulties of verbal expression, unimportant allusions, or technical details.

The books set for this part of the examination are as follows :

For the final examination in 1908 : Shakespeare's *Julius Cæsar ;* Milton's *Lycidas, Comus, L'Allegro,* and *Il Penseroso ;* Burke's *Speech on Conciliation with America ;* Macaulay's *Essay on Addison* and *Life of Johnson.*

For the final examinations in 1909, 1910, and 1911 : Shakespeare's *Macbeth ;* Milton's *Lycidas, Comus, L'Allegro,* and *Il Penseroso ;* either Burke's *Speech on Conciliation with America,* or both Washington's

Farewell Address and Webster's *First Bunker Hill Oration;* either Macaulay's *Life of Johnson* or Carlyle's *Essay on Burns.*

NOTES ON THE ENGLISH REQUIREMENTS

Preparation in English has two main objects: (1) command of correct and clear English, spoken and written; (2) power to read with intelligence and appreciation. To secure these ends, training in grammar and the simpler principles of rhetoric, and the writing of frequent compositions, are as essential as the study of the books specified above. After the year 1908 the English (*b*) paper may contain specific questions upon the essentials of English grammar, including ordinary grammatical terminology, inflections, and syntax. See also the paragraph in italics above, at the head of this section (IV. English).

For candidates who take the complete examination in English at a single session, this examination covers the books set for the final examination in that year, together with those set for the preliminary examination in the preceding year; for example, the complete examination in 1909 will cover the books set for the final examination in 1909, together with those set for the preliminary examination in 1908.

The lists in English (*a*) for 1908, 1909, and 1910, for the classes entering in 1909, 1910, and 1911, are selected from the list adopted by the Conference on Uniform Entrance Requirements in English, at a meeting held at Newark, New Jersey, February 22, 1905. Candidates may make other selections from that list, provided they notify the Registrar of the College before February 1 of the calendar year in which the examination is to be taken.

V. MATHEMATICS

11. Algebra (*a*): fundamental operations, factoring, highest common factor, least common multiple, fractions, equations of the first degree in one or more unknown quantities, problems which lead to equations of the first degree, powers and roots, fractional and negative exponents, reduction of radicals, including the extraction of the square root of numbers.

12. Algebra (*b*): quadratic equations in one or two unknown quantities, ratio and proportion, arithmetical and geometrical progressions, binomial theorem for positive integral exponents.

13. Plane Geometry: demonstrations of theorems and constructions, and demonstrations of problems which are contained in the standard texts; simple exercises in construction and demonstration; numerical problems, of which some are stated in terms of the metric system of weights and measures, relating to the mensuration of the triangle, parallelogram, trapezoid, regular polygons, and circle. For this examination the candidate must provide himself with compasses and ruler.

Special emphasis is laid upon accuracy in reckoning, both in Algebra and in Geometry.

VI. ANCIENT HISTORY

14. Greek and Roman History: from the earliest times to the death of Augustus.

The examination in this subject may not be divided.

COLLEGE ENTRANCE EXAMINATION BOARD EQUIVALENTS

The subjects in the College Entrance Board examination which, as stated above, may be offered as substitutes for the Yale requirements are as follows:

YALE REQUIREMENTS	BOARD EXAMINATION

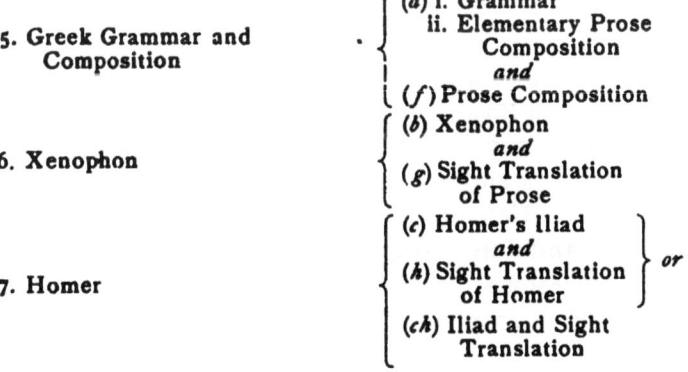

I. LATIN

1. Latin Grammar and Composition
    (*a*) i. Grammar
       ii. Elementary Prose Composition
    and
    (*l*) Prose Composition

2. Cæsar and Nepos
    (*b*) Cæsar
    and
    (*e*) Cornelius Nepos

3. Cicero
    (*c*) Cicero

4. Vergil
    (*d*) Vergil's Æneid
      and either
    (*g*) Ovid *or* (*q*) Sight Translation of Poetry
    (*dq*) Æneid and Sight Translation
    or

II. GREEK OR SUBSTITUTES FOR GREEK:
GREEK

5. Greek Grammar and Composition
    (*a*) i. Grammar
       ii. Elementary Prose Composition
    and
    (*f*) Prose Composition

6. Xenophon
    (*b*) Xenophon
    and
    (*g*) Sight Translation of Prose

7. Homer
    (*c*) Homer's Iliad
      and
    (*h*) Sight Translation of Homer
    (*ch*) Iliad and Sight Translation
    or

SUBSTITUTES FOR GREEK

For Homer,—
Any two of the three parts of Mathematics A1, as follows:
(1) Solid Geometry,
(2) Plane Trigonometry,
(3) Advanced Algebra *or* Analytical Geometry.

For Homer,—
Any two of the three following:
(*d*) Solid Geometry
(*f*) Plane Trigonometry
(*b*) Advanced Algebra

For the entire Greek requirement,—
Both
Elementary French
and
Elementary German
and, in addition, any two of the three following:

French (*b*)

German (*b*)

Any two of the three parts of Mathematics A1 (as above)

For the entire Greek requirement,—
Both
(*a*) Elementary French
and
(*a*) Elementary German
and, in addition, any two of the following groups:
(*b*) Intermediate French
and
(*c*) Advanced French
(*b*) Intermediate German
and
(*c*) Advanced German
(*d*) Solid Geometry,
(*f*) Plane Trigonometry,
and
(*b*) Advanced Algebra

III. FRENCH OR GERMAN

8. French (*a*)
   or
   German (*a*)

(*a*) Elementary French
or
(*a*) Elementary German

IV. ENGLISH

9. English (*a*)
10. English (*b*)

(*a*) Reading and Practice
(*b*) Study and Practice

V. MATHEMATICS

11. Algebra (*a*)
12. Algebra (*b*)
13. Plane Geometry

(*a*) i. Algebra
. ii. Algebra
(*c*) Plane Geometry

VI. ANCIENT HISTORY

14. Greek and Roman History

(*a*) Ancient History

CERTIFICATES OF STANDING ELSEWHERE

Certificates of standing elsewhere are not accepted for admission in lieu of examinations, except in certain cases when a candidate brings evidence that he has passed the whole of Freshman year in good standing at another college. A blank form of application will be furnished by the Registrar of the College upon request. Each application must be accompanied by a certificate of honorable dismission and a detailed statement of the applicant's entrance credits and work completed in college, both signed by the Dean or other proper officer of the college from which the student comes.   Each application is judged on its merits ; in every case the amount of work certified must be more than equivalent to the Yale entrance requirements, usually by a year's work.

ADMISSION TO, AND DIVISION OF, THE EXAMINATION

The examination may be taken either all at one time or in parts, at two or more different times.   Candidates, certificates, and examinations are accordingly designated as either "preliminary" (*i. e.*, other than final) or "final." The requirements for admission to an examination and for the granting of a certificate, together with the regulations under which the examination may be divided, are as follows :

1. Every candidate for admission is expected to send to the Registrar of the College, not later than May 15, a written notification of his intention to take the examination, stating also whether he is a preliminary or a final candidate and at what place he will take the examination. Upon receipt of this notification the Registrar will send a letter of instructions and a blank form for the required recommendation (see paragraph 5, below).

2. At a preliminary examination a candidate, whether he already holds a preliminary certificate or not, must present a definite statement from his instructor or instructors, specifying the subjects in which he is prepared to offer himself for examination.   No candidate is accepted in a subject in which he is not so authorized before the close of the examination.

3. To obtain a preliminary certificate, a candidate must, as a rule, pass at one time in not less than five subjects in which he is duly authorized.   To obtain an addition to the list of subjects credited on such a certificate, he must pass at one time in not less than three authorized subjects.

4. In general there must be an interval of not less than a school year between two parts of an examination ; but a candidate who has received a preliminary certificate at the June examination may at the next September examination add to the list of subjects credited thereon, provided he present evidence of work done during the summer and pass in not less than three subjects.

5. At the final examination a candidate must bring from his instructors satisfactory documents, *covering the whole of the preceding school year, September–June, whether this has all been spent in one school or not,* under the following three heads : (1) the work that has been done by him, (2) the subjects in which he is recommended for examination, (3) his moral character.

DATE AND PLACE OF THE EXAMINATION

The regular examination for admission to the College in 1908 will be held at Alumni Hall, New Haven, on Wednesday, Thursday, Friday, and Saturday, June 24, 25, 26, and 27.

Examinations for admission to the Freshman class (but not to other classes) will be held on the same dates (beginning on Wednesday, June 24, at 2.00 P. M., and closing on Saturday, at 4.00 P. M.) at the following places also :

Albany, N. Y., at the Albany Academy ;
Andover, Mass., at Phillips Academy ;
Asheville, N. C., at the Asheville School ;
Auburn, N. Y., at the High School ;
Berkeley, Cal., inquire of Professor Herbert C. Nutting, 1425 Walnut st. ;
Buffalo, N. Y., at the Central High School ;
Chicago, Ill., at the Bryant & Stratton Business College, northwest corner of Wabash av. and Congress st. ;
Cincinnati, O., at the Hughes High School, Fifth st., head of Mound ;
Cleveland, O., at the University School ;
Concord, N. H., at St. Paul's School ;
Denver, Col., at the East Denver High School ;
Detroit, Mich., at the Central High School ;
Easthampton, Mass., at Williston Seminary ;
Exeter, N. H., at Phillips Academy ;
Garden City, N. Y., at St. Paul's School ;

Groton, Mass., at the Groton School ;

Hartford, Conn., at the Public High School ;

Interlaken, Switzerland, under the supervision of Mr. Howard Copland ;

Kansas City, Mo., at the Central High School ;

Lakeville, Conn., at the Hotchkiss School ;

Lawrenceville, N. J., at the Lawrenceville School ;

Louisville, Ky., at the Male High School ;

Milwaukee, Wisc., at the Milwaukee Academy, 471 VanBuren st.;

Nashville, Tenn., at the Fogg High School ;

New York City, at the Y. M. C. A. building, 215 W. 23d st. ;

Norwich, Conn., at the Free Academy ;

Ossining, N. Y., at Dr. Holbrook's School ;

Philadelphia, Pa., at the Central High School ;

Pittsburg, Pa., at the Shady Side Academy ;

Pomfret, Conn., at the Pomfret School ;

Portland, Oregon, at the Hill Military Academy ;

Pottstown, Pa., at the Hill School ;

St.Louis, Mo., at the Board of Education building, corner 9th and Locust sts. ;

St.Paul, Minn., at the Central High School ;

San Francisco, Cal., see Berkeley, Cal. ;

Scranton, Pa., at the School of the Lackawanna ;

Simsbury, Conn., at the Westminster School ;

Southborough, Mass., at St.Mark's School ;

Tacoma, Wash., at a place to be designated later ;

Washington, Conn., at the Gunnery ;

Watertown, Conn., at the Taft School ;

Worcester, Mass., at Worcester Academy.

The College is prepared to hold an examination also, at the above-named time, in any other city or at any other school where the number of candidates and the distance from other places of examination may warrant it. Applications for such an examination must be sent to the Registrar before May 15.

A detailed schedule of the examination is given below. *All candidates, whether taking the examination in New Haven or elsewhere, must be present at the opening session, at 2.00 P. M. on Wednesday.*

A second examination will be held, *in New Haven only*, on Saturday, Monday, Tuesday, and Wednesday, September 19, 21, 22, and 23, 1908. *All candidates taking this examina-*

tion, except those who hold final certificates (with or without conditions), must be present at Alumni Hall at 10.00 A. M. *on Monday.* A schedule of the examination is given below.

FEE FOR THE EXAMINATION OUTSIDE OF NEW HAVEN

A fee of five dollars (payable at the opening of the sessions) is charged for admission to each examination (whether complete or partial) outside of New Haven.

COPIES OF EXAMINATION PAPERS

A set of the papers given at the examination in June, 1907, will be found at the end of the Academical pamphlet (preceding the indices). Teachers who desire for class use several copies of any paper (for any year since 1900) may obtain them at the rate of ten cents per dozen copies by applying to the Registrar.

SCHEDULE OF THE JUNE EXAMINATION

Wednesday, June 24

Registration	2.00— 2.30
Cæsar and Nepos	2.45— 3.30
Latin Grammar and Composition	3.45— 6.00

Thursday, June 25

English (*b*)	8.30— 9.30
English (*a*)	9.45—10.45
{ Greek Grammar and Composition	11.00—12.45
or	
German (*b*)	11.00— 1.00
Xenophon	2.15— 3.45
Vergil	4.00— 5.00
Cicero	5.15— 6.00

Friday, June 26

Algebra (*a*)	8.30— 9.30
Algebra (*b*)	9.30—10.30
Greek and Roman History	10.45—12.30
German (*a*)	2.15— 3.30
Homer	3.45— 5.15
or	
Mathematics A 1 :	
{ (1) Solid Geometry	3.45— 4.30
(2) Plane Trigonometry.	4.30— 5.15
((3) Advanced Algebra *or* Analytical Geometry	5.15— 6.00
or	
German (*c*)	3.45— 5.45

Saturday, June 27

French (*a*)	. . . . . .	8.30— 9.45
Plane Geometry	. . . . .	10.00—12.00
French (*b*)	. . . . . .	2.00— 4.00

SCHEDULE OF THE SEPTEMBER EXAMINATION
Saturday, September 19

Homer	10.30—12.00

or

Mathematics A 1 :

(1) Solid Geometry	10.30—11.15
(2) Plane Trigonometry. . . .	11.15—12.00
(3) Advanced Algebra *or* Analytical Geometry	12.00—12.45

or

German (*c*)	10.30—12.30
French (*b*)	2.00— 4.00

Monday, September 21

Registration	10.00—10.20
Latin Grammar and Composition . . .	10.30—12.45
Cæsar and Nepos	2.00— 2.45
Vergil	3.00— 4.00
Greek and Roman History	4.15— 6.00

Tuesday, September 22

Plane Geometry	8.30—10.30
Cicero	10.45—11.30
German (*a*)	11.45— 1.00
English (*a*)	2.00— 3.00
English (*b*)	3.15— 4.15
Xenophon	4.30— 6.00

Wednesday, September 23

Algebra (*a*)	8.30— 9.30
Algebra (*b*)	9.30—10.30
Greek Grammar and Composition . . .	10.45—12.30

or

German (*b*)	10.45—12.45
French (*a*)	2.00— 3.15

ANTICIPATION OF FRESHMAN COURSES

Courses regularly offered to the Freshman class (described on later pages) may be anticipated by members of the incoming class under the following regulations: (1) application must be made in writing to the Registrar before September 1; (2) a fee of five dollars for each course (made payable to the College Bursar, Mr. H. M.

Osborn) must accompany the application; (3) the applicant must present himself for examination at the time of the entrance examination in September. If the examination is satisfactorily passed, the student may take in place of the anticipated work an equal number of hours from the courses open to Freshmen or to Sophomores, if he is otherwise qualified to do so; and the anticipated course or courses may, if a grade of C or higher is obtained therein, count as part of the sixty hours required for graduation.

ADMISSION TO ADVANCED STANDING

Examinations for admission to advanced standing will be held at Alumni Hall on Thursday, Friday, and Saturday, June 25, 26, and 27 ; and on Monday, Tuesday, and Wednesday, September 21, 22, and 23, 1908. *All applicants must give evidence of having satisfied the regular requirements for admission to the Freshman class.*

A student from another college is admitted *ad eundem* only on passing a satisfactory examination on the studies of Freshman year, and upon other courses sufficient to make up the number of hours of class-room work already completed by the class which he wishes to enter.

Applications for admission to advanced standing without examination are received from graduates and undergraduates of approved colleges, who expect to fall back one or more years in their class rating. Each case, however, is judged on its merits. Either a diploma of graduation or a statement from the Dean or other proper officer of the college from which the student comes must be handed in with each application. Blank forms of application may be obtained by writing to the Dean of the College.

No one is admitted to the Senior class after the beginning of the second term.

AGE, TESTIMONIAL, AND BOND

No one is admitted to the Freshman class until he has completed his fifteenth year, nor to a higher class without a corresponding increase of age.

A satisfactory testimonial of good moral character is in every case required, before a certificate of admission in full is granted. Students from other colleges, as well as those who have been members of a school at any time during the preceding year, must present certificates of dismission in good standing.

Every person, on being admitted, must give to the College Bursar a bond, executed by his parent or guardian, for five hundred dollars, as security for the payment of charges arising under the laws of the College. A blank form for this purpose is provided at the time of admission.

GOVERNMENT, SCHOLARSHIP, ATTENDANCE, AND CONDUCT

The DEAN OF THE COLLEGE FACULTY has the general supervision, under the Faculty, of the Senior and Junior classes. COMMITTEES ON SOPHOMORE CLASS ADMINISTRATION and ON FRESHMAN CLASS ADMINISTRATION, consisting of instructors of these two classes, respectively, have a similar supervision of the Sophomore and Freshman classes, whose members are assigned in groups to the care of individual members of one or the other Committee.

The COLLEGE RULES FOR SCHOLARSHIP, ATTENDANCE, AND CONDUCT are issued in a separate pamphlet, copies of which are distributed to members of the incoming class and may be obtained at the Dean's Office.

For ATTENDANCE AT PRAYERS AND SUNDAY SERVICE, which is required of Students in the College, see the section on the University Church, on later pages.

TERMS AND VACATIONS

The PUBLIC COMMENCEMENT is held on the last Wednesday in June. The FIRST TERM begins thirteen weeks from the day after Commencement Day and continues twelve weeks. The SECOND TERM begins on the Wednesday after the first Thursday in January and continues until Commencement Day, with a SPRING RECESS of one week (occasionally two weeks, when the exigencies of the College calendar so require) including Easter Sunday. For some purposes the second term is divided into two approximately equal parts, as specified in the College rules.

COLLEGE BUILDINGS
LECTURE AND RECITATION HALLS, LABORATORIES, ETC.

The principal buildings used for the purposes of instruction and administration in the Academical Department are: ALUMNI HALL (for recitations and examinations); COLLEGE STREET HALL (for lectures and concerts); HERRICK HALL (psychological laboratory); KENT CHEMICAL LABORATORY; LAMPSON HALL (for recitations and lectures, and containing the BURSAR'S OFFICE, the DEAN'S OFFICE, and LAMPSON LYCEUM); OSBORN HALL (for recitations and lectures); PHELPS HALL (for recitations and lectures, and containing the BUREAU OF SELF-HELP); PEABODY MUSEUM OF NATURAL HISTORY (containing lecture rooms and laboratories, in addition to extensive collections); and SLOANE PHYSICAL LABORATORY. In some courses open to Academical students exercises are held in the buildings of the ART SCHOOL, the DIVINITY SCHOOL, the LAW SCHOOL, the MEDICAL SCHOOL, the DEPARTMENT OF MUSIC, and the SHEFFIELD SCIENTIFIC SCHOOL. The general administrative building for the University, containing the offices of the President, the Secretary, and the Treasurer, is WOODBRIDGE HALL. The Bicentennial Buildings include MEMORIAL HALL, UNIVERSITY HALL (containing the DINING HALL), and WOOLSEY HALL (containing the NEWBERRY ORGAN). The YALE STATION (University Post Office) is in Fayerweather Hall, which contains also the YALE CO-OPERATIVE STORE. Other buildings, *e. g.*, BATTELL CHAPEL, DWIGHT HALL, UNIVERSITY LIBRARY, GYMNASIUM, and INFIRMARY, are noticed on other pages.

DORMITORIES

The College Dormitories, in the order of date of erection, are as follows: CONNECTICUT HALL (built in 1750–52, long known as SOUTH MIDDLE COLLEGE, restored to its original form and name in 1905) owes its name to the liberal support given by the General Assembly of Connecticut in its construction; FARNAM HALL (built in 1869–70) is named in commemoration of Henry Farnam, Esq., of New Haven, who bore the chief part of the expense of its erection; DURFEE HALL (built in 1870–71) commemorates in like manner the generosity of Bradford M. C. Durfee, Esq., of Fall River, Massachusetts; LAW-RANCE HALL (built in 1885–86) owes its name to a gift for its construction from Mrs. Francis C. Lawrance, of New York City, in memory of her son, Thomas Garner Lawrance, of the class of 1884, who died during his Senior year in College; WELCH HALL (completed in 1892) is the gift of Pierce N. Welch, Esq. (Yale College 1862), of New Haven, in memory of his father, Hon. Harmanus M. Welch, of this city, who died in 1889; VANDERBILT HALL (first occupied in 1894) is the gift of Mr. and Mrs. Cornelius Vanderbilt, of New York City, in memory of their son, William Henry Vanderbilt, a member of the class of 1893, who died in 1892; WHITE HALL (completed in 1894) was erected at the expense of Andrew J. White, M.D. (Yale 1846), of New York City; BERKELEY HALL (completed in 1894) is named in commemoration of Bishop Berkeley, one of the early benefactors of the College; PIERSON HALL (built in 1896) bears the name of the first President (or Rector) of the College; and FAYERWEATHER HALL (completed in 1901) is named in honor of Mr. Daniel B. Fayerweather, of New York City.

The numbers and prices of the rooms in the several dormitories are given in the section on Expenses.

EXPENSES

TUITION

The BILLS FOR TUITION and other charges are made out and delivered to the students (or mailed to the parent or guardian, *if request to that effect is made*) three times a year, namely, at the beginning of each term and at the middle of the second term, at which times they are payable at the Bursar's Office, in Lampson Hall. If a student's account is not settled within the time specified on his bill, he will not be permitted to attend recitations until it has been settled, and in the allotment of College rooms he will not be permitted to retain or choose a room. Drafts on New York, Boston, and Philadelphia are received at par.

The annual charges for tuition are one hundred and fifty-five dollars. Of this amount fifty-five dollars is payable at the beginning of the first term, and fifty dollars at the beginning, and again at the middle, of the second term. An additional charge of eighteen dollars is made in the last bill of the Senior year, to cover expenses of graduation.

A student who is absent from College on account of sickness, or for any other cause, and retains his place in his class, is charged full tuition during his absence ; and payment is required before he can be admitted to examination.

BOARD

BOARD may be obtained at cost at the YALE DINING HALL (described in a later section). Board may be obtained out of College at prices varying from three dollars and a half to eight dollars per week. The average price is under five dollars.

ROOMS

There are in the College buildings (previously described) nearly five hundred rooms occupied by students, at prices varying, according to location, from one dollar to twelve dollars per week, payable each term or half-term in advance. These rooms are not furnished, and the rates charged do not include heat (except in Welch Hall) or light.

Students living out of College are not allowed to room

in any hotel or apartment-house or in any building in which a family does not reside, except by special permission of the Faculty.

Rooms are reserved in May for members of the Freshman class of the year following, and are assigned to applicants in the order of application. Correspondence about College rooms should be addressed to the Dean.

Members of the Junior, Sophomore, and Freshman classes, occupying any of the College rooms, may retain the same rooms for another College year by making application in writing to the Bursar on or before Saturday, May 2, 1908. Rooms not reserved will then be offered to the classes in order. Choices will be allotted to the Junior class on Monday, May 18, to the Sophomore class on Friday, May 22, and to the Freshman class on Friday, May 29.

PRICES PER WEEK OF ROOMS IN COLLEGE FOR 1907–08

When a room is occupied by two persons, each occupant is charged with one-half the price named in this schedule. The prices given for Welch Hall include steam-heat.

$1.00—359, 360, 361, 362, 363, 364, 365, 366 White; 417, 420 Berkeley.

$1.25—418, 419 Berkeley.

$1.50—80, 81, 90, 91 Connecticut; 409, 412, 416, 421 Berkeley.

$2.00—72, 73, 76, 77, 78, 79, 82, 83, 86, 87, 92, 93 Connecticut; 190, 194, 198, 207, 212, 217, 224, 228, 232 Farnam; 401, 404, 408, 410, 411, 413 Berkeley; 527, 529, 591, 593 Pierson.

$2.25—385, 388, 393, 396, 400, 403, 405 Berkeley.

$2.50—70, 71, 74, 75, 84, 85, 88, 89 Connecticut; 144, 145, 151, 152, 161, 162, 171, 172, 176, 177, 182, 183 Lawrance; 196, 197, 213, 214, 215, 216, 229, 230 Farnam; 524, 526, 528, 530, 532, 534, 575, 577, 587, 588, 589, 590, 592, 594, 595, 596, 597, 598 Pierson.

$2.75—384, 386, 387, 389, 392, 394, 395, 397 Berkeley.

$3.00—185, 186, 188, 189, 192, 193, 195, 199, 200, 201, 202, 203, 204, 205, 206, 208, 209, 210, 211, 218, 219, 221, 222, 225, 226, 231 Farnam; 523, 525, 531, 533, 543, 545, 559, 561, 571, 572, 573, 574, 576, 578, 579, 580, 581, 582 Pierson.

$4.00—184, 187, 191, 220, 223, 227 Farnam; 415, 422 Berkeley; 451, 452, 453, 454 Fayerweather; 539, 540, 541, 542, 544, 546, 547, 548, 549, 550, 555, 556, 557, 558, 560, 562, 563, 564, 565, 566 Pierson.

7

$4.50—14, 18 Vanderbilt; 149, 150, 159, 160, 169, 170, 180, 181 Lawrance.

$5.00—22, 26, 40, 56 Vanderbilt; 109, 122, 125, 138 Welch; 142, 143, 147, 148, 153, 154, 157, 158, 163, 164, 167, 168, 173, 174, 178, 179 Lawrance; 240, 247, 248, 255, 256, 263, 264, 271 Durfee; 407, 414 Berkeley; 521, 522, 585, 586, 599, 600 Pierson.

$5.50—44 Vanderbilt; 140, 141 Welch; 341, 342, 379, 380, 381, 382 White; 399, 406 Berkeley; 433, 434, 467, 468, 469, 470 Fayerweather.

$6.00—48, 52 Vanderbilt; 97, 106, 107, 108, 110, 111, 112, 113, 123, 124, 126, 139 Welch; 146, 155, 156, 165, 166, 175 Lawrance; 234, 241, 242, 249, 250, 257, 258, 265 Durfee; 338, 339, 355, 356, 357, 358, 375, 376, 377, 378 White; 430, 431, 447, 448, 449, 450, 463, 464, 465, 466 Fayerweather; 535, 536, 538, 554, 569, 570, 583, 584 Pierson.

$6.25—128, 129 Welch.

$6.50—238, 245, 246, 253, 254, 261, 262, 269 Durfee; 351, 352, 353, 354 White; 383, 390, 391, 398 Berkeley; 443, 444, 445, 446 Fayerweather.

$7.00—2, 3, 13, 15, 41, 43, 45, 58, 60 Vanderbilt; 94, 95, 96, 101, 114, 117, 118, 121, 127, 130, 134 Welch; 233, 235, 236, 237, 243, 244, 251, 252, 259, 260, 267 Durfee; 332, 333, 335, 336, 340, 343, 344, 345, 346, 347, 348, 349, 350, 367, 368, 369, 370, 371, 372, 373, 374 White; 424, 425, 427, 428, 432, 435, 436, 437, 438, 439, 440, 441, 442, 455, 456, 457, 458, 459, 460, 461, 462 Fayerweather; 537, 553 Pierson.

$7.50—133, 136, 137 Welch.

$7.75—132 Welch.

$8.00—1, 11, 12, 16, 25, 27, 29, 36, 42, 55, 57, 59, 67, 69 Vanderbilt, 100, 104, 105, 115, 116, 119, 120, 131, 135 Welch; 266, 268, 270 Durfee; 337 White; 429 Fayerweather; 551, 552, 567, 568 Pierson.

$8.50—5, 8, 17, 19, 21, 23, 47, 49, 51, 53, 63, 66 Vanderbilt; 98, 102 Welch.

$9.00—10, 28, 34, 39, 54, 68 Vanderbilt; 99, 103 Welch; 331 White; 423 Fayerweather.

$10.00—4, 6, 7, 9, 20, 24, 30, 32, 35, 37, 38, 46, 50, 61, 62, 64, 65 Vanderbilt; 334 White; 426 Fayerweather.

$12.00—31, 33 Vanderbilt; 239, 272 Durfee.

ESTIMATES OF EXPENSES

The subjoined table gives estimates of the ordinary annual expenses in College, omitting clothing, vacation expenses, and sundries.

	Lowest	General Average	Very Liberal
Treasurer's bill, tuition	$155	$155	$155
Rent and care of half-room in College .	20	100	140
Board, 36 weeks	117	175	250
Furniture, one-fourth of half-room for 4 years	3	5	10
Fuel (steam-heat) and light, for half-room .	15	20	35
Washing	15	25	40
Text-books and stationery . . .	10	25	40
Subscriptions (to Societies, Sports, Periodicals, etc.)		20	100
Total	**$335**	**$525**	**$770**

SELF-HELP AND BENEFICIARY AID

Besides the Scholarships and Funds noticed in this section, there are many Scholarships and Prizes noticed in the next section which afford material assistance to capable students.

SELF-HELP

Students in any Department of the University are assisted to obtain employment by the Bureau of Self-Help and Appointments (described in a later section), which also has charge of the assignment of beneficiary aid to students in the College.

BENEFICIARY AID

More than thirty thousand dollars is annually applied to the relief of students in the College who need pecuniary aid. Of this sum about twenty thousand dollars is derived from permanent charitable funds, while the remainder is taken from the annual income of the College. This assistance is given in the form of Tuition Scholarships, as Aid to Students Intending to Enter the Ministry, and in Special Beneficiary Scholarships. Needy students are also employed as Monitors, etc., and obtain text-books gratuitously from a Loan Library. As follows:

TUITION SCHOLARSHIPS

Tuition Scholarships are granted to approved students upon the basis of need and of excellence in scholarship, as follows:

For the first term of Freshman year an abatement of

tuition is made at the rate of one hundred and ten dollars a year, from the full annual charge of one hundred and fifty-five dollars, to such students as are judged to be in need of such aid to enable them to pursue their College course. The fact and the degree of the need in each case are determined by the information given by the applicant in filling out a form of application (which may be obtained from the Bureau of Self-Help) in which particular questions are asked as to the financial condition of himself and his family. So far as is practicable this information is regarded as confidential.

After the first term of Freshman year no abatement is allowed to any applicant whose grade in scholarship, in the preceding term or half-term, has fallen below 2.60 on the scale of 0-4.00. To all applicants whose grade in the preceding term or half-term is 2.60 or above Scholarships are assigned, at the beginning of each term or half-term, as follows: to a certain number of those who are found to be at once highest in scholarship and most in need, Scholarships at the rate of one hundred and fifty dollars a year (Group A); to an equal number of those judged to be lowest in scholarship or least in need, Scholarships at the rate of seventy dollars a year (Group C); and to all the rest, Scholarships at the rate of one hundred and ten dollars a year (Group B).

These abatements are made proportionately from each one of the term-bills when due. Assistance is withdrawn from students whose expenditures are not in accordance with the claim of limited means, or who are irregular in attendance, or who have been found guilty of behavior reflecting upon their moral character or subversive of College discipline. Recipients of this aid who join College societies, fraternities, clubs, or other associations, connection with which involves the payment of fees, dues, or other expenses, must arrange with the Bursar of the College in sufficient season to allow the deduction of the amount of expense thus incurred from the amount of the Scholarship.

Those who need this aid should make application to the Bureau of Self-Help, in each year of the College course. A person applying for the first time is required to present evidence in writing that he is worthy to receive assistance and needs it, upon doing which he will receive a form of application, which must be filled out and left at the Bureau on or before October 15.

Tuition Scholarships are derived from the income of funds as follows :

The HARMER FOUNDATION OF SCHOLARSHIPS, the proceeds of a bequest in 1854 from Thomas Harmer Johns (Yale College 1818), of Canandaigua, New York, received in 1858 and now amounting to over eleven thousand dollars, comprises five Scholarships, to be given to deserving students of small means.

The LYON SCHOLARSHIP FUND, of fifty-four hundred dollars, given in 1868–72 by Morris W. Lyon (Yale College 1846), of New York City, benefits four Scholars, selected for their worth and need by the founder or the Faculty.

The MORGAN FUND, bequeathed by Henry T. Morgan, of New York City, received in 1883–84, and now amounting to over eighty-five thousand dollars, has been set apart by the Corporation with the provision that the income shall be divided into Tuition Scholarships, to be assigned by the Faculty for the benefit of indigent and deserving students.

The MARETT FUND, amounting to over one hundred and fifty-two thousand dollars, which was established by the will of Philip Marett, of New Haven, in 1869, and was received in 1889–97, has been appropriated for beneficiary Scholarships, in aid of needy and deserving students.

The CHRISTMAN FUND, amounting to over twenty-two thousand dollars, bequeathed by Joseph A. Christman (Yale College 1857), of New York City, and received in 1891, is devoted to the support of poor and meritorious students.

There is also a FUND, the income of which is used for

Scholarships, which has been constituted from repayments made to the treasury by former students who have received aid during the College course.

There are more than thirty other SCHOLARSHIP FUNDS, most of them of one thousand dollars each, the income of which may be given to such students as shall be selected by the founders or the Faculty. In this number are included Scholarships named in commemoration of William Allen, Charles Atwater, Mills Bordwell, William S. Charnley, Thomas H. and Luther Fuller, Sereno Gaylord, John C. Holley, Charles L. Ives, Elisha C. Jones, William A. Macy, John S. Mitchell, John M. Raymond, John Spaulding, and James M. Whiton.

AID TO STUDENTS INTENDING TO ENTER THE CHRISTIAN MINISTRY

Those who desire this aid should apply to the Bureau of Self-Help on or before October 15 in each year of the College course. A person applying for the first time must present proper testimonials. The applicant is required to sign an agreement (attached to the application for a Tuition Scholarship) that, at the end of his College course, he will give his promissory note to the Bursar of Yale College for an amount equal to all the sums he shall have received on this special account (by which is meant all in excess of what he would have received had he held only a Tuition Scholarship), payable five years from the date of his graduation, if at that time he has not entered upon the work of the Christian ministry.

This aid is generally sufficient to meet the entire charge for tuition. It is derived from the income of funds, as follows:

The LANGDON FUND, of four thousand dollars, was bequeathed in 1835, by Solomon Langdon, of Farmington, Connecticut, to be applied for the instruction of undergraduate students having "the purpose of devoting their lives to the Gospel ministry."

The ELLSWORTH FUND, now about ninety-six thousand

dollars, was received in 1858, from the estate of Hon. Henry L. Ellsworth (Yale College 1810). The Corporation has directed that during the present year the income of this fund be applied to the aid of students in the College who need such assistance, preference being given to those having the purpose of entering the Gospel ministry.

Also devoted to this purpose are the GRATUITY FUND, of over fourteen thousand dollars, and funds named in commemoration of William E. Dodge, Rev. Joel Hawes, D.D., and Rev. Peter Parker, M.D.

SPECIAL BENEFICIARY SCHOLARSHIPS

Certain Beneficiary Scholarship funds have, for one reason or another, been kept distinct from the general Tuition Scholarship funds. They are as follows:

The DEFOREST SCHOLARSHIPS were established in 1823, by David C. DeForest, of New Haven. By the terms of this gift, the fund for which became available in 1852, one thousand dollars is annually appropriated for "the education and support at Yale College, or the University which may grow out of it, of the male descendants of Mehitable Lockwood," the mother of the donor. In default of such descendants the same sum is applied to the education of others of the family of DeForest.

The HOLMES SCHOLARSHIPS, one for each class in College, founded in 1865 by Samuel Holmes, of Montclair, New Jersey, are assigned upon the nomination of the Board of Agents of the Silas Bronson Library of Waterbury to students from the towns of Waterbury, Wolcott, Prospect, and Middlebury, Connecticut, who receive each the income of one thousand dollars per year.

The LUCIUS HOTCHKISS FUND, of ten thousand dollars, a bequest from Lucius Hotchkiss, of New Haven, made and received in 1881, comprises four Scholarships, the income of which is given to indigent and deserving students.

The LEAVENWORTH SCHOLARSHIP FUND, of twelve thousand dollars, was established in 1882, by Hon. Elias W. Leavenworth (Yale College 1824), of Syracuse, New York, with the primary object of defraying in part the expenses of the education of students of good character and promise, bearing the surname of Leavenworth.

The income of the TEELE FUND, of one thousand dollars, given in 1896 by Rev. Albert K. Teele, D.D. (Yale College 1842), is distributed by the President of the University, at his discretion, among needy and deserving undergraduates.

The income of the JAMES MARSHALL SCHOLARSHIP FUND, of about thirteen hundred dollars, established in 1902–04, is used toward paying the tuition annually of some worthy student struggling for an education.

The HENRY PIERSON JOHNES MEMORIAL SCHOLARSHIP FUND, of three thousand dollars, was founded in 1905, by Mr. and Mrs. Goldsmith D. Johnes, of Newburgh, New York, in honor of their son, Henry Pierson Johnes (Yale College 1881), who died in 1898. The income is paid to a student whose home is in the City or Town of Newburgh, New York, if there is in the College such a student, of satisfactory scholarship and high moral character, who is wholly or partly dependent upon his own exertions for support. If at the time of a vacancy in the Scholarship there is more than one student in the College who can satisfy the conditions of the gift, the Dean selects as its recipient the one who, in his judgment, is most worthy. In default of suitable students from Newburgh the income accruing meantime is used by the Bureau of Self-Help for the assistance of students who are at the time wholly or partially supporting themselves in College.

MONITORSHIPS, ETC.

There are also opportunities for students in need of aid to render service to the College as monitors, members of the Chapel choir, etc. In this way about fifteen hundred dollars is disbursed annually. Applications for monitorships should be made to the Registrar of the College.

In general it may be said that the other means of self-help at the command of the students are sufficient to enable many of those who have spare time to provide for the larger part of their College expenses.

LOAN LIBRARY

By the liberality of William L. Andrews, Esq., of New York City, and as a memorial of his son, Loring W. Andrews (Yale College 1883), a well furnished library has been established, containing text-books and works of reference, to be lent gratuitously to those students who have need to avoid the expense of purchasing books. Permission to use this library is obtained from the Bureau of Self-Help.

SCHOLARSHIPS, FELLOWSHIPS, AND PRIZES
UNDERGRADUATE SCHOLARSHIPS

The BRISTED SCHOLARSHIP, founded in 1848 by Charles Astor Bristed (Yale College 1839), of New York City, and having the income of a fund of over two thousand dollars, is awarded, whenever there is a vacancy, to the student in the Sophomore or Junior class who passes the best examination in the Classics and Mathematics. The successful candidate receives the annuity (forfeiting one-third in case of non-residence) until the end of the third year after graduation.

* The WOOLSEY SCHOLARSHIPS, each having the income of a fund of one thousand dollars, given by President Woolsey in 1846–48, are awarded in successive years, one to the student in each Freshman class who passes the best examination in Latin Composition (excellence in which is essential to success), in the Greek of the year, and in the solution of problems in the mathematical subjects required prior to Easter of Freshman year. The examination is held on the third Monday in May and the following Tuesday and Wednesday. The successful candidate receives the annuity during the four years of

his College course, provided he maintain a good standing in character and scholarship, and in Sophomore or Junior year make himself acquainted with the Differential and Integral Calculus.

The student who stands second at the examination for the Woolsey Scholarship receives for one year the income of the HURLBUT SCHOLARSHIP FUND, of one thousand dollars, established by Henry A. Hurlbut, of New York City, in 1858–59.

The student who stands third at the above examination receives the income for one year of the RUNK SCHOLARSHIP FUND, of one thousand dollars, given by Charles M. Runk, Esq. (Yale College 1845), of Allentown, Pennsylvania, in 1864.

The SCOTT HURTT SCHOLARSHIP was established in 1889, in memory of Burgess Scott Hurtt (Yale College 1878), by his classmates and friends. The income of a fund of five thousand dollars is assigned in June of each year to a member of the Sophomore class, who is selected by the Faculty on the ground of approved scholarship. One-half of the income is paid to the incumbent during his Junior year, and one-half during his Senior year, provided he continue to be in need of this assistance.

The THOMAS GLASBY WATERMAN FUND, of forty thousand dollars, was received in 1890, from the estate of Thomas Glasby Waterman (Yale College 1886). The income is given to not more than three Scholars, of manly character and limited means, who have distinguished themselves in their studies and give promise of achieving distinction in the line of work which they have chosen. The incumbents are elected annually by the Faculty from the Senior or Junior class, or from graduates of the College of not more than two years' standing.

The ALFRED BARNES PALMER SCHOLARSHIP FUND, of over five thousand dollars, was given in 1892, by Rev. Charles Ray Palmer, D.D. (Yale College 1855), in memory of his son, Alfred Barnes Palmer (Yale College 1892).

The annual income is paid, during his College course, to a student in avowed need of beneficiary aid, of unexceptionable character, and of high rank in scholarship.

The DANIEL LORD, JR., MEMORIAL FUND, of five thousand dollars, was established in 1894, by Daniel Lord, Esq., of New York City, in memory of his son, Daniel Lord, Jr. (Yale College 1892). The annual income is given to a deserving and needy student in the College, preferably a member of the Senior class, who shall be selected by the Faculty.

The LEARNED SCHOLARSHIPS, two in number, each having the income of a fund of two thousand dollars, established in 1895 by Hon. William L. Learned, LL.D. (Yale College 1841), are awarded, whenever there is a vacancy, at the close of Freshman year, to students in the College who have been markedly successful in their studies. The incumbents receive the income of the fund through the last three years of the course.

The JOHN J. COX SCHOLARSHIP, established in 1898 by the gift of two thousand dollars from Mrs. John J. Cox, of Peekskill, New York, in memory of her son, John J. Cox (Yale College 1891), is awarded yearly to some needy and worthy student in the College, of high character, selected by the Faculty.

The ROBERT CALLENDER SCHOLARSHIP was established in 1901, by a gift of six thousand dollars from W. R. Callender (Yale College 1894) and J. A. Callender (Yale College 1902), in memory of their brother, Robert Callender (Yale College 1898). The income is awarded annually by the Faculty to some needy student in the College.

The JOHN BENNETTO SCHOLARSHIP FUND, of five thousand dollars, was established in 1902, by the class of 1887, in memory of their classmate, John Bennetto. One-half of the income is given each year to a student in the College who has two more years of study before graduation, and who may hold the Scholarship during two years. The recipient must be a person of sound and strong character, marked ability, and high standing in the College world and in the estimation of his classmates; but in judging of a candidate's qualifications very high scholarship shall not be regarded as indispensable. Should any recipient of the income of this fund return to the College the sum received, or any part thereof, the amount returned shall be added to the fund.

The MAHLON LONG SCHOLARSHIP, established in 1902 by Rev. George Wells Ely, of Columbia, Pennsylvania, and yielding four hundred dollars a year, is open to undergraduate members of either the Academical or the Scientific Department of the University, and is intended to be given yearly during the entire course to the same student, though the appointment or reappointment is made each year.

The MEAD SCHOLARSHIP, having a foundation of over fifteen thousand dollars, established in 1902 by the gift of Solomon Mead, Esq., of Greenwich, Connecticut, is awarded to a student in the College, of good ability and undoubted piety, preparing for the Christian ministry. By recommendation of the President and Professors of the College the income may be continued to the beneficiary during his theological course in New Haven. It is expected that the recipients of this benefaction will repay the amount which they shall receive, if they shall ever be able to do so without embarrassing themselves, and any money so returned will be used for the benefit of other Scholars of similar character and intentions.

The BENJAMIN F. BARGE SCHOLARSHIP FUND, of five thousand dollars, was established in 1903. The income is used for the assistance of students in any class or Department of the University who have shown by their industry and attainments that they are worthy of aid in meeting the expenses of the course which they are pursuing.

The WALTER JOSEPH AUSTRIAN SCHOLARSHIP FUND was established in 1904, by a gift of six thousand dollars from Mr. Joseph Austrian, of Chicago, and Mr. Henry Block, of

New York City, in memory of Walter Joseph Austrian, of the class of 1907, who lost his life in the disaster at the Iroquois Theater on December 30, 1903. The income is awarded in June, whenever there is a vacancy, to a Freshman in the College, who shall hold the Scholarship, if worthy, until the date of his graduation. In the selection of a candidate stress is laid primarily upon qualities of manly character and influence, and secondarily upon ability and promise of distinction.

The ANTHONY D. STANLEY MEMORIAL FUND, of ten thousand dollars, was established in 1904, by the will of Walter Stanley Pitkin (Yale College 1858), of Washington, D. C., in memory of Anthony D. Stanley (Yale College 1830), formerly Professor of Mathematics in Yale College. One-half of the income of the fund is given to a needy and deserving student in the College.

The PLAINFIELD SCHOLARSHIP FUND was established in 1907, by Edwin Milner, of Plainfield, Connecticut, by a gift of two hundred and fifty shares of the capital stock of the New York, New Haven, and Hartford Railroad Company. The income of this fund is used in helping worthy students from the County of Windham (preference being given to students from the Town of Plainfield) in securing an education in any Department of Yale University. A Scholarship of five hundred dollars is given each year to a student then entering, and may be held four years.

The LISPENARD STEWART WITHERBEE SCHOLARSHIP FUND was established in 1907, by Mr. and Mrs. Frank S. Witherbee, of New York City, by a gift of ten thousand dollars in five per cent. securities, in memory of their son, Lispenard Stewart Witherbee, of the class of 1907, who died in Senior year. The income of this fund is awarded each year, on the advice of the Dean, to two or more deserving students in the College who are in need of financial assistance, preference being given to members of the Senior class. The recipients must be persons of sound

and strong character, marked ability, and high standing
in the College world; but in judging of a candidate's
qualifications very high scholarship shall not be regarded
as indispensable. Should any recipient of the income of
this fund return to the University the sum received, or
any part thereof, the amount returned shall be added at
the time to the available income balance of the fund.

CHICAGO SCHOLARSHIPS, in the form of annual loans of
six hundred dollars, are offered by the Yale Scholarship
Trust of Chicago, a corporation founded January 16, 1903,
to be distributed in installments to young men of Illinois,
carefully chosen on the basis of personal character and
scholarship, who enter Yale College or the Sheffield Scientific School.

The CLEVELAND SCHOLARSHIP was established in 1907,
by the Yale Alumni Association of Cleveland, to be
offered in competition to boys residing within the limits
of the Association who would otherwise be unable to
obtain the advantages of an undergraduate course at Yale
University. The Scholarship Committee of the Association selects from the successful competitors in the examination the one whom they deem best fitted to be the
recipient of the Scholarship, and advances to him the sum
of four hundred dollars for each year of his course as a
student in Yale College or the Sheffield Scientific School,
with the understanding that he shall at some future time
repay the sums so received, if he can do so without hard-
ship or self-denial, but no legal obligation of repayment
is imposed. The first recipient of the Scholarship will
enter Yale in September, 1908.

A number of UNDERGRADUATE SCHOLARSHIPS are noticed
in the section on Beneficiary Aid.

GRADUATE FELLOWSHIPS AND SCHOLARSHIPS
FELLOWSHIPS

The MACY FELLOWSHIP, being the income of a fund of
ten thousand dollars, received in 1865 from a bequest by
Rev. William A. Macy (Yale College 1844), of Shanghai,

China, who died in 1859, is awarded, whenever there is a vacancy, to a recent graduate of the College, of distinguished scholarship, who may hold it for a term of three years. He shall reside in New Haven, pursuing a course of non-professional study, and shall at the close of each College year present a meritorious thesis in evidence of his work during the previous year.

The DOUGLAS FELLOWSHIP, having the income of a fund of ten thousand dollars, was founded in 1873, by Mrs. Samuel Miller, of New Haven, and named in memory of her brothers, Rev. Sutherland Douglas (Yale College 1821) and George II. Douglas (Yale College 1828). The incumbent, who must be a recent graduate of the College, pursuing non-professional studies in New Haven, is elected annually, but no person shall hold the Fellowship for more than three years.

The FOOTE FELLOWSHIPS, being the income of a fund of twenty-five thousand dollars, established in 1873 by a bequest from Harry W. Foote (Yale College 1866), of New Haven, are awarded annually to two or more graduates of the College, selected by the Corporation, who remain in New Haven for one or more years pursuing studies in the graduate courses of the Department of Philosophy and the Arts.

The SOLDIERS' MEMORIAL FELLOWSHIP, with a foundation of ten thousand dollars, was established in 1875, by Mrs. Theodosia D. Wheeler, of New Haven, in honor of the alumni who fell in battle as Union soldiers in the war of 1861–65, and in special remembrance of William Wheeler (Yale College 1855). The incumbent must be, at the time of his election, a graduate of the College of not more than three years' standing. He shall pursue non-professional studies, and may hold the Fellowship for a period not exceeding five years. In selecting the incumbent the President and Professors are to give preference to one who has shown special proficiency in Greek; and, for the further prosecution of Greek study, the Fellow may spend a part or the whole of the time of his incumbency in Athens, in connection with the American School of Classical Studies, instead of in New, Haven.

The SILLIMAN FELLOWSHIP, for which the first installment of funds was received in 1875, was founded in memory of Benjamin Silliman (Yale College 1796), Professor of Chemistry, Mineralogy, and Geology in Yale College from 1802 until his death in 1864. It has the income of a fund of ten thousand dollars, and is awarded to a graduate of the College who has given evidence of proficiency and promise in some branch of physical science. The incumbent is elected annually, but no person shall hold the Fellowship for more than three years.

The LARNED FELLOWSHIPS, three in number, each having a fund of seven thousand dollars, were founded in 1877, by a bequest from Mrs. Irene Larned, of New Haven, and were augmented in 1888 by a bequest from Mrs. Urania B. Humphrey, of Norfolk, Connecticut. One Fellowship is awarded in each Senior class in the College. The incumbent must reside in New Haven, pursuing a course of advanced study under the direction of the Faculty.

The JOHN SLOANE FELLOWSHIP IN PHYSICS, established in 1889 by the gift of ten thousand dollars from John Sloane, Esq., of New York City, is awarded annually by the Faculty to a graduate of the College who has shown marked proficiency in the study of Physics, and gives promise of success in the prosecution and application thereof. The incumbent shall reside in New Haven for at least thirty-six weeks in each College year, pursuing a course of study in Physics and the related branches of science, and acting as an assistant in the Sloane Physical Laboratory ; he may be reëlected, but shall not hold the Fellowship for more than three consecutive years.

The SCOTT HURTT FELLOWSHIP, with a foundation of twelve thousand dollars, was established in June, 1893, by Mrs. Sarah I. Hurtt, of New York City, in memory of her son, Burgess Scott Hurtt (Yale College 1878). The incumbent must be a graduate of the College, of not more than four years' standing at the time of his first appointment, and may hold the Fellowship for three years by annual reëlection. In addition to having a good moral character, the person appointed must have maintained a satisfactory standing in scholarship and must purpose to pursue a scholastic, professional, or scientific career, in which he gives promise of success. He shall, if required by the President and Professors, reside in New Haven for at least one year of his incumbency, during thirty-six weeks of the year, pursuing his studies there; but with this exception may have the privilege of prosecuting his studies at any foreign University, or at the American School of Classical Studies in Athens, or at the American School of Classical Studies in Rome.

The ELLEN BATTELL ELDRIDGE FELLOWSHIPS, two in number, each having the income of a fund of twelve thousand dollars, were established in 1894, by a bequest from Mrs. Azariah Eldridge, of Yarmouth, Massachusetts. The incumbents must be graduates of the College, selected by the President and Professors, and must reside in New Haven, pursuing such a course of study as they may select and the Faculty approve. No Fellow shall continue on the foundation for more than three years.

The CUYLER FELLOWSHIP was established in 1900, by Thomas DeWitt Cuyler, Esq. (Yale College 1874), Cornelius C. Cuyler, Esq., and Miss Eleanor de Graff Cuyler, in memory of their brother Theodore Cuyler (Yale College 1882). The income of a fund of ten thousand dollars is awarded each year to a graduate of the College who is pursuing a course of study under the direction of the Faculty.

The JOHN ADDISON PORTER MEMORIAL FELLOWSHIP was established in 1901, by a gift of ten thousand dollars from Mrs. Josephine S. Porter, in memory of her husband, Professor John Addison Porter (Yale College 1842), and of her son, John Addison Porter (Yale College 1878).

8

The incumbent must be a graduate of Yale College or of the Sheffield Scientific School, selected for distinguished excellence and promise in the department of English. The Fellowship may be held for three years, and the incumbent is allowed to pursue studies, under the direction of the Professors in the Department of Philosophy and the Arts, "in the English language and literature and cognate subjects," either at New Haven or elsewhere.

The JOHN J. ABERNETHY FELLOWSHIP, with a foundation of ten thousand dollars, was established in 1907, by a provision in the will of Dr. John Jay Abernethy (Yale College 1825), who died in New York City in 1879, to be awarded to recent graduates of the College by the President and Professors.

The WILLIAM BORDEN FELLOWSHIP, yielding eight hundred dollars annually, is offered to the Phi Beta Kappa Society for five years, by Mr. John Borden, of the class of 1906, in memory of his father, William Borden, of Chicago, who died in 1906. It is to be awarded in May of the years 1908, 1909, 1910, 1911, and 1912 to a member of the Phi Beta Kappa Society who is then in the graduating class. The selection is to be made by a Committee consisting of the Graduate and Undergraduate Presidents of the Society and the Dean of the College, and the recipient of the Fellowship is to spend the following year in study in a European university, to be determined by said Committee.

Other FELLOWSHIPS, not restricted to Yale graduates, are noticed in the section on the Graduate School.

SCHOLARSHIPS

The BERKELEY SCHOLARSHIP, founded in 1733 by Rev. George Berkeley, Dean of Derry and afterwards Bishop of Cloyne, Ireland, and yielding about seventy dollars a year, is awarded to the student in each Senior class who passes the best examination (which must be a creditable one) in the Greek Testament (*Pauline Epistles*), the first book of Thucydides, the first six books of Homer's

Iliad, Cicero's *Tusculan Questions*, Tacitus (except the *Annals*), and Horace; provided he remain in New Haven as a graduate one, two, or three years.

The CLARK SCHOLARSHIP, being the income of a fund of two thousand dollars, given in 1824 for this purpose by Mr. Sheldon Clark, of Oxford, Connecticut, is awarded in each Senior class to the applicant who has attained the highest rank in the studies of the course; provided he remain in New Haven for one year or two years immediately after graduation, pursuing a course of non-professional study under the direction of the Faculty.

The W. W. DeFOREST SCHOLARSHIP, being the income of a fund of two thousand dollars, bequeathed in 1867 by William Wheeler DeForest, of New York City, is awarded to a student in each Senior class who has attained distinction in the study of French while in College, provided he pursue for the year after graduation a further course of study in the modern languages, especially French, Spanish, Portuguese, or Italian, under the direction of the Faculty.

The DANIEL C. EATON · GRADUATE SCHOLARSHIP IN BOTANY is endowed with the income of a fund of two thousand dollars, given by Mrs. Eaton in 1897 to establish a Graduate Scholarship in Botany in commemoration of her husband, Professor Daniel C. Eaton (Yale College 1857). This Scholarship is open for competition to members of the Senior classes in Yale College and the Sheffield Scientific School, on conditions to be prescribed by the Governing Board of the Sheffield Scientific School.

The following SCHOLARSHIPS announced in the sections on Beneficiary Aid and on Undergraduate Scholarships may be continued or awarded to graduates :

The DeFOREST SCHOLARSHIPS ;
The BRISTED SCHOLARSHIP ;
The WATERMAN SCHOLARSHIPS ;
The MEAD SCHOLARSHIP ;
The BARGE SCHOLARSHIP.

Other SCHOLARSHIPS, not restricted to Yale graduates, are noticed in the section on the Graduate School.

UNDERGRADUATE PRIZES AND PREMIUMS
NOT RESTRICTED TO A SINGLE CLASS

The LUCIUS F. ROBINSON LATIN PRIZES, from the income of a fund of five thousand dollars given in 1887 by the daughters of the late Lucius F. Robinson (Yale College 1843), of Hartford, will be awarded the present year to students showing special proficiency in Latin—one series of prizes (of fifty, thirty, and twenty dollars, respectively) being open to members of the Senior and Junior classes who are taking at least two hours of work per week in Latin; and a second series, of the same amounts, to members of the Sophomore class who have elected Latin. The awards will be based on the regular class-room work in Latin for the entire year, and on a special written examination (to be held on Monday, June 1, 1908) in translation at sight and on *The Civil War* of Julius Cæsar.

The THACHER MEMORIAL FUND, of three thousand dollars, established in 1892 by gifts from members of the class of 1842 and named in honor of their former instructor, Professor Thomas A. Thacher (Yale College 1835), is devoted to the encouragement of the practice of extemporaneous debate.

The JOHN HUBBARD CURTIS PRIZE, the income of a fund of twenty-five hundred dollars, established in 1900 by Mrs. Virginia H. Curtis, in memory of her son, John Hubbard Curtis (Yale College 1887), is awarded each year to that student in the College who shows the highest excellence in literary or rhetorical work upon assigned subjects. For the year 1907–08 competitors may select any one of the following topics:

1. A sequel to *A Doll's House*. A one-act play, showing the adventures of Nora after she left her husband.
2. Original metrical versions of the *Vexilla Regis*, the 23d or 24th Psalm of David, and Horace's *Integer Vitæ*.
3. The diary of a man marooned for a month in the South Seas.
4. An essay on the life of Joan of Arc as dramatic material.

5. The Poet of the Tontine. Notes on the life and writings of Dr. Thomas Holley Chivers.

6. A satire in the verse and manner of *Hudibras* on a subject chosen by the writer. (Not to exceed five hundred lines.)

7. A poem or short prose romance on the lost colony of Roanoke.

Pieces in competition should be left with Professor Beers or Professor W. L. Phelps on or before May 1, 1908.

The BENJAMIN F. BARGE MATHEMATICAL PRIZES, established in 1900–01 and amounting to two hundred dollars, are given annually from funds provided by Benjamin F. Barge, Esq. (Yale College 1857). A series of three prizes (first prize, fifty dollars ; second, thirty dollars; third, twenty dollars) is awarded in each of the two lower classes in the College. The prizes are awarded, in general, for the solution of original problems.

The JOHN ADDISON PORTER PRIZE IN AMERICAN HISTORY, founded in 1901 by Amy Betts Porter, in memory of her husband, John Addison Porter (Yale College 1878), and consisting of the income of two thousand dollars, will be awarded for the year 1907–08 for the best original essay by a member of the Senior or Junior class in the College on one of the following subjects :

1. The United States and China.
2. Silver in American Politics.
3. The Attitude of England toward the United States in the Civil War.
4. Franklin's Diplomatic Career.
5. The Right of Petition in our System of Government.

To the essays should be prefixed a classified bibliography of the authorities consulted, and precise references in foot-notes to these authorities should be given for all important statements made in the text. Each essay must be typewritten, signed by a fictitious name, and handed in under cover, accompanied by a sealed envelope containing the assumed name and the real name of the writer. The essays must be deposited with the Secretary of the University not later than February 22, 1908.

The ANTHONY D. STANLEY MATHEMATICAL PRIZES were

established in 1904, by the will of Walter Stanley Pitkin
(Yale College 1858), of Washington, D. C., in memory of
Anthony D. Stanley (Yale College 1830), formerly Professor of Mathematics in Yale College. One-half of the
income of a fund of ten thousand dollars is awarded in
prizes to students in the College for proficiency in mathematical study and research.

The ANDREW D. WHITE HISTORY PRIZE, of twenty-five
dollars, was founded in 1907, by an anonymous donor, to
be offered annually to Sophomores and Freshmen in the
College for highest excellence in the library work of
History A1.

See also the BRISTED SCHOLARSHIP, in the section on
Undergraduate Scholarships. Most of the UNIVERSITY
PRIZES, too, described on later pages, are open for com-
petition to all students in the College.

FOR SENIORS

The DEFOREST PRIZE, founded in 1823 by David C.
DeForest, of New Haven, and consisting of a gold medal,
of the value of one hundred dollars, is awarded " to that
scholar of the Senior class who shall write and pronounce
an English Oration in the best manner," the President and
Professors being judges.

TOWNSEND PREMIUMS, five in number, of twelve dollars
each, founded in 1843 by the gift of Isaac H. Townsend
(Yale College 1822), of New Haven, are awarded in each
Senior class for the best specimens of English Composition. All compositions receiving premiums must be read
in public. The following are the subjects for the year
1907–08 :

1. The Naval Efficiency of the United States.
2. Martinique.
3. The Congo To-day.
4. Tennyson at Cambridge.
5. Immigration in the Southern States.
6. The Tristram Story as a Theme of Art.
7. The Tariff as a Political Issue in 1908.
8. The Commerce of the United States with Brazil.

9. The Discoveries of Sir William Ramsay.
10. Marcelin Albert.
11. The Change of Ideal in the Perceval Romances.
12. The Labor Problem in the Philippines.
13. Castro.
14. Mississippi Steamboats.
15. The Consular Service as a Career for College Men.
16. The Idea of Filial Piety among the Latin Races.
17. Some Traditions of the *Yale Literary Magazine*.
18. The Rhodes Scholarships.
19. The Drama as a College Study.
20. The Theory of Employers' Liability.

Within the limits of reasonable implication these subjects may be divided or adapted. Manuscripts in competition are due at 15 White Hall on Wednesday, April 8, 1908, at noon. They should be written for effective oral delivery in about fifteen minutes. Attached to each essay should be a sealed envelope containing the writer's name. The date for the competition in speaking is Monday, May 4, 1908, at 7.30 P. M.

The DeForest Mathematical Prizes were established in 1855, by Dr. John DeForest (Yale College 1826), and were augmented in 1886 by his son, E. L. DeForest (Yale College 1854), of Watertown, Connecticut. A first prize of one hundred dollars and three second prizes of fifty dollars each are offered to the Senior class for worthy solutions of problems in Pure and Applied Mathematics.

See also the Berkeley Scholarship and the Daniel C. Eaton Graduate Scholarship in Botany, in the section on Graduate Scholarships; Prizes and Premiums not restricted to a single class, above; and the James Gordon Bennett Prize, in the section on University Prizes.

FOR JUNIORS

Winthrop Prizes, the income of a fund of five thousand dollars, given in 1871 by Buchanan Winthrop, Esq. (Yale College 1862), of New York City, are annually offered to the Junior class "for the most thorough acquaintance with the Greek and Latin poets," particular attention being paid to elegance of scholarship and appreciation of the spirit of the poetry, as shown at an examination held on the third Monday in May and the following Tuesday. The first prize is two hundred dollars, and the second prize is the balance of the income for the year. The subjects for examination for the class of 1909 are as follows: (Greek) The *Olympian* and the first four *Pythian Odes* of Pindar, the *Odes* of Bacchylides, and the *Prometheus* of Æschylus ; (Latin) The *Odes* of Horace and the *Elegies* of Propertius.

SCOTT PRIZES for excellence in German and in French are offered to the Junior class; they are of the value of thirty dollars each, and are given in books. The prizes were founded by a bequest from Henry W. Scott (Yale College 1863), of Philadelphia, received in 1873.

In the year 1907–08, and thereafter until further notice, the Scott Prize in German will be awarded to that member of the Junior class who shall pass the best examination (to be held during the latter half of the second term) in the following dramas : Lessing's *Nathan der Weise ;* Goethe's *Egmont* and *Iphigenie auf Tauris ;* Schiller's *Wallenstein-Trilogie;* H. von Kleist's *Käthchen von Heilbronn* and *Prinz Friedrich von Homburg.* Students may at any time apply to Professor Palmer for information in detail.

In the year 1907–08, and thereafter until further notice, the Scott Prize in French will be awarded to that member of the Junior class who shall pass the best examination (to be held during the latter half of the second term) in the following dramas : Corneille's *Cid* and *Horace ;* Racine's *Andromaque* and *Athalie ;* Molière's *Misanthrope* and *Femmes Savantes ;* Beaumarchais's *Barbier de Séville ;* Victor Hugo's *Ruy Blas.* Students may at any time apply to Professor Sanderson for information in detail.

The HENRY JAMES TENEYCK PRIZES, the income of a fund of twenty-six hundred dollars, established in 1888 by the Kingsley Trust Association, in memory of Henry James TenEyck (Yale College 1879), are awarded to the successful competitors at the Junior Exhibition, in the second term of each year. The following are the subjects for the year 1908 :

1. Linonia.
2. Italy in Argentina.
3. The Legend of the Fair Unknown.
4. The Development of Unions in the Steel Trades of the United States.
5. The Japanese on the Pacific Coast.
6. The Battle of Saratoga.
7. The Church in Corinth.
8. Mark Twain.
9. New Orleans.
10. The Hudson Bay Company.
11. The Spanish Main.
12. Immigrant Children in the Public School.
13. Arizona and New Mexico.
14. The Carrying Trade of the St. Lawrence.
15. Scandinavians in Minnesota.
16. *La Marseillaise.*
17. *The Leatherstocking Tales.*
18. The Development of Alaska.
19. Walt Whitman.
20. Yale in China.

Within the limits of reasonable implication these subjects may be divided or adapted. Manuscripts in competition are due at 15 White Hall on Saturday, March 21, 1908, at noon. They should be written for effective oral delivery in about twelve minutes. Attached to each manuscript should be a sealed envelope containing the writer's name. The date for the competition in speaking is Friday, April 10, 1908, at 7.30 P. M.

See also Prizes and Premiums not restricted to a single class, above.

FOR SOPHOMORES

The C. WYLLYS BETTS PRIZE, established in 1890 by the Phelps Association, being the income of a fund of one thousand dollars given by L. F. H. Betts, Esq. (Yale College 1891), in memory of his uncle, C. Wyllys Betts, Esq. (Yale College 1867), of New York City, is offered to the Sophomore class for excellence in English

Composition. The prize is awarded annually to that member of the class who has exhibited the most meritorious work in the required compositions of the year and in a special essay on a prescribed subject. The special essay prescribed for the class of 1910 will be on one of the following topics :

1. A Study of a City (for both expository and descriptive interpretation).
2. Socrates and Aristophanes (a contrast of types).
3. Don Quixote.
4. The Puritans of the *Scarlet Letter*.
5. The Development of Artistic Appreciation in College.

Essays in competition are due at 15 White Hall on Friday, May 29, 1908, at noon.

COLLEGE PREMIUMS are given each year in the Sophomore class for Declamation.

See also Prizes and Premiums not restricted to a single class, above.

FOR FRESHMEN

BERKELEY PREMIUMS, in books, for excellence in Latin Composition are offered annually to the Freshman class, from the surplus income of the Berkeley Scholarship Fund. The examination is held on the Tuesday following the third Monday in May.

The McLAUGHLIN MEMORIAL FUND, consisting of eleven hundred dollars, established in 1893 as a memorial of Edward Tompkins McLaughlin (Yale College 1883), Professor of Rhetoric and Belles Lettres in Yale College at the time of his death in 1893, is devoted to the encouragement of English Composition in the Freshman class. From the income of this fund a first and second prize, in books, are offered for the current year.

The WINSTON TROWBRIDGE TOWNSEND PRIZES, given by Judge William K. Townsend (Yale College 1871), in memory of his son, a member of the class of 1901, are annually awarded for excellence in English Composition in the Freshman class.

The McLAUGHLIN MEMORIAL PRIZES and the WINSTON

TROWBRIDGE TOWNSEND PRIZES will be awarded in 1908 for the best essays on any of the following topics :

1. The Botticelli in the Jarves Collection.
2. The Italian Plays of Shakespeare.
3. Tennyson's *In Memoriam*.
4. Queen Elizabeth and Queen Mary ;

or for a translation into English verse of one hundred lines from one of the following :

1. The *Cid* of Corneille.
2. The *Maria Stuart* of Schiller.
3. The *Epistles* of Horace.
4. The *Acharnians* of Aristophanes.

Manuscripts in competition are due at 15 White Hall on Saturday, April 11, 1908, at noon. Attached to each essay should be a sealed envelope containing the writer's name.

See also the WOOLSEY, HURLBUT, and RUNK SCHOLARSHIPS, in the section on Undergraduate Scholarships ; and Prizes and Premiums not restricted to a single class, above.

FOR EXCELLENCE IN ENTRANCE EXAMINATIONS

The HUGH CHAMBERLAIN GREEK PRIZE, being the income of one thousand dollars given for this purpose, in 1886, by Hon. Daniel H. Chamberlain (Yale College 1862), is awarded annually to that member of the Freshman class who has passed the best examination in the Greek required (of those who do not offer substitutes) for admission to the College. Candidates for this prize are required to pass the whole examination in Greek in June of the year of their entrance into College, even though they may have passed in some or all of the Greek subjects in a previous year.

The SAMUEL HENRY GALPIN LATIN PRIZE, being the income of one thousand dollars given for this purpose, in 1901, by Samuel Arthur Galpin, LL.B., in memory of his father, Samuel Henry Galpin (Yale College 1835), is awarded annually to that member of the Freshman class who has passed the best examination in the Latin required for admission to the College. Candidates for this prize are required to pass the whole examination in Latin in June of the year of their entrance into College, even though they may have passed in some or all of the Latin subjects in a previous year.

Two KANSAS CITY PRIZES, of twenty-five dollars each, one in Yale College and one in the Sheffield Scientific School, were established in 1907, by the Yale Alumni Association of Kansas City, to be awarded to candidates who reside in the territory covered by this Association, for the best examination for admission. The examinations, whether preliminary or final, must be taken in Kansas City. The candidate must be admitted without conditions, and must enter as a member of the class with which he has been examined.

See also the CLEVELAND SCHOLARSHIP, in the section on Undergraduate Scholarships.

APPOINTMENTS AND HONORS

To promote the rational choice of electives and give due recognition to good scholarship, Honors in Special Studies are conferred, and there are issued each year Junior and Senior Appointment Lists (on the work of the first half and of the whole of the College course, respectively) and Honor Lists on the studies of Freshman and of Junior year.

The Honors in Special Studies are conferred at the end of Senior year in the following groups of studies :

Classical Languages and Literature ;
Biblical Literature and Semitic Languages ;
Romance Languages and Literature ;
Germanic Languages and Literature ;
English Language and Literature ;
Mathematics ;
Physical Sciences ;
Natural Sciences ;
Philosophy ;
History ;
Social Sciences ;
Music.

A candidate for special honors must pursue with distinction courses aggregating nine hours of work of B and C grades, of which at least three hours must be of C grade, and must present a meritorious thesis embodying the results of individual research. The instructor under whose direction the thesis is to be written must be consulted before December 1 of Senior year ; notification of candidacy must be filed (by the candidate) at the Dean's Office before May 1 ; and the thesis, which must be typewritten, must be presented before June 1.

Courses in Sanskrit and in Classical Archæology may be counted as a part of the work in the Classical Languages.

Courses in Old and Middle English may be counted as a part of the work in the Germanic Languages.

Honors in Music are given for distinguished work in all the courses offered to undergraduates.

A candidate's whole work in courses of grades B and C in any group, though it may be more than the minimum requirement for honors, is taken into account in conferring honors in that group.

DEGREE

The degree of BACHELOR OF ARTS is conferred by the Corporation on those persons who have completed the course of Academical exercises, as appointed by law, and have been approved on examination at the end of the course as candidates for the same. Candidates are required to pay their dues to the Bursar as early as the Saturday before Commencement.

For various University Privileges of interest to students in the College, including The Dining Hall, The Gymnasium, The Infirmary, Libraries, etc., see a later section of the catalogue.

COURSES OF INSTRUCTION
GENERAL AIM AND SCOPE OF INSTRUCTION IN THE SEVERAL SUBJECTS OF STUDY

I. LATIN. It is intended that by the close of Freshman year the student who has taken Latin shall have gained clear conceptions of the genius of the language and its relations to other ancient and to modern tongues, a good knowledge of the characteristics of Latin literature and the essential facts of Roman history, and some appreciation of the position of Rome in the history of civilization. That subsequent reading of the language may be more easy and more exact, due attention is given in the early part of the study to forms, constructions. and idioms. From term to term the study of the literature is made more prominent, and particular texts are treated as means for the study of the public and private life of the Romans. Instruction in Freshman year is given mainly by recitations, but such work is supplemented by occasional lectures by the instructors and by conferences on papers presented by the pupils. In connection with the minute study of the authors considerable time is given to oral and written reading at sight; and for those who desire it there is special instruction in Latin prose composition.

For Sophomores, Juniors, and Seniors, who desire to continue their Latin studies, parallel courses are offered by different instructors, with different ends in view and by different methods. The characteristic of a course may be, for example, literature, or history, or philology, or antiquities, or the speaking and writing of Latin ; and the methods of preparation and the class-room treatment vary accordingly. Topics suggested by the nature of the courses, or by individual tastes and intentions, are assigned to students, and papers thus prepared are discussed before the class. Lectures and the rapid reading of large amounts of text are more frequent than in the work of Freshman year. The connections of Latin with English are emphasized, and written translations are from time to time required and criticized with reference both to faithful reproduction of the Latin thought and to idiomatic English. Editions annotated in German are often used, not only for their intrinsic helpfulness, but also to encourage the practical use of that language. Students who give evidence of unusual capacity and attainments may be admitted to membership in graduate classes.

Suggestions as to the choice of Latin courses may be found at the head of the section on Latin in the detailed statement of courses.

II. GREEK. The student who presents Greek in his examination for admission to College may continue the study of Greek during each of the four years of his College course. During the first two years he may read selections from Homer, Herodotus, Thucydides, and

Xenophon, dramas of Æschylus, Sophocles, and Euripides, one or two comedies of Aristophanes, one or more orations of Demosthenes, Isocrates, or Lysias, and the *Apology*, *Crito*, and other dialogues of Plato. These works are selected with a view to making the student familiar with the leading branches of Greek literature and the most interesting phases of Greek life and thought. The most important grammatical principles are reviewed in Freshman year; in Sophomore year grammatical questions are discussed rarely, except as they are necessary for the interpretation and illustration of the author's meaning. In reading the works of the poets less attention is paid to linguistic and grammatical points than to literary quality, to the structure of the poems, to poetic words, forms, arrangement of words, rhythm, and constructions; but the growth and development of the language are discussed, as well as the development of the literature. In reading the orators and historians the connection of thought and of events is made prominent. Greek prose composition is practiced only so far as to aid the student in reading Greek authors and to quicken his perception of nice distinctions in the order and choice of words and in construction.

In the more advanced courses of Junior and Senior years the student has the opportunity of reading the works of the lyric poets, other Greek dramas and other dialogues of Plato, parts of Aristotle, and the *Idylls* of Theocritus; of studying Hellenistic and Patristic Greek, and of doing broader and more critical work on the Homeric poems than is suited to the first College year; and of practicing more advanced Greek composition. Selected dialogues of Lucian are occasionally read, and courses in Platonic and Aristotelian philosophy are offered in the group of courses in Philosophy.

III. CLASSICAL ARCHÆOLOGY. The subjects covered in this group, which is closely allied with the two preceding ones, are Greek Sculpture, Architecture, and Lesser Arts, Topography and Monuments of Athens, and Roman and Etruscan Art.

IV. SANSKRIT, LINGUISTICS, AND COMPARATIVE PHILOLOGY. The courses offered under this head are intended for students of language, including students of the modern languages as well as classical students. The course in Elementary Sanskrit is intended to show the classical student the close connection between this language and Greek and Latin. The courses in Phonetics, Linguistics, and Comparative Syntax aim to give a broader knowledge of language in general and especially of the Indo-European group of languages.

V. BIBLICAL LITERATURE AND SEMITIC LANGUAGES. Work in this field may begin in Sophomore year and continue through Senior year. Some courses—such as Biblical Literature and History, Historical Origin of Christianity, and Life and Literature of the Apostolic Age—are offered primarily for general students of history and literature ; others are intended especially for those who desire to anticipate the work of the first year in the Divinity School or to specialize in Biblical literature and history or in Semitic languages.

VI–VIII. ROMANCE LANGUAGES (FRENCH, ITALIAN, SPANISH). The student who has passed the entrance examination in French may continue the study of that language during each of the four years of his College course, if he so elect ; the student who has not passed the entrance examination in French may, if he desire, begin the study of French in College.

To the properly equipped student, *i. e.*, one who has had two years of French in College, or the equivalent, courses of two different sorts are open, from which he may choose according to his special wants, with the advice of the instructors : (*a*) linguistic courses, conducted in French and combining the study of some literary topic with practice in speaking and writing ; (*b*) literary courses, in each of which the leading writers of some particular period are read and studied.

The study of Spanish and of Italian may be begun in Sophomore and in Junior year, respectively, and may be continued to the end of the College course.

IX, X. GERMANIC LANGUAGES (GERMAN, SCANDINAVIAN). The student who has passed the entrance examination in German may continue the study of German during each of the four years of his College course, if he so elect. The student who has not offered German in the examination for admission may, if he desire, begin the study of German in either Freshman or Sophomore year and pursue it for four or for three years, respectively. No elementary instruction in the language is given to Juniors or Seniors.

The courses for the successive years may be outlined as follows : During the first year the work consists of German grammar, and of the translation of easy English phrases, sentences, and connected prose into German, and of easy German prose into English. Constant sight-translation is used as a means of developing and strengthening the student's vocabulary and of freeing him from dependence upon the lexicon and from the word-by-word methods which its use encourages. Especial care is devoted to pronunciation. The work of the second year continues and extends that of the first year, taking up the translation of more difficult German prose, both with previous preparation and at sight, the study of word-formation, and the translation of more difficult English prose into German. Throughout the two years the aim in reading German is to cover as much ground as possible—from 500 pages upwards—in the belief that thereby the student will acquire better command of the language than if a smaller amount is read with rigid attention to grammatical details. It is expected that at the end of the second year the student will have adequate preparation for the use of the language in his work in other branches of study. Those, therefore, who are studying German solely with this end in view may perhaps discontinue class-study at this point ; but no student should begin the study of the language unless he expects to devote at least two years to it. For the remaining years the courses vary from year to year ; but opportunity is given for the critical study of works of leading authors and for the study of periods in the history of German literature.

There are courses in which German alone is spoken, and, in general, German is constantly read aloud in the class-room, with the object of improving the student's pronunciation and helping him to acquire some facility in expressing his ideas in German. But it is not a leading aim in the instruction in German to enable the student to converse in that language. Training in the ordinary conversational idiom may be had more profitably elsewhere and cannot form any considerable part of the class-room work. The student may acquire the language as a tool for use in other departments of study, and may come in contact with the best works of German literature, studying the form and contents of each and the life and environment of its author ; fluency in conversation must be acquired where the conditions are more fitted to the object which they are to effect.

Under the head of Scandinavian are offered elementary courses in Norwegian and Danish and in Swedish.

Suggestions as to the choice of German and Scandinavian courses may be found at the head of the section on Germanic Languages in the detailed statement of courses.

XI. ENGLISH. The course pursued by those Freshmen who elect English occupies three hours a week, and is based upon the careful study of a few important books. Among the authors read are Shakespeare, Carlyle, Arnold, and Tennyson. The work as a whole has for its object to cultivate in the student the habit of careful, critical reading of the best English literature.

Of the two elementary courses in rhetoric, which are open to, and especially intended for, Sophomores, one aims at a survey of the whole field of prose composition, a general training in fundamental principles and in the habit of expression, and a special training in exposition. The weekly recitations and lectures are auxiliary to the instruction given to each student in conference on frequent essays. The other elementary course deals with the principles and practice of oratory.

Courses in oral expression (declamation and public reading) are open to Freshmen, Sophomores, and Juniors, respectively.

9

The DeForest, Townsend, TenEyck, Betts, McLaughlin, and Winston Trowbridge Townsend prizes (described in an earlier section) are under the superintendence of the Assistant Professor of Rhetoric.

For the present year a prize in poetry, of the value of fifty dollars, is offered to students in the University by Professor Cook.

The more advanced work in English follows six different, though related, lines. Instruction is offered: (1) in the outlines of the history of English literature, with reading of selected authors ; (2) in the earlier stages of the language, with reference as well to the reading of the older literature as to linguistic discipline ; (3) in rhetoric ; (4) in the theory of poetry, involving a consideration of literary criticism in general ; (5) in the evolution of certain literary forms ; (6) in the study of various periods, classes of writers, and individual authors.

(1) The course in the History of English Literature to the Death of Pope is regarded as preparatory to the study of special periods and topics. A text-book is the main reliance for the history up to the Elizabethan period ; beginning with this period, specimen works of about ten authors are read, and supplementary lectures are delivered.

(2) The course in Old and Middle English is intended to impart the elementary knowledge essential to the reading of pre-Chaucerian authors as well as to the fuller understanding of Chaucer himself, and to give the student a sense of the meaning and value of our earliest literature.

(3) The courses in rhetoric are intended to provide systematic practice and criticism in the chief prose forms and in the composition of verse.

(4) The course in Theories of Poetry is designed to give the student a philosophical conception of the nature of poetry and the laws of its chief genera, as expounded by leading critics and deducible from the master works of literature.

(5) The course in English Lyrical Poetry is a study in literary evolution, its origin and its development from Skelton to the present day being considered. That in Early Narrative discusses the nature of the earliest narrative forms.

(6) The chief periods of English literature with reference to which instruction is at present provided are the seventeenth, eighteenth, and nineteenth centuries. The chief classes of writers examined are the dramatists from the mystery plays to the present time, prose authors, and the leading American writers of the past hundred years. The chief individual authors studied are Shakespeare (in three different courses), Milton (and his contemporaries), Tennyson, and Browning, besides Dante in translation.

The larger number of the courses in English are intended to be disciplinary as well as instructive; in other words, they have in view the development of insight and power no less than the imparting of information.

XII. MATHEMATICS. During the first year Solid Geometry, Plane Trigonometry, and Advanced Algebra may be studied. Freshmen and Sophomores who have passed Solid Geometry and Plane Trigonometry may take up the study of Analytical Geometry and Calculus.

The remaining mathematical courses fall into three main groups, namely, Pure Mathematics, Mathematical Physics, and Engineering Sciences. Detailed suggestions as to choice of courses may be found at the head of the section on Mathematics in the detailed statement of courses, and students who intend to pursue graduate studies in any one of the lines mentioned should follow these suggestions rather closely. .

XIII. PHYSICS. The instruction in Physics is begun in Sophomore year. Two alternative courses are offered to the beginner in the subject. The first of these (A 1) is designed to meet the needs of those students who desire only a single course in the subject, as part of a general education. The other course (B 1) requires Mathematics A 1, and is intended for those who desire a more satisfactory introduction to the subject, as a preparation for further work in Physics or in other branches of science. This second course must be taken by all who are to continue the study of Physics in College. Both courses are conducted by recitations, liberally illustrated by means of apparatus and experiments, and by occasional lectures. For students who desire a more detailed acquaintance with experimental methods an elementary laboratory course is offered, which may be taken simultaneously with the general course described above (B 1) or may be deferred until the following year. To those who have taken one or both of these two courses and have adequate mathematical training more advanced courses are open, of which a full description, together with suggestions as to the choice of courses, may be found at the head of the section on Physics in the detailed statement of courses.

XIV. CHEMISTRY. A course in Inorganic Chemistry, Inductive and Descriptive, is open to all classes. Students who wish to master during the College course those branches of Chemistry which are required for admission to medical or technical schools, or which are anticipatory of work otherwise required in such schools, should take this course as early as possible. It is prerequisite to the other courses in this group and to the courses in Mineralogy and in Physiological Chemistry, and is desirable for those who propose to take other courses in science. Instruction is given by lectures and in the laboratory; and frequent examinations, written or practical, serve to review and emphasize essential facts and principles, as· well as to test the progress of the student.

A course in Qualitative Analysis and one in Organic Chemistry are open to students familiar with the subject-matter of the course in Inorganic Chemistry. A course dealing with typical gravimetric and volumetric methods of Quantitative Analysis may follow or accompany the course in Qualitative Analysis, and courses in the Rare Elements, in Inorganic Preparations, and in Physical Chemistry are open by permission to students sufficiently advanced. Besides the courses already mentioned, the plan of which is to teach facts and principles by experimentation and induction, a lecture course, dealing with the relations of the Carbon Compounds, is open to properly qualified undergraduates. In special cases undergraduates may be admitted to other courses, intended primarily for graduates.

Further suggestions as to the choice of courses may be found at the head of the section on Chemistry in the detailed statement of courses.

XV. Geology. The instruction under this head is planned to meet the wants of two classes of students : (1) those who wish a knowledge of the structure and history of the earth as a means of general culture, and (2) those who intend to make Geology or some related science their chief life-work. To this end an introductory course in General Geology is offered, in which are discussed the elementary facts of earth-structure, the geological processes by which the earth has attained its present form and surface features, and the evolution of living beings. These subjects are abundantly illustrated by laboratory and field practice. The courses offered in Mineralogy and Physical Geography are designed to enlarge the scope of study of the elementary earth sciences. Students who have completed one year of study, and wish to continue, may select work in one of the several branches of Geology and will be encouraged to carry on special investigations. The lines of study now open to undergraduates are Mineralogy, Structural Geology, Physiography, and Historical Geology in its many phases, including Paleontology. The collection of minerals, rocks, maps, and other illustrative material is ample for all branches of the subject, and the New Haven region is well suited to give practical field experience.

Suggestions as to the choice of courses may be found at the head of the section on Geology in the detailed statement of courses.

XVI. Biology and Medical Sciences. The courses offered are adapted to meet the needs of students who desire to take up some line of biological work as a general-culture study, as well as of those who look forward to specialization in Biology or to the practice of Medicine. To the former class are addressed particularly courses in

Physiology, Elementary Biology, General Biology, Organic Evolution, and Botany. For the student of Medicine there are also courses in Anatomy (two), Histology and Embryology, Physiological Chemistry, Physiology of Physical and Nervous Functions, Pathology and Bacteriology, and Pharmacology and Toxicology. By taking this latter group of courses a student is able to anticipate two years of work in the Medical School and thus to obtain both the degree of B.A. and the degree of M.D. in six years. Other details about the group of courses as a whole may be found at the head of the section on Biology and Medical Sciences in the detailed statement of courses.

XVII. PHILOSOPHY. The introductory courses in this group are specially planned to meet the needs of students who elect Philosophy for the sake of general culture. They aim to awaken an intelligent interest in the fundamental problems of life and mind, to foster independence of judgment, and to develop the power of methodical and accurate thinking. The course in Logic lays special stress on the nature of reasoning, the conditions of proof, and the principles of science. The introductory course in Psychology includes a general survey of the conscious processes and a consideration of the scientific methods of psychological investigation. The course in History of Philosophy aims to give the student an appreciation of what is permanently significant in the world-views of the greatest philosophers, and thus to prepare him to face present-day problems in the light of the wisdom of the past. In the course in Elements of Philosophy the problems of Philosophy are studied topically. These courses are all open to Sophomores, and students are advised to elect at least one of them in Sophomore year.

For Juniors and Seniors there are, besides a general course in Ethics, advanced courses in the several branches of the subject, including seminary courses specially intended for graduate students and for those who expect either to make Philosophy their life-work or to take up a calling for which training in Philosophy is an important auxiliary.

XVIII. THEORY AND PRACTICE OF EDUCATION. The courses under this head are designed especially for students who expect to teach.

XIX. HISTORY. The courses in History begin with a general survey of European History from the decline of the Roman Empire to the close of the nineteenth century. The work in this course, which is open to Freshmen and is introductory to all the other courses except those which deal with Ancient History, is based upon a syllabus and upon readings in selected sources and in a considerable variety of text-books and more detailed modern narrative histories. To those who take this general course in Freshman year there is open in Sophomore year a course in English Political History.

The work in Junior and Senior years consists of more detailed courses on particular periods in European and American History, and of general courses in Ancient, Medieval, and Modern Oriental History and in the History of Greece and Rome. In all these courses the attempt is made to familiarize the student not only with the present state of knowledge and opinion in the several fields, but also with some of the representative works of modern scholarship which deal with them. In a number of the courses the students have practice in bibliography and in the use of the sources in dealing with precise problems of research and criticism ; in others essays requiring a more general range of reading and designed to arouse interest in the broader aspects of History form an important part of the work.

XX. ANTHROPOLOGY. This group begins with a course, given in common with the Geology group, wherein are set forth the main phases of the influence of physical environment upon man and human society, with especial attention to the controlling conditions of trade. The several topics of this introductory course may be immediately followed out in other courses. A general course in Anthropology, in which an effort is made to familiarize the student with the general character of the evolutionary theory and its special application to man and society, leads up, in a natural sequence, to a course in the Science of Society. From each of these latter courses more special ones branch out, which take up the Natural History of Man, Ethnology, Colonization, Culture-History, and so on. All the courses in this group are designed to rest upon an ultimate basis in natural science, and to furnish, in their various sequences, a progressively extended scientific knowledge of man ; this to be attained, in good part, through a study of the earlier and simpler forms of human society, and of social habitudes and institutions in their less complex terms.

XXI. ECONOMICS AND LAW. An elementary course in Economics is provided, which treats of the general principles of the science and of some of its more important practical applications in finance and legislation. Text-books are supplemented by lectures and discussions. Those who have taken Elementary Economics have an opportunity in Junior and Senior years to become acquainted with the history of the science and the controversies now going on in it, and to study more thoroughly special topics from different points of view, such as the historical and the statistical.

The courses in Law in Junior and Senior years are intended mainly for prospective students of Law as a profession, and deal with Elementary, Constitutional, and International Law, Contracts, Torts, and Evidence.

XXII. THE FINE ARTS. The School of the Fine Arts aims to provide instruction in the arts of design. Instruction is offered to Academical students in Drawing, Architecture (the elements), Painting, and Modeling.

XXIII. MUSIC. This Department aims to provide adequate instruction for those who intend to become professional musicians, either teachers or composers. In all the courses a knowledge of piano-playing is required.

GENERAL STATEMENT OF THE COURSE OF STUDY AMOUNT OF WORK REQUIRED FOR GRADUATION, AND ENROLLMENT

A candidate for the degree of Bachelor of Arts must successfully complete courses aggregating sixty hours per week through a year—Freshmen ordinarily taking fifteen or sixteen hours per week (at least fifteen); Sophomores and Juniors, from fifteen to eighteen hours (at least fifteen); Seniors, at least twelve hours, and, if entering at the beginning of Senior year, at least fifteen. A student who is enrolled as a Freshman a second year may, if he desires, take eighteen hours per week; no student may take more than eighteen without special permission. Extra hours, in addition to the sixty ordinarily required for graduation, may be made necessary by absence, as specified in the College rules for attendance.

A student is enrolled in the Freshman class until he has completed at least eleven hours of work and has removed all entrance conditions (concerning which see the College rules); he is then enrolled in the Sophomore class until he has completed twenty-six hours; then in the Junior class until he has completed at least forty-one hours; then in the Senior class.

In no other way can a student retain or regain enrollment with his original class than by passing satisfactorily in the required number of hours of work. A course that has not been satisfactorily passed is not counted as part of the work for the degree, and the resulting deficiency can be made up only by taking in a later year, in addition to the amount of work otherwise required, a number of hours equal to that covered by the rejected course. (In general, a student may not repeat, in a later year, a course in which he has failed.) Upon satisfactory completion of the whole number of hours of work required to date, a student who has been separated from his class for deficiency of hours regains enrollment therein.

ANTICIPATION OF COURSES

This is a privilege open only to more capable students. It is restricted to those who have an average scholarship standing of C grade or higher on the work of the previous year, and who, furthermore, have no deficiency due to failure in a course taken in the previous year and are not required to take extra hours for absence. A student who desires to anticipate a course must make application in writing to the Dean before September 1, pay the Bursar the fee for a special examination, and present himself for examination at the time of the entrance examination in September. If the examination is satisfactorily passed, the student may take in place of the anticipated course an equal number of hours from the courses open to his own or the next higher class, if he is otherwise qualified to do so ; and the anticipated course may, if a grade of C or higher is obtained therein, count as part of the sixty hours required for graduation. (Anticipation of Freshman courses is noticed on an earlier page.)

COMPLETION OF THE COLLEGE COURSE IN THREE YEARS

As eighteen hours of work may be taken in Sophomore year and again in Junior year, and one or more courses may be anticipated at the beginning of a year, it is possible for a good student to have completed the required sixty hours at the end of his third year. This completion of the course in three years is open only to those who have taken a high rank in Freshman year, and only by special vote of the Faculty in each case.

MAJORS AND MINORS

Every student must complete before graduation two

majors and three minors,† and these must be so arranged that not more than two of these five units shall be in any one of the three following divisions :

(1) LANGUAGE, LITERATURE, AND CLASSICAL ARCHÆOLOGY: comprising Latin ; Greek ; Classical Archæology ; Sanskrit, Linguistics, and Comparative Philology ; Biblical Literature and Semitic Languages ; French ; Italian ; Spanish ; German ; Scandinavian ; and English (including Rhetoric and Oral Expression).

(2) MATHEMATICS AND THE NATURAL AND PHYSICAL SCIENCES: comprising Mathematics ; Physics; Chemistry ; Geology; and Biology and Medical Sciences.

(3) PHILOSOPHY, EDUCATION, HISTORY, AND THE SOCIAL SCIENCES: comprising Philosophy ; Theory and Practice of Education ; History ; Anthropology ; and Economics and Law.

Courses to complete the remaining thirty-one hours of the sixty required for the degree of Bachelor of Arts may be chosen without any other restriction than such as may be found in the printed statements of the individual courses.

FRESHMAN YEAR

Every member of the Freshman class is required to take five of the three-hour courses listed below. Three of the five courses chosen must be in continuation of subjects offered for admission by the student concerned, and within the following limits: Latin, Greek, French, German, English, and Mathematics. The anticipation (explained under Terms of Admission) of a Freshman course that so

---

† A *major* unit consists of connected courses of grades A, B, and C, aggregating at least seven hours a week ; a *minor* unit consists of connected courses of grades A and B, aggregating at least five hours a week. (A course of grade B may count as of grade A, and a course of grade C as of grade B.)

Connected courses are to be understood as those comprised within the limits of a single, numbered group, *e. g.*, I. Latin, II. Greek, etc. It is to be noted, however, that : (1) in the division of Ancient Languages, etc. (groups I-V), courses in group III (Classical Archæology) count as courses in Latin or in Greek, and Freshman Latin and Freshman Greek are to be considered the elementary [A] course for group IV (Sanskrit, Linguistics, and Comparative Philology); (2) the science courses (groups XIII-XVI) are to be treated in this respect as a single group, and Mathematics A 1 may count as an A course for Physics B 1 ; (3) Geology A 1 is to be considered the regular A course in group XX (Anthropology), and Economics and Law A 1 and C 7 may be counted as A and C courses, respectively, in this group. In a few cases courses count as of B or of A grade, according as they are, or are not, taken after certain other courses. In every such case a specific statement is made in connection with the printed announcement of the course.

continues a subject offered for admission is considered as meeting this requirement for that subject. The complete list of courses from which Freshmen may choose is as follows :

Latin—
> *Livy, Tacitus, and Horace*, Course A 1.

Greek—Two courses are offered from which to choose one :
> (i) *Homer, Herodotus, and Plato*, Course A 1.
> (ii) *Thucydides, Xenophon, Lysias, and Plato*, Course A 2.

French†—
> *Elementary French*, Course A 1.
> *Freshman Second-Year French*, Course A 2.
> *Freshman Third-Year French*, Course A 3.

German†—
> *Elementary German*, Course A 1.
> *Freshman Intermediate German*, Course A 2.
> *Freshman Advanced German*, Course A 3.

English—
> *Freshman English*, Course A 1.

Mathematics—
> *Solid Geometry, Plane Trigonometry, and Advanced Algebra*, Course A 1, or *Analytical Geometry and Calculus*, Course B o (the latter for those who have anticipated Solid Geometry and Plane Trigonometry).

Chemistry—
> *Inorganic Chemistry, Inductive and Descriptive*, Course A 1.

History—
> *European History*, Course A 1.

In addition to five of these three-hour courses, a Freshman may take the following one-hour course :

English—
> *Oral Expression*, Course A 1.

GYMNASTICS

From November 1 until April 1 work in gymnastics is required of the members of the Freshman class, except those who are in regular training with the recognized athletic teams. This work may be either two periods a week in class-drill or four periods of individual exercise, at the option of the student.

---

† A Freshman who has failed in the entrance examination in French (a) must, if he elects either language, take German, and *vice versa*. A Freshman who has passed the entrance examination in either language may either (1) continue the study of that language, or (2) begin the study of the other one in case he has not previously pursued it, or (3) continue the study of the one *and* begin the study of the other. Those who have sufficient knowledge of either language are assigned to classes further advanced.

SOPHOMORE YEAR

Every member of the Sophomore class is required to choose fifteen, and may choose eighteen, hours of the following courses :

Latin—   [One course only may be chosen.]
> *Horace, Catullus, and Cicero,* Course B 1.
> *Horace, Catullus, Plautus, and Terence,* Course B 2.
> *Juvenal, Martial, Pliny, and Latin Comedy and Elegy,* Course B 3 (both parts, *a* and *b*).

Greek—*The Athenian Drama,* Course B 1 or B 2.

Biblical Literature—*Biblical Literature and History,* Course A 1.

French or Spanish—
> [One course only may be chosen.]
> *Elementary French,* Course A 1.
> *Second-Year French,* Course A 4.
> *Sophomore Advanced French,* Course B 1a or B 1b.
> *Elementary Spanish,* Course A 1.

German—   [One course only may be chosen.]
> *Elementary German,* Course A 1.
> *Sophomore Second-Year German,* Course A 4.
> *Sophomore Advanced German,* Course B 1a or B 1b.

English—
> *Written Composition,* Course B 1, and *History of English Literature,* Course B 1 (to count together as a single three-hour course for Sophomores) ; or *Oral Composition,* Course B 2, and *History of English Literature,* Course B 1 (to count as five hours toward the sixty required for graduation, but only three hours will be counted among the fifteen required for Sophomore year) ; or *Oral Composition,* Course B 2 (alone).
> *Oral Expression,* Course A 2 (may not be taken as part of the required fifteen hours).

Mathematics—
> *Analytical Geometry and Calculus,* Course B 1, or *Advanced Calculus,* Course C 1 (the latter open as a Sophomore course only to those who have taken B o in Freshman year).

Physics—
> *Elementary Physics,* Course A 1, or *General Physics,* Course B 1.
> *Elementary Laboratory Physics,* Course B 2 (may not be taken as part of the required fifteen hours).

Chemistry—
[One course only may be chosen as part of the required fifteen hours.]
> *Inorganic Chemistry, Inductive ana Descriptive,* Course A 1.

> *Qualitative Analysis,* Course B 1 ⎱ (for those who have taken
> *Organic Chemistry,* Course B 2 ⎰ A 1 in Freshman year).
> *Inorganic Preparations,* Course B 3 (may not be taken as part
> of the required fifteen hours).

Geology—
> *Physical and Commercial Geography,* Course A 1.
> *Mineralogy and Crystallography,* Course B 3 (may not be taken
> as part of the required fifteen hours).

Biology—
> *Elementary Biology,* Course A 2.
> *Physiology,* Course A 1 (may not be taken as part of the
> required fifteen hours).

Philosophy—
[One course only may be chosen as part of the required fifteen hours.]
> *History of Philosophy,* Course A b1 (may not be chosen with
> A b2).
> *Logic and Elements of Philosophy,* Course A b2 (both parts
> *a* and *b*).
> *Psychology,* Course A b3.

History— [One course only may be chosen.]
> *European History,* Course A 1.
> *English Political History,* Course B 12 (for those who have
> taken A 1 in Freshman year).

Anthropology—
> *Physical and Commercial Geography* (Geology A 1) and *Elemen-
> tary Economics* (Economics and Law A 1) may count as
> A courses in Anthropology.

Economics and Law—
> *Elementary Economics,* Course A 1.

PUBLIC SPEAKING

Private instruction in public speaking is given to members of the
Sophomore class who are chosen to contest for the prizes in reading
and speaking.

When a student makes his choice of Sophomore studies,
he is expected also to indicate his plans for Junior and
Senior years, showing how he intends to satisfy the
requirements for the Bachelor's degree.

JUNIOR AND SENIOR YEARS

Every member of the Junior class is required to select
from the list of courses given in the following detailed
statement not less than fifteen, nor more than eighteen,
hours of class-room work per week. A member of the
Senior class is required to select a number of hours per

week which, in addition to those passed satisfactorily at the end of Junior year, will bring the total number of hours up to sixty ; but no member of the Senior class may take less than twelve hours, and a student entering at the beginning of Senior year must take at least fifteen hours. Any excess of hours above the sixty required for the degree of Bachelor of Arts may be devoted to courses in the professional schools.

PUBLIC SPEAKING

Private instruction in public speaking is given in preparation for the TenEyck prize speaking in Junior year and for the DeForest prize speaking in Senior year.

DETAILED STATEMENT OF COURSES
SPECIAL EXPLANATIONS

1. Courses included in brackets are omitted in 1907-08, but probably will be given in 1908-09.

2. An asterisk (*) prefixed to the statement of a course indicates that written permission must be secured from the instructor in order to gain admission to the course.

3. The sequence of courses is, in general, indicated by division into grades A, B, and C. In some cases one course presupposes another, or must be taken in connection with another. Such restrictions, and restrictions to a particular class or to particular classes, are indicated in brackets after the title of the course, *e. g.*, Latin "B 1 *Horace, Catullus, and Cicero* [after A 1]. [Sophomores, Juniors, and Seniors.]"

4. Courses not otherwise limited are open to Juniors and Seniors, and to them only.

5. The number of hours of class-room or laboratory work per week for each course and the number of hours per year for which the course counts (which numbers are sometimes identical, sometimes not) are explicitly indicated after the title (and limitations, if there be any) of the course, *e. g.*, Mathematics " A *2a Descriptive Astronomy* [after A 1]. 3 hrs. first term, *to count as 1 hr. for the year.*" Unless otherwise indicated, the number of hours per week is identical with the number per year.

THE COURSES

(1) LANGUAGE, LITERATURE, AND CLASSICAL ARCHÆOLOGY

ANCIENT LANGUAGES, CLASSICAL ARCHÆOLOGY, LINGUISTICS, AND BIBLICAL LITERATURE (GROUPS I-V)

I. LATIN

Within the groups of Latin and Greek courses students may, with the consent of the instructors, change from one course to another at the end of the first term.

Students who wish to continue the study of Latin after Freshman year as part of a liberal education should take B 1, B 2, or B 3 in Sophomore year. B 3*a* and B 3*b* (which may be taken separately by Juniors and Seniors), B 4, B 5, B 6, B 7, C 1, C 2, C 3, and C 4 are intended to meet the needs of such students in Junior and Senior years. B 8, B 9, B 10, B 11, C 5, C 6, C 7, and C 8 are more special in character.

Students who propose to specialize in Latin with a view to teaching should take B 10 and one of the B or C reading courses in Junior year, and in Senior year C 8 and one of the other C courses, of which C 5 and C 7 are especially intended for those who expect to teach.

C 6 and the graduate courses mentioned in the next paragraph are intended mainly for men who expect to take a year or more of graduate work.

A few Juniors or Seniors who have done superior work in Latin may, with the consent of the instructor, be received into the following graduate courses : *Plautus* (Professor MORRIS) ; *The Italic Dialects and Comparative Grammar of Latin Sounds and Inflections* (Professor OERTEL) ; and *Latin Palæography* (Assistant Professor CLARK). These courses are described in the pamphlet of the Graduate School.

It is to be noted, with regard to the requirements as to majors and minors, that Classical Archæology B 5 (*Roman and Etruscan Art*) counts as a B course in Latin. For

Phonetics, Comparative Syntax, and *Linguistics,* see Sanskrit, etc. B 2, C 1, and C 2.   Certain courses in general or comparative literature are announced in the English group.   For *Outline Survey of Ancient History,* see History B 2*a* and B 2*b*.   For *History of the Roman Republic,* see History B 4.

A 1   *Livy, Tacitus, and Horace.*   [Freshmen.]   3 hrs.
Assistant Professors INGERSOLL and CLARK, Mr. REA, and
   Mr. MENDELL.
> Livy, Books i and ii or selections ; the *Agricola* and *Germania* of Tacitus; the *Satires* of Horace.

B 1   *Horace, Catullus, and Cicero* [after A 1].
          [Sophomores, Juniors, and Seniors.]   3 hrs.
Professor MORRIS.
> The *Odes* of Horace and the poems of Catullus, as illustrations of two types of Roman lyric poetry ; the *De Amicitia* and the *De Senectute* of Cicero.

B 2   *Horace, Catullus, Plautus, and Terence* [after A 1].
          [Sophomores, Juniors, and Seniors.]   3 hrs.
Assistant Professor INGERSOLL.
> The same as B 1, except for the substitution of one play each of Plautus and Terence (probably the *Menæchmi* and the *Phormio*) in place of the *De Amicitia* and the *De Senectute.*

B 3   *Juvenal, Martial, Pliny, and Latin Comedy and Elegy*
          [after A 1].   [Sophomores,† Juniors, and Seniors.]
   a   *Juvenal, Martial, and Pliny's Letters.*   2 hrs.
Professors T. PECK and H. P. WRIGHT.
> Roman private life ; literary and social conditions at Rome in the early empire.

   b   *Latin Comedy and Elegy* [*not* after B 2].   1 hr.   .
Assistant Professor INGERSOLL.
> One play each of Plautus and Terence, and selected *Elegies* of Tibullus and Propertius.

[B 4   *Cicero (Brutus), Quintilian (x and xii), and Tacitus
          (Dialogus)* [after B 1, B 2, or B 3].   2 hrs.

---

† By Sophomores this course may be taken only with the consent of the student's instructor in Freshman Latin, and, if it is to be counted as part of the required fifteen hours, both *a* and *b* must be taken ; otherwise *a* or *b* may be taken separately.

Professor T. PECK.

> The history and characteristics of Roman oratory. Fragments of several Roman orators are studied in connection with readings from the three critics.
>
> Omitted in 1907-08.]

[B 5 *Plautus and Terence* [after B 1, B 2, or B 3]. 2 hrs. Professor MORRIS.

> Two or three plays of each author (not including the *Menæchmi* or the *Phormio*), with study of literary history, form, and influence.
>
> Omitted in 1907-08.]

B 6 *Latin Sight-Reading* [after A 1]. 4 hrs., *to count as 2 hrs.* Assistant Professor CLARK.

> Rapid reading at sight, commencing with Gudeman's *Latin Literature of the Empire.* No outside preparation is required.

[B 7 *Later Roman Historians* [after A 1]. 2 hrs. Assistant Professor CLARK.

> A study of the development of the Roman Empire, based on readings from several authors, beginning with Tacitus.
>
> Omitted in 1907-08.]

B 8 *Latin Literature of the Early Middle Ages* [after B 1, B 2, or B 3]. 2 hrs. Assistant Professor CLARK.

> A review of the intellectual and literary history of the West from Jerome to Charlemagne. The works read are chosen especially to show the development of language and culture. Knowledge of French and German is essential in this course.

[B 9 *Latin Literature of the Late Middle Ages* [after B 1, B 2, or B 3]. 2 hrs. Assistant Professor CLARK.

> This course illustrates the literary transition from medieval to modern times, and the later phases of medieval culture. Knowledge of French and German is essential in this course.
>
> Omitted in 1907-08.]

B 10 *Latin Composition* [after A 1]. 2 hrs. Assistant Professor CLARK.

> An elementary course, leading up to C 8, but thorough enough to serve as final for men who plan to teach immediately after graduating.

[B 11   *Roman Law* [after A 1].   2 hrs.
Assistant Professor INGERSOLL.

> An elementary and general course, for the classical student or
> the student of law.
>
>> Omitted in 1907–08.]

*C 1 *Hexameter Poetry* [after two years of superior work in
        Latin].   2 hrs.
Professor T. PECK.

> Readings in Ennius, Lucretius, the *Georgics* of Vergil, and the
> *Epistles* of Horace.

*C 2   *Cicero de Oratore* [after three years of superior
        work in Latin].   1½ hrs. 1st half-year,
                                        to count as 1 hr. for the year.
Professor T. PECK.

> Cicero's ideals and practice in oratory.   •

[*C 3   *The Character and Reign of Tiberius* [after two years
        of superior work in Latin].   2 hrs.
Professor T. PECK.

> Tacitus (*Annals*, i–vi), Suetonius (*Tiberius*), and Velleius
> Paterculus.   Characteristics of "Silver" Latin.
>
>> Omitted in 1907–08.]

C 4   *Latin Literature* [after B 1, B 2, or B 3, or, if not to be
        counted as part of a major, after A 1].   2 hrs.
Assistant Professor INGERSOLL.

> A general survey of the whole field. Lectures, illustrative
> readings, and direction of the student's private reading.

*C 5   *Early Latin* [after three years of superior work in
        Latin].   2 hrs.
Professor T. PECK.

> Study of inscriptions and of the ante-classical literature.
> The course is largely philological and critical, dealing with
> the development of forms, constructions, and literature, and
> is especially commended to those who expect to teach Latin.

[*C 6   *Latin Epigraphy* [after three years of superior
        work in Latin].   2 hrs.
Professor T. PECK.

> Such inscriptions (including coins) are studied as illustrate
> Roman private and public antiquities.
>
>> Omitted in 1907–08.]

10

*C 7 *Vergil* [after B 1, B 2, or B 3]. 2 hrs.
Professor MORRIS.

> An introduction to Vergil, for students who expect to teach Latin. Practice in the use of the best editions and of other critical and exegetical helps.

*C 8 *Advanced Latin Prose Writing* [after B 10]. 2 hrs.
Professor OERTEL.

> A study of Cicero's *Lælius* from the stylistic point of view; exercises in translation and free composition. Designed especially for those who expect to teach Latin.

II. GREEK

Within the groups of Latin and Greek courses students may, with the consent of the instructors, change from one course to another at the end of the first term. ·

It is to be noted, with regard to the requirements as to majors and minors, that Classical Archæology B 1 (*Greek Art, I*), B 2 (*Greek Art, II*), B 3 (*Greek Architecture*), and B 4 (*Topography and Monuments of Athens*) count as B courses in Greek. For *Phonetics, Comparative Syntax*, and *Linguistics*, see Sanskrit, etc. B 2, C 1, and C 2. For *New Testament Greek*, see also Biblical Literature and Semitic Languages B 8. Certain courses in general or comparative literature are announced in the English group. For *Greek Philosophy*, see also Philosophy C 1 and C 2. For *Outline Survey of Ancient History*, see History B 2*a* and B 2*b*. For *History of Greece*, see History B 3.

A 1 *Homer, Herodotus, and Plato.*   [Freshmen.] 3 hrs.
Professor PERRIN, Dr. W. H. THOMPSON, and Mr. DEWING.

> Selections from Homer's *Odyssey*, xiii–xxiv, and from Herodotus ; Plato's *Apology* and parts of the *Crito* and *Phædo*.

A 2 *Thucydides, Xenophon, Lysias, and Plato.*

[Freshmen.] 3 hrs.
Professor GOODELL.

> Selections from Thucydides, Book i ; rapid reading of Xenophon's *Hellenica*, Book ii ; three or four speeches of Lysias ; Plato's *Apology* and either the *Crito* or the first half of the *Protagoras*.

B 1   *The Athenian Drama* [after A 1 or A 2].
        [Sophomores, Juniors, and Seniors.]   3 hrs.
Professor GOODELL.

> Reading of representative plays of Æschylus, Sophocles, Euripides, and Aristophanes; lectures on the Greek theater and on the Attic drama and its relations to earlier and later literature.

B 2   *The Athenian Drama* [after A 1 or A 2].
        [Sophomores, Juniors, and Seniors.]   3 hrs.
Professor REYNOLDS.

> The *Prometheus* of Æschylus, the *Œdipus Tyrannus* of Sophocles, the *Medea* of Euripides, and the *Frogs* of Aristophanes ; lectures on the Greek theater and on the Attic drama and its ·relations to earlier and later literature.

B 3   *Homer* [after B 1 or B 2].   2 hrs.
Professor REYNOLDS.

> Reading of the entire *Iliad*. This course is intended for the general student of literature.

[B 4   *Greek Drama* [after B 1 or B 2].   2 hrs.
Professor REYNOLDS.

> Five or six plays of Euripides are read, with discussion of special topics and occasional lectures.
>   Omitted in 1907–08.]

B 5   *Plato* [after B 1 or B 2].   2 hrs.
Professor SEYMOUR.

> The *Gorgias ;* selections from the *Republic ;* some of the minor
>   . dialogues.

[B 7   *Demosthenes and Theocritus* [after B 1 or B 2].   2 hrs.
Professor SEYMOUR.
>   Omitted in 1907-08.]

B 8   *Hellenistic and Patristic Greek* [after B 1 or B 2]. 2 hrs.
Professor SEYMOUR.

> A philological study of selections from the *Septuagint*, of St. Paul's *First Epistle to the Corinthians*, and of other documents of the early Christian Church.

[B 9   *Lucian and Greek Romance-Writers* [after B 1 or B 2].
                                                     2 hrs.
Professor REYNOLDS.

(*a*) Lucian's *Dream, Charon, Timon*, and other minor dialogues, with a study of Greek culture under Marcus Aurelius.

(*b*) Lucian's *True History*, parts of Xenophon's *Cyropædia*, and an introductory survey of the precursors of the modern novel and romance.

    Omitted in 1907–08.]

B 10 *Greek Composition* [after B 1 or B 2].   2 hrs.
Dr. W. H. THOMPSON.

   Intended for those who expect to teach.

*C 1 *Æschylus and Pindar* [after B 1 or B 2]. 2 hrs.
Professor SEYMOUR.

   The *Persians* and the *Seven against Thebes* of Æschylus, with attention to their dramatic structure ; the principal extant *Odes* of Pindar, with a comparison of the poems of Bacchylides.

*C 2 *Sophocles* [after B 1 or B 2].   · 3 hrs.
Professor GOODELL.

   Reading of the seven extant plays, with special attention to the artistic form. This includes (*a*) the Sophoclean dramatic type— in formal structure, development of plot, and character-drawing ; (*b*) the use of meters, with much practice in reading aloud ; (*c*) poetic style.

*C 4 *The Testimonies of Aristophanes, Thucydides, and Plutarch to the Career of Alcibiades* [after B 1 or B 2].

                2 hrs.
Professor PERRIN.

   Reading of the *Frogs* of Aristophanes, with investigation of the other comedies ; analysis and reading of Thucydides and of Plutarch's *Alcibiades*.

[C 5 *The Phædo of Plato and Aristotle's Ethics* [after B 1 or B 2].   2 hrs.
Professor SEYMOUR.

    Omitted in 1907–08.]

*C 6 *Greek Composition.*   1 hr.
Professor GOODELL.

   Intended for graduate students and specially qualified Seniors and Juniors. The weekly session lasts from an hour to an hour and a half.

III. CLASSICAL ARCHÆOLOGY

[B 1   *Greek Art, I : Sculpture* [after Greek A, and counted as a B course in Greek].   2 hrs.

Assistant Professor BAUR.

> Lectures and quizzes by the instructor ; special study of the literary sources by the students ; occasional reports from members of the class.
>
> Omitted in 1907–08.]

B 2   *Greek Art, II : The Lesser Arts* [after Greek A, and counted as a B course in Greek].   2 hrs.

Assistant Professor BAUR.

> This course treats briefly of Greek painting, ceramics, terracottas, bronzes and other metal work, coins, and gems.

B 3   *Greek Architecture* [after Greek A, and counted as a B course in Greek].   2 hrs.

Assistant Professor BAUR.

> The various forms of building-construction are successively examined in informal lectures, supplemented by occasional reports from members of the class.

*B 4   *Topography and Monuments of Athens* [after Greek A, and counted as a B course in Greek].   2 hrs.

Assistant Professor BAUR.

> A combination of the historical and the strictly topographical methods of treatment is adopted.

B 5   *Roman and Etruscan Art* [after Latin A, and counted as a B course in Latin].   2 hrs.

Assistant Professor BAUR.

> This course includes such subjects as Roman architecture, Græco-Roman sculpture, topography and monuments of Rome and of Pompeii, and the domestic arts. Selected topics are investigated by the members of the class.

IV. SANSKRIT, LINGUISTICS, AND COMPARATIVE PHILOSOPHY

Freshman Latin and Freshman Greek are to be considered the elementary [A] course for this group.

B 1 *Elementary Sanskrit* [after Latin A and Greek A].

2 hrs.

Professor HOPKINS.

> Instruction in Sanskrit, beginning with Whitney's *Sanskrit Grammar* and passing on to Lanman's *Reader*. Especially recommended to Seniors who plan to take graduate work in classical philology.

*B 2 *Phonetics* [after Latin A and Greek A]. 1 hr.

Professor OERTEL.

> A general and rather elementary introduction to phonetics, based on a study of the English, French, and German sound-systems. Intended mainly for those who expect to teach.

[*C 1 *Introduction to Comparative Syntax* [after Latin A and Greek A]. 1 hr.

Professor HOPKINS.

> For this course a knowledge of Sanskrit is desirable, but not necessary; it may be taken by any classical student.
>
> Omitted in 1907-08.]

*C 2 *Linguistics* [after Latin A and Greek A]. 2 hrs.

Professor OERTEL.

> An introduction to the scientific study of linguistic development.

V. BIBLICAL LITERATURE AND SEMITIC LANGUAGES

Courses A 1, B 1, B 2, C 1, and C 3 are offered primarily for general students of history and literature. A 1 and B 1 together aim to give a complete constructive survey of Biblical and cognate literature, history, and thought, as an introduction to this and related departments of study. B 4, B 5, B 6, B 7, and B 8 (the last two of which are courses in the Divinity School, open to students in the College) are intended especially for those who desire to anticipate the work of the first year in the Divinity School. Such men must have completed by graduation at least eight of the fifteen hours required of Junior Theological students. Students who desire to complete the Hebrew requirement in one year may elect the three-hour elementary course offered by Professor Curtis in the Theological Department.

For *Hellenistic and Patristic Greek* see also Greek B 8.

A 1   *Biblical Literature and History.*

[Sophomores, Juniors, and Seniors.]   3 hrs.
Professor KENT.

> A general course, intended for students who wish to gain a definite, systematic knowledge of the literature, history, and teachings of the Bible on the basis of the best English translations.

B 1   *Historical Origin of Christianity.*   2 hrs.
Professor KENT.

> Study of the origin, history, and characteristics of Judaism; of political and religious conditions in the Græco-Roman world; and of the life, teachings, and work of the Founder of Christianity. Lectures and assigned reading.

B 2   *Life and Literature of the Apostolic Age.*   2 hrs.
Mr. CLAPP.

> A study of the primitive church in Palestine, the early contact of Christianity with the heathen world, and the development of Apostolic teaching. Lectures and assigned reading.

[B 4   *Elementary Hebrew.*   2 hrs.
Mr. CLAPP.

> A study of the elements of the Hebrew language in connection with the reading of *Genesis*, i–viii, and of selected passages of easy Hebrew.
>
> Omitted in 1907–08.]

B 5   *Advanced Hebrew.*   1 hr.
Professor CURTIS.

> Reading of the *Books of Samuel* and a thorough review of the elements of Hebrew grammar and syntax, followed by practice in rapid sight-reading.

B 6   *Elementary Syriac.*   2 hrs.
Professor TORREY.

Those who intend to make a thorough study of the New Testament or of early Church history will find this course valuable. Text-book: Brockelmann's *Syrische Grammatik.*

B 7 *Pauline Epistles and Synoptic Gospels.* 3 hrs.
Professor BACON.

First term: critical interpretation of *Galatians,* with comparison of the other major epistles. Second term: similar study of *Mark,* with comparison of *Matthew* and *Luke.*

B 8 *New Testament Greek.* 2 hrs., *to count as 1 hr.*
Mr. CLAPP.

A course of rapid reading in the *Gospels* and the *Epistles.* Two hours of class-room work to be credited as one hour.

*C 1 *Biblical Seminary* [after A 1 and B 1]. 2 hrs.
Professor KENT.

A course intended to train students for patient, accurate, and independent investigation of Biblical and cognate questions. Subject for 1907-08: The character, work, writings, and teachings of the Hebrew prophets, and the growth of Israel's Messianic hopes.

*C 2 *Hebrew Seminary.* 2 hrs.
Professor KENT.

A knowledge of Hebrew, Hellenistic Greek, Latin, and German is required. Subject for 1907-08: The syntactical and textual problems of the later prophetic books, and the critical translation of the more important sections.

C 3 *Principles and Methods of Biblical Study* [after A 1]. 2 hrs.
Professor KENT and Mr. CLAPP.

Investigation of the problems and existing methods of religious instruction; study of psychological principles and of the Biblical material, with a view to their practical use in religious education; outlining of definite courses of study.

MODERN LANGUAGES AND LITERATURES (GROUPS VI-XI)
ROMANCE LANGUAGES

French A 1 is for beginners in all classes. A 2, A 4, and A 5 are for students who have the minimum French training. A 3 is for Freshmen who have passed entrance French (*b*). Those who choose A 5 may not, during the same year, take any other course in that language; but the courses in Italian and Spanish are open to them.

All the other courses are of general interest and open to both Juniors and Seniors. The selection in each individual case should depend, next to the student's wish, on the relative amount and success of previous training. In the statement of each course the qualifications required are indicated; but consultation with the instructors is strongly advised, when not definitely required.

For *Phonetics, Comparative Syntax,* and *Linguistics,* see Sanskrit, etc. B 2, C 1, and C 2. A course in Dante and certain courses in general or comparative literature are announced in the English group. For *Readings in French Psychology and Philosophy,* see Philosophy C 13.

VI. FRENCH

A 1   *Elementary French.*   [All classes.]   3 hrs.
Professor WARREN and Assistant Professor CURDY.

> A careful study of the main facts of French grammar, with practice in pronunciation. As soon as possible, the reading of easy French prose is taken up.

A 2   *Freshman Second-Year French.*   [Freshmen.]   3 hrs.
Professor WARREN and Dr. LeCOMPTE.

> See the statement of course A 4, with which this course is identical in subject-matter.

A 3   *Freshman Third-Year French.*   [Freshmen.]   3 hrs.
Assistant Professor SANDERSON and Dr. LeCOMPTE.

> See the statement of course B 1*b*, with which this course is identical in subject-matter.

A 4   *Second-Year French.*

[Sophomores, Juniors, and Seniors.]   3 hrs.
Assistant Professor CURDY.

Reading from standard French authors; a short course in French syntax, with exercises in composition and oral practice.

A 5 *Junior and Senior Second-Year French* [after A 1].

3 hrs.

Assistant Professor McKenzie.

Reading from French authors, mainly of the nineteenth century.

B 1 *Sophomore Advanced French* [either *a* or *b* may be taken, but *not both*]. [Sophomores.] 3 hrs.

a French Masterpieces [after A 3, passed with credit].

Assistant Professor Sanderson.

Masterpieces of the last three centuries; reading of French prose and verse without translating; composition. *Conducted in French.*

b French Prose and Poetry [after A 2, passed with credit].

Assistant Professor Sanderson and Dr. LeCompte.

Prose and poetry of the last three centuries; reading without translating; composition. Division II is *conducted in French.*

B 2 *French Comedy* [after A 2, A 4, or A 5, passed with credit]. 2 hrs.

Assistant Professor McKenzie.

Reading of representative French comedies of the last three centuries, with lectures on the development of the drama in France.

B 3 *General View of French Literature, 1630–1900* [after B 1]. 2 hrs.

Assistant Professor Sanderson.

A study of the great writers of the seventeenth, eighteenth, and nineteenth centuries, and of their principal works.

[*C 1 *Molière.* 1 hr.

Assistant Professor Sanderson.

A linguistic and literary study of some of Molière's best plays. *Conducted in English.*
Omitted in 1907-08.]

*C 2 *Masterpieces of French Literature.* 2 hrs.

Assistant Professor Sanderson.

This course covers practically the same ground as B 3, but is *conducted in French.* It is intended for students who can follow a lecture in French.

*C 3 *Practice in Writing and Speaking French.*   2 hrs.
Assistant Professor SANDERSON.

> This course, *conducted entirely in French*, is specially intended for graduates or undergraduates who read French with ease and understand it when they hear it spoken.

VII. ITALIAN

A 1 *Elementary Italian.*   3 hrs.
Assistant Professor MCKENZIE.

> Stress is laid on good pronunciation and on mastery of the grammar. Grandgent's *Italian Grammar;* reading of modern authors.

[A 2 *Italian Literature.*   1 hr.
Assistant Professor MCKENZIE.

> Lectures on Italian literature, with collateral reading. A knowledge of Italian is not required.
> Omitted in 1907–08.]

B 1 *Dante* [after A 1].   2 hrs.
Assistant Professor MCKENZIE.

> Literary study of Dante's *Vita Nuova* (Casini's ed., Firenze, 1891) and *Divina Commedia.*

*C 1 *Petrarch and Boccaccio.*   2 hrs.
Assistant Professor MCKENZIE.

> The works of Petrarch and Boccaccio and their predecessors and contemporaries. This course is primarily for graduates, but is open also to properly qualified undergraduates.

VIII. SPANISH

A 1 *Elementary Spanish.*
    [Sophomores, Juniors, and Seniors.]   3 hrs.
Professor LANG and Assistant Professor SCHEVILL.

> Stress is laid on good pronunciation and on mastery of the grammar. The chief aim of the instruction is to develop the ability to read the language readily and accurately.

B 1 *Reading and Composition in Spanish* [after A 1].   2 hrs.
Assistant Professor SCHEVILL.

> Chiefly for those who require the use of Spanish for practical purposes. The writing of letters, the reading of commercial papers, and fluency in translating and speaking receive special attention.

*B 2. *Spanish Prose of the Sixteenth and Seventeenth*
Centuries [after one year of Spanish]. 2 hrs.
Professor LANG.

> *Lazarillo de Tormes*, Cervantes's *Don Quijote*, etc., are read in class, and additional work is assigned for private study. The student's attention is directed to the relation of Spanish literature in this period to other literatures.

*C 1 *The Spanish Drama of the Sixteenth and Seventeenth*
Centuries [after two years of Spanish]. 2 hrs.
Assistant Professor SCHEVILL.

> Reading in class of selected plays by Lope de Vega, Tirso de Molina, Calderón, etc. ; reports on assigned work ; lectures.

*C 2 *General View of Spanish Literature* [after two years
of Spanish]. 1 hr.
Professor LANG.

> An outline of the development of Spanish literature. In addition to the work done in the class-room, outside reading is required.

GERMANIC LANGUAGES

Juniors and Seniors who have had but one year of German, and wish to continue its study, should choose German A 5, which is open to Juniors and Seniors *only*.

Juniors and Seniors who have had but two years of German, and wish to continue its study, should choose among German B 2, B 4, and B 5 ; but B 3 also is open to them. German B 2, B 4, and B 5 are intended to be parallel courses, differing in subject-matter and vocabulary, and choice between them should be made according to one's interest in this or that subject-matter and vocabulary.

Juniors and Seniors who have already had three years of German should choose among German B 3, C 1, C 2, and C 3 ; but B 2, B 4, and B 5 also are open to them.

Concerning the courses in Scandinavian Professor Palmer may be consulted.

For *Phonetics*, *Comparative Syntax*, and *Linguistics*, see Sanskrit, etc. B 2, C 1, and C 2. Certain courses in general or comparative literature are announced in the English group.   For *Readings in German Psychology and Philosophy*, see Philosophy C 12.

IX. GERMAN

A 1   *Elementary German.*

[Freshmen and Sophomores.]   3 hrs.

Assistant Professor FARR, Dr. GUBELMANN, Dr. VESTLING, and Mr. CHURCH.

> Grammar; translation from German into English of simple narrative prose; elementary exercises in translating into German; practice in pronunciation.

A 2   *Freshman Intermediate German.*   [Freshmen.]   3 hrs.

Professor GRUENER, Assistant Professor FARR, Dr. VESTLING, and Mr. CHURCH.

> See the statement of course A 5, with which this course is identical in subject-matter.

A 3   *Freshman Advanced German.*   [Freshmen.]   3 hrs.

Professor GRUENER and Dr. VESTLING.

> See the statement of course B 1b, with which this course is identical in subject-matter.

A 4   *Sophomore Second-Year German.*   [Sophomores.]   3 hrs.

Dr. VESTLING and Mr. CHURCH.

> See the statement of course A 5, with which this course is identical in subject-matter.

A 5   *Junior and Senior Second-Year German.*   3 hrs.

Dr. GUBELMANN and Dr. VESTLING.

> Reading of short stories and of selections from more difficult prose and poetry; practice in writing German; study of word-formation.

B 1   *Sophomore Advanced German* [either *a* or *b* may be taken, but *not both*].   [Sophomores.]   3 hrs.

a   German Drama.

Professor PALMER and Dr. GUBELMANN.

> Rapid reading of dramas of the eighteenth and nineteenth centuries.

b   Prose of Modern Historians and Critics.

Dr. GUBELMANN.

> Rapid reading of selections from history, political writings and literary criticism; weekly exercises in German composition.

The object of the course is to acquaint the student particularly with the historical and critical vocabularies and styles.

B 2   *Prose of Modern Historians and Critics* [after two
           years of German].   2 hrs.
Dr. GUBELMANN.

> See the statement of course B 1*b*, with which this course is identical in subject-matter, except for the omission of the weekly exercises in composition.

*B 3   *German Composition and Conversation.*   3 hrs.
Assistant Professor FARR.

> For practice in speaking and writing. This course, *conducted in German*, is specially intended for those who look forward to teaching German.

B 4   *The Drama of Schiller and his Contemporaries* [after
           two years of German, and *not* after B 1*a*].   2 hrs.
Professor GRUENER.

> Rapid reading and literary study of Lessing's *Nathan der Weise*, Goethe's *Götz von Berlichingen* and *Iphigenie auf Tauris*, and Schiller's *Wallenstein's Tod ;* lectures on the literature of the period, with special reference to the development of the German drama.

B 5   *German Literature of the Nineteenth Century* [after two
           years of German].   2 hrs.
Assistant Professor FARR.

> A survey of German literature after the death of Goethe. Representative works of the best known authors are read, and occasional lectures are given to show the development of German literature during the nineteenth century.

C 1   *Goethe : Works and Life* [after a B course or its
           equivalent].   3 hrs.
Professor PALMER.

> Outline study of Goethe's life and development in connection with his lyric poems, early prose writings, and principal dramas; reading and discussion of *Faust* (both parts), the later prose works, and Goethe's important utterances in letters, journals, and conversations.

C 2   *History of German Literature, 1624-1832* [after a B
           course or its equivalent].   2 hrs.

Professor PALMER.

The development of German literature from the time of Opitz to Goethe's death. Text-books : Kluge's *Geschichte der deutschen National-Litteratur*, Scherer's *History of German Literature*, Max Müller's *German Classics*, and Hillebrand's *German Thought from the Seven Years' War to Goethe's Death.*

[*C 3   *German Literature from Goethe's Death to the Rise of Naturalism* [after a B course or its equivalent].

3 hrs.

Professor GRUENER.

A somewhat detailed study of German literature from Grillparzer to the naturalistic movement inaugurated by Hauptmann. The course is *conducted in German.*

Omitted in 1907–08.]

X. SCANDINAVIAN

A 1   *Norwegian and Danish* [after one year of German].

2 hrs.

Professor PALMER.

The object of this course is to lay the foundation for a reading and practical knowledge of the language. Study of the grammar and reading of selections from the writings of modern authors.

A 2   *Swedish* [after one year of German].   2 hrs.

Dr. THORSTENBERG.

A course in Swedish similar to course A 1 in Norwegian and Danish.

Elementary Russian.   2 hrs.

Mr. MANDELL.

First term : grammar, vocabulary, and pronunciation. Second term : composition, conversation, and reading of selected modern authors.

XI. ENGLISH

For *Phonetics, Comparative Syntax,* and *Linguistics,* see Sanskrit, etc. B 2, C 1, and C 2.

COURSES IN RHETORIC

Every student who elects English B 1 is required to take also one hour of rhetoric. If a student wishes no more than one hour of rhetoric, or prefers practice exclusively in writing, he elects Rhetoric B 1. If he wishes, in addition to the one hour required with English B 1, two hours of rhetoric for study and practice in public speaking, he may, by written permission of the instructor, elect Rhetoric B 2 *instead of B 1.* In this case the two additional hours of rhetoric, though they count toward the total of sixty hours required for graduation, do not count toward the fifteen hours required for Sophomore year; *i. e.,* a Sophomore who elects Rhetoric B 2 with English B 1 must carry a total of seventeen hours. (It is to be noted, however, that Rhetoric B 2 may be elected without English B 1.) No student is admitted to both Rhetoric B 1 and Rhetoric B 2.

B 1 *Written Composition* [with English B 1].
[Sophomores.] 1 hr.
Dr. BERDAN, Mr. HOOKER, Dr. E. N. S. THOMPSON, and Mr. BLANCHARD.

> General training in composition and expression; recitations for discussion of principles and methods, and for the study of models; fortnightly themes, mainly in essay-writing and description, with regular appointments for the criticism of each.

*B 2 *Oral Composition (Public Speaking).*
[Sophomores.] 3 hrs.
Assistant Professor C. S. BALDWIN and Dr. E. N. S. THOMPSON.

> First term (Dr. Thompson): preparatory training in the general principles of composition. Second term (Assistant Professor Baldwin): study of the principles and practice of oratory. Hereafter this course may be prerequisite to B 6.

*B 3   *Verse Composition.*   1 hr.
Professor LEWIS.

> Regular fortnightly practice in standard verse-forms, with individual appointments for consultation and criticism.

B 4   *Daily Themes* [after B 1 or B 2].   3 hrs. 1st term,
                                        to count as 1 hr. for the year.
Assistant Professor C. S. BALDWIN.

> A course in personal expression, aiming at fluency in focusing daily impressions.   Regular weekly appointments for criticism of individuals.

*B 5   *Story-Writing* [after B 1 or B 2].   3 hrs. 2d term,
                                        to count as 2 hrs. for the year.
Mr. HOOKER.

> Systematic practice in narrative ; lectures and recitations on narrative forms ; regular appointments for criticism.

B 6   *Debating* [after B 1 or B 2†].   [Juniors, and Seniors who are graduates of other colleges.] 2 hrs.
Assistant Professor C. S. BALDWIN and Mr. PIERCE.

> First term (Assistant Professor Baldwin): practice mainly in rebuttal and in individual speeches ; briefs both for class debates and for analysis of selected models of debating.   Second term (Mr. Pierce): further practice in rebuttal ; the construction of a case ; research, brief-drawing, and coherent presentation.

B 7   *Essay-Writing* [after B 1 or B 2].   3 hrs. 2d term,
                                        to count as 2 hrs. for the year.
Dr. BERDAN.

> Analysis of modern essays for the technique of practical prose ; practice in composition, with regular appointments for criticism.

[C 1   *Literary Forms* [after B 4, B 5, B 6, or B 7]. [Seniors.]
            3 hrs. 2d term, *to count as 2 hrs. for the year.*
Assistant Professor C. S. BALDWIN.

> A review of English literature by its principal forms : lectures and class discussions ; six extended essays in criticism.
> Omitted in 1907–08.]

-----

† Beginning with the class of 1910, only those students may be admitted to this course who have completed Rhetoric B 2 ; but this restriction does not apply to the class of 1909.   Seniors who are graduates of other colleges are admitted without having taken either B 1 or B 2.

11

COURSES IN ORAL EXPRESSION

*A 1   *Oral Expression.*   [Freshmen.†]   1 hr.
Mr. WETZEL.

Especial attention is given to vocal training. The student is expected to acquire a correct and refined pronunciation of English and a distinct and natural utterance.

*A 2   *Oral Expression* [after A 1].   [Sophomores.†]   1 hr.
Mr. WETZEL.

This course includes a study of the history of oratory and systematic practice in delivery, with special reference to emphasis, inflection, movement, tone-color, change of pitch, cadence, and gestural expression.

*A 3   *Oral Expression* [after A 2].   [Juniors.]   1 hr.
Mr. WETZEL.

This course includes systematic practice in forensic speaking and in the vocal interpretation of Shakespeare, with special reference to argumentative and dramatic interpretation.

COURSES IN ENGLISH LITERATURE

A 1   *Freshman English.*   [Freshmen.]   3 hrs.
Dr. TINKER, Dr. JOHNSON, Dr. HOLT, and Mr. MASON.

A careful study of a few important books, having as its aim the development of an intelligent appreciation of the best poetry and prose. Among the authors studied are Shakespeare, Carlyle, Arnold, and Tennyson.

B 1   *History of English Literature to the Death of Pope* [with Rhetoric B 1 or B 2].

[Sophomores,§ Juniors, and Seniors.]   2 hrs.
Assistant Professor REED and Dr. J. C. ADAMS.

A general outline course, preparatory to the study (in more advanced courses) of special periods and topics. Among the authors read are Spenser, Shakespeare, Milton, Addison, Steele, Pope, and Swift.

B 2   *Chaucer, Burns, and the English and Scottish Ballads.*

2 hrs.
Professor BEERS.

Selections from the *Canterbury Tales*, from the old minstrel ballads, and from the poems in dialect of Robert Burns.

† May be taken only outside of the required fifteen hours.
§ See the statement preceding the announcement of Rhetoric B 1.

B 4 *Shakespeare.* [Seniors.] 1 hr.
Professor LEWIS.

> A rapid reading of thirty plays. Lectures, with written recitations at each exercise.

[B 5 *Elizabethan Drama.* 2 hrs.
Professor W. L. PHELPS.

> The English drama, from the mystery plays to the closing of the theaters in 1642, studied from both the literary and the dramatic point of view.
> Omitted in 1907-08.]

B 6 *The Modern Drama.* 2 hrs.
Professor BEERS

> A historical review of the acted drama since 1660. Instruction half by lectures and half by recitations.

*B 7 *English Prose.* 2 hrs.
Assistant Professor REED.

> The first half-year is devoted to prose other than fiction, from Sidney to Johnson ; the second half-year to fiction, from the Elizabethan romances to Jane Austen.

B 8 *English Literature of the Eighteenth Century.* 2 hrs.
Dr. TINKER.

> (1) Dr. Johnson and his circle ; (2) the development of fiction ; (3) the history of poetry from the death of Pope to 1800.

B 9 *American Literature.* 1 hr.
Professor W. L. PHELPS.

> A course of lectures on leading American authors of the past hundred years. A large amount of reading is required ; also a weekly one-page critical theme from each member of the class.

B 10 *English Poets of the Nineteenth Century.*
[Juniors.] 2 hrs.
Professor LEWIS.

> Wordsworth, Coleridge, Byron, Shelley, Keats, Tennyson, Browning, Rossetti, Morris, Swinburne, Arnold, Clough, and a few others. Lectures, with written tests.

B 11 *New England Writers.* 2 hrs.
Professor BEERS.

> A study of the literature of New England from 1830 to 1870, with special reference to the contemporary movement in society, politics, and religion.

B 12 *Tennyson and Browning.* 2 hrs.
Professor W. L. PHELPS.

> The study of Tennyson as poet and artist, and of Browning as an interpreter of life. The method of instruction is by recitations and discussions.

B 13 *English Literary Drama of the Nineteenth Century.* 1 hr.
Dr. J. C. ADAMS.

> A study of the modern literary drama, and its relation both to the stage and to other forms of literature.

B 14 *English Prose of the Nineteenth Century.* 2 hrs.
Dr. J. C. ADAMS.,

> A study of the most important prose of the century, excluding fiction. Extensive reading, supplemented by biographical and critical lectures.

[B 15 *English Fiction of the Nineteenth Century* [after B 7].
1 hr.
Assistant Professor REED.

> This course is a continuation of B 7. Among the authors studied are Scott, Reade, Trollope, Thackeray, and Dickens.
> Omitted in 1907-08.]

B 16 *Emerson and Carlyle.* 1 hr.
Dr. JOHNSON.

> A study of the idealistic movement of the nineteenth century; incidental study of Wordsworth, Coleridge, Hawthorne, Thoreau, and others.

C 1 *Milton and his Contemporaries.* 2 hrs.
Professor BEERS.

> The *belles lettres* of the Puritan Revolution. All Milton's English and some of his Latin poems, with his most important prose; the Church poets and Cavaliers, diaries, memoirs, etc.

[*C 2 *English Literary Criticism.* 1 hr.
Dr. J. C. ADAMS.

> A historical survey of literary criticism in England since the middle of the sixteenth century.
> Omitted in 1907-08.]

*C 4 *Theories of Poetry.* [Seniors.] 1 hr., *to count as 2 hrs.*
Professor COOK.

> A course in the theories of poetry in general, and in the prin-

ciples of criticism applicable to its various departments, as the epic, dramatic, and lyric.

*C 5 *Old and Middle English*.   2 hrs.
Professor COOK.

An elementary course in the beginnings and earlier development of the English language and literature.

[*C 6 *Dante in English*. [Seniors.] 1 hr., *to count as 2 hrs*.
Professor COOK.

A course primarily in the *Divina Commedia* and the *Vita Nuova*. Much attention is bestowed upon the historical and literary background of the poet and his works.
Omitted in 1907–08.]

*C 7 *Literary Types*.   [Seniors.] 1 hr., *to count as 2 hrs*.
Professor COOK.

A survey of European literature, with reference to the characterization and illustration of the more important species. Candidates must satisfy the instructor with regard to their proficiency in French, German, and Latin.

*C 8 *English Lyrical Poetry*.   [Seniors.] 2 hrs.
Assistant Professor REED.

A lecture course, with brief papers on assigned reading, on the origin of the English lyric and its development from Skelton to the present day.

*C 9 *Early Narrative*.   1 hr.
Dr. TINKER.

Famous legends and the various narrative forms which they have assumed, such as ballad, tale, saga, epic, and romance. The influence of these forms upon Percy, Scott, Rossetti, and Morris.

*C 10 *Elizabethan Literature*.
                              [Seniors.] 1 hr., *to count as 2 hrs*.
Professor W. L. PHELPS.

Studies in the poetry and prose of the Elizabethan period exclusive of the drama. Lectures, discussions, and preparation of special papers by members of the class.

*C 11 *Shakespeare*.   [Seniors.] 1 hr.
Professor LEWIS.

A minute study of *Macbeth*; miscellaneous problems as to date, authenticity, and genesis of various plays.

[*C 12 *The Contemporary Drama.* 1 hr.
Professor W. L. PHELPS.

> A study of contemporary stage-plays, such as those of Ibsen, Sudermann, Hauptmann, Mæterlinck, Rostand, Mirbeau, Fitch, Pinero, and Jones. No student is permitted to elect this course who cannot read both French and German.
>
> Omitted in 1907-08.]

*C 13 *English Literature of the Seventeenth Century.*
[Seniors.] 1 hr., *to count as 2 hrs.*
Professor W. L. PHELPS.

> A study of English poetry and prose from Donne to Dryden, exclusive of the drama. The social life of the times is discussed in connection with some of the authors read.

C 14 *Shakespeare.* 2 hrs.
Professor BEERS.

> A study of Shakespeare with reference to his handling of dramatic material ; the comparative treatment of identical or similar themes by other dramatists ; the history of Shakespeare criticism. Topics are assigned for individual research.

*C 15 *English Literary Drama of the Nineteenth Century.*
[Seniors.] 1 hr.
Dr. J. C. ADAMS.

> The class-room work is identical with that of B 13. In addition, extra reading is assigned and a thesis embodying the results of individual outside investigation is required of each member of the class.

(2) MATHEMATICS AND THE PHYSICAL AND NATURAL SCIENCES
XII. MATHEMATICS

The mathematical courses described in the following pages fall into three main groups, namely, Pure Mathematics, Mathematical Physics, and Engineering Sciences. The course in *Analytical Geometry and Calculus* (B 0 or B 1) is the foundation of each of these groups, and should be taken not later than Sophomore year. The further sequence of courses desirable for students in the several groups is as follows :

> Students in Pure Mathematics should take the courses in *Algebra and Analytical Geometry* (B 4) and *Mechanics* (C 2) in their Junior year, and those in *Projective Geometry* (C 5) and *Introduction to the Theory of Functions* (C 6) in their Senior year ; students in Mathematical Physics, the courses in *Advanced Calculus* (C 1) and *Mechanics* (C 2) not later than their Junior year, *Theoretical Physics* (Physics C 1) in their Junior or Senior year, and *Advanced Mechanics* (C 7) in their Senior year ; and students in Engineering Sciences, the courses in *Algebra and Analytical Geometry* (B 4), *Descriptive Geometry and Machine-Drawing* (B 6), and *Machine-Designing* (C 4).

It is desirable even for students of Pure Mathematics that they acquire the elements of Descriptive Geometry and facility in the use of drawing instruments.

As modern mathematical literature is largely in French and German, students should acquire as soon as possible a good reading knowledge of these languages.

The rooms of the Mathematical Club and the Mathematical Laboratory, at 90 High street, are open to students taking the more advanced courses.

A 1   *Solid Geometry, Plane Trigonometry, and Advanced Algebra* [may count as an A course in Physics if followed by Physics B 1].   [Freshmen.]   3 hrs.

Professor BEEBE, Assistant Professor HAWKES, Mr. BURGESS, Mr. RAYWORTH, and Mr. SHELDON.

A 2a   *Descriptive Astronomy* [after A 1].   3 hrs. 1st term, *to count as 1 hr. for the year.*

Professor BEEBE.

Intended principally for the study of the historical and physical side of Astronomy. Opportunity is given for the use of the telescope. Text-book : Young's *Elements of Astronomy.*

A 2b *Spherical Trigonometry and Nautical Astronomy* [after
 A 1].   3 hrs. from January to March,
                                   to count as 1 hr. for the year.
Professor BEEBE.

> Application of Trigonometry and Astronomy to Navigation, with instruction in the use of the sextant.

*A 2c *Surveying* [after A 1].   6 hrs. from March to June,
                                   to count as 1 hr. for the year.
Professor BEEBE.

> Field work with level, transit, and plane table ; correction of instrumental errors ; drawing of contour maps. Required of those electing advanced work in Geology, and open to a limited number of others on application.

B o *Analytical Geometry and Calculus.* [Freshmen.] 3 hrs.
Professor BEEBE.

> Instead of A 1 for Freshmen who have anticipated Solid Geometry and Plane Trigonometry.

B 1 *Analytical Geometry and Calculus* [after A 1].
          [Sophomores, Juniors, and Seniors.]   3 hrs.
Professor PHILLIPS.

> Should be taken by all who propose to take advanced courses in Pure and Applied Mathematics, Mathematical Physics, or certain courses in Chemistry, Economics, and Statistics.

B 4 *Algebra and Analytical Geometry* [after B o or B 1]. 2 hrs.
Assistant Professor HAWKES.

> This course treats those facts and methods of Algebra and Analytical Geometry which are indispensable for the pursuit of Pure Mathematics, Physics, or Engineering.

*B 6 *Descriptive Geometry and Machine-Drawing* [after B o
 or B 1].   3 hrs., *to count as 2 hrs.*
Professor C. B. RICHARDS and Assistant Professor MAR-
     SHALL.

> This course includes the principles of orthographic projection, the intersection and development of surfaces, and the elements of machine-drawing. Open only to a limited number and with the written approval of Professor Phillips.

C 1   *Advanced Calculus* [after B 0 or B 1].
        [Sophomores,† Juniors, and Seniors.]   3 hrs.
Professor BROWN.
> This course is a continuation of B 0 and B 1, and treats those parts of the Calculus which àre specially useful in Applied Mathematics.

C 2   *Mechanics* [after B 0 or with or after B 1].   2 hrs.
Professor BROWN.
> The principles of Mechanics, founded on Newton's Laws of Motion ; applications to the simpler physical problems of particles and bodies in equilibrium and in motion.

[C 3   *Geometry* [after B 0 or B 1, and with or after B 4].
        2 hrs.
Assistant Professor HAWKES.
> Historical and critical study of elementary Geometry, especially intended for those who expect to teach.
>   Omitted in 1907–08.]

*C 4   *Machine-Designing* [after B 6]. 7 hrs., *to count as 4 hrs.*
Professor C. B. RICHARDS.
> This course is a continuation of the work in course B 6, and is open only to a limited number of those who have takeñ that course.

C 5   *Projective Geometry* [after B 4].   2 hrs.
Professor PIERPONT.
> Both the analytic and the synthetic methods are used to develop the fundamental properties of points, lines, planes, conics, and quadric surfaces, and the linear transformation in the plane and in space.

C 6   *Introduction to the Theory of Functions.*   2 hrs.
Professor PIERPONT.
> The fundamental concepts of the Calculus ; functions of a complex variable, including a short sketch of the elliptic functions.

[C 7   *Advanced Mechanics* [after C 2].   2 hrs.
Professor PIERPONT.
> Lagrange's equations, D'Alembert's principle, Hamilton's principle, potential spherical harmonics, elasticity, hydrodynamics.   Numerous examples from Physics, Astronomy, and Engineering.
>   Omitted in 1907–08.]

---

† Open as a Sophomore course only to those who have taken B 0 in Freshman year.

THE PHYSICAL SCIENCES (GROUPS XIII, XIV)

Physics and Chemistry are fundamental to all branches of science. They should, therefore, be taken early by all who propose to do any extended work in science or the technical professions, or to study Medicine.

XIII. PHYSICS

The elementary instruction in Physics is divided into two courses, A 1 and B 1. Of these, A 1 is intended for those students who desire only a general acquaintance with the phenomena and fundamental principles of Physics, and *who do not intend to proceed further in the subject.* B 1 presupposes Mathematics A 1 (or its anticipation in the entrance examination), and presents the subject in greater detail and in a manner more satisfactory and more useful to students who expect to continue in Physics or in other scientific studies; it is introductory to, and a necessary preparation for, the other courses in Physics. B 2 should be chosen by those who intend to devote themselves to any branch of science or to the study of Medicine. C 1 and C 2 should be chosen by those who intend to study Engineering in any of its branches or to engage in manufacturing. Students wishing to specialize in Physics should take also Mathematics C 1 (*Advanced Calculus*), C 2 (*Mechanics*), and C 7 (*Advanced Mechanics*). One or more courses in Inorganic Chemistry also are desirable.

Seniors who have completed C 1 and Mathematics C 1 may, with the consent of the instructor, be received into the following graduate courses: *Theory of Errors* (Professor HASTINGS); *Physical Optics* (Professor HASTINGS); *Vectors* (Assistant Professor BEACH); and *Gravitation and Electrostatics* (Assistant Professor L. P. WHEELER). These courses are described in the pamphlet of the Graduate School.

It is to be noted, with regard to the requirements as to majors and minors, that all the science courses (groups xiii-xvi) are treated as a single group in this respect, and that Mathematics A 1 counts as an A course for Physics B 1. For *Physical Chemistry*, see Chemistry C 4.

A 1　*Elementary Physics.*

　　　　　[Sophomores, Juniors, and Seniors.]　3 hrs.

Assistant Professor KREIDER.

> A general course, covering the mechanics of solids. liquids, gases, heat, magnetism, electricity, sound, and light; conducted by recitations and lectures, fully illustrated by apparatus and experiments.

B 1　*General Physics* [after Mathematics A 1, which counts as an A course in Physics in this combination].

　　　　　[Sophomores, Juniors, and Seniors.]　3 hrs.

Assistant Professor KREIDER and Dr. UHLER.

> This course, like the preceding one, assumes no previous knowledge of Physics. It covers essentially the same ground as A 1, but with more extended mathematical development of physical laws and theories.

B 2　*Elementary Laboratory Physics* [with or after B 1].

　　　　　[Sophomores,† Juniors, and Seniors.]　3 hrs.,

　　　　　　　　　　　　　　　　　　to count as 2 hrs.

Assistant Professor BOLTWOOD and Dr. UHLER.

> Elementary laboratory work in mechanics, heat, sound, light, electricity, and magnetism. It is recommended that (when possible) this course be taken *with* B 1 rather than *after* it.

C 1　*Introduction to Theoretical Physics* [after B 1 and Mathematics B 0 or B 1].　　　　　3 hrs.

Professor BUMSTEAD.

> Mechanics, thermodynamics, the kinetic theory of gases, the wave-theory of light, and the elementary mathematical theory of electricity and magnetism. Lectures and recitations.

C 2　*Advanced Laboratory Physics* [after B 2 and with or after C 1].　　　　　6 hrs., *to count as 4 hrs.*

Professor BUMSTEAD and Dr. UHLER.

> An advanced course in the laboratory. Problems of considerable experimental difficulty and involving a knowledge of mathematical Physics such as may be obtained in C 1. It is recommended that (when possible) this course be taken *with* C 1 rather than *after* it.

---

† By Sophomores this course may be taken only outside of the required fifteen hours.

XIV. CHEMISTRY

The first course, *Inorganic Chemistry* (A 1), is intended to meet the needs of those students who desire a general knowledge of the facts and methods of Chemistry, and is a necessary preparation for the higher courses. *Qualitative Analysis* (B 1) and *Organic Chemistry* (B 2) should be taken by those preparing to study Medicine, as well as by all who intend to take advanced courses in Chemistry. The higher courses are for those who wish to teach Chemistry, to fit themselves for the study of applied Chemistry, to enter the technical schools with advanced standing, or to secure for any reason extended training in Chemistry. Other courses, intended primarily for graduates, may, with the instructor's permission, be taken by sufficiently advanced undergraduates and counted as C courses.

> For the laboratory courses a fixed charge is made (to cover the expenditure for chemicals, gas, water, etc.), in addition to the cost of apparatus broken or not returned in serviceable condition. For each of the courses A 1, B 1, B 2, C 1, the fixed charge is $20.00; for course B 3, C 2, or C 4 the fixed charge is $10.00; for the lecture course C 3 no charge is made. The charge for breakage should not exceed, in the average, $5.00 for each laboratory course.

It is to be noted, with regard to the requirements as to majors and minors, that all the science courses (groups xiii-xvi) are treated as a single group in this respect. For *Physiological Chemistry*, see Biology and Medical Sciences C 3.

A 1   *Inorganic Chemistry, Inductive and Descriptive.*
[All classes.]   6 hrs., *to count as 3 hrs.*
Professor GOOCH, Assistant Professor BROWNING, Dr. I. K. PHELPS, and Dr. VANNAME.

> Lectures, laboratory work, and class-room exercises. An introduction to elementary chemical theory, the use of symbols and equations, and the study of the elements and their compounds.

B 1   *Qualitative Analysis* [after A 1].   [Sophomores, Juniors, and Seniors.]   6 hrs., *to count as 3 hrs.*

Assistant Professor BROWNING.

> Laboratory practice in the ordinary processes of Qualitative Analysis, with lectures.

B 2   *Organic Chemistry* [after A 1].   [Sophomores, Juniors, and Seniors.]   5 hrs., *to count as 3 hrs.*

Professor GOOCH and Dr. I. K. PHELPS.

> An introduction to the study of the compounds of carbon. Lectures, written exercises, and laboratory work.

*B 3   *Inorganic Preparations* [after A 1].   [Sophomores,† Juniors, and Seniors.]   4 hrs., *to count as 2 hrs.*

Assistant Professor BROWNING.

> A short course, mainly laboratory work, covering typical methods for the preparation of inorganic salts.

*C 1   *Quantitative Analysis* [with or after B 1].   6 hrs., *to count as 3 hrs.*

Professor GOOCH.

> Lectures, with laboratory practice in the use of the simpler methods of gravimetric and volumetric Quantitative Analysis.

*C 2   *The Rare Elements* [after B 1]. 5 hrs., *to count as 3 hrs.*

Assistant Professor BROWNING.

> Lectures and laboratory work, covering the principal reactions of the elements not included in the general course (A 1). The methods in use for the qualitative determinations of these elements are carefully studied.

*C 3   *The Carbon Compounds, Descriptive and Theoretical* [after B 2].   3 hrs.

Dr. I. K. PHELPS.

> A course of lectures treating systematically the more important compounds of carbon and the theories concerning them.

*C 4   *Physical Chemistry.*   5 hrs., *to count as 3 hrs.*

Dr. VANNAME.

> Lectures on the modern theories of Physical Chemistry, including Electrochemistry, and laboratory practice in typical physico-chemical measurements.

---

† By Sophomores this course may be taken only outside of the required fifteen hours.

THE NATURAL SCIENCES (GROUPS XV, XVI)
XV. GEOLOGY

Those who wish to gain a general knowledge of the facts and methods of Geology and Paleontology are advised to elect :

In Junior or Senior year : Geology B 1 (*General Geology*).

The following courses also are of interest to students who do not intend to specialize in Geology :

Geology B 5 (*Geography of North America*), B 6 (*Geography of South America*), B 7 (*Geography of Asia*), C 7 (*Geographic Controls in History*).

Those who intend to become teachers of Geology, or to become members of state or national surveys, or who for any reason desire extended training in Geology, are advised to elect :

In Freshman and Sophomore years : Mathematics A 1 (*Geometry, Trigonometry, and Algebra*), B 0 or B 1 (*Analytical Geometry and Calculus*); Physics A 1 (*Elementary Physics*) or B 1 (*General Physics*); Chemistry A 1 (*Inorganic Chemistry*), B 1 (*Qualitative Analysis*); Geology A 1 (*Physical and Commercial Geography*), B 3 (*Mineralogy and Crystallography*).

In Junior year: Mathematics A 2c (*Surveying*); Geology B 1 (*General Geology*), B 2 (*Field and Laboratory Work*), B 4 (*Mineralogy and Crystallography*), B 9 (*Organic Evolution*).

In Senior year: Geology B 10 (*Geological Biology*), C 1 (*Advanced Paleontology*), C 2 (*Advanced Stratigraphic Paleontology and Paleogeography*), C 4 (*Structural Geology*), C 6 (*Physiography*), C 8 (*Field Geology*).

Special attention is called to the course in *Surveying* (Mathematics A 2c), which is required of those who undertake advanced work in Geology.

A limited number of Sophomores who intend to specialize in Geology may obtain permission to take *Mineralogy and Crystallography* (B 3) outside of the required fifteen hours.

It is to be noted, with regard to the requirements as to majors and minors, that all the science courses (groups xiii–xvi) are treated as a single group in this respect.

A 1 *Physical and Commercial Geography* [this is also the A course in Anthropology]. [Sophomores.] 3 hrs.

Professor GREGORY, Dr. BISHOP, Mr. BOWMAN, Mr. HUNT-
INGTON, Mr. BOGGS, Mr. BECK, and Mr. H. P.
FAIRCHILD.

> The physical features of the land ; ocean ; climate ; the natural
> distributions of flora, fauna, minerals, etc. ; the conditions of
> human life as affected by natural environment. Text-books and
> laboratory work.

B 1 *General Geology* [not counted as a B course in a
major or minor unless taken after Physics A 1
(or B 1), Chemistry A 1, or Geology A 1]. 2 hrs.
Professor GREGORY and Assistant Professor BARRELL.

> The structural features of the earth ; the forces by which its
> present condition has been attained ; the past history of the
> earth, including the evolution of living forms. Lectures, text-
> books, and excursions.

*B 2 *Geology with Field and Laboratory Work* [not counted
as a B course in a major or minor unless taken
after Physics A 1 (or B 1), Chemistry A 1, or
Geology A 1]. 3 hrs., *to count as 2 hrs.*
Assistant Professor BARRELL and Mr. HUNTINGTON.

> This course is designed to be taken with, and to supplement
> the exercises of, B 1, but may be taken separately by those
> properly prepared.

B 3 *Mineralogy and Crystallography.* [Sophomores,†
Juniors, and Seniors.] 4 hrs., *to count as 2 hrs.*
Professor DANA.

> Practical study of mineral species by means of blowpipe
> analysis and other methods ; mathematical study of the forms
> of crystals. Open to those who have studied or are study-
> ing Chemistry.

B 4 *Mineralogy and Crystallography.* 6 hrs., *to count as 3 hrs.*
Professor DANA.

> This course consists of the exercises of B 3 and, in addition,
> laboratory work to average two hours per week. Those who
> have completed B 3 may take in the following year the additional
> work included in B 4.

B 5 *Geography of North America.* 2 hrs.

----

† By Sophomores this course may be taken only with the permission of the instructor and outside of the required fifteen hours.

Mr. BOWMAN.

> The regional geography of North America in its physical, political, and commercial aspects ; the life relationships of the physiography of North America. Lectures, maps, and library work, with critical discussion.

B 6 *Geography of South America.* 2 hrs. 2d half-year, *to count as 1 hr. for the year.*

Mr. BOWMAN.

> The regional geography of South America in its physical, political, and commercial aspects ; the life relationships of the physiography of South America. Lectures, maps, and library work, with critical discussion. (Course B 7 comes at the same hours as this course during the first half-year.)

B 7 *Geography of Asia.* 2 hrs. 1st half-year, *to count as 1 hr. for the year.*

Mr. HUNTINGTON.

> The regional geography of the Nearer East, India, and Central Asia ; types of physical environment in relation to types of human activity ; the life relationships of the physiography of Asia. Lectures, maps, and library work.

B 9 *Organic Evolution.* 1 hr.
Assistant Professor LULL.

> A course of lectures, illustrated by specimens, charts, and lantern-views, on the evolution of plants, of animals, and of man. It is advised that this course be taken with or after B 1.

B 10 *Geological Biology.* [Seniors.] 2 hrs.
Assistant Professor LULL.

> In this course organisms are the chief objects of study, and their nature, succession, relations to environment, ancestry, and time, and the principles of organic evolution in their geological relations, are examined.

*C 1a *Advanced Paleontology.* 3 hrs., *to count as 2 hrs.*
Professor SCHUCHERT and Assistant Professor LULL.

> This course, similar to C 1b, but necessarily abridged, is given, upon request, for the benefit of those who do not contemplate Paleontology as a major and can devote but three hours a week to the subject.

*C 1b *Advanced Paleontology.* 6 hrs., *to count as 3 hrs.*
Professor SCHUCHERT and Assistant Professor LULL.

> The object of this course is to acquaint the student with the

structure, evolution, and classification of the various classes of invertebrate and vertebrate animals found as fossils.

*C 2a *Advanced Stratigraphic Paleontology and Paleogeography.* 3 hrs., *to count as 2 hrs.*
Professor SCHUCHERT and Assistant Professor LULL.

This course, similar to C 2b, but necessarily abridged, is given, upon request, for the benefit of those who do not contemplate Paleontology as a major and can devote only three hours a week to the subject.

*C 2b *Advanced Stratigraphic Paleontology and Paleogeography.* 6 hrs., *to count as 3 hrs.*
Professor SCHUCHERT and Assistant Professor LULL.

In this course the student is acquainted with the essential or guide fossils which characterize the major divisions of geological time, the appearance, change, and geographical distribution of the leading faunas, and the significance of these in determining the distribution and character of the ancient seas and lands.

*C 3 *Structural Geology.* 2 hrs.
Assistant Professor BARRELL.

An advanced course, dealing with such subjects as ancient sedimentary formations, crustal movements, and the nature and results of igneous and metamorphic activities. Lectures, papers prepared by the students, and occasional excursions.

*C 4 *Structural Geology.* 3 hrs.
Assistant Professor BARRELL.

This course consists of the exercises of C 3 and, in addition, a larger amount of field work and the reading of geological literature, occasionally in foreign languages.

*C 5 *Physiography* [after B 1 or B 2]. 2 hrs.
Mr. BOWMAN.

A study of the origin, development, and classification of land forms, followed by a study of the physiography of the United States. The exercises include lectures, field excursions, and the reading of topographical maps and of physiographical literature.

*C 6 *Physiography* [after B 1 or B 2]. 3 hrs.
Professor GREGORY and Mr. BOWMAN.

This course consists of the class exercises of C 5 and, in addition, a field problem, which must be satisfactorily completed and reported upon in writing.

12

C 7   *Geographic Controls in History.*   2 hrs. 2d half-year,
to count as 1 hr. for the year.

Mr. BOWMAN and Mr. HUNTINGTON.

> The geographic elements of man's environment as a factor in history ; individual study of the geographic conditions affecting the history of a limited region in America or in Asia. Lectures, discussions, theses.

[*C 8   *Field Geology* [after B 2].   Two afternoons weekly,
to count as 3 hrs.

Dr. H. H. ROBINSON.

> Field work upon selected areas in the vicinity of New Haven, supplemented by lectures and laboratory exercises upon the construction and use of topographical and geological maps.
> Omitted in 1907–08.]

XVI. BIOLOGY AND MEDICAL SCIENCES

BIOLOGY AS A GENERAL-CULTURE STUDY

The seven courses, A 1, A 2, A 3, A 4, B 1, B 2, and C 3, admit of the selection of a given line of biological work, without compelling the student to follow work of an allied nature.   A 1 (*Physiology*) is intended especially for Sophomores and Juniors who may desire to gain some knowledge of Physiology, without any intention of pursuing later the study of Medicine; the scope of the course is broad, and it may well be taken as an independent study, without reference to other biological topics.   A 2 (*Elementary Biology*), A 3 (*Organic Evolution*), and B 1 (*General Biology*) are specially adapted to the needs of those students who desire some knowledge of Biology as a part of their general culture, or as a preparation for other lines of biological work, without necessarily having reference to the study of Medicine later.   A 4 (*Elementary Botany*) and B 2 (*Morphology of Plants*) may be taken with advantage in connection with this general course.   C 3 (*Physiological Chemistry*), while of primary importance for medical students, offers many advantages to those interested in the broader aspects of Biology and Chemistry.

COURSES FOR MEDICAL STUDENTS

In addition to the courses described below, the course

in *Pharmacology and Toxicology* in the Yale Medical School is open to Seniors. It will be counted toward the degree of M.D., but not toward the degree of B.A.

Courses A 1, C 1, C 2, C 3, C 4, C 5, and C 6, together with Chemistry A 1 (*Inorganic Chemistry*), B 1 (*Qualitative Analysis*), B 2 (*Organic Chemistry*), and the course in *Pharmacology and Toxicology*, cover the required work of the first two years of the Medical School curriculum. They are offered to Academical undergraduates for the purpose of affording students who are looking forward to the practice of Medicine the opportunity to anticipate, wholly or partly, the pre-clinical studies of the medical course. Juniors and Seniors who have taken Physics A 1 (*Elementary Physics*) or B 1 (*General Physics*) may matriculate in the Medical School. Students matriculating in 1909 must qualify also in Elementary Biology and General Chemistry. The pursuance of a course in Laboratory Physics also is advisable, and a good reading knowledge of German is very important in Medicine.

Those who matriculate in the Medical School and complete Chemistry A 1, B 1, and B 2 and Biology and Medical Sciences A 1, C 1, C 2, and C 3 may receive credit for one year's registration as medical students. Those who matriculate two years and, in addition to the courses just mentioned, complete Biology and Medical Sciences C 4, C 5, C 6, and the course in *Pharmacology and Toxicology* may receive credit for two years' registration as medical students. Upon receiving such credit for two years' registration, a student will be admitted to the Junior class in the Medical School. The two degrees of Bachelor of Arts and Doctor of Medicine may thus be obtained in six years.

It is to be noted, with regard to the requirements as to majors and minors, that all the science courses (groups xiii–xvi) are treated as a single group in this respect. For another course in *Organic Evolution* and for *Geological Biology*, see Geology B 9 and B 10. For *Physiological Psy-*

chology, see Philosophy B 7. For *Natural History of Man,* see Anthropology C 2.

A 1 *Physiology.* [Sophomores† and Juniors.] 1 hr. Professor CHITTENDEN.

> This course is designed to give familiarity with the structure and functions of the body, as part of a general education and, at the same time, as a preparation for more advanced biological work.

A 2 *Elementary Biology.* [Sophomores.] 6 hrs., *to count as 3 hrs.*

Professor HARRISON.

> A laboratory course, including lectures and demonstrations, dealing with the structure, classification, functions, and development of animals and plants.

A 3 *Organic Evolution.* 1 hr. Dr. KUNKEL.

> Illustrated lectures and demonstrations, intended primarily for those who have had little or no training in Biology and who desire merely a broad knowledge of the subject for general culture.

A 4 *Elementary Botany.* 4 hrs., *to count as 2 hrs.* Professor EVANS.

> An elementary course in the botany of flowering plants. Laboratory work and informal lectures. The plant and its various organs are studied with respect to their form, structure, and functions.

B 1 *General Biology.* 6 hrs., *to count as 3 hrs.* Assistant Professor COE and Dr. WOODRUFF.

> Laboratory work, lectures, and demonstrations, on the general principles of Biology, with special reference to the morphology, histology, embryology, and evolution of vertebrate animals. A laboratory fee of ten dollars is charged for this course. This course will be discontinued after 1907-08 and replaced by a course in Comparative Anatomy of Vertebrates.

B 2 *Morphology of Plants.* [Seniors.] 4 hrs., *to count as 2 hrs.*

Professor EVANS.

> Laboratory work and informal lectures. Beginning with the simplest forms, the various groups of plants are taken up in

---

† By Sophomores this course may be taken only outside of the required fifteen hours.

suitable types, and their structure and development are studied and compared.

_____

C 1   *Human Anatomy.*   5 hrs.
Professor FERRIS.

> This is the first year's work in Anatomy in the Medical School. The instruction is given by recitations and by work in the anatomical laboratory.

C 2   *Human Histology and Embryology.*   5 hrs.,
                                                to count as 3 hrs.

Professor FERRIS.

> Recitations and laboratory work in both Histology and Embryology. All the tissues and organs are studied.

*C 3   *Physiological Chemistry, with special reference to the Physiology of Nutrition* [after Chemistry A 1 and Biology and Medical Sciences A 1].   5 hrs.,
                                                to count as 3 hrs.

Professor CHITTENDEN and Assistant Professor UNDERHILL.

> In brief, a course dealing with the chemical side of Physiology. A laboratory fee of fifteen dollars is charged for this course.

C 4   *Physiology of Physical and Nervous Functions.*   5 hrs.,
                                                to count as 3 hrs.

Assistant Professor HENDERSON.

> Recitations, reports by the students on special topics in the literature, and laboratory work on muscle-nerve, nervous system, special senses, circulation, and respiration.

C 5   *Human Anatomy* [after C 1].   [Seniors.]
           3 hrs. and laboratory work, *to count as 3 hrs.*
Professor FERRIS.

> This is the continuation of C 1. It includes visceral and topographical Anatomy, the organs of sense, and the morphology of the vascular, respiratory, and peripheral nervous systems.

C 6   *Pathology and Bacteriology* [after C 2].
           [Seniors.]   13 hrs., *to count as 5 hrs.*
Professor BARTLETT.

> Bacteriological technique, the cultural characteristics of common bacteria, and bacterial lesions are first studied ; followed by general and special Pathology, including the study of both gross and microscopic lesions. (Separate examinations in Bacteriology and Pathology.)

(3) PHILOSOPHY, EDUCATION, HISTORY, AND THE SOCIAL SCIENCES
XVII. PHILOSOPHY

Courses A b1, A b2, and A b3 are all open to Sophomores, but A b1 and A b2 may not both be taken in Sophomore year. Both A b1 and A b3, or both A b2 and A b3, may be taken in Sophomore year and counted toward the sixty hours required for graduation, but only one of them may be counted as part of the fifteen hours required for Sophomore year. A b2 may be taken by Sophomores only as a single three-hour course, but Juniors and Seniors may take either part (*a* or *b*) separately.

For courses in *Plato* and *Plato and Aristotle*, see also Greek B 5 and C 5.

A b1 *History of Philosophy* [counted as a B course if taken after A b3].

> [Sophomores,† Juniors, and Seniors.] 3 hrs.

Professor BAKEWELL.

> The aim is to familiarize the student with the fundamental problems and categories of philosophy, and to prepare him to face present-day problems from the vantage-ground of the history of philosophic thought.

A b2 *Logic and Elements of Philosophy* [counted as a B course if taken after A b3].

> [Sophomores,† Juniors,† and Seniors.†] 3 hrs.

Professor DUNCAN.

a *Logic.* 3 hrs. 1st term,
> *to count as 1 hr. for the year.*

> The elements of logic, deductive and inductive, with especial attention to the nature of reasoning, the conditions of proof, and the principles of science.

b *Elements of Philosophy.* 3 hrs. 2d term,
> *to count as 2 hrs. for the year.*

> An introductory exposition of the problems of general philosophy and an examination of the merits of the solutions of these problems offered by the different schools of thought (Materialism, Idealism, etc.).

---

† See the statement at the head of this group (XVII).

A b3   *Psychology* [counted as a B course if taken after A b1
    or A b2].
       [Sophomores, Juniors, and Seniors.]   3 hrs.
Professor JUDD, Dr. ANGIER, and Dr. CAMERON.

> A general introductory course. Lectures, one hour a week,
> by Professor Judd ; quiz-exercises in small sections, two hours
> a week, under Dr. Angier and Dr. Cameron.

B 1   *Modern Idealism* [after A b1 or A b2].   2 hrs.
Professor BAKEWELL.

> Discussion of recent expressions of idealistic philosophy, both
> in literature and in the systematic works of the philosophers.

B 2   *Philosophical Systems.*   2 hrs.
Professor DUNCAN.

> The principal modern philosophical systems from Descartes
> to the present day, with especial attention to the problems and
> conceptions relating to knowledge and to the theory of reality,
> and to the resulting philosophical schools and tendencies.

B 3 *Ethics* [with or after A b1, A b2, or A b3].   1 hr.
Professor ROYCE.

> An introductory course. General discussion of the problem
> of duty ; the theory of loyalty, and its applications to the prac-
> tical problems of conduct.

B 5 *Experimental Psychology* [after A b3].   3 hrs.
Professor JUDD.

> A laboratory course in which the student performs experi-
> ments and prepares full reports. Once a week there is critical
> discussion of the reports of the preceding week.

[B 6   *Genetic Psychology* [after A b3].   2 hrs.
Professor JUDD.

> A course of lectures, readings, and reports, dealing with the
> facts of mental development.
>   Omitted in 1907-08.]

B 7   *Physiological Psychology.*   3 hrs.
Dr. ANGIER.

> Psychological phenomena in their relations to the sense-organs
> and the central nervous system, and the facts in anatomy and
> physiology which are necessary to show such relations. Lec-
> tures, demonstrations, prescribed readings and reports.

B 8   *Educational Psychology.*   2 hrs.

Dr. CAMERON.

A course of lectures, demonstrations, and reports, dealing with experimental methods as applied to educational problems. The topics treated include training of the senses, observation, memory, quickness of perception, writing, drawing, and fatigue.

B 9 *Æsthetics.*   1 hr.
Dr. ANGIER.

Lectures and assigned readings on the fundamental problems of æsthetics, all of which center in the problem of the nature of beauty.

[*C 1 *Platonic Idealism.*   [Seniors.] 2 hrs.
Professor BAKEWELL.

Reading of a number of the more important dialogues in translation, followed by the critical reading, in the original, of the *Republic*, Book v, 471 C, to end of Book vii. A reading knowledge of German (or French), as well as of Greek, is required. This course alternates with C 2.
Omitted in 1907-08.]

*C 2 *The Philosophy of Aristotle.*   [Seniors.] 2 hrs.
Professor BAKEWELL.

A first-hand study of the philosophy of Aristotle. Critical reading of the *Categories* and parts of the *Psychology* and the *Metaphysics*. This course alternates with C 1.

*C 3 *Problems and Methods of Philosophy.* [Seniors.] 2 hrs.
Professor BAKEWELL.

Development of the principles that underlie all rigorous philosophical procedure, followed by consideration of some of the more fundamental issues in contemporary philosophical discussions. Lectures, discussions, and theses.

*C 4 *Philosophical Criticism.*   1 ½ hrs., *to count as 2 hrs.*
Professor DUNCAN.

Reading and critical discussion of some one or more of the great masterpieces of philosophical literature, with special attention to the problems of epistemology and metaphysics. In 1907-08, Kant's *Critique of Pure Reason* and his *Prolegomena to any Future Metaphysics.*

*C 5 *Principles of Logic.*   [Seniors.] 1 hr.
Professor DUNCAN.

A course treating of the more important problems, and including an examination of the assumptions and criteria of induction; with suggestions regarding the teaching of logic.

*C 6   *Epistemology.*   [Seniors.]   1 ½ hrs., *to count as 2 hrs.*
Professor DUNCAN.

A systematic course, both critical and constructive, in the philosophy of knowledge. All the important problems of epistemology are considered.

*C 7   *Metaphysics.*   [Seniors.]   1 ½ hrs., *to count as 2 hrs.*
Professor DUNCAN.

An advanced course, the aim of which is the construction of a consistent and tenable theory of reality.

*C 8   *Metaphysical Seminary.*   [Seniors.]   2 hrs.
Professor ROYCE.

Pragmatism and idealism ; the nature of truth ; the idealistic interpretation of reality ; the relation between logical and metaphysical problems. Lectures, theses, and class discussions.

[C 9   *Ethical Seminary.*   2 hrs.
Assistant Professor HOCKING.

A critical study of fundamental ethical concepts. For 1908–09 the subject is the English debate in the nineteenth century ; Bentham, Mill, Spencer, Green, Bradley, Taylor.
Omitted in 1907–08.]

[C 10   *Philosophy of the State.*   2 hrs.
Assistant Professor HOCKING.

A course of lectures on the sources, forms, and ends of political control, surveying the important types of political theory and aiming particularly to determine conditions for stability in democratic governments.
Omitted in 1907–08.]

*C 11   *Psychological Theory and Methods.*[Seniors.]   4 hrs.,
to count as 3 hrs.

Professor JUDD, Dr. ANGIER, and Dr. CAMERON.

An advanced course, intended primarily for graduates. A critical study of current psychological problems by means of lectures, readings with reports, and laboratory exercises.

*C 12   *Readings in German Psychology and Philosophy.*
[Seniors.]   1 hr.
Dr. ANGIER.

Reading of a number of German works with a view to giving

the student an acquaintance with current psychological and philosophical discussions in Germany, and at the same time familiarizing him with the technical German terminology.

[C 13 *Readings in French Psychology and Philosophy.*

[Seniors.] 1 hr.

Dr. CAMERON.

> A course in French psychology and philosophy, similar to C 12 in German psychology and philosophy.
> Omitted in 1907–08.]

*C 14 *Psychological Readings.* [Seniors.] 1 hr.

Dr. CAMERON.

> Critical discussion of James's *Principles of Psychology*. Members of the class are required to prepare papers on the works of other writers who deal with problems parallel to those taken up by Professor James.

XVIII. THEORY AND PRACTICE OF EDUCATION

The courses under this head are designed especially to meet the needs of students who expect to teach.

It is expected that courses in this group will be given in 1908–09 and thereafter.

For *Educational Psychology*, see Philosophy B 8.

XIX. HISTORY

All the courses in History, except A 1, B 1, B 2a, B 2b, B 3, and B 4, presuppose such a general knowledge of European History as would be acquired by successfully completing A 1. Students who have not passed A 1 must secure the permission of the instructor to take courses of B grade, except B 1, B 2a, B 2b, B 3, and B 4. Students who expect to do work of C grade in History should take A 1 in Freshman or Sophomore year.

For courses in *Physical and Commercial Geography, Geography of North America, Geography of South America, Geography of Asia,* and *Geographic Controls in History*, see Geology A 1, B 5, B 6, B 7, and C 7. For a course in *Colonization*, see Anthropology B 3 (and C 4).

A 1 *European History.* [All classes.] 3 hrs.,

> *to count as only 2 hrs. for Juniors and Seniors.*

Assistant Professor RICHARDSON, Mr. DURFEE, Dr. FITE, Mr. SCHUYLER, and Dr. MITCHELL.

Introductory to later courses.   A general survey of European History from the fourth century through the nineteenth.

B 1   *Ancient Oriental Nations from the Earliest Times.* 2 hrs.
Professor TORREY.

Devoted entirely to the oldest civilizations of Western Asia and North Africa to Alexander's conquest.   Text-books on Babylonia, Egypt, Phœnicia, and Persia, with collateral reading and lectures.

B 2a   *Outline Survey of Ancient History.*   1 hr.
Professor PERRIN.

Lectures, following manual-study, outlining such general features of ancient history, from the earliest civilization of the Euphrates to the Empire of Charlemagne, as are most helpful for the study of medieval history.   Oriental history is presented only as a background and source for Greek and Roman history.

*B 2b   *Outline Survey of Ancient History.*   2 hrs.
Professor PERRIN.

The same as B 2a, except that private readings are assigned and special examinations are held on these readings.

B 3   *History of Greece to the Roman Conquest.*   2 hrs.
Professor PERRIN.

A detailed and systematic study of the political, intellectual, and artistic history of the ancient Hellenes, with suitable illustrations from their literature and monuments.   Lectures, conferences, and recitations.

[B 4   *The Roman Republic.*   2 hrs.
' Assistant Professor H. B. WRIGHT.

The history of Rome from the beginnings of the Republic to the accession of Octavius.   Manual-study, supplemented by lectures ; detailed study of a single leader or period from the sources.
Omitted in 1907–08.]

[B 7   *Medieval Asia and the Mohammedan Conquest* [after A 1 or with the consent of the instructor].   2 hrs.
Assistant Professor F. W. WILLIAMS.

History of western Asia from Alexander to the fall of Constantinople, embracing the earlier development of Christianity and the spread of Islam.   Supplementary to the history of the Roman Empire and of medieval Europe.
Omitted in 1907–08.]

B 8 *The Renaissance and Reformation* [after A 1 or with the consent of the instructor]. 2 hrs.
Assistant Professor RICHARDSON.

> The Renaissance is treated purely as an intellectual movement. The Reformation is considered in its relations to all the larger problems of modern history.

B 9 *Modern European History to 1789* [after A 1 or with the consent of the instructor]. 2 hrs.
Assistant Professor RICHARDSON.

> Considers such characteristic features of modern history as combined to produce the Europe of the French Revolution and a knowledge of which is essential to the understanding of the history of the nineteenth century.

B 12 *English Political History* [after A 1].
[Sophomores, Juniors, and Seniors.] 3 hrs.
Professor G. B. ADAMS, Dr. C. ROBINSON, and Dr. WALKER.

> From the Saxon Conquest to the nineteenth century. The history of institutions is not studied; but care is taken to make clear the political conditions which influenced the growth of the constitution.

B 13 *Modern European Governments* [after A 1 or with the consent of the instructor]. 2 hrs.
Dr. FITE.

> The present organization and practical working of English parliamentary government, and of the national governments of the more important European countries; municipal govern- ' ments in England and on the Continent.

B 15 *American History, 1492–1763* [after A 1 or with the consent of the instructor]. 2 hrs.
Professor C. H. SMITH.

> This course includes the discoveries, the Spanish and French colonial systems in outline, the political and social development of the English colonies, and the conquest of New France.

B 16 *American History, 1789–1860* [after A 1 or with the consent of the instructor]. 2 hrs.
Professor C. H. SMITH.

> The organization of the Federal government, the rise of parties, the development of democracy, and the influence of expansion and of slavery on politics.

B 17 *American Constitutional History and Government* [after A 1 or with the consent of the instructor]. 2 hrs.
Professor C. H. SMITH.

> A historical study of the Federal constitution, tracing the origin, development, and working of its principal features.

B 18 *Modern Asiatic History* [after A 1 or with the consent of the instructor].   2 hrs.
Dr. ASAKAWA.

> A brief survey of the history of Eastern and Southern Asia during the past three centuries. India, Japan, and China studied with text-books; reading and essays throughout the year.

B 19 *Modern Japan* [after A 1 or with the consent of the instructor].   2 hrs.
Dr. ASAKAWA.

> An outline of the political development of imperial Japan during the past half-century, and a study of its social and economic conditions.

C 3 *History of Europe since 1789.*   [Seniors.] 2 hrs.
Professor A. M. WHEELER.

> Mainly political; introductory to European politics of our day.

C 5 *English Constitutional History to the Present Time.*
                    [Juniors† and Seniors.] 2 hrs.
Professor G. B. ADAMS.

> The purpose of the course is to show how the Anglo-Saxon system of self-government arose, and how the chief features of the present English constitution took form. Of special value to those who intend to study law.

C 7 *History of Spanish America, chiefly in the Nineteenth Century.*   1 hr.
Dr. H. BINGHAM.

> A survey of the Spanish colonies and of the struggle for independence, followed by an outline study of the history of several representative states and of their relations to the United States and Europe.

C 8 *The United States since 1860.*   [Seniors.] 2 hrs.
Professor C. H. SMITH.

---

† Open to Juniors only after B 12 and with the written consent of the instructor.

First half-year: a study of the Civil War. Second half-year: a study of the Reconstruction Period and of some of the important features of our recent history.

C 9   *The United States since 1860.*   [Seniors who are graduates of other colleges.]   2 hrs.
Professor C. H. SMITH.

This is a graduate course, open to Seniors who are graduates of other colleges. In its scope it is essentially the same as C 8.

C 10   *American Civil War.* [Seniors.] 2 hrs. first half-year,
to count as 1 hr. for the year.
Professor C. H. SMITH.

This course is the first half of C 8.

[C 11   *European Colonies in Asia and Africa.*
[Seniors.]   2 hrs.
Assistant Professor F. W. WILLIAMS.

Chiefly a research course in colonization in modern times. History of the acquisition, and examination of the administration, of existing colonies. Assigned subjects discussed in brief theses.
Omitted in 1907-08.]

[C 12   *Chinese Culture and Institutions.*   [Seniors.]   2 hrs.
Assistant Professor F. W. WILLIAMS.

A research and reading course, using as material for study assigned passages in books in the University Library dealing with the history, language, literature, government, arts, and economic and social condition of the Chinese Empire.
Omitted in 1907-08.]

THE SOCIAL SCIENCES (GROUPS XX, XXI)
XX. ANTHROPOLOGY

The basis of this group is *Physical and Commercial Geography* (Geology A 1), which is to be considered the regular A course in Anthropology. Furthermore, Economics and Law A 1 (*Elementary Economics*) and C 7 (*Economic History*) may be counted as A and C courses, respectively, in this group.

For *Organic Evolution*, see Geology B 9 and Biology and Medical Sciences A 3.

B 1 *Anthropology.*   [Juniors.] 2 hrs.
Professor KELLER.

>   Introductory to course B 2 (and C 1). Text-books on anthropology and ethnography ; lectures explanatory of the text-books and on the doctrine of evolution, with its application to man and human society ; environmental influences, etc.

B 2 *The Science of Society.*   [Seniors.] 2 hrs.
Professor SUMNER.

>   An outline, by text-book and lectures, of the systematic science of society, based on ethnography and history. Course B 1 is necessary to give a fund of information about the facts on which the principles set forth in this course are based.

B 3 *Colonization.*   2 hrs.
Professor KELLER.

>   Colonization, from the standpoint of the science of society, in ancient, medieval, and modern times : emigration, acclimatization, colonial trade, frontier society, contact of races, etc.

B 4 *Transportation Systems.*   2 hrs.
Dr. BISHOP.

>   A historical treatment of transportation systems : their adaptation to the life conditions of societies upon various stages of economic development ; trails, roads, canals, ocean-routes, etc. Text-books, lectures, and reports.

*B 5 *Natural History of Commerce.*   2 hrs.
Dr. BISHOP.

>   The nature of the flora and fauna of commerce, and the conditions of their natural distribution ; domestication, breeding, etc. Text-books, lectures, laboratory demonstrations, and reports.

[*B 6 *Markets.*   2 hrs.

Dr. BISHOP.

The factors influencing the marketing of commercial commodities: supply and demand, interferences with the natural course of trade, the handling of goods in transit, influence of nationality, language, superstition, etc. Text-books, lectures, and reports.

Omitted in 1907-08.]

*C1   *The Science of Society.*   2 hrs.
Professor SUMNER.

The class exercises for this course are identical with those for B 2, but additional work in the way of special reports is required.

*C 2   *Natural History of Man* [after B 1]. [Seniors.] 2 hrs.
Professor FERRIS.

A more special treatment of man as an animal: his embryology, vestigial organs, variations of structure and their significance, body-proportions, general adaptation to environment, etc. Text-books, laboratory work, and lectures.

*C 3   *Ethnology.*   2 hrs.
Professor KELLER.

Primarily a course of investigation into the life of selected groups of uncivilized peoples: in 1907-08, the Negroid races. Ability to read easy French or German is required.

C 4   *Colonization.*   2 hrs.
Professor KELLER.

The class exercises for this course are identical with those for B 3, but additional work in the way of special reports involving the use of some foreign language is required.

*C 5   *Culture-History.*   2 hrs.
Professor KELLER.

A critical reading of Lippert's *Kulturgeschichte* (2 vols., Stuttgart, 1887), (a) for its subject-matter, and (b) as a basis for informal instruction in research, scientific method, etc.

[*C 6   *Historical Anthropology* [with or after B 2 or C 1]. 2 hrs.
Professor KELLER.

An analysis of the anthropological evidence of legend and folktale. For 1906-07 the subject was Homer. Ability to read the original is valuable, but is not required.

Omitted in 1907-08.]

[*C 7   *History of Sociology* [with or after B 2 or C 1]. 2 hrs.

Professor KELLER.

> Readings in the forerunners of the science, in Comte and Spencer, and in later writers ; reports and discussions. Ability to read French or German is required.
> Omitted in 1907–08.]

[*C 8   *The Self-Perpetuation of Society.*   [Seniors.] 2 hrs. Professor SUMNER.

> This graduate course is open to selected students who have taken course B 1 with great credit or have otherwise shown preparation for the work required.
> Omitted in 1907–08.]

*C 9 *Beginnings of Industrial Organization.* [Seniors.] 2 hrs. Professor SUMNER.

> See the statement of C 8, which applies also to this course.

XXI. ECONOMICS AND LAW

In addition to the courses in Law described below, the following courses in the Yale Law School are open to Seniors. They will be counted toward the attainment of the degree of LL.B. (as courses A 6, A 7, A 8, B 8, B 9, and B 10 will be), but not toward the attainment of the degree of B.A.

> a. *Public Wrongs* [after or with A 6, B 8, and B 9].
> b. *Use of Law Library* (1st half-year) and *Study of Cases* (2d half-year) [after or with A 6, B 8, and B 9].
> c. *Pleading at Common Law* [after or with A 6, B 8, B 9, and the above courses *a* and *b*].

For a course in *Roman Law*, see Latin B 11. For a course in *Physical and Commercial Geography*, see Geology A 1. For courses in *Transportation Systems, Natural History of Commerce, Markets,* and *Industrial Organization,* see Anthropology B 4, B 5, B 6, and C 9.

A 1   *Elementary Economics* [may count as an A course in Anthropology].

>   [Sophomores, Juniors, and Seniors.] 3 hrs.
Professors EMERY, FISHER, and DAY, Dr. F. R. FAIRCHILD, and Dr. ZARTMAN.

> Lectures, one hour a week, by Professor Emery; quiz-exercises in small sections, two hours a week, under Professors Emery, Fisher, and Day, Dr. Fairchild, and Dr. Zartman.

13

A 2 *Elementary Statistics.* 2 hrs.
Assistant Professor BAILEY.

The principal statistics of sociology and economics are studied, and the manner of conducting a statistical investigation is explained.

A 6 *Elementary Law.* 3 hrs.
Professor WURTS and Assistant Professor CORBIN.

First half-year : instruction by Professor Wurts on the basis of Robinson's *Elementary Law* and Blackstone's *Commentaries.*

Second half-year : instruction by Assistant Professor Corbin on the basis of Anson *On Contracts* (2d American ed. by Huffcut) and the *Yale Cases on Contracts.*

A 7 *American Constitutional Law.* [Seniors.] 2 hrs.
Professor S. E. BALDWIN.

Lectures, with Cooley's *Principles of Constitutional Law* and the *Yale Cases on Constitutional Law.* The origin and scope of both the national and the state constitutions, and the course of legislation and judicial decision serving toward their exposition, are considered.

A 8 *International Law.* [Seniors.] 3 hrs. 2d term, *to count as 2 hrs. for the year.*
Professor HYDE.

Lectures, with written tests, upon the rules governing the intercourse of states, and upon certain topics in American diplomacy. Designed to explain international politics, to train in intelligent citizenship, and to assist legal practice.

B 2 *Financial History of the United States* [after A 1]. 2 hrs.
Dr. F. R. FAIRCHILD.

Especially the history of American currency, banking institutions and practices, and the government revenue system.

*B 3 *Corporation Economics.* 2 hrs.
Assistant Professor NORTON.

The anatomy of a corporation ; its incorporation and organization, advantages and disadvantages ; the formation of industrial combinations and the statistical basis for the capitalization of net earnings.

B 4 *American Social Conditions* [after A 1 or A 2]. 2 hrs.
Assistant Professor BAILEY.

A study of immigration ; the growth and concentration of

population in cities, with the attendant dangers ; the liquor question ; the criminal ; the negro.

*B 6   *Economic History of the United States* [after A 1]. 2 hrs. Professor CALLENDER.

The economic evolution of the United States from the simple agricultural community of colonial times to the highly diversified industrial society of the present (1760-1860).

B 8   *Contracts* [after A 6].   [Seniors.]   3 hrs. Assistant Professor CORBIN and Mr. EDGERTON.

Ten lectures on Partnership by Mr. Edgerton ; a continuation of the study of the law of Contracts under Professor Corbin.   Text-book : Williston's *Cases on Contracts*.

B 9   *Torts* [with A 6].   [Seniors.]   2 hrs. Professor WATROUS.

Recitations from Cooley *On Torts* (students' ed., 1907), with the study of cases, illustrative of the text, from Chase's *Cases on Torts* (2d ed.).

B 10   *Evidence* [after A 6].   [Seniors.]   2 hrs. Professor WURTS and Judge E. PECK.

Text-books : Reynolds's *Theory of Evidence* (first half-year, under Professor Wurts) and Thayer's *Cases on Evidence* (second half-year, under Judge Peck).

B 11   *Insurance* [after A 1].   2 hrs. Dr. ZARTMAN.

The purpose of insurance, computation of rates, different systems, policy conditions, company management, agency work, legal regulation, and other current problems connected with the business.

B 12   *Corporation Accounting*.   2 hrs. Dr. ZARTMAN.

The theory of accounting ; study of systems of administrative control ; cost-accounts, their nature, and their value to the investor, the business man, and the manufacturer.

[C 1   *Theory of the Distribution of Wealth*.   2 hrs. Professor FISHER.

A study—theoretical, statistical, and historical—of the accumulation and dissipation of wealth among social classes.
Omitted in 1907–08.]

C 2 *Theory of Prices and Price-Levels.* 2 hrs.
Professor FISHER.

> A study of the determination of prices, rents, and wages, and of the relation of money and circulating credit to price-levels.

*C 3 *Railroads.* 2 hrs.
Assistant Professor NORTON.

> The location, consolidation, taxation, and financial and industrial problems of railroads ; the Interstate Commerce Commission and its relation to pooling and discrimination ; analysis of railroad reports and statistics.

*C 4 *Labor Problems.* [Seniors.] 1 hr.
Assistant Professor BAILEY.

> The conflicts between labor and capital, and the methods employed to obtain industrial peace.

C 5 *Trade Statistics.* [Seniors.] 2 hrs.
Assistant Professor NORTON.

> The condition of trade viewed from the standpoint of (i) the international movement, (ii) bank clearings, (iii) the money supply, (iv) the outlook for the harvests, and (v) earnings of corporations. Crop forecasts ; visible supplies ; etc.

C 6 *Interpolation.* 1 hr.
Assistant Professor NORTON.

> Methods of fitting curves to series of statistics in analysis of relations among variables ; the theory of correlation of two or more variables ; practice in handling statistical data.

*C 7 *Economic History* [after A 1 or History A 1 ; may count as a C course in Anthropology]. 2 hrs.
Professor DAY.

> Development of the economic organization in Europe in its relation to the political organization; for advanced students of economics and of history. Lectures, reading, and research.

*C 8 *Industrial History of the United States* [with or after B 6]. 2 hrs.
Professor DAY.

> Introductory lectures on methods and bibliography, followed by investigation of a small number of special topics by each member of the class in conference with the instructor.

*C 9 *Commerce and Commercial Policy in the Nineteenth
        Century.*   [Seniors.]   2 hrs.
Professor EMERY.

> A study of the growth of international trade and the changes
> in commercial policy, especially in the leading countries of
> Europe.

[*C 10   *History of Economics, Part I.*   2 hrs.
Professor EMERY.

> The history of economic ideas, with special reference to eco-
> nomic policy, from the Middle Ages to the middle of the nine-
> teenth century. Lectures and readings in contemporary authors.
> Omitted in 1907–08.]

*C 11   *History of Economics, Part II.*   2 hrs.
Professor EMERY.

> A continuation of the above course (C 10), given in alternate
> years.   It deals with the later reactions from the classical
> school, protectionism, socialism, and the historical school.

*C 12   *Economic Organization of Europe.*   2 hrs.
Professor DAY.

> A descriptive course in national political economy, to supple-
> ment courses in general economics.   Lectures on the organiza-
> tion in the separate states; investigation of special topics by
> members of the class.

C 13 *Public Finance.*   2 hrs.
Dr. F. R. FAIRCHILD.

> A study of the principles of government expenditure, govern-
> ment revenue, and government debt, with special reference to
> the problems of taxation in the United States.

THE FINE ARTS AND MUSIC
XXII. THE FINE ARTS

For *Greek, Roman,* and *Etruscan Art,* see Classical Archæology B 1, B 2, B 3, B 4, and B 5.

A 1 *Drawing (Pen and Pencil).* [Juniors.] 4 hrs., *to count as 2 hrs.*

Professor NIEMEYER.

> This course is designed to teach the fundamental principles of art as understood by the artist, and is also adapted to those students who are interested in art only as part of a liberal education.

B 1 *Architecture* [after A 1]. 4 hrs., *to count as 2 hrs.*
Professor NIEMEYER.

> This course teaches, by means of lectures and graphic representation, the classic styles of architecture, and also the history and significance of decoration.

B 2 *Painting* [after A 1]. [Seniors.] 4 hrs., *to count as 2 hrs.*
Professor WEIR.

> Studies in water-color painting from still-life and the living model, with lectures on the grammar of art and studies in composition and in sketching from nature.

B 3 *Modeling* [after A 1]. [Seniors.] 4 hrs., *to count as 2 hrs.*
Professor WEIR.

> Modeling from the antique and the living figure, supplemented by lectures given in course B 2.

XXIII. MUSIC

A 1 *Harmony.* 2 hrs.
Mr. D. S. SMITH.

> The study of chords, progressions, modulation, and non-harmonic notes. The work consists of exercises in figured-hass, the harmonization of melodies, and harmonic analysis.

A 3 *History of Music.* 1 hr.
Professor PARKER.

> Lectures on the development of music from its earliest stages, with biographical sketches of composers, and practical illustrations at the piano. Parry's *The Evolution of the Art of Music.*

A 5 *Practical Music* [with one of the theoretical courses]. 1 hr.

Professors SANFORD and JEPSON, Assistant Professors TROOSTWYK and KNIGHT, Mr. RABOLD, Mr. SCHULZ, Mr. L. WILLIAMS, and Mr. S. D. BINGHAM, Jr.

> Private instruction in piano-, organ-, violin-, and violoncello-playing and in singing. Fees range from $50.00 to $100.00 for the College year. Private piano or organ practice may be obtained for a small fee.

B 1 *Counterpoint* [after A 1].   2 hrs.
Mr. D. S. SMITH.

> Practice in strict counterpoint, both simple and double, harmonization of chorales, composition of short pieces in a freer style, and analysis of simple polyphonic forms. Spalding's *Tonal Counterpoint*.

C 1 *Strict Composition* [after B 1].   2 hrs.
Professor PARKER.

> The writing of canons, fugues, and polyphonic choral movements. Each student is required to submit at the close of the year a complete four-voiced fugue.

*C2 *Instrumentation* [after B 1].   2 hrs.
Mr. HAESCHE.

> Lectures on the characteristics of all the instruments of the modern orchestra, with illustrations of their use by great composers; exercises in practical orchestration, and playing from orchestral scores.

C 3 *Free Composition* [after C 1].   2 hrs.
Professor PARKER.

> The writing of free vocal and instrumental pieces in the smaller forms, and later in the sonata form, either for single instruments or for combinations of instruments. No text-book is used.

*C 4 *Advanced Orchestration and Conducting* [after C 2]. 1 hr.
Professor PARKER.

> The study of old and new orchestral scores; practical instruction in conducting; orchestration of original or other compositions. No text-book is used, but students are required to buy a number of orchestral scores.

For YALE-COLUMBIA COURSES IN PREPARATION FOR FOREIGN SERVICE, see the section on the Graduate School.

Prizes open to students in other Departments of the University, as well as the Academical Department, are described under University Prizes. See Index.

ADDISON EMERY VERRILL, M.A., *Professor of Zoology, Emeritus*

SIDNEY IRVING SMITH, M.A., *Professor of Comparative Anatomy, Emeritus*

WILLIAM GILBERT MIXTER, M.A., *Professor of Chemistry*

AUGUSTUS JAY DuBOIS, C.E., PH.D., *Professor of Civil Engineering*

CHARLES SHELDON HASTINGS, PH.D., *Professor of Physics*

RUSSELL HENRY CHITTENDEN, PH.D., LL.D., Sc.D., *Professor of Physiological Chemistry*

JOHN HAYS HAMMOND, M.A., *Professor of Mining Engineering*

HORACE LEMUEL WELLS, Sc.D., *Professor of Analytical Chemistry and Metallurgy*

LOUIS VALENTINE PIRSSON, M.A., *Professor of Physical Geology*

WILBUR LUCIUS CROSS, PH.D., *Professor of English*

ROBERT NELSON CORWIN, PH.D., *Professor of German*

PERCEY FRANKLYN SMITH, PH.D., *James E. English Professor of Mathematics*

GUY STEVENS CALLENDER, PH.D., *Professor of Political Economy*

LAFAYETTE BENEDICT MENDEL, PH.D., *Professor of Physiological Chemistry*

CHARLES SCHUCHERT, M.A., *Professor of Historical Geology*

ALEXANDER WILLIAM EVANS, M.D., PH.D., *Eaton Professor of Botany*

JOHN DUER IRVING, PH.D., *Professor of Economic Geology*

ROSS GRANVILLE HARRISON, M.D., PH.D., *Bronson Professor of Comparative Anatomy*

PROFESSORS, ASSISTANT PROFESSORS, AND LECTURERS
ADDITIONAL TO THE GOVERNING BOARD

SAMUEL EBEN BARNEY, C.E., *Assistant Professor of Civil Engineering*

FREDERICK ELIJAH BEACH, PH.D., *Assistant Professor of Physics*

HERMAN HAUPT CHAPMAN, M.F. *(Assistant Professor in the Yale Forest School), Instructor in Forestry*

CHARLES CAMERON CLARKE, JR., B.A., *Assistant Professor of French*

WESLEY ROSWELL COE, PH.D., *Assistant Professor of Comparative Anatomy*

HARRY WARD FOOTE, PH.D., *Assistant Professor of Physical Chemistry*

WILLIAM EBENEZER FORD, JR., PH.D., *Assistant Professor of Mineralogy*

CLYDE CHEW GLASCOCK, PH.D., *Assistant Professor of German*

HENRY SOLON GRAVES, M.A. *(Professor in the Yale Forest School), Professor of Forestry*

HERBERT ERNEST GREGORY, PH.D. *(Silliman Professor of Geology in Yale College), Instructor in Physical Geography*

LOUIS DOREMUS HUNTOON, M.E., *Assistant Professor of Mining and Metallurgy*

ALBERT GALLOWAY KELLER, PH.D. *(Professor of the Science of Society in Yale College), Instructor in Anthropology*

EDWIN HOYT LOCKWOOD, M.E., PH.D., *Assistant Professor of Mechanical Engineering*

FREDERICK BLISS LUQUIENS, PH.D., *Assistant Professor of Spanish*

WILLIAM CROSBY MARSHALL, M.E., C.E., *Assistant Professor of Drawing and Descriptive Geometry*

ARTHUR MARVIN, M.A., *Registrar of the Sheffield Scientific School*

MAX MASON, PH.D., *Assistant Professor of Mathematics*

GEORGE HENRY NETTLETON, PH.D., *Assistant Professor of English*

JOHN HENRY NIEMEYER, M.A. *(Professor in the Yale School of the Fine Arts), Instructor in Free Hand Drawing*

LEO FREDERICK RETTGER, PH.D., *Assistant Professor of Bacteriology and Hygiene*

HERBERT EUGENE SMITH, M.D. *(Professor in the Yale Medical School), Lecturer on Water Analysis*

JAMES WILLIAM TOUMEY, M.A., M.S. *(Professor in the Yale Forest School), Professor of Forestry*

JOHN CLAYTON TRACY, C.E., *Assistant Professor of Structural Engineering*

FRANK PELL UNDERHILL, PH.D. *Assistant Professor of Physiological Chemistry*

PERCY TALBOT WALDEN, PH.D., *Assistant Professor of Chemistry*

HENRY LORD WHEELER, PH.D., *Assistant Professor of Organic Chemistry*

LYNDE PHELPS WHEELER, PH.D., *Assistant Professor of Physics*

INSTRUCTORS

HENRY SEIDEL CANBY, PH.D., *Instructor in English*

LEON JACOB COLE, PH.D., *Instructor in Zoology*

WILLIAM JAMES COMSTOCK, PH.B., *Instructor in Organic Chemistry*

FRANK LAWRENCE COOPER, PH.D., *Instructor in Physics*

PAUL CURTS, M.A., *Instructor in German*

HAROUTUNE MUGURDICH DADOURIAN, PH.D., *Instructor in Physics*

WILLARD HIGLEY DURHAM, B.A., *Instructor in English*

CHARLES SHERMAN FARNHAM, C.E., *Instructor in Civil Engineering*

MILTON STAHL GARVER, PH.D., *Instructor in French*

WILLIAM ANTHONY GRANVILLE, PH.D., *Instructor in Mathematics*

ARTHUR HARMOUNT GRAVES, PH.D., *Instructor in Botany*

RALPH CHIPMAN HAWLEY, M.F. *(Instructor in the Yale Forest School)*, *Instructor in Forestry*

LAURENCE ILSLEY HEWES, PH.D., *Instructor in Mathematics*

ELLSWORTH HUNTINGTON, M.A., *Instructor in Physical Geography*

GEORGE SAMUEL JAMIESON, PH.D., *Instructor in Analytical Chemistry*

CARL OSCAR JOHNS, PH.D., *Instructor in Chemistry*

TREAT BALDWIN JOHNSON, PH.D., *Instructor in Chemistry*

RICHARD SHELTON KIRBY, C.E., *Instructor in Sanitary Engineering*

BEVERLY WAUGH KUNKEL, PH.D., *Instructor in Biology*

GEORGE HENRY LANGZETTEL, B.F.A. *(Secretary of the Yale School of the Fine Arts)*, *Instructor in Drawing*

WILLIAM ALBERT LILLEY, JR., M.E., *Instructor in Mechanical Engineering*

WILLIAM RAYMOND LONGLEY, PH.D., *Instructor in Mathematics*

GEORGE BLAKEMAN LOVELL, M.A., *Instructor in German*

CHAMPION HERBERT MATHEWSON, PH.D., *Instructor in Chemistry and Metallography*

STEWART LEA MIMS, B.A., *Instructor in History*

WATSON NICHOLSON, PH.D., *Instructor in English*

HERBERT BRINKERHOFF NORTH, PH.B., *Instructor in Drawing and Descriptive Geometry*

FREDERICK ERASTUS PIERCE, M.A., *Instructor in English*

CHAUNCEY BREWSTER RICE, PH.D., *Instructor in Applied Electricity*

JOHN PIERREPONT RICE, M.A., *Instructor in French*

FREDERICK OSCAR ROBBINS, B.A., *Instructor in French*

JOSEPH WICKHAM ROE, M.E., *Instructor in Mechanical Engineering*

WILLIAM KENT SHEPARD, PH.D., *Instructor in Mechanics*

GEORGE ALBERT THOMPSON, B.F.A. *(Instructor in the Yale School of the Fine Arts)*, *Instructor in Drawing*

EDWARD THORSTENBERG, PH.D., *Instructor in German*

ARTHUR GUSTAVUS WARD, PH.D., *Instructor in German*

FREEMAN WARD, B.A., *Instructor in Geology and Mineralogy*

LORANDE LOSS WOODRUFF, PH.D., *Instructor in Biology*

ASSISTANTS

CLIFFORD WHITMAN BATES, PH.B., *Assistant in Physics*

STANLEY ROSSITER BENEDICT, B.A., *Laboratory Assistant in Biology*

SAMUEL JOHN BERARD, *Assistant in Descriptive Geometry and Machine Design, and Assistant Librarian*

EARL GORDON BILL, M.A., *Assistant in Mathematics*

WALTER MINOR BRADLEY, PH.B., *Assistant in Mineralogy*

CHARLTON DOWS COOKSEY, PH.B., *Assistant in Physics*

JOHN HAMILTON DERBY, JR., PH.B., *Laboratory Assistant in Chemistry*

GEORGE EDWARD GAGE, M.A., *Laboratory Assistant in Bacteriology*

RUSSELL TYNER GARD, PH.B., *Laboratory Assistant in Mining and Metallurgy*

GEORGE FREDERICK GUNDELFINGER, PH.B., *Assistant in Mathematics*

ISRAEL SIMON KLEINER, PH.B., *Assistant in Physiological Chemistry*

CLARENCE MOORE KNOX, PH.B., *Assistant in Drawing*

FRANCIS BAKER LANEY, M.A., *Laboratory Assistant in Mineralogy*

WILLIAM HARDING LONGLEY, B.A., *Laboratory Assistant in Biology*

JOHN FRANKLIN LYMAN, B.S., *Laboratory Assistant in Biology*

KENNETH GERARD MACKENZIE, PH.B., *Laboratory Assistant in Chemistry*

EDWIN CYRUS MILLER, B.A., *Laboratory Assistant in Botany*

FOSTER STEBBINS NAETHING, PH.B., *Laboratory Assistant in Mining and Metallurgy*

GEORGE ELWOOD NICHOLS, B.A., *Assistant in Botany*

CHARLES CURTISS PERRY, PH.B., *Assistant in Physics and Steam Engine*

JOSEPH CHAPPELL RAYWORTH, M.A., *Assistant in Mathematics*

HEATON RIDGEWAY ROBERTSON, B.A., PH.B., *Assistant in Mining and Metallurgy*

HERBERT LEE SEWARD, PH.B., *Assistant in Shop Visiting and Drawing*

EDWIN KINMOUTH SMITH, PH.B., *Laboratory Assistant in Chemistry*

CARL FRANK SPEH, PH.B., *Laboratory Assistant in Chemistry*

RALPH WILLIAM YOUNG, PH.B., *Laboratory Assistant in Mining and Metallurgy*

OTHER OFFICERS

GEORGE MERWIN BEERS, *Clerk in the Treasurer's Office*

JAMES READE HUTCHINSON, *Assistant Clerk in the Treasurer's Office*

JANE A. FORBES, *Clerk in the Registrar's Office*

MARY M. MAYER, *Private Secretary to the Director*

MARSHALL MOORE BARTHOLOMEW, *Secretary of the Young Men's Christian Association of the Sheffield Scientific School*

GENERAL STATEMENT
OBJECTS

THE SHEFFIELD SCIENTIFIC SCHOOL is devoted to instruction and researches in the mathematical, physical, and natural sciences, with reference to the promotion and diffusion of science, and also to the preparation of young men for such pursuits as require special proficiency in these departments of learning. Instruction is also given in French, German, Spanish, English, History, Anthropology, Economics, and Political Science. The Sheffield Scientific School is one of the Departments of the University, like the Law, Medical, Theological, and Art Schools, having its separate funds, buildings, teachers, and regulations, but governed by the Corporation of Yale University, which appoints the professors and confers the degrees. It is, in part, analogous to the Academical Department, or College, and, in part, to the Professional Schools.

The instruction is intended for two classes of students:—

I.—Graduates of this and other universities or colleges, and other persons qualified for advanced or special scientific study.

II.—Undergraduates who desire a training, chiefly mathematical and scientific, in less part linguistic and literary, for higher scientific studies, or for various other occupations to which such training is suited.

HISTORY AND ORGANIZATION

The School was commenced in 1847. In 1860, a convenient building and a considerable endowment were given by Joseph E. Sheffield, of New Haven, whose name, at the repeated request of the Corporation of Yale College, was subsequently attached to the foundation. Mr. Sheffield afterwards frequently and munificently increased his original gifts.

In 1863, by an act of the Connecticut Legislature, the national grant for the promotion of scientific education (under the congressional enactment of July, 1862) was given to this department of Yale University, which thus became the College of Agriculture and the Mechanic Arts for Connecticut. By an act of the State Legislature in 1892 this was revoked and the special relations of the School to the State created by the act of 1863 were terminated.

In 1871, at the request of Mr. Sheffield, certain of the professors in the Sheffield Scientific School and other friends of the institution organized themselves into a body corporate, under the laws of the State of Connecticut, with the following articles of incorporation :

KNOW ALL MEN BY THESE PRESENTS : That we, the undersigned, George J. Brush, Daniel C. Gilman, William P. Trowbridge, and John S. Beach, all of the city and county of New Haven, in the state of Connecticut, William Walter Phelps, of the city, county and state of New York, and Charles J. Sheffield, of the city of Cleveland, in the county of Cuyahoga, and state of Ohio, do hereby associate ourselves under the provisions of the statute laws of the state of Connecticut as a body politic and corporate for scientific purposes, and the following are our articles of association ; to wit :

ARTICLE 1. The name of said corporation shall be THE BOARD OF TRUSTEES OF THE SHEFFIELD SCIENTIFIC SCHOOL.

ARTICLE 2. The object and purpose of said corporation is to promote the study of physical, natural and mathematical sciences in the college or school of science known as the Sheffield Scientific School, located at said city of New Haven.

ARTICLE 3. The property and affairs of said corporation shall be managed and conducted by a board of nine directors,—of whom by virtue of their respective official positions there shall be three, consisting of the Governor of the state of Connecticut, the President of Yale College and the Chairman of the Trustees of the Peabody Museum of Natural History in Yale College ; and the other six directors shall be the above named associates who shall hold said office until others are chosen in their stead ; and whenever a vacancy shall arise from any cause among said six directors, a successor shall be chosen by all the remaining members of said board, but at least three of said directors, not including any of the ex-officio trustees, shall at all times be professors in the said Sheffield Scientific School, and the other elected directors shall be persons especially interested in promoting the welfare of the Sheffield Scientific School, and shall be chosen without regard to their residence or non-residence in the state of Connecticut, and without regard to their ecclesiastical preferences.

Dated at New Haven, Connecticut, Feb. 8, 1871.

This incorporation of the Board of Trustees of the Sheffield Scientific School was confirmed by Act of the General Assembly in 1882.

ACT OF INCORPORATION

Resolved by this Assembly :

SECTION 1. That the Board of Trustees of the Sheffield Scientific School shall be and remain a body politic and corporate under the provisions herein contained, and shall have the right to and enjoy all the rights, powers, and privileges herein granted, and shall own and possess all the estate and assets now vested in said corporation, or that may hereafter accrue to it as devisee or legatee, to the same extent in all respects as if said corporation had been originally organized under a charter containing the provisions of this act.

SEC. 2. The object and purpose of said corporation is, and shall continue to be, to promote the study of physical, natural, and mathematical sciences, in the college or school of science known as the Sheffield Scientific School, located at the city of New Haven, and to that end the said corporation may do all acts necessary and proper for the well ordering of its affairs, and may receive, hold, or convey any estate, real or personal, that may be conveyed to it, or that it now possesses, and said property, while so used for the promotion of science, shall be free from taxation.

SEC. 3. The property and affairs of said corporation shall be managed and conducted by a board of nine directors, of whom, by virtue of their respective official positions, there shall be three, consisting of the Governor of the state of Connecticut, the President of Yale College, and the Chairman of the Trustees of the Peabody Museum of Natural History in Yale College, and whenever a vacancy shall arise from any cause among the other six directors, a successor shall be chosen by all the remaining members of said board, but at least three of said directors, not including any of the ex-officio trustees, shall at all times be persons who are or who have been professors in the said Sheffield Scientific School, and the other elected directors shall be persons especially interested in promoting the welfare of the Sheffield Scientific School, and shall be chosen without regard to their residence or non-residence in the state of Connecticut, and without regard to their ecclesiastical preferences.

SEC. 4. The present officers of said corporation shall continue in their offices respectively until others shall be chosen under the provisions of this act.

SEC. 5. A majority of said directors, who are resident in New Haven, when met shall constitute a quorum.

SEC. 6. The directors, for the time being, shall have power to fill any vacancy which may happen in their board by death, resignation, or otherwise ; they may appoint and employ such officers as they may deem necessary or desirable to effectuate the purpose and object above mentioned, and may make such by-laws and rules and regulations for the government and management of the affairs of said corporation as they deem reasonable and necessary : provided the same be not inconsistent with the laws of this state or of the United States, and the present by-laws of said corporation shall remain in force until they be altered or amended.

In addition to the bequests made by Mr. Sheffield, numerous liberal gifts have been received, for the endowment of the School and the increase of its buildings and collections, by which the facilities of the institution have been greatly enlarged. Special mention is made of some of these gifts in the descriptions of buildings, apparatus, collections, scholarships and prizes.

The Governing Board consists of the President of the University and the professors who are permanently attached to the School. There are many other instructors associated with them, some of whom are connected with other departments of the University.

INSTRUCTION FOR GRADUATE AND SPECIAL STUDENTS

Students who have completed undergraduate courses of study, here or elsewhere, may avail themselves of the facilities of the School for more special professional training in the natural and physical sciences and their applications, gaining in one, two, or three years the degree of BACHELOR OF PHILOSOPHY, or in two additional years of engineering study that of CIVIL ENGINEER, MECHANICAL ENGINEER, or that of MINING ENGINEER. (See pp. 211 to 213.)

Those who desire to engage in studies of a less exclusively technical character, may become candidates for the degree of MASTER OF SCIENCE or DOCTOR OF PHILOSOPHY. The instruction in such cases will be adapted to the particular needs and capacities of each student, and may be combined with that given by instructors in other departments of the University.

The degree of MASTER OF SCIENCE is conferred upon graduates of this or other universities, of two years' standing or upwards, who have taken their first degree in science, and who have pursued successfully a higher course of study in science under the direction of the Governing Board. Such a course will involve at least one year of resident graduate study, followed by an examination and the presentation of a satisfactory thesis in some department of science. A committee of the Faculty is appointed (consisting for the present year of Professors Chittenden and Richards) to whom all candidates for this degree must submit their proposed courses of study for approval before the end of October of each year. The fee for graduation is ten dollars.

The degree of DOCTOR OF PHILOSOPHY is conferred upon those students (of either sex) who show the results of resident graduate work by a thesis giving evidence of high attainment and power of investigation, and by passing an examination on studies whose grade and amount meet the approval of the Faculty. Under ordinary circumstances two or more years of work in residence is required, but in exceptional cases work of equal grade at another University may take the place of a year's residence here. Whenever the course of undergraduate study has been less than four years, three years of graduate work will be required. The thesis must be deposited at the Library for public inspection not later than May 1. A good knowledge of Latin, German, and French is required in all cases, unless, for some very exceptional reasons, the candidate be excused by the Faculty. Evidence of sufficient attainments in these languages must be presented at least two years before the degree is given. The fee for graduation is ten dollars.

A detailed statement of the graduate instruction of the University, including more than 500 courses, is printed in a separate pamphlet, and may be had on application to the Secretary of the University. The principal courses offered

14

in the Sheffield Scientific School are given by the following instructors:

Professor RICHARDS, in Mechanical Engineering.

Assistant Professor LOCKWOOD, in Thermodynamics and Mechanics of Heat Engines.

Dr. SHEPARD, in Mechanics of Materials.

Professor DuBois, in Civil Engineering.

Assistant Professor BARNEY, in Municipal and Sanitary Engineering.

Assistant Professor TRACY, in Graphic Statics.

Assistant Professor HUNTOON, in Mining and Metallurgy.

Professor HASTINGS, Assistant Professors BEACH, L. P. WHEELER, and Dr. DADOURIAN, in selected subjects in Physics, and guidance in laboratory work.

Professor P. F. SMITH, Assistant Professor MASON, Dr. GRANVILLE, Dr. LONGLEY, and Dr. HEWES, in Advanced Mathematics.

Professor MIXTER, in Chemical Physics.

Professor WELLS, in Analytical Chemistry, Inorganic Chemistry, and Metallurgy.

Dr. MATHEWSON, in Metallography.

Assistant Professor H. L. WHEELER, Mr. COMSTOCK, and Dr. JOHNSON, in Organic Chemistry.

Assistant Professor FOOTE, in Physico-Chemical Measurements, Electro-Chemistry, and Physical Chemistry.

Dr. JAMIESON, in Sanitary Water Analysis.

Assistant Professor FORD, in Mineralogy and Crystallography.

Professor PIRSSON, in Physical Geology and Petrology.

Professor IRVING, in Economic Geology.

Professor HARRISON and Assistant Professor COE, in General Biology, Comparative Anatomy, Embryology, and Cytology.

Dr. WOODRUFF, in General Physiology of the Lower Organisms, and Protozoology.

Dr. COLE, in Invertebrate Zoology.

Dr. KUNKEL, in Organic Evolution.

Professor SCHUCHERT, in Invertebrate Paleontology.

Professor CHITTENDEN, Professor MENDEL, and Assistant Professor UNDERHILL, in Physiology, Physiological Chemistry, and Toxicology.

Professor EVANS and Dr. GRAVES, in Structural and Systematic Botany with special reference to the Microscopic Anatomy of Phanerogamous and Cryptogamous Plants.

Assistant Professor RETTGER, in Bacteriology and Hygiene.

Professor CALLENDER, in Applied Economics.

Professor CROSS, Assistant Professor NETTLETON, Dr. CANBY, and Dr. NICHOLSON, in English Literature.

Professor CORWIN and Assistant Professor GLASCOCK, in the German Language and Literature.

Assistant Professor CLARKE, in French Phonetics and Literature.

Assistant Professor LUQUIENS, in French and Spanish Literature.

Dr. THORSTENBERG, in Swedish.

REQUIREMENTS FOR THE DEGREES OF CIVIL, MECHANICAL, AND MINING ENGINEER

Students who have taken the degree of Bachelor of Philosophy may obtain the degree of CIVIL, MECHANICAL, or MINING ENGINEER at the end of two academical years, by pursuing the following higher courses of study and professional training.   •

THE DEGREE OF CIVIL ENGINEER

The course of study for this degree will comprise :—

1. Scientific Computation, Problems in the Calculus, Harmonic Analysis, each course of one hour per week both terms ; or the equivalent of these courses.
2. Mechanics applied to Engineering.
3. Practical Astronomy, with use of instruments, computations, etc.
4. Construction and Design.
5. Selected subjects in Civil Engineering.
6. Preparation of Theses on special subjects in Engineering.

The course will occupy two years.   During one of these years candidates may, with the consent of the Professor of Civil Engineering, engage in professional practice.

To secure the requisite amount of professional knowledge and practice, the candidate will be required to furnish a comprehensive report of the results of an examination into the existing condition of some special line of
constructive art ; or to present proper evidence that he
has had actual charge in the field, for several months,
of construction or surveying parties, or has held some
responsible position deemed equivalent to this.

A design must also be submitted of some projected
work, based upon data obtained by the candidate, and
comprising all the requisite calculations, and the necessary detailed drawings, accompanied by specifications.

The fee for graduation is five dollars.

THE DEGREE OF MECHANICAL ENGINEER

The course of study for this degree will comprise:—

1. Scientific Computation, Elementary Differential Equations, Problems in the Calculus ; or the equivalent of these courses.
2. Construction of Machines.   Designs.
3. Thermodynamics and Mechanics of Heat Engines.
4. Mechanics of Materials.
5. Preparation of Theses on special subjects in Mechanical Engineering.

The course will occupy two years.   During one of
these, candidates will be permitted to employ such portion
of their time as may be deemed advisable or necessary
in the examination of engineering works and manufacturing establishments, and may also have the privilege of
entering upon professional practice, provided it is done
with the consent of the Professor of Mechanical Engineering, and under such circumstances as shall appear to
him to be favorable to professional progress.

An elaborate thesis on some professional subject, with
an original design, or project, accompanied by proper
working drawings, will be required at the end of the
second year.

The fee for graduation is five dollars.

THE DEGREE OF MINING ENGINEER

The full course for the degree of Mining Engineer consists of three years of undergraduate study and two addi-

tional years of graduate work. A synopsis of the under-graduate work will be found on pp. 240 and 241.

During the two graduate years the course of study will comprise:—

1. Railroad and Mine Surveying.
2. Courses in Mechanical Engineering.
3. Courses in Electrical Engineering.
4. Metallurgy.
5. Selected courses in Geology and Mineralogy.
6. Selected courses in Mining and Ore dressing.
7. Preparation of Thesis.

The student will have the choice in these two years of study of a course in which the emphasis is laid on the general engineering side of mining, thus fitting him especially for mine management ; or of one in which greater stress is laid on geological studies, thus fitting him especially for mine examination or geological survey work. The subjects, however, which form the foundation of a mining education are the same in both alternatives, so that the selection of either will still enable the student to gain a thorough working knowledge of the principles of the other.

The student will be required during a portion of the last year of the course to engage in active professional work with a view to studying methods and gathering material for an original thesis. Such work may consist, if the candidate has selected the engineering alternative, of an apprenticeship in some mine, milling plant or metallurgical works ; or if he has selected the geological alternative, of work upon some geological survey or mine examination.

The fee for graduation is five dollars.

REQUIREMENTS FOR ADMISSION OF SPECIAL STUDENTS

Those students who, being fully qualified, desire to pursue particular studies without reference to the obtaining of a degree, are received in most of the departments of the School as special students ; not, however, in the

Course in Selected Studies in Language, History, and the Natural and Social Sciences, nor in the Freshman class. It should be distinctly understood, however, that these opportunities are designed especially to aid those who, having received a sufficient preliminary education elsewhere, desire to increase their proficiency in special branches.

To gain admission to such a special course of study, it is necessary for the student to show, either by examination or by submitting credentials from other scientific schools or colleges, that he has the preliminary training requisite for the successful pursuit of the course chosen. The plan of studies elected must meet with the approval of the professor in charge of the course. A special student may at any time become a regular student and candidate for a degree, by making up all deficiencies in the requirements for admission and in the required course subjects.

REQUIREMENTS FOR ADMISSION TO THE FRESHMAN CLASS
SUBJECTS OF EXAMINATION*

All candidates for admission to the Freshman class are examined in the following subjects :†

1. *English Grammar*– Whitney's *Essentials of English Grammar*, or an equivalent.
2. *English Literature (A)*.

The candidate should read the books prescribed below with a view to understanding and enjoying them. The examination is designed especially to test the candidate's power of clear and accurate expression, but calls also for a reasonable degree of familiarity with the substance of the books read. The form of the examination is usually the writing of a paragraph or two on each of several topics, to be chosen by the candidate from a considerable number set before him in the examination paper.

The books set for this part of the examination are as follows :

For the preliminary examination in 1907, for the class entering in 1908 : Shakespeare's *Macbeth* and *Merchant of Venice ;* the Sir Roger de Coverley Papers in *The Spectator ;* Irving's *Life of Goldsmith ;*

---

* Specimens of the Examination papers may be obtained of the Registrar.
† Certificates of examination of the College Entrance Examination Board of the Middle States and Maryland are accepted so far as such certificates cover the requirements here set forth. (See p. 224.)

Coleridge's *Ancient Mariner;* Scott's *Ivanhoe* and *Lady of the Lake;* Tennyson's *Gareth and Lynette, Lancelot and Elaine,* and *Passing of Arthur;* Lowell's *Vision of Sir Launfal;* George Eliot's *Silas Marner.*

For the preliminary examination in 1908, for the class entering in 1909: Shakespeare's *Merchant of Venice* and *Julius Cæsar;* Bunyan's *Pilgrim's Progress, Part I;* the Sir Roger de Coverley Papers in *The Spectator;* Scott's *Ivanhoe* and *Lady of the Lake;* Irving's *Sketch Book;* Macaulay's *Lays of Ancient Rome;* Tennyson's *Gareth and Lynette, Lancelot and Elaine,* and *Passing of Arthur;* George Eliot's *Silas Marner.*

For the preliminary examination in 1909, for the class entering in 1910: Shakespeare's *Merchant of Venice* and *Julius Cæsar;* the Sir Roger de Coverley Papers in *The Spectator;* Franklin's *Autobiography;* Scott's *Ivanhoe* and *Lady of the Lake;* either Irving's *Sketch Book* or Hawthorne's *House of the Seven Gables;* Macaulay's *Lays of Ancient Rome;* Tennyson's *Gareth and Lynette, Lancelot and Elaine,* and *Passing of Arthur;* either George Eliot's *Silas Marner* or Dickens's *Tale of Two Cities.*

For the preliminary examination in 1910, for the class entering in 1911: Shakespeare's *Merchant of Venice* and *Julius Cæsar;* the Sir Roger de Coverley Papers in *The Spectator;* either Franklin's *Autobiography* or Goldsmith's *Vicar of Wakefield;* Scott's *Ivanhoe* and *Lady of the Lake;* Hawthorne's *House of the Seven Gables;* Macaulay's *Lays of Ancient Rome;* Tennyson's *Gareth and Lynette, Lancelot and Elaine,* and *Passing of Arthur;* either George Eliot's *Silas Marner* or Dickens's *Tale of Two Cities.*

3. *English Literature (B).*

The candidate should read the books prescribed for this part of the examination with the view of acquiring such knowledge of their contents as will enable him to answer specific questions with accuracy and some detail. The examination tests also the candidate's ability to express his knowledge with clearness and accuracy. It is not designed, however, to acquire minute drill in difficulties of verbal expression, unimportant allusions, or technical details.

The books set for this part of the examination are as follows:

For the final examination in 1908: Shakespeare's *Julius Cæsar;* Milton's *Lycidas, Comus, L'Allegro,* and *Il Penseroso;* Burke's *Speech on Conciliation with America;* Macaulay's *Essay on Addison* and *Life of Johnson.*

For final examinations in 1909, 1910, and 1911: Shakespeare's *Macbeth;* Milton's *Lycidas, Comus, L'Allegro,* and *Il Penseroso;* either Burke's *Speech on Conciliation with America,* or both Washington's *Farewell Address* and Webster's *First Bunker Hill Oration;* either Macaulay's *Life of Johnson* or Carlyle's *Essay on Burns.*

NOTES ON THE ENGLISH REQUIREMENTS.

Preparation in English has two main objects : (1) command of correct and clear English, spoken and written ; (2) power to read with intelligence and appreciation. To secure these ends, training in grammar and the simpler principles of rhetoric, and the writing of frequent compositions, are as essential as the study of the books specified above. After the year 1908 the English (*B*) paper may contain specific questions upon the essentials of English grammar, including ordinary grammatical terminology, inflections, and syntax.

No candidate is accepted in either English (*A*) or English (*B*) whose work is notably defective in point of spelling, capitalization, punctuation, idiom, or division into paragraphs. An entrance condition in English (*A*) is removed only upon evidence of marked improvement in the ability to write English correctly.

For candidates who take the complete examination in English at a single session, this examination covers the books set for the final examination in that year, together with those set for the preliminary examination in the preceding year ; for example, the complete examination in 1908 will cover the books set for the final examination in 1908 together with those set for the preliminary examination in 1907.

The lists in English (*A*) for 1908, 1909, and 1910, for the classes entering in 1909, 1910, and 1911, are selected from the list adopted by the Conference on Uniform Entrance Requirements in English, at a meeting held at Newark, New Jersey, February 22, 1905. Candidates may make other selections from that list, provided they notify the Registrar of the Sheffield Scientific School before February 1 of the calendar year in which the examination is to be held.

4. *History of England*—The student should have some acquaintance with the leading facts of *English History* from the landing of Julius Cæsar (55 B. C.) down to the conclusion of Beaconsfield's ministry (1880). Special attention should be given to incidents from the Norman Conquest onwards. It is recommended that, so far as possible, the attention of the student be directed to the importance not only of the development of English government, but of English industry, and English literature. Montgomery's *Leading Facts of English History*, or an equivalent.

[In view of the importance of a knowledge of the History of England as a preparation for the study of English in Freshman year, no equivalent is accepted for this requirement.]

5. *History of the United States* or *Roman History* or *Greek History*.

In *History of the United States*, a thorough acquaintance is expected with some one of the more recent text-books such as Johnston's *History of the United States*, revised edition,

Montgomery's *Students' American History*, Channing's *Students History of the United States* or McLaughlin's *History of the American Nation.*

In *Greek History* the examination will cover the period to the death of Alexander (323 B. C.). Myers's *A History of Greece*, or Botsford's *History of Greece*, or an equivalent.

In *Roman History* the student should be particularly familiar with the Roman Republic (509 B. C. to the death of Julius Cæsar), though he will be held responsible for some knowledge of the development of the Empire to the death of Augustus (14 A. D.). Myers's *Rome: its Rise and Fall*, or Botsford's *History of Rome*, or an equivalent. In Greek and Roman history the importance of historical geography should not be overlooked.

The examinations in history will be framed to discourage hasty memorizing and to encourage careful preparation at the hands of teachers. Stress should be laid in preparation upon a knowledge of historical geography, and upon a clear understanding of the more salient dates and facts.

6. *Latin Grammar and Composition*—The examination in Latin Grammar will be based on connected passages taken from the first and second books of Cæsar's *Gallic War*. The exercises set for translation from English into Latin will involve the vocabulary and idioms of these two books.

7. *Cæsar* or *Nepos*—The first four books of Cæsar's *Gallic War*.

The first twelve of Nepos's *Lives* as they appear in the Teubner edition, will be accepted as an equivalent for the third and fourth books of Cæsar. For the first and second books of Cæsar no equivalent is accepted.

8. *Virgil* or *Cicero*—The first three books of the *Æneid*. This requirement involves ability to scan Latin hexameters.

Cicero's orations against Catiline and for Archias may be offered in place of Virgil.

In order to allow preparatory schools still further freedom in arranging their courses of work, examination papers will be prepared on other equivalents of the texts mentioned above, provided application for a sufficient number of candidates be made to the Registrar of the Sheffield Scientific School before February 1.

9. *German* or *French*—Candidates will be required to translate at sight simple prose selections from German or French authors, and to have such a knowledge of grammar as will enable them to read the selections intelligently. This implies familiarity with the declensions of nouns, adjectives, and pronouns, with the con-

jugation of verbs, and with the syntax of cases. The ability to translate simple sentences from English into German or French will also be requisite, as well as an intelligible pronunciation of the language offered.

10. *Algebra A, Elementary (through Quadratics)* — The four fundamental operations for rational algebraic expressions; factoring, determination of the highest common factor and least common multiple by factoring; fractions, including complex fractions and ratio and proportion; linear equations both numerical and literal, containing one or more unknown quantities; problems depending on linear equations; radicals, including the extraction of the square root of polynomials and of numbers; exponents, including the fractional and negative. Quadratic equations, both numerical and literal; simple cases of equations with one or more unknown quantities that can be solved by the methods of linear and quadratic equations; problems depending on quadratic equations; binomial theorem for positive integral exponents; formulas for the nth term and the sum of n terms of arithmetical and geometrical progressions, with applications.

11. *Algebra B, Advanced*—Permutations and combinations, limited to simple cases. Numerical equations of higher degree, and so much of the theory of equations with graphical methods as is necessary for their treatment, including Descartes's Rule of Signs and Horner's method, but not Sturm's functions or multiple roots.

A syllabus of the requirement in Advanced Algebra may be obtained from the Treasurer of the Sheffield Scientific School, New Haven, Conn., on payment of ten cents.

It is expected that candidates presenting themselves in Algebra will have covered all the subjects above specified. The examination, however, is especially designed to test the *thoroughness* of the candidate's training and preparation. Those questions, therefore, whose solution involves only the fundamental operations must be worked out rapidly and accurately.

Much time should be devoted to the statement and solution of problems, and the student should be taught the importance of the interpretation and verification of his results.

The required topics in Algebra are adequately treated in *Advanced Algebra* by H. E. Hawkes.

12. *Plane Geometry*—Demonstration of the theorems and constructions contained in any standard text, and solution of original propositions and problems.

The examination in this subject will test not only the candidate's acquaintance with the theorems of any standard text, but also his ability to solve original exercises and problems. Two hours will be allowed for the examination, and it is expected that aptitude will be shown in attacking questions of reasonable difficulty. As much time as possible should be devoted in the student's preparation to originals. The student should learn therefore that knowledge of Geometry means not merely familiarity with propositions proven in the text, but rather the possession of keenness and readiness in space perception as well as the power to reason logically and deductively.

13. *Solid Geometry*—The usual text demonstrations, including the relations of planes and lines in space, the properties and mensuration of prisms, pyramids, cylinders and cones, the sphere and spherical triangle.

In selecting a text-book in Geometry, it is especially important that one be chosen which encourages and develops independent thought and work on the part of the student, and which does not reduce the study of the science to an exercise in memorizing. Knowledge of propositions and constructions is not the only aim of geometric instruction, but training in logical thinking and deductive reasoning as well. The student should acquire power in applying the methods which he has been taught to the solution of original exercises and problems. The examination is intended to test the power of the candidate in this respect, and also his acquaintance with the text.

14. *Trigonometry and Logarithms* — Fundamental definitions, properties and analytical theory of the trigonometric functions, with the usual formulæ ; applications to the solution of simple problems, and, in particular, to the formal solution of plane oblique triangles. Theory and principles of logarithms (without the introduction of work involving infinite series), solution of right and oblique plane triangles, and of numerical problems in Algebra.

Preparation in Trigonometry should include exercises in applying the formulæ to a variety of reductions and transformations, and the solution of trigonometrical equations involving either direct or inverse functions. Of fundamental importance is a thorough drill in the reduction of functions of any angle to functions of an acute angle. Accuracy in results and neatness in the arrangement of computations are insisted upon.

The student should be familiar with the tables furnished at the examination. These are entitled *Four-Place Logarithmic Tables*, and may be obtained from the publishers, Henry Holt

& Company, New York City.   The necessary formulæ for the
solution of plane oblique triangles are given in these tables.

15. *Botany* or *Chemistry* or *Physics*—In *Botany* the requirements include a knowledge of the structure and of the more important
physiological processes of flowering plants, together with matters
pertaining to pollination and the dissemination of seeds.   Leavitt's
Outlines of Botany, or Bergen's *Foundations of Botany*, is recommended as a suitable aid in preparing for the examination.   It
is desirable that the candidate should have had some experience
in the analysis of common flowering plants.

In *Chemistry* the requirement will involve (a) a knowledge of
hydrogen, oxygen, the halogens, sulphur, nitrogen, phosphorus,
arsenic, carbon, silicon, sodium, potassium, ammonium, cal-
cium, barium, magnesium, zinc, mercury, silver, copper, tin,
lead, iron, and aluminium, together with their simple compounds.
This will include ability to describe the occurrence in nature of
such substances, their simple physical properties, the more important or typical chemical changes in which they take part, the
important methods of preparation and a knowledge of the common names ; also, ability to describe accurately the phenomena
observed in experiments and to make deductions from those
observations.

(b) Ability to sketch and describe simple pieces of apparatus
used in the laboratory.

(c) Ability to write equations of simple reactions and to make
calculations of the quantities involved, atomic weights being
supplied ; also, ability to calculate volumes of gases from their
weights or the reverse and to calculate the quantity per unit
volume of a substance in solution from the density and percent-
age composition of the solution.

(d) Familiarity with the fact that elements combine in fixed
ratios or multiples thereof, and a knowledge of the atomic
theory ; also, ability to apply the laws of Boyle, Charles, and
Avogadro and to write equations representing the reactions by
volume of the common gases and vapors.

It is strongly recommended that the preparation for this
requirement should be by a course of class room and laboratory
work in which particular emphasis is laid upon the systematic
study of the elements in natural groups or by the use of Men-
delejeff's classification.   Fundamental principles, such as reduction, oxidation, the reaction of acids, bases, etc., should be
given special attention, and the more important test reactions
should be made familiar.

No candidate will be accepted in this subject unless he has had a laboratory course. Every candidate must attach to his answer paper in chemistry a statement signed by his instructor of the work he has done in this subject.

In *Physics* the examination will be designed to test the candidate's familiarity with the general phenomena of mechanics, sound, light, heat, magnetism, and electricity, and his knowledge of the simpler laws governing these phenomena.

DIVISION OF EXAMINATION

Preliminary Examination—Candidates are allowed to divide the examination between two *successive* years. For the first or *preliminary examination* the candidate may present himself at any regular examination in either June or September and may offer any five or more of the above mentioned subjects. At this examination, each candidate must submit a recommendation from his principal instructor regarding the subjects which he is authorized to offer.*

A *certificate of preliminary examination* will not be granted unless at least five of these subjects have been satisfactorily passed. A preliminary certificate given in June cannot be completed until the following year; but a candidate who has received a preliminary certificate at the June examination may at the next September examination add to the list of subjects credited thereon, provided he present evidence of work done during the summer.

Final Examination—Final candidates, whether presenting themselves for the first time or for completing the credits not included in a certificate of preliminary examination, may take the examinations at any regular session. A final candidate who desires to postpone examination in any subject from June until September should submit with his request the authorization of his principal instructor.

A *final* candidate who has been rejected in June may try the whole examination again in September of the same year.

---

* Blank forms for this purpose will be sent upon application to the Registrar of the Sheffield Scientific School.

Deficiencies—Students are admitted conditionally with certain deficiencies, if their record of examinations is such as to make it appear that they are fitted to pursue the courses of the School successfully. The number of conditions which shall exclude a candidate from admission is not fixed. The record of each candidate is considered with a view to deciding whether his preparation is adequate, and whether the deficiencies are of such a nature as to admit of their being made up within the time allotted. All deficiencies in subjects required for admission must be made up before the student is allowed to enter upon the work of the second (Junior) year.

Testimonials—Candidates for final examinations must present satisfactory testimonials of character and scholarship, covering the whole of the school year preceding the examination. Students from other colleges must present certificates of dismissal in good standing.*

Age—No one is admitted to the Freshman class who is less than sixteen years of age.

TIME AND PLACES OF EXAMINATION

Two regular examination sessions are held each year,— the first, at the close of the college year in June; the second, at the beginning of the college year in September.

In 1908, the first (or June) session will be held on Thursday, Friday and Saturday, June 25, 26, and 27. Attendance, for the purpose of registration, is required at the opening of the session at 8.30 A. M.

In June, 1908, examinations (for the Freshman class only) will be held at the places mentioned on pp. 88–89.

Candidates who propose to present themselves for examination elsewhere than in New Haven are requested to send their names to the Registrar of the School, before May 15.

The School is prepared to hold examinations for entrance, at the above-named time, in any city or at any school

* Blank forms for this purpose will be sent upon application to the Registrar of the Sheffield Scientific School.

where the numbers of candidates and the distance from other places of examination may warrant it.   Applications for this purpose must be sent to the Registrar before May 15.

Fee—A fee of five dollars, payable at the opening of the session at the place of examination, is charged for admission to all examinations (whether complete or partial) held outside of New Haven.

The second (or September) examinations in 1908 will be held in New Haven only, on Monday, Tuesday, and Wednesday, September 21, 22, and 23.   Candidates should present themselves for registration before their first examination.

In general, examinations for admission to the incoming Freshman class can be held only in June and September as specified; if in any case sufficient reason exists for an exception to this rule, a special fee (not exceeding fifty dollars) will be charged.

ADMISSION THROUGH EXAMINATIONS OF THE COLLEGE ENTRANCE EXAMINATION BOARD

Candidates for admission to the Sheffield Scientific School may meet the entrance requirements by passing with satisfactory grades the equivalent subjects in the examinations set by the College Entrance Board and by presenting the Board certificates for credit.   The Sheffield Scientific School requirements are given below, and opposite are placed the subjects in the Board examination which may be offered as substitutes.

SHEFFIELD SCIENTIFIC SCHOOL	COLLEGE ENTRANCE EXAMINATION BOARD
English Grammar*	
English Lit. A (Reading and Practice)	Reading and Practice
English Lit. B (Study and Practice)	Study and Practice .
History of England	English History
History of U. S., or Roman History, or Greek History	American History, or Mediæval and Modern European History, or Ancient History
Latin Grammar and Composition	Grammar Elementary Prose Comp.
Cæsar	Cæsar
Virgil, or Cicero	Virgil's Æneid, or Cicero
German, or French	Elementary German, or Elementary French
Chemistry	Chemistry
Botany	Botany
Physics	Physics
Algebra A	Algebra I, II
Algebra B	Advanced Algebra
Plane Geometry	Plane Geometry
Solid Geometry	Solid Geometry
Trigonometry and Logarithms	Plane Trigonometry

Board certificates should be sent to the Registrar of the Sheffield Scientific School, New Haven, Conn., so that the credits obtained may be recorded.

Requests for blank applications for admission to the Board examinations should be sent to the Secretary of the College Entrance Examination Board, Sub-station 84, New York, N. Y.

REQUIREMENTS FOR ADVANCED STANDING

All candidates for advanced standing are examined in the subjects required for admission as well as in the studies already pursued by the class which they wish to enter, except where satisfactory credits, covering the required subjects, are presented from some other university or college of good standing. No candidate for a degree is admitted later than the beginning of the Senior year.†

* In case the candidate passes the C. E. E. B. examinations in English, the Sheffield Scientific School examination in English Grammar will be waived.

† Blank forms of application for advanced standing will be sent upon request by the Registrar of the Sheffield Scientific School.

INSTRUCTION
FOR UNDERGRADUATE STUDENTS
COURSES OF INSTRUCTION

Courses of instruction, occupying three years, are arranged to suit the requirements of various classes of students. The work of the first year is a general preparation for the advanced and special work of the later courses. The instruction of this year has a general scientific basis of mathematics, chemistry, and physics. In addition to these studies special attention is given to English and the modern languages. For the later years, the instruction is chiefly arranged in Special Courses. Modern languages are, however, studied by all students, irrespective of the special course which they may elect. Either French or German is offered as a requisite for admission by each student. The language taken in the entrance examinations is continued through Freshman and Junior years, while the other language is begun in Junior year and continued through Senior year. Opportunity is also afforded for the study of Spanish.

The Courses of study most distinctly marked out are :

    I. Chemistry ;
    II. Chemistry preparatory to Metallurgy ;
    III. Civil Engineering ;
    IV. Mechanical Engineering ;
    V. Electrical Engineering ;
    VI. Municipal and Sanitary Engineering ;
    VII. Engineering preparatory to Mining ;
    VIII. Zoology and Botany ;
    IX. Mineralogy and other Studies preparatory to Geology ;
    X. Biology preparatory to Medical Studies ;
    XI. Selected Studies in Language, Literature, History, and the Natural and Social Sciences.
    XII. Studies preparatory to the Study of Forestry.
    XIII. Mathematics, Pure and Applied.

A fuller statement of the methods and character of the instruction will be found under SUBJECTS OF INSTRUCTION, pp. 254 to 283.

15

FRESHMAN YEAR: INTRODUCTORY TO ALL COURSES

CHOICE OF COURSE

The class is divided into two groups at the opening of the year. *Students are expected to indicate upon their registration blanks which group they intend to enter.* The groups are :—

THE ENGINEERING SCIENCE GROUP, preparatory to the courses in
> Civil Engineering
> Mechanical Engineering
> Municipal and Sanitary Engineering
> Electrical Engineering
> Engineering preparatory to Mining
> Mathematics, Pure and Applied

THE NATURAL SCIENCE GROUP, preparatory to the courses in
> Chemistry*
> Chemistry preparatory to Metallurgy*
> Biology preparatory to Medical Studies
> Zoology and Botany
> Mineralogy and other Studies preparatory to Geology
> Selected Studies in Language, Literature, History, and the Natural and Social Sciences
> Studies preparatory to the Study of Forestry

The *final choice of course* within the two groups must be made immediately after the Easter recess. The purpose of the division of the Freshman class into two general groups is to permit a suitable preparation for the work of the special courses. With this in view, the students electing the Engineering Group pursue such studies in Mathematics as are demanded by the advanced mathematical studies of the engineering courses. Students in the Natural Science Group pursue a briefer course of a more general nature, including Elementary Calculus, designed to complete their general training. In place of part of the Mathematics and Mechanical Drawing required of the candidates for the engineering courses, the students in the Natural Science Group receive instruction in General Biology in a course especially planned to meet the needs of the general student of science and

---

* Students intending to enter the courses in Chemistry or Metallurgy in Junior year may elect either group.

literature, and intended to contribute to a broad culture, rather than a specialized training.

The arrangement of studies in Freshman year is indicated in the annexed scheme. Unless otherwise specified, the number of hours given means hours per week.

INSTRUCTORS

In Mathematics : Professor P. F. SMITH, Assistant Professor MASON, Dr. GRANVILLE, Dr. HEWES, Dr. W. R. LONGLEY, and assistants.

In Physics : Professor HASTINGS, Assistant Professor BEACH, Dr. COOPER, and assistants.

In Chemistry : Professor MIXTER, Assistant Professor WALDEN, Dr. MATHEWSON, Dr. JOHNS, and assistants.

In English : Professor CROSS, Assistant Professor NETTLETON, Dr. CANBY, Dr. NICHOLSON, Mr. PIERCE, and Mr. DURHAM.

In Foreign Languages : Professor CORWIN, Assistant Professors CLARKE and GLASCOCK, Dr. THORSTENBERG, Dr. GARVER, Dr. CURTS, Mr. ROBBINS, Mr. J. P. RICE, and Mr. LOVELL.

In Free-hand Drawing : Professor NIEMEYER, Mr. LANGZETTEL, and Mr. THOMPSON.

In Mechanical Drawing : Mr. NORTH and assistants.

In Biology : Professors HARRISON, EVANS, Assistant Professors COE, RETTGER, Dr. KUNKEL, Dr. WOODRUFF, and assistants.

SCHEME OF STUDIES
ENGINEERING SCIENCE GROUP

FIRST TERM :—

> *German* or *French*—3 hrs.
>
> *Mathematics*—Plane Analytical Geometry, 3 hrs.
>
> *Physics*—Recitations, 2 hrs.; Experimental lectures, 2 hrs.
>
> *Chemistry*—Recitations, 2 hrs.; Lectures and laboratory work, 3 hrs. for division A. Qualitative Analysis, recitation, 1 hr. ; Lectures and laboratory work, 5 hrs. for division B.
>
> *English*—Shakespeare, 2 hrs.
>
> *Free-hand Drawing*—Practical lessons in the Art School, 3 hrs.

SECOND TERM :—

> *German* or *French*—3 hrs.
>
> *Physics*—Recitations, 2 hrs.; Experimental lectures, 2 hrs.
>
> *Chemistry*—Recitations, 2 hrs.; Lectures and laboratory work, 2 hrs. for division A. Qualitative Analysis, recitation, 1 hr.; Lectures and laboratory work, 5 hrs. for division B.

Mathematics—Plane Analytical Geometry, continued, 3 hrs. Winter half-term.   Analytic Geometry of Space, 3 hrs. Spring half-term.

English—Nineteenth Century Literature, 2 hrs.

Drawing—Principles of Orthographic, Isometric, and Cabinet Projection ; Intersection and Development of Surfaces, 3 hrs.

NATURAL SCIENCE GROUP

FIRST TERM :—

German or *French*—3 hrs.

Mathematics—Analytics and Calculus, 3 hrs.

Physics—Recitations, 2 hrs. ; Experimental Lectures, 2 hrs.

Chemistry—Recitations, 2 hrs. ; Lectures and laboratory work, 2 hrs, for division A.   Qualitative Analysis, recitation, 1 hr.; Lectures and laboratory work, 5 hrs. for division B.

English—Shakespeare, 2 hrs.

Free-hand Drawing—Practical Lessons in the Art School, 3 hrs.

SECOND TERM :—

German or *French*—3 hrs.

Mathematics—Elementary Calculus, 3 hrs. Winter half-term.

Physics—Recitations, 2 hrs. ; Experimental Lectures, 2 hrs.

Chemistry—Recitations, 2 hrs.; Lectures and laboratory work, 3 hrs. for division A.   Qualitative Analysis, recitations, 1 hr. ; Lectures and laboratory work, 5 hrs. for division B.

English—Nineteenth Century Literature, 2 hrs.

Biology—Laboratory, 4 hrs.; Lectures, 1 hr.

Drawing—Principles of Orthographic Projection, 3 hrs. Spring half-term.

At the beginning of the second term an honor section is formed in the Freshman class, consisting of all students whose scholarship during the Fall term has been exceptionally high.   An opportunity is thus afforded for the more proficient to make rapid progress in their studies.

Particular attention is called to the fact that the field work in Surveying for the Junior year begins on the first Monday in September of each year.*

INSTRUCTION IN JUNIOR AND SENIOR YEARS

The aims and scope of the Special Courses in which the instruction is arranged for the Junior and Senior years, are outlined below.   More detailed information regarding the character of the instruction offered will be found under SUBJECTS OF INSTRUCTION, pp. 254 to 283.

---

* In 1908 the Surveying for the Junior year will begin on Monday, August 31.

I. CHEMISTRY

Professors WELLS, PIRSSON ; Assistant Professors H. L. WHEELER, FOOTE, FORD ; Mr. COMSTOCK, Dr. JOHNSON, Dr. JAMIESON, Dr. MATHEWSON, and assistants.

The aim of the instruction in this course is to provide a training which will serve as a basis for a career in any branch of pure or applied chemistry. With this end in view, the general and fundamental principles of the science receive much attention, in the belief that exact scientific knowledge is preferable to mere drill in the practical applications of the subject, since the principles can always be used, while the details of practice are continually changing.

The practical side of the science is not neglected in the course, for much instruction is given in such branches as can be profitably studied in the laboratory. In analytical chemistry—both qualitative and quantitative—much time is devoted to the attainment of skill in manipulation and a knowledge of the more important methods used in practical work. Likewise, much of the laboratory work in organic and inorganic preparations is so chosen as to illustrate important technical operations. In these and in other practical courses particular attention is paid to the scientific principles involved in the operations.

The more theoretical studies of the course are dealt with by recitations and lectures in organic chemistry, general and theoretical chemistry, physical chemistry and chemical calculations. Most of these subjects are introductory to laboratory work, or are carried on in connection with it.

The course gives an opportunity for specializing in several branches, such as in the analysis of food-products, sanitary water analysis, and physico-chemical laboratory work. It includes also the study of metallurgy, considered chiefly from a chemical standpoint, as well as a course in applied chemistry.

Students who have pursued this course successfully will obtain a good foundation of knowledge in several important branches of chemistry. They will be able to‐undertake work in teaching the subject and in practical analytical chemistry ; and they will be well equipped to master rapidly the principles of operations connected with chemical manufacturing.

A more detailed description of the subjects of instruction in this course is given on pp. 259 to 262.

SCHEME OF STUDIES

JUNIOR YEAR :

FIRST TERM :—

Organic Chemistry—Lectures and recitations, 3 hrs.

Qualitative Analysis—Recitations and lectures, 4 hrs. ; Laboratory work, 13 hrs.

Determinative Mineralogy—3 hrs.

English Composition—1 hr.

German—3 hrs.

French—3 hrs.

SECOND TERM :—

Organic Chemistry—Lectures and recitations, 1 hr.; Laboratory work, 6 hrs. Winter half-term ; Lectures and recitations, 3 hrs. Spring half-term.

Quantitative Analysis (Gravimetric)—Laboratory work, 14 hrs. ; Lectures and recitations, 1 hr.

Chemical Calculations—1 hr.

Determinative Mineralogy—3 hrs.

Crystallography and Descriptive Mineralogy—Lectures, 2 hrs.

English Composition—1 hr.

German—3 hrs.

French—3 hrs.

SENIOR YEAR :

FIRST TERM :—

Applied Chemistry—Lectures and recitations, 2 hrs.

General and Theoretical Chemistry—Recitations, 3 hrs.

Quantitative Analysis (Volumetric)—Laboratory work, 14 hrs.; Lectures and recitations, 1 hr.

Chemical Calculations—1 hr.

Geology—Recitations, 3 hrs.

Mineralogy—(optional).

French or *German*—3 hrs.

SECOND TERM :—

Physical Chemistry—Recitations, 3 hrs.

Inorganic Preparations followed by *Organic Preparations*—Laboratory work, 14 hrs. ; Recitations, 1 hr. [Optional : *Proxi-*

mate Analysis of Vegetable and Animal Products ; Physico-Chemical Measurements ; or Sanitary Water Analysis—14 hrs. for part of term.]

Metallurgy, Assaying, and Gas Analysis—3 hrs.

Historical Geology—3 hrs. Winter half-term.

Economic Geology—3 hrs. Spring half-term.

Mineralogy (optional).

Elementary Petrology—Lectures (optional), 1 hr.

French or *German*—3 hrs.

II. CHEMISTRY PREPARATORY TO METALLURGY

Professors WELLS, PIRSSON, IRVING ; Assistant Professors MARSHALL, HUNTOON, FOOTE, TRACY, FORD; Dr. JOHNSON, Dr. JAMIESON, Dr. MATHEWSON, and assistants.

This course is related to that in Chemistry and is intended to provide a training suitable for an understanding of metallurgical operations, particularly from a chemical point of view. Drawing, ore dressing, metallurgical analysis, and a more elaborate course in assaying are taken up in the place of organic chemistry. A course in surveying is also required.

The quantitative chemical analysis given in this course is particularly extensive, since it includes that of the course in chemistry, and also additional work in the analysis of ores, furnace products, etc. The same attention to theoretical principles is given here as in the course in chemistry, and the same instruction is given in general and theoretical chemistry, physical chemistry and chemical calculations, as in that course.

The graduate of this course should be competent to undertake work as a metallurgical chemist or assayer, and he should be in a position to master quickly the details of any metallurgical operation. Those who are desirous of obtaining a more intimate knowledge of the closely related subject of mining, as an aid in a metallurgical career, are advised to pursue a year of graduate work in studies relating to mining.

A more detailed description of the subjects of instruction in this course is given on pp. 259 to 262.

SCHEME OF STUDIES
JUNIOR YEAR :

FIRST TERM :—

Surveying—Field work, 3 weeks, beginning Monday, August 31, in 1908.

Surveying—Office work ; Mapping and Calculations, 4 hrs.

Qualitative Chemical Analysis—Laboratory work, 13 hrs.; Lectures and recitations, 4 hrs.

Determinative Mineralogy—3 hrs.

English Composition—1 hr.

French—3 hrs.

German—3 hrs.

SECOND TERM :—

Quantitative Analysis (Gravimetric)—Laboratory work, 14 hrs.; Lectures and recitations, 1 hr.

Chemical Calculations—1 hr.

Determinative Mineralogy—3 hrs.

Crystallography and Descriptive Mineralogy—Lectures, 2 hrs.

Descriptive Geometry and Drawing—3 hrs.

English Composition—1 hr.

French—3 hrs.

German—3 hrs.

SENIOR YEAR :

FIRST TERM :—

Volumetric Chemical Analysis—Laboratory work, 14 hrs.; Lectures and recitations, 1 hr.

Chemical Calculations—1 hr.

General Chemistry—3 hrs.

Ore Dressing—2 hrs.

Geology—3 hrs.

Mineralogy (optional).

French or *German*—3 hrs.

SECOND TERM :—

Inorganic Preparations and *Physico-Chemical Measurements*, followed by *Assaying* and *Metallurgical Analysis*—14 hrs.

Metallurgy, followed by *Gas Analysis*—3 hrs.

Historical Geology—3 hrs. Winter half-term.

Economic Geology—3 hrs. Spring half-term.

Ore Dressing—2 hrs.

Petrology—1 hr. Winter half-term.

Physical and Electro-Chemistry—3 hrs.

Mineralogy (optional).

French or *German*—3 hrs.

III. CIVIL ENGINEERING

Professors DuBois, Pirsson, P. F. Smith ; Assistant Professors Barney, Tracy, Marshall, Ford, Mason, Rettger ; Dr. Granville, Dr. Hewes, Dr. Longley, Mr. Farnham, Mr. Kirby, and assistants.

The object of this course is to give, first of all, a thorough preparation in the principles of the various sciences involved, and afterwards, as extensive practice in the application of those principles as the time at disposal, the ability of the students, and the facilities and plant permit.

Under the first head are included such subjects as mathematics, physics, mechanics, thermodynamics, astronomy, geology, mineralogy, and chemistry; and under the second head, drawing, surveying, strength and properties of materials, and designs and construction of various kinds, such as bridges, roofs, foundations, arches, retaining walls, dams, water works, railroads, improvement of rivers and harbors, sewerage and drainage, motors, hydraulics and sanitary engineering.

The first division includes Civil Engineering as a Science, the other, Civil Engineering as an Art. The ground covered by the first is definite, and the instruction is made as thorough as possible. The ground covered by the second is of almost indefinite extent. Here, by a careful selection of practical examples, such as occur in engineering practice, the application of principles is illustrated, and together with the analytical or algebraic methods, the student is also instructed in practical graphic solutions, wherever such solutions present a special value. Much time is devoted to geodetic operations and to surveying in the field.

The method of teaching is by means of practical exercises, lectures, and recitations, so combined as to develop as far as possible the mental powers of the student. Visits of inspection are made at suitable intervals to private and public works of engineering interest.

The entire course requires five years, three years of undergraduate and two of graduate instruction ; and a thesis of merit upon some approved subject, accompanied by designs and estimates, is required upon the completion of the course.

The requirements for the degree of CIVIL ENGINEER will be found on pp. 211 and 212. A more detailed description of the subjects of instruction in this course is given on pp. 263 and 264.

SCHEME OF STUDIES

JUNIOR YEAR:

FIRST TERM :—

Surveying—Field work, 3 weeks, beginning Monday, August 31, in 1908.

Mathematics—Differential Calculus, with applications to Geometry and Analysis, 5 hrs.

Descriptive Geometry—6 hrs.

Spherical Trigonometry—2 hrs.

Determinative Mineralogy—3 hrs.

English Composition—1 hr.

German—3 hrs.

French—3 hrs.

SECOND TERM :—

Mathematics—Integral Calculus with applications to Geometry, 5 hrs. Winter half-term. Theoretical Mechanics—5 hrs. Spring half-term.

Surveying—Office work; Mapping and Calculations, 5 hrs. Winter half-term.

Drawing—Bridge details, 6 hrs. Spring half-term.

Mapping and Lettering—4 hrs. Winter half-term.

Railway Engineering—Curves, earthwork, economic location, 4 hrs.

Determinative Mineralogy—3 hrs. Winter half-term.

English Composition—1 hr.

German—3 hrs.

French—3 hrs.

SENIOR YEAR:

FIRST TERM :—

Field Engineering—Location of line of Railroad; three weeks in June and July.

Office Work—Mapping; calculation of earthwork, 5 hrs.

Mechanics—Statics, Kinematics, Kinetics, 3 hrs.

Civil Engineering—Mechanics applied to Engineering; Strength of Materials; Bridges and Roofs; 4 hrs.

Roads and Pavements—Lectures, 1 hr.

Adjustment of Observations—3 hrs.

Public Hygiene and Bacteriology (optional)—1 hr.

Geology—Recitations, 3 hrs.

French or *German*—3 hrs.

SECOND TERM :—

Civil Engineering—Bridges and Roofs; Building Materials; Stability of Arches and Walls; Foundations; 4 hrs.

Railroad Economics—Lectures, 2 hrs. Winter half-term.

Mechanics—Applied Mechanics, 4 hrs. Winter half-term.

Hydraulics—Hydraulics and Hydraulic Motors, 3 hrs. Spring half-term.

Designing—Practical Problems; Specifications and Estimates; 7 hrs. after February 15.

Forest Hydrography—Lectures (optional), 4 to 6 in number during Spring half-term.

Specifications—1 hr. Spring half-term (optional).

Astronomy—Practical Astronomy, with field work, 3 hrs.

Geology—3 hrs. until February 15.

Elementary Petrology—Lectures (optional), 1 hr.

French or *German*—3 hrs.

IV. MECHANICAL ENGINEERING

Professors RICHARDS, P. F. SMITH; Assistant Professors LOCKWOOD, MARSHALL, MASON, FORD; Dr. GRANVILLE, Dr. LONGLEY, Dr. SHEPARD, Dr. HEWES, Mr. LILLEY, Mr. NORTH, and assistants.

The objects aimed at in the plan of instruction in this course are, to give the student a thorough training in elementary and advanced mathematics and physics, and their application to the science of construction; to make him familiar with the general principles of Engineering and, as far as possible, with the practical details of mechanical construction through which these principles are made useful; and to enable him ultimately, in beginning the work of his profession, to bring to bear upon it a well-balanced store of theoretical knowledge, and a mind trained in correct habits of thought and work.

The complete course covers five years, three of which are spent in undergraduate study, and two in a graduate course, a portion of which may be given to actual practical work. A more detailed description of the subjects of instruction in this course is given on pp. 264 to 266. The requirements for the degree of MECHANICAL ENGINEER are given on p. 212.

SCHEME OF STUDIES

JUNIOR YEAR :

FIRST TERM :—

> *Mathematics*—Differential Calculus, 5 hrs.
> *Thermodynamics*—2 hrs.
> *Principles of Mechanism*—2 hrs.
> *Descriptive Geometry*—3 hrs.
> *English Composition*—1 hr.
> *German*—3 hrs.
> *French*—3 hrs.

SECOND TERM :—

> *Mathematics*—Integral Calculus, 5 hrs. Winter half-term ; Theoretical Mechanics, 5 hrs. Spring half-term.
> *Shop-Visiting*—1¾ hrs.
> *Thermodynamics*—2 hrs. until about March 20.
> *Applied Mechanics*—2 hrs. after March 20.
> *Drawing*—3 hrs.
> *English Composition*—1 hr.
> *German*—3 hrs.
> *French*—3 hrs.

·SENIOR YEAR :

FIRST TERM :—

> *Mechanics*—3 hrs.
> *Steam Engineering*—4 hrs.
> *Strength of Materials*—2 hrs.
> *Machine. Designing*—7 hrs.
> *Determinative Mineralogy* (optional)—3 hrs.
> *French* or *German*—3 hrs.

SECOND TERM :—

> *Mechanics*—continued, 3 hrs.
> *Steam Engineering*—continued until about March, 3 hrs.
> *Stresses in Structures*—3 hrs. after February.
> *Hydrostatics and Hydrodynamics*—3 hrs.
> *Machine Designing*—continued, 7 hrs.
> *French* or *German*—3 hrs.
> *Determinative Mineralogy* (optional)—3 hrs.

V. ELECTRICAL ENGINEERING

Professors HASTINGS, P. F. SMITH ; Assistant Professors BEACH, · L. P. WHEELER, MARSHALL, MASON ; Dr. GRANVILLE, Dr. C. B. RICE, Dr. HEWES, Dr. LONGLEY, Dr. DADOURIAN, Dr. COOPER, and assistants.

The aim of this course is to impart a sound knowledge of the extensive theories which form the scientific basis of applied electricity, rather than a familiarity with the ever-changing practice of the manufacturers of electrical machinery. A more detailed description of the method pursued and the subjects of instruction appear on pp. 268 to 270.

SCHEME OF STUDIES

JUNIOR YEAR:

FIRST TERM :—

Mathematics—Differential Calculus, with applications to Geometry and Analysis, 5 hrs.

Theory of Heat—3 hrs.

Descriptive Geometry—3 hrs.

Mechanism—2 hrs.

English Composition—1 hr.

German—3 hrs.

French—3 hrs.

SECOND TERM :—

Mathematics—Integral Calculus, with applications to Geometry, 5 hrs. Winter half-term ; Theoretical Mechanics, 5 hrs. Spring half-term.

Theory of Heat, followed by *Theory of Electricity*—3 hrs.

Descriptive Geometry and *Drawing*—3 hrs.

Analytical Mechanics—3 hrs.

English Composition—1 hr.

German—3 hrs.

French—3 hrs.

SENIOR YEAR:

FIRST TERM :—

Theory of Physical Instruments and Measurements—5 hrs.

Laboratory Work—6 hrs.

Machine Designing—6 hrs.

Steam Engine—2 hrs.

Shop-Visiting—2 hrs.

French or *German*—3 hrs.

SECOND TERM :—

Theory of Electricity—5 hrs.

Laboratory Work—6 hrs.

Dynamo Construction—3 hrs.

Machine Designing—6 hrs.

Steam Engine—2 hrs.

French or *German*—3 hrs.

VI. MUNICIPAL AND SANITARY ENGINEERING

Professors DuBois, Pirsson, P. F. Smith, H. E. Smith; Assistant
Professors Barney, Tracy, Mason, Rettger ; Mr. Farnham,
Mr. Kirby, Dr. Granville, Dr. Hewes, Dr. Longley, Dr.
Woodruff, and assistants.

The object of this course is to afford a training for
students who wish to devote attention especially to those
branches of Civil Engineering that concern the public
health and convenience, such as Water Supply, Sewerage
and Pavements, with due regard to both the engineering
and economic features involved.   This calls first of all for
a thorough training in the general principles of the various
sciences, the applications of which constitute the art of
Civil Engineering; second, for a sufficient knowledge of
Chemistry and Bacteriology and their relations to those
engineering problems dealing with sanitation, to enable
the engineer to design the various municipal works with
due regard to their effect upon the public health.

In the course of study outlined below it is the aim in
each subject first to give as thorough a preparation in the
principles involved as the time at command will allow,
before illustrating their use in applied engineering by
means of carefully selected examples.   The instruction is
intended, above all, to develop in the student that mental
power which will enable him, in the future, to design engineering works, to meet satisfactorily the constantly varying conditions of practice, and to gain the ability to present
his work to the consideration of others in a clear and con-
vincing manner.   The method of teaching is by means of
recitations, lectures and practical exercises, supplemented
by visits to works of engineering and sanitary interest.

A more detailed description of the subjects of instruction in this course is given on pp. 266 to 268.

SCHEME OF STUDIES
JUNIOR YEAR:
First Term :—
>   *Surveying*—Field work, 3 weeks, beginning Monday, August 31,
>   in 1908.

Mathematics—Differential Calculus, with applications to Geometry, Kinematics, and Analysis, 5 hrs.

Spherical Trigonometry—2 hrs.

Cement Testing—2 hrs.

Descriptive Geometry—6 hrs.

English Composition—1 hr.

German—3 hrs.

French—3 hrs.

SECOND TERM :—

Mathematics—Integral Calculus with applications to Geometry, 5 hrs. Winter half-term ; Theoretical Mechanics, 5 hrs. Spring half-term.

Surveying—Office work ; Mapping and calculations, 5 hrs. Winter half-term.

Drawing—Bridge details, 4 hrs. Spring half-term.

Masonry Construction—2 hrs. Winter half-term.

Railway Engineering—3 hrs. Winter half-term.

Hydraulics—3 hrs. Spring half-term.

English Composition—1 hr.

German—3 hrs.

French—3 hrs.

SENIOR YEAR :

FIRST TERM :—

Field Engineering—Topographical and Hydrographical Surveying, three weeks in June and July.

Office Work—Calculations and mapping, 5 hrs.

Water-Supply Engineering—3 hrs.

Mechanics—3 hrs.

Stresses—4 hrs.

Adjustment of Observations—3 hrs.

Roads and Pavements—1 hr.

Public Hygiene and Bacteriology (optional)—1 hr.

Physical Geology—3 hrs.

German or *French*—3 hrs.

SECOND TERM :—

Stresses—Bridges and Roofs, 4 hrs. to February 15.

Designing—Roofs and Bridges, 5 hrs. after February 15.

Sewer Design and Construction—3 hrs. Winter half-term.

Chemistry—Water Analysis, 7 hrs. Winter half-term.

Bacteriology—6 hrs. Spring half-term.

Sewage Disposal—3 hrs. Spring half-term.

Practical Astronomy—3 hrs.

Specifications—1 hr. Spring half-term.

Water Supply and Drainage of Modern Buildings—1 hr. Spring half-term.

Interpretation of Water Analysis—1 hr. Spring half-term.

General Physiology of the Lower Organisms (optional)—2 hrs.

German or *French*—3 hrs.

VII. ENGINEERING PREPARATORY TO MINING

Professors RICHARDS, IRVING, PIRSSON, P. F. SMITH ; Assistant Professors HUNTOON, LOCKWOOD, MARSHALL, FORD, BARNEY, TRACY, MASON ; Dr. GRANVILLE, Dr. HEWES, Dr. LONGLEY, Mr. ROE, and assistants.

This undergraduate course consists largely of studies in mathematics and in several lines of civil and mechanical engineering, and aims to give the student a satisfactory basis for a training in mining. Considerable attention is paid to qualitative and quantitative chemical analysis, mineralogy and crystallography during the Junior year, while the subjects of geology, petrology, ore deposits, ore dressing, and assaying are taken in the Senior year.

A graduate course of two years in advanced work in geology, mineralogy, ore dressing, and chemical, metallurgical, and mining subjects is desirable for those who wish to acquire a broad education in mining. A complete course (covering five years with inclusion of those spent in undergraduate study) is arranged to lead to the degree of MINING ENGINEER. The requirements for this degree are given on pp. 212 and 213.

A more detailed description of the subjects of instruction in this course is given on pp. 270 and 271.

SCHEME OF STUDIES
JUNIOR YEAR :

FIRST TERM :—

Surveying—Field work, 3 weeks, beginning Monday, August 31, in 1908.

Surveying—Office work ; Mapping and calculations, 4 hrs.

Qualitative Chemical Analysis—Laboratory work, 13 hrs.; Lectures and recitations, 4 hours.

Calculus—2 hrs.

Determinative Mineralogy—Laboratory work, 3 hrs.

English Composition—1 hr.

German—3 hrs.

French—3 hrs.

SECOND TERM :—

Quantitative Analysis (Gravimetric and Volumetric)—Laboratory work, 14 hrs.; Lectures and recitations, 1 hr.

Chemical Calculations—1 hr.

Calculus—2 hrs.

Descriptive Geometry—3 hrs.

Determinative Mineralogy—3 hrs.

Crystallography and Descriptive Mineralogy—2 hrs.

English Composition—1 hr.

French—3 hrs.

German—3 hrs.

SENIOR YEAR :

FIRST TERM :—

Surveying—Field work, 3 weeks in June and July.

Mapping—4 hrs.

Assaying and Ore Dressing—Laboratory work, 9 hrs.; Lecture on Assaying, 1 hr.

Mechanics—3 hrs.

Strength of Materials—2 hrs.

Machine Designing—4 hrs.

Ore Dressing—Lectures, 2 hrs.

Geology—3 hrs.

Mineralogy (optional).

French or *German*—3 hrs.

SECOND TERM :—

Assaying and Ore Dressing (until March)—Laboratory work, 9 hrs.; Lecture on Assaying, 1 hr.

Mechanics—3 hrs.

Stresses in Structures—3 hrs. after February.

Hydraulics—3 hrs.

Machine Designing—6 hrs.

Ore Dressing—Lectures, 2 hrs.

Historical Geology—3 hrs. Winter half-term.

Economic Geology—3 hrs. Spring half-term

Petrology—1 hr. Winter half-term.

Mineralogy (optional).

French or *German*—3 hrs.

VIII. ZOOLOGY AND BOTANY

Professors CHITTENDEN, PIRSSON, EVANS, WELLS, SCHUCHERT, HARRISON, GREGORY; Assistant Professors COE, UNDERHILL, FOOTE, FORD, RETTGER; Mr. COMSTOCK, Dr. COLE, Dr. KUNKEL, Dr. WOODRUFF, Dr. A. H. GRAVES, and assistants.

This course aims to prepare students for the work of teaching or investigation in zoology and botany, and may be introductory to advanced work in paleontology. Either zoology or botany may be made the principal laboratory study, as indicated in the scheme where two alternative sets of hours are given in the same subject.

By means of lectures and laboratory work the students are taught the structures of typical animals and plants and the principles of classification, together with the more important phenomena of animal and plant physiology and the relations of organisms to environment. The special methods employed in the study of organisms and in the collection and preparation of objects for microscopical study and dissections are considered. When sufficient proficiency is ˙shown by students, opportunity will be given for the investigation of original problems in zoology or botany, in connection with which the extensive collections of the University are available.

Details regarding the studies of this course are given under SUBJECTS OF INSTRUCTION, pp. 273 and 275.

SCHEME OF STUDIES

JUNIOR YEAR:

FIRST TERM :—

> *Qualitative Analysis*—Recitations and lectures, 4 hrs.; Laboratory work, 13 hrs.
> *Determinative Mineralogy*—3 hrs.
> *Elementary Botany*—Lectures and laboratory work, 3 hrs.
> *Physical Geography*—4 hrs.
> *Physiology*—1 hr.
> *English Composition*—1 hr.
> *German*—3 hrs.
> *French*—3 hrs.

SECOND TERM :—

> *Zoology* (for those specializing in the subject)—Laboratory work, recitations and lectures, 15 hrs.; Excursions (land and marine).
> *Elementary Botany*—Lectures and laboratory work, 4 hrs. or 15 hrs.
> *Physiology*—1 hr.
> *Determinative Mineralogy*—3 hrs. Winter half-term.

English Composition—1 hr.
German—3 hrs.
French—3 hrs.

SENIOR YEAR:

FIRST TERM :—

Zoology—Laboratory work, lectures, and recitations, 3 hrs. or 15, hrs.; Excursions.

Embryology—Lectures and demonstrations, 4 hrs.

Morbhology of Plants—Lectures and laboratory work, 4 hrs. or 15 hrs.

Geology—Recitations, 3 hrs.

French or *German*—3 hrs.

SECOND TERM :—

Zoology—Laboratory work, recitations and lectures, 4 hrs. or 15 hrs.

Morphology of Plants—Lectures and laboratory work, 4 hrs. or 15 hrs.

Historical Geology—3 hrs. Winter half-term.

Bacteriology (optional).

General Physiology of the Lower Organisms—2 hrs.

Plant Physiology (optional)—Lectures and laboratory work.

French or *German*—3 hrs.

IX. MINERALOGY AND OTHER STUDIES PREPARATORY TO GEOLOGY

Professors PIRSSON, IRVING, WELLS ; Assistant Professors FORD, H. L. WHEELER, FOOTE ; Mr. COMSTOCK, Dr. JAMIESON, Dr. JOHNSON, and assistants.

Chemistry is an essential foundation for the study of Mineralogy, hence the course here offered is simply a modification of that in Chemistry, enabling students during the last half of their Senior year to specialize in subjects pertaining to mineralogy. The course is not intended for a large number of students, but rather for the few who may wish to pursue mineralogy as a science, to make practical use of it in teaching or in connection with geological work. The course, therefore, is open only to students who have shown special aptitude in this particular field of work and have maintained a high scholarship standing in the mineralogical and chemical studies of Junior year.

Details regarding the studies of this course are given under SUBJECTS OF INSTRUCTION, pp. 276 to 279.

SCHEME OF STUDIES

JUNIOR YEAR:

In Junior year the course is identical with that in Chemistry preparatory to Metallurgy.

SENIOR YEAR:

FIRST TERM:—

During the first term the course is identical with that in Chemistry preparatory to Metallurgy.

SECOND TERM:—

Crystallography, including the use of the Reflecting Goniometer, and the drawing and calculation of Crystals.

Optical Properties of Crystals and the use of the Polarizing Microscope—Laboratory work, 20 hrs.

Mineralogy—Lectures, 2 hrs.

General Chemistry, Metallurgy, Assaying, and Gas Analysis—2 hrs.

Elementary Petrology—Lectures, 1 hr.

Historical Geology—3 hrs. Winter half-term.

Economic Geology—3 hrs. Spring half-term.

French or *German*—3 hrs.

X. BIOLOGY PREPARATORY TO MEDICINE

Professors CHITTENDEN, WELLS, MENDEL, PIRSSON, SCHUCHERT, EVANS, HARRISON; Assistant Professors BEACH, COE, FOOTE, RETTGER, UNDERHILL; Mr. COMSTOCK, Dr. COLE, Dr. WOODRUFF, Dr. A. H. GRAVES, Dr. KUNKEL, and assistants.

The study of biology, together with chemistry and physics, constitutes the best and most natural line of preparatory work for the study of medicine. The Course in Biology was, accordingly, organized in recognition of the fundamental importance which such preparatory training assumes for the most complete appreciation and intelligent understanding of the science of medicine in its broadest sense. To the prospective medical student the special knowledge as well as the general training afforded are of distinct value; for the biological sciences so closely underlie the science of medicine and are so plainly the substructure on which the latter rests, that a broad and intelligent comprehension of the subject is almost impossible without some acquaintance with one or more of the biological sciences.

With these facts in view, less attention is given to systematic zoology and botany than to morphology and physiology. In morphology, special emphasis is directed to those subjects of which a knowledge is essential to the clear understanding of the physiological work which follows and of medical science in general. On the physiological side, the course provides more extensive study than is ordinarily offered. Considerable attention is devoted to laboratory work in physiological chemistry, thus producing familiarity with the chemical as well as with the physical and morphological aspects of biology. The laboratory method of instruction is introduced wherever feasible in order to develop the powers of observation and train the hand and senses. It is the aim to teach the student self-reliance and the habit of independent observation and deduction while he is acquiring the knowledge needed to enable him to pursue with profit the professional studies of the Medical School.

This course is also pursued by those who desire a liberal training with a view to teaching various branches of biological science, without specializing as extensively as is done in the course in Zoology and Botany. Students are also fitted (especially after an additional year or two of graduate study) to take positions in research laboratories, hygienic institutions connected with Boards of Health, commercial laboratories for the preparation or analysis of foods, for serum manufacture, etc., as well as in Experiment Stations and the other Government laboratories.

Details regarding the studies pursued are given under SUBJECTS OF INSTRUCTION, pp. 271 to 276.

SCHEME OF STUDIES
JUNIOR YEAR:

FIRST TERM:—

Organic Chemistry—Lectures and recitations, 3 hrs.

Qualitative Analysis—Laboratory work, 13 hrs.; Recitations and lectures, 4 hrs.

Elementary Botany—Lectures and laboratory work, 3 hrs.

English Composition—1 hr.

Physiology—1 hr.

German—3 hrs.

French—3 hrs.

SECOND TERM :—

Organic Chemistry—Lectures and recitations, 1 hr.; Laboratory work, 6 hrs. Winter half-term ; Lectures and recitations, 3 hrs. Spring half-term.

Comparative Anatomy and General Biology—Laboratory work, with lectures and demonstrations, 15 hrs.

Physiology—1 hr.

Laboratory Physics—3 hrs. Spring half-term.

Elementary Botany—Lectures and laboratory work, 3 hrs.

English Composition—1 hr.

French—3 hrs.

German—3 hrs.

SENIOR YEAR :

FIRST TERM :—

Physiological Chemistry and Physiology—Recitations and lectures, 1 hr.; Laboratory work with demonstrations, 13 hrs.

Zoology—Lectures and laboratory work, 5 hrs.

Embryology—Lectures and laboratory work, 4 hrs.

Geology—3 hrs.

French or *German*—3 hrs.

SECOND TERM :—

Physiological Chemistry and Physiology—Illustrative lectures and recitations, 4 hrs.; Laboratory work and demonstrations, 13 hrs.

Experimental Toxicology—Lectures, 3 hrs. Spring half-term.

Historical Geology—3 hrs. Winter half-term.

Zoology—Lectures and laboratory work, 3 hrs. Winter half-term.

Bacteriology—Laboratory work with lectures and recitations, 9 hrs. Winter half-term and 5 hrs. Spring half-term.

Plant Physiology—Lectures and laboratory work (optional), Spring half-term.

General Physiology of the Lower Organisms (optional)—2 hrs.

French or *German*—3 hrs.

XI. SELECTED STUDIES IN LANGUAGE, LITERATURE, HISTORY, AND THE NATURAL AND SOCIAL SCIENCES

Professors CROSS, CALLENDER, GREGORY, SCHUCHERT, KELLER ; Assistant Professors RETTGER, NETTLETON ; Mr. MIMS, Dr. KUNKEL, Dr. BISHOP, Mr. HUNTINGTON, Mr. BOGGS, Dr. CANBY, Mr. PIERCE, and assistants.

This course is intended for men who desire the essentials of a liberal education, with a leaning toward science, as a preparation for business or the study of law. While it is based largely upon history, literature, and the social sciences, it also includes the necessary instruction in mathematics, language, and natural science. In the Freshman year, the student continues his preparatory training in mathematics and the modern languages, and gains a knowledge of the elements of physics, chemistry, and biology. For the next two years his time is devoted mainly to English literature, American and modern European history, and a group of social sciences, comprising government, economics, anthropology, and social evolution. Along with this work, he carries on at the same time scientific studies in those branches that are most closely related to the social sciences, such as organic evolution, physical and commercial geography, and public hygiene. In English literature he pursues a continuous course which extends over three years; while in English composition an opportunity is given him to gain practice in debate. Including the entrance requirement, he has ordinarily two years in both French and German; but for one of these languages he may substitute, if it is deemed advisable, two years in Spanish. Men who wish to complete the scientific part of the course in a different manner are permitted to elect historical geology in place of social evolution. It is believed that a well selected course of studies designed to secure general training rather than specialization should include all of these subjects, and that it is adapted to the needs of men who expect to engage in business, manufacturing, and banking, to enter professions like law and journalism, or to seek administrative positions in corporations or the public service.

This training can be taken to advantage under the conditions which prevail in the Sheffield Scientific School. In the first place, it enables students who so desire to shorten the period devoted to general studies to three years. They can then either pass to further work here or elsewhere in the professional schools where specialization can always be done to greater advantage than in college, or go at once into practical affairs if they are to seek a business or administrative career. Second, the course, while not devoted primarily to science, is sufficient to give the student a training in the scientific method of study and accustom his mind to the scientific point of view. This is believed to be an element of great value in the training of men for business careers as well as for those professions which deal with the less exact and definite subjects of history, literature, and the social sciences. Finally, the prevailing method of instruction has many advantages. As the students are usually met in divisions of twenty-five or thirty men, the instructor may know his students individually and have free discussion with them in the class-room. It is not necessary for him to sacrifice the disciplinary value of his subject to the mere acquiring of information, as is the case where the lecture system must be largely used in the instruction of immature students. It is possible therefore, in this course, for students to combine the advantages of life in a large university with those which are usually supposed to belong to the smaller college alone.

Through the generosity of Mr. Edward D. Page, a graduate of the class of 1875, a series of five lectures has been arranged for the Senior class, dealing with commercial ethics or the ethical side of business life. These lectures, which are to be given by men of experience in mercantile, financial, and legal pursuits, will embrace the following or similar topics: the morals and ethics of production and transportation ; the morals and ethics of purchase and sale ; the morals and ethics of credit and banking ; the morals and ethics of public service ; the morals and ethics of corporate and other trusts. It is plain that such a course of lectures coming at the end of Senior year, especially when the presentation is made by men trained in business methods and inspired by a desire to spread abroad among young men correct principles governing business transactions, will prove of the greatest advantage and profit.

Details regarding the studies of the course are given under SUBJECTS OF INSTRUCTION, pp. 279 to 281. ·

SCHEME OF STUDIES

JUNIOR YEAR :

FIRST TERM :—

> *Physical Geography*—3 hrs.
> *English Literature*—3 hrs.
> *History—Mediæval*—3 hrs.
> *Anthropology*—2 hrs.
> *English Composition* – 2 hrs.
> *French***—3 hrs.
> *German***—3 hrs.

SECOND TERM :—

> *Physical and Commercial Geography*—3 hrs.
> *Anthropology*—2 hrs.
> *English Literature*—3 hrs.
> *History—Modern European*—3 hrs.
> *English Composition*—2 hrs.
> *French***—3 hrs.
> *German***—3 hrs.

SENIOR YEAR :

FIRST TERM :—

> *Organic Evolution*—3 hrs.
> *English Literature*—3 hrs.
> *American History*—3 hrs.
> *Economics*—3 hrs
> *Modern Government*— 2 hrs.
> *French, German,* or *Spanish*—3 hrs.

SECOND TERM :—

> *Organic Evolution*—3 hrs. Winter half-term
> *Social Evolution*†—3 hrs. Spring half-term.
> *Public Hygiene*—2 hrs. Winter half-term.
> *English Literature*—3 hrs.
> *American History*—3 hrs.
> *Economics*—3 hrs.
> *Modern Government*—2 hrs.
> *French, German,* or *Spanish*—3 hrs.
> *Commercial Ethics*—5 lectures.

---

* Spanish may be substituted for one of the modern languages on petition and for satisfactory reasons.

† Historical Geology may be substituted for Social Evolution.

XII. STUDIES PREPARATORY TO THE STUDY OF FORESTRY

Professors GRAVES, TOUMEY, EVANS, PIRSSON, CALLENDER, PINCHOT; Assistant Professors TRACY, COE, BARNEY, CHAPMAN, FORD; Dr. A. H. GRAVES, Mr. FARNHAM, Mr. HAWLEY, and assistants.

This course comprises all the subjects necessary for the pursuit of advanced technical studies in Forestry. The work of Forestry at Yale prepares men to meet the large problems of forest organization at present confronting American foresters. Forestry in this country is in its infancy, and it is necessary that foresters should be equipped to organize large public and private forests, to assist in legislative work, to interest public opinion by writing and public speaking, and to teach in forest schools, as well as to carry on practical work in the woods.

The profession of Forestry demands not only a knowledge of botany, geology, zoology, physics, chemistry, engineering and mathematics, but also a liberal training in economics, English, French, German, and similar subjects.

Details regarding the studies of this course are given under SUBJECTS OF INSTRUCTION, pp. 281 to 283.

SCHEME OF STUDIES

JUNIOR YEAR :

FIRST TERM :—

> *Surveying*—Field work, 3 weeks, beginning Monday, August 31, in 1908.
> *Surveying*—Office work ; Mapping and calculations, 5 hrs.
> *Mechanics*—3 hrs.
> *Determinative Mineralogy*—3 hrs.
> *Elementary Botany*—Lectures and laboratory work, 4 hrs.
> *Physical Geography*—4 hrs.
> *English Composition*—1 hr.
> *German*—3 hrs.
> *French*—3 hrs.

SECOND TERM :—

> *Mechanics*—3 hrs. Winter half-term.
> *Strength of Materials*—2 hrs. Winter half-term.
> *Spherical Trigonometry*—2 hrs. Winter half-term

Timber Construction—3 hrs. Spring half-term.

Hydraulics—3 hrs. Spring half-term.

Determinative Mineralogy—3 hrs. Winter half-term.

Elementary Botany—Lectures and laboratory work, 4 hrs.

Botany of Flowering Plants—Laboratory work, 4 hrs. Spring half-term.

English Composition—1 hr.

German—3 hrs.

French—3 hrs.

SENIOR YEAR:

FIRST TERM :—

Field Engineering—3 weeks in June and July.

Mapping—4 hrs.

Physical Geology—3 hrs.

Morphology of Plants—Laboratory work and informal lectures, 4 hrs.

Forest Botany—Field work, 4 hrs.

Dendrology—1 hr.

Silviculture, Silvics (optional)—Lectures, 2 hrs.; Field work.

Economics—3 hrs.

French or *German*—3 hrs.

SECOND TERM :—

Diseases of Trees—Lectures, laboratory work, and excursions, 3 hrs. Winter half-term.

Morphology of Plants—Laboratory work ; informal lectures, 4 hrs.

Plant Physiology—Laboratory work and lectures, 6 hrs. Spring half-term after Easter.

Dendrology—1 hr.

Silviculture, Treatment of Woodlands (optional)—Lectures, 2 hrs.; Field work.

Forest Entomology—4 hrs. Winter half-term.

Petrology—1 hr. Winter half-term.

Silviculture, Seeding and Planting—Lectures and field work, 10 hrs. Spring half-term.

Geology—3 hrs. for six weeks of Winter half-term.

State Forest Law (optional)—2 hrs. Winter half-term.

Government—3 hrs.

Forest Policy (optional)—6 hrs. Winter half-term.

Methods of Field Work in Forestry (optional)—4 lectures, Winter half-term.

Forest Hydrography (optional)—6 lectures, Winter half-term.

French or *German*—3 hrs.

X. MATHEMATICS PURE AND APPLIED

Professors [...] Pierce, P. F. Smith, Assistant Professors [...] Beard, Nichols, Marshall, Dr. Longley, Dr. Hull, Dr. Swartwout, Mr. North, and assistants.

The curriculum of this course for Junior year differs from one studies pursued in the Engineering Courses by the omission of such subjects as belong to technical engineering. Specialization along mathematical lines begins in Senior year.

The course makes it possible for students especially interested in mathematics and science to advance further in these subjects than is possible in the other courses. The subjects offered suffice for a thorough acquaintance with the elements of exact science and prepare for advanced work in either pure or applied mathematics.

A more detailed description will be found on pp. 257 to 259.

SCHEME OF STUDIES
JUNIOR YEAR:

First Term:

  Descriptive Geometry—3 hrs.
  Theory of Heat—3 hrs.
  Mathematics—Differential Calculus, with applications to Geometry and Analysis, 5 hrs.
  General Astronomy—2 hrs.
  German 3 hrs.
  French 3 hrs.
  English Composition—1 hr.

Second Term:

  Descriptive Geometry 3 hrs. until February 15th.
  Sound and Light 3 hrs. after February 15th.
  Theory of Electricity—3 hrs.
  Mathematics Integral Calculus, with applications to Geometry, 5 hrs. Winter half-term; Theoretical mechanics, 5 hrs. Spring half term.
  General Astronomy— 2 hrs.
  German 3 hrs.
  French 3 hrs.
  English Composition 1 hr.

SENIOR YEAR:

FIRST TERM :—

    Geology—3 hrs.

    Differential Equations—1 hr.

    Vector Analysis—2 hrs.

    Higher Analysis—2 hrs.

    Higher Geometry—2 hrs.

    Advanced Mechanics—2 hrs.

    German or *French*—3 hrs.

SECOND TERM :—

    Geology—3 hrs.

    Vector Analysis—2 hrs. until February 15th.

    Differential Equations—1 hr.

    Higher Analysis—2 hrs. ; after February 15th, 3 hrs.

    Higher Geometry—2 hrs. ; after February 15th, 3 hrs.

    Advanced Mechanics—2 hrs.

    German or *French*—3 hrs.

SUBJECTS OF INSTRUCTION
ENGLISH LITERATURE AND COMPOSITION

Professor CROSS, Assistant Professor NETTLETON, Dr. CANBY, Dr. NICHOLSON, Mr. PIERCE, Mr. DURHAM.

ENGLISH LITERATURE—The courses in English literature are designed, first of all, to lay the foundation for that culture which comes from direct acquaintance with literary masterpieces. To this end representative authors of different periods are read and studied for their art and their thought rather than for any of the extraneous purposes that may enter into the study of literature. At the same time, these authors are taken up in chronological order with the view to keeping the proper historical perspective and to calling attention to some of the main lines in literary developments.

During Freshman year English Literature is required of all students. The fall term is devoted to careful study of three plays of Shakespeare—usually comedies or historical plays. The reading of the winter term begins with several of the eighteenth century comedies, such as Goldsmith's *She Stoops to Conquer* and Sheridan's *Rivals* and *School for Scandal*. The drama is succeeded by selections from nineteenth century authors, usually from Scott, Byron, Carlyle, Browning, and Tennyson. From year to year, the reading varies considerably in detail, but it remains the same in spirit and in general scope.

In the Course of Select Studies, English Literature is one of the prescribed subjects for the entire Junior and Senior years. The work of the two years constitutes a single and continuous course of study of the leading authors, both in prose and in verse, from Chaucer to Tennyson. Among the earlier authors always studied are Chaucer, Bacon, Spenser, Shakespeare, Milton, Dryden, Pope, Gray, and Goldsmith. Other authors, such as Marlowe and Ben Jonson, are usually included to represent more fully the Elizabethan drama. In nineteenth century literature the authors chosen vary considerably from year to year, but the aim is always to acquaint the student, so far as time permits, with representative works of the period. Especial attention is paid to Wordsworth, Byron, Keats, Shelley, Browning, Arnold, and Rossetti.

ENGLISH COMPOSITION—Throughout Junior year English composition is required of all students. The class is divided into groups of about twenty-five men each for text-book instruction and practical class-room drill in the fundamental principles of writing. These recitations are supplemented with fortnightly appointments for personal criticism of the required themes. The work of the first term deals chiefly with exposition, and aims to teach first the essentials of structure. In the Winter and Spring half-terms, description, narration, and argumentation are successively studied. The simpler methods of the first term are continued with more advanced study of structure and with increasing attention to style. Selections from representative authors are read and analyzed in connection with the regular recitation work, while the personal theme-criticisms are continued to the end of the course.

In the Course of Select Studies, the work in English Composition is carried out with especial thoroughness, the extra hour alloted to it permitting both more extended theme writing and more collateral reading in nineteenth century prose. A special course in debating, conducted by the University instructor in argumentation, is open, after Christmas, to those who have proved their ability in the fall term work in composition. Another course, involving extensive reading, is open to men who desire to supplement their practice in narrative writing with critical study of the best narrative writers.

Considerable freedom is allowed to the individual student in choice of subject for themes and in method of treatment, and especial help is given to contributors to the different undergraduate publications. Though the primary aim of the course is to impart the ability to write simple, forceful English, the attempt is also made to increase the student's knowledge of the best English prose and to enable him to criticise it intelligently.

FOREIGN LANGUAGES

German : Professor CORWIN, Assistant Professor GLASCOCK, Dr. THORSTENBERG, Dr. A. G. WARD, Mr. LOVELL, Mr. CURTS.

French : Assistant Professors CLARKE, LUQUIENS; Mr. ROBBINS, Mr. J. P. RICE, Dr. GARVER.

Spanish : Assistant Professor LUQUIENS.

German and French are studied for two years by every member of the School. That language which the student offers at his examination for entrance is studied until the end of Junior year. The other language is begun at the opening of Junior year and studied until the end of the course. Thus each student has either German or French during Freshman and Senior years, and both languages during Junior year.

GERMAN—This department has a twofold purpose, to prepare the student to use the language easily and intelligently for those purposes which his course may require, and to supplement the practical training of his special studies by securing some of the important disciplinary results of linguistic and literary study. A systematic and thorough study of the structure of the language is made the point of departure and essential basis for all work. This consists chiefly in the study of assigned texts, in written and oral translation into German, in translation at sight and in constant reading aloud, with the ultimate purpose of making the rendering into English unnecessary. In the work of translation careful attention is given to exactness and form of expression, and the student is made acquainted with the resources of his own language. The subjects of derivation, composition, and the relation of German and English are systematically studied with reference both to their practical aid in the acquisition of a vocabulary and to their scientific value in the establishment of correct ideas of the nature and growth of language. While it is not a primary aim, the course seeks to lay the foundation for the colloquial use of the language by imparting a familiar knowledge of grammatical forms, by the reading aloud of German texts, both by instructor and student, and by oral exercises based on the reading of the day.

· The cycle of texts used differs somewhat with each class. The plan is to familiarize the student with some of the best specimens of modern prose and poetry, aiming in this selection to introduce him to a sufficient number and variety of works to overcome the usual difficulties of style and vocabulary, and give him some insight into the most important phases of German life and literature. With the more advanced divisions, towards the end of the course, some masterpiece of German literature is critically studied, and incidentally some knowledge is gained of the history and present state of German literature.

Opportunity for advanced or special work is offered as occasion requires.

FRENCH—The chief purpose of the instruction in French is to give a ready and accurate reading knowledge of the language, such as will be of use to the student in scientific or other investigation, both while in the University and in after life. At the same time, most careful attention is devoted to imparting a correct pronunciation and to colloquial forms, so that in case of foreign travel or subsequent study of French no time need be lost in the repetition of elementary work. The value of the course as a disciplinary drill and as a means to general culture is always kept clearly in view.

With those beginning the subject, grammar is reduced to its simplest terms ; only the grammatical forms and the few main principles are insisted upon, without which no accurate translation is possible. Some continuous text of interesting character is taken up early in the first year. Then follows translation of representative authors, generally modern, alternating with prose composition, further acquirements in grammar, and such attention to the Latin origin of the language as may help to fix vocabulary in mind.

Students offering French at entrance are assumed to have been sufficiently grounded in the rudiments. They, therefore, are required to read a somewhat greater amount of text, including specimens of the classic period. With both categories of students attention is given to scientific French of a general nature, and its vocabulary is especially impressed.

At the discretion of the instructor, students sufficiently advanced are admitted to a course of reading, known as Higher French, which will familiarize them with the representative authors of the seventeenth, eighteenth, and nineteenth centuries. Some outside reading is required and a short series of lectures on French Literature is given for members of the course and for such other students as may be interested. While a dry list of names and dates is avoided, a connected account of the development of French life and letters and of the salient literary periods is presented.

SPANISH—This course extends through two years. The first year (Elementary Spanish) consists of three recitations a week from January to June ; the second (Advanced Spanish), of three recitations a week throughout the whole college year.

The aim of the course is to give those students who are looking forward to work in Mexico, the West Indies, or the Philippine Islands, the ability to read modern Spanish easily and accurately, in order that later they may be able to put this power to a practical use, either as an aid in business affairs, or as a solid foundation for the attainment of speaking power.

The Hills and Ford Spanish Grammar is used. As soon as the first elements of grammar are mastered, reading is commenced, and thenceforth throughout the first year of the course each lesson is a combination of grammar work and reading of modern authors. A good pronunciation is insisted upon, inasmuch as it aids greatly in the acquirement of a vocabulary, and will also be of practical use in case of travel or residence in Spanish-speaking countries.

During the second year the reading work is supplemented by practice in composition. Especial attention is given to commercial Spanish, the students being exercised in the reading and writing of business advertisements and letters.

MATHEMATICS

Professor P. F. SMITH, Assistant Professor MASON, Dr. GRANVILLE, Dr. HEWES, Dr. LONGLEY, and assistants.

The studies in Mathematics are based upon thorough preparation in all mathematical subjects required for entrance. No review in any of these is given, but all students in the Freshman class begin at once the study of Plane Analytic Geometry.

17

For students in the ENGINEERING GROUP the work in mathematics for Freshman year is in Analytic Geometry, the Fall and Winter half-terms being devoted to Plane, the Spring half-term to Solid Geometry. The instruction is arranged to prepare for the courses in Junior year, and includes many elaborate exercises in drawing. The mathematical subjects for Junior year are Differential Calculus (Fall term), Integral Calculus (Winter term), and Theoretical Mechanics (Spring term).

The course in Mathematics for students in NATURAL SCIENCE is limited to sixty exercises in the Fall and Winter half-terms of Freshman year. So much of Plane Analytics is studied as is necessary for an understanding of Elementary Calculus, this topic being taught chiefly for the sake of its increasing importance to students of experimental and natural science.

Undergraduate instruction in mathematics in Freshman and Junior years is carried on entirely by recitations from the following text-books :—*Elements of Analytic Geometry*, by P. F. Smith and A. S. Gale ; *Elementary Calculus*, by P. F. Smith ; *Elements of Differential and Integral Caculus*, by W. A. Granville.

Students are required to do a large amount of problem work in note-books made specially for this purpose. These books are handed in at each recitation for reading and correction by assistants. The aim of the instruction is primarily to train and drill the student so that he can acquire skill and facility in using mathematics as a tool. It is believed that the engineer should be a practical rather than theoretical mathematician.

A brief description of the special courses in Pure and Applied Mathematics follows :—

GENERAL ASTRONOMY—This course is designed to meet the needs of students interested in Astronomy. Practical work is included but the emphasis is laid upon the theory. The subject matter is the following :—(1) introduction to spherical trigonometry with applications to the transformation of coördinates on the celestial sphere, determination of the time of sunrise, etc. ; (2) determination of time, latitude and longitude from observations with the sextant, surveyor's transit, and meridian transit; (3) descriptive astronomy covering approximately the material contained in F. R. Moulton's *Introduction to Astronomy* or C. A. Young's *General Astronomy* ; (4) applications of the calculus in the discussion of the theory of the heat of the sun, the potential and attraction of bodies, and the problem of two bodies.

DIFFERENTIAL EQUATIONS—This course consists of lectures and recitations on methods of solution and geometrical interpretation of ordinary and partial differential equations.

HIGHER ANALYSIS—In this course a variety of topics in Algebra and Analysis is presented in lectures, including the theory and applications of determinants, definite integrals, series, and the elements of the theory of functions of a complex variable.

HIGHER GEOMETRY—This course is based upon the Analytic Geometry of Freshman year, and includes lectures on systems of conics, elementary transformations, and various topics in Analytic Geometry of Three Dimensions.

ADVANCED MECHANICS—This course is a continuation of the Theoretical Mechanics of Junior year, and includes the dynamics of a system of particles and a rigid body.

The remaining courses under Course XIII are described elsewhere, under SUBJECTS OF INSTRUCTION.

All courses enumerated above are open to students in other courses properly qualified who may desire to take optional studies in mathematics. In addition a course of especial value to students in engineering, entitled Graphical Computation, is offered. This is a one-hour lecture course concerned primarily with the general theory of graphics. Students who wish to take optional courses should arrange at the beginning of the college year with the head of the department of mathematics.

CHEMISTRY

Professors MIXTER, WELLS, CHITTENDEN, MENDEL, IRVING; Assistant Professors H. L. WHEELER, WALDEN, FOOTE; Mr. COMSTOCK, Dr. JOHNSON, Dr. JAMIESON, Dr. JOHNS, Dr. MATHEWSON, and assistants.

The instruction in the various branches of chemistry is for the most part given in the SHEFFIELD CHEMICAL LABORATORY, the courses in Physiological Chemistry and Toxicology being given in the laboratory of physiological chemistry in the SHEFFIELD BIOLOGICAL LABORATORY.

CHEMISTRY OF FRESHMAN YEAR—There are two courses in chemistry offered to the members of the Freshman class:

(A) For those who do not offer chemistry as a subject for entrance, or who fail to show by their entrance examination special proficiency in this subject.

(B) For those who show by their entrance examination a sufficiently thorough preparation to warrant their entering upon advanced work.

A candidate may satisfy the entrance requirement in Chemistry without becoming eligible for the advanced course. Such students will pursue course A.

Course A. Elementary Chemistry—The exercises consist in recitations from a text-book, lectures, and laboratory work. The object of the experimental work is to facilitate the study, and to train the students in the observation of phenomena, and in manipulation. Notes are required and the students are questioned on the experiments.

Course B. Qualitative Analysis—This course is designed to be the equivalent of the regular course in this subject given to the students in Chemistry, Mining, Metallurgy, Biology, Zoology and Botany, and Mineralogy during the fall term of Junior year. Toward the end of the year it will be supplemented by a short course of lectures and recitations on the essentials of Theoretical Chemistry.

The Juniors in the Chemical, Biological, Mining, Metallurgical, and Mineralogical courses who have satisfactorily completed the qualitative analysis of course B will begin quantitative work at the opening of the fall term and thus be able to devote more time to special work later in the course.

ANALYTICAL CHEMISTRY—*Qualitative Analysis.* This subject is taken during the whole of the first term of Junior year in the courses in Chemistry, Metallurgy, Mining, Biology, Zoology and Botany, and Mineralogy. The student spends at least fourteen hours per week in laboratory work, and the laboratory is open all day for the benefit of graduate students and others who desire to devote more time to the subject. There are also four class-room exercises per week, consisting of experimental and explanatory lectures, and recitations. Every effort is made to avoid mere thoughtless, mechanical laboratory work on the part of the student, and to give him an insight into the chemical principles involved in the processes studied.

There is probably no branch of chemical study as important as qualitative analysis in its use in developing the reasoning faculties, and enabling the student to generalize and to classify chemical phenomena. Besides this, a practical knowledge is gained of methods which are applicable to scientific or technical researches.

Quantitative Analysis—This subject is pursued for a year or more in the Chemistry, Metallurgy, and Mineralogy courses, and for two half-terms of the Mining course. It involves fourteen hours per week of laboratory work as a minimum, supplemented by lectures and recitations. Analyses by both gravimetric and volumetric methods are carried out in the laboratory. The methods selected are such as appear to be most typical and important in their practical applications. Much attention is paid to accurate and skillful manipulation, and to the proper understanding of the scientific principles involved.

This general course of quantitative work is followed in the course in Metallurgy by Metallurgical Analysis, in which some of the important technical methods for the analysis of ores, slags, fuels, metals, alloys, etc., are learned practically.

INORGANIC PREPARATIONS—This is a course of laboratory work, with lectures and recitations, which gives experience in the preparation and purification of many inorganic compounds, illustrating important chemical principles as well as commercial operations. The student acquires practice here in working with larger quantities than in analytical operations, and has a different object in view, namely, to obtain good products without the necessity of avoiding slight losses of substance.

CHEMICAL CALCULATIONS—This subject is taught in close connection with quantitative analysis, for it treats chiefly of the arithmetical side of this work. An effort is made to develop the student's reasoning-power, and to make him quick and accurate in the use of figures.

APPLIED CHEMISTRY AND GAS CALCULATIONS—This course occupies two hours per week during the first term of Senior year, in the Chemistry course. Its object is to give familiarity with some of the more important chemical manufacturing processes, and also to familiarize the student with the applications of the laws of gases, particularly in practical calculations.

SANITARY WATER ANALYSIS—This subject is required in the course in Sanitary Engineering, and is optional for the students in Chemistry. It comprises a complete practical course of laboratory work, supplemented by lectures and recitations.

GENERAL AND PHYSICAL CHEMISTRY—This subject occupies three hours a week during the entire Senior year in the courses of Chemistry and Metallurgy. Smith's *General Inorganic Chemistry* is used as a text-book, and regular recitation work is supplemented by lectures as occasion demands. Special attention is given to the laws and theories which form the basis of chemistry ; and a knowledge of elements, their compounds and their reactions is obtained as far as possible by using them to illustrate and explain the laws and theories.

PHYSICO-CHEMICAL MEASUREMENTS—This subject includes laboratory practice in the more important methods of Physical or Electro-Chemistry. About twenty-five exercises of three hours each, in the second term of Senior year, are devoted to this subject. Opportunities for special laboratory work are given to students who are sufficiently advanced.

ORGANIC CHEMISTRY—The course in Organic Chemistry is a combination of text-book work with experimental lectures. The class, including the members of the courses in Chemistry and Biology, has three exercises weekly through the Junior year. Laboratory work in this department of Chemistry is required during the second term of Junior year and is required of the members of the Chemical course during the latter half of the second term of Senior year. Opportunity is also afforded for the carrying on of original investigations in this subject, either in connection with theses, or as a part of the regular work in the case of advanced students.

PROXIMATE ORGANIC ANALYSIS—The purpose of this course is partly to familiarize the student with the chemical and microscopical methods for determining the value and purity of vegetable and animal products and partly to give him a general idea of their nature and composition. During five weeks of the second term of the Senior year, twenty-five exercises of three hours each are devoted to the determination of protein, oil, starch, cellulose and other constituents of vegetable materials, and also to the appearance of these constituents under the microscope and the identification of adulterants by microscopic examination. To those properly qualified the opportunity to carry on further work in this line is offered.

PHYSIOLOGICAL CHEMISTRY and TOXICOLOGY—For details regarding the courses in these subjects see p. 274. For reference to instruction on the chemistry of plants, consult p. 275, under Plant Physiology.

METALLURGY—This subject is included in the Chemistry course and in the course preparatory to Metallurgy. The class-room work consists of three exercises a week during both halves of the second term of Senior year. A text-book is used, but this is supplemented to a considerable extent by lectures. Particular attention is paid to the chemical principles involved in the processes used for the extraction of all the important metals from their ores. A short course on Metallography is included here.

ASSAYING—A series of lectures is given to the members of the Chemistry and Metallurgy courses on the fire-assay of ores, particularly those of gold and silver, and the students in the Metallurgy course are required to take an extensive course of practical work in fire-assaying in the Hammond Metallurgical Laboratory.

GAS ANALYSIS—The more important methods of technical gas analysis are taught in a practical manner in connection with the study of metallurgical analysis in the course in Metallurgy. The students of the Chemistry course are also required to attend the lectures on this subject.

ENGINEERING STUDIES

The work of instruction in the courses in Engineering is carried out in the well equipped laboratories, apparatus, engine and boiler rooms in WINCHESTER HALL and in the HAMMOND METALLURGICAL LABORATORY. WINCHESTER HALL was erected in 1892 by Mrs. Jane Ellen Winchester as a memorial of her husband, Oliver Fisher Winchester, one of the earliest friends and benefactors of the Sheffield Scientific School.

CIVIL ENGINEERING

Professor DuBois, Assistant Professors BARNEY, TRACY; Mr. FARN-
HAM, Mr. KIRBY, and assistants.

The School has leased a large tract of land in the town of Orange, on the line of the Derby Railroad, for the use of the classes in Surveying. The department is adequately equipped for the special work which it aims to teach.

SURVEYING AND FIELD ENGINEERING—A three weeks' course of practical instruction in field-work is given in both the Junior and Senior years. This instruction during the year 1908 for the Senior class begins on Monday, June 15, and for the Junior class on Monday, August 31.

In the Junior year, the three weeks before the beginning of the fall term are spent in uninterrupted work in the field. The course is then continued, three exercises a week, with lectures, recitations, and work in the drawing room.

Land, topographical, stadia, and city surveys are made, plotted, checked, traced, and blue-printed. Levels are run and profiles drawn. Special problems likely to occur in practice are taken up in the field and in the class-room. The field-work is arranged so that each student receives a thorough drill in the use of the instruments, including the transit and the level.

DRAWING AND DESCRIPTIVE GEOMETRY—Drawing is begun at once in the first term of Freshman year, under the charge of the Professor of Drawing in the Art School, and includes practice in free-hand drawing. In the second term, under the Instructor in Engineering, the students take isometric drawing with application to drawing from models and structures by measurements, shading, tinting, conventional use of colors, principles of orthographic projections, and practice in making simple working-drawings, 4 hours both terms.

The Drawing of Junior year, 16 hours both terms, includes Descriptive Geometry, the drawing of structures from measurement, and elements of design for simple structures. The instruction is by recitations, lectures, practical exercises, and models, and is under the charge of the Professor and Assistant in Civil Engineering. Included in the work of this year is also the mapping of surveying field-notes, 7 hours, first term.

In Senior year, the drawing consists of the mapping of the surveys of that year, and the designing of structures and finished drawings, designs, and estimates, under the charge of the Professor and Assistant in Civil Engineering, 6 hours both terms.

RAILWAY ENGINEERING—In the three weeks in June and July before the beginning of the first term of Senior year, a line of railroad is located and set out from a contour map previously obtained, grades and curves established and set out, and computations made. The theory of economic location is taught by lectures and recitations in connection with the field-work. The work is arranged so that each student has sufficient practice in all the various operations. The course is under the charge of the Professors in Civil Engineering, aided by several assistants.

MECHANICS OF ENGINEERING—Senior year, 6 to 8 hours, both terms. The method of instruction is by means of text-books in connection with lectures and solutions of practical problems in illustration of the various topics. The course includes thorough instruction in the strength of materials, the stability of foundations, retaining walls, dams and embankments, and masonry arches, by lectures and graphic methods. Questions of hydraulics, water-supply, the measurement of discharge, and the theory and construction of water-motors receive attention.

CONSTRUCTION AND DESIGN—Senior year, 4 hours second term. A thorough course is given in the determination of stresses and the detailed design of roofs, bridges, etc., with working-drawings, specifications, and estimates. Visits of inspection are made, and recitations and lectures held in connection with the work in the drawing room.

ROADS AND PAVEMENTS—This course consists of a series of lectures on the different methods of road and pavement construction and their adaptability to varying local conditions.

ADJUSTMENT OF OBSERVATIONS AND ASTRONOMY—This course covers the adjustment of the usual class of precise field observations by the method of least squares, together with the methods of determining time, latitude, and azimuth adapted to the sextant and field transit.

Students of Civil and Sanitary Engineering during the second half of the second term of their Senior year, and students in the course preparatory to the study of Forestry in their Senior year, have 4 hours per week including practical experience in the determination of time, azimuth, latitude, longitude, etc.

Reference to the instruction in MASONRY and in SPECIFICATIONS is made on p. 268.

MECHANICAL ENGINEERING

Professor RICHARDS, Assistant Professors LOCKWOOD, MARSHALL ; Dr. SHEPARD, Mr. LILLEY, Mr. NORTH, and assistants.

THERMODYNAMICS (Junior Year)—Instruction is given by recitations and lectures on the mechanical theory of heat and the application of the theory to the discussion of the behavior of steam, air, and explosive gases as they are used in the production of power. The principles involved in the action of refrigerating apparatus are also discussed.

PRINCIPLES OF MECHANISM—This is a course in applied Kinematics. Instruction is by text-books and lectures, illustrated by diagrams and models, an extensive collection of which belongs to the School and is accessible to the student.

DESCRIPTIVE GEOMETRY is taught in the draughting room by lectures and recitations and by exercises at the drawing board, where problems are solved graphically by the student. Applications of the principles are made to the representation of intersections of curved surfaces, the penetrations of solids and the envelopes of solids which penetrate each other.

DRAWING (Junior Year)—The exercises in drawing are at the drawing board, where instruction is given to the student, individually, in methods of designing and representing machine elements and simple apparatus. Text-books, models and cartoons are used representing examples of approved practice.

SHOP-VISITING—The student, accompanied by the instructor, is employed in studying machinery in use and in process of construction in different machine-shops in the city. He is required to make satisfactory, carefully dimensioned sketches, from measurements taken by himself, of the complete machines and their parts, and to describe the tools and mechanical operations used in producing the simpler pieces.

APPLIED MECHANICS (Junior Year)—The Mechanics of Machinery is the dominant subject of this course, and much attention is given to the solution, by graphical methods, of problems relating to link work in which the forces acting upon the mechanism are taken into account and the angular velocities of the links determined.

MECHANICS (Senior Year)—This course comprises a continuation of the analytical treatment of mechanical principles to which the Theoretical Mechanics of the Junior year relates ; but the subject is carried into advanced fields, and numerous applications to practical problems are made, special attention being given to those in which the friction of mechanisms is taken into account.

STRENGTH OF MATERIALS—This is a course on the theory of the subject as applied to the strength and elasticity of structural elements such as riveted pieces, beams, columns and shafts, and to the strength of boilers and pipes. Demonstrations of the operation of testing machines are given in the testing laboratory.

STRESSES IN STRUCTURES—Graphical and analytical methods for determining stresses in the members of simple framed structures such as roofs, cranes, etc., are taught in this course.

MACHINE DESIGN—The course in this subject consists chiefly in practical exercises at the drawing board, and partly in lectures on the functions of machines and the mechanical principles which are applied in determining the proportions of machinery. The student, under the guidance of experienced instructors, is employed in making complete working-drawings of machines, many examples of which are in the drawing rooms and the basements of the School. He does not copy the examples, but is required to change the dimensions and in many cases to alter the design, and is ultimately taught to make partly new designs of important machinery, such as cranes, yacht engines, machine tools, boilers, etc. The discipline the student receives is such as he would obtain in the drawing office of an engineering establishment, while he is also carefully instructed in the theory of the subject he deals with, and in the practical bearing of all his work.

STEAM ENGINEERING AND HEAT ENGINES IN GENERAL—Recitations and lectures on these subjects relate to the application of thermodynamics to the discussion of practical problems presented in the design of steam, hot air and gas engines, and deal with the mechanical principles involved in the mechanism of such engines. The study of steam boilers follows that of engines.

Indicator practice affords opportunities to the student to apply the indicator to various engines in operation and gives him experience in reading indicator cards, measuring them by the planimeter and computing indicated power. Complete Boiler Tests, in connection with Indicator and Brake Tests of an engine, all conducted by the students themselves, form part of the course.

HYDROSTATICS AND HYDRODYNAMICS—This course deals, by lectures, recitations, and drawing exercises, with the theory of the subject and with its application to practical problems, a special example of which is the determination of the displacement of ships and of the power required to propel them. The study of water wheels and turbines receives special attention.

In the laboratory, experiments upon the flow in channels and pipes and through apertures, and tests of the power and efficiency of small water wheels and turbines, are made by the students. In this connection, correct methods of measurement are carefully taught.

MUNICIPAL AND SANITARY ENGINEERING

Professor DuBois, Assistant Professors BARNEY, TRACY ; Mr. FARNHAM, Mr. KIRBY, and assistants.

The instruction in the subjects pertaining directly to Municipal and Sanitary Engineering is given in the lecture rooms and laboratories of WINCHESTER HALL, with the exception of the chemical and bacteriological studies.

The latter are taught in the SHEFFIELD CHEMICAL LABORA-
TORY and in the Bacteriological and Hygienic Laboratory
in SHEFFIELD HALL.   With reference to the work in Surveying, more detailed statements will be found in the
description of the studies in Civil Engineering.

DRAWING—In addition to the free-hand and instrumental drawing of
the Freshman year, instruction in Descriptive Geometry, by recitations
and the graphical solution of problems on the drawing board, is given
in the Junior year, personal instruction being given to each student.
Included in the work of both Junior and Senior years is also the
mapping of all surveys made by the class, and the bridge drafting.

FIELD ENGINEERING—The entire available time for three weeks in
both Junior and Senior years is devoted to a course of practical instruction in field work.   This course during the year 1908 for the Senior
class begins on Monday, June 15, and for the Junior class on Monday, August 31.

In Junior year the work covers the use and adjustment of instruments, the making of land, topographical, stadia, city surveys, and
leveling.   The field work is so arranged as to give each student a
thorough drill in the use of the instruments.   In the second term of
the year a course consisting of lectures and recitations is given dealing
with the calculation of earthwork and with track work, giving especial
attention to street railway requirements.

In Senior year a system of triangulation is laid out over a convenient watershed and with this as a basis a topographical and hydrographical survey is made; all the principal methods for locating
topographical or other details, as by transit, stadia, or plane table,
being employed in different parts of the work, the leveling being done
with the Y-level, hand-level, and vertical angles.   A portion of the
time is also devoted to staking out curves, switches, etc., with especial
reference to street railway requirements.   The work is arranged so as
to give each student sufficient practice in each of the methods
employed under the immediate supervision of an instructor and then
to throw him gradually upon his own responsibility.

In the course in Forestry the work in Surveying at the Summer
Session of the Yale Forest School, at Milford, Pa., may be substituted
for the requirement in Field Engineering.

ROOFS AND BRIDGES—The course of instruction in roofs and bridges
consists of two parts; first, the computation of stresses in all the
standard forms of simple roof trusses and bridge trusses by both the
algebraic and graphic methods; second, the fundamental principles of
design applied to beams, girders, floor-systems, riveted connections,
pin-connections, railway trusses, highway trusses, and roof trusses.

Visits of inspection and lectures supplement the work in the drawing room, but the larger part of the time is spent by the student in actually computing and designing under the direction of the instructor.

MECHANICS—The method of instruction is by means of text-books in connection with lectures and solutions of practical problems in illustration of the various topics.

WATER SUPPLY ENGINEERING—This course treats of the varying quantity of water required by different classes of cities and towns, the methods of collecting and distributing the same, methods of judging its quality and its effect on the public health, sources of contamination and methods of filtration, and in connection with hydraulics the designing of pipe systems.

HYDRAULICS—The method of instruction is by means of recitations and lectures supplemented by illustrative experiments on the apparatus available. Special attention is given to questions in regard to the flow and discharge of streams, pipes, and sewers.

SEWER DESIGN—In this course instruction is given, by lectures, in the various methods of sewer design and construction suited to typical cases, illustrated by existing systems, and followed by requiring the student to design a system to meet simple requirements.

SEWAGE DISPOSAL—This subject is treated by lectures on the various methods adopted in practice with their results, considered both from an engineering and sanitary point of view, supplemented by visits to plants in operation in the immediate vicinity.

MASONRY CONSTRUCTION—The course includes instruction in the properties of the component materials, the details of the construction and calculation of the stability of foundations, retaining walls, dams, and arches. Each student is also required to make the usual tests of cement and mortar.

CHEMISTRY AND BACTERIOLOGY—In these subjects practice is given in the chemical and bacteriological laboratories, the student is instructed in the methods of water analysis, and is taught to observe and identify the various organisms present in natural and contaminated waters ; the main object being to give such instruction as will enable the student to interpret properly the results of water analysis.

SPECIFICATIONS—The laws governing the preparation of engineering specifications are outlined in lectures supplemented by recitations, and illustrative examples from the best practice are reviewed.

Reference to the instruction in ADJUSTMENT OF OBSERVATIONS, ROADS AND PAVEMENTS, and ASTRONOMY is made under the Studies of Instruction in CIVIL ENGINEERING, on p. 264.

PHYSICS AND ELECTRICAL ENGINEERING

Professor HASTINGS, Assistant Professors BEACH, L. P. WHEELER, Dr. C. B. RICE, Dr. DADOURIAN, Dr. COOPER, and assistants.

The instruction in these subjects is given in the lecture rooms and laboratories of WINCHESTER HALL.

PHYSICS—The course in Physics may be regarded as extending through the three years of undergraduate study, although after the first year the work, in accordance with the general plan of the institution, is so specialized that practically only engineering students find it within their reach.

In Freshman year all students attend lectures and recitations on General Physics throughout the year. In the recitations a text-book is used which covers the whole subject, as ordinarily understood, with rather unusual emphasis upon the elementary theory of mechanics, on account of its universal utility as well as its educational value. The subjects of Heat and Electricity follow in the order named. In these the aim is to impart a general philosophical knowledge of the phenomena and of the laws governing them rather than a knowledge of the methods used in laboratories of research and of the technical applications.

The subjects of Sound and Light are associated on account of their intimate relationship as sensations ; thus, less obviously founded upon the basis of mechanics, they receive a different treatment in which more stress is placed upon the physiological aspects of the phenomena.

The lectures are especially designed to enable the student to become familiar by personal observation with nearly all of the phenomena of physics which have proved important in the development of physical theories.

A brief course in elementary laboratory work is given to classes in Biology in their Junior year. The following two courses are offered to students in Course XIII in Junior year.

Sound and Light—The phenomena of these branches of Physics are developed as consequences of the assumption of a wave motion as the cause of our sensations.

Vectors—The relations between directed quantities are developed with reference to their importance in Physics, rather than as a study of the analysis of Hamilton (quaternions) or that of Grassmann (*Ausdehnungslehre*). The later portion of the course involves a discussion of the theory of attractions and the electric field.

ELECTRICAL ENGINEERING—Although the General Physics of the Freshman year may be regarded as preliminary to all courses in applied science, it attaches itself more intimately to that in Electrical Engineering. The time in the Junior year, as far as it has immediate bearing on applied science, is spent in acquiring a necessary knowledge of mathematics and the means of employing such knowledge in the study of advanced Physics. The courses in *Theory of Heat* and *Theory of*

Electricity, which together extend through the year, serve this purpose as also to enlarge the student's knowledge in these important fields.

In the Senior year, students who pursue Electrical Engineering, as well as such others as are properly qualified and apply for the privilege, have a thorough course in the physical laboratory, where they may become proficient in the command of all the more important instruments and methods used in measuring physical magnitudes. The theory and use of typical instruments are taught in a series of lectures simultaneously with the laboratory practice. This course is followed by one on the Theory of Electricity with special attention to the application of the science to the arts.

The later portion of the laboratory work is largely given to the study of electrical machinery such as is in actual use. This work is supplemented by a course on *Dynamo Construction*.

A course on the *Theory of Observations*, including the method of least squares as applied to physical investigations, is given every year. This is open to Graduate Students and to Seniors in Electrical Engineering.

The other subjects, such as : *Machine Design*, *Shop-Visiting*, *Steam Engine*, etc., which are taught in connection with the course in Electrical.Engineering, are referred to under the subjects of instruction in MECHANICAL ENGINEERING, pp. 265 and 266.

MINING STUDIES

Professors HAMMOND, RICHARDS, IRVING; Assistant Professor HUNTOON, and assistants.

The various studies more directly connected with Mining Engineering and Metallurgy will be taught the present year in the HAMMOND METALLURGICAL LABORATORY, which is now practically completed. This building, the gift of Professor John Hays Hammond (Sheffield Scientific School 1876), is devoted entirely to the subjects of Mining, Metallurgy, and Ore Dressing. It contains well-equipped laboratories and research rooms, as well as a departmental library and a museum illustrating the various features of the applied sciences. The laboratories have been planned to give a thorough training in the practical work of assaying and the treatment of ores.

The equipment in the assay department consists of individual desks, pulp balances, coal and gas muffle furnaces, and a sufficient number of bullion balances to accommodate a large class.

There are two ore testing laboratories. The first is equipped with small dressing machinery consisting of jigs, classifiers, tables, and accessories. In this laboratory the theory of ore dressing will be exemplified. The second laboratory is equipped with large machinery where complete mill runs can be made, or the work of an individual machine can be studied under varying conditions of adjustment.

ORE DRESSING—This course includes lectures, recitations, and laboratory work. The lectures cover the general principles, theory of dressing, physical properties of minerals and the application of these properties in separations, the ordinary operations including hand dressing, crushing, sizing, jigging, classifying, and slime treatment. Typical dressing works are described and discussed so as to impress upon the student the necessity of different treatment with different ores.

The laboratory work will consist of sampling, panning of gold-bearing gravel, and studying the effect of crushing an ore containing brittle minerals. The latter will cover screen tests, hand picking, jigging, classifying, and slime treatment. Assays in this department will be made by vanning and fire assay.

ASSAYING—This course includes lectures, recitations, and practical work in the fire-assay of gold, silver, and lead ores. The students are instructed in the various methods of assaying used in practice and before completing the course will be required to make several determinations in one day on unknown ores. This latter is to prepare them for the requirements of practice.

The work in Field Engineering for the year 1908 begins on Monday, June 15, for the Senior year, and on Monday, August 31, for the Junior year.

Further details regarding the subjects of instruction will be found under the studies in MECHANICAL ENGINEERING, pp. 264 to 266.

BIOLOGICAL SCIENCES

Professors CHITTENDEN, MENDEL, EVANS, HARRISON; Assistant Professors RETTGER, COE, UNDERHILL; Dr. COLE, Dr. WOODRUFF, Dr. KUNKEL, and assistants.

The instruction in the various biological sciences is given in laboratories and lecture rooms located in the following buildings: PEABODY MUSEUM, containing the laboratories for Zoology and Paleontology, in connection with the extensive collections belonging to the Museum;

SHEFFIELD HALL, containing the laboratories for Botany, Plant Physiology, Bacteriology and Hygiene, as well as the herbarium and botanical library of the late Professor Eaton, the Swan herbarium and the herbarium of Professor Brewer; SHEFFIELD BIOLOGICAL LABORATORY, in which are located the laboratories for Physiological Chemistry, Toxicology and Physiology (first floor), and the laboratories for General Biology, Comparative Anatomy, Morphology and Embryology (second floor). An experimental green-house is situated near by.

ELEMENTARY BIOLOGY—In the second term of Freshman year an introductory course in Biology is given to students of the Natural Science group. The course consists of lectures and laboratory work designed to acquaint the student with the structure, classification, functions, development, life histories, and evolution of animals and plants, as illustrated by special types. Attention is devoted to the study of protoplasm, cells, and unicellular organisms, including those which cause fermentation, putrefaction, and disease.

COMPARATIVE ANATOMY AND GENERAL BIOLOGY—Instruction in these subjects is given by practical laboratory work supplemented by illustrated lectures and demonstrations. The regular course of instruction, intended especially for students in the Biological course, extends through the second term of Junior year.

The structure of the vertebrate type is first studied and illustrated by careful dissections of the frog and the mammal. Then follows the practical study of some of the more simple plants and of several types of unicellular and other simple animals, with a review of their methods of life, growth, and multiplication. A discussion of the structure and properties of protoplasm and the nature of the animal cell leads to the study of the elementary tissues and the histological structure of the organs of the vertebrate body. Finally the classification of vertebrate animals and the comparative morphology of the different systems of organs in the various groups are discussed with special reference to the theories of evolution. The work of the whole course is supplemented by the study of elementary physiology, which is pursued at the same time.

Although this course is especially planned for students who are preparing for medical studies, it is well adapted for those who wish a practical acquaintance with the general principles of biology and vertebrate anatomy, either for general culture or as preparation for advanced work in zoology, physiology, physiological chemistry, or psychology.

ZOOLOGY—The instruction in Zoology includes a course of illustrated lectures and laboratory exercises on the structure and classification of animals, with particular reference to those forms which are of economic importance or of more general interest. Such groups, particularly invertebrates, as are represented by fossil remains are also discussed at length because of their bearing on the study of Paleontology.

Students in the course in Zoology and Botany also pursue laboratory instruction during the second term of Junior and all of Senior year. This generally occupies from two to four hours a day on four days of each week. It includes dissections of various classes and orders of animals, with microscopic studies of the finer structures and of minute animal forms, as well as work in Systematic Zoology. A briefer course in the laboratory is given to students in Biology during their Senior year.

Special laboratory work on the classification of animals, in preparation for, or in connection with, the study of Paleontology, as well as additional courses of recitations or lectures on particular subjects, are also given when desirable.

EMBRYOLOGY—Lectures and demonstrations are accompanied by practical work in the laboratory. The development and structure of the sexual cells, the fertilization and cleavage of the egg, and the formation of the principal organs of the body are studied in various groups, both of invertebrates and vertebrates, but with special reference to the mammals. The more important theories of heredity, sex determination, and histological differentiation are incidentally discussed.

ENTOMOLOGY—A practical course dealing with the insects injurious to forests is described on p. 283.

ORGANIC EVOLUTION—Instruction is given to the Select course by means of illustrated lectures and recitations during the first half of the Senior year. The course begins with a general study of protoplasm and the fundamental processes of living organisms, with special attention to reproduction. It includes also a consideration of the principles of inheritance and breeding, together with the structure, development, distribution, habits, and instincts of organisms and their relation to their environment in the light of the Darwinian and later theories. The course concludes with a more detailed study of the structure of man, with a view to his proper position in a natural system of classification of animals and the application of the principle of natural selection to his evolution.

GENERAL PHYSIOLOGY OF THE LOWER ORGANISMS—The course will comprise a general survey of the physiology of the lower organisms, particularly the Protozoa, including the problems of general cell-structure, growth and regeneration, development, inheritance, origin of sex, reactions to stimuli, and the relation of Protozoa to disease.

18

The Sedgwick-Rafter method of microscopical examination of water will be employed in the laboratory work, thus affording familiarity with a number of representative types of lower organisms, chiefly unicellular.

PHYSIOLOGY—Elementary Physiology is taught by recitations, lectures, and demonstrations, being designed especially for Junior students in the Biological course. In Senior year a more extensive and detailed study is made of the physiology of nutrition—respiration, digestion, and metabolism—in connection with the study of physiological chemistry.

In a course in Experimental Physiology, designed primarily for graduate students, the various graphic methods are illustrated and applied to the study of the phenomena of the muscular and nervous systems, the circulation, respiration, etc. The work in the laboratory involves the use of the ordinary apparatus for physiological investigation. Stress is laid not alone upon the phenomena of the animal functions, but the topics selected are intended to familiarize the student with the problems and methods of scientific research in this domain. The more advanced students are kept in touch with progress in physiology by a physiological seminary.

PHYSIOLOGICAL CHEMISTRY—Physiological Chemistry is taught by laboratory exercises, illustrative lectures, and recitations. Each student is provided with a suitable working place in the laboratory, well equipped with all needed apparatus and material. The regular course of work, designed especially for Senior students in the Biological course, extends through one year and embraces a thorough study of the chemical composition of the food stuffs and the various tissues and fluids of the body, together with a study of the chemical and physiological processes of respiration, digestion, secretion, excretion, and nutrition in general.

Beginning with a study of the proteins, the more important carbohydrates, and fats, the experimental work extends through the epithelial, connective, contractile, and nervous tissues. Proceeding then to digestion, the various digestive fluids are studied, artificial digestions are made, and the products of digestive action isolated and examined. The blood, milk, and urine are next considered ; and students are taught the applications of quantitative analytical methods to the problems of metabolism and to the identification and estimation of biological products.

EXPERIMENTAL TOXICOLOGY—In connection with a series of lectures and demonstrations on this subject given to Senior students in the Biological course, a portion of one term may also be devoted to a study of the chemical reactions of the more important mineral and organic poisons, and their physiological action is determined experimentally. Advanced students are also taught how to separate poisons from organic tissues and fluids, and to identify them, both by chemical and physiological reactions.

During the second term of Senior year, opportunity is afforded for the carrying on of investigations on some selected subject in either physiology, physiological chemistry or toxicology, in connection with the preparation of honor theses. To those who have the necessary qualifications to undertake original investigations, independently or under guidance, the facilities of the Laboratory of Physiological Chemistry and Physiology are available at all times.

BOTANY—In the courses in Biology and in Zoology and Botany, as well as in the course preparatory to Forestry, a detailed study of typical green flowering plants is pursued in the laboratory, with special reference to the structure and functions of their various organs. This is followed by a general survey of the vegetable kingdom, in which selected types of the different classes of plants, beginning with the lowest, are examined in order. The structure, development, and relationships of these types are discussed in informal lectures. Frequent written tests are required in all the courses.

For those who may desire to pursue the science professionally, the work is arranged to suit individual requirements, whether it be in the direction of morphology or systematic botany, as applied to either flowering plants or cryptogams.

PLANT PHYSIOLOGY—Instruction in plant physiology is offered to those students familiar with the elements of vegetable morphology and histology who possess some knowledge of physics and chemistry. An acquaintance with organic chemistry is also very desirable. Particular attention is devoted to such topics as the composition of the plant body, plant nutrition, the synthesis of proteids and carbohydrates, the distribution and significance of vegetable enzymes, and other features of metabolism. The experimental method is emphasized wherever practicable. Opportunity is offered for research work in plant physiology, especially with reference to its chemical aspects.

BACTERIOLOGY AND HYGIENE—Two courses of instruction are offered in these subjects. The first, briefer course, extends over a period of ten weeks, three afternoons each week, and is designed especially for students in Municipal and Sanitary Engineering. Particular attention is given to such topics as the bacteriology and the purification of water supplies.

The second or longer course covers a period of twenty weeks, fifty exercises. The work is particularly planned to suit the needs of students in Chemistry and Biology, and hence presupposes at least an elementary knowledge of those subjects. Practical instruction is given in the preparation of culture media, the cultivation of bacteria, staining and microscopic technique. The classification of a large number of non-pathogenic and pathogenic bacteria is made, and a careful study is also made of the relation of bacteria to the various industries and to disease. Considerable time is devoted to the study of diseases from the bacteriological and hygienic standpoint. Both courses consist of laboratory work supplemented by lectures and recitations. Ample opportunity is afforded for original investigation.

BACTERIOLOGY OF WATER AND SEWAGE—A course of ten lectures, with demonstrations, given in the first term consists of a discussion of bacteriological methods and micro-organisms in their relation to the safeguarding of water supplies against dangerous pollution.

PUBLIC HYGIENE—In a series of twenty lectures given to Seniors in the course in Select studies special emphasis is placed on hygiene from the public health standpoint. Such topics as the following are presented : bacteria and other microscopic organisms in their relation to disease ; the hygiene of tuberculosis, typhoid fever, etc.; the manufacture and use of vaccine virus and antitoxin ; isolation and quarantine regulations ; foods ; and the hygiene of occupations and of dwellings.

GEOLOGICAL SCIENCES

Professors PIRSSON, SCHUCHERT, GREGORY, IRVING ; Assistant Professor FORD, Mr. F. WARD, and assistants.

Instruction in Mineralogy, Geography and the Geological Sciences is given in KIRTLAND HALL, a building donated by Mrs. Lucy W. Boardman, of New Haven, in memory of her uncle, the late Jared P. Kirtland, LL.D. The first floor is devoted to Mineralogy, and has a large fire-proof room containing the Brush Mineral Collection and Library, a lecture room, laboratories for research work in crystallography and mineral chemistry, and a large laboratory for determinative mineralogy. In 1904 Professor George Jarvis Brush gave to the Trustees of the Sheffield Scientific School his private collection of minerals, his mineralogical library, and a fund to provide for their growth and maintenance, thus placing the department in possession of a wealth of material for study and investigation.

The second floor of Kirtland Hall is devoted to Geology and has a lecture room, laboratories for geological and petrographical research, and a room containing the library and petrographical collection.   On the third floor is the lecture room for Geography and the room containing the collections and library, and the laboratory of Economic Geology.   The instruction in Anthropology is also given on this floor.   All of these varied departments are amply equipped with the collections, libraries, and apparatus necessary for instruction and the most advanced research work.

The instruction in Historical Geology and Paleontology is given in PEABODY MUSEUM, and the large and important collections of the late Professors O. C. Marsh and C. E. Beecher are available for this purpose, as well as for the use of advanced students under the direction of the professor in charge.

GEOLOGY—The course in Geology includes recitations, lectures, and oral instruction, extending through the year.   During the first term the recitations are attended by the entire Senior class, except those in the Mechanical and Electrical Engineering and Select courses.   This part of the course includes Structural and Dynamical Geology and is illustrated by maps, lantern views, photographs, diagrams, and specimens.

During the Winter half-term the Seniors in the Civil Engineering course and in Forestry extend the work of the first term into stratigraphical and historical geology.

Historical Geology and Paleontology—During the Winter half-term the sequence and distribution of the sedimentary formations are studied, together with the introduction and succession of the various types of life during past geological ages.   This part of the course is pursued by the Seniors in Mining, Metallurgy, Mineralogy, Chemistry, Biology, and Zoology and Botany.   Suitable collections of rocks, fossils, lantern views, etc., are used to illustrate the subject.

Opportunities are afforded for geological excursions during the warmer months.   Additional and advanced work in geology, petrology, and paleontology is offered in the list of graduate courses.

ECONOMIC GEOLOGY—The course in Economic Geology is given to the Senior Mining Engineering, Metallurgical, Chemical and Mineralogical divisions during the Spring half-term following directly after the course in Historical Geology.   Instruction is given chiefly by means of lectures, which are illustrated by the use of lantern slides and by specimens from the collection of Economic Geology.   The course includes a discussion of the general features of ore bodies, with the theories of their formation, together with descriptions of the most important and typical ore occurrences in North America. The occurrences and uses of the non-metallic minerals are also described.

ELEMENTARY PETROLOGY—A series òf lectures of an elementary nature and without the use of the microscope, on the history, origin, and classification of rocks with especial reference to their geologic relations and economic properties, is given one hour a week in the second term. This course is illustrated by collections and is offered as an optional to all students in the Senior class and in graduate courses who may desire to take it.

MINERALOGY AND CRYSTALLOGRAPHY—Instruction in Mineralogy in the courses in Chemistry, Metallurgy, Civil Engineering, Mining, Zoology and Botany, Mineralogy, and Forestry, is carried on by means of both lectures and practical work in laboratories especially fitted up for the purpose, the methods of instruction being such that students acquire familiarity with the common minerals, by making chemical and physical tests upon them, as also by seeing and handling a large number of typical specimens. Attention is devoted especially to those species which are of economic, geological, or scientific import- ance. To better understand and appreciate the chemical aspects of the subject, students are first made familiar with the simple chemical tests and blowpipe reactions which are best adapted for testing minerals, and later this knowledge is applied to the determination of unknown species. Students have free access to a labeled collection of carefully selected, typical mineral specimens, where the crystallization and other physical properties of the different species may be studied, and where comparisons may be made with specimens which have been determined. There are also extensive unlabeled collections for study, arranged especially to give students practice and facility in the correct identi- fication of minerals. In addition to laboratory work, instruction is given in Crystallography, illustrated by collections of models and natural crystals. Lectures in Descriptive Mineralogy are illustrated by the extensive collection presented by Professor Brush. The labor- atories are provided with apparatus for the thorough chemical and physical investigation of minerals and with an extensive library to which students have access. The laboratories are open seven hours each day to accommodate any who desire to devote more time to the subject than is laid out in any of the prescribed courses.

PHYSICAL GEOGRAPHY—The course in Physical Geography is devoted to a study of those topics which are of most importance for the understanding of the relation of man to his natural environment. The topics which receive the most attention are the ocean, topography, soils, climate, and the distribution of plants, animals and useful minerals. In the course of this study the student is made acquainted with the dominant features—structural and scenic—of the earth's surface and with the forces and conditions which have brought these features into existence. The regions of the earth are studied in their physical relations involving a consideration of climatic control, plant and animal migrations and habitats, avenues of trade and commerce and explorations. The instruction is by means of text-books, maps, quizzes and informal lectures.

This course combined with Commercial Geography (see p. 280) is a study of the influence upon man of his physical environment and of the efforts of human beings to render nature subservient to their life needs.

SOCIAL SCIENCE AND HISTORY
Professors CALLENDER, KELLER, Mr. MIMS.

GOVERNMENT—The object of this course is to give the student a general knowledge of the governmental machinery of Great Britain and the United States as the two great examples of popular government—the one of the cabinet form, the other of the presidential. Attention is directed chiefly to the actual working of government rather than to the historical development of political institutions, with the view of giving the student some understanding and appreciation of the practical problems of government as they exist in this country at present. The instruction is given by means of text-books, supplemented by lectures and assigned reading in various books on selected topics. The text-books used this year are Moran's *The English Government*, Bagehot's *English Constitution*, and Bryce's *American Commonwealth*.

The course in American history serves as a preparation for this course.

ECONOMICS—The work in this subject is designed primarily to explain the social process by which wealth is produced in a modern community and distributed as income among the different individuals and classes. The social organism so far as it has to do with this process is described in detail and the relation of actual business activity to the process pointed out, to the end that the student may recognize and understand the working of cause and effect in the business world. A secondary purpose is the training of his mind in economic reasoning. One text-book is read by the student and thoroughly discussed in class. This is supplemented by assigned reading in several other standard works on the general principles of Economics. The text-book used this year is Laughlin's *Elements of Political Economy*, supplemented by Mill's *Principles of Political Economy*. Selected topics, such as money, banking, public finance, trusts, transportation, and labor problems, are then treated more in detail, with a view of giving the student a knowledge of the more important current economic questions.

A small library, containing the principal authorities on these subjects, has been provided, in order that the students may be able to familiarize themselves somewhat with the literature of the subject. These books may be used by the student in the reading room of Byers Memorial Hall. The instruction in the later part of the course is given partly by means of text-books and partly by lectures.

ANTHROPOLOGY—This subject occupies two hours per week in the Select Course, during the Junior year. In connection with comprehensive text-books such subjects will be studied as the antiquity of man, the relation of man to other animals, racial differences, language, the arts of life, the spirit world, etc. Lectures will briefly outline the earliest forms of the industrial organization, marriage and the family, property, religion, and government. The anthropological collections of Peabody Museum and other illustrative material will be utilized as far as practicable. Outside reading will be assigned to those desiring it.

SOCIAL EVOLUTION—This subject follows directly upon Organic Evolution (p. 273), the two constituting in reality a single, unbroken course; it occupies three hours a week for the second half of the second term in Senior year. It is designed to treat of the applicability to man and to human society of the ideas and principles derived from the study of Organic Evolution. The topics include: human variation and heredity, selection, the struggle for existence, counter-selective factors, "eugenics," etc.; and the evolutionary system in its application to the institutions of society. Lectures and collateral reading.

COMMERCIAL GEOGRAPHY—This subject follows directly upon Physical Geography (p. 279), the two constituting a single unbroken course; it occupies three hours per week during the second half of the Junior year. The general idea of the course is to exhibit the efforts put forth by men, under various environmental conditions, in the meeting of their life-needs; and this object is designed to be attained through a study and analysis of the stream of trade. The data or statistics of commerce are interpreted in the light of anthropological and economic principles, and some attention is given to the history and development of exchange. Considerable emphasis is laid upon the trade relations of civilized and partly civilized countries, and in particular upon trade with South America. Map-work is required, and as much use as possible is made of the collections in the Yale Commercial Museum. Text-books and informal lectures.

HISTORY—Two courses in History are given to the students in the Select Course, one in European History during the Junior year, one in the History of the United States in the Senior year, an outline of which is given below.

I. *European History*—The work of the Junior year is devoted to the study of some of the more interesting and important movements and epochs in European History since the fall of Rome, such as the Barbarian Invasions, the Rise and Development of the Medieval Empire, the Growth and Importance of the Medieval Church, the Crusades, Feudalism, the Rise of Nationalities, the Renaissance, the Reformation, the French Revolution, etc. Very little effort is made to give a continuous chronological outline of the periods studied. Facts and dates are stressed only so far as they are considered advisable for a better comprehension of the subject matter in hand. The principal aim of the course is to stimulate the student to become acquainted with books which will prove of permanent interest and profit, to so acquaint him with some chapters in the History of Europe as to inspire him to read others for himself and to equip him to understand more intelligently the life of present-day Europe.

The following books form the basis of the work: Emerton's *Introduction to the Middle Ages* and *Medieval Europe*, Robinson's *Readings in European History*, Adams' *Civilisation during the Middle Ages*, Adams' *Growth of the French Nation*, Robinson's *History of Western Europe*, Robinson and Rolfe's *Petrarch*, Emerton's *Erasmus*, Henderson's *French Revolution*, Johnston's *Napoleon*.

II. *History of United States*—The work of the Senior year is devoted to the study of some of the more important phases of the political history of the United States. By the way of introduction, a somewhat thorough study is made of the causes of the American Revolution, the new political ideas which it emphasized, the types of leaders which it produced. The general character of the course is indicated by the following books which are used as a basis for the work: W. E. H. Lecky's *American Revolution* (Woodburn ed.), Fiske's *Critical Period of American History*, Walker's *The Making of the Nation*, Channing's *The Jeffersonian System*, Schurz's *Henry Clay*, MacDonald's *Jacksonian Democracy*, Smith's *Parties and Slavery*, Morse's *Abraham Lincoln*, Dunning's *Reconstruction, Political and Economic*.

Definite provision has been made in Byers Memorial Hall for a working library in these courses which will make assignments in a wide range of books possible.

FORESTRY

Professors GRAVES, TOUMEY, PINCHOT ; Assistant Professor CHAPMAN, Dr. A. H. GRAVES, Mr. HAWLEY, and assistants.

The instruction in the various subjects related to Forestry is given in the lecture rooms and laboratories of the SHEFFIELD SCIENTIFIC SCHOOL and in MARSH HALL, the School building of the Yale Forest School located in the Yale Botanical Garden. Supplementary work is conducted in the woodlands of New Haven and vicinity, as well as at Milford, Pa., during the summer session of the Yale Forest School.

For the course in Field Engineering, described on p. 267, the work in surveying at the summer session of the Yale Forest School, at Milford, Pa., may be substituted.

Students who take the summer term of the Forest School at Milford and complete the optional courses during the Senior year are able to finish the work in the Forest School in a single year of graduate study. Students are urged to take the summer term at Milford at the end of the Junior year instead of the end of the Senior year.

FOREST BOTANY—This course is designed especially for those intend-ing to enter upon the study of Forestry. The instruction is divided as follows : (1) a course in dendrology, consisting of illustrated lectures dealing with the distribution, habits, taxonomic, and silvical char-acters of the economic trees of the United States ; (2) a series of field excursions in New Haven and vicinity for the purpose of acquainting the student with the names, habits, and uses of the local trees and shrubs ; (3) the study of tree diseases, by means of lectures, labora-tory work, and excursions.

SILVICULTURE—During the Fall term a study is made of the forest and of the elements which enter into its composition. The lectures discuss the principles underlying the life history of trees, the concep-tion of forest types, and the methods employed in studying the silvical characteristics of trees and of forests. During the remainder of the year attention is given to the treatment of woodlands, the lectures considering the principles of maintaining forests by means of skillful cuttings, the various systems of forest management, and the practical silvicultural problems in American forest regions. The work in for-estry already accomplished in the United States and Canada is also described. Throughout the course the lectures are supplemented by extensive field work, several tracts of woodland in the vicinity of New Haven being reserved for this purpose.

FOREST SEEDING AND PLANTING—The course includes a careful study of tree seeds with respect to their structure, dissemination, vital-ity, etc. The field work is devoted to practical exercises illustrating the various methods of seeding and planting, and attention is also given to the planting and care of trees in streets and parks.

FOREST ENTOMOLOGY—A course of lectures and practical exercises on such groups of insects as are of economic importance in the man-agement of forests and in the utilization of forests products. It is expected that the student will become familiar with the structure, habits, and life histories of the more injurious species, as well as with such predatory and parasitic insects and other organisms as naturally limit their increase. This work is accompanied by a discussion of the methods by which the attacks of insects upon trees, lumber, and finished products may be most successfully controlled.

STATE FOREST LAW—A study of the forest laws of different states, with particular reference to forest protection and forest reserves.

METHODS OF FIELD WORK—A course of lectures describing the policy of the United States Forest Service in its field studies.

FOREST HYDROGRAPHY—A course of lectures considering the variations in the flow of streams, giving particular attention to irrigation economics, and to the work of the Reclamation Service of the United States Geological Survey in the construction and administration of irrigation systems in the arid West.

FOREST POLICY—A course of lectures describing the origin of forest policy, its objects and principles; legislation and its causes before 1891, and from 1891 to 1903; national organization in Forestry; the forest and other land laws in relation to economic and industrial development; and State forest problems.

GENERAL INFORMATION
DEGREES

Students of this Department, on the recommendation of the Governing Board, are admitted by the Corporation of Yale University to the following degrees which are publicly conferred by the President and Fellows of the University on Commencement Day:

1. BACHELOR OF PHILOSOPHY: This degree is conferred on those who complete any of the three-year courses of study, passing all the examinations in a satisfactory manner.

2. MASTER OF SCIENCE: The requirements for this degree are stated on page 209.

3. CIVIL ENGINEER, MECHANICAL ENGINEER, AND MINING ENGINEER: The requirements for these degrees are stated on pages 211 to 213.

4. DOCTOR OF PHILOSOPHY: The requirements for this degree are stated on page 209.

GOVERNMENT AND DISCIPLINE

All routine questions relating to the discipline of the student body are acted upon by a Committee on Discipline, responsible to the Governing Board and other Professors and Instructors, who form the General Faculty of the School.

Each class is presided over by a special Faculty consisting of a Class Officer and such others of the teaching force as are engaged in the instruction of members of the class. The function of the Class Faculty is to superintend the general and individual progress as well as conduct of the class under its charge, and to recommend to the General Faculty, at convenient intervals, such measures as seem expedient.

Every student is provided at the opening of each scholastic year with a copy of the Regulations of the Sheffield Scientific School. These contain all necessary information regarding scholarship requirements, deportment, attendance etc.

The classes are divided into small sections, each of which is supervised by an instructor, called its Division Officer, whose duty is to advise or direct the members of his Division desiring to consult him, and through whom the student addresses all communications to the Faculty.

TERMS

For purposes of administration and instruction the scholastic year is divided into two terms, the first extending from the beginning of the year to the Winter Vacation, and the second from the end of the Winter Vacation to Commencement. The second term is subdivided into two equal parts, the Winter half-term and Spring half-term.

EXPENSES

The TREASURER'S BILLS are made out and delivered to the students three times a year, viz : at the beginning of each term or half-term, at which time they are payable. The annual charge for tuition for undergraduate students is one hundred and fifty dollars. An additional charge of six dollars for each term or half-term is made for incidentals, including the use of libraries, public rooms, gymnasium, etc. The student in the Chemical, Metallurgical, Mining, and Biological Courses has an additional charge of fifteen dollars per term, or half-term, for chemicals and the use of apparatus in the chemical and metallurgical laboratories. He also supplies himself at his own expense with special apparatus and materials, the cost of which should not exceed ten dollars a term.

For the summer courses in surveying of the Junior and Senior years a fee of fifteen dollars is charged each year.

For graduate students the charge for tuition is one hundred dollars per year.

The fee for graduation as Bachelor of Philosophy, including the fee for Commencement Dinners, etc., is ten dollars unless the person taking the degree is also an Academical graduate, when it is five dollars.

BUILDINGS
LABORATORIES AND RECITATION HALLS

The buildings in which the work of instruction in the Scientific School is mainly carried on are : Sheffield Hall, North Sheffield Hall, Sheffield Biological Laboratory, Winchester Hall, Kirtland Hall, Sheffield Chemical Laboratory, and Hammond Metallurgical Laboratory. Instruction in mineralogy, physical geology, petrology, and physiography is given in Kirtland Hall ; in zoology and historical geology in the Peabody Museum, and in free-hand drawing in the Art School; while instruction in forestry is given at the Yale Forest School. Winchester Hall is intended chiefly for the engineering sections, containing appliances and machinery for their special use. Sheffield Hall, in which the administrative offices of the School and the laboratories for botany, plant physiology, and bacteriology are situated, affords also a number of recitation rooms, but the majority of such rooms devoted to mathematics, the languages, history, and economics will be found in North Sheffield Hall. The names of the other buildings indicate their respective purposes. These buildings contain a large number of recitation and lecture rooms, halls for public assemblies and lectures, chemical, physical, biological, physiological, and metallurgical laboratories, besides studies for some of the professors, where their private technical libraries are kept.

BYERS MEMORIAL HALL

This building, a gift from Mrs. Martha F. Byers, of Pittsburg, Pa., in memory of Alexander MacBurney Byers, the husband of the donor, and their son, Alexander Mac-Burney Byers, Jr., a graduate of the School in the class of 1894, is used for promoting the social and religious life of the Sheffield Scientific School, and provides the comforts of a social club for all Scientific School students.

The basement floor contains billiard rooms, lunch room, toilet rooms with shower baths, and a publication office for the Scientific Monthly. On the main floor of the building is a library and reading room, while on the opposite side of the hall is a large social room, adjoining which is a coat room, office, etc. On the second floor are the rooms of the Young Men's Christian Association of the Sheffield Scientific School, with an assembly hall for the various needs of the student-body. The upper floor of the building is given up to students' rooms (fourteen in number), arranged around a large sitting room, thus constituting a small dormitory.

The building is administered under the advice of a board.of six members, three from the Governing Board of the School and three from its graduates outside of this Board, chosen for their sympathy with the objects of the building and understanding of the needs connected therewith.

The active management of the building is placed as far as practicable in the hands of a committee of students of the Sheffield Scientific School ; the responsible control of the floor occupied by the Young Men's Christian Association being in the hands of those members of the committee who are chosen by the students as representatives of the Young Men's Christian Association of the Sheffield Scientific School.

DORMITORIES

Through the generosity of Mr. Frederick W. Vanderbilt (Sheffield Scientific School 1876), of New York City, a dormitory system for the Sheffield Scientific School has been started on a portion of land called Vanderbilt Square, directly opposite Sheffield Square. Two dormitory buildings known as VANDERBILT-SCIENTIFIC, in memory of the donor's brother, Cornelius Vanderbilt, who died in 1899, are already completed and occupied. These buildings are handsome Gothic stone structures, fire-proof, heated by steam, lighted by electricity, and provided with open fire-places, and all modern conveniences. They contain twenty-eight single rooms, eighteen suites adapted for two persons, and thirty-nine suites capable of accommodating three men each. The rooms in these dormitories are not furnished, and the rates stated below do not include heating.

Students occupying rooms in these dormitories may retain the same rooms for another academic year by making application in writing to the Director of the School, on or before March 1, 1908. Rooms not reserved will then be offered to the classes in order of seniority.

PRICES PER WEEK OF ROOMS IN VANDERBILT-SCIENTIFIC

The prices appended are for a suite of rooms or single rooms, per week, the rental for the college year being for thirty-six weeks. When a suite of rooms is occupied by two or more persons, each occupant will be charged with one-half or one-third the price named in the schedule.

$4.00—Rooms 134, 135, 136, 137, 172, 173, 190, 191.

$5.00—Rooms 117, 118, 119, 122, 123, 124, 125, 128, 129, 130, 131, 164, 165, 168, 169, 176, 177, 182, 183, 186, 187.

$6.50—Rooms 105, 106, 174, 175.

$8.00—Rooms 114, 115, 132, 133, 139, 150, 151.

$8.50—Rooms 120, 126, 142, 146.

$9.00—Rooms 121, 127, 143, 147, 152, 153.

$10.00—Rooms 101, 104, 107, 113, 140, 141, 144, 145, 148, 149, 160, 161, 170, 171, 178, 188, 189.

$11.00—Rooms 102, 103, 109, 111, 112, 162, 163, 166, 167, 180, 181, 184, 185.

$11.50—Rooms 108, 110.

The dormitory floor of BYERS MEMORIAL HALL contains fourteen rooms, arranged around a large sitting room, which is used in common by all the occupants of this floor. These rooms are partially furnished, are lighted by electricity, heated by steam, and provided with commodious toilet facilities closely adjacent on the same floor. The price of these rooms is five dollars per week, for the college year of thirty-six weeks, and includes light and heat.

According to a rule of the Governing Board of the School, students are not allowed to room in any hotel, apartment-house, or building in-which a family does not reside, except by special permission of the Faculty.

UNIVERSITY PRIVILEGES
LIBRARIES AND READING ROOMS

The Special Technical Library of the Scientific School consists of about 7,500 volumes. Included in this is the HILLHOUSE MATHEMATICAL LIBRARY of 2,400 volumes, collected during a long series of years by Dr. William Hillhouse, and in 1870 purchased and presented to the institution by Mr. Sheffield. A catalogue of this collection forms a supplement to the Annual Report of the Governing Board of 1870. Students have access to all the prominent scientific journals, and the proceedings of academies and scientific societies, which can be found either in this library or in the University Library.

There is also a CHEMICAL LIBRARY in the Sheffield Chemical Laboratory, in which the principal chemical journals and periodicals may be found. A compact working library of History, Economics, and Political Science, for the use of students pursuing these subjects, is situated in Byers Memorial Hall, where also there is a collection of books of reference of a general nature, including dictionaries in several languages, encyclopedias, etc., besides other volumes technical and technological in character. A small consulting library of Biology is maintained in the Biological Laboratory and private technical libraries on the subjects of Geology and Mineralogy are in Kirtland Hall; under suitable restrictions these may be used by students.

Members of the Scientific School have a convenient and commodious reading room in Byers Memorial Hall, where they will find the daily and weekly newspapers and reviews, and the standard monthly magazines.

For information regarding the University Library, Peabody Museum of Natural History, Gymnasium, Yale Field, Yale Dining Hall, Bureau of Self-Help, Infirmary, Yale Station, United States Post Office, and University Lectures and Concerts, see Part IV of this Catalogue.

19

CHURCH SITTINGS

Free sittings for students in this department of Yale University are provided as follows : in the Center Church and United Church (Congregational) ; in Trinity Church and Christ Church (Episcopal) ; and in the First Methodist Church.

Those who prefer to pay for a sitting for one year, more or less, in the churches above mentioned, or in any other church of any denomination, may apply to the Director of the School.

Sittings in the College Chapel (Battell Chapel) are free, as heretofore, to the students of this Department. Several pews in the South Gallery are reserved on Sundays for students of the Sheffield Scientific School. The ushers in attendance will indicate which they are.

The Sunday services are occasionally held in Woolsey Hall, where there is ample accommodation for students in all Departments.

For list of University Preachers, see Part IV.

SHEFFIELD LECTURES

A course of ten lectures, under the auspices of the Sheffield Scientific School, is delivered annually between January 15 and April 1 in College Street Hall. The subjects of the course, which is now offered for the forty-second year, are of a scientific nature, of general interest, and are treated by men eminent in their respective lines of work. The lectures are as a rule illustrated. Course tickets are nominal in price, and the topics are announced in the Bulletin of the University and in the local press.

HONORS

Two-year General Honors are awarded at the end of Senior year to those members of the class who have shown a high degree of proficiency in all the studies of their course during Junior and Senior years. A candidate for such honors must present, on or before June 10 of Senior year, a meritorious thesis on some subject approved by his Division Officer.

ONE-YEAR GENERAL HONORS are awarded at the end of Junior year to such students as have maintained a high standing for the year in all the studies of their course.

SPECIAL HONORS are awarded at the end of Junior and Senior years to students, not recipients of general honors, who have shown special excellence in any particular study or studies. Seniors who are candidates for such honors must present an acceptable thesis, unless excused by the Governing Board.

SCHOLARSHIPS

The HOLMES SCHOLARSHIP, founded by Mr. Samuel Holmes, amounts to fifty dollars per year. The recipient must be a citizen of Middlebury, Prospect, Waterbury, or Wolcott, Connecticut; the appointments are made by the Board of Agents of the Bronson Library in Waterbury.

The ROGERS SCHOLARSHIP, founded in 1899, by a gift of five thousand dollars from Mr. William A. Rogers (class of 1874), of Buffalo, New York, is awarded, whenever there is a vacancy, at the end of Junior year, to a student of the course in Biology or Chemistry who has attained high rank in the studies of the course. The annual income from this fund will be paid to the incumbent during his Senior year, and if the holder of the scholarship desires, he may retain the scholarship for one year of graduate study, providing he maintains, during Senior year, high rank in his studies.

The PAGE SCHOLARSHIPS, founded in 1901, in memory of Henry A. Page, a merchant of the city of New York, by his son (class of 1875), consist of the income of a fund of seven thousand dollars. This income is loaned by the Director of the School in amounts of one hundred dollars annually to deserving members of the Junior and Senior classes.

The MOORE SCHOLARSHIPS, five in number, of fifty dollars each, founded in 1906 by a gift of five thousand dollars from Mr. E. J. Moore, of Philadelphia, are awarded each year to deserving students of good scholarship standing. The money so advanced is to be considered in the light of a loan, to be repaid after graduation.

The GAYLORD SCHOLARSHIP. See page 102.

The MAHLON LONG SCHOLARSHIP. See page 108.

The DEFOREST SCHOLARSHIP FUND. See page 103.

Applications for aid from this fund may be made before the first of June to the Director of the Sheffield Scientific School.

THE CLASS OF 1904 SCHOLARSHIP of one hundred dollars is awarded to a member of the Junior class who wholly or in part supports himself and maintains a good scholarship standing and engages in some form of wholesome undergraduate activity.

The LEAVENWORTH SCHOLARSHIP FUND. See page 104.

The BENJAMIN F. BARGE SCHOLARSHIP FUND. See page 108.

The Yale Alumni Association of Kansas City offers two prizes of twenty five dollars each to be awarded to the two boys who pass the best examinations for admission to the Academical and Scientific Departments.

SCHOLARSHIPS in the form of annual loans of six hundred dollars are offered by the Yale Scholarship Trust of Chicago, a corporation formed January 16, 1903, to be distributed in installments to young men of Illinois, carefully chosen on the basis of personal character and scholarship, who enter Yale College or the Sheffield Scientific School.

SHEFFIELD GRADUATE SCHOLARSHIPS.—Six scholarships of one hundred dollars each (covering the charges for tuition) are awarded, on application, to those members of the graduating class of the Sheffield Scientific School who have attained high proficiency in the special studies of their respective courses, and who desire to spend one or more years in graduate study. Each scholarship will be available for one year only. Application for these scholarships must be made in writing, on or before June

1st, to the head of the department to which the student belongs, with a statement as to the character of the graduate study to be pursued.

The DANIEL C. EATON GRADUATE SCHOLARSHIP IN BOTANY. See page 115.

The JOHN ADDISON PORTER MEMORIAL FELLOWSHIP. See page 113.

THE LOOMIS FELLOWSHIP IN PHYSICS. See page 304.

THE LOOMIS FELLOWSHIP IN CHEMISTRY. See page 304.

PRIZES

PRIZES are offered annually, to members of the Senior class, for excellence in Civil Engineering, in Mechanical Engineering, in Mining Engineering, in Sanitary Engineering, and in Electrical Engineering; to members of the Junior and Senior Classes in the Select Course, for excellence in History, as determined by special examination on assigned topics; to members of the Freshman class for excellence in all the studies of the year, in Physics, in German, in French, in Spanish, in English, in Chemistry, in Mathematics, in Biology, and in Drawing.

The WILLIAM R. BELKNAP PRIZES, founded by Mr. William R. Belknap of the class of 1869, are awarded for excellence in the Natural History studies of Senior year. There are two prizes, one for excellence in Geological studies, and one for excellence in Biological studies.

The BLAKE STONE BREAKER PRIZE, founded in 1902 by Mr. Henry T. Blake, representing the heirs of Eli W. Blake, of New Haven, as a memorial to Eli Whitney Blake, the inventor of the Blake Stone Breaker. This prize, consisting of not less than fifty dollars, is awarded to the author of any treatise deemed worthy of such award on some subject connected with Mining or Civil Engineering, and preferably with some branch of those pursuits in which the use of broken stone or ores is an important feature. In the award of said prize, preference shall be given to the work of students, graduate or undergraduate, in the Sheffield Scientific School.

The WILLIAM C. TUCKER PRIZE IN SANITARY ENGINEER-ING, consisting of fifty dollars, is awarded at the end of Senior year to a student in the Sanitary Engineering course who has attained General Honors in said course, and who presents the best thesis on some original work relating to Sanitary Engineering.

The SAMUEL LEWIS PENFIELD PRIZE, for proficiency in Mineralogy, of twenty-five dollars, founded in 1906 by a gift of five hundred dollars from Mr. Morris B. Belknap, of the class of 1877, is awarded at the end of Junior year.

The JAMES GORDON BENNETT PRIZE. See page 575.

The COBDEN CLUB SILVER MEDAL. See page 576.

The GEORGE WASHINGTON EGLESTON HISTORICAL PRIZE. See page 577.

The JOHN A. PORTER ESSAY PRIZE. See page 575.

GRADUATE SCHOOL
OFFICERS OF INSTRUCTION
FACULTY

ARTHUR TWINING HADLEY, LL.D., *President*

ANDREW WHEELER PHILLIPS, PH.D., *Dean, and Professor of Mathematics*

WILLIAM HENRY BREWER, PH.D., LL.D., *Norton Professor of Agriculture, Emeritus*

ARTHUR MARTIN WHEELER, LL.D., *Durfee Professor of History, Emeritus, and Lecturer on European History*

JOHN FERGUSON WEIR, M.A., N.A., *William Leffingwell Professor of Painting and Design, and Director of the School of the Fine Arts*

CHARLES BRINCKERHOFF RICHARDS, M.A., *Higgin Professor of Mechanical Engineering*

JOHN HENRY NIEMEYER, M.A., A.N.A., *Street Professor of Drawing*

TRACY PECK, LL.D., *Professor of the Latin Language and Literature*

WILLIAM GRAHAM SUMNER, LL.D., *Pelatiah Perit Professor of Political and Social Science*

CHARLES HENRY SMITH, LL.D., *Larned Professor of American History*

WILLIAM GILBERT MIXTER, M.A., *Professor of Chemistry*

HENRY PARKS WRIGHT, PH.D., LL.D., *Dunham Professor of the Latin Language and Literature, and Dean of the College Faculty*

HENRY AUGUSTIN BEERS, M.A., *Professor of English Literature*

AUGUSTUS JAY DuBOIS, C.E., PH.D., *Professor of Civil Engineering*

BERNADOTTE PERRIN, PH.D., LL.D., *Lampson Professor of Greek Literature and History*

EDWARD SALISBURY DANA, PH.D., *Professor of Physics, and Curator of the Mineralogical Collection*

THOMAS DAY SEYMOUR, LL.D., *Hillhouse Professor of the Greek Language and Literature*

CHARLES SHELDON HASTINGS, PH.D., *Professor of Physics*

FRANK AUSTIN GOOCH, PH.D., *Professor of Chemistry, and Director of the Kent Chemical Laboratory*

ALBERT STANBURROUGH COOK, PH.D., L.H.D., LL.D., *Professor of the English Language and Literature*

WILLIAM BEEBE, M.A., *Professor of Mathematics, and Instructor in Astronomy*

GEORGE BURTON ADAMS, PH.D., LITT.D., *Professor of History*

SAMUEL SIMONS SANFORD, M.A., *Professor of Applied Music*

HENRY WALCOTT FARNAM, R.P.D., *Professor of Political Economy*

EDWARD PARMELEE MORRIS, L.H.D., *Professor of the Latin Language and Literature*

HENRY ROSEMANN LANG, PH.D., *Benjamin F. Barge Professor of the Romance Languages and Literature*

RUSSELL HENRY CHITTENDEN, PH.D., LL.D., SC.D., *Professor of Physiological Chemistry, and Director of the Sheffield Scientific School*

JOHN HAYS HAMMOND, M.A., *Professor of Mining Engineering*

HORACE LEMUEL WELLS, M.A., *Professor of Analytical Chemistry and Metallurgy*

THOMAS DWIGHT GOODELL, PH.D., *Professor of the Greek Language and Literature*

EDWARD WASHBURN HOPKINS, PH.D., LL.D., *Professor of Sanskrit and Comparative Philology*

ARTHUR HUBBELL PALMER, M.A., *Professor of the German Language and Literature*

HORATIO MCLEOD REYNOLDS, M.A., *Talcott Professor of the Greek Language and Literature*

FREDERICK MORRIS WARREN, PH.D., L.H.D., *Street Professor of Modern Languages*

GEORGE MARTIN DUNCAN, LL.D., *Professor of Logic and Metaphysics*

LOUIS VALENTINE PIRSSON, M.A., *Professor of Physical Geology*

EDWARD GAYLORD BOURNE, PH.D., *Professor of History*

GUSTAV GRUENER, PH.D., *Professor of German*

CHARLES CUTLER TORREY, PH.D., D.D., *Professor of Semitic Languages*

HORATIO WILLIAM PARKER, MUS.D., *Battell Professor of the Theory of Music, and Dean of the Department of Music*

WILBUR LUCIUS CROSS, PH.D., *Professor of English, and Librarian of the Sheffield Scientific School*

CHARLTON MINER LEWIS, PH.D., *Emily Sanford Professor of English Literature*

WILLIAM LYON PHELPS, PH.D., *Lampson Professor of English Literature*

ROBERT NELSON CORWIN, PH.D., *Professor of German*

ERNEST WILLIAM BROWN, SC.D., *Professor of Mathematics*

IRVING FISHER, PH.D., *Professor of Political Economy*

JAMES PIERPONT, PH.D., *Professor of Mathematics*

HANNS OERTEL, PH.D., *Professor of Linguistics and Comparative Philology*

PERCEY FRANKLYN SMITH, PH.D., *James E. English Professor of Mathematics*

JAMES WILLIAM TOUMEY, M.A., M.S., *Professor of Forestry, and Director of the Yale Botanical Garden*

CHARLES FOSTER KENT, PH.D., *Woolsey Professor of Biblical Literature*

GIFFORD PINCHOT, SC.D., *Professor of Forestry*

CHARLES MONTAGUE BAKEWELL, PH.D., *Professor of Philosophy*

ALEXANDER WILLIAM EVANS, M.D., PH.D., *Eaton Professor of Botany*

CHARLES SCHUCHERT, M.A., *Professor of Paleontology, Curator of the Geological Collection, and Professor of Historical Geology in the Sheffield Scientific School*

GUY STEVENS CALLENDER, PH.D., *Professor of Political Economy*

LAFAYETTE BENEDICT MENDEL, PH.D., *Professor of Physiological Chemistry*

HENRY ANDREWS BUMSTEAD, PH.D., *Professor of Physics, and Director of the Sloane Physical Laboratory*

HENRY SOLON GRAVES, M.A., *Pinchot Professor of Forestry, and Director of the Forest School*

HENRY CROSBY EMERY, PH.D., *Professor of Political Economy*

CLIVE DAY, PH.D., *Professor of Economic History*

HARRY BENJAMIN JEPSON, M.A., MUS.B., *Professor of Applied Music, and University Organist*

CHARLES HUBBARD JUDD, PH.D., *Professor of Psychology, and Director of the Psychological Laboratory*

HERBERT ERNEST GREGORY, PH.D., *Silliman Professor of Geology*

JOHN DUER IRVING, PH.D., *Professor of Economic Geology*

ALBERT GALLOWAY KELLER, PH.D., *Professor of the Science of Society*

OTHER INSTRUCTORS

JOHN CHESTER ADAMS, PH.D., *Instructor in English*

ROSWELL PARKER ANGIER, PH.D., *Instructor in Psychology*

KAN-ICHI ASAKAWA, PH.D., *Instructor in the History of Japanese Civilization*

Rev. BENJAMIN WISNER BACON, D.D., LL.D., LITT.D., *Buckingham Professor of New Testament Criticism and Interpretation*

WILLIAM BACON BAILEY, PH.D., *Assistant Professor of Political Economy*

CHARLES SEARS BALDWIN, PH.D., *Assistant Professor of Rhetoric*

Hon. SIMEON EBEN BALDWIN, LL.D., *Professor of American Constitutional and Private International Law*

SAMUEL EBEN BARNEY, C.E., *Assistant Professor of Civil Engineering*

JOSEPH BARRELL, PH.D., *Assistant Professor of Geology*

PAUL VICTOR CHRISTOPHER BAUR, PH.D., *Assistant Professor of Classical Archæology*

FREDERIC ELIJAH BEACH, PH.D., *Assistant Professor of Physics*

JOHN MILTON BERDAN, PH.D., *Instructor in Rhetoric*

HIRAM BINGHAM, PH.D., *Lecturer on South American Geography and History*

SETH DANIELS BINGHAM, JR., B.A., *Assistant in Organ-Playing*

AVARD LONGLEY BISHOP, PH.D., *Instructor in Commercial Geography*

THEODORE HARDING BOGGS, M.A., *Instructor in Commercial Geography*

BERTRAM BORDEN BOLTWOOD, PH.D., *Assistant Professor of Physics*

EDWARD AUGUSTUS BOWERS, B.A., LL.B., *Lecturer on Forest Law*

ISAIAH BOWMAN, B.S., *Instructor in Geography*

PHILIP EMBURY BROWNING, PH.D., *Assistant Professor of Chemistry*

EDWARD HERBERT CAMERON, PH.D., *Instructor in Psychology*

HENRY SEIDEL CANBY, PH.D., *Instructor in English*

HERMAN HAUPT CHAPMAN, M.F., *Assistant Professor of Forestry*

RAYMOND GILMORE CLAPP, M.A., B.D., *Instructor in Biblical Literature, and Director of Religious Work in the Divinity School*

CHARLES UPSON CLARK, PH.D., *Assistant Professor of Latin*

CHARLES CAMERON CLARKE, JR., B.A., *Assistant Professor of French*

WESLEY ROSWELL COE, PH.D., *Assistant Professor of Comparative Anatomy*

LEON JACOB COLE, PH.D., *Instructor in Zoology*

WILLIAM JAMES COMSTOCK, PH.B., *Instructor in Organic Chemistry*

ALBERT EUGENE CURDY, PH.D., *Assistant Professor of French*

Rev. EDWARD LEWIS CURTIS, PH.D., D.D., *Holmes Professor of the Hebrew Language and Literature, and Acting Dean of the Divinity School*

HAROUTUNE MURGURDICH DADOURIAN, PH.D., *Instructor in Physics*

GEORGE FRANCIS EATON, PH.D., *Instructor in Comparative Osteology, Curator of the Osteological Collection, and Associate Curator in Vertebrate Paleontology*

FRED ROGERS FAIRCHILD, PH.D., *Instructor in Political Economy*

HOLLON AUGUSTINE FARR, PH.D., *Assistant Professor of German*

HARRY BURR FERRIS, M.D., *Hunt Professor of Anatomy*

HARRY WARD FOOTE, PH.D., *Assistant Professor of Physical Chemistry*

WILLIAM EBENEZER FORD, JR., PH.D., *Assistant Professor of Mineralogy*

JOHN PIERREPONT CODRINGTON FOSTER, M.D., *Instructor in Anatomy*

CLYDE CHEW GLASCOCK, PH.D., *Assistant Professor of German*

WILLIAM ANTHONY GRANVILLE, PH.D., *Instructor in Mathematics*

ARTHUR HARMOUNT GRAVES B.A., *Instructor in Botany*

WILLIAM EDWIN HAESCHE, MUS.B., *Instructor in Instrumentation*

HERBERT EDWIN HAWKES, PH.D., *Assistant Professor of Mathematics*

YANDELL HENDERSON, PH.D., *Assistant Professor of Physiology*

LAURENCE ILSLEY HEWES, PH.D., *Instructor in Mathematics*

WILLIAM ERNEST HOCKING, PH.D., *Assistant Professor of Philosophy*

ELLSWORTH HUNTINGTON, M.A., *Instructor in Geography*

LOUIS D'OREMUS HUNTOON, M.E., *Assistant Professor of Mining and Metallurgy*

Professor CHARLES CHENEY HYDE, LL.B., M.A., *Lecturer on International Law*

JAMES W. D. INGERSOLL, PH.D., *Assistant Professor of Latin*

GEORGE SAMUEL JAMIESON, PH.D., *Instructor in Analytical Chemistry*

TREAT BALDWIN JOHNSON, PH.D., *Instructor in Chemistry*

ANDREW KEOGH, M.A., *Reference Librarian, and Lecturer on Bibliography*

HENRY STANLEY KNIGHT, *Assistant Professor of Applied Music*

BEVERLY WAUGH KUNKEL, PH.D., *Instructor in Biology*

GEORGE HENRY LANGZETTEL, B.F.A., *Instructor in Drawing, and Secretary of the Art School*

IRVILLE CHARLES LeCOMPTE, PH.D., *Instructor in French*

EDWIN HOYT LOCKWOOD, M.E., PH.D., *Assistant Professor of Mechanical Engineering*

WILLIAM RAYMOND LONGLEY, PH.D., *Instructor in Mathematics*

RICHARD SWANN LULL, PH.D., *Assistant Professor of Vertebrate Paleontology, and Associate Curator in Vertebrate Paleontology*

FREDERICK BLISS LUQUIENS, PH.D., *Assistant Professor of Spanish*

GEORGE GRANT MacCURDY, PH.D., *Lecturer on Anthropology, and Curator of the Anthropological Collection*

KENNETH McKENZIE, PH.D., *Assistant Professor of Italian*

MAX SOLOMON MANDELL, *Instructor in Russian*

MAX MASON, PH.D., *Assistant Professor of Mathematics*

CHAMPION HERBERT MATHEWSON, PH.D., *Instructor in Chemistry and Metallography*

GEORGE HEWITT MYERS, M.F., *Lecturer on Forestry Abroad*

GEORGE HENRY NETTLETON, PH.D., *Assistant Professor of English*

FREDERICK HAYNES NEWELL, B.S., *Lecturer on Forest Hydrography*

WATSON NICHOLSON, PH.D., *Instructor in English*

JOHN PEASE NORTON, PH.D., *Assistant Professor of Political Economy*

ISAAC KING PHELPS, PH.D., *Instructor in Chemistry*

Rev. FRANK CHAMBERLIN PORTER, PH.D., D.D., *Winkley Professor of Biblical Theology*

CHARLES RABOLD, *Instructor in Singing*

EDWARD VILETTE RAYNOLDS, D.C.L., *Professor of Comparative Law*

EDWARD BLISS REED, PH.D., *Assistant Professor of English*

LEO FREDERICK RETTGER, PH.D., *Assistant Professor of Bacteriology and Hygiene*

OLIVER HUNTINGTON RICHARDSON, PH.D., *Assistant Professor of History*

HENRY HOLLISTER ROBINSON, C.E., PH.D., *Instructor in Geology*

Professor JOSIAH ROYCE, PH.D., LL.D., *Lecturer on Philosophy*

ROBERT LOUIS SANDERSON, M.A., *Assistant Professor of French*

RUDOLPH SCHEVILL, PH.D., *Assistant Professor of the Spanish Language and Literature*

HERMANN VON SCHRENK, PH.D., *Lecturer on Diseases of Trees*

LEO SCHULZ, *Instructor in Violoncello-Playing*

WILLIAM KENT SHEPARD, PH.D., *Instructor in Mechanics*

CHARLES PHINEAS SHERMAN, D.C.L., *Assistant Professor of Roman Law, and Librarian of the Law School*

DAVID STANLEY SMITH, B.A., MUS.B., *Instructor in the Theory of Music, and Secretary of the Department of Music*

GEORGE ALBERT THOMPSON, B.F.A., *Instructor in Painting*

WILMOT HAINES THOMPSON, JR., PH.D., *Tutor in Greek*

EDWARD THORSTENBERG, PH.D., *Instructor in German*

CHAUNCEY BREWSTER TINKER, PH.D., *Instructor in English*

JOHN CLAYTON TRACY, C.E., *Assistant Professor of Structural Engineering*

ISIDOR TROOSTWYK, *Assistant Professor of Applied Music, and Instructor in Violin-Playing*

FRANK PELL UNDERHILL, PH.D., *Assistant Professor of Physiological Chemistry*

ALBERT WILLIAM VANBUREN, B.A., *Instructor in the History of Roman Religion*

RALPH GIBBS VANNAME, PH.D., *Instructor in Chemistry*

WILLISTON WALKER, PH.D., D.D., *Titus Street Professor of Ecclesiastical History*

HENRY LORD WHEELER, PH.D., *Assistant Professor of Organic Chemistry*

LYNDE PHELPS WHEELER, PH.D., *Assistant Professor of Physics*

FREDERICK WELLS WILLIAMS, B.A., *Assistant Professor of Modern Oriental History*   .

LEWIS WILLIAMS, *Assistant in Piano-Playing*

LORANDE LOSS WOODRUFF, PH.D., *Instructor in Biology*

HENRY BURT WRIGHT, PH.D., *Assistant Professor of Roman History and Latin Literature*

LESTER WILLIAM ZARTMAN, PH.D., *Instructor in Insurance and Political Economy*

ADMINISTRATIVE COMMITTEE
WITH CONSULTATION HOURS

ARTHUR TWINING HADLEY, LL.D., *President,*
    absent until about March 10, thereafter, Woodbridge Hall, daily, 8.30 A. M. to 1.00 P. M.

ANDREW WHEELER PHILLIPS, PH.D., *Dean, and Professor of Mathematics,* 90 High st., daily, ex. Saturday, 10.30 A. M. to 12.00 M.

CHARLES BRINCKERHOFF RICHARDS, M.A., *Professor of Mechanical Engineering,* 111 Winchester Hall, Wednesday, 10.30 ; Friday, 10.00 to 11.00 A. M.

THOMAS DAY SEYMOUR, LL.D., *Professor of the Greek Language and Literature,* 22 Phelps Hall, daily, 11.00 A. M. to 12.00 M.

ALBERT STANBURROUGH COOK, PH.D., L.H.D., *Professor of the English Language and Literature,* C₁ Osborn Hall, Tuesday, 11.20 A. M. ; D, 135 Elm street, Tuesday, 5.00 P. M.

HENRY WALCOTT FARNAM, R.P.D., *Professor of Political Economy.* Absent.

RUSSELL HENRY CHITTENDEN, PH.D., LL.D., SC.D., *Professor of Physiological Chemistry, and Director of the Sheffield Scientific School,* 3 Sheffield Hall, daily, 9.00 A. M. to 1.00 P. M.

GENERAL STATEMENT
HISTORY AND ORGANIZATION

The Graduate School of Yale University, first formally organized in 1847, is a section of the Department of Philosophy and the Arts and is under the combined Faculty of that Department, the other sections of which are Yale College, the Sheffield Scientific School, the School of the Fine Arts, the Department of Music, and the Forest School.

The degrees of Doctor of Philosophy and Civil Engineer were first offered in 1860, the degree of Dynamical or Mechanical Engineer in 1873, that of Master of Arts (previously given without evidence of study) in 1874, that of Master of Science in 1897, and that of Mining Engineer in 1907.

The general oversight of graduate instruction and graduate students is entrusted to the Dean and the Administrative Committee of the Graduate School, who may be called upon for information and advice. Students are expected to report to the Dean soon after reaching New Haven.

ADMISSION AND REGISTRATION

Graduates of this and other Colleges and Universities, and (in exceptional cases, by special permission) other persons of liberal education who are at least eighteen years old, are received as students for longer or shorter periods, with or without reference to the attainment of a degree. The degree of Doctor of Philosophy, with the courses of the Graduate School leading thereto, is open to candidates without distinction of sex.

All students who take courses in the Graduate School are required to register their names at the office of the Dean at the beginning of each year of study.

FEES AND EXPENSES

The fee for instruction is generally one hundred dollars per year; but it may be more, or less, according to the courses pursued and the amount of instruction received.

The fee for graduation with the degree of Doctor of Philosophy, Master of Arts, or Master of Science is ten dollars ; with the degree of Civil Engineer, Mechanical Engineer, or Mining Engineer, five dollars.

Board is obtained at prices varying from three and a half to eight dollars per week.   The average price is about five dollars.   A list of suitable rooms is kept at the Dean's office.

A special fee of five dollars is charged to those who use the Gymnasium.

FELLOWSHIPS AND SCHOLARSHIPS

Candidates for appointment to Fellowships and Scholarships should send their applications, accompanied by letters of recommendation and other evidence of the excellence of their work already accomplished, to the Dean, Professor Andrew W. Phillips, as soon as possible after March 1.   The limit for all applications is April 15.

FELLOWSHIPS
OPEN TO GRADUATES OF ALL COLLEGES

Five University FELLOWSHIPS, yielding four hundred dollars each (but not exempting the holders from charges for tuition), are open to graduates of all colleges ; but preference is given to those who have already spent at least one year in graduate study and have shown capacity for original work.   .

The HENRY C. ROBINSON FELLOWSHIP was founded in 1900 in the name of Mrs. Mary Robinson Cheney, of Hartford, Connecticut, and her sister, Miss Eliza Robinson, in memory of their uncle, Henry C. Robinson (Yale College 1853), by the gift of five thousand dollars.   The income is awarded annually to a student of the Graduate School, selected on the ground of ability and attainments.

The BULKLEY FELLOWSHIP IN AMERICAN HISTORY was established in 1901 by the gift of ten thousand dollars from Mr. Jonathan Bulkley (Yale College 1879) and other members of his family, in memory of Helena Perry Bulkley.   The income, four hundred dollars, is awarded annually to a student of high character and marked ability, who will pursue graduate studies in American History or Administration under the direction of the Professors of History.

The LOOMIS FELLOWSHIP IN PHYSICS was established in 1902 by Professor Francis E. Loomis (Yale College 1864), by the gift of ten thousand dollars. This Fellowship is open to the graduates of the Academical and Scientific Departments of Yale University, and to graduates of other Universities who have spent at least one year in the study of Physics in the Graduate School of Yale University. It is granted to the candidate who passes the best competitive examination in Physics (descriptive, mathematical, and laboratory practice). The holder of this Fellowship must be a candidate for the degree of Doctor of Philosophy and must make Physics his chief study.

The HENRY BRADFORD LOOMIS FELLOWSHIP IN CHEMISTRY was established in 1905 by Mr. Henry Bradford Loomis (Yale College 1875), by the gift of ten thousand dollars. This Fellowship is open to the graduates of the Academical and Scientific Departments of Yale University, and to graduates of other Universities who have spent at least one year in the study of Chemistry in the Graduate School of Yale University. It is granted to the candidate who passes the best competitive examination in Chemistry (inorganic, organic, chemical analysis, and laboratory practice). The holder of this Fellowship must be a candidate for the degree of Doctor of Philosophy and must make Chemistry his chief study.

RESTRICTED TO GRADUATES OF CERTAIN INSTITUTIONS

The JOHN ADDISON PORTER MEMORIAL FELLOWSHIP (see page 113) is open only to graduates of Yale College or of the Sheffield Scientific School.

The following Fellowships are, by the terms of the donations, open to graduates of Yale College only :

The MACY FELLOWSHIP ;
The DOUGLAS FELLOWSHIP ;

The Foote Fellowships (two or more) ;
The Soldiers' Memorial Fellowship ;
The Silliman Fellowship ;
The Larned Fellowships (three) ;
The John Sloane Fellowship in Physics ;
The Scott Hurtt Fellowship ;
The Ellen Battell Eldridge Fellowships (two) ;
The Cuyler Fellowship ;
The John J. Abernethy Fellowship.

The Yale Alumni Association of California Fellowship, of three hundred dollars, is given to a graduate of one of the California Universities, pursuing studies at Yale in the Graduate School. The incumbent is selected by the Association.

SCHOLARSHIPS

OPEN TO GRADUATES OF ALL COLLEGES

Twenty University Scholarships, yielding one hundred dollars each, are open to graduates of all colleges.

The Arthur Twining Hadley Scholarship yields an income of two hundred and twenty-five dollars a year, which sum may be awarded annually to one or more students of the University, to assist in the publication of meritorious theses or other results of investigation.

RESTRICTED TO GRADUATES OF CERTAIN INSTITUTIONS

The Daniel C. Eaton Graduate Scholarship in Botany (see page 115) is open for competition to members of the Senior classes in Yale College and the Sheffield Scientific School only.

The following Scholarships (see pages 114–115) are open to graduates of Yale College only :
The Berkeley Scholarship ;
The Clark Scholarship ;
The W. W. DeForest Scholarship.

The following Scholarships (primarily for Academical undergraduates), may be continued or awarded to graduates of Yale College :
The DeForest Scholarships ;
The Bristed Scholarship.

20

Six SHEFFIELD SCHOLARSHIPS (see page 292) are awarded to members of the graduating class of the Sheffield Scientific School.

The ROGERS SCHOLARSHIP (see page 291) may be continued to a graduate of the Sheffield Scientific School who has held it during his Senior year.

PUBLICATION OF THESES

The sum of fifty dollars is appropriated by the University towards defraying the cost of publication of each thesis submitted for the degree of Doctor of Philosophy which is recommended for such purpose by the expert readers of the thesis in question, provided that such thesis is actually published, in separate form, by the first day of March following the graduation of the candidate, and that fifty copies have been presented to the University. See also the ARTHUR TWINING HADLEY SCHOLARSHIP, above.

DEGREES

The DEGREE OF DOCTOR OF PHILOSOPHY is conferred upon those students (of either sex) who show the results of resident graduate work by a thesis giving evidence of high attainment and power of investigation, and by passing an examination on studies whose grade and amount meet the approval of the Faculty. Under ordinary circumstances two or more years of work in residence are required, but in exceptional cases work of equal grade at another University may take the place of a year's residence here. The thesis must be deposited at the Library, for public inspection, not later than May 1. A good knowledge of Latin, German, and French is required in all cases, unless, for some very exceptional reasons, the candidate be excused by the Faculty. Evidence of sufficient attainments in these languages must be presented to the Dean at least two years before the degree is given. For fees for instruction and graduation, see page 303.

The DEGREE OF MASTER OF ARTS is conferred on Bachelors of Arts of Yale College (and on Bachelors of Arts

of other colleges whose course of study is equivalent
to that of Yale College) who have given to the College Faculty evidence of satisfactory progress in liberal
studies after receiving their first degree.   Such evidence may be furnished by one year of systematic study
(not professional) in New Haven, under the direction of
the College Faculty, followed by an examination.   Graduates of other colleges can obtain the degree only by
residence as thus described.   For fees see page 303.

Such Bachelors of Arts *of Yale College* as may not choose
to reside at the College for study may, at any time not
less than three years after graduation, show, in either
of the two following ways, that they have spent a year in
liberal (and non-professional) study and are worthy of
recommendation for this degree: (1) Such candidates
may apply to the Faculty for the designation of a course
of study, on which an examination shall be taken.   This
application must be accompanied by a fee of twenty-five
dollars. (2) Or a candidate may submit as evidence of
his fitness for this degree a printed essay, for the examination of which a fee of twenty-five dollars (to be paid in
advance) is required.   An additional fee of ten dollars
is charged in all cases for the degree.

A committee of the Faculty is appointed, to whom candidates for this degree must submit their proposed courses
of study for approval by the end of October in each year ;
and the evidence of a year's study must be submitted to
the same committee by June 1.

The DEGREES OF CIVIL ENGINEER AND OF MECHANICAL
ENGINEER are conferred on Bachelors of Philosophy who
have taken the first degree in Engineering study and
who pursue a higher course under the direction of the
Governing Board of the Sheffield Scientific School for
at least two years, sustaining a final examination and
giving evidence of their ability to design important constructions and to make the requisite drawings and calculations.

The DEGREE OF MINING ENGINEER is conferred on Bachelors of Philosophy who pursue a higher course of study under the direction of the Governing Board of the Sheffield Scientific School for at least two years, sustaining a finâl examination and presenting a satisfactory thesis.

The DEGREE OF MASTER OF SCIENCE is conferred on graduates of this or other Universities, of two years' standing or upwards, who have taken their first degree in science and who pursue successfully a higher course of study in science under the direction of the Governing Board of the Sheffield Scientific School. Such a course involves at least one year of resident graduate study, followed by an examination and the presentation of a satisfactory thesis in some department of science. A committee of the Faculty is appointed, to whom candidates for this degree must submit their proposed courses of study for approval before the end of October of each year.

For fees for instruction and the degrees above mentioned, see pages 302 and 303.

For various University Privileges of interest to graduate students, such as the Bureau of Self-Help and Appointments, the Dining Hall, the Gymnasium, the Infirmary, Libraries, and University Prizes, see later pages.

INSTRUCTION
SCOPE AND METHOD
Courses of study are offered in the following departments :

A. LANGUAGE, LITERATURE, AND THE ARTS:

I. CLASSICAL AND INDO-IRANIAN PHILOLOGY, etc.; (Pages 310–321.)

II. SEMITIC LANGUAGES AND BIBLICAL LITERATURE ; (Pages 322–327.)

III. MODERN LANGUAGES AND LITERATURES ; (Pages 328–339.)

IV. THE FINE ARTS ; (Pages 339–340.)

V. MUSIC ; (Pages 340–341.)

B. THE PHYSICAL AND NATURAL SCIENCES, MATHEMATICS, AND ENGINEERING:

    VI.   THE PHYSICAL AND NATURAL SCIENCES; (Pages 342–359.)

    VII.   MATHEMATICS; (Pages 360–366.)

    VIII.   ENGINEERING; Pages 366–368.)

C. THE SOCIAL SCIENCES, LAW, HISTORY, PHILOSOPHY, AND EDUCATION:

    IX.   THE SOCIAL SCIENCES, LAW, AND HISTORY; (Pages 369–380.)

    X.   PHILOSOPHY; (Pages 380–384.)

    XI.   THE THEORY AND PRACTICE OF EDUCATION; (Page 384.)

Instruction is given partly by lectures, partly in recitations and by criticism of oral and written discussions, partly by directing courses of reading, and partly by the direction of work in the laboratories and with instruments. In the several departments the instructors and students meet periodically, in various voluntary associations, for the reading of papers, oral discussions, etc. Such associations (individually described in the statements of the several departments) are as follows, named in the order of organization :

The CLASSICAL CLUB;

The MATHEMATICAL CLUB;

The POLITICAL SCIENCE CLUB;

The PHILOSOPHICAL CLUB;

The EDUCATIONAL CLUB;

The SEMITIC AND ·BIBLICAL CLUB;

The MODERN LANGUAGE CLUB;

The GERMAN JOURNAL CLUB;

The ROMANCE CLUB;

The ENGLISH CLUB;

The PHYSICS JOURNAL CLUB;

The ENGINEERS' CLUB;

The CHEMICAL CLUB;

The HISTORY CLUB;

The PHYSICAL CLUB;

The GEOLOGICAL CLUB;

The BIOLOGICAL CLUB;

The ANTHROPOLOGY CLUB.

A. LANGUAGE, LITERATURE, AND THE ARTS†

I. CLASSICAL AND INDO-IRANIAN PHILOLOGY

TRACY PECK, LL.D.   HENRY P. WRIGHT, PH.D., LL.D.
BERNADOTTE PERRIN, PH.D., LL.D. THOMAS D. SEYMOUR, LL.D.
EDWARD P. MORRIS, L.H.D.   HENRY R. LANG, PH.D.
THOMAS D. GOODELL, PH.D.   E. W. HOPKINS, PH.D., LL.D.
HORATIO M. REYNOLDS, M.A.   HANNS OERTEL, PH.D.
JAMES W. D. INGERSOLL, PH.D.   PAUL V. C. BAUR, PH.D.
CHARLES U. CLARK, PH.D.   WILMOT H. THOMPSON, JR., PH.D.
ALBERT W. VAN BUREN, B.A.

Students in this department have unrestricted use of its LIBRARY. This is in Phelps Hall, near the CLASSICAL SEMINARY ROOMS, in a large and well lighted apartment supplied with tables and private lockers. It contains nearly four thousand volumes, and additions are made each year, so that the student finds here practically everything needed for ordinary work in the courses in classical philology, except some periodicals and expensive illustrated works, which are accessible in the University Library. Special purchases of books will be made for students who are carrying on investigations either in connection with their theses or otherwise.

The University possesses an unusually good Numismatic Collection and the beginnings of a Collection for the Illustration of other Branches of Classical Archæology, as well as a considerable Collection of Photographs.

The CLASSICAL CLUB, consisting of the instructors and students in this department, meets in the library room every Saturday evening to hear reports and papers in

---

† Courses included in brackets are omitted in 1907-08. Most of the courses thus omitted will probably be offered in 1908-09; others are given at longer intervals or in accordance with the needs of the students in attendance.

Courses marked with an asterisk (*) are undergraduate courses; they are open to graduate students who have the consent of the instructor and the approval of the Faculty.

The number of hours stated, when not otherwise specified, means hours of classroom attendance or laboratory work each week throughout the year.

the field of classical philology, or to read and discuss the work of some Greek or Latin author. During the year 1907–08 the club will read the remains of the Alexandrian Greek literature and the writings of the younger Seneca.

Graduate students of this University who are approved by the classical instructors are admitted without charge to the American Schools of Classical Studies at Athens and at Rome.

SUGGESTIONS TO STUDENTS

The instruction in this department is adapted to the needs of those who desire to spend one or two years in advanced study without reference to a degree, as well as of those who are candidates for the degree of M.A. or Ph.D.

At the outset of his work the student should form two habits: (1) the habit of extensive private reading in Greek and Latin literature; (2) that of following current philological thought in the journals. These habits should be persistently maintained, however strong may be the claims of other work.

Graduate work is not the completion of philological study, but a preparation for further study. To the graduate student, therefore, in the selection of his courses, method is more important than information, and work which requires a large library and the counsel of an instructor should be taken in preference to work which can be done privately.

The individual courses offered fall into three groups, as follows : courses in literature, courses in language, and courses of a more special character. No one of these three groups can wisely be neglected entirely. The courses in literature are of two kinds: (1) those in which the student learns the method of interpretation and gets an intimate knowledge of a small portion of an author; (2) those in which a wider field is covered, to give a general view, bring out the larger features of an author or a period, and suggest a pattern for private reading. The courses in language—except those in Greek and Latin composition—bear less directly on elementary teaching, but they are useful even there and are indispensable as a preparation for later productive work. The courses of a more special character are partly for method (source-criticism, text-criticism, interpretation), partly for information (epigraphy, palæography, archæology, current philological literature). These subjects are for the most part of such character that they cannot be studied to the best advantage without an instructor and a large library.

The number of hours of instruction that may wisely be taken depends upon previous training and the character of the courses. Students are advised to plan a combination of heavier courses with those which require less preparation. For this purpose the student may visit a large number of courses at the beginning of the year and postpone his final selection two or three weeks.

Courses are arranged under five heads: Greek; Latin; Classical Archæology; Indo-Iranian Philology; Comparative Grammar, Phonetics, and Linguistics. A candidate for the degree of Ph.D. in this department will select one of these five subjects as his major subject of study and one or two others as his minor subject. To the minor subject must be given not less than one-third of the student's time. If either Latin or Greek is the major subject, it should be remembered that classical philology, rather than Latin alone or Greek alone, is the true field of study and that some acquaintance with archæology and linguistics is most desirable. For advanced work in language, and for work in comparative philology, Sanskrit should be taken early, so that it may be used in other courses in this group.

All candidates for the doctorate must have had one year in the classical seminary. The final test for the degree consists of a thesis and, after the thesis has been accepted, an oral examination conducted by a committee of the department.   All further details regarding the requirements for the degree of Ph.D. in this department are contained in a pamphlet which may be obtained upon application to the Dean of the Graduate School.

CLASSICAL SEMINARY

The members are expected to have read widely in Greek and Latin literature, and to be able to read French and German freely.

Professor SEYMOUR :—

1 (a) *Pindar and Bacchylides.*   2 hrs. 1st half-year.

Critical, exegetical, and historical studies in selected *Odes* of Pindar and Bacchylides.   .

Professor OERTEL :—

1 (b) *A Study of some Topic in Latin Semantics.*

2 hrs. 2d half-year.

GREEK

GREEK LITERATURE

See also 1 (a), above, courses X, 1 and 2 (*Greek Philosophy*), and some of the courses in Biblical Literature (group II).   Certain courses in general or comparative literature are announced in the English group (III).

Professor SEYMOUR :—

2 *Greek Epic Poetry.*   ·   3 hrs.

Introduction to the critical study of Homer.   Lectures, followed by a critical interpretation (and exercises in interpretation) of portions of the *Odyssey* and of the later Greek epics.

[3 *Æschylus.*   3 hrs.

Omitted in 1907–08.]

[4 *The Greek Orators.*   3 hrs.

Omitted in 1907–08.]

[5 *Plato.*   ·   3 hrs.

The *Republic*, and portions of the other dialogues which are most important for its elucidation.

Omitted in 1907–08.]

Professor GOODELL :—

6 *Sophocles.* 3 hrs.

Reading of the seven extant plays with special attention to the artistic form. This includes (*a*) the Sophoclean dramatic type— in formal structure, development of plot, and character-drawing; (*b*) the use of meters, with much practice in reading aloud; (*c*) poetic style.

Professor REYNOLDS :—

7 *Aristotle's Poetics: Literary Criticism in Ancient Times.* 1 hr.

Interpretation of the *Poetics* and parts of the *Rhetoric*, with selections from Plutarch, Pseudo-Longinus, and Lucian.

[8 *Late Greek Poetry.* 1 hr.

A survey of Alexandrian and later Greek poetry. The *Mimes* of Herondas, selections from the *Anthology* and from the *Hymns* of Callimachus, and other fugitive poetry.

Omitted in 1907-08.]

Professor SEYMOUR :—

*9 *Æschylus and Pindar.* 2 hrs.

[See Course II, C 1, page 148.]

*10 *Plato.* 2 hrs.

[See Course II, B 5, page 147.]

[*11 *Plato and Aristotle.* 2 hrs.

[See Course II, C 5, page 148.]
Omitted in 1907-08.]

[*12 *Demosthenes and Theocritus.* 2 hrs.

[See Course II, B 7, page 147.]
Omitted in 1907-08.]

*13 *Hellenistic and Patristic Greek.* 2 hrs.

[See Course II, B 8, page 147.]

Professor REYNOLDS :—

*14 *Homer.* 2 hrs.

[See Course II, B 3, page 147.]

[*15 *Euripides.* 2 hrs.

[See Course II, B 4, page 147.]
Omitted in 1907-08.]

[*16 *Lucian and Greek Romance-Writers.* 2 hrs.

[See Course II, B 9, page 147.]
Omitted in 1907-08.]

THE GREEK LANGUAGE

See also courses 67 (*Comparative Syntax*), 68 (*Phonetics*), 69 (*Indo-European Phonology*), 70 and 71 (*Comparative Grammar*), and 72 (*Linguistics*).

Professor GOODELL :—

17 *Greek Composition.*   1 hr.

> The weekly session lasts from an hour to an hour and a half.

Professor OERTEL :—

[18 *Greek Dialects and Comparative Grammar of Greek Sounds and Inflections.*   3 hrs.

> Text-book : F. Solmsen's *Inscriptiones Græcæ ad inlustrandas dialectos selectæ* (Leipzig, 1905).
> Omitted in 1907–08.]

Dr. W. H. THOMPSON :—

*19 *Greek Composition.*   2 hrs.

> [See Course II, B 10, page 148.]

COURSES OF A MORE SPECIAL CHARACTER

See also courses 48 (*Interpretation and Criticism*), 50 (*Text-Criticism*), 51 (*Palæography*), 55–59 (*Archæology*), III, 82 (*Bibliography*), and IX, 67 (*Ancient History*).

Professor PERRIN :—

20 *Thucydides.*   1 hr.

> An introduction to the more advanced work of the Classical Seminary in text-criticism and interpretation.

Professor OERTEL :—

21 *Current Philological Literature.*   1 hr.

> Weekly conference for the informal discussion of recent philological publications.

Professor PERRIN :—

*22 *The Testimonies of Aristophanes, Thucydides, and Plutarch to the Career of Alcibiades.*   2 hrs.

> [See Course II, C 4, page 148.]

LATIN
LATIN LITERATURE

Certain courses in general or comparative literature are announced in the English group (III).

Professor PECK :—

[23　*Lucretius.*　　　　　2 hrs.
　　Minute study of the second book ; rapid reading of the other books.
　　Omitted in 1907–08.]

24　*Horace (Epistles) and Persius.*　　　　2 hrs.
　　Literary and ethical studies of the two poets and of their periods.

[25　*Pliny (Letters and Panegyric) and Tacitus (Dialogus de Oratoribus).*　　　　2 hrs.
　　Critical study, the first term ; rapid reading, the remainder of the year.
　　Omitted in 1907–08.]

Professor MORRIS :—

26　*Plautus.*　　　　　2 hrs.
　　Lectures introductory to the study of Plautus, followed by a careful study of the *Bacchides.*

[27　*Terence.*　　　　　2 hrs.
　　A careful study of one play, followed by more rapid reading of the other five plays.　Practice in metrical reading.
　　Omitted in 1907-08.]

28　*Private Reading.*　　　　　1 hr.
　　Weekly conferences on the private reading of the students.

Assistant Professor INGERSOLL :—

29　*Latin Literature.*　　　　　2 hrs.
　　A general survey of the whole field.　Lectures, illustrative readings, and direction of the student's private reading.

Professor PECK :—

*30　*Hexameter Poetry.*　　　　　2 hrs.
　　[See Course I, C 1, page 145.]

*31　*Cicero de Oratore.*　　　1 ½ hrs. 1st half-year.
　　[See Course I, C 2, page 145.]

[*32　*Roman Oratory.*　　　　　2 hrs.
　　[See Course I, B 4, page 143.]
　　Omitted in 1907–08.]

[*33　*The Character and Reign of Tiberius.*　　　　2 hrs.
　　[See Course I, C 3, page 145.]
　　Omitted in 1907–08.]

Professors PECK and H. P. WRIGHT :—
*34 *Juvenal, Martial, and Pliny's Letters.*   2 hrs.
     [See Course I, B 3a, page 143.]

Professor MORRIS :—
[*35 *Plautus and Terence.*   2 hrs.
      [See Course I, B 5, page 144.]
      Omitted in 1907–08.]

*36 *Vergil.*   .   2 hrs.
     [See Course I, C 7, page 146.]

Assistant Professor INGERSOLL :—
*37 *Latin Comedy and Elegy.*   1 hr.
     [See Course I, B 3b, page 143.]

Assistant Professor CLARK :—
*38 *Latin Sight-Reading.*   4 hrs., *to count as 2 hrs.*
     [See Course I, B 6, page 144.]

[*39 *Later Roman Historians.*   2 hrs.
      [See Course I, B 7, page 144.]
      Omitted in 1907–08.]

THE LATIN LANGUAGE

See also 1 (*b*), above, and courses 67 (*Comparative Syntax*), 68 (*Phonetics*), 69 (*Indo-European Phonology*), 70 and 71
(*Comparative Grammar*), and 72 (*Linguistics*).

Professor PECK :—
[40 *Early Latin.*   2 hrs.
     Study of inscriptions and of the ante-classical literature, based
     on Allen's *Remnants of Early Latin*, Merry's *Fragments*, and
     Smith's *Selections*, and dealing with the development of forms,
     constructions, and literature.
       Omitted in 1907–08.]

Professor MORRIS :—
[41 *Latin Syntax.*   2 hrs.
     Introductory lectures on the history of syntactical study and
     on the principles and methods of investigation ; discussion of
     syntactical systems in grammars and text-books.
       Omitted in 1907–08.]

Professor OERTEL :—

[42　*Selections from Latin Authors on the Latin Language.*
　　　　　　　　　　　　　　　　　　　　　　　2 hrs.
　　Passages from Cicero, Quintilian, Aulus Gellius, Varro, and
　　others, which bear on questions of Latin grammar, are read and
　　interpreted.
　　　　　Omitted in 1907–08.]

43　*The Italic Dialects and Comparative Grammar of Latin
　　Sounds and Inflection.*　　　　　　　　　3 hrs.
　　Text-books : Buck's *Grammar of Oscan and Umbrian* (Ginn
　　& Co., 1904) and Sommer's *Handbuch der lateinischen Laut- und
　　Formenlehre* (Heidelberg, 1902).

44　*Characteristics of Latin.*　　　　2 hrs. 1st half-year.

45　*Practice in Writing Latin Prose (Advanced Course).* 2 hrs.
　　Text-books : Cicero's *Lælius* and Menge's *Repetitorium der
　　lateinischen Syntax und Stilistik* (7th ed., 1900).

Assistant Professor CLARK :—

*46　*Latin Composition.*　　　　　　　　　2 hrs.
　　　　　[See Course I, B 10, page 144.]

COURSES OF A MORE SPECIAL CHARACTER

　　See also courses 21 (*Current Philological Literature*), 59
and 60 (*Archæology*), III, 82 (*Bibliography*), and IX, 67 and
68 (*Roman History*).

Professor PECK :—

[47　*Latin Epigraphy.*　　　　　　　　　2 hrs.
　　Study of such inscriptions (including coins) as illustrate the
　　development of the language, and private and public antiqui-
　　ties. Egbert's *Introduction* is the basis of the work, supple-
　　mented by constant use of the *Corpus Inscriptionum Latinarum.*
　　　　　Omitted in 1907–08.]

Professor MORRIS :—

48　*Interpretation and Criticism.*　　　　　　1 hr.
　　Exposition and illustration of the principles of interpretation
　　and text-criticism, with practice in the use of the standard
　　critical editions of eight or ten authors.

Professor LANG :—

49　*Low Latin.*　　　　　　　　　　　　　1 hr.
　　The aim of this course is to give a historical account of the
　　popular speech of Rome and of the Roman provinces, and also
　　an outline of its grammar and syntax

Assistant Professor CLARK :—

[50 *Introduction to Text-Criticism.*   2 hrs.
> Reconstruction of the text of Ammianus Marcellinus in the light of Wilhelm Meyer's Law and on the basis of new collations. Omitted in 1907–08.]

51 *Latin Palæography.*   2 hrs.
> Facility in reading and dating MSS. is acquired by systematic study of the rich University collections of facsimiles. The origin and the bearing upon text-criticism of MS. errors are constantly observed.

Assistant Professor INGERSOLL :—

[*52 *Roman Law.*   2 hrs.
> [See Course I, B 11. page 145.]
> Omitted in 1907–08.]

Assistant Professor CLARK :—

*53 *Latin Literature of the Early Middle Ages.*   2 hrs.
> [See Course I, B 8, page 144.]

[*54 *Latin Literature of the Late Middle Ages.*   2 hrs.
> [See Course I, B 9, page 144.]
> Omitted in 1907–08.]

CLASSICAL ARCHÆOLOGY

Assistant Professor BAUR :—

[55 *Greek Art, I.   Sculpture.*   2 hrs.
> Lectures and quizzes by the instructor ; special study of the literary sources by the students.
> Omitted in 1907–08.]

56 *Greek Art, II.   The Lesser Arts.*   2 hrs.
> Greek painting, ceramics, terra-cottas, bronzes and other metal work, coins, and gems.

57 *Greek Architecture.*   2 hrs.
> The various forms of building-construction are successively examined in informal lectures, supplemented by occasional reports from members of the class.

58 *Topography and Monuments of Athens.*   2 hrs.
> A combination of the historical and the strictly topographical methods of treatment is adopted. Those who take this course should be provided with the Teubner text of Pausanias.

59 *Archæological Exercises.* 2 hrs.
Exercises in the interpretation of archæological monuments, as illustrating classic life and literature. The monuments are selected largely with reference to the courses offered in Greek and Latin authors. No preparation is required.

60 *Roman and Etruscan Art.* 2 hrs.
This course includes Roman architecture, Græco-Roman sculpture, topography and monuments of Rome and of Pompeii; also the domestic arts, such as household utensils, glass, coins, frescoes, mosaics, textiles, terra-cottas.

Mr. VAN BUREN :—

61 *History of Roman Religion.* 2 hrs.
An introduction to the history of Roman Religion, from the earliest times to the supremacy of Christianity, with special reference to its relation to social conditions.

INDO-IRANIAN PHILOLOGY

Professor HOPKINS :—

*62 *Elementary Sanskrit.* 2 hrs.
[See Course IV, B 1, page 150.]

63 *Advanced Sanskrit.* 2 hrs.
Selections from the *Rig-Veda* and Brahmanic texts. The first half-year is occupied with the *Vedic Hymns*, the second with portions of the first Brahmanic works and the early *Upanishads*.

64 *History of Sanskrit Literature.* 1 hr.
This course consists in a review of Vedic and classical Sanskrit literature from the earliest times to the Puranic period, with extracts to illustrate the various phases of literary development.

65 *Pali Language and Literature.* 1 hr.
Intended for those who desire to begin the study of Buddhistic scriptures. Pali is easy for advanced Sanskrit students, and offers much of interest in literature and religion.

66 *Avestan Language and Literature.* 1 hr.
For advanced students of Sanskrit.

Professor Hopkins's *Lectures on Comparative Religion* are announced in the group of courses in Philosophy (X, 18).

COMPARATIVE GRAMMAR, PHONETICS, AND LINGUISTICS

Professor HOPKINS :—

[67 *Introduction to Comparative Syntax.*   1 hr.

This course is intended for students of these languages who desire a more thorough acquaintance with the problems of comparative syntax. To solve these problems a knowledge of Sanskrit syntactical phenomena is necessary, and the lectures are planned accordingly.

Omitted in 1907-08.]

Professor OERTEL :—

68 *Phonetics.*   1 hr.

A general and rather elementary introduction to Phonetics, based on a study of the English, French, and German sound-systems, and intended to furnish a basis both for the study of the historical phonology and for the practical teaching of the various languages. Text-book : Jespersen's *Lehrbuch der Phonetik* (1904).

69 *Eighteen Lectures on Indo-European Phonology.*   1 hr.

An outline of the most important facts of Indo-European phonology : the vowel-system, the problems of ablaut, the gutturals, and accent.

[70 *Comparative Grammar, I.*   1st term.

A short comparative survey of the declensions in Sanskrit, Greek, Latin, and Germanic.

Omitted in 1907-08.]

71 *Comparative Grammar, II.*   2d term.

A short comparative survey of the conjugations in Sanskrit, Greek, Latin, and Germanic.

72 *Linguistics.*   2 hrs.

An introduction to the scientific study of linguistic development. Intended for both students of the classics and students of the modern languages who wish to become acquainted with the general principles and chief problems of linguistic science, modern methods of linguistic research, etc.

II. SEMITIC LANGUAGES AND BIBLICAL LITERATURE

EDWARD L. CURTIS, PH.D., D.D.   FRANK C. PORTER, PH.D., D.D.
B. W. BACON, D.D., LITT.D., LL.D. CHAS. C. TORREY, PH.D., D.D.
CHARLES F. KENT, PH.D.   RAYMOND G. CLAPP, M.A., B.D.

Connected with the department are the Reading Room, the Seminary Room, the Reference Libraries, the Special Collections, and the Semitic and Biblical Club.

The READING ROOM, in 9 Fayerweather Hall, adjoins the SEMINARY ROOM used by the department. It contains a good Reference Library in Biblical Literature and may be used for purposes of study at all times.

The TROWBRIDGE REFERENCE LIBRARY of the Divinity School, situated near the special library of the department proper, is also available for students in this department. It contains more than 3,000 carefully selected volumes and is particularly rich in works of reference for Biblical study.

The SALISBURY COLLECTION of Oriental manuscripts, books, and works of reference, the LIBRARY OF THE AMERICAN ORIENTAL SOCIETY, the LANDBERG COLLECTION of rare and valuable Arabic manuscripts, and the well stocked Semitic Sections of the University Library furnish exceptional advantages and opportunities for independent research to the student of Semitic literature.

The SEMITIC AND BIBLICAL CLUB, composed of the instructors, the students who are candidates for an advanced degree, and others who are interested in the work, holds fortnightly meetings, in Room A, East Divinity Hall, at which papers on subjects of interest to Biblical students are presented and discussed.

The courses in this department are arranged in three groups: Hebrew; Other Semitic Languages; Biblical Literature, but the groups are not entirely mutually exclusive.

See also courses I, 13 (*Hellenistic and Patristic Greek*), III, 82 (*Bibliography*), and Professor Walker's courses in *Church History* and *Christian Literature* (IX, 69, 70, 73, 74).

HEBREW

Professor CURTIS :—

1 *Elementary Hebrew.*   3 hrs.
> The year's work includes a mastery of the elements of Hebrew and the translation of *Genesis*.

2 *The Book of Job.*   1 hr.
> The grammatical and historical exegesis of the Hebrew text. Lectures and recitations.

[3 *Selections from Proverbs, and the Five Megilloth.*   1 hr.
> The grammatical and historical exegesis of the Hebrew text. Lectures and recitations.
> Omitted in 1907–08.]

4 *Selections from the Psalter.*   2 hrs. 1st term.
> The grammatical and historical exegesis of the text, with New Testament interpretation and homiletical application.

[5 *The Book of Isaiah.*   2 hrs. 2d term.
> The grammatical and historical exegesis of the Hebrew text.
> Omitted in 1907–08.]

6 *The Books of Chronicles.*   1 hr. 2d term.
> The grammatical and historical exegesis of the Hebrew text.

Professor KENT :—

7 *Hebrew Seminary.*   2 hrs.
> A knowledge of Hebrew, Hellenistic Greek, and German is required.   Subject for 1907–08 : the syntactical and textual problems of the later prophetic books and the critical translation of important sections.

OTHER SEMITIC LANGUAGES

Advanced courses in Classical and Palestinian Syriac, Old Babylonian, Ethiopic, and Sabæan and Minæan Inscriptions will be given according to the needs of students.   Instruction in modern colloquial Arabic (Syrian dialect) will be offered to those who intend to spend a year or more in the American School in Palestine.

Professor TORREY :—

[*11 *Elementary Arabic.*   2 hrs.
> The elements of Arabic grammar, including exercises in writing ; rapid reading of easy prose extracts.   Text-books : Socin's *Grammar* (2d ed.) Brünow's *Chrestomathy*.
> Omitted in 1907–08.]

12   *The Koran.*   2 hrs. 1st half-year.
Reading of selected suras, with a supplementary study of the life of Mohammed.

13   *Classical Arabic Prose.*   2 hrs. 2d half-year.
Reading of Torrey's *Selections from The Ṣaḥīḥ of al-Buḥārī*, for the main purpose of gaining familiarity with the classical vocabulary and style. The course serves also as an introduction to the *Ḥadīth* literature.

[14   *Arabic Poetry.*   2 hrs. 2d half-year.
Reading of selections from Nöldeke's *Delectus Veterum Carminum Arabicorum.*
Omitted in 1907–08.]

*15   *Elementary Syriac.*   2 hrs.
[See course V, B 6, page 151.]

[16   *Syriac (Advanced Course).*   2 hrs. 1st term.
Reading of the *Chronicle of Joshua the Stylite* (Wright's ed.). The class reads the whole *Chronicle*, which is one of the oldest and most interesting of the works of its kind.
Omitted in 1907–08.]

17   *The Old Syriac Gospels.*   2 hrs.
Reading of a considerable portion of the Lewis palimpsest, with attention to both linguistic and critical phenomena. Students who have taken course 15, or its equivalent, are qualified to enter this course.

[18   *Biblical and Palestinian Aramaic.*   2 hrs. 2d term.
Reading of the Aramaic portions of *Daniel* and *Ezra*, and other specimens of early Palestinian Aramaic. Text-books: Marti's *Grammatik der Biblisch-Aramäischen Sprache* and Dalman's *Aramäische Dialektproben.*
Omitted in 1907–08.]

19   *Elementary Assyrian.*   2 hrs. 1st half-year.
The text-books used are Lyon's *Assyrian Manual* (2d ed.) and Delitzsch's *Lesestücke* (4th ed., 1900).

[20   *Old Babylonian Texts.*   2 hrs. 2d half-year.
The documents studied are the *Law-Code* of Hammurabi, and selected *Letters* from the Amarna correspondence.
Omitted in 1907–08.]

21   *North Semitic Inscriptions.*   1 hr.
The Moabite stone ; the Siloam inscription ; the Zenjīrlī monuments, and other Old Aramaic remains ; selected Phœnician and Palmyrene inscriptions ; coins with old Semitic legends.

[22   *General Introduction to Semitic Philology.*   1 hr. 1st term.
A general view of the Semitic languages and peoples, including a brief survey of their literatures.   No previous knowledge
of the Semitic languages is required, though some acquaintance with at least the Hebrew language is desirable.
Omitted in 1907–08.]

23   *The History of Old Semitic Art.*   1 hr.
The fine arts in Babylonia and Assyria.   Hittite monuments ;
Phœnician art and its sources ; remnants of Palestinian art ; the
Hebrews ; the Western Aramaic peoples ; South Arabian monu-
ments.   Illustrated lectures,supplemented by prescribed reading.

BIBLICAL LITERATURE

Professor CURTIS :—

[31   *Ancient Traditions and History of the Jewish People.* 1 hr.
Studies in history and archæology, with the view of determin-
ing the meaning and historical value of the Biblical records.
Omitted in 1907–08.]

32   *Analysis and Exposition of Isaiah, Jeremiah, and Ezekiel
(English Bible).*   2 hrs. 2d term.

[33   *Analysis and Exposition of the Twelve Minor Prophets
and Daniel (English Bible).*   2 hrs. 2d term.
Omitted in 1907–08.]

34   *Old Testament Introduction.*   2 hrs.
A survey of the history of the canon, text, and versions, followed by a special introduction to the historical books of the Old
Testament and exegesis of their contents.   Lectures and required
reading.

Professor PORTER :—

[36   *Theology of the Pre-exilic Prophets.*   2 hrs. 1st term.
A course of lectures on the religious and ethical conceptions
of Amos, Hosea, Micah, Isaiah, and Jeremiah, based on a critical use of the books that bear their names.
Omitted in 1907–08.]

37   *The Theology of Judaism.*   2 hrs. 1st term.
Lectures on the religious history of the Jews from *Deuteronomy*
to the Maccabean era.

38   *The Jewish Religion of the Time of Christ.* 2 hrs. 2d term.
The history of the Jewish religious life from the Maccabean
period to the writing of the *Mishna (i. e.,* from about 175 B. C.
to 200 A. D.).

[39 *Biblical Theology of the New Testament.* 3 hrs.
The central aim of the course is the right understanding and estimation of the Teaching of Jesus. The Apostolic Teaching is then studied, with emphasis on the distinctive character and influence of the thought of Paul.
Omitted in 1907–08.]

40 *Problems in Theology.* 2 hrs.
Lessons and discussions on the Doctrine of the Sacred Scripture, the Spirit of God, the Person of Christ, and the Future Life.
To be carried forward, after March 1, by Professor Bowne of Boston University.

Professor BACON :—

*41 *The Pauline Epistles.* 3 hrs. 1st term.
[See Course V, B 7, page 152].

42 *The Christological Epistles.* 1 hr. 1st term.
A study of the origin and nature of the Christology of Paul in *Ephesians,* with a comparison of *Colossians, Philemon,* and *Philippians.* Lectures ; preparation of theses by the students.

*43 *Synoptic Gospels.* 3 hrs. 2d term.
[See Course V, B 7, page 152.]

44 *The Teaching of Jesus.* 1 hr. 2d term.
Comparison and interpretation of synoptic reports of the discourses of Jesus, using Bacon's *The Sermon on the Mount.* Lectures and collateral reading.

45 *New Testament Introduction.* 1 hr.
Lectures on the philological and historical apparatus for New Testament exegesis and text-criticism, followed (2d term) by discussion of the problems of the origin and canonization of the books of the New Testament.

46 *Historical Origins of the Church.* 2 hrs.
Critical discussion of the *Book of Acts,* with application of the principles of historical and documentary criticism. Seminar method.

47 *Theological German.* 2 hrs. 1st term.
Reading and discussion of standard German treatises, for practice and information.

48 *Hebrews and Catholic Epistles.* 2 hrs. 2d term.
A critical and exegetical study of the non-Pauline epistles in their origin and historical environment. Courses 48 and 49 are not both given in the same year.

49 *The Johannine Literature.*   2 hrs., 2d term.
    A critical study of the origins of the *Fourth Gospel* and the *Johannine Epistles*. Seminar method.   Courses 48 and 49 are not both given in the same year.

50 *Patristic Greek.*   1 hr. 1st term.
    Exegesis of selected passages from the Apostolic Fathers bearing on problems of the higher criticism.   Seminar method.

51 *Problems of Text-Criticism.*   1 hr. 2d term.
    A critical comparison of the Alexandrian with the Western form of the text, aiming to exhibit the history of the principal variants, beginning with the Lucan writings.   Seminar method.

Professor KENT :—

*52 *Biblical Literature and History.*   3 hrs.
    [See Course V, A 1, page 151.]

*53 *Historical Origin of Christianity.*   2 hrs.
    [See Course V, B 1, page 151.]

54 *Biblical Seminary.*   2 hrs.
    Intended to train students for patient, accurate, and independent investigation of Biblical and cognate questions.   It is open only to those who have a general acquaintance with the field of Biblical history and literature.   For 1907-08 the subject is the character, work, writings, and teachings of the Hebrew prophets, and the growth of Israel's Messianic hopes.

Professor KENT and Mr. CLAPP :—

55 *Principles and Methods of Biblical Study.*   2 hrs.
    Investigation of the problems and existing methods of religious instruction ; study of psychological principles and of the Biblical material, with a view to their practical use in religious education ; outlining of definite courses of study.

Mr. CLAPP :—

[56 *Introduction to the Jewish Pseudepigraphical Literature.*
                                                    2 hrs.
    Consideration of the historical background, origin, date, authorship, and contents of the Jewish pseudepigraphical writings, and their relation to the literature and thought of the Old and New Testaments.   Lectures, supplemented by papers and discussions.
    Omitted in 1907-08.]

*57 *Life and Literature of the Apostolic Age.*   2 hrs.
    [See Course V, B 2, page 151.]

III. MODERN LANGUAGES AND LITERATURES

HENRY A. BEERS, M.A.   ALBERT S. COOK, PH.D.,L.H.D.,LL.D.
HENRY R. LANG, PH.D.   ROBERT L. SANDERSON, M.A.
ARTHUR H. PALMER, M.A.   FRED'K M. WARREN, PH.D., L.H.D.
CHARLES C. CLARKE, JR., B.A.GUSTAV GRUENER, PH.D.
WILBUR L. CROSS, PH.D.   ALBERT E. CURDY, PH.D.
CHARLTON M. LEWIS, PH.D.   WILLIAM L. PHELPS, PH.D.
ROBERT N. CORWIN, PH.D.   CHARLES S. BALDWIN, PH.D.
KENNETH MCKENZIE, PH.D.   CLYDE C. GLASCOCK, PH.D.
WATSON NICHOLSON, PH.D.   EDWARD B. REED, PH.D.
MAX S. MANDELL   HOLLON A. FARR, PH.D.
GEORGE H. NETTLETON, PH.D.RUDOLPH SCHEVILL, PH.D.
JOHN C. ADAMS, PH.D.   JOHN M. BERDAN, PH.D.
FREDERICK B. LUQUIENS, PH.D. IRVILLE C. LeCOMPTE, PH.D.
CHAUNCEY B. TINKER, PH.D.   HENRY S. CANBY, PH.D.
EDWARD THORSTENBERG,PH.D. KAN-ICHI ASAKAWA, PH.D.
ANDREW KEOGH, M.A.

As auxiliary to the regular courses in modern languages and literatures, four clubs hold regular sessions throughout the year. These are The MODERN LANGUAGE CLUB, The ROMANCE CLUB, The GERMAN JOURNAL CLUB, and The ENGLISH CLUB. The first and the last in particular aim to deal with subjects not too technical in character, and thus to promote a sense of comity among all the workers in the same field.

The MODERN LANGUAGE CLUB, formed of instructors and students in the departments of Romance Languages, German, and English, holds meetings regularly each month, for the reading and discussion of original papers and for reports of progress in the field of these studies.

The ROMANCE CLUB, consisting of the instructors and students in the department of Romance Languages and Literatures, meets in 14 Lampson Hall, every other Saturday morning, to report on, and discuss, the results of recent scientific research in this field of study.

The GERMAN JOURNAL CLUB meets on alternate Tuesday evenings, in 12 Lampson Hall, for the presentation of reports on the most interesting periodicals published in German and devoted to Germanic philology.

The ENGLISH CLUB, to which are invited all persons, whether members of the University or not, who are interested in the study or teaching of the English language or literature, meets on alternate Monday evenings at seven o'clock, at 135 Elm street, to listen to the presentation of some topic and engage in the informal discussion of it. The club never remains in session over an hour, and thus other engagements for the same evening are not interfered with.

The GERMAN SEMINARY ROOM in Lampson Hall, where the Journal Club meets, contains a working library for the use of advanced students in the Germanic languages. It also serves as a general study and working room for such students.

The ENGLISH SEMINARY ROOM, at 135 Elm street, which has lately been enlarged for the better accommodation of graduate students in English, contains the nucleus of a working library. This room is general headquarters for the graduate students in English, and serves for the meetings of the English Club and for similar purposes.

ROMANCE LANGUAGES

See also courses I, 49 (*Low Latin*), 51 (*Latin Palæography*), 53 and 54 (*Latin Literature of the Middle Ages*), 67 (*Comparative Syntax*), 68 (*Phonetics*), 69 (*Indo-European Phonology*), 72 (*Linguistics*), III, 82 (*Bibliography*), and X, 26 (*Readings in French Psychology and Philosophy*). Certain courses in general or comparative literature are announced in the English group, below.

Professor LANG :—

1 *Seminary Course in Romance Languages and Literatures.*

1 hr.

This course is designed to give competent students guidance in original research. In 1907–08 the work will center on the study of the origin and growth of medieval lyric poetry in Provence, France, and other Romance countries.

FRENCH LINGUISTICS AND PHONETICS

Assistant Professor CURDY :—

2 *Old French Phonology and Morphology.*   2 hrs.

A study of the historical grammar of the French language from the earliest times.

3 *French Dialects.*   1 hr.

The phonology and morphology of the dialects of northern France before the fifteenth century. A discussion of the various theories regarding the origin and spread of dialects serves as introduction. A knowledge of French historical grammar is requisite.

[4 *Old French Syntax.*   1 hr.

Lectures on the syntax of the Old French period, with reference to the Latin and Modern French rules of syntax. A knowledge of French historical grammar is requisite.

Omitted in 1907–08.]

Dr. LeCOMPTE :—

5 *Old French Readings.*   1 hr.

A two years' course in systematic reading of Old French texts, with literary study of the period. A knowledge of French historical grammar is requisite.   •

Assistant Professor LUQUIENS :—

6 *Old French.*   2 hrs.

Study of Old French grammar, reading of texts, and lectures on the literary development of the period. This course is especially designed for students of English.

Assistant Professor SANDERSON :—

7 *Practice in Writing and Speaking French.*   2 hrs.

This course is *conducted entirely in French.* It is especially intended for graduates or undergraduates who read French with ease and understand it when they hear it spoken.

Assistant Professor CLARKE :—

8 *Phonetics of Modern French.*   1 hr.

Lectures and exercises on the phonetics of the cultivated Parisian speech. Attention is directed to the development of French pronunciation since the fifteenth century. Previous study of general phonetics is required.

FRENCH LITERATURE

Professor WARREN :—

[9   *Medieval Lyric Poetry.*   2 hrs.
   Lectures on the medieval French lyric, its origin and forms.
   Omitted in 1907-08.]

[10   *Romantic School.*   1 hr.
   A course of weekly lectures.
   Omitted in 1907-08]

Assistant Professor SANDERSON :—

11   *Masterpieces of French Literature, 1630-1900.*   2 hrs.
   A study of the great writers of the seventeenth, eighteenth,
   and nineteenth centuries. *Conducted in French.*

[12   *Molière.*   1 hr.
   A linguistic and literary study of some of Molière's best plays.
   Conducted in English.
   Omitted in 1907-08.]

Assistant Professor CLARKE :—

13   *French Poetry of the Nineteenth Century.*   1 hr.
   Lectures and readings intended to familiarize the student with
   the work of representative poets. The evolution of French
   poetry is discussed and some exposition of the versification
   offered. *Conducted in French.*

PROVENÇAL

Professor LANG :—

14   *Provençal Language and Literature.*   2 hrs.
   A study of the historical grammar of medieval Provençal
   and of the poetry of the Troubadours. Appel's *Provenzalische
   Chrestomathie* (2d ed., Leipzig) is used for the beginning.

SPANISH

Professor LANG and Assistant Professor SCHEVILL :—

*15   *Spanish (Elementary Course).*   3 hrs.
   [See Course VIII, A 1, page 155.]

Assistant Professor SCHEVILL :—

*16   *Reading and Composition in Spanish.*   2 hrs.
   [See Course VIII, B 1, page 155.]

Professor LANG :—

17   *Spanish Prose of the Sixteenth and Seventeenth Centuries.*

                                                       2 hrs.

Assistant Professor SCHEVILL :—

*18   *The Spanish Drama of the Sixteenth and Seventeenth Centuries.*   2 hrs.
    [See Course VIII, C 1, page 156.]

Professor LANG :—

19   *General View of Spanish Literature.*   1 hr.

20   *Beginnings of Spanish Literature.*   1 hr.
    A study of Spanish literature previous to the fifteenth century. As often as may be possible, the class will be taken to the Museum of the Hispanic Society in New York City.

PORTUGUESE

Professor LANG :—

21   *Old Portuguese Literature.*   1 hr.
    Given at the discretion of the instructor.

ITALIAN

Assistant Professor MCKENZIE :—

*22   *Italian (Elementary Course).*   3 hrs.
    [See Course VII, A 1, page 155.]

[*23   *Italian Literature.*   1 hr.
    [See Course VII, A 2, page 155.]
    Omitted in 1907–08.]

24   *Dante.*   2 hrs.
    Thorough study of Dante's life and works, particularly his *Vita Nuova* and *Divina Commedia*. (For a course in *Dante in English*, see 59, below.)

25   *Petrarch and Boccaccio.*   2 hrs.
    The works of Petrarch and Boccaccio and their predecessors and contemporaries. Text-book : D'Ancona e Bacci's *Manuale della Letteratura Italiana*, vol. I.

26   *Italian Literature of the Thirteenth Century.*   1 hr.
    Reading of texts, with reference both to their literary qualities and to the history of the language. Text-book : Wiese's *Altitalienisches Elementarbuch* (Heidelberg, 1904).

27   *Fable-Literature in the Middle Ages.*   1 hr.
    The history of Æsopic fables ; their relation to the bestiaries and the beast-epic. Conferences and reports.

GERMAN

For courses in general or Indo-European *Grammar, Linguistics, Phonetics*, and *Syntax*, see I, 67–72. For *Theological German* and *Readings in German Psychology and Philosophy*, see II, 47, and X, 21. A general course in *Bibliography* and certain courses in general or comparative literature are announced in the English group, below.

Professor PALMER :—

The following courses, 34, 35, 46, and 47, will be given in 1907-08 according to circumstances and the needs of the graduate students in attendance.

34 *Introduction to Germanic Philology.* 2 hrs.

> A course introductory to the general study of Germanic philology, dealing with its history, methods, fields, and fundamental facts.

35 *Gothic.* 2 hrs.

> An introductory course, especially for those who intend to study German or English historically, in the study of Gothic and its phonological relations to both earlier Indo-Germanic and later Germanic languages.

*36 *Goethe : Works and Life.* 3 hrs.

> [See Course IX, C 1, page 158.]

*37 *History of German Literature, 1624–1832.* 2 hrs.

> [See Course IX, C 2, page 158.]

Professor GRUENER :—

[38 *Middle High German.* 3 hrs.

> Hartmann's *Der Arme Heinrich* and *Iwein;* the *Nibelungenlied;* selected poems of Walther von der Vogelweide ; selections from Wolfram von Eschenbach's *Parsival.* Lectures and papers. Omitted in 1907–08.]

39 *German Literature of the Reformation Period (1500–1624).* 3 hrs.

> The development of German literature from the beginning of the Reformation to the time of Opitz.

*40 *The Drama of Schiller and his Contemporaries.* 2 hrs.

> [See Course IX, B 4, page 158.]

[*41 *German Literature from Goethe's Death to the Rise of Naturalism.* 3 hrs.

> [See Course IX, C 3, page 159.]
> Omitted in 1907–08.]

Professor Palmer :—

42 *Old High German.* 3 hrs.

A rather detailed course in the oldest High German dialects and literature. Braune's *Althochdeutsche Grammatik* and *Althoch-deutsches Lesebuch*, and the collateral literature for reference.

Professor CORWIN :—

[43 *History of New High German.* 2 hrs.

The earlier periods of the language are first surveyed, for the purpose of gaining a comprehensive idea of the chief linguistic phenomena and their causes. Upon this basis a more special study is made of the origin and development of New High German.

Omitted in 1907-08.]

Assistant Professor GLASCOCK :—

44 *Sudermann and Hauptmann.* 2 hrs.

Reading and critical analysis of all the dramas of Sudermann and Hauptmann, with full discussion of their relations to both earlier and contemporary authors.

Assistant Professor FARR :—

*45 *German Literature of the Nineteenth Century.* 2 hrs.

[See Course IX, B 5, page 158.]

SCANDINAVIAN

Professor PALMER :—

46 *Old Norse (Icelandic).* 3 hrs.

Grammar, and reading in the *Sagas* and the *Elder Edda*.

47 *Norwegian and Danish.* 2 hrs.

The object of this course is to lay the foundation for a reading and practical knowledge of the language.

Dr. THORSTENBERG :—

48 *Swedish.* 2 hrs.

This course is intended as a foundation for a reading and practical knowledge of the language. Together with the study of the grammar, selections from the writings of modern authors are read.

RUSSIAN

Mr. MANDELL :—

*49 *Elementary Russian.* 2 hrs.

[See Course X, page 159.]

JAPANESE

Dr. ASAKAWA :—

50 *Japanese.* 2 hrs.

An introductory course in the written language.

ENGLISH

Two years before taking the degree of Ph.D. in English, a candidate must have obtained from one of the English Professors a certificate of his proficiency in Latin, French, and German.

The candidate for the degree of Ph.D. must pass two oral examinations : (1) a general examination, covering the field of modern English literature from the accession of Queen Elizabeth to the death of Queen Victoria ; (2) a special examination, upon some one period of English literature (or some one phase of it). The subject of the special examination will be designated by the candidate himself, but notice of the subject selected must be given to the Chairman of the Administrative Committee of the English Faculty at least a year beforehand, and the subject selected must receive the Committee's approval. Subjects for graduation theses must also receive the Committee's approval in advance.

While no fixed number of courses is prescribed for candidates for the degree of Ph.D., an aggregate credit of eighteen hours is indicated as most likely to meet the requirements in ordinary cases. It is usual for a student to undertake about eight hours in each of his first two years of residence, and (if he has shown the required proficiency) to devote most of his third year to the completion of his thesis. All students have free election (subject, however, to the approval of the Administrative Committee) among the courses offered in the English department of the School, and with the Committee's approval may choose courses in related subjects in other departments. But every candidate for the degree of Ph.D. must take at least one two-hour course in Old English, unless he has taken the subject as an undergraduate and gives satisfactory evidence of proficiency.

For courses in general or Indo-European *Grammar, Linguistics, Phonetics,* and *Syntax,* see I, 67–72. For a course in *Old French* designed especially for students of English, see 6, above.

Professor BEERS:—

55 *Milton and his Contemporaries.* 2 hrs.

The *belles lettres* of the Puritan Revolution.

56 *Shakespeare.* 2 hrs.

A study of Shakespeare with reference to his handling of dramatic material.

Professor COOK :—

The strictly graduate courses announced below are given according to circumstances and the needs of the graduate students in attendance ; and special attention is given to the supervision of individual research in any part of the general field.

57 *The Method of English Study.* 2 hrs.

A course in the principles and methods of English study, including a general survey of its scope. A knowledge of German is essential in this course.

58 *Theories of Poetry.* 2 hrs.

A course in the theories of poetry in general, and in the principles of criticism applicable to its various departments, as the epic, the drama, and the lyric.

[59 *Dante in English.* 2 hrs.

A course primarily in the *Divina Commedia* and the *Vita Nuova*, though selections from other works are also read. Much attention is bestowed upon the historical and literary background of the poet and his works.

Omitted in 1907–08.]

60 *Literary Types.* 2 hrs.

A survey of European literature, with reference to the characterization and illustration of the more important species. Candidates must satisfy the instructor with regard to their proficiency in French, German, and Latin.

61 *Advanced Old and Middle English.* 2 hrs.

Selected works are read with reference especially to the acquisition of scholarly method. A knowledge of German is essential in this course.

62 *Seminary in English Literature.* 3 hrs.

A critical study of some representative writer or department of literature.

63 *Old and Middle English.* 2 hrs.

An elementary course in the beginnings and earlier development of the English language and literature.

Professor CROSS :—

64 *English Prose Fiction, with Special Reference to the
Nineteenth Century.* 1 hr.

Instruction is mainly by lectures. Each student is required
to read and report on a list of books, and to prepare in the latter part of the second term a paper on an assigned topic.

[65 *Romantic Verse since 1850.* 1 hr.

This course deals mainly with the so called Pre-Raphaelites,
such as Dante Gabriel Rossetti and William Morris. These and
other poets are studied in connection with the medieval
romances from which they drew.

Omitted in 1907–08.]

Professor LEWIS :—

66 *Verse Composition.* 1 hr.

Fortnightly practice in composition, with regular appointments for consultation and criticism.

67 *Prosody.* 1 hr.

Special topics and problems, such as the English hexameter,
English and French Alexandrines, four-time and three-time
measures, etc.

68 *Shakespeare.* 1 hr.

First term : a minute study of *Macbeth*. Second term : miscellaneous problems as to date, authenticity, and genesis of
various plays.

69 *Nineteenth Century Poets.* 2 hrs.

Research work in poetry, biography, and criticism, under the
direction of the instructor.

Professor W. L. PHELPS :—

70 *English Literature of the Seventeenth Century.* 2 hrs.

A study of English poetry and prose from Donne to Dryden,
exclusive of the drama. The social life of the times is discussed
in connection with some of the authors mentioned above. Milton is not included in this course.

71 *Elizabethan Literature.* 2 hrs.

Studies in the poetry and prose of the Elizabethan period,
exclusive of the drama. Lectures, discussions, and preparation
of special papers by members of the class.

22

[*72 *Elizabethan Drama*, 2 hrs.
[See Course XI, B 5, page 163.]
Omitted in 1907-08.]

[73 *The Contemporary Drama*. 1 hr.
A study of contemporary stage-plays in Europe and in America. A good reading knowledge of both French and German is prerequisite to this course.
Omitted in 1907-08.]

Assistant Professor C. S. BALDWIN :—

74 *Rhetoric*. 1 hr.
Regular conferences : (1) for technical criticism of creative composition ; (2) for research in the theory of rhetoric.

Assistant Professor REED :—

75 *English Lyrical Poetry, its History and Development*. 1 hr.
This course extends over two years, but each half is complete in itself. The first year is devoted to the study of the English lyric from 1066 to 1625. Special attention is paid to the influence of the Italian and French lyrics on English verse.

Assistant Professor NETTLETON :—

76 *The English Drama Since the Restoration*.
This course is divided into two parts, given in alternate years, but each part is complete in itself. It is primarily a course of lectures on the history of English drama, with critical study of representative dramatists. It is divided as follows :

[*a English Drama from Dryden to Goldsmith*. 1 hr.
Omitted in 1907-08.]

b English Drama from Goldsmith to Tennyson. 1 hr.

Dr. NICHOLSON :—

77 *English Literature of the First Half of the Eighteenth Century*. 2 hrs.
A study of English literature, exclusive of the drama, from Dryden to the death of Pope, based on the social, political, and intellectual life of the age.

Dr. J. C. ADAMS :—

[78 *English Literary Criticism*. 1 hr.
A historical survey of literary criticism in England since the middle of the sixteenth century.
Omitted in 1907-08.]

Dr. Berdan :—

79 *Poetry of the Renaissance.*   2 hrs.

> Non-dramatic English literature studied in connection with European movements. The effects of the Chaucerian tradition, Humanism, and Petrarchism discussed. Latin, French, and Italian read.

Dr. Tinker :—

80 *Early Narrative.*   1 hr.

● > Beowulf, the *Saga of the Volsungs*, the *Nibelungenlied*, *The Song of Roland* (all in translation), and English and Scottish popular ballads are read. The influence of these works upon Percy, Scott, Rossetti, and Morris.

Dr. Canby :—

81 *Types of Short Narrative.*   1 hr.

> A course in the history and development of the various types of short narrative in English literature. In each group and period stories and collections of stories are studied for their literary value and for their relation to the development of fiction.

THE USE OF THE LIBRARY

Mr. Keogh :—

82 *Bibliography.*

> Ten lectures on certain practical aspects of bibliography. Discussion of general reference books; the means of finding what has been published on a subject; the reviewing of books; the classification and cataloguing of libraries; the taking and filing of notes and references; the compilation of bibliographies; the printing of theses.

IV. THE FINE ARTS

John F. Weir, M.A., N.A.	John H. Niemeyer, M.A., A.N.A.
John P. C. Foster, M.D.	George H. Langzettel, B.F.A.

G. Albert Thompson, B.F.A.

The charge for instruction in the Art Course is twenty-five dollars for the College year, entitling the student to all the privileges of the School as arranged for students from other Departments of the University.

For courses in *Greek, Roman, Etruscan,* and *Old Semitic Art,* see I, 55–60, and II, 23.

Professor WEIR :—

1 *Painting.*

> Technical course in painting from the living model ; composition ; lectures on the grammar of art. Only those students who have been qualified by a course in drawing may take this course.

2 *Modeling.*

> Studies from casts and the living model, with lectures on the grammar of art.

Professor NIEMEYER :—

3 *Drawing.*

> Technical course in drawing from the antique and the living model ; from the portrait and the nude model ; lectures on perspective and composition.

Dr. FOSTER :—

4 *Anatomy.*

> Lectures on artistic anatomy.

Mr. LANGZETTEL :—

5 *Drawing.*

> Drawing from casts.

•Mr. G. A. THOMPSON :—

6 *Painting.*

> Painting from still-life.

Mr. LANGZETTEL and Mr. G. A. THOMPSON :—

7 *Illustration and Decorative Design.*

> Evening class.

V. MUSIC

SAMUEL S. SANFORD, M.A. ISIDOR TROOSTWYK
HORATIO W. PARKER, MUS.D. LEO SCHULZ
HARRY B. JEPSON, M.A., MUS.B. WILLIAM E. HAESCHE, MUS.B.
CHARLES RABOLD H. STANLEY KNIGHT
D. STANLEY SMITH, B.A., MUS.B. LEWIS WILLIAMS
SETH DANIELS BINGHAM, JR., B.A.

Mr. D. S. SMITH :—

1 *Harmony.*   2 hrs.

> The study of chords, progressions, modulation, and non-harmonic notes. The work consists of exercises in figured-bass, the harmonization of melodies, and harmonic analysis.

2 *Counterpoint.* 2 hrs.

Practice in strict counterpoint, both simple and double, harmonization of chorales, composition of short pieces in a freer style, and analysis of simple polyphonic forms.

Professor PARKER :—

3 *Strict Composition.* 2 hrs.

The writing of canons, fugues, and polyphonic choral movements. Each student is required to submit at the close of the year a complete four-voiced fugue.

4 *History of Music.* 1 hr.

Lectures on the development of music from its earliest stages, with biographical sketches of composers and practical illustrations at the piano.

Mr. HAESCHE :—

5 *Instrumentation.* 2 hrs.

Lectures on the characteristics of all the instruments of the modern orchestra, with illustrations of their use by great composers. Exercises in practical orchestration, and playing from orchestral scores.

Professor PARKER :—

6 *Free Composition.* 2 hrs.

The writing of free vocal and instrumental pieces in the smaller forms, and later in the sonata form, either for single instruments or for a combination of instruments.

7 *Advanced Orchestration and Conducting.* 1 hr.

The study of old and new orchestral scores; practical instruction in conducting; orchestration of original or other compositions.

Professors SANFORD and JEPSON, Assistant Professors TROOSTWYK and KNIGHT, Mr. RABOLD, Mr. SCHULZ, Mr. L. WILLIAMS, and Mr. S. D. BINGHAM, Jr :—

8 *Practical Music.* 1 hr.

Private instruction in piano-, organ-, violin-, and violoncello-playing and in singing. Fees range from fifty to one hundred dollars for the College year. No student is admitted to this course who has not been admitted to one of the theoretical courses.

B. THE PHYSICAL AND NATURAL SCIENCES, MATHEMATICS, AND ENGINEERING

VI. THE PHYSICAL AND NATURAL SCIENCES

WILLIAM H. BREWER, PH.D.,LL.D. WILLIAM G. MIXTER, M.A.
EDWARD S. DANA, PH.D. CHARLES S. HASTINGS, PH.D.
FRANK A. GOOCH, PH.D. RUSSELL H. CHITTENDEN, LL.D , SC.D.
HORACE L. WELLS, M.A. WILLIAM J. COMSTOCK, PH.B.
EDWARD A. BOWERS, B.A., LL.B. LOUIS V. PIRSSON, M.A.
FREDERICK E. BEACH, PH.D. FREDERICK H. NEWELL, B.S.
HARRY B. FERRIS, M.D. PHILIP E. BROWNING, PH.D.
JAMES W. TOUMEY, M.A., M.S. GIFFORD PINCHOT, SC.D.
ROSS G. HARRISON, M.D., PH.D. ALEXANDER W. EVANS, M.D.,PH.D.
HENRY L. WHEELER, PH.D. CHARLES SCHUCHERT, M.A.
LAFAYETTE B. MENDEL, PH.D. HENRY A. BUMSTEAD, PH.D.
HENRY S. GRAVES, M.A. WESLEY R. COE, PH.D.
JOSEPH BARRELL, PH.D. BERTRAM B. BOLTWOOD, PH.D.
RICHARD S. LULL, PH.D. HERMANN VON SCHRENK, PH.D.
ISAAC K. PHELPS, PH.D. LYNDE P. WHEELER, PH.D.
GEORGE F. EATON, PH.D. HARRY W. FOOTE, PH.D.
YANDELL HENDERSON, PH.D. HENRY H. ROBINSON, PH.D.
HERBERT E. GREGORY, PH.D. LEO F. RETTGER, PH.D.
JOHN D. IRVING, PH.D. ELLSWORTH HUNTINGTON, M.A.
TREAT B. JOHNSON, PH.D. GEORGE H. MYERS, M.F.
RALPH G. VANNAME, PH.D. WILLIAM E. FORD, JR., PH.D.
HERMAN H. CHAPMAN, M.F. FRANK P. UNDERHILL, PH.D.
ARTHUR H. GRAVES, PH.D. BEVERLY W. KUNKEL, PH.D.
GEORGE S. JAMIESON, PH.D. LEON J. COLE, PH.D.
LORANDE L. WOODRUFF, PH.D. CHAMPION H. MATHEWSON, PH.D.
HAROUTUNE M. DADOURIAN,PH.D. ISAIAH BOWMAN, B.S.

The work in PHYSICS is carried on in the Sloane Physical Laboratory of the Academical Department and in the Physical Laboratory of the Sheffield Scientific School (in Winchester Hall); the work in CHEMISTRY, in the Sheffield Chemical Laboratory and in the Kent Chemical Laboratory of the Academical Department; the work in PHYSIOLOGY, PHYSIOLOGICAL CHEMISTRY, COMPARATIVE ANATOMY, and GENERAL BIOLOGY, in the Sheffield Biological Laboratory; the work in BOTANY, in the Eaton Herbarium (in Sheffield Hall); the work in FORESTRY, in the Forest School; the work in THE GEOLOGICAL SCIENCES and ZOOLOGY, in the Peabody Museum of Natural History and in Kirtland Hall of the Sheffield Scientific School.

The PHYSICS JOURNAL CLUB, open to graduate students in Physics, meets weekly, in 121 Winchester Hall, for the review and discussion of the current literature in this department of study.

The PHYSICAL CLUB, organized for study, criticism, and discussion, holds fortnightly meetings in the Sloane Laboratory, open to graduates and other advanced students in Physics.

The CHEMICAL CLUB, composed of instructors, graduate students, and others interested in Chemistry, holds fortnightly meetings in the Kent Laboratory, for the discussion of current chemical literature and the presentation of papers.

The BIOLOGICAL CLUB, composed of instructors, graduate students, and others interested in Biology, meets fortnightly, in the Sheffield Biological Laboratory, for the presentation and discussion of papers and reviews of recent work.

The GEOLOGICAL CLUB is an association of the instructors and graduate students, for the purpose of encouraging the students to prepare papers, and to aid in the discussion of current topics of interest in geological subjects.

PHYSICS

Professor HASTINGS and Assistants :—

1 *Physics.*   3 hrs. lectures, 6 hrs. laboratory work.
   Laboratory work in the Sheffield Physical Laboratory, supplemented by lectures on the theory of instruments and on the theory of electricity and electrical machinery.

2 *Physical Optics.*   2 hrs. 2d half-year.
   The object of the course is to give the student a critical knowledge of the essential optical instruments and of the fundamental phenomena of light.

3 *Theory of Errors.*   1 hr. 1st half-year.
   This includes the Method of Least Squares and is developed with special attention to the requirements of the student of Physics.

Professor BUMSTEAD and Assistants :—

*4   *Introduction to Theoretical Physics.*   3 hrs.
     [See Course XIII, C 1, page 171.]

5   *Advanced Laboratory Physics.*   6 hrs., *to count as 4 hrs.*
     Laboratory work in the Sloane Laboratory.   Problems of con-
     siderable experimental difficulty and involving a knowledge of
     mathematical Physics such as may be obtained in course 4.

6   *Electricity and Magnetism.*   2 hrs.
     The mathematical theory of Electricity and Magnetism, based
     on Maxwell's Treatise, with explanation of the modifications
     and additions to the theory developed by J. J. Thomson, Lorentz,
     Larmor, and others.

Assistant Professor BEACH :—

7   *Vectors.*   2 hrs.
     The relations between directed quantities are developed with
     reference to their importance in Physics rather than as a study
     of the analysis of Hamilton (quaternions) or that of Grassmann
     (*Ausdehnungslehre*).

Assistant Professor BOLTWOOD :—

8   *Radioactivity.*   1 hr. 2d term.
     Lectures on the chemical and physical properties of radio-
     active substances, and the discussion of these with respect to
     their bearing on the hypothesis of atomic disintegration.

Assistant Professor L. P. WHEELER :—

9   *Theory of Electrons.*   1 hr.
     The lectures treat of that explanation of certain of the prop-
     erties of matter and of the phenomena of electro-magnetism
     which is based on the hypothesis of a molecular structure of
     electricity.

The following courses, given by Professors in the
department of Mathematics, but falling properly within
the field of physical study, are announced in detail in
the group of courses in Mathematics: *Mechanics* and
Celestial Mechanics (Professor BROWN) ; *Advanced Mechanics*
and *Elasticity and Hydromechanics* (Professor PIERPONT) ;
Advanced Dynamics (Dr. DADOURIAN) ; and *Gravitation and
Electrostatics* (Assistant Professor L. P. WHEELER).

See also VI, 15 (*Chemical Physics*), 28 and 50 (*Physical
Chemistry*), 29 and 51 (*Physico-Chemical Measurements and
Methods*), and some of the courses in Engineering.

CHEMISTRY

For a course in *Radioactivity*, see 8, above. For courses in *Physiological Chemistry*, see 71, 72, and 74, below.

COURSES IN THE SHEFFIELD CHEMICAL LABORATORY

The analytical laboratories of the Sheffield Scientific School are open to students in term time from 9.00 A. M. to 1.00 P. M. and from 2.00 to 5.00 P. M. every week day except Saturday. The greater part of the instruction is given in the laboratory, to each student separately, but the various classes have, in addition, two or more lectures or recitations a week, in connection with the studies pursued in the laboratory.

Professor MIXTER :—

15 *Chemical Physics.*

> Especially the methods employed in calorimetry and in the determination of specific heat.

Professor WELLS :—

16 *Qualitative Analysis.*	1st term.

> Embraces a study of the commonly occurring elements in their qualitative relations, and includes a systematic course of analysis for the same. A good knowledge of elementary Chemistry is a necessary preparation for this. If desired, the course is extended to include a study of many of the rare elements.

17 *Quantitative Analysis.*

> This is open only to those who have taken course 16 or its equivalent. (*a*) Gravimetric Analysis : embraces a series of exercises involving a considerable number of important methods. (*b*) Volumetric Analysis : includes the most important and typical methods. (*c*) Ultimate Organic Analysis.

18 *Inorganic Preparations.*	2d term, 1st half.

> A course of laboratory work, with lectures and recitations. About thirty or forty compounds are prepared, which give a variety of important and instructive processes.

19 *Advanced Quantitative Analysis.*

> (*a*) Metallurgical Chemistry : the analysis of ores, fuels, fluxes, alloys, metals, and other furnace products. (*b*) Mineralogical Chemistry : the analysis of minerals for scientific purposes.

20 *Metallurgy.*	2d term.

> A course of recitations and lectures on elementary Metallurgy.

21 *Technical Gas-Analysis.* 2d term, 2d half.

A short practical course, including the principal methods.

22 *Investigations in Inorganic Chemistry.*

Opportunities are offered, to those who have had sufficient preparation, to make researches upon analytical methods, the preparation of chemical compounds, and other scientific problems.

Mr. COMSTOCK :—

23 *Elementary Organic Chemistry.* 3 hrs.

Lectures and recitations through the year, with six hours per week of laboratory work from January to March.

Assistant Professor H. L. WHEELER and Dr. JOHNSON :—

24 *Advanced Organic Chemistry.*

This offers an opportunity for more extended study and original investigation to those who have proper preparation.

25 *Organic Preparations.* 2d term, 2d half.

Laboratory work, consisting of five exercises per week, of about three hours each, in the preparation of such compounds as will give familiarity with the most important synthetical methods.

26 DR. JOHNSON :—

Ultimate Organic Analysis.

Quantitative determinations of carbon, hydrogen, sulphur, and the halogens in organic compounds.

Professor MENDEL :—

27 *Proximate Organic Analysis.* 2d term, 1st half.

Lectures on the chemical composition of vegetable and animal substances (including foods) and laboratory practice in the detection and quantitative determination of the various constituents.

Assistant Professor FOOTE :—

28 *General and Physical Chemistry.* 3 hrs.

Recitations and lectures on General and Physical Chemistry.

29 *Physico-Chemical Measurements.* 2d term.

Laboratory practice in the more important methods of Physical Chemistry.

30 *Electrochemistry.* 2d term.

Experimental work in Electrochemistry, including the usual measurements, quantitative electro-analysis, and the synthesis of organic and inorganic compounds.

Dr. JAMIESON :—

31 *Sanitary Water-Analysis.*   2d term.

   A practical course in the chemical examination of drinking-waters. Three exercises of two and one-half hours each per week, and subsequent opportunity for more extended study of the subject.

32 *Technical Water-Analysis.*   2d term.

   A practical course in the examination of water for use in boilers, of mineral waters, etc.

33 *Metallurgical Analysis.*   2d term, 2d half.

   A laboratory course, including the analysis of ores, alloys, slags, and fuels. Laboratory open Monday–Friday, 9.15–12.15.

COURSES IN THE KENT CHEMICAL LABORATORY

The Kent Chemical Laboratory is open from 9.00 A. M. to 1.00 P. M., and (Saturday excepted) from 2.00 to 5.00 P. M., to students who are taking strictly graduate courses.

Professor GOOCH, Assistant Professor BROWNING, Dr. I. K. PHELPS, and Dr. VANNAME :—

*35 *Inorganic Chemistry, Inductive and Descriptive.*   6 hrs.

   [See Course XIV, A 1, page 172.]

Assistant Professor BROWNING :—

*36 *Qualitative Analysis.*   6 hrs.

   [See Course XIV, B 1, page 172.]

Professor GOOCH and Dr. I. K. PHELPS :—

*37 *Organic Chemistry.*   5 hrs.

   [See Course XIV, B 2, page 173.]

Professor GOOCH :—

*38 *Quantitative Analysis.*   6 hrs.

   [See Course XIV, C 1, page 173.]

39 *Quantitative Analysis (Second Course).*

   Practice in the more complex processes of gravimetric, volumetric, and electrolytic Analysis.

40 *Chemical Theory.*   -   1 hr.

   The historical development of the theories of Chemistry.

41 *Research in Inorganic Chemistry.*

   The critical examination of reactions.

42 *Research in Analytical Chemistry.*

Problems of Analysis—either experimental criticism of known processes or constructive work looking towards the development of new methods.

Assistant Professor BROWNING :—

43 *Inorganic Preparations.* 4 hrs.

A short course, mainly laboratory work, covering typical methods for the preparation of inorganic salts.

44 *The Rare Elements.* 5 hrs.

Lectures and laboratory work, covering the principal reactions of the elements not included in the general course (35).

45 *Research in the Chemistry of the Rare Elements.*

Special problems involving separation of the rare earths and metals.

Dr. I. K. PHELPS :—

46 *The Carbon Compounds, Descriptive and Theoretical.* 3 hrs.

A course of lectures treating systematically the more important compounds of carbon and the theories concerning them. An elementary knowledge of Organic Chemistry is desirable as a preparation.

47 *Organic Analysis.*

Laboratory practice in the methods of Organic Analysis, including gas-analysis.

48 *Organic Preparations.*

Laboratory practice in processes too complicated to be included in the experimental work of course 37, and in processes leading to research.

49 *Research in Organic Chemistry.*

The study of reactions and of the constitution of organic compounds.

Dr. VANNAME :—

50 *Physical Chemistry.* 1 hr.

An elementary course of lectures covering the more important theories of Physical Chemistry, including Electrochemistry.

51 *Physico-Chemical Methods.* 4 hrs.

A laboratory course affording practice in a number of the typical processes and measurements of Physical Chemistry, including Electrochemistry.

52   *Electrochemical Preparations.*   3 hrs.
     The preparation, by electrical means, of various inorganic and
     organic compounds.

BIOLOGY

For other biological or semi-biological courses, see VI,
126 (*Organic Evolution*), 127 (*Geological Biology*), 128 (*Comparative Osteology*), IX, 6 (*The Natural History of Man*), 14
(*Physical Anthropology*), and some of the courses in Psychology (group X).

ZOOLOGY, GENERAL BIOLOGY, ANATOMY, EMBRYOLOGY,
PHYSIOLOGY, PHYSIOLOGICAL CHEMISTRY, TOXI-
COLOGY, BACTERIOLOGY, HYGIENE

Dr. COLE :—

53   *Invertebrate Zoology.*   3 hrs.
     Lectures and laboratory work. A systematic survey of the
     invertebrates, designed to give a fundamental knowledge of
     their structure, habits, and relationships.

54   *Animal Behavior.*   3 hrs.
     Lectures and demonstrations. Essentially a study of the
     physiology of the sense organs and nervous system, correlating
     the simpler types of reactions with reflexes, associative pro-
     cesses, instincts and habits, and the psychic phenomena of
     higher forms.

Professor HARRISON :—

*55   *Elementary Biology.*   6 hrs., *to count as 3 hrs.*
      [See Course XVI, A 2, page 180.]

Assistant Professor COE and Dr. WOODRUFF :—

*56   *General Biology.*   6 hrs., *to count as 3 hrs.*
      [See Course XVI, B 1, page 180.]

Professor HARRISON, Assistant Professor COE, and Dr.
      KUNKEL :—

*57   *Comparative Anatomy and General Biology.*
      [See page 272.]

Assistant Professor COE :—

*58   *Embryology of Vertebrates.*   1st term.
      [See page 273.]

Dr. KUNKEL :—

*59   *Organic Evolution.*   1 hr.
      [See Course XVI, A 3, page 180.]

Professor HARRISON :—

60 *General Anatomy of the Nervous System.* 1 hr.

Lectures upon the structure and development of the nervous elements, including histogenesis, growth, regeneration, degeneration, and structural changes due to functional activity. By special arrangement laboratory work may be done in connection with this course.

61 *Experimental Embryology.*

Research work for those qualified by previous training. By special arrangement.

Professor HARRISON and Assistant Professor COE :—

62 *Biological Seminary and Journal Club.* 1-2 hrs.

Reports and reviews of books and current periodical literature.

63 *Comparative Anatomy and Embryology.*

Graduate students who have had sufficient elementary training are provided with special advanced courses of instruction leading up to original investigation. To such students the laboratory is open daily.

Assistant Professor COE :—

64 *Biology of the Cell.*

Laboratory work and informal lectures on the animal cell, with special attention to maturation, fertilization, and cleavage of the ovum, and to the problems of growth, heredity, and evolution.

65 *General Embryology.*

A practical study of the development of certain types of invertebrates, followed by the elementary principles of vertebrate embryology.

Dr. WOODRUFF :— 3 hrs.

66 *General Physiology of the Lower Organisms.*

A general survey of the physiology of the lower organisms, particularly the Protozoa, including cell-structure, growth and regeneration, development, inheritance, origin of sex, reactions to stimuli, and the relation of Protozoa to disease. Lectures and laboratory work.

Professor FERRIS:—

67 *Comparative Morphology of the Vertebrate Brain.* 1 hr.

A course extending through the year, consisting of dissections, demonstrations, and lectures, on the Embryology and general Morphology of the Vertebrate Brain, with special reference to the human brain.

Professor CHITTENDEN and Assistant Professor UNDERHILL :—

*68　*Physiology.*　　　　　　　　　　　　　　1 hr.

Lectures, illustrated with demonstrations, etc., Huxley's *Lessons in Elementary Physiology* being used as a basis.

Professor CHITTENDEN :—

69　*Physiology of Nutrition.*　　3 hrs. 2d term, 1st half.

Professor MENDEL :—

70　*Experimental Physiology.*　　4 hrs., *to count as 3 hrs.*

A laboratory course, intended to afford experimental acquaintance with certain departments of Physiology and giving particular attention to general physiological methods.

Professor CHITTENDEN and Assistant Professor UNDERHILL :—

*71　*Physiological Chemistry (Shorter Course).*　　5 hrs.,
　　　　　　　　　　　　　　　　　　　to count as 2½ hrs.
[See Course XVI, C 3, page 181.]

Professor MENDEL :—

72　*Physiological Chemistry.*

A course planned for graduate students who have sufficient knowledge of analytical and organic Chemistry and elementary Physiology or general Biology.

Professor CHITTENDEN :—

73　*Experimental Toxicology.*　　　　2d term, 2d half.

A course of about twenty lectures, with demonstrations, on the physiological action of the more important mineral and alkaloidal poisons.

Professors CHITTENDEN and MENDEL :—

74　*Research Work in Physiological Chemistry.*

Opportunity for undertaking research work independently or under guidance is given ; and investigations are planned with reference to the needs and attainments of the individual.

75　*Physiological Seminary.*　　　　　　　　2 hrs.

An informal study of the recent advances in Physiology and Physiological Chemistry is undertaken. The participants are required to prepare reports and reviews of papers appearing in current physiological literature.

Assistant Professor HENDERSON :—

76 *Hæmodynamics.* 3 hrs.

Primarily a laboratory course—with research work—in the study of the circulation. Open only to those who have already had thorough training in the general principles of Physiology.

Assistant Professor RETTGER :—

77 *Bacteriology and Hygiene.* 2d term.

Laboratory work, supplemented by lectures and recitations. The course covers a period of twenty weeks, fifty exercises, and is designed for students of Chemistry and Biology. Ample opportunity is afforded for advanced work and research.

78 *Bacteriology and Hygiene (Shorter Course).*

6 hrs. 2d term, 2d half.

Shorter course, adapted to the needs of students in municipal and sanitary engineering. Special attention is given to such topics as the bacteriology and the purification of water supplies.

*79 *Public Hygiene.* 2 hrs. 2d term, 1st half.

[See page 276.]

80 *Sanitary Science.* 1 hr. 1st term.

Ten lectures, with demonstrations. Essentially a course on the modern methods of bacteriological and biological study of water and the purification of water supplies and sewage.

81 *Tropical Hygiene.* 2 hrs. 1st term.

Twenty lectures, with demonstrations. Discussion of climatic conditions, foods and clothing, and their bearing on the health of the individual. Considerable attention is given to the more important tropical diseases and methods of prevention.

BOTANY AND FORESTRY

Professor EVANS :—

*82 *Elementary Botany.* 4 hrs.

[See Course XVI, A 4, page 180.]

*83 *Morphology of Plants.* 4 hrs.

[See Course XVI, B 2, page 180.]

84 *Advanced Morphology and Taxonomy of Plants.*

The botanical laboratory is open throughout the year to properly qualified graduate students who may wish to pursue advanced studies along some special line in morphological or taxonomic Botany.

Professor EVANS and Assistant Professor UNDERHILL :—

85 *Plant Physiology.*

Opportunity for study in Plant Physiology, particularly in its chemical features, is offered to graduate students who have a knowledge of plant morphology and histology.

Dr. A. H. GRAVES :—

86 *Dendrology.*   4 hrs. 1st term.

Field excursions in New Haven and vicinity, devoted to ecological and taxonomic studies of our trees and shrubs, especial attention being given to the characteristics by which they may be most readily recognized at all seasons of the year.

87 *Diseases of Trees.*   3 hrs. 2d term, 1st half.

Lectures and laboratory work on the destructive diseases of the timber trees of the United States, their causes, nature, and · remedies ; field excursions.

Dr. VON SCHRENK :—

88 *Preservation of Timber.*   2d term, 1st half.

The decay of structural timber, lasting powers of various species, seasoning of wood, methods of preserving timber in America and Europe, description of preserving plants. Twelve lectures.

Professor BREWER :—

90 *Forest Physiography.*   Special lectures, winter term.

General conditions necessary to forests ; elementary meteorology ; forests as related to various elements; the geographical distribution of forests ; the geologic history of forests ; forests in relation to public health and public recreation.

Mr. NEWELL :—

91 *Forest Hydrography.*   4 lectures, winter term.

A course of lectures considering the variations in the flow of streams, giving particular attention to irrigation economies, and to the work of the United States Reclamation Service in the construction and administration of irrigation systems in the arid West.

Assistant Professor CHAPMAN :—

92 *State Forest Law.*   2 hrs. 2d term, 1st half.

A study of the forest laws of different States, with particular reference to those dealing with forest protection. A comparison of the laws of the United States and those abroad.

23

Professor PINCHOT :—

93 *U. S. National Forests.* Special lectures, winter term.

Economic growth and present industrial situation of the West ; settlement and disposal of public lands ; origin, administration, and management of the Forest Reserves.

94 *Forest Policy.* 6 lectures, fall term.

Origins of Forest Policy; its objects and principles ; forest legislation ; the forest and other land laws in relation to economic and industrial development ; State forest problems.

Mr. BOWERS :—

95 *Forest Administration and Law.* 2 hrs. fall term.

The development of the public domain with special reference to laws relating thereto, including rules and regulations governing public lands, forest reserves, and national parks.

96 *Elementary Law for Foresters.* 2 hrs. 1st term.

Treats of contracts, damages, real estate, riparian rights, and abstracts of title.

Professor GRAVES and Mr. MYERS :—

97 *Forestry Management Abroad.* 2 hrs. winter term.

History and practice of forestry in Europe, India, and Japan, with a brief reference to forestry in other foreign countries.

THE GEOLOGICAL SCIENCES
ELEMENTARY COURSES

Professor DANA :—

100 *Mineralogy and Crystallography.* 6 hrs., *to count as 3 hrs.*

Practical study of mineral species by means of blowpipe analysis and other methods ; mathematical study of the forms of crystals.

Assistant Professor FORD :—

101 *Determinative Mineralogy.* 3 hrs. or more.

The object of this course is to gain familiarity with the common minerals, together with facility in their identification. The subject is treated mainly from a chemical standpoint, and it is assumed that all who take the course have some familiarity with the principles of elementary Chemistry.

102 *Crystallography and Descriptive Mineralogy.*

2d term, 2 hrs.

These two subjects are treated together, a group or class of crystals being first studied and then the mineral compounds belonging to that class. Instruction is given by means of lectures and practical demonstrations.

Professor PIRSSON :—

103 *Elementary Petrology.*   1 hr. 2d term, 1st half.

   Lectures of an elementary nature on rocks with reference to their geological relations and economic properties.

104 *Elementary Structural and Dynamical Geology.*

3 hrs. 1st half-year.

   This course of lectures and recitations includes the elements of Structural and Dynamical Geology; gives a general knowledge of the subject, and serves as an introduction to more advanced geology.

Professor GREGORY and Assistant Professor BARRELL :—

*105 *General Geology.*   2 hrs.

   [See Course XV, B 1, page 175.]

Assistant Professor BARRELL and Mr. HUNTINGTON :—

106 *Geology with Field and Laboratory Work.*   3 hrs.,

to count as 2 hrs.

   Practice in determining rock-making minerals and simple types of rocks, and in using and interpreting topographical and geological maps. Field work consisting of the collection of rock-types, study of structures, and the drawing of a detailed geological map of a restricted area.

Professor GREGORY, Mr. HUNTINGTON, and Mr. BOWMAN :—

*107 *Physical Geography.*   3 hrs. 1st half-year.

   [See Course XV, A 1, page 174.]

Mr. BOWMAN :—

*108 *The Geography of North America.*   2 hrs.

   [See Course XV, B 5, page 175.]

*109 *The Geography of South America.*   2 hrs. 2d half-year,

to count as 1 hr. for the year.

   [See Course XV, B 6, page 176.]

Mr. HUNTINGTON :—

*110 *Geography of Asia.*   2 hrs. 1st half-year,

to count as 1 hr. for the year.

   [See Course XV, B 7, page 176.]

Assistant Professor FORD :—

111 *Experimental Work in Crystallography.*

The chief features of this course are the measurement of the angles of crystals with the reflection goniometer, the plotting of the forms of crystals in the stereographic and linear projections, the calculation of axial ratios of crystals and of the symbols of their faces, and the drawing of crystal forms and combinations.

112 *Experimental Work in the Optical Properties of Minerals.*

In this course the optical properties of crystals are studied and determined. Students learn to use the refractometer, total reflectometer, polariscope, polarizing microscope, axial angle apparatus, and other optical appliances. A knowledge of Optics is indispensable.

113 *Original Investigation in Mineralogy and Crystallography.*

Those who are sufficiently advanced may undertake research work in Mineralogy and Crystallography. Such work may be along the lines of analytical Chemistry, or the crystallographic and optical properties of minerals may be studied.

Professor PIRSSON :—

114 *Petrology.*   3 hrs. 2d term.

A course of fifty lectures on the history, origin, properties, and classification of rocks, commencing with the igneous ones and passing into the crystalline schists.

115 *Petrology.*

(*a*) Study and determination of the rock-making minerals by optical and chemical methods.

(*b*) Systematic Petrography. The study of typical rock specimens and of thin sections under the microscope,

(*c*) Study of collections, with specimens and sections, from localities investigated and described.

(*d*) Original investigation. In sequence to (*a*), (*b*), and (c), some special object or locality may be made the subject of investigation.

STRUCTURAL GEOLOGY

Assistant Professor BARRELL :—

116	*Dynamic and Structural Geology.*		2 or 3 hrs.

A course dealing with such subjects as : ancient sedimentary formations, crustal movements, and the nature and results of igneous and metamorphic activities. A large amount of field work and library work is required.

117	*Problems in Structural Geology.*

A study of folds, faults, veins, metamorphism, mountain-making, etc., for those who wish to specialize in Geology. Problems for investigation in preparation of theses for advanced degrees. A knowledge of Petrography is required.

118	*Principles of Metamorphism and their Geological Application.*

In this course the chemical and physical principles of Metamorphism and the structural problems presented by the action of dynamic Metamorphism are studied. A good knowledge of general Geology and of microscopic Petrography is required.

PHYSIOGRAPHY

Professor GREGORY and Mr. BOWMAN :—

119	*Physiography (A).*		5 hrs., *to count as 3 hrs.*

A study of the origin, development, and classification of land forms, followed by a study of the physiography of the United States. The exercises include lectures, field excursions, and the reading of topographical maps and of geological literature.

120	*Physiography (B).*

The origin, development, and classification of land forms, as illustrated by some area selected for special study.

Mr. BOWMAN and Mr. HUNTINGTON :—

121	*Geographic Controls in History.*		2 hrs. 2d half-year,
to count as 1 hr. for the year.

Geographic environment as affecting man's distribution, conditions of life, and institutional development ; study of a limited region, considering the bearing of its topography, drainage, soils, climate, and natural resources upon the history of its people.

ECONOMIC GEOLOGY

Professor IRVING :—

122	*Economic Geology.*		3 hrs. 2d term.

The principles of ore-deposition, and the structural relations, genesis, and geological occurrence of the ores.

123 *Advanced Economic Geology.*

(*a*) This course deals with the distribution, chemistry, geology, and production of the ores of the metals and non-metallic products, and the relation between mining processes and geological occurrence.

(*b*) Original investigation. Some special study or problem in economic Geology.

PALEONTOLOGY

Professor SCHUCHERT and Assistant Professor LULL:—

124 *Advanced Paleontology.* 6 hrs., *to count as 3 hrs.*

The object of this course is to acquaint the student with the structure, evolution, and classification of the various classes of invertebrate and vertebrate animals found as fossils.

125 *Advanced Stratigraphic Paleontology and Paleogeography.* 6 hrs., *to count as 3 hrs.*

In this course the student becomes acquainted with the essential or guide fossils which characterize the major divisions of geological time, and the distribution and character of the ancient seas and lands.

Assistant Professor LULL :—

*126 *Organic Evolution.* 1 hr.

[See Course XV, B 9, page 176.]

127 *Geological Biology.* 2 hrs.

In this course organisms are the chief objects of study, and their nature, succession, relations to environment, ancestry, and time, and the principles of organic evolution in their geological relations, are examined.

Dr. EATON :—

128 *Comparative Osteology.* 2 hrs.

An elementary course, especially designed as a preparation for the study of Vertebrate Paleontology. Laboratory work in which the most important types of the vertebrate skeleton are studied and compared.

METALLOGRAPHY

Dr. MATHEWSON :—

129 *Metallography.* 1 hr. 2d term.

A course of twelve lectures during the first part of the second term, covering methods used in alloy study, discussion of typical physical and chemical metal and alloy structure, and illustrative examples.

130   *Metallographical Laboratory Practise.*

Open to those taking course 129 simultaneously. A laboratory course of six hours a week for twelve weeks, devoted to the preparation and structure study of three to six simple series of alloys.

131   *Metallographical Investigation.*

Advanced research on metals and alloys. Adequate preparation in Organic Chemistry, Physical Chemistry, and Metallography is required for this work.

GENERAL COURSES

Professor GREGORY :—

132   *Geology of Connecticut.*

With special reference to the surface features. Lectures, laboratory work, and field work.

Dr. ROBINSON :—

[133   *Field Geology.*   6 hrs., *to count as 3 hrs.*

This course consists of field work upon selected areas in the vicinity of New Haven, supplemented by lectures and laboratory exercises on the construction and use of topographical and geological maps.

Omitted in 1907–08.]

VII. MATHEMATICS

WILLIAM BEEBE, M.A. ANDREW W. PHILLIPS, PH.D.
ERNEST W. BROWN, Sc.D. JAMES PIERPONT, PH.D.
PERCEY F. SMITH, PH.D. WILLIAM A. GRANVILLE, PH.D.
HERBERT E. HAWKES, PH.D. LAURENCE E. HEWES, PH.D.
MAX MASON, PH.D. WILLIAM R. LONGLEY, PH.D.

Connected with the department are the Seminary Rooms, the Reference Library, the Mathematical Laboratory, the Collection of Models, and the Mathematical Club.

The SEMINARY ROOMS, which are at 90 High street, may be used by all students in Mathematics. They afford a place for students to meet for the discussion of mathematical questions and for study. There is a good departmental Reference Library, and also a collection of drawings and models made by students of previous years illustrating various theories. Many of the lectures in this department in past years have been reported and are here to be found bound and ready for consultation.

The MATHEMATICAL LABORATORY occupies a commodious room on the floor below the seminary rooms. It is well equipped with tools and drawing instruments necessary to construct mathematical models. Students are given direction and advice for the proper and expeditious construction of models more or less elaborate, illustrating the subjects they are studying. Such models and drawings serve to develop the student's geometrical intuition as well as to make more clear the particular theory in hand. Students who expect to become teachers will find the laboratory most useful in acquiring facility in preparing simple models to illustrate subjects which they may later have to teach.

The COLLECTION OF MATHEMATICAL MODELS is one of the most extensive in the country and is constantly growing. Besides a very complete selection of plaster and thread models from Brill, Schilling, and others, the collection contains a large number of models, which have been made under the direction of instructors of the department, illustrating the teaching of Solid Geometry, the Theory of Equations, and various kinematical principles, as well as the theory of twisted curves and surfaces.

The MATHEMATICAL CLUB holds fortnightly meetings in Sloane Laboratory, at which are presented summaries of articles in current periodicals and of recent works on pure and applied Mathematics, descriptions and models of new apparatus, also papers containing the results of the original investigations of the instructors and advanced students in this department. All students are encouraged to prepare papers which, if not original, give a comprehensive survey of some field of Mathematics or treat from a new standpoint some question of general interest to the members of the club. Lectures are occasionally given before the club by professional experts.

GENERAL STATEMENT OF THE COURSES

The courses fall into three groups, as follows: Introductory Courses; Advanced Courses; One-Hour Courses.

The INTRODUCTORY COURSES are intended for students who have completed a year's work in the Calculus and wish to obtain a broad and thorough knowledge of the elements of higher Mathematics.

The ADVANCED COURSES, to which the introductory courses are prerequisite, are adapted to the needs of students specializing in Mathematics and kindred branches. Special topics are treated in detail and the results of modern research are presented, the aim being to develop the student's powers and equip him for independent investigation.

The acquisition of a broad knowledge of modern methods and results in the various fields of Mathematics being difficult, a number of ONE-HOUR COURSES are annually offered, each consisting of one lecture a week throughout the year. In these the range of topics of the advanced courses is covered in a less special way and, in addition, certain subjects are treated which do not naturally lie within the scope of any of the advanced courses. The object sought in all one-hour courses is to give the student breadth of information without making too great demands upon his time.

DESCRIPTION OF THE COURSES
INTRODUCTORY COURSES

Assistant Professor HAWKES :—

*1 *Algebra and Analytical Geometry.* 2 hrs.
[See Course XII, B 4, page 168.]

Professor PIERPONT :—

*2 *Introduction to the Theory of Functions.* 2 hrs.
[See Course XII, C 6, page 169.]

*3 *Projective Geometry.* 2 hrs.
[See Courses XII, C 5, page 169.]

Dr. HEWES :—

4 *Differential Equations.* 1 hr.
Elementary methods of integration, with solution of problems by the students ; applications to Geometry and Mechanics ; geometric study of solutions of equations of the first order.

5 *Geometrical Transformations of the Plane and of Space.*
2 hrs.
Properties of Euclidian transformations, collineations, correlations, inversions, dilatations, and birational transformations, including resolution and composition into groups.

Dr. GRANVILLE :—

6 *Differential Geometry.* 2 hrs.
Parametric representation of plane and skew curves and surfaces, theory of contact, curvature, differential invariants, intrinsic equations, trajectories, conformal and spherical representation, map-projection.

Professor BROWN :—

*7 *Mechanics.* 2 hrs.
[See Course XII, C 2, page 169.]

*8 *Advanced Calculus.* 3 hrs.
[See Course XII, C 1, page 169.]

Assistant Professor HAWKES :—

[*9 *Teachers' Course in Geometry.* 2 hrs.
[See Course XII, C 3, page 169.]
Omitted in 1907-08.]

Professor PIERPONT :—

[15   *Advanced Mechanics.*   •   2 hrs.

Lagrange's equations, D'Alembert's principle, Hamilton's principle, potential, spherical harmonics, elasticity, hydrodynamics. Numerous examples from Physics, Astronomy, and Engineering.

Omitted in 1907–08.]

16   *Elasticity and Hydromechanics.*   2 hrs.

The general theory is illustrated by numerous applications of a practical nature, such as the strength and stiffness of various structures, the steadiness of ships, the dynamic theory of the tides, organ pipes, and vibrating membranes.

[17   *Advanced Theory of Functions.*   2 hrs.

Selected topics, such as the theory of aggregates, transfinite numbers, infinite series, analysis of geometric notions, development of functions.

Omitted in 1907–08.]

[18   *Theory of Numbers.*   2 hrs.

Divisibility, congruences, quadratic residues, Diophantine equations, quadratic forms, algebraic numbers.

Omitted in 1907–08.]

[19   *Finite Groups and Galois's Theory.*   2 hrs.

Substitution groups, abstract groups, linear groups, the icosahedron, Galois's theory, solution of the quintic, geometrical applications.

Omitted in 1907–08.]

20   *Elliptic Functions.*   2 hrs.

Functions of Jacobi and Weierstrass, transformation theory, modular functions, applications to Geometry and mathematical Physics, introduction to the theory of Abelian functions.

[21   *Ordinary Differential Equations.*   2 hrs.

The analytic character of solutions of linear and algebraic equations treated from the standpoint of the theory of functions ; special study of particular equations, as the hypergeometric, Bessel's, Riccati's, etc.

Omitted in 1907–08.]

Assistant Professor HAWKES :—

22   *Advanced Algebra.*   2 hrs.

Systems of linear equations, linear transformations, invariants, quadratic forms, elementary divisors, theory of elimination.

[23 *Linear Associative Algebra.* 2 hrs.

Comparative study from the various points of view suggested by the theory of bilinear forms, matrices, continuous groups, and the work of Benjamin Peirce.

Omitted in 1907–08.]

Assistant Professor MASON :—

24 *Differential Equations.* 2 hrs.

A general course in the theory of Differential Equations, ordinary and partial.

[25 *Linear Differential Equations.* 2 hrs.

Real solutions of ordinary and partial Linear Differential Equations of the second order, with special attention to boundary-value problems.

Omitted in 1907–08.]

[26 *Calculus of Variations.* 2 hrs.

The modern theory, with applications to Geometry and Mechanics.

Omitted in 1907–08.]

[27 *Potential Theory and Harmonic Analysis.* 2 hrs.

Elements of the theory of Newtonian and logarithmic potential; Fourier's series, spherical harmonics, and Bessel's function, with application to numerous physical problems.

Omitted in 1907–08.]

28 *Integral Equations.* 1 hr.

Discussion of recent advances in the theory of functional equations.

29 *Conformal Mapping and Riemann Surfaces.* 1 hr.

An elementary course, based on the introductory courses in theory of functions.

Professor P. F. SMITH :—

[30 *Advanced Analytical Geometry.* 2 hrs.

Singularities of curves and surfaces, the geometry of reciprocal radii, line geometry, and the spherical geometry of Sophus Lie.

Omitted in 1907–08.]

31 *Higher Geometry.* 2 hrs.

A continuation of course 30, including advanced work in the topics of that course, together with a study of the linear systems of curves on algebraic surfaces.

32   *Geometrical Analysis.*   1 hr.

Exposition of Grassmann's *Ausdehnungslehre* and applications; relations to the barycentric calculus of Möbius, vector analysis, quaternions, etc.

[33   *Continuous Groups of Transformations.*   2 hrs.

A study of Sophus Lie's theory of finite continuous groups, and applications to ordinary differential equations.
Omitted in 1907–08.]

[34   *Geometry of Contact Transformations.*   2 hrs.

A study of contact transformations following Sophus Lie with applications to partial differential equations.
Omitted in 1907–08.]

Dr. LONGLEY :—

35   *Differential Geometry.*   2 hrs.

Invariant theory of binary quadratic differential forms, equations of Gauss and Codazzi, theory of applicability, infinitesimal deformation, rectilinear congruences, orthogonal systems.

Dr. HEWES :—

36   *Graphical and Numerical Computation.*   1 hr.

Including an exposition of the theory and practice of d'Ocagne's *Nomographie*, and various topics in numerical approximation.

Professor BROWN :—

37   *Celestial Mechanics.*   2 hrs.

The problems of two and three bodies; the motions of planets and satellites;· general methods, especially the variation of arbitrary constants.

Dr. DADOURIAN :—

38   *Advanced Dynamics.*   2 hrs.

Equations of force, moment, impulse, and work. Later, discussion and application of the Lagrangian and Hamiltonian equations and the principle of least action.

Assistant Professor L. P. WHEELER :—

39   *Gravitation and Electrostatics.*   1 hr.

Elementary theorems and problems in Newtonian fields of force.

COURSES ANNOUNCED UNDER PHYSICS

The following courses, given by Professors in the department of Physics, but falling also under the head of

Mathematics, are announced in detail in the group of courses in Physics; *Physical Optics* and *Theory of Errors* (Professor HASTINGS); *Introduction to Theoretical Physics* and *Electricity and Magnetism* (Professor BUMSTEAD); *Vectors* (Assistant Professor BEACH); *Theory of Electrons* (Assistant Professor L. P. WHEELER).

See also the section on Engineering.

VIII. ENGINEERING

CHARLES B. RICHARDS, M.A.	A. JAY DUBOIS, C.E., PH.D.
JOHN H. HAMMOND, M.A.	SAMUEL E. BARNEY, C.E.
EDWIN H. LOCKWOOD, PH.D.	JOHN C. TRACY, C.E.
LOUIS D. HUNTOON, M.E.	W. K. SHEPARD, PH.D.

Special Reference Libraries, composed chiefly of Engineering Journals and the Transactions of Engineers' Societies, are connected with the department. They contain complete series of the most valuable of these Journals, and a large number of others are received as issued, forming a valuable collection of current journal literature on Engineering.

The Laboratories in Winchester Hall afford facilities for research in various lines of Engineering work, and the HAMMOND METALLURGICAL LABORATORY affords ample facilities in assaying, metallurgy, ore-dressing, etc.

The ENGINEERS' CLUB meets at intervals, in North Sheffield Hall, for the reading and discussion of papers on subjects relating to the different branches of Engineering. Lectures are occasionally given before the club by professional experts.

MECHANICAL ENGINEERING

Courses 1, 2, and 3, arranged for candidates for the degree of Mechanical Engineer, are open also to special graduate students, who are allowed in certain cases to take selected parts. Candidates for the degree of Mechanical Engineer are required to take also courses 4 and 36 in Mathematics (*Differential Equations* and *Graphical and Numerical Computation*), to sustain a final examination, and to present a satisfactory thesis on a subject approved by the Professor in charge of the courses in Mechanical Engineering.

Professor RICHARDS :—

1 *Machine-Designing.*

> In this course the student is engaged in practical exercises under the guidance of the Professor in charge, investigating and designing machinery, and making working-drawings, specifications, and estimates for machines and manufacturing plants.

Assistant Professor LOCKWOOD :—

2 *Thermodynamics and Mechanics of Heat Engines.*

> An advanced course in the study of Steam and Gas Engines, Steam Boilers, etc., supplementary to the courses given in these subjects to the undergraduate students in Mechanical Engineering. Lectures (two hours a week), investigations, and experimental work.

Dr. SHEPARD :—

3 *Mechanics of Materials.*   2 hrs.

> An advanced course, supplementary to the course given in this subject to the undergraduate students in Mechanical Engineering.

CIVIL ENGINEERING

Candidates for the degree of Civil Engineer are required to take, in addition to courses 4 and 5 (which are primarily for regular candidates for the degree of Civil Engineer, but are open also to other graduate students who are properly qualified), a selected course in Applied Mathematics and, when the facilities in the physical laboratory permit, a course of laboratory work under the superintendence of the Professors in charge. They are also required to sustain a final examination, and to present a satisfactory thesis upon a subject approved by the Professor in charge of the course. To special students, not candidates for the degree of Civil Engineer, a selection of special topics is allowed.

Professor DuBois :—

4 *Mechanics of Engineering.*

5 *Construction and Design.*

Assistant Professor BARNEY :—

6 *Geodesy and Practical Astronomy.* 2d term.
> Methods of observation ; theory of least squares ; adjustment of observations. The study of Practical Astronomy embraces the use of the sextant and engineer's transit for determining time, latitude, azimuth, and needle-variation.

7 *Railway Surveying.* Three weeks in June and July.
> A preliminary line for a railroad is run out, and from the contour map so obtained a final line is located and cross-sectioned, and estimates are made for construction. The final maps and estimates are made in October.

8 *Sanitary Engineering.*
> First term: Water Supply. Methods of collecting and distributing water ; designing of reservoirs, pipe systems, and filtration plants. Second term: Sewerage. Design and construction of sewer systems, plants for sewage disposal, etc.

Assistant Professor TRACY :—

9 *Graphic Statics.*
> A rapid review of fundamental principles, followed by a discussion of those problems in which the methods of Graphic Statics can be used to advantage.

MINING AND METALLURGY

Instruction in Mining and Metallurgy is in charge of John Hays Hammond, M.A., Professor of Mining Engineering, and Louis Doremus Huntoon, M.E., Assistant Professor of Mining and Metallurgy. The HAMMOND METALLURGICAL LABORATORY of the Sheffield Scientific School is devoted entirely to the subjects of Mining, Metallurgy, and Ore-Dressing. It contains well equipped laboratories, research rooms, and collections, as well as a departmental library. The laboratories have been planned to give a thorough training in the practical work of assaying and the treatment of ores, and contain small-sized dressing appliances for ore-dressing on a commercial scale.

C. THE SOCIAL SCIENCES, LAW, HISTORY, PHILOSOPHY, AND EDUCATION

IX. THE SOCIAL SCIENCES, LAW, AND HISTORY

ARTHUR M. WHEELER, LL.D.   SIMEON E. BALDWIN, LL.D.
WILLIAM G. SUMNER, LL.D.   CHARLES H. SMITH, LL.D.
BERNADOTTE PERRIN, PH.D., LL.D. GEORGE B. ADAMS, PH.D., LITT.D.
HENRY W. FARNAM, M.A., R.P.D.   F. WELLS WILLIAMS, B.A.
EDWARD V. RAYNOLDS, D.C.L.   EDWARD G. BOURNE, PH.D.
WILLISTON WALKER, PH.D., D.D.   CHARLES C. TORREY, PH.D., D.D.
HARRY B. FERRIS, M.D.   IRVING FISHER, PH.D.
IRVING S. BASSETT, PH.D.   OLIVER H. RICHARDSON, PH.D.
GUY S. CALLENDER, PH.D.   HENRY C. EMERY, PH.D.
CLIVE DAY, PH.D.   GEORGE GRANT MACCURDY, PH.D.
WILLIAM B. BAILEY, PH.D.   CHARLES C. HYDE, LL.B., M.A.
ALBERT G. KELLER, PH.D.   CHARLES P. SHERMAN, D.C.L.
HENRY B. WRIGHT, PH.D.   HIRAM BINGHAM, PH.D.
FRED R. FAIRCHILD, PH.D.   JOHN P. NORTON, PH.D.
KAN-ICHI ASAKAWA, PH.D.   AVARD L. BISHOP, PH.D.
LESTER W. ZARTMAN, PH.D.   THEODORE H. BOGGS, M.A.

The BOOCOCK LIBRARY (founded in 1896 by Mr. and Mrs. S. W. Boocock) is a departmental library in the Social Sciences, which supplies students with rare and special works in those subjects which the University Library does not contain. Any books needed by special students will be obtained. Students of all degrees of advancement will find reference books in the Boocock Library, and are invited to apply for access to it to Professor Sumner.

A BIBLIOGRAPHY OF ECONOMIC AND KINDRED SUBJECTS is maintained by the instructors in Economics, and is available to students in the University Library. The department of Economics also collects statistical charts, tables, and slides, which are preserved in E, Osborn Hall.

The COMMERCIAL MUSEUM, including the exhibit of the U. S. Bureau of Plant Industry at the World's Fair in Portland, Oregon, is available for the study of the materials of commerce.

The ANTHROPOLOGY CLUB meets, generally on alternate Tuesday evenings in Room 1, Herrick Hall, for papers

24

and discussions in A**n**thropology (Historical and Somatic), Ethnology, Sociology, and Demography.

The POLITICAL SCIENCE CLUB, comprising the graduate students and instructors in the Social Sciences, has its headquarters in E Connecticut Hall, which are open to members at all times. The departmental library there installed contains a collection of economic works generally required by advanced students. Fortnightly meetings are held during term time. Students have opportunities to visit such charitable and penal institutions and agencies of social betterment as are in New Haven or within easy access of it.

The HISTORICAL SEMINARY ROOM, at 90 High street, contains a reference library to which graduate students may have access at all hours.

The HISTORY CLUB meets fortnightly, for the reading and discussion of papers and for reports on current periodicals.

ANTHROPOLOGY AND SOCIOLOGY

For a course in *Bibliography*, see III, 82. For *Organic Evolution* and certain other courses bearing on Anthropology, see group VI.

Professor SUMNER :—

*1　*The Science of Society*.　　　　　2 hrs.
　　　[See Course XX, C 1, page 192.]

[2　*Anthropology*.　　　　　2 hrs.
　　　A careful study of Ranke's *Der Mensch* (2d ed.).
　　　Omitted in 1907-08.]

3　*The Self-Perpetuation of Society*.　　　　　2 hrs.
　　　(Section II of Systematic Societology.) A historical and ethnological study of the evolution of the marriage institution, the family, and population.

4　*The Mental Reactions*.　　　　　2 hrs.
　　　(Section IV*a* of Systematic Societology.) An ethnological study of the development of the mental processes and of the growth and contents of the mental outfit of the human race in the earlier stages.

5   *The Beginnings of the Industrial Organization.*   2 hrs.
>   An ethnological study of the industrial organization from its earliest beginnings.

Professor FERRIS :—

*6   *The Natural History of Man.*   2 hrs.
>   [See Course XX, C 2, page 192.]

Professor KELLER :—

*7   *Anthropology.*   2 hrs.
>   [See Course XX, B 1, page 191.]

8   *Culture-History.*   2 hrs.
>   A critical reading of Lippert's *Kulturgeschichte* (2 vols., Stuttgart, 1887), for its subject-matter and as a basis for informal instruction in research, scientific method, etc.

*9   *Colonization.*   2 hrs.
>   [See Course XX, B 3, page 191.]

*10   *Ethnology.*   2 hrs.
>   [See Course XX, C 3, page 192.]

[11   *Historical Anthropology.*   2 hrs.
>   An analysis of the anthropological evidence of legend and folk-tale. The last year was devoted to Homer. Ability to read the original is valuable, but is not required.
>   Omitted in 1907–08.]

[12   *History of Sociology.*   2 hrs.
>   Readings in the forerunners of the science, in Comte and Spencer, and in later writers. Reports and discussions.
>   Omitted in 1907–08.]

Dr. BISHOP and Mr. BOGGS:—

*13   *Commercial Geography.*   3 hrs. 2d half-year.
>   [See Course XV, A 1, page 174.]

Dr. MACCURDY :—

14   *Physical Anthropology.*   2 hrs. 1st half-year.
>   Characters of race, age, sex, etc. Lectures and demonstrations. Students have access to suitable collections as well as practice in the use of laboratory apparatus. This course is primarily intended for those who have taken course 6.

15   *Prehistoric Archæology of Europe.*   2 hrs. 2d half-year.
>   Physical characters of the earliest known races, their environment and stages of culture. Illustrated by specimens from the Museum collections.

16 *American Archæology.*   2 hrs. 2d half-year.
     Lectures and reading, with access to the Museum collections.
Dr. BISHOP :—

*17 *Transportation Systems.*   2 hrs.
      [See Course XX, B 4, page 191.]

*18 *Natural History of Commerce.*   · 2 hrs.
      [See Course XX, B 5, page 191.]

[*19 *Markets.*   2 hrs.
      [See Course XX, B 6, page 191.]
      Omitted in 1907–08.]

ECONOMICS AND LAW

For a course in *Bibliography*, see III, 82. For *Forestry Law*, see VI, 95, and 96.

Professor FARNAM :—
[25 *The Principles of Public Finance.*   2 hrs.
      Omitted in 1907–08.]

[26 *Social Politics.*   2 hrs.
      Omitted in 1907–08.]

[27 *Pauperism and Crime.*   1 hr.
      Omitted in 1907–08.]

[28 *The Modern Labor Movement.*   2 hrs.
      Omitted in 1907–08.]

Professor FISHER :—
[29 *Theory of the Distribution of Wealth.*   2 hrs.
      A study—theoretical, statistical, and historical—of the accumulation and dissipation of wealth among social classes.
      Omitted in 1907–08.]

30 *Theory of Prices and Price-Levels.*   2 hrs.
      A study of the determination of prices, rents, and wages, and of the relation of money and circulating credit to price-levels.

Professor CALLENDER :—
31 *Economic History of the United States.*   2 hrs.
      This course describes the economic evolution of the United States from the simple agricultural communities of colonial times to the highly diversified industrial society of the present.

Professor EMERY :—
*32 *Elementary Economics.*   .   1 or 3 hrs.
      [See Course XXI, A 1, page 193.]

33 *Commerce and Commercial Policy in the Nineteenth Century.*   2 hrs.

> A study of the growth of international trade and the changes in commercial policy, especially in the leading countries of Europe.

[34 *History of Economics, Part I.*   2 hrs.

> The history of economic ideas, with special reference to economic policy, from the Middle Ages to the middle of the nineteenth century. Lectures and readings in contemporary authors. Omitted in 1907–08.]

35 *History of Economics, Part II.*   2 hrs.

> A continuation of the above course, given in alternate years. It deals with the later reactions from the classical school, protectionism, socialism, and the historical school.

Professor DAY :—

36 *Economic Organization of Europe.*   2 hrs.

> A descriptive course in national political economy, to supplement courses in general economics. Lectures on the organization of the separate states ; investigation of special topics by the students.

37 *Economic History of Europe.*   2 hrs.

> Development of the economic organization in Europe in its relation to the political organization : for advanced students in economics and history. Lectures, readings, and investigation.

38 *Industrial History of the United States.*   2 hrs.

> Introductory lectures on methods and-bibliography, followed by investigation of a small number of special topics by each member of the class in conference with the instructor.

Assistant Professor BAILEY :—

*39 *Elementary Statistics.*   2 hrs.

> [See Course XXI, A 2, page 194.]

*40 *American Social Conditions.*   2 hrs.

> [See Course XXI, B 4, page 194.]

41 *Labor Problems.*   1 hr.

> The conflicts between labor and capital, and the methods employed to obtain industrial peace.

42 *Practical Philanthropy.*   2 hrs.

> The aim of this course is, by means of lectures and individual work in the various charitable organizations of the city, to fit men to take charge of such associations or of the welfare work for factories.

43 *Immigration.*   1 hr.
> A course in economic research, for which the subject to be
> investigated during the year is immigration.

Assistant Professor NORTON :—

*44 *Trade Statistics.*   2 hrs.
> [See Course XXI, C 5, page 196.]

*45 *Interpolation.*   1 hr.
> [See Course XXI, C 6, page 196.]

*46 *Corporation Economics.*   2 hrs.
> [See Course XXI, B 3, page 194.]

*47 *Railroads.*   2 hrs.
> [See Course XXI, C 3, page 196.]

Dr. FAIRCHILD :—

*48 *Financial History of the United States.*   2 hrs.
> [See Course XXI, B 2, page 194.]

*49 *Public Finance.*   2 hrs.
> [See Course XXI, C 13, page 197.]

Dr. ZARTMAN :—

*50 *Insurance.*   2 hrs.
> [See Course XXI, B 11, page 195.]

[*51 *Corporation Accounting.*
> [See Course XXI, B 12, page 195.]
> Omitted in 1907-08.]

Professor S. E. BALDWIN :—

*52 *American Constitutional Law.*   2 hrs.
> [See Course XXI, A 7, page 194.]

Professor HYDE :—

*53 *International Law.*   3 hrs. 2d term.
> [See Course XXI, A 8, page 194.]

Professor RAYNOLDS :—

54 *Comparative Constitutional Law.*   2 hrs.
> A comparative study of the typical forms of state organization
> and of constitutional law and practice as developed in modern
> constitutional states.   Special attention is given to the subject
> of Federal States and other State-complexes.

55 *The French Codes.*   2 hrs.
> A study of the civil and penal codes with references to com-
> mentaries and judicial decisions. Text-books: *Les Codes
> Français*, or *Le Code Civil* and *Le Code Penal*, any recent edition.

56 *The German Imperial Code.* 1 hr.

A study of the civil code of the German Empire, with explanation in regard to the division of legislative power between the Empire and the several States, and some consideration of the supplementary legislation of the latter. Text-book : *Das Bürgerliche Gesetzbuch für das Deutsche Reich.*

57 *Spanish Law.* 1 hr.

The Spanish codes and Spanish legal institutions, with special reference to our colonial dependencies. Text-books : *Códigos Civil Español* or Walton's *Civil Law in Spain and Spanish America.*

Assistant Professor SHERMAN :—

*58 *Roman Law.* (See page 502.) 1 hr.

*59 *Roman Law.* (See page 505.) 1 hr.

60 *Roman Law.* 2 hrs.

Readings from and consideration of Gaius, Theodosian Code, *Corpus Iuris Civilis,* and *Basilica*; study of selected cases and leading titles. Krueger, Mommsen, and Schoell's *Corpus Iuris Civilis* and Sohm's *Institutes.* Open only to those who have a reading knowledge of Latin.

For another course in *Roman Law,* see I, 52.

61 *Canon Law.* 1 hr.

Lectures on the origin and development of Canon law, with special attention to the *Corpus Juris Canonici* and its influence on English and American law.

HISTORY

A few of the courses in Classical and Indo-Iranian Philology and in Semitic Languages and Biblical Literature are mainly or partly historical in character, dealing with *Greek, Roman, Semitic,* and *Church History.* For courses in *Latin Palæography* and in *Bibliography,* see I, 51, and III, 82. For *Physical Geography, Geography of North America, Geography of South America, Geography of Asia,* and *Geographic Controls in History,* see VI, 107, 108, 109, 110, and 121.

Professors G. B. ADAMS and BOURNE :—

65 *Methods of Historical Research and Criticism.* 1 hr.

The first half consists of a discussion of the principles of historical criticism. Several typical problems of internal and external criticism are examined by the class and thoroughly analyzed. The second half, conducted by Professor Adams, consists of practical exercises in the study of selected historical documents.

Professor TORREY :—

*66　*Ancient Oriental Nations from the Earliest Times.*　2 hrs.
　　　[See Course XIX, B 1, page 187.]

Professor PERRIN :—

*67　*Outline Survey of Ancient History.*　　　1 hr. or 2 hrs.
　　　[See Course XIX, B 2*b*, page 187.]

Assistant Professor H. B. WRIGHT :—

[*68　*The Roman Republic.*　　　　　　　　　2 hrs.
　　　[See Course XIX, B 4, page 187.]
　　　Omitted in 1907-08.]

Professor WALKER :—

69　*General Church History (First Course).*　　　2 hrs.
　　　The aim of this course for the year 1907-08 is to present an outline of Church history from the beginnings of Christianity to the end of the great Papal schism.

70　*Christian Literature from Clement of Rome to Eusebius.*
　　　　　　　　　　　　　　　　　　　　　　　1 hr.
　　　The attempt is made to familiarize the student with characteristic examples of the writings of the chief authors of the post-Apostolic period, and especially to gain a conception of Christianity as it was understood by them.

Professors G. B. ADAMS and WALKER :—

71　*Medieval Institutions.*
　　　A two or three years' course. The seminary method is employed throughout and large use is made of the original material. A rapid-reading knowledge of Latin, German, and French is required.

a　Professor G. B. ADAMS.　　　　　　　　　2 hrs.
　　　From later Roman and early German institutions to and including the origin of feudalism.

b 1　Professor WALKER.　　　　　　　　　　　1 hr.
　　　Second year's course covering the French institutions of the feudal period in general and with special reference to their development from Louis VI to Louis IX.

[*b* 2   Professor G. B. ADAMS.   2 hrs.

The second year's course opens with a somewhat detailed study of feudal institutions of the tenth and eleventh centuries, and then follows the institutional development in England from the Norman conquest to the establishment of parliament.
Omitted in 1907–08.]

Assistant Professor F. W. WILLIAMS :—

[*72   *Medieval Asia and the Mohammedan Conquest.*   2 hrs.
[See Course XIX, B 7, page 187.]
Omitted in 1907–08.]

Professor WALKER :—

73   *General Church History (Second Course).*   2 hrs.

This course is in continuation of course 69, but may be taken independently of it. Pursuing the same general method, its attempt is to trace the history of the Church from the Renaissance to the present.

74   *Four Eminent Theologians : Augustine, Aquinas, Calvin, Edwards.*   1 hr. 2d term.

In this course a brief outline of the life of each of these theologians is given ; but the chief endeavor is to acquaint the student with their theological and philosophical significance. Characteristic portions of the writings of each are examined.

Assistant Professor RICHARDSON :—

*75   *The Renaissance and Reformation.*   2 hrs.
[See Course XIX, B 8, page 188.]

*76   *Modern European History to 1789.*   2 hrs.
[See Course XIX, B 9, page 188.]

77   *Seminar in French History.*   1 hr.

An examination of the fundamental constitutional enactments, practices, and theories of the Old Régime.

[78   *Studies in the History of Brandenburg-Prussia.*   1 hr.

Especial attention is given to economic and constitutional developments under the Great Elector.
Omitted in 1907–08.]

Professor A. M. WHEELER :—

79   *History of Treaties, 1763–1815.*   1 hr.
A research course.

*80   *History of Europe since 1789.*   2 hrs.
[See Course XIX, C 3, page 189.]

Professor G. B. ADAMS :—

*81 *English Constitutional History to the Present Time.* 2 hrs.
[See Course XIX, C 5, page 189.]

Assistant Professor RICHARDSON :—

82 *English History from the Accession of the Tudors to the Reign of William and Mary.*
A research course extending through two years.

[a *From 1485 to 1603 (First Year).* 2 hrs.
Particular attention is paid to Henry VII and to constitutional developments under Henry VIII and Elizabeth.
Omitted in 1907-08.]

b *From 1603 to 1688 (Second Year).* 2 hrs.
The reign of James I and the constitutional history of the Puritan Revolution receive especial attention.

Professor A. M. WHEELER :—

83 *Constitutional and Political History of England since 1760.*
2 hrs.
Lectures and required reading.

Professor C. H. SMITH :—

*84 *American History, 1492-1763.* 2 hrs.
[See Course XIX, B 15, page 188.]

*85 *American History, 1763-1860.* 2 hrs.
[See Course XIX, B 16, page 188.]

Professor J. S. BASSETT :—

86 *American Political Development, 1815-1845.* 2 hrs.
A seminary course in the history of internal affairs, from the Treaty of Ghent to the annexation of Texas. Students will submit reports from original sources, and emphasis will be laid on bibliography and the development of the critical faculty.

Professor BOURNE :—

[87 *Diplomatic History of the United States.* 2 hrs.
History of the foreign relations of the United States from the end of the Revolution to the close of the Civil War. Special attention is given to the relations with Spanish America and to the annexations of territory.
Omitted in 1907-08.]

Professor C. H. SMITH :—

88 *American History (Constitutional).*   2 hrs.

 (*a*) A study of the Federal Constitution from the historical point of view, tracing the origin, purpose, and working of its principal provisions. Lectures and collateral reading, with an examination at the close of the course.

 (*b*) An extended course of reading in speeches and writings of statesmen and jurists, and decisions of the Supreme Court, whereby the constitution has been expounded and developed. For individual study, with occasional reports and examinations, and an elaborate paper at the close of the course.

89 *The United States since 1860.*   2 hrs.

 The first half-year is given to a study of the Civil War ; the second half, to a study of Reconstruction and some other important features of our recent history. A research course, with weekly reports and discussions.

90 *American State Constitutions.*   1 hr.

 A historical study of the origin and development of the State constitutions, beginning with the Colonial charters and coming down to the present time.

Dr. BINGHAM :—

*91 *History of Spanish America, chiefly in the Nineteenth Century.*   1 h1

 [See Course XIX, C 7, page 189.]

Dr. ASAKAWA :—

*92 *Modern East-Asiatic History.*   2 hrs.

 [See Course XIX, B 18, page 189.]

Assistant Professor F. W. WILLIAMS :—

[*93 *European Colonies in Asia and Africa.*   2 hrs.

 [See Course XIX, C 11, page 190.]
 Omitted in 1907–08.]

[94 *Diplomatic Intercourse with Asiatic Nations.*   2 hrs.

 A special study of the relations between the states of Eastern Asia, Europe, and America, chiefly during the nineteenth century.

 Omitted in 1907–08.]

[95　*Chinese Culture and Institutions.*　　　　　　2 hrs.
A research and reading course, using as material for study assigned passages in books in the University Library dealing with the history, language, literature, government, arts, and economic and social condition of the Chinese Empire.
Omitted in 1907-08.]

Dr. ASAKAWA :—
*96　*History of Japan.*　　　　　　　　　　2 hrs.
[See Course XIX, B 19, page 189.]

97　*Japanese Institutions.*　　　　　　　　2 hrs.
A history of the civilization of ancient Japan and of the evolution of its social and political institutions.

Professor BOURNE :—
[98　*Historiography in America.*　　　1 hr. 2d half-year.
A critical survey of historical writing and scholarship in America. The principles of historical criticism are applied (1) to narrative histories which are classed as sources and (2) to selected secondary authorities.
Omitted in 1907-08.]

[99　*Modern European and English Historiography.*
1 hr. 2d half-year.
History of modern historical literature and investigation from the middle of the eighteenth century.
Omitted in 1907-08.]

X. PHILOSOPHY

CHARLES M. BAKEWELL, PH.D.　　GEORGE M. DUNCAN, LL.D.
CHARLES H. JUDD, PH.D.　　　　E. W. HOPKINS, PH.D., LL.D.
JOSIAH ROYCE, PH.D., LL.D.　　ROSWELL P. ANGIER, PH.D.
WILLIAM E. HOCKING, PH.D.　　EDWARD H. CAMERON, PH.D.

The PHILOSOPHICAL SEMINARY ROOM, 4 Herrick Hall, is fitted up for the use of graduate students in Philosophy. It contains the departmental library (described below) and may be utilized for purposes of study at all times.

The HEALY PHILOSOPHICAL LIBRARY, founded by a gift of ten thousand dollars from Mrs. Susie Healy Camp, of Hartford, as a memorial of her father, William Arnold Healy, and located in the philosophical seminary room, consists of 1,500 volumes (to which additions are constantly being made), besides the current philosophical and psychological periodicals. It aims to afford all the advantages of a well selected consulting library for the students of philosophy.

The PSYCHOLOGICAL LABORATORY, in Herrick Hall, is thoroughly equipped for both instruction and original research. In addition to the provisions for work in experimental psychology, there are sections for work in experimental pedagogy. Each student pursuing investigations is provided with space and apparatus. The results of accepted investigations are published in the *Yale Psychological Studies.*

The PHILOSOPHICAL CLUB, composed of the instructors in the department and all graduate students who take courses in philosophy, holds regular meetings fortnightly. It is designed to afford opportunity for the presentation and discussion of the results of original research by its members, and for hearing addresses and papers on philosophical subjects from distinguished authorities who are not connected with the department as teachers. Addresses have been delivered before the Club by Professors Lloyd Morgan, John Watson, W. T. Harris, J. G. Schurman, William James, J. McKeen Cattell, Josiah Royce, Borden P. Bowne, John Dewey, G. H. Palmer, Hugo Münsterberg, and others.

For other courses in *Plato* and *Aristotle*, see I, 5, 10, and 11. For a course in *Bibliography*, see III, 82. For a course in *Mental Reactions*, see IX, 4.

Professor BAKEWELL :—

[1 *Platonic Idealism.* 2 hrs.

All the more important dialogues are read in translation, followed by the critical reading, in the original, of the *Republic*, Book v, 471 C, to end of Book vii.
Omitted in 1907–08.]

2 *The Philosophy of Aristotle.* 2 hrs.

A first-hand study of the philosophy of Aristotle. Critical reading of the *Categories*, the *Psychology*, Book iii, and the *Metaphysics*, Book xi. Familiarity with Greek is required.

3 *Problems and Methods of Philosophy.* 2 hrs.

Development of the principles that underlie all rigorous philosophical procedure, followed by consideration of some of the more fundamental issues in contemporary philosophical discussions. Lectures, theses, and informal discussions.

*4 *History of Philosophy.* 3 hrs.

[See Course XVII, A b1, page 182.]

*5 *Modern Idealism.* 2 hrs.

[See Course XVII, B 1, page 183.]

Professor DUNCAN :—

6 *Principles of Logic.* 1 hr.

A course treating of the more important problems, and including an examination of the assumptions and criteria of induction ; with suggestions regarding the teaching of logic.

7 *Epistemology.* 1½ hrs., *to count as 2 hrs.*

A systematic course, both critical and constructive, in the philosophy of knowledge. All the important problems of epistemology are considered.

8 *Metaphysics.* 1½ hrs., *to count as 2 hrs.*

An advanced course, the aim of which is to construct a consistent and tenable theory of reality.

9 *Philosophical Criticism.* 1½ hrs., *to count as 2 hrs.*

Reading and discussion of one or more of the great masterpieces of philosophical literature, with especial attention to the problems of epistemology and metaphysics. In 1907–08, Kant's *Critique of Pure Reason* and his *Prolegomena to any Future Metaphysics.*

*10 *Logic.* 3 hrs. 1st term.

[See Course XVII, A b2, *a*, page 182.]

*11 *Elements of Philosophy.* 3 hrs. 2d term.

[See Course XVII, A b2, *b*, page 182.]

*12 *Philosophical Systems.* 2 hrs.

[See Course XVII, B 2, page 183]

Professor JUDD :—

13 *Experimental Psychology (Laboratory Course).* 2 hrs.

A laboratory course in which the student carries on for himself a series of typical psychological experiments. Once a week the class meets for critical discussion of reports.

[14   *Genetic Psychology.*   3 hrs.
    A course of lectures, readings, and reports, dealing with the
facts of mental development.   .
    Omitted in 1907–08.]

Professor JUDD, Dr. ANGIER, and Dr. CAMERON :—

15   *Psychological Theory and Methods.*   4 hrs.
    Lectures on the development of psychological problems and
methods, reports by members of the class on current discussions,
and laboratory exercises. Admission to this course is conditioned on completion of course 13 or its equivalent.

*16   *Psychology.   General Introduction.*   3 hrs.
    [See Course XVII, A b3, page 183.]

Assistant Professor HOCKING:—

[17   *Ethical Seminary.*   2 hrs.
    A critical study of fundamental ethical concepts. In each
year a section of the history of ethical thought is chosen as a
basis of especial reference for the discussions. For 1908–09 the
subject is the English debate in the nineteenth century ; Bentham,
Mill, Spencer, Green, Bradley, Taylor.
    Omitted in 1907–08.]

[17a   *Philosophy of the State.*   2 hrs.
    A course of lectures on the sources, forms, and ends of
political control, surveying the important types of political
theory and aiming particularly to determine conditions for
stability in democratic governments.
    Omitted in 1907–08.]

Professor HOPKINS :—

18   *Lectures on Comparative Religion.*   1 hr.
    These lectures are in two parts. The first part takes up the
study of religion from the comparative point of view. The
second part consists of lectures on special religions. Open to
all graduate students and members of the Divinity School.

Professor ROYCE :—

19   *Metaphysical Seminary.*   2 hrs.
    Pragmatism and idealism ; the nature of truth ; the idealistic
interpretation of reality ; the relation between logical and metaphysical problems. Lectures, theses, and class discussions.

*20   *Ethics.*   1 hr.
    [See Course XVII, B 3, page 183]

Dr. ANGIER :—

21 *Readings in German Psychology and Philosophy.* 1 hr.

Reading of a number of German works in order to give students an acquaintance with current psychological and philosophical discussions in Germany, and to familiarize them with technical German terminology.

*22 *Æsthetics.* 1 hr.

[See Course XVII, B 9, page 184.]

*23 *Physiological Psychology.* 3 hrs.

[See Course XVII, B 7, page 183.]

Dr. CAMERON :—

24 *Psychological Readings.* 1 hr.

Critical discussion of James's *Principles of Psychology.*

*25 *Educational Psychology.* 2 hrs.

A course of lectures, demonstrations, and reports, dealing with the results of experimental methods as applied to educational subjects.

[26 *Readings in French Psychology and Philosophy.* 1 hr.

A course in French psychology and philosophy similar to course 21 in German psychology and philosophy.

Omitted in 1907-08.]

XI. THE THEORY AND PRACTICE OF EDUCATION

Courses in this department are designed to meet the needs of teachers, and of students who expect to teach.

These courses are omitted for the present year.

The EDUCATIONAL CLUB. At the meetings of this club the results of researches in the educational field are presented and discussed, critical reviews of the more recent literature in education are given, and addresses are occasionally delivered by men distinguished in educational work.

For a course in *Bibliography*, useful to students in all departments, see III, 82.

SCHOOL OF THE FINE ARTS

OFFICERS OF INSTRUCTION

FACULTY

ARTHUR TWINING HADLEY, LL.D., PRESIDENT

JOHN FERGUSON WEIR, M.A., N.A., *Director, and Professor of Painting*

JOHN HENRY NIEMEYER, M.A., A.N.A., *Professor of Drawing*

JOHN PIERREPONT CODRINGTON FOSTER, M.D., *Instructor in Anatomy*

OTHER INSTRUCTORS

GEORGE HENRY LANGZETTEL, B.F.A., *Secretary, and Instructor in Drawing*

GEORGE ALBERT THOMPSON, B.F.A., *Instructor in Painting*

JOHN IRELAND HOWE DOWNES, B.F.A., *Librarian*

TROWBRIDGE LECTURERS

FRANK MILES DAY, Recent President of the American Institute of Architects.

CASS GILBERT, President of the American Institute of Architects.

JOHN MERVEN CARRÈRE, A.I.A.

WALTER COOK, A.I.A.

FREDERICK LAW OLMSTED, JR., Charles Eliot Professor of Landscape Architecture in Harvard University.

CHARLES HOWARD WALKER, A.I.A.

COURSE OF STUDY

The School aims to provide thorough technical instruction in the Arts of Design, viz: Drawing, Painting, Sculpture, Architecture, and in Illustration, Decoration and Copperplate Etching; it also aims to afford a knowledge of such branches of learning as relate to the Philosophy, History, and Criticism of Art. As a professional School of Art the aim is to furnish a thorough course of study in the practice of the studios, and as a Department of the University to provide instruction in the Fine Arts as a constituent part of a scheme of general culture. These departments, of Practice and Criticism, may be regarded as distinct or correlative.

THE TECHNICAL COURSE

The technical instruction, for professional students, is based upon methods well adapted to discipline the faculties and ground the pupil in the elements and fundamental principles which constitute a grammar of Art, as a foundation for all forms of special application. This instruction is arranged as follows:

IN DRAWING, the work is distributed over a three years' course. During the first year the practice of the studio is confined to drawing from the "Antique," from plaster casts; during the second year, to drawing from casts and the living model; and during the third year, to drawing from the living model, nude and draped. The classes under the supervision of the Instructor in this department are the antique, portrait, nude-model, and sketching classes. Students showing the requisite proficiency in any class will be advanced to the work of the second or third year according to individual ability. Instruction in this department precedes all special courses in the various branches of Art; no pupil is allowed to enter any of the advanced classes without this necessary qualification in that degree of proficiency which is deemed essential as a preliminary ground for such studies. Lectures on the principles of decoration, as applied in the various branches of Decorative Art, are included in this department.

IN ANATOMY, instruction is given in the form of lectures, and by drawings made from specimens and casts. The course comprises the study of such portions of the human body as manifestly affect the external forms, the aim being to familiarize the pupil with the characteristics of those parts, independently of their combined action in modifying the external forms. Drawings of these parts are made by the pupils, in connection with the subjects discussed by the lecturer. Advanced studies include the whole structure of the human form in its plastic anatomy and mechanism. The skeleton and muscular system are viewed as a whole, and the modification of the external forms studied in action and repose. The subjects of proportion, equipoise and motion, and expression, are studied, and original drawings required in illustration, made from life, or from Greek sculptures, by reducing the same to their anatomical structure by the imagined removal of the integument.

IN PERSPECTIVE, the instruction is likewise given in the form of lectures, illustrated by examples drawn on the blackboard, explaining the principles under discussion. The lectures are supplemented by practical exercises. The student is required to work out examples in the interim between the lectures. Objects are treated with reference to their true dimensions, as preliminary to their correct representation on a flat surface, as seen in perspective, at various distances, and from different points of view, including the study of shadows and reflections, and the application of the general principles of perspective to interior and exterior views. The pupil is required to work out problems in illustration of all the principles involved in linear perspective in its application to the various branches of art.

IN PAINTING, the work is divided into an elementary and an advanced course of study. The first studies are devoted to the acquisition of a knowledge of the elements of technical practice, by painting from still-life. When the pupil has acquired some knowledge of the means in representing objects in color, as to their values and relations, the remainder of the course is given to studies of the living model, in portrait, figure, and composition. This is continued while the pupil remains in the School. The course in painting implies, on the part of the pupil, a requisite knowledge of drawing, and drawing from the living model is continued throughout the course in connection with the work in color. The practice of the studio is supplemented by illustrated lectures on Color, Chiaroscuro, Composition, and such other special topics relating to the principles and means of Art as are comprehended in its theory and practice.

IN MODELING, a course is provided, including the anatomical lectures and drawing. The work in this branch of instruction consists in first modeling in clay, from casts of Greek fragments, the head and other extremities of the human form, and then the whole figure. When the student has sufficient command of the method and means, the rest of the course is devoted to modeling from the living subject.

IN ARCHITECTURE. Until the organization of a Department of Architecture shall have been completed, provisional instruction only is now given in this art, intended chiefly as an elective for undergraduates and for those who wish some preparation for entering an architect's office. The course consists in the study of representative examples of styles and orders in their architectural and historic developments, with technical practice relating to the means and methods adapted for the conventional rendering of architectural design with pencil and brush. These technical studies are supplemented by readings in the history of architecture, on which an examination is held for those taking the course as an elective. What is now provided may be considered as a course preparatory to a course in architecture.

The course includes a general and comprehensive view of the historic development of the various architectures, with a comparative analysis of the same with respect to their principles of construction and decoration.

Courses are provided in ILLUSTRATION and in DECORATIVE DESIGN, with technical instruction in the use of various mediums for magazine, book, and newspaper illustration, and modeling in clay or wax.

IN COPPERPLATE ETCHING, a course is provided, and a room set apart for this special study, containing all the necessary appliances of this art, including a press.

COURSE IN THE HISTORY AND CRITICISM OF ART

The instruction in this Department includes courses of lectures by the various Instructors of the School, and other invited Lecturers, arranged to include professional students in the regular course, and classes from other Departments of the University where it is recognized as an "elective" study.

A course of technical lectures in the Principles and Means of Art is provided, fully illustrated, embracing the subjects of Line, Chiaroscuro, Color, Composition, and Expression, discussing the technical methods of the Painter, the Sculptor, the Architect, and the Engraver, including an historic account of the technical development of these arts.

The regular prescribed course of study, for professional students, covers a period of three years, but pupils are encouraged to remain in the School and pursue advanced studies after the expiration of the prescribed term. The fees are thirty dollars per term of three months, with an annual fee of ten dollars for the use of the University Library and the appliances of the class-rooms. No pupil is received for less than one term. The tuition fee for a fourth year's attendance is one-half the usual rate; pupils remaining for a longer period are classed as "honorary students"; as such they are exempt from the payment of a tuition fee, but are charged an annual fee of fifteen dollars. The School is open to both sexes; no pupil is received under fifteen years of age. All applications for admission should be made through the Director. The

School opens on the last Thursday in September, and the closing exercises are held on the first of June. At the end of the School year an exhibition of the work of the various classes of pupils is held, continuing open through the summer months.

ELECTIVE COURSES are provided for the Junior and Senior classes in the Academical Department, as set forth on page 198. Also, a course in Architectural Drawing, and a special course in Free-hand Drawing arranged to meet the requirements of students in the Sheffield Scientific School.

Members of all Departments of the University may enter the Art School, and enjoy its privileges, as " Special Students," on the payment, in advance, of an annual fee of twenty-five dollars.

CERTIFICATES are awarded to pupils remaining in the School through the regular course of three years ; and the Degree of BACHELOR OF FINE ARTS is conferred by the University upon those students who have fulfilled the requirements of a prescribed course of advanced studies in the several departments of instruction, and have submitted an approved original composition in painting, sculpture, or architecture, and a satisfactory thesis on some topic relating to the Fine Arts. Students from other Art Schools, who have passed through the requisite elementary course in Art, may enter this advanced course, ending in the conferring of the above degree, on passing the requisite examinations.

The WILLIAM WIRT WINCHESTER FELLOWSHIP, for study abroad, supported by the income derived from a fund of twenty thousand dollars, will be competed for every two years, provided a preliminary examination of the work of candidates shall warrant the holding of a competition at the regular time. Competing students must have been pupils of the Yale School of Fine Arts, or of some other Art School of equal standing, for at least two years before entering this competition, which will extend through one year's work in the several departments of instruction. From candidates for this competition, not more than four will be chosen for a final competition, for which a specified subject in composition will be required, in addition to the class-work for the year. The award will be made at the Anniversary of the School, the jury being composed of three well-known artists chosen by the Faculty. The successful competitor may hold this Fellowship for a two years' residence abroad, subject to certain specified requirements. The right is reserved to withhold the award should the work of the competing students fall below the required standard of merit.

The ALICE KIMBALL ENGLISH PRIZES, the income from a foundation of three thousand dollars, are awarded annually to students taking the regular courses of study in the School, under such conditions as the Faculty may prescribe.

The ETHEL CHILDE WALKER PRIZE, the income from a foundation of two hundred dollars, is also awarded annually, under certain restrictions.

The JOHN FERGUSON WEIR SCHOLARSHIP, founded by Mr. and Mrs. Carl Stoeckel, will hereafter be awarded to pupils who have been in the School not less than two years.

The ALICE KIMBALL ENGLISH SCHOLARSHIP will be awarded to pupils who have been in attendance not less than one year.

TROWBRIDGE LECTURES

The TROWBRIDGE LECTURE COURSE provides lectures on Art by various invited speakers outside of the Faculty. This course is open to all members of the University.

EVENING CLASSES

EVENING CLASSES in ILLUSTRATION, MODELING, and DECORATIVE DESIGN, are held from half-past seven to half-past nine o'clock during four evenings of the week.

The evening classes afford opportunity for those who cannot attend the School during the day, to pursue special studies in Illustration, Decorative Design, and Modeling; with technical instruction in the various mediums for magazine, book, and newspaper illustration, such as pen-and-ink, pencil or crayon, and brush-work in India-ink or monochrome, also modeling in clay or wax. Instruction is also given in Perspective and Composition, and living models are provided when required.

The fees are six dollars per month, or twenty dollars for a term of four months, payment in advance.

Students in regular attendance in the day classes may attend the evening classes at one-half the above rates.

COLLECTIONS

The ART LIBRARY, containing a collection of technical handbooks, current art periodicals, and portfolios of etchings and engravings and other works of art, is open, during specified hours, for the use of students. The pupils of the school are entitled to the use of the University Library, and to such other privileges, under the usual restrictions, as are granted to students in the other Departments.

The COLLECTIONS embrace the JARVES GALLERY OF ITALIAN ART, numbering one hundred and twenty-two paintings dating from the eleventh to the seventeenth centuries; the TRUMBULL GALLERY of historical portraits and other works, numbering fifty-four pictures; the ALDEN COLLECTION of Belgian wood-carvings, of the sixteenth century, comprising about one hundred and twenty feet of wainscoting and three confessionals, from a chapel in Ghent; a collection of contemporaneous art, numbering about fifty paintings; a small collection of original sketches by old masters; a collection of about one hundred and fifty casts and marbles, representative of the various periods of Greek and Renaissance Art; a valuable collection of Chinese porcelains and bronzes, loaned by Professor Frederick Wells Williams; and a collection of Braun autotypes, and other reproductions, numbering about two hundred.

The Collections of the School are open daily, without charge, from 1.00 to 5.00 P. M., during term time; also during the summer vacation from 9.00 A. M. to 5.00 P. M., when a fee of twenty-five cents is charged. This fee is also charged when special loan exhibitions are organized, in order to meet incidental expenses.

DEPARTMENT OF MUSIC
FACULTY

ARTHUR TWINING HADLEY, LL.D., PRESIDENT

HORATIO WILLIAM PARKER, M.A., MUS.D., *Dean, and Battell Professor of the Theory of Music*

SAMUEL SIMONS SANFORD, M.A., *Professor of Applied Music*

HARRY BENJAMIN JEPSON, M.A., MUS.B., *Professor of Applied Music and University Organist*

ISIDOR TROOSTWYK, *Assistant Professor of Applied Music, and Instructor in Violin-Playing*

HENRY STANLEY KNIGHT, *Assistant Professor of Applied Music, and Instructor in Piano-Forte Playing*

DAVID STANLEY SMITH, B.A., MUS.B., *Instructor in the Theory of Music, and Secretary*

WILLIAM EDWIN HAESCHE, MUS.B., *Instructor in Instrumentation*

CHARLES RABOLD, *Instructor in Singing*

LEO SCHULZ, *Instructor in Violoncello-Playing*

LEWIS WILLIAMS, *Instructor in Piano-Playing*

SETH DANIEL BINGHAM, JR., B.A., *Assistant in Organ-Playing*

CAROLYN QUINTIN, *Private Secretary to the Dean of the Department of Music*

AIMS AND REQUIREMENTS

The Department of Music aims to provide adequate instruction for those who intend to become musicians by profession, either as teachers or as composers, and to afford a course of study for such as intend to devote themselves to musical criticism and the literature of music.

In all the courses, except that in singing, a knowledge of piano-playing is required, though in a less degree if the student plays well some other musical instrument.

The work in the Department is divided into theoretical and practical courses of study. The Department is open to undergraduates and graduates, also to special students

Admission is granted without distinction of sex. No student under 16 years of age will be admitted. The theoretical studies consist of the courses mentioned below from 1 to 7 inclusive. The practical courses consist of instruction in Piano-, Organ-, Violin- and Violoncello-playing, in Singing and in the playing of Chamber music (Ensemble-playing). No student will be admitted to any practical course except that in Singing and Violoncello-playing, unless he shall already have been admitted to one or more of the theoretical courses.

All applicants for admission to the Department other than Academical undergraduates, or members of the Graduate School, will be required to pass an examination in "The Rudiments of Music," by W. H. Cummings, published by Novello, Ewer & Co., of New York. Candidates will not be examined on Chapters I, III, VIII or IX.

The examination will be held on the Wednesday before College opens.

THEORY OF MUSIC

The theoretical courses are subdivided into elementary and advanced. Courses 1, 2, and 3 are considered elementary. At the close of the academic year, students who have completed course 2 may become candidates for a CERTIFICATE OF PROFICIENCY IN THE THEORY OF MUSIC, which will be issued on the completion of course 4, after passing an examination in four-part harmony and counterpoint, in the history of music, and in the structure of song and sonata forms. An unprepared analysis of classical works will be required in addition. Academic students on the completion of the same course, and passing the same examination with distinction, will receive one-year honors in Music.

The advanced courses are numbered 4, 5, 6, and 7. They are open only to students who are able to pass the examination required preliminary to becoming a candidate for the Certificate of Proficiency in Theory mentioned above. Members of these classes at the end of two years' work, or

its equivalent, may become candidates for the degree of
BACHELOR OF MUSIC. Candidates for this degree must give
their names to the Professor of the Theory of Music at the
beginning of the college year. The candidate will be
required to pass an examination before a Board of Examiners, consisting of the Faculty of the Department of
Music. Satisfactory evidence of proficiency in the theory
of music and in any two of the following languages (one
of which must be a modern language), Greek, Latin,
French, German, Italian, shall be given to the Professor
of the Theory of Music prior to the examination. The
equivalent of two years' work is required in modern languages. In the case of Greek and Latin the requirements
for entrance into Yale College must be met. (See pages
77–79.) An original composition in one of the forms to be
designated by him must also be submitted. The examination will be in advanced Counterpoint, Canon, Fugue,
the higher forms of Musical Composition, and impromptu
Orchestration. Academic undergraduates, on passing this
examination with distinction, will receive two-year honors
in Music. The degree of Bachelor of Music will not be
conferred excepting for at least two years' work done
after the student is entitled to the Certificate of Proficiency in Theory.

The fees for instruction are from fifty to two hundred
dollars per year. The fee for the theoretical courses only
is fifty dollars per year. These fees may be remitted in
whole or in part when the student needs the relief and
shows natural talent in such degree as to warrant it, in
the opinion of the Faculty. The fee for a Certificate of
Proficiency in the Theory of Music is five dollars. The
fee for a degree is ten dollars.

Mr. SMITH :—

1 *Harmony.*   2 hrs.

The study of chords, their construction, relations, and progressions. This course covers the following subjects: Intervals, triads, seventh chords, modulations, chromatically altered chords, suspension, organ point, passing and changing notes. Figured bass is used only as a means of designating chords. Attention is turned at once to the harmonizing of melodies. The original principles from which rules are derived are discussed and students are encouraged to exercise and cultivate their own judgment in the application of these principles. Particular attention is given to the natural melodic and harmonic tendencies of tones and intervals. The subject of modulation is treated with special care and at length. Exercises are corrected in the class-room with explanations and illustrations. G. W. Chadwick's *Harmony* is used as text-book.

2 *Counterpoint.*   2 hrs.

A thorough knowledge of Harmony is required of students in this course. The work is the harmonizing and supplying melodious additional voices to choral and other melodies used as *Canti Firmi*. Examples of the different orders of Counterpoint in two, three, and four voices are required ; also double counterpoint, and more or less free imitative writing. Students in this course are encouraged to try the simpler forms of free composition. Spalding's Tonal *Counterpoint* is used as a text-book.

Professor PARKER :—

3 *The History of Music.*   1 hr.

Lectures are given on the development of music from its earliest stages ; history of Church Music from the time of Gregory; history of Opera and Oratorio ; biographical sketches of famous composers, with description and analysis of their principal works ; history of purely instrumental music, showing the growth and development of musical forms up to their culmination in Beethoven. Practical illustrations of the lectures on musical forms are given in the class-room. *The Evolution of the Art of Music*, by Sir C. Hubert H. Parry, is used as a text-book.

4 *Strict Composition.*   2 hrs.

The more severe kinds of composition form the basis of work in this course : Harmony in Five and more parts ; Threefold and Fourfold Counterpoint ; Four- and Three-part Fugues for voices or for instruments; Canons of various kinds, with or without accompaniment of free voices; Free treatment of different kinds of thematic material. This course is preparatory to course 6. No text-book is used.

Mr. HAESCHE :—

5 *Instrumentation.*   *   2 hrs.

This course is open only to students who have done the work of courses 1 and 2, and it is strongly recommended that course 4 also should precede it. Lectures are given on the nature, compass, tone-color, and other characteristics of all the instruments of the modern orchestra, with illustrations of their use by great composers. Exercises in the practical orchestration of short pieces from the works of classic and modern composers, in analyzing, reading, and playing from orchestral scores, beginning with Haydn and Mozart Symphonies, and embracing modern works of various kinds. Prout's *Instrumentation* and Berlioz's *Orchestration* are used as text-books. (See also under the New Haven Symphony Orchestra, on p. 401.)

Professor PARKER :—

6 *Free Composition.*   2 hrs.

This course is open only to students who have done the work of courses 1, 2, 4, and 5, and have shown unmistakable talent for original composition. Several of the smaller forms of free instrumental and vocal music are composed by the students, and studies are made for larger compositions, which are finished in case the thematic material offered is of sufficient merit. At the close of the year the student is required to produce an extended work, probably in sonata form. No text-book is used.   .

7 *Advanced Orchestration and Conducting.*   1 hr.

Students in this course must have done the work of course 5 and be able to write fluently and correctly for all orchestral instruments. Ancient and modern orchestral scores, of which a large number are available, are studied in detail. Orchestration by the students of original or other compositions is examined and criticized. Explanations are given of the principles by which conductors should be guided in the selection and performance of orchestral or choral works. In case the talent of the student warrants it, opportunity is furnished for practice in actual conducting. No text-book is used, but students are required to buy a number of orchestral scores for study.

PRACTICAL MUSIC

The courses in practical music consist of instruction in playing the Pianoforte, the Organ, the Violin, and the Violoncello, in Singing and in playing Chamber music.

No student is admitted to a course in practical music, except in singing and violoncello-playing, who has not been admitted to one of the theoretical courses.

Assistant Professor KNIGHT and Mr. WILLIAMS :—

Piano.   One exercise weekly.

Candidates for admission to courses in piano-playing other than graduate or undergraduate students in the University are required to pass an examination which will include, (1) knowledge of and ability to play all major and minor scales ; (2) at least two of Bach's two-part inventions ; (3) a sonata by Haydn or Mozart, and (4) a modern pianoforte piece which may be selected by the applicant. Some proficiency in sight-reading is required.

Professor JEPSON and Mr. BINGHAM :—

Organ.   One exercise weekly.

No student is admitted to the courses in playing the organ until he has acquired a satisfactory knowledge of pianoforte technique. The work includes careful study of organ technique, and of works by representative classic and modern composers in Sonata form and in Polyphonic and Free styles, graded according to the needs of the individual student. Especial attention is given to the pitch, quality, and possible combinations of the various registers, and to transposition and playing from vocal-score. The mechanism of the instrument is explained and studied in detail.

Assistant Professor TROOSTWYK :—

Violin.   One exercise weekly.

Students in violin-playing are received in all stages of proficiency. Beginners are limited to members of undergraduate classes in the University. Others are required to be able to play : (1) the major and minor scales ; (2) a study by Kreutzer ; (3) concerto No. 23 by Viotti or some composition of equal difficulty.

Mr. Schulz :—
Violoncello.   One exercise weekly.
> Students in violoncello-playing will be received in all stages of proficiency, but beginners must be members of undergraduate classes in the University.

Mr. Rabold :—
Singing.   One exercise weekly.
> Students of singing are required to show that they possess a good or promising voice and an accurate ear. Apart from this they are received in all degrees of proficiency. Especial attention is given to a proper method of breathing, and it is desired to develop the natural voice of the individual rather than to make it conform to any conventional pattern. The work consists at first of sustained tones, scales, and arpeggios. Classic and modern songs and arias will be used as they are needed.

Assistant Professor Troostwyk :—
Chamber Music.   2 hrs.
> Instruction is given in concerted playing of chamber music, using representative trios, string quartets, and sonatas by classic and modern composers as the material for study. Admission to this course is granted only to those students of violin, violoncello, and piano who have attained proficiency in the use of their respective instruments.

Diplomas are awarded to those students of practical music who, having successfully completed a three-years' course of instrumental study, are qualified to act as teachers or to appear as soloists.

Three rooms in Woolsey Hall have been furnished with pianos, and may be used as practice-rooms by students in the Department of Music   The fee for one hour's daily use of such a room during term-time is fifteen dollars for the college year, or twenty-five dollars for two hours daily.

Two organs in College Street Hall are available for practice by students of organ-playing. The fee for one hour's daily use of an organ during term-time is eighteen dollars for the college year.

The fees for instruction in instrumental music are as follows :

For Piano (for University students, graduate or undergraduate),	.	$ 50.00 for the college year.
For Piano (for other persons),	.	100.00 " " "
For Organ (for University students, graduate or undergraduate),	.	50.00 " " "
For Organ (for other persons),	.	75.00 " " "
For Violin (for University students, graduate or undergraduate),	.	100.00 " " "
For Violin (for other persons),	.	150.00 " " "
For Violoncello, . .	.	100.00 " " "
For Singing (for University students, graduate or undergraduate),	.	75.00 " " "
For Singing (for other persons),	.	100.00 " " "
For Ensemble-playing (for persons not otherwise connected with the Department of Music), .	.	25.00 " " "

These fees are exclusive of the fee for instruction in the theoretical courses, which is fifty dollars for the college year.

Fees in the Department of Music are payable as follows: One-half the amount of all charges for the college year on or before October 15 ; one-half of the balance on or before January 15, and the remainder on or before April 15.

SCHOLARSHIPS AND PRIZES

The LOCKWOOD SCHOLARSHIPS, founded by the bequest of five thousand dollars from Miss Julia A. Lockwood, of Norwalk, Connecticut, in 1897, are offered annually to two students in the Department who shall pass the best examinations in the theory and practice of instrumental music (organ or pianoforte), and in the theory and practice of vocal music, respectively. The Lockwood scholarship in 1907 will be awarded to students of piano-playing and singing.

Through the liberality of Mr. Morris Steinert, of New Haven, an annual prize of one hundred dollars is offered for the best original composition in one of the larger musical forms by a student in the theoretical courses.

A prize of fifty dollars will be given to the student of organ-playing whose work is most satisfactory. The decision will be given at a competitive examination which will be held near the close of the college year.

Two prizes of twenty dollars and ten dollars, respectively, will be awarded to the two students of piano-playing who pass the best entrance examinations in the autumn.

ALLIED MUSICAL SOCIETIES.

The NEW HAVEN SYMPHONY ORCHESTRA, under the direction of the Professor of the Theory of Music, gives a series of concerts during the winter, to which students in any Department of the University are admitted for a small fee. This organization is a complete and well-equipped orchestra of about sixty players, and is a valuable adjunct to the Department of Music.

Students of orchestration are afforded an opportunity to hear their work actually performed, and any composition which is original and of sufficient merit may be performed publicly.

The same orchestra affords an opportunity to acquire orchestral routine to those students of the violin who are able to pass the examination for admission to the orchestra.

The most advanced students of piano-playing as well as violin-playing are allowed to rehearse with the orchestra, and to perform publicly, if fitted to do so in the judgment of the Faculty of the Department.

Informal recitals by students will be given in College Street Hall from time to time after January 1, and at the end of the college year a concert by students in the Department with the orchestra will be given in Woolsey Hall. At this concert the award of the Lockwood scholarships will be announced and those students whose work during the year has been most satisfactory will appear publicly as composers, conductors, or performers.

The NEW HAVEN ORATORIO SOCIETY, incorporated in October, 1903, "To promote the cultivation of Choral Singing in coöperation with the Department of Music in Yale University," is a large chorus of mixed voices which gives concerts from time to time with the New Haven Symphony Orchestra. Students are admitted to these concerts for a small fee, and are encouraged to take the voice trials prescribed for admission to the chorus that they may sing with the Society if fitted to do so.

DEPARTMENTAL LIBRARY

A LIBRARY has been formed for the use of students in the Department, consisting chiefly of orchestral scores, trios, quartets, sextets, etc., and a large number of four-hand piano arrangements of works for orchestra and chamber music. Up to the present time about 500 works have been acquired and additions are constantly being made. By the use of the library students can familiarize themselves with compositions which are about to be performed at the Orchestra, Chamber-music, and Oratorio concerts, preparatory to attending the concerts. They can in this manner study classic and modern works which are otherwise not readily accessible.

STEINERT COLLECTION

Of special interest to all students of music is the M. Steinert collection of musical instruments and manuscripts. It contains a large number of ancient keyed and stringed instruments in a state of excellent preservation, and shows the development of these instruments during a period extending over several centuries. This collection, which also contains a number of ecclesiastical manuscripts, is of much historical importance. It was given to the University by Mr. Morris Steinert, of New Haven, and is kept in Memorial Hall.

DEPARTMENT OF FORESTRY
(YALE FOREST SCHOOL)
OFFICERS
GOVERNING BOARD

ARTHUR TWINING HADLEY, LL.D., PRESIDENT

HENRY SOLON GRAVES, M.A., *Director, and Pinchot Professor of Forestry*

WILLIAM HENRY BREWER, LL.D., *Professor of Agriculture, Emeritus*

GIFFORD PINCHOT, SC.D., *Professor of Forestry*

JAMES WILLIAM TOUMEY, M.S., *Professor of Forestry*

ADDITIONAL INSTRUCTORS AND ASSISTANTS

HERMAN HAUPT CHAPMAN, M.F., *Assistant Professor of Forestry*

RALPH CLEMENT BRYANT, F.E., *Instructor in Forestry*

RALPH CHIPMAN HAWLEY, M.F., *Instructor in Forestry*

ALEXANDER WILLIAM EVANS, M.D., PH.D., *Eaton Professor of Botany*

ARTHUR HARMOUNT GRAVES, PH.D., *Instructor in Botany*

GEORGE ELWOOD NICHOLS, B.A., *Assistant in Botany*

SAMUEL EBEN BARNEY, C.E., *Assistant Professor of Civil Engineering*

JOHN CLAYTON TRACY, C.E., *Assistant Professor of Structural Engineering*

CHARLES SHERMAN FARNHAM, C.E., *Instructor in Civil Engineering*

HERBERT BRINKERHOFF NORTH, PH.B., *Instructor in Drawing and Descriptive Geometry* .

HERBERT ERNEST GREGORY, PH.D., *Professor of Geology*

JOSEPH BARRELL, PH.D., *Assistant Professor of Geology*

ISAIAH BOWMAN, B.S., *Instructor in Geography*

WESLEY ROSWELL COE, PH.D., *Assistant Professor of Comparative Anatomy*

HARRY DONALD TIEMANN, M.E., M.F., *Lecturer on Forest Technology*

EDWARD AUGUSTUS BOWERS, LL.B., *Lecturer on Forest Law*

HERMANN VON SCHRENK, PH.D., *Lecturer on Wood Preservation*

FREDERICK HAYNES NEWELL, B.S., *Lecturer on Forest Hydrography*

This list does not include the names of special lecturers on Lumbering, Law, Grazing, Forest Fires, and other subjects, for which arrangements have not yet been completed.

OVERTON WESTFELDT PRICE, B.A., *Lecturer on Government Forestry*
GEORGE HEWITT MYERS, M.F., *Lecturer on Forestry Abroad*
MRS. GEORGENE LOUISE MILLER, *Librarian and Clerk*

GRADUATE ADVISORY BOARD
JAMES GIRVIN PETERS, M.F., Chairman, Washington, D. C.
WILLIAM BUCKHOUT GREELEY, M.F., San Francisco, Cal.
GEORGE HEWITT MYERS, M.F., Washington, D. C.
EDWARD SEYMOUR WOODRUFF, M.F., Wawbeek, N. Y.
THEODORE SALISBURY WOOLSEY, JR., M.F., Washington, D. C.

EQUIPMENT OF THE SCHOOL
GENERAL ENDOWMENT

The Yale Forest School was founded in 1900 by the gift of one hundred and fifty thousand dollars from Mr. and Mrs. James W. Pinchot and their sons, Gifford Pinchot and Amos R. E. Pinchot. The gift provided for the establishment of a Department in the University to be known as the Yale Forest School, for instruction and research in Forestry. The gift also provides for a Summer School of Forestry in Milford, Pike County, Pennsylvania, at Grey Towers, the estate of Mr. James W. Pinchot.

The endowment of the School was increased in 1903 by an additional gift of fifty thousand dollars from Mr. and Mrs. James W. Pinchot, and Professor Gifford Pinchot.

In 1905 the National Lumber Manufacturers' Association voted to raise a fund among the lumbermen of the country to establish a Chair of Applied Forestry and Lumbering at the Forest School. The first installment, fifty thousand dollars, was presented to the School by the Association in the fall of 1907.

EQUIPMENT IN NEW HAVEN

Marsh Hall, the residence of the late Professor Othniel C. Marsh, 360 Prospect St., is used as the School building. It is equipped with lecture rooms, a library and reading room, and botanical and wood-testing laboratories.

The library contains about seven thousand books and pamphlets. It includes the important works on Forestry in English, French, and German.

In the reading room about forty periodicals, including the important lumber journals and the technical forest journals published in this country and abroad, are placed at the disposal of the students.

The botanical laboratory is equipped with simple and compound microscopes, and other apparatus and material useful in botanical instruction and research. The laboratory is provided with modern facilities for photographic and photo-micrographic work.

An herbarium, containing six thousand mounted sheets of native and exotic trees and shrubs and the more important forest herbs, is arranged for the use of students engaged in research. A large collection of forest tree fruits and seeds is available for students of Forest Botany.

The technological laboratory is equipped for research and instruction in the physical, structural, and mechanical properties of wood. The equipment includes Riehle and Olsen testing machines; planers, lathes, and saws for shaping material for testing; xylometers, drying ovens, chipping machines, and a dry kiln; as well as a large amount of smaller machinery and tools useful in timber testing. The present arrangement of coöperative work with the Federal Forest Service gives students of Forest Technology exceptional facilities for research in the strength and other mechanical properties of timber.

A large collection of domestic and exotic woods is available for students' use. This collection contains boards and planks of most of the important economic species. In addition, nearly all the American species are represented by small hand specimens. Among exotic species, the Central American, West Indian, and Philippine woods are particularly well represented.

Transits, levels, plane tables, compasses, barometers, calipers, height measures, chains, tapes, and other instruments, are provided for the courses in Surveying, Forest Mensuration, Silviculture, and Forest Management.

The following institutions connected with the University are open to Forest students: The University Library, the Yale Dining Hall, the University Gymnasium, the Yale Infirmary, and the Bureau of Self-Help.

The field work in the fall and winter terms, and that of the Junior class in the spring, is conducted in the forests near New Haven. The New Haven Water Company has granted to the Forest School for practical field work the use of its extensive holdings. The School has the entire management of a portion of this area, Maltby Park, where experiments in planting, thinning, reproduction cuttings, and other work are conducted.

EQUIPMENT IN MILFORD, PENNSYLVANIA

In addition to the plant in New Haven, the School is provided with a complete equipment in the field for instruction and research. This is located at Milford, Pike Co., Penn., where the work of the Summer School is conducted. Milford lies on the west bank of the Delaware river, eight miles below Port Jervis, New York, whence it is reached by stage running regularly twice a day. Port Jervis is on the direct line of the Erie railroad.

A number of buildings have been erected by Mr. James W. Pinchot on his country estate and placed at the disposal of the School. Mr. Pinchot has also provided a tract of about 200 acres for experimental work.

THE STONE COTTAGE.—This building contains a lecture hall, a botanical laboratory, and a small library and reading room.

FOREST HALL.—This is a large stone and concrete building erected by Mr. James W. Pinchot and Mr. Gifford Pinchot for the use of the Forest School. It is located in the village of Milford, Penn., and is especially designed for lectures which are open to the public. The building contains a spacious hall, 60 by 30 feet, capable of accommodating about 200 persons.

JUNIOR HALL.—This is a frame building containing a single large lecture room for the work of the Junior class in the courses in Forest Mensuration and Surveying.

THE CLUB HOUSE.—This building is designed as a gathering place for evening study and recreation.

THE SCHOOL CAMP.—A fully equipped camp is provided for those who desire to live in tents. It is situated on high dry ground, about 800 feet above sea level, a location which is exceedingly healthful. The tents are erected on board floors and each is furnished with a cot, table, chairs, washstand, and crockery. Students are required to provide bed linen and towels. The students take their meals together in a large mess hall.

TRACTS FOR FIELD WORK.—Field work is conducted partly on the tract of 200 acres provided by Mr. James W. Pinchot, and partly in the forests in the immediate neighborhood, which offer excellent opportunities for practical work. One of the Pennsylvania State Forest Reservations is but a short distance from Milford.

EXPERIMENT STATION.—A gift of Mr. James W. Pinchot enables the School to conduct at Milford a Forest Experiment Station. The purpose of this station is to conduct research in the life history of trees and forests and to afford facilities for students who wish to carry on original studies. The work done so far comprises the establishment of experimental plantations and the laying out of permanent sample plots for repeated observation of the effect of different methods of treatment on the native forests.

THE WORK OF THE SCHOOL

TERMS OF ADMISSION

The Forest School is a graduate department requiring for admission a college training. Graduates of universities, colleges, or scientific institutions of high standing are admitted upon presentation of their diplomas, provided they have had courses in Botany and Geology,

Inorganic Chemistry, Mathematics through Trigonometry, Economics, and Modern Languages. Undergraduates who expect to enter the Forest School after graduation are advised to take also courses in advanced Botany, advanced Geology including Mineralogy, Zoology, Meteorology, Physical Geography, and higher Mathematics including elementary Calculus.

Candidates for advanced standing may take examinations in any subject, but in case of Forest Management, Forest Mensuration, Silviculture, Lumbering, Forest Botany, Forest Technology, and other technical subjects, they are required, in addition, to present evidence of a specified amount of work done in the field or laboratory. Information regarding the special requirements in each of the above mentioned courses may be obtained from the Director.

COURSE PREPARATORY TO THE STUDY OF FORESTRY

A course preparatory to the study of Forestry is given at the Sheffield Scientific School of Yale. This course is designed to give a complete preparation for advanced technical work at the Forest School. It comprises not only the requisite training in Mathematics, Natural Sciences, Economics, Languages, etc., but the Senior class participates in the technical work of the Forest School. It is possible for members of this course who do extra work in the Senior year to finish at the Forest School in one year after graduation. It is necessary for those intending to complete the work at the Forest School in one year to take the summer term at Milford, Penn., at the end of the Junior year, and to take the course in Silviculture at the Forest School as an optional in their Senior year.

REGISTRATION

There are four terms in the Junior year and three terms in the Senior year. Juniors are required to register in Milford, Penn., in July at the opening of the summer term.   Seniors register in New Haven in October, when the fall term for the Junior class also opens.   In 1908 the summer term begins July 7 and continues ten weeks. The fall term in 1908 begins October 1.

FEES AND EXPENSES

The annual charge for tuition for the Junior class is one hundred and fifty dollars, including the summer term, and for the Senior class one hundred and twenty-five dollars.   Juniors are required to pay the first installment of the tuition, namely thirty-seven dollars and a half, when they register in July.   Bills are sent from the Treasurer's office for the other installments of the Junior tuition and for all payments of the Senior tuition.

Frequent excursions are taken to points of interest near New Haven, involving an annual expense of less than sixty dollars.   The last half of the Senior year is spent in the lumber woods.   This necessitates traveling expenses which vary from year to year, according to the locality in which the work is conducted.   Ordinarily these do not exceed sixty dollars.   The students live in camp, so that living expenses are reduced to a minimum.   Required text-books cost about twenty dollars each year.   Other incidentals, including surveying material, drawing instruments, field maps, etc., amount to about fifteen dollars a year.   Satisfactory board and lodgings can be obtained in New Haven at prices ranging from seven dollars per week upwards.

A charge of twenty-five dollars is made for the use and care of a tent during the regular summer term at Milford. If two persons occupy one tent, the charge is seventeen dollars and a half for each person.   Students who wish to secure the reservation of a tent must apply to the Director before June 1 and make a deposit of five dollars. Board in camp is charged at cost and varies from four dollars and a half to five dollars per week.   Students are required to make deposits on board in advance.   The first installment of twenty dollars is payable at registration.

The fee for graduation is five dollars.

DEGREE

Graduates of the Forest School, who have previously received a Bachelor's degree from a collegiate institution of high standing, or have had a training which, in the judgment of the Corporation, is equivalent to that obtained in such institutions, are granted the degree of Master of Forestry.

THESES

Students are encouraged to carry on original work and to write theses under the supervision of the professors and instructors. Special credit is given for such work, but a thesis is not required for the degree.

CURRICULUM

The regular course covers a period of two years. The work is of an advanced and technical character and is designed for college graduates who already have had a thorough collegiate training in Mathematics and Natural Science. The regular two years' course gives a training for all professional work of Forestry, including a preparation not merely for practical work in the woods, but also for the broad work of forest organization in Government and State service, for handling large tracts of forest land, for consultation work for railroads, lumbermen, water companies, and other owners, for the work of public lecturing and writing, for teaching and for scientific research. Special facilities for study are offered to men preparing for Government service in the Philippine Islands, Hawaiian Islands, or Porto Rico; and for students from foreign countries who wish to prepare themselves for the work of organization in regions where Forestry has not yet been thoroughly established.

Excursions and field work form an important part of the instruction in Forestry. In the Junior year, the whole summer term, five half-days a week in the fall term, and three days a week in the spring term, are devoted to practical work in the field. The Senior class devotes between four and five months of the college year to field work.

The last half of the Senior year is spent in the lumber woods, where the students are trained in the management of logging operations and milling, and are given their final training and practice in topographic surveying, preparation of forest maps, working plans on a large scale, estimating of timber, valuation of land, laying out roads and trails, running lines, projecting plans for lumber operations, etc. In 1906 the work was carried on at Waterville, N. H., on the lands of the International Paper Company. The spring term of 1907 was spent in southern Missouri on the lands owned by the Missouri Lumber & Mining Company. Through the generosity of Mr. J. B. White, of Kansas City, a member of the company, special opportunities were afforded for practical work, both at the mill and in the woods.

The School offers abundant facilities for research work in all branches of Scientific Forestry. The botanical and wood-testing laboratories and the engineering equipment are placed at the disposal of students desiring to do original work. There are excellent opportunities for carrying on research work in Silviculture in the field, both at New Haven and at Milford, and for studying the results of Forestry in this country and abroad from the books and records in the library.

COURSES OF INSTRUCTION
JUNIOR YEAR

Summer Term: Field Surveying; Forest Mensuration; Dendrology.

Fall Term: Silviculture; Dendrology; Diseases of Trees; Forest Physiography; Surveying (Office Work); Mechanical Drawing.

Winter Term: Silviculture; Dendrology; State Forest Law; Morphology of Plants; Forest Physiography; Surveying (Office Work); Mechanical Drawing; Forest Entomology.

Spring Term: Silviculture; Dendrology; Plant Physiology; Morphology of Woody Plants; Forest Physiography.

SENIOR YEAR

Fall Term: Forest Technology; Forest Management; Practice of Forestry in the United States; Federal Forest Law; Elementary Law for Foresters; Lumbering; Forest Policy.

Winter Term: Forest Technology; Forest Management; United States National Forests; Lumbering; Road Construction; Forest Management Abroad; Preservation of Timber.

Spring Term: Field work in the lumber woods, comprising extensive topographic surveying, forest maps, forest working plans, projection of roads and trails, preparation of plans for lumbering; practice in scaling, location of old surveys, grading and other work at the sawmill.

DESCRIPTION OF THE COURSES

1 *General Morphology of Plants.* 6 hrs. in two laboratory periods, winter term.

Professor EVANS, Dr. A. H. GRAVES, and Mr. NICHOLS.

> Laboratory work and informal lectures. Beginning with the simplest forms, the various groups of plants are taken up in suitable types, and their structure, development, and mode of life studied and compared.

2 *Morphology of Woody Plants.* 6 hrs. in two laboratory periods, spring term.

Dr. A. H. GRAVES.

> Special attention is given to the external morphology of the vegetative organs of woody plants, and to the structure and development of wood.

3 *Plant Physiology.* 6 hrs. in two laboratory periods, spring term.

Professor EVANS and Assistant Professor UNDERHILL.

> Chemical composition of plants and soils; formative and metabolic changes of carbohydrates, fats, proteids, and inorganic elements of plants; absorption and transportation of water and food materials; the action of enzymes. A knowledge of the section on Physiology in the Text-Book of Botany by Strasburger, Noll, Schenck, and Schimper will be required.

4 *Dendrology.* 1½ hrs. throughout the year, field work additional.

Professor TOUMEY and Dr. A. H. GRAVES.

> A general taxonomic and biologic study is made of the forest trees of the United States, special attention being given to the species of economic importance.

5 *Diseases of Trees.*   6 hrs. in two periods, fall term.
Dr. A. H. GRAVES.

Lectures on the destructive diseases of the timber trees of the United States, their causes, nature, and remedies, with special attention to those of fungous origin; a period also devoted to wounds and correct methods of tree pruning; laboratory study of the microscopic structure of fungi and the manner in which they attack and decompose wood; field excursions in the study of fungi growing in the forests about New Haven.

6 *Preservation of Timber.*   15 lectures, winter term.
Dr. VON SCHRENK, Shaw Botanical Garden.

The decay of structural timber; lasting powers of various species; seasoning of wood; methods for preserving timber in America and Europe; description of preserving plants. ·

7 *Forest Technology.*   2 hrs. lectures, 6 hrs. laboratory,
                                             fall and winter terms.
Professor TOUMEY and Mr. TIEMANN.

The histology of wood leading to the identification and classification of the economic woods of the United States and the more important exotic species. Normal and abnormal characteristics which are harmful in timber, and abnormal characteristics, such as burls, bird's eye and curly grain, which give it a special economic value.

The appearance and material condition of wood based upon its physical constitution. The importance of color, gloss, grain, texture, odor, and resonance as an aid to identification and in giving value to wood. Wood in its relation to moisture, density, shrinking, warping, swelling, etc., and their effect upon the use of timber.

Dendro-chemistry or the properties of wood based upon its chemical constitution. The chemical constitution of various woods from a qualitative and quantitative standpoint. The carbohydrates of wood, cellulose and lignin, fuel value, pulping qualities, etc. The extractive materials, such as tannin and resin, and the destructive distillates, such as gas, alcohol, acids, and tar, charcoal, etc.

The mechanical properties of wood, viz., elasticity, flexibility, hardness, toughness, compression, cross-bending, and shearing strength of timber.

Factors which actually determine the use of the various economic woods in the United States. The uses to which woods are best suited as determined from their structural, physical, and mechanical properties.

8 *Forest Entomology.* 2 hrs. winter term.
Assistant Professor COE.

A course of lectures and practical exercises on such groups of insects as are of economic importance in the management of forests and the utilization of forests products. It is expected that the student will become familiar with the structure, habits, and life histories of the more injurious species as well as with such predatory and parasitic insects and other organisms as naturally limit their increase. This work is accompanied by a discussion of the methods by which the attacks of insects upon trees, lumber, and finished products may be most successfully controlled.

9 *Forest Physiography.* 2 hrs., field and laboratory work additional.
Professor GREGORY, Assistant Professor BARRELL, and Mr. BOWMAN.

Under this general head are included three closely related subjects,—physiography, lithology, and soils—a study of which is designed to supply a knowledge of the general physical conditions affecting plant growth. The fall term is devoted to physiography, the winter term to physiography and lithology, and the spring term to physiography and soils.

A. *Physiography.* A study of the origin, development, and classification of land forms, including those conditions which affect insolation, water supply, formation of soils, etc. An application of physiographic principles is made to the United States. Each physiographic province is made the subject of detailed study in which the student examines the topography, drainage, climate, and soils of the region. Text-books are used ·in this part of the course but the instruction is chiefly by field exercises, map study, and assigned readings of physiographic literature.

B. *Lithology.* Laboratory exercises supplemented by field excursions and lectures dealing with the composition, structure, and classification of rocks. Particular attention is paid to the method of weathering and decomposition of the various rock types.

C. *Soils.* Laboratory and field exercises with occasional lectures on the origin, classification, and relative value of soils. A study is made of the chemical and physical properties of the various soil types, with special reference to their bearing on the habits and distribution of trees. Each student is required to prepare a soil map of an area of about six square miles, accompanied by a report describing soils, their relation to plant growth, ground water, etc. King's *Soils*, Hilgard's *Soils*, and *Reports of the United States Soil Survey* are used as texts.

10 *Forest Physiography.*   Special lectures, winter term. Professor BREWER.

General conditions necessary to forests ; elementary meteorology ; forests as related to temperature and its range, to rainfall and its range, to excess of weather and climate, to the mechanical and chemical nature of soil and ground water, to the geological character of the surface, to the relief-forms of the land, to other geographical features ; the geographical distribution of forests ; the relation of physiography to the geographical distribution of species of trees ; the reaction of forests upon physiography ; the aspects of forests as related to climate and topography ; the geologic history of forests ; the forests in relation to public health and public recreation.

11 *Forest Hydrography.*   4 lectures, winter term. Mr. F. H. NEWELL, Chief Engineer, Reclamation Service, U. S. Geological Survey.

This course of lectures, illustrated by lantern slides, considers : Flow of streams ; diurnal and seasonable variations non-periodic fluctuations ; regimen of various rivers ; effects of forest and cultural conditions on available flow ; underground water. Particular attention is given to irrigation economics, and to the work of the Reclamation Service of the United States Geological Survey in the construction and administration of irrigation systems in the arid West.

12 *Silviculture (Silvics).*   2 hrs. fall term, field
                                          work additional.
Professor GRAVES, Assistant Professor CHAPMAN, and Mr. HAWLEY.

Principles underlying the life history of trees and forests. The lectures are supplemented by extensive field work.

13 *Silviculture (Treatment of Woodlands).*
                      2 hrs. winter and spring terms, field work
                                                    additional.
Professor GRAVES and Mr. HAWLEY.

Principles of reproducing forests by skillful cuttings. Theoretical discussion of the different silvicultural systems of management. Practical silvicultural problems in this country. The field work consists of practice in marking thinnings and reproduction cuttings.

14   *Silviculture (Forest Seeding and Planting).*

2 hrs. lectures, and 8 hrs. field work, spring term. Professor TOUMEY.

The study of tree seeds ; storage and germination of seeds ; tree planting and the factors governing success.

15   *Surveying (Field Work).* 2½ days a week, summer term. Assistant Professor TRACY and Mr. FARNHAM.

Practically all the methods of surveying are introduced in this work, portions of the ground being covered several times by different methods, thus affording an excellent opportunity for observing the advantages and disadvantages of each method. The work in the field is supplemented throughout the course by lectures and class-room discussions. See also course 21.

16   *Surveying (Office Work).*   6 hrs. fall term, 3 hrs.
                                              winter term.

Assistant Professor TRACY and Mr. FARNHAM.

Plotting and mapping of the data collected during the summer at Milford, Pa.

17   *Mechanical Drawing.*   3 hrs. fall term.
Mr. NORTH.

Preparatory to the work in mapping, followed by the making of simple working drawings in orthographic projection.

18   *Forest Mensuration.*   2 days a week, summer term. Professor GRAVES and Assistant Professor CHAPMAN.

Methods of determining the contents of logs and other parts of felled trees. During the term the students are required to complete an investigation of the growth and yield of some one species. This investigation includes the preparation of volume tables for standing trees, tables of growth in diameter, height, and volume, and tables of present stand and future yield.

19   *Methods of Field Work.*   4 lectures, winter term. Mr. O. W. PRICE, Associate Forester U. S. Dept. of Agriculture.

The policy of the Forest Service in its field studies ; the organization of its several lines of field work ; and the methods under which its field work is conducted upon public and private forest lands and in independent investigations.

20 *Road Construction.*   1 hr. winter term.
Assistant Professor BARNEY.

> A course of lectures dealing with the principles of road construction. This course is supplemented by field work in the spring term.

21 *Lumbering.*

Mr. BRYANT, Assistant Professor CHAPMAN, and special lecturers engaged in the lumber business.

> The object of this course is to give the students a thorough understanding of the chief features of the lumber business and the main principles underlying its successful conduct.
>
> The first half of the fall term and all of the spring term is devoted to field work, supplemented by lectures throughout the year, on topics pertinent to the industry. During the fall term each student prepares a plan for logging a woodlot near New Haven. This includes the following points: consumption and price of native timber in the local market, an estimate of the standing timber and its stumpage value, description of methods of logging adapted to the tract, type of portable sawmill used for small operations, local methods of manufacturing lumber, a detailed statement of the cost of logging the tract and manufacturing the timber into lumber and other products.
>
> A series of lectures is given during the latter part of the fall term and through the winter term on the lumber industry and interests of the United States.
>
> About March 1st the work is transferred from New Haven to the field where the remainder of the year is spent studying the logging and manufacturing methods employed in one of the typical forest regions of the United States.
>
> Excellent facilities are afforded for actual practice in grading rough and finished lumber, and the students become acquainted with the methods of organization and management of all departments of the business.
>
> Final instruction is given by the field work in preparing plans for the management of forest lands.

22 *Forest Management.*   3 hrs. fall and winter terms.
Assistant Professor CHAPMAN.

> Economic principles underlying the management of forest property; working plans for European and American conditions. For field work in Forest Management, see course 21.

27

23 *The Practice of Forestry in the United States.*
                                              3 hrs. fall term.
Mr. HAWLEY.
> Problems of management typical of the various forest regions
> are taken up and discussed at length. Practical forest man-
> agement is considered in all its relations.

24 *U. S. National Forests.*   3 hrs. winter term.
WILLIAM BUCKHOUT GREELEY, Forest Supervisor, U. S.
Forest Service.
> A study of the U. S. National Forests, including a detailed
> description of them, their location, their character, practical
> problems of lumbering and forest management, market condi-
> tions, and methods of management and administration.

25 *U. S. National Forests.* Special lectures, winter term.
Professor PINCHOT.
> Economic growth and present industrial situation of the West ;
> settlement and disposal of public lands ; origin, administration,
> and management of the National Forests.

26 *Forest Policy.*   6 lectures, fall term.
Professor PINCHOT.
> Origins of forest policy ; its objects and principles ; legisla-
> tion and its causes before 1891 ; legislation and its causes from
> 1891 to 1903 ; national organization in Forestry ; the forest and
> other land laws in relation to economic and industrial develop-
> ment ; State forest problems.

27 *Forest Management Abroad.**   2 hrs. winter term.
Professor GRAVES and Mr. MYERS.
> Early forest ordinances in Europe ; beginnings of technical
> forestry ; development of the technical branches ; history of
> Government forest administration ; history of forest education
> in Europe. The systems of Forest Administration in foreign
> countries ; organization of the administrative departments ;
> force of officers ; duties of each ; effectiveness of the service ;
> cost ; civil service regulations ; relation to the army.

28 *State Forest Law.*   2 hrs. winter term.
Assistant Professor CHAPMAN.
> A study of the forest laws of different States, with particular
> reference to forest protection and reserves. History of forest
> legislation and forest policy of the important States.

* This course was formerly entitled History of Forestry.

29   *Forest Administration and Law.*   2 hrs. fall term.
Mr. E. A. BOWERS.

    A. The development of the public domain with reference to the creation of a forest policy by the United States and a consideration of laws relating thereto, including rules and regulations governing public lands and forest reserves, and Federal and State decisions on subjects relating to Forestry.

    B. Elementary Law for Foresters, treating of contracts, damages, real estate, riparian rights, and abstracts of title.

SHORT COURSE OF THE SUMMER SCHOOL

The Short Course, which is conducted at Milford, Penn., is designed to provide instruction in Forestry for those who do not wish to take, or who are not ready for, the more advanced technical courses at a regular Forest School. The course is especially suited to the following classes of students:

I. Students of Forestry who expect later to enter a more advanced technical school.

II. Students who contemplate entering the profession of Forestry, and are unable to make a definite decision.

III. Advanced students of Forestry who desire to carry on independent research work or to study methods of forest experimentation. The Forest Experiment Station affords excellent facilities for such students.

IV. Owners of woodland. Farmers, lumbermen, and others who wish to obtain a knowledge of the principles of Forestry and a practical acquaintance with the care of woodlands and with tree planting, receive instruction to meet their special requirements.

V. Forest Rangers. The course is particularly adapted to persons who wish to fit themselves for work as forest rangers.

VI. Teachers. Instruction in Forestry is now given in a considerable number of Agricultural Colleges, Industrial Schools, and other institutions, both in connection with the study of Horticulture and as separate courses, and it would doubtless form part of the instruction in

Botany and Nature Study in public and private schools, if the teachers were properly qualified. The attention of teachers is especially called to the course offered at the Yale Summer School of Forestry.

VII. All persons who desire to acquire a general knowledge of Forestry, or any of its branches.

EQUIPMENT

The equipment at Milford is described on pp. 406–07.

ADMISSION

Candidates for admission to the short course of the Summer School must be at least seventeen years of age. There are no entrance examinations.

TERM

The course covers a period of seven weeks, beginning, in 1908, on Tuesday, July 7.

EXPENSES

The tuition fee is twenty-five dollars. A charge of seventeen dollars is made for the use of a tent and the privileges of the school camp. If two persons occupy one tent, the charge is twelve dollars each. Both the tuition and tent fees are payable at registration.

CURRICULUM

The instruction is devoted chiefly to Forest Botany, Silviculture, and Forest Mensuration. Students may take any or all of the courses. Those who wish to carry on special research work receive personal direction in their studies.

Practical work in the woods forms an important part of the instruction. In connection with the course in Forest Botany, frequent excursions are made to train the students in identifying native and exotic trees and shrubs. A large part of the work in Silviculture is devoted to practice in selecting trees for thinnings, in making reproduction and improvement cuttings, and in the study of forest planting. In the course in Forest Mensuration the students are given practice in studying the growth of trees and whole stands, making estimates of standing timber, etc.

DESCRIPTION OF THE COURSES

1. FOREST BOTANY

Particular attention is given to Forest Botany. This course embraces laboratory work, field work, and lectures. An important feature of the course is the field work, designed to familiarize the students with the trees near the School, and their habits of growth. The effect of plant parasites upon tree growth and the part taken by herbage and shrubs in the forest are also studied in the field.

The lectures cover a systematic account of the trees of the United States, with particular reference to those of importance in Forestry.

The course comprises also a certain amount of laboratory work to acquaint the students with the fundamental principles of structural botany.

2. SILVICULTURE

The object of this course is to give, as thoroughly as the length of the session will permit, a training in the principles and the practical methods of establishing and treating woodlands. The work is conducted largely in the field, and students are given practice not only in studying the characteristics of trees, but in sowing and planting, and in making improvement and reproduction cuttings.

3. FOREST MENSURATION

This course takes up in a practical way the methods used in determining the contents of felled and standing trees and of whole forests, the methods of making rough and accurate estimates of standing timber, the use of American log rules, and the methods of determining the age and growth of individual trees and of whole stands. Practice is given in running lines with the compass, and making simple maps.

4. RESEARCH WORK IN FORESTRY

This course is designed for advanced students who desire to study the work carried on at the Forest Experiment Station or to study the work done in the European Stations. Students wishing to conduct independent investigations are given individual instruction to meet their requirements.

5. FOREST REGIONS OF THE UNITED STATES

This course consists of a series of weekly lectures, illustrated with the stereopticon, upon the characteristic forest regions of the United States. The course is given by the different members of the teaching staff in Forest Hall in the village of Milford and is open to the public.

DEPARTMENT OF THEOLOGY
(YALE DIVINITY SCHOOL)
OFFICERS
FACULTY AND INSTRUCTORS

ARTHUR TWINING HADLEY, LL.D., PRESIDENT.

Rev. GEORGE PARK FISHER, D.D., LL.D., *Titus Street Professor of Ecclesiastical History, Emeritus*

Rev. LEWIS ORSMOND BRASTOW, D.D., *Professor of Practical Theology, Emeritus*

Rev. EDWARD LEWIS CURTIS, PH.D., D.D., *Holmes Professor of the Hebrew Language and Literature, and Acting Dean of the Faculty*

Rev. HARLAN PAGE BEACH, M.A., *Professor of the Theory and Practice of Missions*

Rev. FRANK CHAMBERLIN PORTER, PH.D., D.D., *Winkley Professor of Biblical Theology*

Rev. BENJAMIN WISNER BACON, LITT.D., D.D., LL.D., *Buckingham Professor of New Testament Criticism and Interpretation*

WILLISTON WALKER, PH.D., D.D., *Titus Street Professor of Ecclesiastical History*

REV. AMBROSE WHITE VERNON, D.D., *Professor of Practical Theology*

WILLIAM BACON BAILEY, PH.D. *(Assistant Professor of Statistics in Yale University), Instructor in Sociology*

REV. MARION LEROY BURTON, PH.D., *Assistant Professor of Systematic Theology*

REV. EDWARD SACKETT HUME, M.A., *Instructor in Missions*

CHARLES CUTLER TORREY, PH.D., D.D. *(Professor of the Semitic Languages in Yale University), Instructor in Semitic Languages*

CHARLES FOSTER KENT, PH.D. *(Woolsey Professor of Biblical Literature in Yale University), Instructor in Biblical Literature*

EDWARD MORGAN LEWIS, M.A., *Instructor in Elocution*

RAYMOND GILMORE CLAPP, M.A., B.D., *Instructor in New Testament Greek and Director of Religious Work*

REV. ALBERT ALONZO MADSEN, PH.D., *Instructor in Palestinian Geography*

REV. ERNEST FRANK' MCGREGOR, M.A., B.D., *Instructor in Sociology*

—422—

HON. SIMEON EBEN BALDWIN, LL.D. *(Professor of Constitutional Law and Private International Law in Yale University), Instructor in Law*

RICHARD SWANN LULL, PH.D. *(Assistant Professor of Vertebrate Paleontology in Yale University), Instructor in Organic Evolution*

BEVERLY WAUGH KUNKEL, PH.D. *(Instructor in Biology in Yale University), Instructor in Organic Evolution*

SPECIAL LECTURERS

REV. WILLIAM HERBERT PERRY FAUNCE, D.D., LL.D., President of Brown University
Lyman Beecher Lecturer

PROFESSOR GEORG WOBBERMIN, PH.D., of the University of Breslau, Germany
Nathaniel William Taylor Lecturer

REV. BORDEN PARKER BOWNE, LL.D., Professor in Boston University
Lecturer on Systematic Theology

REV. HERBERT ATCHINSON JUMP, B.D., of Brunswick, Me.
Alumni Lecturer

OTHER OFFICERS

MAY B. LYON, *Private Secretary to the Faculty*

EZRA PECK MERRIAM, *Superintendent of the Divinity Buildings*

GENERAL STATEMENT

RELATION OF THE DIVINITY SCHOOL TO THE UNIVERSITY

The YALE DIVINITY SCHOOL is one of the coördinate Departments of Yale University. The general advantages of the University are enjoyed by all its members. The graduates of the Divinity School who have received the degree of Bachelor of Divinity since that degree was first conferred by the University in 1867 are enrolled in the Catalogue of the Officers and Graduates of the University and take part in the election of the alumni members of the Corporation. They are also themselves eligible to membership in the Corporation.

CONDITIONS OF ADMISSION

The Divinity School is open, on equal terms, to students of every Christian denomination. The conditions of admission are membership in some evangelical Church, or other satisfactory evidence of Christian character, and a liberal education at some College or University, or, in exceptional cases, an equivalent preparation for theological studies. Some knowledge of the Hebrew language on the part of those entering the Junior class, and expecting to pursue that study, is desirable.

By an arrangement with the Academical Department of Yale University, it is possible for Seniors in that Department to elect as part of their work for the B.A. degree the prescribed courses of the Junior year in the Divinity School, thereby preparing themselves to enter the Middle class on graduation and thus to complete their Theological course in two years. Such students, however, are expected to maintain a high grade of scholarship.

The following rules determine the admission of students to candidacy for the degree of Bachelor of Divinity :

1. Bachelors of Arts whose course of study has included Greek are admitted without examination as candidates for the degree of B.D.

2. Bachelors of Arts whose course of study has not included Greek, and graduates holding other literary degrees—such as B.S., B.L., and Ph.B.—are required to pass the examination in Greek, referred to below (paragraph 2), before being admitted as candidates for the degree of B.D.

3. Applicants for admission who hold no collegiate degree are required to show by certificate and by examination* that they have received the substantial equivalent of a college training. Full statements from their instructors, showing the subjects and the range of

---

* Such applicants will be examined in the following subjects :—

(1) *Latin.* Sight reading of easy prose, and the text of at least three standard authors. Three years' study of Latin would ordinarily be necessary to the passing of this examination.

(2) *Greek.* The same general requirements as are made in Latin. Sight reading of the New Testament.

(3) *English Literature.* The examination will require a good degree of familiarity with the chief English and American writers in prose and poetry. The more exact range of the examination, in any particular case, may be agreed upon between the applicant and the Faculty.

(4) *History.* A careful study of one or more historical periods.

(5) *Philosophy.* A fair knowledge of logic, psychology, ethics, and the history of philosophy.

(6) German, French, political or social science may be offered in addition to, or, in special cases, in lieu of one or more of the above subjects, except Greek and Philosophy.

their previous studies, will be taken into account by the Faculty in determining their fitness for admission. They may be admitted to membership in the institution without becoming at the outset candidates for the degree of B.D.

4. Such non-graduates as show superior scholarship in the actual work of the course may, at any time, by vote of the Faculty, become candidates for the degree of B.D.

5. Students from other Seminaries will be received to advanced standing upon the same terms as applicants for admission at the beginning of the course, but none will be received as candidates for the degree of B.D. after the opening of the first term of the Senior year.

ADMISSION TO ADVANCED STANDING

Students from other theological schools whose course of study, in the judgment of the Faculty, is substantially equivalent to that of this institution, will be received *ad eundem* upon presenting regular certificates of dismission and recommendation. Applicants whose previous training has been received in Colleges which provide a mixed course of literary and biblical (or theological) studies, will not be received to a standing beyond that of Middle year, except upon condition of passing a satisfactory examination in the required studies of that year, or their equivalent.

GRADUATE STUDY

Those who have completed a course of three years in this or some other Theological School can be admitted to Graduate standing in the Divinity School,—a recognition which carries with it registration as a member of the Graduate Department of the University, and, in case of those who hold a bachelor's degree equivalent to that of Yale University, the privilege of working for the M.A. or Ph.D. degrees. This opportunity is designed to meet the needs of three classes of theological graduates: those who desire to pursue an advanced course of general theological study; those who desire to pursue, for a year or two, special subjects of reading or investigation in any of the departments of theology under the advice and direction of the Professors, and with the help furnished by the Reference and University Libraries; and those who are desirous of winning an advanced degree. Candidates for membership in this class are admitted by vote of the Faculty.

From the connection of the Divinity School with the other Departments of the University, special advantages for the prosecution of linguistic and other studies are open to students preparing for service as foreign missionaries.

Members of the Graduate class are required, in all ordinary cases, to take at least three Divinity courses and are expected to continue their studies at the Divinity School during the entire year. Their fees and privileges in respect to rooms, on vote of the Faculty, are the same as those of the undergraduates (see p. 446). A limited number of scholarships are open to members of this class (see p. 451).

Members of this class who have a degree of B.A. equivalent to that of Yale University, may be enrolled in the Graduate Department of the University and become candidates for the degree of M.A. (requiring one year of residence), or that of Ph.D. (requiring at least two years of residence). The proposed course of study must have the approval of a committee of the Academical Faculty in case of M.A., and of the Graduate Faculty in case of Ph.D.

STUDENTS PURSUING SELECTED STUDIES

The privileges of attendance at the lectures and use of the libraries of the Divinity School and University are granted, on application to the Faculty, to young men who desire to pursue special studies throughout the year. A fee of ten dollars for Library and incidental expenses will be charged in such cases. Rooms will be furnished to students thus enrolled and pursuing at least three of the Divinity courses at one-half the price charged occupants who are not members of the Divinity School.

TERMS OF STUDY

Each year is divided into two terms of study by the Christmas vacation. The second term extends to the first Tuesday in June, with a short recess at Easter. Examinations precede each recess. It is expected that every student will be present at the beginning of each session.

Catalogues and forms of application for admission may be obtained by addressing Professor Edward L. Curtis, Yale Station, New Haven, Conn.

LICENSE TO PREACH

Licenses to preach are granted by local and other Associations to students sustaining a satisfactory examination.

The regular time for applying for licensure is near the close of the Middle year, before which time the members of the Divinity School are not expected to accept regular appointments to preach, without special permission of the Faculty.

DEGREES

The degree of Bachelor of Divinity is conferred by the President and Fellows of the University on all members of the School who, having been admitted by the Faculty as candidates for this degree (see pp. 424 and 425), satisfactorily complete the prescribed course of study and present an approved thesis on some topic of theology. A fee of five dollars is charged for a diploma.

Students who have completed two years of study in this School, and who, at the close of the Middle year, desire to forego candidacy for the degree of B.D. and enter the Graduate School as candidates for the degree of Ph.D. in the Departments of Biblical Literature and Semitic Languages or Philosophy, will be enrolled as members of the Senior class, and allowed its privileges, provided they pursue the prescribed studies of that year.

COURSES OF STUDY

Beginning with the class entering at the opening of the academic year 1907–08, the studies pursued in the Divinity School are grouped into three courses, each leading to the degree of B.D., and known as Historical ("Course A"), Philosophical ("Course B"), and Practical ("Course C"). The study of Hebrew is required only in the Historical course, which corresponds substantially to the outline of studies formerly pursued in the Divinity School.

The aim of the Philosophical course is not merely to emphasize acquaintance with the historic and theoretic exposition of Theology, but to ground the students thoroughly in modern scientific and philosophical conceptions of the world viewed from the Christian standpoint. As a preliminary discipline for this course the students are required to take special studies in the Junior Year in Philosophy and Science. These are furnished in part by the Divinity School Faculty, but the Departments of Philosophy and Science in the University assist in this instruction.

In a similar way the Practical course emphasizes the relation of the minister to the problems of modern society, giving special attention to Christian Sociology, Ethics, and Methods of Christian Activity. As a preliminary discipline, students who take this course receive in Junior Year special instruction in Sociology and instruction in Elementary Law in one of the courses furnished by the University for Law students.

Certain studies of the Divinity School in the Old and New Testaments, Biblical and Systematic Theology, Church History and Homiletics, are required of all students. For those courses in which Hebrew is not obligatory provision is made for the study of the Old Testament in English.

Students of ability who so desire may by the use of electives obtain substantially the advantages offered by all three of these courses during a three years' residence as candidate for the degree of B.D.

GENERAL DESCRIPTION OF THE COURSES OF STUDY BY DEPARTMENTS

DEPARTMENT OF OLD TESTAMENT LITERATURE AND HISTORY

PROFESSOR CURTIS AND DR. MADSEN

The prescribed work in this department for the degree of B.D. for students taking the Historical course (see p. 427) consists of one hundred and sixty hours on the Hebrew language and the Hebrew text; but by use of electives one can read critically nearly the entire Old Testament in the Hebrew, and also obtain an elementary knowledge of one or more of the cognate languages during his theological course. Students who do not take Hebrew have an equal opportunity, on the basis of the English text, by means of electives, to familiarize themselves with the Old Testament. Special attention is given to the problems of Old Testament Introduction. In this, sixty-four hours are required of all students during their Junior year.

I. PRESCRIBED COURSES
PROFESSOR CURTIS
JUNIOR YEAR

1 *Elementary Hebrew and Exegesis* (required in Course A).
3 hrs. throughout the year.

The elements of Hebrew are taught with the use of Harper's *Hebrew Method and Manual* and *Elements of Hebrew* as textbooks.

2 *Old Testament Introduction* (required in Courses A, B, and C). 2 hrs. throughout the year.

This course treats briefly the topics of General Introduction and then the history of Biblical criticism with special reference to determining the character of the Pentateuch. It then surveys the Old Testament literature with reference to its historical background, familiarizing the student with the political history of Israel and the geography of Palestine.

DR. MADSEN

3 *Palestinian Geography* (required in Courses A, B, and C).

This course, designed to familiarize the student with the topography of Palestine, is given in connection with course 2 above and counts as part of that course.

MIDDLE YEAR

4 *Hebrew Language and Exegesis* (required in Course A).
2 hrs.

This course consists of the translation and exegesis, by the student, during the first term, of selected passages of Hebrew prose with special reference to Hebrew syntax, and during the second term of selected Psalms with a method of instruction in general that of a seminar. A critical or exegetical paper is required from each student.

5 *The Old Testament (English)* (required in Courses B and C). 2 hrs. throughout the year.
An exposition of the Old Testament Prophetic and Poetic Literature with a view to their use in the pulpit and the Bible class. [To be given in 1908-09.]

II. ELECTIVE COURSES
PROFESSOR CURTIS

6 *The Wisdom Literature (Hebrew).*
1 hr. throughout the year.
A course in translation and exegesis. The Book of Job will be studied in 1907-08; portions of Proverbs, Ecclesiastes, and Canticles, in 1908-09.

7 *The Book of Isaiah (Hebrew).* 2 hrs. 2d term.
Translation and exegesis of selected portions of Isaiah xl-lxvi, in 1907-08; and of Isaiah i-xxxix, in 1908-09.

III. GRADUATE COURSES
PROFESSOR CURTIS

[8 *Old Testament History and Archæology.*
1 hr. throughout the year.
A series of studies in Biblical criticism, history, and archæology, with the view of determining the meaning and historical value of the Old Testament records.
Omitted in 1907-08.]

9 *First and Second Chronicles.* 1 hr. throughout the year.
Translation and exegesis with special reference to the later forms of the Hebrew language and the Midrashic literature.

DEPARTMENT OF NEW TESTAMENT LITERATURE AND HISTORY
PROFESSOR BACON and MR. CLAPP

In this department it is assumed that the student has already mastered the elements of the Greek language and aims at expert interpretation of the Greek New Testament. The first year, accordingly, is devoted to a practical application of the principles of historical Exegesis, first to the Pauline Epistles, afterwards to the Synoptic Gospels, with lectures on the methods and apparatus of the science. The second year is devoted to Introduction, or the study of the origins of the New Testament books.

By the use of the electives in the Undergraduate and Graduate Departments of the University, a thorough training may be obtained in the peculiarities of Hellenistic Greek, and on the grammatical and philological side of the subject generally. The prescribed work of the regular Divinity Course, accordingly, is mainly directed toward Criticism and Exegesis, the Divinity electives supplementing the regular course by a more extensive exegesis of the New Testament writings, a wider outlook into their relations to contemporary Hellenistic thought and literature, and a deeper historical study of their origins.

In view of the fact that many colleges no longer require Greek as part of their curricula, provision has been made whereby college graduates of promise may substitute during the Junior year, for the courses in Greek numbered 10 and 11 below, the course in Church History regularly assigned to the Middle year and numbered 26, taking these courses in Greek during the Middle year. That they may be prepared for these courses, instruction in Elementary Greek has been provided to the amount of two hours a week throughout Junior year, which may be taken as an elective study; but, owing to its rudimentary character, it will be counted as only one hour of credit.

I. PRESCRIBED COURSES

PROFESSOR BACON

JUNIOR YEAR

10   *The Pauline Epistles* (required in Courses A, B, and C).
3 hrs. 1st term.
[See Course V, B 7, page 152.]

11   *The Synoptic Gospels* (required in Courses A, B, and C).
3 hrs. 2d term.
[See Course V, B 7, page 152.]

12   *New Testament Introduction* (required in Courses A, B, and C).
1 hr.
A series of lectures, taking up consecutively the methods and apparatus of New Testament Philology and Archæology, History and Criticism of the Text, History of the Formation of the

Canon, and History of the Science of Introduction or the Higher Criticism, followed (2d term) by discussions of the origin of the several New Testament books in the light of critical investigation.

II.   ELECTIVE COURSES
OPEN TO ALL CLASSES

13   *The Christological Epistles.*   1 hr. 1st term.

A lecture course presenting the origin and nature of the Pauline Christology.   A thesis will be prepared by each member of the class.

14   *The Teaching of Jesus.*   1 hr. 2d term.

Historico-critical exegesis of the principal discourses of Jesus, embodied in Matthew and Luke.   Book reviews by the class.

15   *Theological German.*   2 hrs. 1st term, *to count as 1 hr.*

Reading and discussion of standard German treatises for practice and information.

16   *Hebrews and Catholic Epistles.*   2 hrs. 2d term.

A critical and exegetical study of the non-Pauline epistles in their origin and historical environment.

17   *Origin of the Johannine Writings.*   2 hrs. 2d term.

.[See Course II, 49, page 327.]

OPEN TO THE MIDDLE, SENIOR, AND GRADUATE CLASSES

18   *Historical Origins of the Church.*   2 hrs.

Historico-critical analysis of the Book of Acts.   The method will be to assign consecutive sections of the book to members of the class for discussion from the standpoint of the critical historian, treating it as the fundamental source for a critical history of the Apostolic Age.

III.   GRADUATE COURSES

19   *Patristic Greek.*   1 hr. 1st term.

[See Course II, 50, page 327.]

20   *Problems of Textual Criticism.*   1 hr. 2d term.

A seminar course in textual criticism.

SPECIAL ELECTIVE
Mr. CLAPP

21   *New Testament Greek* (required in certain cases; see p. 431).   2 hrs. throughout the year, *to count as 1 hr.*

A grammatical and philological course to prepare graduates of colleges who have not taken Greek as a part of their college course for the regular work of the department of the New

Testament and to give further practice to any whose proficiency is insufficient for proper participation in the regular New Testament studies.

DEPARTMENT OF BIBLICAL THEOLOGY
PROFESSOR PORTER

In this department the religious thought and life of the Old and New Testaments are studied from the point of view and with the methods of the science of religious history. The effort is not to construct a Biblical Dogmatics, nor merely to set forth in a systematic way the theological conceptions of the several books, but, on the one hand, to understand the religious history out of which the books came, and gain a right appreciation of its persons and events, its shaping forces and the continuity and progress of its movements; and, on the other hand, to study some of the ruling religious ideas of the Bible in their historical orfgin, and the various stages of their development, and in their meaning and value for religious faith and life.

I.   PRESCRIBED COURSES
MIDDLE YEAR

22   *The Theology of Judaism* (required in Courses A, B, and C).   2 hrs. 1st half year.
   [See Course II, 37, page 325.]

SENIOR YEAR

*23   *Biblical Theology of the New Testament* (required in Courses A, B, and C).   3 hrs. throughout the year.
   [See Course II, 39, page 326.]

24   *Problems in Theology* (required in Courses A, B, and C).
                                                    2 hrs., until March 1.

A course of lectures, readings, and discussions on some of the leading theological subjects, including the Doctrine of Sacred Scripture, the Spirit of God, the Person of Christ, with special attention to the Christology of Paul and of John, and the Doctrine of the Future Life. During the months of March, April, and May, 1908, this course will be carried forward by Professor Borden P. Bowne of Boston University, who will discuss especially problems connected with the Theistic and Christian interpretation of the world.

---

* This course was given in the year 1906-07 to the Middle and Senior classes, and will therefore be omitted in 1907-08.

28

25 *The Jewish Religion of the Time of Christ* (required in Courses A and B). 2 hrs. 1st half year.

A course of lectures on the history of Jewish religious life and thought from the Maccabean period until the writing of the Mishna, or about 175 B.C.–200 A.D. The study will include both Palestinian and Hellenistic Judaism, and will aim to set forth the historical background of New Testament Theology.

DEPARTMENT OF CHURCH HISTORY
PROFESSOR WALKER

The aim in this department is to guide the student to a conception of Christian history as the development of the Kingdom of God on earth. While no line is drawn between the sacred and the secular in history, and all historic progress is regarded as essentially one divinely guided process, the primary themes in this department are necessarily the origin, growth, principles, divisions, and leaders of the Christian Church. The development and history of Christian Doctrine is considered in chronological connection with the narrative of the progress of the Church, and also in a supplementary special course. An effort is made to acquaint the student with proper methods of historical investigation and criticism, and to give him some facility in their use.

I. PRESCRIBED COURSES
MIDDLE YEAR

26 *Church History from the Apostolic Age to the Close of the Papal Schism* (required in Courses A, B, and C).
2 hrs. throughout the year.
[See Course IX, 69, page 376.]

SENIOR YEAR

27 *Church History from the Beginnings of the Reformation to the present Age* (required in Courses A, B, and C). 2 hrs. throughout the year.
[See Course IX, 73, page 377.]

28 *History of Christian Doctrine* (required in Courses A and B). 1 hr. throughout the year.

A survey of the development of Christian thought from the Apostolic age to the present.

II. ELECTIVE COURSES

OPEN TO THE MIDDLE AND SENIOR CLASSES

29   *The History of Congregationalism.*   1 hr. 2d term.

A rapid survey designed to familiarize the student with the origins and leading events of Congregational history.

OPEN TO THE SENIOR CLASS ONLY

30   *Four Eminent Theologians: Augustine, Aquinas, Calvin, . Edwards.*   1 hr. 2d term.

In this course an attempt is made to present an outline of the lives of these great theologians; but the chief portion of the time of the class will be devoted to the consideration and comparison of their theological systems.

III. GRADUATE COURSE

31   *Christian Literature from Clement of Rome to Eusebius.*
1 hr. throughout the year.

This course is intended to acquaint the student with the principal ecclesiastical authors of the period from the close of the Apostolic Age to the Conversion of the Roman Empire.

A student desiring to specialize in Church History will find the courses offered by the University in History, Paleography, and Epigraphy of much advantage. The more important of these courses are indicated on pp. 375 ff.

DEPARTMENT OF SYSTEMATIC THEOLOGY
ASSISTANT PROFESSOR BURTON

The aim in this department is to set forth the grounds and content of the Christian faith by a method at once historical, critical, and constructive. The first year is devoted to the consideration of the philosophical and historical bases of Christian theology. During the second year a systematic investigation of theology is undertaken, including the study of each doctrine in its biblical elements and chief historical forms. Ample opportunity is afforded for collateral reading and informal class discussions.

I. PRESCRIBED COURSES
JUNIOR YEAR

32   *The Philosophical Basis of Christian Theology* (required in Course B).   3 hrs. throughout the year.

The aim of this course is to prepare the student to approach the required work of the middle year in Systematic Theology

(Course 33) with an adequate knowledge of the history of philosophic thought. The history of theistic thought will be emphasized throughout the course. Discussions, reviews, and papers.

MIDDLE YEAR

33 *The Science of the Christian Faith* (required in Courses
A, B, and C).   3 hrs. throughout the year.
The course includes the investigation and discussion of such
topics as the Presuppositions of Systematic Theology, the Doctrine of Sacred Scripture, the Christian Ideas of God and of
Man, the Origin, Nature, and Consequences of Sin, the Person
of Christ, the Work of the Holy Spirit, the Trinity, the Atone-
ment, the Christian Life, the Church, and the Consummation of
the Kingdom of God. Lectures, reviews, and discussions.

DEPARTMENT OF PRACTICAL THEOLOGY
PROFESSOR VERNON

The aim in this department is to guide the student to a
large and distinctively Christian message and to aid him
in presenting it effectually to men.

For this year the instruction in the department will be
confined to the necessary courses in Homiletics.

PRESCRIBED COURSES
MIDDLE YEAR

34 *Elementary Homiletics* (required in Courses A, B, and
C).   2 hrs. throughout the year.
The emphasis in this course will be placed upon the form
rather than upon the content of preaching. The work assigned
to the student will be fitted to his individual needs, and the
object of the course is to assist him to that presentation of the
gospel which will grant him the greatest power and freedom.

SENIOR YEAR

35 *Advanced Homiletics* (required in Courses A, B, and C.)
            2 hrs. throughout the year.
The emphasis in this course will be placed rather upon the
content than the form of preaching, though the latter will not be
ignored. The object of the course is to insure a definite and
consistent message that shall be thought out as thoroughly as
possible by the student and that shall be adapted to our present age.

Besides these courses, debates under the auspices of the
LEONARD BACON DEBATING CLUB, and addresses by the

students, are alternately held under the supervision of this department each Wednesday.

DEPARTMENT· OF MISSIONS
PROFESSOR BEACH AND MR. HUME

The establishment of the Chair of the Theory and Practice of Missions enables the Divinity School to make more prominent than in the past this study, so essential in the preparation of the minister for the missionary activities of the modern church, and more important still for the increasing number of men who are looking forward to actual service on the foreign field. As the foundation of the professorship calls for periodical tours of visitation and study of missions in the non-Christian countries, and as the first of these began in March, 1907, and will not be completed till September, 1908, Professor Beach will give no courses during the academic year 1907–08.

The Library of Foreign Missions, containing about 7,500 titles, as well as a complete set of the current periodicals and reports, affords an opportunity unequalled in America for original research and for unrestricted reading.

Candidates for foreign missionary service will find in elective courses open to them in the University exceptional opportunities for broadening their preparation. Thus Arabic, Chinese, Japanese, Sanskrit, Pali, and Spanish will be an aid in language preparation, so far as this may be done profitably in America. Special biblical courses, pedagogy, international law, anthropology, and Oriental history are other studies which will helpfully supplement the work of the Divinity School.

I.　PRESCRIBED COURSES
JUNIOR YEAR

[36　*Mission Fields and Problems.*

　　　　　　　　　　　　　　1 hr. throughout the year
Omitted in 1907–08.]

MIDDLE YEAR

(Elective for Seniors)

[37 *Missions in Relation to the Non-Christian Religions.*

1 hr. throughout the year.

Omitted in 1907–08.]

II. ELECTIVE COURSES

OPEN TO ALL CLASSES

[38 *Sinitic Ethics and Religions.* 1 hr. throughout the year.

Omitted in 1907–08.]

[39 *Course for Missionary Candidates.*

2 hrs. throughout the year.

Omitted in 1907–08.]

MR. HUME

During the absence of Professor Beach the following course, required of the Seniors and elective to the other classes, is offered :

40 *The Making of the Missionary.* 1 hr.

The aim of this course is to give, by means of lectures, classroom exercises and required readings, practical views regarding preparation for Missionary service and the results of experience in various departments of Missionary effort.

DEPARTMENT OF CHRISTIAN SOCIOLOGY

ASSISTANT PROFESSOR BAILEY AND MR. McGREGOR

It is intended that the courses offered in this department shall be taken in their proper order by the members of the various classes, as it is assumed that the students of the Senior class are familiar with the principles laid down during the Junior and Middle years.

The department offers exceptional opportunities for the student who wishes special training in applied philanthropy or welfare work. New Haven affords in Lowell House a social settlement, and in the various charitable organizations excellent examples of modern methods of charity.

There have recently been added over five hundred lantern slides to illustrate the lectures before the department.

In connection with the regular work of the courses, lectures are delivered by men who have made a special study of some related topic.

The theoretical work is supplemented by an annual visit of two or three days to the charitable and correctional institutions of New York City, under Professor Bailey's direction, and is taken also by the members of the Senior class who elect the course in Practical Sociology.

ASSISTANT PROFESSOR BAILEY AND MR. MCGREGOR

JUNIOR YEAR

41 *Systematic Sociology* (required in Course C).   3 hrs.
    Lectures one hour weekly on the historical development of the theories of the leading writers upon this subject. The doctrine of evolution, the organization of society, the formation of the social classes, the conflict of the individual with society, the ethical aspects of social and economic problems will be treated. Two hours per week will be devoted to quiz exercise and discussion upon assigned reading.

ASSISTANT PROFESSOR BAILEY

MIDDLE YEAR

42 *Practical Sociology* (required in Course C).   2 hrs.
    The problems connected with the negro, the concentration of population in cities with the attendant dangers, crime, immigration, the liquor question, and other important American questions will be studied.

SENIOR YEAR

43 *Practical Philanthropy* (required in Course C).   2 hrs.
    The purpose of this course is to enable the student to take charge of the charitable work of a community. To this end the causes of poverty, the means for its prevention, the modern methods of poor relief are studied.

For the University elective courses in Economics and Sociology, see pp. 370–375.

ELOCUTION

MR. LEWIS

The aim of these courses is to fit men to read and speak effectively. They form a progressive series and consist of two distinct lines of work : the practice of technical exercises for the development of voice and body ; the practice of the specific problems presented by the art of reading and speaking. Class-room work will be supplemented by individual work throughout.

For a statement regarding the Downes and Mersick prizes, founded to stimulate an interest in the work of this department, see pages 449 and 450.

JUNIOR YEAR

44 *Voice Training and Vocal Expression* (required in Courses A, B, and C). 1 hr. throughout the year.

This course aims to develop the voice and body as expressive agents.

MIDDLE YEAR

45 *Advanced Vocal Expression and Voice Training* (required in Courses A, B, and C). 1 hr. throughout the year.

This course offers practice in the reading of different forms of literature, including Bible and Hymn reading.

SENIOR YEAR

46 *Advanced Reading and Speaking* (required in Courses A, B, and C). 1 hr. throughout the year.

The aim of this course is to meet the need of each man as a preacher in the delivery of selections from the student's own sermons.

MUSICAL TRAINING

The courses of instruction in the Department of Music are open to Divinity students on the conditions stated in the University Catalogue. These courses, under Professors Parker, Sanford, Jepson, and Knight, include Harmony, Counterpoint, History of Music, Composition, and Instrumentation, affording the fullest opportunities for any one who seeks to perfect his training as a director of church music.

SUPPLEMENTARY PRACTICAL TRAINING

In addition to the more systematic and theoretical courses of study, provision is made by lectures and conferences, and through opportunities for observation and experience, for students to become acquainted with such various forms of administrative work as are required in the life of a pastor.

SCIENCE AND LAW

As preliminary disciplines of high value in themselves, and as especially preparatory to the Philosophical and

Practical courses, members of the Junior class choosing those courses will be required to pursue studies as indicated below.

ORGANIC EVOLUTION
ASSISTANT PROFESSOR LULL

47   *Organic Evolution* (required in Course B).

1 hr. throughout the year.

[See Course XV, B 9, page 176].

For this course the following may be substituted:

DR. KUNKEL

48   *Organic Evolution* (required in Course B).

1 hr. throughout the year.

[See Course XVI, A 3, page 180].

CONSTITUTIONAL LAW
PROFESSOR BALDWIN

49   *American Constitutional Law* (required in Course C).

2 hrs. throughout the year.

[See page 375].

UNIVERSITY ELECTIVES

OPEN TO ALL CLASSES IN THE DIVINITY SCHOOL

The Graduate Courses of Instruction in the University are open to the students of the Divinity School without charge, on conditions prescribed by the Theological Faculty. Undergraduate courses in the University are also open to students of the Divinity School with the consent of the instructor in each case and likewise under conditions prescribed by the Theological Faculty.

For a full list of these courses see Graduate School.

SUBSIDIARY MEANS OF INSTRUCTION
LIBRARIES

The UNIVERSITY LIBRARY contains about 400,000 volumes and many thousands of unbound pamphlets. The Library is particularly strong in theology. The LINONIAN AND BROTHERS LIBRARY contains about 25,000 volumes in general literature. To these Libraries the Divinity students, in common with the other members of the University, have access.

In addition to the periodicals received at the University Library, there will be found in the Reading Rooms nearly two hundred newspapers and current periodicals.

The REFERENCE LIBRARY OF THE DIVINITY SCHOOL, established by the late Henry Trowbridge, Esq., of New Haven, and placed in the Leonard Bacon Memorial Hall, is open for consultation throughout the day and evening. It contains about 4,500 carefully selected volumes, in every department of theological literature, and additions are constantly being made.

The valuable LIBRARY OF CHURCH MUSIC belonging to the late Dr. Lowell Mason was given to the Divinity School by his family. This library contains about 8,000 titles in 4,000 volumes.

The HISTORICAL LIBRARY OF FOREIGN MISSIONS numbers over 7,500 volumes, including pamphlets. It is now an ample collection of the entire body of the Foreign Mission Literature of Europe and America, and with this comprehensive character has become one of the largest special libraries of the kind in the world.

The REFERENCE LIBRARY OF BIBLICAL LITERATURE of the Department of Semitic Languages and Biblical Literature in the University is available to members of the Divinity School.

The SALISBURY COLLECTION of Oriental manuscripts, books, and works of reference, the library of the American Oriental Society, the collection of rare and valuable Arabic manuscripts, made by Count Landberg, acquired for Yale University through the munificence of Morris K. Jesup, Esq., of New York City, and the well-stocked Semitic sections of the general Library, furnish exceptional advantages and opportunities for independent research to the student of Semitic literature.

DIVINITY SCHOOL LECTURESHIPS

The LYMAN BEECHER LECTURESHIP on Preaching (or other topic appropriate to the work of the ministry) was founded in 1871 by a gift of ten thousand dollars from

Mr. Henry W. Sage, then of Brooklyn, N. Y., as a memorial to the great divine whose name it bears. The lectureship is of unique importance in the field of practical
theology, as evidenced by the series of lectures published
in successive volumes. Among the incumbents of the
lectureship may be mentioned Henry Ward Beecher, 1872,
Phillips Brooks, 1877, Robert W. Dale, 1878, Washington
Gladden, 1887 and 1902, James Stalker, 1891, A. M. Fair-
bairn, 1892, R.. F. Horton, 1893, John Watson (Ian
McLaren), 1897, George Adam Smith, 1899, George A.
Gordon, 1902, Lyman Abbott, 1903, Francis Greenwood
Peabody, 1904, Charles R. Brown, 1906, and Principal
Peter T. Forsyth, 1907. The series this year is to be given
by President Faunce, of Brown University.

The NATHANIEL WILLIAM TAYLOR LECTURESHIP in Theology was created in 1902 by the gift of five thousand
dollars from Mrs. Rebecca Taylor Hatch, of Brooklyn,
N. Y., in memory of her father, professor of divinity in
this institution from 1822 to 1858. The lecturers on
this foundation have been, Professor George W. Knox,
1903, President William D. Mackenzie, 1904, Professor
William N. Clarke, 1905, Professor Samuel Satthianad-
han, 1906, President Henry C. King, 1907. The series
this year has been given by Professor Georg Wobbermin,
of the University of Breslau, Germany.

The ALUMNI LECTURESHIP was created in 1902 by vote
of the Faculty. It provides for one or more lectures
each year to be given by an alumnus in recognition of
research carried by him to a successful issue. The next
lecturer will be Rev. Herbert A. Jump, '99.

CLUBS

A number of voluntary associations of instructors and
students exist in the University, whose meetings for the
reading and discussion of papers are open to all students.
Membership in these clubs is open to those who are qualified. Of special interest to divinity students are the

SEMITIC AND BIBLICAL CLUB, the GEORGE B. STEVENS THEOLOGICAL CLUB, the BIBLICAL RESEARCH CLUB, and the PHILOSOPHICAL CLUB.

EXERCISES IN PUBLIC SPEAKING

A rhetorical exercise for all the classes is held every Wednesday, in Marquand Chapel, in the presence of the Faculty, and under the general supervision of the Professor of Practical Theology. Once in two weeks an address is delivered, followed by criticism and discussion. On each alternate week there is an exercise, designed for the cultivation of the power of the students in extemporaneous speaking, as well as for the discussion of subjects of practical importance. These biweekly debates are held under the auspices of the LEONARD BACON DEBATING CLUB.

RELIGIOUS AND SOCIAL PRIVILEGES
PUBLIC WORSHIP

There is daily worship in Marquand Chapel at 12.30 o'clock.

A general prayer meeting of the Divinity School, led by members of the Divinity Faculty or by students, is held on Thursday evenings in Marquand Chapel.

On the Lord's day students have the privilege of listening to many of the most eminent, preachers of this and other countries.

On Friday of each week, in place of the usual chapel service, there is substituted a very brief service with an accompanying address. The speakers represent visitors, resident clergymen, members of the University and Divinity faculties. On Tuesdays the service is largely of a musical character.

CONCERTS

Many opportunities of hearing the best music are open to all students of the University, at moderate cost.

YOUNG MEN'S CHRISTIAN ASSOCIATION

The Young Men's Christian Association of the Divinity School has for its object to deepen the spiritual life of the students, to increase their interest in missions, and to bring them into fellowship with similar associations throughout the world. Occasional addresses are given by persons especially engaged in and familiar with missionary work. Deputation work, in the interest of foreign missions, is carried on by students among churches in adjacent counties of Connecticut.

SOCIAL LIFE

The Lowell Mason Library Room, in West Divinity Hall, is furnished as a Social Room, and serves as a center for the common life of the students. It contains magazines and daily papers, a piano, and other means of recreation.

PHYSICAL EXERCISE

The University Gymnasium, which is complete in all its appointments, is open to the students of this Department at a small charge. The Yale Field is available for baseball and football.

Within the Divinity School enclosure are tennis courts carefully graded and well maintained, with reasonable space for other out-of-door recreation.

INFIRMARY

The Yale Infirmary is open in case of sickness to students of all Departments of the University, affording the best medical attendance and nursing at a minimum cost.

ROOMS AND EXPENSES

BUILDINGS

The buildings of the Divinity School are East and West Divinity Halls, which contain furnished rooms for students; Marquand Chapel, and the Leonard Bacon Memorial Hall, containing the Trowbridge Reference Library.

ASSIGNMENT OF ROOMS

The buildings will be ready for students on Monday of the opening week of the Fall term, and temporary accommodations will be provided for new students whose applications have been received. The assignment of permanent rooms to new students is made on Wednesday, the day before that on which the term opens, at 2 o'clock P. M., in the Lowell Mason Room. The suites, which include a separate bedroom, are designed, for the most part, for one occupant, but a considerable number afford accommodation for two. They are provided with all necessary furniture, except bed-clothes, which may be brought by the occupants, or will be furnished at a moderate charge. Questions regarding location of rooms, disposal of baggage, furniture, bedding, and the like, should be addressed to the Superintendent of the Divinity Buildings, Mr. Ezra P. Merriam, East Divinity Hall.

EXPENSES

The fixed charges for each undergraduate student for the annual session of thirty-two weeks are five dollars for the University Library fee, ten dollars for the care of room, twenty dollars for heating of room (divided in case of two or more occupants), and five dollars for general administrative expenses. Each room is in addition charged for the gas consumed, as indicated by the room meter. No charge is made for tuition.

The University Dining Hall furnishes board at cost (approximating four dollars and a half per week). Board may be obtained at private eating-clubs in the city at about three dollars and a half and upward per week.

The expenses of a student for the school year, exclusive of clothing and sundries, may be estimated as follows :

Care of room	$10.00
Heating of room	10.00 or 20.00
Board, 32 weeks (not counting 4 vacation weeks)	112.00 to 144.00
Incidentals	10.00
Rent of bedding	1.50
Laundry	18.00
Text-books and stationery	20.00 to 50.00
Gymnasium, tennis-courts, etc.	5.00 to 10.00
Subscriptions	5.00
Total	$191.00 to $266.00

By rigid economy the cost of board and of items other than fixed charges may be somewhat reduced.

The charges for an undergraduate student who does not room in the Divinity buildings will be five dollars for the University library fee and five dollars for general administration expenses.

SCHOLARSHIPS AND PRIZES
OPPORTUNITIES FOR SELF-HELP

The long summer vacation is designed to enable students to engage in preaching under the Home Missionary societies, or in other remunerative employment.

During the latter part of the course, a portion of the students receive remuneration for preaching in places easily accessible. The other opportunities for self-help are work in the library, assistance to Professors, service in eating establishments, and those ordinarily open to University students.

GENERAL SCHOLARSHIPS CONDITIONED ON RELIGIOUS WORK

General scholarship funds have been given to the Divinity School by various donors, to enable students of promise to prepare for the Christian ministry, in cases where without such assistance they are unable to do so. By cultivating the spirit of independence, and, at the same time, promoting the practical efficiency of the students themselves, the intention of the donors will be best fulfilled. Scholarship aid is therefore considered not as a gift, but as a means of livelihood obtained by a definite amount of religious work, under competent supervision.

Members of the undergraduate classes whose circumstances require it may make application for scholarship employment, at the beginning of the year. After personal consultation with the Director of Religious Work, each man, whose application is approved, is assigned to service under one of the pastors or mission workers of the city. The assignment and general supervision are in charge of the Director of Religious Work. In consideration for the service received, the pastor or mission worker agrees to give to the student working under him direct supervision and the benefit of his experience. The average amount of time required is six hours per week. The usual remuneration is one hundred dollars per year, payable in semi-annual installments. In cases where the quantity or quality of the work proves conspicuously above or below the standard, the remuneration will be graded accordingly. Regular reports are required from both students and pastors at the end of each term, and payments are made as soon as the work of the student has been pronounced satisfactory.

As one object of the system is to supplement the training given in the Department of Practical Theology, only those employments are selected which involve personal contact with the cases and types which a future pastor is likely to meet, and a study of the personal and parish problems with which he will be confronted. Teaching and public speaking are placed in the background, to leave room for some form of visiting under the guidance of a mature worker. In most cases the student is given a small parish of a few families, for whose religious growth he is largely responsible.

Students whose circumstances do not require scholarship aid, but who desire to have the benefit of the practical training which the system gives, may volunteer for similar work, with the same privilege of mature supervision.

EDUCATION SOCIETY GRANTS

Students intending to enter the Congregational ministry if their circumstances require it, may receive fifty dollars per year, as a grant or loan, from the Congregational Education Society. This aid is conditioned upon good scholarship and high general merit, and requires an examination and certificate by the local committee of the Society.

PRIZE SCHOLARSHIPS

A limited number of prize scholarships of one hundred dollars and fifty dollars each, the former known as the FOGG and the latter as the ALLIS SCHOLARSHIPS, are awarded, on the basis of high scholarship, to members of the several classes at the beginning of each half-year. Candidates for these scholarships for the first half of the Junior year are required to pass an examination in Greek (at sight), Philosophy, and English Literature (in addition Hebrew, History, or Economics may also be offered), on entering the Divinity School, or as may be otherwise arranged with the Faculty. Testimonials and other evidence of previous scholarship will have weight in determining the award. The grade of scholarship required in a candidate for a Fogg Scholarship is that of the Philosophical Oration at Yale College. The regular examinations at the end of each term determine the award of these scholarships for the next succeeding term. A corresponding entrance examination in theological studies equivalent to those of the first or second year is required of candidates for these scholarships who enter the Middle or Senior class as new students.

The Allis Scholarships of fifty dollars each stand in the relation of second prizes to the Fogg Scholarships.

Young men of superior ability and attainments, whose circumstances require it, may thus, through the general and prize scholarships, receive two hundred dollars a year throughout their Divinity course.

Honorary rank is in all cases given to students who are equal in merit to the holders of the Fogg and Allis Scholarships, but whose circumstances are such that they do not require pecuniary assistance.

PREMIUMS

The DOWNES PRIZES, founded in 1896 by the late William E. Downes, Esq., of New Haven, will be awarded to the students of the Senior and Middle classes who shall attain to the highest proficiency in the public reading of the

Scriptures and of Hymns. A first prize of fifty dollars and a second prize of forty dollars will be assigned by a committee appointed by the Faculty to the two successful competitors in each of these classes.

The MERSICK PRIZES, founded in 1906 in memory of the late Charles S. Mersick, Esq., of New Haven, are designed to promote the attainment of effective public address, especially in preaching. For the year 1907–08 prizes will be awarded as follows:

1. Two prizes, of thirty and twenty dollars respectively, are offered to members of the Junior class who have faithfully pursued the course in Elocution, for the best rendering of a selection from a sermon.

2. Three prizes, of twenty-five, fifteen, and ten dollars respectively, are offered to each of the undergraduate classes in the Divinity School, viz., Junior, Middle, and Senior, to be awarded to those members of the classes who exhibit the greatest proficiency in the Department of Elocution.

3. Five prizes of twenty dollars each will be awarded to the Anniversary speakers in the following manner: each of the four speakers selected to represent the Divinity School at its Anniversary shall receive a prize of twenty dollars, and a further prize of twenty dollars shall be awarded to the speaker whose address at the Anniversary shall be deemed best by a committee of judges.

In addition to the Downes and Mersick prizes above described, the John A. Porter University prize, the Cook prize in poetry, the Jacob Cooper prize in Greek Philosophy, the George Washington Egleston historical prize, and the Philo Sherman Bennett prize, are open to students of the Divinity School as well as to students of other Departments of the University.

GRADUATE FELLOWSHIPS

A GRADUATE FELLOWSHIP was established in 1876, as a memorial of the late Mrs. Aurelia D. Hooker, of New Haven. It is assigned at graduation to that member of the class to which it is offered, who, having been connected with the School during, at least, two years of the course, and being of approved Christian character, has, in the judgment of the Faculty, acquired such proficiency in theological studies as best to qualify him for the advantages offered by this foundation for the further prosecution of the same. The person to whom the fellowship is given receives the annual income (six hundred dollars) for two years after graduation, and is expected to pursue a course of theological study under the direction of the Faculty, either as a resident at the School, or, in case he may prefer to do so, in Europe or Palestine. The HOOKER FELLOWSHIP is offered to the classes graduating from the Divinity School in 1909 and in 1911.

A similar GRADUATE FELLOWSHIP yielding five hundred dollars, which has been established as a memorial of the late Mrs. Susan B. Dwight, of New Haven, and will afford to the student who shall receive it the same privileges for one year after graduation, is offered on the same conditions to the classes graduating from the Divinity School in 1908 and 1910.

The Yale Divinity School is a contributor to the schools of the American Institute of Archæology at Rome and Jerusalem. No examinations for entrance are required of the graduates of contributing institutions. A Fellowship in each school is annually assigned, on the basis of competitive examination.

GRADUATE SCHOLARSHIPS

Scholarship aid for the pursuit of fourth-year studies in the Graduate class will, at the discretion of the Faculty, be offered to such members of the Senior class of this School, and to such graduates of other theological schools, as shall, in the judgment of the Faculty, give promise of special success in advanced theological study. Some equivalent service is required.

DEPARTMENT OF MEDICINE
(YALE MEDICAL SCHOOL)
FACULTY

ARTHUR TWINING HADLEY, LL.D., PRESIDENT

HERBERT EUGENE SMITH, M.D., *Dean of the Medical School, and Professor of Chemistry*

WILLIAM HENRY CARMALT, M.D., *Professor of the Principles and Practice of Surgery, Emeritus*

THOMAS HUBBARD RUSSELL, M.D., *Professor of Clinical Surgery, and Lecturer on Surgical Anatomy*

MAX MAILHOUSE, M.D., *Clinical Professor of Neurology*

OLIVER THOMAS OSBORNE, M.D., M.A., *Professor of Materia Medica and Therapeutics, and Clinical Professor of Medicine*

HENRY LAWRENCE SWAIN, M.D., *Clinical Professor of Laryngology and Otology*

ARTHUR NATHANIEL ALLING, M.D., *Clinical Professor of Ophthalmology*

HARRY BURR FERRIS, M.D., *E. K. Hunt Professor of Anatomy*

OTTO GUSTAF RAMSAY, M.D., *Professor of Obstetrics and Gynecology*

RALPH AUGUSTINE MCDONNELL, M.D., *Clinical Professor of Dermatology*

GEORGE BLUMER, M.D., *Professor of the Theory and Practice of Medicine*

CHARLES JOSEPH BARTLETT, M.D., *Professor of Pathology*

JOSEPH MARSHALL FLINT, M.D., *Professor of the Principles and Practice of Surgery*

YANDELL HENDERSON, PH.D., *Assistant Professor of Physiology*

RUSSELL HENRY CHITTENDEN, PH.D., LL.D., SC.D., *Professor of Physiological Chemistry*

FRANK PELL UNDERHILL, PH.D., *Assistant Professor of Physiological Chemistry*

FRANCIS BACON, M.D., SC.D., *Lecturer on Medical Jurisprudence*

EVERETT JAMES MCKNIGHT, M.D., *Instructor in Surgery*

EDWARD KING ROOT, M.D., *Lecturer on Life Insurance Examinations*

WILLIAM GIBBONS DAGGETT, M.D., *Clinical Lecturer on Medicine*

EDWARD MICHAEL MCCABE, M.D., *Clinical Instructor in Ophthalmology*

LOUIS BENNETT BISHOP, M.D., *Instructor in Pediatrics*

WILLIAM HILL BEAN, M.D., *Instructor in Materia Medica*

CHARLES DICKINSON PHELPS, M.D., *Instructor in Physical Diagnosis*

LEONARD CUTLER SANFORD, M.D., *Instructor in Operative Surgery*

WILLIAM SPRENGER, M.D., *Demonstrator of the Uses of X-Rays*

ERNST HERMANN ARNOLD, M.D., *Instructor in Orthopedic Surgery*

ALLEN ROSS DIEFENDORF, M.D., *Lecturer on Psychiatry*

FREDERICK NOYES SPERRY, M.D., *Clinical Instructor in Laryngology*

LOUIS MICHAEL GOMPERTZ, M.D., *Clinical Instructor in Medicine*

DWIGHT MILTON LEWIS, M.D., *Clinical Instructor in Medicine*

CLARENCE GILMAN SPALDING, PH.B., *Demonstrator of Pharmacy*

DAVID RUSSELL LYMAN, M.D., *Clinical Lecturer on Tuberculosis*

ROSWELL PARKER ANGIER, PH.D., *Lecturer on the Physiology of the Special Senses*

THOMAS VINCENT HYNES, M.D., *Clinical Instructor in Obstetrics*

CARLE WILLIAM HENZE, M.D., *Clinical Instructor in Medicine*

CARLTON HOWARD MARYOTT, B.A., *Instructor in Chemistry*

FLORENCE BINGHAM KINNE, M.A., *Laboratory Assistant in Pathology*

HENRY FREDERICK KLENKE, M.D., *Clinical Assistant in Dermatology*

HARRY MERRIMAN STEELE, M.D., *Clinical Assistant in Pediatrics*

HARRY LITTLE WELCH, M.D., *Clinical Assistant in Gynecology*

JOHN EDWARD LANE, M.D., *Clinical Assistant in Medicine*

WILLIS HANFORD CROWE, M.D., *Clinical Assistant in Ophthalmology*

WILLIS ELLIS HARTSHORN, M.D., *Clinical Assistant in Surgery*

RICHARD FOSTER RAND, M.D., *Clinical Assistant in Gynecology and in Surgery*

THOMAS AUGUSTINE O'BRIEN, M.D., *Clinical Assistant in Neurology*

HAROLD SEARS ARNOLD, M.D., *Assistant in Pathology and Bacteriology*

ROBERT GRAHAM TRACY, M.D., *Clinical Assistant in Surgery*

WALTER SIDDERS LAY, M.D., *Clinical Assistant in Pediatrics*

BURTON ISAAC TOLLES, M.D., *Assistant in Anatomy*

FREDERICK GEORGE BECK, M.D., *Clinical Assistant in Gynecology*

ARCHIBALD CECIL HERBERT, M.D., *Clinical Assistant in Medicine*

LOUIS ADOLPH NOTKINS, M.D., *Assistant in Physical Diagnosis*

Frank Billings Standish, M.D., *Clinical Assistant in Medicine*

Seymour Leopold Spier, M.D., *Clinical Assistant in Surgery*

Joseph Leo Gilmore, M.D., *Clinical Assistant in Pediatrics*

Eugene Maurice Blake, M.D., *Clinical Assistant in Ophthalmology*

Mrs. Aleph Kimball Thompson, *Clerk of the Medical School, and Private Secretary to the Dean*

GENERAL STATEMENT

HISTORY

In the fall of 1810 a charter was granted to the President and Fellows of Yale College and the President and Fellows of the Connecticut Medical Society, authorizing them to unite according to the terms of certain "Articles of Union," before agreed upon, for the establishment of a medical seminary, to be styled the Medical Institution of Yale College. Two years later the School was organized, and in the fall of 1813 instruction was begun. The professors of the Faculty were appointed by the College Corporation from nominations by the Medical Society. Degrees were conferred by the College on the recommendation of the board of examiners, consisting of the members of the Faculty and an equal number appointed by the Medical Society. This dual government continued until 1884, when by an amicable arrangement with the Medical Society, the College authorities assumed entire control of the School.

The Medical School now constitutes the Medical Department of the University, and is governed by the Professors of the Faculty of Medicine under the authority of the President and Fellows of the University.

In the early years the instruction consisted of didactic and clinical lectures and dissections during a short winter course. As time passed, changes in the relations between practitioners and students of medicine, and even greater changes in the art and science of medicine, demanded a different kind of instruction, and the course was altered from time to time to meet the varying conditions. In 1879 there had been established a graded course, extending through three years of eight months each and including considerable laboratory instruction. In 1896 the extension of the course to four years permitted a more complete and satisfactory grading of the studies which has formed the basis of the curriculum now in force.

BUILDINGS AND EQUIPMENT

The School owns and occupies three buildings, Medical Hall, the Laboratory Building, and the new University Clinic.

MEDICAL HALL contains the general lecture rooms, the museum, and laboratories of anatomy, histology, pathology, and bacteriology. The lecture rooms are provided with modern electric projection lanterns, and in other ways are well equipped for the lectures and recitations held in them. The laboratories are equipped with the necessary number of modern microscopes as well as with complete outfits for bacteriological research, and for the study of blood, sputum, and other objects of clinical interest. The collections of anatomy, pathology, and materia medica supply material for the class-room demonstrations, and for individual study by students in the laboratories.

The LABORATORY BUILDING contains the lecture rooms and laboratories of physiology and chemistry. The lecture rooms are well equipped for the special work carried on in them, and the laboratories are abundantly supplied with apparatus and materials for the class work as well as for research.

The UNIVERSITY CLINIC has been recently erected and equipped by the University at a cost of about one hundred thousand dollars. It is opposite the New Haven Hospital, and is a three-story building admirably arranged and fully equipped for the work carried on in it. The greater part of the first and second stories is occupied by the New Haven Dispensary. This portion consists of two large waiting rooms, and twenty-five consulting, examining, and operating rooms which are equipped for the special requirements of the different clinics. In the third story is a comfortably furnished dormitory for the use of students attending the out-patient obstetrical service. The building also contains an amphitheatre and lecture room for general and clinical lectures in the practical branches. ·

Aside from the general University endowment, the advantages of which the Medical School shares with the other Departments, the Medical School has a special endowment fund of somewhat over two hundred thousand dollars. This includes the Hunt and Ely memorial professorship endowments. The first was founded in 1896 by a bequest of twenty-five thousand dollars from Mrs. E. K. Hunt as an endowment of the Chair of Anatomy in memory of Ebenezer K. Hunt, M.D., a graduate of Yale College in 1833. In 1906 the School received a gift of fifty thousand dollars from an anonymous donor to endow a professorship in memory of John Slade Ely, M.D., Professor of the Theory and Practice of Medicine in the Medical Faculty from 1897 to 1906.

CLINICAL FACILITIES

The NEW HAVEN HOSPITAL, with a capacity of about 200 beds, is situated but a short distance from the Medical School buildings and offers abundant opportunity for clinical instruction. The service is an active one, as the Hospital is the principal one in the city, which is a large manufacturing and railroad center. The Farnam Operating Theatre is modern in all its equipments, and was planned with special reference to making the operations available for purposes of instruction to students. A Clinical Amphitheatre has been added recently to the Hospital for the better accommodation of the medical clinics and affords the best facilities for the demonstration of cases, and of special methods of examination. The Maternity Building, which has been completed recently, is closely connected with the other hospital buildings and affords the most modern appliances for the obstetrical service.

The NEW HAVEN DISPENSARY occupies a part of the University Clinic. The service consists of more than 17,000 consultations annually, and furnishes ample clinical facilities for the demonstration of disease processes, and is especially valuable in giving students an opportunity to see the ambulant types of disease. The service is divided into the following departments : Internal medicine ; surgery ; orthopedic surgery ; ophthalmology ; laryngology, otology and rhinology ; neurology ; gynecology and obstetrics, including an out-patient department ; pediatrics ; dermatology; and the X-Ray Laboratory. Besides the general clinics which are held in all of these departments, the Dispensary furnishes abundant material for the classes in physical diagnosis, and numerous courses of demonstrations to small groups of students. The Seniors participate in the regular work of all the clinics, to which they are appointed as assistants in rotation.

The STATE HOSPITAL FOR THE INSANE, situated at Middletown, accommodates about 2000 patients. By a recent arrangement the instruction in psychiatry will be combined with clinics at this Hospital. The large number of patients give ample facilities for the demonstration for all forms of insanity, and allied ailments.

The GAYLORD FARM SANATORIUM, located at Wallingford, is devoted to the treatment of Tuberculosis, and accommodates about 60 patients. During each year the Seniors attend a series of clinical demonstrations by Dr. Lyman and receive special instruction on the sanatorium treatment of this class of patients.

LIBRARY FACILITIES

The LIBRARIES—The University Library contains about 400,000 volumes and includes the Medical Library. The University subscribes annually for the most important of the French, German, English, and American journals. The Medical Library is an important part of the facilities of this School, as it gives the student ample opportunities of working in special lines. Medical students have the same privileges of consulting and drawing books as students in the other Departments of the University. A small circulating library of recent medical books is maintained in the alumni room in Medical Hall by the editors of the Yale Medical Journal.

PREPARATION FOR MEDICAL STUDY

The Faculty would urge those intending to find their life work in the profession of medicine to consider the advantages to be derived from first pursuing a baccalaureate course in some good college.

Attention is also called to the possibility of combining the College and Medical School courses. Such a combined course has been provided in this University by placing the studies comprising the first two years of the Medical School course among the elective studies offered students of Yale College. An Academical student, therefore, may pursue one or all of the studies required in the first two years of the Medical School course, and thus advance himself in his preparation for clinical studies while still retaining the benefits of the Academical training and associations. If he elects all of these studies he may register as a student of the Medical School, and on graduation from the College will be able to proceed at once to the clinical studies of the Junior year of the Medical School, thus being eligible for the degree of M.D. in two years after receiving the B.A.

Attention is also called to the desirability of pursuing adequate courses in physics, chemistry, and general biology before beginning the study of medicine. Arrangements have been made in the University by which students of the Medical School who elect to devote five years to the course may pursue certain courses in the Academical Department, among which are French, German, Physics, Chemistry, and elementary Biology.

ADMISSION
CHANGE IN REQUIREMENTS

Candidates for admission to the 97th Annual Session beginning in September, 1909, must qualify in the educational requirements in one of the following ways:

1. Candidates who have received degrees in Arts or Science from approved universities or colleges will be admitted on presenting their diplomas or other satisfactory testimonials.

2. Other candidates must present evidence that they have complied with the entrance requirements of some collegiate institution of good standing or have passed equivalent examinations before some recognized examining board such as the College Entrance Examination Board. They must also present evidence that they have performed with credit the equivalent of at least two full years of work of collegiate grade of fifteen hours per week. Such evidence may be furnished by certificate from an institution of good standing. Candidates from institutions not able to give this certificate but who have otherwise fitted themselves for the study of medicine by work of corresponding grade may qualify by examination in this University on payment of a fee of ten dollars.

All candidates for admission must furnish evidence that they have a satisfactory preparation in Physics, General Inorganic Chemistry, and General Biology.

MATRICULATION REQUIREMENTS FOR STUDENTS ENTERING IN 1908

Candidates for admission to the first year of the course leading to the degree of Doctor of Medicine must present satisfactory testimonials of moral character from former instructors or physicians in good standing, and must qualify in the educational requirements in one of the ways stated below.

1. Candidates who have received degrees in Arts or Science from approved universities or colleges will be

admitted on presenting their diplomas or other satisfactory testimonials.

2. Other candidates must show by certificates that they have qualified in the required subjects as indicated in the list of subjects of examination given below, and in enough elective studies to make up the necessary fifteen units. To be acceptable the certificates of qualification must be based: (a) On examinations for admission to Yale College, the Sheffield Scientific School, or other approved academic institutions, or on examinations conducted by the College Entrance Examination Board. (b) On graduation from a course covering four years in an approved high school, academy, or preparatory school. Blank qualification certificates may be obtained' by applying to the Dean.

Candidates whose certificates being otherwise satisfactory do not cover the required subject, Physics, may qualify in this branch by examination before a committee of the Medical Faculty.

Candidates who desire to qualify in whole, or in part, by examination before the College Entrance Examination Board are informed that these examinations are held each year about the middle of June in many cities throughout the United States. Information concerning the requirements for admission to these examinations and the places and dates of holding them may be obtained by application to the Dean. Candidates are urged to make their applications as early as possible, and not later than May 1.

SUBJECTS FOR EXAMINATION

Candidates entering on certificates must qualify in all of the required subjects amounting to six units, and in elective studies amounting to nine units, making the necessary total of fifteen units.

Required subjects:

   1. English Readings (The equivalent of Yale College
       English a and b or The College Entrance Examination Board a and b) . :   .   .   3 units

    2. Latin Grammar and Elementary Latin Prose,   .   1 unit
    3. Algebra to Quadratics, ...   1 unit
    4. Physics, ...   1 unit

Elective subjects:

    5. Cæsar, books I–IV, ...   1 unit
    6. Vergil's Aeneid, books I–VI, ...   1 unit
    7. Ovid—Metamorphoses, 2,500 lines, .   .   .   ½ unit
    8. Cicero—Six Orations, ...   1 unit
    9. Advanced Prose Composition,   .   .   .   ½ unit
    10. Greek Grammar and Elementary Prose Composition,   1 unit
    11. Xenophon—Anabasis, books I–IV, .   .   .   1 unit
    12. Homer—Iliad, books I–III, ...   1 unit
    13. Advanced Prose Composition,   .   .   .   ½ unit
    14. Ancient History, ...   1 unit
    15. Medieval and Modern European History,   .   .   1 unit
    16. English History, ...   1 unit
    17. American History and Civil Government,   .   .   1 unit
    18. Elementary French (Yale College a),   .   .   1 unit
    19. Advanced French (Yale College b), .   .   .   2 units
    20. Elementary German (Yale College a),   .   .   1 unit
    21. Advanced German (Yale College b),   .   .   2 units
    22. Advanced Algebra (Yale College b),   .   .   1 unit
    23. Plane Geometry, ...   1 unit
    24. Solid Geometry, ...   1 unit
    25. Trigonometry, ...   ½ unit
    26. Chemistry, ...   1 unit
    27. Botany, ...   1 unit
    28. Zoology, ...   1 unit
    29. General Biology, ...   1 unit
    30. Astronomy, ...   ½ unit
    31. Geology, ...   ½ unit
    32. Physical Geography, ...   ½ unit
    33. Physiology, ...   ½ unit

ADMISSION TO ADVANCED STANDING

Students who have studied one year in some other recognized medical institution may be admitted to the Second Year class, and those who have studied two years may be admitted to the Junior class, but students are not received from other schools into the Senior class. Students applying for advanced standing must meet the matriculation requirements, must have pursued studies reasonably equivalent to those already pursued by the class to which they seek admission, and must pass the examinations of the First Year for admission to the Second Year class, and of the First and Second Years for admission to the Junior class. These examinations may be taken in June with the class by applying to the Dean at least four weeks before Commencement, or they may be taken at the time of the autumn examinations, just before the beginning of the school year in September. Graduates in Arts, Philosophy, or Science, who have pursued studies in chemistry, physiology, anatomy, or histology during their undergraduate courses, may receive credit for such work as is the equivalent of the courses in these studies in the First year, and may fill out the number of hours required of First year students by pursuing certain advanced studies with the Second Year class, or by pursuing studies in the Graduate School.

TERMS AND VACATIONS

The annual sessions of the School are divided into three terms, covering thirty-five weeks, exclusive of a vacation of three weeks at Christmas and a recess at Easter usually of one week.

The first term begins with the last Thursday in September, and continues twelve weeks. The second term begins on the Wednesday after the first Thursday in January, and continues twelve weeks. The third term is eleven weeks in length, ending with Commencement. (See Calendar.)

INSTRUCTION
METHODS

The instruction in this School is conducted by recitations and lectures in the class-room, and by personal work in the laboratories and clinics.

The class-room work of the first and second years is chiefly by recitations from assigned readings, with which are combined frequent demonstrations and explanatory lectures. In the third and fourth years, lectures are more employed, but the instruction is still based for the most part on assigned readings in text-books.

The curriculum of the first two years contains a very large proportion of laboratory work which extends to the third and fourth years, but is largely replaced in the latter period by personal clinical work. The laboratories are thoroughly equipped for systematic and accurate work, and such work is exacted from the student. In the clinical instruction less dependence is placed upon formal clinical lectures, and more upon personal instruction to small classes, and to individual students.

Advancement from one class to the next depends not only on the results of examinations but also on the records of the student's daily work as expressed in his term standing.

THE CURRICULUM

The curriculum of this School is graded to furnish in four years a systematic presentation of the various subjects of medical study. When a subject is pursued two years the course is a progressive one, in which the work of the second year is not a repetition of that of the first.

The arrangement of the curriculum is such that the student spends the first and second years on the fundamental branches, chemistry, physiology, anatomy, histology, pathology, and materia medica.

The third year he devotes chiefly to a systematic study of medicine, surgery, obstetrics, and pharmacology.

In the Senior year he continues the study of medicine and surgery and has a systematic presentation of the chief specialties in a series of recitations and lectures, combined with general clinics and section work.

SYNOPSIS OF THE CURRICULUM

N. B.   The number of hours means hours per week.

FIRST YEAR

ANATOMY — *Recitations, Lectures,* and *Demonstrations,* Osteology, Arthrology, Myology, 3 hours throughout the year, Professor Ferris. *Laboratory, Dissections,* 15 hours second term, Professor Ferris and Dr. Tolles.

HISTOLOGY — *Recitations* and *illustrated Lectures,* 1 hour first and second terms, Professor Ferris. *Laboratory,* Microscopical technique and histology of normal tissues, 4 hours first and second terms, Professor Ferris, Dr. H. S. Arnold, and assistants.

EMBRYOLOGY — *Recitations* and *Lectures*, 2 hours third term, Professor Ferris. *Laboratory*, 4 hours third term, Professor Ferris, Dr. H. S. Arnold, and assistant s.

PHYSIOLOGY—*Elementa ryPhysiology*, *Lectures*, 1 hour throughout the year, Professor Chittenden ; *Recitations*, 2 hours first term, 3 hours first half second term, Professor Henderson. *Physiological Chemistry*, *Lectures*, 3 hours second half-year, Professor Chittenden ; *Laboratory*, 9 hours, Professor Underhill and Mr. Maryott.

GENERAL CHEMISTRY—*Recitations* and *experimental Demonstrations*. The elements and their compounds, 4 hours first term, 2 hours first half of second term, Professor Smith and Mr. Maryott. *Analytical Chemistry*, *Class-room*, 1 hour first term, Mr. Maryott. *Laboratory*, 12 hours first term, 9 hours first half of second term, Professor Smith and Mr. Maryott. *Theoretical* and *Physical Chemistry*, *Recitations* and *Demonstrations*, 2 hours second half-year, Mr. Maryott.

ORGANIC CHEMISTRY — *Recitations*, Constitution and properties of organic compounds, 3 hours second and third terms, Professor Smith.

ANNUAL EXAMINATIONS—(1) General Chemistry, including a laboratory examination at the end of the first term. (2) Organic Chemistry. (3) Physiology and Physiological Chemistry. (4) Anatomy. (5) Histology and Embryology. .

SECOND YEAR

ANATOMY—Continued. *Recitations* and *Demonstrations*, Angeiology, Neurology, Splanchnology, Topographical Anatomy, 3 hours throughout the year, Professor Ferris. *Laboratory*, *Dissections*, 15 hours first or second term, Professor Ferris and Dr. Tolles.

PHYSIOLOGY—Finished. *Lectures* and *Recitations*, 2 hours first and second terms, 4 hours, third term, Professor Henderson, 2 hours first and second term, Dr. Angier. *Laboratory*, 4 hours first and second terms, Professor Henderson.

PHARMACY AND MATERIA MEDICA—*Demonstration* of pharmaceutical methods, 2 hours, second half second term, Mr. Spalding. *Recitations* and *Demonstrations*, Classification of drugs, local therapeutic measures, prescription writing, 2 hours third term, Professor Osborne and Dr. Bean.

PHARMACOLOGY — *Laboratory*, Experimental demonstrations of the methods of studying the action of drugs, in the laboratory course in physiology, Professor Henderson. *Lectures* with *Demonstrations* in toxicology, 20 lectures third term, Professor Chittenden.

PATHOLOGY—*Recitations* and *Demonstrations*, General and special Pathology, 2 hours first term, 4 hours second and third terms, Professor Bartlett. *Laboratory*, Histology of morbid tissues, 6 hours second and third terms, Professor Bartlett and Dr. H. S. Arnold.

BACTERIOLOGY—*Recitations*, 2 hours first term, Professor Bartlett. *Laboratory*, Technique, preparation of media, pure cultures, etc., 9 hours first term, Professor Bartlett and Dr. H. S. Arnold.

EXAMINATIONS—(1) Anatomy. (2) Physiology. (3) Materia Medica. (4) Pathology. (5) Bacteriology.

JUNIOR YEAR

PHARMACOLOGY—*Recitations* and *Lectures*, Action and therapeutic uses of drugs, 3 hours throughout the year, Professor Osborne.

THERAPEUTICS—*Lectures*, History of Medicine, physical therapy, climatology, dietetics, 1 hour third term, Professor Osborne.

PATHOLOGY—Autopsies, Professor Bartlett.

MEDICINE—*Recitations* and *Lectures*, 3 hours first, second, and third terms, Professor Blumer. *Clinics*, General medical, New Haven Hospital, 3 hours, Professor Blumer and Dr. Daggett. University Clinic, daily, Professors Blumer and Osborne and Drs. Gompertz, Lewis, and Henze. *Laboratory*, Clinical microscopy, 2 hours second and third terms, Professor Blumer and Dr. Lewis. *Physical Diagnosis*, Systematic practical study of physical signs and methods of examination, 3 hours half a year, in sections, Dr. Phelps. *Neurology*, *Recitations*, 1 hour second and third terms, Professor Mailhouse. *Dermatology*, 1 hour second and third terms, Professor McDonnell.

SURGERY—*Recitations* and *Lectures*, 3 hours, Professor Flint and Dr. McKnight. *Bandaging*, Practical work in sections, 1 hour third term, Dr. Hartshorn. *Surgical Anatomy*, *Lectures*, 1 hour first term, Professor Russell. *Clinics*, General surgical, 2 hours at the University Clinic, Professor Carmalt and Professor Flint, 3 hours at the New Haven Hospital, Professor Carmalt, Professor Flint, and Professor Russell.

OBSTETRICS—*Recitations* and *Lectures*, 2 hours throughout the year, Professor Ramsay. *Demonstrations* with the manikin, mechanism of labor, Dr. Hynes.

GYNECOLOGY—*Recitations*, 2 hours first term, 1 hour second and third terms, Professor Ramsay.

ANNUAL EXAMINATIONS—(1) Pharmacology. (2) Obstetrics and Gynecology. (3) Medicine. (4) Surgery.

SENIOR YEAR

THERAPEUTICS—*Recitations* and *Lectures*, 1 hour throughout the year, Professor Osborne. *Therapeutic Clinics*, Applied therapeutics, with *Section work*, throughout the year, University Clinic, Professor Osborne.

OBSTETRICS—*Demonstrations* with the manikin and *Obstetric Surgery*, in sections, first term. *Midwifery Clinic, Demonstrations,* and *Section work,* with reports of cases attended by students, Professor Ramsay and Dr. Hynes.

GYNECOLOGY—*Clinics, Lectures, Section work,* Diagnosis and treatment, throughout the year, University Clinic and New Haven Hospital, Professor Ramsay.

SURGERY—*Lectures,* special topics, Professor Flint. *Clinics,* General surgical, 2 hours throughout the year, University Clinic, Professor Carmalt and Professor Flint. *Section work,* throughout the year, Professor Carmalt. *Ward Classes* and *Operations,* 3 hours throughout the year, New Haven Hospital, Professor Carmalt, Professor Flint, and Professor Russell.

OPERATIVE SURGERY—*Recitations,* 2 hours first term, Dr. Sanford. *Section work,* Operations on the cadaver, second term, Dr. Sanford.

GENITO-URINARY SURGERY—*Recitations* and *Lectures,* 1 hour second and third terms, Professor Russell.

ORTHOPEDIC SURGERY—*Lectures* and *Section work,* throughout the year, University Clinic, Dr. E. H. Arnold.

OPHTHALMOLOGY — *Lectures,* 1 hour first term, Professor Alling. *Clinics* and *Section work,* throughout the year, University Clinic, Professor Alling and Dr. McCabe.

LARYNGOLOGY AND RHINOLOGY—*Lectures,* 2 hours first term, 1 hour second term, Professor Swain. *Section work* and *Manikin Practice,* throughout the year, University Clinic, Dr. Sperry.

MEDICINE—*Lectures,* 2 hours, Professor Blumer. *Clinics,* general, New Haven Hospital, 3 hours, Professor Blumer and Dr. Daggett. *Special* and *Section work,* daily throughout the year, University Clinic, Professors Blumer and Osborne, and assistants.

DERMATOLOGY—*Clinics, Lectures,* and *Demonstrations,* 1 hour throughout the year, University Clinic, Professor McDonnell.

PEDIATRICS—*Recitations,* 2 hours first term, Dr. Bishop. *Section work,* throughout the year, University Clinic, Dr. Bishop.

NEUROLOGY—University Clinic, *Section work* and *Special Clinics,* throughout the year, Professor Mailhouse; New Haven Hospital, *Clinics,* 1 hour second term, Professor Mailhouse.

PSYCHIATRY—*Recitations,* 1 hour first term, with *Clinics* at the State Hospital, Dr. Diefendorf.

SANITARY SCIENCE—*Lectures,* 1 hour second and third terms, Professor Smith.

LIFE INSURANCE EXAMINATIONS — *Six Lectures,* second term, Dr. Root.

MEDICAL JURISPRUDENCE—*Lectures,* 2 hours second term, Dr. Francis Bacon, Professors Smith and Bartlett, and Dr. Diefendorf.

ANNUAL EXAMINATIONS—(1) Therapeutics. In Medicine (2) Clinical Examination of Cases; (3) Medicine I (Psychiatry, Pediatrics, Neurology); (4) Medicine II (Dermatology, Sanitary Science, Medical Jurisprudence); (5) (Senior Surgery, Operative Surgery, Genito-urinary Surgery); (6) Special Surgery (Orthopedic Surgery, Otology and Rhino-laryngology, Ophthalmology); (7) A Thesis.

CHEMISTRY

The instruction in this department is given by laboratory work, combined with recitations and explanatory lectures, very completely illustrated by experimental demonstrations and specimens.

The department has two large working laboratories fully equipped for analytical and physiological chemistry. In them each student is supplied with a desk and ample apparatus for systematic and accurate experimental work. The lecture room is furnished with a projection lantern, abundant apparatus for demonstration, and a large chemical collection. The research laboratory is well equipped and is open to advanced students.

GENERAL CHEMISTRY—During the first half-year the instruction is given in a course of recitations and experimental demonstrations covering the reactions and characters of the more common elements and compounds. In the second half-year the time is devoted to a fuller presentation of theoretical chemistry and of physical chemistry.

ORGANIC CHEMISTRY—This subject is taught during the second and third terms in a course of recitations and experimental demonstrations. Much attention is devoted to the constitution and relations of the different classes of organic compounds, and many of the typical bodies are prepared before the class as demonstrations. The course includes also a special study of the compounds of physiological interest.

ANALYTICAL CHEMISTRY—*Qualitative Analysis* is taught so far as to enable the students to analyze a mixture of the salts of the common metals. The course is systematic and is well adapted to cultivate habits of observation and the analytical method of thought. In *Quantitative Analysis* each student makes a number of typical determinations by volumetric and gravimetric methods.

PHYSIOLOGICAL AND CLINICAL CHEMISTRY—Physiological Chemistry is taught in the chemical laboratories as a part of the course in physiology, and clinical chemistry is a part of the laboratory course in medicine of the Junior year.

Two examinations are held in this department, one in general chemistry, including analytical chemistry, and one in organic chemistry. The results of these examinations, together with the records of the student's practical work, determine his standing for the year.

ANATOMY

SYSTEMATIC ANATOMY—The course in this subject is graded and extends through the first two years. The instruction is given by means of dissections, recitations, class and section demonstrations, and lectures illustrated by charts, models, wet and dry preparations, and lantern slides. The lectures are intended to be explanatory and supplemental and for the elucidation of the general principles of morphology. The laboratory is well equipped, and ample material, well preserved by embalming and refrigeration, is furnished. Each student is required to make a careful dissection of the three parts of the body at least once. At the completion of a part a quiz is held with each student, which, with the recitations and written examination at the end of the year, determines his standing.

First Year—The work of the first year is devoted to osteology, arthrology, and myology. Each student is furnished with a box containing a skeleton for home study. The study of the soft structures is prosecuted in the laboratory under constant supervision, and two parts at least must be dissected, occupying a period of about twelve weeks.

Second Year—The dissection of at least one part is required this year. The anatomy of the peritoneum, the thoracic and abdominal viscera, and of the eye and brain, are carefully demonstrated to the students in small groups. The study of surface form and topography in the cadaver and model is an important part of the work. The embryology of each organ is reviewed in connection with its structure, and the salient facts of comparative morphology, especially of the brain, alimentary, circulatory, and respiratory organs, are explained. During the second term a special course in the anatomy of the brain is given. The examination at the end of the year includes angeiology, neurology, splanchnology, and topographical anatomy.

HISTOLOGY—Instruction in histology is given by recitations and lectures illustrated by charts, blackboard drawings, and lantern slides, but chiefly by laboratory work. The recitations and lectures precede and prepare for the better interpretation of the specimens in the laboratory. The laboratory is large, well lighted and equipped, and each student is furnished a microscope and locker containing a box with all necessary apparatus and reagents. First the elementary tissues and their morphological units are studied by fresh and unstained specimens as well as by stained ones, then the various organs are systematically taken up. The student prepares, stains, and mounts the specimens so far as is practicable, making drawings of each with explanatory notes. At the beginning of each laboratory exercise, the specimens for the day are demonstrated by an excellent electric projection apparatus experience having shown this method of instruction to be very helpful

Systematic instruction is given in the methods of fixing, embedding, and sectioning tissues, and in the structure and functions of the various parts of the microscope and accessory optical appliances.

A practical and written examination is held at the end of the year covering the subJects of histology and the microscope and microscopical technology, which together with the recitations, laboratory work, and drawing books determines the student's standing.

Facilities are offered and assistance given to students who are making original investigations in connection with their theses.

. EMBRYOLOGY—The method of instruction in this branch is similar to that in histology. The laboratory work consists of a study of the early development of the chick by surface views and serial sections, of a pig of ten millimeters in length and of the structure of the human decidua, placenta, and cord. The cabinet furnishes serial sections of the human embryo which are used for reference. Congenital malformations and vestigial structures are considered and explained. Some attention is given to embryological technology and reconstructions. The examination is incorporated with that of histology and is of a similar nature.

TOPOGRAPHICAL AND SURGICAL ANATOMY—The Junior students receive instruction in the topographical and special surgical relationships of anatomy in a course of lectures, with demonstrations on the living model and the cadaver.

PHYSIOLOGY

The work in this department is given during the first two years and is arranged in five courses.

(1) The introductory courses of the first year are elementary in character, but of such scope as to cover practically the whole field of human physiology. They are designed to afford a general acquaintance with the various aspects of physiology as a broad basis for the specialized courses which follow. The work consists of recitations supplemented by informal lectures and abundant demonstrations of the fundamental phenomena of physiological functions.

(2) The laboratory course in physiological chemistry, of a minimum of nine hours per week during the second half-year, is devoted to the study of the chemistry of the principal tissues and secretions, of the food substances and digestive processes, of respiration, and metabolism. A metabolism experiment extending over one week is also performed by each student upon himself. In connection with this course the instructor demonstrates many of the more important experiments upon secretion and the mechanism of its control in the submaxillary gland, stomach, pancreas, and kidney, and upon the alimentary canal, etc.

(3) The physiology of muscle and nerve, the circulation, and the mechanics and nervous control of respiration, are worked out in the laboratory during the first and second terms of the second year. After the student has acquired proficiency in the technique of graphic methods by experiments upon the frog, he is instructed in the methods of hæmodynamics. Each student then performs many of the more important experiments demonstrating the hydraulic principles and nervous control of the circulation.

Further training in the application of experimental methods is obtained by the study of the physiological action of drugs. The student works out for himself in the laboratory the action on the circulation, respiration, and nervous system, of at least one example of each of the chief classes of drugs.

Each student is assigned a topic to be studied in the original literature, and is required to present a report before the class. These reports are then discussed by the class under the guidance of the instructor. Topics which can not be conveniently treated in this manner are discussed by the instructor in informal lectures. The information gained by the various methods above indicated is reviewed and summarized in connection with assigned lessons in a text-book.

(4) The organs of the special senses and the psychic functions of the central nervous system are taken up in a special course in the Psychological Laboratory of Yale College during the first and second terms. The method of instruction consists in lectures, experiments, the reading of a text-book and assigned papers, and by special demonstrations.

(5) During the third term the subject of pathological physiology is pursued by means of lectures, demonstrations, assigned lessons in a text-book, and reports by the students on special topics in the literature.

MATERIA MEDICA AND THERAPEUTICS

Instruction in this department begins in the second term of the Second year and extends through the remainder of this year and through the whole of the Junior and Senior years.

PHARMACY—This subject is begun in the latter half of the Second year with a series of laboratory demonstrations and lectures. A text-book on pharmacy and prescription writing is begun in this course, and a written examination is held as soon as the course is completed.

During the next six months each student in turn is required to spend at least fifty hours working under instruction in the prescription department of a drug store selected by the demonstrator of pharmacy. In this course each student is required to make various pharmacopœial preparations and compound various prescriptions.

He is also required to watch the preparation of the various prescriptions that come into the store.   Students are also encouraged to spend fifty more hours in the prescription department of some drug store or hospital some time during the Junior year.

MATERIA MEDICA—The study of this subject is begun in the last term of the Second year, and is taught by demonstrations of crude drugs and their preparations, and by recitations from a text-book.   The various methods and apparatus used in all local therapeutic measures are taught by text-book recitation, and by demonstration.

PRESCRIPTION WRITING is taught by text-book recitations in the last term of the Second year, and by blackboard exercises during this term and throughout the Junior year.   During the Senior year the students are appointed to act as clerks in the Dispensary clinics and write prescriptions under the supervision of the assistants.

PHARMACOLOGY—Instruction in this subject begins during the Second year, in the physiological laboratory, with demonstrations of the action of the most important drugs.   The students are assigned in turn to take active part in these pharmacological experiments, and all are required to keep notes and to take quizzes on the work done.   The study of this subject is continued by lectures, and by recitations from a text-book during the Junior year.

TOXICOLOGY—This subject is chiefly studied in the course on pharmacology, but is specially treated in a course of lectures and demonstrations during the last term of the Second year, and from the chemical side in the course in medical jurisprudence in the Senior year.

THERAPEUTICS—This subject is introduced in the latter part of the Junior year by a series of lectures on the history of medicine from the earliest times, particular attention being given to the gradual evolution of scientific rational treatment.   Lectures are then given on electricity, massage, hydrotherapy, organotherapy, climatology, and dietetics.   The subject is continued throughout the Senior year by lectures and recitations on the treatment and results of treatment of internal diseases.   In the therapeutic clinic the treatment and results of treatment are especially emphasized.

Written examinations are held at the end of the Second, Junior, and Senior years.   Advancement depends on these examinations and the term standing.

PATHOLOGY

Instruction in pathology is given in the Second and Junior years. The systematic course in the subject comes in the Second year.   It consists of a recitation and lecture course combined with laboratory work.   The first part of the course is devoted to general pathology, including the study of bacterial lesions and tumors.   This is followed by a detailed review of the special pathology of the important organs. The class-room exercises are illustrated by specimens from the autopsies and the museum.

The laboratory has an excellent equipment, being abundantly supplied with modern microscopes, which are furnished each student, together with the requisite apparatus and reagents. The laboratory course in pathological histology is systematic, and includes a study of the more important pathological processes and morbid tissues. Each student prepares a large collection of typical specimens, which becomes his own property. During the second term of the Second year, one exercise each week is devoted to the demonstration and study of gross pathological specimens. Particular attention is given to pathological technique. The various methods of preserving tissues both for gross and microscopic purposes are emphasized. Material obtained from cases in the clinics, and from the more interesting autopsies of the year, is used by the class for gross and microscopic purposes. In the Junior year attendance at the morgue of the New Haven Hospital is required, and the members of the class assist in performing the autopsies.

BACTERIOLOGY—A laboratory course in this subject with recitations and lectures is given during the first term of the Second year. This is preliminary to the study of the lesions produced by bacteria, which is taken up in the systematic course in pathology. Each student is provided with a desk and apparatus, and receives instruction in the principles and methods of sterilization, the preparation of the ordinary culture media, and the methods of growing, staining, and studying the various bacteria. Especial attention is given to such bacteriological methods as have been found of value in clinical diagnosis.

Facilities are offered for original research by this department both in the microscopical and bacteriological laboratories.

OBSTETRICS AND GYNECOLOGY

The instruction in this department extends through the Junior and Senior years.

THEORY AND PRACTICE OF OBSTETRICS—The principles are thoroughly taught in a course of recitations and lectures extending through the Junior year.

PRACTICAL OBSTETRICS—The theoretical instruction is supplemented by manikin and clinical work. The various positions of the foetus *in utero* and the mechanism of labor are taught in a manikin course during the Junior year. This course is preparatory to the clinical work of the Senior year. The symptoms and signs of pregnancy are demonstrated in the midwifery clinic at the University Clinic. Each member of the graduating class is required to attend at least two cases of

labor, and to present a written report on them.   Provision is made
for this service at the University Clinic, where lodgings are provided
for students in attendance.

OBSTETRIC SURGERY—The various obstetrical operations are taught
in the first half of the Senior year in a course of lectures and demonstrations on the manikin.

GYNECOLOGY—The principles of gynecology are taught in a course
of recitations during the Junior year.   This theoretical work is supplemented by clinical lectures in the Senior year, and by a course in
diagnosis and treatment taken by the students in small sections as
they are assigned to the clinics.

MEDICINE

The instruction in the branches belonging to this department begins
in the third term of the Second year and continues through the Junior
and Senior years.

PATHOLOGICAL PHYSIOLOGY—During the third term of the Second
year a course of lectures with demonstrations is given, discussing the
relations of normal to pathological physiology, and covering substantially the ground gone over in Krehl's well known work on pathological physiology.

THE PRINCIPLES AND PRACTICE OF MEDICINE—During the Junior
year systematic instruction in the Principles and Practice of Medicine
is given.   The student is made familiar with the important diseases by
means of recitations, based on an approved text-book, supplemented
by explanatory talks.   At the same time he is taught the methods of
examination in a course of practical instruction in physical diagnosis,
supplemented by courses in history-taking and medical technics.   He
also attends general medical clinics at the University Clinic, and at
the New Haven Hospital.   During the second and third terms of the
year a course in Clinical Microscopy is added, in which instruction is
given in the chemical and microscopical methods employed in the
examination of the blood, exudates, transudates, sputum, stomach
contents, urine, and fæces.

During the Senior year text-book instruction is discarded.   During
the first term the more unusual diseases, not covered during the systematic course of the Junior year, are discussed in a weekly seminar,
the students looking up literature on assigned subjects, and reading
brief reports on the same to the class.   Throughout the year one hour
a week is devoted to so-called " case teaching," *i. e.*, training in the
methods of reaching a diagnosis from the study of the history and
physical findings in a given case.   During the third term a short lantern slide course illustrating the diseases recognizable on sight, such
as acromegaly, cretinism, etc., is given.

In the Hospital two medical clinics are held weekly. These clinics are devoted to the discussion of the diagnosis, prognosis, and treatment of medical cases which have been studied by the Senior students, who present them before the Senior and Junior classes under the guidance of the instructor.

At the University Clinic the Senior students attend two clinical lectures a week, but most of their time is devoted to section work. Each student serves a stated time in the medical clinic, during which he receives instruction in case taking, and is required to take histories of, examine, and prescribe for patients under the direction of an instructor. Each student also serves a stated time in the clinical laboratory, where he is required to examine the urine, blood, sputum, stomach contents, etc., of the dispensary patients, this course supplementing the formal course in Clinical Microscopy of the Junior year.

PHYSICAL DIAGNOSIS—A practical course in the methods of physical examination is conducted at the University Clinic during the Junior year. The course is a systematic one, and the class is divided into small sections, thus permitting individual attention on the part of the instructors, and abundant practice by the student in the methods taught. This course is supplemented by a recitation course on the same subject, and by a demonstration course on Medical Technics, and clinical talks on case taking and methods of handling patients.

NEUROLOGY—In addition to the instruction in the anatomy of the nervous system, which is a part of the regular anatomy course, special work in the gross structure of the brain is given in the Second year, as is also special laboratory teaching in the pathology of the central nervous system. The systematic instruction in the diseases of the nervous system is given by a course of recitations from a text-book in the second and third terms of the Junior year. During the Senior year the instruction consists of clinical lectures, and section work at the New Haven Hospital and the University Clinic. Here special attention is paid to the demonstration of methods employed in the diagnosis and treatment of diseases of the nervous system, including electro-diagnosis and electro-therapeutics.

PSYCHIATRY—A course of recitations on insanity is given during the first term of the Senior year. These are combined with and illustrated by a series of clinics at the State Hospital for the Insane.

PEDIATRICS—The special instruction in children's diseases is given in a course of recitations during the first term of Senior year, and in the children's clinic at the University Clinic. In the section work attention is first given to the demonstration of the development of the normal child and to special methods of examination, and then to the important subject of infant feeding and to the study and treatment of pathological cases.

DERMATOLOGY—The instruction in this subject is begun with a course of recitations and lectures during the latter part of the Junior year, and is continued during the Senior year at the University Clinic, where a weekly clinic throughout the year affords a good opportunity to become familiar with the clinical appearances and treatment of the various diseases of the skin.

SANITARY SCIENCE AND PUBLIC HYGIENE receive attention in a course of lectures which include a study of the air, soil, water supply, sewage disposal, house construction and ventilation, personal and school hygiene, sanitary administration, and vital statistics.

MEDICAL JURISPRUDENCE is treated in a course of lectures especially from the standpoint of the medical practitioner. The student is provided with a printed syllabus to guide his readings in connection with the lectures.

SURGERY

The instruction in surgery extends through the Junior and Senior years, and includes instruction in the recognized surgical specialties.

THE PRINCIPLES AND PRACTICE OF SURGERY—In the Junior year the class-room instruction consists of a systematic course of lectures and recitations on general surgery. Clinical instruction is also begun at this time with attendance on the surgical clinics and operations at the Hospital and at the University Clinic, where the Junior students also serve in sections as clerks and dressers.

In the Senior year, instruction in general surgery is continued in lectures on special topics during the second half-year, but the major part of the instruction is clinical. At the University Clinic, the Seniors are assigned to the several surgical services in turn to act as assistants. In performing their duties as dressers and general assistants they have an excellent opportunity to become familiar with the practices of modern aseptic methods. Patients needing attention at their home are assigned to students, who are required as a part of their regular duties to visit them and to make full reports concerning them.

Clinics and ward classes are regularly held during the year at the New Haven Hospital. In them the students are shown selected cases during their whole stay in the Hospital, and are afforded an opportunity of studying the causes which necessitate operations, where such are necessary, of seeing the operations, and of observing the results of treatment.

OPERATIVE SURGERY—The instruction in this subject extends through the first half of the Senior year. The first term is devoted to recitations and lectures, all of the more important operations of general surgery being studied in detail. In the second half the class is divided into sections, which perform, under the guidance of the instructor, as many operations as can be conveniently executed on the cadaver. Some few selected operations will be performed by the instructor as demonstrations before the whole class.

BANDAGING—The art of applying bandages is taught during the third term of the Junior year in a practical course, which includes all the more useful methods.

SURGICAL PATHOLOGY—Students will be given an opportunity of becoming familiar with the gross and microscopic appearance of specimens obtained from operations. These exercises will be held either in connection with the clinics or at special hours in the surgical laboratory.

SEMINAR AND JOURNAL CLUB—A few advanced students, especially interested in surgery, will be admitted to the seminar where the more recent literature on special problems in surgery will be discussed.

ORTHOPEDIC SURGERY is taught in the Senior year by section work in the clinic and by lectures on the etiology, symptomatology, diagnosis, and prognosis of deformities. In the discussion of treatment, special attention is paid to mechano-therapy (massage and gymnastics), mechanical appliances (bandages, casts, etc.), and orthopedic apparatus, and to operative procedures.

GENITO-URINARY SURGERY—The special instruction in this subject is given in a course of recitations, with demonstrations of the instruments and appliances used in treatment. The clinical instruction is included in the work of the general surgical clinic.

OPHTHALMOLOGY—The instruction in this department is given in the Senior year. It consists in a systematic course of lectures and recitations, with a practical demonstration of the methods used in the examination of the eye.

During the year attendance is required in the Dispensary eye clinic, and the students in sections have an opportunity to serve as assistants and thus acquire facility in diagnosis and experience in treatment, including the use of the ophthalmoscope and the correction of errors of refraction and motility. They are also invited to witness operations at the New Haven Hospital. Each student is required to make an examination of a number of typical cases and to present reports of them before the class.

LARYNGOLOGY, OTOLOGY, AND RHINOLOGY—The didactic instruction in these subjects is given in a course of lectures and recitations during the first and second terms of Senior year, and by section work in the clinic.

The section work begins with a manikin course on the technique of examinations of the ear, nose, and throat, after which the students receive individual instruction in the examination of patients and the simpler routine methods of treatment. In their work in the clinic they gain facility and experience in these procedures and have the opportunity to see all the usual operations of these specialties.

REQUIREMENTS FOR ADVANCEMENT

Students are advanced from one class to the next by a vote of the Faculty, based on their standing in the examinations, and on the record of their work for the year.

The annual examinations are held in June in the studies of each year, and are open to students of the School and to candidates for admission to advanced standing. The subjects of the examinations of each class are fully shown in the statement of the curriculum. Examinations are also held just before the opening of the School year in September, in the studies of the First, Second, and Junior years. These autumn examinations are open only to students conditioned in June, and to candidates for admission to advanced standing. They are optional, and a fee is required for admission to them.

REQUIREMENTS FOR A DEGREE

To be eligible for the degree of Doctor of Medicine, every candidate must fulfill the following conditions:

I. He must be at least twenty-one years of age, and must sustain a good reputation for moral character.

II. He must have pursued medical studies for four years, and have been a student in this School for at least two years. If he has not pursued the four years' curriculum in this School, he must have taken such studies in some other recognized institution as are equivalent to the remainder of the full term of study.

III. He must have passed, to the satisfaction of the Faculty, the prescribed examinations of the course, and must have presented a satisfactory thesis on some subject relating to medicine. The thesis should be presented to the Dean on the third Wednesday before Commencement.

HONORS AND PRIZES

The degree of Doctor of Medicine *magna cum laude* will be conferred on students whose examinations and school work show distinguished merit.

The degree of Doctor of Medicine *cum laude* will be conferred on students whose examinations and school work show unusual merit.

The CAMPBELL GOLD MEDAL is a memorial of James Campbell, M.D., Professor of Diseases of Women and Children 1886–99, and is awarded to that member of the graduating class who secures the highest rank in the examinations of the course.

The KEESE PRIZE—The income of the fund for the Keese Prize, a memorial of Hobart Keese, M.D., of the class of 1855, amounting to about one hundred and twenty dollars annually, is awarded by the Faculty to that member of the graduating class who presents the best thesis.

Any of these honors may be withheld at the option of the Faculty.

FEES AND EXPENSES

FIRST YEAR:

Matriculation (paid but once), . . .	$ 5.00
Tuition, ...	150.00
Practical Anatomy (including instruction and material),	10.00

SECOND YEAR:

Tuition, ...	$150.00
Practical Anatomy (including instruction and material),	5.00

JUNIOR YEAR:

Tuition, ...	$150.00

SENIOR YEAR:

Tuition, ...	$150.00
Graduation, ...	10.00

A rental fee of three dollars for the use of a microscope is charged in the laboratory courses of the First and Second years. Students may, however, supply their own microscopes, in which case this fee is remitted. A fee of three dollars is also required for the out-patient obstetrical course of the Senior year.

Laboratory deposits are required as follows : First year, Chemical Laboratory, five dollars; Histology Laboratory, one dollar ; Second year, Pathology Laboratory, two dollars. Junior year, Clinical Laboratory, two dollars. These deposits are to cover the cost of apparatus broken by the student, and any excess above such breakage will be returned at the end of the course.

These fees give entrance to all the instruction in the School, including not only the lectures and quizzes but the practical courses in all departments. The curriculum does not need to be supplemented by private quiz-classes.

The matriculation fee is payable to the Dean on admission to the School. The tuition fees are payable in three installments of fifty dollars each, which are due on October 15, February 1, and April 15. Fees are payable to the University Treasurer on or before the dates specified. - If not then paid they will bear interest from the dates when due, and must be paid to the Dean. The graduation fee is payable to the Dean three weeks before Commencement.

Students who do not pay in advance can continue their studies for the year by giving an endorsed note satisfactory to the Dean. No degrees can be conferred, nor any certificate of attendance of examination furnished, until all bills due the University are paid.

Students will be assisted in finding board and lodging by the Janitor of Medical Hall, Mr. William Blackwood, 148 York St. Prices range from five dollars a week upwards.

GRADUATE AND SPECIAL STUDENTS NOT CANDIDATES FOR A DEGREE

The instruction here offered to graduates in medicine is intended to meet the requirements of two classes of students : first, those who wish to review or supplement their knowledge of the regular studies of the medical curriculum, as taught in this School ; and second, those who wish to fit themselves in special lines of medical work, as for the duties of a Medical Examiner or Public Health Officer.

SPECIAL STUDENTS are not taken in the practical branches of medicine, but the general studies of the course are open to such persons as may wish to pursue them, if by their previous studies they are prepared to profit by the instruction. Special courses may also be arranged in Anatomy, Physiology, Pathology, Bacteriology, Experimental Toxicology and Medico-legal Examination, Sanitary Analysis, including the analysis of food, water, sewage, etc., and in the special laboratory methods of Medical and Surgical Diagnosis. The charges for instruction will depend on the courses taken, and can be ascertained for any particular line of study by applying to the Dean.

For further information, address Professor HERBERT E. SMITH, Dean. Office hours from 9.00 to 11.00 A. M., Room No. 25, Medical School, 150 York St.

DEPARTMENT OF LAW
(YALE LAW SCHOOL)

OFFICERS

FACULTY

ARTHUR TWINING HADLEY, LL.D., PRESIDENT

HENRY WADE ROGERS, LL.D., *Dean, and Professor of Equity and Corporations*

Hon. SIMEON EBEN BALDWIN, LL.D., *Professor of American Constitutional and Private International Law*

†THEODORE SALISBURY WOOLSEY, LL.D., *Professor of International Law*

Hon. SAMUEL OSCAR PRENTICE, B.A., LL.B., *Professor of Pleading*

Hon. EDWIN BAKER GAGER, M.A., *Professor of General Jurisprudence Mortgages, and the Law of Public Service Companies*

GEORGE DUTTON WATROUS, D.C.L., *Professor of Torts*

EDWARD VILETTE RAYNOLDS, D.C.L., *Professor of Comparative Law*

JOHN WURTS, M.A., M.L., *LaFayette S. Foster Professor of the English Common Law*

GEORGE EMERSON BEERS, M.A., M.L., *Assistant Professor of Elementary Law and Real Property*

ARTHUR LINTON CORBIN, B.A., LL.B., *Assistant Professor of Contracts*

GEORGE ZAHM, M.L., *Assistant Professor of Mercantile Law and Insurance*

CHARLES PHINEAS SHERMAN, D.C.L., *Assistant Professor of Roman Law, and Librarian*

JOHN WARREN EDGERTON, M.A., LL.B., *Instructor in Mercantile Law, and Secretary of the Faculty*

SPECIAL LECTURERS AND INSTRUCTORS

WILLIAM DAMERON GUTHRIE, M.A., *William L. Storrs Lecturer*

Hon. JOHN HOYT PERRY, M.A., LL.B., *Lecturer on Parliamentary Law.*

THOMAS THACHER, LL.D., *Lecturer on Corporations*

---

† Absent during 1907-08.

JAMES MULFORD TOWNSEND, B.A., LL.B., *Lecturer on Transfer of Monetary Securities*

CYRUS LARUE MUNSON, M.A., LL.B., *Lecturer on General Legal Practice*

JAMES HENRY WEBB, B.S., LL.B., *Instructor in Criminal Procedure and Criminal Law*

JOHN KIMBERLY BEACH, B.A., LL.B., *Lecturer on Patents, Admiralty, Copyright, and Trade Mark*

ROGER FOSTER, M.A., LL.B., *Lecturer on Federal Jurisprudence*

Hon. MACGRANE COXE, B.A., LL.B., *Lecturer on Bankruptcy*

Hon. EPAPHRODITUS PECK, LL.B., *Instructor in Evidence, Civil Procedure, and Domestic Relations*

LEONARD MAYHEW DAGGETT, B.A., LL.B., *Instructor in Wills*

† HOWARD HOYT KNAPP, B.A., LL.B., *Lecturer on Connecticut Practice*

ROBERT CLARK MORRIS, D.C.L., *Lecturer on International Arbitration*

JAMES EVERETT WHEELER, B.A., LL.B., *Lecturer on Looking up the Law* *

EDWARD AVERY HARRIMAN, B.A , LL.B., *Instructor in Comparative Administrative Law*

CHARLES CHENEY HYDE, M.A., LL.B. *(Associate Professor of Law in Northwestern University), Lecturer on International Law*

JOHN WESLEY WETZEL, PH.B., *Instructor in Public Speaking*

ANDREW TEW BIERKAN, D.C.L., *Instructor in Commercial Accounts*

BENEDICT EDWARD LYONS, B.A., *Registrar*

ARTHUR LAUREN MALTBY, B.L., *Assistant Registrar*

ORGANIZATION AND INSTRUCTION
HISTORY

The Yale catalogue for 1824 contained a list of law students, although no announcement was made concerning the course of instruction. The catalogue for 1826 described the work of the Law School for the first time. While the work of the School has been carried on since 1824, no degrees were conferred until 1843.

The law course, from the founding of the School down to 1896, was one of two years. It was then extended to

---
† Absent.

three years. The graduate course was established in 1876. The Yale Law School was the first law school in America or in England to establish a course leading to the degree of Doctor of Civil Law.

In 1880 the Hon. LaFayette S. Foster, who represented Connecticut in the Senate of the United States, died leaving a will in which he provided a sum, now amounting to eighty thousand dollars, to found a Professorship of English Common Law in the Yale Law School. This gift was subject to a life interest, but the University came into possession of the fund in 1903.

In 1887 Mr. Junius S. Morgan of London gave the Corporation the sum of twenty-five thousand dollars for a Professorship of Contracts and Commercial Law, and in 1891 Mr. J. Pierpont Morgan of New York City augmented this amount by a gift of twenty-five thousand dollars, thereby creating the " Morgan Fund," and establishing the " Edward J. Phelps Professorship." Mr. Phelps was a Professor of Law in this School and previously Minister to England.

The will of Mr. Augustus E. Lines, of New Haven, which was probated in 1902, provides a sum of fifty thousand dollars for a chair of Testamentary Law in the Law School. This gift, being subject to a life interest, is not at the present time available.

PURPOSE OF THE SCHOOL

It is the aim of the School to give to all students in its regular undergraduate course a thorough acquaintance with the general principles and rules of American law, so as to fit them for the Bar of any State ; to extend to those who do not propose to become practicing lawyers but wish to pursue some particular branches of legal or political knowledge, such assistance as they may desire ; and to offer to advanced students further instruction in all that belongs to law as a science in its widest sense. Such instruction is given in an undergraduate course, a graduate course, and special courses.

ACADEMIC YEAR

The Academic year 1907–08 began on Thursday, September 26, 1907, and will end on Wednesday, June 24, 1908.

There will be a recess from Wednesday, December 18, 1907, to Wednesday, January 8, 1908; and also from 1.00 P. M. Wednesday, April 15, 1908, to 8.00 A. M. Thursday, April 23, 1908.

Class exercises are suspended on Thanksgiving day (the recess begins Wednesday at 1.00 P. M. and ends Friday at 8.00 A. M.) and on Memorial day.

ATTENDANCE

All students, whether candidates for a degree or special students, are required to be in actual attendance. The work of the Law School cannot be done *in absentia*, nor satisfactorily carried by students who are irregular in their attendance upon the exercises of the Department. Academic standing will be forfeited and registration cancelled whenever a student becomes so irregular in his attendance as to satisfy the Faculty that it is unwise for him to continue his connection with the School.

SYSTEM OF INSTRUCTION

Law has been taught in the law schools of the United States by three distinct methods, by lectures, by text-book, and by cases. The Yale Law School does not adopt any one of these to the exclusion of the others. Experience has seemed to indicate that the best results are attained by a combination of the three methods.

It is the conviction of the Faculty of Law, as well as the tradition of the University, that definite and permanent impressions concerning the principles and rules of legal science are best acquired by the study of standard text-books and the careful analysis of leading cases, followed by the examinations and explanations of the recitation room. Hence, although certain subjects are separately taught by lectures, either because the want of proper manuals, or the constant and rapid advance of learning, or economy of time, requires the adoption of that method, care is taken that the same topics as far as practicable shall be covered by recitation work in connection with the wider branches of the law to which they belong.

The recitation hours, however, are only in part devoted to questioning the student. While this is done with sufficient thoroughness to hold him up to his work of preparation, matters not fully treated in the text-book used or cases to be analyzed are presented at greater length; ample opportunity is also afforded for a free colloquial discussion of the subject of the lesson and for the presentation and solution of the difficulties which he may have encountered in his private study. In this manner each student is brought into personal communication with the instructor in reference to his daily work and, as far as practicable, receives the benefits which would be obtained if he were placed under the individual instruction of his professor.

INSTRUCTION IN OTHER DEPARTMENTS OF THE UNIVERSITY

The share of the School in the general advantages of the University gives the students many opportunities of broadening their views and acquiring knowledge in regard to matters outside of their strictly professional work. They may, on application to the Dean, obtain permission to be present at one or more of the special courses of instruction in the Department of Philosophy and the Arts, or the lectures on Anatomy, Insanity, etc., in the Medical School, on payment of a moderate fee.

THE WILLIAM L. STORRS LECTURESHIP

In 1889 the Misses E. T. and M. A. Robinson of Hartford established a Lectureship in the Law School in memory of William Lucius Storrs. Judge Storrs was a Professor in the Law School and Chief-Justice of the Supreme Court of Connecticut.

A course of five or six lectures is given annually on this foundation. The course is open to graduate or undergraduate students alike.

In the year 1907–08 the William L. Storrs Lectures will be delivered by William Dameron Guthrie, M.A., of New York City, a constitutional lawyer who delivered the course in 1902–03.

UNDERGRADUATE COURSE

The Undergraduate course extends through three years of nine months each. It is mainly devoted to the practical side of legal education, but also gives an introduction to the general ideas and sources of Jurisprudence. In the opinion of the Faculty the progress of the student in the study of the law in its different branches is very much facilitated by a previous examination of those branches collectively and with reference to their relations to each other. The undergraduate course is arranged with a view to acquainting the student, at the beginning of his study, with the nature and scope of the science of the law. The course is designed to give him a knowledge of the elementary principles and doctrines of the law exhibited in their logical and practical connections with each other. Thus prepared, he proceeds to study more in detail the several branches of the law.

The undergraduate course leads either to the degree of Bachelor of Laws, or to that of Bachelor of Civil Law. The same amount of work is required for each of these degrees, but applicants for the latter degree are required to take work in Roman Law not required for the former degree, and are permitted, upon consultation with the Faculty, to substitute certain studies in Political Science for certain of the law subjects.

A candidate for the degree of Bachelor of Laws must pass examinations upon all the required subjects of the first two years of the undergraduate course, and upon seven hours of required and eight hours of elective work in the third year.

DIRECTIONS TO CANDIDATES FOR ADMISSION

An applicant for admission to the Law School must present to the Dean, at his office in Hendrie Hall, formal application for admission on a blank which will be furnished for the purpose. It is essential, prior to making this application, that the applicant should pay to the Treasurer of the University, at his office in Woodbridge Hall, a registration fee of ten dollars, the receipt for which must be exhibited at the time application for admission is made. This fee is not additional to the charge for tuition, but will be credited on the bill of the first term.

An examination fee of ten dollars, which fee is additional to the charge for tuition and must be paid to the Treasurer of the University in advance of obtaining permission to take entrance examinations, is required in the following cases :

1. When application for admission is made after the academic year 1908–09 and the applicant is obliged to take an entrance examination because unable to present a diploma from some approved College or Scientific School, or a certificate from an institution of like character certifying to the fact that he has performed with credit the equivalent of at least two years of work of collegiate grade of fifteen hours per week.

2. When application for admission to advanced standing is made, and it is necessary to take examination on law subjects. But a student who brings credits from a school which is a member of the Association of American Law Schools may be admitted to advanced standing without examination on law subjects for which the credits have been obtained.

On presentation to the Treasurer of the University of a certificate signed by the Dean showing that an applicant has failed to pass the entrance examinations, the money paid as a registration fee, but not the money paid as an examination fee, will be refunded.

ADMISSION TO UNDERGRADUATE COURSE

It is important for law students as a class to have the maturity, culture, and ethical ideals for which an American college education stands. All those who are able to complete a college course before entering the Yale Law School are advised to do so; and if a college makes provision for the effective teaching of subjects contained in the Yale Law School course itself, credit will be given to students here for work which they have previously done in those subjects. The Faculty does not require a college degree, because such a requirement, in view of the differences in standing and merit of colleges in the United States, becomes to some extent an arbitrary one, and is also one which may bear unfairly upon men who, possessing much ability but little time or money, can reach the same grade of preparation by a different road.

ADMISSION TO THE FIRST-YEAR CLASS. Persons wishing to be admitted to the First-Year class of the Yale Law School as candidates for the degree of Bachelor of Laws must be eighteen years of age, and present satisfactory testimonials of good moral character. *Prior to the academic year 1909-10 the rules governing the admission of students will be as follows:*

The persons named below will be admitted without examination upon producing their certificates:

1. Graduates from an approved college, or persons who have been enrolled as regular students in any such college and bring letters of honorable dismissal therefrom.

2. Graduates from a preparatory school approved by the Faculty.

3. Holders of a certificate issued by the Board of Regents of the University of the State of New York, showing that they have passed the Regents' Examination for Law Students, will be excused from any preliminary examinations so far as the English branches are concerned.

4. Holders of a certificate of examination of the College Entrance Examination Board of the Middle States and Maryland will be excused from any preliminary examination so far as such certificates cover the requirements here set forth.

All other applicants are required to pass a satisfactory examination in the following subjects :

1. *English Grammar*—Whitney's *Essentials of English Grammar*, or an equivalent.

2. *English Literature A.*

READING AND PRACTICE—A certain number of books will be set for reading. The candidate will be required to present evidence of a general knowledge of the subject-matter, and to answer simple questions on the lives of the authors. The form of examination will usually be the writing of a paragraph or two on each of several topics, to be chosen by the candidate from a considerable number—perhaps ten or fifteen—set before him in the examination paper. The treatment of these topics is designed to test the candidate's power of clear and accurate expression, and will call for only a general knowledge of the substance of the books.

In preparation for this part of the requirement, it is important that the candidate shall have been instructed in the fundamental principles of rhetoric.

The books set for this part of the examination will be :—

Shakespeare's *Macbeth* and *Merchant of Venice ;* The Sir Roger de Coverley Papers in *The Spectator;* Irving's *Life of Goldsmith;* Coleridge's *Ancient Mariner ;* Scott's *Ivanhoe* and *Lady of the Lake ;* Tennyson's *Gareth and Lynette, Lancelot and Elaine,* and *Passing of Arthur ;* Lowell's *Vision of Sir Launfal ;* George Eliot's *Silas Marner.*

3. *English Literature B.*

STUDY AND PRACTICE—This part of the examination presupposes more careful study of each of the works named below. The examination will be upon subject-matter, form, and structure, and will also test the candidate's ability to express his knowledge with clearness and accuracy. In addition, the candidate may be required to answer questions involving the essentials of English grammar, and questions on the leading facts in those periods of English literary history to which the prescribed works belong.

The books set for this part of the examination will be :—

Shakespeare's *Julius Cæsar;* Milton's *Lycidas, Comus, L'Allegro,* and *Il Penseroso;* Burke's *Speech on Conciliation with America ;* Macaulay's *Essay on Addison,* and *Life of Johnson.*

No candidate will be accepted in English whose work is notably defective in point of spelling, punctuation, idiom, or division into paragraphs.

4. *History of England*—Montgomery's *Leading Facts of English History*, or an equivalent.

The student should have some acquaintance with the leading facts of English history from the landing of Julius Cæsar (55

B. C.) down to the conclusion of Beaconsfield's ministry (1880). Special attention should be given to incidents from the Norman Conquest onwards. It is recommended that, so far as possible, the attention of the student be directed to the importance not only of the development of English government, but of English industry and English literature. No adequate preparation can be made without practice in written statement. A mere reading acquaintance with the story of English history is not sufficient ; the student must be helped to reason upon the subject and to base his reasoning on precise statements of the facts.

5. *History of the United States.*

In *History of the United States*, a thorough acquaintance with some one of the more recent and accurate text-books (such as Johnston's *History of the United States*, revised edition, Montgomery's *Students' American History*, Channing's *Students' History of the United States*, or McLaughlin's *History of the American Nation*) is expected.

The examination is not designed as a memory test merely, but will call for comparison, the exercise of judgment, and will be framed on the supposition that the student has done systematic note-book work and has an adequate knowledge of historical geography. For the purpose of arousing interest in the subject, it is strongly recommended that the student be urged to follow, under his teacher's guidance, a course of supplementary reading, so arranged as to cover the more important periods and events, and to call attention to social development, constitutional growth, and the principles of government.

6. *Latin Grammar and Composition*—The examination in Latin Grammar will be based on connected passages taken from the first and second books of Cæsar's *Gallic War*. The exercises set for translation from English into Latin will involve the vocabulary and idiom of these two books.

7. *Cæsar or Nepos*—The first four books of Cæsar's *Gallic War*.

The first twelve of Nepos's *Lives*, as they appear in the Teubner edition, will be accepted as an equivalent for the third and fourth books of Cæsar.

8. *Vergil or Cicero*—The first three books of the *Æneid*.

Cicero's Orations against Catiline and for Archias may be offered in place of Vergil.

9. *German or French*—Candidates will be required to translate at sight simple prose selections from German or French authors, and to have such a knowledge of grammar as will enable them to read the selections intelligently. This implies familiarity with the declensions of nouns, adjectives, and pronouns, with the conjugation of verbs, and with the syntax of cases.

10. *Algebra.*
11. Plane, Solid, and Spherical Geometry—Phillips and Fisher's *Geometry*, or an equivalent.
12. *Trigonometry and the use of Logarithms*—so much, for example, as is contained in the first six chapters of Newcomb's *Larger Trigonometry*, and in Articles 77–78 of Chapter 8.
13. *Botany or Chemistry or Physics*—Gray's or Bergen's *Elements of Botany* is recommended. If Chemistry be offered, there will be required a knowledge of the common elements and their compounds, ability to write equations of simple reactions, and familiarity with the laws of chemical combination. If Physics be offered, a familiarity with the general phenomena of mechanics, sound, light, heat, magnetism, and electricity will be expected.

Upon application to the Secretary of the Faculty at least four weeks before the date of each examination, equivalents may be offered for subjects nine to twelve inclusive.

In the case of foreign students having a properly accredited knowledge of their own language and literature such knowledge will be accepted in lieu of the requirement of a knowledge of French or German. In all cases Greek may be substituted for Latin.

In choosing equivalents, the following subjects are suggested: General History, Fiske's "Civil Government of the United States" together with the text of the United States Constitution, Physiology, Physical Geography, Geology, Italian, Spanish, Greek, Greek History, and Roman History. In preparation for an examination in General History, Swinton's "Outlines of the World's History," or Fisher's "Brief History of the Nations," is recommended.

ADMISSION TO ADVANCED STANDING. Applicants for admission to the Second-Year class must be at least nineteen years of age, and those seeking admission to the Third-Year class must be at least twenty years of age. All applicants must meet the educational requirement specified for admission to the First-Year class. Persons who have pursued their studies for one or more years in a Law

School belonging to the Association of American Law Schools, or in one which in the opinion of the Dean is of substantially equal standing, will be admitted upon certificate from such school without examination upon the subjects required for admission to the school from which they come, but will be required to pass examination in any other subjects required for admission to this School. Those who present certificates from a Law School above described showing that they have passed satisfactory examinations in law studies there pursued, may be excused from further examination in those studies, and will be classed accordingly ; but students so admitted to the Second-Year or Third-Year class, who have not taken other topics previously pursued by such class, must pass examinations on such topics, at or before the close of the year, as the Dean may in each case decide.

Graduates of approved Law Schools and Attorneys at Law who have been admitted to the Bar after such preliminary or final examinations as attest their proper preparation for the profession, may be allowed to enter without examination, and their class rating will be determined upon consideration of the studies they have pursued and the time they have given to legal study.

ADMISSION OF SPECIAL STUDENTS. Persons who do not desire to pursue the regular work of the School, and those whose preliminary education is not sufficiently extended to justify their admission as candidates for a degree but who satisfy the Dean that they are qualified to study certain branches of the law, may be admitted without examination as special students. Special studies may be taken by students who desire some acquaintance with law as a preparation for business pursuits, and also by those who, not intending to engage in active business, desire to acquire an enlarged acquaintance with our political and legal systems and the rules by which they are governed.

Beginning with the academic year 1909–10, students applying for admission as candidates for the degree of LL.B., or that of B.C.L., will be subject to the following requirements:

Candidates for admission will be required to present either a diploma from some approved College or Scientific School, or evidence that they have performed with credit the equivalent of at least two full years of work, of collegiate grade, of fifteen hours per week.

Such evidence may be furnished by a certificate from an institution of good standing. Candidates who have not attended institutions able to give this certificate, but who have otherwise fitted themselves for the study of the law by work of corresponding grade, are admitted to examination on payment of a fee of ten dollars. The examination will include: 1. Questions on the college entrance requirements included in the schedule which appears on pages 90–91, subject to the modification noted below in the English Literature Requirements, or their equivalent, unless the candidate can present evidence that he has already passed such a test. 2. Questions which will call for attainments such as might fairly be expected to result from not less than two full years of class-room work covering fifteen hours per week, under competent instructors on subjects selected from the following list:

History, Ancient, Medieval, or Modern; studied in a way to involve knowledge of constitutional principles and social movements.
Advanced studies in some language or languages, ancient or modern.
Rhetoric, Literary Criticism, or History of Literature.
Logic, Psychology, Ethics, or History of Philosophy.
Advanced Mathematics.
Physics, Chemistry, or Natural Science; studied in such manner as to be theoretical as well as descriptive.
Physiography, Commercial Geography, or Political Economy.

The candidate must offer subjects from at least three of these groups. With this restriction, the selection of subjects may be made by each applicant at his option, provided written notice of his selection is given by him to the Secretary of the Faculty of the Law Department three weeks before the opening day of the examinations.

For the class entering in 1909 the requirements in English Literature A will be: Shakespeare's *The Merchant of Venice* and *Julius Cæsar*; Bunyan's *The Pilgrim's Progress, Part I*; The Sir Roger de Coverley Papers in *The Spectator*; Scott's *The Lady of the Lake* and *Ivanhoe*; Irving's *Sketch Book*; Macaulay's *Lays of Ancient Rome*; Tennyson's *Gareth and Lynette*, *Lancelot and Elaine*, and *The Passing of Arthur*; George Eliot's *Silas Marner*.

For the class entering in 1910: Shakespeare's *The Merchant of Venice* and *Julius Cæsar*; The Sir Roger de Coverley Papers in *The Spectator*; Franklin's *Autobiography*; Scott's *The Lady of the Lake* and *Ivanhoe*; Irving's *Sketch Book*; Macaulay's *Lays of Ancient Rome*; Tennyson's *Gareth and Lynette*, *Lancelot and Elaine*, and *The Passing of Arthur*; George Eliot's *Silas Marner*.

For the class entering in 1911: Shakespeare's *The Merchant of Venice* and *Julius Cæsar*; The Sir Roger de Coverley Papers in *The Spectator*; Goldsmith's *The Vicar of Wakefield*; Scott's *The Lady of the Lake* and *Ivanhoe*; Hawthorne's *House of Seven Gables*; Macaulay's *Lays of Ancient Rome*; Tennyson's *Gareth and Lynette*, *Lancelot and Elaine*, and *The Passing of Arthur*; George Eliot's *Silas Marner*.

The requirements in English Literature B will be:

In 1909, 1910, and 1911: Shakespeare's *Macbeth*; Milton's *Lycidas*, *Comus*, *L'Allegro*, and *Il Penseroso*; Burke's *Speech on Conciliation with America*, or Washington's *Farewell Address* and Webster's *First Bunker Hill Oration*; Macaulay's *Life of Johnson*, or Carlyle's *Essay on Burns*.

TIME AND PLACE OF EXAMINATIONS FOR ADMISSION. In 1908 examinations in New Haven for admission to the First-Year class will be held at Hendrie Hall on Thursday, June 25 (the day after Commencement), and on Monday, September 21 (three days before the opening of the Academic year). The examinations begin at 9.00 A. M. and those who desire to be examined must be in attendance at the opening.

Examinations outside New Haven for admission to Yale will be held on June 25, 1908, at 8.30 A. M., and at the places mentioned on pages 88–89.

Applicants for admission to the First-Year class of the Law School (but not to higher classes) may arrange to take the examination at any of the places named. But those who propose to take the examination elsewhere than at New Haven should communicate their intention to the

Secretary of the Law Faculty before June 1. A fee of five dollars (payable at the opening of the session) is charged for admission to examinations outside of New Haven.

Examinations for admission to advanced standing will be held in the Law School Building on Monday, Tuesday, and Wednesday, September 21, 22, and 23, 1908. Persons intending to take the examination for advanced standing will find it necessary to be present on each of the days named.

LAW STUDIES COMBINED WITH THOSE OF OTHER DEPARTMENTS.

Students in the Academical Department of Yale University may so combine their work in that Department with the work of the Law School as to obtain the degree in Arts and in Law in six years. Students in the Junior year in the Academical Department may elect three hours of class-room work in the Law School, and in their Senior year may elect eleven hours of such work, thus obtaining a credit of fourteen hours on the sixty hours required for the degree in Arts, and on the forty-five hours required for the degree in Law. Students who obtain this credit while in the Academical Department are enabled to complete the Law School course in two additional years.

The course, in the Law School which is open to Academical Juniors and counts on both the degree in Arts and in Law, is that on *Elementary Law*. The courses open to Academical Seniors which likewise count on both degrees, are as follows: *American Constitutional Law; Contracts; Evidence; International Law;* and *Torts.* Academical students must have completed the course in Elementary Law before they enter upon the study of other law courses. The following additional law subjects are open to Academical Seniors, although they can be counted only on the degree in Law: *Common Law Pleading; Criminal Law;* and the *Study of Cases.*

The course in *Elementary Law* above mentioned includes not only the *Elementary Law* course described below in the Program of Undergraduate Instruction but a special course in the *Law of Contracts*.

The course in *Mining Law* is open to students in the Sheffield Scientific School who are studying Engineering and who present to the Dean of the Law School the written consent of the Director of the Scientific School to their registration for the course.

The course in *American Constitutional Law* is open to students in the Divinity School who present to the Dean of the Law School the written consent of the Dean of the Divinity School to their registration for this course.

Graduates of approved colleges who have taken while in college what amounts to not less than five hours a week of strictly legal studies during an entire college year and have passed a creditable examination in such studies at such college, may, so far as such studies form part of the regular First-Year curriculum, substitute for them certain courses of the Second-Year curriculum ; and, in such case, during their second year may take some of the courses offered in the Third-Year curriculum ; thus becoming enabled to take, if they desire, during the Second and Third years, all the courses offered in those years instead of being restricted to an election between them. Or, if they desire and feel able to do the work which would be thus required, they may register provisionally in the Second-Year class and be advanced from that in the regular course into the Third-Year class in case they pass, at the close of the Second year, examinations both on their Second-Year work and on such studies of the First year as were not covered by them while in college, taking a high stand in both.

MASTER OF ARTS DEGREE

Bachelors of Arts of Yale College, and Bachelors of Arts of other colleges whose course of study is equivalent to that of Yale College, may, while pursuing their Law School studies, obtain the degree of Master of Arts of Yale University. Students of the Law School may, on paying the regular fees to the Graduate School for the courses taken, take courses in the Graduate School which do not count for the degree in Law and may have these courses count towards the attainment of the degree of Master of Arts.

PROGRAM OF UNDERGRADUATE INSTRUCTION

The number of hours stated, when not otherwise specified, means hours of recitations or lectures each week throughout the year.

FIRST YEAR.

Professor BALDWIN :—

American Law.   8 lectures in 1st half-year.

> The course gives an outline sketch of the sources, divisions, and character of the law of the States and the United States, both substantive and adJective.

Professor WURTS :—

Elementary Law.   3 hrs. to end of calendar year.

> The course is designed to introduce the student to underlying principles and to preparation for their application.
>
> Robinson's *Elementary Law*, and Lectures.

Mr. EDGERTON :—

Agency.   2 hrs 2d half-year.

> The course treats of law of principal and agent, their mutual rights and liabilities, and those in favor of and against third persons, in contract and in tort.
>
> Mecham's *Agency*, and *Cases.*

Mr. EDGERTON :—

Bailments and Carriers.   2 hrs. 2d half-year.

> A study of the different classifications of bailments, and of the rights, duties, and liabilities of the parties to the various transactions, both *inter se* and as to third persons.
>
> Goddard's *Bailments and Carriers*, and *Cases.*

Professor PRENTICE : —

Common Law Pleading.   1 hr.

> The course considers theory and principles of the common law system of pleading as it now exists, and attempts to bring practical application of these principles within comprehension of the student.
>
> Heard on *Civil Pleading*, and Lectures.

Assistant Professor CORBIN :—

Contracts. 4 hrs.

The course treats of the elements required for the formation of a valid contract ; of fraud, mistake, duress, and undue influence ; of the interpretation, performance, and discharge of contracts ; and of the Statute of Frauds.

Huffcut's *Anson on Contracts* (2d ed.) ; Williston's *Cases on Contracts.*

Assistant Professor BEERS and Mr. WEBB :—

Criminal Law. 1 hr.

(*a*) To the end of the calendar year the course is under the direction of Assistant Professor Beers, and is devoted to a study of the elementary principles of Criminal Law.

Robinson's *Elementary Law.*

(*b*) From the end of the calendar year the course is under the direction of Mr. Webb. The common law felonies and misdemeanors are considered, as well as the general principles governing statutory offenses.

Kenny's *Outlines of Criminal Law, Webb's Edition.*

Judge PECK : —

Domestic Relations and the Law of Persons. 1 hr.

The course considers marriage and divorce, husband and wife, infancy, parent and child, guardian and ward, employer and employee, persons under the disabilities of insanity, alienage, etc.

Lectures and Cases.

Professor WURTS :—

Evidence. 2 hrs. 1st half-year.

An elementary course in which the student is required to memorize the principal rules and their exceptions governing production and admissibility of evidence.

Reynold's *Theory of Evidence.*

Professor WURTS :—

Property. (Subject commenced.)

2 hrs. beginning in January.

The course covers the entire field of estates in real and personal property, rights incident to ownership, powers, trusts, rights to the use or profits of another's land, and fraudulent disposition of property.

Tiffany on *Real Property*, vol. 1, and Lectures.

Professor WATROUS :—

Torts. 2 hrs.

This course includes private wrongs (other than those which consist of breaches of contract), liability for tort and remedies therefor, and specific torts.

Cooley on *Torts* (Students' edition) and Chase's *Cases on Torts.*

THE FOLLOWING COURSES ARE OPTIONAL :

Dr. BIERKAN :—

Commercial Accounts. 1 hr.

The course explains systems of accounts used in commercial establishments and considers accounts as evidence in court and accounts from the standpoint of the counselor.

Mr. J. E. WHEELER :—

Looking up the Law. 5 lectures in 2d half-year.

The student is shown how to find legal authorities. The use of text-books and decisions, and the proper method of analysis and classification of statements of fact, are explained.

Mr. WETZEL :—

Elocution. 1 hr.

Especial attention is given to vocal training. The student is expected to acquire a correct and refined pronunciation of English, and an absolutely distinct and natural utterance.

Cumnock's *Choice Readings.*

Mr. EDGERTON :—

Study of Cases. 1 hr. 2d half-year.

The course considers headnotes and digests, weight to be given cases, dicta, and text-books as authorities; modes of criticizing a case, and the writing of briefs.

Wambaugh on *The Study of Cases.*

Assistant Professor SHERMAN :—

Use of the Library. 1 hr. 1st half-year.

The course explains different kinds of law books, abbreviation and citation, use of unofficial series of reports, methods of searching for authorities, use of bibliographies and printed guides to legal literature.

Lectures and Practical Exercises.

SECOND YEAR.

Professor BALDWIN :—

American Constitutional Law. 2 hrs.

This course considers the foundations of constitutional law laid in colonial times ; the general nature of constitutional government ; and its development both in the States and the United States.

Cooley's *Principles of Constitutional Law, the Yale Cases on Constitutional Law,* and Lectures.

Judge PECK :—

Civil Procedure. 1 hr.

The course considers fundamental principles of procedure, constitution and powers of courts, Jurisdiction, venue, institution and conduct of actions, trial and argument of causes, the Jury, verdicts, Judgments, proceedings in error, etc.

Lectures and Moot Courts.

Professor PRENTICE :—

Code Pleading. 1 hr.

The course gives an intelligent understanding of those distinctive features of code pleading which are common to the several Jurisdictions in this country where the code system has been adopted.

Bryant on *Code Pleading.*

Professor ROGERS:—

Equity Jurisprudence. 2 hrs.

The course gives the student a knowledge of the development and present condition of equity Jurisprudence, includes a careful study of equitable titles, equitable rights, and equitable remedies.

Bispham on the *Principles of Equity.*

Judge PECK :—

Evidence. (Subject continued.) 2 hrs. 2d half-year.

The student is required to apply the principles of evidence to facts and situations which might arise in the course of trial. The work is intended to be thoroughly practical.

Thayer's *Cases on Evidence* (the book begun).

Professor HYDE :—

International Law. 2 hrs. 1st half-year.

Exposition of the rules which govern the relations of States in peace and in war.

Lectures.

Professor ROGERS :—

Private Corporations. ·· 2 hrs.

This course considers the manner of creating, managing, and dissolving corporations, the rights and duties of officers, directors, and stockholders, the rights and remedies of creditors, etc.

Marshall on *Private Corporations*, and the *Yale Cases on Private Corporations*.

. Assistant Professor ZAHM :—

Promissory Notes and Bills of Exchange. 2 hrs. 1st half-year.

A consideration of the formal and essential requirements of negotiable instruments, their acceptance, indorsement, transfer, presentment and notice of dishonor, and the nature of the liability of the respective parties thereto.

Norton on *Bills and Notes, 3d edition*, Selected Cases and Lectures.

Professor WATROUS :—

Quasi-Contracts. 1 hr. 1st half-year.

This course deals with contracts implied in law, so-called, as distinguished from express contracts and those implied in fact, and covers the recovery of money paid by mistake, unjust enrichment at another's expense, etc.

Professor WURTS ;—

Property. 2 hrs.

A continuation of the first-year course on vols. I and II, on the same subject. It covers the entire field of title, except title by private grant (see *Titles and Conveyancing*) and title by devise (see *Wills*), prescriptive rights, mortgages, and liens both equitable and statutory.

Tiffany on *Real Property*.

Assistant Professor BEERS :—

Titles and Conveyancing. 1 hr.

A course on private grant, including execution of deeds, capacity to convey, covenants, registration, examination of title and abstract of title, with practical exercises in conveyancing.

Tiffany on *Real.Property*, Lectures and practical exercises.

THE FOLLOWING COURSES ARE OPTIONAL :

Professor WURTS :—

Damages. 1 hr. 2d half-year.

Hale on *Damages*.

Mr. WETZEL :—

Elocution, Vocal and Gestural Expression. 1 hr.

> The course includes the vocal interpretation of Julius Cæsar. Students are expected to acquire the ability to interpret thought readily through the harmonious blending of the elements of expression.
>
> Cumnock's *Choice Readings.*

Mr. WEBB :—

Medical Jurisprudence. 1 hr. 1st half-year.

> The course considers the symptoms produced by poisons, and explains the methods of their determination. Insanity and the rules of law applicable thereto are considered, and expert and opinion testimony.
>
> Lectures.

Assistant Professor SHERMAN :—

Roman Law. 1 hr.

> The outlines of Roman Law in its developed form as well as the leading features of its historical growth.
>
> Bernard's *First Year of Roman Law* (Sherman's edition), and Lectures.

THIRD YEAR.

The courses in Evidence, Mortgages, Municipal Corporations, Practice in United States Courts, Sales, and Wills, are required of all students not specially excused. The student will elect at least eight additional year-hours.

Mr. BEACH :—

Admiralty, Copyrights, Patents, and Trademarks. 1 hr.

> The course covers history and principles of admiralty, copyright, patent, and trademark law. About half the course is devoted to patent law.
>
> Lectures and Cases.

Professor HYDE :—

American Diplomatic History. 1 hr.

> The course considers Diplomacy of the Revolution, U. S. Foreign Relations from 1793 to 1815, Boundary questions, Fishery questions, Civil War diplomacy, relations with Cuba, and the War with Spain.
>
> Lectures.

Mr. COXE :—

The Law and Practice of Bankruptcy. ˙   1 hr. 2d half-year.

An historical review of the bankruptcy systems of foreign nations. An examination of the United States bankruptcy laws, constitutionally and historically considered as a regulation of commerce, and the study of the law as it exists today, and of the practice thereunder.

Lectures. Leading Cases.

Judge PECK :—

Civil Procedure.   1 hr.

The course deals with the actual conduct of cases in code states, from the standpoint of helpful suggestions rather than of theoretical law. The conduct of actions in Yale Moot Court is required.

Lectures and Moot Courts.

Mr. WEBB :—

Criminal Procedure.   1 hr.

The course treats of the principles especially applicable to the trial of a criminal cause, including the practice, pleading, and evidence. The essential averments of the accusation are especially considered.

Clark's *Criminal Procedure.*

Professor ROGERS :—

Equity Jurisprudence.   2 hrs.

The course supplements the course on the same subject in the Second year. It is based on a study of leading cases illustrating the maxims and most important doctrines of equity.

Ames's *Cases in Equity Jurisdiction.*

Professor WATROUS :—

Estates.   1 hr. for 10 weeks in 2d half-year.

The course is chiefly devoted to the consideration of the history and extent of the probate Jurisdiction, and the practice in probate courts.

Lectures.

Judge PECK :—

Evidence. (Subject concluded.)   1 hr.

The aim of this course is not only to reach a clear understanding of the principles, but also to learn something of their historical development and the reason for their existence.

Thayer's *Cases on Evidence.*

Professor WURTS :—

Extraordinary Legal Remedies.　　14 lectures in 2d half-year.
　　An examination and discussion of the common law principles
　　of *habeas corpus, mandamus, quo warranto,* and prohibition.
　　Lectures.

Assistant Professor ZAHM :—

Insurance.　　　　　　　　　　　　　　　　　　　1 hr.
　　A thorough, comprehensive, and critical study of the princi-
　　ples of fire, life, marine, accident, guaranty, credit, and liability
　　insurance law.
　　Vance on *Insurance.*

Professor GAGER :—

Jurisprudence.　　　　　　　　　　　　　　　　　1 hr.
　　In this course law is studied historically as a development,
　　and philosophically as a formal science.
　　Maine's *Ancient Law* and Holland's *Jurisprudence.*

Professor Gager :—

Mortgages.　　　　　　　　　　　　　　　　　　1 hr.
　　This course considers the history of mortgages, and gives a
　　practical working knowledge of the fundamental principles of
　　the law of mortgages in force in the United States.
　　Kirchwey's *Cases on Mortgages.*

Professor ROGERS :—

Municipal Corporations.　　　　　　　　　　　　1 hr.
　　The course considers the creation and dissolution of munici-
　　pal corporations, municipal charters and ordinances, municipal
　　elections and officers, the liability of municipal corporations for
　　contracts and torts, the control of the legislature over them, etc.
　　Smith's *Cases on Municipal Corporations.*

Mr. EDGERTON :—

Partnership.　　　　　　　　　　　　　　　　　　1 hr.
　　An examination and thorough study of all of the principles
　　connected with the partnership relation, including Joint stock
　　companies and limited partnerships.
　　Mecham's *Elements* and Mecham's *Cases on the Law of Part-
　　nerships.*

Mr. KNAPP :—

Practice in Connecticut.　　　　　　10 lectures in 2d half-year.
　　A study of the principles and rules relative to the bringing of
　　actions and preparation for trial in Connecticut.
　　Lectures.

Judge PECK :—
Practice Act of Connecticut.   2 hrs. 1st half-year.

> A study of the history, theory, and practical working of the Practice Act and the rules under it with reference to leading cases.
>
> Lectures and *Connecticut Practice Act with Rules.*

Assistant Professor ZAHM :—
Practice in New York Courts.   1 hr.

> The course covers the several steps in a civil action from its inception to Judgment, together with the various proceedings incidental thereto, and with especial emphasis upon pleading, under the New York Code.
>
> Lectures and the *New York Code of Civil Procedure.*

Professor WURTS :—
Practice in the United States Courts.

                                  2 hrs. 2d half-year.

> A course of lectures on pleading and practice in the Federal Courts, especially in equity.
>
> Wurts's *Cases.*

Professor BALDWIN :—
Railroad Law.   1 hr.

> The discussion is mainly confined to what is distinctive in Railroad Law, but also includes the application to railroad companies of the general rules of corporation law.
>
> Lectures and Baldwin's *Cases on Railroad Law.*

Assistant Professor BEERS :—
Remedies.   1 hr.

> Covering the subject of remedies and remedial rights in the common law and equity systems briefly and under the Codes at length ; embracing the essential elements of the cause of action, pleading, parties, and procedure.
>
> Pomeroy on *Remedies and Remedial Rights.*

Assistant Professor SHERMAN :—
Roman Law.   1 hr.

> The history of Roman Law prior and subsequent to its codification by Justinian. A systematic study of Roman Law, special attention being given to the Institutes and Digest.
>
> Bernard's *First Year of Roman Law* (Sherman's edition), *Yale Cases on Roman Law,* Moyle's *Institute of Justinian,* and Lectures.

Mr. EDGERTON :—

Sales of Personal Property. 2 hrs.

A thorough study of the nature and formalities of the contract of bargain and sale, future sale and conditional sale, and of the rights, duties, and liabilities of the respective parties to the contract.

Lectures and Burdick's *Cases on the Law of Sales.*

Assistant Professor CORBIN :—

Suretyship. 1 hr.

A study of the obligations, the rights, and the defenses of a surety, in relation to the creditor, co-sureties, and others, in equity and at law, whether the surety's contract be regarded as collateral or original.

Ames's *Cases on Suretyship.*

Professor WURTS :—

Taxation. 1 hr. 2d half-year.

This course deals with the exercise of the power of taxation and its limitations, with the remedies of property owners and the rights and liabilities of property owners *inter se.*

Lectures.

Professor ROGERS :—

Trusts. 2 hrs.

The course treats of appointments, substitution, resignation, and removal of trustees, relation of trustees to trust estates, powers, duties, and obligations of trustees, rights and remedies of *cestui que trust* and extinguishment of trusts.

Ames's *Cases on Trusts.*

Mr. DAGGETT :—

Wills. 2 hrs. 1st half-year.

The course includes history, nature of power, testamentary capacity, undue influence, requirements of execution, extended study of leading principles and more frequent problems of construction, and exercises in the drafting of wills.

Gardner on *Wills* and Selected Cases.

Mr. MUNSON :—

Beginnings of Legal Practice. 7 lectures in 2d half-year.

Generally speaking, these lectures are intended to acquaint the novitiate with the practical side of his profession, and with that which is acquired only by actual experience at the bar.

Dr. THACHER :—

Special Topics in Corporation Law.

5 lectures in 2d half-year.

The course is intended to show the nature of incorporation or the franchise of corporate being, the use and abuse of the fiction of the legal entity, the various relations to which incorporation gives rise, and the special difficulties of corporation law.

Mr. WETZEL :—

Forensic Oratory.   1 hr.

Students are instructed in composition and delivery of forensic oratory. This course is open to those who have had the course in vocal culture of the first year.

Robinson's *Forensic Oratory.*

Dr. MORRIS :—

International Arbitration and Procedure.   3 lectures.

Professor BALDWIN :—

Legal Ethics.   5 lectures in 2d half-year.

Mr. FOSTER :—

Liberty of Contract.   5 lectures in 2d half-year.

The course includes a discussion of the constitutionality of labor legislation or laws intended to better the condition of the manual working classes.

Judge PERRY :—

Parliamentary Law.   12 lectures in 1st half-year.

The course considers origin of parliamentary law and modern common law on the subject. It explains changes commonly made by special rules, and gives directions for the conduct of deliberative bodies.

Mr. TOWNSEND :—

Transfer of Monetary Securities.   5 lectures.

The course treats of the history and growth of corporate securities, and their negotiability and "quasi negotiability" as developed by necessities of commerce, estoppel, custom, etc. The longer course, when given, takes up gambling contracts, usury, and history, and methods of London and New York Exchanges and Paris Bourse.

Assistant Professor ZAHM :—

Conflict of Laws.   5 lectures.

EXAMINATIONS

The rules relating to written examinations are as follows:

1. The members of the First-Year class, at the end of the first term, will be examined upon all subjects studied during the term. This examination is intended to test the student's progress and is not final upon the topics covered. If the result discloses a student's inability to satisfactorily carry the work of the School, his registration will be cancelled.

2. The members of all classes will be given final examinations at the time the study of a subject is concluded, provided the work is completed prior to the Easter recess. If concluded thereafter it is optional with the instructor to give the examination upon the completion of the work or postpone it to the end of the academic year.

3. Examination will include not only the prescribed subjects in the first and second years, and the elected subjects in the third and fourth years, but also such optional courses as the student may have pursued. Marks obtained in examinations on optional subjects will be considered in determining relative rank at the close of the year.

4. When a student's unexcused absences in any study amount to 15 per cent. of the total requirement in that study, his registration in that subject is cancelled and the privilege of examination therein is denied.

The student should present his excuse for absence in writing to the Dean.

5. A member of the First-Year class cannot be advanced to the Second-Year class until he shall have removed all entrance conditions, if any; satisfactorily passed examinations on subjects requiring at least eleven (11) hours of work per week; attained at least a pass mark on a general average of all the required studies of the year; and been deemed worthy of advancement by the Faculty.

6. A member of the Second-Year class cannot be advanced to the Third-Year class until he shall have removed all conditions on First-Year subjects, if any; obtained credit for at least twenty-six (26) hours of required work; and complied with the other provisions of Rule 4.

7. No student is admitted to an examination in a subject for which he did not regularly register.

* 8. Special examinations cannot be given except by vote of the Faculty and under special circumstances.

9. The examination of conditioned students will be held at Hendrie Hall on September 21, 22, and 23, 1908, at 9.00 A. M.

PRACTICE COURTS

The intention is that students shall acquire as thorough a knowledge of actual practice as can be derived in a law school. With this end in view the YALE MOOT COURT and the SUPREME COURT OF THE YALE LAW SCHOOL have been established.

The YALE MOOT COURT is presided over by the instructor in Court Procedure, who has himself had actual experience as a judge of a trial court. The court is provided with a full corps of officers, a clerk, assistant clerk, sheriff and the necessary deputies. It is divided into two departments, known as the First Department and the Second Department. The members of the Third-Year class constitute the bar of the First Department, and the members of the Second-Year class that of the Second Department.

The purpose is to give practical instruction in pleading and practice at law and in equity, both under the common law system and the "reformed" or "code" procedure. Pleading and practice in the Second Department is according to the common law; and in the First Department is under the New York Code of Civil Procedure in all civil cases assigned to students not resident in Connecticut, and under the Connecticut Practice Act and the Connecticut Rules of Court in all civil cases assigned to students resident in Connecticut. Any student may, however, be transferred from Connecticut to New York practice, or *vice versa*, upon application to the instructor in Court Procedure.

Equity cases are governed by the rules of equity practice in the United States courts.

Printed statements of facts are prepared and assigned upon which process is to be issued, pleadings drawn, and the case conducted to an issue. When there is a question of fact it is submitted to trial by jury, the jurors being summoned from the First-Year class. Questions of law are argued and disposed of upon the facts submitted.

Writs of error, or appeals, from the judgments of the Yale Moot Court may be taken to the Supreme Court of the Yale Law School, which is composed of some of the members of the Faculty of Law.

Students issue, serve, and return the process, prepare and file the proper pleadings, conduct the trial (when it is necessary to have a trial) and make the legal argument upon the facts involved. When a judgment is obtained the successful party enters it upon the court records. Writs of error, executions, or other writs are prepared by the students and signed by the clerk of the court.

In this way the student is given practical experience in the commencement of suits, the preparation of pleadings, the argument of the law, the trial of the case, the entry of judgment, the taking out of execution, and the appealing of the case to the court of last resort.

CONVEYANCING

A COURSE IN CONVEYANCING has been established with the view of extending the practical instruction given in the Law School. The purpose of the course is not merely to give systematic instruction in the substantive law of the subject, but also to afford a thorough drill in the drafting of deeds, mortgages, wills, contracts, and other instruments which the lawyer in actual practice is likely to be called upon to prepare. The work of the student is submitted to the instructor, and is reviewed and commented upon by him.

STUDENTS' ORGANIZATIONS

There are two flourishing debating societies—the KENT CLUB and the WAYLAND CLUB—which are conducted by the law students, and afford a good opportunity for practice in public speaking.

Class Quiz clubs also exist and hold their meetings in rooms provided for their use in the Law School. Those formed in the first year are under the special direction of a competent instructor appointed by the Governing Board.

The YALE FORUM and the YALE POLITICAL CLUB have been formed by the students of the Law School. The organizations are non-partisan and are addressed from time to time by men prominent in political affairs.

The YALE SENATE is composed of students in the Graduate Course in the Law School who have organized themselves into a body patterned after the Senate of the United States. Bills are introduced and discussed as in a legislative body.

THE YALE LAW JOURNAL

The YALE LAW JOURNAL is a legal periodical conducted by an editorial board of students. The members of this board are chosen by competition, the results of which are passed on by a committee of the Faculty, which reports to that body its findings and recommendations. The Journal contains about seventy-five pages in each issue, and appears once a month during the academic year. Each issue is made up of five chief departments: First, leading articles upon important and interesting legal subjects; second, comments upon significant occurrences in the legal world; third, abstracts and digests of the most important recent cases with a citation of leading authorities previously decided upon the same points; fourth, reviews of books; and fifth, alumni notes.

GRADUATE COURSE

The graduate course is designed to afford to the advanced student an opportunity to round out his legal acquirements and to investigate the philosophic principles of human law in a more comprehensive manner than is possible in the undergraduate course. The primary conceptions to which the student was introduced at the commencement of his studies are again taken up and developed in a scientific method, and examined in the light of various systems of practical jurisprudence now or heretofore prevailing.

Graduate instruction, besides continuing some of the lines of study pursued in the undergraduate course, comprehends many of a more scientific and philosophical character, including Comparative Jurisprudence, Legislation and Government, Legal History, Economics, Roman Law, Foreign European Codes, and Private International Law. The regular course of study for candidates for the degree of Master of Laws covers a period of one year, but students are at liberty to take a part of the course one year and part another year, being examined at the close of each year on the studies pursued and dividing the tuition fees in like proportion. Two years of study will generally be found necessary in order to complete the work for the degree of Doctor of Civil Law.

ADMISSION TO GRADUATE COURSE

The following persons will be admitted to the graduate course as candidates for the degree of Master of Laws (M.L. or LL.M.):

1. Persons who are graduates of some Law School which is a member of the Association of American Law Schools.

2. Persons who are graduates of some Law School in a foreign country, which Law School is of recognized standing and requires at least three (3) years' study of Law as a condition of graduation.

3. Persons who have been admitted to the Bar, either in this country or another, and who have been actively engaged in practice for not less than five (5) years, and who present a recommendation from one of the judges of the highest court of the State or Country in which they have practiced.

The following persons will be admitted as candidates for the degree of Doctor of Civil Law (D.C.L.):

1. Persons who have a degree in Arts or Science from a College or University of recognized standing, or have had an education equivalent to that required for that degree, and who are also graduates of some Law School which is a member of the Association of American Law Schools, or of some Law School in a foreign country,

which Law School is of recognized standing and requires at least a three (3) years' study of Law as a condition of graduation.

2. Persons who are graduates of the Yale Law School and are unable to meet the' requirements as established in the preceding paragraph but who have obtained a law degree at Yale, either *cum laude*, *magna cum laude*, or *summa cum laude*.

3. But no person can be admitted as a candidate for the degree of Doctor of Civil Law without passing a preliminary examination upon the subjects following :

(A) The outlines of Roman Law and History unless the applicant received his degree at a Law School where Roman Law constituted one of the studies upon which he there passed a satisfactory examination, which fact shall be duly certified.

(B) Latin, and either French or German.

The examination is designed to test the candidate's ability to translate at sight.

In the case of students from foreign and non-English speaking countries, a good knowledge of the English language may be accepted as an equivalent for that of French or German.

Examinations for admission to the graduate course will be held on the second day after the University Commencement, beginning at 9.00 A. M., in the Law School Building.

GRADUATE COURSES OF INSTRUCTION

A graduate student must elect and satisfactorily complete at least twelve hours of class-room work. He must select a major course of study and such number of minor courses as may be approved by the Faculty. The major course must occupy at least two hours a week throughout the year. Several minor courses, on cognate subjects, may be taken as together constituting a major course. The major and minor courses may be upon the same or different topics, in the six groups stated, but courses covering

33

at least three hours a week, throughout the year, must be selected from one or more of Groups II, III, V, and VI.

One intending to apply for the degree of Doctor of Civil Law must make Course 9 in Roman Law his major study.

Roman Law is made the principal topic for those who desire the degree of D.C.L. The Institutes of Justinian and a considerable part of the Commentaries of Gaius are read. Illustrative cases are studied from the Digest, including some as treated in Eckert's *Chrestomathie*, and Hess's *Achtzehn Rechtsfälle*. Roby's *Introduction to the Digest* is used and leading titles of the Digest, Code, and Novels made the subject of investigation.

The lectures on Political and Social Science, Economics, etc., are given in connection with the graduate courses in the Philosophical Department of the University, and are attended by the graduate students of the Law School in common with the members of that Department.

Elections may be made by graduate students from the following topics and courses:

GROUP I

The Organization and Working of Human Society

Professor GREGORY, Dr. BISHOP, Mr. BOWMAN, Mr. HUNTINGTON, and Mr. BOGGS :—

1 *Physical and Commercial Geography.*   3 hrs.
  [See Course XV, A 1, page 174.]

Professors ADAMS and WALKER :—

2 *Medieval Institutions.*   2 hrs. 1st year, 1 hr. 2d year.
  [See Course IX, 71, page 376.]

Professor FARNAM :—

[3 *Social Politics.*   2 hrs.
  [See Course IX, 26, page 372.]
  Omitted in 1907–08.]

Professor SUMNER :—

4 *The Self-Perpetuation of Society.*   2 hrs.
  [See Course IX, 3, page 370.]

Professor SUMNER :—

5 *The Science of Society.* 2 hrs.
   [See Course XX, C 1, page 192.]

GROUP II

General Jurisprudence and Ancient Law

Professor GAGER :—

6 *General Jurisprudence.* 1 hr.
   This is an undergraduate course open to graduates. See p. 504.

Professor GAGER :—

7 *General Jurisprudence.* 1 hr.
   This is an advanced course upon special topics in legal history and legal theory which may be selected according to the needs of those taking it. Primary consideration is given to English and American law. Holmes's *Common Law* may be referred to as indicating the nature and scope of the work required.

Assistant Professor CHARLES P. SHERMAN :—

8 *Roman Law.* 1 hr.
   An undergraduate course open to graduates. See p. 505.

9 *Roman Law.* 2 hrs.
   [See Course IX, 60, page 375.]

10 *Canon Law.* 1 hr. 2d half 2d term.
   [See Course IX, 61, page 375.]

GROUP III

Comparative Jurisprudence and Government

Professor KELLER :—

10 *Colonization.* 2 hrs.
   [See Course XX, B 3, page 191.]

Mr. HARRIMAN :—

11 *Comparative Administrative Law.* 1 hr.

Professor RAYNOLDS :—

12 *Comparative Constitutional Law.* 2 hrs.
   [See Course IX, 54, page 374.]

Professor BALDWIN :—

13 *Private International Law.*   1 hr.

This is a seminary class for the conversational discussion of the various topics covered by this branch of law, and examination of the present attitude towards them of the principal nations of the world. Leading cases in the American courts, bearing on the conflict of laws, are studied, and Wharton's *Private International Law* is read.

Professor RAYNOLDS :—

14 *The French Codes.*   2 hrs.

[See Course IX, 55, page 374.]

Professor RAYNOLDS :—

15 *The German Imperial Code.*   1 hr.

[See Course IX, 56, page 375.]

Professor RAYNOLDS :—

16 *Spanish Law.*   1 hr.

[See Course IX, 57, page 375.]

GROUP IV
American and English Constitutional Law and History

Professor BALDWIN :—

17 *American Constitutional Law.*   2 hrs.

An undergraduate course open to graduates. See p. 500.

Professor CHARLES H. SMITH :—

18 *American (Constitutional) History.*   2 hrs.

[See Course IX, 88, page 379.]

Professor BASSETT :—

15 *American Political Development, 1815-1845.*   2 hrs.

[See Course IX, 86, page 378.]

Professor CHARLES H. SMITH :—

20 *The United States since 1860.*   2 hrs.

[See Course IX, 89, page 379.]

Professor ARTHUR M. WHEELER :—

21 *Constitutional and Political History of England since 1760.*

[See Course IX, 83, page 378.]   2 hrs.

Professor ADAMS :—

22 *English Constitutional History to the present time.*   2 hrs.

[See Course XIX, C 5, page 189.]

Assistant Professor RICHARDSON :—

23 *English History 'from the accession of the Tudors to the reign of William and Mary.* ·   2 hrs.
[See Course IX, 82, page 378.]

Professor WOOLSEY :—

[24 *International Law in American History.*   1 hr.
A seminary course.
Omitted 1907–08.]

GROUP V
American Jurisprudence and Legislation
PUBLIC LAW

Professor ROGERS :—

25 *Municipal Corporations.*   1 hr·
An undergraduate course open to graduates.   See p. 504.

Judge PERRY :—

26 *Parliamentary Law and Drafting of Statutes.*
12 lectures.

PRIVATE LAW

Assistant Professor BEERS :—

27 *Attorneys.*   1 hr.
A course upon the rights, duties, and liabilities of attorneys at law in all the States, embracing the history of the office of attorney, and a study of the leading cases upon the subject.

Mr. BEACH :—

28 *Admiralty, Copyrights, Patents, and Trademarks.*   1 hr.
An undergraduate course open to graduates.   See p. 502.

Mr. COXE :—

29 *Bankruptcy.*   1 hr. 2d half year.
An undergraduate course open to graduates.   See p. 503.

Mr. BOWERS :—

30 *Forest Administration and Law.*   2 hrs. fall term.
[See Course VI, 95, page 354.]

Assistant Professor ZAHM :—

31 *Insurance.*   ·   1 hr.
An undergraduate course open to graduates.   See p. 504.

Mr. WEBB :—   •

32 *Medical Jurisprudence.*   1 hr. 1st term.
An undergraduate course open to graduates.   See p. 502.   ·

Assistant Professor CORBIN :—

33　*Mining, Irrigation, and Public Lands.*　　　　　1 hr.

A study of the Federal mining law applicable to the public lands, including State legislation and local and land office rules; of the law of irrigation in the arid land States; and of the homestead and other public land laws.

Lectures and Illustrative Cases.

Mr. EDGERTON :—

34　*Partnership.*　　　　　　　　　1 hr.

An undergraduate course open to graduates. See p. 504.

Professor ROGERS :—

35　*Private Corporations.*　　　　　　2 hrs.

An undergraduate course open to graduates. See p. 501.

Professor GAGER :—

36　*Public Service Corporations.*　　　　1 hr.

The laws special to the conduct of those kinds of business classed as public service business and public utilities are investigated through the medium of selected cases and informal lectures. The nature of such business, the methods of incorporation and public control, and the rights and obligations of those conducting such business, at common law and under statutes, together with some attention to the laws concerning combinations and monopolies, are the leading topics.

Lectures.

Professor BALDWIN :—

37　*Railroad Law.*　　　　　　　　1 hr.

An undergraduate course open to graduates. See p. 505.

Professor ROGERS :—

38　*Receivers.*　　　　　　　　　1 hr.

The course treats of the general principles relating to the law of receivers. It considers among other topics the appointment of receivers, conflicts between courts in making appointments, suits by and against receivers, effects of their appointment, the duties and liabilities of receivers, receivers of corporations, including railroads, of partnerships, of mortgaged property, and in Judgment creditors suits.

Lectures and Selected Cases.

Assistant Professor BEERS :—

39　*Remedies.*　　　　　　　　　1 hr.

An undergraduate course open to graduates. See p. 505.

Assistant Professor CORBIN :—

40 *Suretyship.*   1 hr.
    An undergraduate course open to graduates. See p. 506.

Professor ROGERS :—

41 *Trusts and Trustees.*   2 hrs.
    An undergraduate course open to graduates. See p. 506.

GROUP VI
International Law and Diplomacy

Professor BOURNE :—

[42 *Diplomatic History of the United States.*   2 hrs.
    [See Course IX, 87, page 378.]
    Omitted in 1907–08.]

Professor WILLIAMS :—

[43 *Diplomatic Intercourse with Asiatic Nations.*   2 hrs.
    [See Course IX, 94, page 379.]
    Omitted in 1907–08.]

Professor WHEELER :—

44 *History of Treaties, 1763–1815.*   1 hr.
    [See Course IX, 79, page 377.]

Professor HYDE :—

45 *American Diplomatic History.*   1 hr.
    An undergraduate course open to graduates. See p. 502.

Professor WOOLSEY :—

[46 *International Law.*   1 hr.
    Research and advanced work.
    Omitted in 1907–08.]

Any courses from the undergraduate Law School curriculum, other than those above named, may be substituted for any of the courses named on American Jurisprudence and Legislation (Group V), by permission of the Faculty. Graduates of other Law Schools are recommended to make substitutions of undergraduate in place of some of the strictly graduate courses, in respect to such topics as they may not previously have pursued to the same extent or in the same manner as taught here. •

Other courses in Political Science, Finance, History, etc., in the Department of Philosophy and the Arts, may also be substituted for some of those named in Groups I and IV, on consultation with the Faculty.

The courses above outlined are subject to change from time to time, and books should not be purchased until the work is entered upon.

In all cases the Faculty reserves the right to withdraw a course if less than three students elect it.

THE GRADUATE THESIS

Each graduate student is required to prepare a thesis upon some topic, preferably one connected with his major subject, which topic must be approved by the Dean.

The subject of this thesis must be filed with the Secretary of the Faculty on or before the first Monday in December.

Each thesis must contain :

1. An introductory statement of the position to be maintained, or proposition to be contended for, and also a final *résumé* of results.

2. An analytical outline of its contents with reference to the pages of the thesis.

3. A bibliography of the works consulted, as well as an alphabetical list of the cases cited, giving their respective dates and a reference to the pages of the thesis whereon they are cited.

4. A statement as to the period for which the cases have been examined.

Cases must be cited by name and volume and year. The student is expected to exhaust the cases decided during the period covered by his thesis, including the latest accessible cases upon the subject.

The thesis submitted for the degree of Doctor of Civil Law is regarded as of especial importance and cannot be accepted unless it is of marked excellence, evinces original research, and amounts to a contribution to legal scholarship. While its acceptance depends more upon its subject matter than upon its literary form, it must exhibit creditable literary ability.

The thesis must be typewritten on linen sheets, 8½ by 11 inches in size. There must be double spaces between the typewritten lines, and a clear margin of two inches at the left, and a like margin of one and one-half inches at the top and bottom. A thesis cannot be accepted unless the typewriting is neatly and accurately done.

An original typewritten copy must be filed with the Secretary of the Faculty on or before May 1.

All accepted theses will be bound by the School and deposited in the Law Library.

GENERAL INFORMATION
EQUIPMENT

HENDRIE HALL, the Law School building, faces the Green, near the College Campus. It was erected for the Law School's exclusive use and was completed in 1900. The building and grounds are valued at one hundred and seventy-five thousand dollars. The building is named after John W. Hendrie, a graduate of Yale College in 1851, now deceased, who gave sixty-five thousand dollars of the fund which the friends of the School raised for its erection. It contains ample rooms for the law library, and has, together with the executive offices and professors' rooms, six large lecture halls, and reading, conversation, and consultation rooms for the use of the students. The building is within two blocks of the Court House of New Haven County, in which two terms of the Supreme Court of Errors of Connecticut are held annually; while the Superior Court and Court of Common Pleas (the principal civil and criminal courts of the State) are also in session there almost daily during each of the School terms, thus affording the students peculiar facilities for observing actual practice in court.

LAW LIBRARY. The Law Library embraces all the reports of Great Britain and America, with an extensive collection of text-books, and the leading legal periodicals. It contains about 30,000 volumes, and 1,600 pamphlets.

Students are not allowed to take the books from the building, but are encouraged to examine the books on the shelves for themselves, without the intervention of the librarian. The familiarity with the reports and authorities thus gained, the Faculty deem of great importance in accustoming the student to prepare his cases intelligently and thoroughly in his future practice.

The Library includes the Albert Sproull Wheeler Library of Roman Law, now containing 1,837 volumes and being constantly increased as new works on Roman Law appear. These books constitute a separate collection, are in charge of the Law Librarian, and are accessible on request.

The Library also contains the T. L. Cole collection of Statutory Law, numbering some 4,000 volumes and constituting one of the most complete collections ever made of the Session Laws of the various States and Territories of the United States. Those desiring access to this collection should apply to the Law Librarian.

The Library is open daily, except Sundays, from 8.00 A. M. to 10.00 P. M. during the academic year, and during the Christmas vacation and Easter recess from 9.00 A. M. to 10.00 P. M. In the summer vacation it is open Tuesdays only from 9.00 A. M. to 1.00 P. M., and from 2.00 to 5.00 P. M.

A permanent endowment for the support of the Library was established in 1873 by Hon. James E. English, M.A.

For various University privileges of interest to students of the Department, including the University Library, Dining Hall, Gymnasium, Infirmary, etc., see a later section of the catalogue.

PRIZES

Essays submitted in competition for a prize must be typewritten, signed by a fictitious name and handed in under cover, which should be plainly marked on the outside to indicate the prize intended. An essay must be accompanied by a sealed envelope containing the assumed name and the real name of the writer. The essays, except those for the John A. Porter Prize, must be deposited with the Secretary of the Faculty on or before May 1. In no case will a prize be awarded if none of the competing essays is of sufficient merit.

The following prize is open to competition to any person who has been pursuing a regular course for a degree in any Department during the whole of the current College year:

The JOHN A. PORTER PRIZE, being the income of a fund of five thousand dollars, established by the Kingsley Trust Association in 1872, is offered for the best English Essay on a prescribed subject. For fuller information see page 575.

The following prizes are open to competition to Law students only:

The JOSEPH PARKER PRIZE of one hundred and twenty-five dollars, established by the will of Miss Eliza T. Parker in 1898, is awarded for the best thesis on a subject connected with Roman Law. This prize is open to any member of the School at graduation from either the undergraduate or graduate course.

For the year 1908, competitors may write on any of the following subjects:

1. The Roman Roots of the Institution of the Jury.
2. Code Theodosius I, II. *De Jurisdictione et ubiquis conveniri debeat.*
3. The Evolution and Scope of the Roman Law of Evidence.
4. A Comparison of the Legal Status of the Roman *Peregrini* with that of the Native Inhabitants of the United States Colonies of Spanish Origin.

The TOWNSEND PRIZE of one hundred dollars, established by the Hon. James M. Townsend in 1874, is awarded that member of the Third-Year class who shall write and pronounce the best oration at the public anniversary exercises on graduation.

No oration shall contain over twelve hundred words. Students will write on every other page, leaving a full margin on the left of the page. No oration shall, as delivered, occupy more than ten minutes.

Orations must be handed to the Secretary of the Law School on or before April 1, 1908.

The selection of the final contestants will be determined by a preliminary contest of those whose orations are approved by the committee.

For the year 1908, competitors may write on any one of the following subjects :

1. The Limitations of International Arbitration.
2. Roger B. Taney.
3. The Mending or the Ending of the House of Lords.
4. The Growth of the Constitution by Construction.
5. The Lawyer's Present Relation to Society.
6. The Forty-sixth State.
7. The Hague Conference of 1907.
8. Federalism of To-day.

The MONTGOMERY PRIZE of fifty dollars established by Phelps Montgomery, B.A., LL.B., in 1904, is awarded to that member of the Third-Year class who receives the highest marks at his annual examination.

The JEWELL PRIZE of fifty dollars, established by the Hon. Marshall Jewell, M.A., in 1871, is awarded to that member of the Second-Year class who receives the highest marks at his annual examination.

The BETTS PRIZE of fifty dollars, established by Frederic H. Betts, LL.D., in 1875, is awarded to that member of the First-Year class who receives the highest marks at his annual examination.

The WAYLAND PRIZES, one of fifty dollars, one of thirty dollars, and one of twenty dollars, established by Professor Francis Wayland in 1890, are awarded to those three members of the Yale Kent Club who, at a public competitive debate, are pronounced first, second, and third in excellence as debaters.

The MUNSON PRIZES, one of fifty dollars, one of thirty dollars, and one of twenty dollars, established in 1905 by Cyrus LaRue Munson, M.A., LL.B., of Williamsport, Pennsylvania, a graduate of the Law School of the class of 1875, are awarded to those three members of the Wayland Club who, at a public competitive debate, are pronounced first, second, and third in excellence as debaters.

HONORS

Honors are awarded in each class, at the end of the year, to those students who have maintained a high standing in all the studies of the year.

CERTIFICATE OF ATTENDANCE

A regular student who has been connected with the Department for a period not entitling him to graduate, or a special student who is not a candidate for a degree, may, on application to the Secretary of the Faculty, receive an official certificate, which states the time of his attendance and the subjects on which he has passed examination.

DEGREES

The law degrees are conferred at the Commencement of the University, which is held on the last Wednesday in June. On this occasion all candidates for degrees are required to present themselves in person.

The rules relating to degrees are as follows :

1. Degrees are granted by the Corporation of Yale University to those persons who have completed the course of law study, with the requirements prescribed, and been recommended by the Faculty of the Department.

2. No student may be a candidate for a degree on less than a full year of residence and study, or on less than a complete year's work.

3. Any student who has not complied with the requirements for a degree before the end of his Law School course may be recommended for his degree in a subsequent year when all his deficiencies are made up.

4. No student who fails to obtain his degree in due course because of conditions, will be permitted to remove those conditions later than two years after the graduation of his regular class, unless permission is granted by special vote of the Faculty.

5. Candidates for the degree of BACHELOR OF LAWS must, to the satisfaction of the Faculty, complete courses amounting to fifteen hours per week for three years.

6. Candidates for the degree of BACHELOR OF CIVIL LAW must, to the satisfaction of the Faculty, attain a like credit under the conditions specified on p. 485.

7. Candidates for the degree of MASTER OF LAWS must, in like manner, attain a credit of at least twelve hours per week for one year, and comply with the conditions specified on p. 512.

8. Candidates for the degree of DOCTOR OF CIVIL LAW are required to satisfy the Faculty that they possess high attainments in scholarship and that they have complied with the conditions specified on pp. 512–13 and on p. 520.

9. Degrees are awarded, in cases of students of unusual merit, *cum laude, magna cum laude,* or *summa cum laude.*

EXPENSES

The annual fees for tuition and use of the University and Law libraries are one hundred and fifty dollars for all students studying for a degree. Bills for tuition will be made out and delivered to the students, or (*request to that effect being made*) mailed to the parent or guardian, three times a year, fifty dollars being payable at the beginning of the first·term, and fifty dollars at the beginning, and again at the middle, of the second term, at the office of the Treasurer of the University in Woodbridge Hall. If not paid before the end of the month following the month in which they are issued, the student's registration will be cancelled and his name removed from all class lists. A student whose registration is cancelled is required at once to cease attending lectures or recitations, using the Libraries or Gymnasium, boarding at the University Dining Hall, and making use of any other privileges as a student until his indebtedness to the University has been arranged satisfactorily and his registration restored. Failure to comply with this rule is cause for final separation of the student from the University. Registration cannot be restored without the payment of an additional registration fee of five dollars.

The tuition charged for special students will be on the basis charged students studying for a degree, but proportioned to the amount of instruction and supervision required.

An additional charge of five dollars is made for graduation and is included in the last bill of the third year.

The following table exhibits the scale of annual expenditures :

	Low	Average	Liberal
Tuition	$150	$150	$150
Board, 36 weeks	125	175	250
Half room, heat and light.	35	120	175
Washing	15	25	40
	$325	$470	$615

The student may expect to expend for text- and case-books in the first year about thirty dollars; in the second year twenty-five dollars, and in the third year from twenty to forty dollars, according to the subjects elected. As the books used for purposes of instruction will be found, for the most part, essential in subsequent practice, no loss will be incurred in their purchase.

Board at cost can be obtained at the University Dining Hall by members of the Law School. Applications for seats should be addressed to the Superintendent of the Yale University Dining Hall.

The following dormitories, which are under University supervision, are open to law students: Pierson Hall, and East and West Divinity Halls. Students who desire to secure rooms in any one of the dormitories named will find it necessary to make early application. Communications concerning rooms in Pierson Hall should be addressed to Professor Henry Parks Wright, Dean of Yale College, and communications concerning rooms in the Divinity Halls should be addressed to the Superintendent of the Yale Divinity Halls.

Kent Hall, though not under University supervision, is not far removed from Hendrie Hall, and is specially open to Law students. Communications concerning rooms in this dormitory should be addressed to the Manager of Kent Hall.

Those who desire more detailed information concerning the Law School may address letters of inquiry to the Secretary of the Yale Law School.

YALE-COLUMBIA COURSES IN PREPA-
RATION FOR FOREIGN SERVICE

The system of .COURSES FOR FOREIGN SERVICE inaugurated by Yale University and Columbia University is designed to prepare students for practical work in foreign countries, either in the service of the United States Government, or in business enterprises, or in missionary or scientific lines. The course of study includes seven divisions: (1) Languages, (2) Geography, (3) Ethnography, (4) History, (5) Religions, (6) Economics, (7) Law.

Students registering for this work are expected to have completed successfully at least two years of undergraduate work. If this preliminary work does not include six hours of college French or German and the regular college course in the general principles of economics, in American history, and in European history of the nineteenth century, the student must either pass special examinations on these subjects before admission or pursue them subsequently in addition to the courses otherwise required for the certificate.

A considerable number of the individual courses (see detailed list below) may be taken by undergraduates and counted both toward the Bachelor's degree and toward the Yale-Columbia certificate. The successful completion of the courses offered, which (as a whole and by itself) will normally occupy three years in the case of candidates for the consular service, and two years in the case of candidates for other foreign service in special fields, will entitle the student, on recommendation of the joint committee in charge of the course of study, to an appropriate certificate, signed by the Presidents of Yale University and Columbia University. The fee for registration for the certificate is five dollars.

A special shelf has been reserved in the University Library, where the student will find printed information regarding consular and commercial service in foreign countries.

Students who contemplate working for the Yale-Columbia certificate should consult Professor Emery or Professor Phillips, and should apply to the latter for the separate pamphlet containing a full list of courses and other detailed information, including the provisions of the new law regarding consular positions and the rules for promotion.

The full list of courses open to Yale undergraduates under this head is as follows:

French A 1 (*Elementary French*), A 2, A 4, or A 5 (*Second-Year French*), B 1a (*French Masterpieces*), C 3 (*Practice in Writing and Speaking French*).

Italian A 1 (*Elementary Italian*), A 2 (*Italian Literature*).

Spanish A 1 (*Elementary Spanish*), B 1 (*Reading and Composition in Spanish*), C 2 (*General View of Spanish Literature*).

German A 1 (*Elementary German*), A 2, A 4, or A 5 (*Second-Year German*), B 1b (*Prose of Modern Historians and Critics*), B 3 (*German Composition and Conversation*). .

Geology A 1 (*Physical and Commercial Geography*), B 5 (*Geography of North America*), B 6 (*Geography of South America*), B 7 (*Geography of Asia*), C 7 (*Geographic Controls in History*).

History B 7 (*Medieval Asia and the Mohammedan Conquest*), B 18 (*Modern Asiatic History*), C 7 (*History of Spanish America, chiefly in the Nineteenth Century*), C 11 (*European Colonies in Asia and Africa*), C 12 (*Chinese Culture and Institutions*).

Anthropology B 1 (*Anthropology*), B 3 or C 4 (*Colonization*), B 4 (*Transportation Systems*), B 5 (*Natural History of Commerce*), B 6 (*Markets*), C 3 (*Ethnology*).

Economics and Law A 2 (*Elementary Statistics*), A 6 (*Elementary Law*), A 8 (*International Law*), B 6 (*Economic History of the United States*), C 5 (*Trade Statistics*), C 9 (*Commerce and Commercial Policy in the Nineteenth Century*).

PART IV

INSTITUTIONS CONNECTED WITH THE UNIVERSITY

LIBRARIES

JOHN CHRISTOPHER SCHWAB, PH.D., *Librarian*

ADDISON VANNAME, M.A., *Librarian Emeritus*

FRANKLIN BOWDITCH DEXTER, LITT.D., *Assistant Librarian*

ANDREW KEOGH, M.A., *Reference Librarian*

CURATORS

KAN-ICHI ASAKAWA, PH.D. (*Japanese and Chinese Collections*)

EDWARD THEODORE NEWELL, B.A. (*Numismatic Collections*)

CATALOGUERS

Mrs. JENNIE CAMPBELL

RUTH LOUISE COMES

A. PAMELIA DINGMAN

JOEL NELSON ENO, M.A.

Mrs. JESSIE CRAIG HARGER

ELLEN A. HEDRICK, B.A., *Reviser*

ARABELLA ENSIGN HORTON

ANNIE ELIZA HUTCHINS, *Reviser*

SARA GARDNER HYDE, *Reviser*

CONSTANCE KERSCHNER

ARNE KILDAL, PH.B., B.L.S., *Reviser*

ANNA MARIE MONRAD, B.S.

CORNELIA E. NOTZ, B.A.

JESSIE AGNES PARSONS

HARRIET BENTON PHELPS

ISABELLA MAUDE TISDALE

ADRIENNE VAN WINKLE, *Reviser*

ALICE AMELIA WOOD, B.S.

ASSISTANTS

HENRY ROBERT GRUENER (*Order and Accession Department*)

Mrs. HENRIETTA CLARK GILBERT (*Order and Accession Department*)

GEORGE ALEXANDER JOHNSON (*Linonian and Brothers Library*)

MAYNARD RAY SANBORN (*Order and Accession Department*)

EDNA MAY GILLETTE (*Private Secretary to the Librarian*)

JAMES ALOYSIUS DELACEY *(Order and Accession Department)*
ELIZABETH DESHLER BOYLES *(Order and Accession Department)*
CHARLES DAVID FAIRMAN *(Delivery Desk)*
KARL DIEHL *(Reading Room)*

The Standing Committee in charge of the University Library, appointed by the Corporation, consists of President HADLEY, the Librarian (Secretary), Director RUSSELL H. CHITTENDEN, Professors EDWARD S. DANA, THOMAS D. SEYMOUR, GEORGE B. ADAMS, and CLIVE DAY.

The whole number of books in the several libraries of the University is about 500,000. This number includes both bound and unbound volumes, but does not include many thousands of unenumerated pamphlets. The annual accessions exceed 20,000, and include more than 1,000 periodical publications and publications of learned societies, about half of which are foreign.

The UNIVERSITY LIBRARY proper contains about 400,000 volumes. These are preserved in the Old Library Building and in the Chittenden Library, the latter erected by the munificence of the late Hon. Simeon B. Chittenden. The recent generous bequest of William Baldwin Ross, B.A. 1852, has enabled the University to erect a third building between these two, which contains offices for the Librarians, a series of study rooms, and a book-stack sufficient to hold a maximum of 400,000 volumes.

While designed especially for the use of the officers and students of the University, the privileges of the Library are open to graduates of the University, residents of New Haven, and visitors in general, who, as investigators, may have occasion to consult it.

The Yale University Library has among its notable collections the following:—The Edward E. Salisbury collection of Oriental books and manuscripts; the Count Landberg collection of Arabic manuscripts; the collection of Chinese literature, including the collection of the late

Professor S. Wells Williams; a collection of 3,000 volumes of Japanese literature; the J. Sumner Smith Russian library, including general periodicals and publications of learned societies, and aggregating over 6,000 volumes; the Henry M. Dexter library of Congregational history; the Ezra Stiles manuscript diaries and itineraries; the Jonathan Edwards manuscripts; an extensive collection of American newspaper files, and of earlier English periodical and dramatic literature since the Restoration; a collection of coins; the Foreign Missions library, recently bequeathed to the University by the late Professor George E. Day; the Marsh Paleontological library, the bequest of the late Professor Othniel C. Marsh; the Wheeler Roman Law library, bequeathed by the late Professor Albert S. Wheeler; the William Loring Andrews collection of incunabula; the Scandinavian library of Count Riant; the Curtius library of Classical Literature, especially of Classical Archæology; the R. von Mohl library of Political Science.

The University Library is open on week days throughout the year with the exception of the seven leading holidays. On Saturdays during vacations it is closed after 1.00 P. M. The Library hours during term time are from 8.30 A. M. to 5.00 P. M.; during vacations, from 9.00 A. M. to 1.00 P. M. and from 2.15 to 5.00 P. M.

The UNIVERSITY READING ROOM, containing books of reference, the leading scholarly periodicals, and such books as are reserved for special use in connection with different courses of study, is open during term time from 8.30 A. M. to 9.00 P. M.; during vacations, from 9.00 A. M. to 1.00 P. M. and from 2.15 to 5.00 P. M.

The LINONIAN AND BROTHERS LIBRARY contains about 25,000 volumes, to which additions of several hundred volumes, chiefly of the best current literature, are annually made. It is designed primarily for the use of the officers and students of the University, but others may be admitted to its privileges at the discretion of the Librarian. It is open during term time from 9.00 A. M. to 5.00 P. M.; during vacations, from 9.00 A. M. to 1.00 P. M.

The COLLEGE READING ROOM, in Dwight Hall, is open during term time from 7.30 A. M. to 9.00 P. M., and on Sundays from 1.00 to 9.00 P. M. It contains the leading daily newspapers, American and foreign, and the lighter periodicals, weekly, monthly, and quarterly.

The LIBRARY OF BYERS HALL, some 500 volumes, comprises general works of reference, and books reserved for the use of students of the Sheffield Scientific School in connection with their courses of study. The current newspapers and periodicals are also taken.

The ANDREWS MEMORIAL LIBRARY supplies needy Academical students with many of the necessary textbooks. A similar Loan Library is maintained by the Department of the Social Sciences.

The LIBRARY OF THE MEDICAL SCHOOL and that of the CONNECTICUT ACADEMY OF ARTS AND SCIENCES are incorporated in the University Library.

The LIBRARY OF THE AMERICAN ORIENTAL SOCIETY, consisting of about 6,000 books and manuscripts, is deposited in the University Library.

The SHEFFIELD SCIENTIFIC SCHOOL LIBRARY in Sheffield Hall contains chiefly the Hillhouse collection of mathematical works, aggregating about 7,500 volumes.

The following special libraries are connected with the various departments of the University, and serve the use of the officers and students of its departments.

Name	Location	Approximate Number of Books
LAW	Hendrie Hall	25,000 (see pp. 521–22)
HEALY	Herrick Hall	1,750, standard philosophical works and periodicals
BIOLOGY	Sheffield Biological Laboratory	300, chiefly bound periodicals
CHEMISTRY	Sheffield Chemical Laboratory	3,600, chiefly bound periodicals

Name	Location	Approximate Number of Books
CHEMISTRY	Kent Chemical Laboratory	800, manuals and periodicals
BOTANY	Sheffield Hall	ᴣ,500, periodicals and herbarium
MINERALOGY, GEOLOGY AND PHYSIOGRAPHY	Kirtland Hall	7,000
GEOLOGY AND MINERALOGY	Peabody Museum	16,000
ASTRONOMY	Observatory	4,500
FORESTRY	Forest School	6,000, standard works and periodicals
MATHEMATICS	Sheffield Hall	7,500 (see above)
MATHEMATICAL CLUB	90 High Street	600, chiefly manuals
ENGINEERING	Winchester Hall	1,500
PHYSICS	Sloane Laboratory	800, periodicals and manuals
PHYSICS	Winchester Hall	1,000, chiefly bound periodicals
BOOCOCK	Herrick Hall	800, chiefly anthropological
HISTORICAL CLUB	90 High Street	1,600
POLITICAL SCIENCE CLUB	Connecticut Hall	800
CLASSICAL CLUB	Phelps Hall	2,800
ROMANCE DEPARTMENT	Lampson Hall	200
GERMANIC DEPARTMENT	Lampson Hall	800
ENGLISH DEPARTMENT	135 Elm Street	
BIBLICAL LITERATURE DEPARTMENT	Fayerweather Hall	500
BIBLICAL LITERATURE AND MISSIONS	Dwight Hall	1,450
TROWBRIDGE REFERENCE LIBRARY	Divinity Hall	7,000, standard theological works
FOREIGN MISSIONS	Divinity Hall	7,500 (see above)
LOWELL MASON LIBRARY	West Divinity Hall	4,000, chiefly hymnological standard musical works
MUSIC DEPARTMENT	126 College Street	500
ART LIBRARY	Art School	700

PEABODY MUSEUM OF NATURAL HISTORY

In 1866, George Peabody, of London, but of Massachusetts birth, entrusted to a board of Trustees, selected by himself, the sum of one hundred and fifty thousand dollars "to found and maintain a Museum of Natural History, especially in the departments of Zoology, Geology, and Mineralogy, in connection with Yale College." Of this sum, one hundred thousand dollars was devoted by Mr. Peabody to the erection, "on land to be given for that purpose by the President and Fellows of Yale College, of a fire-proof building," "planned with special reference to its subsequent enlargement," to be, "when completed, the property of Yale College." Of the remainder of the gift, twenty thousand dollars was set apart to "accumulate as a building fund," and thirty thousand dollars to meet by its income from investment the expenses attending "the care of the Museum, the increase of its collections, and the general interests of the departments of science before named."

Ten years later, in 1876, the first wing of the Museum—the part now standing—was completed and furnished with cases at a cost of one hundred and seventy-five thousand dollars, the whole outlay being met by the accumulated building fund. The central part of the projected structure and the south wing—which will extend it to Library street—remain to be built whenever the means available for the purpose shall be adequate. The central part is much needed, as only a small part of the specimens secured can now be placed on exhibition.

The first floor of the building is devoted to the departments of Mineralogy and Geology, and contains also a large lecture room. The minerals occupy cases in the west room, the door of which fronts the entrance to the Museum. The minerals of the Gibbs collection, deposited by Col. George Gibbs with the College in 1809-10, and purchased in 1825 at a cost of twenty thousand dollars, and the extensive accumulations since made, are here preserved and for the most part on exhibition, making one of the largest public collections of the kind in the country. Besides minerals, the exhibition room contains one of the largest collections of meteorites in the country. Among the specimens, there are the famous mass of meteoric iron from Texas, weighing 1635 pounds ; some hundreds of meteorites, large and small, all of which came from a single fall in Iowa, in May, 1879; the interesting Weston meteorite, which fell in Weston, Connecticut, in 1807, and was soon after described at length by Professors Silliman and Kingsley; besides many others of special interest. An important recent addition is a collection of meteorites numbering nearly one thousand, which came from the great meteoric fall of May 2, 1890, in Winnebago county, Iowa. Another valuable specimen is the Jerome (Gove co.), Kansas, meteorite weighing 65 pounds. On the occasion of the recent Bicentennial celebration, the collection of meteorites brought together by Professor H. A. Newton during the latter part of his life, was presented to the Museum by his daughters as a memorial of him. This collection numbers about one hundred falls, and includes many rare specimens, a number of which are not otherwise represented in the Museum. The collection has not only a large intrinsic value, but is also particularly interesting because of the contributions which Professor Newton made to the department of Meteoric Astronomy. The specimens are preserved together in a special case. A case in the center of the room contains a large and beautiful collection of Chinese artistic work in stone, chiefly in jade and agate, with other like objects, bequeathed by Dr. S. Wells Williams, who was for forty-three years in China and for some years before his decease was the Professor of Chinese in the University. Two adjacent rooms on this floor are used for the mineralogical and geological laboratories.

The second floor is given up to Paleontology. The southern exhibition room contains vertebrate fossils. These collections were mainly made by Professor Marsh, in the Rocky Mountain region and other parts of the West, and presented to the University. On entering this room the first object to attract attention is the gigantic pelvis and hind limbs of the thunder saurian (*Brontosaurus*), one of the largest of the Dinosaurs. To the left, in the center of the room, is a large slab containing the skeleton of a Cretaceous Dinosaur (*Claosaurus*), measuring more than twenty-nine feet in length by thirteen feet in height. Adjoining in a small vertical case is shown the mounted skeleton of an early Eocene Creodont (*Dromocyon*) related to the Dog family. In the large central case against the south wall are two fine skulls and the vertebral column of *Triceratops*, a large Dinosaur having a monstrous head with three horns, also from the Cretaceous of Wyoming. On the other side of the central area, a large slab of chalk is seen, with the skeleton, as found, of a fish-eating marine reptile, and nearby a life-sized restoration of the great flying reptile or pterodactyl (*Pteranodon*), both from the chalk deposits of Kansas. Near the entrance of the room, again, in the first table case on the left are shown many fossil fishes from the oldest to the more recent. In the second table case are seen fossil birds (*Hesperornis* and *Ichthyornis*), while on the top of the corner case is one of the largest fossil birds known to geologists (*Dinornis*), from New Zealand. The other wall cases on this side of the room have a Mastodon from the Post-Pliocene of southern New York, several fish-eating reptiles (*Ichthyosaurus*), crocodiles, and turtles. On the other side of the room, in one of the table cases, are three skeletons of Dinosaurs from the Connecticut River sandstone, near Manchester, Connecticut; a portion of the armor of a crocodilian reptile from New Haven, and great dermal plates and spines of another Dinosaur (*Stegosaurus*) from the Jurassic of Wyoming, measuring about thirty feet in length. (The remainder of the skeleton is in one of the wall cases.) The other table case has fossil horse remains, beginning with small forms no larger than a fox, with three or four toes, and ending in the existing horse, with one toe on each foot. In the wall cases of this side of the room are shown many skulls of Mammals, some very large, from the Tertiary of Dakota and Nebraska.

Over the entrance is the skull of the extinct Irish Elk, with the very large antlers complete.

Of the large collection of foot-prints belonging to the University, only a few fine slabs are on exhibition. These are on the north and east walls above the cases. One of the most interesting is a slab about twelve feet long, covered throughout with raindrop impressions, and besides these, two series of foot-prints of biped reptiles.

The western exhibition room is occupied by a collection of plant and invertebrate fossils. On the lower floor the fossils are arranged according to affinity, and in the gallery there is to be a collection arranged stratigraphically or according to age. The first two alcove cases on the south are devoted chiefly to fossil sponges. Then follow two cases of corals. The succeeding eighteen alcove cases contain crinoids, starfishes, brittlestars, echinoids, worms, bryozoans, brachiopods, mollusca, and crablike animals. One table case exhibits an extensive collection of recent brachiopods, assembled by the late Professor C. E. Beecher, while the other two table cases have trilobites and insects. Along the east wall are shown three large slabs of crinoids, or feather-star animals. The largest of these slabs is unique, and is from the Lower Devonian formation, near Syracuse, New York ; another is from the Lower Carboniferous at Crawfordsville, Indiana, and the third from the chalk deposits of Kansas. In this room are also shown many large Cycad trunks from the Black Hills of South Dakota, plants related to the living sago palms.

The third story is occupied with the zoological collections, so far as there is room for their exhibition. The general zoological collection, nearly the whole of which has been accumulated since Professor Verrill took charge of the department, occupies the western room. The specimens are well arranged for exhibition and all labelled. Facing the south door stands a vertical case devoted to the sponges, among which are many species of the siliceous or glass sponges (*Euplectella*, etc.). Beyond the sponges, twelve cases are filled with the collection of corals, which is one of the most extensive in the country. These are followed by the echinoderms, etc. Several cases are devoted to a nearly complete collection of the marine invertebrates of New England. Other cases contain special collections of the shells and corals of the Pacific Coast of America, of the corals of Bermuda, of the shells of Florida, etc. The collections are rich in species from the deep-sea dredgings in the Atlantic, but only a small part is on exhibition. Overhead are models of two of the huge Cephalopods of the world; one, of twice the natural size, an Octopus from California, twenty-eight feet in diameter (between the tips of the opposite arms), and the other, of natural size, a species of the Newfoundland seas, related to the squids, having enormous eyes, and a length, from the posterior extremity to the tips of the longer arms, of forty-two feet. The models were made for the zoological department by Mr. J. H. Emerton.

The southern exhibition room of the zoological story contains a collection of skeletons in cases on its east and south sides, beginning near the door. These were presented by Professor Marsh. The skeletons of mammals, beginning with man and the apes, occupy all the east side, being followed by the birds, reptiles, and fishes. The rest of the cases are occupied with collections of vertebrates, both mounted and alcoholic, including a nearly complete series of the species inhabiting New England.

The second and third stories have also large laboratories and workrooms, devoted to the department represented in the exhibition rooms of the same floor. Those of the second or geological story are in charge of Professor Schuchert; and of the third or zoological story, besides serving for workrooms, are for the laboratory exercises and instruction of students in General Zoology. These rooms contain also large collections of specimens arranged in drawers and trays, which are open to special students in the department.

In the fourth story is a large Anthropological collection, much of which was presented to the University by Professor Marsh. The arranged collections comprise : a classified series of objects representing the Stone Age ; the Egyptian collections received from the Egyptian Exploration Fund and the Barringer collection; the collection of Indian basketry made by Mr. and Mrs. William H. Moseley ; the Benjamin Hoppin collection from Greenland, and other smaller series. The remaining rooms on the fourth floor and in the attic are in use for storage purposes.

The basement is devoted to workrooms and storerooms, and contains a very large number of specimens, especially in the departments of Paleontology and Zoology. This part of the building is closed to visitors.

The exhibition rooms are open from 9.00 A. M. to 6.00 P. M., except in the winter, when the hours are from 9.00 A. M. to 5.00 P. M. The janitor of the building is Mr. J. Rice, 92 High street.

THE OBSERVATORY

The OBSERVATORY was built from the avails of the gift .of the late Hon. Oliver F. Winchester, of New Haven, on land given by the late Mrs. Cornelia L. Hillhouse and her daughters. The principal astronomical instruments now in use are a six-inch Heliometer constructed by Messrs. Repsold, of Hamburg, an eight-inch Equatorial by Messrs. Grubb, of Dublin, given by the late Mr. Edward M. Reed, of New Haven, and an equatorially mounted set of Cameras for photographing meteors.

Besides its ordinary astronomical work, the Observatory maintains two public services. Continuous time-signals are transmitted from the distributing clock at the Observatory to the railroads and elsewhere. The Observatory offers facilities also to persons interested in accurate thermometry for the comparison of thermometers with standard instruments.

For the proper performance of these services the following equipment is in use :

1. Standard clocks, a transit instrument, chronographs, and the accessories for refined accuracy in the determination and transmission of time.

2. Apparatus for research and comparison in thermometry, including a collection of the best thermometers obtainable of the foreign makers and observatories which · devote special attention to thermometric standards.

Descriptive circulars of the thermometric service may be obtained by addressing the Observatory.

By the will of Professor Elias Loomis, who died in 1889, the Observatory receives one-third of the income, and will ultimately receive the entire income, of a fund established by him and called the *Loomis Fund*. The income received is to be applied to one or more of the following objects only, namely, the payment of the salaries of observers whose time is exclusively devoted to the making of observations for the promotion of the science of astronomy, the reduction of astronomical observations, and the defraying of the expense of publishing these observations and of publishing investigations based upon astronomical observations. The principal of the Loomis Fund is over three hundred thousand dollars.

THE BOTANICAL GARDEN

JAMES WILLIAM TOUMEY, M.A., M.S., *Director*

JOHN HILL MURRAY, *Head Gardener*

The BOTANICAL GARDEN was established in 1900 on the estate of the late Professor Othniel C. Marsh, who bequeathed his place to the University for this purpose. Prof. Marsh was deeply interested in trees, shrubs, and flowers, and by the extensive plantings, particularly of trees and shrubs, laid the foundation of the present Botanical Garden.

No serious attempt has as yet been made to introduce a large variety of exotic and indigenous herbaceous species such as are found in the larger Botanical Gardens of the country, although additional plants are introduced as funds are available.

Approximately 150,000 plants of coniferous species are growing in the forestry nursery. For the most part these are one- and two-year old seedlings of white pine. The Garden serves an important purpose in training the students in nursery practice.

The work of the Garden has expanded to a considerable extent during the year. The care of Sachem's Wood has been entrusted to the Garden ; also the care of other large land possessions of the University. The Garden also has general care of the street and campus trees, and undertakes the planting of trees and other decorative plants for the University.

During the past year the income has been increased by several hundred dollars from outside work, and has enabled the Garden to employ additional permanent help. This has worked not only to the advantage of the Garden, but to the advantage of the various Departments of the University as well.

THE UNIVERSITY CHURCH

The privileges of THE CHURCH OF CHRIST IN YALE UNIVERSITY are extended to all students of the University. · The services, except for the monthly University services in Woolsey Hall, are held in the BATTELL CHAPEL, a building completed in 1876, and erected mainly through the generosity of Mr. Joseph Battell of New York City.

The services in the Chapel are threefold:

(1.) PRAYERS are held daily (Sunday excepted) at 8.10 A. M. The attendance of all students in the Academical Department is required. The services, which consist of Reading of the Scriptures, Prayer, and Singing, are conducted this year by the following officers of the University:

Dean Wright.	Professor Seymour.
Professor Perrin.	Mr. Stokes.
Professor Phelps.	Professor Vernon.
Professor Reed.	Professor Walker.

(2.) PUBLIC WORSHIP is held every Sunday at 10.30. Attendance of students in the Academical Department is required, unless they obtain special permission from the Dean to worship elsewhere. Appointments for the Sunday services are made by a Joint Committee of the Corporation and Faculty, who endeavor to select as preachers those who, by their daily contact with active life and their knowledge of young men, are especially fitted to reach and influence a College audience. The income of the Chittenden Professorship of Divinity fund is at present used to maintain the Sunday preaching, the preachers having also pastoral duties in connection with their work. The preachers for the present year, as far as arranged at the date of the publication of this Catalogue, are as follows:

1907.
Sept.   29.   President Hadley.
Oct.   6.   Rev. William Douglas Mackenzie, D.D., President of the Hartford Theological Seminary, Hartford, Conn.

Oct.	13.	Rt. Rev. A. F. W. Ingram, D.D., Lord Bishop of London, London, England. •
	20.	Rev. Lyman Abbott, D.D., LL.D., Editor of *The Outlook*, New York City.
	27.	Rt. Rev. Charles H. Brent, D.D., Bishop of the Philippines, Manila, P. I.
Nov.	3.	Rev. Professor Ambrose W. Vernon, D.D., Acting Pastor of the Church of Christ in Yale University.
	10.	Rev. George Hodges, D.D., Dean of the Episcopal Theological School, Cambridge, Mass.
	17.	John R. Mott, M.A., Secretary of the World's Student Christian Federation, New York City.
	24.	Rev. Professor Paul VanDyke, D.D., Princeton University, Princeton, N. J.
Dec.	1.	John R. Mott, M.A., Secretary of the World's Student Christian Federation, New York City.
	8.	Rev. Charles E. Jefferson, D.D., New York City.
	15.	Rev. Henry Sloane Coffin, D.D., New York City.

1908.

Jan.	12.	Rev. Sherrard Billings, M.A., Groton School, Groton, Mass.
	19.	Rev. Endicott Peabody, D.D., Groton School, Groton, Mass.
	26.	Rt. Rev. Charles H. Brent, D.D., Bishop of the Philippines, Manila, P. I.
Feb.	2.	Rev. Professor Ambrose W. Vernon, D.D.
	9, 16.	Robert E. Speer, M.A., Secretary of the Presbyterian Board of Foreign Missions, New York City.
March	1, 8.	Rev. Hugh Black, D.D., Union Theological Seminary, New York City.
	22, 29.	Rev. Rush Rhees, D.D., LL.D., President of the University of Rochester, Rochester, N. Y,
April	5.	Rev. William R. Richards, D.D., New York City.
	12.	Rev. Roswell Bates, New York City.
	26.	Rev. Joseph H. Twichell, M.A., Hartford, Conn.
May	10.	Rev. Bishop William F. McDowell, D.D., Chicago, Ill.
	17.	Rev. J. O. S. Huntington, O.H.C., West Park, N. Y.
	24.	Rev. William James Dawson, Taunton, Mass.
	31.	Rev. George A. Gordon, D.D., Boston, Mass.
June	7.	Rev. James G. K. McClure, D.D., President of the McCormick Theological Seminary, Chicago, Ill.
	14.	Rev. Henry Sloane Coffin, D.D., New York City.
	21.	President Hadley.

(3.) A COMMUNION SERVICE is held on the first Sunday of each month in term time. It is conducted by the Acting Pastor of the University Church, Rev. Professor Vernon, assisted by the preacher of the morning. The invitation to it is extended by the President to "all who have professed and would profess themselves followers of the Lord Jesus Christ."

THE INFIRMARY

THE YALE INFIRMARY is situated on Prospect street in a healthful and beautiful part of the city. It was built in 1892 at a cost of about forty thousand dollars, raised by subscription among friends of the University. An extension costing fifteen thousand dollars, the gift of Mrs. Charles P. Taft, of Cincinnati, was added in 1906. One dollar is charged on the Treasurer's bill for each day that a student remains in the Infirmary. A competent matron and nurse are in residence, but the choice of physician rests with the patient.

THE DINING HALL

THE YALE DINING HALL, situated in University Hall and containing seats for nearly eleven hundred persons, furnishes board at cost to members of the University. Each boarder is charged three dollars and a quarter per week, which pays for linen, service, tea, coffee, cocoa, bread, butter, milk, and vegetables. In addition there is an *à la carte* service from which anything in season may be ordered to be paid for extra. A vegetarian may live well on the fixed charge of three dollars and a quarter per week ; a reasonable amount of meats may be added for one dollar and a. half per week. The bills for board of students are rendered and payable monthly. Meals will be furnished to visiting graduates, and to friends of the regular boarders, at a reasonable rate. Application for board should be made at the office of the Superintendent, at the east end of University Hall.

THE GYMNASIUM
ADVISORY COMMITTEE

LEE McCLUNG, M.A.

WALTER CAMP, B.A.

WILLIAM GILBERT ANDERSON, M.D., M.A., *Director*

EUGENE LAMB RICHARDS, M.A.

JOHN EDWARD HEATON, Esq.

LAFAYETTE BENEDICT MENDEL, PH.D.

The GYMNASIUM, presented by graduates to the University in 1892, is located on Elm street, between York and High. It is one of the largest buildings in the country devoted exclusively to gymnastics and athletics, having a frontage of one hundred and thirty-eight feet, a depth of eighty-six feet, and a height of four stories. The equipment is most complete and includes the best devices from the German and Swedish gymnasia, as well as the American developing appliances. The porte-cochère leads to a large "gymnasium lot," which may be used for out-of-door sports.

The basement contains the heating, ventilating, drying, and pumping apparatus, as well as the bowling alleys, shower baths, and special rooms for the football and baseball teams.

On the first floor will be found the Turkish bath and swimming pool with all accessories, rowing tanks, handball courts, dressing rooms and shower baths for visiting teams, crew rooms, and service quarters for the janitors.

The second floor contains the principal dressing rooms with about one thousand lockers, new and very much improved shower baths, wrestling, fencing and boxing rooms, and the offices of administration.

The trophy room occupies the eastern portion of the second floor, and is reached by the large marble staircase from the main entrance off the porte-cochère.

The main hall or exercise room (11,000 square feet) occcupies the third and fourth floors. It is remarkably well lighted, and is heated and ventilated by special air conduits.

The Director of the Gymnasium is a trained physician who has made a study of physical education and hygiene. With him are associated a Medical Assistant who is always present at the gymnasium, and an Instructor in gymnastics who will be found on the main floor from 9.30 A. M. to 12.00 M. and from 2.00 to 6.00 P. M. daily.

The gymnastic training is designed to be progressive from year to year. The members of the different classes may take exercises in the various forms of gymnastics under the supervision of the Director, and any student may enter the classes in general gymnastics. Instructors are always present in the main exercise-hall to direct individual or class work. All students requiring such care are assigned exercises suited to their special needs.

A thorough physical examination and measurement is offered each student yearly, and a record of the results is kept as a basis of advice as to exercise and regimen. An examination of these records shows that the standard of health of the average student improves during his college course.

For the welfare of the students the following rule has been passed by the Corporation :

Required that every man who presents himself for exercise in the gymnasium, or who desires to use its privileges, should first submit to a physical examination by the Medical Director ; or, in default of such an examination, should bring from his physician a written certificate (the form to be furnished by the Director) that he is physically sound, or a written certificate from his parent or guardian that he wishes the student excused from the examination and that he himself will take the responsibility of exercise without a previous examination.

Special attention is paid to the art of swimming. All Freshmen who cannot swim are given lessons free of charge. It is expected that the new Carnegie Swimming

Pool will be ready in the fall of 1908. It will be the most complete of its kind, and will have an amphitheater for spectators seating one thousand persons.

During the months of October and November a course of lectures on health topics are given members of the Academical Freshman class, attendance being compulsory, by several members of the faculty who have made a specialty of personal health and hygiene. All members of the Scientific Freshman class are invited to attend these lectures.

The Gymnasium is open from 9.30 A. M. to 6.30 P. M.

A charge for the use of the Gymnasium is included in the term bills of students in the Academical Department and Sheffield Scientific School. Students of other Departments may use the Gymnasium upon payment of the regular fee of five dollars.

THE ATHLETIC FIELD

WALTER CAMP, B.A., *Treasurer*

The Athletic Grounds of the University, known as the YALE FIELD, are open to the students of all departments. A quarter of a century ago the project was advanced of securing a suitable field where the students might obtain the physical exercise so conducive to health and to the best mental effort. A committee consisting partly of graduates and partly of undergraduates was then formed, and it was decided to purchase a tract of land, consisting of some thirty acres, lying just beyond the Orange town line, and a mile from the Campus. Subscriptions were started, and in 1882 the field was purchased, the cost being about twenty-two thousand dollars for the land itself, and thirty-one thousand dollars more for its immediate grading and preparation. It was necessary, in addition to subscriptions, to borrow an amount of twenty-one thousand dollars. The field thus purchased lies on the bank of West River on a bluff some forty feet above the river bed and extending westward. Just beyond it rises Edgewood Hill, and to the north stands West Rock, while towards the south is Long Island Sound, and east is the city and the University. The trolley cars run to the gate.

One of the original articles of incorporation provided for the turning over of the field to the University, and it was towards this end that the Yale Field Corporation worked for many years. It was impossible that the University should accept the property while it was mortgaged or in debt. The final payment on the eight thousand dollar mortgage was at last accomplished and the field deeded over to the University,—a property representing an original expenditure of some fifty-three thousand dollars, to which, for maintenance and improvements, a sum of about one hundred thousand dollars has been added, the bulk of which has come from the athletic associations in gate receipts.

The Yale Field has several baseball and football fields, a quarter mile running track with a 220-yard straight away, football grandstands accommodating over 30,000 people, and a covered baseball stand seating over 3,000. There is a small section to the southwest not yet fully graded which will be made available for athletic purposes as soon as funds can be provided.

The articles under which the Corporation was formed provide that the grounds shall be managed by persons connected with Yale University for athletic games and exercises, and for out-door recreation, to encourage such games, exercises, and recreation in the University, and to take, buy, own, and hold property necessary or proper therefor. The University, having taken over the property, will see that the purposes for which it was purchased are duly protected and the athletic interests properly conserved.

THE YALE UNIVERSITY CHRISTIAN ASSOCIATION

The headquarters of the Academical, Graduate, Law, and Medical Departments of the YALE UNIVERSITY CHRISTIAN ASSOCIATION are in Dwight Hall, which was erected in 1886 through the generosity of Mr. Elbert B. Monroe, of Southport, Connecticut. Dwight Hall is a stone building situated on the College Square and is admirably adapted to be the center of the religious and social life of the University. It contains a convenient reading room, a grill room, a pool and billiard room, a library, an auditorium for general religious services, separate rooms for the Bible classes and prayer meetings of the various College classes, as well as quarters for the University General Secretary and the Academical General Secretary.

The Secretaries, who are recent graduates, are elected annually and have immediate supervision respectively of the graduate and professional schools and of such Association work as is common to all the University, and such as relates to the Academical Department exclusively. The Academical General Secretary has immediate supervision of the building.

The "management and control" of Dwight Hall rest, in accordance with the expressed wish of the donor, in the Corporation of the University. There is, however, a Graduate Advisory Committee known as the Board of Directors, elected by the members of the Association and consisting at present of the following: Mr. William Sloane, '95 (term expires 1913), Chairman ; Mr. E. S. Harkness, '87 S. (term expires 1909), Secretary ; Mr. S. H. Fisher, '89 (term expires 1910), Treasurer ; and Messrs. R. C. Morse, '62 (term expires 1912), J. B. Reynolds, '84 (term expires 1910), M. H. Bowman, Jr., '05 S. (term expires 1911), and V. C. McCormick, '93 S. (term expires 1908). The actual planning and carrying out of the organized religious work of the University is in the hands of the various executive committees of the different departments of the Association. This work consists of classes for Bible study, prayer, and the study of missions; deputations to preparatory schools, colleges, and churches; aid for new students in obtaining board and rooms; the conduct of city missions, Sunday schools, and boys' clubs; together with other philanthropic and church supply work. The class Deacons of the Academical Department, elected by the members of each class in Sophomore year, and the class Deacons of the Sheffield Scientific School, elected by the members of each class at the end of Freshman year, assume the general direction of the religious work in their classes, while for special activities committees are appointed.

The headquarters of the Sheffield Association are on the second floor of Byers Memorial Hall (see pages 286–87). An auditorium, a carefully selected library, and separate class rooms are devoted to the various uses of the Association. There are also on this floor quarters for the Sheffield Scientific School General Secretary.

The different departments of the Association are bound together by a University Council composed of the chief officers of the departments.

THE YALE STATION, UNITED STATES POST OFFICE

The YALE STATION, a branch of the New Haven Post Office, was established October 1, 1900, for the purpose of affording the best possible mail service for members of Yale University. The office is equipped with one thousand lock boxes, there being no carrier delivery. Each college room is assigned a lock box for which a nominal rental is charged on the term bill. Members of the University residing outside of the dormitories may be assigned a box upon application to the Superintendent of the Station, Mr. Thomas F. Clark. All box holders are obliged to procure a box key. There are five mails received and the same number despatched each week day, one on Sunday and two on legal holidays. These mails are arranged to meet the important trains. The schedule of arrival and departure of mails can be found on the official bulletin-board in the Post Office corridor.

The office conducts all branches of the postal·service and is entitled to all the privileges of a first-class office, including the sale of stamps and stamped paper, a registered mail department, and postal money order service, both Domestic and International.

The station is located in Fayerweather Hall, and is central to all departments of the University.

THE BUREAU OF SELF-HELP AND APPOINTMENTS

ADVISORY COMMITTEE

ARTHUR TWINING HADLEY, LL.D.

ANSON PHELPS STOKES, Jr., M.A.

HENRY·PARKS WRIGHT, PH.D., LL.D.

RUSSELL HENRY CHITTENDEN, PH.D., LL.D., Sc.D.

ANDREW WHEELER PHILLIPS, PH.D.

HERBERT EUGENE SMITH, M.D.

HENRY WADE ROGERS, LL.D.

C. L. KITCHEL, M.A., B.D., *Secretary of the Bureau*

The BUREAU OF SELF HELP represents all the agencies and opportunities which the University affords in its various departments and activities by which students of insufficient means obtain compensation for services rendered. It is open to students in any department of the University. The office is at 4 Phelps Hall.

The work of the Secretary of the Bureau is to obtain employment for students of the University and for graduates, and the assignment of beneficiary aid to students in the Academical Department. All students who desire employment in order to assist in paying their way may leave their names at this Bureau, and all persons who have work of any sort which students can do are requested to leave their orders here. Students who are about to graduate, and graduate students who desire positions especially as teachers, should apply to this bureau, where also applications for teachers may be made. Also those students in the Academical Department who need abatement of tuition should make application for it to this Bureau before October fifteenth in each year of the College course.

A pamphlet, entitled "Self-Help at Yale," giving an account of the various means by which students help work their own way through college, will be sent on application.

ALUMNI ASSOCIATIONS
UNIVERSITY ALUMNI ASSOCIATIONS

Alabama, Yale Alumni Association of
President, William I. Grubb, 1st National Bank Bldg., Birmingham, Ala.
Secretary, Paul A. Savage, care Court House, Birmingham, Ala.

Boston, Yale Alumni Association of
President, Alfred L. Ripley, M.A., Andover, Mass.
Secretary,

Boston, Yale Club of
President, H. S. Frazer, 8 Exchange pl., Boston, Mass.
Secretary, Henry C. Stetson, 84 State st., Boston, Mass.

Bristol, Conn., Yale Club of
President, Hon. Epaphroditus Peck, 130 Main st., Bristol, Conn.
Secretary, Charles T. Treadway, 72 Bellevue av., Bristol, Conn.

Buffalo, Yale Alumni Association of
President, William E. Foster, Box 195, Buffalo, N. Y.
Secretary, G. Barrett Rich, Jr., 723 Main st., Buffalo, N. Y.

California, Yale Alumni Association of
President, Prof. Edward B. Clapp, 2225 Hearst av., Berkeley, Cal.
Secretary, James A. Ballentine, Piedmont, Cal.

Central Pennsylvania, Yale Alumni Association of
President, Lyman D. Gilbert, Harrisburg, Pa.
Secretary, H. M. Gross, 23 N. Front st., Harrisburg, Pa.

Central and Western Massachusetts, Yale Alumni Association of
President, Denison B. Tucker, 115 Exchange st., Worcester, Mass.
Secretary, Thomas B. Shaw, M.D., 47 Pleasant st., Worcester, Mass.

Central Ohio, Yale Alumni Association of
President, Henry T. Chittenden, Columbus, O.
Secretary, William H. Page, 1068 Franklin av., Columbus, O.

Chicago, Yale Club of
President, Thomas E. Donnelley, 149 Plymouth pl., Chicago, Ill.
Secretary, George B. Carpenter, R. R. Donnelly & Sons Co., Chicago, Ill.

China, Yale Alumni Association of
President, Taotai S. T. Laisun.
Secretary,

Cincinnati, Yale Club of
President, Frank J. Jones, Fosdick Bldg.; Cincinnati, O.
Secretary, Ralph E. Clark, 1325 Union Trust Bldg , Cincinnati, O.

Cleveland, Yale Alumni Association of
President, Frederick S. Dickson, 1712 Prospect st., Cleveland, O.
Secretary, George A. Welch, 1015 Garfield Bldg., Cleveland, O.

Colorado, Yale Alumni Association of
President, Theron R. Field, 737 Clarkson st., Denver, Colo.
Secretary, Frederick H. Morley, 409 McPhee Bldg., Denver, Colo.

Essex County, N. J., Yale Alumni Association of
President, Hon. Austen Colgate, 53 John st., N. Y. City.
Secretary, Andrew S. Taylor, 103 Scotland road, South Orange,
   N. J.

Fairfield County (Conn.), Yale Alumni Association
● *President*, Hon. George W. Wheeler, Bridgeport, Conn.
Secretary, George E. Hill, 3 Sanford Bldg., Bridgeport, Conn.

Florida, Yale Alumni Association of
Secretary, Russell E. Colcord, 31 Monroe pl., Brooklyn, N. Y.

Fulton and Montgomery Counties (N. Y.), Yale Alumni Association of
President, Hallock C. Alvord, 61 N. Main st., Gloversville, N. Y.
Secretary, Abraham R. Brubacher, Ph.D., 2 N. Wendell av., Sche-
   nectady, N. Y.

Georgia, Yale Alumni Association of
President, C. Morris Brandon, 488 Peachtree st , Atlanta, Ga.
Secretary, William J. Tilson, 1201 Century Bldg., Atlanta, Ga.

Hartford Yale Alumni Association
President, Archibald A. Welch, 21 Woodland st., Hartford, Conn.
Secretary, Walter L. Goodwin, 783 Main st., Hartford, Conn.

Indiana, Yale Alumni Association of
President, Merrill Moores, 1025 Law Bldg , Indianapolis, Ind.

Iowa, Yale Alumni Association of
President, Rev. Edmund M. Vittum, D.D., 1109 Park st., Grinnell,
   Iowa.
Secretary, Rev. John O. Stevenson, D.D., Waterloo, Iowa.

Japan, Yale Association of
President, Marquis Hiroboumi Ito, LL.D., Tokyo, Japan.
Secretaries, Prof. John T. Swift, Tokyo Higher Normal School,
   Tokyo, Japan.
   Taro Yamada, *Japan Times*, Tokyo, Japan.

Kansas City, Yale Alumni Association of
  President, Frederick N. Sewall, 1009 W. 8th st., Kansas City, Mo.
  Secretary, Porter B. Godard, 607 N. Y. Life Bldg., Kansas City,
    Mo.
Kentucky Yale Alumni Association
  President, Col. Morris B. Belknap, Louisville, Ky.
  Secretary and Treasurer, Gilbert S. Cowan, 435 W. Main st.,
    . Louisville, Ky.
Long Island Yale Alumni Association
  President, Hon. William B. Davenport, 189 Montague st., Brook-
    lyn, N. Y.
  Secretary, Morris U. Ely, 43 Cedar st., N. Y. City.
Louisiana Yale Alumni Association
  Secretary, Harry H. Clark, Round Table Club, Jackson av., New
    Orleans, La.
Maryland, Yale Alumni Association of
  President, Harvey Cushing, M.D., 3 West Franklin st., Baltimore,
    Md.
  Secretary, Albert H. Buck, 1623 St. Paul st., Baltimore, Md.
Meriden Yale Alumni Association
  President, Edward T. Bradstreet, M.D., 170 Colony st., Meriden,
    Conn.
  Secretary, Charles T. Dodd, 79 Colony st., Meriden, Conn.
Michigan, Yale Alumni Association of
  President,
  Secretary, George B. Perry, Moffat Bldg., Detroit, Mich.
New York City, Yale Club of
  President, Julian W. Curtiss, 126 Nassau st., N. Y. City.
  Secretary, J. McLean Walton, 358 5th av., N. Y. City.
Northeastern New York, Yale Alumni Association of
  President, John K. Howe, 37 State st., Albany, N. Y.
  Secretary, William L. L. Peltz, 82 State st., Albany, N. Y.
Northeastern Pennsylvania, Yale Alumni Association of
  President, F. E. Donnelly, 907 Mears Bldg., Scranton, Pa.
  Secretary, Charles H. Welles, Jr., 322 Connell Bldg., Scranton, Pa.
Northwestern Yale Alumni Association
  President, Burnside Foster, M.D., Lowry Bldg., St. Paul, Minn.
  Secretary, R. M. Newport, Jr., 433 Ashland av., St. Paul, Minn.
Onondaga Yale Alumni Association
  President, Charles W. Bardeen, 406 S. Franklin st., Syracuse, N. Y.
Oregon Yale Alumni Association
  Secretary, John D. Carson, 6 N. Front st., Portland, Oregon.

Philadelphia, Yale Alumni Association of
President, Edward S. Duer, M.D., 1606 Locust st., Philadelphia, Pa.
Secretary, John S. Evans, 701 Arcade Bldg., Philadelphia, Pa.

Pittsburg, Yale Alumni Association of
President, John C. Oliver, Termon av., Allegheny, Pa.
Secretary, Berne H. Evans, 1045 S. Negley av., Pittsburg, Pa.

Plainfield, N. J., Yale Club
President, Thomas M. Day, 62 Cedar st., N. Y. City, or Plainfield,
N. J.
Secretary, Lewis A. Williams, Jr., 428 Lafayette pl., N. Y. City, or
Plainfield, N. J.

Reading, Pa., Yale Club of
President, Herbert R. Green, 612 Washington st., Reading, Pa.
Secretary, Frederic R. Stauffer, 1513 Hill Road, Reading, Pa.

Rhode Island, Yale Alumni Association of
President, Hon. LeBaron B. Colt, 105 Waterman st., Providence,
R. I.
Secretary, Thomas B. Owen, 110 Bowen st., Providence, R. I.

Savannah Yale Club
President, Rev. Charles H. Strong, 503 Whitaker st., Savannah, Ga.
Secretary, C. Wayne Cunningham, 118 E. 36th st., Savannah, Ga.

Seattle, Wash., Yale Alumni Association of
Secretary, Corwin S. Shank, 632 36th av. N., Seattle, Wash.

St. Louis, Yale Alumni Association of
President, Joseph G. Holliday, 410 Laclede Bldg , St. Louis, Mo.
Secretary, George V. Reynolds, 617 Roe Bldg., St. Louis, Mo.

South Carolina, Yale Alumni Association of
President, John C. Simonds, Jr., 29 E. Battery st., Charleston, S. C.
Secretary, Henry Buist, 30 Broad st., Charleston, S. C.

Southern California, Yale Alumni Association of
President, Francis B. Kellogg, M.D., 328 Douglass Bldg., Los
Angeles, Cal.
Secretary, Charles M. Latimer, 516 E. 1st st., Los Angeles, Cal.

Tennessee Yale Alumni Association
President, Hon. Luke W. Finlay, Memphis, Tenn.
Secretary, Prof. Charles S. Brown, Vanderbilt University, Nash-
ville, Tenn.

Texas Yale Association
President, Alexander S. Cleveland, Commerce st., Houston, Texas.
Secretary, William M. Jones, 314 Slaughter Bldg., Dallas, Texas.

Utica, Yale Club of
   President, Beecher M. Crouse, 6 Miller st., Utica, N. Y.
   Secretary, Walter F. Roberts, 420 Genesee st., Utica, N. Y.

Washington, D. C., Yale Alumni Association of
   President, Hon. Victor H. Metcalf, Washington, D. C.
   Secretary, George X. McLanahan, D.C.L., Bond Bldg., Washington, D. C.

Associated Western Clubs
   President, Hon. William H. Taft, LL.D., Washington, D. C.
   Secretary, Walter W. Heffelfinger, North Star Shoe Co., Minneapolis, Minn.

Wisconsin, Yale Alumni Association of
   President, Hon. John M. Whitehead, Jackman Block, Janesville, Wisc.
   Secretary, James H. Niedecken, 673 Cass st., Milwaukee, Wisc.

Wyoming Valley, Pa., Yale Alumni Association
   President, Hon. F. W. Wheaton, 24 Coal Exchange, Wilkes-Barre, Pa.
   Secretary, A. A. Beaumont, 54 W. Union st., Wilkes-Barre, Pa.

DIVINITY SCHOOL ALUMNI ASSOCIATION
President, Rev. Prof. Irving F. Wood, Ph.D., 251 Franklin st., Northampton, Mass.
Secretary, Rev. Jason Noble Pierce, 139 Greene st., New Haven, Conn.
Treasurer, Rev. John H. Grant, Meriden, Conn.

Connecticut Branch
   President, Rev. Edward M. Chapman, Lyme, Conn.
   Vice-President, Rev. Harry E. Peabody, Hartford, Conn.
   Secretary and Treasurer, Raymond G. Clapp, New Haven, Conn.

Eastern Massachusetts Branch
   President, Rev. Frank R. Shipman, Andover, Mass.
   Vice-President, Rev. Jay T. Stocking, Newtonville, Mass.
   Secretary and Treasurer, Rev. Frank B. McAllister, Cohasset, Mass.

Iowa Branch
   President, —— ——
   Secretary. Rev. John O. Stevenson, D.D., Waterloo, Iowa.

New York Branch
   President, Rev. Edward A. George, Ithaca, N. Y.
   Secretary, Rev. Alfred E. Thistleton, Schenectady, N. Y.

Western Massachusetts Branch
President, Rev. John Pierpont, Williamsburg, Mass.
Secretary and Treasurer, Rev. Herbert P. Woodin, Chicopee Mass.
Member of Executive Committee, Rev. Charles H. Hamlin, East-hampton, Mass.
Wisconsin ·Branch
President, Rev. Philip H. Ralph, Antigo, Wisc.
Secretary and Treasurer, Rev. Jesse E. Sarles, Baraboo, Wisc.

PART V

UNIVERSITY LECTURE COURSES
AND PRIZES

THE PUBLIC LECTURE COURSE

UNDER THE AUSPICES OF

YALE UNIVERSITY

AND THE

NEW HAVEN UNIVERSITY EXTENSION CENTER

A series of twenty-seven lectures under the above title has been arranged for the season of 1907–08. This course, established in 1900, is under the joint auspices of Yale University and the New Haven University Extension Center. It represents a popular presentation of systematic instruction in Literature, Science, History, Art, and Music. The subjects in general are treated in a more scholarly manner than in the magazines, although they are presented in popular language. A number of the lectures, especially those in Science and Art, are illustrated by lantern slides and apparatus, while musical lectures are usually accompanied by vocal and instrumental selections.

These lectures are given in College Street Hall, Yale University. The price of a season ticket is three dollars. This also admits to the course of Sheffield Lectures.

Letters of inquiry may be addressed to Mr. Willis K. Stetson, Free Public Library, where circulars may always be found giving dates of lectures, etc.

The list of lectures in this course for the year, not including the ten Sheffield Lectures, follows:

RUSSELL H. CONWELL,
    Personal Glimpses of Celebrated Men and Women—Lessons from Life.

ARTHUR K. PECK,
    The Yellowstone National Park. (Illustrated.)

CHARLES D. KELLOGG,
    Lecture Recital and Talks with Birds by the Bird Warbler.

LELAND POWERS,
    (Dramatic Recital.) Tarkington's "Monsieur Beaucaire."

THOMAS E. GREEN,
    The Key to the Twentieth Century.

GEORGE E. VINCENT,
  Democracy, Cynicism, or Faith.

EARL BARNES,
  The Power of Work—A Study on Cecil Rhodes.

EARL BARNES,
  The Power of Love—A Study on St. Francis of Assisi.

EARL BARNES,
  The Power of Ideas—A Study on Robert Owen.

WILLIAM LYON PHELPS,
  John Greenleaf Whittier. (The 100th anniversary of his birth.)

EARL BARNES,
  Children as seen in Art.

ERNEST THOMPSON SETON,
  Northern Travels in the Rocky Mountains. (Illustrated.)

GEORGE KIERNAN,
  (Dramatic Recital.) Joseph Jefferson's "Rip Van Winkle."

JOHN CALVIN GODDARD,
  The Art of Being Interesting.

RUDOLPH SCHEVILL,
  Spanish Cities and Highways. (Illustrated.)

FRANK SPEAIGHT,
  (Dramatic Recital.) Charles Dickens's "Nicholas Nickleby."

J. C. POWYS, Oxford, England,
  English Novelists, Hardy and Kipling.

UNIVERSITY LECTURES AND CONCERTS
LECTURE COURSES

In addition to the Yale Public Lectures and the lectures regularly offered in connection· with the Curriculum, there is a large number of LECTURE COURSES given under the auspices of the various University Departments and organizations. These lectures are open to all students of the University.

The LYMAN BEECHER LECTURES ON PREACHING. This lectureship was founded in 1871 by a gift of ten thousand .dollars from the late Henry W. Sage, then of Brooklyn, N. Y. It is filled by the appointment, by the President and Fellows, of a minister of the Gospel or layman, of any evangelical denomination, who has been markedly successful in the special work of the Christian ministry. The lecturer for this year is Rev. William Herbert Perry Faunce, D.D., LL.D., President of Brown University. ·

The SILLIMAN MEMORIAL LECTURES, on subjects connected with "the natural and moral world," were established by the will of the late Augustus Ely Silliman, of Brooklyn, N. Y., who died in 1884. The Mrs. Hepsa Ely Silliman Memorial Fund which supports this lectureship, amounting to eighty-five thousand dollars, did not come into the possession of the University until 1901. The five courses on this foundation have been given by Professor Thomson of Cambridge University, England, Professor Sherrington of the University of Liverpool, Professor Rutherford of McGill University, Professor Walter Nernst of the University of Berlin, and William Bateson, M.A., F.R.S., of Cambridge University, England.

The DODGE LECTURES ON THE RESPONSIBILITIES OF CITIZENSHIP. This lectureship, founded in 1900 by a gift of thirty thousand dollars from William E. Dodge, Esq., of New York City, has as its object the promoting among "students and graduates, and among educated men of the United States, an understanding of the duties of Christian citizenship and a sense of personal responsibility for the performance of those duties."

The TROWBRIDGE LECTURE COURSE. This course was established in 1899 through a gift of five thousand dollars from Rutherford Trowbridge, Esq., of New Haven. The gift constitutes the Thomas R. Trowbridge Fund. The lectures are given every year in the School of the Fine Arts. The present year the course will consist of six lectures by eminent architects on "Civic Improvement."

The BROMLEY LECTURES ON JOURNALISM, LITERATURE, AND PUBLIC AFFAIRS. These lectures are provided for by. the gift to the University in 1900 of five thousand dollars. It is the wish of the donor, Mrs. Adelaide E. Bromley, that the lectureship should be a memorial to her husband, the late Isaac H. Bromley, of the class of 1853. Two or more lectures are given annually by men of distinction, on subjects connected with Journalism, Literature, or Public Affairs, it being understood that a lecture on Journalism be arranged as often as once in four years. The next lecturer is Mr. George Harvey, Editor of the Harpers publications.

The HARVARD LECTURES were established in 1905 by the gift of ten thousand dollars from an anonymous Harvard graduate. The income of this fund is to be employed in securing members of the Harvard faculty to give lectures or instruction at Yale. The first lecture on this foundation was given by President Eliot.

DANIEL S. LAMONT MEMORIAL LECTURESHIP was established in 1906 by the gift of one thousand dollars, the income of which is to be used for an annual lecture on English Letter Writers and Letter Writing, by a member of the English Department of the University.

The STANLEY WOODWARD LECTURESHIP FUND, established in 1907, provides an income which is to be used to secure occasionally lectures from distinguished foreigners visiting this country. Two lectures on this foundation have been given by Mr. James Fitzmaurice-Kelly, of London, on Spanish Literature, and it is hoped that Mr. Cobden-Sanderson, the distinguished English printer, will lecture later.

The SHEFFIELD LECTURES (formerly the Mechanics' Course) are provided by the authorities of the Sheffield Scientific School. The subjects cover a broad field, and the lectures are usually illustrated.

The DWIGHT HALL LECTURES, arranged for by the Yale University Christian Association, are given from time to time by men of distinction.

The MEDICAL ALUMNI LECTURES, two in number, are given annually.

The PHI BETA KAPPA Society, the LEONARD BACON CLUB of the Theological School, and the SIGMA XI Society, also arrange for public lectures from time to time.

The BERKELEY SERMONS are given under the auspices of the Berkeley Association of the University, in one of the Episcopal churches of the city. The list of preachers for this year is as follows:

1. Rt. Rev. William N. McVickar, D.D., LL.D., Bishop of Rhode Island.
2. Rev. Hugh Birckhead, Rector of St. George's Church, New York City.
3. Rt. Rev. Chauncey Brewster, D.D., Bishop of Connecticut.
4. Rev. Ernest M. Stires, D.D., Rector of St. Thomas's Church, New York City.
5. Archdeacon Stuck, Fairbanks, Alaska.

CONCERTS

The following opportunities in Music are open to all students of the University on payment of moderate admission fees, which are so adjusted as to meet the unavoidable expenses of such undertakings with as small a margin as possible.

The UNIVERSITY CHAMBER CONCERTS.—Three concerts will be given during the winter months by the Kneisel Quartet of Boston, and one by the Adamowski Trio. The present season is the twenty-first of these concerts.

FACULTY TRIO CONCERTS.—Three concerts of chamber music for piano, violin, and violoncello, will be given, probably toward the end of January, February, and March, by Professors Knight and Troostwyk and Mr. Schulz.

The SYMPHONY CONCERTS.—These concerts, five in number, are given by the New Haven Symphony Orchestra. Programs of classical and modern compositions are played and the assistance of eminent soloists is secured.

The ORATORIO SOCIETY CONCERTS.—At the first of the two concerts of the present season, Handel's Oratorio of The Messiah, and at the second concert, Sir Edward Elgar's Dream of Gerontius, will be sung by the New Haven Oratorio Society.

ORGAN RECITALS.—Recitals are given in Woolsey Hall on the Newberry Memorial Organ by Professor Jepson on Monday afternoons during the winter term. Following these a supplementary series is given by visiting organists of note.

ARTIST'S CONCERTS by musicians of the highest standing are given from time to time.

UNIVERSITY PRIZES

The JOHN A. PORTER PRIZE, being the income of a fund of five thousand dollars, established by the Kingsley Trust Association in 1872, is offered annually for the best English essay on a prescribed subject. Any person who is pursuing a regular course for a degree in any Department during the whole of the current College year, may compete for this prize. The award is announced on Commencement Day. If in any year none of the competing essays is of sufficient merit, the prize is not awarded. The subjects for essays in 1908 are as follows :

1. The Present Position of the Executive in National and State Government.
2. The Relation of the American University to the Religious, Political, and Social Issues of American Life.
3. Contributions of Modern Psychical Research to the Belief in Immortality.
4. Foreign Missions.
5. Augustus St. Gaudens.
6. Walt Whitman.

Essays for the John A. Porter Prize should be plainly marked on the outside, "John A. Porter University Essay for 1908," and should be mailed addressed to the John A. Porter University Prize Essay Committee, in care of the Secretary of Yale University, New Haven. Each essay must be typewritten, signed by an assumed name, and accompanied by the author's real name in a sealed envelope. The essays are due on or before May 1, 1908.

The JAMES GORDON BENNETT PRIZE, being the income of a fund of one thousand dollars, given in 1893 by James Gordon Bennett, Esq., of New York City, is awarded annually, on Commencement Day, to that member of the Senior class in either the Academical Department or the Sheffield Scientific School who has pursued courses in Political Science and English Literature and has prepared the best essay, in English prose, upon some subject of contemporaneous interest in the domestic or foreign policy of the United States government, selected by the Faculty.

Essays in competition for this prize must be presented at the University Library, Monday, June 1, 1908, before 12.00 M. The subject will be one of the following :

1. Socialism in the United States as contrasted with Other Types of Socialism.
2. The Treasury and the Money Market.

The COBDEN CLUB SILVER MEDAL is awarded annually to that undergraduate of either the Academical Department or the Sheffield Scientific School who shows the greatest proficiency in the elements of Political Economy. Subjects for theses the present year are the following :

1. Should the American States adopt an Employers' Liability Act similar to that of Great Britain ?
2. The Tariff on Forest Products.
3. Do Recent Changes in Transportation Conditions justify an Extensive Program of Federal Improvement of Internal Waterways ?
4. A Comparison of the Panics of 1893 and 1907.
5. The Trust Companies and the Banks.

A student desiring to substitute another subject for one of those given above must apply for permission to the committee before March 1. Theses are due at the University Library on or before June 1.

The ALBERT STANBURROUGH COOK PRIZE IN POETRY, of the value of fifty dollars, is offered for the present year by Professor Cook for the best unpublished poem. Competition is open to students of the University in all Departments. If none of the competing poems is of sufficient merit, the prize will not be awarded. Before receiving the prize, the winner must print the successful poem in a manner acceptable to the donor. The poems, each of which should be signed by an assumed name and accompanied by a sealed envelope containing the writer's full name, are due on April 1, and may be handed in at the University Library.

The JACOB COOPER PRIZE IN GREEK PHILOSOPHY, established in 1900 by the gift of five hundred dollars from

Professor Albert S. Cook, is awarded in any year by the Professors of Greek and of Philosophy to that student of the University, being a person of high attainments and ability, who passes the best examination in the *Metaphysics* and *Organon* of Aristotle, and submits the best thesis upon some topic drawn from one of these works and announced publicly at a convenient time in advance.

The GEORGE WASHINGTON EGLESTON HISTORICAL PRIZE, the income of one thousand dollars, founded in 1901 by George Washington Egleston, Esq., of Eardisley, Herefordshire, England, is awarded annually to a student of the University who during the preceding year, by research, has discovered some new fact or facts relating to American History ; or, from existing data, has brought to bear some information, or criticism, sufficiently notable to be useful from a literary point of view. .

The PHILO SHERMAN BENNETT PRIZE is the income of a fund of four hundred dollars, given in 1905 by Hon. William ·J. Bryan as trustee under the will of Philo Sherman Bennett, Esq., of New Haven, for the best essay discussing the principles of free government. The subject for this year will be "The Principles of Free Government with Respect to the Constitution of the Executive Power." Essays must be typewritten, and must be left at the Secretary's office, Yale University, on or before May 1, 1908. Students in all Departments may compete.

PART VI

DEGREES AND HONORS, 1907

DEGREES CONFERRED IN COURSE
BACHELORS OF ART

Gordon Wilson Abbott
Fred Davis Abrams
Fritz George Achelis
George Morris Adams
George Elmer Anderson
Edgar Hobbs Arnold
Nelson Irving Asiel
Edward Parsons Bagg, Jr.
Ernest Schwefel Ballard
William Deluce Barnes, Jr.
Edward Morgan Barradale
Edward Hudson Barstow
Morris Lyon Beard
George Elbert Beck
Douglas Jerrold Abbey Bell
Edwin Bendheim
Howard Francis Bishop
Kenneth McLeod Bissell
William McCormick Blair
William Carmichael Blyth
Philip Waldron Boardman
George Borup
Richard Hassard Boswell
Howard Boulton
Carl Hammer Breaker
Ernest Milford Bristol
Alexander Cushing Brown
Burt Layton Brown
Earl Brown, PH.B.
   University of Iowa 1905
Richmond Lennox Brown
James White Bruce
Leroy Ewalt Brunner
Morgan Gardner Bulkeley, Jr.
Ludlow Seguine Bull
Edward Hubert Butler, Jr.
Arthur Goodwin Camp
Rumsey Campbell
Winthrop Lakey Carter

Clarence Edward Chaney
Edward Barton Chapin
Ralph Waldo Chase
William Bowen Church
Joseph Herendeen Clark
Norman Parsons Clement
William Ellsworth Clow, Jr.
George Hamilton Colket, Jr.
William Welch Collin, Jr.
William Ernest Collins
Willoughby Francis Colton, B.A.
   Center College 1906
Charles Williams Comfort, Jr.
Arthur Milton Comley
Lawrence Merritt Connell
Leland Church Covey
Joseph Graham Crane
Seth Turner Crawford
Benjamin Franklin Crenshaw, B.A.
   Western College 1906
James Cunningham
Robert Howe Cunningham
Daniel Joseph Curran
*Harry Alban Leonard Curran
Ralph Dennis Cutler
Forrest Leonard Daniels
Richard Ely Danielson
Charles Lowell Davidson
Charles Julius Davis
Richard Douglas Davis, Jr.
Franklin Augustus Dean, Jr.
Clinton Demas Deming
Richard Henry Deming
Chester Merritt Deuel
William Hughes Diller
Theodore Polhemus Dixon
Dunham Brown Dodge
Philip Lyndon Dodge
Liguori Alphonsus Doherty

* Deceased

— 581 —

Frederic Russell Dolbeare
William Stanton Donoho, B.A.
  Baylor University 1906
Blatchford Downing
Theodore Ives Driggs
Paul Alexander Drucklieb
Edward Lee Dummer
Ralph Henry Dunning
Russell Stearns Dwight
Rolland Mooney Edmonds
Paul Bradley Elmore
Arthur Edwin Ely
Harold Pegram Fabian
Henry Robertson Failing
William Everett Fay
Charles Milton Fessenden
William Sherman Fisher
Henry Fleischner
Bainbridge Doty Folwell
Robert Wilson Forbes
Frederick Clifford Ford
Henry Albert Foster
Talton Turner Francis
Julius Walter Freiberg
Robert Henry Fruin
William Spencer Fuller
George Napoleon Gaboury
Bertram Adolph Gabriel
Umberto Dante Garfield
Charles Pew Garland
Milton Washington Garrette, PH.B.
  Illinois Wesleyan College 1904
Lorin Henry Gates
Thomas Theron Giffen, B.A.
  Pomona College 1906
Prentiss Bailey Gilbert, PH.B.
  University of Rochester 1906
Hugh Gillis
George Brette Glaenzer
Barzilla Parks Gooden
Philip Lippincott Goodwin
Bradley Goodyear
James W. Green, Jr.
Albert Byron Gregory

Arthur Robbins Griswold
William Francis Gunn, Jr.
Milton Bruce Hadley
Charles Herbert Halcomb, Jr.
Charles Walter Hall, B.A.
  Doane College 1904
Clarence Russell Hall
Benjamin Pomeroy Hamlin
Howard Edmiston Hannum
Charles Edwin Hart, Jr.
Edward Henry Hart
Mortimer Hall Hartwell
Edwin Deeks Harvey
Roemer Benjamin Hathaway
Harold Hauenstein
Frank Anderson Hayes
Harry Clifton Heaton
Dona Benjamin Heil
Charles Bingham Heisler
Charles Erle Hibbard
Graham Shields Hislop
Percy William Holter
Charles Roberts Hopkins
Bayard Cushing Hoppin
Charles Melvin Horton
William Irving Howbert
Henry Martyn Hoyt, Jr.
James Lanman Hubbard
James Howard Hull
Roger Benton Hull
Rutherford Hayes Hunter
Horace Lyman Huson
Walter Waters Husted
Anson Blake Jackson, Jr.
Charles Balfe Jackson
Isaac Lamson Jennings
Stephen Jennings
Gerard Edward Jensen
Frank Elmer Johnson
Jeremiah Howard Jones
Richard Michael Joy
William Oded Keirstead, B.A.
  Bates College 1906
LeRoy Mervyn Kellas

Hal Rowe Kellogg
Frederick Trowbridge Kelsey
James Madison Kennedy
Whitney Kernochan
Horace Ogden Kilbourn
Charles Porter Kimball
Clarence Hopkins King
Joseph Casimir Kircher
John Colby Kitchen
James Walter Knott
Hugh Smith Knox
William Francis Knox
Ralph Damon Kochersperger
Harold Kountze
Stephen Lesher Landon
William James Larkin, Jr.
Robert Cathcart Latimer
Edward Elliott Lattin
John Harold Lawrence
Harold Dimock Lee
Norman Alvah Leonard
Edmund Harris Lewis
Lester Sweet Lewis
Nathan Everett Lincoln
Mitchell Stuart Little
Leighton Lobdell
Manice DeForest Lockwood, Jr.
Robert Ralph Lockwood
William Harding Longley, B.A.
   Acadia University 1901
Henry Stow Lovejoy
John Gilbert Lowe
Tasker Gantt Lowndes
Maurice Francis Lyons
George McAuliff
Paul Ely McChesney
Bowdoin Updike McClintock
Frank Stockton McClintock
Chauncey Brooks McCormick
Constantine Joseph McGuire, Jr.
Sumner Thomas McKnight, Jr.
Raymond Richard McOrmond
John James Maddox
Rufus Sherrell Maddox

Herbert Lawrence Malcolm
Howard Jones Mandell
Francis Edgerton Manierre
Francis Hartman Markoe, Jr.
Robert Davies Marshall
Amasa Stone Mather
Harold Mead
Dwight Raymond Meigs
Charles Goodwin Merriam
Schuyler Merritt Myer
Robert Middlebrook, Jr.
William Henry Milholland
Edwin Cyrus Miller
James Raglan Miller
James Lynn Mitchell
John Fowler Mitchell, Jr., B.A.
   Butler College 1906
William Crittenden Mooney, Jr.
Francis William Moore
Henry Butler Moore, Jr.
Raymond Bartlett Morris
Reuben Henry Morrish
Philip Lefèvre Morrison
Samuel Finley Brown Morse
Edward Theodore Newell
Douglas Keefer Noyes
Frederick Kinney Noyes
Irving Sands Olds
Marshall Johnson Olds
Charles Oliver
Bertice Henry Olmstead
Elbert Ellery Orcutt
Minott Augur Osborn
Charles Pomeroy Otis
Howard Earle Palmer
Fred Amasa Parker
Arthur Newbury Parmelee
Eli Burton Parsons
Simon Truby Patterson
William Marline Pearce
Nicholas Elias Peieff
Karlton Goodsell Percy
Hervey Bates Perrin
William Augustine Perry

Robert Edward Pfeiffer
Howard Phipps
Livingston Platt
Ernest Marcus Porter
George Boardman Potter
Edward Leander Pratt
Robert Hamilton Prentice
Karl Preston
Edward Jerome Quinlan
George Goble Quirk
Oren Mitchell Ragsdale
Harrison Pierce Rich
Morgan Thomas Riley
Sam Tom Robb, PH.B.
  Baylor University 1905
Charles Francis Robbins, Jr.
Graham Robinson
Randolph Preston Rogers
Howard LeChevalier Roome
Harold Arthur Rosenbaum
Milton Alexis Rosenfeld
Benjamin Irving Rouse
Albert Billings Ruddock
Donald Mitchell Ryerson
Albert Godfrey Sanders, B.A.
  Southwestern University 1904
James Cox Sanderson
Ansley Wilcox Sawyer
Frederick Hirsheal Schmidt
George Schaefer Scott
Harold Bartlett Scott
Walter Hawley Scott
Richard Frank Seidensticker
Clarence William Seymour
Henry Earl Sheffield
Ernest Wilson Sheldon, B.A.
  McGill University 1904
George Clarence Sherwood
Albert William Shields
John Elbert Shirk
Frank Ronald Simmons
Lewis Edmond Sisson
Malcolm Douglas Sloane
George Washington Small

Alexander Wyley Smith, Jr., B.A.
  University of Georgia 1906
Charles Paget Smith
Everett Robbins Smith
Frank Butts Smoyer
George Mark Sneath
Donald McLean Somers .
Gilbert Little Stark
Edward Burgis Starr
Henry Harmon Stevens
Elias Robert Stevenson
Henry Bartlett Stimson
Arthur Purdy Stout
McNeil Seymour Stringer
Stuart Robinson Strong
William George Sullivan
Cyril Sumner
George Lewis Sutherland
Edward Francis Sweeney
Stanley Adams Sweet
Henry Hawley Swords
Walbridge Smith Taft
Senjiro Takagi
Spencer Jay Teller, M.E.
  Cornell University 1906
James Harl Tener
Stephen Dows Thaw
Frederick Herrick Thomas
Gaylord Thomas
Hubert Fletcher Thomas
Guy Van Zandt Thompson
Roy Smith Thompson
Lauren Scott Thomson
Montgomery Hunt Throop
Charles Frederick Todd
Douglas Jay Torrey
Richard Rodermond Townsend
Ernest Bell Tracy
Roger Culver Tredwell
Calvin Truesdale
Thomas Allen Tully
George Coolidge Tuttle
Reuel Lincoln Twitchell
William Finney Tyler

John Adolf Vietor
Arthur Hill Vincent
Daniel Eligius Wade
Herbert Hamilton Wagenhals
Wayne Winslow Waite
Henry Freeman Walradt
Ira Davenport Waterman
James Watson Webb
Ralph Eugene Weber
Benjamin Webster
George Harold Weiss
Harold Sherman Wells
Cortlandt Stuyvesant Wheeler
Ernest Cousins Wheeler
Robert Campbell Wheeler
Frank Elbert Wheelock, B.A.
  Acadia University 1905

John Alan White
Robert George White
Lewis Bliss Whittemore
William Sheldon Whittlesey
Alfred Williams, B.A.
  Tarkio College 1902
Arthur Robinson Williams
Arthur Putnam Williamson
George Wilshire
* Lispenard Stewart Witherbee
Walter Bertram Wolf
Brainard Hardy Woodward
Heathcote Muirson Woolsey
Henry Haight Wright
Thomas Goddard Wright
William Francis Wrynn
Bayard Daniel York

BACHELORS OF PHILOSOPHY

Henry Alphonse Alker
Leon Hudson Andrews
Samuel Walter Avis
Clifford Myron Baker
John Alexander Baker
Harry Garwood Baldwin
Charles Thurston Ballard, Jr.
William Newell Bannard, Jr.
Robert Daniels Bardwell
Denise Barkalow
Marshall Moore Bartholomew
Frank Lemuel Baxter
Stanley Drew Beard
William Rose Benêt
Mark John Bennett
Charles Van Denbergh Benton
Louis Berman
Charles Eddy Betcher
Carl Welch Bettcher
David Edward Bigwood
Walter Babcock Binnian
Harold Law Blakeslee
Francis Hervey Bradley
Edward Ainslie Brewer

Robert Lee Brewer
Harry Farnsworth Brown
Aldis Jerome Browne
Frederick Herbert Brundage
Ralph William Burnet
Harry Walter Burr
Edwin Converse Butler
Charles Eben Canada
Hiram Bissell Carey
Harold Frank Carlton
Earle Buell Carter
· Valentine Burt Chamberlain
Charles VanWycke Chamberlin
Charles Hall Chapin
John Pierce Cheney
John Oren Christian
Elias Treat Clark
Ernest Dwight Clark
Robert Eli Clark
Talcott Hunt Clarke
Eugene Ellsworth Clements
Raymond Savage Coe
William Thomas Coholan
John Archibald Campbell Colston

* Deceased

Johns Hopkins Congdon, Jr.
John Hamilton Derby, Jr.
James E. Diamond
Lewis Acker Dibble
Burgess Dickinson
Joseph Dilworth
Raymond Jones Doty
Augustus Cornwall Downing, Jr.
Henry Gibbs Ellis
Walter Joseph Feder
Rufus Flynt
Benjamin Rossiter Foote
Samuel Elbert Ford
William Edward Foster, 2d
Edward Griffin Beckwith Fox
William Dixon Fullerton
Frederick Riley Gagel
George Thomas Gambrill, Jr.
Russell Tyner Gard
Karl Knox Gartner
John Gilbert George
William Carey Gibson
Harold Moffett Gould
Carl Emil Green
Fairfax Hall
Lamont Andrew Hall
Floyd Linsley Hamilton
Clarence Piper Hanly
Francis Howe Hardy
William Bibb Hartshorne
Samuel Clarke Harvey
Henry Peter Hass
Rolland Miles Hastings
Philip Moulton Hatheway
Philip Ferguson Hawley
Warner Searle Hays
Milton Alfred Hellman
Elton Brigham Hill
Harold Lucius Hoadley
Clarence William Hockenberger
James Allen Hoffman
Leigh Irving Holdredge
Joseph Foster Hoss

Yuen-li Hsia
    Nanyang College, Shanghai
Stanley Bailey Ineson
Charles Richard Irvin
Jacob Louis Jacobs
John Joseph Jennings
Emory Lyon Johnson
Douglas Turner Johnston
Carlton Benjamin Jones
Walter Edward Joyce
William Dennis Kennedy
Thomas Sylvester Keveney
Edward Dyer Kingman
Gilmore Kinney, Jr.
Theodore Engelmann Kircher
Harold Bennett Kline
Clarence Moore Knox
Robert Bidwell Lattin
Veader Newton Leonard
Commodore Dunlap Lester, B.S.
    Baylor University 1906
Howard Linn
Leslie Hays Lord
Cyrus Henry Loutrel
Richard Leonard Lovell
Fred H. McCulloch
John Stokes McCune
Harold Orville Mackenzie
Kenneth Gerard Mackenzie
Stanley Robinson MacLane, B.A.
    Yale University 1906
Forman Taylor McLean
Lawrence Riley McWeeney
John William Madden
Henry Swan Manning, Jr.
Ralph Julian Marsh
James Waller Marshall
Norman Andrews Martin
Charles Wesley Meloney
Merritt B. Merwin
Alfred Charles Meyer
Hugh Irving Millerd
Ellsworth Frost Miner

Clifford Joseph Monahan
Paul Seiberling Mosser
Wilfred Eaton Murchie
Sidney Charles Murray
Foster Stebbins Naething
Herbert Lewis Nichols
Frank John O'Donnell
Louis Albert Oldershaw
John Gilman Ordway
Roswell Park, Jr.   .
Roy Taylor Parker
Herbert Arthur Parsons
Earl Partridge
John Sherman Peck
Heman J. Pettengill, Jr.
Lawrence Clinton Phipps
Walter D. Pinkus
William A. Pond
Louis Robert Porteous
Charles Talbot Porter, 2d
Lawrence Copeland Porter
Waldo Todd Pratt
Marshall Prentiss
Frank Taylor Quinlan
James McHenry Rauers
Karl Vernon Raymond
James MacGregor Renfrew
Carroll Ridgway
Stanley Pickett Rockwell
Thomas Rodd, Jr.
William Starling Sullivant Rodgers,
   Jr.
Joseph Rosenbaum
Samuel Barnell Rosenbaum
George Vallandigham Rotan
Julian Eastman Rothery
Aretas Andrews Saunders
Leon Ewart Savage
Howard Sheafer Schall
Leonard Hawxhurst Searing
Horatio Seymour, Jr.
Kent Shaffer
George Bradstreet Shaw

Arthur Carr Sherman
Chester Peter Siems
Oliver Martin Smart
Edwin Kinmouth Smith
George Colmore Smith, Jr.
Philip Seabury Smith
Reynold Webb Smith
David Benton Snow
Harold Fowler Sperry
Radcliff Evans Sprott
William Wetmore Stanley
Horace William Staples
Edward Walter Steele
Joseph Clayton Stephenson
John Stilwell
Charles Buchanan Stuart
George Amory Thomas
Arthur VanRensselaer Thompson
Cleveland May Thorne
Carl Perkins Tomlinson
Morris English Tuttle
Clifford Andrew Upson
Thornton Edwin Vail
George Warren VanBrunt
John Martin VanHarlingen
Herbert Francis Vanorden
Paul Lansing Veeder
Boynton Stephen Voorhees
Ralph Bickerton Wainwright
Frederick Hemingway Waldron, Jr.   .
Walter Treat Walker
Robert Wallace
Evans Ward
William Wayne, Jr.
Harold Edward Webster
Alden Wells
Frank Everts Werneken
Jacob Wershow
Edwin Blake Whiting
Lucian Thames Wilcox
Lee Charles Wilson
Henry H. Wittstein
Ralph William Young

BACHELOR OF FINE ARTS
William Adams Delano, B.A.
Yale University 1895

BACHELOR OF MUSIC
Walter Ruel Cowles, B.A.
Yale University 1906

BACHELORS OF LAWS

Harry Hall Atwater, B.A.
Yale University 1905
Thorpe Babcock
Louis Hyde Bauman
Ralph Turner Beers
. Michael Vincent Blansfield, LL.B.
Vanderbilt University 1905
Spencer Gilson Brown, B.A.
Blackburn College 1903,
M.A. Princeton University 1904
Robert Burton, B.A.
Blackburn College 1904,
M.A. Yale University 1906
Robert Harold Butterfield, *cum laude*
William Kernan Camblos, B.A.
St. Joseph's College 1904,
M.A. Yale University 1906
John Francis Clark
Luther Gardner Coburn, B.S.
Wesleyan University 1901
John Aloysius Cohan
Robert Newton Crane
James Augustin Cummings
Marion Roscoe Davis, B.A.
Hamilton College 1904
Russell Deudney, LL.B.
New York Law School 1906
John Bernardine Dillon
William Brewster Ely, B.A.
Yale University 1904, *cum laude*
Albert Jeffreys Evans
Charles William Evarts
Ray Henry Everett
Joseph Marion Forsyth, B.A.
Yale University 1905
Pierrepont Beers Foster, B.A.
Yale University 1903

John Morrison Fox
Howard Garrett Fuller, Jr.
Abe Saul Geduldig
Garnett Andrews Green, B.L.
University of Georgia 1906
Daniel Myron Greene, B.A.
West Virginia University 1905,
LL.B. West Virginia University 1906
George Thacher Guernsey, Jr., B.A.
University of Kansas 1904
Maurice E. Holzman
Charles Arthur Hopwood
George Charles Howard
Charles Hadlai Hull, B.A.
Yale University 1905
Francis Dustin Hurtt
Mahlon Hensley Jefferson, LL.B.
Grant University 1906
Newell Jennings, B.A.
Yale University 1904, *cum laude*
Joshua Lervy Johns, LL.B.
Grant University 1906
William Alexander Johnson
Bernard Israel Kamen
Thomas Henry Kirkland, B.A.
Yale University 1904
Frederick William Lang
Francis James McCoy
Frank Patrick McEvoy
Arthur Packer McKinstry, B.A.
Yale University 1905, *magna cum laude*
William James Maher, M.A.
Saint Viateur's College 1906
George Frazier Mara
Charles Everett Moore, B.A.
Yale University 1904
Albert Clayton Moss

Edgar Munson, B.A.
Yale University 1904
George Sharp Munson, B.A.
Yale University 1904, *magna cum laude*
Hugh Joseph Murphy, B.A.
Yale University 1904
George Nicholas
George Elton Parks, B.A.
Yale University 1904, *magna cum laude*
Eugene James Phillips, B.A.
Yale University 1905
Alvin LaFayette Richards, LL.B.
Valparaiso University 1906
Milton William Sametz, B.L.
New York University 1906
Harry John Schmidt
Joseph George Shapiro, *cum laude*
Adelbert Arthur Skeel, PH.B.
Yale University 1904

Arthur Henry Slack
John Carroll Slade, B.A.
Yale University 1905, *cum laude*
George Groot Snow
Robert Gordon Starr
George Arthur Stokes, LL.B.
Vanderbilt University 1905
Gaylord Bacon VanKirk
George Slingerland VanSchaick, *magna cum laude*
Thomas George Wall, PH.B.
. Drake University 1905
Erskine Donahue Warren
George Price Whitman, B.L.
University of Georgia 1906
Orrin Arthur Wing
Charles Herbert Woods, B.A.
Blackburn College 1904, *cum laude*
Maxwell Wyckoff, B.L.
New York University 1906

BACHELORS OF DIVINITY

Hugh Elmer Brown, B.S.
Whitman College 1904, *cum laude*
Charles Melanchthon Calderwood, PH.B.
Iowa College 1900
Charles Martin Good, B.A.
Otterbein University 1904
Raymond Rogers Gregory, B.A.
Franklin and Marshall College 1904
William Henry Harris
Wesleyan Theological College, Montreal

Darwin Ashley Leavitt, B.A.
Beloit College 1904, *magna cum laude*
George Douglas Milbury, B.A.
Bates College 1905
William Henry Smith, B.A.
Hiram College 1901
Wilbur Kelsey Thomas, B.A.
Friends University 1904
Karl Owen Thompson, B.A.
Amherst College 1904, *cum laude*
Arthur Ewen Westenberg, B.A.
Beloit College 1904

MASTERS OF ARTS
WITH SUBJECTS OF STUDY

Raymond Garfield Aylsworth, B.A.
Cotner University 1896, M.A. 1906
Semitic Languages and Biblical Literature
Preston A. Barba, B.A.
Muhlenberg College 1906
English
Harry Annesley Beadle, B.A.
Bowdoin College 1900
Biblical Literature

Otis Munro Bigelow, B.A.
Yale University 1904
French
David Verner Brunstrom, B.A.
Bethany College 1903,
B.A. Yale University 1905
History
Horace Thomas Burgess, B.A.
National Normal University 1905,
B.A. Yale University 1906
Mathematics

Ernest Wilfred Bysshe, B.A.
Columbia University 1901,
B.D. Drew Theological Seminary 19 6
Biblical Literature

Charles Carver, Jr., B.A.
Yale University 1906
English

Howard Wadsworth Church, B.A.
Yale University 1904
German

Robert Lincoln Clark, B.A.
Yale University 1906
English

Raymond Eugene Cook, B.A.
Williams College 1905
History

Paul Curts, B.A.
Yale University 1905
German

Thomas Frederick Davies, Jr., B.A.
Yale University 1894
Philosophy

George Stuart Dole, B.A.
Yale University 1906
Economics

Louis Alexander Dole, B.A.
Yale University 1906
Economics

Robert John Drysdale, B.A.
Knox College (Canada) 1905
Semitic Languages and Biblical Literature

Richard Grenville Ely, B.A.
Amherst College 1906
History

Robert Louis Ervin, B.A.
Ohio Northern University 1903,
M.A. Defiance College 1906
History and Economics

James Fraser Evans, B.A.
Toronto University 1893
Biblical Literature and English

William Abraham Evans, B.A.
Yale University 1902
English

James Linwood Fawley, B.A.
Yale University 1906
Chemistry

Ch'i-hao Fei, B.A.
Oberlin College 1906
Education

James Fulton Ferguson, B.A.
Monmouth College 1903,
B.A. Yale University 1906
Classics

Charles Franklin, B.A.
Central College 1894, M.A. 1895,
B.D. Vanderbilt University 1901
Biblical Literature

George Edward Gage, B.A.
Clark University 1906
Bacteriology

Asa Russell Gifford, B.A.
Wesleyan University 1904
Philosophy

Ernest Hausberg, B.A.
Yale University 1901
English

Norman Elwood Henry, B.A.
Bucknell University 1905, M.A. 1905
Classical Philology

Charles Hjerpe, B.A.
Bethany College 1902,
B.A. Yale University 1905
History

Isaac Henry Hughes, B.A.
National Normal University 1896,
B.A. Yale University 1906
Modern Languages

Marion Bertram Hunter, B.A.
Maryville College 1904,
B.A. Yale University 1906
Literature and History

Teizaburo Inomata, B.A.
Tokyo Imperial University 1903
English

D L James, B.A.
Yale University 1902
Modern Languages

Frank Oscar Jones, B.A.
Brown University 1897
Philosophy

Tviichi Kairiyama, PH.B.
Cornell University 1898
Philosophy

Mihran Tatios Kalaidjian, B.A.
St. Paul's Institute, Tarsus, 1900,
B.D. Yale University 1905
Philosophy of Religion

Junichiro Kinoshita, B.L.
  Doshisha College 1897,
  Meiji University 1898
  Economics
Lucian Swift Kirtland, B.A.
  Yale University 1903
  English
James Atsutoshi Kumon
  Kansai Law School 1898
  Economics
Hsiang-hsi K'ung, B.A.
  Oberlin College 1906
  Chemistry
George Christopher Lambert, B.D.
  Hartford Theological Seminary 1906
  Biblical Literature
Kenneth Scott Latourette, B.S.
  McMinnville College 1904,
  B.A. Yale University 1906
  History
Henry Wells Lawrence, Jr., B.A.
  Yale University 1906
  History
Darwin Ashley Leavitt, B.A.
  Beloit College 1904
  Semitic Languages and Biblical Lit-
  erature
William Pitt McCune, B.A.
  Yale University 1906
  English
Alfred Arundel May, B.A.
  University of Wooster 1900
  English
Morgan Millar, B.A.
  Harvard University 1897
  Biblical Literature
John Milton Miller, B.A.
  Yale University 1904
  Physics
Charles Everett Moore, B.A.
  Yale University 1904
  English
Henry Thomas Moore, B.A.
  Missouri University 1903, M.A. 1904
  Psychology
Shozi Murakawa
  Doshisha College 1905
  Economics
Suyekichi Nakagawa
  Waseda University 1899
  Economics

Charles Washburn Nichols, B.A.
  Yale University 1905
  English
Levi Fatzinger Noble, B.A.
  Yale University 1905
  Geology
Haralambus Michaelides Pappado-
poulos, B.A.
  Oberlin College 1904
  Greek
Harvey Whitefield Peck, B.A.
  Oberlin College 1905
  English
Joseph Chappell Rayworth, B.A.
  Acadia University 1903,
  B.A. Yale University 1906
  Mathematics
Albert Edward Roraback, B.A.
  Yale University 1902
  Church History
Daniel Crehange Rosenthal, B.A.
  Syracuse University 1906
  Romance Languages
Harold Roy Sampson, B.A.
  Westminster College 1903
  Latin
Iwao Segawa
  Keiogijiku University 1904
  Economics
Ryonosuke Seita, B.A.
  Kenyon College 1904
  English
Guy Andrew Simmons, B.A.
  McFerrin College 1897,
  M.A. DePauw University 1902
  Latin
Milton Simpson, B.A.
  Acadia University 1905,
  B.A. Yale University 1906
  English
William Ernest Andrew Slaght, B.A.
  Toronto University 1898,
  B.D. Yale University 1902
  Biblical Literature
Benjamin Augustus Thaxter, B.A.
  Yale University 1897
  English
Archie Toothaker, B.A.
  Highland University 1903,
  B.D. Pacific Theological Seminary 1904
  Biblical Literature

Warren Gookin Waterman, B.A.
  Yale University 1892
  Geology

Robert Day Williams, B.S.
  Pomona College 1903
  Philosophy

Selah Howell Wright, B.A.
  Yale University 1906
  Economics

MASTERS OF LAWS

Terence Byrne Cosgrove, B.A.
  St. Viateur's College 1903, M.A. 1906,
  LL.B. University of Notre Dame 1906,
  cum laude

José Escaler, B.A.
  Liceo de Manila 1902, LL.B. 1905, *magna
  cum laude*

Lawrence Kirby Fulton, PH.B.
  Kansas City School of Law 1906

Martin John Hurley, LL.B.
  University of Minnesota 1906

Mariano Honrade de Joya, LL.B.
  Indiana University 1906, *cum laude*

MASTERS OF SCIENCE

James Osborne Hopwood, B.S.
  University of Pennsylvania 1904

Chester Albert Reeds, B.S.
  University of Oklahoma 1905

MECHANICAL ENGINEERS

Joseph Wickham Roe, PH.B.
  Yale University 1895

William Klein Simpson, PH.B.
  Yale University 1905

CIVIL ENGINEERS

Charles Sherman Farnham, PH.B.
  Yale University 1902

Herbert Vincent Olds, PH.B.
  Yale University 1905

Guy Louis Winthrop, B.A.
  Florida State College 1903,
  PH.B. Yale University 1905

MASTERS OF FORESTRY

William Burnett Barrows, B.A.
  Columbia University 1905

Avila Bédard, B.A.
  Laval University 1905

John Bentley, Jr., B.S.
  Wesleyan University 1904, *magna cum
  laude*

Ovid McOuat Butler, B.A.
  Butler College 1902

Philip Tripp Coolidge, B.A.
  Harvard University 1905

Stephen Miller Crowell, B.S.
  Connecticut Agricultural College 1905

Samuel Trask Dana, B.A.
  Bowdoin College 1904, *summa cum
  laude*

Raymond Davis, B.A.
  Bowdoin College 1905

Nils Bonnevie Eckbo
  Stenkjar Skogskole 1904

John Harold Foster, B.S.
  Norwich University 1903

Bartle Trott Harvey, B.S.
  University of Maine 1905

Charles Sheldon Judd, B.A.
  Yale University 1905, *cum laude*

Francis Bentley Kellogg, B.A.
  University of California 1905

Kingsley Rich MacGuffey, B.A.
  Yale University 1905

Clyde Sayers Martin, B.S.
  DePauw University 1905

David Townsend Mason, B.S.
  Rutgers College 1905
Louis Sutliffe Murphy, B.S.
  Tufts College 1901, *cum laude*
Gustave Clodomir Piché
Colin Charles Robertson, *cum laude*
Alfred Senn
  Swiss French College 1881
William Chambers Shepard, F.E.
  Cornell University 1907

William Hoyt Weber, B.A.
  Wesleyan University 1903
Charles Parker Wilber, B.A.
  Rutgers College 1905
Hugo August Winkenwerder, B.S.
  University of Wisconsin 1902, *cum laude*
Edward Seymour Woodruff, B.A.
  Yale University 1899, *cum laude*

DOCTORS OF MEDICINE

David Nils Ahlstrom
Horace Doolittle Bellis, *cum laude*
George Houghton Bodley, *cum laude*
Patrick Joseph Brennan
Felix Percy Chillingworth
James Ryle Coffey, B.A.
  Yale University 1903, *cum laude*
Charles Clarence Davis
Hugh Francis Flaherty
Philip Frank
Samuel James Goldberg, *cum laude*
Rufus Warren Hall
Albert Ludwig Hendricks
George Francis Herrity
Samuel Francis Jackson
Robert Francis Lawless
Emmett Judson Lyman

John Joseph MacDonald
Edmund Lowell Marcy
Anthony Joseph Mendillo, *cum laude*
Matthew Nigohos Nahigan
William Orrin Rice, PH.B.
  Brown University 1903
Clyde Augustus Roeder
Charles Arthur Ruickoldt
Thomas Francis Scanlon
Marvin McRae Scarbrough, B.A.
  University of Oregon 1902,
  M.A. Yale University 1905, *cum laude*
John Walter Sweeney
George Edward Teehan
Frank William Thompson
Benedict Nolasco Whipple

DOCTORS OF PHILOSOPHY
WITH SUBJECTS OF STUDY

Luther Anderson, B.A.
  Bethany College 1899,
  B.A. Yale University 1903, M.A. 1904
  History
Gilbert Giddings Benjamin, PH.B.
  Syracuse University 1899,
  M.A. Yale University 1904
  History
Marion LeRoy Burton, B.A.
  Carleton College 1900
  Philosophy
Marian Dickinson Campbell, B.A.
  Radcliffe College 1899
  English

George DeWitt Castor, B.A.
  Drury College 1898, M.A. 1903,
  B.D. Yale University 1903, M.A. 1905
  Biblical Literature
Henry H. Conover, B.S.
  Rutgers College 1900,
  M.S. Yale University 1902
  Mathematics
Loring Holmes Dodd, B.A.
  Dartmouth College 1900,
  M.A. Columbia University 1901
  English

38

Arthur Harmount Graves, B.A.
    Yale University 1900
    Botany
Albert Edward Gubelmann, B.A.
    University of Rochester 1897, M.A. 1900,
    M.A. Yale University 1902
    German
Herbert Franklin Hamilton, B.A.
    Amherst College 1897,
    M.A. Yale University 1899
    English
William Barri Kirkham, B.A.
    Yale University 1904, M.A. 1906
    Biology
Albert Alonzo Madsen, B.A.
    Moravian College 1900, B.D. 1902,
    B.D. Yale University 1903, M A. 1904
    Biblical Literature and Semitic Languages
Philip Henry Mitchell, PH.B.
    Yale University 1904
    Physiological Chemistry
Sidney Knox Mitchell, B.A.
    Yale University 1898
    History

David Lindsey Randall, B.A.
    Yale University 1904, M.A. 1905
    Chemistry
William Drown Rorer, B.A.
    Yale University 1891
    History
Tadasu Saiki, M.D.
    Okayama Medical College 1898
    Physiological Chemistry
Oscar Emil Staaf, B.A.
    Bethany College 1900,
    M.A. Yale University 1902
    Romance Languages
George Bremner Tennant, B.A.
    Yale University 1900, M.A. 1903
    English
Harry Brown VanDeventer, B.A.
    Yale University 1903, M.A. 1904
    Latin
Axel Ebenezer Vestling, B.A.
    Bethany College 1900,
    B.A. Yale University 1903, M.A. 1905
    German
Arthur Gustavus Ward, B.A.
    Yale University 1898, M.A. 1904
    German

HONORARY DEGREES CONFERRED JUNE, 1907

DOCTORS OF DIVINITY

Rev. William Adams Brown, B.A.
    Yale University 1886

Rev. William Douglas Mackenzie, M.A.
    University of Edinburgh 1881

DOCTORS OF LAWS

Frederick Newton Judson, B.A.
    Yale University 1886
Philander Chase Knox, B.A.
    Mount Union College 1872

Herbert Putnam, B.A.
    Harvard University 1883
Henry Pickering Walcott, B.A.
    Harvard University 1858

DOCTOR OF LETTERS

Francis Hopkinson Smith

DOCTORS OF SCIENCE

Joseph Paxson Iddings, PH.B.
    Yale University 1877

Archibald Byron Macallum, B.A.
    University of Toronto 1880

MASTERS OF ARTS

Frederick Trevor Hill, B.A.
　Yale University 1887

Vance Criswell McCormick, PH.B.
　Yale University 1893

Everett James McKnight

Lewis Frank Tooker, B.A.
　Yale University 1877

Henry Vaughan

(Officers of Yale University given the degree of Master of Arts *privatim* by vote of the Corporation conferring this in the case of all members of the Corporation and Professors who have no previous Yale degree or no Yale degree higher than the Bachelor's.)

JUNE AND OCTOBER, 1907

George Blumer, M.D.
　Cooper Medical College 1891

Ernest William Brown, B.A.
　Christ's College, Cambridge, 1887

Guy Stevens Callender, B.A.
　Oberlin College 1891

Joseph Marshall Flint, B.S.
　University of Chicago 1895

Hon. Edwin Baker Gager, B.A.
　Yale University 1877

Ross Granville Harrison, B.A.
　Johns Hopkins University 1889

John Duer Irving, B.A.
　Columbia University 1896

Harry Benjamin Jepson, B.A.
　Yale University 1893

Charles Hubbard Judd, B.A.
　Wesleyan University 1894

Payson Merrill, B.A.
　Yale University 1865

Henry Wade Rogers, B.A.
　University of Michigan 1874

Henry Bradford Sargent, PH.B.
　Yale University 1871

James William Toumey, B.S.
　Michigan Agricultural College 1889

Rev. Ambrose White Vernon, B.A.
　Princeton University 1891

Frederick Morris Warren, B.A.
　Amherst College 1880

HONORS IN THE SEVERAL DEPARTMENTS

THE ACADEMICAL DEPARTMENT
SENIOR APPOINTMENTS
(FOR THE WORK OF THE WHOLE COLLEGE COURSE†)
CLASS OF 1907

PHILOSOPHICAL ORATIONS

HOWARD FRANCIS BISHOP
RICHMOND LENNOX BROWN
WILLIAM ERNEST COLLINS
LIGUORI ALPHONSUS DOHERTY
FREDERICK TROWBRIDGE KELSEY
FRANK STOCKTON McCLINTOCK
FREDERICK KINNEY NOYES
JOHN ALAN WHITE
WILLIAM SHELDON WHITTLESEY
ARTHUR ROBINSON WILLIAMS
BAYARD DANIEL YORK

GEORGE ELBERT BECK
CHARLES LOWELL DAVIDSON
MILTON WASHINGTON GARRETTE
THOMAS THERON GIFFEN
RUTHERFORD HAYES HUNTER
WILLIAM HARDING LONGLEY
JOHN JAMES MADDOX
EDWIN CYRUS MILLER
WILLIAM MARLINE PEARCE
ERNEST WILSON SHELDON
JAMES HARL TENER
FRANK ELBERT WHEELOCK

HIGH ORATIONS

Kenneth McLeod Bissell
Seth Turner Crawford
Philip Lyndon Dodge
Edward Lee Dummer
Rolland Mooney Edmonds
Clarence Russell Hall
Edward Henry Hart
Norman Alvah Leonard
Henry Stow Lovejoy
Herbert Lawrence Malcolm
William Crittenden Mooney, Jr.
Edward Theodore Newell
Elbert Ellery Orcutt
Charles Pomeroy Otis
Howard Earle Palmer
Robert Edward Pfeiffer

Morgan Thomas Riley
James Cox Sanderson
Frederick Hirsheal Schmidt
Clarence William Seymour
Everett Robbins Smith
Henry Harmon Stevens
Senjiro Takagi
Montgomery Hunt Throop
Thomas Allen Tully

Dona Benjamin Heil
Albert Godfrey Sanders
George Clarence Sherwood
Spencer Jay Teller
Alfred Williams

ORATIONS

Edward Barton Chapin
Joseph Herendeen Clark
William Welch Collin, Jr.
Richard Douglas Davis, Jr.
Blatchford Downing
Paul Alexander Drucklieb
Arthur Edwin Ely
Harold Pegram Fabian
William Everett Fay
Henry Fleischner

Howard Edmiston Hannum
Edwin Deeks Harvey
Harry Clifton Heaton
Gerard Edward Jensen
William Francis Knox
Ralph Damon Kochersperger
Robert Cathcart Latimer
Nathan Everett Lincoln
Rufus Sherrell Maddox
Donald Mitchell Ryerson

† The subdivision of a group by a dash indicates that the men whose names are below the dash were students in Yale College only during Senior year.

ORATIONS—*continued*

Albert William Shields
Henry Bartlett Stimson
Roy Smith Thompson
Charles Frederick Todd
George Coolidge Tuttle
Henry Hamilton Wagenhals
Henry Freeman Walradt

Ernest Cousins Wheeler
Brainard Hardy Woodward
-

Prentiss Bailey Gilbert
Charles Walter Hall'
Alexander Wyly Smith, Jr.

DISSERTATIONS

Gordon Wilson Abbott
Fred Davis Abrams
Fritz George Achelis
Edward Parsons Bagg, Jr.
Ernest Schwefel Ballard
Carl Hammer Breaker
Ernest Milford Bristol
Alexander Cushing Brown
Norman Parsons Clement
George Hamilton Colket, Jr.
Ralph Dennis Cutler
Richard Ely Danielson
Henry Albert Foster
Philip Lippincott Goodwin
James Lanman Hubbard

Frank Elmer Johnson
Horace Ogden Kilbourn
Harold Dimock Lee
Marshall Johnson Olds
Albert Billings Ruddock
Ansley Wilcox Sawyer
Stuart Robinson Strong
George Lewis Sutherland
Robert Campbell Wheeler
Lewis Bliss Whittemore
Thomas Goddard Wright

Willoughby Francis Colton
William Stanton Donoho

FIRST DISPUTES

Edward Morgan Barradale
Leroy Ewalt Brunner
Clarence Edward Chaney
Charles Williams Comfort, Jr.
Robert Howe Cunningham
Charles Julius Davis
Russell Stearns Dwight
Paul Bradley Elmore
Charles Milton Fessenden
Bainbridge Doty Folwell
Bertram Adolf Gabriel
Mortimer Hall Hartwell
Howard Jones Mandell
Amasa Stone Mather
Philip Lefèvre Morrison
Douglass Keefer Noyes
Irving Sands Olds

Nicholas Elias Peieff
Hervey Bates Perrin
Livingston Platt
Charles Francis Robbins, Jr.
Howard LeChevalier Roome
Harold Arthur Rosenbaum
John Elbert Shirk
Malcolm Douglas Sloane
Gilbert Little Stark
Elias Robert Stevenson
Arthur Purdy Stout
Stanley Adams Sweet
William Finney Tyler
Wayne Winslow Waite
Arthur Putnam Williamson

John Fowler Mitchell, Jr.

SECOND DISPUTES

Morris Lyon Beard
Philip Waldron Boardman
Clinton Demas Deming
Henry Robertson Failing
Julius Walter Freiberg
George Napoleon Gaboury
George Brette Glaenzer
Bradley Goodyear
Benjamin Pomeroy Hamlin
Charles Bingham Heisler

Roger Benton Hull
Charles Porter Kimball
Joseph Casimir Kircher
Robert Ralph Lockwood
George McAuliff
Francis William Moore
Bertice Henry Olmstead
Minott Augur Osborn
Karlton Goodsell Percy
George Boardman Potter

SECOND DISPUTES—*continued*

Edward Jerome Quinlan
Oren Mitchell Ragsdale
Harrison Pierce Rich
Randolph Preston Rogers
Benjamin Irving Rouse
Frank Butts Smoyer
McNeil Seymour Stringer

Cyril Sumner
Ralph Eugene Weber
Heathcote Muirson Woolsey
Henry Haight Wright
___
Earl Brown
Benjamin Franklin Crenshaw

FIRST COLLOQUIES

George Elmer Anderson
Douglas Jerrold Abbey Bell
Edwin Bendheim
George Borup
Howard Boulton
Winthrop Lakey Carter
Arthur Milton Comley
Frederic Russell Dolbeare
William Spencer Fuller
Umberto Dante Garfield
Charles Edwin Hart, Jr.
Roemer Benjamin Hathaway
Harold Hauenstein
Frank Anderson Hayes
Charles Erle Hibbard
William Irving Howbert
Henry Martyn Hoyt, Jr.
James Howard Hull
Isaac Lampson Jennings
LeRoy Mervyn Kellas

James Madison Kennedy
Mitchell Stuart Little
Francis Edgerton Manierre
Charles Goodwin Merriam
James Raglan Miller
Raymond Bartlett Morris
Fred Amasa Parker
Eli Burton Parsons
George Schaefer Scott
Harold Bartlett Scott
Richard Frank Seidensticker
Edward Burgis Starr
Guy VanZandt Thompson
Lauren Scott Thomson
Ernest Bell Tracy
Ira Davenport Waterman
Benjamin Webster
Robert George White
___
William Obed Keirstead

SECOND COLLOQUIES

George Morris Adams
Nelson Irving Asiel
William Deluce Barnes, Jr.
James White Bruce
Rumsey Campbell
Richard Henry Deming
William Hughes Diller
Barzilla Parks Gooden
Arthur Robbins Griswold
Milton Bruce Hadley
Charles Herbert Halcomb, Jr.
Charles Roberts Hopkins
Anson Blake Jackson, Jr.
Richard Michael Joy
Whitney Kernochan
James Waller Knott
Harold Kountze
Stephen Lesher Landon
William James Larkin, Jr.
Edward Elliott Lattin

Edmund Harris Lewis
Tasker Gantt Lowndes
Bowdoin Updike McClintock
Chauncey Brooks McCormick
Robert Davies Marshall
Dwight Raymond Meigs
Robert Middlebrook, Jr.
William Henry Milholland
Henry Butler Moore, Jr.
William Augustine Perry
Howard Phipps
Walter Hawley Scott
Henry Earl Sheffield
Frank Ronald Simmons
George Washington Small
Donald McLean Somers
William George Sullivan
Douglas Jay Torrey
James Watson Webb
Cortlandt Stuyvesant Wheeler

·HONORS IN SPECIAL STUDIES
CLASS OF 1907

CLASSICAL LANGUAGES AND
LITERATURE
THOMAS ALLEN TULLY

GERMANIC LANGUAGES AND
LITERATURE
EVERETT ROBBINS SMITH

ENGLISH LANGUAGE AND
LITERATURE
HENRY STOW LOVEJOY
CHARLES POMEROY OTIS
STUART ROBINSON STRONG
CHARLES FREDERICK TODD

MATHEMATICS
ERNEST WILSON SHELDON
JOHN ALAN WHITE
BAYARD DANIEL YORK

PHYSICAL SCIENCES
JOHN LANMAN HUBBARD
HOWARD EARLE PALMER

HISTORY
HENRY STOW LOVEJOY
MORGAN THOMAS RILEY
CLARENCE WILLIAM SEYMOUR

HONORS IN THE STUDIES OF JUNIOR YEAR
CLASS OF 1908

CARLETON MANSFIELD ALLEN
ALBERT EDWIN AVEY
JAMES CORBETT BARRY
FORREST BEYER
REGINALD MCINTOSH
CLEVELAND
RAYMOND VERE CONGDON
GEORGE DAHL
LEWIS CHARLES EVERARD
HAROLD THOMAS FULLER
HUSTED

HENRY HOLLISTER JACKSON
KARL WINDELL KIRCHWEY
ROBERT WILLIAM ROSENBERG
CHARLES SEYMOUR
RAYMOND BATES SMALL
WILLIAM NORWOOD SPARHAWK
RALPH FERNHEAD STODDARD
THOMAS ANTHONY THACHER
LEWIS HILL WEED
ARTHUR HAROLD WESTON
HOWARD VERNON YERGIN

Everett Lee Baker
William Burke Belknap
Earl Edward Beyer
Andrew Linn Bostwick
Ronald Muirhead Byrnes
Starr Gardiner Cooper
Eugene Delano, Jr.
David Ferguson
Sydney Joseph Frank
Ralph Edward Goodwin
Walter Earle Hartley
Davenport Hooker
Samuel Lamson Howell
Otis Scott Humphrey
Donald Lines Jacobus

William Rockwell Leete
Howard Bishop Lewis
William Benjamin Lipphardt
Charles Fisher Luther
Homer Chidsey Neal
Francis Ely Norris
Patrick Brett O'Sullivan
Edward Hartman Reisner
John Harold Ryan
Robert Alphonso Shackleton
Frederick Nelson Stevens
Horace VanSands Taylor
Laurence Vail Updegraff
William Stix Weiss
James Willard Williams

Samuel Alpert
Clifford Hershey Bissell
Charles Sherman Bodwell
Lewis Samuel Boothe
Rowland Sherwood Bosworth
Wendell Stanton Brooks
Hamilton Mabie Brush
Thomas James Camp

Oscar Henry Cooper, Jr.
Walter Goodwin Davis, Jr.
Leonard Henry Freiberg
Chauncey Brewster Garver
Charles Howard Gilbert
Frederick Augustus Godley
John Irving Hull
George Metcalf Johnson

Charles Whittemore Knapp
Geoffrey Konta
Julius Ansgar Larsen
Isaac Loewenthal
Philip Rogers Mallory
Alan Newhall Mann
Wilford Wolfie Naman
Frank Hermon Nettleton

Arthur Dimon Osborne, 2d
William Richmond Peters, Jr.
Graham Cummings Porter
Walter Richardson
Harold Wade Riggs
Richard Roy Smith
Kenneth Brakeley Welles
Ernest Lionel Wismer

JUNIOR APPOINTMENTS
(FOR THE WORK OF THE FIRST HALF OF THE COURSE)
CLASS OF 1909
PHILOSOPHICAL ORATIONS.

PAUL THOMPSON ARNOLD
WILLIAM RIDER BABCOCK
RICHARD HERBERT BENNETT
JOHN KINGSLEY BIRGE
HARVEY HOLLISTER BUNDY
CHARLES SOUTTER CAMPBELL
FRANK THOMPSON CASE
CHARLES VANDERVEER GRAHAM
CLARENCE FLACK GRAHAM
ROBERT NOAH GRISWOLD
JESSE McMILLAN HARDING
WILSON McCLAUGHRY HUME

ELIAS ALFRED JOHNSON
ALEXANDER COMSTOCK KIRK
ALLEN TRAFFORD KLOTS
DICKSON HAMMOND LEAVENS
KARL EUGENE MURCHEY
WILLIAM ADOLPH NOTKINS
LEONARD BACON PARKS
JOHN BATES PERRIN
HOWARD BENJAMIN SLIDER
JOHN MINOR STETSON
CARL HAMMOND THURSTON
RAYMOND LOWREY WALKLEY

HIGH ORATIONS

Paul Shipman Andrews
William Whiting Borden
Francis Peabody Butler
Douglas Treat Davidson
Allen Robert Dodd
Thomas Perkins Durell
Jackson Annan Dykman
Daniel Higgins Fenton
Leon Godchaux
Ralph Volney Harlow
Frank Edward Jones
Joseph Paul Kaufman
Courtland Kelsey

James Lukens McConaughy
Benjamin Harrison McKee
Robert Moses
Lawrence Benjamin Pagter
Sidney Marcellus Phelan, Jr.
Edward Otis Proctor
Stuart Craig Rand
Harold Cady Reynolds
Cleaveland Jocelyn Rice
Henry Brush Richardson
Frank Jay Scribner
Rowland Gregory Wright

ORATIONS

Frank August Assmann
Wheaton Augur
Paul Howie Benedict
Harold Edward Chittenden
Chauncey Haseltine Clarke
Paul Howard McGregor Converse
Samuel Foree Dennis
Harold Ransom Edwards
Arthur Olney Friel
Laurence Wilcoxson Gregory
Birch Helms

Bernhard Eliot Hoffman
Harris Monroe Humason
George Albert Hurd
Robert Louis Levy
Wilber McKee
Stephen Willis Ryder
Peter Benjamin Sarason
Harold Phelps Stokes
Malcolm Burt Vilas
John Benjamin Westcott
Thorne Lake Wheeler
Edward Luther White

DISSERTATIONS

Willis Lloyd Allen
Harold Stanley Bates
Gerald Morton Butler
Alexander Colin Campbell, Jr.
Carolus Thomas Clark
Frederick Hull Cogswell, Jr.
Charles Canfield Cunningham, Jr.
James Benton Grant, Jr.
Henry Booth Hitchcock
Roland Werner Klupfel
Robert Stell Lemmon

Milton Charles Lightner
Rufus Monroe Meroney
Leonard Oechsli
Arthur Ward Ruff
William Sharp
Joseph Byron Sieber
Mortimer Clark Terrill
Walker Moore VanRiper
Melvin Harvey Walker, Jr.
William Corcoran Welling
George Glendining Wyant

FIRST DISPUTES

Herbert Burr Alvord
Claude Gillette Beardslee
Bennet Bronson
William Leroy Burdick
DeWitt Scoville Clark, Jr.
Charles Hollister Davis
Malcolm Taylor Dougherty
Arthur Gotzian Driscoll
John Conner Failing
Patrick Joseph Healey
Burrell Richardson Huff
Allan Farrand Kitchel

Irvin Edward Margulies
Harry Meixell, Jr.
Edward McDonell O'Brien
Clarence Appleton Peirce
Lawrence Tyler Post
Henry Lewis Read
William Payne Roberts
Robert Selden Rose
Walter Pearson Smart
James Platt Sweeney
Nelson Case Taintor
Aubrey Richardson Watzek

SECOND DISPUTES

Edward Paul Alker
John Kendrick Bangs, Jr.
Carroll Teller Brown
Clay Crawford
Trevor Arnold Cushman
Howard Carter Davis
Lyall Dean
James Connelly Edwards, Jr.
Douglas Fitch Guilford Eliot
Stanley Egbert Ellis
Robert Otis Hayward
Paul Hilsdale
Thomas Carrington Hood
Edward Francis Jefferson

Charles Chesebrough Jones
Daniel Lathrop Lawton
Henry Hopkins Livingston
Grant Street Macartney
Robert Mallory, Jr.
Frederic Ogden Mason
Harold Talmadge Messenger
Jeremiah Milbank, 2d
Edward Kendall Morse
Francis Wisner Murray, Jr.
Morgan Porter
Horace Winston Stokes
Morton Charnleigh Stone
Raymond Fuller Swett

FIRST COLLOQUIES

Earle Wilson Bachman
John Frederick Baker
Henry Augustin Beers, Jr.
Herbert Hawthorne Benedict
Harold Wilson Brooks
Ralph Hodge Clark
Harry Frederick Cole
Aims Chamberlain Coney
John Favill
Horace Barnes Hewlett
Robert Coit Johnson
Henry Lippitt

Clinton Merrick
Clark Goodell Mitchell
Charles Milton Olcott
Henry Noyes Otis
Herbert Payne
Charles Henry Raymond, 2d
Franklyn Thomas Raymond
Daniel Seltzer
Arthur MacCartney Shepard
Boetius Henry Sullivan
Floyd Wallace
Morton Weeks

SECOND COLLOQUIES

Clarence Hayden Allis
Robert Barlow
Rufus Bradford Burnham
George Edward Cantine
Sydney Buchanan Carragan
Frank Andrew Cellar
Eugene Judson Curtis
Arthur Leete Davison
Julian French Devereux
Gayer Gardner Dominick
Peter Francis Joseph Fuchs
Bryant Burwell Glenny, Jr.
William Brown Glover
Joseph Kilbourne Hooker
Charles Wadsworth Howard
Stephen Tomlinson Kelsey
George Dimmick Kittredge

Franklin Drake Lightner
Alfred Lee Loomis
Reginald Carman MacKnight Peirce
Theodore Pomeroy
Elisha Francis Riggs, Jr.
James Sidney Schmertz
Edwin Lewis Scofield, Jr.
Charles Eugene Selover, Jr.
George Herman Seybold
Ralph Smillie
Herbert Mason Southworth
William Howard Taft
Robert James Tearse
Robert Stevens Whitlock
Perry Swearingen Young

HONORS IN ENGLISH COMPOSITION
CLASS OF 1909

PAUL THOMPSON ARNOLD
FRANCIS PEABODY BUTLER
PAUL HOWARD McGREGOR CONVERSE
ALLEN ROBERT DODD
JESSE McMILLAN HARDING
ROBERT LOUIS LEVY
JAMES LUKENS McCONAUGHY

WILBER McKEE
KARL EUGENE MURCHEY
JOHN BATES PERRIN
SIDNEY MARCELLUS PHELAN, JR.
STUART CRAIG RAND
FRANK JAY SCRIBNER
HAROLD PHELPS STOKES
CARL HAMMOND THURSTON

HONORS IN THE STUDIES OF FRESHMAN YEAR
CLASS OF 1910

DONALD ANNIS
CHARLES DUDLEY ARMSTRONG
JOHN EDWIN BARBER
MORRIS HARRY BEHRMAN
CHARLES RAYMOND BENTLEY
PERCY WELLS BIDWELL
SAMUEL MICHAEL COHEN
DONALD RYDER DICKEY
ARTHUR ROBERTSON FERGUSSON
JOHN WILLARD FORD
ROBERT DUDLEY FRENCH
CHARLES MARK GILL

RICHARD DWIGHT HILLIS
LEWIS ORRIN HUTCHINSON
GEORGE GORDON HYDE
ELMER DAVENPORT KEITH
LYNDON MARRS KING
BENJAMIN LIONEL LIBERMAN
CARL ALBERT LOHMANN
EDGAR MENDERSON
ROBERT ALPHONSO TAFT
ARTHUR VANBRUNT
WAYLAND WELLS WILLIAMS

Paul Duane Bailey
Leonard Cutter Bigelow
Clayton Tilton Cochran
Warren Gilbert Davis
James Harold Flye
Collin Ford
Perrin Comstock Galpin
Nathan Flower George
Charles Frederic Jefferson
Harry Jacob Kugel
Frank Coe Lewis

John Joseph MacCarthy
Henry Darius McCord
Buckingham Parsons Merriman
Julius Christian Peter
Graham Llewellyn Raynolds
George Adams Richardson
Henry Montague Smith, Jr.
Edward Douglas Snyder
Philip Moen Stimson
Edwin A Whitman

Arthur Edward Baker
Byron George Bliss
Theodore Henry Brown
Henry Clarence Cloud
Kent Sarver Clow .
Edward Ely Curtis
Walter Herman Dietz
Frederick Morris Drew, Jr.
William Young Duncan
John Gilbert Dunn
Howard Alfred Dye
Charles Pascal Franchot

Nathan Henry Gellert
Arthur Benson Gilbert
Rufus Bartlett Hall, Jr.
George Leslie Harrison
Stephen Edwards Keeler, Jr.
Robert Burr King
John Joseph Lane
Harold Bishop Reid
Frank Guiles Roth
Victor Sobell Shear
Howard DeForest Widger

THE SHEFFIELD SCIENTIFIC SCHOOL
CLASS OF 1907
GENERAL TWO-YEAR HONORS FOR EXCELLENCE IN ALL STUDIES.

BIOLOGICAL COURSE
SAMUEL CLARKE HARVEY

CHEMICAL COURSE
JOHN STOKES MCCUNE
KENNETH GERARD MACKENZIE
RALPH JULIAN MARSH

CIVIL ENGINEERING COURSE
LOUIS BERMAN
CHARLES VAN WYCKE CHAMBER-
LIN
CARL EMIL GREEN
LOUIS ALBERT OLDERSHAW

ELECTRICAL ENGINEERING COURSE
CHARLES EBEN CANADA
BENJAMIN ROSSITER FOOTE
YUEN-LI HSIA

MECHANICAL ENGINEERING
COURSE
LAWRENCE RILEY MCWEENEY
CHARLES TALBOT PORTER, 2d
FRANK TAYLOR QUINLAN
JOSEPH ROSENBAUM

MINING ENGINEERING COURSE
JOHN ALEXANDER BAKER
RUSSELL TYNER GARD

SELECT COURSE
DOUGLAS TURNER JOHNSTON
THEODORE ENGELMANN KIRCHER
CARROLL RIDGWAY

HONORS IN SPECIAL STUDIES AWARDED TO STUDENTS NOT RECIPIENTS
OF GENERAL HONORS

BIOLOGY
STANLEY DREW BEARD
VEADER NEWTON LEONARD

CHEMISTRY
CLIFFORD JOSEPH MONAHAN

FORESTRY
FORMAN TAYLOR MCLEAN

HISTORY AND SOCIAL SCIENCES
DAVID EDWARD BIGWOOD
GEORGE VALLANDIGHAM ROTAN

METALLURGY
EDWIN KINMOUTH SMITH

SANITARY ENGINEERING
HIRAM BISSELL CAREY

CLASS OF 1908
HONORS FOR EXCELLENCE IN ALL STUDIES OF THE JUNIOR YEAR

BIOLOGICAL COURSE
SELIM WALKER MCARTHUR

CHEMICAL COURSE
CONSTANTINE M. CONSTANTIAN, B.A.
MORRIS SEIDE FINE
HERBERT HARTLEY GUEST

CIVIL ENGINEERING COURSE
HAROLD CRUSIUS BIRD
HOWARD EMERSON CHURCH
VALENTINE ODELL KETCHAM
WILLIAM THORP STURGES

ELECTRICAL ENGINEERING COURSE
RAYMOND LESTER BROWN
ROGER BALDWIN COLTON
HAROLD TURNBULL PRITCHARD

FORESTRY COURSE
FREDERICK ALAN GAYLORD

MECHANICAL ENGINEERING COURSE
FREDERIC QUINTARD BOYER
LESTER AMBLER NOTHNAGLE

MINING ENGINEERING COURSE
CARRYL ARTHUR ASHER
LOUTFI HAGOP BABIKIAN, B.A.
WESLEY EARL DUNKLE
NATHANIEL HERZ
DAVID DURYEA IRWIN
LEWIS A. PARSONS
LAURENCE BALLARD ROBBINS
HENRY DEWITT SMITH
WILLIAM WALTER TAYLOR

SELECT COURSE
CLARENCE HOLLOWAY COGSWELL
GEORGE LEWIS EMMONS
CHARLES S. HART
THOMAS ALBERT DWIGHT JONES
JOHN NEWTON PEYTON
MEDARY WILSON STARK

HONORS IN SPECIAL STUDIES AWARDED TO STUDENTS NOT RECIPIENTS OF GENERAL HONORS

ENGLISH HISTORY AND SOCIAL SCIENCES
EDWARD F. CONGDON

FORESTRY
MEYER HENRY WOLFF

FRENCH
GEORGE FRANKLIN ATWATER
HOWARD HARDING JONES
EDWARD NESBITT MILLAN
FRANK LANSING GRINNELL PAGE

FRENCH AND GERMAN
JOSEPH ALLEN PECK

GERMAN
EDWIN SELDEN LANE
ALDO LEOPOLD
HOWARD ELMER PHELPS
HARRY ARNOLD SAUTTER
ALBIN CHAMPLIN SWENSON
CHARLES GALLUP WILLIAMS
HERMAN LEWIS WITTSTEIN

MATHEMATICS
NATHAN ROSCOE FRANCIS, B.A.

THE DIVINITY SCHOOL
DEGREE OF B.D., *magna cum laude*
Darwin Ashley Leavitt, B.A. Beloit College 1904
DEGREE OF B.D., *cum laude*
Hugh Elmer Brown, B.S. Whitman College 1904
Karl Owen Thompson, B.A. Amherst College 1904

THE MEDICAL SCHOOL
DEGREE OF M.D., *cum laude*

Horace Doolittle Bellis
George Houghton Bodley
James Ryle Coffey, B.A. Yale University 1903   ·
Samuel James Goldberg
Anthony Joseph Mendillo
Marvin McRae Scarbrough, M.A. Yale University 1905

THE LAW SCHOOL
DEGREE OF M.L., *magna cum laude*
José Escaler, Liceo de Manila 1902, LL.B. 1905

DEGREE OF M.L., *cum laude*

Terence Byrne Cosgrove, B.A. St. Viateur's College 1903, M.A.
 1906, LL.B. University of Notre Dame 1906
Mariano Honrade de Joya, LL.B. Indiana University 1906

DEGREE OF LL.B., *magna cum laude*

Arthur Packer McKinstry, B.A. Yale University 1905
George Sharp Munson, B.A. Yale University 1904
George Elton Parks, B.A. Yale University 1904
George Slingerland VanSchaick

DEGREE OF LL.B., *cum laude*

Robert Harold Butterfield
William Brewster Ely, B.A. Yale University 1904
Newell Jennings, B.A. Yale University 1904
Joseph George Shapiro
John Carroll Slade, B.A. Yale University 1905
Charles Herbert Woods, B.A. Blackburn College 1904

HONORS IN SECOND YEAR CLASS

Walter Preston Armstrong, B.A. Yale University 1906
William Edward Egan   ·
Richard Carley Hunt
Harold Burton Jamison, B.A. Yale University 1906
Clifton Junius O'Hara, B.A. Carthage College 1906
Nathaniel Paul Sterne
Charles Lyman Stewart

HONORS IN FIRST YEAR CLASS

Howard Daniels Atkins
William Emil Greenbaum
Edward Robert McGlynn
Dennis Thomas O'Brien
Lewis Jack Somers
Edward Colpitts Weyman, B.A. University of New Brunswick
 1902, B.A. Harvard Univ. 1903, M.A. Yale Univ. 1905
Frederick Holme Wiggin, Jr., B.A. Yale University 1904

Awards of Prizes and Scholarships
UNIVERSITY PRIZES
AWARDED IN 1907

John A. Porter Prize—Graduate Class in the Divinity School, Charles Franklin, with honorable mention of Albert Thomas Steele, a member of the Class of 1907 in the Divinity School.

James Gordon Bennett Prize—Class of 1907, divided between Roger Benton Hull and Robert Ralph Lockwood.

Cobden Club Silver Medal—Class of 1907, Henry Freeman Walradt.

Albert Stanburrough Cook Prize in Poetry—Class of 1905, Charles Washburn Nichols.

GRADUATE FELLOWS AND SCHOLARS, 1907–08
[See pages 50–52]

UNDERGRADUATE SCHOLARS OF THE HOUSE
YALE COLLEGE, 1907–08

Bristed Scholar—Class of 1908, Henry Hollister Jackson.

Woolsey Scholars—Class of 1908, Albert Edwin Avey; Class of 1909, Karl Eugene Murchey; Class of 1910, Robert Alphonso Taft.†

Hurlbut Scholar—Class of 1910, Samuel Michael Cohen.†

Runk Scholar—Class of 1910, Charles Raymond Bentley.

Scott Hurtt Scholars—Class of 1908, Ralph Fernhead Stoddard; Class of 1909, Charles Soutter Campbell.

Thomas Glasby Waterman Scholars—Class of 1908, Albert Edwin Avey and George Dahl.

Alfred Barnes Palmer Scholar—Class of 1908, Hillier McClure Burrowes.

Daniel Lord, Jr., Scholar—Class of 1908, Lewis Charles Everard.

Learned Scholars—Class of 1908, Ronald Muirhead Byrnes; Class of 1909, Karl Eugene Murchey.

John J. Cox Scholar—Class of 1910, Samuel Michael Cohen.

Robert Callender Scholar—Class of 1908, Henry Hollister Jackson.

John Bennetto Scholars—Class of 1908, Lewis Charles Everard; Class of 1909, James Lukens McConaughy.

Mahlon Long Scholar—Class of 1908, Robert Bruner Umberger.

†The two leading contestants, Mr. Cohen and Mr. Taft, being judged equal, the award was made by lot.

— 606 —

MEAD SCHOLAR—Class of 1907, EDWIN DEEKS HARVEY.

BENJAMIN F. BARGE SCHOLAR—Class of 1908, CLARKE STANLEY HURLBUT.

WALTER JOSEPH AUSTRIAN SCHOLAR—Class of 1910, JAMES HAROLD FLYE.

ANTHONY D. STANLEY SCHOLARS—Class of 1908, DONALD LINES JACOBUS and HOWARD VERNON YERGIN; Class of 1909, HOWARD BENJAMIN SLIDER.

PLAINFIELD SCHOLARS—Class of 1909, JOHN BENJAMIN WESTCOTT; Class of 1910, GEORGE HENRY SANDERSON.

LISPENARD STEWART WITHERBEE SCHOLARS—Class of 1908, HOWARD BISHOP LEWIS; Class of 1909, EDWARD FRANCIS JEFFERSON.

CHICAGO SCHOLARS—Class of 1908, GEORGE DAHL; Class of 1909, ELIAS ALFRED JOHNSON.

UNDERGRADUATE PRIZES AND PREMIUMS
AWARDED IN YALE COLLEGE IN 1907
PRIZES NOT RESTRICTED TO A SINGLE CLASS

LUCIUS F. ROBINSON LATIN PRIZES—Class of 1907, 2d Prize, THOMAS ALLEN TULLY; 3d Prize, ELBERT ELLERY ORCUTT.—Class of 1908, 1st Prize, HAROLD THOMAS FULLER HUSTED; 2d Prize, HENRY HOLLISTER JACKSON; 3d Prize, ARTHUR HAROLD WESTON.—Class of 1909, 1st Prize, KARL EUGENE MURCHEY; 2d Prizes, WILLIAM RIDER BABCOCK and EDWARD OTIS PROCTOR; 3d Prize, DANIEL HIGGINS FENTON.

THACHER PRIZES—Class of 1907, ROGER BENTON HULL (two prizes).

JOHN HUBBARD CURTIS PRIZE—Class of 1907, WILLIAM SHELDON WHITTLESEY.

BENJAMIN F. BARGE MATHEMATICAL PRIZES—Class of 1909, 1st Prize, CARL HAMMOND THURSTON; 2d Prize, WILLIAM McCLAUGHRY HUME; 3d Prize, ROBERT MOSES.—Class of 1910, 1st Prizes, ROBERT ALPHONSO TAFT and EDWIN A WHITMAN; 2d Prize, GRAHAM LLEWELLYN RAYNOLDS.

JOHN ADDISON PORTER PRIZE IN AMERICAN HISTORY—Class of 1907, 1st Prize, HENRY STOW LOVEJOY.—Class of 1908, 2d Prize, LEWIS CHARLES EVERARD.

ANDREW D. WHITE HISTORY PRIZE—Class of 1909, FREDERICK LAMONT GATES, with honorable mention of WILLIAM YOUNG DUNCAN, Class of 1910.

SENIOR PRIZES

DEFOREST PRIZE MEDAL—Class of 1907, ROGER BENTON HULL.

TOWNSEND PREMIUMS—Class of 1907, HOWARD FRANCIS BISHOP, EDWARD HENRY HART, MARSHALL JOHNSON OLDS, ALBERT BILLINGS RUDDOCK, and CLARENCE WILLIAM SEYMOUR.

DeForest Mathematical Prizes—Class of 1907, Ernest Wilson Sheldon, John Alan White, and Bayard Daniel York.

JUNIOR PRIZES

Winthrop Prizes—Class of 1908, 1st Prize, Henry Hollister Jackson; 2d Prize, divided between Albert Edwin Avey and Charles Seymour.

Scott Prize in German—Class of 1908, Frederick Nelson Stevens.

Scott Prize in French—Class of 1908, divided between Geoffrey Konta and Clifford Hershey Bissell.

Henry James TenEyck Prizes—Class of 1908, 1st Prize, Joseph William Murphy; 2d Prizes, Wilford Wolfie Naman, Charles Seymour, Laurence Vail Updegraff, and William Wilford Wynkoop; 3d Prizes, Ronald Muirhead Byrnes, Thomas James Camp, Sydney Joseph Frank, Irving Goldenburg, and Lester William Perrin.

SOPHOMORE PRIZES

C. Wyllys Betts Prize—Class of 1909, James Lukens McConaughy.

College Premiums in Declamation—Class of 1909, 1st Prize, Irvin Edward Margulies; 2d Prize, Edward Otis Proctor.

FRESHMAN PRIZES

Berkeley Premiums in Latin Composition—Class of 1910, 1st Grade, Charles Raymond Bentley, Samuel Michael Cohen, Charles Frederic Jefferson, and Robert Alphonso Taft; 2d Grade, Elmer Davenport Keith and Harry Jacob Kugel.

McLaughlin Prizes—Class of 1910, no award.

Winston Trowbridge Townsend Prizes—Class of 1910, no award.

ENTRANCE PRIZES

Hugh Chamberlain Greek Prize—Class of 1911, Ewing Reginald Philbin, of New York City, who prepared at the Westminster School; with honorable mention of Joel Ellis Fisher, of New York City, who prepared at the Browning School, and of Bernard Wertheimer Scharff, of Natchez, Miss., who prepared at Phillips Exeter Academy.

Samuel Henry Galpin Latin Prize—Class of 1911, Rodney Dean, of Orange, N. J., who prepared at Carteret Academy.

PRIZES AWARDED IN THE SHEFFIELD SCIENTIFIC SCHOOL IN 1907

RECIPIENTS OF THE SHEFFIELD GRADUATE SCHOLARSHIPS, CLASS OF 1907

Stanley Drew Beard, Samuel Clarke Harvey, Jacob Lewis Jacobs, John William Madden, Clifford Joseph Monahan, Joseph Rosenbaum.

SHEFFIELD UNDERGRADUATE PRIZES
CLASS OF 1907

For EXCELLENCE IN MECHANICAL ENGINEERING—CHARLES TALBOT PORTER, 2d, with honorable mention of LAWRENCE RILEY McWEENEY.

For EXCELLENCE IN ELECTRICAL ENGINEERING—CHARLES EBEN CANADA.

For EXCELLENCE IN MINING ENGINEERING—RUSSELL TYNER GARD.

For EXCELLENCE IN HISTORY—THEODORE ENGELMANN KIRCHER.

The TUCKER PRIZE IN SANITARY ENGINEERING—LOUIS ALBERT OLDER-SHAW.

The WILLIAM R. BELKNAP PRIZE IN GEOLOGICAL STUDIES—KENNETH GERARD MACKENZIE.

CLASS OF 1908

The ROGERS SCHOLARSHIP, for excellence in the studies of the Chemical Course—HERBERT HARTLEY GUEST.

The PENFIELD PRIZE, for excellence in Mineralogy—NATHANIEL HERZ, with honorable mention of WILLIAM WALTER TAYLOR and LEWIS A. PARSONS.

For EXCELLENCE IN HISTORY—CHARLES S. HART.

CLASS OF 1909

For EXCELLENCE IN ALL THE STUDIES OF FRESHMAN YEAR—ROBERT PRINCE WINTON, with honorable mention of BURTIS BARTON McCARN and CARLETON RUFUS HEWITT.

For EXCELLENCE IN PHYSICS—CARLETON RUFUS HEWITT.

For EXCELLENCE IN GERMAN—HENRY WALTER ROUTENBERG.

For EXCELLENCE IN FRENCH—WILFRED ATTWOOD BEARDSLEY, with honorable mention of DELANO FULLER WOODCLIFFE DOUGLASS.

For EXCELLENCE IN CHEMISTRY—In Chemistry B: HARLEY TAYLOR PECK, with honorable mention of ZAI-ZIANG ZEE. In Chemistry A: RAY HAMILTON SKELTON, with honorable mention of BURTIS BARTON McCARN.

For EXCELLENCE IN MECHANICAL DRAWING—RAY HAMILTON SKELTON, with honorable mention of ALFRED BRYANT SEELEY and ROBERT PRINCE WINTON.

For EXCELLENCE IN MATHEMATICS—WILLIAM HENRY HUBBARD, with honorable mention of BURTIS BARTON McCARN.

For EXCELLENCE IN ENGLISH—WILFRED ATTWOOD BEARDSLEY, with honorable mention of BURTIS BARTON McCARN.

For EXCELLENCE IN SPANISH—In Advanced Spanish: WILLIAM JOSEPH LINN, PH.B., Yale University 1906. In Elementary Spanish: NATHANIEL HERZ, Class of 1908; WILLIAM BYERS DENTON, Class of 1909.

39

PRIZES AWARDED IN THE SCHOOL OF THE FINE ARTS, 1907

ALICE KIMBALL ENGLISH PRIZES—ALBERT CARL LOHMANN, JOSEPH JOHN MCKEON, and FRANKLIN EARLE KNOTTS, with honorable mention of ·FREDERICK AMOS OSBORNE MAYER.

FOR EXCELLENCE IN COMPOSITION—Honorable mention of JOHN DOWNES WHITING and ANNE HARRIET PIERCE.

ETHEL CHILDE WALKER PRIZE—WILLIAM CHESTER MACLANE.

PRIZES AWARDED IN THE DEPARTMENT OF MUSIC, 1907

LOCKWOOD SCHOLARSHIPS—Vocal Music, MARGUERITE CECELIA MAC-DONALD; Piano Music, divided between JENNIE MARGARET HAWLEY and BESSIE ALICE PIERCE.

PRIZE IN ORGAN-PLAYING—WALTER EARLE HARTLEY.

STEINERT PRIZE—WALTER RUEL COWLES, B.A. Yale University 1906.

PRIZES AWARDED IN THE MEDICAL SCHOOL, 1907

CAMPBELL GOLD·MEDAL—MARVIN MCRAE SCARBROUGH, M.A., with honorable mention of SAMUEL JAMES GOLDBERG.

KEESE PRIZE—FELIX P. CHILLINGWORTH, with honorable mention of JAMES RYLE COFFEY, B.A. Yale University 1903, SAMUEL JAMES GOLDBERG, MARVIN MCRAE SCARBROUGH, M.A. Yale University 1905.

PRIZES AWARDED IN THE DIVINITY SCHOOL

DOWNES PRIZES in Scripture and Hymn Reading, June 4, 1907—Class of 1907, 1st, HUGH ELMER BROWN, B.S. Whitman College 1904; 2d, CHARLES MELANCHTHON CALDERWOOD, PH.B. Iowa College 1900.—Class of 1908, 1st, ERNEST EUGENE YOUTZ, B.A. Simpson College 1904; 2d, HARRY GRIMES, B.A. Beloit College 1905.

MERRICK PRIZES for effective Public Address—Class of 1907, Anniversary Prizes, 1st, HUGH ELMER BROWN, B.S. Whitman College 1904; 2d, DARWIN ASHLEY LEAVITT, B.A. Beloit College 1904, KARL OWEN THOMPSON, B.A. Amherst College 1904, ARTHUR EWEN WESTENBERG, B.A. Beloit College 1904.—Class of 1907, Prizes for Class Work, 1st, GEORGE D. MILBURY, B.A. Bates College 1905; 2d, HUGH ELMER BROWN, B.S. Whitman College 1904; 3d DARWIN ASHLEY LEAVITT, B.A. Beloit College 1904.—Class of 1908, 1st, DANIEL WEBSTER KURTZ, B.A. Juniata College 1905 ; 2d, JOHN LUTHER DICKSON ; 3d, HARRY GRIMES, B.A. Beloit College 1905.—Class of 1909, 1st, HERMAN HENRY LINDEMAN, B.A. University of Nebraska 1903 ; 2d, ELMER EDWIN BURTNER, B.A. Otterbein University 1906 ; 3d, BENJAMIN DAUGHERTY ROJAHN, B.A. Lebanon Valley College 1905. Prizes for Sermonic Delivery.—Class of 1909, 1st, THOMAS BENJAMIN POWELL, B.A. Bucknell University 1906 ; 2d, WASHINGTON IRVING MAURER, B.A. Beloit College 1906.

FIRST TERM, 1906–07

FOGG SCHOLARSHIPS—Class of 1907, DARWIN ASHLEY LEAVITT, B.A. Beloit College 1904 ; Class of 1908, DANIEL WEBSTER KURTZ. B.A. Juniata College 1905.

ALLIS SCHOLARSHIPS—Class of 1907, HUGH ELMER BROWN, B.S. Whitman College 1904, ALBERT THOMAS STEELE, B.A. Adrian College 1896, KARL OWEN THOMPSON, B.A. Amherst College 1904, ARTHUR EWEN WESTENBERG, B.A. Beloit College 1904 ; Class of 1908, THEODORE BURGER LATHROP, B.A. Beloit College 1903, PEARL EUGENE MATHIAS, B.A. Lebanon Valley College 1905.

SECOND TERM, 1906–07

FOGG SCHOLARSHIPS—Class of 1907, DARWIN ASHLEY LEAVITT, B.A. Beloit College 1904 ; Class of 1908, DANIEL WEBSTER KURTZ, B.A. Juniata College 1905 ; Class of 1909, LUTHER BATEMAN HENDERSON, B.S. New York University 1906.

ALLIS SCHOLARSHIPS—Class of 1907, HUGH ELMER BROWN, B.S. Whitman College 1904, KARL OWEN THOMPSON B.A. Amherst College 1904 ; Class of 1908, THEODORE BURGER LATHROP, B.A. Beloit College 1903, PEARL EUGENE MATHIAS, B.A. Lebanon Valley College 1905 ; Class of 1909, WASHINGTON IRVING MAURER, B.A. Beloit College 1906.

PRIZES AWARDED IN THE LAW SCHOOL, JUNE, 1907

THE TOWNSEND PRIZE—JOHN CARROLL SLADE, B.A. Yale University 1905.

THE PHELPS MONTGOMERY PRIZE—ARTHUR PACKER MCKINSTRY, B.A. Yale University 1905.

THE JEWELL PRIZE—NATHANIEL PAUL STERNE.

THE BETTS PRIZE—EDWARD COLPITTS WEYMAN, B.A. University of New Brunswick 1902, B.A. Harvard University 1903, M.A. Yale University 1905.

The WAYLAND PRIZES
  First Prize.   GEORGE PRICE WHITMAN, B.L. University of
                  Georgia 1906.
  Second Prize.   CLIFTON JUNIUS O'HARA, B.A. Carthage Col-
                  lege 1906.
  Third Prize.   TERENCE BYRNE COSGROVE, B.A. St. Viateur's
                  College 1903, M.A. 1906, LL.B. University of
                  Notre Dame 1906.
The MUNSON PRIZES
  First Prize.   HAROLD BURTON JAMISON, B.A. Yale Univer-
                  sity 1906.
  Second Prize.   WALTER PRESTON ARMSTRONG, B.A. Yale Uni-
                  versity 1906.
  Third Prize.   THOMAS JOSEPH MOLLOY.
KENT CLUB PRIZES FOR THE BEST EXAMINATION IN PARLIAMENTARY
  LAW
  First Prize.   JOSEPH GEORGE SHAPIRO.
  Second Prize.   NEWELL JENNINGS, B.A. Yale University 1904.
KENT CLUB DIPLOMAS
                  JOHN BERNADINE DILLON
                  JOSEPH GEORGE SHAPIRO
                  ADELBERT ARTHUR SKEEL
                  GEORGE PRICE WHITMAN
                  NEWELL JENNINGS
                  TERENCE BYRNE COSGROVE
                  BERNARD ISRAEL KAMEN
                  FERDINAND D'ESOPO

PART VII

LISTS OF STUDENTS, DIRECTORY, AND INDEX

LISTS OF STUDENTS
DEPARTMENT OF PHILOSOPHY AND THE ARTS
GRADUATE SCHOOL

[The major subject of study is stated in each case. Students marked "A." are pursuing courses of study in absence, under the direction of the Faculty, for the degree of Master of Arts, Mechanical Engineer, or Civil Engineer.]

Rose Abel, B.A.   *Montesano, Wash.*   142 York st.
University of Kansas 1901   Latin and English

Harry Leslie Agard, B.A.   *New Britain, Conn.*   711 W. D.
Wesleyan University 1904   Mathematics

Unosuke Akatsuka   *Mie, Japan*   720 W. D.
Formosan Association College 1904   Political Economy

Sarkis Manoog Albarian, B.A.   *Hadjin, Turkey*   614 Yale P. O.
St. Paul's Institute, Tarsus, 1901,   Philosophy
B.D. Hartford Theol. Seminary 1907

Charles Roberts Aldrich, B.A.   *El Paso, Texas*
Yale University 1903   English

Arthur Dwight Allen, B.A.   *Glen View, Ky.*
Yale University 1901   Economics

May Alice Allen, B.A.   *Yarmouth, Me.* 256 Edgewood av.
Smith College 1901   Classics

William Talbot Allison, B.A.   *Middlefield, Conn.*   Middlefield
University of Toronto 1899, M.A. 1900,   English
B.D. Yale University 1901

Coleman Emanuel Andel, B.A.   *Belleville, Ill.*
Yale University 1902   German

Christopher Magee Anderson, B.A. *Pittsburg, Pa.*
Yale University 1904   English

William Gilbert Anderson, M.D.   *New Haven, Conn.*   G.
Western Reserve University 1883,   Physiology
B.A. Yale University 1902, M.A. 1903

Clarence Edward Andrews, B.A.   *Norwalk, Conn.*   1026 Yale P. O.
Yale University 1906   English

Lewis Elmer Armstrong, PH.B.   *New Haven, Conn.* 175 East Rock rd.
Yale University 1906   Mathematics

Frances Arnold, B.A.   *Galesburg, Ill.*   25 Norton st.
Knox College 1895,   English
M.A. Wellesley College 1900

Edward Monroe Bailey, Jr., PH.B. *New Haven, Conn.* 168 Sheffield av.
Yale University 1902, M.S. 1905   Physiological Chemistry

William Deluce Barnes, Jr., B.A.   *Mansfield, Mass.*   DW.
Yale University 1907   Biology and Chemistry

Arthur Herbert Basye, B.A.   *Lawrence, Kans.*   204 F.
University of Kansas 1904, M.A. 1906   History

Clifford Whitman Bates, PH.B.   *Cleveland, O.*   293 York st.
Yale University 1905   Mechanical Engineering

Laura Lorraine Batson, B.A.   *Longview, Texas*   166 York st.
University of Texas 1904   German

John Bauer, B.A.   *Crete, Nebr.*   565 P.
Doane College 1904,   Sociology and Economics
B.A. Yale University 1906

Robert James Beach, B.A.   *So. Meriden, Conn.*   So. Meriden
Wesleyan University 1890,   English
B.D. Drew Theological Seminary 1893,
M.A. New York University 1899

Harry Beal, B.A.   *Concord, N. H.*
Yale University 1906   English

George Elbert Beck, B.A.   *Bethel, O.*   7 Library st.
National Normal University 1903,   Geology
B.A. Yale University 1907

George Loomis Beecher, PH.B.   *New Haven, Conn.* 201 Sherman av.
Yale University 1906   Civil Engineering

Sara Elizabeth Beecher, B.A.   *New Haven, Conn.* 220 Davenport av.
Smith College 1903   Modern Languages

Stanley Rossiter Benedict, B.A.   *Cincinnati, O.*   77 Grove st.
University of Cincinnati 1906   Physiological Chemistry

Earl Gordon Bill, B.A.   *Wolfville, N. S.*   122 Howe st.
Acadia University 1902,   Mathematics
B.A. Yale University 1906, M.A. 1906

Frederick Thomas Blanchard, B.L.   *National City, Cal.*   650 E. D.
University of California 1904   English

Herbert Luther Bodman, B.A.   *New York City*
Yale University 1905   English

Theodore Harding Boggs, B.A.   *Wolfville, N. S.*   115 Park st.
Acadia University 1902, M.A. 1904,   Social Science
B.A. Yale University 1905

John Sidney Boman, B.A.   *Columbia, Mo.*   MEM.
University of Missouri 1902   Mathematics

Isaiah Bowman, B.S.   *Brown City, Mich.*   203 York st.
Harvard University 1905   Geology

Charles Henry Boyer, B.A.   *Raleigh, N. C.*
Yale University 1896   English

Walter Minor Bradley, PH.B.   *New Haven, Conn.* 1346 Chapel st.
Yale University 1899   Mineralogy

Charles Andrew Brautlecht, PH.B.   *New Haven, Conn.*   130 Front st.
Yale University 1906   Physiological Chemistry

Earl Brown, PH.B.   *Emmetsburg, Ia.*   315 York st.
State University of Iowa 1905,   Economics and Law
B.A. Yale University 1907

Harry Gunnison Brown, B.A.   *Troy, N. Y.*   82 Whalley av.
Williams College 1904   Economics

Herbert Stanley Brown, B.A.   *Darien, Conn.*   Darien
Yale University 1881, B.D. 1886, M.A. 1906   Biblical Literature

Mable Electa Buland, B.A.   *Castle Rock, Wash.*   N. Y. City
University of Washington 1904   English

Otis Gridley Bunnell, PH.B.   *Burlington, Conn.*   132 Howe st.
Yale University 1892, M.S. 1900   Romance Languages

Horace Thomas Burgess, B.A.   *Waynesville, O.*   700 Yale P. O.
National Normal University 1905,   Mathematics
B.A. Yale University 1906, M.A. 1907

Josephine May Burnham, PH.B.   *Chicago, Ill.*   142 York st.
University of Chicago 1901   English

Freeman Foster Burr, B.S.   *East Haven, Conn.* State Normal School
Harvard University 1900   Geology

William Burrows, B.A.   *New Haven, Conn.*   68 Grand av.
St.Stephen's College 1902,   Semit. Lang. and Bibl. Lit.
B.D. Berkeley Divinity School 1905,
M.A. Yale University 1906

Katharine Jeannette Bush, PH.D.   *New Haven, Conn.*   133 Howe st.
Yale University 1901   Natural Science

Lucy Peck Bush   *New Haven, Conn.*   133 Howe st.
                                                   Botany

Henry Holland Carter, B.A.   *Brecksville, O.*   129 Mansfield st.
Oberlin College 1907   •   English

Leonard Joshua Carter, B.A.   *Danville, Va.*   602 E. D.
Holiness University 1907   Biblical Literature

Gerald Chittenden, B.A.   *Simsbury, Conn.*
Yale University 1904   History

Howard Wadsworth Church, B.A.   *Meriden, Conn.*   78 Lake pl.
Yale University 1904, M.A. 1907   German

Raymond Gilmore Clapp, B.A.   *Boston, Mass.*   613 E. D.
Boston University 1900,   Biblical Literature
B.D. Yale University 1903, M.A. 1904

Samuel Hopkins Clapp, B.A.   *New Haven, Conn.*   98 York sq.
Yale University 1901   Chemistry

Lois Clark, B.A.   *Seattle, Wash.*   130 Howe st.
University of Washington 1907   Botany

Elizabeth Whittlesey Cleaveland, PH.B. *Lakeville, Conn.*   133 Howe st.
University of Chicago 1902   English

Norman Parsons Clement, B.A.   *Buffalo, N. Y.*
Yale University 1907   English

Charles Alexander Cockayne, B.A. *Tiffin, O.*   105 Park st.
Heidelberg University 1901, M.A. 1903,   Philosophy and Education
M.A. Yale University 1906

Erma Eloise Cole, B.A.   *Fayette, Ia.*   142 York st.
Upper Iowa University 1900   Greek and Latin

Howard Garfield Connelly, B.A.   *Baltimore, Md.*   623 E. D.
Bethany College (W. Va.) 1905   Biblical Literature

Curtis Edward Cook, B.A.   *Newtown, Conn.*   Newtown
Pennsylvania College 1903   English

Charlton Dows Cooksey, PH.B.   *New Haven, Conn.* 284 Orange st.
Yale University 1905   Physics

Darrah Corbet, PH.B.   *Brookville, Pa.*
Yale University 1905   Mechanical Engineering

Urban Cronan, B.A.   *New Haven, Conn.* 455 Orange st.
Yale University 1906   Spanish

Paul Curts, B.A.   *Coldwater, Mich.* 3 Hillhouse av.
Yale University 1905   German

David Edward Dangler, B.A.   *Cleveland, O.*
Yale University 1905   English

George Eugene Davis, B.A.   *Hartford, Conn.*   Hartford
Yale University 1902   Classics

Pierpont VanDerveer Davis, B.A.   *New York City*
Yale University 1905   English

William Dwight Dean, B.A.   *Evanston, Ill.*
Yale University 1905   English

John Bellows DeForest, B.A.   *Bridgeport, Conn.*   Cheshire
Yale University 1905   French

Chester Rhoades DeLaVergne, B.A. *New York City*
Yale University 1905   Social Science

John Hamilton Derby, Jr., PH.B.   *Sandy Hill, N. J.*   110 Wall st.
Yale University 1907   Chemistry

Henry Bronson Dewing, B.A.   *Berkeley, Cal.*   219 F.
University of California 1903, M.A. 1905   Classics

James Edward Diamond, PH.B.   *New Haven, Conn.* 173 Whalley av.
Yale University 1907   Electrical Engineering

Sherwood Owen Dickerman, B.A.   *New Haven, Conn.*   Germany
Yale University 1896   Classics

Henry Groff Dodge, B.A.   *Cleveland, O.*
Yale University 1905   English

George Stuart Dole, B.A.   *Wilmington, Del.*   644 E. D.
Yale University 1906, M.A. 1907   Economics

Louis Alexander Dole, B.A.   *Wilmington, Del.*   644 E. D.
Yale University 1906, M.A. 1907   Economics

Arthur Wayland Dox, B.S.   *Storrs, Conn.*   Storrs
University of Pennsylvania 1904,   Physiological Chemistry
M.A. Columbia University 1905

William Allen Drushel, B.S.   *Lebanon, O.*   47 Lake pl.
National Normal University 1896, LL.B. 1900,   Chemistry
B.A. Yale University 1905

Waldo Hilary Dunn, B.A. *Middletown, O.*
Yale University 1906 **English**

Willard Higley Durham, B.A. *Holland Patent, N. Y.* 701 W. D.
Yale University 1904 **English**

Herbert William Eales, B.A. *Bridgeport, Conn.* 7 Library st.
Yale University 1904 **Physics**

Graham Edgar, B.S. *Lexington, Ky.* 144 Dwight st.
Kentucky State College 1907 **Chemistry**

Marion Graham Elkins, B.S. *Amesbury, Mass.* 568 Chapel st.
Rhode Island Coll. of Agric. and Mech. Arts 1906 **Botany**

Joseph Roy Ellis, B.A. *Kansas City, Mo.* 679 W. D.
Oberlin College 1905 **English**

William Dean Embree, B.A. *New York City*
Yale University 1902 **Romance Languages**

José Escaler, B.A. *Apalit, P. I.* 14' Whalley av.
Liceo de Manila 1902, LL.B. 1905, **Sociology**
M.L. Yale University 1907

James Fraser Evans, B.A. *Falls Village, Conn.* 10 University pl.
University of Toronto 1893, **Biblical Literature and English**
M.A. Yale University 1907

William Abraham Evans, B.A. *New Haven, Conn.* 399 Elm st.
Yale University 1902, M.A. 1907 **English**

Henry Pratt Fairchild, B.A *Crete, Nebr.* 1233 Chapel st.
Doane College 1900 **Sociology**

James Linwood Fawley, B.A. *Philadelphia, Pa.* 205 F.
Yale University 1906 **Chemistry**

James Fulton Ferguson, B.A. *Xenia O.* 197 F.
Monmouth College 1903, **History**
B.A. Yale University 1906, M.A. 1907

Edna Louise Ferry, B.A. *New Haven, Conn.* 24 Edgewood av.
Mt. Holyoke College 1905 **Physiological Chemistry**

Arthur Sargent Field, B.A. *St. Johnsbury, Vt.* 100 Howe st.
Dartmouth College 1902, M.A. 1903 **Economics**

Theodore Adolph Fischer, D.D. *New Haven, Conn.* 409 Edgewood av.
Tufts College 1896 **Economics**

Everett Henry Fitch, B.A. *New Haven, Conn.* 148 Whalley av.
Colgate University 1893, M.A. 1896 **Latin**

William Ruthven Flint, B.A. *New Haven, Conn.* 121 Dwight st.
Yale University 1898, M.A. 1906 **Chemistry**

Charlotte Starkweather Fowler, B.A. *New Haven, Conn.* 205 Whalley av.
University of Michigan 1905 **French**

Alan Fox, B.A. *New York City*
Yale University 1903 **History**

George Levi Fox, B.A. *New Haven, Conn.* 7 College st.
Yale University 1874, LL.B. 1879, M.A. 1885 **Classics**

Charles Franklin, B.A. *North Haven, Conn.* North Haven
Central College 1894, M.A. 1895, Philosophy
B.D. Vanderbilt University 1901,
M.A. Yale University 1907

Victor Oscar Freeburg, B.A. *Lindsborg, Kans.* 295 York st.
Bethany College 1904, English
B.A. Yale University 1905

Frank Nugent Freeman, B.A. *Ontario, Cal.* 227 F.
Wesleyan University 1904, Psychology
M.A. Yale University 1906

Roy Leon French, PH.B. *Attica, N. Y.* 210 F.
Syracuse University 1906 English

Andrew Chesley Furbush, B.A. *Georgetown, Conn.* Georgetown
Yale University 1897, M.A. 1899, Philosophy
B.D. Andover Theological Seminary 1900

George Edward Gage, B.A. *Springfield, Mass.* 642 E. D.
Clark University 1906, Bacteriology and Physiol. Chemistry
M.A. Yale University 1907

Frederick Riley Gagel, PH.B. *Dayton, O.* 124 Prospect st.
Yale University 1907 Mining

Herbert Draper Gallaudet, B.A. *Washington, D. C.*
Yale University 1898 English

Arthur James Gammack, B.A. *West Haven, Conn.* West Haven
Trinity College (Toronto) 1891, M.A. 1902 Biblical Literature

Russell Tyner Gard, PH.B. *Frankfort, Ind.* 685 W. D.
Yale University 1907 Mining

Thomas Theron Giffen, B.A. *Fowler, Cal.* 213 F.
Pomona College 1906, Philosophy
B.A. Yale University 1907

Asa Russell Gifford, B.A. *New Haven, Conn.* 227 F.
Wesleyan University 1904, Philosophy
M.A. Yale University 1907

Hiram Gillespie, B.A. *Lincoln, Ill.* 219 F.
University of Chicago 1898, Greek and Latin
M.A. Yale University 1902

Frederick Augustus Godley *New York City* 334 WH.
Yale University English

Charles Martin Good, B.A. *Harrisonburg, Va.* 612 Yale P. O.
Otterbein University 1904, Philosophy
B.D. Yale University 1907

Aubrey Ward Goodenough, B.A. *Johannesburg, So. Africa*
Oberlin College 1906 25 Edwards st.
 English

Bradley Goodyear, B.A. *Buffalo, N. Y.*
Yale University 1907 English

Crawford Greene, B.A. *Nordhoff, Cal.* A.
Yale University 1906 English

George Frederick Gundelfinger, PH.B. *Sewickley, Pa.* 124 Wall st.
Yale University 1906 Mathematics

Charles Walter Hall, B A. *Stockville, Nebr.* 81 Yale P. O.
Doane College 1904, History
B.A. Yale University 1907

Alfred Ernest Hamill, B.A. *Chicago, Ill.*
Yale University 1905 English

George Washington Hanners, B.A. *Newport, N. J.* 59 Broadway
Syracuse University 1905 Greek and Latin

Austin Morris Harmon, B.A. *Brockport, N. Y.* Rome, Italy
Williams College 1902 Classics

Samuel Milby Harrington, B.A. *New York City*
Yale University 1906 English

Isaac Faust Harris, B.S. *New Haven, Conn.*
University of North Carolina 1900, M.S. 1903 Physiol. Chemistry

William Henry Harris, B.D. *Wardsville, Ont.* Beacon Falls
Yale University 1907 Philosophy

Edwin Deeks Harvey, B.A. *Cheshire, England* 625 E. D.
Yale University 1907 Sociology

Ruth Sawyer Harvey, B.A. *Cincinnati, O.* 142 York st.
University of Cincinnati 1905 Geology

Samuel Clarke Harvey, PH.B. *Woodbury, Conn.* 114 High st.
Yale University 1907 Bacteriology and Hygiene

Wells Southworth Hastings, B.A. *Englewood, N. J.*
Yale University 1902 English

Yasujiro Hayakawa *Oita, Japan* 55 Prospect st.
Oita Agricultural School 1899 Economics

Jessie Hays, B.A. *Kansas City, Mo.* 158 York st.
Drury College 1900, M.A. 1907 Latin and Greek

Fred Harvey Heath, B.S. *Warner, N. H.* 712 W. D.
New Hampshire Coll. Agr. and Mech. Arts 1905 Chemistry

Harry Clifton Heaton, B.A. *Waterbury, Conn.* Paris, France
Yale University 1907 Romance Languages

Laurent Heaton, B.A. *Poughkeepsie, N. Y.*
Yale University 1902 Electricity

Samuel Burdett Hemingway, B.A. *New Haven, Conn.* 327 Temple st.
Yale University 1904, M.A. 1905 English

Frederick William Heyl, PH.B. *New Haven, Conn.* 137 Blatchley av.
Yale University 1904 Chemistry

Warren Witherell Hilditch, PH.B. *Thompsonville, Conn.* 90 Lake pl.
Yale University 1905 Physiological Chemistry

Alfred Reed Hill, B.A. *Cambridge, Mass.*
Yale University 1902 English

Francis Jerome Holder, B.S. *LaCrosse, Fla.* 23 Lynwood pl.
National Normal University 1896, Mathematics
M.A. Yale University 1905

John Dean Holm, B.S.   *Stillwater, Minn.*   47 Lake pl.
Carleton College 1906, M.S. 1907   Mineralogy

Percy K. Holmes, B.P.T.   *Bridgeport, Conn.*   Bridgeport
Y. M. C. A. Training School 1907   English

Charles Roberts Hopkins, B.A.   *Philadelphia, Pa.*   245 York st.
Yale University 1907   English

James Osborne Hopwood, B.S.   *Philadelphia, Pa.*
University of Pennsylvania 1904   Botany and Chemistry

Edward Traill Horn, B.A.   *Reading, Pa.*   616 E. D.
Muhlenberg College 1907   History

Philip Mead Howe, B.A.   *Rockville, Conn.*   Rockville
Yale University 1902   History

William Rabon Howell, PH.B.   *Wilson, N. C.*   634 Yale P. O.
Milligan College 1904, B.A. 1905   Biblical Literature and History

Albert Wallace Hull, B.A.   *Torrington, Conn.*   120 York st.
Yale University 1905   Physics

Charles Hadlai Hull, B.A.   *New London, Conn.*   New London
Yale University 1905, LL.B. 1907   Social Science

Lon Lewis Hutchison, B.A.   *Norman, Okla.*   127 Dwight st.
University of Oklahoma, 1907   Geology

Harry Neal Hyde, B.A.   *Syracuse, N. Y.*
Yale University 1895   History

Seimin Inaoka, B.A.   *Tokyo, Japan*   350 George st.
University of Minnesota 1907   Economics

Tora Inouye   *Tokyo, Japan*   333 York st.
Keio University   Economics

William Johnson Jack, B.A.   *Indiana, Pa.*
Yale University 1905   History

Katherine Jackson, B.A.   *London, Ky.*   South Hadley
Ohio Wesleyan University 1898, M.A. 1900,   English
PH.D. Columbia University 1906

Jacob Louis Jacobs, PH.B.   *New Haven, Conn.* 1066 Yale P. O.
Yale University 1907   Civil Engineering

Ross Jewell, PH.B.   *Newtown, Conn.*   Newtown
Syracuse University 1897   English

John Francis Johnston, B.A.   *Seymour, Conn.*   Yale P. O.
Illinois Wesleyan Univ. 1898, M.A. 1901, PH.D. 1902
M.A. Yale University 1905   Philosophy

Blanche Adaline Jones, B.A.   *Pittsburg, Pa.*   Bridgeport
Vassar College 1896   English

David Breese Jones, B.A.   *Cambria, Wisc.*   103 Park st.
Ripon College 1904   Chemistry

Alexander Corbin Judson, B.A.   *Bostonia, Cal.*   716 W. D.
Pomona College 1907   English

Margaret Judson, B.A.   *New York City*   37 Howe st.
Vassar College 1903   English

Mihran Tatios Kalaidjian, B.A.   *Everek, Asia Minor* 619 Yale P. O.
St. Paul's Institute, Tarsus, 1900,   Philosophy
B.D. Yale University 1905, M.A. 1907

Kannosuke Kawanaka, B.A.   *Toba, Japan*   637 E. D.
Tohoku Gakuin 1889,   Semitic Lang. and Bibl. Lit.
B.D. Pacific Theol. Seminary 1906,
M.A. Columbia University 1907

Robert Porter Keep, B.A.   *Farmington, Conn.*
Yale University 1903   German

William Oded Keirstead, B.A.   *Cornhill, N. B.*   Montowese
Bates College 1906,   Sociology
B.A. Yale University 1907

Chauncey Clark Kennedy, B.A.   *New York City*
Yale University 1904   Biblical Literature

Virginia Wadlow Kennedy, B.A.   *Baltimore, Md.*   146 Norton st.
Woman's College of Baltimore 1896   English

Adeline Katherine Kerlin, B.S.   *New Haven, Conn.*   7 Library st.
St. Lawrence University 1905   English

Robert Thomas Kerlin, M.A.   *New Haven, Conn.*   7 Library st.
Central College 1890,   English
PH.D. Yale University 1906

John Ervin Kirkpatrick, B.D.   *Oxford, Conn.*   Oxford
Chicago Theological Seminary 1895,   History
M.A. Yale University 1906

Israel Simon Kleiner, PH.B.   *New Haven, Conn.*   39 Howe st.
Yale University 1906   Physiological Chemistry

Clarence Moore Knox, PH.B.   *Hartford, Conn.*   685 Yale P. O.
Yale University 1907   Mechanical Engineering

Saburo Koshiba, B.A.   *Tokyo, Japan*   639 E. D.
Union Christian College (Indiana) 1904,   Bibl. Literature and Philosophy
B.D. Oberlin College 1907

James Atsutoshi Kumon   *Osaka, Japan*   993 Yale P. O.
Kansai Law School 1898,   Economics
M.A. Yale University 1907

Daniel Webster Kurtz, B.A.   *Lake, O.*   655 Yale P. O.
Juniata College 1905   Philosophy

Arthur Burton LaCour, B.A.   *New Orleans, La.*   A.
Yale University 1904   English

Walter Edwards Lagerquist, B.A.   *Clarinda, Ia.*   198 Hamilton st.
Simpson College 1903,   Economics and Social Science
B.A. Yale University 1905, M.A. 1906

John Kenyon Lamond, B.S.   *Usquepaugh, R. I.*   103 Park st.
Rhode Island Coll. Agric. and Mech. Arts 1907, M.A. 1907
Mathematics

Francis Baker Laney, B.S.   *Chapel Hill, N. C.* 1305 Chapel st.
Drury College 1902,   Geology
M.A. University of Wisconsin 1905

Theodore Burger Lathrop, B.A.   *Ashland, Wisc.*   626 E. D.
Beloit College 1903   Biblical Literature

William Gilbert Lathrop, B.A.   *Shelton, Conn.*   Shelton
Brown University 1889,   Social Science
B.D. Yale University 1892, M.A. 1905

Kenneth Scott Latourette, B.S.   *Oregon City, Oregon*   197 F.
McMinnville College 1904,   History
B.A. Yale University 1906, M.A. 1907

Henry Wells Lawrence, Jr., B.A.   *White Plains, N. Y.*   125 Dwight st.
Yale University 1906, M.A. 1907   History

Henry Barrett Learned, B.A.   *New Haven, Conn.* 50 Cold Spring st.
Harvard University 1890, M.A. 1897   History

Eugene Heitler Lehman, B.A.   *New York City*   453 FW.
Yale University 1902   Semitic Languages

Leonard Merritt Liddle, B.S.   *Walker, Ia.*   88 C.
Cornell College 1906   Chemistry

William Harding Longley, B.A.   *Paradise, N. S.*   120 York st.
Acadia University 1901,   Biology
B.A. Yale University 1907

William Hayes Longsworth, B.A.   *Cheshire, Conn.*   687 W. D.
West Lafayette College 1906   Biblical Literature and History

Louis Eleazer Lord, B.A.   *Oberlin, O.*   35 Sherland av.
Oberlin College 1897, M.A. 1897,   Greek
M.A. Harvard University 1900

Herman Samuel Lovejoy, B.S.   *Branford, Conn.*   Branford
Dartmouth College 1894   Education

George Blakeman Lovell, B.A.   *New Haven, Conn.* 765 Whitney av.
Yale University 1901, M.A. 1903   German

Tasker Gantt Lowndes, B.A.   *Baltimore, Md.*
Yale University 1907   English

Frederick Bliss Luquiens, B.A.   *New Haven, Conn.* 595 Orange st.
Yale University 1897, PH.D. 1905   English

John Franklin Lyman, B.S.   *Amherst, Mass.*   706 W. D.
Massachusetts Agricultural College 1905   Physiological Chemistry

Ernest Barnes Lytle, B.S.   *Urbana, Ill.*   120 York st.
University of Illinois 1901, M.A. 1904   Mathematics

Donald McBride, B.A.   *Cleveland, O.*
Yale University 1906   English

William Pitt McCune, B.A.   *Columbus, O.*   384 B.
Yale University 1906, M.A. 1907   English

Ernest Frank McGregor, B.A.   *Clinton, Conn.*   760 Yale P. O.
University of Minnesota 1901,   Social Science
B.D. Yale University 1904, M.A. 1906

Kenneth Gerard Mackenzie, PH.B.   *Westport, Conn.*   162 S. C. L.
Yale University 1907   Chemistry

John William Madden, PH.B.   *Deposit, N. Y.*   88 Wall st.
Yale University 1907   Mechanical Engineering

John Lee Maddox, B.A.   *Deering, N. D.*   675 W. D.
Denison University 1904   History

Constantine Frithiof Malmberg, B.A. *St. Peter, Minn.*   293 York st.
Bethany College 1903   Philosophy

Max Solomon Mandell   *New Haven, Conn.*   101 Orange st.
     English

Francis Hartman Markoe, Jr., B.A. *New York City*
Yale University 1906   English

Harriette Parnal Marsh, PH.B.   *New Haven, Conn.* 89 Whalley av.
University of Chicago 1904   History

Thomas Randolph Marshall, PH.B. *Philadelphia, Pa.*   144 Dwight st.
Brown University 1907

Norman Andrews Martin, PH.B.   *New Castle, Pa.*   684 W. D.
Yale University 1907   Chemistry

Carlton Howard Maryott, B.A.   *Springfield, Mass.*   U. C.
Brown University 1904   Chemistry

Lawrence Mason, B.A.   *Chicago, Ill.*   245 York st.
Yale University 1904   English

Samuel Livingston Mather, B.A.   *Ishpeming, Mich.*
Yale University 1905   English

Alfred Arundel May, B.A.   *Wooster, O.*   17 Whalley av.
University of Wooster 1900,   English
M.A. Yale University 1907

Clarence Whittlesey Mendell, B.A. *Boston, Mass.*   86 C.
Yale University 1904, M.A. 1905   Greek

George Douglas Milbury, B.A.   *Lewiston, Me.*   627 Yale P. O.
Bates College 1905,   Biblical Literature
B.D. Yale University 1907

Edwin Cyrus Miller, B.A.   *Baltimore, O.*   728 Yale P. O.
National Normal University 1906,   Botany
B.A. Yale University 1907

Jesse William Miller, B.A,   *Arizpe, Mex.*
Yale University 1900   English

John Milton Miller, B.A.   *Bridgeport, Conn.* Washington, D. C.
Yale University 1904   Physics

Stewart Lea Mims, B.A.   *Durham, N. C.*   701 W. D.
Yale University 1904   History

Michael Minassian, PH.B.   *Boston, Mass.*   754 Yale P. O.
Yale University 1900   Chemistry

Isabel Stewart Mitchell, B.A.   *New Haven, Conn.* 152 Whalley av.
Maryville College 1905   Romance Languages

Clifford Joseph Monahan, PH.B. *New Haven, Conn.*   686 W. D.
Yale University 1907   Chemistry

40

Marie Guenther Mussaeus, B.A.   *Front Royal, Va.*   90 Whalley av.
Smith College 1906   Romance Languages

Victor Caryl Myers, B.A.   *Buskirk Bridge, N. Y.*   707 W. D.
Wesleyan University 1905, M.A. 1907   Physiological Chemistry

Foster Stebbins Naething, PH.B.   *New York City*   124 Prospect st.
Yale University 1907   Mining

Robert Welden Neeser, B.A.   *New York City*   Paris, France
Yale University 1906   History

John Strong Newberry, B.A.   *Cleveland, O.*
Yale University 1906   English

Howard Douglass Newton, B.S.   *Interlaken, Mass.*   117 Wall st.
Massachusetts Agricultural College 1904   Chemistry

George Elwood Nichols, B.A.   *New Haven, Conn.*   569 P.
Yale University 1904   Botany

Levi Fatzinger Noble, B.A.   *Auburn, N. Y.*   90 Wall st.
Yale University 1905   Paleontology

Herbert Brinkerhoff North, PH.B.   *New Haven, Conn.* 250 Whalley av.
Yale University 1901   Mechanical Engineering

John Arthur Northcott, B.A.   *Toronto, Canada*   Cheshire
Trinity University (Toronto) 1904,   Mathematics
M.A. University of Toronto 1905

Wallace Notestein, B.A.   *Lawrence, Kans.*   1157 Chapel st.
University of Wooster 1900,   History
M.A. Yale University 1903

Charles Reinold Noyes, B.A.   *St.Paul, Minn.*
Yale University 1905   English

Daniel Raymond Noyes, B.A.   *St.Paul, Minn.*
Yale University 1905   English

Kenzaburo Okamoto   *Tokyo, Japan*   128 High st.
Keiogijiku University 1907   English

Irving Sands Olds, B.A.   *Erie, Pa.*
Yale University 1907   English

Raymond William Osborne, B.A.   *Berea, Ky.*   846 Yale P. O.
Yale University 1906   Chemistry and Mineralogy

George Washington Page, B.A.   *Nacogdoches, Texas* 1157 Chapel st.
Bethel College 1899, M.A. 1903,   History
Baylor University 1905

Sidney Paige   *Washington, D. C.*   217 York st.
     Geology

Howard Earle Palmer, B.A.   *Branford, Conn.*   Branford
Yale University 1907   Chemistry

Willis Nathaniel Parker, B.A.   *Philadelphia, Pa.*
Yale University 1891,   Education
M.A. Univ. of Pa. 1897. PH.D. 1898

Eli Burton Parsons, Jr., B.A.   *Troy, Pa.*   1076 Chapel st.
Yale University 1907   Mathematics and Physics

Nicholas Elias Peieff, B.A. ·   *Macedonia*   122 Dwight st.
Yale University 1907   History and Economics

Claude Clair Perkins, B.A.   *Pine Island, Minn.*   118 Howe st.
University of Minnesota 1907   Chemistry

Perry Blaine Perkins, B.A.   *Connell, N. B.*   102 DeWitt st.
University of New Brunswick 1902,   Physics
B.A. Harvard University 1903,
M.A. Yale University 1904

Hervey Bates Perrin, B.A.   *Indianapolis, Ind.*
Yale University 1907   English

Clarence Curtiss Perry, PH.B.   *New Britain, Conn.*   121 Maple st.
Yale University 1904   Physics

Walter Hart Perry, B.A.   *Oxford, Conn.*   111 Dwight st.
Yale University 1901   History

Walter Petersen, B.A.   *Grand Island, Nebr.*   58 Dixwell av.
Grand Island College 1900,   Linguistics and Sanskrit
M.A. University of Nebraska 1902

Clyde Pharr, B.A.   *Ridgeway, Texas*   98 York sq.
Yale University 1906   Greek

Max Patten Philbrick, B.A.   *Hartford, Conn.*   Hartford
Colby College 1902   French

Frederick Erastus Pierce, B.A.   *So. Britain, Conn.*   ·West Haven
Yale University 1904, M.A. 1905   English

Frederick Williams Pierce, PH.B.   *Baldwin, Kans.*   373 Crown st.
Baker University 1906   German

Frank Wesley Pitman, PH.B.   *New Haven, Conn.*   646 George st.
Yale University 1904, M.A. 1906   History

Joseph Ezekiel Pogue, Jr., B.A.   *Raleigh, N. C.*   1305 Chapel st.
University of North Carolina 1906, M.S. 1907   Geology

Bryant Hawk Prentice, B.A.   *Buffalo, N. Y.*
Yale University 1905   History

George Ellsworth Putnam, B.A.   *Ottawa, Kans.*   176 Meadow st.
University of Kansas 1907   Political Science

Katharine Mordaunt Quint, B.A.   *Boston, Mass.*   90 Whalley av.
Wellesley College 1890,   Greek and Latin
M.A. Dartmouth College 1896

Ethel Ziveley Rather, B.A.   *Gonzales, Texas*   133 Howe st.
University of Texas 1902, M.A. 1903   History

Henry Augustus Raymond, B.A.   *Cleveland, O.*
Yale University 1905   English

Joseph Chappell Rayworth, B.A.   *Upper Sackville, N. B.* 120 York st.
Acadia University 1903,   Mathematics
B.A. Yale University 1906, M.A. 1907

John Dougan Rea, B.A.   *Richmond, Ind.*   351 Crown st.
Yale University 1903, M.A. 1905   Latin

Chester Albert Reeds, B.S.   *Norman, Okla.*   204 F.
University of Oklahoma 1905,   Paleontology
M.S. Yale University 1907

Ray John Reigeluth   *Carbondale, Pa.*   29 V.
Yale University   Economics

John Pierrepont Rice, B.A.   *Northampton, Mass.*   77 Elm st.
Yale University 1900, M.A. 1901   Romance Languages

Howard MacMillan Richard, B.A.   *New Haven, Conn.* 504 Whitney av.
Wesleyan University 1904,   Biblical Literature
B.A. Yale University 1905

Frank Stanley Rickcords, B.A.   *Chicago, Ill.*
Yale University 1905   English

Henry Martyn Robert, Jr., B.A.   *New York City*
Yale University 1896   Mathematics

Edwin Jay Roberts, B.S.   *Laconia, N. H.*   712 W. D.
New Hampshire Coll. Agr. and Mech. Arts 1906   Chemistry

Richmond Grout Roberts, B.H.   *Bradford, Mass.*   152 Temple st.
Y. M. C. A. Training School 1907   English

Francis Clapp Robertson, B.A.   *New York City*
Yale University 1906   English

Heaton Ridgeway Robertson, B.A.   *New Haven, Conn.*
Yale University 1904, PH.B. 1906   Mining

Thomas Markoe Robertson, B.A.   *New York City*
Yale University 1901   English

Charles Prescot Robinson, B.A.   *New York City*
Yale University 1900   English and History

William Goodwin Robinson, B.A.   *Williamsport, Pa.*
Yale University 1906   English

Anton Richard Rose, B.S.   *Geneva, N. Y.*   342 Crown st.
University of Minnesota 1904   Physiological Chemistry

William Cumming Rose, B.S.   *Laurinburg, N. C.*   91 Park st.
Davidson College 1907   Chemistry

Joseph Rosenbaum, PH.B.   *New Haven, Conn.*   68 Park st.
Yale University 1907   Mathematics

John Rossiter, B.A.   *Guilford, Conn.*
Yale University 1882   Psychology

Edith Sutherland Russell, B.A.   *West Haven, Conn.*   West Haven
Vassar College 1899

Tadasu Saiki, M.D.   *Kitayamasaki Iyo, Japan*   462 Elm st.
Okayama Medical College 1898,   Physiological Chemistry
PH.D. Yale University 1907

George Paull Torrence Sargent, B.A.   *New York City*
Yale University 1905   History

Thomas Edmund Savage, B.A.	*Urbana, Ill.*	West Haven
Iowa Wesleyan University 1895,	Geology
B.S. State University of Iowa 1897, M.S. 1898

Samuel Scoville, B.A.	*Philadelphia, Pa.*
Yale University 1893,	Icelandic
LL.B. New York Law School 1895

Howard Arnold Seckerson, B.A.	*Brooklyn, N. Y.* 178 Ellsworth av.
Wesleyan University 1907	English

Nobuji Sekido	*Tokyo, Japan* 385 Winthrop av.
Waseda University 1907	English

William Edward Selin, B.A.	*Cynthiana, Ky.* 671 W. D.
Yale University 1898, M.A. 1900	English

Edward Burt Sellew, B.A.	*New Haven, Conn.* 809 Orange st.
Williams College 1890	English

Herbert Lee Seward, PH.B.	*New Haven, Conn.* 116 V-S.
Yale University 1906	Mechanical Engineering

Ernest Wilson Sheldon, B.A.	*Cornwall, Ont., Canada* 542 P.
McGill University 1904,	Mathematics
B.A. Yale University 1907

William Arthur Shelton, B.A.	*Columbia, Conn.* 680 W. D.
Hargrove College 1905	English

George Clarence Sherwood, B.S.	*Ewing, Ky.* 276 Elm st.
National Normal University 1899,	English
B.A. Yale University 1907

Guy-Andrew Simmons, B.A.	*Martin, Tenn.* 142 Edgewood av.
McFerrin College 1897,	Latin
M.A. De Pauw University 1902,
M.A. Yale University 1907

William Ernest Andrew Slaght, B.A.	*New Haven, Conn.* 980 Whalley av.
National Normal University 1905,	Philosophy
M.A. Yale University 1907

Arthur Wells Smith, B.A.	*Cañon City, Colo.* 529 Elm st.
National Normal University 1905	Biology and Chemistry

Edwin Kinmouth Smith, PH.B.	*Morristown, N. J.* 51 Prospect st.
Yale University 1907	Chemistry

Jesse Fowler Smith, B.A.	*Silver Lane, Conn.* 1068 Yale P. O.
Brown University 1896	Sanskrit

Mary Winslow Smyth, B.L.	*New Haven, Conn.* 328 Temple st.
Smith College 1895, M.A. 1905	English

Carl Frank Speh, PH.B.	*New Haven, Conn.* 63 Crown st.
Yale University 1906	Chemistry

Albert Thomas Steele, B.A.	*Bethel, Conn.*	Bethel
Adrian College 1896,	Philosophy
B.D. Yale University 1907

Jessie Mae Stokely, B.A.	*Newport, Tenn.* 90 Park st.
Virginia Institute 1904	History

Walter Frederick Storey, PH.B.   *New Haven, Conn.*   172 Lloyd st.
  Yale University 1906   Chemistry

Frederick Azel Sumner, B.A.   *Milford, Conn.*   Milford
  Oberlin College 1891,   Biblical Literature
  B.D. Hartford Theological Seminary 1894   *1169*

Nizzo Suruda, B.L.   *Kishu, Japan*   ~~416 Crown st.~~
  Bethany College (W. Va.) 1906   English

Mary Davies Swartz, B.L.   *Wooster, O.*   25 Whalley av.
  Denison University 1901,   Physiol. Chemistry and Bacteriology
  B.S. Columbia University 1906

Ludwig Emil Swenson, B A.   *Lindsborg, Kans.*   376 Elm st.
  Bethany College 1905   German

James Spencer Taintor, B.A.   *Hartford, Conn.*
  Yale University 1901   History

Senjiro Takagi, B.A.   *Yokohama, Japan*   228 Crown st.
  Yale University 1907   Social Science

Seijiro Takahashi   *Seattle, Wash.*   652 E. D.
  Keiogijiku University 1900   History and Social Science

Arthur Harrington Taylor, B.A.   *Kentville, N. S.*   892 Yale P. O.
  Acadia College 1903,   Economics and Social Science
  B.A. Yale University 1905, M.A. 1906

Thomas Smith Taylor, B.A.   *Peoli, O.*   687 W. D.
  Yale University 1906   Physics

Wyatt Warner Taylor, PH.B.   *Stamford, Conn.*
  Yale University 1900   Mechanical Engineering   •

Clifford Griffith Thompson, B.A.   *Bogart, Ga.*   647 E. D.
  Young Harris College 1903   Philosophy

Edwin Ward Tillotson, Jr., B.A.   *Farmington, Conn.* 846 Yale P. O.
  Yale University 1906   Chemistry

John Ker Towles, B.S.   *New Orleans, La.*   706 W. D.
  Tulane University 1902, M.A. 1904   Economics

Thomas Allen Tully, B.A.   *Stapleton, N. Y.*   130 Howe st.
  Yale University 1907   Classical Philology

Charles Eugene Underwood, B.A. *Indianapolis, Ind.* 585 Howard av.
  Butler College 1903, M.A. 1904   Biblical Literature

Albert William VanBuren, B.A.   *New Haven, Conn.* 9 Trumbull st.
  Yale University 1900   Classics

Orlin Hale Venner, PH.B.   .   *Corydon, Ind.*   1233 Chapel st.
  Berea College 1902,   •   English
  B.A. University of West Virginia 1905

Mary Emma Wadlington, B.A.   *Norman, Okla.*   166 York st.
  University of Mississippi 1902   English

Mary Shore Walker, B.A.   *Columbia, Mo.*   North Haven
  University of Missouri 1903, M.A. 1904   Mathematics

Roosevelt Pruyn Walker, B.A.   *Macon, Ga.*   79 Howe st.
Mercer University 1905   English

James Harold Wallis, B.A.   *Dubuque, Ia.*
Yale University 1906   English

Henry Freeman Walradt, B.A.   *Whitman, Mass.*   417 B.
Yale University 1907   Economics

Evans Ward, PH.B.   *Port Chester, N. Y.*   88 Wall st.
Yale University 1907   Mechanical Engineering

Freeman Ward, B.A.   *Yankton, S. D.*   106 Howe st.
Yale University 1903   Geology

Hiram Lee Ward, B.A.   *Unadilla, N. Y.*   205 F.
Yale University 1906   Chemistry

Ella Pardee Warner, PH.B.   *Highwood, Conn.*   914 Dixwell av.
Wesleyan University 1906, M.S. 1907   English

Edward Colpitts Weyman, B.A.   *Apohaqui, N. B.*   189 F.
University of New Brunswick 1902,   Economics
B.A. Howard University 1903,
M.A. Yale University 1905

Frank Elbert Wheelock, B.A.   *Lawrencetown, N. S.* 120 York st.
Acadia University 1905,   Physics
B.A. Yale University 1907

Henry Adelbert White, B.A.   *Middletown, Conn.* 82 Whalley av.
Wesleyan University 1904, M.A. 1905   English

John Alan White, B.A.   *Walton, N. Y.*   82 C.
Yale University 1907   Mathematics

Raymond Henry White, B.A.   *New Haven, Conn.*   411 B.
Yale University 1905, M.A. 1906   Greek

Philip Barrows Whitehead, B.A.   *Janesville, Wisc.*   641 E. D.
Beloit College 1906   History

Dean Rockwell Wickes, PH.B.   *Chicago, Ill.*   638 E. D.
University of Chicago 1905   Biblical Literature

Robert Day Williams, B.S.   *Redlands, Cal.*   213 F.
Pomona College 1903,   Philosophy
M.A. Yale University 1907

Thomas Aber Williams, B.A.   *Criccieth, Wales*   628 E. D.
Marietta College 1905   Sociology

Mark Skinner Willing, B.A.   *Chicago, Ill.*
Yale University 1902   English

Harold Moffat Wilson, B.A.   *New York City*
Yale University 1898   Church History

Wallace Alvin Wilson, B.A.   *Branford, Conn.*   Branford
Yale University 1905   Mathematics

Milton Frederick Wittler, B.A.   *Seattle, Wash.*   716 W. D.
Pomona College 1907   Philosophy

Roger Henry Wolcott, B.A.   *Denver, Col.*
Yale University 1905   English

William Hamilton Wood, B.A.   *Iroquois, Ont.*   Berlin, Germany
University of Toronto 1901,   Biblical Literature
B.D. Yale University 1905

George Edward Woodbine, B.A.   *Harding, Mass.*   245 York st.
Yale University 1903   History

Euphemia Richardson Worthington, B.A.
Wellesley College 1904   *Troy, N. Y.*   37 Howe st.
          Mathematics

Thomas Goddard Wright, B.A.   *Phelps, N. Y.*   74 C.
Yale University 1907   English

Benjamin Franklin Wyland, PH.B. *Harlan, Ia.*   702 W. D.
State University of Iowa 1905   Sociology and Philosophy

Yukichi Yanagi, B.A.   *Wakayama, Japan*   91 Dwight st.
Keio University 1907   Economics

Harry Clinton York, B.A.   *Leonard Bridge, Conn.* 125 Dwight st.
Yale University 1905, M.A. 1906   Semit. Lang. and Bibl. Lit.

Ralph William Young, PH.B.   *West Upton, Mass.*   665 W. D.
Yale University 1907   Mining

TEACHERS NOT HOLDING DEGREES ADMITTED TO GRADUATE COURSES

Anna I. Baldwin   *New Haven, Conn.* 78 Whalley av.
       Biblical Literature

Jessica A. Cutting   *New Haven, Conn.* 821 Whitney av.
       Biblical Literature

Jessie E. Holt   *New Haven, Conn.*   68 Clark st.
       Biblical Literature

John Kielle Hooper   *New Haven, Conn.*   33 Lake pl.
       Physics

Friend Edward Hoyt   *Shelton, Conn.*   964½ Chapel st.
     Economics and Social Science

Hortense Metzger   *New Haven, Conn.*   23 Grove st.
       English

Camille Tenney   *New Haven, Conn.*   21 Home pl.
       English

Samuel Watson Warden   *Meriden, Conn.*   Meriden
     Educational Psychology

GRADUATE SCHOOL, 357

ACADEMICAL DEPARTMENT
(YALE COLLEGE)
SENIOR CLASS, 1908

Albert Parker Abbe	*New Britain, Conn.*	25 V.
Robert Abbott	*Plainfield, N. J.*	30 V.
Thomas Achelis	*New York City*	368 WH.
Clifton LeBarron Adams	*Rochester, Vt.*	78 Dwight st.
Carleton Mansfield Allen	*Hartford, Conn.*	434 FW.
Herman Alofsin, 2d	*Norwich, Conn.*	715 W. D.
Samuel Alpert	*New Haven, Conn.*	96 Washington av.
Frank Altschul	*New York City*	251 D.
Danforth Fletcher Alvord	*Winsted, Conn.*	425 FW.
Gordon Auchincloss	*New York City*	426 FW.
James Coates Auchincloss	*New York City*	426 FW.
Joseph Howland Auchincloss	*New York City*	51 V.
Albert Edwin Avey	*Cincinnati, O.*	84 C.
Oswald Prentiss Backus, Jr.	*Rome, N. Y.*	88 C.
Everett Lee Baker	*Webster, N. Y.*	97 W.
Donald Campbell Bakewell	*Pittsburg, Pa.*	5 V.
Samuel Alexander Baldwin	*Sprecklesville, H. I.*	24 V.
Simeon Baldwin	*New Haven, Conn.*	659 W. D.
Malcolm Sterling Banks	*Brooklyn, N. Y.*	1 V.
Earl Morton Barnum	*Naugatuck, Conn.*	234 D.
David Nye Barrows	*New York City*	368 WH.
James Corbett Barry	*Rochester, N. Y.*	20 V.
Philip Curtis Kibling Bartlett	*St. Joseph, Mo.*	345 WH.
Chauncey Perry Beadleston	*New York City*	32 V.
Henry Sartwell Beardsley	*Auburn, N. Y.*	42 V.
Roderick Beebe	*New York City*	354 WH.
William Burke Belknap	*Louisville, Ky.*	334 WH.
Shelley Edward Bennett, Jr., B.A.	*Sturgis, Ky.*	249 Crown st.
Lincoln College 1907		
Edward Bennetto, Jr.	*Stratford, Conn.*	331 WH.
George Reis Bart Berger	*Pittsburg, Pa.*	62 V.
Earl Edward Beyer	*Rochester, Ind.*	9 V.
Forrest Beyer	*Kendallville, Ind.*	9 V.
Lucius Horatio Biglow, 3d	*Brooklyn, N. Y.*	30 V.
Clifford Hershey Bissell	*New York City*	45 V.
Willard Samuel Bissell	*Waterville, N. Y.*	63 V.
Joseph Clarence Black	*Seattle, Wash.*	7 V.
Carl William Blegen, B.A.	*Minneapolis, Minn.*	364 George st.
University of Minnesota 1907		

Charles Sherman Bodwell	*New Haven, Conn.*	202 F.
Lewis Samuel Boothe	*Shelton, Conn.*	202 F.
Andrew Linn Bostwick	*Montclair, N. J.*	358 WH.
Rowland Sherwood Bosworth	*Providence, R. I.*	43 V.
Jonathan Sawyer Bradley	*Dover, N. H.*	24 V.
Caleb Smith Bragg	*Cincinnati, O.*	101 W.
Frank Eugene Bridgett	*Wallingford, Conn.*	Wallingford
Ralph Shepherd Bromer	*Schwenkville, Pa.*	3 V.
Wendell Stanton Brooks	*Chicago, Ill.*	85 C.
Baird Broomhall	*Troy, O.*	265 D.
Rollin Broughton, B.A.	*Madison, Ga.*	126 W.
University of Georgia 1907		
Hamilton Mabie Brush	*Greenwich, Conn.*	356 WH.
Richard Beaumaris Bulkeley	*Hartford, Conn.*	346 WH.
Nathan Hollister Bundy	*Grand Rapids, Mich.*	19 V.
Hillier McClure Burrowes	*Coeymans, N. Y.*	45 V.
Ronald Muirhead Byrnes	*Norwich, Conn.*	336 WH.
Thomas James Camp	*Seymour, Conn.*	266 D.
George Edward Catlin	*New Haven, Conn.*	176 York st.
Reginald Woodward Catlin	*Brooklyn, N. Y.*	28 V.
Francis Deraismes Childs	*Hartford, Conn.*	15 V.
Hugh Joseph Chisholm, Jr.	*New York City*	40 V.
Clinton Clark	*Buffalo, N. Y.*	370 WH.
Loyal Brown Clark	*Cornwall, Conn.*	695 W. D.
Guy Cory Cleveland	*Orange, N. J.*	46 V.
Reginald McIntosh Cleveland	*New York City*	22 V.
Alfred Horace Cohen	*Brooklyn, N. Y.*	73 C.
Philip Hamilton Collins	*Cleveland, O.*	69 V.
Edward Chester Congdon	*Duluth, Minn.*	6 V.
Raymond Vere Congdon	*Yantic, Conn.*	418 B.
Oscar Henry Cooper, Jr.	*Abilene, Texas* •	89 C.
Starr Gardiner Cooper	*Brooklyn, N. Y.*	455 FW.
Leonard Jacob Crawford, Jr.	*Fort Thomas, Ky.*	50 V.
Charles Templeton Crocker	*San Mateo, Cal.*	348 WH.
Walter Morgan Crunden	*St. Louis, Mo.*	350 WH.
William Smith Culbertson, B.A.	*Emporia, Kans.*	691 W. D.
Emporia College 1907		
Charles Gould Curtiss	*Buffalo, N. Y.*	39 V.
William Strong Cushing	*Simsbury, Conn.*	4 V.
John Dicks Cutter, Jr.	*Brooklyn, N. Y.*	1 V.
George Dahl	*Chicago, Ill.*	29 V.
Edward Stiles Davey	*Jersey City, N. J.*	7 V.
Walter Goodwin Davis, Jr.	*Portland, Me.*	33 V.
Lewis Henry DeBaun　　　.	*Brooklyn, N. Y.*	295 York st.

Sydney Beauclerc DeGolyer	*Springfield, Mass.*	339 WH.
Eugene Delano, Jr.	*New York City*	53 V.
Harmar Denny Denny, Jr.	*Allegheny, Pa.*	367 WH.
John Maurice Deyo	*Fairfield, Conn.*	85 C.
Conway Wing Dickson	*Berwick, Pa.*	23 V.
Chandler Diehl	*Highland Park, Ill.*	110 Wall st.
Tyson Manzey Dines	*Denver, Colo.*	11 V.
Courtlandt Palmer Dixon	*New York City*	33 V.
Malcolm Graham Douglas	*Chestnut Hill, Pa.*	346 WH.
Charles Bigelow Drake	*St. Paul, Minn.*	433 FW.
Walter Remy Dray	*Chicago, Ill.*	8 V.
Prescott Dudley	*Chicago, Ill.*	8 V.
Charley Meredith DuPuy	*Allegheny, Pa.*	64 V.
Arthur Delma Dyess, PH.B.	*Holland, Texas*	147 L.
Baylor University 1906		
Ernest Arthur Eddy	*St. Louis, Mo.*	344 WH.
Robert Bacon English	*Hartford, Conn.*	66 V.
Joseph Sherman Euans	*Watseka, Ill.*	443 FW.
Lewis Charles Everard	*New Orleans, La.*	75 C.
Haliburton Fales, Jr.	*New York City*	112 W.
David Ferguson	*Manchester, Conn.*	72 C.
John Elliott Field	*New Haven, Conn.*	33 Lynwood pl.
John Henry Fitzgerald, Jr.	*Hebron, Conn.*	436 FW.
Joseph Taylor Foster	*Scranton, Pa.*	10 V.
Sydney Joseph Frank	*Chicago, Ill.*	382 WH.
Leonard Henry Freiberg	*Cincinnati, O.*	442 FW.
Sydney Dodd Frissell	*Hampton, Va.*	354 WH.
William Gammell, Jr.	*Providence, R. I.*	37 V.
John Arthur Gardner	*New York City*	400 B.
Chauncey Brewster Garver	*New York City*	343 WH.
Charles Howard Gilbert	*Brooklyn, N. Y.*	53 V.
Frederick Augustus Godley	*New York City*	334 WH.
Irving Goldenburg	*New Haven, Conn.*	35 Nash st.
Francis Yarrington Goodell	*Montclair, N. J.*	435 FW.
Ralph Edward Goodwin	*East Hartford, Conn.*	382 WH.
Frank Gosnell, Jr.	*Baltimore, Md.*	47 V.
George Jackson Grammer, Jr.	*Cleveland, O.*	58 V.
Donald Greene	*St. Louis, Mo.*	62 V.
Dwight Torrey Griswold	*Erie, Pa.*	42 V.
Joseph Thomas Hagan	*Piqua, O.*	265 D.
Jule Murat Hannaford, Jr.	*St. Paul, Minn.*	428 FW.
Walter Earle Hartley	*Grand Rapids, Mich.*	267 D.
Cornelius DeForest Haskell	*Wakefield, Nebr.*	65 V.
Richard Withington Hawes	*Somerville, Mass.*	56 V.

Vincent Eugene Healy	*Chicago, Ill.*	428 FW.
Frederick Chase Heck	*Bismarck, Mo.*	142 Dwight st.
Arly Luther Hedrick	*Kansas City, Mo.*	54 V.
James Pendleton Helm, Jr.	*Louisville, Ky.*	347 WH.
Louis Lee Hemingway	*New Haven, Conn.*	59 V.
William Emanuel Hendricks	*St. Croix, Danish W. I.*	152 L.
Joe Martin Higginbotham, Jr., B.S.	*Dublin, Texas*	147 L.
Baylor University 1907		
Samuel Newton Holliday, 2d	*St. Louis, Mo.*	. 68 V.
Burton Johnson Hollister	*Evansville, Wisc.*	356 WH.
Nathaniel Holmes	*Pittsburg, Pa.*	69 V.
Davenport Hooker	*Brooklyn, N. Y.*	92 C.
Thomas Hooker	*Hartford, Conn.*	354 WH.
Charles Robert Housum	*Cleveland, O.*	58 V.
Chapin Howard	*Grafton, Vt.*	13 V.
Samuel Lamson Howell	*Philadelphia, Pa.*	41 V.
Edward Kenneth Hoyt	*New York City*	32 V.
DeForest Hulburd	*Chicago, Ill.*	352 WH.
Otis Scott Humphrey	*Springfield, Ill.*	20 V.
Roy Bryant Hunter	*Bridgeport, O.*	700 W. D.
Clarke Stanley Hurlbut	*Philadelphia, Pa.*	18 V.
Harold Thomas Fuller Husted	*Westfield, N. Y.*	45 V.
John Cornelius Hyde	*Westfield, Mass.*	60 V.
Charles Elliott Ide	*Syracuse, N. Y.*	367 WH.
Raymond Ives	*New York City*	51 V.
Henry Hollister Jackson	*Barre, Vt.*	434 FW.
Donald Lines Jacobus	*New Haven, Conn.*	87 C.
George Metcalf Johnson	*New Haven, Conn.*	92 C.
John Quincy Adams Johnson, Jr.	*Yonkers, N. Y.*	234 D.
Benjamin Franklin Jones	*Nanticoke, Pa.*	137 Dwight st.
Clarence Drummond Jones	*St. Louis, Mo.*	428 FW.
Howard Kenworthy	*Poughkeepsie, N. Y.*	423 FW.
Harold Brown Keyes	*Hartford, Conn.*	25 V.
Carl Kincaid	*Galveston, Texas*	338 WH.
Robert Saxe Kinsey	*Cincinnati, O.*	439 FW.
Karl Windell Kirchwey	*New York City*	3 V.
Russell Dyer Kittredge	*Westfield, Mass.*	60 V.
Charles Whittemore Knapp	*Poughkeepsie, N. Y.*	357 WH.
Ellis Knowles	*Pensacola, Fla.*	347 WH.
Geoffrey Konta	*New York City*	21 V.
Julius Ansgar Larsen	*New Haven, Conn.*	406 B.
William Rockwell Leete	*New Haven, Conn.*	29 V.
Howard Bishop Lewis	*Southington, Conn.*	74 C.
Sinclair Lewis	*New York City*	14 Whalley av.

William Benjamin Lipphardt	*Buffalo, N. Y.*	81 C.
Isaac Loewenthal	*New York City*	443 FW.
John Louis Lowe	*New Haven, Conn.*	362 Grand av.
Charles Fisher Luther	*Milton, Mass.*	355 WH.
Theodore Bird Lyon	*New Haven, Conn.*	425 FW.
William Howard Lyon	*Cincinnati, O.*	35 V.
John Charles McCarthy	*McLean, N. Y.*	71 C.
Irving J. MacDuffie, Jr.	*LeMars, Ia.*	65 V.
Daniel Carroll McEuen	*East Orange, N. J.*	28 V.
Charles James McGraw	*Augusta, Me.*	344 WH.
Delivan Alexander McGregor	*Sardis, Miss.*	86 Howe st.
Ralph Porter Mackenzie	*Lima, O.*	26 V.
William Holmes Mackenzie	*Lima, O.*	17 V.
Philip Rogers Mallory	*Brooklyn, N. Y.*	10 V.
Alan Newhall Mann	*Buffalo, N. Y.*	44 V.
Frank Gilbert Marsh	*Winsted, Conn.*	344 WH.
Thomas Mercer Marshall, 3d	*Pittsburg, Pa.*	34 V.
Samuel Francis Melcher	*Salem, Mass.*	82 C.
Austin Cook Merrill	*Carthage, N. Y.*	360 WH.
Charles Edward Messerly, Jr.	*Sedalia, Mo.*	66 V.
Douglas Miller	*Glen Ridge, N. J.*	63 V.
Lawrence Vernon Miller	*Baltimore, Md.*	49 V.
James Thacker Milliken	*Traverse City, Mich.*	267 D.
Mark Lincoln Mitchell	*Cincinnati, O.*	426 FW.
August Charles Mitke	*Freeland, Pa.*	27 V.
Albert John Mohlman	*Brielle, N. J.*	35 V.
John Warner Moore	*Carlisle, Pa.*	71 C.
Paul Moore	*New York City*	5 V.
Frederic Timothy Murphy	*New York City*	62 V.
Joseph William Murphy	*Brooklyn, N. Y.*	36 V.
Gilbert Nairn	*Hartford, Conn.*	39 V.
Wilford Wolfie Naman	*Waco, Texas*	442 FW.
Homer Chidsey Neal	*Southington, Conn.*	406 B.
Frank Hermon Nettleton	*New Haven, Conn.*	158 Blatchley av.
Henry Dutton Noble, Jr.	*Auburn, N. Y.*	61 V.
Francis Ely Norris	*Boonton, N. J.*	21 V.
Oliver Burnham North	*New Haven, Conn.*	54 V.
Haskell Noyes	*Milwaukee, Wisc.*	346 WH.
Robert Hale Noyes	*St. Paul, Minn.*	6 V.
Emmet O'Neal, B.A. Central College 1907	*Louisville, Ky.*	335 WH.
Philip Scudder Ordway	*Winchester, Mass.*	28 V.
Samuel Gilman Ordway	*St. Paul, Minn.*	16 V.
Arthur Dimon Osborne, 2d	*New Haven, Conn.*	55 V.

Patrick Brett O'Sullivan	*Derby, Conn.*	60 V.
Sidney Rollins Overall	*St.Louis, Mo.*	37 V.
George Albert Peirce	*Winterport, Me.*	429 FW.
Lester William Perrin	*New Haven, Conn.*	11 V.
John Punnett Peters, Jr.	*New York City*	3 V.
William Richmond Peters, Jr.	*New York City*	44 V.
Chester Arthur Phillips, B.A.	*Huntington, Ind.*	276 Elm st.
Central College 1904		
Duncan Clinch Phillips, Jr.	*Washington, D. C.*	. 349 WH.
James Laughlin Phillips	*Washington, D. C.*	349 WH.
Otto Carl Pickhardt	*New York City*	429 FW.
Philip Hale Pierson	*Wellesley Hills, Mass.*	97 W.
John Thomas Pigott, Jr.	*Helena, Mont.*	24 V.
Harold Sackett Pond	*Washington, Conn.*	1233 Chapel st.
Donald Wallace Porter	*New Haven, Conn.*	59 V.
Eliot Hale Porter	*New Britain, Conn.*	266 D.
Graham Cummings Porter	*Kyoto, Japan*	67 V.
Edwin Pugsley	*Buffalo, N. Y.*	334 WH.
William Lutkins Rae	*Jersey City, N. J.*	333 WH.
Ray John Reigeluth	*Carbondale, Pa.*	29 V.
Edward Hartman Reisner	*McConnellsburg, Pa.*	267 D.
Walter Richardson	*St.Paul, Minn.*	357 WH.
Harold Wade Riggs	*Hartford, Conn.*	57 V.
Henry Alsop Riley	*New York City*	371 WH.
Wright Haffards Robertson	*Fall River, Mass.*	50 V.
Robert William Rosenberg	*Springfield, Mass.*	87 C.
Gustave Jennings Rosenn	*Bridgeport, Conn.*	57 V.
Beekman Oliver Rouse	*Rochester, N. Y.*	2 V.
Schuyler Humphrey Rust	*New Brunswick, N. J.*	13 V.
John Harold Ryan	*Toledo, O.*	455 FW.
Arnold Schmidt	*So. Manchester, Conn.*	72 C.
William David Scholle	*New York City*	339 WH.
Robert Enos Scragg	*Scranton, Pa.*	333 WH.
Joseph Lionel Seligman	*New York City*	105 W.
George Alexander Seligmann	*New York City*	14 V.
Nathaniel Burton Sewell	*London, Ky.*	529 Elm st.
Charles Seymour	*New Haven, Conn.*	30 V.
Robert Alphonso Shackleton	*Riverhead, L. I., N Y.*	436 FW.
Archie McDaniels Sheldon	*Rutland, Vt.*	358 WH
Roger Bulkley Shepard	*St.Paul, Minn.*	34 V.
Harold Briggs Sherman	*Newtonville, Mass.*	15 V.
Roger Sherman	*Salt Lake City, Utah*	427 FW.
Joseph Byron Sieber	*Akron, O.*	1076 Chapel st.
Vinton D. Singer, B.A.	*Dayton, O.*	226 F.
Otterbein University 1907		

John Wyness Skinner	*Holyoke, Mass.*	1076 Chapel st.
Raymond Bates Small	*Hartwell, O.*	439 FW.
Charles McLean Smith	*Hartford, Conn.*	375 WH.
Richard Roy Smith	*Chicago, Ill.*	36 V.
Henry Burgess Snyder	*Piqua, O.*	67 V.
George Henry Soule, Jr.	*Stamford, Conn.*	23 V.
William Norwood Sparhawk	*West Swanzey, N. H.*	406 B.
Albert Tenney Spaulding	*Santa Barbara, Cal.*	427 FW.
Morry William Spitz	*Chicago, Ill.*	110 Wall st.
William Marshall Walter Splawn, B.A.	*Greenwood, Texas*	147 L.
Baylor University 1906		
Harold Stanley	*Great Barrington, Mass.*	35 V.
Maurice Stanley	*New Britain, Conn.*	266 D.
Henry Bascom Stapler	*Pelham Manor, N. Y.*	46 V.
Roswell Hiram Steele	*Brooklyn, N. Y.*	268 D.
James Hale Steinman	*Lancaster, Pa.*	355 WH.
Frederick Nelson Stevens	*Kendall, N. Y.*	75 C.
Donald Barton Stewart	*New York City*	19 V.
Ralph Fernhead Stoddard	*Belleville, N. J.*	434 FW.
Leonard Sullivan	*New York City*	61 V.
Samuel Swift	*New York City*	424 FW.
Edgar Wendell Tait	*Bradford, Pa.*	2 V.
Horace Van Sands Taylor	*Hartford, Conn.*	70 C.
Thomas Anthony Thacher	*New Haven, Conn.*	355 WH.
Gordon Chatfield Thayer	*Brooklyn, N. Y.*	337 WH.
Miles Gordon Thompson	*Lebanon, O.*	105 Park st.
James Carlton Thornton	*Bedford, Ind.*	343 WH.
Dennis Bascombe Tilson	*Grapevine, N. C.*	332 WH.
Vernon Victor Tilson	*Grapevine, N. C.*	332 WH.
Charles Augustus Tournier	*Auburn, N. Y.*	70 C.
George Henry Townsend, 2d	*New Haven, Conn.*	64 V.
James Mulford Townsend, Jr.	*New York City*	4 V.
Henry Carlisle Tuttle	*Naugatuck, Conn.*	52 V.
William Henry Twenhofel	*Kenton, Ky.*	122 Derby av.
Robert Bruner Umberger	*Wyoming, Pa.*	30 V.
Kennard Underwood	*Auburn, N. Y.*	352 WH.
Laurence Vail Updegraff	*Chicago, Ill.*	67 V.
William Stephen VanRensselaer	*New York City*	348 WH.
Paul Lansing Veeder, PH.B.	*Chicago, Ill.*	64 V.
Yale University 1907		
Elmer Chester Louis Wagner	*Waterbury, Conn.*	54 V.
Pike Powers Waldrop, B.A.	*Owenton, Ky.*	210 F.
Georgetown College 1907		
Thomas Joseph Walker	*St. Louis, Mo.*	338 WH.

William John Walker	*Albany, N. Y.*	41 V.
William Kay Wallace	*Florence, Colo.*	345 WH.
Clarke Washburne	*Chicago, Ill.*	47 V.
Joshua Boone Waterworth	*Brooklyn, N. Y.*	34 V.
Charles Law Watkins	*Scranton, Pa.*	12 V.
Henry Walter Webb	*New York City*	48 V.
Lewis Hill Weed	*Cleveland, O.*	370 WH.
William Stix Weiss	*New York City*	371 WH.
Kenneth Brakeley Welles	*Scranton, Pa.*	12 V.
Donald Breckenridge Wells	*Hartford, Conn.*	25 V.
Thomas Perry Wells	*Kingston, R. I.*	17 V.
Arthur Harold Weston	*Mount Vernon, Me.*	74 C.
Harvey S Whitacre	*Blanchester, O.*	105 Park st.
Rollin Thomas White	*Brattleboro, Vt.*	438 FW.
Arthur Murray Whitehill	*Newburgh, N. Y.*	332 WH.
Isadore David Whitestone	*Bradford, Pa.*	83 C.
Warren Ball Wilkes	*Buffalo, N. Y.*	435 FW.
James Willard Williams	*Glastonbury, Conn.*	30 V.
Ernest Lionel Wismer	*North Branford, Conn.*	412 B.
Eugene Clark Worman, B.A.	*Brookville, O.*	226 F.
Otterbein University 1907		
Arthur Wren	*Bridgeport, Conn.*	331 WH.
Herbert David Wright	*Cleveland, O.*	337 WH.
William Josiah Wright, B.S.	*Bear River, N. S.*	348 Crown st.
Acadia University 1907		
William Wilford Wynkoop	*Tacoma, Wash.*	43 V.
Howard Vernon Yergin	*Auburn, N. Y.*	436 FW.

SENIORS, 317

JUNIOR CLASS, 1909

Edward Paul Alker	*New York City*	377 WH.
Willis Lloyd Allen	*Shirley, Mass.*	414 B.
Charles Boothe Alling	*Montclair, N. J.*	269 D.
Clarence Hayden Allis	*Derby, Conn.*	133 W.
Herbert Burr Alvord	*Gloversville, N. Y.*	218 F.
Paul Shipman Andrews	*Syracuse, N. Y.*	238 D.
William McClure Andrews	*Youngstown, O.*	68 V.
Paul Thompson Arnold	*Ridgway, Pa.*	449 FW.
Frank August Assmann	*East Orange, N. J.*	381 WH.
Wheaton Augur	*Chicago, Ill.*	270 D.
William Rider Babcock	*Brookline, Mass.*	446 FW.
Earle Wilson Bachman	*Auburn, N. Y.*	94 W.
John Frederick Baker	*Willimantic, Conn.*	246 D.
John Kendrick Bangs, Jr.	*New York City*	243 D.
Robert Barlow	*Corry, Pa.*	469 FW.
Harold Erwin Barnes	*New Haven, Conn.* 26 Lynwood pl.
Harold Stanley Bates	*Mt. Vernon, N. Y.*	461 FW.
Edgar Farrar Bateson	*New York City*	238 D.
Claude Gillette Beardslee	*Windsor, Conn.*	247 D.
Charles Carrington Beeman	*Fairfield, Conn.*	250 D.
Henry Augustin Beers, Jr.	*New Haven, Conn.*	342 WH.
Frederick Wilder Bellamy	*Brooklyn, N. Y.*	103 W.
Herbert Hawthorne Benedict	*North Abington, Mass.*	79 C.
Paul Howie Benedict	*Utica, N. Y.*	445 FW.
David VerNooy Bennett	*Newburgh, N. Y.*	89 C.
Richard Herbert Bennett	*Fall River, Mass.*	449 FW.
Alfred Alexander Biddle	*Philadelphia, Pa.*	239 D.
John Kingsley Birge	*Bristol, Conn.*	464 FW.
Chauncey Buckley Blair	*Chicago, Ill.*	377 WH.
Francis Malbone Blodget	*East Greenwich, R. I.*	374 WH.
William Whiting Borden	*Chicago, Ill.*	380 WH.
Bennet Bronson	*Waterbury, Conn.*	383 B.
Harold Brooks	*Tenafly, N. J.*	268 D.
Harold Wilson Brooks	*New York City*	447 FW.
Carroll Teller Brown	*Denver, Colo.*	467 FW.
Harvey Hollister Bundy	*Grand Rapids, Mich.*	131 W.
Robert Boyd Burch	*Cincinnati, O.*	239 D.
Edgar Bartow Burgess	*Garden City, L. I., N. Y.*	116 W.
Samuel Parkes Burnam	*Richmond, Ky.*	398 B.
Edward Neufville Tailer Burnett	*New York City*	462 FW.
Rufus Bradford Burnham	*Norwich, Conn.*	116 W.
Raymond Marcy Burnham	*Hartford, Conn.*	124 W.
Francis Peabody Butler	*Chicago, Ill.*	262 D.

41

Gerald Morton Butler	*Evanston, Ill.*	173 L.
Charles Soutter Campbell	*Essex Fells, N. J.*	379 WH.
George Edward Cantine	*Albany, N. Y.*	387 B.
Charles Bronson Carpenter	*New York City*	404 B.
Sydney Buchanan Carragan	*Brooklyn, N. Y.*	106 W.
Eliot Avery Carter	*West Newton, Mass.*	253 D.
Frank Thompson Case	*Hartford, Conn.*	445 FW.
Gordon Case	*Peconic, N. Y.*	78 C.
Frank Andrew Cellar	*Sewickley, Pa.*	466 FW.
Neal Townley Childs	*New York City*	104 W.
Harold Edward Chittenden	*East River, Conn.*	448 FW.
Ponson Carles Chu	*Shanghai, China*	386 B.
Avery Artison Clark	*Middlebury, Conn.*	180 L.
Carolus Thomas Clark	*Westfield, N. J.*	445 FW.
DeWitt Scoville Clark, Jr.	*Salem, Mass.*	269 D.
Ralph Hodge Clark	*Derby, Conn.*	133 W.
Chauncey Haseltine Clarke	*Springfield, Mo.*	120 W.
Waldo Park Clement, Jr.	*New York City*	16 V.
Frederick Hull Cogswell, Jr.	*New Haven, Conn.*	79 C.
Harry Frederick Cole	*Newburyport, Mass.*	244 D.
Frank Burnett Condon	*Unionville, Conn.*	463 FW.
Aims Chamberlain Coney	*Orange, N. J.*	240 D.
Gilbert Maurice Congdon	*Providence, R. I.*	271 D.
Paul Howard McGregor Converse	*Rochester, N. Y.*	238 D.
Chester Jules Copmann	*Yokohama, Japan*	239 D.
Clay Crawford	*Fort Thomas, Ky.*	113 W.
Charles Canfield Cunningham, Jr.	*Washington, Ia.*	249 D.
Eugene Judson Curtis	*Clinton, Ia.*	272 D.
Trevor Arnold Cushman	*Winchester, Mass.*	373 WH.
Walter Dallas	*Waterbury, Conn.*	107 W.
Allen Sturges Davenport	*Yonkers, N. Y.*	395 B.
Douglas Treat Davidson	*Warren, Pa.*	466 FW.
Charles Hollister Davis	*Manchester, Conn.*	247 D.
Howard Carter Davis	*Elizabeth, N. J.*	341 WH.
Arthur Leete Davison	*Thompsonville, Conn.*	76 C.
Lyall Dean	*New York City*	460 FW.
Samuel Foree Dennis	*Louisville, Ky.*	108 W.
William Andrew DeWitt	*Wilton, Conn.*	336 WH.
Allen Robert Dodd	*Upper Montclair, N. J.*	127 W.
Gayer Gardner Dominick	*New York City*	447 FW.
William Minton Donnelly	*Detroit, Mich.*	242 D.
Malcolm Taylor Dougherty	*Brooklyn, N. Y.*	178 L.
Arthur Gotzian Driscoll	*St. Paul, Minn.*	374 WH.
Samuel Ellis Dunham	*Stamford, Conn.*	412 B.

Thomas Perkins Durell	*Somerville, Mass.*	414 B.
Jackson Annan Dykman	*Brooklyn, N. Y.*	235 D.
Thomas Collyer Eastman	*New York City*	241 D.
Elford Welles Eddy	*New Britain, Conn.*	264 D.
Harold Ransom Edwards	*Granby, Conn.*	255 D.
James Connelly Edwards, Jr.	*Russellville, Ky.*	107 W.
Douglas Fitch Guilford Eliot	*Irvington-on-Hudson, N. Y.*	132 W.
Stanley Egbert Ellis	*St. Albans, Vt.*	257 D.
James Murdock Ethridge, Jr.	*Rome, N. Y.*	468 FW.
John Conner Failing	*Portland, Oregon*	119 W.
Robert Fairbanks	*Indianapolis, Ind.*	130 W.
Albert Day Farwell	*Lake Forest, Ill.*	262 D.
Edward Spottiswoode Faust	*New York City*	49 V.
John Favill	*Chicago, Ill.*	173 L.
Daniel Higgins Fenton	*Holyoke, Mass.*	140 W.
Henry Theodore Fleitmann	*New York City*	432 FW.
Thomas Coolidge Fowler	*Glens Falls, N. Y.*	337 WH.
Arthur Olney Friel	*Manchester, N. H.*	259 D.
Peter Francis Fuchs	*Brooklyn, N. Y.*	452 FW.
Walter Emery Gard	*South Orange, N. J.*	353 WH.
Frederick Lamont Gates	*New York City*	340 WH.
Francis Dwight Gilbert	*Grand Rapids, Mich.*	462 FW.
Percy Macaulay Gilbert	*Brooklyn, N. Y.*	469 FW.
Bryant Burwell Glenny, Jr.	*Sheffield, Mass.*	131 W.
William Brown Glover	*Fairfield, Conn.*	388 B.
Leon Godchaux	*New Orleans, La.*	440 FW.
Charles Vanderveer Graham	*Brooklyn, N. Y.*	134 W.
Clarence Flack Graham	*Albany, N. Y.*	392 B.
Harvey Graham	*New York City*	242 D.
James Benton Grant, Jr.	*Denver, Colo.*	341 WH.
Laurence Wilcoxson Gregory	*Norwalk, Conn.*	441 FW.
Robert Noah Griswold	*Hartford, Conn.*	390 B.
William Cleveland Haley	*Brooklyn, N. Y.*	363 WH.
Francis Bacon Hamlin	*Washington, D. C.*	180 L.
Jesse McMillan Harding	*Omaha, Nebr.*	369 WH.
Ralph Volney Harlow	*Southbridge, Mass.*	450 FW.
Robert Otis Hayward	*Bronxville, N. Y.*	272 D.
Patrick Joseph Healey	*Waterbury, Conn.*	366 WH.
Birch Helms	*Pottsville, Pa.*	464 FW.
Horace Barnes Hewlett	*New Haven, Conn.*	451 FW.
Paul Hilsdale	*Sauk Center, Minn.*	437 FW.
Henry Booth Hitchcock	*Jamestown, N. Y.*	410 B.
Melville Espe Hitchcock	*Ansonia, Conn.*	527 P.
Bernhard Eliot Hoffman	*New Haven, Conn.*	107 Dixwell av.

George Lyon Hollett	*Chicago, Ill.*	109 W.
Stanley Westcott Holmes	*Saratoga Springs, N. Y.*	135 W.
Joseph Kilbourne Hooker	*Hartford, Conn.*	253 D.
Richard Schiller Hosford	*Moline, Ill.*	272 D.
Charles Wadsworth Howard	*Brooklyn, N. Y.*	241 D.
James Merrian Howard	*Montclair, N. J.*	254 D.
Henry Almy Howe	*So. Orange, N. J.*	468 FW.
Burrell Richardson Huff	*Greensburg, Pa.*	99 W
Harris Monroe Humason	*New Britain, Conn.*	264 D.
Wilson McClaughry Hume	*Ahmednagar, India*	178 L
Ralph Dresser Hunting	*Cedar Rapids, Ia.*	43 V.
John Aloysius Hurley, Jr.	*Bridgeport, Conn.*	244 D.
Jefferson Gotherford Ish, Jr.	*Little Rock, Ark.*	658 W. D.
Edward Francis Jefferson	*South Dennis, N. J.*	181 L.
Nelson Holland Jewett	*Buffalo, N. Y.*	395 B.
Allan Macfarlan Johnson	*Boston, Mass.*	115 W.
Elias Alfred Johnson	*Chicago, Ill.*	458 FW.
Frank Leonard Johnson	*Norwich, Conn*	136 W.
Robert Coit Johnson	*Norwich, Conn.*	372 WH.
Charles Chesebrough Jones	*New Hartford, Conn.*	95 W.
Frank Edward Jones	*Unionville, Conn.*	413 B.
Joseph Paul Kaufman	*Norwich, Conn.*	419 B.
Samuel Jerman Keator, Jr.	*Rock Island, Ill.*	254 D.
Hudson Kelley	*Chicago, Ill.*	256 D.
Courtland Kelsey	*East Orange, N. J.*	240 D.
Stephen Tomlinson Kelsey	*East Orange, N. J.*	236 D.
Leonard Kennedy	*Brooklyn, N. Y.*	260 D.
Alexander Comstock Kirk	*Chicago, Ill.*	241 Lawrence st.
Allan Farrand Kitchel	*East Liverpool, O.*	100 W.
Allen Trafford Klots	*Huntington, N. Y.*	108 W.
Roland Werner Klupfel	*New York City*	114 W.
Daniel Lathrop Lawton	*New York City*	96 W.
Dickson Hammond Leavens	*Norwich, Conn.*	446 FW.
Hugh Ledyard	*Detroit, Mich.*	55 V.
Robert Stell Lemmon	*Englewood, N. J.*	394 B.
Robert Louis Levy	*New York City*	174 L.
Nestor Searle Light	*So. Coventry, Conn.*	403 B.
Franklin Drake Lightner	*St.Paul, Minn.*	129 W.
Milton Charles Lightner	*St.Paul, Minn.*	132 W.
Henry Lippitt	*Providence, R. I.*	271 D.
Henry Hopkins Livingston	*Catskill Station, N. Y.*	174 L.
Alfred Lee Loomis	*New York City*	430 FW.
Francis Percy Loveland	*Denver, Colo.*	423 FW.
Grant Street Macartney	*St.Paul, Minn.*	460 FW.

James Lukens McConaughy	*Mount Hermon, Mass.*	257 D.
Hubert McDonnell	*New York City*	457 FW.
Benjamin Harrison McKee	*New York City*	430 FW.
Wilber McKee	*Lakeville, Conn.*	120 W.
Arthur Perkins McWilliams	*Norwich, Conn.*	136 W.
Robert Mallory, Jr.	*Brooklyn, N. Y.*	262 D.
Irvin Edward Margulies	*Brooklyn, N. Y.*	421 B.
Simon Seelig Marks	*Meridian, Miss.*	122 W.
Frederic Ogden Mason	*Chicago, Ill.*	135 W.
Harry Meixell, Jr.	*Reading, Pa.*	454 FW.
Rufus Monroe Meroney	*Chicago, Ill.*	28 Gill st.
Clinton Merrick	*Evanston, Ill.*	181 L.
Harold Talmadge Messenger	*Winsted, Conn.*	94 W.
Jeremiah Milbank, 2d	*New York City*	391 B.
Clark Goodell Mitchell	*Denver, Colo.*	263 D.
Edgar James Moch	*Cincinnati, O.*	110 W.
Frederick Augustus Morrell, Jr.	*Putnam, Conn.*	389 B.
Edward Kendall Morse	*Carbondale, Pa.*	372 WH.
Robert Moses	*New York City*	246 D.
Arthur Parsons Mullins	*Salem, O.*	456 FW.
Karl Eugene Murchey	*Detroit, Mich.*	259 D.
Francis Wisner Murray, Jr.	*New York City*	102 W.
Leroy Russell Myers	*Auburn, N. Y.*	224 F.
Sherman Brown Neff	*Ridgeway, Mo.*	100 Howe st.
Edward McDonell O'Brien	*Plattsburgh, N. Y.*	408 B.
Charles Milton Olcott	*Montclair, N. J.*	369 WH.
Henry Noyes Otis	*Andover, Mass.*	393 B.
Lawrence Benjamin Pagter	*New Haven, Conn.*	50 Admiral st.
Allan Douglas Parker	*Lowell, Mass.*	260 D.
Leonard Bacon Parks	*Cleveland, O.*	373 WH.
Maxwell Oswald Parry	*Indianapolis, Ind.*	242 D.
Judson Aspinwall Parsons	*Troy, Pa.*	256 D.
Herbert Payne	*Menlo Park, Cal.*	235 D.
Clarence Appleton Peirce	*Methuen, Mass.*	463 FW.
Reginald Carman MacKnight Peirce	*Montclair, N. J.*	103 W.
John Bates Perrin	*Indianapolis, Ind.*	261 D.
Norman Francis Peters	*Newside, Pa.*	454 FW.
Sidney Marcellus Phelan, Jr.	*St. Louis, Mo.*	129 W.
Theodore Pomeroy	*Chicago, Ill.*	263 D.
Morgan Porter	*Pittsburg, Pa.*	459 FW.
Lawrence Tyler Post	*St. Louis, Mo.*	123 W.
Edward Otis Proctor	*Wakefield, Mass.*	257 D.
Stuart Craig Rand	*Newton Center, Mass.*	124 W.
Charles Henry Raymond, 2d	*Morristown, N. J.*	243 D.

Franklyn Thomas Raymond	*New York City*	432 FW.
Henry Lewis Read	*Brooklyn, N. Y.*	248 D.
Paul Whedon Redfield	*Madison, Conn.*	448 FW.
Gomer Henry Rees	*Paris, Texas*	433 FW.
Donald Louis Reynolds	*Toledo, O.*	378 WH.
Harold Cady Reynolds	*Danbury, Conn.*	390 B.
Cleaveland Jocelyn Rice	*New Haven, Conn.* 410 Winthrop av.
Welles Kennon Rice	*New York City*	456 FW.
Henry Brush Richardson	*Derby, Conn.*	218 F.
Elisha Francis Riggs, Jr.	*Washington, D. C.*	99 W.
William Payne Roberts	*Brooklyn, N. Y.*	178 L.
Paul Goodwin Robison	*Curwensville, Pa.*	27 V.
Robert Selden Rose	*Geneva, N. Y.*	239 D.
Arthur Ward Ruff	*Schenectady, N. Y.*	420 B.
Stephen Willis Ryder	*New York City*	450 FW.
Benjamin Bethen Sanderson	*Portland, Me.*	469 FW.
Peter Benjamin Sarason	*New Haven, Conn.*	48 Broad st.
Theodore Schulze	*St.Paul, Minn.*	376 WH.
Raymond Joseph Schweizer	*New York City*	270 D.
Edwin Lewis Scofield, Jr.	*Stamford, Conn.*	119 W.
Frank Jay Scribner	*Wallingford, Vt.*	127 W.
Mortimer Ashmead Seabury	*Wellesley Hills, Mass.*	271 D.
Arthur Warren Selleck	*White Plains, N. Y.*	80 C.
Charles Eugene Selover, Jr.	*Auburn, N. Y.*	179 L.
Daniel Seltzer	*Denver, Colo.*	450 FW.
William Sharp	*Cranford, N. J.*	470 FW.
Arthur MacCartney Shepard	*Nome, Alaska*	401 B.
Stanley Stokes Shepard	*Syracuse, N. Y.*	249 D.
Eustace Morrow Sheppard	*Pittsburg, Pa.*	118 W.
Charles Delanzon Simmons	*Norwalk, O.*	397 B.
Howard Benjamin Slider	*Loag, Pa.*	451 FW.
Walter Pearson Smart	*Allegheny, Pa.*	449 FW.
Ralph Smillie	*New York City*	383 B.
Huntington Smith, Jr.	*St.Louis, Mo.*	440 FW.
Herbert Mason Southworth	*Wakefield, Mass.*	106 W.
Joel Andrew Sperry, 2d	*New Haven, Conn.*	438 FW.
Roland Adelbert Spitzer	*Toledo, O.*	378, WH.
William Spoerle	*Brooklyn, N. Y.*	137 W.
Alfred Springer, Jr.	*Norwood, O.*	459 FW.
John Minor Stetson	*New Haven, Conn.* 76 Mansfield st.
Sanford Delwin Stockton, Jr.	*Poughkeepsie, N. Y.*	381 WH.
Harold Phelps Stokes	*New York City*	237 D.
Horace Winston Stokes	*New York City*	132 W.
Morton Charnleigh Stone	*New Haven, Conn.*	250 D.

Howard Sturges	*Providence, R. I.*	350 WH.
Boetius Henry Sullivan	*Chicago, Ill.*	467 FW.
James Platt Sweeney	*Naugatuck, Conn.*	441 FW.
Raymond Fuller Swett	*Medina, N. Y.*	138 W.
William Howard Taft	*New York City*	239 D.
Nelson Case Taintor	*Hartford, Conn.*	252 D.
Harrison Wood Talcott	*South Bend, Ind.*	375 WH.
Robert James Tearse	*Winona, Minn.*	465 FW.
Mortimer Clark Terrill	*Ansonia, Conn.*	94 W.
Raymond Thatcher	*Pueblo, Colo.*	467 FW.
Carl Hammond Thurston	*Worcester, Mass.*	446 FW.
Francis Berger Trudeau	*Saranac Lake, N. Y.*	237 D.
Ye-tsung Tsur	*Shanghai, China*	651 Yale P. O.
John Screven Turnbull	*New York City*	A.
Moore Caldwell Tussey	*Salina, Pa.*	27 V.
Walker Moore VanRiper	*St. Louis, Mo.*	470 FW.
Charles Edmund VanVleck, Jr.	*Montclair, N. J.*	376 WH.
Malcolm Burt Vilas	*Cleveland, O.*	380 WH.
Charles Carter Walbridge	*Philadelphia, Pa.*	457 FW.
Melvin Harvey Walker, Jr.	*Westboro, Mass.*	104 W.
Raymond Lowrey Walkley	*Southington, Conn.*	396 B.
Floyd Wallace	*Wallingford, Conn.*	179 L.
Chester Alan Wardwell	*Haverhill, Mass.*	123 W.
Joseph Bradford Wardwell	*Stamford, Conn.*	100 W.
Aubrey Richardson Watzek	*Davenport, Ia.*	463 FW.
Hicks Arnold Weatherbee	*New York City*	117 W.
William Seward Webb, Jr.	*Shelburne Farms, Vt.*	31 V.
Morton Weeks	*Brookline, Mass.*	115 W.
William Corcoran Welling	*Hartford, Conn.*	458 FW.
John Benjamin Westcott	*Wauregan, Conn.*	390 B.
Edwin Adolph Wetzlar	*New York City*	424 FW.
Thorne Lake Wheeler	*Chatham, N. Y.*	259 D.
Inness Whitaker	*New York City*	141 W.
Edward Luther White	*Waterbury, Conn.*	175 L.
Norman Ogden Whitehouse	*Newport, R. I.*	31 V.
Robert Stevens Whitlock	*Naugatuck, Conn.*	441 FW.
Henry Clarence Wick, Jr.	*Cleveland, O.*	339 WH.
Dudley Willcox	*Lawrenceville, N. J.*	1 V.
Jacob Farrand Williams	*Detroit, Mich.*	353 WH.
Rowland Gregory Wright	*Hancock, Mich.*	465 FW.
George Glendining Wyant	*Stamford, Conn.*	444 FW.
Perry Swearingen Young	*Abilene, Texas*	141 W.

JUNIORS, 305

SOPHOMORE CLASS, 1910

Roy Montgomery Andrew	*East Arlington, Vt.*	379 Crown st.
Donald Annis	*Detroit, Mich.*	8 College st.
Charles Dudley Armstrong	*Pittsburg, Pa.*	8 College st.
Louis Girard Audette	*Jamestown, N. Y.*	379 WH.
Roswell Mears Austin	*Highgate Center, Vt.*	164 L.
Andrew Meech Avery	*Norwich, Conn.*	136 W.
Henry Gerhardt Baars, Jr.	*Pensacola, Fla.*	251 Crown st.
Leonard Bacon	*Peacedale, R. I.*	342 WH.
Frank Trowbridge Bailey	*Montclair, N. J.*	111 W.
George Ezra Bailey	*Ottawa, O.*	122 Dwight st.
Paul Duane Bailey	*Middletown, Conn.*	215 F.
Arthur Edward Baker	*Bridgeport, Conn.*	250 Crown st.
Herbert Howard Baker	*Toledo, O.*	22 College st.
Howard Clifton Baker	*Providence, R. I.*	260 Crown st.
John Edwin Barber	*Toledo, O.*	18 College st.
Lawrence Luther Barber	*Danielson, Conn.*	170 L.
Edward Shippen Barnes	*New York City*	143 L.
Fuller Forbes Barnes	*Bristol, Conn.*	225 Crown st.
Thomas Sloane Barnes	*New York City*	22 College st.
Walter Barnum	*Mamaroneck, N. Y.*	22 College st.
Stanhope Bayne-Jones	*New Orleans, La.*	260 Crown st.
Harold Weymouth Bean	*Framingham, Mass.*	254 Crown st.
Morris Harry Behrman	*Worcester, Mass.*	221 F.
Walter Beincke	*Oscawana-on-Hudson, N. Y.*	22 College st.
David Bellamy	*New York City*	260 Crown st.
Hildreth Benner	*Tarrytown, N. Y.*	22 College st.
Charles Raymond Bentley	*Rochester, N. Y.*	236 Crown st.
Percy Wells Bidwell	*So. Manchester, Conn.*	170 L.
Leonard Cutter Bigelow	*Framingham, Mass.*	254 Crown st.
Henry Payne Bingham	*Cleveland, O.*	8 College st.
Gould Shelton Bissell	*Shelton, Conn.*	128 W.
Joseph Bloom Blackburn	*Pittsburg, Pa.*	8 College st.
George Bleistein, Jr.	*Buffalo, N. Y.*	22 College st.
Byron George Bliss	*Warrensburg, Mo.*	8 College st.
John deKoven Bowen	*Chicago, Ill.*	22 College st.
Thomas Wilson Bowers	*Chicago, Ill.*	8 College st.
Frank Silver Brainard	*New York City*	22 College st.
Harold Brewster Bretz	*Brooklyn, N. Y.*	214 Crown st.
John Northmore Brigham	*Glencoe, Ill.*	11 College st.
Theodore Henry Brown	*Darien, Conn.*	159 L.
George Lamb Buist, Jr.	*Charleston, S. C.*	160 L.

Howard Cordis Carter	*Norfolk, Conn.*	166 L.
George Wells Chency	*So. Manchester,Conn.*	260 Crown st.
Douglas Chisholm	*Cleveland, O.*	437 FW.
Yii Ying Chu	*Tientsin, China*	114 High st.
Martin Lee Clark	*Buffalo, N. Y.*	225 Crown st.
Stephen Merrell Clement, Jr.	*Buffalo, N. Y.*	22 College st.
Robert Coyne Clifford	*St. Louis, Mo.*	270 Crown st.
Henry Clarence Cloud	*Winnebago, Nebr.*	169 L.
Kent Sarver Clow	*Chicago, Ill.*	22 College st.
Arthur Pierce Coates	*Upper Montclair, N. J.*	11 College st.
Clayton Tilton Cochran	*Bridgeport, Conn.*	236 Crown st.
Samuel Michael Cohen	*Hartford, Conn.*	161 L.
Brevard Mays Connor	*Dallas, Texas*	260 Crown st.
Carroll Trowbridge Cooney	*Brooklyn, N. Y.*	22 College st.
Edward Boies Cowles	*Rye, N. Y.*	22 College st.
Edward Harris Coy	*New Haven, Conn.*	22 College st.
Reuben Bernard Crispell	*Kingston, N. Y.*	236 Crown st.
Edward Ely Curtis	*New Haven, Conn.*	663 W. D.
Rosewell Mansing Curtis	*Lenox, Mass.*	166 L.
David Lewis Daggett	*New Haven, Conn.*	22 College st.
Frank Damrosch, Jr.	*New York City*	250 Crown st.
Edward John Davin	*New York City*	155 L.
Warren Gilbert Davis	*Worcester, Mass.*	254 Crown st.
Wilbur Fisk Davis	*Meriden, Conn.*	184 F.
Thompson Dean	*Katonah, N. Y.*	8 College st.
Kilbourn Smith Dennis	*Louisville, Ky.*	8 College st.
Albert DeSilver	*Brooklyn, N. Y.*	22 College st.
Julian French Devereux	*Cleveland, O.*	457 FW.
Donald Ryder Dickey	*Dubuque, Ia.*	8 College st.
Warren Wallace Diehl	*Springfield, O.*	236 Crown st.
Walter Herman Dietz	*Holyoke, Mass.*	140 W.
Sidney Philip Dine	*Cincinnati, O.*	43 College st.
Geoffrey Dodge	*New York City*	98 W.
Frederick Morris Drew, Jr.	*Ansonia, Conn.*	167 L.
Louis Goethe Dreyfus, Jr.	*Santa Barbara, Cal.*	407 B.
Arthur Howard Drisko	*Roxbury, Mass.*	236 Crown st.
William Young Duncan	*Jersey City, N. J.*	169 L.
Howard Alfred Dye	*Gloversville, N. Y.*	646 E. D.
David Jay Ely	*New York City*	8 College st.
Charles Leverett English	*New Haven, Conn.*	142 L.
Albert Jeffreys Evans	*Pittsburg, Pa.*	1062 Yale P. O.
John Meiggs Ewen, Jr.	*Chicago, Ill.*	22 College st.
Wilson Lear Eyre	*New Rochelle, N. Y.*	8 College st.
Samuel Henry Fancher, Jr.	*Walton, N. Y.*	251 Crown st.

Russell Sargent Fenn	*New Haven, Conn.*	22 College st.
Arthur Robertson Fergusson	*Manila, P. I.*	250 Crown st.
Gilbert Bishop Ferris	*Westchester, N. Y.*	8 College st.
George Baldwin Field	*Newton Center, Mass.*	260 Crown st.
William Kountz Fitch	*Rockford, Ill.*	8 College st.
James Harold Flye	*Winter Park, Fla.*	212 F.
Collin Ford	*Toledo, O.*	1151 Chapel st.
John Willard Ford	*Youngstown, O.*	260 Crown st.
Edwin Louis Fouts	*Stamford, Conn.*	8 College st.
Denton Fowler, 3d	*Haverstraw, N. Y.*	272 D.
Charles Pascal Franchot	*Olean, N. Y.*	8 College st.
Robert Dudley French	*New Haven, Conn.*	225 Bishop st.
George Gregg Fuller	*Rochester, N. Y.*	8 College st.
Albert Sydney Gaffney	*West Newton, Pa.*	49 Goffe st.
Perrin Comstock Galpin	*New Haven, Conn.*	236 Crown st.
Stanley Lincoln Gedney, Jr.	*Maplewood, N. J.*	231 F.
Nathan Henry Gellert	*Colchester, Conn.*	1193 Chapel st.
Nathan Flower George	*Danbury, Conn.*	8 College st.
Arthur Benson Gilbert	*Mt. Kisco, N. Y.*	713 W. D.
Charles Mark Gill	*St.Louis, Mo.*	45.Park st.
Charles Carroll Glover, Jr.	*Washington, D. C.*	22 College st.
Charles Allen Goddard	*Salisbury, Conn.*	165 L.
William Arthur Goebel	*Phœnix, Ariz.*	254 Crown st.
Gerald Blenkiron Gould	*New York City*	236 Crown st.
Havens Grant	*Jamestown, N. Y.*	8 College st.
Tappan Gregory	*Chicago, Ill.*	22 College st.
Millen Griffith	*Ross, Cal.*	22 College st.
Milton Wright Griggs	*St.Paul, Minn.*	8 College st.
Lyle Gillis Hall	*Ridgeway, Pa.*	8 College st.
Rufus Bartlett Hall, Jr.	*Cincinnati, O.*	250 Crown st.
Charles Glover Hammond	*New Haven, Conn.*	347 Orchard st.
Miles Carrington Hannah	*Lake Forest, Ill.*	102 W.
George Leslie Harrison	*Fort Monroe, Va.*	22 College st.
Albert McClellan Haskell	*Wakefield, Nebr.*	22 College st.
Richard Kingsley Hawes	*Fall River, Mass.*	22 College st.
Wellington Burt Hay	*London, England*	22 College st.
Michael Conran Hayes	*Waterbury, Conn.*	57 Lake pl.
Roger Russ Hayes	*Buffalo, N. Y.*	254 Crown st.
Robert Young Hayne	*San Mateo, Cal.*	254 Crown st.
Walter Frank Hayward, Jr.	*Brooklyn, N. Y.*	159 L.
James Drayton Heard	*Pittsburg, Pa.*	22 College st.
Morgan Hebard	*Philadelphia, Pa.*	22 College st.
Henry Glen Heedy	*Youngstown, O.*	22 College st.
John Heron	*Pittsburg, Pa.*	8 College st.

Thomas Hewes	*Hartford, Conn.*	22 College st.
Arthur Sturgess Hildebrand	*Hartford, Conn.*	260 Crown st.
Richard Dwight Hillis	*Brooklyn, N. Y.*	22 College st.
Edward BenJamin Hinckley	*Hinckley, Me.*	152 Temple st.
Lyman Northrop Hine	*New York City*	22 College st.
Lin Ho	*Foochow, Fookien, China*	66 Whalley av.
Chalmers Holbrook	*New York City*	165 L.
Howard Keys Hollister	*Cincinnati, O.*	8 College st.
Henry Gilbert Holt	*Grand Rapids, Mich.*	22 College st.
Thomas Carrington Hood⁻	*Chester, Conn.*	255 D.
Sherman Abbey Hooker	*Fredonia, N. Y.*	251 Crown st.
Stephen VanCulen Hopkins	*Brooklyn, N. Y.*	·214 Crown st.
Fred Augustus Hotchkiss	*Millerton, N. Y.*	8 College st.
Harold Jacob Hotton	*Franklinville, N. Y.*	156 L.
Elton Hoyt, 2d	*Cleveland, O.*	22 College st.
Eugene Hall Humphrey	*Winchester, Conn.*	713 W. D.
Lewis Orrin Hutchinson	*Bristol, Conn.*	646 W. D.
George Gordon Hyde	*New York City*	154 L.
Edward Ingraham	*Bristol, Conn.*	225 Crown st.
Charles Frederic Jefferson	*New York City*	158 L.
Francis Bates Jennings	*Brooklyn, N. Y.*	163 L.
Richard Jente	*New Haven, Conn.*	86 Henry st.
Oliver Seymour Jewell	*New Hartford, Conn.*	95 W.
Carlton Clarke Jewett	*Buffalo, N. Y.*	22 College st.
James Ford Johnson, Jr.	*Dobbs Ferry, N. Y.*	22 College st.
Elliot Penrose Jones	*West Chester, Pa.*	230 F.
Frank Williams Jones, Jr.	*New Hartford, Conn.*	236 Crown st.
Stephen Edwards Keeler, Jr.	*New Canaan, Conn.*	159 L.
Elmer Davenport Keith	*Brooklyn, N. Y.*	207 F.
William Abraham Kincaid, Jr.	*Galveston, Texas*	405 B.
Arthur Godwyn King	*Norfolk, Va.*	8 College st.
Lyndon Marrs King	*Minneapolis, Minn.*	22 College st.
Robert Burr King	*Hartford, Conn.*	228 Crown st.
Max David Kirjassoff	*Waterbury, Conn.*	724 W. D.
George Dimmick Kittredge	*Fishkill-on-Hudson, N. Y.*	369 WH.
Augustus Knight	*Evanston, Ill.*	22 College st.
Harry Jacob Kugel	*New Haven, Conn.*	33 Oak st.
Frederick Clinton Lake, Jr.	*St.Louis, Mo.*	260 Crown st.
Judson Stuart Landon	*Schenectady, N. Y.*	148 L.
John Joseph Lane	*Brooklyn, N. Y.*	359 WH.
Earl Langstroth	*Glen Ridge, N. J.*	254 D.
Dana Turley Leavenworth	*Hotchkissville, Conn.*	156 L.
Louis Heitler Lehman	*Pueblo, Colo.*	206 F.
Frank Coe Lewis	*New Britain, Conn.*	8 College st.

BenJamin Lionel Liberman	*St. Joseph, Mo.*	35 High st.
Walter Seth Logan, Jr.	*Washington, Conn.*	22 College st.
Carl Albert Lohmann	*Akron, O.*	22 College st.
James Taber Loree	*New York City*	175 L.
George Hale Lowe, Jr.	*Wellesley, Mass.*	8 College st.
Yin Chu Ma	*Shanshiang, Chehkiang, China*	66 Whalley av.
Richard Holloway Mabbatt, Jr.	*Chicago, Ill.*	8 College st.
Earl Clarence MacArthur	*McCollum, N. Y.*	167 L.
Ralph Richard Macartney	*St. Paul, Minn.*	22 College st.
Sydney Clement McCall	*New York City*	98 W.
John Joseph MacCarthy	*North Brookfield, Mass.*	93 C.
Henry Darius McCord	*New York City*	254 Crown st.
Nelson Whitaker McCormick	*Cleveland, O.*	260 Crown st.
Charles Ramsey McCulloch	*Gloversville, N. Y.*	247 D.
Roy Leighton McFarland	*St. Joseph, Mo.*	122 Dwight st.
John T. McGraw	*Grafton, W. Va.*	254 Crown st.
Charles Patrick McKiernan	*Union City, Conn.*	385 B.
William MacLane	*New Haven, Conn.*	33 Howe st.
Donald Bentley McLaury	*Chicago, Ill.*	251 Crown st.
John Harper Mallory	*Pittsburg, Pa.*	261 D.
John Joseph Mann	*Buffalo, N. Y.*	22 College st.
Thomas Linder Marshall	*Charlestown, Ill.*	160 L.
Thomas Means	*New Haven, Conn.*	356 Humphrey st.
Edgar Menderson	*Cincinnati, O.*	254 Crown st.
Buckingham Parsons Merriman	*Waterbury, Conn.*	22 College st.
Paul Gurley Merrow	*Hartford, Conn.*	236 D.
John Trumbull Metcalf	*New Haven, Conn.*	119 College st.
Buckingham Miller	*Newton Highlands, Mass.*	225 F.
Meade Minnigerode	*Paris, France*	260 Crown st.
Louis David Minsk	*Colchester, Conn.*	1193 Chapel st.
Erwin Albert Morse	*New York City*	22 College st.
Oliver Cromwell Morse, Jr.	*New York City*	170 L.
Daniel Mungall, Jr.	*South Hadley Falls, Mass.*	221 F.
Frederick James Murphy	*Westboro, Mass.*	164 L.
Arthur Murray, Jr.	*Auburn, N. Y.*	169 L.
Daniel Herman Myers	*Albany, N. Y.*	236 Crown st.
Ralph Emerson Myers	*Buskirk Bridge, N. Y.*	707 W. D.
Arthur Theodore Nabstedt	*Davenport, Ia.*	214 Crown st.
Frank Thayer Nelson	*Detroit, Mich.*	22 College st.
Lawrence Harper Norton	*Cleveland, O.*	18 College st.
Garnett Morgan Noyes	*Warren, Pa.*	8 College st.
George Otto Oberhelman	*Norwood, O.*	229 F.
Harold Obernauer	*Pittsburg, Pa.*	249 Crown st.

Howard Vincent O'Brien	*Chicago, Ill.*	214 Crown st.
Walter Thomas O'Donohue	*Hartford, Conn.*	Hartford
Francis Howard Olmsted	*Lakeville, Conn.*	241 D.
Francis Ward Paine	*Boston, Mass.*	236 Crown st.
George Fish Parsons, Jr.	*New York City*	22 College st.
William Henry Parsons, Jr.	*New York City*	22 College st.
Ward Edgerly Pearson	*Great Barrington, Mass.*	461 FW.
J. Lanphear Penoyar	*Bay City, Mich.*	
Julius Christian Peter	*Seymour, Ind.*	254 Crown st.
Richardson Phelps	*Minneapolis, Minn.*	11 College st.
Stephen Holladay Philbin	*New York City*	8 College st.
Ralph Harlan Pierce	*Brockton, Mass.*	172 L.
Joseph Curtis Platt	*Scranton, Pa.*	22 College st.
Henry Kerr Plumb	*Brooklyn, N. Y.*	142 L.
George Stewart Pomeroy, Jr.	*Wernersville, Pa.*	251 Crown st.
John Gooden Poore	*Willow Grove, Del.*	61 Wolcott st.
Marsh Klock Powers	*Cleveland, O.*	214 Crown st.
Warren Cone Pratt	*Hartford, Conn.*	444 FW.
Charles Baird Price	*Louisville, Ky.*	8 College st.
Lawrence Avery Rankin	*Peekskill, N. Y.*	22 College st.
Randolph Raynolds	*New Haven, Conn.*	139 W.
William Howard Read	*Brooklyn, N. Y.*	248 D.
Harold Bishop Reid	*Walden, N. Y.*	163 L.
Graham Llewellyn Reynolds	*Pasadena, Cal.*	236 Crown st.
George Adams Richardson	*Auburn, N. Y.*	22 College st.
Truman Post Riddle	*St. Louis, Mo.*	18 College st.
Thomas Lawrason Riggs	*Washington, D. C.*	8 College st.
Edward Constant Roberts	*Hartford, Conn.*	22 College st.
Joseph Stone Roberts	*Salem, Mass.*	22 College st.
Philip Roberts	*Hartford, Conn.*	22 College st.
Arthur Frederic Robinson	*Norwich, Conn.*	91 C.
William Silliman Rogers	*Buffalo, N. Y.*	22 College st.
Reginald Roome	*New York City*	22 College st.
Frank Guiles Roth	*Harrisburg, Pa.*	156 L.
Guy Meredith Russell	*New Haven, Conn.*	162 L.
George Henry Sanderson	*Moosup, Conn.*	171 L.
Frank Dyckman Scudder	*New York City*	167 L.
Clarence Eugene Secor, Jr.	*Yonkers, N. Y.*	128 W.
Arthur Sewall	*Bath, Me.*	22 College st.
George Herman Seybold	*Mansfield, O.*	224 F.
Edward Palmer Seymour	*Highland Park, Ill.*	260 Crown st.
Victor Sobel Shear	*Warren, Pa.*	228 Crown st.
Roger Sherman	*Rye, N. Y.*	22 College st.

William Hawthorne Shields, Jr.	*Norwich, Conn.*	90 C.
Michael Nathaniel Slotnick	*Holyoke, Mass.*	161 L.
David Parker Smith	*Meriden, Conn.*	223 F.
Douglas Tracy Smith	*Hartford, Conn.*	214 Crown st.
Emery Holland Smith	*New York City*	398 B.
Gilbert Max Smith	*Evanston, Ill.*	22 College st.
Henry Montague Smith, Jr.	*Morristown, N. J.*	236 Crown st.
Edward Douglas Snyder	*Rockford, Ill.*	158 L.
James Brookes Spencer	*St. Louis, Mo.*	22 College st.
Charles Messinger Steele	*Brooklyn, N. Y.*	22 College st.
Scott Sterling	*Lawrence, Kans.*	171 L.
Robert Bernhard Stern	*Irvington-on-Hudson, N. Y.*	228 Crown st.
Neil Campbell Stevens	*Morristown, N. J.*	251 Crown st.
Philip Moen Stimson	*New York City*	22 College st.
William Stricker, Jr.	*Brooklyn, N. Y.*	47 Lake pl.
John Martin Sweeney, Jr.	*Naugatuck, Conn.*	77 C.
Robert Alphonso Taft	*Washington, D. C.*	8 College st.
Hsüan Tang	*Tientsin, China*	142 Dwight st.
Waldo Elliot Tillinghast	*Vernon, Conn.*	203 F.
Alexander Berthold Timm	*New Haven, Conn.*	106 York sq.
John Campbell Townsend	*New York City*	22 College st.
Thomas Rufus Tracy	*Whitney Pt., N. Y.*	183 L.
William Allen Underhill	*Bath, N. Y.*	236 Crown st.
Ralph Palmer Uptegrove	*Brooklyn, N. Y.*	8 College st.
John Edwin Urquhart, Jr.	*Ashfield, Mass.*	260 Crown st.
Arthur VanBrunt	*New York City*	154 L.
Adrian VanSinderen	*Brooklyn, N. Y.*	8 College st.
Frederick Glade Wacker	*Chicago, Ill.*	22 College st.
Ernest Ross Warren	*Killingly, Conn.*	172 L.
Harvey Tracy Warren	*Bridgeport, Conn.*	11 College st.
Edwin Morey Waterbury	*Corning, N. Y.*	162 L.
Francis Melzar Watrous	*New Haven, Conn.*	252 D.
Henry Crouch Webb	*Dover, Del.*	249 Crown st.
William Bakewell Wharton	*Pittsburg, Pa.*	251 Crown st.
Ralph Dean Whipple	*Bridgeport, Conn.*	Bridgeport
Francis Joseph Whitcomb	*Bridgeport, Conn.*	249 Crown st.
Edwin A. Whitman	*Moravia, N. Y.*	151 L.
James Moro Whittaker	*Cincinnati, O.*	398 B.
Howard DeForest Widger	*Cortland, N. Y.*	151 L.
Arthur Williams, Jr.	*Mt. Vernon, N. Y.*	250 Crown st.
Earl Trumbull Williams	*Brooklyn, N. Y.*	22 College st.
Wayland Wells Williams	*New Haven, Conn.*	22 College st.
George Charles Wilson	*Delhi, N. Y.*	151 L.

Ruthven Adriance Wodell	*Poughkeepsie, N. Y.*	22 College st.
William Herbert Wood	*Syracuse, N. Y.*	214 Crown st.
Harold Perrine Woodford	*New York City*	22 College st.
Edward Farrand Wright	*Detroit, Mich.*	22 College st.
Chung Lui Yao	*Tientsin, China*	142 Dwight st.
Sheldon Smith Yates	*Brooklyn, N. Y.*	8 College st.
Tsu En Yin	*Soochow, China*	66 Whalley av.
Louis Bradstreet Zacher	*Branford, Conn.*	155 L.
Ralph Snyder Zimmerman	*Somerset, Pa.*	148 L.

SOPHOMORES, 311

FRESHMAN CLASS, 1911

Cary Abbott	*Cheyenne, Wyo.*	250 York st.
Harold Duncan Aikman	*Terre Haute, Ind.*	545 P.
John Alden	*Rochester, N. Y.*	1076 Chapel st.
Francis Olcott Allen	*Milwaukee, Wisc.*	242 York st.
Philip Thompson Allen	*Montrose, Pa.*	163 York st.
Robert Bruce Anderson	*Salem, O.*	200 York st.
Howard Daniel Atkins	*Denver, Colo.*	364 WH.
Thomas Joseph Aubrey	*Norwich, Conn.*	53 Prospect st.
Frederick Rowe Avery	*Westbrook, Conn.*	217 York st.
Benjamin Selden Bacon	*New Haven, Conn.*	576 P.,
Paul Bradford Badger	*Winchester, Mass.*	200 York st.
Hamill Wood Baker	*Terre Haute, Ind.*	250 York st.
James Lenox Banks, Jr.	*New York City*	238 York st.
William Nimmo Bartlett	*St. Joseph, Mo.*	231 York st.
Joseph Wickliff Beach	*Bangor, Me.*	581 P.
Samuel Birdsey Beardsley	*Bridgeport, Conn.*	Bridgeport
Victor Augustus Beede	*New Haven, Conn.*	236 Crown st.
Thomas Beer	*Yonkers, N. Y.*	248 York st.
Edward Berman	*Bayonne, N. J.*	63 York st.
William Darius Bishop, Jr.	*Bridgeport, Conn.*	242 York st.
Edward Seymour Blair	*Chicago, Ill.*	238 York st.
Charles Edgar Blake	*Hartford, Conn.*	554 P.
Samuel Sikes Board	*Montclair, N. J.*	536 P.
Malcolm Bogue	*San Francisco, Cal.*	250 York st.
Howard Bonbright	*New York City*	242 York st.
Robert Bowman	*Chicago, Ill.*	563 P.
Horace Rollin Boynton, Jr.	*Los Angeles, Cal.*	537 P.
Walter Perley Bradford	*Lyndeboro, N. H.*	196 F.
Herbert Newton Bradley	*New York City*	8 College st.
Robert Franklin Bradley	*New Haven, Conn.*	432 Whitney av.
Joseph Henry Bragdon	*Brooklyn, N. Y.*	242 York st.
Samuel Henry Braude	*Rockville, Conn.*	586 P.
Ericsson Bushnell Broadbent	*New Haven, Conn.*	911 Dixwell av.
Ulysses Hayden Brockway, Jr.	*Hartford, Conn.*	550 P.
Wilbur Birdsey Bronson	*Winchester, Conn.*	West Haven
George Percy Brown	*Barre, Mass.*	584 P.
Orlando Cobden Brown	*Danbury, Conn.*	570 P.
Reed McClellan Brown	*Germantown, O.*	266 York st.
Stanley Ernest Brown	*Darien, Conn.*	182 L.
Walter Leroy Brown	*Erwin, Tenn.*	22 College st.
Horace DeWitt Brush	*Brookline, Mass.*	254 York st.

George Burgess	*Garden City, L. I., N. Y.*	574 P.
John Mansfield Burrill	*New York City*	238 York st.
Ellsworth Bushnell	*Minneapolis, Minn.*	577 P.
Beth Vincent Butterfield	*Wilmington, Vt.*	589 P.
Thomas Elton Canfield	*Thomaston, Conn.*	225 Crown st.
James Theodore Carney	*Bridgeport, Conn.*	Bridgeport
Robert John Carpenter	*Winchester, Mass.*	200 York st.
Thomas Walker Carter	*Lexington, Mass.*	596 P.
John Rendall Chandler	*Auburndale, Mass.*	709 W. D.
David Everett Chantler	*Pittsburg, Pa.*	22 College st.
Harold Benjamin Chapman	*Hartford, Conn.*	159 Elm st.
Kortright Church	*Washington, D. C.*	217 York st.
Harold Clinton Clapp	*Berryville, Va.*	250 York st.
Charles Edward Clark	*Orange, Conn.*	961 Yale P. O.
Edward Goddard Clark	*Westfield, N. J.*	591 P.
Sidney Tuttle Clark	*Binghamton, N. Y.*	231 York st.
Tyler Clark	*Buffalo, N. Y.*	200 York st.
George Steele Clarke	*New Orleans, La.*	266 York st.
Lewis Strong Clarke, Jr.	*New Orleans, La.*	266 York st.
Robert Clement	*Rutland, Vt.*	22 College st.
Mather Cleveland	*Denver, Colo.*	231 York st.
Clifton Cromwell Clough	*Vineyard Haven, Mass.*	200 York st.
Samuel Coan	*New Haven, Conn.*	2 West st.
Albert Presby Colburn	*Sharon, Mass.*	188 F.
Ralph Elliott Coleman	*Saranac Lake, N. Y.*	250 York st.
Carleton Alexander Connell	*Scranton, Pa.*	242 York st.
Joseph Connolly	*Roxbury, Mass.*	7 Library st.
Harry Coombe	*Cincinnati, O.*	22 College st.
Joseph Addison Copp	*Groton, Conn.*	538 P.
Frank Marion Coppock, Jr.	*Cincinnati, O.*	254 Crown st.
Alan Lyle Corey	*New York City*	170 York st.
Chanter Cornish	*Yonkers, N. Y.*	299 York st.
Francis William Crandall	*Westfield, N. Y.*	250 York st.
John Douglas Crawford	*Randolph, Mass.*	562 P.
William Anthony Curran	*Holyoke, Mass.*	126 High st.
Henry Tomlinson Curtiss	*Greenwich, Conn.*	22 College st.
Eliot Daggett	*Minneapolis, Minn.*	242 York st.
James McLellan Dain	*Peekskill, N. Y.*	200 York st.
Frederic Joseph Daly	*Cambridge, Mass.*	200 York st.
James Dwight Dana	*New Haven, Conn.*	583 P.
Mitchell Lyon Danforth	*Grand Rapids, Mich.*	295 York st.
George Webster Darr	*Wilkinsburg, Pa.*	170 York st.
Clinton Wildes Davis	*Portland, Me.*	242 York st.
George Reuling Davis	*Wilkes-Barré, Pa.*	1076 Chapel st.

42

Henry Barnard Davis	*Grand Rapids, Mich.*	549 P.
Malcolm Waters Davis	*Hartford, Conn.*	237 York st.
Sherwood Sunderland Day	*Catskill, N. Y.*	200 York st.
Rodney Dean	*Orange, N. J.*	567 P.
Charles Shaver DeLong	*Chicago, Ill.*	250 York st.
Robert Champion Deming	*New Haven, Conn.*	583 P.
John Bourne Dempsey	*Cleveland, O.*	242 York st.
Scoville Thomas Devan	*Stamford, Conn.*	529 P.
Edward Jordan Dimock	- *Elizabeth, N. J.*	568 P.
John Templeman Doneghy, Jr.	*Macon, Mo.*	238 York st.
Francis Drake	*Chicago, Ill.*	535 P.
Charles Holland Duell, Jr.	*New York City*	242 York st.
William McKee Dunn	*Hot Springs, Va.*	250 York st.
William Brooke Dunwoody	*Philadelphia, Pa.*	525 P.
Ralph Brintnall Durell	- *Somerville, Mass.*	231 York st.
Thomas William Durkin	*Brookfield, Mass.*	192 F.
Sydney Dunham Dyer	*Cleveland, O.*	558 P.
Lawrence Waldo Eames	*Providence, R. I.*	8 College st.
Frederick Eckstein	*New Haven, Conn.*	237 York st.
Symund Mason Ehrman	*Portland, Oregon*	571 P.
Charles Clement Elwell, Jr.	*New London, Conn.*	588 P.
Andrew Jefferson Ely	*New Haven, Conn.*	198 F.
Wilson Barton Emery	*New Haven, Conn.* 213 Blatchley av.
Franklin Alfred Ethridge, Jr.	*Rome, N. Y.*	231 York st.
Rowland Evans, Jr.	*Haverford, Pa.*	242 York st.
James Hollyday Stone Fair	*Grand Rapids, Mich.*	248 York st.
Clinton Ellsworth Farnham	*Westfield, Mass.*	149 L.
Robert Leslie Ficks	*Cincinnati, O.*	250 York st.
John W. Field	*Washington, D. C.*	585 P.
Joel Ellis Fisher, Jr.	*New York City*	552 P.
William Hasty Flint	*Larchmont Manor, N. Y.*	251 Crown st.
Henry Lloyd Folsom	*Orange, N. J.*	237 York st.
Stanhope Foster	*Westport, Conn.*	692 W. D.
Howard Tallmadge Foulkes	*Milwaukee, Wisc.*	200 York st.
Sidney Rowland Francis	*St. Louis, Mo.*	250 York st.
Waldo David Frank	*New York City*	200 York st.
Howard Brooks Freeman	*Plainfield, N. J.*	200 York st.
Stuart Fox Freeman	*Plainfield, N. J.*	200 York st.
Seth Barton French, 2d	*New York City*	238 York st.
Elliott Frost	*Waltham, Mass.*	531 P.
Leo Charles Fuller	*St. Louis, Mo.*	250 York st.
Arthur Amory Gammell	*Providence, R. I.*	238 York st.
James Prentice Garland	*Saco, Me.*	250 York st.

Frederick Lawrence Gay	*Los Angeles, Cal.*	537 P.
Charles William Gaylord	*Branford, Conn.*	7 Library st.
Arthur Vincent Geary	*New Haven, Conn.*	479 Orange st.
Henry Gemmer	*Hackensack, N. J.*	598 P.
Robert Alexander Gibney	*New York City*	242 York st.
James Parke Gillespie	*Orange, N. J.*	250 York st.
Ansel Whiting Gillis	*Mt. Pleasant, Ia.*	551 P.
Robert Philip Goldman	*Cincinnati, O.*	547 P.
Stanley A. Goldsmith	*New London, Conn.*	544 P.
Fisher Goodhue	*New York City*	250 York st.
Lawrence Manche Goodman	*Youngstown, O.*	594 P.
George Arthur Goodson, Jr.	*Minneapolis, Minn.*	7 Library st.
Charles Edwin Graves	*New Haven, Conn.*	14 Lincoln st.
Clifford Hendryx Graves	*New Haven, Conn.*	232 Bradley st.
Eugene Hollister Gray	*Maine, N. Y.*	183 L.
Carlos Stockwell Greeley	*St.Louis, Mo.*	8 College st.
Giles Pollard Greene	*Honesdale, Pa.*	250 York st.
John Greenebaum	*Chicago, Ill.*	200 York st.
George Newton Gregory	*New York City*	236 Crown st.
Stephen Strong Gregory, Jr.	*Chicago, Ill.*	250 York st.
Martin Hall Griffing	*Danbury, Conn.*	570 P.
Robert Kalman Haas	*New York City*	242 York st.
James Augustus Haight, Jr.	*Seattle, Wash.*	250 York st.
Mark Anthony Hall	*Cedar Rapids, Ia.*	530 P.
Richard Ware Hall	*Omaha, Nebr.*	556 P.
Thomas Lyon Hamilton, Jr.	*Bayside, L. I., N. Y.*	242 York st.
Edward Harrah	*New York City*	250 York st.
L'Engle Hartridge	*Jacksonville, Fla.*	8 College st.
Arthur Mowry Hartwell	*Albany, N. Y.*	523 P.
Harold Talbot Hartwell	*Danbury, Conn.*	553 P.
Justus Miller Hartwell	*Upper Troy, N. Y.*	200 York st.
Merrill George Hastings	*Winchendon, Mass.*	534 P.
Robert Day Hastings	*Hartford, Conn.*	555 P.
Clarence Bolton Hawke	*Warren, Pa.*	8 College st.
Henry William Heinrich	*Clinton, Mass.*	586 P.
Erastus Henry Hewitt	*Williamstown, Mass.*	578 P.
Charles Virgil Hickox, Jr.	*Springfield, Ill.*	250 York st.
Henry Morrison Hille	*Bath, N. Y.*	186 F.
James Theodore Hillhouse	*Willimantic, Conn.*	584 P.
Carroll Clark Hincks	*Andover, Mass.*	551 P.
Carl Hitchcock	*Ansonia, Conn.*	527 P.
John Marshall Holcombe, Jr.	*Hartford, Conn.*	242 York st.
Reuben Andrus Holden, Jr.	*Cincinnati, O.*	237 York st.

John Baker Hollister	*Cincinnati, O.*	250 York st.
Joseph Horne	*Pittsburg, Pa.*	242 York st.
Edward Gillette Hotchkiss	*Millerton, N. Y.*	250 York st.
Guy Morris Howland	*Asheville, N. C.*	250 York st.
Allen Skinner Hubbard	*Auburn, N. Y.*	250 York st.
Maxwell Crouse Hughes	*West Pittston, Pa.*	1076 Chapel st.
Treat Clark Hull	*Danbury, Conn.*	553 P.
Clarke Fox Hunn	*Rochester, N. Y.*	557 P.
Albert Emery Hutchins	*New Haven, Conn.*	234 Division st.
Frederick Walton Hyde, Jr.	*St. Albans, Vt.*	200 York st.
George Frederic Ingersoll	*Sioux City, Ia.*	560 P.
Harry Stuart Irons	*Elkins, W. Va.*	526 P.
James Lowry Jack	*Indiana, Pa.*	231 York st.
Waldemar Hubbell Jacob	*Cincinnati, O.*	250 York st.
Walter Jamison	*Hazleton, Pa.*	163 York st.
John James Jansen, Jr.	*Albany, N. Y.*	236 Crown st.
Reuben Jeffery, Jr.	*Norwich, N. Y.*	250 York st.
Ralph Herbert Jewell	*Washington, D. C.*	238 York st.
Alexander Bryan Johnson	*Yonkers, N. Y.*	114 High st.
Thomas Slater Johnston, Jr.	*Rochester, N. Y.*	8 College st.
Ernest Sherwin Kavanagh	*Plymouth Union, Vt.*	595 P.
Arthur Thomas Keefe	*New London, Conn.*	254 Crown st.
John Lawrence Keenan	*Boston, Mass.*	186 F.
Malcolm Kemper	*Cincinnati, O.*	163 York st.
Frederick Boughton Keppy	*Brooklyn, N. Y.*	559 P.
Austin Jerome Kilbourn	*Hartford, Conn.*	600 P.
Jonathan Francis Kilbourn	*Hartford, Conn.*	600 P.
Edward Jones Kilduff	*Waterbury, Conn.*	587 P.
John Reed Kilpatrick	*New York City*	200 York st.
William Turney Kimber	*Springfield, Ill.*	250 York st.
Richard Ransom King	*Hartford, Conn.*	237 York st.
Henry Wright Kirby	*Cleveland, O.*	242 York st.
Francis William Kittredge, Jr.	*Boston, Mass.*	250 York st.
Davis Laird Krebs, Jr.	*Clearfield, Pa.*	231 York st.
Floyd Eugene Lamb	*Auburn, N. Y.*	182 L.
Harrold Morton Landon	*New York City*	248 York st.
Thomas Armitage Larremore	*New York City*	567 P.
Frank Waldo Lathrop	*New London, Conn.*	538 P.
Frederick Abraham Laubscher	*Rockville, Conn.*	195 F.
Kenneth LeBlanc	*New Orleans, La.*	250 York st.
Charles Taylor Lee	*New Milford, Conn.*	185 F.
Solomon Lester Levy	*Wilmington, Del.*	521 P.
Frank Grassy Lewis	*Newport, R. I.*	237 York st.
Harold Mayo Lewis	*Somerville, Mass.*	231 York st.

James McKeen Lewis	*Morristown, N. J.*	250 Crown st.
Raymond Williams Lewis	*New Britain, Conn.*	250 York st.
Joseph Prescott Little	*Manchester, Conn.*	149 L.
Edmund Pendleton Livingston	*Catskill Station, N. Y.*	237 York st.
Arthur M. Loewenthal	*Rochester, N. Y.*	579 P.
Cornelius Ennis Lombardi	*Berkeley, Cal.*	250 York st.
Bert Harry Long	*Cincinnati, O.*	199 F.
Abbot Augustus Low, Jr.	*Brooklyn, N. Y.*	231 York st.
Robert Barrie Luchars	*Montclair, N. J.*	248 York st.
Joseph Matthew Lynch	*Meriden, Conn.*	164 L.
William Archibald McAfee	*New Haven, Conn.*	573 P.
Shirley McAndrew	*Ojai Valley, Ventura Co., Cal.*	561 P.
Britt MacConnell	*Morristown, N. J.*	238 York st.
John Vincent McDonnell	*New York City*	238 York st.
James Harold Machette	*Scranton, Pa.*	214 Crown st.
Alexander Lawton Mackall	*Baltimore, Md.*	250 Crown st.
William Glenn McKee	*Pittsburg, Pa.*	599 P.
James Edward McKnight	*Waterbury, Conn.*	587 P.
William Erle McMicken	*Seattle, Wash.*	200 York st.
James Fergus McRee	*St. Louis, Mo.*	254 Crown st.
Paul Griswold Macy	*Newington, Conn.*	159 Elm st.
Harry James Malony	*Dundee, N. Y.*	121 York st.
William DeForest Manice	*New York City*	242 York st.
George Walter Mannel	*Rockville, Conn.*	192 F.
Alexander Drummond Marks	*Brooklyn, N. Y.*	237 York st.
Irving Wolff Marshall	*Auburn, N. Y.*	1169 Chapel st.
Frank Russell Mason	*Groton, Mass.*	34 Hillhouse av.
Orion Augustus Mason	*Medway, Mass.*	200 York st.
George Matthews	*Buffalo, N. Y.*	22 College st.
Stanley Penfield Mead	*New Canaan, Conn.*	193 F.
Nathan Mears	*Evanston, Ill.*	200 York st.
Egbert Mesereau	*Portland, Oregon*	248 York st.
Robert James Milholland	*Newburgh, N. Y.*	383 Crown st.
Robert Anderson Miller, Jr.	*Ponce, Porto Rico*	248 York st.
William Cammack Miller	*Cleveland Park, D. C.*	585 P.
Walter Hall Mills	*Dorchester Center, Mass.*	237 York st.
Russell Mitcheltree	*West Middlesex, Pa.*	7 Library st.
Miles Anson Morgan	*Ilion, N. Y.*	592 P.
Edward Thomas Morrill	*New York City*	242 York st.
Effingham Buckley Morris, Jr.	*Ardmore, Pa.*	242 York st.
Lawrence Stillman Morrison	*Redlands, Cal.*	200 York st.
Karl Mosser	*Boston, Mass.*	237 York st.
George Ray Nettleton	*Milford, Conn.*	Milford
Samuel Johnson Newman	*New Haven, Conn.*	41 Park st.

Paul Cos Nicholson	*Providence, R. I.*	250 York st.
William Porter Norcom	*Portsmouth, Va.*	175 Goffe st.
Morgan John Gray O'Brien	*New York City*	242 York st.
Edward O'Bryan, Jr.	*Chicago, Ill.*	535 P.
Kirk Bassett O'Ferrall	*Piqua, O.*	236 Crown st.
Rene Mead Pardee	*Orange, N. J.*	231 F.
Merrill Olstead Parker	*Auburn, N. Y.*	238 York st.
Edward William Brown Parkinson	*Brooklyn, N. Y.*	216 F.
Paul Patterson	*Pittsburg, Pa.*	599 P.
Robert Alexander Patterson	*Bristol, Conn.*	597 P.
Stuyvesant Peabody	*Chicago, Ill.*	242 York st.
Frederic Arnold Pease	*Pittsfield, Mass.*	250 York st.
Allen Danforth Pettee	*Cleveland, O.*	188 F.
George Emerson Pettit	*Far Rockaway, N. Y.*	126 High st.
Ewing Reginald Philbin	*New York City*	238 York st.
Howard Francis Phipps	*Waterbury, Conn.*	575 P.
Lawrence W. Phipps	*Waterbury, Conn.*	575 P.
William Trigg Pigott, Jr.	*Helena, Mont.*	231 York st.
Gardner Carter Porter	*Arlington, Mass.*	200 York st.
Arthur Leo Price	*New York City*	248 York st.
William Albert Prime, Jr.	*New York City*	248 York st.
George DuBois Proctor	*Randolph, Mass.*	266 York st.
Erving Hascall Rand	*Lawrence, L. I., N. Y.*	238 York st.
George Mulford Randell	*New York City*	22 College st.
Francis Fitz Randolph	*Baltimore, Md.*	231 York st.
Dudley Eley Raymond	*Norwalk, Conn.*	254 York st.
Fred Carl Reckert	*Terre Haute, Ind.*	533 P.
Charles Lawson Reed	*Cincinnati, O.*	242 York st.
Thomas Pattison Reid	*Shelton, Conn.*	Shelton
John Henry Reisner	*McConnellsburg, Pa.*	7 Library st.
Merle DeForest Richard	*New Haven, Conn.*	504 Whitney av.
Stanley Richardson	*Berkeley, Cal.*	548 P.
Francis Bayard Rives	*New York City*	238 York st.
Edward Lewelyn Roberts, Jr.	*Chicago, Ill.*	8 College st.
William Meade Robinson, Jr.	*Louisville, Ky.*	200 York st.
Charles Phinney Rodenbach	*Naugatuck, Conn.*	231 York st.
Harry Louis Rosenberg	*New Britain, Conn.*	14 Gold st.
Roy Ross	*Cowan, Tenn.*	362 WH.
Zeno Carl Ross	*Beverly, Mass.*	200 York st.
Lippman Levy Rothschild	*Buffalo, N. Y.*	521 P.
John Eliot Rowland	*Plainfield, N. J.*	242 York st.
John Tilghman Rowland	*Greenwich, Conn.*	200 York st.
Joseph Franck Rumsey, Jr.	*Lake Forest, Ill.*	250 York st.
Clarence Wardell St. John	*Simsbury, Conn.*	554 P.

James Waugh Sanders	*Montclair, N. J.*	536 P.
Richard Collier Sargent	*New Haven, Conn.*	256 Edwards st.
Bernard Wertheimer Scharff	*Natchez, Miss.*	231 York st.
Stanley Franklin Schwaner	*New London, Conn.*	560 P.
Otto Henry.Schwarz	*St.Louis, Mo.*	238 York st.
Henry Pepper Scott, Jr.	*Wilmington, Del.*	540 P.
Raymond Seabrook	*New York City*	231 York st.
Fidardo Reuben Serri	*Proctor, Vt.*	186 F.
Kenneth Hanna Sessions	*Pittsburg, Pa.*	200 York st.
Frederick Dwight Seward	*Binghamton, N. Y.*	586 P.
Alex Wessel Shapleigh	*St.Louis, Mo.*	242 York st.
Charles Shartenberg	*Pawtucket, R. I.*	200 York st.
Howard Francis Shattuck	*Columbus, O.*	526 P.
Edward Ely Sherman	*New Baltimore, N. Y.*	564 P.
John Homer Sherman	*Fremont, O.*	250 York st.
Henry Knox Sherrill	*Brooklyn, N. Y.*	524 P.
Sturges Bradford Shields	*New York City*	1076 Chapel st.
Arthur Meyer Sidenberg	*New York City*	233 York st.
Isaac Silberstein	*Denver, Colo.*	206 F.
Archer Roberts Simpson	*Orange, Mass.*	590 P.
Carlton Stedman Smith	*Newtown, Conn.*	80 Stanley st.
Harold Ellsworth Smith	*New York City*	532 P.
Oliver Harrison Smith	*Hartford, Conn.*	237 York st.
Felix Brunot Snowdon	*Brownsville, Pa.*	254 Crown st.
Leslie Soule	*Dorchester Center, Mass.*	237 York st.
Leonard Lovejoy Stanley	*Great Barrington, Mass.*	22 College st.
Edmund Courtlandt Stanton	*New York City*	705 W. D.
Mason Brayman Starring, Jr.	*Chicago, Ill.*	250 York st.
Earl Ledgerwood Steele	*Kansas, Ill.*	528 P.
Carl Isaac Stix	*Cincinnati, O.*	539 P.
John Cameron Stoddart	*Englewood, N. J.*	1076 Chapel st.
Frederick Brett Stokes	*New York City*	231 York st.
James Cashmon Sweeney	*New York City*	546 P.
Wallace Nathaniel Sweet	*Lebanon, Conn.*	371 Crown st.
Albert Day Swords	*Morristown, N. J.*	22 College st.
Thomas William Symons, Jr.	*Washington, D. C.*	250 York st.
George Hamlet Taylor	*Rochester, N. Y.*	541 P.
Ralph Emerson Taylor	*Dennisville, N. J.*	195 F.
John Taylor Terry, 3d	*New York City*	242 York st.
Henry Nelson Tetreault	*Augusta, Me.*	572 P.
Clarence Proctor Thomas	*New York City*	250 York st.
Benjamin Casper Thompson	*St.Paul, Minn.*	200 York st.
Horace Thompson	*New Haven, Conn.*	238 York st.
Harold Hayward Thresher	*Norwich, Conn.*	593 P.

Orrin Herbert Tilson	*Grapevine, N. C.*	524 P.
Benjamin Hartshorne Trask	*Highlands, N. J.*	248 York st.
Morton Candee Treadway	*Bristol, Conn.*	225 Crown st.
Yun-siang Tsao	*Shanghai, China*	143 York st.
Gouverneur Morris Wilkins Turnbull	*New York City*	242 York st.
Cyrus Calhoun Turner, Jr.	*New York City*	580 P.
Henry Turner	*St. Louis, Mo.*	254 York st.
Herbert Orvin Tuttle	*Warren, Mass.*	590 P.
Dixon VanBlarcom	*St. Louis, Mo.*	595 P.
Harry Brinsmade VanSinderen	*New Haven, Conn.*	242 York st.
John David Wachman	*Cincinnati, O.*	566 P.
Robert Coleman Walker	*Richmond, Va.*	242 York st.
Benjamin Franklin Bean Wallis	*Dorchester Center, Mass.*	22 College st.
Frederic Lozier Walters	*Buffalo, N. Y.*	416 Crown st.
Everett Oyler Waters	*New York City*	582 P.
James Webster Waters	*Buffalo, N. Y.*	250 York st.
John Charles Weibel	*New Haven, Conn.*	114 Sherman av.
Arthur Weil	*New Haven, Conn.*	352 Orange st.
Charles Aloysius Welch	*New Haven, Conn.*	23 Bradley st.
Alexander Royal Wheeler	*Endeavor, Pa.*	250 York st.
Edward Curtis Wheeler	*Westerleigh, S. I., N. Y.*	200 York st.
Lawrence Raymond Wheeler	*Portville, N. Y.*	250 York st.
William Reginald Wheeler	*Endeavor, Pa.*	250 York st.
William Preston White	*St. Paul, Minn.*	8 College st.
Josiah Macy Willets	*White Plains, N. Y.*	242 York st.
Stanley Thomas Williams	*Meriden, Conn.*	231 York st.
Frank Miller Willis	*Worcester, Mass.*	543 P.
Alexander Augustus Wilson	*San Francisco, Cal.*	254 Crown st.
Holden Wilson	*Cincinnati, O.*	242 York st.
Silas Hemenway Witherbee	*Port Henry, N. Y.*	254 York st.
Harold Irving Wood	*Gardner, Mass.*	225 F.
Edgar Montillion Woolley	*New York City*	248 York st.
Clifford Ramsey Wright	*Cincinnati, O.*	242 York st.
Philip North Wright	*Detroit, Mich.*	242 York st.
Walter Esher Yaggy	*Hutchinson, Kans.*	250 York st.

FRESHMEN, 382

SUMMARY

SENIORS	.	.	.	.	.	317
JUNIORS	.	.	.	.	.	305
SOPHOMORES	.	.	.	.	.	311
FRESHMEN	.	.	.	.	.	382
						1315
STUDENTS FROM OTHER DEPARTMENTS	.				.	255
TOTAL UNDER INSTRUCTION	.			.	.	1570

SHEFFIELD SCIENTIFIC SCHOOL
GRADUATE STUDENTS
WITH THEIR MAJOR SUBJECTS OF STUDY

Rose Abel, B.A.   *Montesano, Wash.*   142 York st.
University of Kansas 1901   French

Harry Leslie Agard, B.A.   *Andover, Mass.*   711 W. D.
Wesleyan University 1904   Mathematics

William Talbot Allison, B.A.   *Middlefield, Conn.*   Middlefield
University of Toronto 1899, M.A. 1900,   English
B.D. Yale University 1901

Clarence Edward Andrews, B.A.   *Norwalk, Conn.*   1026 Yale P. O.
Yale University 1906   English

Edward Monroe Bailey, Jr., PH.B.   *New Haven, Conn.* 168 Sheffield av.
Yale University 1902, M.S. 1905   Physiological Chemistry

Oliver Edwin Baker, B.S.   *Tiffin, O.*   182 Mansfield st.
Heidelberg University 1903, M.S. 1904,   Botany
M.A. Columbia University 1905

William Deluce Barnes, Jr., B.A.   *Mansfield, Mass.*   DW.
Yale University 1907   Biology and Chemistry

Arthur Herbert Basye, B.A.   *Lawrence, Kans.*   204 F.
University of Kansas 1904, M.A. 1906   Economics

Clifford Whitman Bates, PH.B.   *Cleveland, O.*   299 York st.
Yale University 1905   Physics and Mathematics

Laura Lorraine Batson, B.A.   *Longview, Tex.*   166 York st.
University of Texas 1904   German

George Elbert Beck, B.A.   *Bethel, O.*   7 Library st.
Yale University 1907   Mineralogy

Fredrik Ferdinand Woods Beckman *Altoona, Pa.*   717 W. D.
Högre Realläroverk, Stockholm 1905   Surveying and Mapping, and Botany

George Loomis Beecher, PH.B.   *New Haven, Conn.* 201 Sherman av.
Yale University 1906   Civil Engineering

Stanley Rossiter Benedict, B.A.   *Cincinnati, O.*   78 Lake pl.
University of Cincinnati 1906   Physiological Chemistry

Earl Gordon Bill, B.A.   *Wolfville, N. S.*   122 Howe st.
Acadia University 1902,   Mathematics
B.A. Yale University 1905, M.A. 1906

Frederick Howell Billard, B.A.   *Meriden, Conn.*   315 York st.
Yale University 1896   Botany

Walter Minor Bradley, PH.B.   *New Haven, Conn.* 1346 Chapel st.
Yale University 1899   Mineralogy

Charles Andrew Brautlecht, PH.B. *New Haven, Conn.*   130 Front st.
Yale University 1906   Physiological Chemistry

Harry Gunnison Brown, B.A.   *Troy, N. Y.*   82 Whalley av.
Williams College 1904   Economics

Horace Thomas Burgess, B.A.   *Waynesville, O.*   700 W. D.
Yale University 1906, M.A. 1907   Mathematics

Josephine May Burnham, PH.B.   *Chicago, Ill.*   142 York st.
University of Chicago 1901   French

Henry Holland Carter, B.A.   *Brecksville, O.*   129 Mansfield st.
Oberlin College 1907   English

Samuel Hopkins Clapp, B.A.   *New Haven, Conn.*   98 York sq.
Yale University 1901   Organic and Physiol. Chemistry

Lois Clark, B.A.   *Seattle, Wash.*   130 Howe st.
University of Washington 1907   Botany and Biology

Ralph Oakley Clock, PH.B.   *New York City*
Yale University 1901,   Biology
M.D. University of Pennsylvania 1904

Arthur Mayhew Cook, B.A.   *Laconia, N. H.*   333 York st.
Harvard University 1906   Surveying and Mapping

Charlton Dows Cooksey, PH.B.   *New Haven, Conn.*   284 Orange st.
Yale University 1905   Physics

Darrah Corbet, PH.B.   *Brookville, Pa.*
Yale University 1905   Mechanical Engineering

John Hamilton Derby, Jr., PH.B.   *Sandy Hill, N. Y.*   110 Wall st.
Yale University 1907   Chemistry

James Edwards Diamond, PH.B.   *New Haven, Conn.* 173 Whalley av.
Yale University 1907   Electrical Engineering

Louis Alexander Dole, B.A.   *Wilmington, Del.*   644 E. D.
Yale University 1906   Economics and Biology

William Allen Drushel, B.S.   *Lebanon, O.*   47 Lake pl. ·
National Normal University 1896, LL.B. 1900,   Physiological Chemistry
B.A. Yale University 1905

Arthur Wood DuBois, B.A.   *Hallstead, Pa.*   333 York st.
Cornell University 1907   Botany

Willard Higley Durham, B.A.   *Holland Patent, N. Y.*   701 W. D.
Yale University 1904   English

Marion Graham Elkins, B.S.   *Amesbury, Mass.*   568 Chapel st.
Rhode Island College of Agric. and Mechanic Arts 1906   Botany

Joseph Roy Ellis, B.A.   *Kansas City, Mo.*   679 W. D.
Oberlin College 1905   French

Henry Pratt Fairchild, B.A.   *Crete, Nebr.*   1233 Chapel st.
Doane College 1900   Economics

Herman Edgar Fegley, B.A.   *Auburn, Pa.*   8 Prospect pl.
Franklin and Marshall College 1904   Botany

Edna Louise Ferry, B.A.   *New Haven, Conn.* 24 Edgewood av.
Mt. Holyoke College 1905   Physiological Chemistry

Arthur Sargent Field, B.A.   *St. Johnsbury, Vt.*   100 Howe st.
Dartmouth College 1902   Economics

Victor Oscar Freeburg, B.A.   *Lindsborg, Kans.*   295 York st.
Bethany College 1904,   French
B.A. Yale University 1905

Roy Leon French, PH.B.   *Attica, N. Y.*   210 F.
Syracuse University 1906   English

George Edward Gage, B.A.   *Springfield, Mass.*   642 E. D.
Clark University 1906,   Bacteriology and Hygiene
M.A. Yale University 1907

Frederick Riley Gagel, PH.B.   *Dayton, O.*   124 Prospect st. ·
Yale University 1907   Mining

Russell Tyner Gard, PH.B.   *Frankfort, Ind.*   685 W. D.
Yale University 1907   Mining

Belknap Chittenden Goldsmith, B.S. *Berkeley, Cal.*   70 Whalley av.
University of California 1906   Botany

Aubrey Ward Goodenough, B.A.   *New Haven, Conn.* 25 Edwards st.
Oberlin College 1906   English

James W. Green, Jr., B.A.   *Gloversville, N. Y.*   689 W. D.
Yale University 1907   Metallurgy

George Frederick Gundelfinger, PH.B. *Sewickley, Pa.*   124 Wall st.
Yale University 1906   Mathematics

Charles Walter Hall, B.A.   *Stockville, Nebr.*   81 C.
Doane College 1904,   Economics
B.A. Yale University 1907

Isaac Faust Harris, B.S.   *New Haven, Conn.*
University of North Carolina 1900, M.S. 1903   Physiological Chemistry

Edwin Deeks Harvey, B.A.   *Rock Ferry, England*   625 E. D.
Yale University 1907   Economics

Ruth Sawyer Harvey, B.A.   *Cincinnati, O.*   142 York st.
University of Cincinnati 1905   Petrology

Samuel Clarke Harvey, PH.B.   *Woodbury, Conn.*   114 High st.
Yale University 1907   Bacteriology and Hygiene

Yasujiro Hayakawa   *Oita, Japan*   55 Prospect st.
Oita Agricultural School 1899   Economics

Frederick William Heyl, PH.B.   *New Haven, Conn.* 137 Blatchley av.
Yale University 1904   Physiological Chemistry

Warren Witherell Hilditch, PH.B.   *Thompsonville, Conn.*   90 Lake pl.
Yale University 1905   Physiological Chemistry

Edgar Clarkson Hirst, B.A.   *Yellow Springs, O.* 60 Whalley av.
Ohio State University 1907   Botany

Francis Jerome Holder, B.S.   *Lacrosse, Fla.*   23 Lynwood pl.
National Normal University 1896,   Mathematics
M.A. Yale University 1905

John Dean Holm, B.S.   *Stillwater, Minn.* 1032 Yale P. O.
Carleton College 1906, M.S. 1907   Geology

Percy K. Holmes, B.P.T.   *Bridgeport, Conn.*   Bridgeport
Y.M.C.A. Training School 1907   English

Albert Wallace Hull, B.A.   *Torrington, Conn.* 120 York st.
Yale University 1905   Physics

Lon Louis Hutchison, B.A.   *Norman, Okla.* 127 Dwight st.
University of Oklahoma 1907   Geology

Oswald Drew Ingall, B.A.   *Montclair, N. J.*   718 W. D.
Cornell University 1907   Botany

Jacob Louis Jacobs, PH.B.   *New Haven, Conn.* 128 Lafayette st.
Yale University 1907   Civil Engineering

Henry Langley Johnson, B.A.   *Boston, Mass.* 17 Compton st.
Cornell University 1907   Botany

David Breese Jones, B.A.   *Cambria, Wisc.* 103 Park st.
Ripon College 1904   Chemistry

Richard Chapin Jones, B.A.   *Montclair, N. J.* 60 Whalley av.
Vanderbilt University 1904   Surveying and Mapping

Margaret Judson, B.A.   *New York City* 37 Howe st.
Vassar College 1903   French

William Oded Keirstead, B.A.   *Oakland, Me.*   Montowese
Bates College 1906,   Economics
B.A. Yale University 1907

Joseph Casimir Kircher, B.A.   *Belleville, Ill.* 1076 Chapel st.
Yale University 1907   Botany

Israel Simon Kleiner, PH.B.   *New Haven, Conn.* 39 Howe st.
Yale University 1906   Physiological Chemistry

Clarence Moore Knox, PH.B.   *Hartford, Conn.*   685 W. D.
Yale University 1907 ·   Mechanical Engineering

James Atsutoshi Kumon   *Osaka, Japan* 993 Yale P. O.
Kansai Law School 1898,   Economics
M.A. Yale University 1907

John Kenyon Lamond, B.S.   *Kingston, R. I.* 103 Park st.
Rhode Island College of Agric. and Mech. Arts 1907   Mathematics

Francis Baker Laney, B.S.   *Chapel Hill, N. C.* 1305 Chapel st.
Drury College 1902,   Geology
M.A. University of Wisconsin 1905

Kenneth Scott Latourette, B.S.   *Oregon City, Oregon*   197 F.
McMinnville College 1904,   Economics
B.A. Yale University 1906, M A. 1907

Henry Wells Lawrence, Jr., B.A.   *White Plains, N. Y.* 125 Dwight st.
Yale University 1906   Economics

Charles Stanley Leavenworth, PH.B.   *Hamden, Conn.* 2 Hillhouse av.
Yale University 1902   Physiological Chemistry

Leonard Merritt Liddle, B.S.	*Walker, Ia.*	88 C.
Cornell College 1906	Chemistry

William Harding Longley, B.A.	*Paradise, N. S.*	120 York st.
Acadia University 1901,	Biology
B.A. Yale University 1907

George Blakeman Lovell, B.A.	*New Haven, Conn.* 765 Whitney av.
Yale University 1901, M.A. 1903	German

John Franklin Lyman, B.S.	*Amherst, Mass.*	7c6 W. D.
Massachusetts Agricultural College 1905,	Physiological Chemistry
B.S. Boston University 1905

William Pitt McCune, B.A.	*Columbus, O.*	384 B.
Yale University 1906, M.A. 1907	French

Everett Herman MacDaniels, B.A.	*Oberlin, O.*	716 W. D.
Oberlin College 1906	Botany

John William Madden, PH.B.	*Deposit, N. Y.*	88 Wall st.
,Yale University 1907	Mechanical Engineering

Rufus Sherrell Maddox, B.A.	*Coldwater, Tenn.*	664 W. D.
Yale University 1907	Botany

Harriette Parnal Marsh, PH.B.	*New Haven, Conn.* 89 Whalley av.
University of Chicago 1904	Economics

Thomas Randolph Marshall, PH.B.	*Philadelphia, Pa.*	144 Dwight st.
Brown University 1907	Economics

Norman Andrews Martin, PH.B.	*New Castle, Pa.*	684 W. D.
Yale University 1907	Chemistry

Edwin Cyrus Miller, B.A.	*Baltimore, Md.*	7 Library st.
Yale University 1907	Botany

Stewart Lea Mims, B.A.	*Durham, Conn.*	701 W. D.
Yale University 1904	History

Michael K. Minassian, PH.B.	*Boston, Mass.*	11 Lake pl.
Yale University 1900	Chemistry

Isabel Stewart Mitchell, B.A.	*New Haven, Conn.* 152 Whalley av.
Maryville College (Tenn.) 1905	French and German

Axel Erik Teodor Moberg	*Upsala, Sweden*	919 Howard av.
Upsala University 1906	Botany

Clifford Joseph Monahan, PH.B.	*New Haven, Conn.*	686 W. D.
Yale University 1907	Chemistry

Frederick Franklin Moon, B.A.	*Nazareth, Pa.*	664 W. D.
Amherst College 1901	Botany

Victor Caryl Myers, B.A.	*Buskirk Bridge, N. Y.* 707 W. D.
Wesleyan University 1905, M.A. 1907	Physiological Chemistry

Foster Stebbins Naething, PH.B.	*New York City*	124 Prospect st.
Yale University 1907	Mining

George Elwood Nichols, B.A.	*New Haven, Conn.*	569 P.
Yale University 1904	Botany

Levi Fatzinger Noble, B.A.   *Auburn, N. Y.*   90 Wall st.
Yale University 1905   Geology

Herbert Brinkerhoff North, PH.B.   *New Haven, Conn.* 250 Whalley av.
Yale University 1901   Mechanical Engineering

Kenzaburo Okamoto, B.A.   *Tokyo, Japan*   128 High st.
Keiogijiku University 1907   English

William Bushnell Osborne, Jr., B.A.   *Victor, N. Y.*   17 Compton st.
Williams College 1907   Surveying and Mapping

Howard Earle Palmer, B.A.   *Branford, Conn.*   Branford
Yale University 1907   Mineralogy

Eli Burton Parsons, B.A.   *Troy, Pa.*   1076 Chapel st.
Yale University 1907   Electrical Engineering

Percy Jerould Paxton, B.A.   *Princeton, Ind.*   159 Elm st.
Williams College 1906   Botany

Nicholas Elias Peieff, B.A.   *Macedonia*   Yale P. O.
Yale University 1907   Economics

Claude Clair Perkins, B.A.   *Pine Island, Minn.* 118 Howe st.
University of Minnesota 1907   Mineralogy

Clarence Curtiss Perry, PH.B.   *New Britain, Conn.* 121 Maple st.
Yale University 1904   Physics

Frederick Erastus Pierce, B.A.   *South Britain, Conn.*
Yale University 1904, M.A. 1905   622 Washington av., West Haven
     English

Joseph Ezekiel Pogue, Jr., B.A.   *Raleigh, N. C.*   1305 Chapel st.
University of North Carolina 1906, M.S. 1907   Mineralogy

Robert Hamilton Prentice, B.A.   *Buffalo, N. Y.*
Yale University 1907   Surveying and Mapping

Reuben Parker Prichard, B.S.   *Somerville, Mass.*   719 W. D.
Dartmouth College 1907   Botany

Joseph Chappell Rayworth, B.A.   *Upper Sackville, N. B.* 120 York st.
Acadia University 1903,   Mathematics
B.A. Yale University 1906, M.A. 1907

Chester Albert Reeds, B.S.   *Norman, Okla.*   204 F.
University of Oklahoma 1905,   Paleontology
M.S. Yale University 1907

Heaton Ridgeway Robertson, B.A. *New Haven, Conn.*
Yale University 1904, PH.B. 1906   Mining

Anton Richard Rose, B.S.   *Geneva, N. Y.*   403 Elm st.
University of Minnesota 1904   Physiological Chemistry

William Cumming Rose, B.S.   *Laurinburg, N. C.*   91 Park st.
Davidson College 1907   Chemistry and Biology

Joseph Rosenbaum, PH.B.   *New Haven, Conn.*   68 Park st.
Yale University 1907   Mathematics

Tadasu Saiki, M.D. *Kitayamasaki, Iyo, Japan* 462 Elm st.
Okayama Medical College 1898, Physiological Chemistry
PH.D. Yale University 1907

Thomas Edmund Savage, B.A. *Urbana, Ill.* 7 Holmes st., West Haven
Iowa Wesleyan University 1895, Paleontology
M.S. State University of Iowa 1898

Howard Arnold Seckerson, B.A. *Brooklyn, N. Y.* 178 Ellsworth av.
Wesleyan University 1907 English

William Edward Selin, B.A. *Cynthiana, Ky.* 671 W. D.
Yale University 1898, M.A. 1900 English and French

Herbert Lee Seward, PH.B. *New Haven, Conn.* 116 V-S.
Yale University 1906 Mechanical Engineering

George Clarence Sherwood, B.S. *Ewing, Ky.* 276 Elm st.
National Normal University, Lebanon, O., 1899, English
B.A. Yale University 1907

Robert Simmons, B.A. *New York City* 196 Mansfield st.
College of the City of New York 1905 Botany

Arthur Wells Smith, B.A. *Cañon City, Colo.* 529 Elm st.
National Normal University 1905 Biology

Edwin Kinmouth Smith, PH.B. *Morristown, N. J.* 51 Prospect st.
Yale University 1907 Chemistry

Mary Winslow Smyth, B.L. *New Haven, Conn.* 328 Temple st.
Smith College 1895, M.A. 1905 French

Thomas Elliott Snyder, B.A. *New York City* 8 Prospect pl.
Columbia University 1907 Botany

Carl Frank Speh, PH.B. *New Haven, Conn.* 63 Crown st.
Yale University 1906 Chemistry

Willard Springer, Jr., C.E. *Wilmington, Del.* 60 Whalley av.
Lafayette College 1907 Botany

Jessie Mae Stokely, B.A. *Newport, Tenn.* 90 Park st.
Virginia Institute 1904 Economics

Walter Frederick Storey, PH.B. *New Haven, Conn.* 172 Lloyd st
Yale University 1906 Chemistry

Nizzó Suruda, B.L. *Kishu, Japan* 416 Crown st.
Bethany College (W. Va.) 1906 English

Mary Davies Swartz, B.L. *Wooster, O.* 25 Whalley av.
Denison University 1901, Physiol. Chemistry and Bacteriology
B.S. Columbia University 1906

Senjiro Takagi, B.A. *Yokohama, Japan* 417 B.
Yale University 1907 Economics

Thomas Smith Taylor, B.A. *Peoli, O.* 687 W. D.
Yale University 1906 Physics

Wyatt Warner Taylor, PH.B. *Stamford, Conn.*
Yale University 1900 Mechanical Engineering

Orlin Hale Venner, PH.B.	*Corydon, Ind.*	1233 Chapel st.
Berea College 1902,	English	
B.A. West Virginia University 1905		
Mary Emma Wadlington, B.A.	*Norman, Okla.*	166 York st.
University of Mississippi 1902	French	
Henry Freeman Walradt, B.A.	*Whitman, Mass.*	417 B.
Yale University 1907	Economics	
Evans Ward, PH.B.	*Port Chester, N. Y.*	88 Wall st.
Yale University 1907	Mechanical Engineering	
Freeman Ward, B.A.	*Yankton, S. D.*	106 Howe st.
Yale University 1903	Geology	
Ella Pardee Warner, PH.B.	*New Haven, Conn.*	914 Dixwell av.
Wesleyan University 1906, M.S. 1907	English	
Ernest Cousins Wheeler, B.A.	*Norwalk, Conn.*	1076 Chapel st.
Yale University 1907	Botany	
Frank Elbert Wheelock, B.A.	*Lawrencetown, N. S.*	120 York st.
Acadia University 1905,	Physics	
B.A. Yale University 1907		
Henry Adelbert White, B.A.	*Middletown, Conn.*	82 Whalley av.
Wesleyan University 1904, M.A. 1905	English	
John Alan White, B.A.	*Walton, N. Y.*	82 C.
Yale University 1907	Physics	
Chester Harvey Wilcox, C.E.	*Center Moriches, N. Y.*	13 Lake pl.
Lehigh University 1907	Botany	
Addison Wetherald Williamson, PH.B.	*Waterport, N. Y.*	91 Lake pl.
Wesleyan University 1907	Botany	
Thomas Goddard Wright, B.A.	*Phelps, N. Y.*	74 C.
Yale University 1907	English and French	
Ralph William Young, PH.B.	*West Upton, Mass.*	665 W. D.
Yale University 1907	Mining	

GRADUATE STUDENTS, 154

[Students marked "A" are candidates for the degree of Master of Science, Mechanical Engineer or Civil Engineer, who, having had one year of resident graduate study, are now pursuing courses of study in absence under the direction of the Faculty.]

SHEFFIELD SCIENTIFIC SCHOOL
SENIOR CLASS

Clarence Frank Alcott	*Cleveland, O.*	111 Grove st.
Ralph John Andrews	*Clinton, Conn.*	373 Crown st.
Mortimer Reynolds Anstice	*Rochester, N. Y.*	96 Wall st.
Carryl Arthur Asher	*New Haven, Conn.*	59 Grove st.
George Franklin Atwater	*New Haven, Conn.*	1776 State st.
Loutfi Hagop Babikian, B.A.	*Aintab, Turkey*	391 Temple st.
Central Turkey College 1905		
Carl Conrad Baker	*Zanesville, O.*	70 Trumbull st.
John Lawrance Barker	*Evanston, Ill.*	180 v-s.
Joseph Nicolson Barrett	*Newport, R. I.*	181 v-s.
Lawrence Marsh Bartlett	*Buffalo, N. Y.*	110 Wall st.
Lyman Earle Bassett	*New Haven, Conn.*	275 Humphrey st.
Gaspard d'Audelot Belin	*Scranton, Pa.*	131 Grove st.
Walter Kingsbury Belknap	*Louisville, Ky.*	125 v-s.
Ray Graham Biglow	*New York City*	124 Prospect st.
Harold Crusius Bird	*Hartford, Conn.*	948 Yale P. O.
Lawrence Hubbert Blinn	*New Haven, Conn.*	184 Blatchley av.
William Jarvis Boardman, 2d	*Cleveland, O.*	111 Grove st.
Frank Armstrong Boder	*St. Joseph, Mo.*	70 Trumbull st.
George Raymond Boggs	*Landore, Idaho*	131 Grove st.
William Purinton Bomar	*Fort Worth, Texas*	17 Hillhouse av.
Frederick Boone Bostwick	*New Haven, Conn.*	220 Lawrence st.
Arthur Harding Bosworth	*Denver, Colo.*	184 v-s.
Frederic Quintard Boyer	*Norwalk, Conn.*	182 v-s.
John Smith Bradley, Jr.	*New Haven, Conn.*	41 High st.
John Akin Branch	*Richmond, Va.*	96 Wall st.
Carl Brewer, B.A.	*New Haven, Conn.*	418 Orange st.
Yale University 1905		
Wallace Seymour Brinsmade	*Shelton, Conn.*	191 v-s.
.Joshua Twing Brooks	*Shields, Pa.*	131 Grove st.
Harold Ross Brown	*Salt Lake City, Utah*	111 Grove st.
Robert Ervin Brown	*Yalesville, Conn.*	Yalesville.
Raymond Lester Brown	*Campville, Conn.*	373 Crown st.
James Herbert Browning	*New York City*	180 v-s.
Gerard Louis Buhrman	*Cincinnati, O.*	131 Grove st.
Amasa Cobb Bull	*New York City*	176 v-s.
George Haring Bunker .	*Yonkers, N. Y.*	124 Prospect st.
Laidlaw Boswell Burger	*Litchfield, Conn.*	96 Wall st.
Arthur Killam Burwell	*New Haven, Conn.*	24 Maple st.
Harwood Byrnes	*Norwich, Conn.*	126 Wall st.

43

Carleton Strong Cairoli	*Milford, Conn.*	Milford
Henry Coffin Carlisle	*New Rochelle, N. Y.*	186 v-s.
James Richardson Carpenter	*El Paso, Texas*	115 v-s.
Samuel Laurence de Carteret	*Auckland, New Zealand* 976 Yale P. O.
Russell Estes Chatfield	*New Haven, Conn.*	175 v-s.
Ju Hsiang Chen	*Tientsin, China*	690 w. D.
James Henderson Childs, B.S.	*Forsyth, Ga.*	166 v-s.
Alabama Polytechnic Institute 1904		
Tsung Hua Chow	*Tientsin, China*	674 w. D.
Leroy Christy	*Montclair, N. J.*	167 v-s.
Howard Emerson Church	*Rockville, Conn.*	177 v-s.
Bernard Stearns Clark	*New York City*	124 Prospect st.
James Joseph Clifford	*Naugatuck, Conn.* 17 Hillhouse av.
Clarence Holloway Cogswell	*New Haven, Conn.*	175 v-s.
Roger Baldwin Colton	*Campbellsville, Ky.*	177 v-s.
Edwin Chesney Colwell	*New York City*	111 Grove st.
Edward Fratus Congdon	*New Haven, Conn.* 470 Orchard st.
Constantine M. Constantian, B.A.	*New Haven, Conn.* 1069 Yale P. O.
Central Turkey College 1902		
Harry Holmes Coolidge	*Minneapolis, Minn.* 124 Prospect st.
Algernon Booth Corbin, Jr.	*New Haven, Conn.*	185 v-s.
George Hyland Crofton	*New York City*	109 v-s.
Wells Sargent Dickinson	*New York City*	111 Grove st.
Hiram Waldemar Dodd	*Wiconisco, Pa.*	78 Lake pl.
Albert Lee Donnelly	*New Haven, Conn.*	57 Pearl st.
David Dows	*New York City* 17 Hillhouse av.
Conrad Gotzian Driscoll	*St. Paul, Minn.*	131 Grove st.
Noel Maxton Swezey Dunbar	*Port Washington, L. I., N. Y.* 147 v-s.
William Edwin Dunham	*Warren, Pa.*	174 v-s.
Wesley Earl Dunkle	*Pittsburg, Pa.*	174 v-s.
Stanley Lane Eddy	*Bay City, Mich.*	379 Temple st.
George Lewis Emmons	*Schenectady, N. Y.*	96 Wall st.
Fred Engelhardt	*Naugatuck, Conn.*	176 v-s.
Herman Walker Farrar	*Springfield, Mass.* 1023 Yale P. O.
Lyle Gordon Fear	*Portland, Oregon*	176 v-s.
Morris S. Fine	*New Haven, Conn.* 45 Stevens st.
George Morris Fosdick	*Springfield, L. I., N. Y.* 333 York st.
Lee Nathaniel Foster	*Fairchild, Wisc.*	135 Wall st.
Nathan Roscoe Francis, B.A.	*Winchester, Tenn.* 156 Grove st.
Yale University 1902		
Lawrence Percival Galt	*Newburgh, N. Y.*	162 v-s.
Paul Smith Gates	*West Haven, Conn.*	West Haven
Frederick Alan Gaylord	*Ansonia, Conn.*	165 v-s.
Ferdinand LaMotte Gilpin, Jr.	*Wilmington, Del.*	189 v-s.

William Barns Given, Jr.	*Chicago, Ill.*	96 Wall st.
Franklin Thomas Griswold	*New Britain, Conn.*	395 Temple st.
Herbert Hartley Guest	*New Haven, Conn.*	99 Scranton st.
George Charles Haas	*New York City*	163 V–S.
Willis Worthington Hale	*Cleveland, O.*	162 V–S.
Edward Bigelow Hall	*Evanston, Ill.*	96 Wall st.
Harry Breden Ham	*Mexico City, Mexico*	96 Wall st.
Frank Watrous Hamilton	*Groton, Conn.*	133 College st.
BenJamin Pomeroy Hamlin, B.A.	*Easthampton, Mass.*	38 Lynwood pl.
Yale University 1907		
Henry Dennis Hammond	*Nashville, Tenn.*	228 Crown st.
Foster Hannaford.	*St.Paul, Minn.*	111 Grove st.
Charles S. Hart	*Dayton, O.*	159 Elm st.
George Frederick Hendricks	*New Haven, Conn.*	239 George st.
Lucius Felix Herz	*New Haven, Conn.*	118 Edwards st.
Nathaniel Herz	*New Haven, Conn.*	118 Edwards st.
Donald York Hill	*Cincinnati, O.*	110 Wall st.
Hou Wei Ho	*Tientsin, China*	114 High st.
William Patton Hopkins	*Lock Haven, Pa.*	184 V–S.
William Israel Howland, Jr.	*Evanston, Ill.*	108 V–S.
Yü Peng Hua	*Tientsin, China*	55 Prospect st.
Clayton Harwood Huckans	*Gloversville, N. Y.*	646 E. D.
Frank W. Hulett	*New Haven, Conn.*	910 Whalley av.
John Irving Hull	*South Coventry, Conn.*	84 C.
Henry Julian Correll Humphrey	*Brooklyn, N. Y.*	105 V–S.
Burdon Pelton Hyde	*Waterbury, Conn.*	131 Grove st.
Edward Terence Hyland	*New Haven, Conn.*	144 Bradley st.
David Duryea Irwin	*Boston, Mass.*	133 College st.
Nejib Hovhanness Jebejian, B.A.	*Aintab, Turkey*	945 Yale P. O.
Central Turkey College 1903		
Edgar Mayer Johnson	*Cincinnati, O.*	70 Trumbull st.
Carleton Hill Jones	*New Haven, Conn.*	367 Howard av.
Howard Harding Jones	*Excello, O.*	133 College st.
Stanley Howell Jones	*Napa, Cal.*	170 V–S.
Thomas Albert Dwight Jones	*Excello, O.*	133 College st.
William Strother Jones, Jr.	*Red Bank, N. J.*	133 College st.
John I. Kane	*Ossining, N. Y.*	111 Grove st.
Ben Chapman Keator, Jr.	*New Haven, Conn.*	96 Wall st.
Alexis Augustus Kelsey	*Westbrook, Conn.*	106 V–S.
Aaron Lufkin Kelsey	*Toledo, O.*	96 Wall st.
Julian Kennedy, Jr.	*Pittsburg, Pa.*	141 V–S.
Peter Maximus Kennedy	*Derby, Conn.*	Derby
Elmore Coe Kerr	*New York City*	108 V–S.
Valentine Odell Ketcham	*Stamford, Conn.*	173 V–S.

Maurice Land	*New Haven, Conn.*	9 Arch st.
Edwin Selden Lane	*Philadelphia, Pa.*	183 v-s.
Frank Robert Langdale, Jr.	*New Haven, Conn.*	28 Edgewood av.
Kenneth William Leighton	*New Haven, Conn.*	227 Sherman av.
Norman Alvah Leonard, B.A.	*Willimantic, Conn.*	416 B.
Yale University 1907		
Aldo Leopold	*Burlington, Ia.*	172 v-s.
Oskar Liebig	*Brooklyn, N. Y.*	124 Prospect st.
Sidney Henry Lincoln	*Springfield, Mass.*	17 Hillhouse av.
Robert Bruce Lindsay	*Rochester, N. Y.*	111 Grove st.
George Granville Lobdell	*Wilmington, Del.*	111 Grove st.
Stuart Logan	*Chicago, Ill.*	108 v-s.
Allan Loudon	*Norwalk, Conn.*	126 Wall st.
Clarence Henry Lyman	*Avon, Conn.*	159 Elm st.
Duane Shuler Lyman	*Buffalo, N. Y.*	147 v-s.
Albert Sephton Lynch	*Rowayton, Conn.*	82 Wall st.
Stanley Lyon	*Sewickley, Pa.*	70 Trumbull st.
Selim Walker McArthur	*Chicago, Ill.*	110 Wall st.
Herbert McCuen	*Westville, Conn.*	West Rock av.
Neil Atkinson McGill	*Ely, Nev.*	110 Wall st.
William Francis McKone	*Hartford, Conn.*	57 v.
Tai Cheng Ma	*Tientsin, China*	333 York st.
William Edward Mahoney	*Hopkinton, Mass.*	85 Sachem st.
Robert Newton Manross	*New Haven, Conn.*	118 v-s.
Stuart Clarke Merwin	*New Britain, Conn.*	70 Trumbull st.
William Flagg Middlemass	*New Britain, Conn.*	153 v-s.
Edward Nesbitt Millan	*St. Joseph, Mo.*	17 Hillhouse av.
Thomas Woodnutt Miller	*Wilmington, Del.*	111 Grove st.
Winfield Clarence Miller	*Indianapolis, Ind.*	82 Wall st.
Harry Joseph Moakley	*New Haven, Conn.*	171 Franklin st.
Cary Brownell Moon	*Cleveland, O.*	111 Grove st.
Edgar Dwight Moore	*New Haven, Conn.*	175 Hallock av.
John Upshur Moorhead	*Washington, D. C.*	133 College st.
William James Morden	*Chicago, Ill.*	181 v-s.
Jared Kirtland Morse	*Evanston, Ill.*	184 v-s.
George Henry Mosely	*Barnet, England*	126 v-s.
Franklin Gilman Neal	*Springfield, Mass.*	190 v-s.
Richard Edgar Needham	*Charleston, W. Va.*	174 v-s.
William Wallace Newcomb, Jr.	*Brooklyn, N. Y.*	110 Wall st.
Harold Pierrepont Newton	*Brooklyn, N. Y.*	171 v-s.
Jesse Brooks Nichols	*Tarrytown, N. Y.*	131 Grove st.
Ralph Wilbur Nichols	*North Haven, Conn.*	59 Dwight st.
Lester Ambler Nothnagle	*Bridgeport, Conn.*	293 York st.
William Henry Joseph O'Brien	*New Haven, Conn.*	438 Oak pl.

Howard Taylor Oliver	*Covington, Ky.*	126 High st.
Thomas Francis O'Neill	*New Haven, Conn.*	251 Washington av.
Allen Starr Page	*Oakland, N. J.*	166 v-s.
Frank Lansing Grinnell Page	*New York City*	189 v-s.
H. Ray Paige	*Painesville, O.*	131 Grove st.
William Parker, Jr.	*Cedartown, Ga.*	166 v-s.
Lewis A. Parsons	*Grand Rapids, Mich.*	110 Wall st.
Claude Jewell Peck	*Washington, D. C.*	133 College st.
Joseph Allen Peck	*New Haven, Conn.*	538 Elm st.
Philip Field Wythe Peck	*Chicago, Ill.*	133 College st.
James Vincent Perrin	*North Woodstock, Conn.*	159 Elm st.
John Newton Peyton	*Duluth, Minn.*	96 Wall st.
Howard Elmer Phelps	*Danbury, Conn.*	574 George st.
Morris Curtis Pigott	*Helena, Mont.*	124 Prospect st.
Robert Pike	*New Haven, Conn.*	775 Yale P. O.
Tillotson Beach Platt	*Washington, D. C.*	96 Wall st.
Solomon Colman Poriss	*Hartford, Conn.*	715 W. D.
Ellsworth St. John Prentice	*New Haven, Conn.*	78 Trumbull st.
Harold Turnbull Pritchard	*Waukegan, Ill.*	796 Yale P. O.
Curtis Prout	*Nutley, N. J.*	131 Grove st.
George Wenner Quentin	*Whitneyville, Conn.*	973 Yale P. O.
William Richards, Jr.	*Norwich, Conn.*	119 Wall st.
Laurence Ballard Robbins	*Springfield, Mass.*	131 Grove st.
Empey Arthur Robertson, B.S.	*Newark, N. J.*	393 Temple st.
Lafayette College 1907		
Arthur James Robin	*Denver, Colo.*	105 v-s.
Fred Alexander Rogers	*Providence, R. I.*	111 Grove st.
Herbert Morse Root	*Denver, Colo.*	133 College st.
Robert Stephen Rose	*New Haven, Conn.*	288 N. Front st.
Harry Rosenbaum	*New Haven, Conn.*	68 Park st.
Frank Alexander Ross	*No. Woodbury, Conn.*	153 v-s.
Edward Larned Ryerson, Jr.	*Chicago, Ill.*	133 College st.
Harry Arnold Sautter	*New Britain, Conn.*	153 v-s.
John Hannon Schoolfield	*Danville, Va.*	17 Hillhouse av.
Carl Trueworthy Schuneman	*St. Paul, Minn.*	111 Grove st.
Lawrence Williams Scudder	*New York City*	178 v-s.
Alexander Clifford Scully	*Chicago, Ill.*	161 v-s.
Washington Kyle Sheffield	*New London, Conn.*	131 Grove st.
George Willis Shubert	*New Haven, Conn.*	20 Avon st.
Abbott Beecher Silva	*Chattanooga, Tenn.*	333 York st.
William Wood Skinner	*St. Paul, Minn.*	111 Grove st.
George Dresser Smith	*Chicago, Ill.*	164 v-s.
Henry DeWitt Smith	*New London, Conn.*	126 High st.
Joseph Newton Smith	*Lynn, Mass.*	139 v-s.

Bogart Greenwood Southack	*New York City*	167 v-s.
Henry Boardman Spalding	*New York City*	124 Prospect st.
Allen Conkling Staley	*New York City*	188 v-s.
Medary Wilson Stark	*Mansfield, O.*	135 v-s.
Harlin Melville Steely, Jr.	*Danville, Ill.*	180 v-s.
Holland Newton Stevenson, 2d	*Pittsfield, Mass.*	141 v-s.
Glenn Stewart	*Pittsburg, Pa.*	124 Prospect st.
Ralph Holmes Stone	*Hollidaysburg, Pa.*	96 Wall st.
Willard Frost Story	*Chillicothe, O.*	161 v-s.
William Thorp Sturges	*Shelton, Conn.*	698 w. D.
Albin Champlin Swenson	*New York City*	133 College st.
Theodore VanKleek Swift	*Poughkeepsie, N. Y.*	131 Grove st.
Edward Brooks Taylor	*Binghamton, N. Y.*	96 Wall st.
William Walter Taylor	*New Haven, Conn.*	136 Spring st.
George Ross Templeton	*West Haven, Conn.*	West Haven
Arthur Philo Terrill	*New Haven, Conn.*	147 Dwight st.
Charles Dunning Thompson	*Honesdale, Pa.*	133 College st.
Charles Pomroy Thompson, Jr.	*New Haven, Conn.*	. 185 v-s.
Paul Thompson	*New Haven, Conn.*	60 Grove st.
Douglas Hotchkiss Thomson	*Hartford, Conn.*	17 Hillhouse av.
Clifton Edmun Visel	*Highwood, Conn.*	967 Yale P. O.
Philip Stanley Wainwright	*Hartford, Conn.*	395 Temple st.
Henry Erwin Walker	*New Rochelle, N. Y.*	56 Grove st.
John Morton Walker, Jr.	*Denver, Colo.*	120 College st.
Ching Chun Wang	*Peking, China*	66 Whalley av.
Paul Milo Watrous	*Grove Beach, Conn.*	373 Crown st.
Cornelius Bushnell Watson	*Parkersburg, W. Va.*	133 College st.
Jacob Weinstein	*New Haven, Conn.*	27 Rose st.
Joseph Francis Weller	*Newburgh, N. Y.*	96 Wall st.
Bishop White	*West Hartford, Conn.*	110 Wall st.
Frank Whitney	*Morristown, N. J.*	111 Grove st.
Stephen Whitney	*New Haven, Conn.*	133 College st.
Francesco Bianchi Whittemore	*New York City*	107 v-s.
Morris Leggett Willets	*Flushing, N. Y.*	169 v-s.
Charles Gallup Williams	*Hartford, Conn.*	17 Hillhouse av.
Howard Benjamin Wilson	*Norwalk, Conn.*	104 Wall st.
William Porter Witherow	*Allegheny, Pa.*	133 College st.
Herman Lewis Wittstein	*New Haven, Conn.*	392 Congress av.
Edgar Clinton Wolcott	*Rochester, N. Y.*	96 Wall st.
Meyer Henry Wolff	*Brooklyn, N. Y.*	724 w. D.
George Edgar Wood	*Branford, Conn.*	Branford
Templeton Woolston Wood	*St. Louis, Mo.*	17 Hillhouse av.
Edward Alexander Gill Wylie	*New York City*	131 Grove st.
In Young	*Canton, China*	132 Wall st.

SENIORS, 251

JUNIOR CLASS

William Jacques Adams	*Palo Alto, Cal.*	112 V-S.
Joseph Arthur Allard, Jr.	*Stratford, Conn.*	Stratford
George Milton Allerton, Jr.	*Naugatuck, Conn.*	111 V-S.
Frank Gorman Almquist	*New Rochelle, N. Y.*	132 V-S.
Clement Gould Amory	*New York City*	82 Wall st.
Sprague Walton Ashley	*Hornell, N. Y.*	184 F.
Joseph Gerrish Ayers, Jr.	*Port Jervis, N. Y.*	108 High st.
John Leonard Bagg	*Holyoke, Mass.*	82 Wall st.
Benton Baker	*Bismarck, N. D.*	129 V-S.
Godfrey Vaughan Baker	*Philadelphia, Pa.*	119 Grove st.
John Mayhew Baldwin	*Torrington, Conn.*	124 Wall st.
Gustave Breaux Ballard	*Louisville, Ky.*	17 Hillhouse av.
Leslie Avery Banker	*Cranford, N. J.*	111 Grove st.
Herbert Woodward Barlow	*Bridgeport, Conn.*	1011 Yale P. O.
Kenneth Tuttle Barnaby	*New York City*	111 V-S.
William Hoyt Bartlett	*Peoria, Aris.*	78 Whalley av.
Edgar Leidy Beaty	*Warren, Pa.*	111 Grove st.
Fritz William Beinecke	*Oscawana-on-Hudson, N. Y.*	122 Wall st.
Clinton Percival Bernard	*New Haven, Conn.*	131 Maple st.
John Fedor Bernhardi	*Jamaica, N. Y.*	333 York st.
Oliver Frederick Bishop	*New Haven, Conn.*	174 Grand av.
Roland Stevens Boardman	*Branford, Conn.*	391 Temple st.
Carleton Ward Bonfils	*Jamaica, N. Y.*	114 V-S.
Benjamin Noble Booth	*New Haven, Conn.*	660 George st.
Seymour Mersick Bradley	*New Haven, Conn.*	104 V-S.
Delos Judson Bristol, Jr.	*New Haven, Conn.*	519 George st.
George Farnam Brown	*Philadelphia, Pa.*	110 V-S.
Henry Lee Bunce, Jr.	*Hartford, Conn.*	124 Prospect st.
Frank Gains Burke, Jr.	*New York City*	111 Grove st.
Isaac Sidney Burnett	*Seattle, Wash.*	140 V-S.
Gerald Burnham	*Chicago, Ill.*	96 Wall st.
Julian Penfield Burr	*Westport, Conn.*	178 V-S.
Stanley Mainville Burroughs	*West Newton, Mass.*	111 Grove st.
George Goodrich Byrnes	*Boston, Mass.*	181 V-S.
Walton Thaddeus Carpenter	*Katonah, N. Y.*	126 Wall st.
James Dunbar Cass	*New York City*	133 College st.
Harold Montford Cathcart	*Newburgh, N. Y.*	120 High st.
William Pomeroy Champney, Jr.	*Cleveland, O.*	110 Wall st.
George Mottu Chandlee	*Baltimore, Md.*	122 Wall st.
Tatsung Chang	*Kashing, Chekiang, China*	9 Library st.
William Octave Chanute	*Chicago, Ill.*	17 Hillhouse av.

Joseph Morris Chapin	*Norfolk, Conn.*	694 w. d.
Walter William Cheney, Jr.	*Manlius, N. Y.*	96 Wall st.
Norman King Clarke	*New Haven, Conn.*	114 College st.
Stanley Newton Clarke	*Milford, Conn.*	25 Wooster pl.
James Insley Coddington	*East Orange, N. J.*	70 Trumbull st.
Clifford Stuart Condon	*Oswego, Kans.*	119 Grove st.
Maurice Diehl Cooper	*Buffalo, N. Y.*	103 v-s.
Frank John Cox	*West Haven, Conn.*	110 Wall st.
George Almon Coy	*Milford, Conn.*	Milford
James Brewer Crane	*Westfield, Mass.*	111 Grove st.
Edward Henry Croll	*Buffalo, N. Y.*	128 High st.
Edward Livingston Wells Curtis	*Southport, Conn.*	110 Wall st.
Nathan Alfred Curtiss	*Wallingford, Conn.*	Wallingford
Wilbur Alonzo Curtiss	*East Haven, Conn.*	211 F.
Robert Edward Dakin	*Gaylordsville, Conn.*	694 w. d.
John Grant Daley	*Harlan, Ia.*	315 York st.
Charles Joseph Daly	*New Haven, Conn.*	8 Mechanic st.
Frank Barker Dangler	*Cleveland, O.*	111 Grove st.
Fred Harold Daniels	*Worcester, Mass.*	70 Trumbull st.
Harold Frederick DeLacour	*Stratford, Conn.*	146 v-s.
William Byers Denton	*Denver, Colo.*	8 Prospect pl.
Alonzo Nelson Dewey	*Springfield, Mass.*	131 Grove st.
Elihu Elias Dickerman	*North Haven, Conn.*	119 Wall st.
Robert John Dickey	*Brooklyn, N. Y.*	693 w. d.
Alan Carson Dixon	*Chicago, Ill.*	82 Wall st.
James Donegan	*New Haven, Conn.*	22 Ward st.
Charles Henry Doolittle	*Meriden, Conn.*	140 v-s.
William Dorenbaum	*Hartford, Conn.*	120 High st.
Forbes Franklin Dougherty	*Buffalo, N. Y.*	136 v-s.
Delano Fuller Woodcliffe Douglass	*Worcester, Mass.*	70 Trumbull st.
Charles Raymond Downs	*New Haven, Conn.*	813 Quinnipiac av.
Luke Cantwell Doyle	*Worcester, Mass.*	124 Prospect st.
Emanuel Louis Dreyfus	*Santa Barbara, Cal.*	407 B.
John Gilbert Dunn	*Schenectady, N. Y.*	40 Lake pl.
Elbridge Griswold Dyer	*Cleveland, O.*	103 v-s.
William Blake Earnshaw	*Dayton, O.*	131 Grove st.
Lloyd Searing Emory	*Hempstead, L. I., N. Y.*	130 v-s.
Leo Englander	*New Haven, Conn.*	34 Sylvan av.
Himon William Evans	*New Haven, Conn.*	22 Oak st.
William Farson	*Oak Park, Ill.*	131 Grove st.
Grover Cleveland Fels	*Lowell, Mass.*	131 Grove st.
Frederick Clarkstone Fletcher	*Ansonia, Conn.*	Ansonia.
Hervey Lytton Foster	*Brooklyn, N. Y.*	107 v-s.
Thomas Fox	*Wyoming, O.*	119 Wall st.

William Llewellyn Fox	*New Haven, Conn.*	507 Orange st.
Samuel Judah Frankfurt	*New Haven, Conn.*	27 Silver st.
Southgate Bowne Freeman	*Morristown, N. J.*	148 V-S.
Charles Gillette Frisbie •	*Hartford, Conn.*	131 Grove st.
Frank William Gallagher	*New Haven, Conn.*	1081 Chapel st.
William Hallowell Gallaher	*Santa Barbara, Cal.*	126 Wall st.
Colin Gardner, Jr.	*Middletown, O.*	133 College st.
Robert Edward Gaylord	*Winsted, Conn.*	124 Prospect st.
William Edward Geary	*New Haven, Conn.*	479 Orange st.
George Edward Gillespie	*Newburgh, N. Y.*	70 Trumbull st.
Maurice Hope Givens, B.S.	*Pittsburg, Ky.*	529 Elm st.
National Normal University 1907		
James Gerber Gorman	*Elizabeth, N. J.*	126 Wall st.
Dabney Grant	*Kansas City, Mo.*	112 V-S.
Stanley Holland Graves	*Buffalo, N. Y.*	133 College st.
Charles Wesley Griggs	*New Haven, Conn.*	178 Lawrence st.
Seymour Dwight Hall	*Wallingford, Conn.*	115 V-S.
Donald Adams Hallock	*Derby, Conn.*	110 Wall st.
Samuel Jackson Hammitt	*Apollo, Pa.*	110 Wall st.
Henry Morris Hartmann	*Morris, N. Y.*	110 Wall st.
Allen Graves Haskell	*Pittsfield, Mass.*	124 Wall st.
Benjamin Rawls Hawley	*Hartford, Conn.*	120 High st.
John Terrill Hawley	*Danbury, Conn.*	666 W. D.
Andrew King Haxstun	*Fort Edward, N. Y.*	106 V-S.
Philip Hawley Hedges	*Newark, N. J.*	110 Wall st.
Walter Clarke Hemingway	*New Haven, Conn.*	25 Hotchkiss st.
Louis John Henes	*New York City*	126 High st.
Earle Chapman Herrick	*Norwich, Conn.*	119 Wall st.
Carleton Rufus Hewitt	*Torrington, Conn.*	124 Wall st.
Erastus Hodges	*Torrington, Conn.*	124 Wall st.
Harold Newton Hooghkirk	*New Haven, Conn.*	286 Norton st.
Lucien Ball Horton	*Binghamton, N. Y.*	90 Wall st.
Raymond Hewlett Hotchkiss	*Ansonia, Conn.*	Ansonia
Edgar Billings Howard	*New Orleans, La.*	133 College st.
Leonard Vernon Howe	*Minneapolis, Minn.*	96 Wall st.
William Henry Hubbard, Jr.	*Auburn, N. Y.*	121 V-S.
George Franklin Huff, Jr.	*Greensburg, Pa.*	315 York st.
Frank Carley Hunt	*Hot Springs, S. D.*	131 Grove st.
William Henry Hunt, Jr.	*Helena, Mont.*	101 V-S.
Harold Larned Hutchins	*New Haven, Conn.*	234 Division st.
Frank Burch Ijams	*Terre Haute, Ind.*	17 Hillhouse av.
Gerald Breck Jackson	*Paterson, N. J.*	110 Wall st.
Loring Kenneth Jordan	*St. Joseph, Mo.*	126 Wall st.
James Stanley Joyce	*Chicago, Ill.*	187 V-S.

Pao-vung Jui	*Shanghai, China*	56 Grove st.
George Hughes Kaercher	*Pottsville, Pa.*	149 v-s.
Charles Emmanuel Kaufmann	*Sioux Falls, So. Dak.*	128 Wall st.
Paul Independence Keeler	*Tunkhannock, Pa.*	133 v-s.
Forest Bowns Kellogg	*Chicago, Ill.*	132 v-s.
Oliver Stuart Kelly	*Springfield, O.*	126 Wall st.
Richard Albert Kenworthy, Jr.	*Poughkeepsie, N. Y.*	96 Wall st.
Frederick Harold Kenyon	*Hartford, Conn.*	104 Wall st.
John Kerr	*New York City*	145 v-s.
George Russell King	*Elmhurst, Ill.*	207 Bishop st.
Robert Snyder King	*Dayton, O.*	131 Grove st.
Stephen Vincent Klem	*New Haven, Conn.*	15 Lake pl.
Joseph Whitmore Knapp	*Newburyport, Mass.*	150 v-s.
Bedross Sahag Koshkarian, B.A.	*Harpoot, Armenia*	7 Library st.
Euphrates College 1903		
Robert Weir LaMontagne	*New York City*	17 Hillhouse av.
William Shelden Lawson, Jr.	*New York City*	133 College st.
Joseph Allen Lee	*Chicago, Ill.*	128 Wall st.
James Luther Leeper, Jr.	*Summit, N. J.*	126 Wall st
Frederic Bradley Lewis	*Stratford, Conn.*	Stratford
Henry Leroy Lewis	*Stratford, Conn.*	146 v-s.
Maxfield Crosby Lewis	*New Haven, Conn.* 391 Winthrop av.	
Robert Curtis Lewis	*Stratford, Conn.*	Stratford
John Leavens Lilley	*Waterbury, Conn.*	101 v-s.
Paul Parkes Llewellyn	*Evanston, Ill.*	160 v-s.
Charles Edwin Lockhart	*Greenwich, Conn.*	122 Wall st.
Thomas Thomson Logie	*New Haven, Conn.*	106 Bishop st.
John William Lowe, Jr.	*Woodmont, Conn.*	Woodmont
Henry Hall Lyman	*Middlefield, Conn.*	148 v-s.
Thomas Lynn	*Camden, N. J.*	96 Wall st.
Burtis Barton McCarn	*Chicago, Ill.*	391 Temple st.
Edward Michael McDonough	*New Haven, Conn.*	38 Hallock st.
Drury Albert McMillen	*Alton, Ill.*	104 Wall st.
William Bennett Malone	*Denver, Colo.*	149 v-s.
Richard Leach Mann	*Buffalo, N. Y.*	124 v-s.
Edward Ward Manning	*New Haven, Conn.*	32 Stevens st.
Mervyn Mason Manning	*Groton, Mass.*	128 High st.
Tomás Augusto Mazier, B.A.	*Tegucigalpa, Hond., C. A.* 399 Orange st.	
El Porvenir College, Honduras, 1904		
William Henry Mead	*Hinsdale, N. H.*	51 Trumbull st.
Frederick Abraham Merlis	*New Haven, Conn.*	132 Hill st.
Arthur Royden Merritt	*Grandview, N. Y.*	17 Hillhouse av.
Haines Rennyson Merritt	*East Aurora, N. Y.*	120 v-s.
Robert Ira Merwin	*New Haven, Conn.*	68 Clark st.

Charles Ferdinand Mills	*Savannah, Ga.*	133 College st.
Laurence Lewis Moore	*Redlands, Cal.*	168 v-s.
Robert Royster Moore	*Kansas City, Mo.*	665 w. d.
Vernon Starr Morehouse	*Stratford, Conn.*	Stratford
Thomas Clayton Mott	*Rouse's Point, N. Y.*	106 v-s.
Raymond Burton Munson	*Stratford, Conn.*	Stratford
Richard VanWyck Negley	*San Antonio, Texas*	17 Hillhouse av.
Horace Albert Newbury	*New London, Conn.*	47 Lake pl.
Axel Hjahnar Nicander	*New Haven, Conn.*	49 Winthrop av.
Martin William Nill	*Rockville, Conn.*	391 Temple st.
Alexander Nimick	*Pittsburg, Pa.*	150 v-s.
Edward Champlin Osborn	*New Haven, Conn.*	167 Ellsworth av.
Ralph Rand Parish	*Meriden, Conn.*	177 Norton st.
Wendell Lawrence Paul	*Montreal, Canada*	59 Wall st.
Harley Taylor Peck	*Newtown, Conn.*	391 Temple st.
Earl Stanley Peirce	*Frankfort, Me.*	96 Wall st.
Arthur Paul Peterson	*Ansonia, Conn.*	Ansonia
Norman Philip Pierce	*Honey Grove, Texas*	119 Grove st.
Dwight Warren Pond	*Terryville, Conn.*	124 Wall st.
Raymond Augustus Pond	*Unionville, Conn.*	124 Wall st.
James Poole	*New Haven, Conn.*	126 Columbus av.
Paul Ragnet Preston	*Davenport, Ia.*	17 Hillhouse av.
William Eversole Prosser	*St. Louis, Mo.*	104 Wall st.
William Johns Ralston	*New York City*	379 Temple st.
Herbert Hartley Ramsay	*Los Angeles, Cal.*	133 College st.
John Patterson Ramsey	*St. Louis, Mo.*	133 College st.
Jonathan Sanford Randle	*Redding, Conn.*	39 Lynwood pl.
Charles Denman Raymond	*Ridgefield, Conn.*	82 Wall st.
John Reimann	*New Haven, Conn.*	113 Lawrence st
Frank Anthony Rend	*Chicago, Ill.*	88 Wall st.
George Fullerton Renton, Jr.	*Honolulu, H. I.*	112 v-s.
Earle Hay Reynolds	*Chicago, Ill.*	96 Wall st.
Edward Carrington Mayo Richards	*New York City*	131 v-s.
Robert Annan Riley	*Philadelphia, Pa.*	149 v-s.
George W. Rittenour	*Piketon, O.*	161 v-s.
Douglass Raymond Robbins	*Middletown, O.*	133 College st.
Caryl Roberts	*Philadelphia, Pa.*	111 Grove st.
Walter Gregory Rodiger	*Chicago, Ill.*	124 Prospect st.
Walter Francis Roesler	*Great Neck, L. I., N. Y.*	145 v-s.
Frederick James Root	*New Haven, Conn.*	65 Foote st.
Roswell J. Roth	*Watertown, N. Y.*	133 College st.
Henry Walter Routenberg	*Keene, N. H.*	124 Wall st.
Donald Gardner Russell	*Wallingford, Conn.*	137 v-s.
Wilbur Barlow Ruthrauff	*New York City*	111 Grove st.

John Francis Sagarino	*Hartford, Conn.*	74 Howe st.
Arthur John St. Lawrence	*West Haven, Conn.*	77 Olive st.
Donald Stuart Sammis	*Stratford, Conn.*	Stratford
Truman Frank Sanford	*Unionville, Conn.*	124 Wall st.
Edward Johnson Sanger	*Naugatuck, Conn.*	96 Wall st.
Joseph Alexander Scarlett, Jr.	*Cincinnati, O.*	124 Prospect st.
James Edward Schall, Jr.	*New Haven, Conn.*	167 Livingston st.
Henry Seymour Scott	*New York City*	70 Trumbull st.
Alfred Bryant Seeley	*New Haven, Conn.*	147 Blatchley av.
Roupen Nazareth Serabian	*Shelton, Conn.*	152 Grove st.
Norman Fisk Shailer	*Chester, Conn.*	109 V-S.
Ray Hamilton Skelton .	*Brooklyn, N. Y.*	144 V-S.
Bryan Hooker Smith	*Montclair, N. J.*	120 College st.
Herbert Scott Snead	*Montclair, N. J.*	114 High st.
Chester Raymond Snow	*Hackensack, N. J.*	8 Prospect pl.
Horace Adams Soper	*Bloomington, Ill.*	133 College st.
Charles Reginald Southey	*Schoombie, Cape Colony, South Africa*	
		96 Wall st.
Alfred Brim Southworth	*Brooklyn, N. Y.*	102 V-S.
Karl Conrad Stadtmiller	*Meriden, Conn.*	120 College st.
Rudolph Stanley-Brown	*Cold Spring Harbor, L. I., N. Y.*	104 V-S.
Burt Stearns	*Denver, Colo.*	17 Hillhouse av.
Howard Voorheis Stephens	*Cincinnati, O.*	96 Wall st.
Frederick Archibald Stewart	*Ansonia, Conn.*	391 Temple st.
John Thomas Stoddart	*Buffalo, N. Y.*	82 Wall st.
Russell Wheeler Strong	*Setauket, L. I., N. Y.*	171 V-S.
James Breden Stuart .	*New York City*	124 Prospect st.
Benjamin Thaw, Jr.	*New York City*	119 V-S.
Joseph Dio Thomas	*Pittsburg, Pa.*	82 Wall st.
Ralph Emerson Thompson	*Rockford, Ill.*	133 College st.
John Montgomery Toucey	*New York City*	124 Prospect st.
Glenn Wood Traer, Jr.	*Chicago, Ill.*	101 V-S.
Frank Henry Villie	*Milford, Conn.*	96 Wall st.
Talbot Cyrus Walker	*San Francisco, Cal.*	170 V-S.
Thomas Hay Walker	*Sewickley, Pa.*	131 Grove st.
John Bryant Wallace, Jr.	*Ansonia, Conn.*	111 V-S.
James Farley Walton	*Allegheny, Pa.*	17 Hillhouse av.
Warren Leland Ward	*Port Chester, N. Y.*	88 Wall st.
Howard Thomas Ware	*Covington, Ky.*	119 Wall st.
Lee Gilbert Warren	*Piqua, O.*	119 Wall st.
William Joseph Waters	*Derby, Conn.*	117 Wall st.
Roy Stuart Watson	*Milwaukee, Wisc.*	85 Sachem st.
Theodore Stout Watson	*Short Hills, N. J.*	131 Grove st.
Lawrence Watts	*Brooklyn, N. Y.*	102 V-S.

David Tolner Weinerman	*Hartford, Conn.*	649 E. D.
John Herbert Weiss, Jr.	*Chicago, Ill.*	110 Wall st.
George Gregg Welch	*Dover, N. H.*	134 V-S.
Frederic Hart Wells	*Amityville, L. I., N. Y.*	113 V-S.
Henry Myers Wheaton	*Philadelphia, Pa.*	131 Grove st.
John Robert Whiting	*New Haven, Conn.*	83 Mansfield st.
Warren Corning Wick	*Cleveland, O.*	131 Grove st.
Richard Ernst Wiles	*Kansas City, Mo.*	117 V-S.
Edmund Farrington Williams	*Syracuse, N. Y.*	84 Trumbull st.
Gurth Williams	*Plainfield, N. J.*	82 Wall st.
Robert Prince Winton	*New Haven, Conn.*	136 Canner st.
Edward Collins Wood	*Kansas City, Mo.*	110 V-S.
Eric Fisher Wood	*New York City*	143 V-S.
Harold Spry Woods	*Portsmouth, N. H.*	666 W. D.
Clarence Aldro Wright	*Washington, D. C.*	217 York st.
William Yale	*Alder Creek, N. Y.*	110 V-S.
George LeRoy Young	*Orient, L. I., N. Y.*	119 Wall st.
Zai-Ziang Zee	*Shanghai, China*	365 WH.

JUNIORS, 275

FRESHMAN CLASS

Robert Mims Aldrich	*Greenfield, Mass.*	281 Crown st.
Kenneth Leland Allen	*Cleveland, O.*	117 Wall st.
Lloyd Seward Allen	*Auburn, N. Y.*	86 Wall st.
Kenneth Slade Alling	*Montclair, N. J.*	122 Wall st.
Eliott Landon Alvord	*Winsted, Conn.*	118 College st.
Joseph Alfred Ambler	*Norwich, Conn.*	9 Library st.
Hamlin Foster Andrus	*Yonkers, N. Y.*	423 Temple st.
Edward Percy Apgar	*Jersey City, N. J.*	423 Temple st.
Shreve Maclaren Archer	*Minneapolis, Minn.*	128 High st.
Harold Ralph Bacon	*Derby, Conn.*	120 College st.
Collier Whittemore Baird	*South Orange, N. J.*	122 Wall st.
Dudley Mills Baker	*New Haven, Conn.*	210 St. Ronan st.
Frank Albert Baker	*Zanesville, O.*	128 High st.
Delavan Munson Baldwin	*New York City*	133 College st.
Samuel Gunn Barker	*Scranton, Pa.*	125 High st.
Terry Earle Barker	*Coronado Beach, Cal.*	125 High st.
Edward Lewis Barlow	*Bridgeport, Conn.*	Bridgeport
Starr Hickok Barnum, 2d	*New Haven, Conn.*	160 v-s.
Bradley White Bartholomew	*Springfield, Mass.*	55 Prospect st.
Edmund Benton Bartlett	*New London, Conn.*	10 B. M. H.
Jay B. Bassett	*Minneapolis, Minn.*	119 Wall st.
Howard C. Bates	*Providence, R. I.*	125 High st.
Lindell Theodore Bates	*New York City*	119 Wall st.
Gordon Battelle, 2d	*Columbus, O.*	188 v-s.
Howard Wood Beardsley	*Hartford, Conn.*	104 Wall st.
Robert Oglesby Beardsley	*Middletown, O.*	125 High st.
Charles Elliott Beaumont	*New Haven, Conn.*	391 Howard av.
Harold Clark Beebe	*New Haven, Conn.*	89 Gregory st.
Robert Bengis	*New Haven, Conn.*	271 Cedar st.
Edward Whittemore Benner	*Englewood, N. J.*	128 High st.
Jacob Berman	*Hartford, Conn.*	214 F.
Howard Bird	*New Haven, Conn.*	244 Orchard st.
William Franklin Bishop, Jr.	*Norwalk, Conn.*	132 Wall st.
Malcolm Havens Bissell	*New York City*	125 High st.
Milton Elvin Blanchard, Jr.	*Newark, N. J.*	4 B. M. H.
Chandler Wells Bleistein	*Buffalo, N. Y.*	413 Temple st.
Ralph Elmer Boggs	*Tacoma, Wash.*	120 High st.
Daniel Berger Boyer	*Boyertown, Pa.*	124 Wall st.
Donald Stuart Boynton	*Highland Falls, Ill.*	395 Temple st.
Henry Franklin Bradley	*Salt Lake City, Utah*	82 Wall st.

Howard Stanford Brainerd	*Mt. Vernon, N. Y.*	610 E. D.
Emmett Raymond Brann	*Warren, Pa.*	82 Wall st.
Jacob Reuben Brenner	*New Haven, Conn.*	113 Bradley st.
William Henry Brevoort, Jr.	*New York City*	3 Hillhouse av.
William Edwards Brewster	*Iron Mountain, Mich.*	117 Wall st.
Jarvis Adams Britton	*Cleveland, O.*	117 Wall st.
William Almet Broadhead	*Jamestown, N. Y.*	387 Temple st.
Joseph Edward Brody	*Perth Amboy, N. J.*	21 William st.
Sydney Freeman Brown	*Reading, Mass.*	117 Wall st.
Carl Reed Brownell	*Worcester, Mass.*	7 B. M. H.
Henry Clay Bughman, Jr.	*Pittsburg, Pa.*	409 Temple st.
Arthur William Burgess	*New Haven, Conn.*	871 Grand av.
Charles Allen Burleson	*Jewett City, Conn.*	114 High st.
Fred Enos Burnside	*Seattle, Wash.*	110 Wall st.
Philip Laurence Buttrick	*New Haven, Conn.*	296 Columbus av.
Bruce Eldon Cameron	*Toronto, Canada*	19 Whitney av.
William Allen Camp	*Bridgeport, Conn.*	Bridgeport
George Henry Campbell	*Great Falls, Mont.*	333 York st.
Louis James Campbell	*Youngstown, O.*	480 Winthrop av.
Andrew Haley Candee	*Ft. Dodge, Ia.*	367 Union av., West Haven
Raymond Bishop Canfield	*New Haven, Conn.*	314 Crown st.
Wooster Canfield	*Bridgeport, Conn.*	82 Wall st.
Robert Cartmell	*New York City*	3 Hillhouse av.
William Harrison Caruthers	*Norwich, Conn.*	114 High st.
Robert Hart Cary	*North Platte, Nebr.*	120 York st.
Lowell Mead Chapin	*Chicago, Ill.*	131 Grove st.
Alfred Floss Cherry	*Colony, Okla.*	227 Crown st.
Joseph Du Barry Childs	*Pittsburg, Pa.*	120 College st.
Arthur Amos Clapp	*St. Paul, Minn.*	114 V-s.
Hale Austin Clark	*So. Norwalk, Conn.*	So. Norwalk
Robert Varney Clay	*Glenville, O.*	405 Temple st.
Thomas C. Coffin	*Nampa, Idaho*	119 Wall st.
Viott Myers Cole	*East Orange, N. J.*	13 B. M. H.
George Robb Collins	*Chicago, Ill.*	120 College st.
Glen Moore Comstock	*Denver, Colo.*	364 WH.
Edwin Dillingham Crowell, Jr.	*East Dennis, Mass.*	48 Lake pl.
John Adam Crowley	*West Haven, Conn.*	West Haven
Loftus Brookman Cuddy	*Cleveland, O.*	96 Wall st.
Frank Addison Cutler	*New Haven, Conn.*	119 Washington av.
William Frye Cutler	*Suffern, N. Y.*	40 Lake pl.
Harry Eliott Daggett	*New Haven, Conn.*	240 View st.
Morris James Dale	*Cincinnati, O.*	128 High st.
Walter Julius Damtoft	*Bridgeport, Conn.*	Bridgeport
Charles Loomis Dana, Jr.	*New York City*	114 High st.

William McClure Dandy, Jr.	*Chicago, Ill.*	151 V-S.
Nelson Davidson	*Lancaster, Pa.*	395 Temple st.
William Treat Davidson	*Warren, Pa.*	128 High st.
George Germaine Dearborn	*Seattle, Wash.*	110 Wall st.
William Frederick Dexheimer	*New Haven, Conn.*	183 Dixwell av.
Claude Mc Conaha Dibble	*New Haven, Conn.*	37 Fairmont av.
John Calvert Donaldson	*Philadelphia, Pa.*	118 College st.
Walter Cooley Douglas	*New York City*	333 York st.
Hudson Downs Dravo	*Pittsburg, Pa.*	59 Grove st.
Charles Doyle Drynan	*Sewickley, Pa.*	144 Dwight st.
Charles Henry Dunlap	*New Haven, Conn.*	493 Dixwell av.
Charles Hutchinson Dunning	*Auburn, N. Y.*	96 Wall st.
Robert Ernest Dwyer	*New Haven, Conn.*	8 Prospect pl.
William Wallace Eastman	*Minneapolis, Minn.*	409 Temple st.
John Nicholas Eckle	*West Haven, Conn.*	West Haven
Charles Dudley Eldred	*Joliet, Ill.*	122 Wall st.
Arthur Dana Elliot	*New York City*	133 Wall st.
Matthew Griswold Ely	*New York City*	397 Temple st.
Rufus Dodd Woods Ewing	*Enfield, Mass.*	379 Temple st.
Adison Morgan Farley	*Fairfield, Conn.*	114 High st.
Roy Emerson Farnham	*New Haven, Conn.*	238 Grand av.
Frederick Charles Fearing	*New York City*	11 B. M. H.
Carl Ferguson	*Logansport, Ind.*	413 Temple st.
Joseph Patrick Fleming	*Wallingford, Conn.*	Wallingford
Clarence Jean Fraissinet	*New York City*	119 Wall st.
Bernard Barney Frankel	*New Haven, Conn.*	346 George st.
Philip Mansfield Freeman	*Plainville, Conn.*	110 Wall st.
Walter Clifford French	*Derby, Conn.*	333 York st.
William Shepard French	*Saratoga Springs, N. Y.*	14 B. M. H.
Myron Elmer Fuller	*New York City*	110 Wall st.
Dwight Lyman Fullerton	*Chillicothe, O.*	387 Temple st.
Edwin Baker Gager, Jr.	*Derby, Cônn.*	333 York st.
Arthur Gardner	*Washington, D. C.*	117 Wall st.
Edwin Gisbon Gaynor	*Bridgeport, Conn.*	132 Wall st.
George Charles Gerner	*New Haven, Conn.*	12 Nicoll st.
Bennett Edward Glazer	*New Haven, Conn.*	250 George st.
James Joseph Gleason	*New Haven, Cônn.*	241 Hamilton st.
Paul Goldberg	*Bridgeport, Conn.*	Bridgeport
Elsworth Helbert Goldschmidt	*New York City*	128 Wall st.
Henry Karl Goldstein	*Hartford, Conn.*	120 High st.
Donald Goodrich	*Minneapolis, Minn.*	132 Wall st.
Charles Goodwin	*Brooklyn, N. Y.*	120 College st.
Sheppard Bliss Gordy	*Derby, Conn.*	333 York st.
Joseph Marion Goss	*Centerville, Ia.*	113 Wall st.

Raymond Willis Gowdy	*Thompsonville, Conn.*	333 York st.
Douglas Grant	*Burlingame, Cal.*	108 High st.
William McKinnie Green	*Cleveland, O.*	117 Wall st.
Harry Paul Greenough	*Missoula, Mont.*	120 High st.
Theodore Morris Greer	*Denver, Colo.*	150 Grove st.
Samuel Adams Griswold	*Wethersfield, Conn.*	82 Wall st.
Harry Frank Guggenheim	*New York City*	1 B. M. H.
Kenneth Stone Hall	*Portland, Oregon*	333 York st.
Richard Nash Hall	*Topeka, Kans.*	82 Wall st.
William Storrs Hoyt Hamilton	*New Haven, Conn.*	28 Norton st.
John Hays Hammond, Jr.	*New York City*	128 v-s.
Marcus Alonzo Hanna	*Ravenna, O.*	400 Temple st.
James Ely Harding, Jr.	*Lyme, Conn.*	55 Prospect st.
William Allen Harris, Jr.	*Springfield, Mass.*	130 Wall st.
Berthold Francis Hastings	*Bridgeport, Conn.*	Bridgeport
Harold W. Hatch	*New Britain, Conn.*	113 Wall st.
Harrison Rountree Hathaway	*East Orange, N. J.*	127 v-s.
Loomis Havemeyer	*Hartford, Conn.*	117 Wall st.
John Ryan Hayes	*Waterbury, Conn.*	55 Prospect st.
Arthur Grant Heidrich	*Peoria, Ill.*	131 Grove st.
Carl Constantine Heisen, Jr.	*Chicago, Ill.*	150 Grove st.
Wilmer Du Pont Hemming	*Colorado Springs, Colo.*	120 High st.
John Philip Henderson	*Sharon, Pa.*	9 B. M. H.
Arthur Joseph Hill	*Meriden, Conn.*	Meriden
Earl Alton Hinkley	*Stony Creek, Conn.*	Stony Creek
Arthur B. Hinterleiter	*Kutztown, Pa.*	118 College st.
Harold Peckham Hobart	*Cleveland, O.*	119 Wall st.
Henry Homer Hobbs	*New York City*	423 Temple st.
Russell John Holden	*Danville, Ill.*	111 Grove st.
Joseph DuBois Holloway	*Wheeling, W. Va.*	397 Temple st.
Arthur Downing Holmes	*New Haven, Conn.*	32 Gilbert st.
Albert William Honywill, Jr.	*Hartford, Conn.*	53 Lake pl.
Edgar Malin Hoopes, Jr.	*Wilmington, Del.*	127 v-s.
Bayard Hopkins	*Ridgewood, N. J.*	110 Wall st.
Henry Stanley Horn	*East Orange, N. J.*	110 Wall st.
John Crompton Horsfall	*New Britain, Conn.*	217 York st.
Osborn Ensign Horton	*New Haven, Conn.*	202 Crown st.
Willard Porter Hovey	*Kansas City, Mo.*	59 Grove st.
Alvin Pike Howard	*New Orleans, La.*	3 Hillhouse av.
Thomas Franklin Hoxsey	*Paterson, N. J.*	110 Wall st.
Preston Southworth Hoyt	*Danbury, Conn.*	37 Lake pl.
Yao-chang Henry Hsin	*Shanghai, China*	114 High st.
John Giddings Hughes	*Bridgeport, Conn.*	Bridgeport
Henry Hull	*Savannah, Ga.*	400 Temple st.

44

Harold Hunsiker	*London, England*	96 Wall st.
Robert Edward Hunter	*Chicago, Ill.*	152 Grove st.
Carroll Solomon Hurlbutt	*Gales Ferry, Conn.*	37 College st.
James Richard Hyde	*Brooklyn, N. Y.*	126 High st.
James Arthur Ingalls	*Brooklyn, N. Y.*	1371 Chapel st.
Hamilton Ingersoll	*Islip, N. Y.*	133 Wall st.
Andrew Jerome Jackson	*Waterbury, Conn.*	126 Wall st.
Gilbert Nelson Jerome	*New Haven, Conn.*	24 Gilbert av.
Oswald Jimenis	*New York City*	110 Wall st.
Birger Lawrence Johnson	*Chicago, Ill.*	96 Wall st.
Alfred Murphy Jones	*New Haven, Conn.*	367 Howard av.
Frank Rowland Jones	*Brooklyn, N. Y.*	405 Temple st.
Percy Wonson Jones	*Christmas, Ariz.*	147 Dwight st.
Giles Bernard Keeny	*Meriden, Conn.*	Meriden
Lawrence Kidder Kelley	*Nyack, N. Y.*	113 v-s.
Charles Daniel Hanford Kellogg, Jr.	*Bridgeport, Conn.*	130 Wall st.
Albert Kerr	*Newport, R. I.*	704 W. D.
Chester Munson Kerr	*New Rochelle, N. Y.*	82 Wall st.
William Geoffrey Kimball	*New York City*	3 Hillhouse av.
Louis Solomon Kirjassoft	*Waterbury, Conn.*	724 W. D.
Harry Joseph Klarman	*New Haven, Conn.*	279 Lombard st.
Alfred Carl Kluepful	*New York City*	266 York st.
Henry Martyn Knight	*Sharon, Conn.*	105 College st.
Carl Alexis Krah	*New Haven, Conn.*	315 York st.
Veste Cornelius Kylberg	*Milburn, N. J.*	534 State st.
Dwight Morgan Kyle	*Danbury, Conn.*	295 York st.
Edward Allyn Lambert	*Bridgeport, Conn.*	124 Prospect st.
Perin Langdon, Jr.	*Cincinnati, O.*	150 Grove st.
Alfred Emanuel Langfeld	*Philadelphia, Pa.*	796 Yale P. O.
William Boice Langford	*Chicago, Ill.*	704 W. D.
Robert Morrow Larimore	*Mt. Vernon, N. Y.*	615 E. D.
Alexander Laughlin, Jr.	*Sewickley, Pa.*	117 Wall st.
Oscar Cobb Lautz	*Buffalo, N. Y.*	110 Wall st.
John Bailey Lawrence	*Mastic, N. Y.*	391 Temple st.
Harry George Legg	*Minneapolis, Minn.*	8 B. M H.
Benjamin Leopold	*Waterbury, Conn.*	18 Howe st.
Vyvyan Paul Letcher	*Plainfield, N. J.*	333 York st.
Charles Grandison Lewis	*New Haven, Conn.*	205 Whitney av.
Joseph Warren Lewis	*Philadelphia, Pa.*	425 Temple st.
Edward Harold Liebman	*New Haven, Conn.*	186 Willow st.
Theodore Lilley	*Waterbury, Conn.*	405 Temple st.
Albert Curtis Lockwood	*Seymour, Conn.*	Seymour
Howard Hancock Logan	*Chicago, Ill.*	152 Grove st.
Nelson Johnson Lomax	*St. Joseph, Mo.*	128 Wall st.

Cassius Lopez deVictoria	*New York City*	122 Howe st.
Russell Lord	*Chicago, Ill.*	117 Wall st.
John Titley Lounsbury	*Seymour, Conn.*	Seymour
Cecil Earl Lovejoy	*Kansas City, Mo.*	150 Grove st.
Toy Kay Lowe	*Oakland, Cal.*	114 High st.
John Francis Lynch	*West Haven, Conn.*	West Haven
William Joseph Lynch	*West Haven, Conn*	West Haven
Albert Porter McCarthy	*Oswego, N. Y.*	124 Wall st.
Daniel Joseph McCormick, Jr.	*Norwich, Conn.*	91 c.
Samuel Rowley MacDonald	*Yonkers, N. Y.*	122 Wall st.
Otis Edwin McIntyre	*Colorado Springs, Colo.*	130 Wall st.
Frederick Lee McNally	*Chicago, Ill.*	88 Wall st.
Allen Fletcher Marsh	*Chicago, Ill.*	393 Temple st.
Harold Emmons Marsh	*Branford, Conn.*	Branford
Bayard Martin	*Buffalo, N. Y.*	123 v-s.
Stirling Martin	*Brooklyn, N. Y.*	113 Wall st.
Thomas Wade Mather	*New Haven, Conn.*	225 Bishop st.
Hugh M. Matheson	*Huntington, N. Y.*	124 Prospect st.
George Mathews, Jr.	*New York City*	3 Hillhouse av.
Charles E. Maxwell, Jr.	*Chicago, Ill.*	152 Grove st.
Albert Younglove Meriam	*East Cleveland, O.*	117 Wall st.
Asa Suydam Merrell	*Flemington, N. J.*	140 v-s.
Kenneth Newton Merritt	*Grand View, N. Y.*	88 Wall st.
John Clifford Merwin	*New Haven, Conn.*	25 Tryon st.
John Edgar Meyer	*Montclair, N. J.*	117 Wall st.
Richard Kirby Miles	*Lakeville, Conn.*	105 College st.
Victor Milkowski	*Schenectady, N. Y.*	33 Rose st.
Charles George Mills	*Bradford, Pa.*	133 v-s.
Wilson Waddingham Mills	*East Las Vegas, N. M.*	119 Wall st.
Abner Wheeler Mitchell	*Washington, Conn.*	53 Lake pl.
John Philip Mitchell	*Cleveland, O.*	132 Wall st.
Leroy Bradley Mitchell•	*Southbury, Conn.*	128 High st.
Spencer Frank Moore	*Schenectady, N. Y.*	40 Lake pl.
Walter Ronald Morse	*Waterbury, Conn.*	126 Wall st.
Spencer Latham Murfey	*East Cleveland, O.*	119 Grove st.
Joseph Bradley Murray	*Brooklyn, N. Y.*	393 Temple st.
Oliver Murray	*Davenport, Ia.*	407 Temple st.
Theodore Charles Naedele	*Hartford, Conn.*	82 Wall st.
Clyde Ross Newell	*Orange, Conn.*	Orange
Paul Curtis Newkom	*Corry, Pa.*	135 Wall st.
William Monypeny Newsom	*Columbus, O.*	152 v-s.
Sih-Zung Nie	*Shanghai, China*	37 Lynwood pl.
St. John's College, Shanghai, 1901		
Warren Arthur Norris	*Troy, N. Y.*	413 Temple st.

Carl Gottfried Ortmayer	*Chicago, Ill.*	407 Temple st.
Eugene Osborn	*Montclair, N. J.*	5 B. M. H.
Rutherford Page	*New York City*	427 Temple st.
Francis Strickland Page	*Brooklyn, N. Y.*	133 College st.
Elwell Palmer	*Brooklyn, N.Y.*	117 Wall st.
Dwight Boyce Pangburn	*New Haven, Conn.*	731 Elm st.
Andrew Giles Parker, Jr.	*New Haven, Conn.*	652 Dixwell av.
James Parker, 3d	*Harrisburg, Pa.*	1317 Boulevard
Felicano Primo Paterno, B.A.	*Manila, P. I.*	114 High st.
University of Manila 1905		
George S. Patterson	*White Plains, N. Y.*	379 Temple st.
John William Patton	*Curwensville, Pa.*	82 Wall st.
Francis Frederick Peck	*West Haven, Conn.*	Box 44, West Haven
Sanford Benham Perkins	*Torrington, Conn.*	656 W. D.
Sherman Hickox Perry	*Waterbury, Conn.*	148 V-S.
Leon Jay Phillips	*New Milford, Conn.*	53 Prospect st.
Francis Frith Pickslay	*Warwick, N. Y.*	70 Trumbull st.
Joseph Pierpont	*North Haven, Conn.*	North Haven
Orlando Bronson Potter	*Ossining, N. Y.*	113 Wall st.
Donald Bishop Prentice	*Hartford, Conn.*	117 Wall st.
Jansen Hasbrock Preston	*Kingston, N. Y.*	421 Temple st.
Thomas Harold Prosser	*Brooklyn, N. Y.*	133 College st.
Maxwell Lewis Rafferty	*New York City*	120 High st.
Jack Adincourt Rainier	*New York City*	150 Grove st.
Harry Brooks Rathbun	*Noank, Cohn.*	148 Whalley av.
Homer Reed, Jr.	*Kansas City, Mo.*	150 Grove st.
John Chapin Reed	*Springfield, Mass.*	6 B. M. H.
Harold Wily Reeder	*Detroit, Mich.*	379 Temple st.
John Charles Reilly, Jr.	*Derby, Conn.*	333 York st.
Charles Edward Richardson	*Salem, Mass.*	119 Wall st.
David Munson Ricks	*Bethel, Conn.*	132 Wall st.
Clyde Albert Risdon	*Kane, Pa.*	126 High st.
Archer Egbert Roberts	*Mt. Kisco, N. Y.*	117 Wall st.
Philip Rogers	*Greenfield, Mass.*	117 Wall st.
Leo D. Rothensies	*Walton, N. Y.*	684 W. D.
William Beardslee Rudd	*Media, Pa.*	389 Temple st.
Louis Spring Runciman	*Portland, Me.*	397 Temple st.
Raymond Warren Rush	*Oil City, Pa.*	117 Wall st.
Harry Salzstein	*Milwaukee, Wisc.*	333 York st.
Oscar Adolph Sandquist	*New Haven, Conn.*	153 St. John st.
Selden Bradley Sanford	*Brooklyn, N. Y.*	110 Wall st.
Charles Adam Sattig	*New Haven, Conn.*	65 Foster st.
Albert Wilcox Savage	*Meriden, Conn.*	113 Wall st.
Herman George Scharmann	*Brooklyn, N. Y.*	118 College st.

Ernest Carl Schnuck	*Ansonia, Conn.*	299 York st.
Harold Moore Seitz	*Kansas City, Mo.*	59 Grove st.
Abraham Morris Shapiro	*Hartford, Conn.*	40 Broad st.
Norman Arthur Shepard	*New Haven, Conn.*	159 Blatchley av.
George Kendall Shields	*Colorado Springs, Colo.*	61 Trumbull st.
George Webb Shillingford	*Clearfield, Pa.*	3 Hillhouse av.
Sidney Elbert Short	*New York City*	333 York st.
Jacob Shulansky	*Hartford, Conn.*	649 E. D.
William Simpson Sloan	*New York City*	144 V-S.
Benjamin Harrison Smith	*West Haven, Conn.*	West Haven
Harrison Braxton Smith	*Cincinnati, O.*	12 B. M. H.
Oliver Ledlie Smith	*Pittsburg, Pa.*	120 College st.
Philip Augustus Smith	*New Haven, Conn.*	123 Carmel st.
William Howard Smith	*Philadelphia, Pa.*	114 High st.
William Penn Snyder, Jr.	*Sewickley, Pa.*	120 College st.
Burt Kellogg Spencer	*Suffield, Conn.*	373 Crown st.
Roger Sherman Sperry	*Waterbury, Conn.*	427 Temple st.
Joel Spitz	*Chicago, Ill.*	110 Wall st.
Louis Roemmer Stadtmiller	*Stamford, Conn.*	126 Wall st.
Alfred Russell Starr, Jr.	*New York City*	113 V-S.
George Whitney Stephenson	*Allegheny, Pa.*	120 High st.
George Albert Stetson	*New Haven, Conn.*	76 Mansfield st.
Edgar Alden Stevens	*Buffalo, N. Y.*	391 Temple st.
John F. Stevens, Jr.	*New Haven, Conn.*	250 Church st.
Addison Stillwell	*Chicago, Ill.*	152 Grove st.
Irving Davis Stone	*Troy, N. Y.*	413 Temple st.
Jeffrey Alexander Stone	*Danbury, Conn.*	333 York st.
Norman Luman Stone	*New Haven, Conn.*	119 Wall st.
Richard Lawton Strobridge	*Stamford, Conn.*	104 Wall st.
Henry Holt Sturges	*Shelton, Conn.*	698 W. D.
Thomas Bonser Summers	*Springfield, O.*	3 Hillhouse av.
John Swan	*Pittsburg, Pa.*	120 High st.
Arthur Darling Sykes	*Rockville, Conn.*	152 Grove st.
Thomas Douglas Taggart	*Indianapolis, Ind.*	96 Wall st.
Harold Elstner Talbot, Jr.	*Dayton, O.*	150 Grove st.
Donald Forrester Taylor	*Morristown, N. J.*	395 Temple st.
Irving Howland Taylor	*Summit, N. J.*	110 Wall st.
Walter Willard Taylor	*Chicago, Ill.*	400 Temple st.
Lawrence Aldrich Teasdale	*New Haven, Conn.*	121 Nicoll st.
Joe Crisler Terrill	*Dallas, Texas*	8 Prospect pl.
Walter Scott Thatcher	*Waverly, N. Y.*	55 Prospect st.
Joseph Paul Thomas	*Denver, Colo.*	15 Sylvan av.
Harold Wilson Thompson	*New Haven, Conn.*	719 Orange st.
John Henry Thompson, Jr.	*Kansas City, Mo.*	59 Grove st.

Landon Ketchum Thorne	*Babylon, L. I., N. Y.*	119 Wall st.
Harold C. Tiebout •	*Brooklyn, N. Y.*	387 Temple st.
Norman Edwin Titus	*New York City*	333 York st.
Andrew Edward Bernard Tommers	*New Haven, Conn.*	
		103 Thompson st.
Charles Solberg Traer	*Chicago, Ill.*	407 Temple st.
Robert Treat	*Bridgewater, Conn.*	397 Crown st.
Henry Elisha Trowbridge	*New Haven, Conn.*	76 Gregory st.
William Abbey Turner	*Housatonic, Mass.*	421 Temple st.
Warren William Upson	*Kensington, Conn.*	114 High st.
Ezra Read Vail	*New York City*	17 Hillhouse av.
Dudley Blanchard Valentine	*Berkeley, Cal.*	393 Temple st.
William Thomas VanAlstyne	*Albany, N. Y.*	122 V·S.
Benedict VanVoorhis	*Monterey, Mexico*	117 Wall st.
Philip Osborn Viall	*Painesville, O.*	117 Wall st.
Charles Ridgely Vincent	*Chicago, Ill.*	82 Wall st.
Morris Roderick Volck	*New York City*	135 Wall st.
Robert Strong Wadsworth	*Warehouse Point, Conn.*	76 C.
Stanley Byron Waite	*Yonkers, N. Y.*	132 Wall st.
Carroll Kennon Warmoth	*Lawrence, La.*	2 B. M. H.
Winfred Clark Warner	*New Haven, Conn.*	10 Clinton av.
Lewis Baker Warren	*New York City*	133 Wall st.
Charles Cutler Waterman	*Roxbury, Mass.*	389 Temple st.
Charles Harlan Watzek	*Davenport, Ia.*	119 Wall st.
Richard Wayne	*Cincinnati, O.*	125 High st.
Chester Louis Weil	*New Haven, Conn.*	352 Orange st.
Joseph Mahon Wells	*Newell, W. Va.*	266 York st.
Harold Andrews White	*New Britain, Conn.*	114 High st.
Hubert Knapp Whitmer	*Goshen, Ind.*	86 Wall st.
Russell Whittlesey	*Pittsfield, Mass.*	59 Grove st.
Ward Alington Wickwire	*Cortland, N. Y.*	133 College st.
Wilbur Elliott Wilder, Jr.	*Auburn, N. Y.*	86 Wall st.
Livingston Evans Wilkeson	*Tacoma, Wash.*	110 Wall st.
Albert Nathaniel Williams	*Denver, Colo.*	610 E. D.
Milton Sanborn Williams	*Derby, Conn.*	120 College st.
Samuel Guy Williams	*Cochranville, Pa.*	333 York st.
Myron Henry Wilson, Jr.	*Cleveland, O.*	119 Grove st.
Carroll Dana Winslow	*New York City*	427 Temple st.
Francis Winslow, Jr.	*Hartford, Conn.*	82 Wall st.
Francis H. Wittstein	*Chicago, Ill.*	132 Wall st.
Wing Dan Wong	*Ichang, China*	56 Grove st.
St. John's College, Shanghai, 1907		
Fletcher Hegeman Wood	*Mt. Vernon, N. Y.*	615 E. D.
Richard Gilpin Wood, Jr.	*Bryn Mawr, Pa.*	114 High st.

William Janeway Wood, Jr.	*Westport, Conn.*	692 w. d.
Donald Woodward	*Washington, D. C.*	3 Hillhouse av.
Gerald Lockwood Wright	*Hancock, Mich.*	3 Hillhouse av.
Cecil George Young	*Norwich, Conn.*	37 College st.
Charles Sidney Young	*Johnstown, N. Y.*	Derby, Conn.
Nathan Young	*Kansas City, Mo.*	425 Temple st.
Harry Yudowitch	*Hartford, Conn.*	9᾿ Prince st.
Abraham Zimmerman	*Bridgeport, Conn.*	Bridgeport

FRESHMEN, 396

SPECIAL STUDENTS

Douglass Cole Arnold	*Westfield, N. J.*	142 v-s.
Samuel John Berard	*New Haven. Conn.*	813 Orange st.
Pierrepont Bigelow	*New Haven, Conn.*	17 Hillhouse av.
John Manvers Briscoe	*Pottsville, Pa.*	39 Lynwood pl.
Charles Rollin Clark	*Carthage, Ill.*	13 Lake pl.
Earl Adna Cryne	*New Britain, Conn.*	62 Lake pl.
Rex W. Dunlap	*Kansas City, Mo.*	125 High st.
Richard Cunningham Eggleston	*Philadelphia, Pa.*	47 Lake pl.
Samuel Banon Flauman	*New Haven, Conn.*	53 Prince st.
Tetsutaro Hasegawa	*Tokyo. Japan*	479 Elm st.
Herman Gardner Herrick	*New Haven, Conn.*	37 Pearl st.
Allen Harrison Hodgson	*Chico, Cal.*	718 w. d.
Anthony Michael Ingram	*St. Mary's, Pa.*	686 w. d.
Seth Sidney Langley, ph.b.	*New Haven, Conn.*	229 Blatchley av.
Yale University 1903		
Albert Arthur Lawrence	*New Haven, Conn.*	87 Trumbull st.
Rodolfo Orgarrio, Jr.	*Mexico City, Mex.*	85 Sachem st.
Francis McLeod Patton	*Asheville, N. C.*	129 Mansfield st.
Edmund Chase Prouty	*Spencer, Mass.*	70 Trumbull st.
John William Shea	*Holyoke, Mass.*	423 Temple st.
Gustavus Nor Dhal Snow	*Rye, N. Y.*	122 Wall st.
Stephen Leslie Tyler	*New Haven, Conn.*	33 Pearl st.
William Joseph Whiting	*New Haven, Conn.*	83 Mansfield st.
Ellwood Coggeshall Wilder	*Honolulu, H. I.*	329 Whalley av.

SPECIAL STUDENTS, 23

STUDENTS FROM OTHER DEPARTMENTS

Harry Louis Abramson	*St. Joseph, Mo.*	35 High st.
Edward Paul Alker	*New York City*	377 WH.
Charles Boothe Alling	*Montclair, N. J.*	269 D.
Clarence Hayden Allis	*Derby, Conn.*	133 W.
Samuel Alpert	*New Haven, Conn.* 96 Washington av.	
Robert Bruce Anderson	*Salem, O.*	200 York st.
Frank August Assmann	*East Orange, N. J.*	381 WH.
Wheaton Augur	*Chicago, Ill.*	270 D.
John Frederick Baker	*Willimantic, Conn.*	246 D.
Charles Gardiner Barnum, B.A.	*Cornwall, Vt.* 344 Humphrey st.	
Middlebury College 1905, M.A. 1907		
Earl Morton Barnum	*Naugatuck, Conn.*	234 D.
David Nye Barrows	*New York City*	368 WH.
Harold Stanley Bates	*Mt. Vernon, N. Y.*	461 FW.
Edgar Farrar Bateson	*New York City*	238 D.
Frederick Wilder Bellamy	*Brooklyn, N. Y.*	103 W.
Earl Edward Beyer	*Rochester, Ind.*	9 V.
Forrest Beyer	*Kendallville, Ind.*	9 V.
Alfred Alexander Biddle	*Philadelphia, Pa.*	239 D.
John Kingsley Birge	*Bristol, Conn.*	464 FW.
Clifford Hershey Bissell	*New York City*	45 V.
Willard Samuel Bissell	*Waterville, N. Y.*	63 V.
Chauncey Buckley Blair	*Chicago, Ill.*	377 WH.
Francis Malbone Blodget	*East Greenwich, R. I.*	374 WH.
Lewis Samuel Boothe	*Shelton, Conn.*	202 F.
William Whiting Borden	*Chicago, Ill.*	380 WH.
Frank Eugene Bridgett	*Wallingford, Conn.*	Wallingford
Bennet Bronson	*Waterbury, Conn.*	383 B.
Harold Brooks	*Tenafly, N. J.*	268 D.
Harold Wilson Brooks	*New York City*	447 FW.
Carroll Teller Brown	*Denver, Colo.*	467 FW.
James Ignatius Bryan	*Bridgeport, Conn.*	
Robert Emmett Buckley	*New Britain, Conn.*	217 York st.
Nathan Hollister Bundy	*Grand Rapids, Mich.*	19 V.
Edgar Bartow Burgess	*Garden City, N. Y.*	116 W.
Samuel Parkes Burnam	*Richmond, Ky.*	398 B.
Edward Neufville Tailer Burnett	*New York City*	462 FW.
Raymond Marcy Burnham	*Hartford, Conn.*	124 W.
Rufus Bradford Burnham	*Norwich, Conn.*	116 W.
Gerald Morton Butler	*Evanston, Ill.*	173 L.
George Francis Cahill	*New Haven, Conn.* 8 Cedar Hill av.	
Charles Soutter Campbell	*Essex Fells, N. J.*	379 WH.

George Edward Cantine	*Albany, N. Y.*	387 B.
Charles Bronson Carpenter	*New York City*	404 B.
George Edward Catlin	*New Haven, Conn.*	176 York st.
Frank Andrew Cellar	*Sewickley, Pa.*	466 FW.
Francis Deraismes Childs	*Hartford, Conn.*	15 V.
Hugh Joseph Chisholm, Jr.	*New York City*	40 V.
Avery Artison Clark	*Middlebury, Conn.*	180 L.
DeWitt Scoville Clark, Jr.	*Salem, Mass.*	269 D.
Ralph Hodge Clark	*Derby, Conn.*	133 W.
John Daniel Coffman	*New Haven, Conn.*	91 Lake pl.
Frank Burnett Condon	*Unionville, Conn.*	463 FW.
Gilbert Maurice Congdon	*Providence, R. I.*	271 D.
Harry Albert Conte	*New Haven, Conn.*	183 Hamilton st.
Frank Marion Coppock, Jr.	*Cincinnati, O.*	254 Crown st.
Ralph Edward Costanzo	*New Haven, Conn.*	100 Greene st.
James Francis Coughlan	*New Haven, Conn.*	196 Wallace st.
Forrest Glenmore Crowley	*Galion, O.*	384 Crown st.
Charles Canfield Cunningham, Jr.	*Washington, Ia.*	249 D.
William Francis Cunningham	*Norwich, Conn.*	53 Prospect st.
Eugene Judson Curtis	*Clinton, Ia.*	272 D.
Trevor Arnold Cushman	*Winchester, Mass.*	373 WH.
Walter Dallas	*Waterbury, Conn.*	107 W.
Edward Chellis Daoust	*Defiance, O.*	120 V-S.
Allen Sturges Davenport	*Yonkers, N. Y.*	395 B.
Edward Stiles Davey	*Jersey City, N. J.*	7 V.
Douglas Treat Davidson	*Warren, Pa.*	466 FW.
Edward John Davin	*New York City*	155 L.
Charles Hollister Davis	*Manchester, Conn.*	247 D.
Herbert Frederick Day	*Hartford, Conn.*	199 F.
Sydney Beauclerc DeGolyer	*Springfield, Mass.*	339 WH.
Samuel Foree Dennis	*Louisville, Ky.*	108 W.
Joseph Laudium Desrosiers	*New Haven, Conn.*	42 Shelter st.
Julian French Devereaux	*Cleveland, O.*	457 FW.
Allen Robert Dodd	*Upper Montclair, N. J.*	127 W.
Geoffrey Dodge	*New York City*	98 W.
Gayer Gardner Dominick	*New York City*	447 FW.
William Minton Donnelly	*Detroit, Mich.*	415 B.
Charles Bigelow Drake	*St. Paul, Minn.*	433 FW.
Arthur Gotzian Driscoll	*St. Paul, Minn.*	374 WH.
Edward Thomas Dwyer	*Ansonia, Conn.*	Ansonia
Jackson Annan Dykman	*Brooklyn, N. Y.*	235 D.
Thomas Collyer Eastman	*New York City*	242 D.
Harold Ransom Edwards	*Granby, Conn.*	255 D.

James Connelly Edwards, Jr.	*Russellville, Ky.*	107 W.
Douglas Fitch Guilford Eliot	*Irvington-on-Hudson, N. Y.*	132 W.
Stanley Egbert Ellis	*St. Albans, Vt.*	257 D.
Edward Amedeo Esposito	*New Haven, Conn.*	337 George st.
Joseph Vincent Esposito	*New Haven, Conn.*	15 Summer st.
James Murdock Ethridge, Jr.	*Rome, N. Y.*	468 W.
Tracy Farnam	*New Haven, Conn.*	37 Hillhouse av.
Albert Day Farwell	*Lake Forest, Ill.*	262 D.
Edward Spottiswoode Faust	*New York City*	49 V.
John Favill	*Chicago, Ill.*	173 L.
David Ferguson	*Manchester, Conn.*	72 C.
Henry Theodore Fleitmann	*New York City*	432 FW.
Charles Thomas Flynn	*New Haven, Conn.*	175 Orchard st.
William Ralph Fogerty	*Ansonia, Conn.*	Ansonia
Denton Fowler, 3d	*Haverstraw, N. Y.*	272 D.
Peter Francis Fuchs	*Brooklyn, N. Y.*	452 FW.
Frederick Lamont Gates	*New York City*	340 WH.
Arthur Benson Gilbert	*Mt Kisco, N. Y.*	713 W. D.
Francis Dwight Gilbert	*Grand Rapids, Mich.*	462 FW.
Leon Godchaux	*New Orleans, La.*	440 FW.
Ralph Edward Goodwin	*East Hartford, Conn.*	382 WH.
Charles Vanderveer Graham	*Brooklyn, N. Y.*	134 W.
George Clifford Graham	*Bristol, Conn.*	63 Pond st.
Joseph Oliver Guerra	*New Haven, Conn.*	750 Grand av.
Francis Bacon Hamlin	*Washington, D. C.*	180 L.
John Francis Hanifin	*Belchertown, Mass.*	236 James st.
Joseph Edwards Harris	*New Haven, Conn.*	233 Oak st.
Patrick Joseph Healey	*Waterbury, Conn.*	366 WH.
Horace Barnes Hewlett	*New Haven, Conn.*	451 FW.
John Lawrence M. Higgins	*New Haven, Conn.*	652 Congress av.
Melville Espe Hitchcock	*Ansonia, Conn.*	527 P.
John Francis Hogan	*New Haven, Conn.*	44 Winchester av.
Stanley Wescott Holmes	*Saratoga Springs, N. Y.*	135 W.
Thomas Carrington Hood	*Chester, Conn.*	255 D.
Davenport Hooker	*Brooklyn, N. Y.*	92 C.
Richard Schiller Hosford	*Moline, Ill.*	272 D.
Charles Wadsworth Howard	*Brooklyn, N. Y.*	241 D.
Henry Almy Howe	*South Orange. N. J.*	468 FW.
Burrell Richardson Huff	*Greensburg, Pa.*	99 W.
Wilson McClaughry Hume	*Ahmednagar, India*	178 L.
Horatio Norsworthy Humphreys	*New York City*	333 York st.
Oliver Seymour Jewell	*New Hartford, Conn.*	95 W.
Allan Macfarlan Johnson	*Boston, Mass.*	115 W.
Arthur Edward Johnson	*Ansonia, Conn.*	Ansonia

Frank Leonard Johnson	*Norwich, Conn.*	136 W.
Robert Coit Johnson	*Norwich, Conn.*	372 WH.
Frank Edward Jones	*Unionville, Conn.*	413 B.
Samuel Jerman Keator, Jr.	*Rock Island, Ill.*	254 D.
Joseph Francis Keegan	*New Haven, Conn.*	1331 Chapel st.
Hudson Kelley	*Chicago, Ill.*	256 D.
Courtland Kelsey	*East Orange, N. J.*	240 D.
Stephen Tomlinson Kelsey	*East Orange, N. J.*	230 D.
Leonard Kennedy	*Brooklyn, N. Y.*	260 D.
Harold Brown Keyes	*Hartford, Conn.*	25 V.
Allan Farrand Kitchel	*East Liverpool, O.*	100 W.
Roland Werner Klupfel	*New York City*	114 W.
Charles Whittemore Knapp	*Poughkeepsie, N. Y.*	357 WH.
John Francis Krasnye	*Yonkers, N. Y.*	716 Howard av.
Earl Langstroth	*Glen Ridge, N. J.*	254 D.
Julius Ansgar Larsen	*New Haven, Conn.*	406 B.
Maurice Farvish Lautman	*New Britain, Conn.*	553 Oak st.
Daniel Lathrop Lawton	*New York City*	96 W.
Maxwell Lear	*New Haven, Conn.*	307 George st.
Dickson Hammond Leavens	*Norwich, Conn.*	446 FW.
Hugh Ledyard	*Detroit, Mich.*	55 V.
Frederick Patrick Lee	*New Britain, Conn.*	1081 Chapel st.
William Rockwell Leete	*New Haven, Conn.*	29 V.
Louis H. Levy, PH.B.	*New Haven, Conn.*	64 Congress av.
Yale University 1904, M.S. 1906		
Robert Louis Levy	*New York City*	174 L.
William Levy	*New Haven, Conn.*	91 Greene st.
William David Levy	*New Haven, Conn.*	69 Audubon st.
Franklin Drake Lightner	*St. Paul, Minn.*	129 W.
Henry Lippitt	*Providence, R. I.*	271 D.
Alfred Lee Loomis	*New York City*	430 FW.
Theodore Bird Lyon	*New Haven, Conn.*	425 FW.
Sydney Clement McCall	*New York City*	98 W.
John Charles McCarthy	*McLean, N. Y.*	71 C.
Grant Street Macartney	*St. Paul, Minn.*	460 FW.
James Lukens McConaughy	*Mount Hermon, Mass.*	257 D.
Benjamin Harrison McKee	*New York City*	430 FW.
James Patrick McManus	*New Haven, Conn.*	97 Orchard st.
Arthur Perkins McWilliams	*Norwich, Conn.*	136 W.
Robert Mallory, Jr.	*Brooklyn, N. Y.*	262 D.
Harry Meixell, Jr.	*Reading, Pa.*	454 FW.
Clinton Merrick	*Evanston, Ill.*	181 L.
Paul Gurley Merrow	*Hartford, Conn.*	236 D.
John Simon Message	*Brooklyn, N. Y.*	1081 Chapel st.

Harold Talmadge Messenger	*Winsted, Conn.*	94 W.
Jetemiah Milbank, 2d	*New York City*	391 B.
Lawrence Vernon Miller	*Baltimore, Md.*	49 V.
Clark Goodell Mitchell	*Denver, Colo.*	263 D.
Arthur Allen Mitten	*Chicago, Ill.*	475 Whitney av.
Edgar James Moch	*Cincinnati, O.*	110 W.
Frederick Augustus Morrell, Jr.	*Putnam, Conn.*	388 B.
Arthur Parsons Mullins	*Salem, O.*	. 456 FW.
Francis Wisner Murray, Jr.	*New York City*	102 W.
Ralph Emerson Myers	*Buskirk Bridge, N. Y.*	707 W. D.
Arthur Theodore Nabstedt	*Davenport, Ia.*	214 Crown st.
Homer Chidsey Neal	*Southington, Conn.*	406 B.
Joseph Francis O'Brien	*Meriden, Conn.*	Meriden
Edward McDonell O'Brien	*Plattsburgh, N. Y.*	408 B.
Charles Milton Olcott	*Montclair, N. J.*	369 WH.
Francis Howard Olmsted	*Lakeville, Conn.*	241 D.
Wallace Lyman Orcutt	*West Burke, Vt.*	925 Howard av.
Samuel Gilman Ordway	*St. Paul, Minn.*	16 V.
Patrick Brett O'Sullivan	*Derby, Conn.*	60 V.
Sydney Paige	*Washington, D. C.*	215 York st.
Rene Mead Pardee	*Orange, N. J.*	231 F.
Allan Douglas Parker	*Lowell, Mass.*	260 D.
Maxwell Oswald Parry	*Indianapolis, Ind.*	415 B.
Herbert Payne	*Menlo Park, Cal.*	235 D.
Duncan Clinch Phillips, Jr.	*Washington, D. C.*	349 WH.
James Laughlin Phillips	*Washington, D. C.*	349 WH.
Otto Carl Pickhardt	*New York City*	429 FW.
Donald Wallace Porter	*New Haven, Conn.*	59 V.
Graham Cummings Porter	*Kyoto, Japan*	67 V.
Warren Cone Pratt	*Hartford, Conn.*	444 FW.
Lemuel Eugene Punderson	*Ashtabula, O.*	381 Crown st.
Franklyn Thomas Raymond	*New York City*	432 FW.
Randolph Reynolds	*New Haven, Conn.*	260 Crown st.
Henry Lewis Read	*Brooklyn, N. Y.*	248 D.
Ray John Reigeluth	*Carbondale, Pa.*	29 V.
Edward Hartman Reisner	*McConnellsburg, Pa.*	267 D.
Donald Louis Reynolds	*Toledo, O.*	378 WH.
Harold Cady Reynolds	*Danbury, Conn.*	390 B.
Cleaveland Jocelyn Rice	*New Haven, Conn.*	410 Winthrop av.
Peter Hadley Rich	*Cleveland, O.*	73 C.
Henry Alsop Riley	*New York City*	371 WH.
Edward Constant Roberts	*Hartford, Conn.*	22 College st.
William Payne Roberts	*Brooklyn, N. Y.*	178 L.
Wright Haffards Robertson	*Fall River, Mass.*	50 V.

George Henry Sanderson	*Moosup, Conn.*	171 L.
Peter Benjamin Sarason	*New Haven, Conn.*	48 Broad st.
Robert Frederick Scholl	*New Haven, Conn.*	149 Lombard st.
Raymond Joseph Schweizer	*New York City*	270 D.
Edwin Lewis Scofield, Jr.	*Stamford, Conn.*	119 W.
Frank Dyckman Scudder	*New York City*	167 L.
Richard Frank Seidensticker, B.A.	*Meriden, Conn.*	120 York st.
Yale University 1907		
George Alexander Seligmann	*New York City*	14 V.
Arthur Warren Selleck	*White Plains, N. Y.*	80 C.
William Sharp	*Cranford, N. J.*	470 FW.
Archie McDaniels Sheldon	*Rutland, Vt.*	358 WH.
Eustace Morrow Sheppard	*Pittsburg, Pa.*	335 WH.
Harold Briggs Sherman	*Newtonville, Mass.*	15 V.
Vinton D. Singer	*Dayton, O.*	226 F.
Charles McLean Smith	*Hartford, Conn.*	375 WH.
David Parker Smith	*Meriden, Conn.*	223 F.
Emery Holland Smith	*New York City*	398 B.
Herbert Mason Southworth	*Wakefield, Mass.*	106 W.
William Norwood Sparhawk	*West Swanzey, N. H.*	406 B.
Joel Andrew Sperry, 2d	*New Haven, Conn.*	438 FW.
Alfred Springer, Jr.	*Norwood, O.*	459 FW.
Leonard LoveJoy Stanley	*Great Barrington, Mass.*	22 College st.
Maurice Stanley	*New Britain, Conn.*	266 D.
Neil Campbell Stevens	*Morristown, N. J.*	236 Crown st.
Donald Barton Stewart	*New York City*	19 V.
Harold Phelps Stokes	*New York City*	237 D.
Boetius Henry Sullivan	*Chicago, Ill.*	467 FW.
Grover Cleveland Sweet	*New Haven, Conn.*	710 Howard av.
Samuel Swift	*New York City*	424 FW.
Robert Alphonso Taft	*Washington, D. C.*	8 College st.
William Howard Taft	*New York City*	239 D.
Harrison Wood Talcott	*South Bend, Ind.*	375 WH.
Horace Van Sands Taylor	*Hartford, Conn.*	70 C.
Robert James Tearse	*Winona, Minn.*	465 FW.
Mortimer Clark Terrill	*Ansonia, Conn.*	94 W.
Raymond Thatcher	*Pueblo, Colo.*	467 FW.
Walter Clark Tilden	*New London, Conn.*	381 Crown st.
Francis Berger Trudeau	*Saranac Lake, N. Y.*	237 D.
John Screven Turnbull	*New York City*	A.
Moore Caldwell Tussey	*Salina, Pa.*	27 V.
William Stephen Van Rensselaer	*New York City*	348 WH.
Elmer Chester Louis Wagner	*Waterbury, Conn.*	54 V.
Charles Carter Walbridge	*Philadelphia, Pa.*	457 FW.

George Stephen Walker	*New Haven, Conn.*	79 Lafayette st.
William Little Wallace	*New Haven, Conn.*	151 Canner st.
Edwin Morey Waterbury	*Corning, N. Y.*	162 L.
Aubrey Richardson Watzek	*Davenport, Ia.*	463 FW.
Henry Crouch Webb	*Dover, Del.*	249 Crown st.
Lewis Hill Weed	*Cleveland, O.*	370 WH.
William Corcoran Welling	*Hartford, Conn.*	458 FW.
Donald Breckenridge Wells	*Hartford, Conn.*	25 V.
Thorne Lake Wheeler	*Chatham, N. Y.*	259 D.
Robert Stevens Whitlock	*Naugatuck, Conn.*	441 FW.
James Moro Whittaker	*Cincinnati, O.*	398 B.
Henry Clarence Wick, Jr.	*Cleveland, O.*	339 WH.
Jacob Farrand Williams	*Detroit, Mich.*	353 WH.
George Charles Wilson	*Delhi, N. Y.*	151 L.
Rowland Gregory Wright	*Hancock, Mich.*	465 FW.
William Josiah Wright, B.S.	*Bear River, N. S.*	346 Crown st.
Acadia University 1907		
George Glendining Wyant	*Stamford, Conn.*	444 FW.
Monroe Falk Zunder	*New Haven, Conn.*	583 Whitney av.

STUDENTS FROM OTHER DEPARTMENTS, 276

SUMMARY

GRADUATES	154
SENIORS	251
JUNIORS	275
FRESHMEN	396
SPECIAL STUDENTS	23
TOTAL	1099
STUDENTS FROM OTHER DEPARTMENTS	276
TOTAL UNDER INSTRUCTION . .	1375

YALE SCHOOL OF THE FINE ARTS
REGULAR STUDENTS

Edna Black Adams	*New Haven, Conn.*	544 Whitney av.
Laura Jane Bradley	*New Haven, Conn*	21 Hillside av.
Lorintha Blanche Brown	*Bridgeport, Conn.*	Bridgeport
Hazel Lynn Bulkley	*Ivoryton, Conn.*	384 Crown st.
Theodore Deidrickson, Jr.	*New Haven, Conn.*	288 George st.
Salvatore Epifanio	*New Haven, Conn.*	798 Grand av.
William Edward Fagan	*Wallingford, Conn.*	Wallingford
William Edward Foster, 2d, PH.B.	*New Haven, Conn.*	109 College st.
Yale University 1907		
Charles Heaton Fulton	*New Haven, Conn.*	211 F.
Harry Bruce Griffin	*New Haven, Conn.*	38 Clark st.
Viola Ethel Hyde	*Peekskill, N. Y.*	402 Crown st.
Annie S. Johnson	*New Haven, Conn.*	374 Grand av.
Elizabeth Katherine Atwater Kirkman	*New Haven, Conn.*	
		183 Lawrence st.
Franklin Earle Knotts	*Shawnee, Okla.*	25 High st.
Martin Michael Krakauer	*New York City*	673 W. D.
Eunice Hall Linsly	*Northford, Conn.*	445 George st.
Albert Carl Lohmann	*Meriden, Conn.*	Meriden
Grace Lois Mailhouse	*New Haven, Conn.*	45 Elm st.
Edwin J. Merriam	*Chicago, Ill.*	522 George st.
Helen Zetler Moore	*New Haven, Conn.*	218 Orchard st.
George Andrew Noble	*Waterbury, Conn.*	9 Library st.
James A. Nuckle	*New Haven, Conn.*	1190 Whalley av.
Samuel Solomon Raphael	*New Haven, Conn.*	757 State st.
Harriet Grace Roe	*Bridgeport, Conn.*	Bridgeport
Edna Estelle Smith	*New Haven, Conn.*	95 Howard av.
August Spaenkuch	*New Haven, Conn.*	170 Commerce st.
Ruth Lillian Spalding	*New Haven, Conn.*	70 Grove st.
Arthur Russell Squires	*Akron, O.*	9 Library st.
Mabel Lucy Stevens	*Clinton, Conn.*	Clinton
Paul Taylor Sturges	*Sioux City, Ia.*	152 Temple st.
James Taddeo	*New Haven, Conn.*	329 Cedar st.
Mabelle Humiston Tolles	*Ansonia, Conn.*	Ansonia
Minna Mansfield Walker	*New Haven, Conn.*	162 York st.
Anna Elizabeth Walsh	*Cromwell, Conn.*	Cromwell
Sarah Isabelle Weadick	*New Haven, Conn.*	591 Elm st.
Florence Helen Wood	*Stratford, Conn.*	402 Crown st.
John Henry Wood	*Stratford, Conn.*	228½ Edgewood av.

*Loutfi Daniel Yacobian   *Troy, N. Y.*   Paris, France
Natalie Barbara Zacher   *Branford, Conn.*   Branford
   * Holder of the William Wirt Winchester Fellowship.

                                        REGULAR STUDENTS, 39

STUDENTS FROM OTHER DEPARTMENTS

Thomas Achelis	*New York City*	368 WH.
Herbert Burr Alvord	*Gloversville, N. Y.*	218 F.
Paul Shipman Andrews ·	*Syracuse, N. Y.*	238 D.
Edgar Farrar Bateson	*New York City*	238 D.
Gerald Morton Butler	*Evanston, Ill.*	173 L.
Charles Bronson Carpenter	*New York City*	404 B.
Reginald Woodward Catlin	*Brooklyn, N. Y.*	28 V.
Aims Chamberlain Coney	*Orange, N. J.*	240 D.
Paul Howard McGregor Converse	*Rochester, N. Y.*	238 D.
Allen Robert Dodd	*Upper Montclair, N. J.*	127 W.
Haliburton Fales, Jr.	*New York City*	112 W.
Samuel Lamson Howell	*Philadelphia, Pa.*	41 V.
Ralph Dresser Hunting	*Cedar Rapids, Ia.*	43 V.
Julius Ansgar Larsen	*New Haven, Conn.*	400 B.
Robert Stell Lemmon	*Englewood, N. J.*	394 B.
William Chester MacLane	*New Haven, Conn.*	33 Howe st.
Henry Noyes Otis	*Andover, Mass.*	393 B.
Maxwell Oswald Parry	*Indianapolis, Ind.*	415 B.
Clarence Appleton Peirce	*Methuen, Mass.*	463 FW.
Clarence Eugene Secor, Jr.	*Yonkers, N. Y.*	128 W.
Stanley Stokes Shepard	*Syracuse, N. Y.*	249 D.
Horace Van Sands Taylor	*Hartford, Conn.*	70 C.
Miles Gordon Thompson	*Lebanon, O.*	105 Park st.
Mary Emma Wadlington, B.A.	*Norman, Okla.*	166 York st.
University of Mississippi 1902		
Floyd Wallace	*Wallingford, Conn.*	179 L.
Hicks Arnold Weatherbee	*New York City*	117 W.
Thorne Lake Wheeler	*Chatham, N. Y.*	259 D.

                                                       27

Sheffield Scientific School Freshman Class   .   .   .   340

        STUDENTS FROM OTHER DEPARTMENTS   .   .   367

SUMMARY

REGULAR STUDENTS   39
STUDENTS FROM OTHER DEPARTMENTS   .   367

        TOTAL UNDER INSTRUCTION   406

DEPARTMENT OF MUSIC
REGULAR STUDENTS

Anna Judith Elizabeth Anderson	*West Haven, Conn.*	West Haven
Sheila Jewett Bailey	*New Haven, Conn.*	26 Edgewood av.
Marshall Moore Bartholomew, PH.B.	*New York City*	Byers Hall
Yale University 1907		
Dorothea Bayliss	*New Haven, Conn.*	46 Shelton av.
Leita Tolles Beecher	*New Haven, Conn.*	259 Edgewood av.
Mary Elizabeth Bennett	*New Haven, Conn.*	357 Elm st.
Roy Walter Beron	*Waterbury, Conn.*	Waterbury
Henry Emanuel Bonander	*New Haven, Conn.*	98 Chapel st.
Katherine Somers Bonn	*Waterbury, Conn.*	Waterbury
Nellie May Boynton	*Branford, Conn.*	Branford
Mary Ellen Brosnan	*Wallingford, Conn.*	Wallingford
Charles Edward Burleigh	*West Haven, Conn.*	West Haven
Peter Caporossi	*New Haven, Conn.*	558 Grand av.
Sara Frances Coughlin	*Middletown, Conn.*	Middletown
Helen Reeves Crane	*New Haven, Conn.*	109 Dwight st.
Elsie Davidson Cropper	*Derby, Conn.*	Derby
George Edward Daniels	*New Haven, Conn.*	61 Shelton av.
William Enright Davenport, B.A.	*Bridgeport, Conn.*	Bridgeport
Yale University 1899		
Samuel Davey	*Ansonia, Conn.*	Ansonia
Harold Carter Davies	*New Haven, Conn.*	321 Dixwell av.
Mary Whiting Deming	*New Haven, Conn.*	245 Bradley st.
Dorothea Mary Dexter	*New Haven, Conn.*	178 Prospect st.
Anna Young Fanslow	*New Haven, Conn.*	54 Salem st.
Harriet Lewis Fischer	*New Haven, Conn.*	409 Edgewood av.
Anna Smith Gagel	*West Haven, Conn.*	West Haven
Madelon Schillings Gardner	*New Haven, Conn.*	1079 Chapel st.
Maude Ethel Gordon	*Windsor, N. J.*	1305 Chapel st.
Frederick Burrage Granniss	*Bridgeport, Conn.*	Bridgeport
Effie Ella Grant	*New Haven, Conn.*	12 Edgewood av.
George John Greiner	*New Haven, Conn.*	116 Nash st.
Helen Eugenia Hagan	*New Haven, Conn.*	83 Whalley av.
Arvin Burnham Hall	*New Haven, Conn.*	211 Norton st.
Jennie Margaret Hawley	*Bridgeport, Conn.*	Bridgeport
Dayton Millis Henry	*Waterbury, Conn.*	Waterbury
Clayton Eugene Hotchkiss	*Hartford, Conn.*	Hartford
Ralph Shelton Hudson	*New York City*	713 W. D.
Susan Keefe	*Derby, Conn.*	Derby
Eleanor Alexena Kennedy	*New Haven, Conn.*	45 Houston st.

Rose Mary Kennedy	*Wallingford, Conn.*	Wallingford
Adeline Kerlin	*New Haven, Conn.*	9 Library st.
Frances Louise Kirchoff	*New Haven, Conn.*	75 Maple st.
Laura Adelia Kirkman	*New Haven, Conn.*	183 Lawrence st.
Hattie Lambert	*New Haven, Conn.*	64 Whalley av.
Farnum Howard Lane	*Hartford, Conn.*	Hartford
Ruth Syner Lathrop	*New Haven, Conn.*	130 Howe st.
Prudence Lee	*Orange, Conn.*	Orange
Norma Symes Lewis	*Anniston, Ala.*	West Haven
John Owen Lynch	*New Haven, Conn.*	168 Mansfield st.
Elizabeth Sperry McAfee	*New Haven, Conn.*	94 York sq.
Marguerite Cecelia Macdonald	*Ansonia, Conn.*	Ansonia
Frank Patrick McGovern	*New Haven, Conn.*	109 View st.
Wilhelmina MacGregor	*New Haven, Conn.*	414 Crown st.
Evelyn Corney Mackrille	*West Haven, Conn.*	West Haven
Harry Silas Metzger	*New Haven, Conn.*	92 Avon st.
Martha Curtis Miles	*Milford, Conn.*	Milford
William Hall Miner	*Naugatuck, Conn.*	Naugatuck
Clara Wentworth Mix	*Bridgeport, Conn.*	Bridgeport
Constantina Moeller	*New Haven, Conn.*	349 Crown st.
Julius Eberhardt Neumann	*New Haven, Conn.*	103 Alden av.
Kathryn Augusta O'Connor	*Middletown, Conn.*	Middletown
Bessie Alice Pierce	*South Britain, Conn.*	South Britain
Louise Cornelia Pierpont	*New Haven, Conn.*	42 Mansfield st.
William Stevens Porter	*Brooklyn, N. Y.*	116 Howe st.
Alton Scoville Potter	*Torrington, Conn.*	Torrington
Robert Henry Prutting	*Hartford, Conn.*	Hartford
Clarence Edward Rolfe	*Ansonia, Conn.*	Ansonia
Orton Augustus Rose, Jr.	*New Haven, Conn.*	140 Fulton st.
Arthur Schuckai	*New Haven, Conn.*	33 Elliot st.
Caroline Mary Schumann	*Southington, Conn.*	Southington
Jessie Rhea Starkweather	*New Haven, Conn.*	1452 Boulevard
Emeline Amelia Street	*East Haven, Conn.*	East Haven
Floyd Grant Terry	*New Haven, Conn.*	1304 Chapel st.
Francis David Tiernan	*New Haven, Conn.*	250 Howard av.
William Andrew Tinsley	*Waterbury, Conn.*	Waterbury
George Ira Tompkins	*Waterbury, Conn.*	178 v-s.
Hendrika Troostwyk	*New Haven, Conn.*	179 Bradley st.
Leo Troostwyk	*New Haven, Conn.*	179 Bradley st.
Charles Worthington Vishno, M.D.	*New Haven, Conn.*	23 College st.
Yale University 1885		
Anna Marie Weber	*New Haven, Conn.*	262 Lloyd st.
Ruth Wilson	*New Haven, Conn.*	50 Houston st.
Amalia Veronica Woedtke	*New Haven, Conn.*	6 Olive st.

| Cecil Wright | *Sandy Hook, Conn.* | 542 P. |
| Arthur Frederick Zeidler | *Waterbury, Conn.* | Waterbury |

REGULAR STUDENTS, 83

STUDENTS FROM OTHER DEPARTMENTS

Albert Parker Abbe	*New Britain, Conn.*	25 V.
Robert Abbot	*Plainfield, N. J.*	30 V.
William McClure Andrews	*Syracuse, N. Y.*	238 D.
Lewis Elmer Armstrong, PH.B.	*New Haven, Conn.*	175 East Rock rd.
Yale University 1906		
Paul Thompson Arnold	*Ridgeway, Pa.*	449 FW.
Joseph Howland Auchincloss	*New York City*	426 FW.
Earle Wilson Bachman	*Auburn, N. Y.*	94 W.
Malcolm Sterling Banks	*Brooklyn, N. Y.*	1 V.
Edward Shippen Barnes	*New York City*	143 L.
Earl Morton Barnum	*Naugatuck, Conn.*	234 D.
Henry Sartwell Beardsley	*Auburn, N. Y.*	42 V.
Walter Kingsbury Belknap	*Louisville, Ky.*	125 V-S.
Shelley Edward Bennett, Jr.	*Sturgis, Ky.*	249 Crown st.
Lincoln College		
Francis Malbone Blodget	*East Greenwich, R. I.*	374 WH.
John Northmore Brigham	*Glencoe, Ill.*	11 College st.
Francis Peabody Butler	*Chicago, Ill.*	262 D.
George Edward Catlin	*New Haven, Conn.*	176 York st.
Reginald Woodward Catlin	*Brooklyn, N. Y.*	28 V.
James Henderson Childs, B.S.	*Forsyth, Ga.*	166 V-S.
Alabama Polytechnic Institute 1904		
Samuel Coan	*New Haven, Conn.*	2 West st.
Leonard Jacob Crawford, Jr.	*Fort Thomas, Ky.*	50 V.
Walter Morgan Crunden	*St. Louis, Mo.*	350 WH.
Charles Canfield Cunningham, Jr.	*Washington, Ia.*	249 D.
Charles Gould Curtiss	*Buffalo, N. Y.*	39 V.
Frank Damrosch, Jr.	*New York City*	250 Crown st.
Edward John Davin	*New York City*	155 L.
Harmar Denny Denny, Jr.	*Allegheny, Pa.*	367 WH.
Chandler Diehl	*Highland Park, Ill.*	110 Wall st.
Geoffrey Dodge	*New York City*	98 W.
Gayer Gardner Dominick	*New York City*	447 FW.
Thomas Collyer Eastman	*New York City*	242 D.
Albert Day Farwell	*Lake Forest, Ill.*	262 D.
Edward Spottiswoode Faust	*New York City*	49 V.
Thomas Coolidge Fowler	*Glens Falls, N. Y.*	337 WH.
Waldo David Frank	*New York City*	200 York st.
William Gammell, Jr.	*Providence, R. I.*	37 V.

Dwight Terry Griswold	*Erie, Pa.*	42 V.
Miles Carrington Hannah	*Lake Forest, Ill.*	102 W.
Francis Ely Harris	*Boonton, N. J.*	21 V.
Walter Earle Hartley	*Grand Rapids, Mich.*	267 D.
Vincent Eugene Healy	*Chicago, Ill.*	428 FW.
Nathaniel Holmes	*Pittsburg, Pa.*	69 V.
Charles Wadsworth Howard	*Brooklyn, N. Y.*	241 D.
James Merriam Howard	*Montclair, N. J.*	254 D.
Otis Scott Humphrey	*Springfield, Ill.*	20 V.
George Dimmick Kittredge	*Fishkill-on-Hudson, N. Y.*	369 WH.
Augustus Knight	*Evanston, Ill.*	22 College st.
Ellis Knowles	*Pensacola, Fla.*	347 WH.
Nestor Searle Light	*So. Coventry, Conn.*	403 B.
William BenJamin Lipphardt	*Buffalo, N. Y.*	81 C.
Henry Lippitt	*Providence, R. I.*	271 D.
Sidney Clement McCall	*New York City*	98 W.
Hubert McDonnell	*New York City*	457 FW.
Asa Suydam Merrell	*Flemington, N. J.*	140 V-S.
Jeremiah Milbank, 2d	*New York City*	391 B.
Charles George Mills	*Bradford, Pa.*	133 V-S.
James Thacker Milliken	*Traverse City, Mich.*	267 D.
Mark Lincoln Mitchell	*Cincinnati, O.*	426 FW.
Francis Wisner Murray, Jr.	*New York City*	102 W.
Francis Howard Olmsted	*Lakeville, Conn.*	241 D.
Sidney Rollins Overall	*St.Louis, Mo.*	37 V.
Richardson Phelps	*Minneapolis, Minn.*	11 College st.
Duncan Clinch Phillips, Jr.	*Washington, D. C.*	349 WH.
James Laughlin Phillips	*Washington, D. C.*	349 WH.
George Stewart Pomeroy, Jr.	*Wernersville, Pa.*	251 Crown st.
Donald Wallace Porter	*New Haven, Conn.*	59 V.
Eliot Hale Porter	*New Britain, Conn.*	266 D.
Donald Louis Reynolds	*Toledo, O.*	378 WH.
Howard MacMillan Richard, B.A.	*New Haven, Conn.*	504 Whitney av.
Wesleyan University 1904		
Robert Selden Rose	*Geneva, N. Y.*	239 D.
Frank Alexander Ross	*No.Woodbury, Conn.*	153 V-S.
John Harold Ryan	*Toledo, O.*	455 FW.
Theodore Schulze	*St.Paul, Minn.*	376 WH.
Raymond Joseph Schweizer	*New York City*	270 D.
George Alexander Seligmann	*New York City*	14 V.
Joseph Lionel Seligman	*New York City*	105 W.
Charles Seymour	*New Haven, Conn.*	30 V.
Angelo Eusebius Shattuck, B.A.	*Columbus, O.*	629 E. D.
Beloit College 1905		

Stanley Stokes Shepard	*Syracuse, N. Y.*	249 D.
Eustace Morrow Sheppard	*Pittsburg, Pa.*	335 WH.
George Mark Sneath, B.A.	*New Haven, Conn.*	32 Perkins st.
Yale University 1907		
Huntington Smith, Jr.	*St.Louis, Mo.*	440 FW.
George Henry Soule, Jr.	*Stamford, Conn.*	21 V.
Henry Boardmann Spalding	*New York City*	124 Prospect st.
Morry William Spitz	*Chicago, Ill.*	110 Wall st.
Roswell Hiram Steele	*Brooklyn, N. Y.*	268 D.
Horace Van Sands Taylor	*Hartford, Conn.*	70 C.
James Carlton Thornton	*Bedford, Ind.*	343 WH.
Vernon Victor Tilson	*Grapevine, N. C.*	332 WH.
Laurence Vail Updegraff	*Chicago, Ill.*	67 V.
William Stephen VanRensselaer	*New York City*	348 WH.
Charles Edmund VanVleck, Jr.	*Montclair, N. J.*	376 WH.
Floyd Wallace	*Wallingford, Conn.*	179 L.
Charles Carter Walbridge	*Philadelphia, Pa.*	457 FW.
Hicks Arnold Weatherbee	*New York City*	117 W.
Donald Breckenridge Wells	*Hartford, Conn.*	25 V.
Inness Whitaker	*New York City*	141 W.
Arthur Murray Whitehill	*Newburgh, N. Y.*	332 WH.
Wayland Wells Williams	*New Haven, Conn,*	22 College st.
Perry Swearingen Young	*Abilene, Texas*	141 W.
Monroe Falk Zunder	*New Haven, Conn.*	583 Whitney av.

STUDENTS FROM OTHER DEPARTMENTS, 101

SUMMARY

REGULAR STUDENTS	83
STUDENTS FROM OTHER DEPARTMENTS .	101
TOTAL UNDER INSTRUCTION . .	184

DEPARTMENT OF FORESTRY
(YALE FOREST SCHOOL)
SENIOR CLASS

Raymond Walter Allen, B.S.   *Medford, N. J.*   91 Lake pl.
Rutgers College 1906

Nelson Courtlandt Brown, B.A.   *South Orange, N.J.* 129 Mansfield st.
Yale University 1906

Frank Herbert Brundage, PH.B. *New Haven, Conn.*   145 Franklin st.
Yale University 1907

Elias Treat Clark, PH.B.   *Woodbridge, Conn.*   Woodbridge
Yale University 1907

Ernest Dwight Clark, PH.B.   *Litchfield, Conn.*   699 W. D.
Yale University 1907

Robert Eli Clark   *New Haven, Conn.* 125 DeWitt st.
Yale University 1907

Arthur Mayhew Cook, B.A.   *Laconia, N. H.*   129 Mansfield st.
Harvard University 1906

Chester Boyd Cox   *Santa Maria, Cal.*   609 E. D.

Burgess Dickinson, PH.B.   *Buffalo, N. Y.*   82 Wall st.
Yale University 1907

John Arden Ferguson, B.A.   *Canandaigua, N. Y.*   91 Lake pl.
Hamilton College 1896

Joseph Albert Fitzwater   *Phœnixville, Pa.*   699 W. D.

Walter William Gleason, B.S.   *Johnsonburg, Pa.*   609 E. D.
Allegheny College 1906

Jesse Rexford Hall, B.S.   *Bostonia, Cal.*   642 E. D.
University of California 1905

Rufus Clifford Hall, B.S.   *Chicago, Ill.*   13 Lake pl.
Northwestern University 1906

William Catesby Latané, Jr., B.S.   *Oak Grove, Va.*   699 W. D.
Virginia Polytechnic Institute 1905

Charles Augustus Lewis, B.A.   *New York City*   137 Wall st.
Trinity College 1893

Forman Taylor McLean, PH.B.   *Eatontown, N.J.*   17 Compton st.
Yale University 1907

Harvey Reginald MacMillan, B.A.S. *Aurora, Ont., Canada* 74 Lake pl.
University of Toronto 1906

Willis Norman Millar, B.S.   *Pittsburg, Pa.*   74 Whalley av.
University of Pennsylvania 1906

Robert Barclay Miller, M.A.   *Thorntown, Ind.* 103 Winchester av.
Wabash College 1896

Barrington Moore, B.A.   *New York City*   182 Mansfield st.
Yale University 1906

Thornton Taft Munger, B.A.   *New Haven, Conn.* 202 Prospect st.
Yale University 1905

Wilfred Eaton Murchie, PH.B.   *South Orange, N. J.* 124 Prospect st.
  Yale University 1907
Rutledge Parker   *Charleston, S. C.*   26 Tilton st.
Francis McLeod Patton   *Asheville, N. C.* 129 Mansfield st.
Robert Landon·Rogers, B.A.   *Providence, R. I.* 182 Mansfield st.
  Yale University 1906
Julian Eastman Rothery, PH.B.   *Wellesley, Mass.* 129 Mansfield st.
  Yale University 1907
Aretas Andrews Saunders, PH.B.   *New Haven, Conn.*   125 Maple st.
  Yale University 1907
Edward Burgis Starr, B.A.   *Cornwall, Conn.*   74 Lake pl.
  Yale University 1907
Dillon Parnell Tierney, B.S.F.   *Farmington, Minn.*   91 Lake pl.
  University of Minnesota 1906
Ralph Bickerton Wainright, PH.B. *New Britain, Conn.*   82 Wall st.
  Yale University 1907
Wilford Bennett Willey, B.A.   *Ithaca, N. Y.*   74 Lake pl.
  Cornell University 1907

SENIOR CLASS, 32

JUNIOR CLASS

Oliver Edwin Baker, B.S.   *Tiffin, O.*   182 Mansfield st.
  Heidelberg University 1903, M.S. 1904.
  M.A. Columbia University 1905
Fredrik Ferdinand Woods Beckman *Altoona, Pa.*   717 W. D.
  Stockholm Högre Reallaroverk 1905
Frederick Howell Billard, B.A.   *Meriden, Conn.*   315 York st.
  Yale University 1896
John Manvers Briscoe   *Pottsville, Pa.*   39 Lynwood pl.
Hugh Gilman Calkins, B.S.   *Newport, R. I.*   74 Lake pl.
  University of California 1906
John Daniel Coffman ·   *Redlands, Cal.*   91 Lake pl.
Arthur Wood DuBois, B.A.   *Hallstead, Pa.*   333 York st.
  Cornell University 1907
Herman Edgar Fegley, B.A.   *Auburn, Pa.*   8 Prospect pl.
  Franklin and Marshall College 1904
Belknap Chittenden Goldsmith, B.S. *Berkeley, Cal.*   70 Whalley av.
  University of California 1906
Edgar Clarkson Hirst, B.A.   *Yellow Springs, O.* 60 Whalley av.
  Ohio State University 1907
Allen Harrison Hodgson   *Chico, Cal.*   718 W. D.
Oswald Drew Ingall, B.A.   *Montclair, N. J.*   718 W. D.
  Cornell University 1907
Henry Langley Johnson, B.A.   *Boston, Mass.*   17 Compton st.
  Cornell University 1907
Richard Chapin Jones, B.A.   *Nashville, Tenn.*   60 Whalley av.
  Vanderbilt University 1904
Joseph Casimir Kircher, B.A.   *Belleville, Ill.*   1076 Chapel st.
  Yale University 1907

Richard Leonard Lovell, PH.B.　　*Plainfield, N. J.*　145 Franklin st.
　　Yale University 1907
Everett Herman MacDaniels, B.A.　*Oberlin, O.*　　　　716 W. D.
　　Oberlin College 1906
Rufus Sherrell Maddox, B.A.　　*Coldwater, Tenn.*　.　664 W. D.
　　Yale University 1907
Axel Erik Teodor Moberg　　　*Upsala, Sweden*　919 Howard av.
　　Upsala University 1906
Frederick Franklin Moon, B.A.　　*Nazareth, Pa.*　　664 W. D.
　　Amherst College 1901
William Bushnell Osborne, Jr., B.A. *Victor, N. Y.*　17 Compton st.
　　Williams College 1907
Percy Jerauld Paxton, B.A.　　*Princeton, Ind.*　　159 Elm st.
　　Williams College 1906
Reuben Parker Prichard, B.S.　　*Somerville, Mass.*　719 W. D.
　　Dartmouth College 1907
Robert Simmons, B.A.　　　　*New York City*　196 Mansfield st.
　　College of the City of New York 1905
Thomas Elliot Snyder, B.A.　　*New York City*　8 Prospect pl.
　　Columbia University 1907
Willard Springer, Jr , C.E.　　*Wilmington, Del.*　60 Whalley av.
　　Lafayette College 1907
Ernest Cousins Wheeler, B.A.　　*Norwalk, Conn.*　1076 Chapel st.
　　Yale University 1907
Chester Harvey Wilcox, C.E.　　*Center Moriches, N. Y.* 13 Lake pl.
　　Lehigh University 1907
Addison Wetherald Williamson, PH.B.　*Waterport, N. Y.*　91 Lake pl.
　　Wesleyan University 1907

JUNIOR CLASS, 29

STUDENTS IN THE SHEFFIELD SCIENTIFIC SCHOOL TAKING COURSES AT THE FOREST SCHOOL

Charles Rollin Clark　　　　*Carthage, Ill.*　　13 Lake pl.
William Edwin Dunham　　　*Warren, Pa.*　　174 V-S.
Wesley Earle Dunkle　　　　*Pittsburg, Pa.*　174 V-S.
Frederick Alan Gaylord　　　*Ansonia, Conn.*　165 V-S.
Henry Julian Correll Humphrey　*Brooklyn, N. Y.*　105 V-S.
Aldo Leopold　　　　　　*Burlington, Ia.*　172 V-S.
Edmund Chase Prouty　　　　*Spencer, Mass.*　70 Trumbull st
Abbott Beecher Silva　　　　*Chattanooga, Tenn.*　333 York st.
Meyer Henry Wolff　　　　　*Brooklyn, N. Y.*　724 W. D.

STUDENTS FROM THE SHEFFIELD SCIENTIFIC SCHOOL, 9

STUDENTS TAKING ONLY THE JUNIOR WORK AT THE SUMMER SCHOOL

George Adams Bright　　　　*Vineyard Haven, Mass.*
Donald Robinson Cole　　　　*Rochester, N. Y.*

Clarence Adolph Metzger	*Hartford, Conn.*
Willis Munroe	*Buffalo, N. Y.*
Herbert Stuart Nelson	*New Haven, Conn.*
Robert Hamilton Prentice	*East Aurora, N. Y.*
Guy Eston Yerkes	*Hutchinson, Kans.*

STUDENTS TAKING ONLY THE JUNIOR WORK
AT THE SUMMER SCHOOL, 7

STUDENTS TAKING THE SHORT COURSE IN THE SUMMER SCHOOL

Victor Augustus Beede	*New Haven, Conn.*
Chapin Loyd Brown	*Peekskill, N. Y.*
Harry Philip Brown	*Herkimer, N. Y.*
Algernon Sidney Cadwallader	*Yardley, Pa.*
Robert Edward Eastman	*Manhattan, Kans.*
Edward Woolsey Freeman	*New York City*
James Lippincott Goodwin	*Hartford, Conn.*
Donald Sidney Moister	*Mont Clare, Pa.*
Manlius Jay Post	*Milwaukee, Wisc.*
Ralph Renwick	*Chicago, Ill.*
Harold Louis Russell	*Baltimore, Md.*
William Henry Southworth	*Brooklyn, N. Y.*
Roderick Swift Steele	*Port Edwards, Wisc.*
George Raymond Towne	*Stafford Springs, Conn.*
Richard Chandler Walton	*Avondale, Pa.*
John Robert Whiting	*New Haven, Conn.*

STUDENTS TAKING THE SHORT COURSE
IN THE SUMMER SCHOOL, 16

SUMMARY

SENIOR CLASS	32
JUNIOR CLASS	29
REGULAR STUDENTS	61
STUDENTS FROM OTHER DEPARTMENTS .	9
STUDENTS TAKING ONLY THE JUNIOR WORK AT THE SUMMER SCHOOL . . ˙	‒
STUDENTS TAKING THE SHORT COURSE AT THE SUMMER SCHOOL	16
TOTAL UNDER INSTRUCTION	93

DEPARTMENT OF THEOLOGY

(YALE DIVINITY SCHOOL)

GRADUATE CLASS

HOOKER FELLOW FOR 1907

Darwin Ashley Leavitt, B.A.   *Beloit, Wisc.*   Berlin, Germany
Beloit College 1904,
B.D. Yale University 1907

———

Sarkis Manoog Albarian, B.A.   *Hajin, Asia Minor*   614 E. D.
St. Paul's Institute, Tarsus, 1901,
B.D. Hartford Theological Seminary 1906

William Herbert Alexander   *Derby, Conn.*   Derby
Cheshunt College 1901,
B.D. Yale University 1905

William Talbot Allison, B.A.   *Middlefield, Conn.*   Middlefield
University of Toronto 1899, M.A. 1900,
B.D. Yale University 1901

Herbert Stanley Brown, B.A.   *Darien, Conn.*   Darien
Yale University 1881, B.D. 1886

William Burrows, B.A.   *New Haven, Conn.*   68 Grand av.
St. Stephen's College 1902,
B.D. Berkeley Divinity School 1905,
M.A. Yale University 1906

Ernest W. Bysshe, B.A.   ·   *Rowayton, Conn.*   Rowayton
Columbia University 1901,
B.D. Drew Theological Seminary 1906

Raymond Gilmore Clapp, B.A.   *Boston, Mass.*   613 E. D.
Boston University 1900,
B.D. Yale University 1903, M.A. 1904

James Fraser Evans, B.A.   *Georgetown, Ont., Canada* 10 University pl.
University of Toronto 1893,
M.A. Yale University 1907

Charles Franklin, M.A.   *North Haven, Conn.* North Haven
Central College 1895,
B.D. Vanderbilt University 1901,
M.A. Yale University 1907

Charles Martin Good, B.A.   *Bethlehem, Conn.*   612 E. D.
Otterbein University 1904,
B.D. Yale University 1907

William Henry Harris   *Wardsville, Ont., Canada* Beacon Falls
Wesleyan Theological College, Montreal,
B.D. Yale University 1907

Mihran Tatios Kalaidjian, B.A.   *Everek, Asia Minor*   619 E. D.
St. Paul's Institute, Tarsus, 1900,
B.D. Yale University 1905, M.A. 1907

Kannosuke Kawanaka   *Toba, Japan*   637 E. D.
    Tohoku Gakuin 1899,
    B.D. Pacific Theological Seminary 1906,
    M.A. Columbia University 1907

Saburo Koshiba, B.A.   *Azabu, Tokyo, Japan*   639 E. D.
    Union Christian College (Indiana) 1904,
    B.D. Oberlin Theological Seminary 1907

Ernest Frank McGregor, B.A.   *Clinton, Conn.*   670 W. D.
    University of Minnesota 1901,
    B.D. Yale University 1904, M.A. 1906

Albert Alonzo Madsen, B.A.   *Durham, Conn.*   Durham
    Moravian College 1900,
    B.D. Yale Univ. 1903, M.A. 1904, PH.D. 1907

George D. Milbury, B.A.   *Bethany, Conn.*   627 E. D.
    Bates College 1905,   .
    B.D. Yale University 1907

Charles Benjamin Franklin Pease, B.A.   *New Haven, Conn.*   622 E. D.
    Williams College 1886,
    B.D. Yale University 1889

Jason Noble Pierce, B.A.   *New Haven, Conn.*   139 Greene st.
    Amherst College 1903,
    B.D. Yale University 1906

William Ernest Andrew Slaght, B.A. *New Haven, Conn.* 980 Whalley av.
    University of Toronto 1898,   .
    B.D. Yale University 1902

Willard Learoyd Sperry, B.A.   *Reading, Mass.*   648 E. D.
    Olivet College 1903,
    B.A. Oxford University 1907

Albert Thomas Steele, B.A.   *Bethel, Conn.*   Bethel
    Adrian College 1896,
    B.D. Yale University 1907

Frederick Azel Sumner, B.A.   *Milford, Conn.*   Milford
    Oberlin College 1891,
    Hartford Theol. Sem. 1904

GRADUATE CLASS, 24

SENIOR CLASS

Robert Bell   *New Haven, Conn.*   600 Chapel st.
Howard Garfield Connelly, B.A.   *Baltimore, Md.*   623 E. D.
    Bethany College 1905
John Luther Dickson   *Pleasant Valley, Conn.* 27 Tryon st.
Harry Grimes, B.A.   *Brodhead, Wisc.*   626 E. D.
    Beloit College 1905
Arthur Jones, B.A.   *Tonganoxie, Kans.*   604 E. D.
    Friends University 1903
Daniel Webster Kurtz, B.A.   *Lake, O.*   655 W. D.
    Juniata College 1905
Theodore Burger Lathrop, B.A.   *Ashland, Wisc.*   626 E. D.
    Beloit College 1903

Robert Bryan McCord, B.A.   *Tallahassee, Fla.*   624 E. D.
    Florida State College 1905
John Lee Maddox, B.A.   *Deering, No. Dak.*   675 W. D.
    Denison University 1904
Pearl Eugene Mathias, B.A.   *Highspire, Pa.*   620 E. D.
    Lebanon Valley College 1905
Howard MacMillan Richard, B.A. *New Haven, Conn.* 504 Whitney av.
    Wesleyan University 1904
Angelo Eusebius Shattuck, B.A.   *Columbus, O.*   629 E. D.
    Beloit College 1905
William Arthur Shelton, B.A.   *Poteau, Okla.*   680 W. D.
    Hargrove College 1905
Thomas Aber Williams, B.A.   *Criccieth, Wales*   628 E. D.
    Marietta College 1905
Benjamin Franklin Wyland, PH.B. *Harlan, Ia.*   702 W. D.
    State University of Iowa 1905

SENIOR CLASS, 15

MIDDLE CLASS

Carlo Altarelli   *Newark, N. J.*   696 W. D.
Lorne Webster Barclay, B.A.   *Poplar Hill, Ont., Canada*   633 E. D.
    Bethany College, 1906, M.A. 1907
Elmer Edwin Burtner, B.A.   *Hinton, Va.*   635 E. D.
    Otterbein University 1906
Walter Lewis Ferris, B.A.   *Oak Park, Ill.*   636 E. D.
    Beloit College 1905
Luther Bateman Henderson, B.S.   *Newport, N. J.*   617 E. D.
    New York University 1906
William Rabon Howell, PH.B.   *Wilson, N. C.*   634 E. D.
    Milligan College 1904, B.A. 1905
William Hayes Longsworth, B.A.   *Freeport, O.*   687 W. D.
    West Lafayette College 1906
Harry Stratton Martin, B.A.   *Spring Valley, Wisc.*   603 E. D.
    Carleton College 1903
Washington Irving Maurer, B.A.   *Beloit, Wisc.*   631 E. D.
    Beloit College 1904
Thomas Benjamin Powell, B.A.   *Scranton, Pa.*   630 E. D.
    Bucknell University 1906
Samuel Ross Swift, B.S.   *Beaver Falls, Pa.*   641 E. D.
    Geneva College 1906
Philip Barrows Whitehead, B.A.   *Janesville, Wisc.*   641 E. D.
    Beloit College 1906
Dean Rockwell Wickes, PH.B.   *Chicago, Ill.*   638 E. D.
    University of Chicago 1905

MIDDLE CLASS, 13

JUNIOR CLASS '

Eli Jacob Arnot, B.A.	*Monrovia, Ind.*	126 Park st.
Indiana University 1907		
John Kivett Arnot, B.A.	*Monrovia, Ind.*	126 Park st.
Indiana University 1907		
Leonard Joshua Carter, B.A.	*Danville, Va.*	602 E. D.
Holiness University 1907		
Robert Elmer Chandler, B.A.	*Auburndale, Mass.*	709 W. D.
Yale University 1904		
Arthur Raymond Clippinger, B.A.	*Shippensburg, Pa.*	96 Dwight st.
Lebanon Valley College 1905		
Augustus William Gidart, B.A.	*Nybygget, Barnarp,*	643 E. D.
University of Chicago 1907	*Jönköping, Sweden*	
Fred Lyman Hall, B.A.	*Danbury, Nebr.*	657 W. D.
Doane College 1905		
Edwin Deeks Harvey, B A.	*Rock Ferry, England*	625 E. D.
Yale University 1907		
Mark Gordon Inghram, B.A.	*Waynesburg, Pa.*	646 E. D.
Waynesburg College 1904		
Roderick Colin Jackson	*Roger's Hill, N. S., Canada*	618 E. D.
Queen's University		
William Adrian Jenkins, PH.B.	*Colerain, N. C.*	678 W. D.
University of North Carolina 1907		
Samuel Richard Morsell, B.A.	*Baltimore, Md.*	106 Goffe st.
Oberlin College 1907		
Algoth Ohlson	*Brevik Hvena, Sweden*	645 E. D.
Chicago Theological Seminary 1907		
George Mark Sneath, B.A.	*New Haven, Conn.*	32 Perkins st.
Yale University 1907		
Clifford Griffith Thompson, B.A.	*Bogart, Ga.*	647 E. D.
Young Harris College 1903		
Milton Frederick Wittler, B.A.	*Seattle, Wash.*	716 W. D.
Pomona College 1907		

JUNIOR CLASS, 16

SPECIAL STUDENTS

Angelo di Domenica	*New Haven, Conn.*	301 George st.
Theodore A. Fischer, B.D.	*New Haven, Conn.*	409 Edgewood av.
Tufts College 1896		
Robert Nelson Harris	*New Haven, Conn.*	137 Shelton av.
Roy Mac Houghton, B.A.	*Derby, Conn.*	Derby
Olivet College 1902,		
B.D. Yale University 1905		
Friend Edward Hoyt	*Shelton, Conn.*	964½ Chapel st.
James M. Lent	*So. Windsor, Conn.*	So. Windsor
John Gillespie Magee, B.A.	*Pittsburg, Pa.*	2 DW.
Yale University 1906		
Per Albin Nelson	*Clinton, Ia.*	61 Winchester av.

Victor Manly Patterson	*Brooklyn, N. Y.*	721 W. D.
BenJamin Lee Roberts	*Thornwell, La.*	616 E. D.
Charles George Smith	*New Haven, Conn.*	304 Exchange st.
Christopher Hubert Yearwood	*Georgetown, Brit. Guiana*	99 Dixwell av.

SPECIAL CLASS, 12

STUDENTS FROM OTHER DEPARTMENTS

Arthur Herbert Basye, B.A.	*Lawrence, Kans.*	204 F.
University of Kansas 1904, M.A. 1906		
Richard Herbert Bennett	*Fall River, Mass.*	449 FW.
John Maurice Deyo	*Fairfield, Conn.*	135 W.
George Stuart Dole, B A.	*Wilmington, Del.*	644 E. D.
Yale University 1906		
Louis Alexander Dole, B.A.	*Wilmington, Del.*	644 E. D.
Yale University 1906		
José Escaler, B.A.	*Apalit, P. I.*	14 Whalley av.
Liceo de Manila, 1902, LL. B. 1905		
Sydney Joseph Frank	*Chicago, Ill.*	382 W.
Charles Walter Hall, B.A.	*Stockville, Nebr.*	81 C.
Doane College 1904		
William Emanuel Hendricks	*St. Croix, Danish W. I.*	152 L.
Jessie E. Holt	*New Haven, Conn.*	68 Clark st.
William Oded Keirstead, B.A.	*Oakland, Me.*	Montowese
Bates College 1906, B.A. Yale University 1907		
Kenneth Scott Latourett, B.S.	*Oregon City, Oregon*	197 F.
McMinnville College 1904, B.A. Yale University 1906		
Eugene Heitler Lehman, B.A.	*New York City*	453 FW.
Yale University 1902		
Jessie Mae Stokely, B.A.	*Newport, Tenn.*	90 Park st.
Virginia Institute 1904		
Ernest Lionel Wismer	*North Branford, Conn.*	412 B.
Harry Clinton York, B.A.	*Leonard Bridge, Conn.*	125 Dwight st.
Yale University 1905, M.A. Yale University 1907		

STUDENTS FROM OTHER DEPARTMENTS, 16

SUMMARY

GRADUATE CLASS	. . . .	24
SENIOR CLASS	. . . . .	15
MIDDLE CLASS	. . . . .	13
JUNIOR CLASS	. . . . .	16
SPECIAL CLASS	. . . . .	12
REGULAR STUDENTS	. . . .	80
STUDENTS FROM OTHER DEPARTMENTS	.	16
TOTAL UNDER INSTRUCTION		96

DEPARTMENT OF MEDICINE
(YALE MEDICAL SCHOOL)
SENIOR CLASS

Robert Robertson Agnew	*East Haven, Conn.*	East Haven
Alfonso Louis Avitabile	*New Haven, Conn.*	476 Chapel st.
Abraham Bernstein	*Ansonia, Conn.*	163 York st.
John Eugene Black, PH.B.	*Bridgeport, Conn.*	120 York st.
Yale University 1903		
Robert Joseph Boyle	*New Haven, Conn.*	974 State st.
Thomas Frederick Broderick, Jr.	*Jamaica Plain, Mass.*	925 Howard av.
Paul Morgan Butterfield, B.A.	*Wilmington, Vt.*	589 P.
Yale University 1905		
Perley Bickford Chandler, B.A.	*Ladora, Ia*	63 Grove st.
Yale University 1905		
Clifton Mather Cooley	*Norwalk, Conn.*	371 Crown st. .
Alfred Carlton Gilbert	*Portland, Oregon*	120 York st.
Abram Aron Hershman	*New Haven, Conn.*	6 High st.
Hugh Francis Keating	*Wallingford, Conn.*	371 Crown st.
Joseph Edwards Kerney	*New Haven, Conn.*	67 Howe st.
George Conklin Kinne	*Ypsilanti, Mich.*	209 York st.
Joseph Irving Linde	*New Haven, Conn.*	540 Whitney av.
William Edward Lippman	*New Haven, Conn.*	134½ Olive st.
John Henry McGrath	*Waterbury, Conn.*	925 Howard av.
Arthur Drought Marsh	*Westville, Conn.*	1015 Whalley av.
Clement Channing Nevin	*Edgartown, Mass.*	373 Crown st.
Ira Hart Noyes	*Stonington, Conn.*	371 Crown st.
John Francis O'Brien	*Meriden, Conn.*	1081 Chapel st.
Sumpat Kevork Pachanian, B.A.	*Marash, Armenia*	11 Lake pl.
St. Paul's Institute, Tarsus, 1899		
Michael Antonio Parlato	*Derby, Conn.*	Derby
George James Schuele	*Chicago, Ill.*	925 Howard av.
Joseph Eastman Sheehan	*Wallingford, Conn.*	249 Crown st.
Goodrich Truman Smith	*Woodbury, Conn.*	70 Trumbull st.
Emil Maurice Soroch	*Bay City, Mich.*	279 Crown st.
Paul Titus	*Syracuse, N. Y.*	70 Trumbull st.
Mendel Volkenheim	*New Haven, Conn.*	40 Spruce st.
Edward Joseph Whalen	*Northampton, Mass.*	413 B.

SENIOR CLASS, 30

JUNIOR CLASS

Jacques Louis Buttner	*Douai, France*	78 Dwight st.
Daniel Joseph Byrne	*Waterbury, Conn.*	114 High st.

Robert Sheffield Clark	*Woodbury, Conn.*	114 High st.
Benjamin Brooks Finkelstone	*Bridgeport, Conn.*	38 High st.
Claude Vincent Flaherty	*Ansonia, Conn.*	Ansonia
Charles Lawrence Furcolow	*New Haven, Conn.*	792 Grand av.
Carl Johannes Gade	*New Haven, Conn.*	307 George st.
Thomas Humphrey Gallivan	*Norwich, Conn.*	1076 Chapel st.
William Joseph Good	*Norwich, Conn.*	1076 Chapel st.
John Joseph Horgan	*Worcester, Mass.*	911 Howard av.
Charles Elias Hyde	*New Haven, Conn.*	81 Newhall st.
Vincent Joseph Irwin, Jr.	*Springfield, Mass.*	1 Sylvan av.
Edward Charles Kiernan	*New Haven, Conn.*	98 St. John st.
George Washington King	*Ansonia, Conn.*	911 Howard av.
Israel Kleiner	*New Haven, Conn.*	288 Willow st.
William Charles McGuire	*New Haven, Conn.*	909 Howard av.
Walter Irving Russell	*Mystic, Conn.*	925 Howard av.
Abraham Albert Smernoff	*New Haven, Conn.*	71 Washington av.
John Newell Waggoner	*Jerseyville, Ill.*	925 Howard av.
Niles Wescott, M.A.	*Oak Lawn, R. I.*	219 York st.
Brown University 1905		
Foh-chung Yen	*Shanghai, China*	662 W. D.

JUNIOR CLASS, 21

SECOND YEAR CLASS

William Henry Beardsley	*Roxbury Station, Conn.*	710 W. D.
Isidore Morton Brenner	*New Haven, Conn.*	44 Bishop st.
Arthur Edward Brides	*Brockton, Mass.*	70 Trumbull st.
Genesis Frank Carelli	*New Haven, Conn.*	138 St. John st.
Charles Williams Comfort, Jr., B.A.	*Norristown, Pa.*	144 L.
Yale University 1907		
Jacob Julius Epstein	*New York City*	911 Howard av.
Edward Brendon Farley	*Derby, Conn.*	Derby
Edward James Finn	*Shelton, Conn.*	Shelton
William John Henry Fischer	*Danbury, Conn.*	911 Howard av.
John Francis Flynn	*Bridgeport, Conn.*	Bridgeport
George Goldman	*New Haven, Conn.*	64 Prince st.
James Francis Gorman	*So. Manchester, Conn.*	121 York st.
John Davis Greenberg	*Hartford, Conn.*	116 High st.
James Hamilton, Jr., PH.B.	*Howard, R. I.*	193 York st.
Brown University 1906		
George Richard James	*New Haven, Conn.*	141 Greene st.
Frank Elmer Johnson, B.A.	*Orange, Conn.*	45 Third st.
Yale University 1907		
Harold Brown Keyes	*Hartford, Conn.*	25 V.
John Albert Kimzey	*Detroit, Mich.*	287 York st.
Herman Clarke Little	*Manchester, Conn.*	710 W. D.

John Charles Malony	*Dundee, N. Y.*	121 York st.
Alexander Louis Prince	*Paterson, N. J.*	280 Elm st.
Harry St.Clair Reynolds	*New Haven, Conn.*	317 Grand av. -
Thomas Hubbard Russell, Jr., PH B.	*New Haven, Conn.*	137 Elm st.
Yale University 1906		
Mark Thomas Sheehan	*Wallingford, Conn.*	Wallingford
Eugene Johnson States	*Springville, Pa.*	27 High st.
Harry Eaton Stewart	*New Haven, Conn.* 191	Edgewood av.
George Emanuel Thielcke	*Danbury, Conn.*	1 Sylvan av.
Herbert King Thoms	*Torrington, Conn.*	656 W. D.
Henry Smith Turrill, PH B.	*New Milford, Conn.*	293 York st.
Yale University 1906		
Harry St.John Williams	*Bridgeport, Conn.*	Bridgeport
Leslie Adams Wilson	*Meriden, Conn.*	78 Lake pl.
Wells Warren Wilson	*New Haven, Conn.*	230 Portsea st.

SECOND YEAR CLASS, 32

FIRST YEAR CLASS

Harry Louis Abramson	*St.Joseph, Mo.*	35 High st.
Charles Gardiner Barnum, B.A.	*Cornwall, Vt.*	344 Humphrey st.
Middlebury College 1905, M.A. 1907		
Lewis Samuel Boothe	*Shelton, Conn.*	202 F.
Robert Emmett Buckley	*New Britain, Conn.*	217 York st.
George Francis Cahill	*New Haven, Conn.*	53 Houston st.
Harry Albert Conte	*New Haven, Conn.*	183 Hamilton st.
Ralph Edward Costanzo	*New Haven, Conn.*	100 Greene st.
James Francis Coughlan	*New Haven, Conn.*	196 Wallace st.
Forrest Glenmore Crowley	*Galion, O.*	384 Crown st.
William Francis Cunningham	*Norwich, Conn.*	53 Prospect st.
Herbert Frederick Day	*Hartford, Conn.*	199 F.
Joseph Laudium Desrosiers	*New Haven, Conn.*	42 Shelter st.
Edward J. Donovan	*Quincy, Mass.*	35 High st.
Edward Thomas Dwyer	*Ansonia, Conn.*	Ansonia
Edward Amedeo Esposito	*New Haven, Conn.*	337 George st.
Joseph Vincent Esposito	*New Haven, Conn.*	15 Summer st.
Tracy Farnam	*New Haven, Conn.*	37 Hillhouse av.
Samuel Banon Flauman	*Wallingford, Conn.*	53 Prince st.
Charles Thomas Flynn	*New Haven, Conn.*	175 Orchard st.
William Ralph Fogarty	*Ansonia, Conn.*	Ansonia
George Clifford Graham	*Bristol, Conn.*	63 Pond st.
Joseph Oliver Guerra	*New Haven, Conn.*	750 Grand av.
John Francis Hanifin	*Belchertown, Mass.*	236 James st.
Joseph Edwards Harris	*New Haven, Conn.*	233 Oak st.
Samuel Clark Harvey, PH.B.	*Woodbury, Conn.*	114 High st.
Yale University 1907		

John Lawrence M. Higgins	*New Haven, Conn.*	652 Congress av.
John Francis Hogan	*New Haven, Conn.*	44 Winchester av.
- Horatio Norsworthy Humphreys	*New York City*	333 York st.
Arthur Edward Johnson	*Ansonia, Conn.*	Ansonia
Joseph Francis Keegan	*New Haven, Conn.*	1331 Chapel st.
John Francis Krasnye	*Yonkers, N. Y.*	716 Howard av.
Maurice Farvish Lautman	*New Britain, Conn.*	553 Oak st.
Maxwell Lear	*New Haven, Conn.*	307 George st.
Frederick Patrick Lee	*New Britain, Conn.*	1081 Chapel st.
Louis Henry Levy, M.S.	*New Haven, Conn.*	64 Congress av.
Yale University 1906		
William Levy .	*New Haven, Conn.*	91 Greene st.
William David Levy	*New Haven, Conn.*	69 Audubon st.
James Patrick McManus	*New Haven, Conn.*	97 Orchard st.
John Simon Message	*Brooklyn, N. Y.*	1081 Chapel st.
Arthur Allen Mitten	*Chicago, Ill.*	475 Whitney av.
Joseph Francis O'Brien	*Meriden, Conn.*	Meriden
Wallace Lyman Orcutt	*West Burke, Vt.*	925 Howard av.
Otto Carl Pickhardt	*New York City*	429 FW.
Lemuel Eugene Punderson	*Ashtabula, O.*	381 Crown st.
Henry Alsop Riley	*New York City*	371 WH.
Peter Benjamin Sarason	*New Haven, Conn.*	48 Broad st.
Robert Frederick Scholl	*New Haven, Conn.*	149 Lombard st.
Richard Frank Seidensticker, B.A.	*Meriden, Conn.*	. 120 York st.
Yale University 1907		
Grover Cleveland Sweet	*New Haven, Conn.*	710 Howard av.
Walter Clark Tilden	*New London, Conn.*	381 Crown st.
George Stephen Walker	*New Haven, Conn.*	79 Lafayette st.
William Little Wallace	*New Haven, Conn.*	151 Canner st.
Monroe Falk Zunder	*New Haven, Conn.*	583 Whitney av.

FIRST YEAR CLASS, 53

SPECIAL STUDENT

Daniel Tony Banks	*New Haven, Conn.*	258 Fairmont av.

SPECIAL STUDENT, 1

SUMMARY

SENIOR CLASS	.	.	.	.	30
JUNIOR CLASS	.	.	.	.	21
SECOND YEAR CLASS	.	.	.	.	32
FIRST YEAR CLASS	.	.	.	.	53
SPECIAL STUDENT	.	.	.	.	1

137

DEPARTMENT OF LAW
(YALE LAW SCHOOL)
GRADUATE CLASS

William Henry Beeler, LL.B. — *Bloomington, Ind.* — 354 Whalley av.
Indiana University 1903

William Kernan Camblos, B.A. — *Philadelphia, Pa.* — 271 Crown st.
St. Joseph's College 1904,
M.A. Yale University 1906, LL.B. 1907

Timothy James Campbell, B.A. — *Newton, Ia.* — 34 Howe st.
Monmouth College 1904, M.A. 1907,
LL.B. Drake University 1907

Ira T. Crask, LL.B. — *Lebanon, Ind.* — 1079 Chapel st.
Indiana University 1907

Alexander Cumming, PH.B. — *New Haven, Conn.* 1032 Chapel st.
University of Michigan 1894,
LL.B. Harvard University 1902, M.A. 1903,
M.L. Yale University 1906

Francisco Aban Delgado, LL.B. — *Manila, P. I.* — 14 Whalley av.
Indiana University 1907

Claude Chesterfield Fogel, B.A. — *Lancaster, Mo.* — 1076 Chapel st.
University of Missouri 1903,
LL.B. University of Michigan 1907

Harry Scheuer Haas, LL.B. — *St. Louis, Mo.* — 333 York st.
Washington University 1907

Lester Irving Heyman, LL.B. — *St. Louis, Mo.* — 333 York st.
Washington University 1907

Francis Dustin Hurtt, LL.B. — *New York City* — 661 W. D.
Yale University 1907

Harry LeRoy Laurens, LL.B. — *Livingston, Mont.* — 109 York st.
Kansas City School of Law 1907

David Ignatius McCahill, LL.B. — *Des Moines, Ia.* — 57 Grove st.
Drake University 1907

Samuel Stephen McCahill, LL.B. — *San Francisco, Cal.* 405 Temple st.
University of Southern California 1906

Emilio Mapa, LL.B. — *Ililo, P. I.* — 14 Whalley av.
St. Thomas University 1906

Wayne Montgomery Musgrave, LL.B. *New York City* 152 Temple st.
New York Law School 1899,
M.L. Yale University 1906

Frederick Lord Perry, LL.B. — *New Haven, Conn.* — 68 Dwight st.
Yale University 1897

Thompson Morris Rector, B.S. — *Bastrop, Texas* — 141 Dwight st.
University of Texas 1905, LL.B. 1907

Sidney William Solomon, LL.B. — *St. Louis, Mo.* — 333 York st.
Washington University 1907

— 723 —

John Carlyle Wilkes, LL.B.   *Sharon, Pa.*   688 W. D.
   University of Michigan 1907
Carleton Hutchins Woodward, LL.B.   *Council Bluffs, Ia.*   315 York st.
   State University of Iowa 1907
                         GRADUATE CLASS, 20

THIRD YEAR CLASS

Chester Adraine Adams   *Akron, Ia.*   1076 Chapel st.
Donald Allison Adams, B.A.   *New York City*   569 P.
   Carleton College 1903
William Mathew Aiken   *Greensville, Miss.* 142 Edgewood av.
John Quincy Ames   *New Haven, Conn.*   479 Elm st.
Walter Preston Armstrong, B.A. *Coffeeville, Miss.*   155 Elm st.
   Yale University 1906
Leonard Woods Baker   *New Haven, Conn.* 210 St. Ronan st.
John Joseph Bartek, Jr.   *Wallingford, Conn.*   Wallingford
Arthur Willis Blackman, B.A.   *New Haven, Conn.*   691 W. D.
   Yale University 1905
Clarence J. Blinn   *New Brighton, Pa.*   688 W. D.
William Andrew Bree   *New Haven, Conn.*   712 State st.
Charles Philip Brewer   *Vineland, N. J.*   333 York st.
Martin Leonard Caine   *Naugatuck, Conn.*   105 Park st.
Samuel Campner   *New Haven, Conn.*   214 F.
Arnold Plack Carr   *Trenton, Ill.*   722 W. D.
Paul Stanley Chapman   *Bridgeport, Conn.*   281 Crown st.
Chauncey Irving Clark   *New Haven, Conn.*   17 Bishop st.
Edward Claxton   *Rensselaer, N. Y.*   130 Wall st.
Richard William Cronecker   *Sea Isle City, N. J.*   108 High st.
Frank Quinn Cronin, B.A.   *New London, Conn.* 364 George st.
   Yale University 1905
Roy Edwin Cubbage, PH.B.   *Ida Grove, Ia.*   409 Temple st.
   Drake University 1907
Joseph Irving Davidson   *Pittsburg, Pa.*   104 York sq.
Ferdinand D'Esopo   *Hartford, Conn.*   Hartford
James Henry Dixon   *Boston, Mass.*   36 Elm st.
Walter Vincent Donovan   *Brooklyn, N. Y.*   137 W.
Harold Espe Drew, B.A.   *Ansonia, Conn.*   155 Elm st.
   Yale University 1906
Edwin Jason Dryer, B.A.   *Clarence, N. Y.*   293 York st.
   Randolph-Macon College 1905, M.A. 1905
William Edward Egan   *Southington, Conn.* 925 Howard av.
James Edwin Ewers, B.A.   *Fredericktown, O.*   125 Dwight st.
   Yale University 1906
Percy Coleman Field, LL.B.   *Kansas City, Mo.*   109 York st.
   Kansas City School of Law 1907
William Henry Fogerty   *Hartford, Conn.*   109 York st.

Forrest LeBest Forbes	*Dalton, Mass.*	70 Trumbull st.
Graham Foster	*Anthony, Kans.*	293 York st.
Herbert Bradley Foster	*Fairchild, Wisc.*	36 Elm st.
Wilson David Frederick	*Chicago, Ill.*	152 Temple st.
William Gamble	*San Francisco, Cal.*	817 Yale P. O.
Andrew William Gardella	*Bridgeport, Conn.*	104 York st.
Benjamin Jacob Garfunkel	*Melrose, N. Y.*	820 Yale P. O.
Karl Goldsmith	*Sac City, Ia.*	36 Elm st.
George Basil Gordon	*Glendora, Cal.*	271 Crown st.
William Vincent Griffin	*New Haven, Conn.*	70 Edgewood av.
Charles Nelson Harmon	*Frankford, Del.*	289 York st.
Cramer Chesterfield Hegeman	*Bridgeport, Conn.*	670 W. D.
John Frederick Hauck	*New York City*	159 Elm st.
Stanton Higgins	*New Haven, Conn.*	19 Broad st.
Robert Caspar Hoerle	*Johnstown, Pa.*	130 Wall st.
Richard Carley Hunt	*Hot Springs, S. D.*	36 Elm st.
Harold Burton Jamison, B.A.	*Gloversville, N. Y.*	559 W. D.
Yale University 1906		
George Foster Jones, B.L.	*Oroville, Cal.*	271 Crown st.
University of California 1906		
Thomas Alexander Keating	*Danbury, Conn.*	424 George st.
Irenus Prime Keith, B.A.	*Winchester, Tenn.*	333 York st.
Yale University 1906		
Gunther Rudolph Lessing	*El Paso, Texas*	442 FW.
Benedict Edward Lyons, B.A.	*Thomaston, Conn.*	155 Elm st.
Yale University 1905		
William Joseph McKenna	*New Haven, Conn.*	166 Davenport av.
Raymond Peter McNulty	*Brooklyn, N. Y.*	137 W.
Charles Joseph Martin	*New Haven, Conn.*	109 York st.
Benjamin Heath Mead, B.A.	*New Canaan, Conn.*	193 F.
Yale University 1906		
Paul Lathrop Miller	*Bridgeport, Conn.*	631 E. D.
Charles Francis Mitchell	*New Haven, Conn.*	191 DeWitt st.
Thomas Joseph Molloy	*Hartford, Conn.*	29 Court st.
Charles Edward Moore	*Stamford, Conn.*	94 Crown st.
Harry Augustin Moran	*Hartford, Conn.*	29 Court st.
Aurelio Narganes	*New York City*	271 Crown st.
Clifton Junius O'Hara, Jr., B.A.	*Carthage, Ill.*	287 York st.
Carthage College 1906		
Arthur Bernard O'Keefe	*New Haven, Conn.*	147 Clay st.
Dwight Partridge	*Bedford, N. Y.*	36 Elm st.
Louis Mario Petruccelli	*Bridgeport, Conn.*	Bridgeport
Walter Mason Pickett	*New Haven, Conn.*	23 Lynwood pl.
Adrian Abraham Pierson	*West Burlington, N. Y.*	293 York st.
John Harry Pohlman, Jr., LL.B.	*St.Louis, Mo.*	422 B.
Benton Law School 1907		

Joseph Quittner	*New York City*	333 York st.
David Michael Reilly	*New Haven, Conn.*	13 Winthrop av.
Harry Woodward Ritter	*Tippecanoe City, O.*	266 York st.
Maury Robinson, LL.B.	*Charleston, W. Va.*	335 W. H.
Central University 1907		
Maurice Downs Rowland	*Milton, Ia.*	109 York st.
George Henry Rowley, B.A.	· *Greenville, Pa.*	392 Temple st.
Yale University 1906		
Paul Augustus Schlafly, B.A.	*St.Louis, Mo.*	36 Elm st.
St.Mary's College 1905		
Harrison Tweed Sheldon, B.A.	*New Haven, Conn.*	235 Lawrence st.
Yale University 1905		
George Matthew Skene	*Norwalk, Conn.*	130 Wall st.
Charles Alston Smythwick, B.A.	*Fairfield, Conn.*	65 Edgewood av.
Shaw University 1904		
Harold Gordon Spencer	*Honolulu, H. I.*	120 High st.
James Jefferson Stanton	*Bridgeport, Conn.*	Bridgeport
Theodore Emil Steiber	*Bridgeport, Conn.*	265 Orange st.
Nathaniel Paul Sterne	*Anniston, Ala.*	925 Howard av.
Carleton Hickox Stevens, B.A.	*New Haven, Conn.*	23 Asylum st.
Yale University 1906		
Lester Barber Stevens	*Milwaukee, Wisc.*	35 V.
Charles Lyman Stewart	*No. Stonington, Conn.*	925 Howard av.
Doran Hollister Sutphen, LL.B.	*Miller, S. D.*	1081 Chapel st.
University of South Dakota 1907		
Percy Truman Sutphen, LL.B.	*Miller, S. D.*	1081 Chapel st.
University of South Dakota 1907 ·		
Harold Wood Thatcher	*New Haven, Conn.*	23 Norton st.
Beverly Blolock Thomasson, B.L.	*Carrollton, Ga.*	137 Dwight st.
University of Georgia 1907		
Harry Griffy Tolliver	*New Haven, Conn.*	56 Foote st.
Rupert Beach Turnbull	*New Haven, Conn.*	486 Dixwell av.
Donald Judson Warner, B.A.	*Salisbury, Conn.*	36 Elm st.
Yale University 1906		
Herbert Joel Wilcox	*Waterbury, Conn.*	27 High st.
Huston Hobart Wright	*New Haven, Conn.*	146 York st.

THIRD YEAR CLASS, 95

SECOND YEAR CLASS

Robert Walpole Adams	*Washington, D. C.*	890 Chapel st.
Alfred Winchester Andrews	*East Haven, Conn.*	East Haven
Earle Andrew Barker	*Branford, Conn.*	Branford
Frank Barnes	*Norwich, N. Y.*	423 Temple st.
John Robert Beecher	*Bridgeport, Conn.*	Bridgeport
William Cooke Beers, PH.B.	*New Haven, Conn.*	279 Willow st.
Yale University 1895		

Joseph A. Bergens	*Waterbury, Conn.*	9 Library st.
Saul Berman	*Hartford, Conn.*	214 F.
Henry Winchester Bickford	*Memphis, Tenn.*	264 York st.
Samuel Henry Bowman, Jr.	*Minneapolis, Minn.*	36 Elm st.
Henry Joseph Calnen	*Hartford, Conn.*	287 York st.
Harry Anthony Campbell	*Kane, Pa.*	36 Elm st.
Vahan Cardashian	*New York City*	349 Elm st.
Arthur Woodburne Chambers	*New Haven, Conn.*	173 Sherman av.
Franklin Willard Cohen	*Ansonia, Conn.*	163 York st.
Arthur Earl Conner	*Walton, N. Y.*	714 W. D.
Joseph Lea Connor	*Manchester, N. H.*	120 High st.
Arthur Irving Cook	*Waterbury, Conn.*	38 Lynwood pl.
Theodore Marburg Crisp	*New York City*	36 Elm st.
Charles Rollin Crossett, Jr.	*Salem, Mass.*	130 Wall st.
Mitchell Leon Danforth	*Grand Rapids, Mich.*	295 York st.
Edward Chellis Daoust	*Defiance, O.*	120 V-S.
Henry Fleischner, B.A.	*New Haven, Conn.*	151 Bradley st.
Yale University 1907		
John Francis Foley	*So. Manchester, Conn.*	10 York st.
Lea David Freeman	*New Orleans, La.*	119 Wall st.
Lorin Henry Gates, B.A.	*Thomaston, Conn.*	409 B.
Yale University 1907		
Julius Getzelsohn	*New York City*	722 W. D.
William Emil Greenbaum	*Bridgeport, Conn.*	265 Orange st.
Henry Herbert Harbison	*Dayton, O.*	451 FW.
William Henry Hitchings	*New Haven, Conn.*	313 Howard av.
Ernest Franklin Hodgdon	*Townsend, Vt.*	333 York st.
Perry Joseph Hollandersky	*New London, Conn.*	37 Lake pl.
Loring Revere Hoover	*Elkhart, Ind.*	86 Wall st.
Joshua Edmund James	*Ocean View, Del.*	298 York st.
Cheney Church Jones, B.A.	*Trenton, Nebr.*	1233 Chapel st.
Doane College 1904		
Robert Guthrie Jordan	*New Haven, Conn.*	36 Mansfield st.
Matthew Patrick Kelly	*Windsor Locks, Conn.*	111 Greenwood st.
Clayton Leopold Klein	*Union City, Conn.*	124 Park st.
John Baptist LaCava	*Hartford, Conn.*	Hartford
William James Larkin, Jr., B.A.	*Waterbury, Conn.*	1076 Chapel st.
Yale University 1907		
Edward Robert McGlynn	*Orange, N. J.*	120 High st.
J. Donald McGregor	*Newark, N. J.*	119 Wall st.
Rol Hunter McQuistion	*Butler, Pa.*	143 L.
Humbert Emmanuel Mangini	*Waterbury, Conn.*	105 Park st.
Wesley Cornell Martin	*Providence, R. I.*	1151 Chapel st.
John William Mason	*Fairmont, W. Va.*	119 Wall st.
Ivan Lee Morehouse	*Stratford, Conn.*	Stratford

John Leo Murphy	*Steelton, Pa.*	150 L.
Dennis Thomas O'Brien	*Meriden, Conn.*	925 Howard av.
Charles O'Connor	*Waterbury, Conn.*	9 Library st.
Arthur Stuart Page	*East Haven, Conn.*	833 Yale P. O.
Charles Henry Platt	*Brooklyn, N. Y.*	452 FW.
Walter George Pond	*Branford, Conn.*	Branford
John Randolph Powelson	*Norwich, Conn.*	119 Wall st.
Edward Jerome Quinlan, B.A.	*New Haven, Conn.*	542 George st.
Yale University 1907		
James Jackson Ragan, B.S.	*Atlanta, Ga.*	1076 Chapel st.
University of Georgia 1906		
Lee Roy Robbins	*Norwich, Conn.*	119 Wall st.
Randolph Preston Rogers, B.A.	*Ft. Smith, Ark.*	1076 Chapel st.
Yale University 1907		
Howard Irving Russell	*New Haven, Conn.*	41 Howe st.
Abraham Schneider	*Monticello, N. Y.*	397 Temple st.
Ephraim Samuel Shill	*New York City*	1079 Chapel st.
Gerald Freeman Sibley	*Cuba, N. Y.*	126 Wall st.
Alexander Wyley Smith, Jr., B.A.	*Atlanta, Ga.*	1076 Chapel st.
Yale University 1907		
John William Festus Smith	*Cañon City, Colo.*	264 York st.
Mark Carleton Smith	*Altoona, Pa.*	670 W. D.
William Armstrong Smith	*Bridgeport, Conn.*	677 W. D.
Lewis Jack Somers	*New Haven, Conn.*	140 St. John st.
Richard Edgar Stillman	*Pensacola, Fla.*	271 Crown st.
Earl Augustine Sweeney	*Dedham, Mass.*	85 Sachem st.
Edward Francis Sweeney, B.A.	*Naugatuck, Conn.*	77 C.
Yale University 1907		
Philip Manual Thorne, Jr.	*Charleston, S. C.*	658 W. D.
John Francis Vail	*Hartford, Conn.*	150 L.
William Webb, B.A.	*Nauvoo, Ill.*	155 Elm st.
Carthage College 1906		
George LeRoy Weekes	*Harwich, Mass.*	1076 Chapel st.
Hermann John Weisman	*Union City, Conn.*	39 Lynwood pl.
Francis Patrick Welch	*Norwich, Conn.*	53 Prospect st.
Edward Colpitts Weyman, B.A.	*Apohaqui, N. B.*	189 F
University of New Brunswick 1902, B.A. Harvard University 1903, M.A. 1905		
Frederick Holme Wiggin, Jr., B.A.	*Litchfield, Conn.*	155 Elm st.
Yale University 1904		
David Arthur Wilson	*Hartford, Conn.*	287 York st.

SECOND YEAR CLASS, 79

FIRST YEAR CLASS

John Stanley Addis	*New Milford, Conn.*	105 Dwight st.
Murray Mansfield Ashbaugh	*Washington, D. C.*	216 Orange st.

Abram Bachner	*Gloversville, N. Y.*	43 College st.
Howard Francis Bishop, B.A.	*Chicago, Ill.*	1076 Chapel st.
Yale University 1907		
Samuel William Botwick	*New Haven, Conn.*	24 Arch st.
Hopkins Payne Breazeale	· *Natchitoches, La.*	137 Dwight st.
Rasselas Wilcox Brown	*Corry, Pa.*	168 L.
Harry Burnstine	*Bridgeport, Conn.*	Bridgeport
Alexander Bass Campbell	*Worcester, Mass.*	333 York st.
George A. Carr	*Cheshire, Conn.*	Cheshire
Tateh Clarence Chen	*Shanghai, China*	25 High st.
Roy Alexander Cheney	*Syracuse, N. Y.*	425 Temple st.
Shunsan Chenchang Chu	*Hankow, China*	25 High st.
Frederick Franklin Coeller	*New Haven, Conn.*	589 Howard av.
William Ernest Collins, B.A.	*Livingston, N. J.*	1076 Chapel st.
Yale University 1907		
Arthur Milton Comley, B.A.	*Bridgeport, Conn.*	Bridgeport
Yale University 1907		
Arthur Leon Connor	*Holyoke, Mass.*	276 Crown st.
James Edward Connor, Jr.	*New Haven, Conn.*	270 Lloyd st.
John Francis Conway	*New York City*	217 York st.
William Stuart Culbertson	*Louisville, Ky.*	379 Temple st.
Arthur Francis Danziger	*New York City*	124 Wall st.
Peter Tracy Dondlinger, B.A.	*New Haven, Conn.*	23 Lynwood pl.
National Normal University 1899,		
PH.D. Yale University 1904		
Russell Keresy Dougherty	*Brooklyn, N. Y.*	242 York st.
Milton Matthew Eisenberg	*New York City*	333 York st.
Louis Anthony Faverio	*Westerly, R. I.*	107 York st.
Salvatore Emmanuel Fiore	*Collinsville, Conn.*	222 F.
William Malcolm Ford	*Cazenovia, N. Y.*	152 Temple st.
Edward Earle Garlick	*Bridgeport, Conn.*	Bridgeport
Archibald Samuel Goldflam	*St. Joseph, Mo.*	35 High st.
William Harold Goodman	*New Haven, Conn.*	340 George st.
Thomas Cullen Gordon	*Brockport, N. Y.*	133 College st.
John G. Gottesman	*Springfield, Mass.*	683 W. D.
Lewis David Gross	*Hartford, Conn.*	128 Wall st.
Anthony Haines	*Rockford, Ill.*	411 Temple st.
George Hains, Jr., B.A.	*Augusta, Ga.*	137 Dwight st.
University of Georgia 1906		
Burton Boule Hall	*Wallingford, Conn.*	Wallingford
Clarence Russell Hall, B.A.	*Woodstock, Conn.*	1076 Chapel st.
Yale University 1907		
Frederick Hanson	*Seattle, Wash.*	110 Wall st.
Charles Edwin Hart, Jr., B.A.	*New Britain, Conn.*	New Britain
Yale University 1907		
Lawrence Albert Hart	*Muncie, Ind.*	108 High st.

Eldon Lewis Hilditch	*Thompsonville, Conn.*	90 Lake pl.
Clarence Edward Hirschfield	*New York City*	159 Elm st.
Maximilian Carl Hoegen	*New Haven, Conn.*	227 Columbus av.
Clarence Arthur Hoomkeek	*Napanoch, N. Y.*	681 w. d.
Harry Orlando Hoyt	*Minneapolis, Minn.*	1071 Yale P. O.
Arunah Crampton Hyde	*West Haven, Conn.*	West Haven
Charles Venantio James	*Norwich, Conn.*	53 Prospect st.
William John Kennedy	*New Haven, Conn.*	51 Clark st.
Matthew Henry Kenealy	*Stamford, Conn.*	209 F.
Arthur Burke Koontz	*Kesslers Lanes, W. Va.*	333 York st.
John Harold Lancaster	*Litchfield, Conn.*	124 Wall st.
Benjamin Daniel Land	*New Haven, Conn.*	9 Arch st.
William Joseph Langdon	*Hartford, Conn.*	421 Temple st.
Alexander Lennox	*Hartford, Conn.*	Hartford
Ralph Hayford Lincoln	*Fall River, Mass.*	1081 Chapel st.
Thomas Francis McGrath	*Waterbury, Conn.*	925 Howard av.
John Daniel MacKay, B.A.	*Saticoy, Cal.*	107 York st.
Santa Clara College 1907		
Frederick Watson McMurray	*Lewiston, Me.*	416 Crown st.
James Louis Malcolm	*Catskill, N. Y.*	132 Wall st.
Samuel Harry Malkan	*New Haven, Conn.*	380 Oak pl.
George Henry Malstedt	*New Rochelle, N. Y.*	333 York st.
Arthur Lauren Maltby	*Belvue, Kans.*	187 F.
Henry Jacal Marks	*Hartford, Conn.*	333 York st.
Louis Bruce Mattison	*South Shaftsbury, Vt.*	135 Wall st.
George Gordon Mead	*Scranton, Pa.*	222 F.
Stanley Morrill	*Chicago, Ill.*	3 Hillhouse av.
Louis Murolo	*New Haven, Conn.*	64 Mill st.
George Washington Myers	*Collinsville, Conn.*	333 York st.
Bentley Nelson	*Buffalo, N. Y.*	86 Howe st.
Ralph Andrew Nicholson	*Southwick, Mass.*	148 York st.
Edwin Thomas Noel	*Nashville, Tenn.*	119 Wall st.
John Hopkins Noel ·	*Nashville, Tenn.*	119 Wall st.
Oscar French Noel	*Nashville, Tenn.*	119 Wall st.
John Vincent O'Brien	*New Haven, Conn.*	783 Orange st.
Benedict Mallon O'Connell	*Wallingford, Conn.*	Wallingford
Timothy Francis O'Connell	*New York City*	319 Wallace st.
Neilson Olcott, 2d	*New York City*	397 Temple st.
James Justin Palmer	*New Haven, Conn.*	35 Redfield st.
Clifford Hayes Pangburn	*New Haven, Conn.*	731 Elm st.
William Selden Pattee	*Bethel, Conn.*	371 Crown st.
Charles Vernon Porter	*Natchitoches, La.*	137 Dwight st.
William Carrol Porter	*Norfolk, Conn.*	703 w. d.
Michael James Quinn	*Meriden, Conn.*	163 DeWitt st.

Bernard Eugene Reilly	*Brockton, Mass.*	266 York st.
Allan Robert Rosenberg	*Brooklyn, N. Y.*	422 B.
Samuel Rosenthal	*Hartford, Conn,*	Hartford
William Milford Ruffcorn	*Ashland, O.*	366 Whalley av.
Robert Stanley Ruthven	*Buffalo, N. Y.*	333 York st.
Richard Holliday Semple •	*Louisville, Ky.*	82 Wall st.
Myers Maurice Shapiro	*New Haven, Conn.*	288 Grand av.
Allan Gleason Siems	*St. Paul, Minn.*	200 York st.
Abraham Herman Slavin	*Springfield, Mass.*	683 W. D.
Frederick Whitmore Smith	*New Britain, Conn.*	New Britain
Wilbur Rush Smith, Jr.	*Lexington, Ky.*	397 Temple st.
Arthur Clinton Spurr	*Valley City, N. D.*	161 York st.
John Laurence Stivers	*Montrose, Colo.*	86 Howe st.
George Andrew Stone -	*New Haven, Conn.* 635 Quinnipiac av.
Thomas Arthur L. Stone	*Concord, N. H.*	107 Temple st.
James Burne Sweeney	*Keene, N. H.*	333 York st.
John Francis Tobin	*Waterbury, Conn.*	333 York st.
William Ward Vars	*Norwich, Conn.*	9 Library st.
George Napoleon Vidal	*Arctic, R. I.*	40 Franklin st.
Walter Henry West	*Boston, Mass.*	416 Crown st.
Charles Wesley Winslow	*New Haven, Conn.*	18 Dwight st.
Samuel Joseph Witz	*New Haven, Conn.*	757 State st.
Charles Davis Wood	*New York City*	333 York st.
Joseph George Woods	*New Britain, Conn.*	New Britain
Charles Kenneth Wynne	*New Haven, Conn.* 327 Edgewood av.
Morse Abraham Yagendorf	*New York City*	307 George st.
William Morris Ziff	*Bridgeport, Conn.*	Bridgeport

FIRST YEAR CLASS, 110

SPECIAL CLASS

Harold Nelson Aikens	*Sioux Falls, S. D.*	155 Elm st.
Charles Mitchell Armstrong	*Katherine, Texas*	36 Elm st.
John Kivett Arnot, B.A.	*Monrovia Ind.*	126 Park st.
Indiana University 1907		
Lorne Webster Barclay, B.A.	*Poplar Hill, Ont., Canada* 633 E. D.
Bethany College 1906, M.A. 1907		
Lionell Fuller Burgess	*Hartford, Conn.*	Hartford
Albert Bernard Cheadle	*New York City*	152 Temple st.
Arthur Raymond Clippinger, B.A.	*Shippensburg, Pa.*	96 Dwight st.
Lebanon Valley College 1905		
Arthur Denton Colyer	*Perth Amboy, N. J.*	35 Sherland av.
James Raymond Costello	*New Haven, Conn.*	7 Summer st.
Joseph Francis Dutton	*Forestville, Conn.*	23 Lynwood pl.

Thomas Francis Gleason	*Worcester, Mass.*	1081 Chapel st.
Morris Goldstone	*New Haven, Conn.*	194 State st.
Charles Martin Good, B.A.	*Harrisonburg, Va.*	612 E. D.
Otterbein University		
Morton Bradshaw Greims	*Lansdowne, Pa.*	135 Wall st.
Michael Patrick Haggarty	*Butte, Mont.*	17 Auburn st.
James Joseph Healy	*Newburyport, Mass.*	70 Trumbull st.
James Christie Johnson	*St. Louis, Mo.*	407 Temple st.
Samuel Percy Landers	*New York City*	1015 Yale P. O.
Sidney Lewis	*New York City*	258 D.
David Joseph McCoy	*New Haven, Conn.*	554 George st.
Robert Hunter MacKay	*Cleveland, O.*	271 Crown st.
Frederick Richard Manning	*Manchester, Conn.*	287 York st.
Manning Martin	*Des Moines, Ia.*	155 Elm st.
Wilford Woolfie Naman	*Waco, Texas*	442 R̃N.
Walter Christopher O'Connell	*New Haven, Conn.*	53 Asylum st.
Alexander Patterson	*Ogden, Utah*	120 High st.
Benjamin Lee Roberts, B.A.	*Thornwell, La.*	616 E. D.
Washington Training College		
Arnold Orestes Schramm, B.A.	*New York City*	146 York st.
Columbia University 1903		
Isadore Shapiro	*Birmingham, Ala.*	333 York st.
Christian Braderson Skan	*Hartford, Conn.*	152 Temple st.
Herbert Wesley Stanton, B.S.	*Los Angeles, Cal.*	125 W.
University of California 1907		
George Richard Sturges	*New Haven, Conn.*	858 Quinnipiac av.
Ezra Crowell Terry	*Willimantic, Conn.*	537 Howard av.
Harold Knapp Watrous	*New Britain, Conn.*	105 Park st.
Earl William Wood, B.A.	*Carthage, Ill.*	27 College st.
Carthage College 1906		

SPECIAL STUDENTS, 35

SUMMARY

GRADUATE CLASS	.	.	.	. 20
THIRD YEAR CLASS	.	.	.	. 95
SECOND YEAR CLASS	.	.	.	. 79
FIRST YEAR CLASS	.	.	.	. 110
SPECIAL STUDENTS	.	.	.	. 35
REGULAR STUDENTS	.	.	.	. 339
STUDENTS FROM OTHER DEPARTMENTS			.	171
TOTAL UNDER INSTRUCTION		.	.	510

SUMMER SCHOOL

Jennette Mantel Adams	*Watertown, N. Y.*
Sister Mary Agnes	*New Haven, Conn.*
Joseph Birchard Allen, B.A.	*Washington, D. C.*
Sherman Alden Allen, B A.	*Castile, N. Y.*
Easter Armstrong	*New Haven, Conn.*
Margaret Barrett	*Brooklyn, N. Y.*
Aida Barton	*Brooklyn, N. Y.*
Irene Barton	*Brooklyn, N. Y.*
Samuel John Berard	*New Haven, Conn.*
Aristide Cleophile Bernard, Jr.	*Jeanerette, La.*
Charles Hubbell Bidwell, B.A.	*Orange, Conn.*
Mary Harriet Bishop	*New Haven, Conn.*
Gould Shelton Bissell	*Shelton, Conn.*
Susan Coe Blauvelt	*N'yack, N. Y.*
Joel Roland Borton	*Woodstown, N. J.*
Mary Grace Breckinridge, PH.B., B.PD.	*Binghamton, N. Y.*
Wendell Stanton Brooks	*Chicago, Ill.*
Louis Lawrence Broussard	*Baton Rouge, La.*
Lucy Pearce Brownell, B.A.	*Newport, R. I.*
Edward Neufville T. Burnett	*New York City*
George Francis Cahill	*New Haven, Conn.*
Walter Chapin Chalker, PH.B.	*New Haven, Conn.*
Ju Hsiang Chen	*Tientsin, China*
Wilfred Leonard Childs	*Andover, Conn.*
Tsung Hua Chow	*Tientsin, China*
Ayala Lucia Churchill	*Portland, Conn.*
Isbel Scoular Clarke	*Montreal, Canada*
Lucy Eugenie Cobey	*Hartford, Conn.*
Harry Albert Conte	*New Haven, Conn.*
George Durkin Corneal	*Philadelphia, Pa.*
Elizabeth Sturgis Cowan	*Waterbury, Conn.*
Geoffrey Curtiss	*Buffalo, N. Y.*
Helen Calhoun Danforth	*Pittsburg, Pa.*
Thomas Callahan Davison, M.D.	*Atlanta, Ga.*
Rosa Warner Dimock	*Merrow, Conn.*
Charles Henry Doolittle	*Meriden, Conn.*
Alice Osborn Dow, B.S.	*Reading, Mass.*
Lawrence Francis Dowd	*Holyoke, Mass.*

Mabel Adelene Duncan, B.L.	*Cedarburg, Wis.*
Joseph Vincent Esposito	*New Haven, Conn.*
Agnes Elsie Falvey	*Meriden, Conn.*
Tracy Farnam	*New Haven, Conn.*
Edward Spottiswoode Faust	*New York City*
Harry Firestone	*McKeesport, Pa.*
Christabel Flood, M.A.	*New York City*
Anne Phelps Foskett	*Meriden, Conn.*
Bertie Hamilton Frantz	*New York City*
Louisa Birckhead Gambrall, B.A.	*Baltimore, Md.*
John Arthur Gardner	*New York City*
William Luther Gaylord	*Pasadena, Cal.*
Charles Mark Gill	*New Haven, Conn.*
George Francis Green	*Philadelphia, Pa.*
Mayme Griffin	*Ogden, Ind.*
Catherine St. J. Noyes Guion	*New Haven, Conn.*
John Henry Hartwell	*Shelton, Conn.*
Richard Withington Hawes	*Somerville, Mass.*
Mary Fiske Heap	*Chicago, Ill.*
Lillie Elizabeth Hedberg	*Newport, R. I.*
Emma Susanna Heilman	*Naperville, Ill.*
Caroline Hendrickson	*Bridgeport, Conn*
Hou Wei Ho	*Tientsin, China*
Karl David Hofer	*Hartford, Conn.*
John Francis Hogan	*New Haven, Conn.*
Levi Llewellyn Hoopes	*West Chester, Pa.*
Philip Mead Howe, B.A.	*Rockville, Conn.*
Yü Peng Hua	*Tientsin, China*
Rebecca Barnett Hubbell	*New Haven, Conn.*
Helen Lou Evelyn James	*Saybrook, Conn.*
Mabel Adelia Jarvis	*Blue Point, N. Y.*
Elizabeth Jasper	*Indianapolis, Ind.*
Stanley Russell Jelliffe	*Brooklyn, N. Y.*
Millicent May Johnson	*New Haven, Conn.*
Matie Lee Jones	*Waukegan, Ill.*
Mariano Honrade de Joya, M.L.	*Batangas, P. I.*
Orrin Lockwood Judd	*Hazardville, Conn.*
John Thomas Kibler	*Chestertown, Md.*
Stanislaus Kobytecki, PH.D.	*Galacia, Austria*
Henry Wells Lawrence, Jr., M.A.	*White Plains, N. Y.*
Eugene Hugo Lehnert, B.S., D.V.S.	*Storrs, Conn.*
Nestor Searle Light	*So. Coventry, Conn.*
Orton Lowe	*Grafton, Pa.*
Marie Elizabeth Lufbery	*New York City*

Edith Mary Luther, M.A.	*South Orange, N. J.*
Tai Cheng Ma	*Tientsin, China*
John Joseph Mann	*Buffalo, N. Y.*
Louise Adele MacNeille	*New York City*
Rosalie Marie Martin	*Niagara Falls, N. Y.*
Daniel Carroll McEuen	*East Orange, N. J.*
Leah Meck	*Naperville, Ill.*
Sister Mary Mercedita	*New Haven, Conn.*
William Stuart Messer, B.A.	*Jersey. City, N. J.*
Ida Madeleine Middleton	*Minneapolis, Minn.*
Mabelle Evalena Miller	*Bristol, Conn.*
Lewis Sprague Mills	*Collinsville, Conn.*
Norma Gray Morison	*Brooklyn, N. Y.*
Ella Hortense Morrison	*New York City*
Homer Chidsey Neal	*Southington, Conn.*
Marguerita Mary O'Brien	*Hartford, Conn.*
Mary Imelda O'Brien	*Hartford, Conn.*
Mary Livia Olds	*Duluth, Minn.*
George Washington Page, PH.D.	*Alpine, Texas*
William Arnold Palmer	*Muskegon, Mich.*
Julia Maria Peacocke	*Litchfield, Conn.*
Augusta Peehl	*Indianapolis, Ind.*
Benjamin Judah Phelps, B.A.	*West Suffield, Conn.*
Josephine Laurian Przelomiec	*New Haven, Conn.*
Ethel Ziveley Rather, M.A.	*Gonzales, Texas*
Randolph Raynolds	*New Haven, Conn.*
Ruth Elizabeth Razee, B.A.	*New Haven, Conn.*
William Reed	*Hartford. City, Ind.*
Eleanor Marie Reilly	*Brooklyn, N. Y.*
Frank H. Remaley, B.A.	*McKeesport, Pa.*
Minna Davis Reynolds, M.A.	*Baltimore, Md.*
Florence Rogers	*Flushing, N. Y.*
Nellie Frances Russell	*Meriden, Conn.*
Arthur Warren Selleck	*White Plains, N. Y.*
Mary Franc Short, B.S.	*New York City*
Josephine Skelley	*Cleveland, O.*
Carl Herring Smith, B.S.	*Gouverneur, N. Y.*
Mary Agnes Sponheimer	*Ansonia, Conn.*
William Howard Sprenkle, B.S.	*McKeesport, Pa.*
Louis Howard Stanley	*Hartford, Conn.*
Edwin Booth Stone	*Brooklyn, Conn.*
Alfred Leon Stowe	*Plainville, Conn.*
Howard Sturges	*Providence, R. I.*
Frances Alice Terrill	*New Haven, Conn.*

William Edward Thoms, B.A.   *Waterbury, Conn.*
Frances Sarah Walkley   *Plantsville, Conn.*
William Little Wallace   *New Haven, Conn.*
Francis Melgar Watrous   *New Haven, Conn.*
Susan Mary James Weston   *Waterbury, Conn.*
Franklin Lyron Wheeler   *Shelton, Conn.*
Emma E. White   *Tonawanda, N. Y.*
Clara Helen Whitmore, M.A.   *New York City*
Henry Clarence Wick, Jr.   *Cleveland, O.*
Dudley Willcox   *Lawrenceville, N. J.*
Alexander James Wood, B.A.   *Branford, Conn.*
Jennie Dearborn Wood   *Meriden, Conn.*
Minnie Velma Yeaw   *Cranston, R. I.*

SUMMER SCHOOL, 139

GENERAL SUMMARY

OFFICERS

PROFESSORS, including other University Officers - 116

ASSISTANT PROFESSORS - - - 55

INSTRUCTORS, including Tutors, Lecturers, etc. - 157

ASSISTANTS IN INSTRUCTION - - - 67

ASSISTANTS IN ADMINISTRATION - 79

TOTAL 474

STUDENTS

DEPARTMENT OF PHILOSOPHY AND THE ARTS:

	Enrollment	Total under Instruction
GRADUATE SCHOOL, Resident -	295	357
Non-resident -	62	
COLLEGE - - ..	1315	1570
SHEFFIELD SCIENTIFIC SCHOOL -	948*	1375
ART SCHOOL - -	39	406
MUSIC SCHOOL	83	184
FOREST SCHOOL -	61	93
	2803	
DEPARTMENT OF THEOLOGY - -	80	96
DEPARTMENT OF MEDICINE	137	
DEPARTMENT OF LAW	339	510
	3359	
Deduct for names inserted twice -	53	
	3306	
TOTAL UNIVERSITY REGISTRATION -	3306	
SUMMER SCHOOL OF FORESTRY - -	23	
SUMMER SCHOOL - -	139	
	3468	
Deduct for Summer School students enrolled in other Departments	35	
TOTAL RECEIVING INSTRUCTION -	3433	

* Besides 151 graduates who are members of the Graduate School or Forest School.

SUMMARY OF STUDENTS
BY STATES OR COUNTRIES

Alabama	.	.	.	3
Alaska	.	.	.	1
Arizona	.	.	.	3
Arkansas	.	.	.	2
California	.	.	.	44
Colorado	.	.	.	30
Connecticut	.	.	1159
Delaware	.	.	.	13
District of Columbia	.	.	23
Florida	.	.	.	7
Georgia	.	.	.	12
Hawaii	.	.	.	4
Idaho	.	.	.	2
Illinois	.	.	.	153
Indiana	.	.	.	34
Iowa	.	.	.	34
Kansas	.	.	.	16
Kentucky	.	.	.	30
Louisiana	.	.	.	17
Maine	.	.	.	16
Maryland	.	.	.	13
Massachusetts	.	.	.	177
Michigan	.	.	.	32
Minnesota	.	.	.	48
Mississippi	.	.	.	5
Missouri	.	.	.	67

Montana	.	.	.	8
Nebraska	.	.	.	12
Nevada	.	.	.	1
New Hampshire	.	.	15
New Jersey	.	.	120
New Mexico	.	.	.	1
New York	.	.	671
North Carolina	.	.	12
North Dakota	.	.	3
Ohio	.	.	.	172
Oklahoma	.	.	.	5
Oregon	.	.	.	7
Pennsylvania	.	.	201
Philippine Islands	.	.	6
Rhode Island	.	.	30
South Carolina	.	.	3
South Dakota	.	.	7
Tennessee	.	.	14
Texas	.	.	.	24
Utah	.	.	.	4
Vermont	.	.	.	21
Virginia	.	.	.	14
Washington	.	.	15
West Virginia	.	.	9
Wisconsin	.	.	18
Wyoming	.	.	.	1

Austria	.	.	.	1
British Guiana	.	.	1
Canada	.	.	.	21
China	.	.	.	25
England	.	.	.	4
France	.	.	.	2
Honduras	.	.	.	1
India	.	.	.	1
Japan	.	.	.	16

Mexico	.	.	.	4
New Zealand	.	.	.	
Porto Rico	.	.	.	
South Africa	.	.	2
Sweden	.	.	.	3
Turkey	.	.	7
Wales	.	.	.	1
West Indies (Danish)	.	.	

SUMMARY OF STUDENTS
BY CITIES AND TOWNS
[Places represented by five or more students only are mentioned.]

Albany	7	Milford	7
Allegheny	6	Milwaukee	7
Ansonia	24	Minneapolis	16
Auburn (N. Y.)	19	Montclair	20
Baltimore	13	Morristown	10
Berkeley (Cal.).	5	Mt. Vernon (N. Y.).	5
Binghamton	5	Nashville	5
Boston	14	Naugatuck	13
Branford	13	Newark (N. J.).	5
Bridgeport	53	New Britain	26
Bristol	8	Newburgh	7
Brooklyn (N. Y.)	90	New Haven	412
Buffalo	40	New London	12
Chicago	98	New Orleans	11
Cincinnati	38	Newport	7
Cleveland	42	New Rochelle.	6
Columbus	5	New York	243
Danbury	14	Norwalk	10
Davenport (Ia.)	5	Norwich	28
Dayton	7	Orange (N. J.)	8
Denver	22	Philadelphia	26
Derby	19	Pittsburg	35
Detroit	10	Plainfield (N. J.)	7
East Haven	6	Portland (Ore.)	6
East Orange (N. J.).	8	Poughkeepsie	7
Evanston	11	Providence	13
Fairfield	5	Rochester	14
Gloversville	7	Rockville.	7
Grand Rapids	10	St. Joseph.	10
Hartford	93	St. Louis	33
Holyoke	9	St. Paul	23
Indianapolis	9	Salem (Mass.)	5
Kansas City	15	San Francisco.	5
Litchfield	5	Schenectady	6
Louisville	11	Scranton	11
Manchester	5	Seattle	9
Meriden	25	Sewickley	7

Shanghai	9	Torrington	7
Shelton	12	Troy (N. Y.)	6
Somerville (Mass.)	5	Wallingford	15
Southington	5	Warren (Pa.)	8
South Manchester	5	Washington	22
South Orange (N.J.)	6	Waterbury	43
Springfield (Mass.)	15	West Haven	17
Stamford	13	Wilmington (Del.)	9
Stratford	12	Winchester (Mass.)	5
Syracuse	8	Winsted	5
Tientsin	8	Worcester	11
Tokyo	6	Yonkers	11
Toledo	7	Youngstown	5

SUMMARY OF STUDENTS

BY DEGREES REPRESENTED

Acadia University	7	Cheshunt College	1
Adrian College	1	Chicago Theological Seminary	2
Alabama Polytechnic Institute	1	Clark University	1
Allegheny College	1	Colby College	1
Amherst College	2	Colgate University	1
Andover Theological Seminary	1	College of the City of New York	1
Baker University	1		
Bates College	2	Columbia University	7
Baylor University	4	Cornell College	1
Beloit College	6	Cornell University	4
Benton Law School	1	Dartmouth College	4
Berea College	1	Davidson College	1
Berkeley Divinity School	1	Denison University	2
Bethany College (Kans.)	4	DePauw University	1
Bethany College (W. Va)	2	Doane College	5
Bethel College	1	Drake University	3
Boston University	1	Drew Theological Seminary	2
Brown University	6	Drury College	2
Bucknell University	1	El Porvenir College	1
Butler College	1	Emporia College	1
Carleton College	3	Euphrates College	1
Carthage College	3	Florida State College	1
Central College (Mo.)	4	Formosan Association College	1
Central Turkey College	3	Franklin and Marshall College	1
Central University	1	Friends University	1

Geneva College	1	Ohio State University	1
Grand Island College	1	Ohio Wesleyan University	1
Hamilton College	1	Oita Agricultural School	1
Hargrove College	1	Okayama Medical College	1
Hartford Theological Seminary	2	Olivet College	2
Harvard University	8	Otterbein University	4
Heidelberg University	2	Oxford University	1
Holiness University (Texas)	1	Pacific Theological Seminary	1
Howard University	1	Pennsylvania College	1
Illinois Wesleyan University	1	Pomona College	3
Indiana University	5	Queen's University	1
Iowa Wesleyan University	1	Randolph-Macon College	1
Juniata College	1	Rhode Island College	2
Kansai Law School	1	Ripon College	1
Kansas City School of Law	2	Rutgers College	1
Keiogijiku University	4	St. Joseph's College (Phila.)	1
Kentucky State Colllege	1	St. Lawrence University	1
Knox College	1	St. Mary's College	1
Lafayette College	1	St. Paul's Institute	3
Lebanon Valley College	2	St. Stephen's College	1
Lehigh University	1	St. Thomas University	1
Liceo de Manila	1	Santa Clara College	1
Lincoln College	1	Shaw University	1
McFerrin College	1	Simpson College	1
McGill University	1	Smith College	4
McMinnville College	1	State University of Iowa	4
Marietta College	1	Stockholm Högre Realla-	
Maryville College	1	roverk	1
Massachusetts Agricultural		Syracuse University	3
College	2	Tohoku Gakuin	1
Mercer University	1	Trinity College	1
Middlebury College	1	Trinity University	2
Milligan College	1	Tufts College	1
Monmouth College	2	Tulane University	1
Moravian College	1	Union Christian College (Ind.)	1
Mt. Holyoke College	1	University of California	7
Muhlenberg College	1	University of Chicago	6
National Normal University	10	University of Cincinnati	2
New Hampshire College	2	University of Georgia	4
New York Law School	1	University of Illinois	1
New York University	1	University of Kansas	3
Northwestern University	1	University of Manila	1
Oberlin College	8	University of Michigan	4

University of Minnesota	.	8	Vanderbilt University	.	2
University of Mississippi	.	1	Vassar College .	.	3
University of Missouri	.	3	Virginia Institute	.	1
University of Nebraska	.	1	Virginia Polytechnic Institute	1
University of New Brunswick	3	Wabash College	.	1
University of North Carolina	3	Waseda University	.	1
University of Oklahoma	.	2	Washington Training College	1
University of Pennsylvania	3	Washington University	.	3
University of Toronto	.	5	Waynesburg College	.	1
University of Texas	.	3	Wellesley College	.	3
University of South Dakota	2	Wesleyan University	.	10
University of Southern California	.	1	West Lafayette College	.	1
University of Washington	2	Western Reserve University	1
University of West Virginia	1	Williams College	.	6
University of Wisconsin	.	1	Woman's College (Baltimore)	1
University of Wooster	.	2	Yale University	.	306
Upper Iowa University	.	1	Young Harris College	.	1
Upsala University	.	1	Y. M. C. A. Training School	2

The name of every officer is printed in italics and is followed by a reference to the page on which the name occurs in the List of Officers. When more than one page is mentioned the reference is to the page or pages on which the courses given by the officers are described.

The names of students are followed by the designations of their several classes (Grad., Graduate; Sr., Senior; Mid., Middle; Jr., Junior; 2, Second Year; 1, First Year; So., Sophomore; Fr., Freshman; Spec., Special); the names of students have appended also an indication of the Department to which each belongs, viz.: *a*, Academical Department; *d*, Divinity School; *f*, School of the Fine Arts; *for.*, Forest School; *g*, Graduate School; *l*, Law School; *m*, Medical School; *mus.*, Department of Music; *s*, Sheffield Scientific School.*

Abbe, A. P., Sr. *a*	25 V.	Allen, W. L., Jr. *a*	414 B.
Abbott, C., Fr. *a*	250 York st.	Allerton, G. M., Jr., Jr. *s*	111 V-S.
Abbott, R., Sr. *a*	30 V.	*Alling, A. N., Prof.* (pp. 26, 466)	
Abel, R., *g*	142 York st.		199 York st.
Abramson, H. L., 1 *m*	35 High st.	Alling, C. B., Jr. *a*	269 D.
Achelis, T., Sr. *a*	368 WH.	Alling, K. S., Fr. *s*	122 Wall st.
Adams, C. A., 3 *l*	1076 Chapel st.	Allis, C. H., Jr. *a*	133 W.
Adams, C. L., Sr. *a*	78 Dwight st.	Allison, W. T., *g*, Grad. *d*	
Adams, D. A., Proctor (p. 46)	569 P.		Middlefield
Adams, E. B., *f*	544 Whitney av.	Almquist, F. G., Jr. *s*	132 V-S.
Adams, G. B., Prof. (pp. 23, 188-9,		Alofsin, H., 2d, Sr. *a*	715 W. D.
375-8, 514, 516)	57 Edgehill rd.	Alpert, S., Sr. *a*	96 Washington av.
Adams, J. C., Instr. (pp. 32, 162, 164,		Altarelli, C. Mid. *d*	696 W. D.
166, 338) (A, c.)	75 Mansfield st.	Altschul, F., Sr. *a*	251 D.
Adams, R. W., 2 *l*	890 Chapel st.	Alvord, D. F., Sr. *a*	425 FW.
Adams, W. J., Jr. *s*	112 V-S.	Alvord, E. L., Fr. *s*	118 College st.
Addis, J. S., 1 *l*	105 Dwight st.	Alvord, H. B., Jr. *a*	218 F.
Agard, H. L., *g*	711 W. D.	Ambler, J. A., Fr. *s*	9 Library st.
Agnew, R. R., Sr. *m*	East Haven	Ames, J. Q., 3 *l*	479 Elm st.
Aiken, W. M., 3 *l*	142 Edgewood av.	Amory, C. G., Jr. *s*	82 Wall st.
Aikens, H. N., Spec. *l*	155 Elm st.	Andel, C. E., *g*	A.
Aikman, H. D., Fr. *a*	545 P.	Anderson, A. J. E., *mus.*	
Akatsuka, U., *g*	720 W. D.		West Haven
Albarian, S. M., *g*, Grad. *d*	614 E. D.	Anderson, C. M., *g*	A.
Alcott, C. F., Sr. *s*	111 Grove st.	*Anderson, Mrs. E. M., Matron*	
Alden, J., Fr. *a*	1076 Chapel st.	(p. 45)	276 Prospect st.
Aldrich, C. R., *g*	A.	*Anderson, H. S., Instr.* (p. 32)	
Alexander, W. H., Grad. *d*	Derby		350 Humphrey st.
Alker, E. P., Jr. *a*	377 WH.	*Anderson, J., Fellow*	Woodmont
Allard, J. A., Jr., Jr. *s*	Stratford	Anderson, R. B., Fr. *a*	200 York st.
Allen, A. D., *g.*	A.	*Anderson, W. G., Director* (p. 25)	
Allen, C. M., Sr. *a*	434 FW.		(G.) 1151 Chapel st.
Allen, F. O., Fr. *a*	242 York st.	Andrew, R. M., So. *a*	379 Crown st.
Allen, K. L., Fr. *s*	117 Wall st.	Andrews, A. W., 2 *l*	East Haven
Allen, L. S., Fr. *s*	86 Wall st.	*Andrews, C. E., Ass't.* (p. 41)	
Allen, M. A., *g*	256 Edgewood av.	(1026 Yale P. O.)	
Allen, P. T., Fr. *a*	163 York st.		12 France st., Norwalk
Allen, R. W., Sr. *for.*	91 Lake pl.	Andrews, P. S., Jr. *a*	238 D.

* The names of students in the Summer Schools are not included in the Directory.

Andrews, R. J., Sr. *s* 373 Crown st.
Andrews, W. M., Jr. *a* 68 v.
Andrus, H. F., Fr. *s* 423 Temple st.
Angier, R. P., Instr. (pp. 32, 183-5, 383-4, 464) (7 HER.) 44 Elm st.
Annis, D., So. *a* 8 College st.
Anstice, M. R., Sr. *s* 96 Wall st.
Apgar, E. P., Fr. *s* 423 Temple st.
Archer, S. M., Fr. *s* 128 High st.
Armstrong, C. D., So. *a* 8 College st.
Armstrong, C. M., Spec. *l* 36 Elm st.
Armstrong. L. E., *g* 175 East Rock rd.
Armstrong. W. P., 3 *l* 155 Elm st.
Arnold, E. II., Instr. (pp. 32, 466) 46 York sq.
Arnold, F., *g* 25 Norton st.
Arnold, H. S., Ass't. (pp. 41, 464-5) 36 Dwight st.
Arnold, P. T., Jr. *a* 449 FW.
Arnot, E. J., Jr. *d* 126 Park st.
Arnot, J. K., Jr. *d*, Spec. *l* 126 Park st.
Asakawa, K., Instr. and Curator (pp. 32, 189, 334, 379-80) 385 Winthrop av.
Ashbaugh, M. M., 1 *l* 216 Orange st.
Asher, C. A., Sr. *s* 59 Grove st.
Ashley, S. W., Jr. *s* 184 F.
Assmann, F. A., Jr. *a* 381 WH.
Atkins, Howard D., Fr. *a* 364 WH.
Atwater, G. F., Sr. *s* 1776 State st.
Aubrey, T. J., Fr. *a* 53 Prospect st.
Auchincloss, G., Sr. *a* 426 FW.
Auchincloss, J. C., Sr. *a* 426 FW.
Auchincloss, J. H., Sr. *a* 51 V.
Audette. L. G., So. *a* 379 WH.
Augur, W., Jr. *a* 270 D.
Austin, R. M., So. *a* 164 L.
Avery, A. M., So. *a* 136 W.
Avery, F. R., Fr. *a* 217 York st.
Avey, A. E.. Sr. *a* 84 C.
Avitabile, A. L., Sr. *m* 476 Chapel st.
Ayers, J. G., Jr., Jr. *s* 108 High st.

Baars, H. G.. Jr., So. *a* 251 Crown st.
Babcock, W. R., Jr. *a* 446 FW.
Babikian, L. H., Sr. *s* 128 High st.
Bachman, E. W., Jr. *a* 94 W.
Bachner, A., 1 *l* 43 College st.
Backus. O. P., Jr., Sr. *a* 88 C.
Bacon, B. S., Fr. *a* 576 P.
Bacon, B. IV., Prof. (pp. 25, 152, 326, 431) (605 E. D.) 244 Edwards st.

Bacon, F., Lect. (pp. 32, 466) 32 High st.
Bacon, H. R., Fr. *s* 120 College st.
Bacon, L., So. *a* 342 WH.
Badger, P. B., Fr. *a* 200 York st.
Bagg, J. L., Jr. *s* 82 Wall st.
Bailey, E. M., *g* 168 Sheffield av.
Bailey, F. T., So. *a* 111 W.
Bailey, G. E., So. *a* 122 Dwight st.
Bailey, P. D., So. *a* 215 F.
Bailey, S. J., *mus.* 26 Edgewood av.
Bailey, W. B., Ass't. Prof. (pp. 29, 194, 196, 373, 439) 26 Edgewood av.
Baird, C. W., Fr. *s* 122 Wall st.
Baker, A. E., So. *a* 250 Crown st.
Baker, B., Jr. *s* 129 V. S.
Baker, C. C., Sr. *s* 70 Trumbull st.
Baker, D. M., Fr. *s* 210 St. Ronan st.
Baker, E. L., Sr. *a* 97 W.
Baker, F. A., Fr. *s* 128 High st.
Baker, G. M., Instr. (p. 32) A.
Baker, G. V., Fr. *s* 119 Grove st.
Baker, H. C., So. *a* 260 Crown st.
Baker, H. H., So. *a* 22 College st.
Baker, H. W., Fr. *a* 250 York st.
Baker, J. F., Jr. *a* 246 D.
Baker, L. W., 3 *l* 210 St. Ronan st.
Baker, O. E., Jr. *for.*, Grad. *s* 182 Mansfield st.
Bakewell, C. M., Prof. (pp. 27, 182-4, 381) (G, C.) 305 Lawrence st.
Bakewell, D. C., Sr. *a* 5 V.
Baldwin, A. I., *g* 78 Whalley av.
Baldwin, C. S., Ass't. Prof. (pp. 29, 160-1, 338) (15 WH.) 57 Wall st.
Baldwin, D. M., Fr. *s* 133 College st.
Baldwin, J. M., Jr. *s* 124 Wall st.
Baldwin, S., Sr. *a* 659 W. D.
Baldwin, S. A., Sr. *a* 24 V.
Baldwin, S. E., Prof. (pp. 22, 194, 374, 441, 497, 500, 505, 507, 516, 518) (69 Church st.) 44 Wall st.
Ballard, G. B., Jr. *s* 17 Hillhouse av.
Bangs, J. K., Jr., Jr. *a* 243 D.
Banker, L. A.. Jr. *s* 111 Grove st.
Banks, D. T., Spec. *m* 258 Fairmont av.
Banks, J. L., Jr., Fr. *a* 238 York st.
Banks, M. S., Sr. *a* 1 V.
Barber, J. E.. So. *a* 18 College st.
Barber, L. L., So. *a* 170 L.

arclay, L. W., Mid. *d*, Spec. *l*
633 E. D.
Barker, E. A., 2 *l* Branford
arker, J. L., Sr. *s* 180 V-S.
Barker, S. G., Fr. *s* 125 High st.
Barker, T. E., Fr. *s* 125 High st.
Barlow, E. L., Fr. *s* Bridgeport
arlow, H. W., Jr. *s* 1011 Yale P. O.
Barlow, R., jr. *a* 469 FW.
Barnaby, K. T., Jr. *s* 111 V-S.
Barnes, E. S., So. *a* 143 L.
Barnes, F., 2 *l* 423 Temple st.
Barnes, F. F., So. *a* 225 Crown st.
arnes, H. A., Sup't. (p. 45)
(rear HER.) 80 Admiral st.
Barnes, H. E., jr. *a* 26 Lynwood pl.
Barnes, T. S., So. *a* 22 College st.
Barnes, W. D., Jr., Sec'y. Acad.
Dep't. Y. U. C. A. (p. 45)
Dwight Hall
arney, S. E., Ass't. Prof. (pp. 29,
233, 238, 240, 250, 263, 266, 368,
417) (132 WIN.) 346 Whitney av.
arnum, C. G., 1 *m*
344 Humphrey st.
Barnum, C. L., Ass't. (p. 45)
344 Humphrey st.
Barnum, E. M., Sr. *a* 234 D.
Barnum, S. H., 2d, Fr. *s* 160 V-S.
arnum, T. R., Ass't. (p. 45)
(WOOD.) 344 Humphrey st.
Barnum, W., So. *a* 22 College st.
arrell, J., Ass't. Prof. (pp. 29, 175,
177, 355, 357, 414) (1 PEAB.)
85 Avon st.
Barrett, J. N., Sr. *s* 181 V-S.
Barrows, D. N., Sr. *a* 368 WH.
Barry, J. C., Sr. *a* 20 V.
Bartek, J. J., Jr., 3 *l* Wallingford
Bartholomew, B. W., Fr. *s*
55 Prospect st.
Bartholomew, M. M., Sec'y. Sci.
Dep't. Y. U. C. A. (p. 45) B. M. H.
Bartlett, C. J., Prof. (pp. 27, 181,
465-6) 209 York st.
Bartlett, E. B., Fr. *s* 10 B. M. H.
Bartlett, L. M., Sr. *s* 110 Wall st.
Bartlett, P. C. K., Sr. *a* 345 WH.
Bartlett, W. H., Jr. *s* 78 Whalley av.
Bartlett, W. N., Fr. *a* 231 York st.
Bassett, J. B., Fr. *s* 119 Wall st.
Bassett, J. S., Lect. (pp. 378, 516)
(90 High st.) Northampton, Mass.

Bassett, L. E., Sr. *s* 275 Humphrey st.
Basye, A. H., *g* 204 F.
Bates, C. W., Ass't. (p. 41)
293 York st.
Bates, H. C., Fr. *s* 125 High st.
Bates, H. S., Jr. *a* 461 FW.
Bates, L. T., Fr. *s* 119 Wall st.
Bateson, E. F., Jr. *a* 238 D.
Bateson, W., Lect. (p. 32)
Cambridge, England
Batson, L. H., *g* 166 York st.
Battelle, G., 2d, Fr. *s* 188 V-S.
Bauer, J., Proctor (p. 45) 565 P.
Baur, P. V. C., Ass't. Prof. (pp. 29,
149, 319) 246 Church st.
Bayliss, D., *mus.* 46 Shelton av.
Bayne-Jones, S., So. *a* 260 Crown st.
Beach, F. E., Ass't. Prof. (pp. 29, 227,
236, 244, 252, 268, 344)
44 Lyon st.
Beach, H. P., Prof. (pp. 24, 437) A.
Beach, J. K., Lect. (pp. 32, 502, 517)
450 Temple st.
Beach, J. W., Fr. *a* 581 P.
Beach, R. J., *g* So. Meriden
Beadleston, C. P., Sr. *a* 32 V.
Beal, H., *g* A.
Bean, H. W., So. *a* 254 Crown st.
Bean, W. H., Inst. (pp. 32, 464)
252 York st.
Beardslee, C. G., Jr. *a* 247 D.
Beardsley, H. S., Sr. *a* 42 V.
Beardsley, H. W., Fr. *s* 104 Wall st.
Beardsley, R. O., Fr. *s* 125 High st.
Beardsley, S. B., Fr. *a* Bridgeport
Beardsley, W. H., 2 *m* 710 W. D.
Beaty, E. L., Jr. *s* 111 Grove st.
Beaumont, C. E., Fr. *s*
391 Howard av.
Beck, F. G., Ass't. (p. 41)
821 Congress av.
Beck, G. E., Asst. (pp. 41, 175)
7 Library st.
Beckman, F. F. W., Jr. *for.*, Grad. *s*
717 W. D.
Beebe, H. C., Fr. *s* 89 Gregory st.
Beebe, R., Sr. *a* 354 WH.
Beebe, W., Prof. (pp. 23, 167-8)
262 Bradley st.
Beecher, G. L., *g* 201 Sherman av.
Beecher, J. R., 2 *l* Bridgeport
Beecher, L. T., *mus.*
359 Edgewood av.

Beecher, S. E., g   220 Davenport av.
Beede, F. H., Lect. (p. 32)
                        424 Temple st.
Beede, V. A., Fr. a   236 Crown st.
Beeler, W. H., Grad. l
                        354 Whalley av.
Beeman, C. C., Jr. a   250 D.
Beer, T., Fr. a   248 York st.
Beers, G. E., Ass't. Prof. (pp. 29, 498,
    501, 505, 517-18) (15 HEN.)
                        42 Church st.
Beers, G. M., Clerk (p. 45) (3 s. H.)
                        130 Cottage st.
Beers, H. A., Prof. (pp. 23, 162-4, 166,
    336)   65 York sq.
Beers, H. A., Jr., Jr. a   342 WH.
Beers, W. C., 2 l   279 Willow st.
Behrman, M. H., So. a   221 F.
Beinecke, F. W., Jr. s   122 Wall st.
Beinecke, W., So. a   22 College st.
Belin, G. d'A., Sr. s   131 Grove st.
Belknap, W. B., Sr. a   334 WH.
Belknap, W. K., Sr. s   125 V-S.
Bell, R., Sr. d   600 Chapel st.
Bellamy, D., So. a   260 Crown st.
Bellamy, F. W., Jr. a   103 W.
Bellis, H. D., Ass't. (p. 41)   G.
Benedict, H. H., Jr. a   79 C.
Benedict, P. H., Jr. a   445 FW.
Benedict, S. R., Ass't. (p. 41)
    (64 s. B. L.)   77 Grove st.
Bengis, R., Fr. s   271 Cedar st.
Benner, E. W., Fr. s   128 High st.
Benner, H., So. a   22 College st.
Bennett, D. V., Jr. a   89 C.
Bennett, M. E., mus.   357 Elm st.
Bennett, R. H., Jr. a   449 FW.
Bennett, S. E., Jr., Sr. a
                        249 Crown st.
Bennett, T. G., Trustee S. S. S.
    (p. 200)   423 Prospect st.
Bennetto, E., Jr., Sr. a   331 WH.
Bentley, C. R., So. a   236 Crown st.
Berard, S. J., Ass't. (p. 41)
                        813 Orange st.
Berdan, J. M., Instr. (pp. 32, 160-1,
    339)   (11 WH.)   681 Orange st.
Bergens, J. A., 2 l   9 Library st.
Berger, G. R. B., Sr. a   62 V.
Berman, E., Fr. a   63 York st.
Berman, J., Fr. s   214 F.
Berman, S., 2 l   214 F.
Bernard, C. P., Jr. s   131 Maple st.

Bernhardi, J. F., Jr. s   333 York st.
Bernstein, A., Sr. m   163 York st.
Beron, R. W., mus.   Waterbury
Beyer, E. E., Sr. a   9 V.
Beyer, F., Sr. a   9 V.
Bickford, H. W., 2 l   264 York st.
Biddle, A. A., Jr. a   239 D.
Bidleman, H. C., Jr. s   133 College st.
Bidwell, P. W., So. a   170 L.
Bierkan, A. T., Instr. (pp. 32, 499)
                        42 Church st.
Bigelow, L. C., So. a   254 Crown st.
Bigelow, P., Spec. s   17 Hillhouse av.
Biglow, L. H., 3d, Sr. a   30 V.
Biglow, R. G., Sr. s   124 Prospect st.
Bill, E. G., Ass't. (p. 41)
                        122 Howe st.
Billard, F. H., Jr. for., Grad. s
                        315 York st.
Bingham, H., Lect. (pp. 32, 189, 379)
    (201 F.)   58 Everitt st.
Bingham, H. P., So. a   8 College st.
Bingham, S. D., Jr., Ass't. (pp. 41,
    199, 341, 398)   94 Prospect st.
Bird, H., Fr. s   244 Orchard st.
Bird, H. C., Sr. s   948 Yale P. O.
Birge, J. K., Jr. a   464 FW.
Bishop, A. L., Instr. (pp. 32, 175,
    191-2, 246, 371-2)   120 York st.
Bishop, H. F., 1 l   1076 Chapel st.
Bishop, L. B., Instr. (pp. 32, 466, 514)
                        356 Orange st.
Bishop, O. F., Jr. s   174 Grand av.
Bishop, W. D., Jr., Fr. a   242 York st.
Bishop, W. F., Jr., Fr. s   132 Wall st.
Bissell, C. H., Sr. a   45 V.
Bissell, G. S., So. a   128 W.
Bissell, M. H., Fr. s   125 High st.
Bissell, R. M., Lect. (p. 33)   Hartford
Bissell, W. S., Sr. a   63 V.
Black, J. C., Sr. a   7 V.
Black, J. E., Sr. m   120 York st.
Blackburn, J. B., So. a   8 College st.
Blackman, A. W., 3 l   691 W. D.
Blair, C. B., Jr. a   377 WH.
Blair, E. S., Fr. a   238 York st.
Blake, C. E., Fr. a   554 P.
Blake, E. M., Ass't. (p. 41)
                        199 York st.
Blanchard, F. T., Ass't. (pp. 41, 160)
    (15 WH.)   650 E. D.
Blanchard, M. E., Jr., Fr. s   4 B. M. H.
Blegen, C. W., Sr. a   364 George st.

Bleistein, C. W., Fr. *s* 389 Temple st.
Bleistein, G., Jr., So. *a* 22 College st.
Blinn, C. J., 3 *l* 688 w. D.
Blinn, L. H., Sr. *s* 184 Blatchley av.
Bliss, B. G., So. *a* 8 College st.
Blodget, F. M., Jr. *a* 374 WH.
Blumer, G., Prof. (pp. 27, 465-6)
204 York st.
Board, S. S., Fr. *a* 536 P.
Boardman, R. S., Jr. *s* 391 Temple st.
Boardman, W. J., 2d, Sr. *s*
111 Grove st.
Bodman, H. L., *g* A.
Bodwell, C. S., Sr. *a* 202 F.
Boggs, E. D., Ass't. (p. 45) (LIB.)
327 Willow st.
Boggs, G. R., Sr. *s.* 131 Grove st.
Boggs, R. E., Fr. *s* 120 High st.
Boggs, T. H., Instr. (pp. 33, 175, 246,
371, 514) (HER.) 115 Park st.
Bogue, M., Fr. *a* 250 York st.
Boltwood, B. B., Ass't. Prof. (pp. 29,
171, 344) (S. P. L.)
43 Livingston st.
Boman, J. S., *g* MEM.
Bomar, W. P., Sr. *s* 17 Hillhouse av.
Bonander, H. E., *mus.* 98 Chapel st.
Bonbright, H., Fr. *a* 242 York st.
Bonfils, C. W., Jr. *s* .114 V-S.
Bonn. K. S., *mus.* Waterbury
Booth, B. N., Jr. *s* 660 George st.
Boothe, L. S., Sr. *a*, 1 *m* 202 F.
Borden, W. W., Jr. *a* 380 WH.
Born, F. J., Med. Ass't. Gymnasium
(p. 33) 125 High st.
Bostwick, A. L., Sr. *a* 358 WH.
Bostwick. F. B., Sr. *s*
220 Lawrence st.
Bostwick, T. A., Ass't. (p. 45)
(9 PEAB.) 43 Livingston st.
Bosworth, A. H., Sr. *s* 184 V-S.
Bosworth, R. S., Sr. *a* 43 V.
Botwick, S. W., 1 *l* 24 Arch st.
Bourne, E. G., Prof. (pp. 25, 375,
378, 380, 519) A.
Bowen, J. K., So. *a* 22 College st.
Bowers, E. A., Lect. (pp. 33, 354, 419,
517) 209 Crown st.
Bowers, T. W., So. *a* 8 College st.
Bowman, I., Instr. (pp. 33, 175-8,
355, 357, 414, 514) (1 PEAB.)
203 York st.
Bowman, R., Fr. *a* 563 P.

Bowman, S. H., Jr., 2 *l* 36 Elm st.
Bowne, B. P., Lect. (p. 33)
Boston, Mass.
Boyer, C. H., *g* A.
Boyer, D. B., Fr. *s* 124 Wall st.
Boyer, F. Q., Sr. *s* 182 V-S.
Boyle, R. J., Sr. *m* 974 State st.
Boynton, D. S., Fr. *s* 395 Temple st.
Boynton, H. R., Jr., Fr. *a* 537 P.
Boynton, N. M., *mus.* Branford
Bradford, W. P., Fr. *a* 196 F.
Bradley, H. F., Fr. *s* 82 Wall st.
Bradley. H. N., Fr. *a* 8 College st.
Bradley, J. S., Sr. *a* 24 V.
Bradley, J. S., Jr., Sr. *s* 41 High st.
Bradley, L. J., *f* 21 Hillside av.
Bradley, R. F., Fr. *a* ,
432 Whitney av.
Bradley, S. M., Jr. *s* 104 V-S.
Bradley, W. M., Ass't. (p. 41)
1346 Chapel st.
Bragdon, J. H., Fr. *a* 242 York st.
Bragg, C. S., Sr. *a* 101 W.
Brainard, F. S., So. *a* 22 College st.
Brainerd, H. S., Fr. *s* 610 E. D.
Branch, J. A., Sr. *s* 96 Wall st.
Brann, E. R., Fr. *s* 82 Wall st.
Brastow, L. O., Prof. (p. 21)
(601 E. D.) 146 Cottage st.
Braude, S. H., Fr. *a* 586 P.
Brautlecht, C. A., *g* 130 Front st.
Breazeale, H. P., 1 *l* 137 Dwight st.
Bree, W. A., 3 *l* 712 State st.
Brenner, I. M., 2 *m* 44 Bishop st.
Brenner, J. R., Fr. *s* 113 Bradley st.
Bretz, H. B., So. *a* 214 Crown st.
Brevoort, W. H., Jr., Fr. *s*
3 Hillhouse av.
Brewer, C., Sr. *s* 418 Orange st.
Brewer, C. P., 3 *l* 333 York st.
Brewer, W. H., Prof. (pp. 21, 353,
415) 418 Orange st.
Brewster, W. E., Fr. *s* 117 Wall st.
Brides, A. E., 2 *m* 70 Trumbull st.
Bridgett, F. E., Sr. *a* Wallingford
Brigham, J. N., So. *a* 11 College st.
Brinsmade, W. S., Sr. *s* 191 V-S.
Briscoe, J. M., Jr. *for.*, Spec. *s*
39 Lynwood pl.
Bristol, D. J., Jr., Jr. *s* 519 George st.
Britton, J. A., Fr. *s* 117 Wall st.
Broadbent, E. B., Fr. *a*
911 Dixwell av.

Broadhead, W. A., Fr. *s*
387 Temple st.
Brockway, U. H., Jr., Fr. *a*　　550 P.
Broderick, T. F., Jr., Sr. *m*
925 Howard av.
Brody, J. E., Fr. *s*　　21 William st.
Bromer, R. S., Sr. *a*　　3 v.
Bronson, B., Jr. *a*　　422 B.
Bronson, W. B., Fr. *a*　West Haven
Brooks, H., Jr. *a*　　268 D.
Brooks, H. W., Jr. *a*　　447 FW.
Brooks, J. T., Sr. *s*　131 Grove st.
Brooks, W. S., Sr. *a*　　85 C.
Broomhall, B., Sr. *a*　　265 D.
Brosnan, M. E., *mus.*　Wallingford
Broughton, R., Sr. *a*　　126 W.
Brown, C. C., Priv. Sec'y. (p. 45)
(WOOD.)　22 Lynwood pl.
Brown, C. T., Jr. *a*　　467 FW.
Brown, E., *g*　　315 York st.
Brown, E. W., Prof. (pp. 26, 169,
362, 365)　　389 Temple st.
Brown, G. F., Jr. *s*　　110 V-S.
Brown, G. P., Fr. *a*　　584 P.
Brown, H. G., *g*　82 Whalley av.
Brown, H. R., Sr. *s*　111 Grove st.
Brown, H. S., *g*, Grad. *d*　Darien
Brown, L. B., *f*　　Bridgeport
Brown, N. C., Sr. *for.*
129 Mansfield st.
Brown, O. C., Fr. *a*　　570 P.
Brown, R., Sec'y. (p. 21)
Observatory pl.
Brown, R. E., Sr. *s*　　Yalesville
Brown, R. L., Sr. *s*　373 Crown st.
Brown, R. M., Fr. *a*　266 York st.
Brown, R. W., 1 *l*　　168 L.
Brown, S. E., Fr. *a*　·　182 L.
Brown, S. F., Fr. *s*　117 Wall st.
Brown, T. H., So. *a*　　159 L.
Brown, W. L., Fr. *a*　8 College st.
Brownell, C. R., Fr. *s*　7 B. M. H.
Browning, J. H., Sr. *s*　180 V-S.
Browning, P. E., Ass't. Prof. (pp. 29,
172-3, 347-8) (K. C. L.)
23 Edgehill rd.
Brownlow, H. M., Fr. *s*
96 Howe st.
Brundage, F. H., Sr. *for.*　178 V-S.
Brush, G. J., Prof. (pp. 21, 200)
14 Trumbull st.
Brush, H. D., Fr. *a*　254 York st.
Brush, H. M., Sr. *a*　　356 WH.

Bryant, R. C., Instr. (pp. 33, 417)
217 St. Ronan st.
Buckley, R. E., 1 *m*　217 York st.
Bughman, H. C., Jr., Fr. *s*
409 Temple st.
Buhrman, G. L., Sr. *s*　131 Grove st.
Buist, G. L., Jr., So. *a*　　160 L.
Buland, M. E., *g*　　N. Y. City
Bulkeley, R. B., Sr. *a*　　346 WH.
Bulkley, H. L., *f*　384 Crown st.
Bull, A. C., Sr. *s*　　176 V-S.
Bumstead, H. A., Prof. (pp. 27, 171,
344) (S. P. L.) 45 Edgehill rd.
Bunce, H. L., Jr., Jr. *s*
124 Prospect st.
Bundy, H. H., Jr. *a*　　131 W.
Bundy, N. H., Sr. *a*　　19 V.
Bunker, G. H., Sr. *s*
124 Prospect st.
Bunnell, O. G., *g*　132 Howe st.
Burch, R. B., Jr. *a*　　239 D.
Burger, L. B., Sr. *s*　96 Wall st.
Burgess, A. W., Fr. *s*
871 Grand av.
Burgess, E. B., Jr. *a*　　116 W.
Burgess, G., Fr. *a*　　574 P.
Burgess, H. T., Instr. (pp. 33, 167)
700 W. D.
Burgess, L. F., Spec. *l*　Hartford
Burke, F. G., Jr., Jr. *s*　111 Grove st.
Burleigh, C. E., *mus.*　West Haven
Burleson, C. A., Fr. *s*　114 High st.
Burnam, S. P., Jr. *a*　　398 B.
Burnett, E. N. T., Jr. *a*　462 FW.
Burnett, S., Jr. *s*　　140 V-S.
Burnham, G., Jr. *s*　96 Wall st.
Burnham, J. M., *g*　142 York st.
Burnham, R. B., Jr. *a*　　116 W.
Burnham, R. M., Jr. *a*　　124 W.
Burnside, F. E., Fr. *s*　110 Wall st.
Burnstine, H., 1 *l*　　Bridgeport
Burr, F. F., *g*　　2 Howe st.
Burr, J. P., Jr. *s*　　178 V-S.
Burrill, J. M., Fr. *a*　238 York st.
Burroughs, S. M., Jr. *s*
111 Grove st.
Burrowes, H. M., Sr. *a*　　45 V.
Burrows, W., *g*, Grad. *d*
68 Grand av.
Burt, L. A., Fr. *s*　119 Park st.
Burtner, E. E., Mid. *d*　635 E. D.
Burton, M. L., Ass't. Prof. (pp. 29,
435) (607 E. D.) 93 Cottage st.

Burwell, A. K., Sr. *s*   24 Maple st.
Bush, K. J., Ass't. (p. 45)
            (13 PEAB.)   133 Howe st.
Bush, L. P., *g*   133 Howe st.
Bushnell, E., Fr. *a*   577 P.
Butler, F. P., Jr. *a*   262 D.
Butler, G. H., Cashier (p. 45)
            (25 LAM.)   136 Dwight st.
Butler, G. M., Jr. *a*   173 L.
Butterfield, B. V., Fr. *a*   589 P.
Butterfield, P. M., Proctor (p. 45)
            (K. C. L.)   589 P.
Buttner, J. L., Jr. *m*   78 Dwight st.
Buttrick, P. L., Fr. *s*
            296 Columbus av.
Byrne, D. J., Jr. *m*   114 High st.
Byrnes, G. G., Jr. *s*   181 V-S.
Byrnes, H., Sr. *s*   126 Wall st.
Byrnes, R. M., Sr. *a*   ·   336 WH.
Bysshe, E. W., Grad. *d*   Rowayton

Cahill, G. F., 1 *m*   53 Houston st.
Caine, M. L., 3 *l*   105 Park st.
Cairoli, C. S., Sr. *s*   Milford
Calhoun, N. M., Fellow
            181 Edwards st.
Calkins, H. G., Jr. *for.*   74 Lake pl.
Callender, G. S., Prof. (pp. 27, 195,
    246, 250, 279, 372)   (D. C.)
            Forest st.
Calnen, H. J., 2 *l*   287 York st.
Camblos, W. K., Grad. *l*
            271 Crown st.
Cameron, B. E., Fr. *s*   19 Whitney av.
Cameron, E. H., Instr. (pp. 33, 183-6,
    383-4)   (10 HER.)   67 Howe st.
Camp, T. J., Sr. *a*   266 D.
Camp, W., Treasurer of Yale Field
    (p. 25)   New Haven House
Camp, W. A., Fr. *s*   Bridgeport
Campbell, A. B., 1 *l*   333 York st.
Campbell, C. S., Jr. *a*   379 WH.
Campbell, G. H., Fr. *s*   333 York st.
Campbell, H. A., 2 *l*   36 Elm st.
Campbell, Mrs. J., Cataloguer
    (p. 45)   (LIB.)   152 Norton st.
Campbell, L. J., Fr. *s*
            480 Winthrop av.
Campbell, T. J., Grad. *l*   34 Howe st.
Campner, S., 3 *l*   214 F.
Canby, H. S., Instr. (pp. 33, 227, 246,
    254, 339)   105 Mansfield st.
Candee, A. H., Fr. *s*   West Haven

Canfield, R. B., Fr. *s*   314 Crown st.
Canfield, T. E., Fr. *a*   225 Crown st.
Canfield, W., Fr. *s*   82 Wall st.
Cantine, G. E., Jr. *a*   387 B.
Caporossi, P., *mus.*   558 Grand av.
Cardashian, V., 2 *l*   349 Elm st.
Carelli, G. F., 2 *m*   138 St. John st.
Carlisle, H. C., Sr. *s*   186 V-S.
Carmalt, W. H., Prof. (pp. 22, 465-6)
            87 Elm st.
Carney, J. T., Fr. *a*   Bridgeport
Carpenter, C. B., Jr. *a*   404 B.
Carpenter, J. R., Sr. *s*   115 V-S.
Carpenter, R. J., Fr. *a*   200 York st.
Carpenter, W. T., Jr. *s*   126 Wall st.
Carr, A. P., 3 *l*   722 W. D.
Carr, G. A., 1 *l*   Cheshire
Carragan, S. B., Jr. *a*   106 W.
Carter, E. A., Jr. *a*   253 D.
Carter, H. C., So. *a*   166 L.
Carter, H. H., *g*   129 Mansfield st.
Carter, L. J., *g*, Jr. *d*   602 E. D.
Carter, T. W., Fr. *a*   596 P.
Carteret, S. L. de, Sr. *s*
            976 Yale P. O.
Cartmell, R., Fr. *s*   3 Hillhouse av.
Caruthers, W. H., Fr. *s*   114 High st.
Cary, R. H., Fr. *s*   120 York st.
Case, F. T., Jr. *a*   445 FW.
Case, G., Jr. *a*   78 C.
Cass, J. D., Jr. *s*   133 College st.
Cathcart, H. M., Jr. *s*   120 High st.
Catlin, G. E., Sr. *a*   176 York st.
Catlin, R. W., Sr. *a*   28 V.
Cellar, F. A., Jr. *a*   466 FW.
Chambers, A. W., 2 *l*
            173 Sherman av.
Champney, W. P., Jr., Jr. *s*
            110 Wall st.
Chandlee, G. M., Jr. *s*   122 Wall st.
Chandler, J. R., Fr. *a*   709 W. D.
Chandler, P. B., Sr. *m*   63 Grove st.
Chandler, R. E., Jr. *d*   709 W. D.
Chang, T., Jr. *s*   9 Library st.
Chantler, D. E., Fr. *a*   22 College st.
Chanute, W. O., Jr. *s*
            17 Hillhouse av.
Chapin, J. M., Jr. *s*   694 W. D.
Chapin, L. M., Fr. *s*   131 Grove st.
Chapman, H. B., Fr. *a*   159 Elm st.
Chapman, H. H., Ass't. Prof. (pp. 29,
    250, 281, 353, 415-18)   17 Tryon st.
Chapman, P. S., 3 *l*   281 Crown st.

Chase, F. L., Ass't. Astron. (p. 29)
Observatory
Chatfield, R. E., Sr. *s*   175 v-s.
Chatfield, R. M., Ass't. (p. 46)
    (WOOD.)   102 Dwight st.
Cheadle, A. B., Spec. *l*   152 Temple st.
Chen, J. H., Sr. *s*   690 w. D.
Chen, T. C., 1 *l*   25 High st.
Cheney, G. W., So. *a*   260 Crown st.
Cheney, R. A., 1 *l*   425 Temple st.
Cheney, W. W., Jr., Jr. *s*   96 Wall st.
Cherry, A. F., Fr. *s*   227 Crown st.
Childs, F. D., Sr. *a*   15 v.
Childs, J. D. B., Fr. *s*   120 College st.
Childs, J. H., Sr. *s*   166 v-s.
Childs, N. T., Jr. *a*   104 w.
Chisholm, D., So. *a*   437 FW.
Chisholm, H. J., Jr., Sr. *a*   40 v.
Chittenden, G., *g*   A.
Chittenden, H. E., Jr. *a*   448 FW.
Chittenden, R. H., Prof. and Director (pp. 24, 180-1, 241, 244, 259, 271, 351, 464)   (3 S. H.)
        83 Trumbull st.
Chow, T. H., Sr. *s*   674 w. D.
Christy, L., Sr. *s*   167 v-s.
Chu, P. C., Jr. *a*   386 B.
Chu, S. C., 1 *l*   25 High st.
Chu, Y. Y., So. *a*   114 High st.
Church, H. E., Sr. *s*   177 v-s.
Church, H. W., Instr. (pp. 33, 157)
         78 Lake pl.
Church, K., Fr. *a*   217 York st.
Clapp, A. A., Fr. *s*   114 v-s.
Clapp, H. C., Fr. *a*   250 York st.
Clapp, R. G., Instr. and Director of Relig. Work (pp. 33, 151-2, 327)
        613 E. D.
Clapp, S. H., *g*   98 York sq.
Clark, A. A., Jr. *a*   108 L.
Clark, B. S., Sr. *s*   124 Prospect st.
Clark, C., Sr. *a*   370 WH.
Clark, C. E., Fr. *a*   961 Yale P. O.
Clark, C. I., 3 *l*   17 Bishop st.
Clark, C. R., Spec. *s*   13 Lake pl.
Clark, C. T., Jr. *a*   445 FW.
Clark, C. U., Ass't. Prof. (pp. 29, 143-44, 317-19)   (194 F.)
      473 Edgewood av.
Clark, D. S., Jr., Jr. *a*   269 D.
Clark, E. D., Sr. *for.*   699 w. D.
Clark, E. G., Fr. *a*   591 P.
Clark, E. T., Sr. *for.*   Woodbridge

Clark, H. A., Fr. *s*   So. Norwal
Clark, J. E., Prof. (p. 21)
     Longmeadow, Mass.
Clark, L., *g*   130 Howe st.
Clark, L. B., Sr. *a*   695 w. D.
Clark, M. L., So. *a*   225 Crown st.
Clark, R. E., Sr. *for.*   125 DeWitt st.
Clark, R. H., Jr. *a*   133 w.
Clark, R. S., Jr. *m*   114 High st.
Clark, S. T., Fr. *a*   231 York st.
Clark, T., Fr. *a*   200 York st.
Clark, T. F., Sup't. Yale Station,
  U. S. Post Office (p. 559)
    (Yale P. O.)   13 Bishop st.
Clarke, C. C., Jr., Ass't. Prof. (pp. 29, 227, 255, 330-1)   254 Bradley st.
Clarke, C. H., Jr. *a*   120 w.
Clarke, G. S., Fr. *a*   266 York st.
Clarke, L. S., Fr. *a*   266 York st.
Clarke, N. K., Jr. *s*   114 College st.
Clarke, S. N., Jr. *s*   25 Wooster pl.
Claxton, E. A., 3 *l*   130 Wall st.
Clay, R. V., Fr. *s*   405 Temple st.
Cleaveland, E. W., *g*   133 Howe st.
Clement, N. P., *g*   A.
Clement, R., Fr. *a*   22 College st.
Clement, S. M., Jr., So. *a*
        22 College st.
Clement, W. P., Jr., Jr. *a*   16 v.
Cleveland, G. C., Sr. *a*   46 v.
Cleveland, M., Fr. *a*   231 York st.
Cleveland, R. M., Sr. *a*   22 v.
Clifford, J. J., Sr. *s*   17 Hillhouse av.
Clifford, R. C., So. *a*   270 Crown st.
Clippinger, A. R., Jr. *d*, Spec. *l*
       96 Dwight st.
Cloud, H. C., So. *a*   169 L.
Clough, C. C., Fr. *a*   200 York st.
Clow, K. S., So. *a*   22 College st.
Coan, S., Fr. *a*   2 West st.
Coates, A. P., So. *a*   11 College st.
Cochran, C. T., So. *a*   236 Crown st.
Cockayne, C. A., Ass't. (p. 41)   •
       105 Park st.
Coddington, J. I., Jr. *s*
      70 Trumbull st.
Coe, W. R., Ass't. Prof. (pp. 29, 180, 227, 241, 244, 250, 271, 349-50, 414)
    (75 S. B. L.)   484 Orange st.
Coellar, F. F., 1 *l*   589 Howard av.
Coffin, T. C., Fr. *s*   119 Wall st.
Coffman, J. D., Jr. *for.*   91 Lake pl.
Cogswell, C. H., Sr. *s*   175 v-s.

Cogswell, F. H., Jr., Jr. *a*   79 C.
Cohen, A. H., Sr. *a*   73 C.
Cohen, F. W., 2 *l*   163 York st.
Cohen, S. M., So. *a*   161 L.
Colburn, A. P., Fr. *a*   188 F.
Cole, E. E., *g*   •   142 York st.
Cole, H. F., Jr. *a*   244 D.
Cole, L. J., Instr. (pp. 33, 241, 244, 271, 349)   (14 PEAB.)
                              186 Lawrence st.
Cole, V. M., Fr. *s*   13 B. M. H.
Coleman, R. E., Fr. *a*   250 York st.
Collins, G. R., Fr. *s*   120 College st.
Collins, P. H., Sr. *a*   69 V.
Collins, W. E., 1 *l*   1076 Chapel st.
Colton, R. B., Sr. *s*   177 V-S.
Colwell, E. C., Sr. *s*   111 Grove st.
Colyer, A. D., Spec. *l* 35 Sherland av.
Comes, R. L., Cataloguer (p. 533)
           (LIB.)   382 Dixwell av.
Comfort, C. W., Jr., 2 *m*   144 L.
Comley, A. M., 1 *l*   Bridgeport
Comstock, G. M., Fr. *s*   364 W H.
Comstock, W. J., Instr. (pp. 33, 229, 241, 243-4, 259, 346) 43 Trumbull st.
Condon, C. S., Jr. *s*   119 Grove st.
Condon, F. B., Jr. *a*   463 FW.
Coney, A. C., Jr. *a*   240 D.
Congdon, E. C., Sr. *a*   6 V.
Congdon, E. F., Sr. *s* 470 Orchard st.
Congdon, G. M., Jr. *a*   271 D.
Congdon. R. V., Sr. *a*   418 B.
Connell, C. A., Fr. *a*   242 York st.
Connelly, H. G., *g*, Sr. *d*   623 E. D.
Conner, A. E., 2 *l*   714 W. D.
Connolly. J., Fr. *a*   7 Library st.
Connor, A. L., 1 *l*   276 Crown st.
Connor, B. M.. So. *a*   260 Crown st.
Connor, J. E., Jr., 1 *l*   270 Lloyd st.
Connor, J. L., 2 *l*   120 High st.
Constantian, C. M., Sr. *s*
                              1069 Yale P. O.
Conte, H. A.. 1 *m*   183 Hamilton st.
Converse, P. H. M., Jr. *a*   238 D.
Conway, J. F., 1 *l*   217 York st.
Cook, A. I., 2 *l*   38 Lynwood pl.
Cook, A. M., Sr. *for.*, Grad. *s*
                              129 Mansfield st.
Cook, A. S., Prof. (pp. 23, 164-5, 336)   (135 Elm st.)   219 Bishop st.
Cook, C. E., *g*   Newtown
Cooksey, C. D., Ass't. (p. 41)
                              284 Orange st.

Cooley, C. M., Sr. *m*   371 Crown st.
Coolidge, H. H., Sr. *s*
                              124 Prospect st.
Coombe, H., Fr. *a*   22 College st.
Cooney, C. T., So. *a*   22 College st.
Cooper, F. L., Instr.   (pp. 33, 227, 236, 268)   40 Lake pl.
Cooper, J. W., Fellow
           287 Fourth av., New York City
Cooper, M. D., Jr. *s*   103 V-S.
Cooper, O. H., Jr., Sr. *a*   89 C.
Cooper, S. G., Sr. *a*   455 FW.
Copmann, C. J., Jr. *a*   239 D.
Copp, J. A., Fr. *a*   538 P.
Coppock, F. M., Jr., Fr. *a*
                              254 Crown st.
Corbet, D., *g*   A.
Corbin, A. B., Jr., Sr. *s*   185 V-S.
Corbin, A. L., Ass't. Prof. (pp. 29, 194-5, 498, 506, 518-19)
                              285 Willow st.
Corey, A. L., Fr. *a*   170 York st.
Cornish, C., Fr. *a*   299 York st.
Corwin, R. N., Prof. (pp. 26, 227, 255, 334)   A.
Costanzo, R. E., 1 *m*   100 Greene st.
Costello, J. R., Spec. *l*
                              7 Summer st.
Coughlan, J. F., 1 *m*   196 Wallace st.
Coughlin, S. F., *mus.*   Middletown
Cowles, E. B., So. *a*   22 College st.
Cox, C. B., Sr. *for.*   609 E. D.
Cox, F. J., Jr. *s*   110 Wall st.
Coxe, M., Lect. (pp. 33, 503, 517)
           65 Wall st., New York City
Coy, E. H., So. *a*   22 College st.
Coy, G. A., Jr. *s*   Milford
Crandall, F. W., Fr. *a*   250 York st.
Crane, H. R., *mus.*   109 Dwight st.
Crane, J. B., Jr. *s*   111 Grove st.
Crask, I. T., Grad. *l*   1079 Chapel st.
Crawford, C., Jr. *a*   113 W.
Crawford, J. D., Fr. *a*   562 P.
Crawford, L. J., Jr., Sr. *a*   50 V.
Crisp, T. M., 2 *l*   36 Elm st.
Crispell, R. B., So. *a*   236 Crown st.
Crocker, C. T., Sr. *a*   348 W H.
Crofton, G. H., Sr. *s*   109 V-S.
Croll, E. H., Jr. *s*   128 High st.
Cronan, U., *g*   455 Orange st.
Cronecker, R. W., 3 *l*   108 High st.
Cronin, F. Q., 3 *l*   364 George st.
Cropper, E. D., *mus.*   Derby

Cross, W. L., Prof. (pp. 26, 227, 246, 254, 337) (22 s. H.)
24 Edgehill rd.
Crossett, C. R., Jr., 2 l   130 Wall st.
Crowe, W. H., Ass't. (p. 41)
106 Whalley av.
Crowell, E. D., Jr., Fr. s 48 Lake pl.
Crowley, F. G., 1 m   384 Crown st.
Crowley, J. A., Fr. s   West Haven
Crunden, W. M., Sr. a   350 WH.
Cryne, E. A., Spec. s   62 Lake pl.
Cubbage, R. E., 3 l   409 Temple st.
Cuddy, L. B., Fr. s   96 Wall st.
Culbertson, W. S., 1 l 379 Temple st.
Cumming, A., Grad. l
1032 Chapel st.
Cunningham, C. C., Jr., Jr. a 249 D.
Cunningham, W. F., 1 m
53 Prospect st.
Curdy, A. E., Ass't. Prof. (pp. 29, 153, 330)   361 Elm st.
Curran, W. A., Fr. a 126 High st.
Curtis, E. E., So. a   663 W. D.
Curtis, E. J., Jr. a   272 D.
Curtis, E. L., Prof. and Acting Dean (pp. 24, 151, 323, 325, 429-30)
(668 W. D.) 61 Trumbull st.
Curtis, E. L. W., Jr. s 110 Wall st.
Curtis, R. M., So. a   166 L.
Curtiss, C. G., Sr. a   39 V.
Curtiss, H. T., Fr. a 22 College st.
Curtiss, N. A., Jr. s   Wallingford
Curtiss, W. A., Jr. s   211 F.
Curts, P., Instr. (pp. 33, 227, 255)
3 Hillhouse av.
Cushing, W. S., Sr. a   4 V.
Cushman, T. A., Jr. a 373 WH.
Cutler, F. A., Fr. s
119 Washington av.
Cutler, W. F., Fr. s   40 Lake pl.
Cutter, J. D., Jr., Sr. a   1 V.
Cutting, J. A., g   821 Whitney av.

Dadourian, H. M., Instr. (pp. 33, 236, 268, 365)   299 York st.
Daggett, D. L., So. a 22 College st.
Daggett, E., Fr. a   242 York st.
Daggett, H. E., Fr. s 240 View st.
Daggett, L. M., Instr. (pp. 33, 506)
(42 Church st.) 60 Wall st.
Daggett, W. G., Lect. (pp. 34, 465-6)
189 Church st.
Dahl, G., Sr. a   29 V.

Dain, J. M., Fr. a   200 York st.
Dakin, R. E., Jr. s   694 W. D.
Dale, M. J., Fr. s   128 High st.
Daley, J. G., Jr. s   315 York st.
Dallas, W., Jr. a   107 W.
Daly, C. J., Jr. s • 8 Mechanic st.
Daly, F. J., Fr. a   200 York st.
Damrosch, F., Jr., So. a
250 Crown st.
Damtoft, W. J., Fr. s   Bridgeport
Dana, C. L., Jr., Fr. s 114 High st.
Dana, E. S., Prof. and Curator (pp. 23, 175, 354) (4 PEAB.)
24 Hillhouse av.
Dana, J. D., Fr. a   583 P.
Dandy, W. M., Jr., Fr. s 151 V-S.
Danforth, M. L., Fr. a 295 York st.
Dangler, C. S., Sr. s 111 Grove st.
Dangler, D. E., g   A.
Dangler, F. B., Jr. s 111 Grove st.
Daniels, F. H., Jr. s 70 Trumbull st.
Daniels, G. E., mus. 61 Shelton av.
Danziger, A. F., 1 l 124 Wall st.
Daoust, E. C., 2 l   120 V-S.
Darr, G. W., Fr. a   170 York st.
Davenport, A. S., Jr. a 395 B.
Davenport, W. E., mus. Bridgeport
Davey, E. S., Sr. a   7 V.
Davey, S., mus.   Ansonia
Davidson, D. T., Jr. a 466 FW.
Davidson, J. I., 3 l 104 York sq.
Davidson, N., Fr. s 395 Temple st.
Davidson, W. T., Fr. s 128 High st.
Davies, H. C., mus. 321 Dixwell av.
Davin, E. J., So. a   155 L.
Davis, C. H., Jr. a   247 D.
Davis, C. W., Fr. a 242 York st
Davis, G. E., g   Hartfor
Davis, G. R., Fr. a 1076 Chapel st.
Davis, H. B., Fr. a   549 P
Davis, H. C., Jr. a   341 WH
Davis, M. W., Fr. a 237 York st
Davis, P. V., g
Davis, W. F., So. a   184 1
Davis, W. G., So. a 254 Crown s
Davis, W. G., Jr., Sr. a 33 V
Davison, A. L., Jr. a   76 C
Day, C., Prof. (pp. 28, 193, 196-7, 373) (D, C.) 44 Highland st
Day, H. F., 1 m   199 F
Day, S. S., Fr. a   200 York s
Dean, L., Jr. a   460 FW.
Dean, R., Fr. a   567 P.

Dean, T., So. *a*   8 College st.
Dean, W. D., *g*   A.
Dearborn, G. G., Fr. *s*   110 Wall st.
DeBaun, L. H., Sr. *a*   295 York st.
DeForest, J. B., *g*   Cheshire
DeGolyer, S. B., Sr. *a*   339 WH.
Deidrickson, T., Jr., *f*
                               288 George st.
DeLacey, J. A., Ass't. (p 46) (LIB.)
                               179 Exchange st.
DeLacour, H. F., Jr. *s*   146 V-S.
Delano, E., Jr., Sr. *a*   53 V.
De La Vergne, C. R., *g*   A.
Delgado, F. A., Grad. *l*
                               14 Whalley av.
DeLong, C. S., Fr. *a*   250 York st.
Deming, M. W., *mus.* 245 Bradley st.
Deming, R. C., Fr. *a*   583 P.
Dempsey, J. B., Fr. *a*   242 York st.
Dennis, K. S., So. *a*   8 College st.
Dennis, S. F., Jr. *a*   108 W.
Denny, H. D., Jr., Sr. *a*   367 WH.
Denton, W. B., Jr. *s*   8 Prospect pl.
Derby, J. H., Jr., Ass't. (p. 41)
                               110 Wall st.
DeSilver, A., So. *a*   22 College st.
D'Esopo, F., 3 *l*   Hartford
Desrosiers, J. L., 1 *m*   42 Shelter st.
Devan, S. T., Fr. *a*   529 P.
Devereux. J. F., So. *a*   457 FW.
Dewey, A. N., Jr. *s*   131 Grove st.
Dewing, H. B., Instr. (pp. 34, 146)
                               219 F.
DeWitt, W. A., Jr. *a*   336 WH.
Dexheimer, W. F., Fr. *s*
                               183 Dixwell av.
Dexter, D. M., *mus.*   178 Prospect st.
Dexter, F. B., Ass't. Librarian
  (p. 22)   (LIB.)   178 Prospect st.
Deyo. J. M., Sr. *a*   85 C.
Diamond, J. E., *g*   173 Whalley av.
Dibble, C. M., Fr. *s*   37 Fairmont av.
Dickerman, E. E., Jr. *s*   119 Wall st.
Dickerman, S. O., *g*   Germany
Dickey, D. R., So. *a*   8 College st.
Dickey, R. J., Jr. *s*   693 W. D.
Dickinson, B., Sr. *for.*   82 Wall st.
Dickinson, W. S., Sr. *s*   111 Grove st.
Dickson, C. W., Sr. *a*   21 V.
Dickson, J. L., Sr. *d*   27 Tryon st.
Diefendorf, A. R., Lect. (pp. 34,
  466)   Middletown
Diehl, C., Sr. *a*   110 Wall st.

Diehl, K., Ass't. (p. 46) (LIB.)
                               43 Sylvan av.
Diehl, W. W., So. *a*   236 Crown st.
Dietz, W. H., So. *a*   140 W.
Dimock, E. J., Fr. *a*   568 P.
Dimock, H. F., Fellow
                25 E. 60th st., New York City
Dine, S. P., So. *a*   43 College st.
Dines, T. M., Sr. *a*   11 V.
Dingman, A. P., Cataloguer (p. 46)
               (LIB.)   78 Lake pl.
Dixon, A. C., Jr. *s*   82 Wall st.
Dixon, C. P., Sr. *a*   33 V.
Dixon, J. H., 3 *l*   36 Elm st.
Dodd, A. R., Jr. *a*   127 W.
Dodd. H. W., Sr. *s*   78 Lake pl.
Dodge, G., So. *a*   98 W.
Dodge, H. G., *g*   A.
Dole, G. S., *g*   644 E. D.
Dole, L. A., *g*   644 E. D.
Dole, W. C., Ass't. (p. 41)
                               331 Edgewood av.
Domenica, A. di, Spec. *d*
                               301 George st.
Dominick, G. G., Jr. *a*   447 FW.
Donaldson, J. C., Fr. *s* 118 College st.
Dondlinger, P. T., 1 *l* 23 Lynwood pl.
Donegan, J., Jr. *s*   22 Ward st.
Doneghy, J. T., Jr., Fr. *a* 238 York st.
Donnelly, A. L., Sr. *s*   57 Pearl st.
Donnelly, W. M., Jr. *a*   242 D.
Donovan, E. J., 1 *m*   35 High st.
Donovan, W. V., 3 *l*   137 W.
Doolittle, C. H., Jr. *s*   140 V-S.
Dorenbaum. W., Jr. *s*   120 High st.
Dougherty, F. F., Jr. *s*   136 V-S.
Dougherty, M. T., Jr. *a*   178 L.
Dougherty, R. K., 1 *l*   242 York st.
Douglas, M. G., Sr. *a*   346 WH.
Douglas, W. C., Fr. *s*   333 York st.
Douglass, D. F. W., Jr. *s*
                               70 Trumbull st.
Downes, J. I. H., Librarian (p. 46)
                               345 Whitney av.
Downs, C. R., Jr. *s*
                               813 Quinnipiac av.
Dows, D., Sr. *s*   17 Hillhouse av.
Dox, A. W., *g*   Storrs
Doyle, L. C., Jr. *s*   124 Prospect st.
Drake, C. B., Sr. *a*   433 FW.
Drake, F., Fr. *a*   535 P.
Dravo, H. D., Fr. *s*   59 Grove st.
Dray, W. R., Sr. *a*   8 V.

Drew, F. M., Jr., So. *a*   167 L.
Drew, H. E., 3 *l*   155 Elm st.
Dreyfus, E. L., Jr. *s*   407 B.
Dreyfus, L. G., Jr., So. *a*   407 B.
Driscoll, A. G., Jr. *a*   374 WH.
Driscoll, C. G., Sr. *s*   131 Grove st.
Drisko, A. H., So. *a*   236 Crown st.
Drushel, W. A., Ass't. (p. 42)
      47 Lake pl.
Dryer, E. J., 3 *l*   293 York st.
Drynan, C. D., Fr. *s*   144 Dwight st.
DuBois, A. J., Prof. (pp. 23, 233, 238, 263, 266, 368) (129 WIN.)
      334 Edwards st.
DuBois, A. W., Jr. *for.*, Grad. *s*
      333 York st.
Dudley, P., Sr. *a*   8 V.
Dudley, W. A., Cashier (p. 46)
      (G.) Guilford
Duell, C. H., Jr., Fr. *a*   242 York st.
Dunbar, N. M. S., Sr. *s*   147 V-S.
Duncan, G. M., Prof. (pp. 25, 182-5, 382)   299 Edwards st.
Duncan, W. Y., So. *a*   169 L.
Dunham, S. E., Jr. *a*   412 B.
Dunham, W. E., Sr. *s*   174 V-S.
Dunkle, W. E., Sr. *s*   174 V-S.
Dunlap, C. H., Fr. *s*   493 Dixwell av.
Dunlap. R. W., Spec. *s*   125 High st.
Dunn, J. G., Jr. *s*   40 Lake pl.
Dunn, W. H., *g*   A.
Dunn, W. M., Fr. *a*   250 York st.
Dunning, C. H., Fr. *s*   96 Wall st.
Dunwoody. W. B., Fr. *a*   525 P.
DuPuy. C. M., Sr. *a*   64 V.
Durell, R. B., Fr. *a*   231 York st.
Durell, T. P., Jr. *a*   414 B.
Durfee, E. L., Instr. (pp. 34, 186)
      95 Cottage st
Durham, W. H., Instr. (pp. 34, 227, 254)   (701 W. D.)
Durkin, T. W., Fr. *a*   192 F.
Dutton, J. F., Spec. *l*   23 Lynwood pl.
Dwyer. E. T., 1 *m*   Ansonia
Dwyer, R. E., Fr. *s*   8 Prospect pl.
Dye, H. A., So. *a*   646 E. D.
Dyer, E. G., Jr. *s*   103 V-S.
Dyer, S. D., Fr. *a*   558 P.
Dyess, A. D., Sr. *a*   147 L.
Dykman, J. A., Jr. *a*   235 D.

Eales, H. W., *g*   7 Library st.
Eames, L. W., Fr. *a*   8 College st.

Earnshaw, W. B., Jr. *s*   131 Grove st.
Eastman, T. C., Jr. *a*   241 D.
Eastman, W. W., Fr. *s*
      409 Temple st.
Eaton, D. C., Prof. (p. 22)
      218 Prospect st.
Eaton, G. F., Instr. and Curator (pp. 34, 358) (9 PEAB.)
      80 Sachem st.
Eckle, J. N., Fr. *s*   West Haven
Eckstein, F., Fr. *a*   237 York st.
Eddy, E. A., Sr. *a*   344 WH.
Eddy, E. W., Jr. *a*   264 D.
Eddy, S. L., Sr. *s*   379 Temple st.
Edgar, G., *g*   144 Dwight st.
Edgerton, J. W., Instr. and Sec'y. (pp. 34, 195, 497, 499, 504, 506, 518)   (HEN.) 77 Elm st.
Edwards, H. R., Jr. *a*   255 D.
Edwards, J. C., Jr., Jr. *a*   107 W.
Egan, W. E., 3 *l*   925 Howard av.
Eggleston, R. C., Spec. *s*   47 Lake pl.
Ehrman, S. M., Fr. *a*   571 P.
Eisenberg, M. M., 1 *l*   333 York st.
Eldred, C. D., Fr. *s*   122 Wall st.
Eliot, D. F. G., Jr. *a*   132 W.
Elkin, W. L., Director (p. 24)
      477 Prospect st.
Elkins, M. G., *g*   568 Chapel st.
Elliot. A. D., Fr. *s*   133 Wall st.
Ellis, J. R., *g*   679 W. D.
Ellis, S. E., Jr. *a*   257 D.
Elwell, C. C., Jr., Fr. *a*   588 P.
Ely, A. J., Fr. *a*   198 P.
Ely, D. J., So. *a*   8 College st.
Ely, M. G.. Fr. *s*   397 Temple st.
Embree, W. D., *g*   A.
Emery, H. C., Prof. (pp. 27, 193, 197, 372)   270 Crown st.
Emery, W. B., Fr. *a* 213 Blatchley av.
Emmons, G. L., Sr. *s*   96 Wall st.
Emory, L. S.. Jr. *s*   130 V-S.
Engelhardt, F., Sr. *s*   176 V-S.
Englander, L., Jr. *s*   34 Sylvan av.
English, C. L., So. *a*   142 L.
English, R. B., Sr. *a*   66 V.
Eno, J. N., Cataloguer (p. 46)
      (LIB.) 130 Howe st.
Epifanio, S., *f*   798 Grand av.
Epstein, J. J., 2 *m*   911 Howard av.
Escaler, J., *g*, Spec. *d*   14 Whalley av.
Esposito, E. A., 1 *m*   337 George st.
Esposito, J. V., 1 *m*   15 Summer st.

thridge, F. A., Jr., Fr. *a* 231 York st.
Ethridge, J. M., Jr., Jr. *a* 468 ꜰw.
Euans, J. S., Sr. *a* 443 ꜰw.
vans, A. J., So. *a* 1062 Yale P. O.
vans, A. W., Prof. (pp. 27, 180, 227,
241, 244, 250, 271, 352, 412)
(18 s. ʜ.) 67 Mansfield st.
Evans, H. W., Jr. *s* 22 Oak st.
Evans, J. F., *g*, Grad. *d*
10 University pl.
Evans, R., Jr., Fr. *a* 242 York st.
Evans, W. A., *g* 399 Elm st.
Everard, L. C., Sr. *a* 75 ᴄ.
Ewen, J. M., Jr., So. *a* 22 College st.
Ewers, J. E., 3 *l* 125 Dwight st.
Ewing, R. D. W., Fr. *s* 379 Temple st.
Eyre, W. L., So. *a* 8 College st.

Fagan, W. E., *f* Wallingford
Failing, J. C., Jr. *a* 119 w.
Fair, J. H. S., Fr. *a* 248 York st.
Fairbanks, R., Jr. *a* 130 w.
airchild, F. R., Instr. (pp. 34, 193-4,
197, 374) 1233 Chapel st.
airchild, H. P., Ass't. (pp. 42, 175)
(3a ʜᴇʀ.) 1233 Chapel st.
Fairman, C. D., Ass't. (p. 46)
(ʟɪʙ.) 208 Whalley av.
Fales, H., Jr., Sr. *a* 112 w.
Fancher, S. H., Jr., So. *a*
251 Crown st.
Fanslow, A. Y., *mus.* 54 Salem st.
Farley, A. M., Fr. *s* 114 High st.
Farley, E. B., 2 *m* Derby
arnam, H. W., Prof. (pp. 24, 372,
514) A.
Farnam, T., 1 *m* 37 Hillhouse av.
Farnham, C. E., Fr. *a* 149 ʟ.
arnham, C. S., Instr. (pp. 34, 233,
238, 250, 263, 266, 416) 671 w. ᴅ.
Farnham, R. E., Fr. *s* 238 Grand av.
Farr, H. A., Ass't. Prof. (pp. 29,
157-8, 334) 351 wʜ.
Farrar, H. W., Sr. *s* 1023 Yale P. O.
Farson, W., Jr. *s* 131 Grove st.
Farwell, A. D., Jr. *a* 262 ᴅ.
aunce, W. H. P., Lect. (p. 34)
Providence, R. I.
Faust, E. S., Jr. *a* 49 ᴠ.
Faverio, L. A., 1 *l* 107 York st.
Favill, J., Jr. *a* 173 ʟ.
Fawley, T. L., *g* 205 ꜰ.
Fear, L. G., Sr. *s* 176 ᴠ-s.

Fearing, F. C., Fr. *s* 11 ʙ. ᴍ. ʜ.
Fegley, H. E., Jr. *for.*, Grad. *s*
8 Prospect pl.
Fels, G. C., Jr. *s* 131 Grove st.
Fenn, R. S., So. *a* 22 College st.
Fenton, D. H., Jr. *a* 140 w.
Ferguson, C., Fr. *s* 413 Temple st.
Ferguson, D., Sr. *a* 72 ᴄ.
Ferguson, J. A., Sr. *for.* 91 Lake pl.
Ferguson, J. F., *g* 197 ꜰ.
Fergusson, A. R., So. *a* 250 Crown st.
Ferris, G. B., So. *a* 8 College st.
Ferris, H. B., Prof. (pp. 26, 181, 192,
350, 371, 463-4) 395 St. Ronan st.
Ferris, W. L., Mid. *d* 636 ᴇ. ᴅ.
Ferry, E. L., *g* 24 Edgewood av.
Ficks, R. L., Fr. *a* 250 York st.
Field, A. S., *g* 100 Howe st.
Field, G. B., So. *a* 260 Crown st.
Field, J. E.. Sr. *a* 33 Lynwood pl.
Field, J. W., Fr. *a* 585 ᴘ.
Field, P. C., 3 *l* 109 York st.
Fine, M. S., Sr. *s* 45 Stevens st.
Finkelstone, B. B., Jr. *m* 38 High st.
Finn, E. J., 2 *m* Shelton
Fiore, S. E., 1 *l* 222 ꜰ.
Fischer, H. L., *mus.*
409 Edgewood av.
Fischer, T. A., *g*, Spec. *d*
409 Edgewood av.
Fischer, W. J. H., 2 *m*
911 Howard av.
Fisher, E., Fr. *s* 413 Temple st.
Fisher, G. P., Prof. (p. 21) A.
Fisher, Irving, Prof. (pp. 26, 193,
195-6, 372) 460 Prospect st.
Fisher, J. E., Jr., Fr. *a* 552 ᴘ.
Fitch, E. H., *g* 148 Whalley av.
Fitch, W. K., So. *a* 8 College st.
Fite, E. D., Instr. (pp. 34, 186, 188)
85 Cottage st.
Fitzgerald, J. H., Jr., Sr. *a* 436 ꜰw.
Fitzwater, J. A., Sr. *for.* 699 w. ᴅ.
Flaherty, C. V., Jr. *m* Ansonia
Flauman, S. B., 1 *m*, Spec. *s*
53 Prince st.
Fleischner, H., 2 *l* 151 Bradley st.
Fleitmann, H. T., Jr. *a* 432 ꜰw.
Fleming, J. P., Fr. *s* Wallingford
Fletcher, F. C., Jr. *s* Ansonia
Flint, J. M., Prof. (pp. 28, 465-6)
311 Temple st.
Flint, W. H., Fr. *a* 251 Crown st.

Flint, W. R., Ass't. (p. 42)
 121 Dwight st.
Flye, J. H., So. a 212 F.
Flynn, C. T., 1 m 175 Orchard st.
Flynn, J. F., 2 m Bridgeport
Fogarty, W. R., 1 m Ansonia
Fogel, C. C., Grad. l 1076 Chapel st.
Fogerty, W. H., 3 l 109 York st.
Foley, J. F., 2 l 10 York st.
Folsom, H. L., Fr. a 237 York st.
Foote, C. P., Clerk (p. 46)
 (25 LAM.) Stony Creek
Foote, H. W., Ass't. Prof. (pp. 29, 229, 231, 241, 243-4, 259, 346)
 209 Livingston st.
Forbes, J. A., Clerk (p. 40)
 Kimberly av., East Haven
Forbes, F. L., 3 l 70 Trumbull st.
Ford, C., So. a 1151 Chapel st.
Ford, J. W., So. a 260 Crown st.
Ford, W. E., Jr., Ass't. Prof. (pp. 30, 229, 231, 233, 235, 240-1, 243, 250, 276, 354, 356) (183 K.)
 16 Lynwood pl.
Ford, W. M., 1 l 152 Temple st.
Fosdick, G. M., Sr. s 333 York st.
Foster, G., 3 l 293 York st.
Foster, H. B., 3 l 36 Elm st.
Foster. H. L., Jr. s 107 V-S.
Foster, J. P. C., Instr. (pp. 34, 340)
 109 College st.
Foster, J. T., Sr. a 10 V.
Foster, L. N., Sr. s 135 Wall st.
Foster, R., Lect. (pp. 34, 507)
 79 W. 54th st., New York City
Foster, S., Fr. a 692 W. D.
Foster, W. E., 2d, f 109 College st.
Foulkes, H. T., Fr. a 200 York st.
Fouts, E. L., So. a 8 College st.
Fowler, C. S., g 205 Whalley av.
Fowler, D., 3d, So. a 272 D.
Fowler, T. C., Jr. a 337 WH.
Fox, A., g A.
Fox, G. L., g 7 College st.
Fox, T., Jr. s 119 Wall st.
Fox, W. L., Jr. s 507 Orange st.
Fraissinet, C. J., Fr. s 119 Wall st.
Franchot, C. P., So. a 8 College st.
Francis, N. R., Sr. s 156 Grove st.
Francis, S. R., Fr. a 250 York st.
Frank, S. J., Sr. a 382 WH.
Frank, W. D., Fr. a 200 York st.
Frankel, B. B., Fr. s 346 George st.

Frankfurt, S. J., Jr. s 27 Silver st.
Franklin, C., g, Grad. d
 North Haven
Frederick, W. D., 3 l 152 Temple st.
Freeburg, V. O., g 295 York st.
Freeman, F. N., Ass't. and Proctor
 (p. 42) 227 F.
Freeman, H. B., Fr. a 200 York st.
Freeman, L. D., 2 l 119 Wall st.
Freeman, P. M., Fr. s 110 Wall st.
Freeman, S. B., Jr. s 148 V-S.
Freeman, S. F., Fr. a 200 York st.
Freiberg, L. H., Sr. a 442 FW.
French, R. D., So. a 225 Bishop st.
French, R. L., g 210 F.
French, S. B., 2d, Fr. a 238 York st.
French, W. C., Fr. s 333 York st.
French, W. S., Fr. s 14 B. M. H.
Friel, A. O., Jr. a 259 D.
Frisbie, C. G., Jr. s 131 Grove st.
Frissell, S. D., Sr. a 354 WH.
Frost, E., Fr. a 531 P.
Fuchs, P. F., Jr. a 452 FW.
Fuller, G. G., So. a 8 College st.
Fuller, L. C., Fr. a 250 York st.
Fuller, M. E., Fr. s 110 Wall st.
Fullerton, D. L., Fr. s 387 Temple st.
Fulton, C. H., f 211 F.
Furbush, A. C., g Georgetown
Furcolow, C. L., Jr. m 792 Grand av.

Gade, C. J., Jr. m 307 George st.
Gaffney, A. S., So. a 49 Goffe st.
Gage, G. E., Ass't. (p. 42)
 (12 S. H.) 642 E. D.
Gagel, A. S., mus. West Haven
Gagel, F. R., g 124 Prospect st.
Gager, E. B., Prof. (pp. 24, 504, 515, 518) Derby
Gager, E. B., Jr., Fr. s 333 York st.
Gallagher, F. W. Jr. s 1081 Chapel st.
Gallaher, W. H., Jr. s 26 Wall st.
Gallaudet, H. D., g A.
Gallivan, T. H., Jr. m 1076 Chapel st.
Galpin, P. C., So. a 236 Crown st.
Galt, L. P., Sr. s 162 V-S.
Gamble, W. E., 3 l 817 Yale P. O.
Gammack, A. J., g West Haven
Gammell, A. A., Fr. a 238 York st.
Gammell, W., Jr., Sr. a 37 V.
Gard, R. T., Ass't. (p. 42) 685 W. D.
Gard, W. E., Jr. a 353 WH.
Gardella, A. W., 3 l 104 York st.

Gardner, A., Fr. *s*   117 Wall st.
Gardner, C., Jr., Jr. *s*   133 College st.
Gardner, J. A., Sr. *a*   400 B.
Gardner, M. S., *mus.*   1079 Chapel st.
Garfunkel, B. J., 3 *l*   820 Yale P. O.
Garland, J. P., Fr. *a*   250 York st.
Garlick, E. E., 1 *l*   Bridgeport
Garver, C. B., Sr. *a*   343 WH.
Garver, M. S., Instr. (pp. 34, 227, 255)   3 B. M. H.
Gates, F. L., Jr. *a*   340 WH.
Gates, L. H., 2 *l*   409 B.
Gates, P. S., Sr. *s*   West Haven
Gay, F. L., Fr. *a*   537 P.
Gaylord, C. W., Fr. *a*   7 Library st.
Gaylord, F. A., Sr. *s*   165 v-s.
Gaylord, R. E., Jr. *s*   124 Prospect st.
Gaynor, E. G., Fr. *s*   132 Wall st.
Geary, A. V., Fr. *a*   479 Orange st.
Geary, W. E., Jr. *s*   479 Orange st.
Gedney, S. L., Jr., So. *a*   231 P.
Gellert, N. H., So. *a*   1193 Chapel st.
Gemmer, H., Fr. *a*   598 P.
George, N. F., So. *a*   8 College st.
Gerner, G. C., Fr. *s*   12 Nicoll st.
Getzelsohn, J., 2 *l*   722 W. D.
Gibb, H., Ass't. (p. 46)   (26 PEAB.)   229 Lloyd st.
Gibney, R. A., Fr. *a*   242 York st.
Gidart, A. W., Jr. *d*   643 E. D.
Giffen, T. T., *g*   213 F.
Gifford, A. R., Ass't. (p. 42)   227 F.
Gilbert, A. B., So. *a*   713 W. D.
Gilbert, A. C., Sr. *m*   120 York st.
Gilbert, C. H., Sr. *a*   53 V.
Gilbert, F. D., Jr. *a*   462 FW.
Gilbert, Mrs. H. C., Ass't. (p. 46)   (LIB.)   26 Kensington st.
Gilbert, P. M., Jr. *a*   469 FW.
Gill, C. M., So. *a*   45 Park st.
Gillespie, G. E., Jr. *s*   70 Trumbull st.
Gillespie, H., *g*   219 F.
Gillespie, J. P., Fr. *a*   250 York st.
Gillette, E. M., Priv. Sec'y. (p. 46)   (LIB.)   252 Winthrop av.
Gillis, A. W., Fr. *a*   551 P.
Gilmore, J. L., Ass't. (p. 42)   198 Main st., West Haven
Gilpin, F. L., Jr., Sr. *s*   189 v-s.
Given, W. B., Sr. *s*   96 Wall st.
Givens, M. H., Jr. *s*   529 Elm st.
Glascock, C. C., Ass't. Prof. (pp. 227, 255, 334)   138 v-s.

Glazer, B. E., Fr. *s*   250 George st.
Gleason, J. J., Fr. *s*   241 Hamilton st.
Gleason, W. W., Sr. *for.*   609 E. D.
Glenny, B. B., Jr., Jr. *a*   131 W.
Glover, C. C., Jr., So. *a*   22 College st.
Glover, W. B., Jr. *a*   388 B.
Godchaux, L., Jr. *a*   440 FW.
Goddard, C. A., So. *a*   165 L.
Godley, F. A., *g*, Sr. *a*   334 WH.
Goebel, W. A., So. *a*   254 Crown st.
Goldberg, P., Fr. *s*   Bridgeport
Goldenburg, I., Sr. *a*   35 Nash st.
Goldflam, A. S., 1 *l*   35 High st.
Goldman, G., 2 *m*   64 Prince st.
Goldman, R. P., Fr. *a*   547 P.
Goldschmidt, E. H., Fr. *s*   128 Wall st.
Goldsmith, B. C., Jr. *for.*, Grad. *s*   70 Whalley av.
Goldsmith, K., 3 *l*   36 Elm st.
Goldsmith, S. A., Fr. *a*   544 P.
Goldstein, H. K., Fr. *s*   120 High st.
Goldstone, M., Spec. *l*   194 State st.
Gompertz, L. M., Instr. (pp. 34, 465)   1195 Chapel st.
Gooch, F. A., Prof. (pp. 23, 172-3, 347)   (K. C. L.)   291 Edwards st.
Good, C. M., *g*, Grad. *d*, Spec. *l*   612 E. D.
Good, W. J., Jr. *m*   1076 Chapel st.
Goodell, F. Y., Sr. *a*   435 FW.
Goodell, T. D., Prof. (pp. 24, 146-8, 314-15)   35 Edgehill rd.
Goodenough, A. W., *g*   25 Edwards st.
Goodhue, F., Fr. *a*   250 York st.
Goodman, L. M., Fr. *a*   594 P.
Goodman, W. H., 1 *l*   340 George st.
Goodrich, D., Fr. *s*   132 Wall st.
Goodson, G. A., Jr., Fr. *a*   7 Library st.
Goodwin, C., Fr. *s*   120 College st.
Goodwin, R. E., Sr. *a*   382 WH.
Goodyear, B., *g*   A.
Gordon, G. B., 3 *l*   271 Crown st.
Gordon, M. E., *mus.*   1305 Chapel st.
Gordon, T. C., 1 *l*   133 College st.
Gordy, S. B., Fr. *s*   333 York st.
Gorman, J. F., 2 *m*   121 York st.
Gorman, J. G., Jr. *s*   126 Wall st.
Gosnell, F., Jr., Sr. *a*   47 V.
Goss, J. M., Fr. *s*   113 Wall st.
Gottesman, J. G., 1 *l*   683 W. D.

Gould, G. B., So. *a*   236 Crown st.
Gowdy, R. W., Fr. *s*   333 York st.
Graham, C. F., Jr. *a*   392 B.
Graham, C. V., Jr. *a*   134 W.
Graham, G. C., 1 *m*   63 Pond st.
Graham, H., Jr. *a*   242 D.
Grammer, G. J., Sr. *a*   58 V.
Granniss, F. B., *mus.*   Bridgeport
Grant, Dabney, Jr. *s*   112 V-S.
Grant, Douglas, Fr. *s*   108 High st.
Grant, E. E., *mus.*   12 Edgewood av.
Grant, H., So. *a*   8 College st.
Grant, J. B., Jr., Jr. *a*   341 WH.
Granville, W. A., Instr. (pp. 34, 227,
233, 235-6, 238, 240, 252, 257, 362)
(46 N. S. H.)   118 Howe st.
Graver, C. H., Fr. *a*   232 Bradley st.
Graves, A. H., Instr. (pp. 34, 241,
244, 250, 281, 353, 412-13)
97 Grove st.
Graves, C. E., Fr. *a*   14 Lincoln st.
Graves, H. S., Prof. and Director
(pp. 27, 250, 281, 354, 415-16, 418)
(MAR.)   68 Trumbull st.
Graves, S. H., Jr. *s*   133 College st.
Gray, E. H., Fr. *a*   183 L.
Greeley, C. S., Fr. *a*   8 College st.
Greeley, W. B., Lect. (p. 418)
San Francisco
Green, W. M., Fr. *s*   117 Wall st.
Greenbaum, W. E., 2 *l*   265 Orange st.
Greenberg, J. D., 2 *m*   116 High st.
Greene, C., *g*   A.
Greene, D., Sr. *a*   62 V.
Greene, G. P., Fr. *a*   250 York st.
Greenebaum, J., Fr. *a*   200 York st.
Greenough, H. P., Fr. *s*   120 High st.
Greer, T. M., Fr. *s*   150 Grove st.
Gregory, G. N., Fr. *a*   236 Crown st.
Gregory, H. E., Prof. (pp. 28, 175,
177, 241, 246, 276, 355, 357, 359,
414, 514) (6 PEAB.)   399 B.
Gregory, L. W., Jr. *a*   441 FW.
Gregory, S. S., Jr., Fr. *a*   250 York st.
Gregory, T., So. *a*   22 College st.
Greims, M. B., Spec. *l*   135 Wall st.
Greiner, G. J., *mus.*   116 Nash st.
Griffin, H. B., *f*   38 Clark st.
Griffin, W. V., 3 *l*   70 Edgewood av.
Griffing. M. H., Fr. *a*   570 P.
Griffith, M., So. *a*   22 College st.
Griggs, C. W., Jr. *s*   178 Lawrence st.
Griggs, M. W., So. *a*   8 College st.

Grimes, H., Sr. *d*   626 E. D.
Griswold, C. D., Fr. *s*   82 Wall st.
Griswold, D. T., Sr. *a*   42 V.
Griswold, F. T., Sr. *s*   395 Temple st
Griswold, R. N., Jr. *a*   390 B.
Griswold, S. A., Fr. *s*   82 Wall st.
Gross, L. D., 1 *l*   128 Wall st.
Gruener, G., Prof. (pp. 25, 157-9,
333) (146 L.)   78 Pearl st.
Gruener, H. R., Ass't. (p. 46)
(LIB.)   78 Pearl st.
Gubelmann, A. E., Instr. (pp. 34,
157-8)   95 Brownell st.
Guerra, J. O., 1 *m*   750 Grand av.
Guest, H. H., Sr. *s*   99 Scranton st.
Guggenheim, H. F., Fr. *s*   1 B. M. H.
Gundelfinger, G. F., Ass't. (p. 42)
124 Wall st.
Guthrie, W. D., Lect. (p. 34)
New York City

Haas, G. C., Sr. *s*   163 V-S.
Haas, H. S., Grad. *l*   333 York st.
Haas, R. K., Fr. *a*   242 York st.
Hadley, A. T., President (p. 21)
(WOOD.)   93 Whitney av.
Haesche, W. E., Instr. (pp. 35, 199,
341, 397)   19 Whitney av.
Hagan, H. E., *mus.*   83 Whalley av.
Hagan, J. T., Sr. *a*   265 D.
Haggarty, M. P., Spec. *l*   17 Auburn st.
Haight, J. A., Jr., Fr. *a*   250 York st.
Haines, A., 1 *l*   411 Temple st.
Hains, G., Jr., 1 *l*   137 Dwight st.
Hale, W. W., Sr. *s*   162 V-S.
Haley, W. C., Jr. *a*   363 WH.
Hall. A. B., *mus.*   211 Norton st.
Hall, B. B., 1 *l*   Wallingfor
Hall, C. R., 1 *l*   1076 Chapel st.
Hall, C. W., *g*   81 C.
Hall, E. B., Sr. *s*   96 Wall st
Hall, F. L., Jr. *d*   657 W. D.
Hall, J. R., Sr. *for.*   642 E. D.
Hall, K. S., Fr. *s*   333 York st
Hall, L. G., So. *a*   8 College st.
Hall, M. A., Fr. *a*   530 P.
Hall, R. B., Jr., So. *a*   250 Crown st
Hall, R. C., Sr. *for.*   13 Lake pl.
Hall, R. N., Fr. *s*   82 Wall st.
Hall, R. W., Fr. *a*   556 P.
Hall, S. D., Jr. *s*   115 V-S.
Hall, W. L., Lect. (p. 35)
Washington, D. C.

Hallington, A. J., Spec. *d* 105 Ward st.
Hallock, D. A., Jr. *s* 110 Wall st.
Ham, H. B., Sr. *s* 96 Wall st.
Hamill, A. E., *g* A.
Hamilton, F. W., Sr. *s* 133 College st.
Hamilton, J., Jr., *2 m* 193 York st.
Hamilton, T. L., Fr. *a* 242 York st.
Hamilton, W. S. H., Fr. *s* 28 Norton st.
Hamlin, B. P., Sr. *s* 38 Lynwood pl.
Hamlin, F. B., Jr. *a* 180 L.
Hammitt, S. J., Jr. *s* 110 Wall st.
Hammond, C. G., So. *a* 347 Orchard st.
Hammond, H. D., Sr. *s* 228 Crown st.
Hammond, J. H., Prof. (pp. 24, 270) New York City
Hammond, J. H., Jr., Fr. *s* 128 v-s.
Hand, C. W. H., Ass't. (p. 46) 158 York st.
Hanifin, J. F., *1 m* 236 James st.
Hanna, M. A., Fr. *s* 400 Temple st.
Hannaford, F., Sr. *s* 111 Grove st.
Hannaford, J. M., Jr., Sr. *a* 428 FW.
Hannah, M. C., So. *a* 102 W.
Hanners, G. W., *g* 59 Broadway
Hanson, F., *1 l* 110 Wall st.
Harbison, H. H., *2 l* 451 FW.
Harding, J. E., Jr., Fr. *s* 55 Prospect st.
Harding, J. M., Jr. *a* 369 WH.
Harger, Mrs. J. C., Cataloguer (p. 46) (LIB.) 14 University pl.
Harlow, R. V., Jr. *a* 450 FW.
Harmon, A. M., *g* Rome
Harmon, C. N., *3 l* 289 York st.
Harrah, E., Fr. *a* 250 York st.
Harriman, E. A., Instr. (pp. 35, 515) Derby
Harrington, S. M., *g* A.
Harris, I. F., *g* A.
Harris, J. E., *1 m* 233 Oak st.
Harris, R. N., Spec. *d* 137 Shelton av.
Harris, W. A., Jr., Fr. *s* 130 Wall st.
Harris, W. H., *g*, Grad. *d* Beacon Falls
Harrison, G. L., So. *a* 22 College st.
Harrison, R. G., Prof. (pp. 27, 180, 227, 241, 244, 271, 349-50) 306 York st.
Hart, C. E., *1 l* New Britain

Hart, C. S., Sr. *s* 159 Elm st.
Hart, L. A., *1 l* 108 High st.
Hartley, W. E., Sr. *a* 267 D.
Hartmann, H. M., Jr. *s* 110 Wall st.
Hartridge, L., Fr. *a* 8 College st.
Hartshorn, W. E., Ass't. (pp. 42, 465) 1138 Chapel st.
Hartwell, A. M., Fr. *a* 523 P.
Hartwell, H. T., Fr. *a* 553 P.
Hartwell, J. M., Fr. *a* 200 York st.
Harvey, E. D., *g*, Jr. *d* 625 E. D.
Harvey, R. S., *g* 142 York st.
Harvey, S. C., *g*, *1 m* 114 High st.
Hasegawa, T., Spec. *s* 479 Elm st.
Haskell, A. G., Jr. *s* 124 Wall st.
Haskell, A. M., So. *a* 22 College st.
Haskell, C. D., Sr. *a* 65 V.
Hastings, B. F., Fr. *s* Bridgeport
Hastings, C. S., Prof. (pp. 23, 227, 236, 252, 268, 343) (120 WIN.) 248 Bradley st.
Hastings, M. G., Fr. *a* 534 P.
Hastings, R. D., Fr. *a* 555 P.
Hastings, W. S., *g* A.
Hatch, H. W., Fr. *s* 113 Wall st.
Hathaway, H. R., Fr. *s* 127 v-s.
Hauch, J. F., *3 l* 159 Elm st.
Havemeyer, L., Fr. *s* 117 Wall st.
Hawes, R. K., So. *a* 22 College st.
Hawes, R. W., Sr. *a* 56 V.
Hawke, C. B., Fr. *a* 8 College st.
Hawkes, H. E., Ass't. Prof. (pp. 30, 167-9, 362-3) 45 Huntington st.
Hawley, B. R., Jr. *s* 120 High st.
Hawley, J. M., *mus.* Bridgeport
Hawley, J. T., Jr. *s* 666 W. D.
Hawley, R. C., Instr. (pp. 35, 250, 281, 415, 418) 634 E. D.
Haxstun, A. K., Jr. *s* 106 v-s.
Hay, W. B., So. *a* 22 College st.
Hayakawa, Y., *g* 55 Prospect st.
Hayes, C. W., Lect. (p. 35) Washington, D C.
Hayes, J. R., Fr. *s* 55 Prospect st.
Hayes, M. C., So. *a* 57 Lake pl.
Hayes, R. R., So. *a* 254 Crown st.
Hayne, R. Y., So. *a* 254 Crown st.
Hays, J., *g* 158 York st.
Hayward, R. O., Jr. *a* 272 D.
Hayward, W. F., Jr., So. *a* 159 L.
Healey, P. J., Jr. *a* 366 WH.
Healy, J. J., Spec. *l* 70 Trumbull st.
Healy, V. E., Sr. *a* 428 FW.

Heard, J. D., So. *a*   22 College st.
Heath, F. H., Ass't. (p. 42)
     712 W. D.
Heaton, H. C., *g*   Paris
Heaton, L., *g*   A.
Hebard, M., So. *a*   22 College st.
Heck, F. C., Sr. *a*   142 Dwight st.
Hedges, P. H., Jr. *s*   110 Wall st.
Hedrick, A. L., Sr. *a*   54 V.
Hedrick, E. A., Catalogue Reviser
   (p. 46)   (LIB.)   65 Grove st.
Heedy, H. G., So. *a*   22 College st.
Hegeman, C. C., 3 *l*   670 W. D.
Heidrich, A. G., Fr. *s*   131 Grove st.
Heinrich, H. W., Fr. *a*   586 P.
Heisen, C. C., Jr., Fr. *s*   150 Grove st.
Helm, J. P., Jr., Sr. *a*   347 WH.
Helms, B., Jr. *a*   464 FW.
Hemingway, L. L., Sr. *a*   59 V.
Hemingway, S. B., *g*   327 Temple st.
Hemingway, W. C., Jr. *s*
     25 Hotchkiss st.
Hemming, W. D. P., Fr. *s*
     120 High st.
Henderson, J. P., Fr. *s*   9 B. M. H
Henderson, L. B., Mid. *d*   617 E. D.
Henderson, Y., Ass't. Prof. (pp. 30,
   181, 352, 464)   400 Prospect st.
Hendricks, G. F., Sr. *s* 239 George st.
Hendricks, W. E., Sr. *a*   152 L.
Hendrickson, G. L., Prof. (p. 26)   A.
Henes, L. J., Jr. *s*   126 High st.
Henry, D. M., *mus.*   Waterbury
Hense, C. W., Instr. (pp. 35, 465)
     22 Trumbull st.
Herbert, A. C., Ass't. (p. 42)
     159 Elm st.
Heron, J., So. *a*   8 College st.
Herrick, E. C., Jr. *s*   119 Wall st.
Herrick, H. G., Spec. *s*   37 Pearl st.
Hershman, A. A., Sr. *m*   6 High st.
Herz, L. F., Sr. *s*   118 Edwards st.
Herz, N., Sr. *s*   118 Edwards st.
Hewes, L. I., Instr. (pp. 35, 227,
   233, 235-6, 238, 240, 252, 257, 362,
   365)   Hamden
Hewes, T., So. *a*   22 College st.
Hewitt, C. R., Jr. *s*   124 Wall st.
Hewitt, E. H., Fr. *a*   578 P.
Hewlett, H. B., Jr. *a*   451 FW.
Heyl, F. W., *g*   137 Blatchley av.
Heyman, L. I., Grad. *l*   333 York st.
Hickox, C. V., Jr., Fr. *a*   250 York st.

Higginbotham, J. M., Jr., Sr. *a*   147 L.
Higgins, J. L. M., 1 *m*
     652 Congress av.
Higgins, S., 3 *l*   19 Broad st.
Hildebrand, A. S., So. *a*
     260 Crown st.
Hilditch, E. L., 1 *l*   90 Lake pl.
Hilditch, W. W., *g*   90 Lake pl.
Hill, A. J., Fr. *s*   Meriden
Hill, A. R., *g*   A.
Hill, D. Y., Sr. *s*   110 Wall st.
Hille, H. M., Fr. *a*   186 F.
Hillhouse, J. T., Fr. *a*   584 P.
Hillis, R. D., So. *a*   22 College st.
Hilsdale, P., Jr. *a*   437 FW.
Hinckley, E. B., So. *a*   152 Temple st.
Hincks, C. C., Fr. *a*   551 P.
Hine, L. N., So. *a*   22 College st.
Hinkley, E. A., Fr. *s*   Stony Creek
Hinterleiter, A. B., Fr. *s*
     118 College st.
Hirschfield, C. E., 1 *l*   159 Elm st.
Hirst, E. C., Jr. *for.*, Grad. *s*
     60 Whalley av.
Hitchcock, C., Fr. *a*   527 P.
Hitchcock, H. B., Jr. *a*   410 B.
Hitchcock, M. E., Jr. *a*   527 P.
Hitchings, W. H., 2 *l*
     313 Howard av.
Ho, H. W., Sr. *s*   114 High st.
Ho, L., So. *a*   66 Whalley av.
Hobart, H. P., Fr. *s*   125 High st.
Hobbs, H. H., Fr. *s*   423 Temple st.
Hocking, W. E., Ass't. Prof.
   (pp. 30, 185, 383)   A.
Hodgdon, E. F., 2 *l*   333 York st.
Hodges, E., Jr. *s*   124 Wall st.
Hodgson, A. H., Jr. *for.* Spec. *s*
     718 W. D.
Hoegen, M. C., 1 *l*   227 Columbus av.
Hoerle, R. C., 3 *l*   130 Wall st.
Hoffman, B. E., Jr. *a*   107 Dixwell av.
Hogan, J. F., 1 *m*   44 Winchester av.
Hogdon, E. F., 2 *l*   333 York st.
Holbrook, C., So. *a*   165 L.
Holcombe, J. M., Lect. (p. 35)
     Hartford
Holcombe, J. M., Jr., Fr. *a*
     242 York st.
Holden, R. A., Jr., Fr. *a*   237 York st.
Holden, R. J., Fr. *s*   111 Grove st.
Holder. F. J., *g*   23 Lynwood pl.
Hollandersky, P. J., 2 *l*   37 Lake pl.

Hollett, G. L., Jr. *a*   109 w.
Holliday, S. N., 2d, Sr. *a*   68 v.
Hollister, B. J., Sr. *a*   356 WH.
Hollister, H. K., So. *a*   8 College st.
Hollister, J. B., Fr. *a*   250 York st.
Holloway, J. D., Fr. *s*   397 Temple st.
Holm. J. D., *g*   47 Lake pl.
Holmes, A. D., Fr. *s*   32 Gilbert st.
Holmes, N., Sr. *a*   69 v.
Holmes, P. K., *g*   Bridgeport
Holmes, S. W., Jr. *a*   135 w.
Holt, H. G., Fr. *a*   22 College st.
Holt, J. E., *g*   68 Clark st.
Holt, L. H., Instr (pp. 35, 162)
                                   315 Crown st.
Honywill, A. W., Jr., Fr. *s*
                                   53 Lake pl.
Hood, T. C., So. *a*   255 D.
Hooghkirk, H. N., Jr. *s*
                                   286 Norton st.
Hooker, D., Sr. *a*   92 C.
Hooker, J. K., Jr. *a*   253 D.
Hooker, S. A., So. *a*   251 Crown st.
Hooker, T., Sr. *a*   354 WH.
Hooker, W. B., Instr. (pp. 35, 160-1)
                    (15 WH.)   121 w.
Hoomkeek, C. A., 1 *l*   681 W. D.
Hooper, J. K., *g*   33 Lake pl.
Hoopes, E. M., Jr., Fr. *s*   127 V-S.
Hoover, L. R., 2 *l*   86 Wall st.
Hopkins, A. D., Lect. (p. 35)
                                   Washington, D. C.
Hopkins, B., Fr. *s*   110 Wall st.
Hopkins, C. R., *g*   245 York st.
Hopkins, E. W., Prof. (pp. 24, 150,
    320-1, 383)   299 Lawrence st.
Hopkins, S. V., So. *a*   214 Crown st.
Hopkins, W. P., Sr. *s*   184 V-S.
Hopwood, J. O., *g*   A.
Horgan, J. J., Jr. *m*   911 Howard av.
Horn, E. T., *g*   616 E. D.
Horn, H. S., Fr. *s*   110 Wall st.
Horne, J., Fr. *a*   242 York st.
Horsfall, J. C., Fr. *s*   217 York st.
Horton, A. E., Cataloguer (p. 46)
                    (LIB.)   202 Crown st.
Horton, L. B., Jr. *s*   90 Wall st.
Horton, O. E., Fr. *s*   202 Crown st.
Hosford, R. S., Jr. *a*   272 D.
Hotchkiss, A. S., Priv. Sec'y. (p. 47)
                    (WOOD.)   45 Lake pl.
Hotchkiss, C. E., *mus.*   Hartford
Hotchkiss, E. G., Fr. *a*   250 York st.

Hotchkiss, F. A., So. *a*   8 College st.
Hotchkiss, F. E., Sup't. (p. 47)
                                   104 High st.
Hotchkiss, R. H., Jr. *s*   Ansonia
Hotton, H. J., So. *a*   156 L.
Houghton, R. M., Spec. *d*   Derby
Housum, C. R., Sr. *a*   58 v.
Hovey, W. P., Fr. *s*   59 Grove st.
Howard, A. P., Fr. *s*   3 Hillhouse av.
Howard, C., Sr. *a*   13 v.
Howard, C. W., Sr. *a*   241 D.
Howard, E. B. Jr. *s*   133 College st.
Howard, J. M., Jr. *a*   254 D.
Howe, H. A., Jr. *a*   468 FW.
Howe, L. V., Jr. *s*   96 Wall st.
Howe, P. M., *g*   Rockville
Howell, S. L., Sr. *a*   41 v.
Howell, W. R., *g*, Mid. *d*   634 E. D.
Howland, G. M., Fr. *a*   250 York st.
Howland, H. E., Fellow
                    35 Wall st., New York City
Howland, W. I., Jr., Sr. *s*   108 V-S.
Hoxsey, T. F., Fr. *s*   110 Wall st.
Hoyt, E. 2d, So. *a*   22 College st.
Hoyt, E. K., Sr. *a*   32 v.
Hoyt, F. E., *g*, Spec. *d*
                                   964½ Chapel st.
Hoyt, H. O., 1 *l*   1071 Yale P. O.
Hoyt, P. S., Fr. *s*   37 Lake pl.
Hsin, Y. H., Fr. *s*   114 High st.
Hua, Y. P., Sr. *s*   55 Prospect st.
Hubbard, A. S., Fr. *a*   250 York st.
Hubbard, W. H., Jr., Jr. *s*   121 V-S.
Huckans, C. H., Sr. *s*   646 E. D.
Hudson, R. S., *mus.*   713 W. D.
Huff, B. R., Jr. *a*   99 w.
Huff, G. F., Jr., Jr. *s*   315 York st.
Hughes, J. G., Fr. *s*   Bridgeport
Hughes, M. C., Fr. *a*   1076 Chapel st.
Hulburd, D., Sr. *a*   352 WH.
Hulett, F. W., Sr. *s*   910 Whalley av.
Hull, A. W., Ass't. (p. 42)
                                   120 York st.
Hull, C. H., *g*   New London
Hull, H., Fr. *s*   400 Temple st.
Hull, J. I., Sr. *s*   84 C.
Hull, T. C., Fr. *a*   553 P.
Humason, H. M., Jr. *a*   264 D.
Hume, E. S., Instr. (pp. 35, 438)
                    (606 E. D.)   79 Howe st.
Hume, W. M., Jr. *a*   178 L.
Humphrey, E. H., So. *a*   713 W. D.
Humphrey, H. J. C., Sr. *s*   105 V-S.

Humphrey, O. S., Sr. *a* 20 v.
Humphreys, H. N., 1 *m* 333 York st.
Hunn, C. F., Fr. *a* 557 P.
Hunsiker, H., Fr. *s* 96 Wall st.
Hunt, F. C., Jr. *s* 131 Grove st.
Hunt, R. C., 3 *l* 36 Elm st.
Hunt, W. H., Jr., Jr. *s* 101 v-s.
Hunter, R. B., Sr. *a* 700 w. D.
Hunter, R. E., Fr. *s* 152 Grove st.
Hunting, R. D., Jr. *a* 43 v.
Huntington, E., Instr. (pp. 35, 175-6, 178, 246, 355, 357, 514) 708 w. D.
Huntoon, L. D., Ass't. Prof. (pp. 30, 231, 240, 270) 284 Orange st.
Hurlbut, C. S., Sr. *a* 18 v.
Hurlbutt, C., Fr. *s* 53 Prospect st.
Hurley, J. A., Jr., Jr. *a* 244 D.
Hurtt, F. D., Grad. *l* 661 w. D.
Husted, H. T. F., Sr. *a* 45 v.
Hutchins, Albert E., Fr. *a* 234 Division st.
Hutchins, Annie E., Catalogue Reviser (p. 47) Library
Hutchins, H. L., Jr. *s* 234 Division st.
Hutchinson, J. R., Ass't. Clerk (p. 47) (3 s. H.) Branford
Hutchinson, L. O., So. *a* 646 E. D.
Hutchison, L. L., Ass't. (p. 42) (PEAB.) 127 Dwight st.
Hyde, A. C., 1 *l* West Haven
Hyde, B. P., Sr. *s* 131 Grove st.
Hyde, C. C., Lect. (pp. 35, 194, 374, 500, 502, 519) Chicago, Ill.
Hyde, C. E., Jr. *m* 81 Newhall st.
Hyde, F. W., Jr., Fr. *a* 200 York st.
Hyde, G. G., So. *a* 154 L.
Hyde, H. N., *g* A.
Hyde, J. C., Sr. *a* 60 v.
Hyde, J. R., Fr. *s* 126 High st.
Hyde, S. G., Catalogue Reviser (p. 47) (LIB.) 65 Grove st.
Hyde, V. E., *f* 402 Crown st.
Hyland, E. T., Sr. *s* 144 Bradley st.
Hynes, T. V., Instr. (pp. 35, 465-6) 27 College st.

Ide, C. E., Sr. *a* 367 WH.
Ijams, F. B., Jr. *s* 17 Hillhouse av.
Inaoka, S., *g* 350 George st.
Ingall, O. D., Jr. *for.*, Grad. *s* 718 w. D.
Ingalls, J. A., Fr. *s* 1371 Chapel st.

Ingersoll, G. F., Fr. *a* 560 P.
Ingersoll, H., Fr. *s* 133 Wall st.
Ingersoll, J. W. D., Ass't. Prof. (pp. 30, 143, 145, 316-17, 319) (D, C.) 139 York st.
Inghram, M. G., Jr. *d* 646 E. D.
Ingraham, E., So. *a* 225 Crown st.
Ingram, A. M., Spec. *s* 686 w. D.
Inouye, T., *g* 333 York st.
Irons. H. S., Fr. *a* 526 P.
Irving, J. D., Prof. (pp. 28, 231, 240, 243, 259, 270, 276, 357) (191 K.) 76 Wall st.
Irwin, D. D., Sr. *s* 133 College st.
Irwin, V. J., Jr., Jr. *m* 1 Sylvan av.
Ish, J. G., Jr., Jr. *a* 658 w. D.
Ives, R., Sr. *a* 51 v.

Jack, J. L., Fr. *a* 231 York st.
Jack, W. J., *g* A.
Jackson, A. J., Fr. *s* 126 Wall st.
Jackson, G. B., Jr. *s* 110 Wall st.
Jackson, H. H., Sr. *a* 434 FW.
Jackson, K., *g* South Hadley, Mass.
Jackson, R. C., Jr. *d* 618 E. D.
Jacob, W. H., Fr. *a* 250 York st.
Jacobs, J. L., *g* 1066 Yale P. O.
Jacobus, D. L., Sr. *a* 87 C.
James, C. V., 1 *l* 53 Prospect st.
James, G. R., 2 *m* 141 Greene st.
James, J. E., 2 *l* 298 York st.
Jamieson, G. S., Instr. (pp. 35, 229, 231, 243, 259, 347) 162 S. C. L.
Jamison, H. B., 3 *l* 559 w. D
Jamison, W., Fr. *a* 163 York st
Janson, J. J., Jr., Fr. *a* 236 Crown s
Jebejian, N. H., Sr. *s* 945 Yale P. O
Jefferson, C. E., Fellow 121 W. 85th st., New York Ci
Jefferson, C. F., So. *a* 158
Jefferson, E. F., Jr. *a* 181
Jeffery, R., Jr., Fr. *a* 250 York s
Jenkins, W. A., Jr. *d* 678 w.
Jennings, F. B., So. *a* 163
Jente, R., So. *a* 86 Henry s
Jepson, H. B., Prof. and Univ. Organist (pp. 28, 199, 341, 398) (MEM.) 294 Lawrence st.
Jerome, G. N., Fr. *s* 24 Gilbert av.
Jewell, O. S., So. *a* 95 w
Jewell, R., Instr. (p. 35) Newtow
Jewell, R. H., Fr. *a* 238 York s
Jewett. C. C., So. *a* 22 College

Jewett, N. H., Jr. *a*   391 B.
Jimenis, O., Fr. *s*   110 Wall st.
Johns, C. O., Instr. (pp. 35, 227, 259)
                                    162 S. C. L.
Johnson, A. B., Fr. *a*   114 High st.
Johnson, A. E., 1 *m*   Ansonia
Johnson, A. M., Jr. *a*   115 W.
Johnson, A. S., *f*   374 Grand av.
Johnson, B. L., Fr. *s*   96 Wall st.
Johnson, E. A., Jr. *a*   458 FW.
*Johnson, E. C., Sup't. Univ. Dining
  Hall* (p. 47)   1361 Chapel st.
Johnson, E. M., Sr. *s* 70 Trumbull st.
Johnson, F. E., 2 *m*   45 Third st.
Johnson, F. L., Jr. *a*   136 W.
Johnson, G. A., Ass't. (p. 47)
            (LIB.)   1916 State st.
Johnson, G. M., Sr. *a*   92 C.
Johnson, H. L., Jr. *for.,* Grad. *s*
                                   17 Compton st.
Johnson, J. C., Spec. *l* 407 Temple st.
Johnson, J. F., Jr., So. *a*
                                   22 College st.
Johnson, J. Q. A., Jr., Sr. *a*   234 D.
Johnson, R. C., Jr. *a*   372 WH.
Johnson, S. W., Prof. (p. 21)
                                 54 Trumbull st.
Johnson, T. B., Instr. (pp. 35, 229,
  231, 243, 259, 347)   (162 S. C. L.)
                                  120 Dwight st.
Johnson, W. S., Instr. (pp. 35, 162,
  164)   361 Elm st.
Johnston, J. F., *g*   Yale P. O.
Johnston, T. S., Jr., Fr. *a* 8 College st.
Jones, A., Sr. *d*   604 E. D.
Jones, A. M., Fr. *s*   367 Howard av.
Jones, B. A., *g*   Bridgeport, Conn.
Jones, B. F., Sr. *a*   137 Dwight st.
Jones, Charles C., Jr. *a*   95 W.
Jones, Cheney C., 2 *l*   1233 Chapel st.
Jones, C. D., Sr. *a*   428 FW.
Jones, C. H., Sr. *s*   367 Howard av.
Jones, D. B., *g*   103 Park st.
Jones, E. P., So. *a*   230 F.
Jones, F. E., Jr. *a*   413 B.
Jones, F. R., Fr. *s*   405 Temple st.
Jones, F. W., Jr., So. *a* 236 Crown st.
Jones, G. F., 3 *l*   271 Crown st.
Jones, H. H., Sr. *s*   133 College st.
Jones, P. W., Fr. *s*   147 Dwight st.
Jones, R. C., Jr. *for.,* Grad. *s*
                                 60 Whalley av.
Jones, S. H., Sr. *s*   170 V-S.

Jones, T. A. D., Sr. *s*   133 College st.
Jones, W. S., Jr., Sr. *s* 133 College st.
Jordan, L. K., Jr. *s*   126 Wall st.
Jordan, R. G., 3 *l*   36 Mansfield st.
Joyce, J. S., Jr. *s*   187 V-S.
Judd, C. H., Prof. (pp. 28, 183, 185,
  382)   (6 HER.) 318 Willow st.
Judson, A. C., *g*   716 W. D.
Judson, M., *g*   37 Howe st.
Jui, P., Jr. *s*   56 Grove st.
Jump, H. A., Lect. (p. 36)
                                 Brunswick, Me.

Kaercher, G. H., Jr. *s*   149 V-S.
Kalaidjian, M. T., *g*, Grad. *d*
                                       619 E. D.
Kane, J. I., Sr. *s*   111 Grove st.
Kaufman, J. P., Jr. *a*   419 B.
Kavanagh, E. S., Fr. *a*   595 P.
Kavanaugh, E. C., Clerk (p. 47)
                                 14 Compton st.
Kawanaka, K., *g*, Grad. *d*   637 E. D.
Keating, H. F., Sr. *m*   371 Crown st.
Keating, T. A., 3 *l*   424 George st.
Keator, B. C., Jr., Sr. *s*   96 Wall st.
Keator, S. J., Jr., Jr. *a*   254 D.
Keefe, A. T., Fr. *a*   254 Crown st.
Keefe, S., *mus.*   Derby
Keegan, J. F., 1 *m*   1331 Chapel
Keeler, P. I., Jr. *s*   133 V-S.
Keeler, S. E., Jr., So. *a*   159 L.
Keenan, J. L., Fr. *a*   186 F.
Keeny, G. B., Fr. *s*   Meriden
Keep, R. P., *g*   A.
Keirstead, W. O., *g*   Montowese
Keith, E. D., So. *a*   207 F.
Keith, I. P., 3 *l*   333 York st.
Keller, A. G., Prof. (pp. 28, 191-3,
  246, 279, 371, 515) 55 Huntington st.
Kelley, H., Jr. *a*   256 D.
Kelley, L. K., Fr. *s*   113 V-S.
Kellogg, C. D. H., Jr., Fr. *s*
                                  130 Wall st.
Kellogg, F. B., Jr. *s*   132 V-S.
Kelly, M. P., 2 *l*   111 Greenwood st.
Kelly, O. S., Jr. *s*   126 Wall st.
Kelsey, A. A., Sr. *s*   106 V-S.
Kelsey, A. L., Sr. *s*   96 Wall st.
Kelsey, C., Jr. *a*   240 D.
Kelsey, S. T., Jr. *a*   236 D.
Kemper, M., Fr. *a*   163 York st.
Kenealy, M. H., 1 *l*   209 F.
Kennedy, C. C., *g*   A.

Kennedy, E. A., *mus.* 45 Houston st.
Kennedy, J., Jr., Sr. *s* 141 V-S.
Kennedy, L., Jr. *a* 260 D.
Kennedy, P. M., Sr. *s* Derby
Kennedy, R. M., *mus.* Wallingford
Kennedy, V. W., *g* 146 Norton st.
Kennedy, W. J., 1 *l* 51 Clark st.
Kent, C. F., Prof. (pp. 27, 151-2, 323, 327) (145 L.)
406 Humphrey st.
Kenworthy, H., Sr. *a* 423 FW.
Kenworthy, R. A., Jr., Jr. *s*
96 Wall st.
Kenyon, F. H., Jr. *s* 104 Wall st.
Keogh, A., Ref. Libr. and Lect. (pp. 30, 339) (LIB.)
49 Huntington st.
Keppy, F. B., Fr. *a* 559 P.
Kerlin, A. T., *g, mus.* 7 Library st.
Kerlin, R. T., *g* 7 Library st.
Kerney, J. E., Sr. *m* 67 Howe st.
Kerr, A., Fr. *s* 704 W. D.
Kerr, C. M., Fr. *s* 82 Wall st.
Kerr, E. C., Sr. *s* 108 V-S.
Kerr, J., Jr. *s* 145 V-S.
Kerschner, C., Cataloguer (p. 47)
(LIB.) 221 Orchard st.
Ketcham, V. O., Sr. *s* 173 V-S.
Keyes, H. B., Sr. *a, 2 m* 25 V.
Kiernan, E. C., Jr. *m* 98 St. John st.
Kilbourn, A. J., Fr. *a* 600 P.
Kilbourn, J. F., Fr. *a* 600 P.
Kildal, A., Catalogue Reviser (p. 47)
(LIB.) 293 York st.
Kilduff, E. J., Fr. *a* 587 P.
Kilpatrick, J. R., Fr. *a* 200 York st.
Kimball, W. G., Fr. *s*
3 Hillhouse av.
Kimber, W. T., Fr. *a* 250 York st.
Kimzey, J. A., *2 m* 287 York st.
Kincaid, C., Sr. *a* 338 WH.
Kincaid, W. A., Jr., So. *a* 405 B.
King, A. G., So. *a* 8 College st.
King, G. R., Jr. *s* 207 Bishop st.
King, G. W., Jr. *m* 911 Howard av.
King, L. M., So. *a* 22 College st.
King, R. B., So. *a* 228 Crown st.
King, R. R., Fr. *a* 237 York st.
King, R. S., Jr. *s* 131 Grove st.
Kinne, F. B., Ass't. (p. 42)
96 Sherman av.
Kinne, G. C., Sr. *m* 209 York st.
Kinsey, R. S., Sr. *a* 439 FW.

Kirby, H. W., Fr. *a* 242 York st
Kirby, R. S., Instr. (pp. 36, 233, 238, 263, 266) 297 Crown st.
Kircher, J. C., Jr. *for.*, Grad. *s*
1076 Chapel s
Kirchoff, F. L., *mus.* 75 Maple
Kirchwey, K. W., Sr. *a* 3 V.
Kirjassoff, L. S., Fr. *s* 724 W. D.
Kirjassoff, M. D., So. *a* 724 W. D.
Kirk, A. C., Jr. *a* 241 Lawrence st.
Kirkman, E. K. A., *f*
183 Lawrence st.
Kirkman, L. A., *mus.*
183 Lawrence st.
Kirkpatrick, J. E., *g* Oxford
Kitchel, A. F., Jr. *a* 100 W.
Kitchel, C. L., Sec'y. Bur. Self-Help and Appointments (p. 30)
(4 PH.) 253 Lawrence st.
Kittredge, F. W., Jr., Fr. *a*
250 York st.
Kittredge, G. D., So. *a* 369 WH.
Kittredge, R. D., Sr. *a* 60 V.
Klarman, H. J., Fr. *s* 279 Lombard st.
Klein, C. L., 2 *l* 124 Park st.
Kleiner, I., Jr. *m* 288 Willow st.
Kleiner, I. S., Ass't. (p. 42)
39 Howe st.
Klem, S. V., Jr. *s* 15 Lake pl.
Klenke, H. F., Ass't. (p. 42)
11 Wooster pl.
Klots, A. T., Jr. *a* 108 w.
Kluepful, A. C., Fr. *s* 266 York st.
Klupfel, R. W., Jr. *a* 114 W.
Knapp, C. W., Sr. *a* 357 WH.
Knapp, H. H., Lect. (pp. 36, 504)
Bridgeport
Knapp, J. W., Jr. *s* 150 V-S.
Knight, A., So. *a* 22 College st.
Knight, H. M., Fr. *s* 105 College st.
Knight, H. S., Ass't. Prof. (pp. 30, 199, 341, 398) (C. S. H.)
258 Bradley st.
Knotts, F. E., *f* 25 High st.
Knowles, E., Sr. *a* 347 WH.
Knox, C. M., Ass't. (p. 42) 685 W. D.
Konta, G., Sr. *a* 21 V.
Koontz, A. B., 1 *l* 333 York st.
Koshiba, S., *g,* Grad. *d* 639 E. D.
Koshkarian, B. S., Jr. *s* 7 Library st.
Krah, C. A., Fr. *s* 315 York st.
Krakauer, M. M., *f* 673 W. D.
Krasnye, J. F., 1 *m* 716 Howard av.

rebs, D. L., Jr., Fr. *a*   231 York st.
reider, D. A., Ass't. Prof. (pp. 30, 171)   (S. P. L.)   298 Lawrence st.
ugel, H. J., So. *a*   33 Oak st.
umon, J. A., *g*   993 Yale P. O.
unkel, B. W., Instr. (pp. 36, 180, 227, 241, 244, 246, 271, 349, 441)   179 V-s.
urtz, D. W., *g*, Sr. *d*   655 W. D.
ylberg, V. C., Fr. *s*   534 State st.
yle, D. M., Fr. *s*   295 York st.

Cava, J. B., 2 *l*   Hartford
Cour, A. B., *g*   A.
add, G. T., Prof. (p. 22)   204 Prospect st.
agerquist, W. E., *g*   198 Hamilton st.
e, F. C., Jr., So. *a*   260 Crown st.
ib, F. E., Fr. *a*   182 L.
ibert, E. A., Fr. *s* 124 Prospect st.
ibert, H., *mus.*   64 Whalley av.
ond, J. K., *g*   103 Park st.
*l*ontagne, R. W., Jr. *s*   17 Hillhouse av.
caster, J. H., 1 *l*   124 Wall st.
nd, B. D., 1 *l*   9 Arch st.
nd, M., Sr. *s*   9 Arch st.
nders, S. P., Spec. *l*   1015 Yale P. O.
don, H. M., Fr. *a*   248 York st.
ndon, J. S., So. *a*   148 L.
ne, E. S., Sr. *s*   183 V-s.
ne, F. H., *mus.*   Hartford
ne, J. E., Ass't. (p. 42)   203 York st.
e, J. J., So. *a*   359 WH.
ney, F. B., *g*   1305 Chapel st.
ang, H. R., Prof. (pp. 24, 155-6, 318, 329, 331-2)   60 Trumbull st.
angdale, F. R., Jr., Sr. *s*   28 Edgewood av.
angdon, P., Jr., Fr. *s* 150 Grove st.
angdon, W. J., 1 *l*   421 Temple st.
angfeld, A. E., Fr. *s* 796 Yale P. O.
ngford, W. B., Fr. *s*   704 W. D.
ngley, S. S., Spec. *s*   229 Blatchley av.
ngstroth, E., So. *a*   254 D.
ngzettel, G. H., Instr. and Sec'y. (pp. 36, 227, 340)   (A. S.)   725 Whitney av.
rimore, R. M., Fr. *s*   615 E. D.

Larkin, W. J., 2 *l*   1076 Chapel st.
Larremore, T. A., Fr. *a*   567 P.
Larsen, J. A., Sr. *a*   406 B.
Latané, W. C., Sr. *for.*   699 W. D.
Lathrop, F. W., Fr. *a*   538 P.
Lathrop, R. S., *mus.*   130 Howe st.
Lathrop, T. B., *g*, Sr. *d*   626 E. D.
Lathrop, W. G., *g*   Shelton
Latourette, K. S., *g*   197 F.
Laubscher, F. A., Fr. *a*   195 F.
Laughlin, A., Jr., Fr. *s*   117 Wall st.
Laurens, H. L., Grad. *l*   109 York st.
Lautman, M. F., 1 *m*   553 Oak st.
Lautz, O. C., Fr. *s*   110 Wall st.
Lawrence, A. A., Spec. *s*   87 Trumbull st.
Lawrence, H. W., Jr. *g*   125 Dwight st.
Lawrence, J. B., Fr. *s* 391 Temple st.
Lawson, W. S., Jr., Jr. *s*   133 College st.
Lawton, D. L., Jr. *a*   96 W.
Lay, W. S., Ass't. (p. 43) Centerville
Lear, M., 1 *m*   ·   307 George st.
Learned, H. B., *g* 50 Cold Spring st.
Leavens, D. H., Jr. *a*   446 FW.
Leavenworth, C. S., Grad. *s*   2 Hillhouse av.
Leavenworth, D. T., So. *a*   156 L.
Leavitt, D. A., *g*, Grad. *d*   Berlin, Germany
LeBlanc, K., Fr. *a*   250 York st.
LeCompte, I. C., Instr. (pp. 36, 153-4, 330)   316 Crown st.
Ledyard, H., Jr. *a*   55 V.
Lee, C. T., Fr. *a*   185 F.
Lee, F. P., 1 *m*   1081 Chapel st.
Lee, J. A., Jr. *s*   128 Wall st.
Lee, P., *mus.*   Orange
Leepert, J. L., Jr., Jr. *s* 126 Wall st.
Leete, W. R., Sr. *a*   29 V.
Legg, H. G., Fr. *s*   8 B. M. H.
Lehman, E. H., *g*   453 FW.
Lehman, L. H., So. *a*   206 F.
Leighton, K. W., Sr. *s*   227 Sherman av.
Lemmon, R. S., Jr. *a*   394 B.
Lennox, A., 1 *l*   Hartford
Lent, J. M., Spec. *d*
Leonard, N. A., Sr. *s*   416 B.
Leopold, A., Sr. *s*   172 V-s.
Leopold, B., Fr. *s*   18 Howe st.
Lessing, G. R., 3 *l*   442 FW.

Letcher, V. P., Fr. *s*   333 York st.
Levy, L. H., 1 *m*   64 Congress av.
Levy, R. L., Jr. *a*   174 L.
Levy, S. L., Fr. *a*   521 P.
Levy, W., 1 *m*   91 Greene st.
Levy, W. D., 1 *m*   69 Audubon st.
Lewis, C. A., Sr. *for.*   137 Wall st.
Lewis, C. G., Fr. *s*   205 Whitney av.
Lewis, C. M., Prof.   (pp. 26, 161, 163,
   165, 337) (190 F.) 425 St. Ronan st.
Lewis, D. M., Instr.   (pp. 36, 465)
                               438 George st.
Lewis, E. M., Instr.   (pp. 36, 439-40)
   (610 E. D.)   Williamstown, Mass.
Lewis, F. B., Jr. *s*   Stratford
Lewis, F. C., So. *a*   8 College st.
Lewis, F. G., Fr. *a*   237 York st.
Lewis, H. B., Sr. *a*   74 C.
Lewis, H. L., Jr. *s*   146 V-S.
Lewis, H. M., Fr. *a*   231 York st.
Lewis, J. M., Fr. *a*   250 Crown st.
Lewis, J. W., Fr. *s*   425 Temple st.
Lewis, M. C., Jr. *s*   391 Winthrop av.
Lewis, N. S., *mus.*   West Haven
Lewis, R. C., Jr. *s*   Stratford
Lewis, R. W., Fr. *a*   250 York st.
Lewis, Sidney, Spec. *l*   258 D.
Lewis, Sinclair, Sr. *a* 14 Whalley av.
Liberman, B. L., So. *a*   35 High st.
Liddle, L. M., *g*   88 C.
Liebig, O., Sr. *s*   124 Prospect st.
Liebman, E. H., Fr. *s*   186 Willow st.
Light, N. S., Jr. *a*   403 B.
Lightner, F. D., Jr. *a*   129 W.
Lightner, M. C., Jr. *a*   132 W.
Lilley, J. L., Jr. *s*   101 V-S.
Lilley, T., Fr. *s*   405 Temple st.
Lilley, W. A., Jr., Instr.   (pp. 36, 235,
   264)   781 Orange st.
Lincoln, Mrs. C. T., Priv. Sec'y.
   (p. 47)   126 McKinley av.
Lincoln, R. H., 1 *l*   1081 Chapel st.
Lincoln, S. H., Sr. *s* 17 Hillhouse av.
Linde, J. I., Sr. *m*   540 Whitney av.
Lindsay, R. B., Sr. *s*   111 Grove st.
Linsly, E. H., *f*   445 George st.
Lipphardt, W. B., Sr. *a*   81 C.
Lippitt, H., Jr. *a*   271 D.
Lippman, W. E., Sr. *m* 134½ Olive st.
Little, H. C., 2 *m*   710 W. D.
Little, J. P., Fr. *a*   149 L.
Livingston, E. P., Fr. *a*   237 York st.
Livingston, H. H., Jr. *a*   174 L.

Llewellyn, P. P., Jr. *s*   160 V-S.
Lobdell, G. G., Sr. *s*   111 Grove st.
Lockhart, C. E., Jr. *s*   122 Wall st.
Lockwood, A. C., Fr. *s*   Seymour
Lockwood, E. H., Ass't. Prof.
   (pp. 30, 235, 240, 264, 367)
      (110 WIN.)   79 Division st.
Loewenthal, A. M., Fr. *a*   579 P.
Loewenthal, I., Sr. *a*   443 FW.
Logan, H. H., Fr. *s*   152 Grove st.
Logan, S., Sr. *s*   108 V-S.
Logan, W. S., Jr., So. *a* 22 College st.
Logie, T. T., Jr. *s*   106 Bishop st.
Lohmann, A. C., *f*   Meriden
Lohmann, C. A., So. *a*   22 College st.
Lomax, N. J., Fr. *s*   128 Wall st.
Lombardi, C. E., Fr. *a*   250 York st.
Long, B. H., Fr. *a*   199 F.
Longley, W. H., Ass't.   (p. 43)
                               120 York st.
Longley, W. R., Instr.   (pp. 36, 227,
   233, 235-6, 238, 240, 252, 257, 365)
                          121 Brownell st.
Longsworth, W. H., *g*, Mid. *d*
                               687 W. D.
Loomis, A. L., Jr. *a*   430 FW.
Lopez de Victoria, C., Fr. *s*
                          122 Howe st.
Lord, L. E., *g*   35 Sherland av.
Lord, R., Fr. *s*   117 Wall st.
Loree, J. T., So. *a*   175 L.
Loudon, A., Sr. *s*   126 Wall st.
Lounsbury, J. T., Fr. *s*   Seymour
Lounsbury, T. R., Prof.   (p. 22)
                           22 Lincoln st.
Lovejoy, C. E., Fr. *s*   150 Grove st.
Lovejoy, H. S., *g*   Branford
Loveland, F. P., Jr. *a*   423 FW.
Lovell, G. B., Instr.   (pp. 36, 227, 255)
                          765 Whitney av.
Lovell, R. L., Jr. *for.*
                          145 Franklin st.
Low, A. A., Jr., Fr. *a*   231 York st.
Lowe, G. H., Jr., So. *a*   8 College st.
Lowe, J. L., Sr. *a*   362 Grand av.
Lowe, J. W., Jr., Jr. *s*   Woodmont
Lowe, T. K., Fr. *s*   114 High st.
Lowndes, T. G., *g*   A.
Luchars, R. B., Fr. *a*   248 York st.
Lull, R. S., Ass't. Prof. and Assoc.
   Curator (pp. 30, 176-7, 358, 441)
      (9 PEAB.)   327 Willow st.
Lunger, J. B., Lect. (p. 36)   Hartford

Luquiens, F. B., Ass't. Prof. (pp. 30, 255, 330) 595 Orange st.
Luther, C. F., Sr. *a* 355 WH.
Lyman, C. H., Sr. *s* 159 Elm st.
Lyman, D. R., Lect. (p. 36) Wallingford
Lyman, D. S., Sr. *s* 147 V-S.
Lyman, H. H., Jr. *s* 148 V-S.
Lyman, J. F., Ass't. (p. 43) 706 W. D.
Lynch, A. S., Sr. *s* 82 Wall st.
Lynch, J. F., Fr. *s* West Haven
Lynch, J. M., Fr. *a* 164 L.
Lynch, J. O., *mus.* 168 Mansfield st.
Lynch, W. J., Fr. *s* West Haven
Lynn, T., Jr. *s* 96 Wall st.
Lyon, M. B., Priv. Sec'y. (p. 47) (668 W. D.) 100 Howe st.
Lyon, S., Sr. *s* 70 Trumbull st.
Lyon, T. B., Sr. *a* 425 FW.
Lyon, W. H., Sr. *a* 35 V.
Lyons, B. E., Registrar (p. 47) (HEN.) 155 Elm st.
Lytle, E. B., *g* 120 York st.

Ma, T. C., Sr. *s* 333 York st.
Ma, Y. C., So. *a* 66 Whalley av.
Mabbatt, R. H., Jr., So. *a* 8 College st.
McAfee, E. S., *mus.* 94 York sq.
McAfee, W. A., Fr. *a* 573 P.
McAndrew, S., Fr. *a* 561 P.
MacArthur, E. C., So. *a* 167 L.
McArthur, S. W., Sr. *s* 110 Wall st.
Macartney, G. S., Jr. *a* 460 FW.
Macartney, R. R., So. *a* 22 College st.
McBride, D., *g* A.
McCabe, E. M., Instr. (pp. 36, 466) 22 Elm st.
McCahill, D. I., Grad. *l* 57 Grove st.
McCahill, S. S., Grad. *l* 405 Temple st.
McCall, S. C., So. *a* 98 W.
McCarn, B. B., Jr. *s* 391 Temple st.
McCarthy, A. P., Fr. *s* 124 Wall st.
McCarthy, J. C., Sr. *a* 71 C.
MacCarthy, J. J., So. *a* 93 C.
McClelland, J. S., Priv. Sec'y. (p. 47) (WOOD.) 70 Smith st., West Haven
McClung, L., Treasurer (p. 27) (WOOD.) 284 Orange st.

McConaughy, J. L., Jr. *a* 257 D.
MacConnell, B., Fr. *a* 238 York st.
McCord, H. D., So. *a* 254 Crown st.
McCord, R. B., Sr. *d* 624 E. D.
McCormick, D. J., Jr., Fr. *s* 91 C.
McCormick, N. W., So. *a* 260 Crown st.
McCoy, D. J., Spec. *l* 554 George st.
McCuen, H., Sr. *s* West Rock av.
McCulloch, C. R., So. *a* 247 D.
McCune, W. P., *g* 384 B.
MacCurdy, G. G., Lect. and Curator (pp. 36, 371) (10 PEAB.) 237 Church st.
MacDaniels, E. H., Jr. *for.*, Grad. *s* 716 W. D.
MacDonald, M. C., *mus.* Ansonia
MacDonald, S. R., Fr. *s* 122 Wall st.
McDonnell, H., Jr. *a* 457 FW.
McDonnell, J. V., Fr. *a* 238 York st.
McDonnell, R. A., Prof. (pp. 27, 465-6) 1142 Chapel st.
McDonough, E. M., Jr. *s* 38 Hallock st.
MacDuffie, I. J., Jr., Sr. *a* 65 V.
McEuen, D. C., Sr. *a* 28 V.
McFarland, R. L., So. *a* 122 Dwight st.
McGill, N. A., Sr. *s* 110 Wall st.
McGlynn, E. R., *2 l* 120 High st.
McGovern, F. P., *mus.* 109 View st.
McGrath, J. H., Sr. *m* 925 Howard av.
McGrath, T. F., *1 l* 925 Howard av.
McGraw, C. J., Sr. *a* 344 WH.
McGraw, J. T., So. *a* 254 Crown st.
McGregor, D. A., Sr. *a* 86 Howe st.
McGregor, E. F., Instr. (pp. 36, 439) 670 W. D.
McGregor, J. D., *2 l* 119 Wall st.
MacGregor, W., *mus.* 414 Crown st.
McGuire, W. C., Jr. *m* 909 Howard av.
Machette, J. H., Fr. *a* 214 Crown st.
McIntyre, O. E., Fr. *s* 130 Wall st.
Mackall, A. L., Fr. *a* 250 Crown st.
MacKay, J. D., *1 l* 107 York st.
MacKay, R. H., Spec. *l* 271 Crown st.
McKee, B. H., Jr. *a* 430 FW.
McKee, W., Jr. *a* 120 W.
McKee, W. G., Fr. *a* 599 P.
McKenna, W. J., *3 l* 166 Davenport av.

McKenzie, K., Ass't. Prof. (pp. 30, 154-5, 332)   67 Mansfield st.
Mackenzie, K. G., Ass't. (p. 44)   162 S. C. L.
Mackenzie, R. P., Sr. *a*   26 V.
Mackenzie, W. H., Sr. *a*   17 V.
McKiernan, C. P., So. *a*   385 B.
McKnight, E. J., Instr. (pp. 36, 465)   Hartford
McKnight, J. E., Fr. *a*   587 P.
McKone, W. F., Sr. *s*   57 V.
Mackrille, E. C., *mus.*   West Haven
MacLane, W., So. *a*   33 Howe st.
McLaury, D. B., So. *a*   251 Crown st.
McLean, F. T., Sr. *for.*   17 Compton st.
McManus, J. P., 1 *m*   97 Orchard st.
McMicken, W. E., Fr. *a*   200 York st.
MacMillan, H. R., Sr. *for.*   74 Lake pl.
McMillen, D. A., Jr. *s*   104 Wall st.
McMurray, F. W., 1 *l*   416 Crown st.
McNally, F. L., Fr. *s*   88 Wall st.
McNulty, R. P., 3 *l*   137 W.
McQuistion, R. H., 2 *l*   143 L.
McRee, J. F., Fr. *a*   254 Crown st.
McWilliams, A. P., Jr. *a*   136 W.
Macy, P. G., Fr. *a*   159 Elm st.
Madden, J. W., *g*   88 Wall st.
Maddox, J. L., *g*, Sr. *d*   675 W. D.
Maddox, R. S., Jr. *for.*, Grad. *s*   664 W. D.
Madsen, A. A., Instr. (pp. 36, 429)   Durham
Magee, J. G., Univ. Gen. Sec'y. Y. U. C. A. (p. 47)   2 DW.
Mahoney, W. E., Sr. *s*   85 Sachem st.
Mailhouse, G. L., *f*   45 Elm st.
Mailhouse, M., Prof. (pp. 24, 465-6)   45 Elm st.
Malcolm, J. L., 1 *l*   132 Wall st.
Malkan, S. H., 1 *l*   380 Oak pl.
Malley, W. W., Jr. *s*   389 Temple st.
Mallory, J. H., So. *a*   261 D.
Mallory, P. R., Sr. *a*   10 V.
Mallory, R., Jr., Jr. *a*   262 D.
Malmberg, C. F., *g*   293 York st.
Malone, W. B., Jr. *s*   149 V-S.
Malony, H. J., Fr. *a*   121 York st.
Malony, J. C., 2. *m*   121 York st.
Malstedt, G. H., 1 *l*   333 York st.
Maltby, A. L., Assistant Registrar of Law School (p. 47) (HEN.) 187 F.

Mandell, M. S., Instr. (pp. 36, 159, 334)   101 Orange st.
Mangini, H. E., 2 *l*   105 Park st.
Manice, W. D., Fr. *a*   242 York st.
Mann, A. N., Sr. *a*   44 V.
Mann, J. J., So. *a*   22 College st.
Mann, R. L., Jr. *s*   124 V-S.
Mannel, G. W., Fr. *a*   192 F.
Manning, E. W., Jr. *s*   32 Stevens st.
Manning, F. R., Spec. *l*   287 York st.
Manning, M. M., Jr. *s*   128 High st.
Manross, R. N., Sr. *s*   118 V-S.
Mapa, E., Grad. *l*   14 Whalley av.
Margulies, I. E., Jr. *a*   421 B.
Markoe, F. H., Jr. *g*   A.
Marks, A. D., Fr. *a*   237 York st.
Marks, H. J., 1 *l*   333 York st.
Marks, S. S., Jr. *a*   122 W.
Marsh, A. D., Sr. *m*   1015 Whalley av.
Marsh, A. F., Fr. *s*   393 Temple st.
Marsh, F. G., Sr. *a*   344 WH.
Marsh, H. E., Fr. *s*   Branford
Marsh, H. P., *g*   89 Whalley av.
Marshall, I. W., Fr. *a* 1169 Chapel st.
Marshall, T. L., So. *a*   160 L.
Marshall, T. M., 3d, Sr. *a*   34 V.
Marshall, T. R., *g*   144 Dwight st.
Marshall, W. C., Ass't. Prof. (pp. 30, 168, 231, 233, 235-6, 240, 252, 264) (114 WIN.) 201 Edwards st.
Martin, B., Fr. *s*   123 V-S.
Martin, C. J., 3 *l*   109 York st.
Martin, H. S., Mid. *d*   603 E. D.
Martin, M., Spec. *l*   155 Elm st.
Martin, N. A., *g*   684 W. D.
Martin, S., Fr. *s*   113 Wall st.
Martin, W. C., 2 *l*   1151 Chapel st.
Marvin, A., Registrar (p. 30) (1 S. H.) 40 Lake pl.
Maryott, C. H., Instr. (pp. 37, 464)   U. C.
Mason, F. O., Jr. *a*   135 W.
Mason, F. R., Fr. *a* 34 Hillhouse av.
Mason, J. W., 2 *l*   119 Wall st.
Mason, L., Instr. (pp. 37, 162, 233, 235-6, 238, 240, 252, 257, 364)   245 York st.
Mason, M., Ass't. Prof. (pp. 30, 227)   87 Cottage st.
Mason, O. A., Fr. *a*   200 York st.
Mather, S. L., *g*   A.
Mather, T. W., Fr. *s*   225 Bishop st.

Matheson, H. M., Fr. *s*
     124 Prospect st.
Mathewson, C. H., Instr. (pp. 37,
 227, 229, 231, 259, 358)
   (H. M. L.) 666 Chapel st.
Mathias, P. E., Sr. *d* 620 E. D.
Matthews, G., Fr. *a* 22 College st.
Matthews, G., Jr., Fr. *s*
     3 Hillhouse av.
Mattison, L. B., 1 *l* 135 Wall st.
Maurer, W. I., Mid. *d* 631 E. D.
Mautte, J., Engineer (p. 47)
   32 Dudley st., Highwood
Maxwell, C. E., Jr., Fr. *s*
     152 Grove st.
May, A. A., *g* 17 Whalley av.
Mayer, M. M., Priv. Sec'y. (p. 48)
   (3 S. H.) 475 Elm st.
Maynard, W. A., Ass't. (p. 48)
   (25 LAM.) 68 Gilbert av.
Mazier, T. A., Jr. *s* 333 York st.
Mead, B. H., 3 *l* 193 F.
Mead, G. G., 1 *l* 222 F.
Mead, S. P., Fr. *a* 193 F.
Mead, W. H., Jr. *s* 51 Trumbull st.
Means, T., So. *a* 356 Humphrey st.
Mears, N., Fr. *a* 200 York st.
Meixell, H., Jr., Jr. *a* 454 FW.
Melcher, S. F., Sr. *a* 82 C.
Mendel, L. B., Prof. (pp. 27, 244,
 259, 271, 346, 351) (63 S. B. L.)
     18 Trumbull st.
Mendell, C. W., Instr. (pp. 37, 143)
     86 C.
Menderson, E., So. *a* 254 Crown st.
Meriam, A. Y., Fr. *s* 117 Wall st.
Merlis, F. A., Jr. *s* 132 Hill st.
Meroney, R. M., Jr. *a* 28 Gill st.
Merrell, A. S., Fr. *s* 140 V-S.
Merriam, E. J., *f* 522 George st.
Merriam, E. P., Sup't. (p. 48)
     108 College st.
Merrick, C., Jr. *a* 181 L.
Merrill, A. C., Sr. *a* 360 WH.
Merrill, P., Fellow
  31 Nassau st., New York City
Merriman, B. P., So. *a*
     22 College st.
Merritt, A. K., Registrar (p. 30)
   (LAM.) 38 V.
Merritt, A. R., Jr. *s* 17 Hillhouse av.
Merritt, H. R., Jr. *s* 120 V-S.
Merritt, K. N., Fr. *s* 88 Wall st.

Merritt, M. G., Resident Nurse
 (p. 48) 276 Prospect st.
Merrow, P. G., So. *a* 236 D.
Merwin, J. C., Fr. *s* 25 Tryon st.
Merwin, R. I., Jr. *s* 68 Clark st.
Merwin, S. C., Sr. *s* 70 Trumbull st.
Mesereau, E., Fr. *a* 248 York st.
Message, J. S., 1 *m* 1081 Chapel st.
Messenger, H. T., Jr. *a* 94 W.
Messerly, C. E., Jr., Sr. *a* 66 V.
Metcalf, J. T., So. *a* 119 College st.
Metzger, H., *g* 23 Grove st.
Metzger, H. S., *mus.* 92 Avon st.
Meyer, C. F., Jr. *for.*
Meyer, J. E., Fr. *s* 117 Wall st.
Middlemass, W. F., Sr. *s* 153 V-S.
Milbank, J., 2d, Jr. *a* 391 B.
Milbury, G. D., *g*, Grad. *d* 627 E. D.
Miles, M. C., *mus.* Milford
Miles, R. K., Fr. *s* 105 College st.
Milholland, R. J., Fr. *a* 383 Crown st.
Milkowski, V., Fr. *s* 33 Rose st.
Millan, E. N., Sr. *s* 17 Hillhouse av.
Millar, W. N., Sr. *for.*
     74 Whalley av.
Miller, B., So. *a* 225 F.
Miller, D., Sr. *a* 63 V.
Miller, E. C., Ass't. (p. 43)
     7 Library st.
Miller, J. M., *g* Washington, D. C.
Miller, J. W., *g* A.
Miller, L. V., Sr. *a* 49 V.
Miller, P. L., 3 *l* 631 E. D.
Miller, R. A., Jr., Fr. *a* 248 York st.
Miller, R. B., Sr. *for.*
    103 Winchester av.
Miller, T. W., Sr. *s* 111 Grove st.
Miller, William C., Fr. *a* 585 P.
Miller, Winfield C., Sr. *s* 82 Wall st.
Miller, W. C., Fr. *a* 585 P.
Milliken, J. T., Sr. *a* 267 D.
Mills, C. F., Jr. *s* 133 College st.
Mills, C. G., Fr. *s* 133 V-S.
Mills, W. H., Fr. *a* 237 York st.
Mills, W. W., Fr. *s* 119 Wall st.
Mims, S. L., Instr. (pp. 37, 246, 279)
     701 W. D.
Minassian, M., *g* 754 Yale P. O.
Miner, W. H., *mus.* Naugatuck
Minnigerode, M., So. *a*
     260 Crown st.
Minsk, L. D., So. *a* 1193 Chapel st.
Mitchell, A. W., Fr. *s* 53 Lake pl.

Mitchell, C. F., 3 *l* 191 DeWitt st.
Mitchell, C. G., Jr. *a* 263 D.
Mitchell, I. S., *g* 152 Whalley av.
Mitchell, J. P., Fr. *s* 132 Wall st.
Mitchell, L. B., Fr. *s* 128 High st.
Mitchell, M. L., Sr. *a* 426 FW.
Mitchell, S. K., Instr. (pp. 37, 186)
  152 Whalley av.
Mitcheltree, R., Fr. *a* 7 Library st.
Mitke, A. C., Sr. *a* 27 V.
Mitten, A. A., 1 *m* 475 Whitney av.
Mix, C. W., *mus.* Bridgeport
Mixter, W. G., Prof. (pp. 23, 227, 259, 345) (160 S. C. L.)
  250 Edwards st.
Moakley, H. J., Sr. *s* 171 Franklin st.
Moberg, A. E. T., Jr. *for.*, Grad. *s*
  919 Howard av.
Moch, E. J., Jr. *a* 110 W.
Moeller, C., *mus.* 349 Crown st.
Mohlman, A. J., Sr. *a* 35 V.
Molloy, T. J., 3 *l* 29 Court st.
Monahan, C. J., *g* 686 W. D.
Monrad, A. M., Cataloguer (p. 48)
  146 Norton st.
Moon, C. B., Sr. *s* 111 Grove st.
Moon, F. F., Jr. *for.* Grad. *s* 664 W. D.
Moore, B., Sr. *for.* 182 Mansfield st.
Moore, C. E., 3 *l* 94 Crown st.
Moore, E. D., Sr. *s* 175 Hallock av.
Moore, H. Z., *f* 218 Orchard st.
Moore, J. W., Sr. *a* 71 C.
Moore, L. L., Jr. *s* 168 V-S.
Moore, P., Sr. *a* 5 V.
Moore, R. R., Jr. *s* 665 W. D.
Moore, S. F., Fr. *s* 40 Lake pl.
Moorhead, J. U., Sr. *s* 133 College st.
Moran, H. A., 3 *l* 29 Court st.
Morden, W. J., Sr. *s* 181 V-S.
Morehouse, I. L., 2 *l* Stratford
Morehouse, V. S., Jr. *s* Stratford
Morgan, M. A., Fr. *a* 592 P.
Morrell, F. A., Jr., Jr. *a* 389 B.
Morrill, E. T., Fr. *a* 242 York st.
Morrill, S., 1 *l* 3 Hillhouse av.
Morris, E. B., Jr., Fr. *a* 242 York st.
Morris, E. P., Prof. (pp. 24, 143, 144, 146, 316-18) (194 F.)
  53 Edgehill rd.
Morris, R. C., Lect. (pp. 37, 507)
  767 Fifth av., New York City
Morrison, L. S., Fr. *a* 200 York st.
Morse, E. A., So. *a* 22 College st.

Morse, E. K., Jr. *a* 372 WH.
Morse, J. K., Sr. *s* 184 V-S.
Morse, O. C., Jr., So. *a* 170 L.
Morse, W. R., Fr. *s* 126 Wall st.
Morsell, S. R., Jr. *d* 106 Goffe st.
Mosely, G. H., Sr. *s* 126 V-S.
Moses, R., Jr. *a* 246 D.
Mosser, K., Fr. *a* 237 York st.
Mott, T. C., Jr. *s* 106 V-S.
Moxley, J. E., Machinist (p. 48)
  411 Blohm st., West Haven
Mullins, A. P., Jr. *a* 456 FW.
Mungall, D., Jr., So. *a* 221 F.
Munger, T. T., Sr. *for.*
  202 Prospect st.
Munro, J A., Supt. (p. 48)
  (88 High st.) 88 Lake pl.
Munson, C. L., Lect. (pp. 37, 506)
  Williamsport, Pa.
Munson, R. B., Jr. *s* Stratford
Murchey, K. E., Jr. *a* 259 D.
Murchie, W. E., Sr. *for.*
  124 Prospect st.
Murfey, S. L., Fr. *s* 119 Grove st.
Murolo, L., 1 *l* 64 Mill st.
Murphy, F. J., So. *a* 164 L.
Murphy, F. T., Sr. *a* 62 V.
Murphy, J. L., 2 *l* 150 L.
Murphy, J. W., Sr. *a* 36 V.
Murray, A., Jr., So. *a* 169 L.
Murray, F. W., Jr., Jr. *a* 102 W.
Murray, J. B., Fr. *s* 393 Temple st.
Murray, J. H., Head Gardener (p. 48) 227 Mansfield st.
Murray, O., Fr. *s* 407 Temple st.
Musgrave, W. M., Grad. *l*
  152 Temple st.
Mussaeus, M. G., *g* 90 Whalley av.
Myers, D. H., So. *a* 236 Crown st.
Myers, G. H., Lect. (pp. 37, 354, 418)
  Washington, D. C.
Myers, G. W., 1 *l* 333 York st.
Myers, L. M., Jr. *a* 224 F.
Myers, L. R., Fr. *a* 224 F.
Myers, R. E., So. *a* 707 W. D.
Myers, V. C., *g* 707 W. D.

Nabstedt, A. T., So. *a* 214 Crown st.
Naedele, T. C., Fr. *s* 132 Howe st.
Naething, F. S., Ass't. (p. 43)
  124 Prospect st.
Nairn, G., Sr. *a* 39 V.
Naman, W. W., Sr. *a*, Spec. *l* 442 FW.

Narganes, A., 3 *l*   271 Crown st.
Nason, L. B., Accountant (p. 49)
          84 Park st.
Neal, F. G., Sr. *s*   190 v-s.
Neal, H. C., Sr. *a*   406 B.
Needham, R. E., Sr. *s*   174 v-s.
Neeser, R. W., *g*   Paris
Neff, S. B., Jr. *a*   100 Howe st.
Negley, R. V., Jr. *s* 17 Hillhouse av.
Nelson, B., 1 *l*   86 Howe st.
Nelson, F. T., So. *a*   22 College st.
Nelson, P. A., Spec. *d*
          61 Winchester av.
Nettleton, F. H., Sr. *a*
          158 Blatchley av.
Nettleton, G. H., Ass't. Prof.
  (pp. 31, 227, 246, 254, 338)
          339 Prospect st.
Nettleton, G. R., Fr. *a*   Milford
Neumann, J. E., *mus.* 103 Alden av.
Nevin, C. C., Sr. *m*   373 Crown st.
Newberry, J. S., *g*   A.
Newbury, H. A., Jr. *s*   47 Lake pl.
Newcomb, W. W., Jr., Sr. *s*
          110 Wall st.
Newell, C. R., Fr. *s*   Orange
Newell, E. T., Curator Numismatics
  (p. 48) (LIB.)   Kenosha, Wisc.
Newell, F. H., Lect. (pp. 37, 353, 415)
          Washington, D. C.
Newkom, P. C., Fr. *s*   135 Wall st.
Newman, S. J., Fr. *a*   41 Park st.
Newsom, W. M., Fr. *s*   125 v-s.
Newton, H. D., Ass't. (p. 43)
          117 Wall st.
Newton, H. P., Sr *s*   171 v-s.
Nicander, A. H., Jr. *s*
          49 Winthrop av.
ichols, G. E., Ass't. and Proctor
  (pp. 43, 412)   569 P.
ïchols, J. B., Sr. *s*   131 Grove st.
ichols, R. W., Sr. *s*   59 Dwight st.
icholson. P. C., Fr. *a*   250 York st.
icholson, R. A., 1 *l*   148 York st.
icholson, W., Instr. (pp. 37, 227, 254, 338)   329 Whalley av.
ie, S., Fr. *s*   37 Lynwood pl.
iemeyer, J. H., Prof. (pp. 22, 198, 227, 340) (8 A. S.)
          251 Lawrence st.
ill, M. W., Jr. *s*   391 Temple st.
imick, A., Jr. *s*   150 v-s.
oble, G. O., *f*   9 Library st.

Noble, H. D., Jr., Sr. *a*   61 v.
Noble, L. F., *g*   90 Wall st.
Noel, E. T., 1 *l*   119 Wall st.
Noel, J. H., 1 *l*   119 Wall st.
Noel, O. F., 1 *l*   119 Wall st.
Norcom, W. P., Fr. *a*   175 Goffe st.
Norris, F. E., Sr. *a*   21 v.
Norris, W. A., Fr. *s*
          215 Townsend av.
North, H. B., Instr. (pp. 37, 227, 235, 252, 264, 416)   250 Whalley av.
North, O. B., Sr. *a*   54 v.
Northcott, J. A., *g*   Cheshire
Norton, J. P., Ass't. Prof. (pp. 31, 194, 196, 374)   551 Orange st.
Norton, L. H., So. *a*   18 College st.
Notestein, W., *g*   1157 Chapel st.
Nothnagle, L. A., Sr. *s*   293 York st.
Notkins, L. A., Ass't. (p. 43)
          704 Howard av.
Notz, C. E., Cataloguer (p. 48)
          (LIB.) 221 Orchard st.
Noyes, C. R., *g*   A.
Noyes, D. R., *g*   A.
Noyes, G. M., So. *a*   8 College st.
Noyes, H., Sr. *a*   346 WH.
Noyes, I. H., Sr. *m*   371 Crown st.
Noyes, R. H., Sr. *a*   6 v.
Nuckle, J. A., *f*   1190 Whalley av.

Oberhelman, G. O., So. *a*   229 F.
Obernauer, H., So. *a*   249 Crown st.
O'Brien, D. T., 2 *l*   925 Howard av.
O'Brien, E. M., Jr. *a*   408 B.
O'Brien, H. V., So. *a*   214 Crown st.
O'Brien, J. F., 1 *m*   Meriden
O'Brien, J. T., Sr. *m*
          1081 Chapel st.
O'Brien, J. V., 1 *l*   783 Orange st.
O'Brien, M. J. G., Fr. *a*   242 York st.
O'Brien, T. A., Ass't. (p. 43)
          230 Oak st.
O'Brien, W. H. J., Sr. *s*   438 Oak pl.
O'Connell, B. M., 1 *l*   Wallingford
O'Connell, T. F., 1 *l*   319 Wallace st.
O'Connell, W. C., Spec. *l*
          53 Asylum st.
O'Connor, C., 2 *l*   9 Library st.
O'Connor, K. A., *mus.*   Middletown
O'Donohue, W. T., So. *a*   Hartford
Oertel, H., Prof. (pp. 26, 146, 150, 313, 315, 321) (2 PH.)
          New Haven House

O'Ferrall, K. B., Fr. *a*
236 Crown st.
O'Hara, C. J., Jr., 3 *l* 287 York st.
Ohlson, A., Jr. *d* 645 E. D.
Okamoto, K., *g* 128 High st.
O'Keefe, A. B., 3 *l* 147 Clay st.
Olcott, C. M., Jr. *a* 369 WH.
Olcott, N., 2d, 1 *l* 397 Temple st.
Olds, I. S., *g* A.
Oliver, H. T., Sr. *s* 126 High st.
Olmsted, F. H., So. *a* 241 D.
O'Neal, E., Sr. *a* 335 WH.
O'Neill, T. F., Sr. *s*
251 Washington av.
Orcutt, W. L., 1 *m* 925 Howard av.
Ordway, P. S., Sr. *a* 28 V.
Ordway, S. G., Sr. *a* 16 V.
Ortmayer, C. G., Fr. *s*
407 Temple st.
Osborn, E., Fr. *s* 5 B. M. H.
Osborn, E. C., Jr. *s*
167 Ellsworth av.
Osborn, H. M., Bursar (p. 48)
(25 LAM.) 406 Orange st.
Osborne, A. D., 2d, Sr. *a* 55 V.
Osborne, O. T., Prof. (pp. 25, 464-5)
252 York st.
Osborne, R. W., Ass't. (p. 43)
(K. C. L.) 846 Yale P. O.
Osborne, W. B., Jr., Jr. *for.*, Grad. *s*
17 Compton st.
Ostrander, H. J., Clerk (p. 48)
(WOOD.) 328 Humphrey st.
O'Sullivan, P. B., Sr. *a* 60 V.
Otis, H. N., Jr. *a* 393 B.
Overall, S. R., Sr. *a* 37 V.

Pachanian, S. K., Sr. *m* 11 Lake pl.
Page, Allen S., Sr. *s* 166 V-S.
Page, Arthur S., 2 *l* 833 Yale P. O.
Page, F. L. G., Sr. *s* 189 V-S.
Page, F. S., Fr. *s* 133 College st.
Page, G. W., *g* 1157 Chapel st.
Page, R., Fr. *s* 427 Temple st.
Pagter, L. B., Jr. *a* 50 Admiral st.
Paige, H. R., Sr. *s* 131 Grove st.
Paige, S., *g*
Paine, F. W., So. *a* 236 Crown st.
Palmer, A. H., Prof. (pp. 25, 157-9, 333-4) 149 East Rock rd.
Palmer, C. R., Fellow
562 Whitney av.
Palmer, E., Fr. *s* 117 Wall st.

Palmer, H. E., *g* Branford
Palmer, J. J., 1 *l* 35 Redfield st.
Palmer, W. A., Ass't. (p. 43) (G.)
333 York st.
Pangburn, C. H., 1 *l* 731 Elm st.
Pangburn, D. B., Fr. *s* 731 Elm st.
Pardee, R. M., Fr. *a* 231 F.
Parish, R. R., Jr. *s* 177 Norton st.
Parker, A. D., Jr. *a* 260 D.
Parker, A. G., Jr., Fr. *s*
652 Dixwell av.
Parker, E. P., Fellow Hartford
Parker, H. W., Prof. and Dean
(pp. 26, 198-9, 341, 396-7)
(126 College st.) 420 Temple st.
Parker, J., 3d, Fr. *s* 1317 Boulevard
Parker, M. O., Fr. *a* 238 York st.
Parker, R., Jr. *for.* 26 Tilton st.
Parker, W., Jr., Sr. *s* 166 V-S.
Parker, W. N., *g* A.
Parkinson, E. W. B., Fr. *a* 216 F.
Parks, L. B., Jr. *a* 373 WH.
Parlato, M. A., Sr. *m* Derb
Parry, M. O., Jr. *a* 242 D.
Parsons, E. B., *g* 1076 Chapel st.
Parsons, G. F., Jr., So. *a*
22 College st.
Parsons, Jessie A., Cataloguer
(p. 48) (LIB.) 917 Howard av.
Parsons, Judson A., Jr. *a* 256 D.
Parsons, L. A., Sr. *s* 110 Wall st.
Parsons, W. H., Jr., So. *a*
22 College st.
Partridge, D., 3 *l* 36 Elm s
Paterno, F. P., Fr. *s* 114 High s
Pattee, W. S., 1 *l* 371 Crown s
Patterson, A., Spec. *l* 120 High st
Patterson, G. S., Fr. *s*
379 Temple st
Patterson, P., Fr. *a* 599 P
Patterson, R. A., Fr. *a* 597 P
Patterson, V. M., Spec. *d* 721 W. D.
Patton, F. M., Sr. *for.*, Spec. *s*
129 Mansfield s
Patton, J. W., Fr. *s* 82 Wall s
Paul, W. L., Jr. *s* 59 Wall s
Paxton, P. J., Grad. *s*, Jr. *for.*
159 Elm s
Payne, H., Jr. *a* 235 I
Peabody, S., Fr. *a* 242 York s
Pearson, W. E., So. *a* 461 FW
Pease, C. B. F., Grad. *d* 622 E. I
Pease, F. A., Fr. *a* 250 York s

eck, C. J., Sr. *s*	133 College st.	
eck, E., Instr. (pp. 37, 195, 498, 500, 503, 505)	Bristol	
'eck, F. F., Fr. *s*	Box 44, West Haven	
eck, H. T., Jr. *s*	391 Temple st.	
eck, J. A., Sr. *s*	538 Elm st.	
eck, P. F. W., Sr. *s*	133 College st.	
eck, T., Prof. (pp. 22, 143-5, 316-18)	124 High st.	
eieff, N. E., *g*	122 Dwight st.	
eirce, C. A., Jr. *a*	463 FW.	
eirce, E. S., Jr. *s*	96 Wall st.	
eirce, G. A., Sr. *a*	429 FW.	
eirce, R. C. M., Jr. *a*	103 W.	
enoyar, J. L., So. *a*		
erkins, C. C., *g*	118 Howe st.	
erkins, P. B., *g*	102 DeWitt st.	
erkins, S. B., Fr. *s*	656 W. D.	
errin, B., Prof. (pp. 23, 146, 148, 187, 315, 376) (191 F.)	463 Whitney av.	
errin, H. B., *g*	A.	
errin, J. B., Jr. *a*	261 D.	
errin, J. V., Sr. *s*	159 Elm st.	
errin, L. W., Sr. *a*	11 V.	
erry, C. C., Ass't. (p. 43)	121 Maple st.	
'erry, F. L., Grad. *l*	68 Dwight st.	
erry, J. H., Lect. (pp. 37, 507, 517)	Southport	
erry, S. H., Fr. *s*	148 V-S.	
erry, W. H., *g*	111 Dwight st.	
eter, J. C., So. *a*	254 Crown st.	
eters, J. P., Jr., Sr. *a*	3 V.	
eters, N. F., Jr. *a*	454 FW.	
eters, W. R., Jr., Sr. *a*	44 V.	
eterson, A. P., Jr. *s*	Ansonia	
eterson, W., *g*	58 Dixwell av.	
etrucelli, L. M., 3 *l*	Bridgeport	
ettee, A. D., Fr. *a*	188 F.	
ettit, G. E., Fr. *a*	126 High st.	
eyton, J. N., Sr. *s*	96 Wall st.	
harr, C., *g*	98 York sq.	
helan, S. M., Jr., Jr. *a*	129 W.	
helps, C. D., Instr. (pp. 37, 465)	642 Campbell av., West Haven	
helps, H. B., Cataloguer (p. 48) (LIB.)	67 Dwight st.	
helps, H. E., Sr. *s*	574 George st.	
helps, I. K., Instr. (pp. 37, 172-3, 347-8) (K. C. L.)	84 Wall st.	
helps, R., So. *a*	11 College st.	
Phelps, W. L., Prof. (pp. 26, 163-6, 337) (A, c.)	44 High st.	
Philbin, E. R., Fr. *a*	238 York st.	
Philbin, S. H., So. *a*	8 College st.	
Philbrick, M. P., *g*	Hartford	
Phillips, A. W., Prof. and Dean (pp. 23, 67, 168) (90 High st.)	137 Wall st.	
Phillips, C. A., Sr. *a*	276 Elm st.	
Phillips, D. C., Jr., Sr. *a*	349 WH.	
Phillips, J. L., Sr. *a*	349 WH.	
Phillips, L. J., Fr. *s*	53 Prospect st.	
Phipps, H. F., Fr. *a*	575 P.	
Phipps, L. W., Fr. *a*	575 P.	
Pickett, W. M., 3 *l*	23 Lynwood pl.	
Pickhardt, O. C., Sr. *a*, 1 *m*	429 FW.	
Pickslay, F. F., Fr. *s*	70 Trumbull st.	
Pierce, B. A., *mus.*	South Britain	
Pierce, F. E., Instr. (pp. 37, 161, 227, 246, 254)	622 Washington av., West Haven	
Pierce, F. W., *g*	373 Crown st.	
Pierce, J. N., Grad. *d*	139 Greene st.	
Pierce, N. P., Jr. *s*	119 Grove st.	
Pierce, R. H., So. *a*	172 L.	
Pierpont, James, Prof. (pp. 26, 169, 362-3)	42 Mansfield st.	
Pierpont, Joseph, Fr. *s*	North Haven	
Pierpont, L. C., *mus.*	42 Mansfield st.	
Pierson, A. A., 3 *l*	293 York st.	
Pierson, P. H., Sr. *a*	97 W.	
Piggott, J. T., Jr., Sr. *a*	24 V.	
Pigott, M. C., Sr. *s*	124 Prospect st.	
Pigott, W. T., Jr., Fr. *a*	231 York st.	
Pike, R., Sr. *s*	775 Yale P. O.	
Pinchot, G., Prof. (pp. 27, 250, 281, 354, 418)	Washington, D. C.	
Pirsson, L. V., Prof. (pp. 25, 229, 231, 233, 238, 240, 241, 243-4, 250, 252, 276, 355-6) (186 K.)	41 Trumbull st.	
Pitman, F. W., *g*	646 George st.	
Platt, C. H., 2 *l*	452 FW.	
Platt, J. C., So. *a*	22 College st.	
Platt, T. B., Sr. *s*	96 Wall st.	
Plumb, H. K., So. *a*	142 L.	
Pogue, J. E., Jr., *g*	1305 Chapel st.	
Pohlman, J. H., 3 *l*	422 B.	
Pomeroy, G. S., Jr., So. *a*	251 Crown st.	
Pomeroy, T., Jr. *a*	263 D.	

Pond, D. W., Jr. *s*   124 Wall st.
Pond, H. S., Sr. *a*   1233 Chapel st.
Pond, R. A., Jr. *s*   124 Wall st.
Pond, W. G., 2 *l*   Branford
Poole, J., Jr. *s*   126 Columbus av.
Poore, J. G., So. *a*   61 Wolcott st.
Poriss, S. C., Sr. *s*   715 W. D.
Porter, C. V., 1 *l*   137 Dwight st.
Porter, D. W., Sr. *a*   59 V.
Porter, E. H., Sr. *a*   266 D.
Porter, F. C., Prof. (pp. 25, 325, 433)
   (611 E. D.) 266 Bradley st.
Porter, Gardner C., Fr. *a*
   200 York st.
Porter, Graham C., Sr. *a*   67 V.
Porter, M., Jr. *a*   459 FW.
Porter, W. C., 1 *l*   703 W. D.
Porter, W. S., *mus.*   116 Howe st.
Post, L. T., Jr. *a*   123 W.
Potter, A. S., *mus.*   Torrington
Potter, O. B., Fr. *s*   113 Wall st.
Powell, T. B., Mid. *d*   630 E. D.
Powelson, J. R., 2 *l*   119 Wall st.
Powers, M. K., So. *a*   214 Crown st.
Pratt, W. C., So. *a*   444 FW.
Prentice, B. H., *g*   A.
Prentice, D. B., Fr. *s*   117 Wall st.
Prentice, E. S., Sr. *s*   78 Trumbull st.
Prentice, S. O., Prof. (pp. 24, 497, 500)   Hartford
Preston, J. H., Fr. *s*   421 Temple st.
Preston, P. R., Jr. *s*   17 Hillhouse av.
Price, A. L., Fr. *a*   248 York st.
Price, C. B., So. *a*   8 College st.
Price, O. W., Lect. (pp. 37, 416)
   Washington, D. C.
Prichard, R. P., Grad. *s*, Jr. *for.*
   719 W. D.
Prime, W. A., Jr., Fr. *a*   248 York st.
Prince, A. L., 2 *m*   280 Elm st.
Pritchard, H. T., Sr. *s* 796 Yale P. O.
Proctor, E. O., Jr. *a*   257 D.
Proctor, G. D., Fr. *a*   266 York st.
Prosser, T. H., Fr. *s*   133 College st.
Prosser, W. E., Jr. *s*   104 Wall st.
Prout, C., Sr. *s*   131 Grove st.
Prouty, E. C., Spec. *s* 70 Trumbull st.
Prutting, R. H., *mus.*   Hartford
Pugsley, E., Sr. *a*   334 WH.
Punderson, L. E., 1 *m*   381 Crown st.
Putnam, G. E., *g*   176 Meadow st.

Quentin, C., Priv. Sec'y. (p. 48)
   (126 College st.) Whitneyville

Quentin, G. W., Sr. *s*   973 Yale P. O
Quinlan, E. J., 2 *l*   542 George st.
Quinn, M. J., 1 *l*   163 DeWitt st.
Quint, K. M., *g*   90 Whalley av.
Quittner, J., 3 *l*   333 York st.

Rabold, C., Instr. (pp. 38, 199, 341, 399)
   141 E. 16th st., New York City
Rae, W. L., Sr. *a*   333 WH.
Rafferty, M. L., Fr. *s*   120 High st.
Ragan, J. J., 2 *l*   1076 Chapel st.
Rainier, J. A., Fr. *s*   150 Grove st.
Ralston, W. J., Jr. *s*   379 Temple st.
Ramsay, H. H., Jr. *s*   133 College st.
Ramsay, O. G., Prof. (pp. 27, 465-6)
   251 Church st.
Ramsey, John P., Jr. *s*
   133 College st.
Rand, E. H., Fr. *a*   238 York st.
Rand, R. F., Ass't. (p. 43)
   246 Church st.
Rand, S. C., Jr. *a*   124 W.
Randell, G. M., Fr. *a*   22 College st.
Randle, J. S., Jr. *s*   39 Lynwood pl.
Randolph, F. F., Fr. *a*   231 York st.
Rankin, L. A., So. *a*   22 College st.
Raphael, S. S., *f*   757 State st.
Rathbun, H. B., Fr. *s*
   148 Whalley av.
Rather, E. Z., *g*   133 Howe st.
Raymond, C. D., Jr. *s*   82 Wall st.
Raymond, C. H., 2d, Jr. *a*   243 D.
Raymond, D. E., Fr. *a*   254 York st.
Raymond, F. T., Jr. *a*   432 FW.
Raymond, H. A., *g*   A.
Raynolds, E. V., Prof. (pp. 25, 374, 515-16)   168 Prospect st.
Raynolds, R., So. *a*   139 W.
Rayworth, J. C., Instr. (pp. 38, 167)
   120 York st.
Rea, J. D., Instr. (pp. 38, 143)
   351 Crown st.
Read, H. L., Jr. *a*   248 D.
Read, W. H., So. *a*   248 D.
Reckert, F. C., Fr. *a*   533 P.
Rector, T. M., Grad. *l*
   141 Dwight st.
Redfield, P. W., Jr. *a*   448 FW.
Reed, C. L., Fr. *a*   242 York st.
Reed, E. B., Ass't. Prof. (pp. 31, 162-5, 338) (B, C.) 215 Bishop st.
Reed, H., Fr. *s*   150 Grove st.
Reed, J. C., Fr. *s*   6 B. M. II.

Reeder, H. W., Fr. *s*	379 Temple st.	Rickcords, F. S., *g*	A.
Reeds, C. A., *g*	204 F.	Ricks, D. M., Fr. *s*	132 Wall st.
Rees, G. H., Sr. *a*	433 FW.	Riddle, T. P., So. *a*	18 College st.
Reid, H. B., So. *a*	163 L.	Riggs, E. F., Jr., Jr. *a*	99 W.
Reid, T. P., Fr. *a*	Shelton	Riggs, H. W., Sr. *a*	57 V.
Reigeluth, R. J., *g*, Sr. *a*	29 V.	Riggs, T. L., So. *a*	8 College st.
Reilly, B. E., I *l*	266 York st.	Riley, H. A., Sr., *a*, I *m*	371 WH.
Reilly, D. M., 3 *l*	13 Winthrop av.	Riley, R. A., Jr. *s*	149 V-S.
Reilly, J. C., Jr., Fr. *s*	333 York st.	*Ripley, A. L., Fellow*	
Reimann, J., Jr. *s*		State Nat. Bank, Boston, Mass.'	
	113 Lawrence st.	Risdon, C. A., Fr. *s*	126 High st.
Reisner, E. H., Sr. *a*	267 D.	Rittenour, G. W., Jr. *s*	161 V-S.
Reisner, J. H., Fr. *a*	7 Library st.	Ritter, H. W., 3 *l*	266 York st.
Rend, F. A., Jr. *s*	88 Wall st.	Rives, F. B., Fr. *a*	238 York st.
Renton, G. F., Jr., Jr. *s*	112 V-S.	Robbins, D. R., Jr. *s*	133 College st.
Rettger, L. F., Ass't. Prof. (pp. 31, 227, 233, 238, 241, 244, 246, 271, 352) (12 S. H.)	370 Edgewood av.	*Robbins, F. O., Instr.* (pp. 38, 227, 255)	215 Livingston st.
Reynolds, D. L., Jr. *a*	378 WH.	Robbins, L. B., Sr. *s*	131 Grove st.
Reynolds, E. H., Jr. *s*	96 Wall st.	Robbins, L. R., 2 *l*	119 Wall st.
Reynolds, G. L., So. *a*	236 Crown st.	Robert, H. M., Jr., *g*	A.
Reynolds, H. C., Jr. *a*	390 B.	Roberts, A. E., Fr. *s*	117 Wall st.
Reynolds, H. M., Prof. (pp. 25, 147, 314) (3 PH.)	85 Trumbull st.	Roberts, B. L., Spec. *d*, Spec. *l*	616 E. D.
Reynolds, H. S., 2 *m*	317 Grand av.	Roberts, C., Jr. *s*	111 Grove st.
Rice, C. B., Instr. (pp. 38, 236, 268) (56 N. S. H.)	61 Huntington st.	Roberts, E. C., So. *a*	22 College st.
Rice, C. J., Jr. *a*	410 Winthrop av.	*Roberts, E. J., Ass't.* (p. 43)	712 W. D.
Rice, J. P., Instr. (pp. 38, 227, 255)	179 V-S.	Roberts, E. L., Jr., Fr. *a*	8 College st.
Rice, W. K., Jr. *a*	456 FW.	Roberts, J. S., So. *a*	22 College st.
Richard, H. M., *g*, Sr. *d*		Roberts, P., So. *a*	22 College st.
	504 Whitney av.	Roberts, R. G., *g*	152 Temple st.
Richard, M. D., Fr. *a*		Roberts, W. P., Jr. *a*	178 L.
	504 Whitney av.	Robertson, E. A., Sr. *s*	
ichards, C. B., Prof. (pp. 22, 168-9, 235, 240, 264, 270, 367) (III WIN.)	227 Edwards st.		393 Temple st.
		Robertson, F. C., *g*	A.
		Robertson, H. R., Ass't. (p. 43)	A.
ichards, E. C. M., Jr. *s*	131 V-S.	Robertson, T. M., *g*	A.
ichards, E. L., Prof. (p. 22)		Robertson, W. H., Sr. *a*	50 V.
	Woodbridge	Robin, A. J., Sr. *s*	105 V-S.
ichards, W., Jr., Sr. *s*	119 Wall st.	Robinson, A. F., So. *a*	91 C.
ichards, W. R., Fellow		*Robinson, C., Instr.* (pp. 38, 188)	233 Edwards st.
14 E. 37th st., New York City		Robinson, C. P., *g*	A.
ichardson, C. E., Fr. *s*	333 York st.	*Robinson, H. H., Instr.* (pp. 38, 178, 359)	A.
ichardson, G. A., So. *a*	22 College st.	Robinson, M., 3 *l*	335 WH.
ichardson, H. B., Jr. *a*	218 F.	Robinson, W. G., *g*	A.
ichardson, O. H., Ass't. Prof. (pp. 31, 186, 188, 377-8, 517)	284 Orange st.	Robinson, W. M., Jr., Fr. *a*	200 York st.
		Robison, P. G., Jr. *a*	27 V.
ichardson, S., Fr. *a*	548 P.	Rodenbach, C. P., Fr. *a*	231 York st.
'chardson, W., Sr. *a*	357 WH.	Rodiger, W. G., Jr. *s*	124 Prospect st.
		Roe, H. G., *f*	Bridgeport

Roe, J. W., Instr. (pp. 38, 240)
79 Trumbull st.
Roesler, W. F., Jr. *s* 145 v-s.
Rogers, F. A., Sr. *s* 111 Grove st.
Rogers, H. W., Prof. and Dean
(pp. 24, 500-1, 503-4, 506, 517-19)
(HEN.) 413 Orange st.
Rogers, P., Fr. *s* 117 Wall st.
Rogers, R. L., Sr. *for.*
182 Mansfield st.
Rogers, R. P., 2 *l* 1076 Chapel st.
Rogers, W. S., So. *a* 22 College st.
Rolfe, C. E., *mus.* Ansonia
Roome, R., So. *a* 22 College st.
Root, E. K., Lect. (pp. 38, 466)
Hartford
Root, F. J., Jr. *s* 65 Foote st.
Root, H. M., Sr. *s* 133 College st.
Rose, A. R., *g* 342 Crown st.
Rose, O. A., Jr., *mus.* 140 Fulton st.
Rose, R. Selden, Jr. *a* 239 D.
Rose, R. Stephen, Sr. *s*
288 N. Front st.
Rose, W. C., *g* 91 Park st.
Rosenbaum, H., Sr. *s* 68 Park st.
Rosenbaum, J., *g* 68 Park st.
Rosenberg, A. R., 1 *l* 422 B.
Rosenberg, H. L., Fr. *a* 14 Gold st.
Rosenberg, R. W., Sr. *a* 87 c.
Rosenn, G. J., Sr. *a* 57 v.
Rosenthal, G. J., Sr. *a* Hartford
Rosenthal, S., 1 *l* Hartford
Ross, F. A., Sr. *s* 153 v-s.
Ross, R., Fr. *a* 362 WH.
Ross, Z. C., Fr. *a* 200 York st.
Rossiter, J., *g* A.
Roth, F. G., So. *a* 156 L.
Roth, R. J., Jr. *s* 133 College st.
Rothensies, L. D., Fr. *s* 684 w. D.
Rothery, J. E., Sr. *for.*
129 Mansfield st.
Rothschild, L. L., Fr. *a* 521 P.
Rouse, B. O., Sr. *a* 2 v.
Routenberg, H. W., Jr. *s* 124 Wall st.
Rowland, J. E., Fr. *a* 242 York st.
Rowland, J. T., Fr. *a* 200 York st.
Rowland, M. D., 3 *l* 109 York st.
Rowland, W. E., Cashier (p. 48)
(WOOD.) 480 Winthrop av.
Rowley, G. H., 3 *l* 392 Temple st.
Royce, J., Lect. (pp. 38, 183, 185, 383)
Cambridge, Mass.
Rudd, W. B., Fr. *s* 389 Temple st.

Ruff, A. W., Jr. *a* 420 B
Ruffcorn, W. M., 1 *l* 366 Whalley av
Rumsey, J. F., Jr., Fr. *a* 250 York st.
Runciman, L. S., Fr. *s* 397 Temple st.
Rush, R. W., Fr. *s* 117 Wall st.
Russell, D. G., Jr. *s* 137 v-s.
Russell, E. S., *g* West Haven
Russell, G. M., So. *a* 162 L.
Russell, H. I., 2 *l* 41 Howe st.
Russell, T. H., Prof. and Lect.
(pp. 23, 465-6) 137 Elm st.
Russell, T. H., Jr., 2 *m* 137 Elm st.
Russell, W. I., Jr. *m* 925 Howard av.
Rust, S. H., Sr. *a* 13 v.
Ruthrauff, W. B., Jr. *s* 111 Grove st.
Ruthven, R. S., 1 *l* 333 York st.
Ryan, J. H., Sr. *a* 455 FW.
Ryder, S. W., Jr. *a* 450 FW.
Ryerson, E. L., Jr., Sr. *s*
133 College st.
Sagarino, J. F., Jr. *s* 74 Howe st.
Saiki, T., *g* 462 Elm st.
St. John, C. W., Fr. *a* 554 P.
St. Lawrence, A. J., Jr. *s* 77 Olive st.
Salzstein, H., Fr. *s* 333 York st.
Sammis, D. S., Jr. *s* Stratford
Sanborn, M. R., Ass't. (p. 48)
(LIB.) 25 Woodland st.
Sanders, J. W., Fr. *a* 536 P.
Sanderson, B. B., Jr. *a* 469 FW.
Sanderson, G. H., So. *a* 171 L.
Sanderson, R. L., Ass't. Prof.
(pp. 31, 153-5, 330-1) (228 F.)
277 Willow st.
Sandquist, O. A., Fr. *s*
153 St. John st.
Sanford, L. C., Instr. (pp. 38, 466)
347 Temple st.
Sanford, S. B., Fr. *s* 110 Wall st.
Sanford, S. S., Prof. (pp. 24, 199, 341)
50 W. 52d st., New York City
Sanford, T. F., Jr. *s* 124 Wall st.
Sanger, E. J., Jr. *s* 96 Wall st.
Sarason, P. B., Jr. *a*, 1 *m* 48 Broad st.
Sargent, G. P. T., *g* A.
Sargent, H. B., Fellow
247 Church st.
Sargent, R. C., Fr. *a* 256 Edwards st.
Sattig, C. A., Fr. *s* 65 Foster st.
Saunders, A. A., Sr. *for.*
125 Maple st.

Sautter, H. A., Sr. *s*   153 v-s.
Savage, A. W., Fr. *s*   113 Wall st.
Savage, T. E., *g*   West Haven
Scarlett, J. A., Jr., Jr. *s*
                                    124 Prospect st.
Schall, J. E., Jr., Jr. *s*
                                    167 Livingston st.
Scharff, B. W., Fr. *a*   231 York st.
Scharmann, H. G., Fr. *s*
                                    118 College st.
Schevill, R., Ass't. Prof. (pp. 31,
    155-6, 331-2)   431 FW.
Schlafley, P. A., 3 *l*   36 Elm st.
Schmidt, A., Sr. *a*   77 C.
Schneider, A., 2 *l*   397 Temple st.
Schnuck, E. C., Fr. *s*   299 York st.
Scholl, R. F., 1 *m*   149 Lombard st.
Scholle, W. D., Sr. *a*   339 WH.
Schoolfield, J. H., Sr. *s*
                                    17 Hillhouse av.
Schramm, A. O., Spec. *l* 146 York st.
Schrenk, H. V., Lect. (pp. 38, 353,
    413)   St. Louis, Mo.
Schuchert, C., Prof. and Curator
    (pp. 27, 176-7, 241, 244, 246, 276,
    358)   (9 PEAB.)   59 Wall st.
Schuckai, A., *mus.*   33 Elliot st.
Schuele, G. J., Sr. *m* 925 Howard av.
Schulz, L., Instr. (pp. 38, 199, 341,
    399)   Woodcliff, Bergen Co., N. J.
Schulze, T., Jr. *a*   376 WH.
Schumann, C. M., *mus.*   Southington
Schuneman, C. T., Sr. *s* 111 Grove st.
Schuyler, R. L., Instr. (pp. 38, 186)
                                    879 Elm st.
Schwab, J. C., Librarian (p. 26)
    (LIB.)   310 Prospect st.
Schwaner, S. F., Fr. *a*   560 P.
Schwartz, M., Ass't. (p. 43)
                                    465 Dixwell av.
Schwarz, O. H., Fr. *a*   238 York st.
Schweizer, R. J., Jr. *a*   270 D.
Scofield, E. L., Jr., Jr. *a*   119 W.
Scott, H. P., Jr., Fr. *a*   540 P.
Scott, H. S., Jr. *s*   70 Trumbull st.
Scoville, S., *g*   A.
Scragg, R. E., Sr. *a*   333 WH.
Scribner, F. J., Jr. *a*   127 W.
Scudder, F. D., So. *a*   167 L.
Scudder, L. W., Sr. *s*   178 v-s.
Scully, A. C., Sr. *s*   161 v-s.
Seabrook, R., Fr. *a*   231 York st.
Seabury, M. A., Jr. *a*   271 D.

Seckerson, H. A., *g*
                              1-8 Ellsworth av.
Secor, C. E., Jr., So. *a*   128 W.
Seeley, A. B., Jr. *s* 147 Blatchley av.
Seidensticker, R. F., 1 *m*
                                    120 York st.
Seitz, H. M., Fr. *s*   59 Grove st.
Sekido, N., *g*   385 Winthrop av.
Seligman, J. L., Sr. *a*   105 W.
Seligmann, G. A., Sr. *a*   14 V.
Selin, W. E., *g*   671 W. D.
Selleck, A. W., Jr. *a*   80 C.
Sellew, E. B., *g*   809 Orange st.
Selover, C. E., Jr., Jr. *a*   179 L.
Seltzer, D., Jr. *a*   450 FW.
Semple, R. H., 1 *l*   82 Wall st.
Serabian, R. N., Jr. *s*   152 Grove st.
Serri, F. R., Fr. *a*   186 F.
Sessions, K. H., Fr. *a*   200 York st.
Sewall, A., So. *a*   22 College st.
Seward, F. D., Fr. *a*   586 P.
Seward, H. L., Ass't. (p. 43) 116 v-s.
Sewell, N. D., Sr. *a*   529 Elm st.
Seybold, G. H., So. *a*   224 F.
Seymour, C., Sr. *a*   30 V.
Seymour, E. P., So. *a* 260 Crown st.
Seymour, T. D., Prof. (pp. 23, 147-
    8, 313-14)   (22 PH.)
                                    34 Hillhouse av.
Shackleton, R. A., Sr. *a*   436 FW.
Shailer, N. F., Jr. *s*   109 v-s.
Shapiro, A. M., Fr. *s*   40 Broad st.
Shapiro, I., Spec. *l*   333 York st.
Shapiro, M. M., 1 *l*   288 Grand av.
Shapleigh, A. W., Fr. *a* 242 York st.
Sharp, W., Jr. *a*   470 FW.
Shartenberg, C., Fr. *a*   200 York st.
Shattuck, A. E., Sr. *d*   629 E. D.
Shattuck, H. F., Fr. *a*   526 P.
Shea, J. W., Spec. *s*   423 Temple st.
Shear, V. S., So. *a*   228 Crown st.
Sheehan, J. E., Sr. *m*   249 Crown st.
Sheehan, M. T., 2 *m*   Wallingford
Sheffield, W. K., Sr. *s*   131 Grove st.
Sheldon, A. M., Sr. *a*   358 WH.
Sheldon, E. W., Instr. (pp. 38, 167)
                                       542 P.
Sheldon, H. T., 3 *l* 235 Lawrence st.
Shelton, W. A., *g*, Sr. *d.*   680 W. D.
Shepard, A. M., Jr. *a*   401 B.
Shepard, N. A., Fr. *s*
                              159 Blatchley av.
Shepard, R. B., Sr. *a*   34 V.

Shepard, S. T., Jr. *a* 249 D.
Shepard, *W. K.*, *Instr.* (pp. 38, 235, 264, 367) 321 Willow st.
Sheppard, E. M., Jr. *a* 118 W.
Sherman, C. P., Ass't. Prof. and Librarian (pp. 31, 375, 499, 502, 505, 515) 438 Edgewood av.
Sherman, E. E., Fr. *a* 564 P.
Sherman, H. B., Sr. *a* 15 V.
Sherman, J. H., Fr. *a* 250 York st.
Sherman, R., Sr. *a* 427 FW.
Sherman, R., So. *a* 22 College st.
Sherrill, H. K., Fr. *a* 524 P.
Sherwood, G. C., *g* 276 Elm st.
Shields, G. K., Fr. *s* 61 Trumbull st.
Shields, S. B., Fr. *a* 1076 Chapel st.
Shields, W. H., Jr., So. *a* 90 C.
Shill, E. S., 2 *l* 1079 Chapel st.
Shillingford, G. W., Fr. *s*
3 Hillhouse av.
Short, S. E., Fr. *s* 333 York st.
Shubert, G. W., Sr. *s* 20 Avon st.
Shulansky, J., Fr. *s* 649 E. D.
Sibley, G. F., 2 *l* 126 Wall st.
Sidenberg, A. M., Fr. *a* 233 York st.
Sieber, J. B., Sr. *a* 1076 Chapel st.
Siems, A. G., 1 *l* 200 York st.
Silberstein, I., Fr. *a* 206 F.
Silva, A. B., Sr. *s* 333 York st.
Simmons, C. D., Jr. *a* 397 B.
Simmons, G. A., *g* 142 Edgewood av.
Simmons, R., Grad. *s*, Jr. *for.*
196 Mansfield st.
Simpson, A. R., Fr. *a* 590 P.
Singer, V. D., Sr. *a* 226 F.
Shann, C. B., Spec. *l* 152 Temple st.
Skelton, R. H., Jr. *s* 144 V-S.
Skene, G. M., 3 *l* 130 Wall st.
Skinner, J. W., Sr. *a* 1076 Chapel st.
Skinner, W. W., Sr. *s* 111 Grove st.
Slaght, W. E. A., *g*, Grad. *d.*
980 Whalley av.
Slavin, A. H., 1 *l* 683 W. D.
Slider, H. B., Jr. *a* 451 FW.
Sloan, W. S., Fr. *s* 144 V-S.
Slotnick, M. N., So. *a* 161 L.
Small, R. B., Sr. *a* 439 FW.
Smart, W. P., Jr. *a* 449 FW.
Smernoff, A. A., Jr. *m*
71 Washington av.
Smillie, R., Jr. *a* 383 B.
Smith, A. W., *g* 529 Elm st.
Smith, A. W., Jr., 2 *l* 1076 Chapel st.

Smith, Benj. H., Fr. *s* West Haven
Smith, Bryan H., Jr. *s* 120 College st.
Smith, C. G., Spec. *d*
304 Exchange st.
Smith, C. H., Prof. (pp. 22, 188-90, 378-9, 516) (177 L.)
284 Orange st.
Smith, C. M., Sr. *a* 375 WH.
Smith, Carlton S., Fr. *a*
80 Stanley st.
Smith, Charles S., Fr. *s* Bridgeport
Smith, D. P., So. *a* 223 F.
Smith, D. S., Instr. and Sec'y. (pp. 38, 198-9, 340, 396)
(126 College st.) 120 Linden st.
Smith, D. T., So. *a* 214 Crown st.
Smith, E. E., *f* 95 Howard av.
Smith, E. H., So. *a.* 398 B.
Smith, E. K., Ass't. (p. 43)
51 Prospect st.
Smith, F. W., 1 *l* New Britain
Smith, G. D., Sr. *s* 164 V-S.
Smith, G. M., So. *a* 22 College st.
Smith, G. T., Sr. *m* 70 Trumbull st.
Smith, H., Jr., Jr. *a* 440 FW.
Smith, H. B., Fr. *s* 12 B. M. H.
Smith, H. D., Sr. *s* 126 High st.
Smith, Harold E., Fr. *a* 532 P.
Smith, Herbert E., Prof. and Dean (pp. 25, 238, 464, 466) (25 M. S.)
430 George st.
Smith, H. M., Jr., So. *a*
236 Crown st.
Smith, J. F., *g* 1068 Yale P. O.
Smith, J. N., Sr. *s* 139 V-S.
Smith, J. W. F., 2 *l* 264 York st.
Smith, M. C., 2 *l* 610 W. D.
Smith, M. F., Ass't. (p. 49) W. O.
Smith, O. H., Fr. *a* 237 York st.
Smith, O. L., Fr. *s* 120 College st.
Smith, P. A., Fr. *s* 123 Carmel st.
Smith, P. F., Prof. (pp. 26, 227, 233, 235-6, 238, 240, 252, 257, 364)
(26 S. H.) 330 Willow st.
Smith, R. R., Sr. *a* 36 V.
Smith, S. I., Prof. (p. 23)
147 Whalley av.
Smith, W. A., 2 *l* 677 W. D.
Smith, W. Henry, Jr. *s*
70 Trumbull st.
Smith, W. Howard, Fr. *s*
114 High st.
Smith, W. R., Jr., 1 *l* 397 Temple st.

myth, M. W., *g*   328 Temple st.
myth, N., *Fellow*   328 Temple st.
mythwick, C. A., 3 *l*
    65 Edgewood av.
nead, H. S., Jr. *s*   114 High st.
neath, G. M., Jr. *d*   32 Perkins st.
now, C. R., Jr. *s*   8 Prospect pl.
now, G. N. D., Spec. *s*   122 Wall st.
nowdon, F. B., Fr. *a*   254 Crown st.
nyder, E. D., So. *a*   158 L.
nyder, H. B., Sr. *a*   67 v.
nyder, T. E., Grad. *s*, Jr. *for.*
    8 Prospect pl.
nyder, W. P., Jr., Fr. *s*
    120 College st.
solomon, S. W., Grad. *l*   333 York st.
Somers, L. J., 2 *l*   140 St. John st.
oper, H. A., Jr. *s*   133 College st.
oroch, E. M., Sr. *m* .   279 Crown st.
ule, G. H., Jr., Sr. *a*   23 v.
oule, L., Fr. *a*   237 York st.
southack, B. G., Sr. *s*   167 v-s.
outhey, C. R., Jr. *s*   96 Wall st.
outhworth, A. B., Jr. *s*   102 v-s.
outhworth, H. M., Jr. *a*   106 w.
paenkuch, A., *f*   170 Commerce st.
palding, C. G., Demonstrator
(pp. 39, 464)   70 Grove st.
palding, H. B., Sr. *s*
    124 Prospect st.
palding, R. L., *f*   70 Grove st.
parhawk, W. N., Sr. *a*   406 B.
paulding, A. T., Sr. *a*   427 FW.
peh, C. F., Ass't. (p. 43)   (S. C. L.)
    Short Beach
pencer, B. K., Fr. *s*   373 Crown st.
pencer, H. G., 3 *l*   120 High st.
pencer, J. B., So. *a*   22 College st.
perry, F. N., Demonstrator (pp. 39, 466)   42 College st.
perry, J. A., 2d, Jr. *a*   438 FW.
perry, R. S., Fr. *s*   427 Temple st.
perry, W. L., Grad. *d*   648 E. D.
pier, S. L., Ass't. (p. 44)
    359 Crown st.
pitz, J., Fr. *s*   110 Wall st.
pitz, M. W., Sr. *a*   110 Wall st.
pitzer, R. A., Jr. *a*   378 WH.
plawn, W. M. W., Sr. *a*   147 L.
poerle, W., Jr. *a*   137 w.
prenger, W., Demonstrator (p. 39)
    366 George st.
pringer, A., Jr., Jr. *a*   459 FW.

Springer, W., Jr., Grad. *s*, Jr. *for.*
    60 Whalley av.
Spurr, A. C., 1 *l*   161 York st.
Squires, A. R., *f*   9 Liberty st.
Stadtmiller, K. C., Jr. *s*
    120 College st.
Stadtmiller, L. R., Fr. *s*   126 Wall st.
Staley, A. C., Sr. *s*   188 v-s.
Standish, F. B., Ass't. (p. 44)
    312 Elm st.
Stanley, H., Sr. *a*   35 v.
Stanley, L. L., Fr. *a*   22 College st.
Stanley, M., Sr. *a*   266 D.
Stanley-Brown, R., Jr. *s*   104 v-s.
Stanton, E. C., Fr. *a*   705 w. D.
Stanton, H. W., Spec. *l*   125 w.
Stanton, J. J., 3 *l*   Bridgeport
Stapler, H. B., Sr. *a*   46 v.
Stark, M. W., Sr. *s*   135 v-s.
Starkweather, J. R., *mus.*
    1452 Boulevard st.
Starr, A. R., Jr., Fr. *s*   113 v-s.
Starr, E. B., Sr. *for.*   74 Lake pl.
Starring, M. B., Jr., Fr. *a*
    250 York st.
States, E. J., 2 *m*   27 High st.
Stearns, B., Jr. *s*   17 Hillhouse av.
Steele, A. T., *g*, Grad. *d*   Bethel
Steele, C. M., So. *a*   22 College st.
Steele, E. L., Fr. *a*   528 P.
Steele, H. M., Ass't. (p. 44)
    226 Church st.
Steele, R. H., Sr. *a*   268 D.
Steely, H. M., Jr., Sr. *s*   180 v-s.
Steiber, T. E., 3 *l*   265 Orange st.
Steinman, J. H., Sr. *a*   355 WH.
Stephens, H. V., Jr. *s*   96 Wall st.
Stephenson, G. W., Fr. *s*
    120 High st.
Sterling, S., So. *a*   171 L.
Stern, R. B., So. *a*   228 Crown st.
Sterne, N. P., 3 *l*   925 Howard av.
Stetson, G. A., Fr. *s*   76 Mansfield st.
Stetson, J. M., Jr. *a*   76 Mansfield st.
Stevens, C. H., 3 *l*   23 Asylum st.
Stevens, E. A., Fr. *s*   391 Temple st.
Stevens, F. N., Sr. *a*   75 C.
Stevens, J. F., Jr., Fr. *s*
    250 Church st.
Stevens, L. B., 3 *l*   35 v.
Stevens, M. L., *f*   Clinton
Stevens, N. C., So. *a*   251 Crown st.
Stevenson, H. N., 2d, Sr. *s*   141 v-s.

Stewart, C. L., 3 *l*   925 Howard av.
Stewart, D. B., Sr. *a* ·   19 v.
Stewart, F. A., Jr. *s*   391 Temple st.
Stewart, G., Sr. *s*   124 Prospect st.
Stewart, H. E., 2 *m*
    191 Edgewood av.
Stillman, R. E., 2 *l*   271 Crown st.
Stillwell, A., Fr. *s*   152 Grove st.
Stimson, P. M., So. *a*   22 College st.
Stivers, J. L., 1 *l*   86 Howe st.
Stix, C. I., Fr. *a*   539 P.
Stockton, S. D., Jr., Jr. *a*   381 WH.
Stoddard, R. F., Sr. *a*   434 FW.
Stoddart, J. C., Fr. *a*   1076 Chapel st.
Stoddart, J. T., Jr. *s*   82 Wall st.
Stokely, J. M., *g*   90 Park st.
Stokes, A. P., Jr., Secretary (p. 28)
    (WOOD.)   73 Elm st.
Stokes, F. B., Fr. *a*   231 York st.
Stokes, H. P., Jr. *a*   237 D.
Stokes, H. W., Jr. *a*   132 W.
Stone, G. A., 1 *l*   635 Quinnipiac av.
Stone, I. D., Fr. *s*   413 Temple st.
Stone, J. A., Fr. *s*   333 York st.
Stone, M. C., Jr. *a*   250 D.
Stone, N. L., Fr. *s*   119 Wall st.
Stone, R. H., Sr. *s*   96 Wall st.
Stone, T. A. L., 1 *l*   107 Temple st.
Storey, W. F., *g*   172 Lloyd st.
Story, W. F., Sr. *s*   161 V-S.
Street, E. A., *mus.*   East Haven
Stricker, W., Jr., So. *a*   47 Lake pl.
Strobridge, R. L., Fr. *s*   104 Wall st.
Strong, J. P., Accountant (P. 49)
    (WOOD.)   222 Sherman av.
Strong, R. W., Jr. *s*   171 V-S.
Stuart, J. B., Jr. *s*   124 Prospect st.
Sturges, G. R., Spec. *l*
    858 Quinnipiac av.
Sturges, H., Jr. *a*   350 WH.
Sturges, H. H., Fr. *s*   698 W. D.
Sturges, P. T., *f*   152 Temple st.
Sturges, W. T., Sr. *s*   698 W. D.
Sullivan, B. H., Jr. *a*   467 FW.
Sullivan, L., Sr. *a*   61 V.
Summers, T. B., Fr. *s*
    3 Hillhouse av.
Sumner, F. A., *g*, Grad. *d*   Milford
Sumner, W. G., Prof. (pp. 22, 191-3,
    370, 514)   240 Edwards st.
Suruda, N., *g*   ,   416 Crown st.
Sutphen, D. H., 3 *l*   1081 Chapel st.
Sutphen, P. T., 3 *l*   1081 Chapel st.

Swain, H. L., Prof. (pp. 26, 466)
    232 York st.
Swan, J., Fr. *s*   120 High st.
Swartz, M. D., *g*   25 Whalley av.
Sweeney, E. A., 2 *l*   85 Sachem st.
Sweeney, E. F., 2 *l*   77 C.
Sweeney, J. B., 1 *l*   333 York st.
Sweeney, J. C., Fr. *a*   546 P.
Sweeney, J. M., Jr., So. *a*   77 C.
Sweeney, J. P., Jr. *a*   441 FW.
Sweet, G. C., 1 *m*   710 Howard av.
Sweet, W. N., Fr. *a*   371 Crown st.
Swenson, A. C., Sr. *s*   133 College st.
Swenson, L. E., *g*   376 Elm st.
Swett, R. F., Jr. *a*   138 W.
Swift, S., Sr. *a*   424 FW.
Swift, S. R., Mid. *d*   641 E. D.
Swift, T. V., Sr. *s*   131 Grove st.
Swords, A. D., Fr. *a*   22 College st.
Sykes, A. D., Fr. *s*   152 Grove st.
Symons, T. W., Jr., Fr. *a*
    250 York st.

Taddeo, J., *f*   329 Cedar st.
Taft, R. A., So. *a*   8 College st.
Taft, W. H., Fellow
    Washington, D. C.
Taft, W. H., Jr. *a*   239 D.
Taggart, T. D., Fr. *s*   96 Wall st.
Taintor, J. S., *g*   A.
Taintor, N. C., Jr. *a*   252 D.
Tait, E. W., Sr. *a*   2 V.
Takagi, S., *g*   228 Crown st.
Takahashi, S., *g*   652 E. D.
Talbot, H. E., Jr., Fr. *s*   150 Grove st.
Talcott, H. W., Sr. *a*   375 WH.
Tang, H., So. *a*   142 Dwight st.
Taylor, A. H., *g*   892 Yale P. O.
Taylor, D. F., Fr. *s*   395 Temple st.
Taylor, E. B., Sr. *s*   96 Wall st.
Taylor, G. H., Fr. *a*   541 P.
Taylor, H. V. S., Sr. *a*   70 C.
Taylor, I. H., Fr. *s*   110 Wall st.
Taylor, R. E., Fr. *a*   195 F.
Taylor, T. S., Ass't. (p. 44)   687 W. D.
Taylor, Walter W., Fr. *s*
    400 Temple st.
Taylor, William W., Sr. *s*
    136 Spring st.
Taylor, Wyatt W., *g*   A.
Tearse. R. J., Jr. *a*   465 FW.
Teasdale, L. A., Fr. *s*   121 Nicoll st.
Templeton, G. R., Sr. *s*   West Haven

Tenney, C., *g*   21 Home pl.
Terrill, A. P., Sr. *s*   147 Dwight st.
Terrill, J. C., Fr. *s*   105 Dwight st.
Terrill, M. C., Jr. *a*   94 W.
Terry, E. C., Spec. *l*   537 Howard av.
Terry, F. G., *mus.*   1304 Chapel st.
Terry, J. T., 3d, Fr. *a*   242 York st.
Tetreault, H. N., Fr. *a*   572 P.
Thacher, S. E., Accountant (p. 49)
        441 Second av., West Haven
Thacher, T., Lect. (pp. 39, 507)
        62 Cedar st., N. Y. City
Thacher, T. A., Sr. *a*   355 WH.
Thatcher, H. W., 3 *l*   23 Norton st.
Thatcher, R., Jr. *a*   467 FW.
Thatcher, W. S., Fr. *s* 55 Prospect st.
Thaw, B., Jr., Jr. *s*   119 V-S.
Thayer, G. C., Sr. *a*   337 WH.
Thielcke, G. E., 2 *m*   1 Sylvan av.
Thomas, C. P., Fr. *a*   250 York st.
Thomas, J. D., Jr., *s*   82 Wall st.
Thomas, J. P., Fr. *s*   15 Sylvan av.
Thomasson, B. B., 3 *l*   137 Dwight st.
Thompson, Mrs. A. K., Clerk and
  Priv. Sec'y. (p. 49)   96 Park st.
Thompson, B. C., Fr. *a*   200 York st.
Thompson, C. D., Sr. *s*
                              133 College st.
Thompson, C. G., *g*, Jr. *d*   647 E. D.
Thompson, C. P., Jr., Sr. *s*   185 V-S.
Thompson, E. N. S., Instr. (pp. 39,
  160)   (11 WH.)   732 Elm st.
Thompson, G. A., Instr. (pp. 39, 227,
  340)   (A. S.)   79 Clinton av.
Thompson, H., Fr. *a*   238 York st.
Thompson, H. W., Fr. *s*
                              719 Orange st.
Thompson, J. H., Jr., Fr. *s*
                              59 Grove st.
Thompson, M. G., Sr. *a* 105 Park st.
Thompson, P., Sr. *s*   60 Grove st.
Thompson, R. E., Jr. *s*
                              133 College st.
Thompson, W. H., Jr., Tutor
  (pp. 39, 146, 148, 315)   157 L.
Thoms, H. K., 2 *m*   656 W. D.
Thomson, D. H., Sr. *s*
                              17 Hillhouse av.
Thorne, L. K., Fr. *s*   119 Wall st.
Thorne, P. M., Jr., 2 *l*   658 W. D.
Thornton, J. C., Sr. *a*   343 WH.
Thorstenberg, E., Instr. (pp. 39, 159,
  227, 255, 334)   35 Lynwood pl.

Thresher, H. H., Fr. *a*   593 P.
Thurston, C. H., Jr. *a*   446 FW.
Tiebout, H. C., Fr. *s*   387 Temple st.
Tiemann, H. D., Lect. (pp. 39, 413)
                                    MAR.
Tiernan, F. D., *mus.*
                        250 Howard av.
Tierney, D. P., Sr. *for.*   91 Lake pl.
Tilden, W. C., 1 *m*   381 Crown st.
Tillinghast, W. E., So. *a*   203 F.
Tillotson, E. W., Jr., *g*
                              846 Yale P. O.
Tilson, D. B., Sr. *a*   332 WH.
Tilson, O. H., Fr. *a*   524 P.
Tilson, V. V., Sr. *a*   332 WH.
Timm, A. B., So. *a*   106 York sq.
Tinker, C. B., Instr. (pp. 39, 162-3,
  165, 339)   245 D.
Tinsley, W. A., *mus.*   Waterbury
Tisdale, I. M., Cataloguer (p. 49)
              (LIB.)   268 Orchard st.
Titus, N. E., Fr. *s*   333 York st.
Titus, P., Sr. *m*   70 Trumbull st.
Tobin, J. F., 1 *l*   333 York st.
Tolles, B. I., Ass't. (pp. 44, 463-4)
                              196 York st.
Tolles, M. H., *f*   Ansonia
Tolliver, H. G., 3 *l*   ·   56 Foote st.
Tommers, A. E. B., Fr. *s*
                          103 Thompson st.
Tompkins, G. I., *mus.*   178 V-S.
Torrey, C. C., Prof. (pp. 25, 151, 187,
  323-5, 376)   (232 F.)
                          67 Mansfield st.
Toucey, J. M., Jr. *s* 124 Prospect st.
Toumey, J. W., Prof. and Director
  (pp. 26, 250, 281, 412-13, 416)
              (MAR.)   459 Prospect st.
Tournier, C. A., Sr. *a*   70 C.
Towles, J. K., *g*   706 W. D.
Townsend, G. H., 2d, Sr. *a*   64 V.
Townsend, J. C., So. *a* 22 College st.
Townsend, J. M., Lect. (pp. 39, 507)
        318 W. 75th st., New York City
Townsend, J. M., Jr., Sr. *a*   4 V.
Tracy, J. C., Ass't. Prof. (pp. 31, 231,
  233, 238, 240, 250, 263, 266, 368,
  416)   (131 WIN.)
                          345 Winthrop av.
Tracy, R. G., Ass't. (p. 44)
                          407 Howard av.
Tracy, T. R., So. *a*   183 L.
Traer, C. S., Fr. *s*   407 Temple st.

Traer, G. W., Jr., Jr. *s*   101 V-S.
Trask, B. H., Fr. *a*   248 York st.
Treadway, M. C., Fr. *a*
       225 Crown st.
Treat, R., Fr. *s*   397 Crown st.
Troostwyk, H., *mus.*   179 Bradley st.
Troostwyk, I., Ass't. Prof. (pp. 31,
   199, 341, 398-9)   (C. S. H.)
       179 Bradley st.
Troostwyk, L., *mus.*   179 Bradley st.
Trowbridge, H. E., Fr. *s*
       76 Gregory st.
Trudeau, F. B., Jr. *a*   237 D.
Tsao, Y., Fr. *a*   143 York st.
Tsur, Y., Jr. *a*   561 Yale P. O.
Tully, T. A., Recorder (p. 39)
     (LAM.)   130 Howe st.
Turnbull, G. M. W., Fr. *a*
       242 York st.
Turnbull, J. S., Jr. *a*   A.
Turnbull, R. B., 3 *l*   486 Dixwell av.
Turner, C. C., Jr., Fr. *a*   580 P.
Turner, H., Fr. *a*   254 York st.
Turner, W. A., Fr. *s*   421 Temple st.
Turrill, H. S., 2 *m*   293 York st.
Tussey, M. C., Jr. *a*   27 V.
Tuttle, H. C., Sr. *a*   52 V.
Tuttle, H. O., Fr. *a*   590 P.
Twenhofel, W. H., Sr. *a*
       122 Derby av.
Twichell, J. H., Fellow   Hartford
Tyler, S. L., Spec. *s*   33 Pearl st.

Uhler, H. S., Instr. (pp. 39, 171)
     (S. P. L.)   86 Avon st.
Umberger, R. B., Sr. *a*   36 V.
Underhill, F. P., Ass't. Prof. (pp. 31,
   181, 241, 244, 271, 351, 353, 412,
   464)   (63 S. B. L.)   91 Clark st.
Underhill, W. A., So. *a*
       236 Crown st.
Underwood, C. B., Priv. Sec'y.
   (p. 49)   (90 High st.)   130 Howe st.
Underwood, C. U., *g*   585 Howard av.
Underwood, K., Sr. *a*   352 WH.
Updegraff, L. V., Sr. *a*   67 V.
Upson, W. W., Fr. *s*   114 High st.
Uptegrove, R. P., So. *a*   8 College st.
Urquhart, J. E., Jr., So. *a*
       260 Crown st.

Vail, E. R., Fr. *s*   17 Hillhouse av.
Vail, J. F., 2 *l*   150 L.

Valentine, D. B., Fr. *s*
       393 Temple st.
VanAlstyne, W. T., Fr. *s*   122 V-S.
VanBlarcom, D., Fr. *a*   595 P.
VanBrunt, A., So. *a*   154 L.
VanBuren, A. W., Instr. (pp. 39,
   320)   9 Trumbull st.
*Vanderbilt, C., Trustee Peabody
   Museum* (p. 538)
   100 Broadway, New York City
Vanderbilt, F. W., Trustee S. S. S.
   (p. 200)
     459 Fifth av., New York City
VanName, A., Librarian Emeritus
   (p. 22)   (LIB.)   121 High st.
VanName, R. G., Instr. (pp. 39, 172-
   3, 347-8)   (K. C. L.)   121 High st.
VanRensselaer, W. S., Sr. *a*   348 WH.
VanRiper, W. M., Jr. *a*   470 FW.
VanSinderen, A., So. *a*   8 College st.
VanSinderen, H. B., Fr. *a*
       242 York st.
VanVleck, C. E., Jr., Jr. *a*   376 WH.
VanVoorhis, B., Fr. *s*   117 Wall st.
Van Winkle, A., Catalogue Reviser
   (p. 49)   (LIB.)   98 Howe st.
Vars, W. W., 1 *l*   9 Library st.
Veeder, P. L., Sr. *a*   64 V.
Venner, O. H., *g*   1233 Chapel st.
*Vernon, A. W., Prof. and Acting
   Pastor* (pp. 27, 436)   (632 E. D.)
       339 Humphrey st.
Verrill, A. E., Prof. (p. 22)
   (15 PEAB.)   86 Whalley av.
Vestling, A. E., Instr. (pp. 39, 157)
       73 Avon st.
Viall, P. O., Fr. *s*   117 Wall st.
Vidal, G. N., 1 *l*   40 Franklin st.
Vilas, M. B., Jr. *a*   380 WH.
Villie, F. H., Jr. *s*   96 Wall st.
Vincent, C. R., Fr. *s*   82 Wall st.
Visel, C. E., Sr. *s*   967 Yale P. O.
Vishno, C. W., *mus.*   23 College st.
Volck, M. R., Fr. *s*   135 Wall st.
Volkenheim, M., Sr. *m*   40 Spruce st.

Wachman, J. D., Fr. *a*   566 P.
Wacker, F. G., So. *a*   22 College st.
Wadlington, M. E., *g*   166 York st.
Wadsworth, R. S., Fr. *s*   76 C.
Waggoner, J. N., Jr. *m*
       925 Howard av.
Wagner, E. C. L., Sr. *a*   54 V.

Wainwright, P. S., Sr. *s*	395 Temple st.
Wainwright, R. B., Sr. *for.*	82 Wall st.
Waite, S. B., Fr. *s*	132 Wall st.
Walbridge, C. C., Jr. *a*	457 FW.
Walden, P. T., Ass't. Prof. (pp. 31, 227, 259)	(159 S. C. L.)	367 Prospect st.
Waldrop, P. P., Sr. *a*	210 F.
Walker, C. H., Instr. (pp. 39, 188)	399 B.
Walker, G. S., 1 *m*	79 Lafayette st.
Walker, H. E., Sr. *s*	56 Grove st.
Walker, J. M., Jr., Sr. *s*	120 College st.
Walker, M. H., Jr., Jr. *a*	104 W.
Walker, M. M., *f*	162 York st.
Walker, M. S., *g*	North Haven
Walker, R. C., Fr. *a*	242 York st.
Walker, R. P., *g*	79 Howe st.
Walker, T. C., Jr. *s*	170 V-S.
Walker, T. H., Jr. *s*	131 Grove st.
Walker, T. J., Sr. *a*	338 WH.
Walker, W., Prof. (pp. 25, 376-7, 434, 514)	(668 W. D.)	281 Edwards st.
Walker, W. J., Sr. *a*	41 V.
Walkley, R. L., Jr. *a*	396 B.
Wallace, F., Jr. *a*	179 L.
Wallace, J. B., Jr., Jr. *s*	111 V-S.
Wallace, W. K., Sr. *a*	345 WH.
Wallace, W. L., 1 *m*	151 Canner st.
Wallis, B. F. B., Fr. *a*	22 College st.
Wallis, J. H., *g*	A.
Walradt, H. F., *g*	417 B.
Walsh, A. E., *f*	Cromwell
Walters, F. L., Fr. *a*	416 Crown st.
Walton, J. F., Jr. *s*	17 Hillhouse av.
Wang, C. C., Sr. *s*	66 Whalley av.
Ward, A. G., Instr. (pp. 39, 255)	152 Whalley av.
Ward, E., *g*	88 Wall st.
Ward, F., Instr. (pp. 39, 276)	106 Howe st.
Ward, H. L., Ass't. (p. 44)	205 F.
Ward, W. L., Jr. *s*	88 Wall st.
Warden, S. W., *g*	Meriden
Wardwell, C. A., Jr. *a*	123 W.
Wardwell, J. B., Jr. *a*	100 W.
Ware, H. T., Jr. *s*	119 Wall st.
Warmoth, C. K., Fr. *s*	2 B. M. H.
Warner, D. J., 3 *l*	36 Elm st.

Warner, E. P., *g*	914 Dixwell av.
Warner, W. C., F*r. s*	10 Clinton av.
Warren, E. R., So. *a*	172 L.
Warren, F. M., Prof. (pp. 25, 153, 331)	(208 F.)	46 Mansfield st.
Warren, H. T., So. *a*	11 College st.
Warren, L. B., Fr. *s*	133 Wall st.
Warren, L. G., Jr. *s*	119 Wall st.
Washburne, C., Sr. *a*	47 V.
Waterbury, E. M., So. *a*	162 L.
Waterman, C. C., Fr. *s* 389 Temple st.
Waters, E. O., Fr. *a*	582 P.
Waters, J. W., Fr. *a*	250 York st.
Waters, W. J., Jr. *s*	117 Wall st.
Waterworth, J. B., Sr. *a*	34 V.
Watkins, C. L., Sr. *a*	12 V.
Watrous, F. M., So. *a*	252 D.
Watrous, G. D., Prof. (pp. 25, 195, 499, 501, 503)	(121 Church st.)	261 Bradley st.
Watrous, H. K., Spec. *l*	105 Park st.
Watrous, P. M., Sr. *s*	373 Crown st.
Watson, C. B., Sr. *s*	133 College st.
Watson, R. S., Jr. *s*	85 Sachem st.
Watson, T. S., Jr. *s*	131 Grove st.
Watts, L., Jr. *s*	102 V-S.
Watzek, A. R., Jr. *a*	463 FW.
Watzek, C. H., Fr. *s*	119 Wall st.
Wayne, R., Fr. *s*	125 High st.
Weadick, S. I., *f*	591 Elm st.
Weatherbee, H. A., Jr. *a*	117 W.
Webb, H. C., So. *a*	249 Crown st.
Webb, H. W., Sr. *a*	48 V.
Webb, J. H., Instr. (pp. 40, 498, 502-3, 517)	42 Church st.
Webb, W., 2 *l*	155 Elm st.
Webb, W. S., Jr., Jr. *a*	31 V.
Weber, A. M., *mus.*	262 Lloyd st.
Weed, L. H., Sr. *a*	370 WH.
Weekes, G. L., 2 *l*	1076 Chapel st.
Weeks, M., Jr. *a*	115 W.
Weibel, J. C., Fr. *a*	114 Sherman av.
Weil, A., Fr. *a*	352 Orange st.
Weil, C. L., Fr. *s*	352 Orange st.
Weinermann, D. T., Jr. *s*	649 E. D.
Weinstein, J., Sr. *s*	27 Rose st.
Weis, J. F., Prof. and Director (pp. 22, 198, 340)	(9 A. S.)	58 Trumbull st.
Weisman, H. J., 2 *l*	39 Lynwood pl.
Weiss, J. H., Jr., Jr. *s*	110 Wall st.
Weiss, W. S., Sr. *a*	371 WH.
Welch, C. A., Fr. *a*	23 Bradley st.

Welch, F. P., 2 *l*   53 Prospect st.
Welch, G. G., Jr. *s*   134 v-s.
Welch, H. L., Ass't. (p. 44)
                         44 College st.
Weller, J. F., Sr. *s*   96 Wall st.
Welles, K. B., Sr. *a*   12 v.
Welling, W. C., Jr. *a*   458 fw.
Wells, D. B., Sr. *a*   25 v.
Wells, F. H., Jr. *s*   113 v-s.
Wells, H. L., Prof. (pp. 24, 229, 231,
   241, 243-4, 259, 345) (151 s. c. l.)
                         445 Orange st.
Wells, J. M., Fr. *s*   266 York st.
Wells, T. P., Sr. *a*   17 v.
West, W. H., 1 *l*   416 Crown st.
Westcott, J. B., Jr. *a*   390 d.
Westcott, N., Jr. *m*   219 York st.
Weston, A. H., Sr. *a*   74 c.
Wetmore, G. P., Trustee Peabody
   Museum (p. 538)   Newport, R. I.
Wetzel, J. W., Instr. (pp. 40, 162,
   499, 502, 597) (hen.)
                         16 Dwight st.
Wetzlar, E. A., Jr. *a*   424 fw.
Weyman, E. C., 2 *l*   189 f.
Whalen, E. J., Sr. *m*   413 b.
Wharton, W. B., So. *a*   251 Crown st.
Wheaton, H. M., Jr. *s*   131 Grove st.
Wheeler, A. M., Prof. (pp. 21, 189,
   377-8, 516, 519) (h, c.)
                         86 Trumbull st.
Wheeler, A. R., Fr. *a*   250 York st.
Wheeler, Edward C., Fr. *a*
                         200 York st.
Wheeler, Ernest C., Grad. *s*, Jr. *for.*
                         1076 Chapel st.
Wheeler, H. L., Ass't. Prof. (pp. 31,
   229, 243, 259, 346) (s. c. l.)
                         45 Trumbull st.
Wheeler, J. E., Lect. (pp. 40, 499)
                         82 Edgehill rd.
Wheeler, L. P., Ass't. Prof. (pp. 31,
   236, 252, 268, 344, 365)
       (118 win.)   124 Linden st.
Wheeler, L. R., Fr. *a*   250 York st.
Wheeler, T. L., Jr. *a*   259 d.
Wheeler, W. R., Fr. *a*   250 York st.
Wheelock, F. E., Ass't. (p. 45)
                         120 York st.
Whipple, R. D., So. *a*   Bridgeport
Whitacre, H. S., Sr. *a*   105 Park st.
Whitaker, I., Jr. *a*   141 w.
Whitcomb, F. J., So. *a*   249 Crown st.

White, B., Sr. *s*   110 Wall st.
White, E. L., Jr. *a*   175 l.
White, Harold A., Fr. *s*   114 High st.
White, Henry A., *g*   82 Whalley av.
White, J. A., *g*   82 c.
White, R. H., *g*   411 b.
White, R. T., Sr. *a*   438 fw.
White, W. P., Fr. *a*   8 College st.
Whitehead, P. B., *g*, Mid. *d*   641 e. d.
Whitehill, A. M., Sr. *a*   332 wh.
Whitehouse, N. O., Jr. *a*   31 v.
Whitestone, I. D., Sr. *a*   83 c.
Whiting, J. R., Jr. *s*   83 Mansfield st.
Whiting, W. J., Jr. *s*   83 Mansfield st.
Whitlock, R. S., Jr. *a*   441 fw.
Whitman, E. A., So. *a*   151 l.
Whitmer, H. K., Fr. *s*   86 Wall st.
Whitney, E., Fellow 800 Whitney av.
Whitney, F., Sr. *s*   111 Grove st.
Whitney, S., Sr. *s*   133 College st.
Whittaker, J. M., Jr. *a*   398 b.
Whittemore, F. B., Sr. *s*   107 v-s.
Whittler, M. F., *g*   716 w. d.
Whittlesey, R., Fr. *s*   59 Grove st.
Wick, H. C., Jr., Jr. *a*   339 wh.
Wick, W. C., Jr. *s*   131 Grove st.
Wickes, D. R., *g*, Mid. *d*   638 e. d.
Wickwire, W. A., Fr. *s*   133 College st.
Widger, H. D., So. *a*   151 l.
Wieland, G. R., Lect. (p. 40)
       (27 peab.)   Woodmont
Wiggin, F. H., Jr., 2 *l*   155 Elm st.
Wilcox, C. H., Grad. *s*, Jr. *for.*
                         13 Lake pl.
Wilcox, H. J., 3 *l*   27 High st.
Wilder, E. C., Spec. *s* 329 Whalley av.
Wilder, W. E., Jr., Fr. *s*   86 Wall st.
Wiles, R. E., Jr. *s*   117 v-s
Wilkes, J. C., Grad. *l*   688 w. d
Wilkes, W. B., Sr. *a*   435 fw
Wilkeson, L. E., Fr. *s*   110 Wall s
Willcox, D., Jr. *a*   1 v
Willets, J. M., Fr. *a*   242 York st
Willets, M. L., Sr. *s*   169 v-s
Willey, W. B., Sr. *for.*   74 Lake p
Williams, A., Jr., So. *a*   250 Crown
Williams, A. N., Fr. *s*   610 e. i
Williams, C. G., Sr. *s*
                         17 Hillhouse av
Williams, E. F., Jr. *s*   84 Trumbull s
Williams, E. T., So. *a*   22 College s
Williams, F. W., Ass't. Prof.
   (pp. 31, 190, 377, 379, 419) a

Williams, G. Jr. *s*   82 Wall st.
Williams, H. C., Sr. *for.* 119 Grove st.
Williams, H. S., *2 m*   Bridgeport
Williams, J. F., Jr. *a*   353 WH.
Williams, J. W., Sr. *a*   30 V.
Williams, L., Instr. (pp. 41, 199, 341, 398)   284 Orange st.
Williams, M. S., Fr. *s*   120 College st.
Williams, R. D., *g*   213 F.
Williams, S. G., Fr. *s*   333 York st.
Williams, S. T., Fr. *a*   231 York st.
Williams, T. A., *g*, Sr. *d*   628 E. D.
Williams, W. W., So. *a* 22 College st.
Williamson, A. W., Grad. *s*, Jr. *for.*   91 Lake pl.
Willing, M. S., *g*   •   A.
Willis, F. M., Fr. *a*   543 P.
Wilson, A. A., Fr. *a*   254 Crown st.
Wilson, D. A., *2 l*   287 York st.
Wilson, G. C., So. *a*   151 L.
Wilson, H., Fr. *a*   242 York st.
Wilson, H. B., Sr. *s*   104 Wall st.
Wilson, H. M., *g*   A.
Wilson, L. A., *2 m*   78 Lake pl.
Wilson, M. H., Fr. *s*   119 Grove st.
Wilson, R., *mus.*   50 Houston st.
Wilson, W. A., *g*   Branford
Wilson, W. W., *2 m*   230 Portsea st.
Winslow, C. D., Fr. *s*   427 Temple st.
Winslow, C. W., *1 l*   18 Dwight st.
Winslow, F., Jr., Fr. *s*   82 Wall st.
Winton, R. P., Jr. *s*   136 Canner st.
Wismer, E. L., Sr. *a*   412 B.
Witherbee, S. H., Fr. *a*   254 York st.
Witherow, W. P., Sr. *s* 133 College st.
Wittler, M. F., *g*, Jr. *d*   716 W. D.
Wittstein, F. H., Fr. *s*   132 Wall st.
Wittstein, H. L., Sr. *s*
   392 Congress av.
Witz, S. J., *1 l*   757 State st.
Wobbermin, G., Lect. (p. 40)
   Breslau, Germany
Wodell, R. A., So. *a*   22 College st.
Woedtke, A. V., *mus.*   6 Olive st.
Wolcott, E. C., Sr. *s*   96 Wall st.
Wolcott, R. H., *g*   A.
Wolff, M. H., Sr. *s*   724 W. D.
Wong, W. D., Fr. *s*   56 Grove st.
Wood, A. A., Cataloguer (p. 49)
   (LIB.)   1305 Chapel st.
Wood, C. D., *1 l*   333 York st.
Wood, E. C., Jr. *s*   110 V-S.
Wood, E. F., Jr. *s*   143 V-S.

Wood, E. W., Spec. *l*   27 College st
Wood, Fletcher H., Fr. *s*   615 E. D
Wood, Florence H., *f*   402 Crown st
Wood, G. E., Sr. *s*   Branfor
Wood, H. I., Fr. *a*   225 F
Wood, J. H., *f*   228½ Edgewood av
Wood, R. G., Jr., Fr. *s*   114 High st
Wood, T. W., Sr. *s*   17 Hillhouse av
Wood, W. Hamilton, *g*
   Berlin, German
Wood, W. Herbert, So. *a*
   214 Crown st
Wood, W. J., Jr., Fr. *s*   692 W. D
Woodbine, G. E., *g*   245 York st
Woodford, H. P., So. *a* 22 College st.
Woodruff, L. L., Instr. (pp. 40, 180, 227, 238, 241, 244, 271, 349-50)
   (73 S. B. L.)   835 Orange st.
Woods, H. S., Jr. *s*   666 W. D.
Woods, J. G., *1 l*   New Britain
Woodward, C. H., Grad. *l*
   315 York st.
Woodward, D., Fr. *s* 3 Hillhouse av.
Woolley, E. M., Fr. *a*   248 York st.
Woolsey, T. S., Prof. (pp. 23, 517, 519)   A.
Worman, E. C., Sr. *a*   226 F.
Worthington, E. R., *g*   37 Howe st.
Wren, A., Sr. *a*   331 WH.
Wright, A. W., Prof. (p. 22)
   73 York sq.
Wright, C., Proctor (p. 49)   542 P.
Wright, C. R., Fr. *a*   242 York st.
Wright, E. F., So. *a*   22 College st.
Wright, G. L., Fr. *s* 3 Hillhouse av.
Wright, H. B., Ass't. Prof. (pp. 31, 187, 376)   A.
Wright, H. D., Sr. *a*   337 WH.
Wright, H. H., *3 l*   146 York st.
Wright, H. P., Prof. and Dean (pp. 23, 143, 317)   (LAM.)
   128 York st.
Wright, P. N., Fr. *a*   242 York st.
Wright, R. G., Jr. *a*   465 FW.
Wright, T. G., *g*   74 C.
Wright, W. J., Sr. *a*   348 Crown st.
Wurts, E., *f*
   654 Savin av., West Haven
Wurts, J., Prof. (pp. 26, 194-5, 497-8, 501, 504)
   654 Savin av., West Haven
Wyant, G. G., Jr. *a*   444 FW.
Wyland, B. F., *g*, Sr. *d*   702 W. D.

Wylie, E. A. G., Sr. *s*   131 Grove st.
Wynkoop, W. W., Sr. *a*   43 v.
Wynne, C. K., 1 *l*   327 Edgewood av.

Yacobian, L. D., *f*   Paris, France
Yagendorf, M. A., 1 *l*   307 George st.
Yaggy, W. E., Fr. *a*   250 York st.
Yale, W., Jr. *s*   110 v-s.
Yanagi, Y., *g*   91 Dwight st.
Yao, C. L., So. *a*   142 Dwight st.
Yates, S. S., So. *a*   8 College st.
Yearwood, C. H., Spec. *d*
   99 Dixwell av.
Yen, F., Jr. *m*   662 w. D.
Yergin, H. V., Sr. *a*   436 FW.
Yin, T. E. So. *a*   66 Whalley av.
York, H. C., *g*   125 Dwight st.
Young, C. G., Fr. *s*   53 Prospect st.
Young, C. S., Fr. *s*   Derby

Young, G. L., Jr. *s*   119 Wall st.
Young, I., Sr. *s*   132 Wall st.
Young, N., Fr. *s*   425 Temple st.
Young, P. S., Jr. *a*   141 w.
Young, R. W., Ass't. (p. 44) 665 w. D.
Yudowitch, H., Fr. *s*   98 Prince st.

Zacher, L. B., So. *a*   155 L.
Zacher, N. B., *f*   Branford
Zahm, G., Ass't. Prof. (pp. 31, 501,
   504-5, 507, 517)   New York City
Zartman, L. W., Instr. (pp. 40, 193,
   195, 374)   100 Brownell st.
Zee, Z., Jr. *s*   365 WH.
Zeidler, A. F., *mus.*   Waterbury
Ziff, W. N., 1 *l*   Bridgeport
Zimmerman, A., Fr. *s*   Bridgeport
Zimmerman, R. S., So. *a*   148 L.
Zunder, M. F., 1 *m*   583 Whitney av.

	PAGE
Abbreviations	9, 743
Abernethy Fellowship	114
Absence from College	96
Academical Dep't. *See* College.	
Administrative Officers	19
Admission, Terms of, to Art School	388
to College	76-93
to Divinity School	423-25
to Forest School	407-08
to Graduate School	302
to Law School	487-94
to Medical School	459-62
to Department of Music	393-95
to Sheffield Sci.School	213-24
Advanced Standing, Admission to,	
in Art School	389
in College	92
in Divinity School	425
in Law School	491
in Medical School	461
in Sheffield Sci.School	224
Æsthetics	184
Aid to Students in College	99-105
in Divinity School	447-51
in Music Department	395
in Sheffield Sci. School	291-93
Allen, W., Scholarship	102
Allis Scholarships	449
Alumni Associations	561-66
Lectureship	443
Advisory Board	17
American Oriental Society, Library of	536
Anatomy, Comparative	272
Human	181, 468
Andrews, W. L., Memorial (Loan) Library	105, 536
Anthropological Collection	543
Anthropology	134, 191, 280, 370
Anthropology Club	369
Anticipation of College Courses	136
Appointments, Commencem't 1907	596-98
Junior, 1907	600-02
Arabic	323
Archæology, Classical	127, 149, 319
Art School, Collections of	391-92
Course of Instruction in	385-89
Degree in	389
Director, Office hours of	7
Elective Courses	389
Evening Classes	390-91
Faculty of	385
Fees in	388
Library of	391
Prizes in	389-90
Students in	393-94
Terms and vacations in	389
Terms of admission to	388
Trowbridge Lecture Course	390, 572

	PAGE
Arts, Bachelor of, Degree of	125
List of class of 1907	581-85
Master of, Degree of	306, 496
List of graduates, 1907	589-92
Astronomical Observatory	545-46
Astronomy	167, 258
Athletic Field	555-56
Atwater, C., Scholarship	102
Austrian, W. J., Scholarship	108
Awards of Prizes and Scholarships	606-12
Bacteriology	275, 352, 472
Barge, Benjamin F., Mathematical Prizes	117
Scholarship	108
Beecher, Lyman, Lectures	442, 571
Belknap Prizes	293
Beneficiary aid. *See* Aid.	
Bennett, James Gordon, Prize	575
Bennett, Philo Sherman, Prize	577
Bennetto, J., Scholarship Fund	107
Berkeley Premiums	122
Berkeley Scholarship	114
Sermons	573
Betts Prize	524
Betts, C. W., Prize	121
Biblical Literature	127, 150, 325, 428-33
Biblical Research Club	444
Bibliography	353
Biological Club	343
Biology	132, 178, 244, 271, 349
Blake Stone Breaker Prize	293
Board, Cost of	96, 551
Bonds of College students	93
Boocock Library	369
Borden, Wm., Fellowship	114
Bordwell, M., Scholarship	102
Botanical Garden	547
Botany	180, 241, 275, 282, 352, 421
Bristed Scholarship	105
Bromley Lectures	572
Buildings, University, Location of *See* before Title-page.	
Bulkley Fellowship	303
Byers Memorial Hall	286
Calendar for 1907-08	10
California Fellowship, Yale Alumni Association of	305
Callender, Robert, Scholarship	107
Campbell Gold Medal	478
Catalogues	8
Chamber Concerts	573
Chamberlain, Hugh, Greek Prize	123
Chaplains	548
Charnley, W. S., Scholarship	102
Charter of Collegiate School of Yale College	55
Chemical Club	343
Chemistry	131, 172, 220, 228, 229-31, 259-62, 345, 467
Physiological	181, 274, 351, 467

	PAGE
Chicago Scholarships	110, 292
Christman Fund	101
Chronological Table	12
Church History	376-77, 434
Civil Engineer, Degree of	211-12, 307
Civil Engineering	233, 263
Clark Scholarship	115
Classical Archæology	149, 319
Classical Club	310
Cleveland Scholarship Fund	110
Clubs for Research	310, 322, 328-29, 343, 361, 366, 369-70, 381, 384
Cobden Club Medal	576
Cole, T. I., Library	522
College, Appointments and Honors in	124-25
Beneficiary aid in	99-105
Board, price of, in	96, 551
Buildings	94-95
Chapel. *See* Public Worship.	
Church. *See* Univ. Church.	548-50
Course of instruction in	126-199
Courses in Law School	495
in Medical School	458
Dean, office hours of	7
Degrees in	125, 135
Degrees, list of, 1907	581-85
Examinations for	76-93
Expenses in	95-99
Faculty of	67-73
Graduate Fellowships, etc., in	110-16
list of holders of, 1907	50-52
Historical notices of	55-63, 76
Honors in	124-25
Honors, awards of, 1907	596-603
Prizes offered in	116-24
awards of, 1906-07	606-08
Rooms in	96-98
Scholarships offered in	105-10
holders of, 1907	50-52, 506
Standing Committees in	75
Students in	633-64
Terms and vacations in	11, 93
Terms of admission to	76-93
Text-Books, cost of	99
Loan Library of	105
Tuition charges in	95
Commencement Day	11
Commercial Geography	174, 371, 514
Commercial Museum	369
Commons. *See* Dining Hall.	
Communion in University Church	550
Concerts, University	573
Contents, Table of	5-6
Cook Prize in Poetry	576
Cooper Prize in Greek Philosophy	576
Corporation, Charter powers of	55-63
Legal name of	55
Members and officers of	15-16
Council, University, Committees of	20
Courses for Teachers	186, 384
Cox, J. J., Scholarship	107
Curtis, J. H., Prize	116
Cuyler Fellowship	113
Deans, Office hours of the	7
DeForest Mathematical Prizes	119
DeForest Prize	118
DeForest Scholarships	103
DeForest, W. W., Scholarship	115

	PAGE
Degree of Bachelor of Arts	125, 135
of Civil Law	525
of Divinity	424
of Fine Arts	389
of Laws	525
of Music	395
of Philosophy	284
Civil Engineer	211, 307
Doctor of Civil Law	525
of Medicine	477
of Philosophy	209, 284, 306, 427
Master of Arts	306, 496
of Forestry	410
of Laws	525
of Science	209, 284, 308
Mechanical Engineer	212, 307
Mining Engineer	212, 308
Degrees in course, 1907	581-94
Degrees, Honorary, 1907	594
Departments of Instruction	63-64
Honor Students in	596
Dining Hall	551
Directory	743-86
of Living Graduates	8
Divinity School, Admission to advanced standing	425
Alumni Association in	565-66
Buildings	445
Clubs	443
Courses in	427-28
Dean, office hours of	7
Degrees in	427
Degrees given in 1907 in	589
Educational Society Grants in	448
Expenses in	446
Faculty of	422
General Statement of	423
Graduate Fellowships in	450
Scholarships in	451
Study in	425
Lectureships in	442
Libraries of	442
Licensure in	427
Prizes offered in	449-50
Awards of, 1907	610
Rooms	445
Scholarships, General	447
Prize	449
Special Lecturers in	423
Students in	714-18
Students pursuing Selected Studies in	426
Terms and vacations in	426
Terms of admission to	423
Dodge, W. E., Fund	103
Dodge Lectures	571
Douglas Fellowship	111
Downes Prizes	449
Drawing	198, 263, 265, 340
Dwight Hall Lectures	573
Dwight, Susan B., Fellowship	451
Eaton, D. C., Graduate Scholarship	115, 305
Economics	134, 193, 279, 371
Education	384
Educational Club	384
Egleston, G. W., Historical Prize	577
Eldridge, EllenBattell, Fellowships	113

PAGE

Electrical Engineering 236, 268
Ellsworth Fund 102
Elocution 140, 162, 439, 499, 502
Embryology..................181, 273, 350
Engineer, Civil, Degree of.......211, 307
    Mechanical, Degree of 212, 307
    Mining, Degree of.........212, 308
Engineering.... 211-13, 233-41, 262-70, 366
Engineers' Club................... 366
English..................129, 160, 254, 335
English, A. K., Prizes and Schol-
    arship 390
English Club 329
English Seminary Room 329
Epistemology..................185, 382
Ethics 133, 183, 185, 383
Evening Classes in Art School ... 390
Examinations for admission, Places
    where held 88-89
Expenses in Art School........... 388
    College..................... 95-99
    Divinity School............... 446
    Forest School............. 409, 420
    Graduate School............. 302
    Law School................. 526
    Medical School............. 478
    Department of Music 395, 399-400
    Sheffield Scientific School 285
Faculty of Art School 385
    College..................... 67-70
    Divinity School............... 422
    Forest School............. 403
    Graduate School 295-301
    Law School................. 481
    Medical School............. 452
    Music School............. 393
    Sheffield Scientific School..... 200-04
    University................. 21-44
Fees. *See* Expenses.
Fellows 15, 50-52
Fellowships, Graduate, in College
    110-14, 303
    in Divinity School... 450
Fellowships, List of holders of,
    1907-08.................. 50-52
Finance Committee................ 16
Fine Arts.................135, 198, 339
Fine Arts, School of. *See* Art School.
    Bachelor of, Degree of 389
Fogg Scholarships................. 449
Foote Fellowships 111
Foreign Missions, Historical Li-
    brary of.................. 442
Foreign Service, Yale-Columbia
    Courses preparatory to......... 528
Forest School, Courses in 410-21
    Degree in 410
    Degrees given in 1907........ 592
    Equipment 404
    Fees and Expenses......... 409, 420
    Governing Board of 403
    Graduate Advisory Board of 404
    Preparatory Course.......... 408
    Students in 710-13
    Summer School of Forestry
    404, 406, 419-21
    Terms and vacations in....... 408
    Terms of admission to........ 407
    Theses 410
Forestry..................250, 281, 352-54

PAGE

French 128, 153, 256, 330-31
Freshman Studies, Honors in..... 602
Fuller, T. H. and L., Scholarship.. 102
Galpin, S. H., Latin Prize 123
Gaylord Farm Sanatorium 457
Gaylord, S., Scholarship.......... 102
General Assembly, Acts of 55
Geography......174, 175-76, 178, 278, 280,
    355, 357, 371, 514
Geological Club 343
    Collections 539-40
Geology... 132, 174, 243, 276, 355, 357, 359
German 128, 156, 255, 333
German Journal Club 281
German Seminary Room......... 329
Government of the University.... 55-63
Graduate Fellowships and Scholar-
    ships. *See* Fellowships.
Graduate School, Administrative
    Committee of............. 301
    Clubs in. *See* Research Clubs.
Graduate School—
    Courses in.....308, 310 (notes), 310-84
    Dean, office hours of 7
    Degrees in 306-08
    Faculty of................. 295-301
    Fees in 302
    Fellowships 303-05
    Historical notice of......... 302
    Scholarships............. 305-06
    Students in 615-32
    Terms and vacations in....... 11
    Terms of admission to 302
Gratuity Fund.................. 103
Greek 126, 146, 313-15
    Equivalents for admission.... 79
Gymnasium 552-54
Hadley Scholarship.............. 305
Harmer Foundation.......... 101
Harvard Lectures 572
Hawes, J., Fund............. 103
Healy Philosophical Library..... 380
Hebrew 151, 152, 323
Hillhouse Mathematical Library . 289
Histology 181, 468
Historical Seminary Room 370
History 133, 186, 280, 375, 434
    Club 370
Holley, J. C., Scholarship 102
Holmes Scholarships.............103, 291
Honorary degrees, 1907........... 594
Honors in the Several Departments,
    1907.................. 596-605
    in College 124
    in Law School 524
    in Medical School.......... 478
Hooker Fellowship............. 450
Hoppin, Benjamin, Greenland
    collection 543
Hotchkiss, Lucius, Fund......... 103
Hurlbut Scholarship Fund 106
Hurtt, Scott, Fellowship.......... 112
    Scholarship.......... 106
Infirmary..................... 551
Information, general.............. 8
Institutions connected with the Uni-
    versity 531
Instructors. *See* Faculty, Univer-
    sity.
Insurance 195, 374

PAGE

Investments, Committee on 16
Italian 128, 155, 332
Ives, C. L., Scholarship 102
Japanese History 189, 380
Language 334
Jewell Prize..................... 524
Johnes, H. P., Scholarship........ 104
Jones, E. C., Scholarship.......... 102
Junior Appointments in 1907...... 600-02
Exhibition..................... 121
Prizes 119-21
Kansas City Scholarship Fund ..124, 292
Keese Prize 478
Kent Club..................... 510
Lamont Memorial Lectureship... 572
Landberg Collection..............442, 534
Langdon Fund 102
Larned Fellowships 112
Latin....................126, 142, 315
Law School—
Academical and Law Courses
combined....................193, 495
Courses combined with Shef-
field Scientific or Divinity
School..................... 496
Courses in..................497-507
Dean, office hours of 7
Degrees in 496-525
list of, 1907............... 588, 592
Examinations in............... 508
Expenses in 526
Faculty of..................... 481
Graduate Courses 511-21
Instruction, System of 484
Kent Club..................... 510
Library of..................521-22
Practice Courts of........... 509-10
Prizes in..................... 522
awards of, 1907 611
Special Students 492
Students in 723-32
Terms and vacations in....... 484
Terms of admission to........ 487-95
Wayland Club................. 510
Learned Scholarships............. 107
Leavenworth Scholarship Fund .. 104
Lecture courses, University...... 571
Libraries 533-37
Library, Art School 391
Byers Hall................. 536
Divinity School............. 442
Foreign Missions............. 442
Forest School 404, 537
Law School..................521, 536
Linonian and Brothers........ 535
Lowell Mason 442, 537
Medical School 457, 536
Sheffield Scientific School.... 289, 536
University..................... 534
Linguistics..................127, 150, 321
Loan Library of Text-Books 105, 536
Lockwood Scholarships........... 400
Logic.................... 133, 182, 184, 382
Long, M., Scholarship........... 108
Loomis, H. B., Fellowship in
Chemistry..................... 304
Loomis Fellowship in Physics 304
Lord, Daniel, Jr., Memorial Fund 107
Lyon Scholarships................. 101
McLaughlin Memorial Fund 122
Macy Fellowship................. 110

PAGE

Macy Scholarship................. 102
Maps. *See* before Title-page.
Marett Fund 101
Marshall, J., Scholarship Fund ... 104
Mathematical Club............... 361
Mathematical Laboratory 360
Mathematical models, Collection
of 360
Mathematics 131, 167, 252, 257, 360
Mead Scholarship 108
Mechanical Engineer, Degree of 212, 307
Mechanical Engineering..........235, 264
Medical Alumni Lectures 573
Medical School—
Buildings and equipment..... 455
Clinical facilities 456
Course in...................462-77
Dean, Office hours of......... 480
Degrees in 477
Degrees given in 1907 in...... 593
Expenses in 478
Faculty of.................... 452
Graduate and Special Students
in..................... 479-80
Historical notice of........... 454
Honors and Prizes in......... 478
awards of, 1907..............603, 610
Library facilities 457, 536
Preparation. 458
Students in 719-22
Terms and vacations in....... 462
Terms of admission to........ 459-62
Mersick Prizes. 450
Metallography 358
Metallurgy 231, 262, 368
Metaphysics 185, 282
Milner Fund.................... 109
Mineralogical Collections 539
Mineralogy.........175, 243, 278, 354, 356
Mining 240, 270, 308, 446
Mining Engineer, Degree of 212, 308
Missions...................... 437
Mitchell, J. S., Scholarship...... 102
Modern Language Club.......... 328
Modern Languages 153, 328
Monitorships 104
Montgomery Prize 524
Moore Scholarships 291
Morgan Fund 101
Moseley Collection of Indian
Basketry........................... 543
Municipal Engineering 238, 266
Munson Prizes 524
Museum of Natural History, Pea-
body 538-44
Music, Department of............393-402
Academic Honors in 395
Certificate 394
Courses in..................394, 396-99
Dean, office hours of 7
Degree 395
Diplomas. 399
Expenses in 395, 399-400
Library of..................402, 442
Scholarships in 400
Awards of................... 610
Students in 705-07
Music courses 135, 198, 340
Natural Sciences 174, 342-59
New Haven—
Map of. *See* before Title-page.

PAGE

New Haven—
Oratorio Society............402, 574
Symphony Orchestra.........401, 574
New Testament Literature and
History 326,430
Observatory.................... 545–46
Director, office hours of...... 7
Office Hours 7
Officers of the University 13–49
Officers and Graduates of the
University, Catalogue of....... 8
Old Testament Literature and
History....................325,428
Oratorio Society.............402, 574
Organ Recitals 574
Page Lecture Course............. 248
Page Scholarships............... 291
Paleontology 176,277, 358
Palmer, A. B., Scholarship Fund. 106
Parker, Joseph, Prize 523
Parker, Peter, Fund 103
Peabody Museum of Nat. Hist... 538–44
Pecuniary Aid. *See* Aid.
Pedagogy 186, 384
Penfield Prize.................. 294
Petrology.................278, 355, 356
Philology, Classical 310
Comparative.............127, 150
Indo-Iranian............... 320
Philosophical Club 381
Philosophical Seminary Room ... 380
Philosophy 133, 182, 369, 380
Bachelor of, Degree of 284
list of class of 1907........ 585–87
Doctor of, Degree of......209, 306
list of graduates, 1907..... 593–94
Philosophy and the Arts, Dep't of 63–64
Phonetics 150, 321, 330
Physical Club 343
Physical Geography..132, 174, 278, 355, 514
Physical Sciences 170, 342
Physics................131, 171, 269, 343
Physics Journal Club........... 343
Physiography 132, 177, 357
Physiological Chemistry ..181, 274, 351, 467
Physiology............133, 180, 273, 351
Plainfield Scholarship Fund 109
Political Science Club 370
Porter, John A., Memorial Fellow-
ship 113, 304
Porter, John A., Prize in American
History 117
Porter, John A., Essay Prize..... 575
Portuguese..................... 332
Post Office, Yale Station 559
Prayers, College 548
Preachers, Battell Chapel 549
Berkeley 573
Preaching, Lectures on...........442, 571
Preliminary Examinations, College 87
Sheffield Scientific School..... 221
Premiums. *See* Prizes.
President, Office hours of 7
Prizes, Art School 389–90
awards of, 1907 610
College...................116–24
awards of, 1907............ 606–08
Divinity School............449–50
awards of, 1907............ 610
Law School................ 522–24
awards of, 1907............ 611–12

PAGE

Prizes, Medical School 478
awards of, 1907............ 610
Department of Music......... 400–01
awards of, 1907........... 610
Sheffield Scientific School 293–94
awards of, 1907........... 608–09
University................. 575–77
awards of, 1907............ 606
Professorships 21–28
Prudential Committee........... 16
Psychological Laboratory........ 381
Psychology 133, 183, 382–83, 384
Public Lectures 569–70
Public Worship...........93, 444, 548
Raymond, J. M., Scholarship..... 102
Reading Room—
College..................... 536
University.................. 535
Representation by Cities 739–40
by Colleges 740–42
by Departments 737
by States 738
Research Clubs......309, 310, 322, 328–29,
343, 361, 366, 369–70, 381, 384
Robinson, Henry C., Fellowship.. 303
Robinson, L. F., Latin Prizes..... 116
Rogers Scholarship.............. 291
Romance Club 328
Romance Languages 128, 153, 329
Rooms in College 96–98
in Sheffield Scientific School.. 287–88
Numbering of............... 9
Runk Scholarship Fund 106
Russian 159, 334
Salisbury Collection..........322, 442, 534
Sanitary Engineering...........238, 266
Sanskrit 127, 150, 320
Scandinavian 159, 334
Scholarships in College.......... 99–110
Holders of, 1907 606–07
See, also, Aid.
Science, Master of, Degree of 209, 284, 308
Scott Prizes.................... 120
Secretary, Office hours of 7
Select Studies in Science and Lit-
erature 246
Self-Help, Bureau of 99, 560
Semitic and Biblical Club.........322, 444
Semitic Languages.........127, 150, 322–25
Sheffield Graduate Scholarships ..292, 306
Sheffield Lectures 573
Sheffield Scientific School—
Buildings 286
Church Sittings for Students in 290
Courses of instruction in...... 225–53
graduate................... 208–13
special.................... 213
Courses preparatory to For-
estry 250, 408
Degrees in..............208, 584
list of, 1907..........585–87, 592
Director, Office hours of...... 7
Expenses in 285
Governing Board of 200
History and organization of .. 205–08
Honors 290
awards of, 1907 603–04
Lectures................... 299
Libraries of, Technical........ 289
Prizes in................... 293–94
Prizes, awards of, 1907........ 609

PAGE

Sheffield Scientific School—
　Rooms in........................ 287-88
　Scholarships 291-93, 306
　Students in 665-702
　Terms of admission to........ 214-24
　Trustees of 203
Silliman Fellowship................ 112
Silliman Memorial Lectures 571
Sloane, John, Fellowship.......... 112
Social Sciences 191, 279, 369
Sociology, Christian.............. 438
Soldiers' Memorial Fellowship.... 111
Sophomore Declamation Prizes... 122
Southern California Alumni Asso-
　ciation Scholarship.............. 305
Spanish...................128, 155, 257, 331
Spaulding, J., Scholarship 102
Special Students 213, 426, 480, 492
Stanley Mathematical Prize 117
　　　Memorial Fund...........109, 117
Steinert Collection................ 402
Steinert Prize 400
Storrs Lectureship................ 485-86
Students, Summary of—
　　　　by Cities 739-40
　　　　by Degrees.........740-42
　　　　by Departments 737
　　　　by States 738
Summer School of Forestry
　　　　404, 406, 419-20
Surveying 263
Symphony Orchestra............401, 574
Taylor, N. W., Lectureship...... 443
Teachers, Courses for...........186, 384
Teele Fund........................ 104
TenEyck Prizes 120
Term-bills. *See* Expenses.
Terms and Vacations
　　　11, 93, 285, 408, 426, 462, 484
Text-books in College, Cost of.. 99
　Loan Library of 105
Thacher Memorial Fund 116
Theological Department. *See*
　Divinity School.
Theology, Biblical 433
　　　　Practical 436
　　　　Systematic 435
Thesis Publication................ 306
Townsend Premiums 118

PAGE

Townsend Prize................... 523-24
Townsend, W. T., Prizes......... 122
Treasurer, Office hours of 7
Triennial Catalogue 8
Trowbridge Lectures 390, 572
Trowbridge Reference Library..322, 442
Tucker, W. C., Prize.............. 294
Tuition. *See* Expenses.
　Scholarships 99-102
University, Charters of the....... 55-63
　Christian Association.......... 557-58
　Church 548-50
　Corporation 15
　Council 20
　Departments of the........... 63-64
　General Information........... 8
　Lectures and Concerts 571-73
　Legal name of the 55, 64
　Officers of.................... 13-49
Vacations 11
Walker, E. C., Prize............. 390
Waterman, T. G., Fund.......... 106
Wayland Club 510
　Prizes 524
Weir, J. F., Scholarship.......... 390
Wheeler, A. L., Library of Roman
　Law 522
White, Andrew D., History Prize 118
Whiton, J. M., Scholarship....... 102
Winchester, W. W., Fellowship.. 389
Winthrop Prizes 119
Witherbee, Lispenard Stewart,
　Fund 109
Women Students 64, 306
Woolsey Scholarships 105
Yale Botanical Garden........... 547
　Field 555-56
　Public Lectures 569-70
　Station, U. S. Post Office..... 559
　University Christian Associa-
　　tion.......................... 557-58
　　　Scientific School Branch 287
Yale-Columbia Foreign Service
　Courses 528-29
Young Men's Christian Association,
　Divinity School................ 445
Zoological Collections........... 542
Zoology 241, 271, 349